# D'accord! 1

Langue et culture du monde francophone

VISTA
HIGHER LEARNING

Boston, Massachusetts

Cover photos, clockwise from top left: characters from the **D'ACCORD!** **Roman-photo** video program in Aix-en-Provence, France; madeleines; the window of a crêperie; a francophone teen; the Eiffel Tower.

**Publisher:** José A. Blanco

**Senior Project Manager:** Thomas Keon

**Managing Editor for Technology:** Paola Ríos Schaaf

**Editors:** Christian Biagetti (Technology), Nicolas Cosseron, Daniel Finkbeiner, Mónica González

**Production and Design Director:** Marta Kimball

**Design Manager:** Susan Prentiss

**Design and Production Team:** Sarah Cole, Jennifer Christopher, Oscar Díez, Natalia González, Mauricio Henao, Nick Ventullo

Student Text ISBN: 978-1-60576-361-3
Teacher's Annotated Edition ISBN: 978-1-60576-364-4

2 3 4 5 6 7 8 9 RJ 14 13 12 11

# Table of Contents

## UNIT OPENERS
### outline the content and features of each unit.

### La famille et les copains

**UNITÉ 3**

**Leçon 3A**

CONTEXTES
pages 74–77

- Family, friends, and pets
- **L'accent aigu** and **l'accent grave**

ROMAN-PHOTO
pages 78–79

- **L'album de photos**

CULTURE
pages 80–81

- The family in France
- **Flash culture**

STRUCTURES
pages 82–85

- Descriptive adjectives
- Possessive adjectives

SYNTHÈSE
pages 86–87

- **Révision**
- **Le zapping**

**Leçon 3B**

CONTEXTES
pages 88–91

- More descriptive adjectives
- Professions and occupations
- **L'accent circonflexe, la cédille,** and **le tréma**

ROMAN-PHOTO
pages 92–93

- **On travaille chez moi!**

CULTURE
pages 94–95

- Relationships

STRUCTURES
pages 96–99

- Numbers 61–100
- Prepositions of location

SYNTHÈSE
pages 100–101

- **Révision**
- **À l'écoute**

**Pour commencer**

- Combien de personnes y a-t-il?
- Où sont ces personnes?
- Que font-elles?
- Ont-elles l'air agréables ou désagréables?

**Savoir-faire**
pages 102–107

**Panorama:** Paris
**Lecture:** Read a short article about pets.
**Écriture:** Write a letter to a friend.

**Pour commencer** activities jump-start the units, allowing students to use the French they know to talk about the photos.

**Content thumbnails** break down each unit into its two lessons and one **Savoir-faire** section, giving students an at-a-glance summary of the vocabulary, grammar, cultural topics, and language skills on which they will focus.

# CONTEXTES

## presents and practices vocabulary in meaningful contexts.

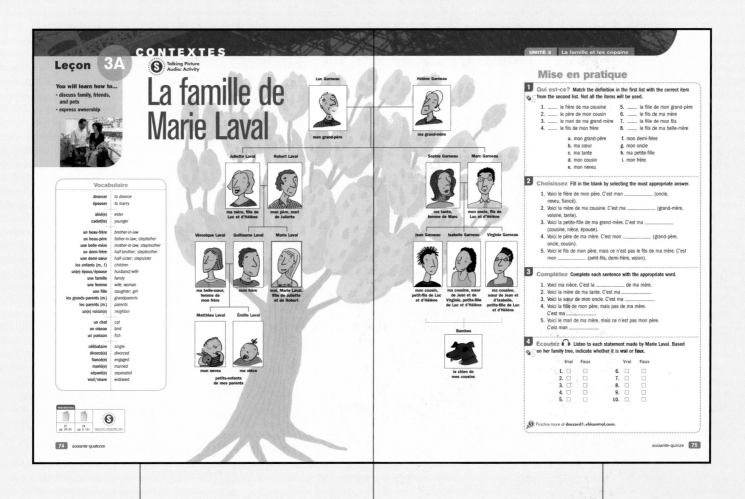

**You will learn how to...** highlights the communicative goals and real-life tasks students will be able to carry out in French by the end of each lesson.

**Illustrations** High-frequency vocabulary is introduced through expansive, full-color illustrations.

**Vocabulaire** boxes call out other important theme-related vocabulary in easy-to-reference French-English lists.

**Ressources** boxes let students know exactly what ancillaries they can use to reinforce and expand on every section of every lesson in their textbook.

**Mise en pratique** activities always practice the new vocabulary in meaningful contexts, and there is always one listening activity among them.

**Mouse icons** identify activities from the book that are on the Supersite with auto-grading.

**Supersite icons** show when additional activities or materials are available online.

## CONTEXTES
### practices vocabulary in a variety of formats.

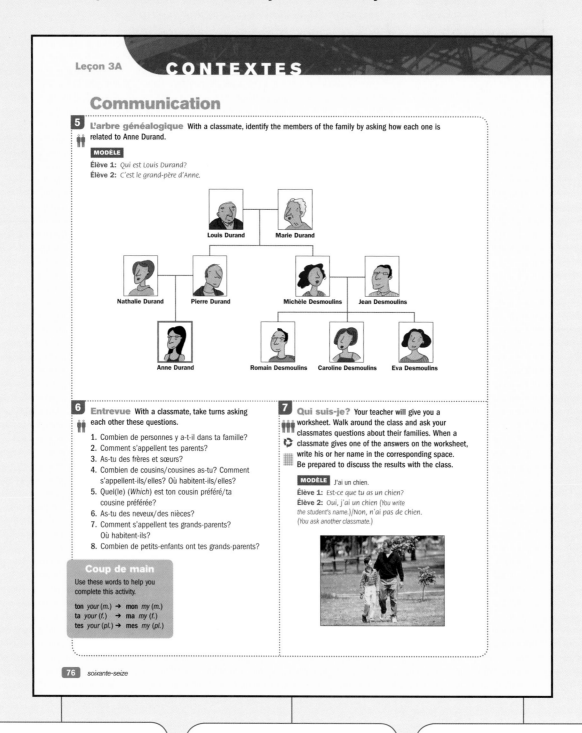

**Coup de main** boxes provide handy, on-the-spot, language or grammar information that helps students complete the activities.

**Communication** activities allow students to use the vocabulary creatively in interactions with a partner, a small group, or the entire class.

**Icons** provide on-the-spot visual cues for various types of activities: pair, small group, recycling, listening-based, video-related, handout-based, and information gap. For a legend explaining all icons used in the student text, see page **xxviii**.

# CONTEXTES
## Les sons et les lettres presents the rules of French pronunciation and spelling.

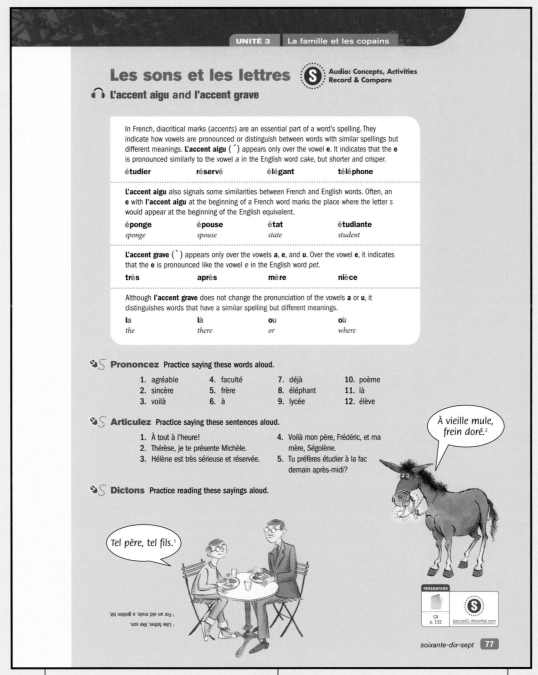

### Les sons et les lettres
**Audio: Concepts, Activities Record & Compare**

🎧 **L'accent aigu and l'accent grave**

In French, diacritical marks (*accents*) are an essential part of a word's spelling. They indicate how vowels are pronounced or distinguish between words with similar spellings but different meanings. **L'accent aigu** ( ´ ) appears only over the vowel **e**. It indicates that the **e** is pronounced similarly to the vowel *a* in the English word *cake*, but shorter and crisper.

**é**tudier        **ré**servé        **é**l**é**gant        **té**l**é**phone

**L'accent aigu** also signals some similarities between French and English words. Often, an **e** with **l'accent aigu** at the beginning of a French word marks the place where the letter *s* would appear at the beginning of the English equivalent.

**é**ponge        **é**pouse        **é**tat        **é**tudiante
*sponge*        *spouse*        *state*        *student*

**L'accent grave** ( ` ) appears only over the vowels **a**, **e**, and **u**. Over the vowel **e**, it indicates that the **e** is pronounced like the vowel *e* in the English word *pet*.

très        après        mère        nièce

Although **l'accent grave** does not change the pronunciation of the vowels **a** or **u**, it distinguishes words that have a similar spelling but different meanings.

la        là        ou        où
*the*        *there*        *or*        *where*

🔊 **Prononcez** Practice saying these words aloud.

1. agréable
2. sincère
3. voilà
4. faculté
5. frère
6. à
7. déjà
8. éléphant
9. lycée
10. poème
11. là
12. élève

🔊 **Articulez** Practice saying these sentences aloud.

1. À tout à l'heure!
2. Thérèse, je te présente Michèle.
3. Hélène est très sérieuse et réservée.
4. Voilà mon père, Frédéric, et ma mère, Ségolène.
5. Tu préfères étudier à la fac demain après-midi?

🔊 **Dictons** Practice reading these sayings aloud.

À vieille mule, frein doré.²

Tel père, tel fils.¹

¹ Like father, like son.
² For an old mule, a golden bit.

**ressources**
CA p. 132 | daccord1.vhlcentral.com

*soixante-dix-sept* **77**

---

**Explanation** Rules and tips to help students learn French pronunciation and spelling are presented clearly with abundant model words and phrases.

**Practice** Pronunciation and spelling practice is provided at the word- and sentence-levels. The final activity features illustrated sayings and proverbs that help practice the pronunciation or spelling point in an entertaining cultural context.

**The headset icon** at the top of the page indicates when an explanation and activities are recorded for convenient use in or outside of class.

## ROMAN-PHOTO
## tells the story of a group of students living
## in Aix-en-Provence, France.

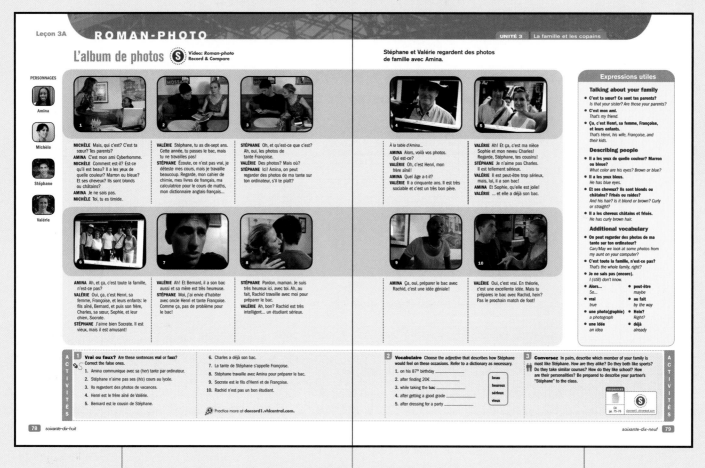

**Personnages** The photo-based conversations take place among a cast of recurring characters—four college students, the landlady of two of them (who owns the café downstairs), and her teenage son.

**Roman-photo video episodes** The **Roman-photo** episode appears in the **Roman-photo** part of the Video Program. To learn more about the video, turn to page xxvi.

**Expressions utiles** organizes new, active words and expressions by language function so students can focus on using them for real-life, practical purposes.

**Conversations** The conversations reinforce vocabulary from **Contextes**. They also preview grammatical structures from the upcoming **Structures** section in context and in a comprehensible way.

# CULTURE
## explores cultural themes introduced
## in CONTEXTES and ROMAN-PHOTO.

**Culture à la loupe** presents a main, in-depth reading about the lesson's cultural theme. Full-color photos bring to life important aspects of the topic, while charts with statistics and/or intriguing facts support and extend the information.

**Le français quotidien** exposes students to current, contemporary language by presenting familiar words and phrases related to the lesson's theme that are used in everyday spoken French.

**Portrait** profiles people, places, and events throughout the French-speaking world, highlighting their importance, accomplishments, and/or contributions to the cultures of the French-speaking people and the global community.

**Supersite video icons** in one of the **Culture** sections of each unit mean that an episode of **Flash culture**, a cultural video related to the lesson's theme, is available for viewing. To learn more about the video, see page **xxvii**.

**Le monde francophone** puts the spotlight on the people, places, and traditions of the countries and areas of the French-speaking world.

**Sur Internet** boxes, with their provocative questions and photos, direct students to the **D'ACCORD!** Supersite where they can continue to learn more about the topics of **Culture**, **Flash culture**, and the lesson's theme.

# D'ACCORD! 1 AT-A-GLANCE

## STRUCTURES
### uses innovative design to support the learning of French.

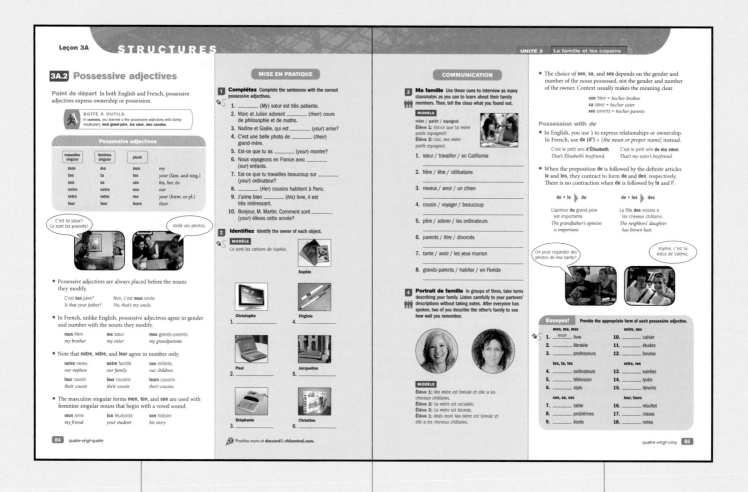

**Text format** For each grammar point, the explanation and practice activities appear on two facing pages. Grammar explanations in the outside panels offer handy on-page support for the activities in the central panels, providing students with immediate access to information essential to communication.

**Charts and diagrams** Within the clear, easy-to-grasp grammar explanations, colorful, carefully designed charts and diagrams call out key grammatical structures and forms, as well as important related vocabulary.

**Graphics-intensive design** Photos from the video program consistently integrate the lesson's video episode and **Roman-photo** section with the grammar explanations. Additional photos, drawings, and graphic devices liven up activities and heighten visual interest.

# STRUCTURES

## provides varied types of directed and communicative practice.

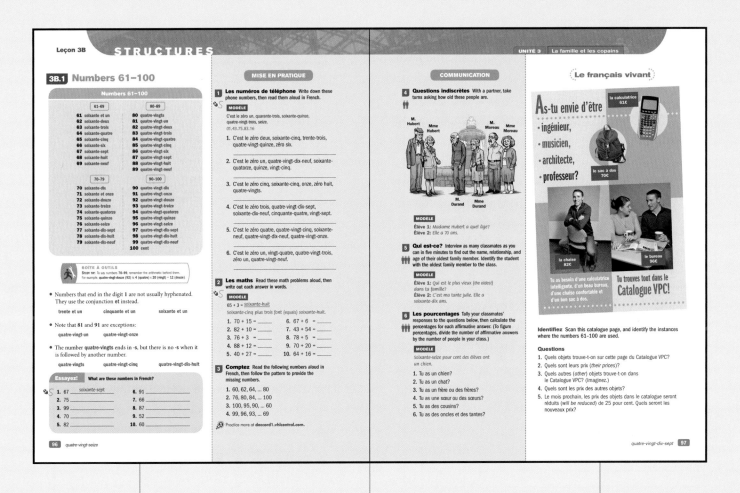

**Essayez!** offers students their first practice of each new grammar point. They get students working with the grammar point right away in simple, easy-to-understand formats.

**Mise en pratique** activities provide a wide range of guided exercises in contexts that combine current and previously learned vocabulary with the current grammar point.

**Le français vivant** activities incorporate documents, like advertisements and posters, into the grammar practice, highlighting the new grammar point in a real-life context.

**Communication** activities offer opportunities for creative expression using the lesson's grammar and vocabulary. Students should do these activities with a partner, in small groups, or with the whole class.

# SYNTHÈSE

## pulls the lesson together with cumulative practice in **Révision**.

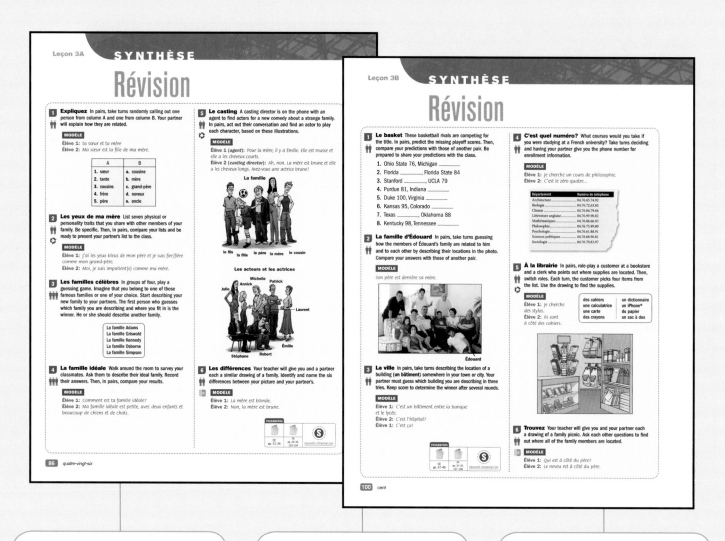

**Révision** activities integrate the lesson's two grammar points with previously learned vocabulary and structures, providing consistent, built-in review and recycling as you progress through the text.

**Pair and group icons** call out the communicative nature of the activities. Situations, role-plays, games, personal questions, interviews, and surveys are just some of the types of activities that students will experience.

**Information gap activities**, identified by the interlocking puzzle pieces, engage students and a partner in problem-solving situations. Each student has only half of the necessary information, so they must work together to accomplish the task at hand.

# SYNTHÈSE

## The second page of the section alternates between **Le zapping** and **À l'écoute**.

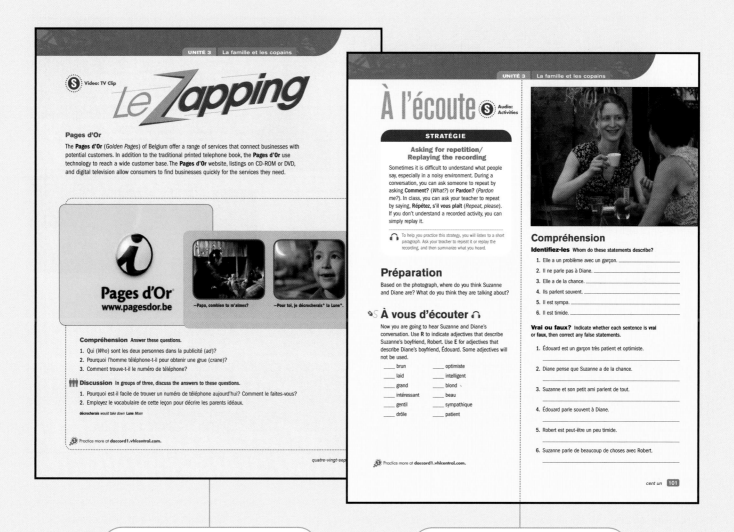

**Le zapping** features television clips in French—commercials, a recipe, a tourism notice for Rennes, and short films—supported by background information, images from the videos and activities to help students understand and to check comprehension of what they see.

**À l'écoute** presents a recorded conversation or narration to develop students' listening skills in French. **Stratégie** and **Préparation** prepare students for listening to the recorded passage.

**À vous d'écouter** tracks students through the recorded passage, and **Compréhension** checks their understanding of what they heard.

## SAVOIR-FAIRE

### Panorama presents the French-speaking world.

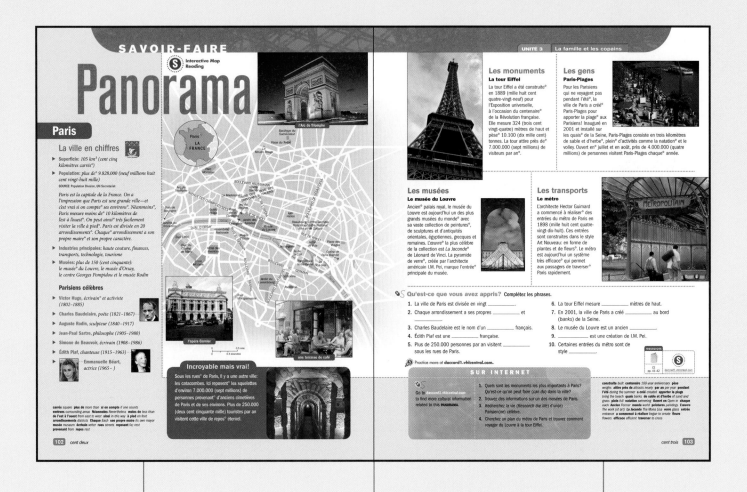

**La ville/Le pays/La région en chiffres** provides interesting key facts about the featured city, country, or region.

**Maps** point out major cities, rivers, and other geographical features and situate the featured place in the context of its immediate surroundings and the world.

**Readings** A series of brief paragraphs explores facets of the featured place's culture such as history, landmarks, fine art, literature, and aspects of everyday life.

**Incroyable mais vrai!** highlights an intriguing fact about the featured place or its people.

**Qu'est-ce que vous avez appris?** exercises check students' understanding of key ideas, and **ressources** boxes reference the additional activities in the student ancillaries.

**Sur Internet** offers Internet activities on the **D'ACCORD!** Supersite for additional avenues of discovery.

# SAVOIR-FAIRE

## Lecture develops reading skills in the context of the unit's theme.

**Avant la lecture** presents valuable reading strategies and pre-reading activities that strengthen students' reading abilities in French.

**Cultural Readings** are directly tied to the unit theme and recycle vocabulary and grammar students have learned.

**Après la lecture** includes post-reading activities that check students' comprehension of the reading.

## SAVOIR-FAIRE
## Écriture develops writing skills in the context
## of the unit's theme.

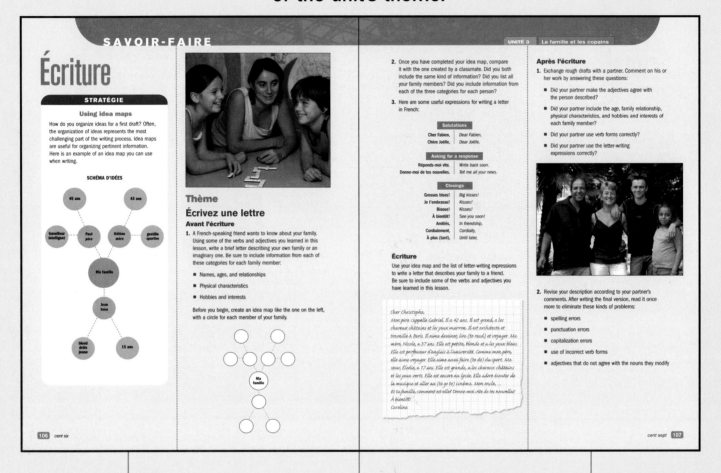

**Stratégie** provides useful strategies that prepare students for the writing task presented in **Thème**.

**Thème** describes the writing topic and includes suggestions for approaching it.

**Process approach** Like **À l'écoute** and **Lecture**, **Écriture** is a skill-building feature. It was developed using a process approach to better guide students' efforts. It has pre-writing tasks (**Avant l'écriture**), a task to use during writing (**Écriture**), and post-writing tasks (**Après l'écriture**).

# VOCABULAIRE
## summarizes all the active vocabulary of the unit.

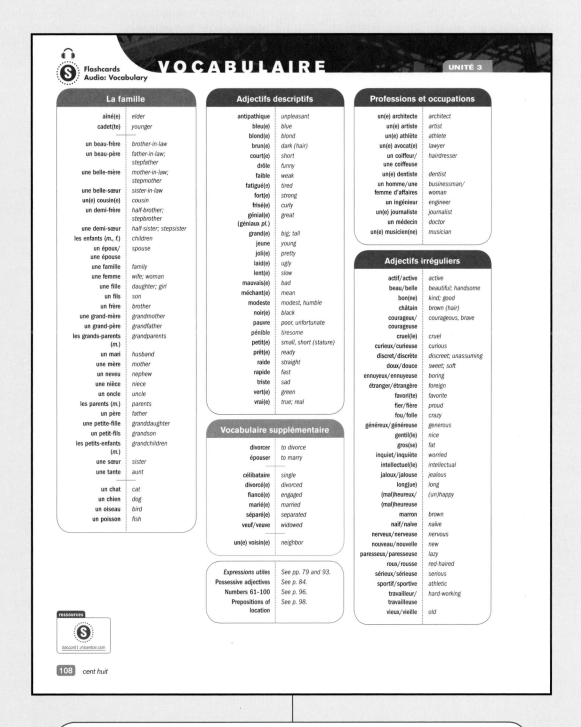

Flashcards
Audio: Vocabulary

# VOCABULAIRE

## La famille

| | |
|---|---|
| aîné(e) | elder |
| cadet(te) | younger |
| un beau-frère | brother-in-law |
| un beau-père | father-in-law; stepfather |
| une belle-mère | mother-in-law; stepmother |
| une belle-sœur | sister-in-law |
| un(e) cousin(e) | cousin |
| un demi-frère | half-brother; stepbrother |
| une demi-sœur | half-sister; stepsister |
| les enfants (m., f.) | children |
| un époux/ une épouse | spouse |
| une famille | family |
| une femme | wife; woman |
| une fille | daughter; girl |
| un fils | son |
| un frère | brother |
| une grand-mère | grandmother |
| un grand-père | grandfather |
| les grands-parents (m.) | grandparents |
| un mari | husband |
| une mère | mother |
| un neveu | nephew |
| une nièce | niece |
| un oncle | uncle |
| les parents (m.) | parents |
| un père | father |
| une petite-fille | granddaughter |
| un petit-fils | grandson |
| les petits-enfants (m.) | grandchildren |
| une sœur | sister |
| une tante | aunt |
| un chat | cat |
| un chien | dog |
| un oiseau | bird |
| un poisson | fish |

## Adjectifs descriptifs

| | |
|---|---|
| antipathique | unpleasant |
| bleu(e) | blue |
| blond(e) | blond |
| brun(e) | dark (hair) |
| court(e) | short |
| drôle | funny |
| faible | weak |
| fatigué(s) | tired |
| fort(e) | strong |
| frisé(e) | curly |
| génial(e) (géniaux pl.) | great |
| grand(e) | big; tall |
| jeune | young |
| joli(e) | pretty |
| laid(e) | ugly |
| lent(e) | slow |
| mauvais(e) | bad |
| méchant(e) | mean |
| modeste | modest, humble |
| noir(e) | black |
| pauvre | poor, unfortunate |
| pénible | tiresome |
| petit(e) | small, short (stature) |
| prêt(e) | ready |
| raide | straight |
| rapide | fast |
| triste | sad |
| vert(e) | green |
| vrai(e) | true; real |

## Vocabulaire supplémentaire

| | |
|---|---|
| divorcer | to divorce |
| épouser | to marry |
| célibataire | single |
| divorcé(e) | divorced |
| fiancé(e) | engaged |
| marié(e) | married |
| séparé(e) | separated |
| veuf/veuve | widowed |
| un(e) voisin(e) | neighbor |

| | |
|---|---|
| *Expressions utiles* | *See pp. 79 and 93.* |
| *Possessive adjectives* | *See p. 84.* |
| *Numbers 61–100* | *See p. 96.* |
| *Prepositions of location* | *See p. 98.* |

## Professions et occupations

| | |
|---|---|
| un(e) architecte | architect |
| un(e) artiste | artist |
| un(e) athlète | athlete |
| un(e) avocat(e) | lawyer |
| un coiffeur/ une coiffeuse | hairdresser |
| un(e) dentiste | dentist |
| un homme/une femme d'affaires | businessman/ woman |
| un ingénieur | engineer |
| un(e) journaliste | journalist |
| un médecin | doctor |
| un(e) musicien(ne) | musician |

## Adjectifs irréguliers

| | |
|---|---|
| actif/active | active |
| beau/belle | beautiful; handsome |
| bon(ne) | kind; good |
| châtain | brown (hair) |
| courageux/ courageuse | courageous, brave |
| cruel(le) | cruel |
| curieux/curieuse | curious |
| discret/discrète | discreet; unassuming |
| doux/douce | sweet; soft |
| ennuyeux/ennuyeuse | boring |
| étranger/étrangère | foreign |
| favori(te) | favorite |
| fier/fière | proud |
| fou/folle | crazy |
| généreux/généreuse | generous |
| gentil(le) | nice |
| gros(se) | fat |
| inquiet/inquiète | worried |
| intellectuel(le) | intellectual |
| jaloux/jalouse | jealous |
| long(ue) | long |
| (mal)heureux/ (mal)heureuse | (un)happy |
| marron | brown |
| naïf/naïve | naïve |
| nerveux/nerveuse | nervous |
| nouveau/nouvelle | new |
| paresseux/paresseuse | lazy |
| roux/rousse | red-haired |
| sérieux/sérieuse | serious |
| sportif/sportive | athletic |
| travailleur/ travailleuse | hard-working |
| vieux/vieille | old |

ressources

daccord1.vhlcentral.com

---

**Recorded vocabulary** The headset icon at the top of the page and the **ressources** box at the bottom of the page highlight that the active lesson vocabulary is recorded for convenient study and practice on the **D'ACCORD!** Supersite.

## TEACHER MATERIALS

- **Teacher's Annotated Edition**
  The unique, extended format of the TAE with its slightly reduced student pages surrounded by side and bottom panels provides comprehensive support for classroom teaching: expansion, variations, teaching tips, cultural information, scripts, and a wide array of additional activities.

- **Textbook Audio Program**
  This audio program, recorded by native French speakers, integrates directly with the **Contextes, Vocabulaire,** and **À l'écoute** sections of the textbook. It is available online and on audio CD to suit your classroom needs.

- **Video Program on DVD**
  Two separate video programs provide linguistic and cultural input. The **Roman-photo** program features a storyline closely integrated with the lesson's content. The thematically based **Flash culture** program expands on the content presented in the **Culture** section of the textbook.

- **Audio Program**
  The Audio Program provides the recordings to be used in conjunction with the audio activities in the **Cahier d'activités**. It is available online and on audio CD to suit your classroom needs.

- **Supersite powered by MAESTRO®**
  The **D'ACCORD!** Supersite utilizes the power of **MAESTRO®** to provide tracking, grading, and monitoring of student performance and to facilitate communication with the class. Teachers have access to the student site, as well as to lesson plans and select instructor resources.

- **Audio and Video Scripts**
  The Audio and Video Scripts contain the Textbook Audio Program and the Audio Program scripts; the video scripts; and English translations of the video scripts.

- **Answer Keys**
  This contains answers to activities in the **Cahier d'exercices**, the **Cahier d'activités,** and in the **Contextes** and **Structures** sections of the textbook.

- **Overhead Transparencies**
  The Overhead Transparencies include maps of the francophone world, drawings to reinforce vocabulary presented in the textbook's **Contextes** sections, and other useful illustrations for presenting or practicing concepts such as telling time. They are available online in PDF format.

- **Testing Program**
  The Testing Program consists of vocabulary & grammar quizzes, lesson & unit tests, cumulative, midterm and final exams, listening scripts, and answer keys. It is provided in ready-to-print PDFs, in RTF (word-processing) files, and in a Test Generator. Testing audio files are also available on audio CD and on the Supersite as MP3s.

## STUDENT MATERIALS

- **Cahier d'exercices**
  The **Cahier d'exercices** provides additional practice of the vocabulary and grammar in each textbook lesson and the cultural information in each unit's **Panorama** section. The **Cahier d'exercices** is a practical homework option for your students.

- **Cahier d'activités**
  The **Cahier d'activités** offers audio activities that build listening comprehension, speaking, and pronunciation skills, as well as video activities for pre-, while-, and post-viewing of the video programs. It also contains the **Feuilles d'activités** and the Info Gap Activities, worksheets for paired communication activities.

- **Cahier interactif**
  The **Cahier interactif** contains the **Cahier d'exercices** and the audio and video activities from the **Cahier d'activités** in an online environment powered by the **MAESTRO®** engine.

- **Supersite powered by MAESTRO®**
  Among the extensive online resources offered on the **D'ACCORD!** Supersite are a wide variety of interactive activities for each section of every lesson of the student text; auto-scored exercises for extra practice of vocabulary, grammar, video, and cultural content; Internet search activities; Information Gap activity and **Feuilles d'activités** handouts; reference tools; the **Le zapping** video clips; the complete Video Program; the Textbook Audio Program; and the Audio Program.

# The Vista Higher Learning Story

## Your Specialized Foreign Language Publisher

Independent, specialized, and privately owned, Vista Higher Learning was founded in 2000 with one mission: to raise the teaching and learning of world languages to a higher level. This mission is based on the following beliefs:

- It is essential to prepare students for a world in which learning another language is a necessity, not a luxury.
- Language learning should be fun and rewarding, and all students should have the tools necessary for achieving success.
- Students who experience success learning a language will be more likely to continue their language studies both inside and outside the classroom.

With this in mind, we decided to take a fresh look at all aspects of language instructional materials. Because we are specialized, we dedicate 100 percent of our resources to this goal and base every decision on how well it supports language learning.

That is where you come in. Since our founding in 2000, we have relied on the continuous and invaluable feedback from language instructors and students nationwide. This partnership has proved to be the cornerstone of our success by allowing us to constantly improve our programs to meet your instructional needs.

The result? Programs that make language learning exciting, relevant, and effective through:

- an unprecedented access to resources
- a wide variety of contemporary, authentic materials
- the integration of text, technology, and media, and
- a bold and engaging textbook design

By focusing on our singular passion, we let you focus on yours.

The Vista Higher Learning Team

# VISTA
### HIGHER LEARNING

31 St. James Avenue Boston, MA 02116-4104 TOLL-FREE: 800-618-7375
TELEPHONE: 617-426-4910 FAX: 617-426-5209 **www.vistahigherlearning.com**

# D'ACCORD! and the *Standards for Foreign Language Learning*

**D'ACCORD!** promotes and enhances student learning and motivation through its instructional design, based on and informed by the best practices of the *Standards for Foreign Language Learning in the 21st Century* as presented by the American Council on the Teaching of Foreign Languages (ACTFL).

**D'ACCORD!** blends the underlying principles of the five Cs (Communication, Cultures, Connections, Comparisons, Communities) with features and strategies tailored specifically to build students' speaking, listening, reading, and writing skills. As a result, right from the start students are given the tools to express themselves articulately, interact meaningfully with others, and become highly competent communicators in French.

**Key Standards** annotations, at the beginning of each section in the TAE, highlight the most important standards met in that section. Below is a complete list of the standards.

## The Five Cs of Foreign Language Learning

### 1. Communication
Students:
1. Engage in conversation, provide and obtain information, express feelings and emotions, and exchange opinions. (Interpersonal mode)
2. Understand and interpret written and spoken language. (Interpretive mode)
3. Present information, concepts, and ideas to an audience of listeners or readers. (Presentational mode)

### 2. Cultures
Students demonstrate an understanding of the relationship between:
1. The practices and perspectives of the culture studied.
2. The products and perspectives of the culture studied.

### 3. Connections
Students:
1. Reinforce and further their knowledge of other disciplines through French.
2. Acquire information and recognize distinctive viewpoints only available through French language and cultures.

### 4. Comparisons
Students demonstrate understanding of:
1. The nature of language through comparisons of the French language and their own.
2. The concept of culture through comparisons of the cultures studied and their own.

### 5. Communities
Students:
1. Use French both within and beyond the school setting.
2. Show evidence of becoming life-long learners by using French for personal enjoyment and enrichment.

Adapted from ACTFL's *Standards for Foreign Language Learning in the 21st Century*

# Good Teaching Practices

The design and format of the presentations and activities in the **D'ACCORD!** program incorporate research-based instructional principles to address your instructional needs and goals.

## Contextualized Vocabulary

Vocabulary concepts are explicitly presented, carefully organized, and frequently reviewed—always in context—to reinforce student understanding. Each lesson provides ample opportunities for students to practice and work with all the vocabulary they have learned up to that point. The **Contextes** section presents vocabulary in meaningful contexts and reinforces new words, phrases, and expressions through varied and engaging practice activities.

## Ongoing Comprehensible Input

The *Roman-photo* Video Program features conversations that reinforce vocabulary from **Contextes.** The video storyboard—the companion script with accompanying visuals in the textbook—provides students with instructional reinforcement and preparation that ensure successful and confident use of French.

## Contextualized Grammar

Grammatical terms are clearly and concisely defined in the **Structures** section. Grammatical structures are carefully called out and modeled with sample context sentences. Students are encouraged to apply their knowledge of English grammar to make comparisons with grammatical concepts in French.

## Communication

The language practice activities provided in the **Contextes** and **Structures** sections are carefully designed to progress from directed to open-ended to fully communicative, all within context-based, personalized activities. The varied activity formats include pair and small-group work, class interaction, and task-based, to name a few. The **D'ACCORD!** program offers ample opportunities for all types of learners to demonstrate what they can do with the vocabulary and grammar they have learned.

## Cultural Context for Learning

Language learning, like any academic subject, requires a context. Without it, the vocabulary and grammar students learn lack real meaning. Culture is the framework that provides the necessary context to students. It adds depth and color to their linguistic landscape, and over time it becomes a powerful incentive for continued study.

Culture is a prominent feature of the **D'ACCORD!** program. Students are continually prompted to use French in different cultural contexts and to use critical thinking skills to make connections and comparisons. In particular, the **Culture** and **Panorama** textbook sections, with their respective emphases on culture from thematic and geographical perspectives, provide opportunities for teaching French in a cultural context. In addition to the cultural material in the textbook, you can enrich your students' learning experience with the *Flash culture* videos and by bringing to the classroom authentic items from different Francophone cultures, such as restaurant menus, songs, poetry, podcasts, documentaries, or films.

# Universal Access

You can build a unique classroom community by engaging all students and encouraging them to participate regularly in class. Knowing how to appeal to learners of different abilities and learning styles will allow you to foster a positive teaching environment and motivate all your students.

Here are some strategies for creating inclusive learning environments for students who are cognitively, emotionally, or physically challenged as well as for heritage language and advanced learners.

## Learners with Special Needs

Learners with special needs include students with attention priority disorders, students with learning disabilities, slower-paced learners, at-risk learners, gifted students, and English-language learners. Some inclusion strategies that work well with the special needs of such students are:

**Clear Structure** By teaching concepts related to language in a predictable or understandable order, you can help students classify language in logical groups. For example, encourage students to keep outlines of materials they read, classify words under categories such as colors, shapes, etc., or follow prewriting steps.

**Frequent Review and Repetition** Preview material to be taught and review material covered at the end of each lesson. Pair proficient learners with less proficient ones to practice and reinforce concepts. Help students retain concepts through continuous practice and review.

**Multi-sensory Input and Output** Use visual, auditory, and kinesthetic tasks and activities to add interest and motivation and achieve long-term retention. For example, vary input with the use of audio recordings, video, guided visualization, rhymes, and mnemonics. Or use specially prepared displays for emphasizing key vocabulary and concepts. Encourage students to repeat words or mime responses to questions.

**Sentence Completion** Provide sentence starters for students who struggle to remember vocabulary or grammar. Emphasize different sentence structures. Write and encourage students to copy cloze sentences before filling in blanks.

**Additional Time** Consider how physical limitations may affect participation in special projects or daily routines. Allow extra time for completing a task or moving around the classroom. Provide additional time and recommended accommodations for hearing-impaired or visually-impaired students.

## Advanced Learners

Advanced learners have the potential to learn language concepts and complete assignments at an accelerated pace. They may be enrolled in school programs such as Advanced Placement or International Baccalaureate that require them to sharpen writing and problem-solving skills, study subjects in greater detail, and develop the study skills needed for tackling rigorous coursework.

As a result, advanced learners may benefit from assignments that are more challenging than the ones given to their peers. Examples include reading a variety of texts and sharing their perspectives with the class, retelling detailed stories, preparing analyses of texts, or adding to discussions. The key to differentiating for advanced learners is adapting or enriching existing activities by adding a degree of challenge to a given task. Here are some strategies for engaging advanced learners:

**Timed Answers** Have students answer questions within a specified time limit.

**Persuading** Adapt activities so students have to write or present their points of view in order to persuade an audience. Pair or group advanced learners to form debating teams and have them present their opinions on a lesson topic to the rest of the class.

**Circumlocution** Prompt students to discover various ways of expressing ideas and of overcoming potential blocks to communication through the use of circumlocution and paraphrasing.

**Identifying Cause and Effect** After reading passages in the text or other types of writing, prompt students to explain why something happened and what followed as a result. Encourage them to vary vocabulary and use precise words and appropriate conjunctions to indicate sequence and the relation between events.

## All Learners

**Use Technology to Reach All Learners** No matter what their ability level or learning style, students are surrounded by technology. Many are adept at using it to understand their world. They use it enthusiastically, but they need your guidance in how to use it for learning French. You can use technology to customize your students' learning experience by providing materials for visual, auditory, and kinesthetic learners, as well as for learners who need more time to accomplish certain tasks.

The **D'ACCORD!** program provides a wide range of technology that is designed to make sure that all your students, no matter what their home or school environment, have equal access to all instructional materials—and to success.

If your students have no access to computers, you can bring audio and video into your classroom with the Textbook and Audio Program CDs and the Video DVDs. Accompanying activities are found in both the textbook and the **Cahier d'activités**. If you wish, you can use the **Cahier d'exercices** for homework to reinforce concepts learned in class.

If students have access to computers through your classroom or a school language lab, they can complete activities on the **D'ACCORD!** Supersite. Activities are motivating, as well as instructional, and include interactive flashcards, games, short self-quizzes, and more. Selected activities are connected to an online gradebook, so you can monitor student performance.

If all students have access to computers at home as well as at school, consider having them use the **Cahier interactif**, which incorporates the **Cahier d'exercices** with the audio and video activities from the **Cahier d'activités** in an online, auto-graded format, connected to a gradebook.

# Classroom Environment

The creators of **D'ACCORD!** understand that there are many different approaches to successful language teaching and that no one method works perfectly for all teachers or all learners. The strategies and tips provided in this Teacher's Annotated Edition take into account the many widely accepted language-teaching methods applied by successful teachers today.

## Strategies for Creating a Communicative Learning Community

The aim of communicative learning is to develop oral and listening proficiency, literacy skills, and cultural knowledge in order to have meaningful exchanges with others through conversation, writing, listening, and viewing. Think of communicative interaction as being an instructional method as well as the ultimate reason for learning French.

Apply the following strategies to address challenges commonly faced by French-language learners. Good strategies will help your students gain confidence to communicate clearly, fully, accurately, personally, and confidently. Always focus on ways to engage students and increase meaningful interaction.

## Maintain the Target Language

As much as possible, create an immersion environment by using French to *teach* French. Encourage the exclusive use of the target language in your classroom, employing visual aids, circumlocution, or gestures to complement what you say. Encourage students to perceive meaning directly through careful listening and observation, and by using cognates and familiar structures and patterns to deduce meaning. Employ mnemonics, and encourage students to develop strategies to expand and retain their knowledge of French.

## Accommodate Different Learning Styles

**Visual Learners** learn best by seeing, so engage them in activities and projects that are visually creative. Encourage them to write down information and think in pictures as a long-term retention strategy; reinforce their learning through visual displays such as diagrams, videos, and handouts.

**Auditory Learners** best retain information by listening. Engage them in discussions, debates, and role-playing. Reinforce their learning by playing audio versions of texts or reading aloud passages and stories. Encourage them to pay attention to voice, tone, and pitch to infer meaning.

**Kinesthetic Learners** learn best through moving, touching, and doing hands-on activities. Involve such students in skits and dramatizations; to infer or convey meaning, have them observe or model gestures such as those used for greeting someone or getting someone's attention.

## Cultivate Critical Thinking

Prompt students to reflect, observe, reason, and form judgments in French. Engaging students in activities that require them to compare, contrast, predict, criticize, and estimate will help them to internalize the language structures they have learned.

## Encourage Cooperative Learning

There are many reasons for encouraging cooperative learning among your students, particularly in the context of French-language learning. Pair or group students of differing abilities and levels of proficiency to encourage peer coaching, promote student self-confidence, help enhance individual and group social skills and promote positive relations in your classroom.

Pair and group work can promote learning and achievement among students, create positive learning experiences, and improve students' abilities to retain information for longer periods of time.

Monitor group interactions and presentations regularly. Allow for flexible grouping and encourage movement within and among groups, so that group leaders and facilitators as well as group members are constantly changing. If possible, match students with common interests to encourage them to engage in conversation and share knowledge. You may want to allow for equal special needs or heritage learner representation among groups where possible to allow for different perspectives.

# The Four Skills

Effective second-language teaching equips students with the ability to recognize, understand, and produce the target language. Think of listening and reading as forms of input, and focus on speaking and writing as student output.

## Listening/Speaking Skills

As students begin to study French, it is likely that they will expect to need to recognize every word they hear in order to understand. The audio and video materials in the **D'ACCORD!** program build on what students have already learned but also introduce words, phrases, and structures to which they will be exposed later. It will be important for you to train students to listen for tone, the gist of the message, and cues that will help them situate meaning, such as **hier** or **demain** to distinguish between past and future.

**Three Stages of Listening** In the first stage, students should read any pre-listening strategies and post-listening activity items before listening to a passage. This will help them anticipate the main ideas as they listen to the passage the first time. Encourage them to listen to it in its entirety while jotting down words and ideas and while keeping in mind what the comprehension items ask. Remind students that they should not expect to understand every word. As students listen to the passage a second time, they should attempt to answer as many of the activity items as they can, leaving the more challenging ones for the final time they listen to the passage. If you choose to do these activities as a class, modeling the various listening stages for students will establish constructive precedents for future listening situations, both in and out of the classroom.

**Mastering Speaking Activities D'ACCORD!** activities progress from guided to open-ended, with speaking opportunities becoming more numerous from one section to the next. Before starting open-ended speaking activities in any section, make sure students have practiced and understood any relevant lexical or grammatical forms by completing guided activities that precede the communicative ones. Practice circumlocution with your students on a regular basis as part of your curriculum so that it is always clear to them that talking their way around an unknown word or expression is a normal communication strategy in French just as in their first language.

## Reading/Writing Skills

As students develop reading comprehension skills in French, encourage them to access texts by applying the reading strategies they learn both within and beyond your classroom. Remind them to predict or infer content by observing supporting information such as pictures and captions. Have them focus on text organization (main idea and details, order of events, and so on).

**Three Stages of Reading** Remind students to look over pre-reading activities or strategies to familiarize themselves with the topic of the reading passage. They should also look at post-reading activities in order to anticipate the reading's theme. They should keep this information in mind as they read the selection through the first time. At this point, their focus should be on understanding the gist of the passage. Remind them that it is fine if they do not understand every word. As students read the passage a second time, they should consult the glosses of unfamiliar words or phrases, and when finished, revisit post-reading activities in order to answer as many items as possible, leaving the more difficult ones for the time being, before beginning a third or subsequent reading of the passage. Most importantly, any reading assignment should be integrated into a broader framework of tasks consisting of all the language skills, giving students the opportunity to speak, listen, and write about the reading selection's topic. To this end, consider using the reading as a springboard for pair or group discussions or a short essay soliciting students' reactions to the reading's theme.

**Writing Activities** Writing skill development should focus on meaning and comprehensibility. As needed, remind students to take into account spelling, mechanics, and a logical structure to their paragraphs.

**D'ACCORD!** offers many opportunities for writing practice. Most prominent of course is the **Écriture** section of **Savoir-faire**, however other activities in strands such as **Culture** and **Structures** provide writing practice via shorter tasks.

# Assessment

As you use the **D'ACCORD!** program, you can employ a variety of assessments to check for student comprehension and evaluate progress. You can also use assessment as a way to identify student needs and modify your instruction accordingly. The program provides both traditional assessments that are comprehensive in scope and elicit discrete answers, as well less traditional ones that offer a more communicative approach by eliciting open-ended, personalized responses.

The **D'ACCORD!** Testing Program provides a variety of quizzes and tests for each lesson. The testing program includes a quiz (with two versions) for the **Contextes** section and for each grammar point. End of lesson and unit tests allow you to assess students' grasp of entire instructional units. Finally, cumulative midterms and final exams reinforce concepts taught over longer periods of time.

You can use the tests just as they appear in the printed Testing Program. They are also available in the Test Generator and as RTF (word-processing) files in the Resources section of the teacher's Supersite. You can customize the tests as you wish, adding, eliminating, or moving items according to your classroom and student needs.

## Portfolio Assessment

Portfolios can provide further valuable evidence of your students' learning. They are useful tools for evaluating students' progress in French and also suggest to students how they are likely to be assessed in the real world. Since portfolio activities often comprise classroom tasks that you would assign as part of a lesson or as homework, you should think of the planning, selecting, recording, and interpreting of information about individual performance as a way of blending assessment with instruction.

You may find it helpful to refer to portfolio contents, such as drafts, essays, and samples of presentations when writing student reports and conveying the status of a student's progress to his or her parents.

At the beginning of the school year, ask students to consider which pieces of their own work they would like to share with family and friends, and help them develop criteria for selecting representative samples of essays, stories, poems, recordings of plays or interviews, mock documentaries, and so on. Prompt students to choose a variety of media in their activities wherever possible to demonstrate development in all four language skills. Encourage them to seek peer and parental input as they generate and refine criteria to help them organize and reflect on their own work.

## Strategies for Differentiating Assessment

Here are some strategies for modifying tests and other forms of assessment according to your students' needs and your own purposes for administering the assessment.

**Adjust Questions** Direct complex or higher-level questions to students who are equipped to answer them adequately and modify questions for students with greater needs. Always ask questions that elicit thinking, but keep in mind the students' proficiency and readiness.

**Provide Tiered Assignments** Assign tasks of varying complexity depending on individual student needs. Refer to the Universal Access section on page TAE-22 for tips on making activities simpler or more challenging.

**Promote Flexible Grouping** Encourage movement among groups of students so that all learners are appropriately challenged. Group students according to interest, oral proficiency levels, or learning styles.

**Adjust Pacing** Pace the sequence and speed of assessments to suit your students' learning needs. Time advanced learners to challenge them and allow slower-paced learners more time to complete tasks or answer questions.

# D'ACCORD! 1 Instructional Design and Pacing Guides

As you plan your lessons with **D'ACCORD!**, trust our research-based instructional design to provide you maximum effectiveness and efficiency in teaching.

- Begin each chapter by asking students to provide, *from their own experience*, words, concepts, categories, and opinions on the context of the chapter. As students progress, they will move from doing this in English to using more and more French.

- Only then turn to the *vocabulary*, inviting students to experience it as a new code to express what they already know and experience about the chapter context.

- Once students see that the new code (French) is a tool for expressing their own ideas, bridge their experiences to that of their francophone peers through the *Roman-photo*.

- Next bring students into the experience of francophone *culture* as seen from the perspective of those living in it. Using their new language tool, they can learn about new cultural experiences as well as effectively share their own.

- Now they can refine and strengthen the accuracy and range of their communication through understanding how to recognize and manipulate language structure, i.e. *grammar* and *syntax*.

## 85-Minute (Block Schedule) Pacing Guide

Assumptions:

- 90 days, *85* minutes per day; *Minus 6 days* for standardized testing, school events; 84 total working days
- 8 **Unités** into 84 days = 10 ½ days per **Unité**

- 4 days per **Leçon** (including incremental quizzes) + 2 days for Savoir-faire and review + ½ day for final unit test = 10 ½ days

| Day | Topic (minutes) | | | | |
|---|---|---|---|---|---|
| 1 | Orientation to **Unité**; *Pour commencer* (5) | **Contextes A** orientation, vocabulary presentation (20) | **Contextes A** *Mise en pratique* (20) | **Contextes A** *Communication* (30) | *Les sons et les lettres* (10) |
| 2 | **Roman-photo A** overview, presentation (15) | **Roman-photo A** viewing (15) | **Culture A** (20) | **Structure A.1** presentation (20) | **Flash Culture** (15) |
| 3 | **Structure A.1** *Mise en pratique* (20) | **Structure A.1** *Communication* (20) | **Structure A.2** presentation (25) | Assessment: **Contextes A** (20) | |
| 4 | **Structure A.2** *Mise en pratique* (15) | **Structure A.2** *Communication* (15) | **Synthèse A** *Révision* (15) **Synthèse A** *Le zapping* (10) | Assessment **Structure A.1** (15) | **Contextes B** orientation, vocabulary presentation (15) |
| 5 | **Contextes B** Mise en pratique (20) | **Contextes B** *Communication* (25) | *Les sons et les lettres* (10) | **Roman-photo B** overview, presentation (15) | Assessment **Structure A.2** (15) |
| 6 | **Roman-photo B** viewing (20) | **Culture B** (20) | **Flash Culture** (15) | Test: **Leçon A** (30) | |
| 7 | **Structure B.1** presentation (20) | **Structure B.1** *Mise en pratique* (25) | **Structure B.1** *Communication* (25) | Assessment: **Contextes B** (15) | |
| 8 | **Structure B.2** presentation (20) | **Structure B.2** *Mise en pratique* (15) | **Structure B.2** *Communication* (15) | **Savoir-faire** Panorama (20) | Assessment **Structure B.1** (15) |
| 9 | **Synthèse B** *Révision* (20) | **Synthèse B** *À l'écoute* (20) | **Savoir-faire** *Lecture* (30) | Assessment **Structure B.1** (15) | |
| 10 | **Savoir-faire** *Écriture* (60) | Test: **Leçon B** (25) | | | |
| 11 | Test: **Unité** (45) | | | | |

# 45-Minute Pacing Guide

**Assumptions:**

- 180 days, *45* minutes per day; ***Minus 12 days*** for standardized testing, school events; 168 total working days
- 8 **Unités** into 168 days = 21 days per **Unité**
- 8 days per **Leçon** (including incremental quizzes) + 4 days for Savoir-faire and review + 1 day for final unit test = 21 days

| Day | Topic (minutes) | | |
|---|---|---|---|
| 1 | Orientation to **Unité**; *Pour commencer* (5) | **Contextes A** orientation, vocabulary presentation (25) | **Contextes A** *Mise en pratique* (15) |
| 2 | *Les sons et les lettres* (10) | **Contextes A** review, practice (15) | **Contextes A** *Communication* (20) |
| 3 | **Roman-photo A** overview, presentation (20) | **Roman-photo A** viewing (10) | Assessment: **Contextes A** (15) |
| 4 | **Roman-photo A** review, activities (10) | **Contextes A** review, practice (10) | **Culture A** with activities (25) |
| 5 | **Structure A.1** presentation (20) | **Structure A.1** *Mise en pratique* (15) | **Flash Culture** (10) |
| 6 | **Structure A.1** review, *Communication* (20) | **Structure A.2** presentation (20) | Review/practice of **Contextes A, Roman-photo A, Culture A** (5) |
| 7 | **Structure A.2** review, *Mise en pratique* (15) | **Structure A.2** *Communication* (15) | Assessment: **Structure A.1** (15) |
| 8 | **Synthèse A** *Révision* (20) | **Synthèse A** *Le zapping* (10) | Assessment: **Structure A.2** (15) |
| 9 | **Contextes B** orientation, vocabulary presentation (15) | **Contextes B** *Mise en pratique* (15) | **Contextes B** *Communication* (15) |
| 10 | *Les sons et les lettres* (15) | Test: **Leçon A** (30) | |
| 11 | **Contextes B** *Communication* (15) | **Roman-photo B** overview, viewing, activities (30) | |
| 12 | Assessment: **Contextes B** (15) | **Culture B** with activities (30) | |
| 13 | **Structure B.1** presentation (15) | **Structure B.1** *Mise en pratique* (15) | **Structure B.1:** *Communication* (15) |
| 14 | Assessment: **Structure B.1** (15) | **Structure B.2** presentation (20) | Review/practice of **Contextes A/B, Roman-photo A/B, Culture A/B** (10) |
| 15 | **Structure B.2** review, *Mise en pratique* (20) | **Structure B.2** *Communication* (25) | |
| 16 | **Synthèse B** *Révision* (15) | **Synthèse B** *À l'écoute* (15) | Assessment: **Structure B.2** (15) |
| 17 | **Savoir-faire** *Panorama* (45) | | |
| 18 | **Savoir-faire** *Lecture* (20) | Test: **Leçon B** (25) | |
| 19 | **Savoir-faire** *Écriture* (25) | **Leçon A/B** review (20) | |
| 20 | **Savoir-faire** *Écriture* (25) | **Leçon A/B** review (20) | |
| 21 | Test: **Unité** (40) | Orientation to next **Unité**; *Pour commencer* (5) | |

# Professional Resources

## Printed Resources

- American Council on the Teaching of Foreign Languages (2006). *Standards for Foreign Language Learning in the 21st Century*. Third Edition. Yonkers, NY: ACTFL.

- Brown, H Douglas (2000). *Principles of Language Learning and Teaching*. Fourth Edition. White Plains, NY: Pearson Education.

- Crawford, L. W. (1993). *Language and Literacy Learning in Multicultural Classrooms*. Boston, MA: Allyn & Bacon.

- Hughes, Arthur (2002). *Testing for Language Teachers*. Second Edition. Cambridge, UK: Cambridge University Press.

- Kramasch, Claire (2004). *Context and Culture in Language Teaching*. Oxford, UK: Oxford University Press.

- Krashen, S.D., & Terrell, T.D. (1996). *The Natural Approach: Language Acquisition in the Classroom*. Highgreen, UK: Bloodaxe Books Ltd.

- Larsen-Freeman, D. (2000). *Techniques and Principles in Language Teaching*. Second Edition. Oxford, UK: Oxford University Press.

- Nunan, D. (1999). *Second Language Teaching and Learning*. Boston: Heinle & Heinle.

- O'Malley, J. Michael and Anna Uhl Chamot (1990). *Learning Strategies in Language Acquisition*. Cambridge, UK: Cambridge University Press.

- Ommagio Hadley, Alice (2000). *Teaching Language in Context*. Third Edition. Boston, MA: Heinle & Heinle.

- Richards, Jack C. and Rodgers, Theodore S (2001). *Approaches and Methods in Language Teaching*. Cambridge, UK: Cambridge University Press.

- Shrum, Judith L. and Glisan, Eileen W. (2005). *Teacher's Handbook: Contextualized Language Instruction*. Third Edition. Boston: Heinle & Heinle.

- Tomlinson, C. A. (1999). *The Differentiated Classroom: Responding to the Needs of Learners*. Alexandria, VA: Association for Curriculum and Supervision Development.

- Tomlinson, C.A. (2001). *How to Differentiate Instruction in Mixed-Ability Classrooms*. Alexandria, VA: Association for Curriculum and Supervision Development.

## Online resources

*American Council on the Teaching of Foreign Languages (ACTFL)*
www.actfl.org

*American Association of Teachers of French (AATF)*
www.frenchteachers.org

*Modern Language Association (MLA)*
www.mla.org

*Center for Applied Linguistics (CAL)*
www.cal.org

*Computer Assisted Language Instruction Consortium (CALICO)*
www.calico.org

*The Center for Advanced Research on Language Acquisition (CARLA)*
www.carla.acad.umn.edu

*The Joint National Committee for Languages and National Council for Languages (JNCL/NCLIS)*
www.languagepolicy.org

*International Association for Language Learning Technology (IALLT)*
http://iallt.org/

*Linguistic Society of America (LSA)*
www.lsadc.org/

*National K-12 Foreign Language Resource Center (NFLRC K-12 )*
http://nflrc.iastate.edu/homepage.html

*National Foreign Language Resource Center (NFLRC)*
http://nflrc.hawaii.edu

*National Capital Language Resource Center (NCLRC)*
http://www.nclrc.org

*Center for Advanced Language Proficiency Education and Research (CALPER)*
http://calper.la.psu.edu/

*Center for Applied Second Language Studies (CASLS)*
http://casls.uoregon.edu/

# D'ACCORD! 1 Index of Cultural References

## Animals
dogs: attitudes in France, 104–105
rooster (symbol of France), 23

## Architecture
arènes de Nîmes (France), 211
Art Nouveau, (French-born art movement), 103
château de Chambord, (France), 174
château de Chenonceau (France), 66
château de Versailles (France), 284
château Frontenac (Canada), 261
hôtel Matignon (Prime Minister's residence, France), 274
housing, styles in the Francophone world, 261
opéra Garnier (opera house, Paris, France), 102
Pagerie, (birthplace of Joséphine de Beauharnais, Martinique), 274
Palais du Prince (residence of the Prince of Monaco), 274
Palais présidentiel de Dakar (presidential residence, Senegal), 274
Palais royal de Rabat, (King's Palace, Morocco), 274

## Arts
Cinema
Bardot, Brigitte (actress, France), 67
Béart, Emmanuelle (actress, France), 102
Besson, Luc (filmmaker, France), 67
Cannes (film festival, France), 247
Deneuve, Catherine (actress, France), 67
Depardieu, Gérard (actor, France), 95, 174
Depardieu, Guillaume (actor, France), 95
Depardieu, Julie (actress, France), 95
Lumière, Auguste and Louis (inventors of cinematography, France), 67
Martinez, Olivier (actor, France), 67
Palmade, Pierre (actor, France), 267
Reno, Jean (actor, France), 30
Tautou, Audrey (actress, France), 67
Pagnol, Marcel (filmmaker, France), 246
Renoir, Jean (filmmaker, writer, France), 67
Sembène, Ousmane (filmmaker, writer, Senegal), 30
Truffaut, François (filmmaker, France), 67

Music
Brassens, Georges (singer, France), 210
Cabrel, Francis (singer, France), 210
Debussy, Claude (composer, musician, France), 66
Dion, Céline (singer, Quebec, Canada), 30
Kaas, Patricia (singer, France), 282
opéra Garnier (opera house, Paris, France), 102
Piaf, Édith (singer, France), 102
Printemps de Bourges (music festival, France), 175

Painters
de La Tour, Georges (painter, France), 282
Doré, Gustave (painter, illustrator, France), 282
Magritte, René (France), 30
Monet, Claude (painter, France), 139
Paul Cézanne (France), 9
Renoir, Auguste (France), 66
de Toulouse-Lautrec, Henri (painter, France), 210

Sculptors
Bartholdi, Auguste (sculptor of Statue of Liberty, France), 282
Claudel, Camille (France), 66
Rodin, Auguste (sculptor, France), 102

## Business and Industry
Airbus (aerospace, France), 67
Century 21 (real estate, France), 267
Citroën (automobile, France), 67
Clairefontaine (paper and stationery), 51
Électricité de France (nuclear power, France), 67
Poste (Belgian mail service), 195
Moulinex, (appliances, France), 15
Pages d'Or (telephone directory, France), 87
Peugeot (automobile, France), 67
Renault (automobile, France), 67
Swiss International Airlines (air carrier, Switzerland), 123
SwissLife (insurance), 159

## Celebrations and Festivals
Aix en Musique (music, Aix-en-Provence, France), 9
Bastille Day, 189
Carnaval (Mardi Gras), 188
Father's Day and Mother's Day, 81
Festival International d'Art Lyrique (music, France), 9
Heiva (annual festival, Papeete, Tahiti), 30
Journée internationale de la Francophonie, 31
Printemps de Bourges (music, France), 175

## Countries and Regions
Algeria, 22, 31
Alsace (France), 282–283
Aquitaine (France), 210–211
Bretagne (France), 138–139
Cambodia, 22
Centre (France), 174–175
ethnicities in France, 22
France (geographical data), 66
Languedoc-Roussillon (France), 210–211
Laos, 22
Lorraine (France), 282–283
Louisiana (USA), 31, 274
Midi-Pyrénées (France), 210–211
Morocco, 22
Normandie (France), 138–139
Pays de la Loire (France), 174–175
Provence-Alpes-Côte d'Azur (France), 246–247
Québec, Canada, 31
Rhône-Alpes, (France), 246–247
Senegal, 22
Tahiti, 224
Vietnam, 22

## Education
Académie française, 66
Association sportive scolaire, 44
bac, 44, 56, 58
études supérieures, 59
grandes écoles, 59
lycée, 44–45
secondary education in francophone countries, 45
université, 59

# D'accord! 1

Langue et culture du monde francophone

VISTA
HIGHER LEARNING

Boston, Massachusetts

Cover photos, clockwise from top left: characters from the **D'ACCORD!** **Roman-photo** video program in Aix-en-Provence, France; madeleines; the window of a crêperie; a francophone teen; the Eiffel Tower.

**Publisher:** José A. Blanco

**Senior Project Manager:** Thomas Keon

**Managing Editor for Technology:** Paola Ríos Schaaf

**Editors:** Christian Biagetti (Technology), Nicolas Cosseron, Daniel Finkbeiner, Mónica González

**Production and Design Director:** Marta Kimball

**Design Manager:** Susan Prentiss

**Design and Production Team:** Sarah Cole, Jennifer Christopher, Oscar Díez, Natalia González, Mauricio Henao, Nick Ventullo

Student Text ISBN: 978-1-60576-361-3
Library of Congress Control Number: 2009935442

3 4 5 6 7 8 9 RJ 14 13 12 11

# D'accord! 1

## Langue et culture du monde francophone

# TABLE OF CONTENTS

| | | contextes | roman-photo | culture |
|---|---|---|---|---|

# TABLE OF CONTENTS

| | | contextes | roman-photo | culture |
|---|---|---|---|---|

# TABLE OF CONTENTS

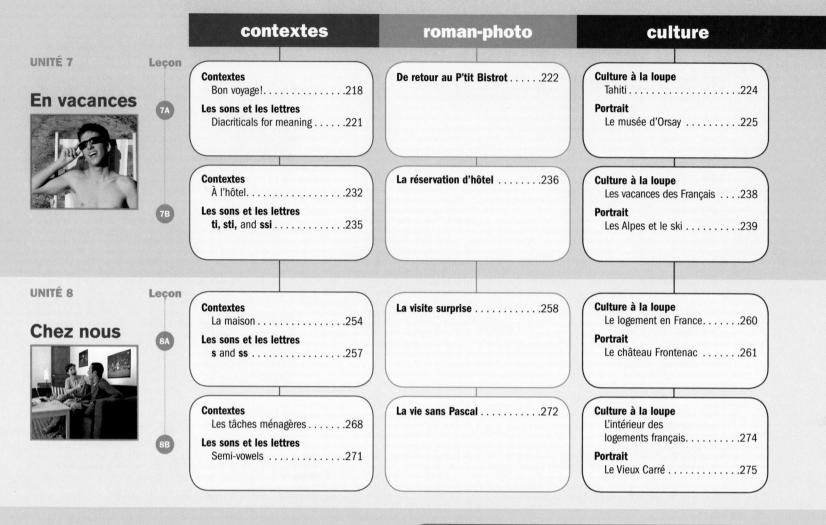

## Le monde francophone

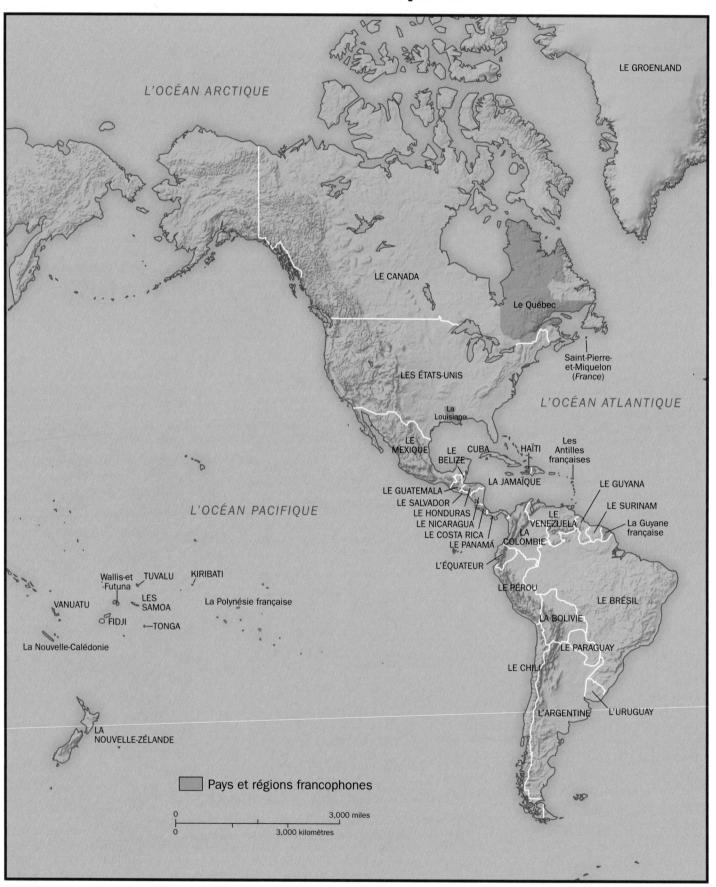

L'OCÉAN ARCTIQUE

LE GROENLAND

LE CANADA

Le Québec

Saint-Pierre-
et-Miquelon
(France)

LES ÉTATS-UNIS

L'OCÉAN ATLANTIQUE

La
Louisiane

LE
MEXIQUE

LE
BELIZE

CUBA

HAÏTI

Les
Antilles
françaises

LA JAMAÏQUE

LE GUYANA

L'OCÉAN PACIFIQUE

LE GUATEMALA

LE SALVADOR

LE HONDURAS

LE NICARAGUA

LE COSTA RICA

LE PANAMÁ

LE
VENEZUELA

LE SURINAM

La Guyane
française

LA
COLOMBIE

L'ÉQUATEUR

Wallis-et
-Futuna

TUVALU

KIRIBATI

LE PÉROU

LE BRÉSIL

VANUATU

LES
SAMOA

La Polynésie française

FIDJI

TONGA

LA BOLIVIE

La Nouvelle-Calédonie

LE PARAGUAY

LE CHILI

L'ARGENTINE

L'URUGUAY

LA
NOUVELLE-ZÉLANDE

Pays et régions francophones

0          3,000 miles

0        3,000 kilomètres

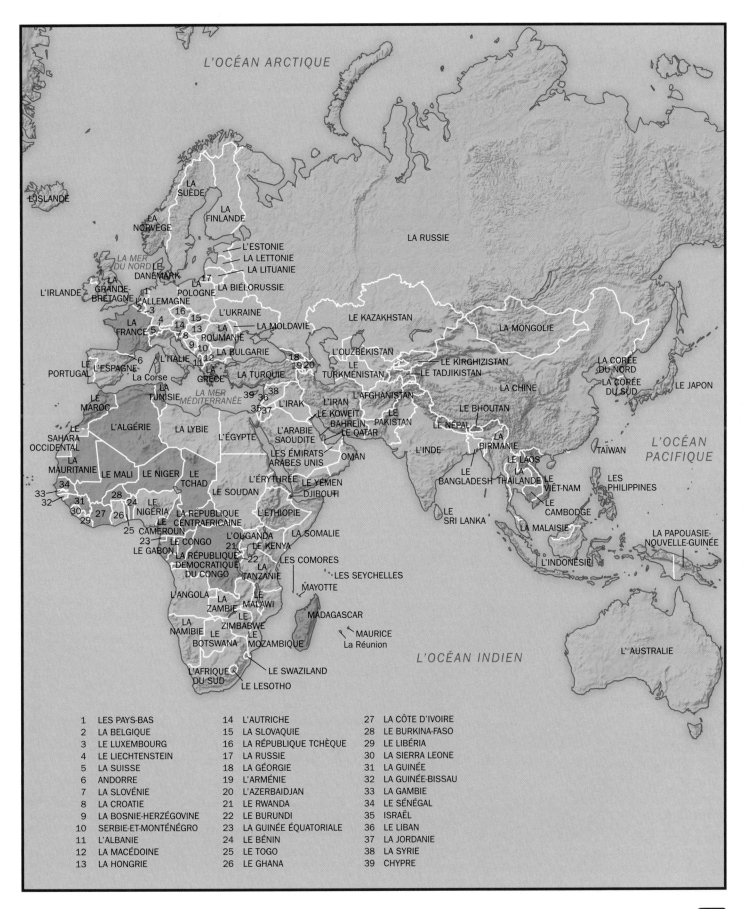

L'OCÉAN ARCTIQUE

L'ISLANDE

LA SUÈDE

LA NORVÈGE

LA FINLANDE

L'ESTONIE

LA LETTONIE

LA LITUANIE

LA RUSSIE

LA MER DU NORD

LE DANEMARK

L'IRLANDE

LA GRANDE-BRETAGNE

LA POLOGNE

LA BIÉLORUSSIE

L'ALLEMAGNE

L'UKRAINE

LE KAZAKHSTAN

LA MONGOLIE

LA FRANCE

LA MOLDAVIE

LA ROUMANIE

LA BULGARIE

L'OUZBÉKISTAN

LE KIRGHIZISTAN

LE TADJIKISTAN

LA CORÉE DU NORD

LA CORÉE DU SUD

LE JAPON

PORTUGAL

L'ESPAGNE

L'ITALIE

La Corse

LA GRÈCE

LA TURQUIE

LE TURKMÉNISTAN

L'AFGHANISTAN

LA CHINE

L'OCÉAN PACIFIQUE

LE MAROC

LA TUNISIE

LA MER MÉDITERRANÉE

L'IRAK

L'IRAN

LE KOWEÏT

LE PAKISTAN

LE BHOUTAN

LE NÉPAL

LA BIRMANIE

TAÏWAN

LE SAHARA OCCIDENTAL

L'ALGÉRIE

LA LYBIE

L'ÉGYPTE

L'ARABIE SAOUDITE

BAHREÏN

LE QATAR

L'INDE

LES LAOS

LE VIÊT-NAM

LES PHILIPPINES

LA MAURITANIE

LE MALI

LE NIGER

LE TCHAD

LES ÉMIRATS ARABES UNIS

OMAN

LE BANGLADESH

LA THAÏLANDE

LE CAMBODGE

LE SÉNÉGAL

L'ÉRYTHRÉE

LE YÉMEN

DJIBOUTI

LE SOUDAN

LE SRI LANKA

LA MALAISIE

LA PAPOUASIE-NOUVELLE-GUINÉE

LE NIGÉRIA

LA RÉPUBLIQUE CENTRAFRICAINE

LE CAMEROUN

L'ÉTHIOPIE

L'OUGANDA

LE KENYA

LA SOMALIE

L'INDONÉSIE

LE CONGO

LE GABON

LA RÉPUBLIQUE DÉMOCRATIQUE DU CONGO

LE RWANDA

LE BURUNDI

LA TANZANIE

LES COMORES

MAYOTTE

LES SEYCHELLES

L'ANGOLA

LA ZAMBIE

LE MALAWI

MADAGASCAR

MAURICE

La Réunion

L'OCÉAN INDIEN

L'AUSTRALIE

LA NAMIBIE

LE ZIMBABWE

LE BOTSWANA

LE MOZAMBIQUE

L'AFRIQUE DU SUD

LE SWAZILAND

LE LESOTHO

| | | | | | |
|---|---|---|---|---|---|
| 1 | LES PAYS-BAS | 14 | L'AUTRICHE | 27 | LA CÔTE D'IVOIRE |
| 2 | LA BELGIQUE | 15 | LA SLOVAQUIE | 28 | LE BURKINA-FASO |
| 3 | LE LUXEMBOURG | 16 | LA RÉPUBLIQUE TCHÈQUE | 29 | LE LIBÉRIA |
| 4 | LE LIECHTENSTEIN | 17 | LA RUSSIE | 30 | LA SIERRA LEONE |
| 5 | LA SUISSE | 18 | LA GÉORGIE | 31 | LA GUINÉE |
| 6 | ANDORRE | 19 | L'ARMÉNIE | 32 | LA GUINÉE-BISSAU |
| 7 | LA SLOVÉNIE | 20 | L'AZERBAIDJAN | 33 | LA GAMBIE |
| 8 | LA CROATIE | 21 | LE RWANDA | 34 | LE SÉNÉGAL |
| 9 | LA BOSNIE-HERZÉGOVINE | 22 | LE BURUNDI | 35 | ISRAËL |
| 10 | SERBIE-ET-MONTÉNÉGRO | 23 | LA GUINÉE ÉQUATORIALE | 36 | LE LIBAN |
| 11 | L'ALBANIE | 24 | LE BÉNIN | 37 | LA JORDANIE |
| 12 | LA MACÉDOINE | 25 | LE TOGO | 38 | LA SYRIE |
| 13 | LA HONGRIE | 26 | LE GHANA | 39 | CHYPRE |

# L'Amérique du Nord et du Sud

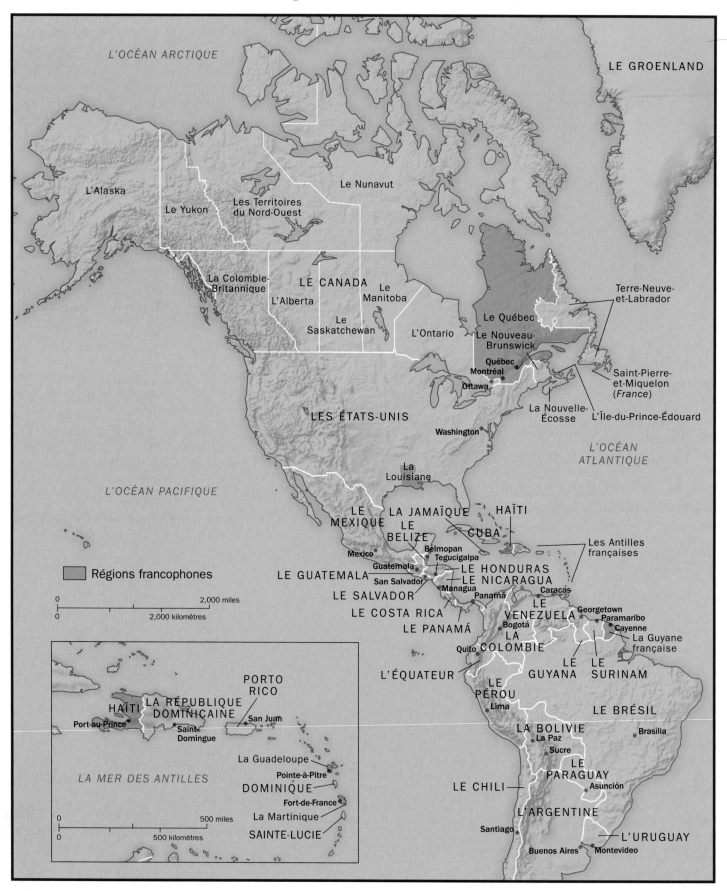

L'OCÉAN ARCTIQUE

LE GROENLAND

L'Alaska

Le Nunavut

Le Yukon

Les Territoires
du Nord-Ouest

La Colombie-
Britannique

LE CANADA

Le Manitoba

L'Alberta

Le Saskatchewan

L'Ontario

Le Québec

Terre-Neuve-
et-Labrador

Le Nouveau-
Brunswick

Québec

Montréal

Ottawa

Saint-Pierre-
et-Miquelon
(France)

La Nouvelle-
Écosse

L'Île-du-Prince-Édouard

LES ÉTATS-UNIS

Washington

L'OCÉAN
ATLANTIQUE

La
Louisiane

L'OCÉAN PACIFIQUE

LE
MEXIQUE

LA JAMAÏQUE

LE
BELIZE

HAÏTI

CUBA

Les Antilles
françaises

Mexico

Belmopan

Tegucigalpa

LE HONDURAS

LE GUATEMALA

Guatemala

San Salvador

LE NICARAGUA

LE SALVADOR

Managua

Panamá

Caracas

LE COSTA RICA

LE
VENEZUELA

Georgetown

Paramaribo

Cayenne

LE PANAMÁ

Bogotá

LA
COLOMBIE

LE
GUYANA

LE
SURINAM

La Guyane
française

L'ÉQUATEUR

Quito

LE
PÉROU

LE BRÉSIL

Lima

Régions francophones

0                    2,000 miles

0              2,000 kilomètres

LA BOLIVIE

La Paz

Sucre

Brasília

PORTO
RICO

LA RÉPUBLIQUE
DOMINICAINE

LE CHILI

LE
PARAGUAY

Asunción

HAÏTI

San Juan

L'ARGENTINE

Port-au-Prince

Saint-
Domingue

LA MER DES ANTILLES

La Guadeloupe

Pointe-à-Pitre

DOMINIQUE

Fort-de-France

La Martinique

SAINTE-LUCIE

L'URUGUAY

Santiago

Buenos Aires

Montevideo

0                500 miles

0           500 kilomètres

# La France

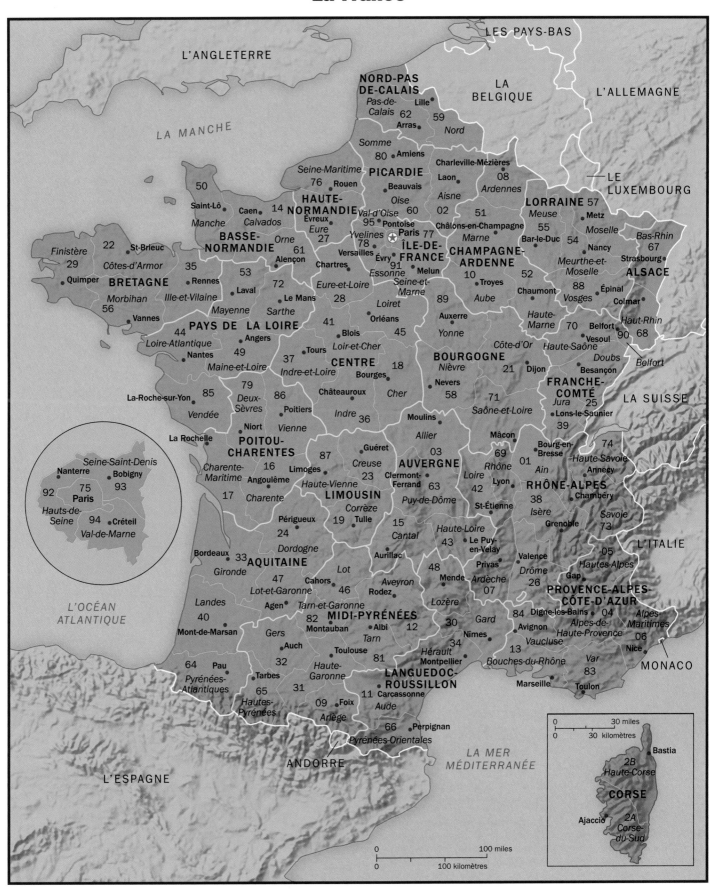

L'ANGLETERRE

LES PAYS-BAS

LA MANCHE

LA BELGIQUE

L'ALLEMAGNE

LE LUXEMBOURG

**NORD-PAS DE-CALAIS**
Pas-de-Calais
62 Lille
Arras 59
Nord

Somme
80 Amiens

Charleville-Mézières

**PICARDIE**
Seine-Maritime
76 Rouen
Beauvais
Oise 60
Val-d'Oise 95
Pontoise

Laon
Aisne 02

08
Ardennes

**LORRAINE** 57
Meuse
51 Metz
Moselle
Bar-le-Duc 55
54 Nancy

Bas-Rhin
67
Strasbourg

50

**HAUTE-NORMANDIE** 14
Saint-Lô Caen
Manche Calvados
Évreux
Eure 27

Yvelines Paris 77
78 Versailles **ÎLE-DE-FRANCE**
Évry 91
Essonne

Châlons-en-Champagne
Marne

**CHAMPAGNE-ARDENNE**
10
Troyes
Aube

52
Chaumont

Meurthe-et-Moselle
88
Vosges

**ALSACE**
Épinal
Colmar

Finistère
29 22 St-Brieuc
Côtes-d'Armor 35
Quimper **BRETAGNE** Rennes
Morbihan Ille-et-Vilaine
56 Vannes

**BASSE-NORMANDIE**
Orne
Alençon 61
Chartres
53 72

Le Mans
Eure-et-Loir
28

Melun
Seine-et-Marne
89

Auxerre
Yonne

Haute-Marne

Côte-d'Or
21 Dijon

Belfort
70 Vesoul 90
Haute-Saône
Doubs 68
Besançon
Haut-Rhin

Belfort

LA SUISSE

Mayenne Sarthe

**PAYS DE LA LOIRE**
44
Loire-Atlantique 49
Nantes
Maine-et-Loire
37 Tours
Indre-et-Loire

41 Blois
Loir-et-Cher 45
**CENTRE** 18
Bourges
Cher

Orléans
Loiret

**BOURGOGNE**
Nièvre
Nevers
58

**FRANCHE-COMTÉ**
Jura 25
Lons-le-Saunier
39

Angers

La-Roche-sur-Yon 85
Vendée

79
Deux-Sèvres
Niort

86
Poitiers
Vienne

Châteauroux
Indre 36

Moulins

Saône-et-Loire
71

Allier

Mâcon

Bourg-en-Bresse
69
Rhône 01
Ain

74
Haute-Savoie
Annecy

La Rochelle

**POITOU-CHARENTES**

Seine-Saint-Denis
Nanterre Bobigny
92 75 93
**Paris**
Hauts-de-Seine 94 Créteil
Val-de-Marne

Charente-Maritime
16
Angoulême

87
Guéret
Creuse
23

Limoges
Haute-Vienne

Clermont-Ferrand
63

**AUVERGNE**

Loire
42 Lyon

**RHÔNE-ALPES**
38
Isère
Grenoble

Chambéry

Savoie
73

17 Charente

**LIMOUSIN**
Corrèze
19 Tulle

15
Cantal

Aurillac

St-Étienne

Puy-de-Dôme

Haute-Loire
43 Le Puy-en-Velay

Valence
Drôme
26

05
Hautes-Alpes
Gap

L'ITALIE

L'OCÉAN
ATLANTIQUE

Bordeaux 33
Gironde **AQUITAINE**

Périgueux
24
Dordogne

Lot
47 Cahors 46
Lot-et-Garonne

Rodez
Aveyron

48
Lozère

Mende
Ardèche
07

Privas

84 Digne-les-Bains 04
Alpes-de-Haute-Provence

**PROVENCE-ALPES-CÔTE-D'AZUR**

06
Nice

Alpes-Maritimes

MONACO

Landes
40
Mont-de-Marsan

Agen
Gers
Auch

Tarn-et-Garonne
82 Montauban
Albi 12
Tarn
Toulouse

**MIDI-PYRÉNÉES**
81

30
Gard
Nîmes
34
Hérault
Montpellier

Avignon
Vaucluse

13
Bouches-du-Rhône

Var
83

Marseille Toulon

64 Pau
Pyrénées-Atlantiques
65
Hautes-Pyrénées

Tarbes
32
31

Haute-Garonne

09 Foix
Ariège

11 Carcassonne
Aude

66 Perpignan
Pyrénées-Orientales

**LANGUEDOC-ROUSSILLON**

LA MER
MÉDITERRANÉE

ANDORRE

L'ESPAGNE

| 0 | 30 miles |
| 0 | 30 kilomètres |

Bastia
2B
Haute-Corse

**CORSE**

Ajaccio
2A
Corse-du-Sud

| 0 | 100 miles |
| 0 | 100 kilomètres |

# L'Europe

0 _____ 500 miles
0 _____ 500 kilomètres

Pays francophones

LA MER DE BARENTS

L'ISLANDE
Reykjavik

LA MER DE NORVÈGE

LA SUÈDE
LA FINLANDE
Helsinki

LA NORVÈGE
LA RUSSIE

Oslo
Stockholm
Tallinn
L'ESTONIE
Moscou

LA MER BALTIQUE

Riga
LA LETTONIE
LA LITUANIE
Vilnius
Minsk

LA MER DU NORD
LE DANEMARK
Copenhague
LA RUSSIE
LA BIÉLORUSSIE

Dublin
L'IRLANDE
LA GRANDE BRETAGNE
LES PAYS-BAYS
La Haye
Berlin
Varsovie
Kiev

Londres
Bruxelles
L'ALLEMAGNE
LA POLOGNE
L'UKRAINE

L'OCÉAN ATLANTIQUE
LA BELGIQUE
Luxembourg
Prague
LA RÉPUBLIQUE TCHÈQUE
LA SLOVAQUIE
LA MOLDAVIE

Paris
LE LUXEMBOURG
LE LIECHTENSTEIN
Bratislava
Vienne
Budapest
Chisinau

Berne
L'AUTRICHE
LA HONGRIE
LA ROUMANIE

LA SUISSE
Ljubljana
LA FRANCE
LA SLOVÉNIE
Zagreb
Belgrade
Bucarest
LA MER NOIRE

LA CROATIE
LA BOSNIE-HERZÉGOVINE
SERBIE-ET-MONTÉNÉGRO

Monte Carlo
Sarajevo
LA BULGARIE

Andorre-la-Vieille
MONACO
L'ITALIE
Sofia
Skopje

LE PORTUGAL
ANDORRE
La Corse
Rome
Tirana
LA MACÉDOINE
LA TURQUIE

Madrid
L'ALBANIE
LA GRÈCE

Lisbonne
L'ESPAGNE

La Sardaigne
Athènes
Nicosie

La Sicile
CHYPRE

MALTE
La Valette

LA MER MÉDITERRANÉE

LE MAROC
LA TUNISIE
L'ALGÉRIE

LA LIBYE
L'ÉGYPTE

# L'Afrique

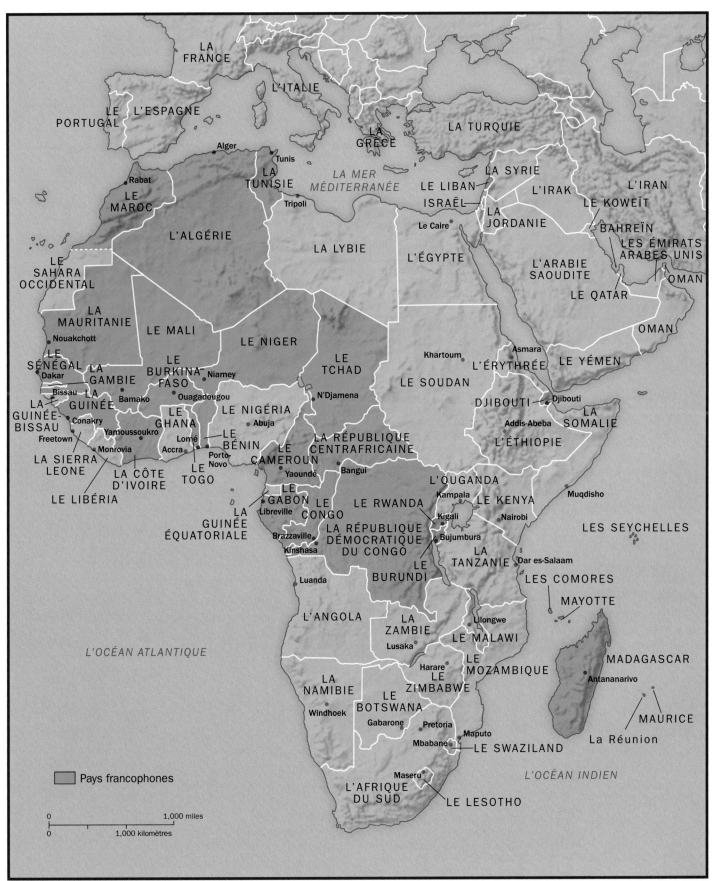

LA FRANCE

L'ITALIE

LE PORTUGAL

L'ESPAGNE

LA GRÈCE

LA TURQUIE

Alger

Tunis

LA TUNISIE

LA MER MÉDITERRANÉE

LA SYRIE

LE LIBAN

L'IRAK

L'IRAN

Rabat

LE MAROC

Tripoli

ISRAËL

LA JORDANIE

LE KOWEÏT

BAHREÏN

LES ÉMIRATS ARABES UNIS

L'ALGÉRIE

LA LYBIE

Le Caire

L'ÉGYPTE

L'ARABIE SAOUDITE

LE QATAR

OMAN

LE SAHARA OCCIDENTAL

LA MAURITANIE

LE MALI

LE NIGER

Khartoum

Asmara

L'ÉRYTHRÉE

LE YÉMEN

OMAN

Nouakchott

LE SÉNÉGAL

Dakar

LA GAMBIE

LE BURKINA FASO

Niamey

LE TCHAD

LE SOUDAN

DJIBOUTI

Djibouti

LA SOMALIE

Bissau

LA GUINÉE

Bamako

Ouagadougou

N'Djamena

Addis-Abeba

LA GUINÉE-BISSAU

Conakry

LE GHANA

Yamoussoukro

Abuja

LE NIGÉRIA

L'ÉTHIOPIE

Freetown

Lomé

LE BÉNIN

LA RÉPUBLIQUE CENTRAFRICAINE

LA SIERRA LEONE

Monrovia

Accra

Porto-Novo

LE CAMEROUN

Yaoundé

Bangui

L'OUGANDA

LE KENYA

Muqdisho

LE LIBÉRIA

LA CÔTE D'IVOIRE

LE TOGO

LE GABON

LE CONGO

LE RWANDA

Kampala

Kigali

Nairobi

LES SEYCHELLES

LA GUINÉE ÉQUATORIALE

Libreville

LA RÉPUBLIQUE DÉMOCRATIQUE DU CONGO

Bujumbura

LA TANZANIE

Brazzaville

Kinshasa

LE BURUNDI

Dar es-Salaam

LES COMORES

Luanda

MAYOTTE

L'ANGOLA

LA ZAMBIE

Lilongwe

LE MALAWI

MADAGASCAR

L'OCÉAN ATLANTIQUE

Lusaka

Harare

LE ZIMBABWE

LE MOZAMBIQUE

Antananarivo

LA NAMIBIE

LE BOTSWANA

MAURICE

Windhoek

Gabarone

Pretoria

Maputo

La Réunion

Mbabane

LE SWAZILAND

L'OCÉAN INDIEN

Maseru

Pays francophones

L'AFRIQUE DU SUD

LE LESOTHO

0 — 1,000 miles

0 — 1,000 kilomètres

# The French-speaking World

Do you know someone who speaks French? Chances are you do! French is the third most commonly spoken language in the U.S., after English and Spanish, and is the second most common language in some states. More than 1 million Americans speak French at home. It is the official language of more than twenty-five countries and an official language of the European Union and United Nations. Along with English, French is one of only two languages that is spoken on every continent of the world.

### The French-speaking World

**Speakers of French**
**(approx. 200 million worldwide)**

- America and the Caribbean — 7%
- Asia and Oceania — 1%
- Europe — 42%
- North Africa and the Middle-East — 11%
- Sub-Saharan Africa and the Indian Ocean — 39%

Source: Organisation internationale de la Francophonie

## The Growth of French

Have you ever heard someone say that French is a Romance language? This doesn't mean it's romantic—although some say it is the language of love!—but that it is derived from Latin, the language of the Romans. Gaul, a country largely made up of what is now France and Belgium, was absorbed into the Roman Empire after the Romans invaded Gaul in 58 B.C. Most Gauls began speaking Latin. In the third century, Germanic tribes including the Franks invaded the Roman territories of Western Europe. Their language also influenced the Gauls. As the Roman empire collapsed in the fifth century, people in outlying regions and frontiers were cut off from Rome. The Latin spoken by each group was modified more and more over time. Eventually, the language that was spoken in Paris became the standard for modern-day French.

## French in the United States

**1500**     **1600**     **1700**

**1534**
Jacques Cartier claims territories for France as he explores the St. Lawrence river, and the French establish fur trading posts.

**1600s**
French exploration continues in the Great Lakes and the Mississippi Valley. La Salle takes the colony of Louisiana for France in 1682.

**1685–1755**
The Huguenots (French Protestants) form communities in America. French Acadians leave Nova Scotia and settle in northern New England and Louisiana.

# French in the United States

French came to North America in the 16th and 17th centuries when French explorers and fur traders traveled through what is now America's heartland. French-speaking communities grew rapidly when the French Acadians were forced out of their Canadian settlement in 1755 and settled in New England and Louisiana. Then, in 1803, France sold the Louisiana territory to the United States for 80 million francs, or about 15 million dollars. Overnight, thousands of French people became citizens of the United States, bringing with them their rich history, language, and traditions.

This heritage, combined with that of the other French populations that have immigrated to the United States over the years, as well as U.S. relations with France in World Wars I and II, has led to the remarkable growth of French around the country. After English and Spanish, it is the third most commonly spoken language in the nation. Louisiana, Maine, New Hampshire, and Vermont claim French as the second most commonly spoken language after English.

You've made a popular choice by choosing to take French in school; it is the second most commonly taught foreign language in classrooms throughout the country! Have you heard people speaking French in your community? Chances are that you've come across an advertisement, menu, or magazine that is in French. If you look around, you'll find that French can be found in some pretty common places. Depending on where you live, you may see French on grocery items such as juice cartons and cereal boxes. In some large cities, you can see French language television broadcasts on stations such as TV5Monde. When you listen to the radio or download music from the Internet, some of the mo_ _rform popular choices are French artists wh_ the in French. In fact, French music sal_ since United States have more than do_ly two 2004. French and English are t_Games. More official languages of the Oly_h language are than 20,000 words in the _nch can create of French origin. Learni_veryday life. opportunities within _

## 1800

## 1900

## 2000

**1803**
The United States purchases Louisiana, where Cajun French is widely spoken.

**19_,**
_ Nand
_ties in
_ nited States
_r courses
_ French as a
foreign language.
It is the second most commonly studied language.

**2009**
French is the third most commonly spoken language in the U.S., with 1.6 million speakers.

# Why Study French?

## Connect with the World

Learning French can change how you view the world. While you learn French, you will also explore and learn about the origins, customs, art, music, and literature of people all around the world. When you travel to a French-speaking country, you'll be able to converse freely with the people you meet. And whether here in the U.S. or abroad, you'll find that speaking to people in their native language is the best way to bridge any culture gap.

## Learn an International Language

There are many reasons for learning French, a language that has spread to many parts of the world and has along the way embraced words and sounds of languages as diverse as Latin, Arabic, German, and Celtic. The French language, standardized and preserved by the **Académie française** since 1634, is now among the most commonly spoken languages in the world. It is the second language of choice among people who study languages other than English in North America.

## Understand the World Around You

Knowing French can also open doors to communities within the United States, and it can broaden your understanding of the nation's history and geography. The very names Delaware, Oregon, and Vermont are French in origin. Just knowing their meanings can give you some insight into, of all things, the history and landscapes for which the states are known. Oregon is derived from a word that means "hurricane," which tells you about the windiness of the Columbia River; and Vermont

| City Name | Meaning in French |
|---|---|
| Bel Air, California | "good air" |
| Boise, Idaho | "wooded" |
| Moines, Iowa | "river of the monks" |
| ir, New | "clear mountain" |

comes from a phrase meaning "green mountain," which is why its official nickname is The Green Mountain State. You've already been speaking French whenever you talk about these states!

## Explore Your Future

How many of you are already planning your future careers? Employers in today's global economy look for workers who know different languages and understand other cultures. Your knowledge of French will make you a valuable candidate for careers abroad as well as in the United States. Doctors, nurses, social workers, hotel managers, journalists, businesspeople, pilots, flight attendants, and many other kinds of professionals need to know French or another foreign language to do their jobs well.

## Expand Your Skills

Studying a foreign language can improve your ability to analyze and interpret information and help you succeed in many other subject areas. When you begin learning French, much of your studies will focus on reading, writing, grammar, listening, and speaking skills. You'll be amazed at how the skills involved with learning how a language works can help you succeed in other areas of study. Many people who study a foreign language claim that they gained a better understanding of English and the structures it uses. French can even help you understand the origins of many English words and expand your own vocabulary in English. Knowing French can also help you pick up other related languages, such as Portuguese, Spanish, and Italian. French can really open doors for learning many other skills in your school career.

# How to Learn French

## Start with the Basics !

As with anything you want to learn, start with the basics and remember that learning takes time!

**Vocabulary** Every new word you learn in French will expand your vocabulary and ability to communicate. The more words you know, the better you can express yourself. Focus on sounds and think about ways to remember words. Use your knowledge of English and other languages to figure out the meaning of and memorize words like **téléphone**, **l'orchestre**, and **mystérieux**.

**Grammar** Grammar helps you put your new vocabulary together. By learning the rules of grammar, you can use new words correctly and speak in complete sentences. As you learn verbs and tenses, you will be able to speak about the past, present, or future; express yourself with clarity; and be able to persuade others with your opinions. Pay attention to structures and use your knowledge of English grammar to make connections with French grammar.

**Culture** Culture provides you with a framework for what you may say or do. As you learn about the culture of French-speaking communities, you'll improve your knowledge of French. Think about a word like **cuisine** and how it relates to a type of food as well as the kitchen itself. Think about and explore customs observed at **le Réveillon de la Saint-Sylvestre** (New Year's Eve) or **le Carnaval** (or Mardi Gras, "fat Tuesday") and how they are similar to celebrations you are familiar with. Observe customs. Watch people greet each other or say good-bye. Listen for sayings that capture the spirit of what you want to communicate!

# Listen, Speak, Read, and Write

**Listening** Listen for sounds and for words you can recognize. Listen for inflections and watch for key words that signal a question such as **comment** (how), **oú** (where), or **qui** (who). Get used to the sound of French. Play French pop songs or watch French movies. Borrow books on CD from your local library, or try to attend a meeting with a French language group in your community. Download a podcast in French or watch a French newscast online. Don't worry if you don't understand every single word. If you focus on key words and phrases, you'll get the main idea. The more you listen, the more you'll understand!

**Speaking** Practice speaking French as often as you can. As you talk, work on your pronunciation, and read aloud texts so that words and sentences flow more easily. Don't worry if you don't sound like a native speaker, or if you make some mistakes. Time and practice will help you get there. Participate actively in French class. Try to speak French with classmates, especially native speakers (if you know any), as often as you can.

**Reading** Pick up a French-language newspaper or a magazine on your way to school, read the lyrics of a song as you listen to it, or read books you've already read in English translated into French. Use reading strategies that you know to understand the meaning of a text that looks unfamiliar. Look for cognates, or words that are related in English and French, to guess the meaning of some words. Read as often as you can, and remember to read for fun!

**Writing** It's easy to write in French if you put your mind to it. Memorize the basic rules of how letters and sounds are related, practice the use of diacritical marks, and soon you can probably become an expert speller in French! Write for fun—make up poems or songs, write e-mails or instant messages to friends, or start a journal or blog in French.

# Tips for Learning French

- **Listen** to French radio shows, often available online. Write down words you can't recognize or don't know and look up the meaning.

- **Watch** French TV shows or movies. Read subtitles to help you grasp the content.

- **Read** French-language newspapers, magazines, Web sites, or blogs.

- **Listen** to French songs that you like—anything from a best-selling pop song by Superbus to an old French ballad by Edith Piaf. Sing along and concentrate on your pronunciation.

- **Seek** out French speakers. Look for neighborhoods, markets, or cultural centers where French might be spoken in your community. Greet people, ask for directions, or order from a menu at a French restaurant in French.

- **Pursue** language exchange opportunities in your school or community. Try to join language clubs or cultural societies, and explore opportunities for studying abroad or hosting a student from a French-speaking country in your home or school.

### Practice, practice, practice!

Seize every opportunity you find to listen, speak, read, or write French. Think of it like a sport or learning a musical instrument—the more you practice, the more you will become comfortable with the language and how it works. You'll marvel at how quickly you can begin speaking French and how the world that it transports you to can change your life forever!

- **Connect** your learning to everyday experiences. Think about naming the ingredients of your favorite dish in French. Think about the origins of French place names in the U.S., like Baton Rouge and Fond du Lac, or of common English words and phrases like *café, en route, fiancé, matinée, papier mâché, petite,* and *souvenir.*

- **Use** mnemonics, or a memorizing device, to help you remember words. Make up a saying in English to remember the order of the days of the week in French (L, M, M, J, V, S, D).

- **Visualize** words. Try to associate words with images to help you remember meanings. For example, think of a **pâté** or **terrine** as you learn the names of different types of meats and vegetables. Imagine a national park and create mental pictures of the landscape as you learn names of animals, plants, and habitats.

- **Enjoy** yourself! Try to have as much fun as you can learning French. Take your knowledge beyond the classroom and find ways to make your learning experience your very own.

# Common Names

Get started learning French by using a French name in class. You can choose from the lists on these pages, or you can find one yourself. How about learning the French equivalent of your name? The most popular French female names are Marie, Jeanne, Françoise, Monique, and Catherine. The most popular male names in French are Jean, Pierre, Michel, André, and Philippe. Is your name, or that of someone you know, in the French top five?

| More Boys Names | More Girls Names |
| --- | --- |
| Thomas | Léa |
| Lucas | Manon |
| Théo | Chloé |
| Hugo | Emma |
| Maxime | Camille |
| Alexandre | Océane |
| Antoine | Marie |
| Enzo | Sarah |
| Quentin | Clara |
| Clément | Inès |
| Nicolas | Laura |
| Alexis | Julie |
| Romain | Mathilde |
| Louis | Lucie |
| Valentin | Anaïs |
| Léo | Pauline |
| Julien | Marine |
| Paul | Lisa |
| Baptiste | Eva |
| Tom | Justine |
| Nathan | Maéva |
| Arthur | Jade |
| Benjamin | Juliette |
| Florian | Charlotte |
| Mathis | Émilie |

| The top five names for boys: | The top five names for girls: |
| --- | --- |
| Jean | Marie |
| Michel | Jeanne |
| Pierre | Françoise |
| André | Monique |
| Philippe | Catherine |

# Useful French Expressions

The following expressions will be very useful in getting you started learning French. You can use them in class to check your understanding, and to ask and answer questions about the lessons. Learn these ahead of time to help you understand direction lines in French, as well as your teacher's instructions. Remember to practice your French as often as you can!

| Expressions utiles | Useful expressions |
|---|---|
| **Corrigez les phrases fausses** | Correct the false statements. |
| **Créez/Formez des phrases…** | Create/Form sentences… |
| **D'après vous/Selon vous…** | According to you… |
| **Décrivez les images/ dessins…** | Describe the images/ drawings… |
| **Désolé(e), j'ai oublié.** | I'm sorry, I forgot. |
| **Déterminez si…** | Decide whether… |
| **Dites si vous êtes/Dis si tu es d'accord ou non.** | Say if you agree or not. |
| **Écrivez une lettre/une phrase.** | Write a letter/a sentence. |
| **Employez les verbes de la liste.** | Use the verbs from the list. |
| **En utilisant…** | Using… |
| **Est-ce que vous pouvez/ tu peux choisir un(e) …** | Can you please choose … |
| **autre partenaire/ quelqu'un d'autre?** | another partner/ someone else? |
| **Êtes vous prêt(e)?/ Es-tu prêt(e)?** | Are you ready? |
| **Excusez-moi, je suis en retard.** | Excuse me for being late. |
| **Faites correspondre…** | Match… |
| **Faites les accords nécessaires.** | Make the necessary agreements. |

| Expressions utiles | Useful expressions |
|---|---|
| **Allez à la page 2.** | Go to page 2. |
| **Alternez les rôles.** | Switch roles. |
| **À tour de rôle…** | Take turns… |
| **À voix haute** | Aloud |
| **À votre/ton avis** | In your opinion |
| **Après une deuxième écoute…** | After a second listening… |
| **Articulez.** | Enunciate.; Pronounce carefully. |
| **Au sujet de, À propos de** | Regarding/about |
| **Avec un(e) partenaire/ un(e) camarade de classe** | With a partner/a classmate |
| **Avez-vous/As-tu des questions?** | Do you have any questions? |
| **Avez-vous/As-tu fini/ terminé?** | Are you done?/Have you finished? |
| **Chassez l'intrus.** | Choose the item that doesn't belong. |
| **Choisissez le bon mot.** | Choose the right word. |
| **Circulez dans la classe.** | Walk around the classroom. |
| **Comment dit-on ____ en français?** | How do you say ____ in French? |
| **Comment écrit-on ____ en français?** | How do you spell ____ in French? |

| Expressions utiles | Useful expressions |
|---|---|
| **Félicitations!** | *Congratulations!* |
| **Indiquez le mot qui n'appartient pas.** | *Indicate the word that doesn't belong.* |
| **Indiquez qui a dit…** | *Indicate who said…* |
| **J'ai gagné!/Nous avons gagné!** | *I won!/We won!* |
| **Je n'ai pas/Nous n'avons pas encore fini.** | *I/We have not finished yet.* |
| **Je ne comprends pas.** | *I don't understand.* |
| **Je ne sais pas.** | *I don't know.* |
| **Je ne serai pas là demain.** | *I won't be here tomorrow.* |
| **Je peux continuer?** | *May I continue?* |
| **Jouez le rôle de…/ la scène…** | *Play the role of…/ the scene…* |
| **Lentement, s'il vous plaît.** | *Slowly, please.* |
| **Lisez…** | *Read…* |
| **Mettez dans l'ordre…** | *Put in order…* |
| **Ouvrez/Fermez votre livre.** | *Open/Close your books.* |
| **Par groupes de trois/ quatre…** | *In groups of three/four…* |
| **Partagez vos résultats…** | *Share your results…* |
| **Posez-vous les questions suivantes.** | *Ask each other the following questions.* |
| **Pour demain, faites…** | *For tomorrow, do…* |

| Expressions utiles | Useful expressions |
|---|---|
| **Pour demain, vous allez/ tu vas faire…** | *For tomorrow you are going to do…* |
| **Prononcez.** | *Pronounce.* |
| **Qu'est-ce que ____ veut dire?** | *What does ____ mean?* |
| **Que pensez-vous/ penses-tu de…** | *What do you think about…* |
| **Qui a gagné?** | *Who won?* |
| **…qui convient le mieux.** | *…that best completes/is the most appropriate.* |
| **Rejoignez un autre groupe.** | *Get together with another group.* |
| **Remplissez les espaces.** | *Fill in the blanks.* |
| **Répondez aux questions suivantes.** | *Answer the following questions.* |
| **Soyez prêt(e)s à…** | *Be ready to…* |
| **Venez/Viens au tableau.** | *Come to the board.* |
| **Vous comprenez?/ Tu comprends?** | *Do you understand?* |
| **Vous pouvez expliquer encore une fois, s'il vous plaît?** | *Could you explain again, please?* |
| **Vous pouvez répéter, s'il vous plaît?** | *Could you repeat that, please?* |
| **Vrai ou faux?** | *True or false?* |

## *ROMAN-PHOTO* VIDEO PROGRAM

Fully integrated with your textbook, the **Roman-photo** Video contains thirty dramatic episodes, one for each lesson of the text in Levels 1 & 2. The episodes present the adventures of four college students who are studying in the south of France at the **Université Aix-Marseille**. They live in apartments above and near **Le P'tit Bistrot**, a café owned by Valérie Forestier. The video tells their story and the story of Madame Forestier and her teenage son, Stéphane.

The **Roman-photo** section in each textbook lesson is actually an abbreviated version of the dramatic episode featured in the video. Therefore, each **Roman-photo** section can be done before you see the corresponding video episode, after it, or as a section that stands alone in its own right.

As you watch each video episode, you will first see a live segment in which the characters interact using vocabulary and grammar you are studying. As the video progresses, the live segments carefully combine new vocabulary and grammar with previously taught language. You will then see a **Reprise** segment that summarizes the key language functions and/or grammar points used in the dramatic episode.

## THE CAST
Here are the main characters you will meet when you watch **Roman-photo**:

Of Senegalese heritage
**Amina Mbaye**

From Washington, D.C.
**David Duchesne**

From Paris
**Sandrine Aubry**

From Aix-en-Provence
**Valérie Forestier**

Of Algerian heritage
**Rachid Kahlid**

And, also from
Aix-en-Provence
**Stéphane Forestier**

## *FLASH CULTURE* VIDEO PROGRAM

For one lesson in each unit, a **Flash culture** segment allows you to experience the sights and sounds of France, the French-speaking world, and the daily life of French speakers. Each segment is from two-to-three minutes long and is correlated to your textbook in one **Culture** section in each unit.

Hosted by narrators Csilla and Benjamin, these segments of specially shot footage transport you to a variety of venues: schools, parks, public squares, cafés, stores, cinemas, outdoor markets, city streets, festivals, and more. They also incorporate mini-interviews with French speakers in various walks of life, for example, family members, friends, students, and people in different professions.

The footage was filmed taking special care to capture rich, vibrant images that will expand your cultural perspectives with information directly related to the content of your textbook. In addition, the narrations were carefully written to reflect the vocabulary and grammar covered in **D'ACCORD!**

# ICONS AND *RESSOURCES* BOXES

## Icons

These icons in **D'ACCORD!** alert you to the type of activity or section involved.

| Icons legend | | |
|---|---|---|
| 🎧 Listening activity/section | Ⓢ | Additional content found on the Supersite: audio, video, and presentations |
| 🔊Ⓢ Activity also on the Supersite | 🖰Ⓢ | Additional practice on the Supersite |
| 👥 Pair activity | ▯ | Information Gap activity |
| 👥👥 Group activity | ▦ | Feuilles d'activités |
| | ♺ | Recycling activity |

- The Information Gap activities and those involving **Feuilles d'activités** (*activity sheets*) require handouts that your instructor will give you.

- The listening icon appears in **Contextes**, **Les sons et les lettres**, **À l'écoute**, and **Vocabulaire** sections.

- The video icon appears in **Roman-photo**, either one of the **Culture** sections, and **Le zapping**.

- The recycling icon tells you that to finish a specific activity you will need to use vocabulary and/or grammar learned in previous lessons.

## *Ressources* Boxes

**Ressources** boxes let you know exactly which print and technology ancillaries you can use to reinforce and expand on every section of every lesson in your textbook. They even include page numbers when applicable.

| *Ressources* boxes legend | | |
|---|---|---|
| 📄 **CE** pp. 29–30 | Cahier d'exercices | Ⓢ daccord1.vhlcentral.com | **D'ACCORD! Supersite** |
| 📄 **CA** p. 17 | Cahier d'activités | | |

# MAESTRO® Supersite

The **D'ACCORD!** Supersite, powered by **MAESTRO**®, provides a wealth of resources for both students and instructors. Icons indicate exactly which resources are available on the Supersite for each section of every lesson.

**(S)** Access to the **Supersite** comes free with the purchase of a new student text.

## LEARNING TOOLS AVAILABLE TO STUDENTS:

### • Practice

- directed practice from the textbook, including audio activities
- additional practice for every textbook section
- open-ended activities to explore and search the Internet

Practice more at **daccord1.vhlcentral.com.**

### • Audio

- Record & Compare audio activities
- All audio material related to the **D'ACCORD!** program (Vocabulary, Activities, Pronunciation Concepts)
- Talking Picture vocabulary activities

### • Streaming Video

- **Roman-photo:** These dramatic video episodes follow a group of students living in Aix-en-Provence, France.
- **Flash culture:** Appearing in one lesson per unit, specially shot footage expands on cultural topics presented in the book.
- **Le Zapping:** Authentic francophone video clips, offered on the **D'ACCORD!** Supersite, provide you with an authentic window into French-language media.

- • MP3 files for the complete **D'ACCORD!** Audio Program 🎧
  - textbook audio files
  - audio program files

- • and more…
  - Interactive Maps
  - Flashcards with audio
  - integration with the **MAESTRO®** Cahier interactif

# ACKNOWLEDGMENTS

On behalf of its authors and editors, Vista Higher Learning expresses its sincere appreciation to the many college professors nationwide who reviewed materials from **D'ACCORD!**. Their input and suggestions were vitally helpful in forming and shaping the program in its final, published form.

We also extend a special thank you to the contributing writer whose hard work was central to bringing **D'ACCORD!** to fruition: Nora Portillo.

We are especially grateful to our National Language Consultant, Norah Jones, for her continued support and feedback regarding all aspects of the text.

## In-depth reviewers

Dorothy E. Diehl
Saint Mary's University of Minnesota

Lynne Wettig
Park University, Kansas

## Reviewers

Ellen Abrams
New England Community College, MA

Norma Alvarez
College of Southern Nevada

Eileen M. Angelini
Canisius College, NY

Christine Armstrong
Denison University, OH

Michael Armstrong
Florida Atlantic University

Kathleen Attwood
Owens Community College, OH

Marty Bandini
Southwestern College, CA

Samira Belaoun
Bunker Hill Community College, MA

Maria Benson
Virginia Commonwealth University

Juan A. Bernabeu
Laramie County Community College, WY

Marie Bertola
West Valley College, CA

Kaye Bletso
Jefferson Community College, KY

Julia Bordeaux
Mansfield University, PA

Christine Boudin-Stoa
Saint Mary's University of Minnesota

Cavella Bullard
Wake Technical Community College, NC

Thomas Buresi
Southern Polytechnic State University, GA

Allegra Clement-Bayard
John Burroughs School, MO

Helene Coignet
Canisius College, NY

Margaret Colvin
Otterbein College, OH

Mary Beth Crane
College of Southern Idaho

LaVerne Dalka
Hanover College, IN

Nathalie Davaut
Rowan Cabarrus Community College, NC

David de Posada
Macon State College, GA

Linda Downing
Diablo Valley College, CA

Beth Droppleman
Columbia College, SC

Kamila Dudley
University of Hawaii

Vicki Earnest
Calhoun College, AL

Paula Egan-Wright
Laramie County Community College, WY

Natasha Engering-Ward
Justin-Siena High School, CA

Lisa C. Franks
Cabrini College, PA

Kerwin Friebel
Muskegon Community College, MI

Barbara I. Friedman
Florida Atlantic University

Trisha Frye
Salem Academy and College, NC

Maria Gardeta-Healey
Mesa Community College, AZ

Sophie Gelaw
University of the Virgin Islands

Virginie Gindoff
Plymouth State University, NH

Martha Grant
Falmouth High School, ME

Stella Greenbaum
The Hun School of Princeton, NJ

Sue Grove
Riverland Community College, MN

Luc Guglielmi
Kennesaw State University, GA

Nathan Guss
Clemson University, SC

Kwaku A. Gyasi
University of Alabama in Huntsville

B. Sabastian Hobson
Northern Virginia Community College

Jessica Hoy
Illinois State University

Rejane Jehanno
Pacific Union College, CA

Zhen Ji
Our Lady of the Lake University, TX

E. Joe Johnson
Clayton State University, GA

Nikki L. Kaltenbach
Indiana University Northwest

Ann Kirkland
Hanover College, IN

Ute S. Lahaie
Gardner-Webb University, NC

Stanley F. Levine
University of South Carolina Aiken

Leanne Lindelof
San Jose State University, CA

Oksana Lutsyshyna
University of South Florida

Olivia Marancy-Ferrer
North Broward Preparatory School, FL

Jackie Mauldin
Gainsville State College, GA

Kitzie McKinney
Bentley College, MA

Mireille McNabb
West Valley College, CA

Sylvie Merlier-Rowen
Shoshana S. Cardin School, MD

Cedric Michel
University of South Florida

Isabelle Miller
Bellevue Community College, WA

Doug Mrazek
Clark College, WA

Martine Motard-Noar
McDaniel College, MD

Shonu Nangia
Louisiana State University at Alexandria

Justin Niati
Houghton College, NY

Eva Norling
Bellevue Community College, WA

Leslie Norman
Gonzaga University, WA

Marie-Noelle Olivier
University of Nevada, Las Vegas

Scooter Pegram
Indiana University Northwest

Christiane E. Reese
Florida Atlantic University, FL

Anna K. Sandstrom
University of New Hampshire

Amy Sawyer
Clemson University, SC

Lisa F. Signori
Erskine College, SC

Virginia Stamanis
The Meadows School, NV

Janis Tansey
Pine Crest School, FL

Maria-Elena Torales
Imperial Valley College, CA

Michael Vermy
Fullerton College, CA

Nirva Vernet
Virginia Commonwealth University

Terri Woellner
University of Denver, CO

Lisa Yigit
North Broward Preparatory, FL

Samuel Zadi
Wheaton College, IL

Elizabeth Zwanziger
Wartburg College, IA

# Salut!

UNITÉ 1

### Pour commencer
- What are these girls saying?
  a. Excusez-moi.  b. Bonjour!  c. Merci.
- How many girls are there in the photo?
  a. une  b. deux  c. trois
- What do you think is an appropriate title for either of these girls?
  a. Monsieur  b. Madame  c. Mademoiselle

## Unit Goals

**Leçon 1A**

In this lesson, students will learn:
- terms for greetings, farewells, and introductions
- expressions of courtesy
- the French alphabet and the names of accent marks
- about shaking hands and **bises**
- more about greetings and farewells through specially shot video footage
- gender of nouns
- articles (definite and indefinite)
- the numbers 0–60
- the expression **il y a**
- about the company Moulinex

**Leçon 1B**

In this lesson, students will learn:
- terms to identify people
- terms for objects in the classroom
- rules for silent letters
- about France's multicultural society
- subject pronouns
- the present tense of **être**
- **c'est** and **il/elle est**
- adjective agreement
- some descriptive adjectives and adjectives of nationality
- to listen for familiar words

**Savoir-faire**

In this section, students will learn:
- cultural, linguistic, and historical information about the francophone world
- to recognize cognates
- strategies for writing in French
- to write a telephone/address book

**Pour commencer**
- b. Bonjour!
- b. deux
- c. Mademoiselle

---

**R E S O U R C E S**

**Student Materials**
**Print:** Student Book, Workbooks (*Cahier d'exercices, Cahier d'activités*)
**Technology:** MAESTRO® *Cahier interactif* and Supersite (Audio, Video, Practice)

**Teacher Materials**
DVDs (*Roman-photo, Flash culture*)
Teacher's Resources (Scripts, Answer Keys, Testing Program)
Audio CDs (Testing Program, Textbook, Audio Program)

MAESTRO® Supersite: Student Supersite Content; Planning and Teaching Resources (Overheads, *PowerPoints*, Lesson Plans, Information Gaps and *Feuilles d'activités*); Learning Management System (Gradebook, Assignments); Audio MP3s and Streaming Video
**D'ACCORD! 1 Supersite:** daccord1.vhlcentral.com

## Section Goals

In this section, students will learn and practice vocabulary related to:
• basic greetings and farewells
• introductions
• courtesy expressions

## Key Standards

1.1, 1.2, 4.1

**Student Resources**
*Cahier d'exercices*, pp. 1–2;
*Cahier d'activités*, p. 115;
Supersite: Activities,
*Cahier interactif*

**Teacher Resources**
Answer Keys; Overheads #13, #14; Audio Script; Textbook & Audio Activity MP3s/CD; Testing program: Vocabulary Quiz

## Suggestions

• To familiarize students with the meanings of headings used in the lessons and important vocabulary for classroom interactions, point students to the frontmatter in their textbooks.
• For complete lesson plans, go to **daccord1.vhlcentral.com** to access the teacher's part of the **D'accord!** companion Supersite.
• With books closed, write a few greetings, farewells, and courtesy expressions on the board, explain their meaning, and model their pronunciation. Circulate around the room, greeting students, making introductions, and encouraging responses. Then, have students open their books to pages 2–3. Ask them to identify which conversations are exchanges between friends and which seem more formal. Then point out the use of **vous** vs. **tu** in each conversation. Give examples of different situations in which each form would be appropriate.

## Successful Language Learning
Encourage students to make flash cards to help them memorize or review vocabulary.

---

**Leçon 1A**

**You will learn how to...**
- greet people in French
- say good-bye

**Talking Picture
Audio: Activity**

# Ça va?

**GEORGES** Ça va, Henri?
**HENRI** Oui, ça va très bien, merci. Et vous, comment allez-vous?
**GEORGES** Je vais bien, merci.

**PAUL** Merci!
**JEAN** Il n'y a pas de quoi.

**MARIE** À plus tard, Guillaume!
**GUILLAUME** À tout à l'heure, Marie!

**JACQUES** Bonjour, Monsieur Boniface. Je vous présente Thérèse Lemaire.
**M. BONIFACE** Bonjour, Mademoiselle.
**THÉRÈSE** Enchantée.

## Vocabulaire

| | |
|---|---|
| Bonsoir. | Good evening.; Hello. |
| À bientôt. | See you soon. |
| À demain. | See you tomorrow. |
| Bonne journée! | Have a good day! |
| Au revoir. | Good-bye. |
| Comme ci, comme ça. | So-so. |
| Je vais bien/mal. | I am doing well/badly. |
| Moi aussi. | Me too. |
| Comment t'appelles-tu? *(fam.)* | What is your name? |
| Je vous/te présente... *(form./fam.)* | I would like to introduce (name) to you. |
| De rien. | You're welcome. |
| Excusez-moi. *(form.)* | Excuse me. |
| Excuse-moi. *(fam.)* | Excuse me. |
| Merci beaucoup. | Thanks a lot. |
| Pardon. | Pardon (me). |
| S'il vous plaît. *(form.)* | Please. |
| S'il te plaît. *(fam.)* | Please. |
| Je vous/t'en prie. *(form./fam.)* | You're welcome.; It's nothing. |
| Monsieur (M.) | Sir (Mr.) |
| Madame (Mme) | Ma'am (Mrs.) |
| Mademoiselle (Mlle) | Miss |
| ici | here |
| là | there |
| là-bas | over there |

**ressources**

CE pp. 1–2 | CA p. 115 | daccord1.vhlcentral.com

**2** *deux*

---

**O P T I O N S**

**Language Notes** Point out that **Salut** and **À plus**, the shortened form of **À plus tard**, are familiar expressions. Explain that the translation of **Je vais bien/mal** is not literal. **Je vais** means *I go*, but **je vais bien** means *I am doing well*.

**Using Games** Divide the class into two teams. Create sentences and questions based on the **Vocabulaire** and the illustrated conversations. Choose one person at a time, alternating between teams. Tell students to respond logically to your statement or question. Award a point for each correct response. The team with the most points at the end of the game wins.

## Attention!

In French, people can be addressed formally or informally. Use the **tu/toi** forms with close friends, family, or children. Use the **vous** forms with groups, a boss, adults, or someone you do not know, unless they ask you to use **tu**.

**MARC** Bonjour, je m'appelle Marc, et vous, comment vous appelez-vous?
**ANNIE** Je m'appelle Annie.
**MARC** Enchanté.

**SOPHIE** Bonjour, Catherine!
**CATHERINE** Salut, Sophie!
**SOPHIE** Ça va?
**CATHERINE** Oui, ça va bien, merci. Et toi, comment vas-tu?
**SOPHIE** Pas mal.

# Mise en pratique

**1** **Chassez l'intrus** Circle the word or expression that does not belong.

1. a. Bonjour.
   b. Bonsoir.
   c. Salut.
   d. Pardon. *(circled)*

2. a. Bien.
   b. Très bien.
   c. De rien. *(circled)*
   d. Comme ci, comme ça.

3. a. À bientôt.
   b. À demain.
   c. À tout à l'heure.
   d. Enchanté. *(circled)*

4. a. Comment allez-vous?
   b. Comment vous appelez-vous? *(circled)*
   c. Ça va?
   d. Comment vas-tu?

5. a. Pas mal. *(circled)*
   b. Excuse-moi.
   c. Je vous en prie.
   d. Il n'y a pas de quoi.

6. a. Comment vous appelez-vous?
   b. Je vous présente Dominique.
   c. Enchanté.
   d. Comment allez-vous? *(circled)*

7. a. Pas mal.
   b. Très bien.
   c. Mal.
   d. Et vous? *(circled)*

8. a. Comment allez-vous?
   b. Comment vous appelez-vous?
   c. Et toi? *(circled)*
   d. Je vous en prie.

**2** **Écoutez** Listen to each of these questions or statements and select the most appropriate response.

| | | | |
|---|---|---|---|
| 1. Enchanté. | ☐ | Je m'appelle Thérèse. | ☑ |
| 2. Merci beaucoup. | ☐ | Je vous en prie. | ☑ |
| 3. Comme ci, comme ça. | ☑ | De rien. | ☐ |
| 4. Bonsoir, Monsieur. | ☑ | Moi aussi. | ☐ |
| 5. Enchanté. | ☑ | Et toi? | ☐ |
| 6. Bonjour. | ☐ | À demain. | ☑ |
| 7. Pas mal. | ☑ | Pardon. | ☐ |
| 8. Il n'y a pas de quoi. | ☑ | Moi aussi. | ☐ |
| 9. Enchanté. | ☐ | Très bien. Et vous? | ☑ |
| 10. À bientôt. | ☑ | Mal. | ☐ |

**3** **Conversez** Madeleine is introducing her classmate Khaled to Libby, an American exchange student. Complete their conversation, using a different expression from **CONTEXTES** in each blank. *Answers will vary.*

**MADELEINE** (1) _____!

**KHALED** Salut, Madeleine. (2) _____?

**MADELEINE** Pas mal. (3) _____?

**KHALED** (4) _____, merci.

**MADELEINE** (5) _____ Libby. Elle est de (*She is from*) Boston.

**KHALED** (6) _____ Libby. (7) _____ Khaled. (8) _____?

**LIBBY** (9) _____, merci.

**KHALED** Oh, là, là. Je vais rater (*I am going to miss*) le bus. À bientôt.

**MADELEINE** (10) _____.

**LIBBY** (11) _____.

Practice more at **daccord1.vhlcentral.com**.

*trois* 3

---

**1 Suggestion** Go over the answers with the class and have students explain why each expression does not belong.

**2 Script**
1. Comment vous appelez-vous?
2. Excusez-moi.
3. Comment allez-vous?
4. Bonsoir, Mademoiselle.
5. Je te présente Thérèse.
6. À bientôt.
7. Comment vas-tu?
8. Merci.
9. Bonjour, comment allez-vous?
10. Au revoir.
*(On Textbook Audio)*

**2 Suggestion** Before students listen, tell them to read the possible responses provided and write down the questions or statements that they think would elicit each response. After completing the listening activity, go over the answers to check whether students' predictions were accurate.

**3 Suggestion** Have students work in groups of three on the activity. Tell them to choose a role and complete the conversation. Then ask groups to act out their conversation for the class.

---

**OPTIONS**

**Scrambled Conversations** Have students work in pairs. Tell them to write an original conversation with six to eight lines. After completing this task, they should rewrite the conversation and scramble the order of the sentences. Have pairs exchange their scrambled conversations and put them in a logical order. Remind students that they should verify the answers.

**Role-playing** Have small groups role-play a conversation in which adults, children, and high school-age people interact. Remind students to use formal and informal expressions in the appropriate situations. Give them time to prepare, and then have a few groups present their conversations to the class.

**4 Suggestions**
- Before beginning the activity, encourage students to use as many different words and expressions as they can from the **Vocabulaire** on page 2 rather than repeating the same expressions in each conversation.
- Have a few volunteers write their conversations on the board. Ask the class to identify, correct, and explain any errors.

**4 Expansions**
- Have students look at the photo, identify the conversation it most likely corresponds to (**Conversation 1**), and explain their reasoning. Point out that nearly all formal greetings are accompanied by a handshake. Tell the class that they will learn more about gestures used in greetings in the **Culture** section of this lesson.
- Have students rewrite **Conversation 1** in the formal register, and **Conversations 2** and **3** in the informal register.

**5 Suggestions**
- Before beginning this activity, ask students if they would use **tu** or **vous** in each situation.
- If class time is limited, assign a specific situation to each pair.
- Call on volunteers to act out their conversations for the class.

**6 Suggestion** Have two volunteers read the **modèle** aloud. Remind students to use **vous** when addressing more than one classmate at a time.

## Communication

**4** **Discutez** With a partner, complete these conversations. Then act them out. Answers will vary.

Conversation 1   Salut! Je m'appelle François. Et toi, comment t'appelles-tu?

_____

Ça va?

_____

Conversation 2   _____

Comme ci, comme ça. Et vous?

_____

Bon (*Well*), à demain.

_____

Conversation 3   Bonsoir, je vous présente Mademoiselle Barnard.

_____

Enchanté(e).

_____

Très bien, merci. Et vous?

_____

**5** **C'est à vous!** How would you greet these people, ask them for their names, and ask them how they are doing? With a partner, write a short dialogue for each item and act it out. Pay attention to the use of **tu** and **vous.** Answers will vary.

1. **Madame Colombier**   2. **Mademoiselle Estèves**

3. **Monsieur Marchand**   4. **Marie, Guillaume et Geneviève**

**6** **Présentations** Form groups of three. Introduce yourself, and ask your partners their names and how they are doing. Then, join another group and take turns introducing your partners. Answers will vary.

**MODÈLE**

**Élève 1:** *Bonjour. Je m'appelle Fatima. Et vous?*
**Élève 2:** *Je m'appelle Fabienne.*
**Élève 3:** *Et moi, je m'appelle Antoine. Ça va?*
**Élève 1:** *Ça va bien, merci. Et toi?*
**Élève 3:** *Comme ci, comme ça.*

**O P T I O N S**

**Using Categories** Read some sentences to the class and ask if they would use them with another student of the same age or an older person. Examples: **1. Je te présente Guillaume.** (student) **2. Merci beaucoup, Monsieur.** (older person) **3. Comment vas-tu?** (student) **4. Bonjour, professeur _____.** (older person) **5. Comment vous appelez-vous?** (older person)

**Mini-conversations** Have students circulate around the classroom and conduct mini-conversations in French with other students, using the words and expressions they learned on pages 2–3. As students are carrying out the activity, move around the room, monitoring their work and offering assistance if requested.

# Les sons et les lettres

Audio: Concepts, Activities
Record & Compare

## 🎧 The French alphabet

The French alphabet is made up of the same 26 letters as the English alphabet. While they look the same, some letters are pronounced differently. They also sound different when you spell.

| lettre | | exemple | lettre | | exemple | lettre | | exemple |
|--------|---|---------|--------|---|---------|--------|---|---------|
| a | (a) | **a**dresse | j | (ji) | **j**ustice | s | (esse) | **s**pécial |
| b | (bé) | **b**anane | k | (ka) | **k**ilomètre | t | (té) | **t**able |
| c | (cé) | **c**arotte | l | (elle) | **l**ion | u | (u) | **u**nique |
| d | (dé) | **d**essert | m | (emme) | **m**ariage | v | (vé) | **v**idéo |
| e | (e) | r**e**belle | n | (enne) | **n**ature | w | (double vé) | **w**agon |
| f | (effe) | **f**ragile | o | (o) | **o**live | x | (iks) | **x**ylophone |
| g | (gé) | **g**enre | p | (pé) | **p**ersonne | y | (i grec) | **y**oga |
| h | (hache) | **h**éritage | q | (ku) | **q**uiche | z | (zède) | **z**éro |
| i | (i) | **i**nnocent | r | (erre) | **r**adio | | | |

Notice that some letters in French words have accents. You'll learn how they influence pronunciation in later lessons. Whenever you spell a word in French, include the name of the accent after the letter. For double letters, use **deux: ss = deux s.**

| accent | nom | exemple | orthographe |
|--------|-----|---------|-------------|
| ´ | *accent aigu* | **identité** | I-D-E-N-T-I-T-E-accent aigu |
| ` | *accent grave* | **problème** | P-R-O-B-L-E-accent grave-M-E |
| ^ | *accent circonflexe* | **hôpital** | H-O-accent circonflexe-P-I-T-A-L |
| ¨ | *tréma* | **naïve** | N-A-I-tréma-V-E |
| ¸ | *cédille* | **ça** | C-cédille-A |

🔊 **L'alphabet** Practice saying the French alphabet and example words aloud.

🔊 **Ça s'écrit comment?** Spell these words aloud in French.

1. judo
2. yacht
3. forêt
4. zèbre
5. existe
6. clown
7. numéro
8. français
9. musique
10. favorite
11. kangourou
12. parachute
13. différence
14. intelligent
15. dictionnaire
16. alphabet

🔊 **Dictons** Practice reading these sayings aloud.

*Grande invitation, petites portions.*[1]

*Tout est bien qui finit bien.*[2]

*Lundi* ∘ *Mardi*

[1] Great boast, small roast.
[2] All's well that ends well.

*cinq* **5**

## Section Goals
In this section, students will learn about:
• the French alphabet and how it contrasts with the English alphabet
• the names of the letters
• the names of the accent marks

## Key Standards
4.1

**Student Resources**
*Cahier d'activités,* p. 116;
Supersite: Activities,
*Cahier interactif*
**Teacher Resources**
Answer Keys; Audio Script;
Textbook & Audio Activity
MP3s/CD

## Suggestions
• Model the pronunciation of the French alphabet and the example words. Have students repeat.
• Point out that vowel sounds can have many different pronunciations when combined with other vowels or when spelled with accents, particularly the **e.**
• Point out the different diacritical marks and model their pronunciation. For a detailed explanation of **l'accent aigu** and **l'accent grave**, see **Leçon 3A**, page 77. For an explanation of **l'accent circonflexe, le tréma,** and **la cédille**, see **Leçon 3B**, page 91.
• Draw attention to any posters, signs, or maps in the classroom. Point out individual letters, and ask the class to identify them in French.
• Write on the board the French abbreviations of several famous organizations (Examples: **ONU, OPEP**), and have students spell them in French. Explain what each abbreviation represents: **ONU** = **l'Organisation des Nations Unies** (*United Nations, UN*); **OPEP** = **l'Organisation des pays exportateurs de pétrole** (*Organization of Petroleum-Exporting Countries, OPEC*).
• Have students work on the **Ça s'écrit comment?** activity in pairs.
• The explanation and exercises are available on the Supersite. You may want to play them in class so students hear French speakers other than yourself.

**OPTIONS**

**Mini-dictée** Do a dictation activity in which you spell out a list of words in French to the class. Spell each word twice to allow students sufficient time to write. After you have finished, write your list on the board or project it on a transparency and have students check their work.

**Making Friends** Tell students to greet two classmates that they haven't met yet, ask each person his or her name, and ask the person to spell the last name as they write it down. Tell them to verify the spelling with the person to make sure it is correct. Before beginning the activity, write this question on the board and model the pronunciation: **Comment s'écrit** *last name*?

## Section Goals

In this section, students will learn functional phrases for making introductions and speaking on the telephone through comprehensible input.

## Key Standards

1.2, 2.1, 2.2, 4.1, 4.2

**Student Resources**
*Cahier d'activités*, pp. 67–68;
Supersite: Activities,
*Cahier interactif*
**Teacher Resources**
Answer Keys; Video Script & Translation; *Roman-photo* video

**Video Synopsis** Sandrine buys a magazine at Monsieur Hulot's newsstand. At **Le P'tit Bistrot**, Rachid introduces David, his American friend, to Sandrine and Amina. Madame Forestier (Valérie), who owns the café, gets a phone call from her son's high school French teacher because he didn't do well on his French exam. Stéphane tells Rachid to introduce David to his mother so he can avoid talking to her.

## Suggestions

• Have students cover the French captions and guess the plot based only on the video stills. Write their predictions on the board.
• Have students volunteer to read the characters' parts in the **Roman-photo** aloud. Then have them get together in groups of eight to act out the episode.
• After students have read the **Roman-photo**, quickly review their predictions, and ask them which ones were correct.
• Point out that 100 centimes = 1 euro, the monetary unit of the European Union, which includes France.

**Au café** Video: *Roman-photo* Record & Compare

**PERSONNAGES**

Amina

David

Monsieur Hulot

Michèle

Rachid

Sandrine

Stéphane

Valérie

*Au kiosque...*
**SANDRINE** Bonjour, Monsieur Hulot!
**M. HULOT** Bonjour, Mademoiselle Aubry! Comment allez-vous?
**SANDRINE** Très bien, merci! Et vous?
**M. HULOT** Euh, ça va. Voici 45 (quarante-cinq) centimes. Bonne journée!
**SANDRINE** Merci, au revoir!

*À la terrasse du café...*
**AMINA** Salut!
**SANDRINE** Bonjour, Amina. Ça va?
**AMINA** Ben... ça va. Et toi?
**SANDRINE** Oui, je vais bien, merci.
**AMINA** Regarde! Voilà Rachid et... un ami?

**RACHID** Bonjour!
**AMINA ET SANDRINE** Salut!
**RACHID** Je vous présente un ami, David Duchesne.
**SANDRINE** Je m'appelle Sandrine.
**DAVID** Enchanté.

**STÉPHANE** Oh, non! Madame Richard! Le professeur de français!
**DAVID** Il y a un problème?

**STÉPHANE** Oui! L'examen de français! Présentez-vous, je vous en prie!

**VALÉRIE** Oh... l'examen de français! Oui, merci, merci Madame Richard, merci beaucoup! De rien, au revoir!

**A C T I V I T É S**

**1** **Vrai ou faux?** Decide whether each statement is **vrai** or **faux**. Correct the false statements. Answers may vary.

1. Sandrine va (*is doing*) bien. Vrai.
2. Sandrine et Amina sont (*are*) amies. Vrai.
3. David est français. Faux. David est américain.
4. David est de Washington. Vrai.
5. Rachid présente son frère (*his brother*) David à Sandrine et Amina. Faux. Rachid présente son ami David à Sandrine et à Amina.

6. Stéphane est étudiant à l'université. Faux. Stéphane est au lycée.
7. Il y a un problème avec l'examen de sciences politiques. Faux. Il y a un problème avec l'examen de français.
8. Amina, Rachid et Sandrine sont (*are*) à Paris. Faux. Amina, Rachid et Sandrine sont à Aix-en-Provence.
9. Michèle est au P'tit Bistrot. Vrai.
10. Madame Richard est le professeur de Stéphane. Vrai.
11. Valérie va mal. Vrai.
12. Rachid a (*has*) cours de français dans 30 minutes. Faux. Rachid a cours de sciences politiques dans 30 minutes.

🛰 Practice more at **daccord1.vhlcentral.com.**

**O P T I O N S**

**Video Tips** General suggestions for using video clips in the classroom can be found in the frontmatter of this Teacher's Annotated Edition.
**Avant de regarder la vidéo** Before showing the video episode, have students brainstorm some greetings and some other expressions that they might hear in an episode in which some of the characters meet each other for the first time.

**Regarder la vidéo** Play the episode once and tell the class to listen for basic greetings. After the video is over, have students recall the greetings they heard and write them on the board. Show the episode again and ask the class to write down all of the courtesy expressions that they hear, including ways to say *pleased to meet you.*

Les étudiants se retrouvent (*meet*) au café.

**DAVID** Et toi..., comment t'appelles-tu?
**AMINA** Je m'appelle Amina.
**RACHID** David est un étudiant américain. Il est de Washington, la capitale des États-Unis.
**AMINA** Ah, oui! Bienvenue à Aix-en-Provence.
**RACHID** Bon..., à tout à l'heure.
**SANDRINE** À bientôt, David.

*À l'intérieur (inside) du café...*
**MICHÈLE** Allô. Le P'tit Bistrot. Oui, un moment, s'il vous plaît. Madame Forestier! Le lycée de Stéphane.
**VALÉRIE** Allô. Oui. Bonjour, Madame Richard. Oui. Oui. Stéphane? Il y a un problème au lycée?

**RACHID** Bonjour, Madame Forestier. Comment allez-vous?
**VALÉRIE** Ah, ça va mal.
**RACHID** Oui? Moi, je vais bien. Je vous présente David Duchesne, étudiant américain de Washington.

**DAVID** Bonjour, Madame. Enchanté!
**RACHID** Ah, j'ai cours de sciences politiques dans 30 (trente) minutes. Au revoir, Madame Forestier. À tout à l'heure, David.

## Expressions utiles

### Introductions
- **David est un étudiant américain. Il est de Washington.**
  *David is an American student. He's from Washington.*
- **Présentez-vous, je vous en prie!**
  *Introduce yourselves, please!*
- **Il/Elle s'appelle...**
  *His/Her name is...*
- **Bienvenue à Aix-en-Provence.**
  *Welcome to Aix-en-Provence.*

### Speaking on the telephone
- **Allô.**
  *Hello.*
- **Un moment, s'il vous plaît.**
  *One moment, please.*

### Additional vocabulary
- **Regarde! Voilà Rachid et... un ami?**
  *Look! There's Rachid and... a friend?*
- **J'ai cours de sciences politiques dans 30 (trente) minutes.**
  *I have political science class in thirty minutes.*
- **Il y a un problème au lycée?**
  *Is there a problem at the high school?*

| | |
|---|---|
| • **Il y a...** *There is/are...* | • **euh** *um* |
| • **Il/Elle est** *He/She is...* | • **bon** *well; good* |
| • **Voici...** *Here's...* | • **centimes** *cents* |
| • **Voilà...** *There's...* | |

**2** **Complétez** Fill in the blanks with the words from the list. Refer to the video scenes as necessary.

1. ___Bienvenue___ à Aix-en-Provence.
2. Il est de Washington, la ___capitale___ des États-Unis.
3. ___Voici___ 45 (quarante-cinq) centimes. Bonne journée!
4. J'___ai___ cours de sciences politiques.
5. David ___est___ un étudiant américain.

| ai | est |
|---|---|
| bienvenue | voici |
| capitale | |

**3** **Conversez** In groups of three, write a conversation where you introduce an exchange student to a friend. Be prepared to present your conversation to the class.

ressources

CA
pp. 67–68

daccord1.vhlcentral.com

A
C
T
I
V
I
T
É
S

**S** Video: *Flash culture*

CULTURE À LA LOUPE

# La poignée de main ou la bise?

**French friends and relatives usually exchange a kiss (la bise) on alternating cheeks whenever they meet and again when they say good-bye.** Friends of friends may also kiss when introduced, even though they have just met. This is particularly true among students and young adults. It is normal for men of the same family to exchange **la bise**; otherwise, men generally greet one another with a handshake (**la poignée de main**). As the map shows, the number of kisses varies from place to place in France. In some regions, two kisses (one on each cheek) is the standard while in others, people may exchange as many as four kisses. Whatever the number, each kiss is accompanied by a slight kissing sound.

Unless they are also friends, business acquaintances and coworkers usually shake hands each time they meet and do so again upon leaving. A French handshake is brief and firm, with a single downward motion.

**Combien de** *How many*

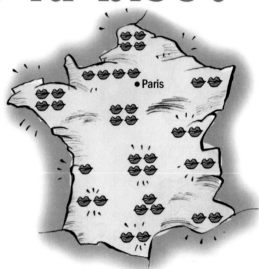

**Combien de° bises?**

**Coup de main**

If you are not sure whether you should shake hands or kiss someone, or if you don't know which side to start on, you can always follow the other person's lead.

**A C T I V I T É S**

**1** **Vrai ou faux?** Indicate whether each statement is **vrai** or **faux**. Correct any false statements.

1. In northwestern France, giving four kisses is common. Vrai.

2. Business acquaintances usually kiss one another on the cheek. Faux. They usually shake hands.

3. French people may give someone they've just met **la bise**. Vrai.

4. **Bises** exchanged between French men at a family gathering are common. Vrai.

5. In a business setting, French people often shake hands when they meet each day and again when they leave. Vrai.

6. When shaking hands, French people prefer a long and soft handshake. Faux. A French handshake is brief and firm.

7. The number of kisses given can vary from one region to another. Vrai.

8. It is customary for kisses to be given silently. Faux. Each kiss is accompanied by a slight kissing sound.

**S** Practice more at **daccord1.vhlcentral.com**.

**OPTIONS**

**La bise** Tell students that, although people in some social circles in the United States commonly kiss each other on the cheek once, this is not common practice in France. It could be considered impolite to give only one **bise** since the other person would be waiting for the second kiss. In some regions of France and Switzerland, people may even give three **bises**, but just one is rare.

**Using Games** Divide the class into two teams. Indicate one team member at a time, alternating teams. Give situations in which people greet each other. Students should say if the people should greet each other with **la poignée de main** or **la bise**. Examples: female friends (**la bise**); male and female business associates (**la poignée de main**). Give a point for each correct answer. The team with the most points at the end wins.

## LE FRANÇAIS QUOTIDIEN

### Les salutations

| | |
|---|---|
| **À la prochaine!** | *Until next time!* |
| **À plus!** | *See you later!* |
| **Ciao!** | *Bye!* |
| **Coucou!** | *Hi there!/Hey!* |
| **Pas grand-chose.** | *Nothing much.* |
| **Quoi de neuf?** | *What's new?* |
| **Rien de nouveau.** | *Nothing new.* |

## LE MONDE FRANCOPHONE

### Les bonnes manières

In any country, an effort to speak the native language is appreciated. Using titles of respect and a few polite expressions, such as **excusez-moi**, **merci**, and **s'il vous plaît**, can take you a long way when conversing with native Francophones.

#### Dos and don'ts in the francophone world:

**France** Always greet shopkeepers upon entering a store and say good-bye upon leaving.

**Northern Africa** Use your right hand when handing items to others.

**Quebec Province** Make eye contact when shaking hands.

**Sub-Saharan Africa** Do not show the soles of your feet when sitting.

**Switzerland** Do not litter or jaywalk.

## PORTRAIT

# Aix-en-Provence: ville d'eau, ville d'art°

Aix-en-Provence is a vibrant university town that welcomes international students. Its main boulevard, **le cours Mirabeau**, is great for people-watching or just relaxing in a sidewalk café. One can see many beautiful fountains, traditional and ethnic restaurants, and the daily vegetable and flower market among the winding, narrow streets of **la vieille ville** (*old town*).

Aix is also renowned for its dedication to the arts, hosting numerous cultural festivals every year such as **le Festival International d'Art Lyrique**, and **Aix en Musique**. For centuries, artists have been drawn to Provence for its natural beauty and its unique quality of light. Paul Cézanne, artist and native son of Provence, spent his days painting the surrounding countryside.

Paris ✵
LA
FRANCE
Aix-en-Provence ●

**ville d'eau, ville d'art** *city of water, city of art*

### SUR INTERNET

**What behaviors are socially unacceptable in French-speaking countries?**

Go to **daccord1.vhlcentral.com** to find more information related to this **CULTURE** section. Then watch the corresponding **Flash culture.**

---

**2** **Les bonnes manières** In which places might these behaviors be particularly offensive?

1. littering
   Switzerland
2. offering a business card with your left hand
   Northern Africa
3. sitting with the bottom of your foot facing your host
   Sub-Saharan Africa
4. failing to greet a salesperson
   France
5. looking away when shaking hands
   Quebec Province

**3** **À vous** With a partner, practice meeting and greeting people in French in various social situations.

1. Your good friend from Provence introduces you to her close friend.
2. You walk into your neighborhood bakery.
3. You arrive for an interview with a prospective employer.

**ressources**

CA
pp. 99–100

Ⓢ
daccord1.vhlcentral.com

**A C T I V I T É S**

---

- Model the pronunciation of each expression and have students repeat.
- Tell students to list all the situations they can think of in which they could use these expressions. Then have them compare their lists in pairs or small groups.

**Portrait** Mention that Aix-en-Provence is often referred to simply as Aix. Ask students why they think Aix is called **ville d'eau, ville d'art** in the title. Tell them that the Romans made Aix famous for its thermal baths. Then ask if they would like to visit Aix, and which aspects of the town attract them the most.

**Le monde francophone** Ask students which dos and don'ts in the francophone world should be followed in the anglophone world, too. Have the class think of logical reasons for following each custom or social convention, especially for North Africa and Sub-Saharan Africa. Example: In North Africa, the left hand is reserved for using the toilets.

**Sur Internet** Point out to students that they will find supporting activities and information at **daccord1. vhlcentral.com.**

**2** **Suggestion** Have students check their answers with a partner.

**3** **Suggestion** Before beginning this activity, ask students if they would use **tu** or **vous** in each situation. Remind them to use appropriate gestures and manners.

**Flash culture** Tell students that they will learn more about greetings and farewells in French by watching a variety of real-life images narrated by Csilla. Show the video segment, then have students jot down in French at least three examples of situations or things they saw. You can also use the activities in the video manual in class to reinforce this **Flash culture** or assign them as homework.

---

**Cultural Activity** Have students choose one of these topics to research on the Internet: **Aix-en-Provence, le Festival International d'Art Lyrique, Aix en Musique,** or **Paul Cézanne.** Tell them to come to the next class with printouts of two photos illustrating their topic and a sentence or two in French, if possible, about each photo. Divide the class into groups of three or four students so that they can present the material to one another while looking at the images.

**Mini-skits** Have students work in groups of three or four. Tell them to create an informal conversation using the expressions in **Le français quotidien** and appropriate gestures. Have a few groups act out their conversations for the class.

## Section Goals

In this section, students will learn:
- gender and number of nouns
- definite and indefinite articles

## Key Standards

4.1, 5.1

**Student Resources**
*Cahier d'exercices*, pp. 3-4;
*Cahier d'activités*, p. 117;
Supersite: Activities,
*Cahier interactif*

**Teacher Resources**
Answer Keys; Audio Script;
Audio Activity MP3s/CD;
*Feuilles d'activités;* Testing
program: Grammar Quiz

## Suggestions

- Explain what a noun is by giving examples of people (**professeur**), places (**café**), things (**examen**), and ideas (**problème**). Then write these nouns on the board: **ami, amie, cours, télévision**. Point out the gender of each noun. Explain that nouns for male beings are usually masculine, and nouns for female beings are usually feminine. All other nouns can be either masculine or feminine. Tell students that they should memorize the gender of a noun along with the word.
- Explain that **étudiant(e)** *usually* refers to a college student, while **élève**, which students will learn in Leçon 1B, refers more commonly to students of high school age or younger.
- Write these nouns on the board: **professeur, professeurs, étudiante, étudiantes**. Ask students to point out the singular and plural nouns. Then have students pronounce the words. Point out that the final **-s** is not pronounced in French.
- Write these words on the board: **le café, les cafés, l'ami, les amis, la personne, les personnes**. Explain the use of the definite article. Point out that singular nouns beginning with a vowel or silent **h** use **l'**.
- Follow the same procedure for indefinite articles using these words: **un café, des cafés, un ami, des amis, une personne, des personnes**. Point out that the **-n** of **un** is pronounced before a vowel.

## 1A.1 Nouns and articles

**Point de départ** A noun designates a person, place, or thing. As in English, nouns in French have number (singular or plural). However, French nouns also have gender (masculine or feminine).

| masculine singular | masculine plural | feminine singular | feminine plural |
|---|---|---|---|
| **le café** | **les cafés** | **la bibliothèque** | **les bibliothèques** |
| *the café* | *the cafés* | *the library* | *the libraries* |

- Nouns that designate a male are usually masculine. Nouns that designate a female are usually feminine.

| masculine | | feminine | |
|---|---|---|---|
| **l'acteur** | *the actor* | **l'actrice** | *the actress* |
| **l'ami** | *the (male) friend* | **l'amie** | *the (female) friend* |
| **le chanteur** | *the (male) singer* | **la chanteuse** | *the (female) singer* |
| **l'étudiant** | *the (male) student* | **l'étudiante** | *the (female) student* |
| **le petit ami** | *the boyfriend* | **la petite amie** | *the girlfriend* |

- Some nouns can be used to designate either a male or a female regardless of their grammatical gender.

| **le professeur** | **la personne** |
|---|---|
| *the (male or female) teacher, professor* | *the (male or female) person* |

- Nouns for objects that have no natural gender can be either masculine or feminine.

| masculine | | feminine | |
|---|---|---|---|
| **le bureau** | *the office; desk* | **la chose** | *the thing* |
| **le lycée** | *the high school* | **la différence** | *the difference* |
| **l'examen** | *the test, exam* | **la faculté** | *the university; faculty* |
| **l'objet** | *the object* | **la littérature** | *literature* |
| **l'ordinateur** | *the computer* | **la sociologie** | *sociology* |
| **le problème** | *the problem* | **l'université** | *the university* |

- You can usually form the plural of a noun by adding **-s**, regardless of gender. However, in the case of words that end in **-eau** in the singular, add **-x** to the end to form the plural. For most nouns ending in **-al**, drop the **-al** and add **-aux**.

| | singular | | plural | |
|---|---|---|---|---|
| typical masculine noun | **l'objet** | *the object* | **les objets** | *the objects* |
| typical feminine noun | **la télévision** | *the television* | **les télévisions** | *the televisions* |
| noun ending in **-eau** | **le bureau** | *the office* | **les bureaux** | *the offices* |
| noun ending in **-al** | **l'animal** | *the animal* | **les animaux** | *the animals* |

**1** **Les singuliers et les pluriels** Make the singular nouns plural, and vice versa.

1. l'actrice
les actrices
2. les lycées
le lycée
3. les différences
la différence
4. la chose
les choses
5. le bureau
les bureaux
6. le café
les cafés
7. les librairies
la librairie
8. la faculté
les facultés
9. les acteurs
l'acteur
10. l'ami
les amis
11. l'université
les universités
12. les tableaux
le tableau
13. le problème
les problèmes
14. les bibliothèques
la bibliothèque

**2** **L'université** Complete the sentences with an appropriate word from the list. Don't forget to provide the missing articles. Answers may vary slightly. Suggested answers below.

| bibliothèque | examen | ordinateurs | sociologie |
|---|---|---|---|
| bureau | faculté | petit ami | |

1. À _____ la faculté _____, les tableaux et _____ les ordinateurs _____ sont (*are*) modernes.
2. Marc, c'est _____ le petit ami _____ de (*of*) Marie. Marc étudie (*studies*) la littérature.
3. Marie étudie _____ la sociologie _____. Elle (*She*) est dans _____ la bibliothèque _____ de l'université.

**3** **Les mots** Find ten words (**mots**) hidden in this word jumble. Then, provide the corresponding indefinite articles. *une amie; des bureaux; un café; une chose; une faculté; un lycée; des objets; des ordinateurs; une librairie; un tableau*

🔮 Practice more at **daccord1.vhlcentral.com**.

**O P T I O N S**

**Rapid Drill** Write ten singular nouns on the board. In a rapid-response drill, call on students to give the appropriate gender. Examples: **bureau** (masculine), **télévision** (feminine). You may also do this activity without writing the words on the board.

**Using Games** Divide the class into groups of three to four students. Bring in photos or magazine pictures, point to various objects or people, and say the French word without saying the article. Call on groups to indicate the person's or object's gender. Give a point for each correct answer. Deduct a point for each wrong answer. The group with the most points at the end wins.

## COMMUNICATION

**4  Qu'est-ce que c'est?** In pairs, take turns identifying each image.

**MODÈLE**
Élève 1: *Qu'est-ce que c'est?*
Élève 2: *C'est un ordinateur.*

1. Ce sont des tables.    4. C'est une télévision.

2. Ce sont des étudiants.    5. C'est une bibliothèque/un étudiant.

3. C'est un tableau.    6. C'est un cafe./Ce sont des cafés.

**5  Identifiez** In pairs, take turns providing a category for each item.

**MODÈLE**
Michigan, UCLA, Rutgers, Duke
*Ce sont des universités.*

1. saxophone  C'est un instrument.
2. lion, tigre, éléphant  Ce sont des animaux.
3. SAT  C'est un examen.
4. Library of Congress  C'est une bibliothèque.
5. Angelina Jolie, Halle Berry, Juliette Binoche  Ce sont des actrices.
6. Céline Dion, Bruce Springsteen  Ce sont des chanteurs.

**6  Pictogrammes** In groups of four, someone draws a person, object, or concept for the others to guess. Whoever guesses correctly draws next. Continue until everyone has drawn at least once.  Answers will vary.

---

- Refer to a group composed of males and females with a masculine plural noun.

les amis          les étudiants
the (male and female) friends    the (male and female) students

- The English definite article *the* never varies for number or gender. However, the French definite article takes different forms according to the gender and number of the noun that it accompanies.

|  | singular noun beginning with a consonant | singular noun beginning with a vowel sound | plural noun |
|---|---|---|---|
| masculine | **le tableau** the picture/ blackboard | **l'ami** the (male) friend | **les cafés** the cafés |
| feminine | **la librairie** the bookstore | **l'université** the university | **les télévisions** the televisions |

- In English, the singular indefinite article is *a/an*, and the plural indefinite article is *some*. Although *some* is often omitted in English, the plural indefinite article cannot be omitted in French.

|  | singular | | plural | |
|---|---|---|---|---|
| masculine | **un instrument** | *an instrument* | **des instruments** | *(some) instruments* |
| feminine | **une table** | *a table* | **des tables** | *(some) tables* |

Il y a **un ordinateur** ici.      Il y a **des ordinateurs** ici.
*There's a computer here.*      *There are (some) computers here.*

Il y a **une université** ici.      Il y a **des universités** ici.
*There's a university here.*      *There are (some) universities here.*

- Use **c'est** followed by a singular article and noun or **ce sont** followed by a plural article and noun to identify people and objects.

Qu'est-ce que c'est?    C'est une librairie.    Ce sont des bureaux.
*What is that?*    *It's a bookstore.*    *They're offices.*

**Essayez!**    Select the correct article for each noun.

**le, la, l' ou les?**
1. __le__ café
2. __la__ bibliothèque
3. __l'__ acteur
4. __l'__ amie
5. __les__ problèmes
6. __le__ lycée
7. __les__ examens
8. __la__ littérature

**un, une ou des?**
1. __un__ bureau
2. __une__ différence
3. __un__ objet
4. __des__ amis
5. __des__ amies
6. __une__ université
7. __un__ ordinateur
8. __des__ tableaux

---

**Essayez!** Have students change the singular nouns and articles to the plural and vice versa.

**1 Suggestion** To check students' answers, have volunteers write them on the board or spell out the nouns orally.

**1 Expansion** Have students close their books. Tell them to change the plural nouns they hear to the singular and vice versa. Then randomly give them the answers to the items in the activity.

**2 Suggestion** Have volunteers read the words in the list aloud. Tell students to read all three items before attempting to start filling in blanks.

**3 Suggestion** This activity can also be done in pairs or groups.

**4 Suggestion** Before beginning this activity, have students identify the objects in the photos. Then read the **modèle** aloud with a volunteer. Remind them that **Ce sont** is used with plural nouns.

**5 Expansion** Have students work in pairs. Tell them to write two more items for the activity. Example: PSAT, GED, GRE (**Ce sont des examens.**) Then have volunteers read their items aloud, while the rest of the class guesses the category.

**6 Suggestions**
- Before beginning the activity, remind students that they must choose something the class knows how to say in French, and that to guess what the picture is, they should say: **C'est un(e) ____? or Ce sont des ____?**
- Tell students they will learn more about **c'est/ce sont** on p. 25.

---

**O P T I O N S**

**Using Movement** Distribute cards preprinted with articles and nouns to each of four students. Then line up ten students, each of whom is assigned a noun. Include a mix of masculine, feminine, singular, and plural nouns. Say one of the nouns (without the article), and that student must step forward. The student assigned the corresponding article has five seconds to join the student with the noun.

**Using Video** Show the video episode again to offer more input on singular and plural nouns and their articles. With their books closed, have students write down every noun and article that they hear. After viewing the video, ask volunteers to list the nouns and articles they heard.

## Section Goals

In this section, students will learn:
- numbers 0–60
- the expression **il y a**

## Key Standards

4.1, 5.1

**Student Resources**
*Cahier d'exercices*, pp. 5-6;
*Cahier d'activités*, p. 118;
Supersite: Activities,
*Cahier interactif*

**Teacher Resources**
Answer Keys; Audio Script;
Audio Activity MP3s/CD;
Testing program: Grammar Quiz

### Suggestions

- Introduce numbers by asking students how many of them can count to ten in French. Hold up varying numbers of fingers and ask students to shout out the corresponding number in French.
- Go through the numbers, modeling the pronunciation of each. Write individual numbers on the board and call on students at random to say each number as you point to it.
- Assign each student a number at random that they must remember. When finished, have the student assigned **un** say his or her number aloud, then **deux**, **trois**, etc. Help anyone who struggles with his or her number.
- Emphasize the variable forms of **un** and **une**, **vingt et un**, and **vingt et une**, giving examples of each. Examples: **vingt et un étudiants, vingt et une personnes.**
- Ask questions like the following: **Il y a combien d'élèves dans la classe?** (**Il y a seize élèves dans la classe.**)

## 1A.2 Numbers 0–60

**Point de départ** Numbers in French follow patterns, as they do in English. First, learn the numbers **0–30**. The patterns they follow will help you learn the numbers **31–60**.

| Numbers 0–30 | | |
|---|---|---|
| **0–10** | **11–20** | **21–30** |
| **0** zéro | | |
| **1** un | **11** onze | **21** vingt et un |
| **2** deux | **12** douze | **22** vingt-deux |
| **3** trois | **13** treize | **23** vingt-trois |
| **4** quatre | **14** quatorze | **24** vingt-quatre |
| **5** cinq | **15** quinze | **25** vingt-cinq |
| **6** six | **16** seize | **26** vingt-six |
| **7** sept | **17** dix-sept | **27** vingt-sept |
| **8** huit | **18** dix-huit | **28** vingt-huit |
| **9** neuf | **19** dix-neuf | **29** vingt-neuf |
| **10** dix | **20** vingt | **30** trente |

- When counting, use **un** for *one*. Use **une** before a feminine noun.

  **un objet**          **une télévision**
  *an/one object*       *a/one television*

- Note that the number **21** (**vingt et un**) follows a different pattern than the numbers **22–30**. When **vingt et un** precedes a feminine noun, add **-e** to the end of it: **vingt et une**.

  **vingt et un objets**     **vingt et une choses**
  *twenty-one objects*       *twenty-one things*

- Notice that the numbers **31–39**, **41–49**, and **51–59** follow the same pattern as the numbers **21–29**.

| Numbers 31–60 | | |
|---|---|---|
| **31–34** | **35–38** | **39, 40, 50, 60** |
| **31** trente et un | **35** trente-cinq | **39** trente-neuf |
| **32** trente-deux | **36** trente-six | **40** quarante |
| **33** trente-trois | **37** trente-sept | **50** cinquante |
| **34** trente-quatre | **38** trente-huit | **60** soixante |

- To indicate a count of **31**, **41**, or **51** for a feminine noun, change the **un** to **une**.

  **trente et un objets**      **trente et une choses**
  *thirty-one objects*         *thirty-one things*

  **cinquante et un objets**   **cinquante et une choses**
  *fifty-one objects*          *fifty-one things*

**12** *douze*

---

### MISE EN PRATIQUE

**1** **Logique** Provide the number that completes each series. Then, write out the number in French.

**MODÈLE**

2, 4, __6__, 8, 10; __six__

1. 9, 12, __15__, 18, 21; __quinze__
2. 15, 20, __25__, 30, 35; __vingt-cinq__
3. 2, 9, __16__, 23, 30; __seize__
4. 0, 10, 20, __30__, 40; __trente__
5. 15, __17__, 19, 21, 23; __dix-sept__
6. 29, 26, __23__, 20, 17; __vingt-trois__
7. 2, 5, 9, __14__, 20, 27; __quatorze__
8. 30, 22, 16, 12, __10__; __dix__

**2** **Il y a combien de...?** Provide the number that you associate with these pairs of words.

**MODÈLE**

lettres: l'alphabet *vingt-six*

1. mois (*months*): année (*year*) *douze*
2. états (*states*): USA *cinquante*
3. semaines (*weeks*): année *cinquante-deux*
4. jours (*days*): octobre *trente et un*
5. âge: le vote *dix-huit*
6. Noël: décembre *vingt-cinq*

**3** **Numéros de téléphone** Your mother left behind a list of phone numbers to call today. Now she calls you and asks you to read them off. Be sure to add the correct definite article. (Note that French phone numbers are read as double, not single, digits.)

**MODÈLE**

*Le bureau, c'est le zéro un, vingt-trois, quarante-cinq, vingt-six, dix-neuf.*

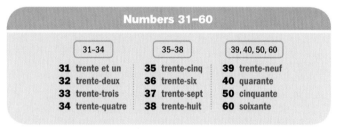

1. *bureau: 01.23.45.26.19*

2. *bibliothèque: 01.47.15.54.17* La bibliothèque, c'est le zéro un, quarante-sept, quinze, cinquante-quatre, dix-sept.

3. *café: 01.41.38.16.29* Le café, c'est le zéro un, quarante et un, trente-huit, seize, vingt-neuf.

4. *librairie: 01.10.13.60.23* La librairie, c'est le zéro un, dix, treize, soixante, vingt-trois.

5. *lycée: 01.58.36.14.12* Le lycée, c'est le zéro un, cinquante-huit, trente-six, quatorze, douze.

 Practice more at **daccord1.vhlcentral.com**.

---

**OPTIONS**

**Using Movement** Assign ten students a number from 0–60 and line them up in front of the class. Call out one of the numbers at random and have the student assigned to that number take a step forward. When two students have stepped forward, ask them to repeat their numbers. Then ask individuals to add (say: **plus**) or subtract (say: **moins**) the two numbers.

**Using Games** Hand out Bingo cards with B-I-N-G-O across the top of five columns. The 25 squares underneath will contain random numbers. From a hat, draw letters and numbers and call them out in French. The first student that can fill in a number in each one of the lettered columns yells "Bingo!" and wins.

## COMMUNICATION

**4** **Sur le campus** Nathalie's little brother wants to know everything about her new college campus. In pairs, take turns acting out the roles.

### MODÈLE

bibliothèques: 3
**Élève 1:** *Il y a combien de bibliothèques?*
**Élève 2:** *Il y a trois bibliothèques.*

1. professeurs de littérature: 22
   *Il y a vingt-deux professeurs de littérature.*
2. étudiants dans (*in*) la classe de français: 15
   *Il y a quinze étudiants dans la classe de français.*
3. télévision dans la classe de sociologie: 0
   *Il n'y a pas de télévision dans la classe de sociologie.*
4. ordinateurs dans le café: 8
   *Il y a huit ordinateurs dans le café.*
5. employés dans la librairie: 51
   *Il y a cinquante et un employés dans la librairie.*
6. tables dans le café: 21
   *Il y a vingt et une tables dans le café.*

**5** **Contradiction** Thierry is describing the new Internet café in the neighborhood, but Paul contradicts everything he says. In pairs, act out the roles using words from the list. *Answers will vary.*

### MODÈLE

**Élève 1:** *Dans (In) le café, il y a des tables.*
**Élève 2:** *Non, il n'y a pas de tables.*

| | |
|---|---|
| actrices | professeurs |
| bureau | tableau |
| étudiants | tables |
| ordinateur | télévision |

**6** **Choses et personnes** In groups of three, make a list of ten things or people that you see or don't see in the classroom. Use **il y a** and **il n'y a pas de**, and specify the number of items you can find. Then, compare your list with that of another pair. *Answers will vary.*

### MODÈLE

**Élève 1:** *Il y a deux étudiants français.*
**Élève 2:** *Il n'y a pas d'ordinateur.*

---

- Use **il y a** to say *there is* or *there are* in French. This expression doesn't change, even if the noun that follows it is plural.

**Il y a un ordinateur** dans le bureau.
*There is a computer in the office.*

**Il y a des tables** dans le café.
*There are tables in the café.*

Il y a deux amies.

Il y a trois étudiants.

- In most cases, the indefinite article (**un**, **une**, or **des**) is used with **il y a**, rather than the definite article (**le**, **la**, **l'**, or **les**).

**Il y a un** professeur de biologie américain.
*There's an American biology teacher.*

**Il y a des** étudiants français et anglais.
*There are French and English students.*

- Use the expression **il n'y a pas de/d'** followed by a noun to express *there isn't a...* or *there aren't any...* Note that no article (definite or indefinite) is used in this case. Use **de** before a consonant sound and **d'** before a vowel sound.

| before a consonant | before a vowel sound |

**Il n'y a pas de tables** dans le café.
*There aren't any tables in the café.*

**Il n'y a pas d'ordinateur** dans le bureau.
*There isn't a computer in the office.*

- Use **combien de/d'** to ask how many of something there are.

Il y a **combien de tables**?
*How many tables are there?*

Il y a **combien d'ordinateurs**?
*How many computers are there?*

| **Essayez!** | Write out or say the French word for each number below. |
|---|---|

1. 15 _quinze_
2. 6 _six_
3. 22 _vingt-deux_
4. 5 _cinq_
5. 12 _douze_
6. 8 _huit_
7. 30 _trente_
8. 21 _vingt et un_
9. 1 _un_
10. 17 _dix-sept_
11. 44 _quarante-quatre_
12. 14 _quatorze_
13. 38 _trente-huit_
14. 56 _cinquante-six_
15. 19 _dix-neuf_

*treize* **13**

---

**Essayez!** Have students write four more numbers from 0–60. Tell them to exchange papers with a classmate and write the numbers as words.

**1 Expansion** Ask the class to list the prime numbers (**les nombres premiers**) up to 30. Explain that a prime number is any number that can only be divided by itself and 1. Prime numbers to 30 are: 1, 2, 3, 5, 7, 11, 13, 17, 19, 23, 29.

**2 Suggestion** Have students form complete sentences using **Il y a** when answering. Example: **Il y a douze mois dans une année.**

**2 Expansion** For additional practice, give students these items. **7. jours: semaine (sept) 8. jours: novembre (trente) 9. minutes: heure** (*hour*) **(soixante) 10. saisons** (*seasons*): **année (quatre)**

**3 Expansion** Write on the board three more telephone numbers for real places, with their area codes, using double digits as in the activity. Call on volunteers to read the numbers aloud. Permit students to say the digits one by one if the numbers exceed 60.

**4 Suggestion** Have two volunteers read the **modèle** aloud. Remind students to use **combien d'** before a noun that begins with a vowel sound.

**5 Suggestion** Have two volunteers read the **modèle** aloud. Remind students that they shouldn't use any article (definite or indefinite) after **Il n'y a pas de/d'**.

**6 Expansion** After groups have compared their answers, convert the statements into questions. Example: **Il y a combien d'étudiants?**

---

**Using Movement** Give ten students a card with a number from 0–60. (You may want to assign numbers in fives to simplify the activity.) The card must be visible to the other students. Then call out simple math problems (addition or subtraction) involving the assigned numbers. When the first two numbers are called, each student steps forward. The student whose assigned number completes the math problem has five seconds to join them.

**My School** Ask questions about your school and the town or city in which it is located. Examples: **Il y a combien de professeurs de français? Il y a combien de professeurs d'anglais? Il y a combien de bibliothèques à ____?** Encourage students to guess the number if they don't know it.

# Révision

## Key Standards

1.1

**Suggestion** Tell students that this section reviews and recycles the lesson vocabulary and grammar points.

**Student Resources**
*Cahier d'activités*, pp. 19-20;
Supersite: Activities,
*Cahier interactif*

**Teacher Resources**
Answer Keys; Info Gap Activities; Testing Program: Lesson Test (Testing Program Audio MP3s/CD)

**1 Suggestion** Before beginning this activity, you may wish to review the alphabet and how to say the accent marks.

**2 Suggestion** Tell students not to accept a guess if the letter is not pronounced correctly in French.

**3 Suggestion** Before beginning the activity, have two volunteers read the **modèle** aloud.

**4 Suggestion** Remind students to use appropriate gestures and encourage them to add information to the introduction, such as the person's hometown.

**5 Suggestions**
• Before beginning this activity, quickly review the numbers 0–60. Hold up cards with various numbers, and have the class or individuals say them in French.
• Read the **modèle** aloud with a volunteer.

**6 Suggestion** Divide the class into pairs and distribute the Info Gap Handouts for this activity. Give students ten minutes to complete the activity.

**1** **Des lettres** In pairs, take turns choosing nouns. One partner chooses only masculine nouns, while the other chooses only feminine. Slowly spell each noun for your partner, who will guess the word. Find out who can give the quickest answers. Answers will vary.

**2** **Le pendu** In groups of four, play hangman (**le pendu**). Form two teams of two partners each. Take turns choosing a French word or expression you learned in this lesson for the other team to guess. Continue to play until your team guesses at least one word or expression from each category. Answers will vary.

1. un nom féminin
2. un nom masculin
3. un nombre entre (*number between*) 0 et 30
4. un nombre entre 31 et 60
5. une expression

**3** **C'est... Ce sont...** Doug is spending a week in Paris with his French e-mail pal, Marc. As Doug points out what he sees, Marc corrects him sometimes. In pairs, act out the roles. Doug should be right half the time. Answers will vary.

**MODÈLE**
**Élève 1:** *C'est une bibliothèque?*
**Élève 2:** *Non, c'est une librairie.*

1. C'est une bibliothèque./
   Ce sont des élèves/étudiants.

4. Ce sont des acteurs.

2. C'est un café.

5. C'est un professeur. /
   Ce sont des élèves/étudiants.

3. C'est une actrice.

6. Ce sont des amies.

**4** **Les présentations** In pairs, introduce yourselves. Together, meet another pair. One person per pair should introduce him or herself and his or her partner. Use the items from the list in your conversations. Switch roles until you have met all of the other pairs in the class. Answers will vary.

| ami | élève |
|---|---|
| c'est | ami(e) |
| ce sont | professeur |

**5** **S'il te plaît** You need help finding your way and so you ask your partner for assistance. He or she gives you the building (**le bâtiment**) and room (**la salle**) number and you thank him or her. Then, switch roles and repeat with another place from the list. Answers will vary.

**MODÈLE**
**Élève 1:** *Pardon... l'examen de sociologie, s'il te plaît?*
**Élève 2:** *Ah oui... bâtiment E, salle dix-sept.*
**Élève 1:** *Merci beaucoup!*
**Élève 2:** *De rien.*

| Bibliothèque | Bâtiment C Salle 11 |
|---|---|
| Bureau de Mme Girard | Bâtiment A Salle 35 |
| Bureau de M. Brachet | Bâtiment J Salle 42 |
| Bureau de M. Grondin | Bâtiment H Salle 59 |
| Examen de français | Bâtiment B Salle 46 |
| Examen d'anglais | Bâtiment E Salle 24 |
| Examen de sociologie | Bâtiment E Salle 17 |
| Salle de télévision | Bâtiment F Salle 33 |
| Salle des ordinateurs | Bâtiment D Salle 40 |

**6** **Mots mélangés** You and a partner each have half the words of a wordsearch (**des mots mélangés**). Pick a number and a letter and say them to your partner, who must tell you if he or she has a letter in the corresponding space. Do not look at each other's worksheet. Answers will vary.

**ressources**

| CE pp. 3-6 | CA pp. 19-20, 117-118 | **S** daccord1.vhlcentral.com |
|---|---|---|

**14** *quatorze*

**OPTIONS**

**Using Visuals** Bring in pictures from newspapers, magazines, or the Internet of nouns that students have learned, and ask them to identify the people or objects. Examples: **C'est un(e) ____? Ce sont des ____? Qu'est-ce que c'est?** You might also ask how many people or objects are in the picture if there are more than one. Example: **Il y a combien de(d') ____?**

**Using Visuals** Bring in family photos or magazine pictures showing people greeting or introducing each other in different situations. Assign a photo to each group or allow them to choose one. Tell students to write a brief conversation based on the photo. Remind the class to use formal and informal expressions as appropriate.

S Video: TV Clip

# Le Zapping

## La Triplette de Moulinex… un, deux, trois!

The story of Moulinex started with an invention. In 1932, Jean Mantelet invented the electric potato masher to help his wife. Later, he invented an electric coffee grinder called **Moulin° X**, which went on to become the company brand. After World War II, Moulinex came up with the famous slogan, **Moulinex libère la femme** (*Moulinex liberates women*). In the 1980s, Moulinex started facing tough competition and in 2001 was bought out by Groupe SEB, another French company specializing in small appliances and kitchen equipment.

### Coup de main

**Moulin X** is a play on words. **Moulin** means *grinder* and you need to pronounce the x the English way, not the French way. That's how you obtain Moulinex.

—Un, deux, trois, elle fait° la raclette°.    —Un, deux, trois, elle fait des crêpes.

**Compréhension**  Answer these questions.  Some answers will vary.

1. What numbers and articles did you recognize?  un, deux, trois, la, des
2. What is special about this device?

👤👤👤 **Discussion**  In groups of four, discuss the answers to these questions. Use as much French as you can.  Answers will vary.

1. Have you ever eaten **raclette** or **crêpes** before? Where?
2. When would one use **la Triplette**?

3. What other appliance can you think of that performs more than one job?
4. If you could invent an appliance with several functions, what would it do? What would you name it?

**Moulin** *grinder* **elle fait** *it makes* **raclette** *dish made from melted cheese scraped onto bread or boiled potatoes*

S Practice more at **daccord1.vhlcentral.com.**

*quinze* **15**

## Section Goals
In this section, students will:
• read about Moulinex, a company that makes small household appliances
• watch the commercial for one of its devices, the **Triplette**
• answer questions about the device and Moulinex

## Key Standards
**1.2, 2.2, 4.2, 5.2**

**Student Resources**
Supersite: Video, Activities
**Teacher Resources**
Video Script & Translation;
Supersite: Video

**Introduction**
To check comprehension, ask these questions.
1. What did Jean Mantelet invent? (He invented an electric potato masher and an electric coffee grinder.)
2. What was Moulinex's slogan after World War II? (**«Moulinex libère la femme»**)
3. Who bought Moulinex in 2001? (Seb, another French company specializing in small appliances and kitchen equipment)

**Avant de regarder la vidéo**
• Have students look at the video stills, read the captions, and describe the device and what it is used for. (It's an electric cooking device that you can use to prepare **raclette** and **crêpes**.)
• Before showing the video, explain to students that they do not need to understand every word they hear. Tell them to listen for numbers, articles, and cognates.

**Compréhension**  Have students work in pairs or groups for this activity. Tell them to write their answers. Then show the video again so that they can check their answers and add any missing information.

**Discussion**
• Have volunteers report their answers to the class.
• Take a quick class survey to find out who likes or would like to try either **raclette** or **crêpes**.

## Section Goals

In this section, students will learn and practice vocabulary related to:
• objects in the classroom
• identifying people

## Key Standards

1.1, 1.2, 4.1

**Student Resources**
*Cahier d'exercices*, pp. 7-8; *Cahier d'activités*, pp. 21-22, 119; Supersite: Activities, *Cahier interactif*

**Teacher Resources**
Answer Keys; Overhead #15; Audio Script; Textbook & Audio Activity MP3s/CD; Info Gap Activities; Testing program: Vocabulary Quiz

## Suggestions

• Introduce vocabulary for classroom objects, such as **un cahier, une carte, un dictionnaire, un stylo**. Hold up or point to an object and say: **C'est un stylo.**
• Hold up or point to an object and ask either/or questions. Examples: **C'est un crayon ou un stylo? C'est une porte ou une fenêtre?**
• Using either objects in the classroom or **Overhead #15**, point to items or people and ask questions, such as **Qu'est-ce que c'est? Qui est-ce? C'est un stylo? C'est un professeur?**
• Have students pick up or point out objects you name. You might want to teach them the expression **Montrez-moi un/une ____.**

**Leçon 1B**

**Talking Picture**
**Audio: Activity**

You will learn how to...
▪ identify yourself and others
▪ ask yes/no questions

# En classe

### Vocabulaire

| | |
|---|---|
| Qui est-ce? | *Who is it?* |
| Quoi? | *What?* |
| une calculatrice | *calculator* |
| une montre | *watch* |
| une porte | *door* |
| un résultat | *result* |
| une salle de classe | *classroom* |
| un(e) camarade de chambre | *roommate* |
| un(e) camarade de classe | *classmate* |
| une classe | *class (group of students)* |
| un copain/ une copine (*fam.*) | *friend* |
| un(e) élève | *pupil, student* |
| une femme | *woman* |
| une fille | *girl* |
| un garçon | *boy* |
| un homme | *man* |

une horloge
un crayon
un sac à dos
une fenêtre
un livre
un cahier
un dictionnaire
un stylo
une feuille (de papier)
une corbeille (à papier)

**ressources**

| CE pp. 7-8 | CA pp. 21-22, 119 | S daccord1.vhlcentral.com |
|---|---|---|

**OPTIONS**

**Making Lists** Have students work in pairs and take an inventory of all the people and items in the classroom. Tell them to write their list in French using the expression **Il y a ____**. After students have finished, tell them to compare their lists with another pair to see if they are the same.

**Using Games** Divide the class into teams. Then, in English, say the name of a classroom object and ask one of the teams to provide the French equivalent. If the team provides the correct term, it gets a point. If not, the second team gets a chance to give the correct term. Alternate giving items to the two teams. The team with the most points at the end of the game wins.

# Mise en pratique

**1 Chassez l'intrus** Circle the word that does not belong.

1. étudiants, élèves, (professeur)
2. un stylo, un crayon, (un cahier)
3. un livre, un dictionnaire, (un stylo)
4. un homme, (un crayon,) un garçon
5. une copine, (une carte,) une femme
6. une porte, une fenêtre, (une chaise)
7. une chaise, (un professeur,) une fenêtre
8. (un crayon,) une feuille de papier, un cahier
9. une calculatrice, une montre, (une copine)
10. une fille, (un sac à dos,) un garçon

**2 Écoutez** 🎧 Listen to Madame Arnaud as she describes her French classroom, then check the items she mentions.

1. une porte ☑           6. vingt-quatre cahiers ☐
2. un professeur ☐       7. une calculatrice ☐
3. une feuille de papier ☐  8. vingt-sept chaises ☑
4. un dictionnaire ☑     9. une corbeille à papier ☑
5. une carte ☑          10. un stylo ☑

**3 C'est...** Work with a partner to identify the items you see in the image.

**MODÈLE**
**Élève 1:** Qu'est-ce que c'est?
**Élève 2:** C'est un tableau.

1. un tableau
2. une porte
3. un crayon/stylo
4. un livre
5. une calculatrice
6. un stylo/crayon
7. une feuille (de papier)
8. un bureau
9. un dictionnaire
10. une corbeille à papier
11. une chaise
12. un professeur

🔎 Practice more at **daccord1.vhlcentral.com.**

*dix-sept* **17**

**une carte**

**une chaise**

**4 Expansion** For additional practice, point to different students' desks that have objects on them and ask: **Qu'est ce qu'il y a sur le bureau de _____?** You might also ask: **Qu'est-ce qu'il y a sur mon bureau?**

**5 Suggestion** Before beginning the activity, have a few volunteers demonstrate what students should do using the **modèle**.

**6 Suggestion** Before beginning the activity, remind students that to guess what the drawing represents, they should say: **C'est un(e) _____?** or **Ce sont des _____?**

**7 Suggestions**
• Divide the class into pairs and distribute the Info Gap Handouts on the Supersite for this activity. Give students ten minutes to complete the activity.
• Have two volunteers read the **modèle** aloud.

**7 Expansion** Have students describe the people and objects in the photo using **Il y a**.

**Successful Language Learning** Remind the class that errors are a natural part of language learning. Point out that it is impossible to speak "perfectly" in any language. Emphasize that their spoken and written French will improve if they make an effort to practice.

# Communication

**4** **Qu'est-ce qu'il y a dans mon sac à dos?** Make a list of six different items that you have in your backpack, then work with a partner to compare your answers. Answers will vary.

Dans mon (*my*) sac à dos, il y a...

1. _____
2. _____
3. _____
4. _____
5. _____
6. _____

Dans le sac à dos de ____*nom*____, il y a...

1. _____
2. _____
3. _____
4. _____
5. _____
6. _____

**5** **Qu'est-ce que c'est?** Point at eight different items around the classroom and ask a classmate to identify them. Write your partner's responses on the spaces provided below. Answers will vary.

**MODÈLE**
**Élève 1:** *Qu'est-ce que c'est?*
**Élève 2:** *C'est un stylo.*

1. _____
2. _____
3. _____
4. _____

5. _____
6. _____
7. _____
8. _____

**6** **Pictogrammes** Play pictionary as a class.
Answers will vary.
• Take turns going to the board and drawing words you learned on pp. 16–17.
• The person drawing may not speak and may not write any letters or numbers.
• The person who guesses correctly in French what the **grand(e) artiste** is drawing will go next.
• Your teacher will time each turn and tell you if your time runs out.

**7** **Sept différences** Your teacher will give you and a partner two different drawings of a classroom. Do not look at each other's worksheet. Find seven differences between your picture and your partner's by asking each other questions and describing what you see.

**MODÈLE**
**Élève 1:** *Il y a une fenêtre dans ma (my) salle de classe.*
**Élève 2:** *Oh! Il n'y a pas de fenêtre dans ma salle de classe.*

**18** *dix-huit*

**OPTIONS**
**Using Games** Divide the class into two teams. Put labels of classroom vocabulary in a box. Alternating between teams, one person picks a label out of the box without showing it to anyone. This person must place the label on the correct person or object in the classroom and say the word aloud. Each player is allowed only 15 seconds and one guess per turn. Award a point for a correct response. If a player is incorrect, the next player on the opposing team may "steal" the point by placing the label on the correct person or object. The team with the most points at the end of the game wins.

# Les sons et les lettres

 **Audio: Concepts, Activities Record & Compare**

🎧 **Silent letters**

> Final consonants of French words are usually silent.
>
> **françai~~s~~**     **spor~~t~~**     **vou~~s~~**     **salu~~t~~**
>
> - - - - - - - - - - - - - - - - - - - - - - - - - - - - - - - - - - - - - - - - - - - - -
>
> An unaccented **-e** (or **-es**) at the end of a word is silent, but the preceding consonant is pronounced.
>
> **français~~e~~**     **américain~~e~~**     **orang~~es~~**     **japonais~~es~~**
>
> - - - - - - - - - - - - - - - - - - - - - - - - - - - - - - - - - - - - - - - - - - - - -
>
> The consonants **-c**, **-r**, **-f**, and **-l** are usually pronounced at the ends of words. To remember these exceptions, think of the consonants in the word **c**a**r**e**f**u**l**.
>
> **par**c          **bonjou**r          **acti**f          **anima**l
>
> **la**c          **professeu**r          **naï**f          **ma**l

✍️ⓢ **Prononcez** Practice saying these words aloud.

1. traditionnel
2. étudiante
3. généreuse
4. téléphones
5. chocolat
6. Monsieur
7. journalistes
8. hôtel
9. sac
10. concert
11. timide
12. sénégalais
13. objet
14. normal
15. importante

✍️ⓢ **Articulez** Practice saying these sentences aloud.

1. Au revoir, Paul. À plus tard!
2. Je vais très bien. Et vous, Monsieur Dubois?
3. Qu'est-ce que c'est? C'est une calculatrice.
4. Il y a un ordinateur, une table et une chaise.
5. Frédéric et Chantal, je vous présente Michel et Éric.
6. Voici un sac à dos, des crayons et des feuilles de papier.

✍️ⓢ **Dictons** Practice reading these sayings aloud.

> *Aussitôt dit, aussitôt fait.*[2]

> *Mieux vaut tard que jamais.*[1]

[1] Better late than never.    [2] No sooner said than done.

**ressources**

CA
p. 120

daccord1.vhicentral.com

*dix-neuf* **19**

---

## Section Goals

In this section, students will learn about:
- silent letters
- a strategy for remembering which consonants are pronounced at the end of words

## Key Standards
**4.1**

**Student Resources**
*Cahier d'activités*, p. 120;
Supersite: Activities,
*Cahier interactif*

**Teacher Resources**
Answer Keys; Audio Script;
Textbook & Audio Activity
MP3s/CD

**Suggestions**
- Write the sentences below on the board or a transparency. Then say each sentence and ask students which letters are silent. Draw a slash through the silent letters as students say them. **Qui est-ce? C'est Gilbert. Il est français. Qu'est-ce que c'est? C'est un éléphant.**
- Work through the example words. Model the pronunciation of each word and have students repeat after you.
- Tell students that the final consonants of a few words that end in **c**, **r**, **f**, or **l** are silent. Examples: **porc** (*pork*), **blanc** (*white*), **nerf** (*nerve*), and **gentil** (*nice*).
- Point out that the letters **-er** at the end of a word are pronounced like the vowel sound in the English word *say*. Examples: **cahier** and **papier**.
- Explain that numbers are exceptions to pronunciation rules. When counting, some final consonants are pronounced. Have students compare the pronunciation of the following: **six, sept, huit; six cahiers, sept stylos, huit crayons**.
- Tell students that the final consonants of words borrowed from other languages are often pronounced. Examples: **snob, autobus**, and **club**. This topic will be presented in Level 2.
- The explanations and exercises are recorded on the Textbook MP3s CD-ROM and are available on the **D'ACCORD!** Supersite. You may want to play them in class so students hear French speakers other than yourself.

# Les copains

 Video: *Roman-photo*
Record & Compare

**PERSONNAGES**

Amina

David

Michèle

Stéphane

Touriste

Valérie

*À la terrasse du café...*
**VALÉRIE** Alors, un croissant, une crêpe et trois cafés.
**TOURISTE** Merci, Madame.
**VALÉRIE** Ah, vous êtes... américain?
**TOURISTE** Um, non, je suis anglais. Il est canadien et elle est italienne.
**VALÉRIE** Moi, je suis française.

*À l'intérieur du café...*
**VALÉRIE** Stéphane!!!
**STÉPHANE** Quoi?! Qu'est-ce que c'est?
**VALÉRIE** Qu'est-ce que c'est! Qu'est-ce que c'est! Une feuille de papier! C'est l'examen de maths! Qu'est-ce que c'est?
**STÉPHANE** Oui, euh, les maths, c'est difficile.

**VALÉRIE** Stéphane, tu es intelligent, mais tu n'es pas brillant! En classe, on fait attention au professeur, au cahier et au livre! Pas aux fenêtres. Et pas aux filles!
**STÉPHANE** Oh, oh, ça va!!

*À la table d'Amina et de David...*
**DAVID** Et Rachid, mon colocataire? Comment est-il?
**AMINA** Il est agréable et très poli... plutôt réservé mais c'est un étudiant brillant. Il est d'origine algérienne.

**DAVID** Et toi, Amina. Tu es de quelle origine?
**AMINA** D'origine sénégalaise.
**DAVID** Et Sandrine?

**AMINA** Sandrine? Elle est française.
**DAVID** Mais non... Comment est-elle?
**AMINA** Bon, elle est chanteuse, alors elle est un peu égoïste. Mais elle est très sociable. Et charmante. Mais attention! Elle est avec Pascal.
**DAVID** Pfft, Pascal, Pascal...

## ACTIVITÉS

**1** **Identifiez** Indicate which character would make each statement: Amina (A), David (D), Michèle (M), Sandrine (S), Stéphane (St), or Valérie (V).

1. Les maths, c'est difficile. St
2. En classe, on fait attention au professeur! V
3. Michèle, les trois cafés sont pour les trois touristes. V
4. Ah, Madame, du calme! M
5. Ma mère est très impatiente! St
6. J'ai (*I have*) de la famille au Sénégal. A
7. Je suis une grande chanteuse! S
8. Mon colocataire est très poli et intelligent. D
9. Pfft, Pascal, Pascal... D
10. Attention, David! Sandrine est avec Pascal. A/V

 Practice more at **daccord1.vhlcentral.com.**

**20** *vingt*

**Amina, David et Stéphane passent la matinée (*spend the morning*) au café.**

*Au bar...*
**VALÉRIE** Le croissant, c'est pour l'Anglais, et la crêpe, c'est pour l'Italienne.
**MICHÈLE** Mais, Madame. Ça va? Qu'est-ce qu'il y a?
**VALÉRIE** Ben, c'est Stéphane. Des résultats d'examens, des professeurs... des problèmes!

**MICHÈLE** Ah, Madame, du calme! Je suis optimiste. C'est un garçon intelligent. Et vous, êtes-vous une femme patiente?
**VALÉRIE** Oui... oui, je suis patiente. Mais le Canadien, l'Anglais et l'Italienne sont impatients. Allez! Vite!

**VALÉRIE** Alors, ça va bien?
**AMINA** Ah, oui, merci.
**DAVID** Amina est une fille élégante et sincère.
**VALÉRIE** Oui! Elle est charmante.
**DAVID** Et Rachid, comment est-il?
**VALÉRIE** Oh! Rachid! C'est un ange! Il est intelligent, poli et modeste. Un excellent camarade de chambre.

**DAVID** Et Sandrine? Comment est-elle?
**VALÉRIE** Sandrine?! Oh, là, là. Non, non, non. Elle est avec Pascal.

## Expressions utiles

### Describing people

- **Vous êtes/Tu es américain?**
  *You're American?*
- **Je suis anglais. Il est canadien et elle est italienne.**
  *I'm English. He's Canadian, and she's Italian.*
- **Et Rachid, mon colocataire? Comment est-il?**
  *And Rachid, my roommate (in an apartment)? What's he like?*
- **Il est agréable et très poli... plutôt réservé mais c'est un étudiant brillant.**
  *He's nice and polite... rather reserved, but a brilliant student.*
- **Tu es de quelle origine?**
  *What's your heritage?*
- **Je suis d'origine algérienne/sénégalaise.**
  *I'm of Algerian/Senegalese heritage.*
- **Elle est avec Pascal.**
  *She's with (dating) Pascal.*
- **Rachid! C'est un ange!**
  *Rachid! He's an angel!*

### Asking questions

- **Ça va? Qu'est-ce qu'il y a?**
  *Are you OK? What is it?/What's wrong?*

### Additional vocabulary

- **Ah, Madame, du calme!**
  *Oh, ma'am, calm down!*
- **On fait attention à...**
  *One pays attention to...*
- **Mais attention!** • **alors**
  *But watch out!* • *so*
- **Allez! Vite!** • **mais**
  *Go! Quickly!* • *but*
- **Mais non...** • **un peu**
  *Of course not...* • *a little*

**2 Complétez** Use words from the list to describe these people in French. Refer to the video scenes and a dictionary as necessary.

1. Michèle always looks on the bright side. ___optimiste___
2. Rachid gets great grades. ___intelligent___
3. Amina is very honest. ___sincère___
4. Sandrine thinks about herself a lot. ___égoïste___
5. Sandrine has a lot of friends. ___sociable___

| | |
|---|---|
| **égoïste** | |
| **intelligent** | |
| **optimiste** | |
| **sincère** | |
| **sociable** | |

**3 Conversez** In pairs, choose the words from this list you would use to describe yourselves. What personality traits do you have in common? Be prepared to share your answers with the class.

| | |
|---|---|
| **brillant** | **modeste** |
| **charmant** | **optimiste** |
| **égoïste** | **patient** |
| **élégant** | **sincère** |
| **intelligent** | **sociable** |

**ressources**

CA
pp. 69-70

daccord1.vhlcentral.com

**A C T I V I T É S**

# CULTURE

## Section Goals

In this section, students will:
- learn about France's multicultural society
- learn some familiar terms for identifying people
- read the mottos of some francophone countries
- read about **Superdupont**, a popular comic-strip character

## Key Standards

**2.1, 2.2, 3.1, 3.2, 4.2**

**Student Resources**
Supersite: Activities
**Teacher Resources**
Answer Keys

**Culture à la loupe**
**Avant la lecture** Have students discuss what their idea of a typical French person is.

**Lecture**
- Point out the regions where Provençal (**Provence**), Breton (**Bretagne**), and Basque (**Le Pays basque**) are spoken on the map of France in the frontmatter.
- Explain that there are other regional languages not mentioned in the text: Alsatian, Caribbean Creole, Catalan, Corsican, Dutch, Gascon, Lorraine German dialect, and Occitan.

**Après la lecture** Ask students what facts in this reading are interesting or surprising to them.

**1 Expansion** For additional practice, give students these items. 11. There are several official languages in France. (**Faux.** French is the only official language.) 12. South Africans represent a significant immigrant population in France. (**Faux.** North and West Africans represent significant immigrant populations.) 13. There are more immigrants in France from both Italy and Spain than from Tunisia. (**Vrai.**) 14. There aren't many Asians in France. (**Faux.** There are significant Indo-Chinese populations.)

# Qu'est-ce qu'un Français typique?

**What is your idea of a typical Frenchman?**
Do you picture a man wearing a **béret**? How about French women? Are they all fashionable and stylish? Do you picture what is shown in these photos? While real French people fitting one aspect or another of these cultural stereotypes do exist, rarely do you find individuals who fit all aspects.

France is a multicultural society with no single, national ethnicity. While the majority of French people are of Celtic or Latin descent, France has significant North and West African (e.g., Algeria, Morocco, Senegal) and Asian (e.g., Vietnam, Laos, Cambodia) populations as well. Long a **terre d'accueil°**, France today has over four million foreigners and immigrants. Even as France has maintained a strong concept of its culture through the preservation of its language, history, and traditions, French culture has been ultimately enriched by the contributions of its immigrant populations. Each region of the country also has its own traditions, folklore, and, often, its own language. Regional languages, such as Provençal, Breton, and Basque, are still spoken in some areas, but the official language is, of course, French.

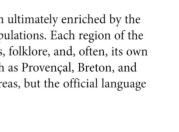

**terre d'accueil** *a land welcoming of newcomers*

| Immigrants in France, by country of birth | |
| --- | --- |
| **COUNTRY NAME** | **NUMBER OF PEOPLE** |
| Algeria | 574,200 |
| Portugal | 571,900 |
| Other European countries | 568,800 |
| Morocco | 522,500 |
| Italy | 378,700 |
| Spain | 316,200 |
| Tunisia | 201,600 |
| Turkey | 174,200 |
| Cambodia, Laos, Vietnam | 159,800 |
| Poland | 98,600 |

SOURCE: INSEE

## ACTIVITÉS

**1 Vrai ou faux?** Indicate whether each statement is **vrai** or **faux**. Correct the false statements.

1. Cultural stereotypes are generally true for most people in France. Faux. Rarely do you find individuals who fit all aspects of a stereotype.
2. People in France no longer speak regional languages. Faux. Regional languages are still spoken in some areas.
3. Many immigrants from North Africa live in France. Vrai.
4. More immigrants in France come from Portugal than from Morocco. Vrai.
5. Algerians and Moroccans represent the largest immigrant populations in France. Faux. Algerians and Portuguese are the largest immigrant populations.
6. Immigrant cultures have little impact on French culture. Faux. French culture has been enriched by immigrant cultures.
7. Because of immigration, France is losing its cultural identity. Faux. France has maintained its culture.
8. French culture differs from region to region. Vrai.
9. Most French people are of Anglo-Saxon heritage. Faux. The majority of French people are of Celtic or Latin descent.
10. For many years, France has received immigrants from many countries. Vrai.

 Practice more at daccord1.vhlcentral.com.

## OPTIONS

**Cultural Activity** Ask students what stereotypical ideas a French person might have of Americans. If students have difficulty answering, then give them a few examples of American stereotypes and ask them if they are true or valid. Examples: Americans are loud and obnoxious. Americans only speak English. Americans are overweight.

**Brainstorming** Divide the class into groups of three or four. Give groups five minutes to brainstorm names of cities, states, lakes, rivers, mountain ranges, and so forth in the United States that have French origins. One member of each group should write down the names. Then have groups share their lists with the class.

## LE FRANÇAIS QUOTIDIEN

### Les gens

| | |
|---|---|
| **ado** (*m./f.*) | *adolescent, teen* |
| **bonhomme** (*m.*) | *fellow* |
| **gars** (*m.*) | *guy* |
| **mec** (*m.*) | *guy* |
| **minette** (*f.*) | *young woman, sweetie* |
| **nana** (*f.*) | *young woman, girl* |
| **pote** (*m.*) | *buddy* |
| **type** (*m.*) | *guy* |

## LE MONDE FRANCOPHONE

### Les devises

Here are the **devises** (*national mottos*) of some francophone countries.

**Belgium** L'union fait la force (*Unity is strength*)

**Ivory Coast** Union, Discipline, Travail (*Unity, Discipline, Work*)

**France** Liberté, Égalité, Fraternité (*Liberty, Equality, Fraternity*)

**Monaco** Avec l'aide de Dieu (*With the help of God*)

**Morocco** Dieu, la Patrie, le Roi (*God, Country, King*)

**Senegal** Un Peuple, un But, une Foi (*One People, one Goal, one Faith*)

**Switzerland** Un pour tous, tous pour un (*One for all, all for one*)

**Tunisia** Liberté, Ordre, Justice (*Liberty, Order, Justice*)

## PORTRAIT

# Superdupont

*Superdupont* is an ultra-French superhero in a popular comic strip parodying French nationalism. The protector of all things French, he battles the secret enemy organization **Anti-France**, whose agents speak **anti-français**, a mixture of English, Spanish, Italian, Russian, and German. *Superdupont* embodies just about every French stereotype imaginable. For example, the name Dupont, much like Smith in the United States, is extremely common in France. In addition to his **béret** and moustache, he wears a blue, white, and red belt around his waist representing **le drapeau français** (*the French flag*). Physically, he is overweight and has a red nose—signs that he appreciates rich French food and wine. Finally, on his arm is **un coq** (*a rooster*), the national symbol of France. The Latin word for rooster (*gallus*) also means "inhabitant of Gaul," as France used to be called.

### SUR INTERNET

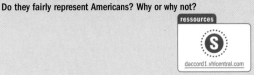

**What countries are former French colonies?**

Go to **daccord1.vhlcentral.com** to find more information related to this **CULTURE** section.

---

**2** **Complétez** Provide responses to these questions.

1. France is often symbolized by this bird: _____the rooster_____
2. _____Blue, white, and red_____ are the colors of the French flag.
3. France was once named _____Gaul_____.
4. The French term _____ado_____ refers to a person aged 15 or 16.
5. _____Liberty, equality, and fraternity_____ are three basic principles of French society.

**3** **Et les Américains?** What might a comic-book character based on a "typical American" be like? With a partner, brainstorm a list of stereotypes to create a profile for such a character. Compare the profile you create with your classmates'. Do they fairly represent Americans? Why or why not?

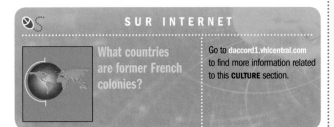

ressources

**S** daccord1.vhlcentral.com

A C T I V I T É S

*vingt-trois* **23**

---

---

**Le français quotidien**
- Point out that this vocabulary is very familiar. These words are usually used in informal conversations among young people.
- Model the pronunciation of each term and have students repeat.

**Portrait**
- Explain that this political comic strip is not unique and that **la bande dessinée (B.D.)** represents serious reading for young and old alike in France. An international comic-book festival takes place every year in the small town of Angoulême, France.
- Ask students why they think *Superdupont* is so popular in France.

**Le monde francophone**
- Have students locate the countries listed here on the world map in **Appendice A**.
- To check comprehension, ask these questions. 1. Which countries' mottos include the word *union*? (Belgium and Ivory Coast) 2. How do other mottos express this same idea? (Senegal: **Un Peuple, un But, une Foi** and Switzerland: **Un pour tous, tous pour un**) 3. Whose motto mentions freedom? (France and Tunisia) 4. Whose motto mentions God? (Monaco and Morocco) 5. What other country considers religion important? (Senegal: **une Foi**) 6. What does Morocco's motto tell you about the country's political structure? (It's a monarchy.)

**Sur Internet** Point out to students that they will find supporting activities and information at **daccord1.vhlcentral.com**.

**2** **Expansion** Have students write four more fill-in-the-blank statements based on the information on this page. Then tell them to exchange papers with a classmate and complete the activity.

**3** **Expansion** Have students draw a picture of their comic-book character or find a photo in a newspaper or magazine to illustrate the character's profile.

## Section Goals

In this section, students will learn:
- subject pronouns
- the verb **être**
- **c'est** and **il/elle est**

## Key Standards

**4.1, 5.1**

**Student Resources**
*Cahier d'exercices*, pp. 9-10;
*Cahier d'activités*, p. 121;
Supersite: Activities,
*Cahier interactif*
**Teacher Resources**
Answer Keys; Audio Script;
Audio Activity MP3s/CD;
Testing program: Grammar Quiz

## Suggestions

- Point to yourself and say: **Je suis professeur**. Then walk up to a student and say: **Tu es…**The student should say: **élève**. Once the pattern has been established, include other subject pronouns and forms of **être** while pointing to other students. Examples: **Il est élève. Elle est élève. Elles sont élèves.**
- Ask students a few simple questions and tell them to respond **Oui** or **Non**. Examples: **Brad Pitt est acteur? Jennifer Aniston est chanteuse?**
- Point out that in French you do not use an article before a profession after **il/elle est** and **ils/elles sont**. You say: **Il est acteur**, not **Il est un acteur**.
- Ask students to give examples of situations in which they would use the **tu** and **vous** forms of **être**.
- Give examples of how **on** can mean *we* in casual conversation: **On est copains.** Explain that **On est copains** is in the plural because it means *We are friends.*
- Point out the liaison in **vous êtes**. Also point out that the **-n** in **on est** is pronounced. Have students pronounce these phrases.
- When teaching the difference between **c'est/ce sont** and **il(s)/elle(s) est/sont**, explain that **c'est/ce sont** is most often followed by a noun and **il(s)/elle(s) est/sont** is most often followed by an adjective. Point out the exceptions: **C'est très bien. Elle est chanteuse.**

### 1B.1 The verb *être*

**Point de départ** In French, as in English, the subject of a verb is the person or thing that carries out the action. The verb expresses the action itself.

SUBJECT ←→ VERB
Le professeur     parle français.
*The professor     speaks French.*

### Subject pronouns

- Subject pronouns replace a noun that is the subject of a verb.

SUBJECT PRONOUN ←→ VERB
Il     parle français.
*He     speaks French.*

**French subject pronouns**

|  | | singular | | plural | |
|---|---|---|---|---|---|
| first person | je | *I* | nous | *we* |
| second person | tu | *you* | vous | *you* |
| third person | il | *he/it* (masc.) | ils | *they* (masc.) |
| | elle | *she/it* (fem.) | elles | *they* (fem.) |
| | on | *one* | | |

- Subject pronouns in French show number (singular vs. plural) and gender (masculine vs. feminine). When a subject consists of both genders, use the masculine form.

**Ils** dansent très bien.
*They dance very well.*

**Ils** sont de Dakar.
*They are from Dakar.*

- Use **tu** for informal address and **vous** for formal. **Vous** is also the plural form of *you*, both informal and formal.

Comment vas-**tu**?          Comment allez-**vous**?
*How's it going?*            *How are you?*

- The subject pronoun **on** refers to people in general, just as the English subject pronouns *one, they,* or *you* sometimes do. **On** can also mean *we* in a casual style. **On** always takes the same verb form as **il** and **elle**.

En France, **on** parle français.     **On** est au café.
*In France, they speak French.*       *We are at the coffee shop.*

**24**   *vingt-quatre*

---

**1** **Pascal répète** Pascal repeats everything his older sister Odile says. Give his response after each statement, using subject pronouns.

**MODÈLE** Chantal est étudiante. *Elle est étudiante.*

1. Les professeurs sont en Tunisie. Ils sont en Tunisie.
2. Mon (*My*) petit ami Charles n'est pas ici. Il n'est pas ici.
3. Moi, je suis chanteuse. Tu es chanteuse.
4. Nadège et moi, nous sommes à l'université. Vous êtes à l'université.
5. Tu es élève. Je suis élève.
6. L'ordinateur est dans (*in*) la chambre. Il est dans la chambre.
7. Claude et Charles sont là. Ils sont là.
8. Lucien et toi, vous êtes copains. Nous sommes copains.

**2** **Où sont-ils?** Thérèse wants to know where all her friends are. Tell her by completing the sentences with the appropriate subject pronouns and the correct forms of **être**.

**MODÈLE** Sylvie / au café *Elle est au café.*

1. Georges / à la faculté de médecine Il est à la faculté de médecine.
2. Marie et moi / dans (*in*) la salle de classe Nous sommes dans la salle de classe.
3. Christine et Anne / à la bibliothèque Elles sont à la bibliothèque.
4. Richard et Vincent / là-bas Ils sont là-bas.
5. Véronique, Marc et Anne / à la librairie Ils sont à la librairie.
6. Jeanne / au bureau Elle est au bureau.

**3** **Identifiez** Describe these photos using **c'est**, **ce sont**, **il/elle est**, or **ils/elles sont**.

1. ___C'est___ un acteur.

4. ___Elle est___ chanteuse.

2. ___Il est___ ici.

5. ___Elle est___ là.

3. ___Elles sont___ copines.

6. ___Ce sont___ des montres.

 Practice more at **daccord1.vhlcentral.com.**

---

## COMMUNICATION

**4 Assemblez** In pairs, take turns using the verb **être** to combine elements from both columns. Talk about yourselves and people you know. *Answers will vary.*

| A | B |
|---|---|
| **Singulier:** | |
| Je | agréable |
| Tu | d'origine française |
| Mon (*My*, masc.) prof | difficile |
| Mon/Ma (*My*, fem.) | élève |
| camarade de classe | sincère |
| Mon cours | sociable |
| **Pluriel:** | |
| Nous | agréables |
| Mes (*My*) profs | copains/copines |
| Mes camarades de | difficiles |
| classe | élèves |
| Mes cours | sincères |

**5 Qui est-ce?** In pairs, identify who or what is in each picture. If possible, use **il/elle est** or **ils/elles sont** to add something else about each person or place. *Answers will vary.*

**MODÈLE**

*C'est Céline Dion. Elle est chanteuse.*

1.

2.

3.

4.

5.

6.

**6 Enchanté** You and your brother are in a local bookstore. You run into one of his classmates, whom you've never met. In a brief conversation, introduce yourselves, ask how you are, and say something about yourselves using a form of **être**. *Answers will vary.*

### The verb *être*

- **Être** (*to be*) is an irregular verb; its conjugation (set of forms for different subjects) does not follow a pattern. The form **être** is called the infinitive; it does not correspond to any particular subject.

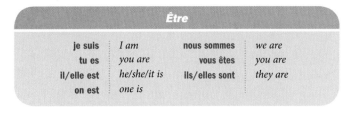

| | | | |
|---|---|---|---|
| **je suis** | *I am* | **nous sommes** | *we are* |
| **tu es** | *you are* | **vous êtes** | *you are* |
| **il/elle est** | *he/she/it is* | **ils/elles sont** | *they are* |
| **on est** | *one is* | | |

- Note that the **-s** of the subject pronoun **vous** is pronounced as an English *z* in the phrase **vous êtes**.

**Vous êtes** à Paris.
*You are in Paris.*

**Vous êtes** M. Leclerc? Enchantée.
*Are you Mr. Leclerc? Pleased to meet you.*

### *C'est* and *il/elle est*

- Use **c'est** or its plural form **ce sont** plus a noun to identify who or what someone or something is. Except with proper names, an article must always precede the noun.

**C'est** un téléphone.
*That's a phone.*

**Ce sont** des photos.
*Those are pictures.*

**C'est** Amina.
*That's Amina.*

- Use the phrases **il/elle est** and **ils/elles sont** to refer to someone or something previously mentioned. Any noun that follows directly must not be accompanied by an article or adjective.

La bibliothèque?
**Elle est** moderne.
*The library?*
*It's modern.*

Voilà M. Richard.
**Il est** professeur.
*There's Mr. Richard.*
*He's a teacher.*

> **BOÎTE À OUTILS**
> Note that in French, unlike English, you cannot use an article before a profession after **il/elle est** and **ils/elles sont**: **il est chanteur** (*he is a singer*); **elles sont actrices** (*they are actresses*).

**Essayez!** Fill in the blanks with the correct forms of the verb **être**.

1. Je ___suis___ ici.
2. Ils ___sont___ intelligents.
3. Tu ___es___ étudiante.
4. Nous ___sommes___ à Québec.
5. Vous ___êtes___ Mme Lacroix?
6. Marie ___est___ chanteuse.

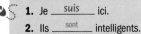

**Essayez!** Have students create additional simple sentences using the verb **être**.

**1 Suggestion** Have students work on this activity in pairs. Tell them to switch roles for items 5–8.

**2 Suggestion** To check students' answers, call on volunteers to read the sentences aloud or write them on the board.

**3 Suggestion** Before beginning the activity, have students quickly identify the items or people in the photos.

**4 Suggestion** Tell students to add two questions of their own to the list and to jot down notes during their interviews.

**5 Suggestion** Tell students to write down their descriptions. After they have completed the activity, call on volunteers to read their descriptions.

**6 Suggestion** Have volunteers act out their conversations for the class.

**OPTIONS**

**Using Video** Replay the video episode, having students focus on subject pronouns and the verb **être**. Ask them to write down as many examples of sentences that use forms of **être** as they can. Stop the video where appropriate to ask comprehension questions about what the characters said.

**Small Groups** Working in small groups, have students invent a story about the people in the photos from **Activité 5**. Tell them to include who the people are, where they are from, and what they do in their story. Circulate around the room and assist with unfamiliar vocabulary as necessary, but encourage students to use terms they already know.

## Section Goals

In this section, students will learn:
- forms, agreement, and position of adjectives
- some descriptive adjectives
- adjectives of nationality

## Key Standards
**4.1, 5.1**

**Student Resources**
*Cahier d'exercices*, pp. 11-12;
*Cahier d'activités*, p. 122;
Supersite: Activities,
*Cahier interactif*
**Teacher Resources**
Answer Keys; Audio Script;
Audio Activity MP3s/CD;
Testing program: Grammar Quiz

## Suggestions

- Write these adjectives on the board: **impatient, impatiente, impatients, impatientes**. Model each adjective in a sentence and ask volunteers to tell you whether it is masculine or feminine and singular or plural.
- Model the pronunciation of adjectives of nationality and have students repeat them. Point out that the feminine forms ending in **-ienne**.
- Go around the room asking **Quelle est votre nationalité?** Also have a few students ask each other their nationalities.
- Use pictures and the names of celebrities to practice other adjectives of nationality. Examples: **Le prince William est-il canadien? (Non, il est anglais.) Julia Roberts est-elle française? (Non, elle est américaine.)**
- Explain that adjectives of nationality can be used as nouns as well. Examples: **La femme anglaise est réservée. L'Anglaise est réservée.**
- Point out that in English most adjectives are placed before the noun, but in French they are placed after the noun. Write the following example on the board, circle the adjective, and draw an arrow pointing to the noun. Example: **C'est un examen difficile.**

### 1B.2 Adjective agreement

**Point de départ** Adjectives are words that describe people, places, and things. In French, adjectives are often used with the verb **être** to point out the qualities of nouns or pronouns.

*Le cours est **difficile**.*

*Je suis **optimiste**.*

- Many adjectives in French are cognates; that is, they have the same or similar spellings and meanings in French and English.

#### Cognate descriptive adjectives

| | | | |
|---|---|---|---|
| agréable | *pleasant* | intelligent(e) | *intelligent* |
| amusant(e) | *fun* | intéressant(e) | *interesting* |
| brillant(e) | *bright* | occupé(e) | *busy* |
| charmant(e) | *charming* | optimiste | *optimistic* |
| désagréable | *unpleasant* | patient(e) | *patient* |
| différent(e) | *different* | pessimiste | *pessimistic* |
| difficile | *difficult* | poli(e) | *polite* |
| égoïste | *selfish* | réservé(e) | *reserved* |
| élégant(e) | *elegant* | sincère | *sincere* |
| impatient(e) | *impatient* | sociable | *sociable* |
| important(e) | *important* | sympathique (sympa) | *nice* |
| indépendant(e) | *independent* | timide | *shy* |

- In French, most adjectives agree in number and gender with the nouns they describe. Most adjectives form the feminine by adding a silent **-e** (no accent) to the end of the masculine form, unless one is already there. Adding a silent **-s** to the end of masculine and feminine forms gives you the plural forms of both.

| MASCULINE SINGULAR   MASCULINE SINGULAR | FEMININE SINGULAR   FEMININE SINGULAR |
|---|---|
| **Henri** est **élégant**. | **Patricia** est **élégante**. |
| *Henri is elegant.* | *Patricia is elegant.* |

| MASCULINE PLURAL   MASCULINE PLURAL | FEMININE PLURAL   FEMININE PLURAL |
|---|---|
| **Henri et Jérôme** sont **élégants**. | **Patricia et Marie** sont **élégantes**. |
| *Henri and Jérôme are elegant.* | *Patricia and Marie are elegant.* |

**BOÎTE À OUTILS**
Use the masculine plural form of an adjective to describe a group composed of masculine and feminine nouns: **Henri et Patricia sont élégants.**

### MISE EN PRATIQUE

**1** **Nous aussi!** Olivier is bragging about himself, but his younger sisters Stéphanie and Estelle believe they possess the same attributes. Tell what they say.

**MODÈLE**

Je suis amusant. Nous aussi, nous sommes *amusantes*.

1. Je suis intelligent. Nous aussi, nous sommes...
   intelligentes.
2. Je suis sincère. Nous aussi, nous sommes...
   sincères.
3. Je suis élégant. Nous aussi, nous sommes...
   élégantes.
4. Je suis patient. Nous aussi, nous sommes...
   patientes.
5. Je suis sociable. Nous aussi, nous sommes...
   sociables.
6. Je suis poli. Nous aussi, nous sommes...
   polies.

**2** **Les nationalités** You are with a group of students from all over the world. Indicate their nationalities according to the cities from which they come.

**MODÈLE**

Monique est de (*from*) Paris. *Elle est française.*

1. Les amies Fumiko et Keiko sont de Tokyo. Elles sont japonaises.
2. Hans est de Berlin. Il est allemand.
3. Juan et Pablo sont de Guadalajara. Ils sont mexicains.
4. Wendy est de Londres. Elle est anglaise.
5. Jared est de San Francisco. Il est américain.
6. Francesca est de Rome. Elle est italienne.
7. Salim et Mehdi sont de Casablanca. Ils sont marocains.
8. Jean-Pierre et Mario sont de Québec. Ils sont québécois/canadiens.

**3** **Voilà Mme...** Your parents are having a party and you point out different people to your friend. Use words and expressions from this grammar point. Answers will vary.

**MODÈLE**

Voilà M. Duval. Il est sénégalais.
C'est un ami.

M. Duval     M. Berthet

Catherine et Jeanne     Georges et Denise     Mme Malbon

 Practice more at **daccord1.vhlcentral.com.**

**Rapid Drill** As a rapid-response drill, say the name of a country and have students respond with the appropriate adjective of nationality. For variation, have students write the adjective on the board or tell them to spell the adjective after they say it.

**Matching** Write each descriptive adjective on two cards or slips of paper and put them in two separate piles in random order. Hand out one card to each student. Tell students they have to find the person who has the same adjective as they do. Example: **Élève 1: Tu es optimiste? Élève 2: Oui, je suis optimiste./Non, je suis sociable.** For variation, this activity can also be used to practice adjectives of nationality.

## COMMUNICATION

**4** **Ils sont comment?** In pairs, take turns describing each item below. Tell your partner whether you agree (**C'est vrai.**) or disagree (**C'est faux.**) with the descriptions. Answers will vary.

### MODÈLE

Johnny Depp
**Élève 1:** *C'est un acteur désagréable.*
**Élève 2:** *C'est faux. Il est charmant.*

1. Beyoncé et Céline Dion
2. les étudiants de Harvard
3. Bono
4. la classe de français
5. le président des États-Unis (*United States*)
6. Tom Hanks et Gérard Depardieu
7. le prof de français
8. Steven Spielberg
9. notre (*our*) lycée
10. Tina Fey et Angelina Jolie

**5** **Interview** Interview someone to see what he or she is like. In pairs, play both roles. Are you compatible as friends? Answers will vary.

### MODÈLE

pessimiste
**Élève 1:** *Tu es pessimiste?*
**Élève 2:** *Non, je suis optimiste.*

1. impatient      5. égoïste
2. modeste        6. sociable
3. timide         7. indépendant
4. sincère        8. amusant

**6** **Au café** You and two classmates are talking about your new teachers, each of whom is very different from the other two. In groups of three, create a dialogue in which you greet one another and describe your teachers. Answers will vary.

- French adjectives are usually placed after the noun they modify when they don't directly follow a form of **être**.

Ce sont des **élèves brillantes**.
*They're brilliant students.*

Bernard est un homme **agréable et poli**.
*Bernard is a pleasant and polite man.*

- Here are some adjectives of nationality. Note that the **-n** of adjectives that end in **-ien** doubles before the final **-e** of the feminine form: **algérienne, canadienne, italienne, vietnamienne**.

### Adjectives of nationality

| | | | |
|---|---|---|---|
| algérien(ne) | *Algerian* | japonais(e) | *Japanese* |
| allemand(e) | *German* | marocain(e) | *Moroccan* |
| anglais(e) | *English* | martiniquais(e) | *from Martinique* |
| américain(e) | *American* | mexicain(e) | *Mexican* |
| canadien(ne) | *Canadian* | québécois(e) | *from Quebec* |
| espagnol(e) | *Spanish* | sénégalais(e) | *Senegalese* |
| français(e) | *French* | suisse | *Swiss* |
| italien(ne) | *Italian* | vietnamien(ne) | *Vietnamese* |

- The first letter of adjectives of nationality is not capitalized.

**Il est américain.**     **Elle est française.**

- An adjective whose masculine singular form already ends in **-s** keeps the identical form in the masculine plural.

Pierre est **un ami sénégalais**.
*Pierre is a Senegalese friend.*

Pierre et Yves sont **des amis sénégalais**.
*Pierre and Yves are Senegalese friends.*

- To ask someone's nationality or heritage, use **Quelle est ta/votre nationalité?** or **Tu es/Vous êtes de quelle origine?**

**Quelle est votre nationalité?**
*What is your nationality?*

**Je suis de nationalité canadienne.**
*I'm of Canadian nationality.*

**Tu es de quelle origine?**
*What is your heritage?*

**Je suis d'origine italienne.**
*I'm of Italian heritage.*

### Essayez!    Write in the correct forms of the adjectives.

1. Marc est ___timide___ (timide).
2. Ils sont ___anglais___ (anglais).
3. Elle adore la littérature ___française___ (français).
4. Ce sont des actrices ___suisses___ (suisse).
5. Elles sont ___réservées___ (réservé).
6. Il y a des universités ___importantes___ (important).
7. Christelle est ___amusante___ (amusant).
8. Les étudiants sont ___polis___ (poli) en cours.

---

**1** **Suggestion** Before beginning the activity, make sure students understand that they should use feminine plural forms of the adjectives. For each item, call on one student to read the sentence in the book and another student to respond.

**2** **Expansion** For additional practice, change the subject of the sentence and have students restate or write the sentences. Examples: **1. Kazumi est de Tokyo. (Il est japonais.) 2. Gerta et Katarina sont de Berlin. (Elles sont allemandes.) 3. Carmen est de Guadalajara. (Elle est mexicaine.) 4. Tom et Susan sont de Londres. (Ils sont anglais.) 5. Linda est de San Francisco. (Elle est américaine.) 6. Luciano et Gino sont de Rome. (Ils sont italiens.) 7. Fatima est de Casablanca. (Elle est marocaine.) 8. Denise et Monique sont de Québec. (Elles sont canadiennes/québécoises.)**

**3** **Expansion** Have students say what each person in the drawing is not. Example: **Madame Malbon n'est pas sociable.**

**4** **Suggestion** Have two volunteers read the **modèle** aloud.

**4** **Expansion** Have small groups brainstorm names of famous people, places, and things not found in the activity and write them in a list. Tell them to include some plural items. Then ask the groups to exchange lists and describe the people, places, and things on that list.

**5** **Suggestions**
- Have students add two more qualities to the list that are important to them.
- After students have completed the activity, ask them if they are compatible roommates and to explain why or why not.

**6** **Suggestion** Tell students to give their teachers names so that it is obvious if they are male or female. Also encourage students to ask each other questions about their teachers during the conversation.

---

**O P T I O N S**

**Using Surveys** Do a quick class survey to find out how many nationalities are represented in your class. As students respond, write the nationality and number of students on the board. Ask: **Combien d'élèves sont d'origine américaine? Mexicaine? Vietnamienne?** If students ask, clarify that the gender of the adjective of nationality agrees with the word **origine**, which is feminine.

**Using Visuals** Have students collect several interesting pictures of people from magazines or newspapers. Have them prepare a description of one of the pictures ahead of time. Invite them to show the pictures to the class and then give their descriptions orally without indicating which picture they are talking about. The class will guess which of the pictures is being described.

**1** **Suggestion** Have pairs act out their conversations for the rest of the class.

**2** **Suggestion** Before students begin to make corrections on their classmates' papers, tell them to check the following: correct use of articles and subject pronouns, subject-verb agreement, and adjective agreement.

**3** **Expansion** Have students repeat the activity and describe their differences this time.

**4** **Suggestion** Because this is the first activity in which the **Feuilles d'activités** are used, tell students that they use the **feuilles** to complete the corresponding activity. Explain that they must approach their classmates with their paper in hand and ask questions following the **modèle**. When they find someone who answers affirmatively, that student signs his or her name.

**5** **Expansion** Have a few volunteers read their descriptions to the class. Then ask the class to point out the differences between the various descriptions.

**6** **Suggestions**
• Divide the class into pairs and distribute the Info Gap Handouts for this activity. Give students ten minutes to complete the activity.
• Have two volunteers read the **modèle** aloud.

---

**1** **Festival francophone** With a partner, choose two characters from the list and act out a conversation between them. The people are meeting for the first time at a Francophone festival. Then, change characters and repeat.
Answers will vary.

**Angélique, Sénégal**     **Abdel, Algérie**

**Laurent, Martinique**     **Sylvain, Suisse**

**Hélène, Canada**     **Daniel, France**

**Mai, Viêt-Nam**     **Nora, Maroc**

**2** **Tu ou vous?** How would the conversations between the characters in **Activité 1** differ if they were all 19-year-old students at a university orientation? Write out what you would have said differently. Then, exchange papers with a new partner and make corrections. Return the paper to your partner and act out the conversation using a new character.
Answers will vary.

**3** **En commun** In pairs, tell your partner the name of a friend. Use adjectives to say what you both (**tous les deux**) have in common. Then, share with the class what you learned about your partner and his or her friend. Answers will vary.

**MODÈLE**

*Charles est un ami. Nous sommes tous les deux amusants.*
*Nous sommes patients aussi.*

---

**4** **Comment es-tu?** Your teacher will give you a worksheet. Survey as many classmates as possible to ask if they would use the adjectives listed to describe themselves. Then, decide which two students in the class are most similar.
Answers will vary.

**MODÈLE**

**Élève 1:** *Tu es timide?*
**Élève 2:** *Non. Je suis sociable.*

| Adjectifs | Noms |
|---|---|
| 1. timide | Éric |
| 2. impatient (e) | |
| 3. optimiste | |
| 4. réservé (e) | |
| 5. charmant (e) | |
| 6. poli (e) | |
| 7. agréable | |
| 8. amusant (e) | |

**5** **Mes camarades de classe** Write a brief description of the students in your French class. What are their names? What are their personalities like? What is their heritage? Use all the French you have learned so far. Your paragraph should be at least eight sentences long. Remember, be complimentary! Answers will vary.

**6** **Les descriptions** Your teacher will give you one set of drawings of eight people and a different set to your partner. Each person in your drawings has something in common with a person in your partner's drawings. Find out what it is without looking at your partner's sheet. Answers will vary.

**MODÈLE**

**Élève 1:** *Jean est à la bibliothèque.*
**Élève 2:** *Gina est à la bibliothèque.*
**Élève 1:** *Jean et Gina sont à la bibliothèque.*

---

**OPTIONS**

**Mini-skits** Have students work in groups of three or four. Tell them to prepare a skit on any situation they wish, provided that they use material presented in this lesson. Possible situations can include meeting at a café (as in **Roman-photo**), meeting in between classes, and introducing friends to teachers. Remind them to use as many adjectives as possible. Encourage students to have fun with the skit and be creative.

**Interview** To practice **vous**, have students ask you yes/no questions. First, have them guess your nationality. Example: **Vous êtes français(e)?** Then have them ask you about your personality. Example: **Vous êtes impatient(e)?**

# À l'écoute  Audio: Activities

## STRATÉGIE

### Listening for words you know

You can get the gist of a conversation by listening for words and phrases you already know.

🎧 To help you practice this strategy, listen to this sentence and make a list of the words you have already learned.

_____ _____

## Préparation

Look at the photograph. Where are these people? What are they doing? In your opinion, do they know one another? Why or why not? What do you think they're talking about?

## À vous d'écouter 🎧

As you listen, circle the items you associate with Hervé and those you associate with Laure and Lucas.

| HERVÉ | LAURE ET LUCAS |
|---|---|
| la littérature | le café |
| l'examen | la littérature |
| le bureau | la sociologie |
| le café | la librairie |
| la bibliothèque | le lycée |
| la librairie | l'examen |
| le tableau | l'université |

 Practice more at **daccord1.vhlcentral.com.**

## Compréhension

**Vrai ou faux?** Based on the conversation you heard, indicate whether each of the following statements is **vrai** or **faux**.

| | Vrai | Faux |
|---|---|---|
| 1. Lucas and Hervé are good friends. | ☐ | ☑ |
| 2. Hervé is preparing for an exam. | ☑ | ☐ |
| 3. Laure and Lucas know each other from school. | ☑ | ☐ |
| 4. Hervé is on his way to the library. | ☐ | ☑ |
| 5. Lucas and Laure are going to a café. | ☑ | ☐ |
| 6. Lucas studies literature. | ☐ | ☑ |
| 7. Laure is in high school. | ☐ | ☑ |
| 8. Laure is not feeling well today. | ☐ | ☑ |

**Présentations** 👥 It's your turn to get to know your classmates. Using the conversation you heard as a model, select a partner you do not know and introduce yourself to him or her in French. Follow the steps below.

- Greet your partner.
- Find out his or her name.
- Ask how he or she is doing.
- Introduce your partner to another student.
- Say good-bye.

## Section Goals

In this section, students will:
- learn to listen for known vocabulary
- listen to sentences containing familiar and unfamiliar vocabulary
- listen to a conversation and complete several activities

## Key Standards
1.2, 2.1

**Student Resources**
Supersite: Activities, Audio
**Teacher Resources**
Answer Keys; Audio Script; Audio Activity MP3s/CD

**Stratégie**
Script Je vous présente une amie, Juliette Lenormand. Elle étudie la sociologie à la faculté.

**Successful Language Learning** Tell your students that many people feel nervous about their ability to comprehend what they learn in a foreign language. Tell them that they will probably feel less anxious if they follow the advice for increasing listening comprehension in the **Stratégie** sections.

**Préparation** Have students look at the photo and describe what they see. Ask them to justify their responses based on the visual clues.

**À vous d'écouter**
Script
HERVÉ: Salut, Laure! Ça va?
LAURE: Bonjour, Hervé. Ça va bien. Et toi?
HERVÉ: Pas mal, merci.
LAURE: Je te présente un copain de l'université. Lucas, Hervé. Hervé, Lucas.
LUCAS: Enchanté.
H: Bonjour, Lucas. Comment vas-tu?
LU: Très bien, merci.
LA: Qu'est-ce que tu fais, Hervé?
H: Je vais à la librairie pour acheter un livre sur la littérature.
LA: Pour un examen?
H: Oui, pour un examen. Et vous?
LA: Nous, on va au café.
H: Alors, à plus tard.
LA: Oui, salut.
LU: Au revoir, Hervé.
H: À bientôt.

**Interactive Map Reading**

# Panorama

## Le monde francophone

### Les pays en chiffres°

Organisation internationale de la Francophonie

- Nombre de pays° où le français est langue° officielle: *28*
- Nombre de pays où le français est parlé°: *plus de° 60*
- Nombre de francophones dans le monde°: *200.000.000 (deux cents millions)*

SOURCE: Organisation internationale de la Francophonie

### Villes capitales

- **Algérie:** *Alger*
- **Cameroun:** *Yaoundé*
- **France:** *Paris*
- **Guinée:** *Conakry*
- **Haïti:** *Port-au-Prince*
- **Laos:** *Vientiane*
- **Mali:** *Bamako*
- **Rwanda:** *Kigali*
- **Seychelles:** *Victoria*
- **Suisse:** *Berne*

### Francophones célèbres

- **Marie Curie**, *Pologne, scientifique, prix Nobel en chimie et physique (1867–1934)*
- **René Magritte**, *Belgique, peintre° (1898–1967)*
- **Ousmane Sembène**, *Sénégal, cinéaste° et écrivain° (1923–2007)*
- **Jean Reno**, *France, acteur° (1948– )*
- **Céline Dion**, *Québec, chanteuse° (1968– )*
- **Marie-José Pérec**, *Guadeloupe (France), athlète° (1968– )*

**chiffres** numbers  **pays** countries  **langue** language  **parlé** spoken  **plus de** more than  **monde** world  **peintre** painter  **cinéaste** filmmaker  **écrivain** writer  **chanteuse** singer  **sur** on  **comme** such as  **l'OTAN** NATO  **Jeux** Games  **deuxième** second  **enseignée** taught  **Heiva** an annual Tahitian festival

**30** *trente*

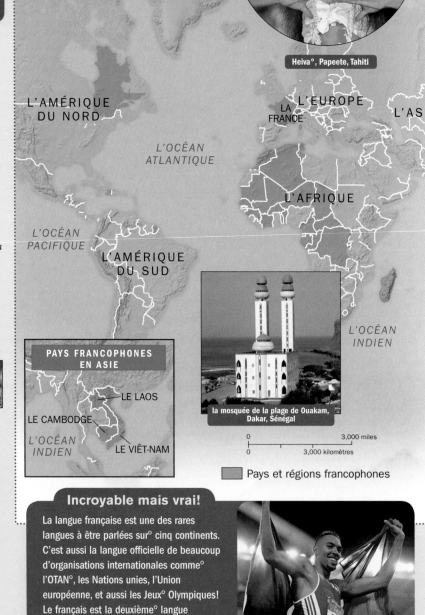

**Heiva°, Papeete, Tahiti**

L'AMÉRIQUE DU NORD

L'EUROPE

LA FRANCE

L'ASIE

L'OCÉAN ATLANTIQUE

L'AFRIQUE

L'OCÉAN PACIFIQUE

L'AMÉRIQUE DU SUD

L'OCÉAN INDIEN

**PAYS FRANCOPHONES EN ASIE**

LE LAOS

LE CAMBODGE

L'OCÉAN INDIEN

LE VIÊT-NAM

la mosquée de la plage de Ouakam, Dakar, Sénégal

| 0 | 3,000 miles |
| 0 | 3,000 kilomètres |

■ Pays et régions francophones

### Incroyable mais vrai!

La langue française est une des rares langues à être parlées sur° cinq continents. C'est aussi la langue officielle de beaucoup d'organisations internationales comme° l'OTAN°, les Nations unies, l'Union européenne, et aussi les Jeux° Olympiques! Le français est la deuxième° langue enseignée° dans le monde, après l'anglais.

## La société

### Le français au Québec

Au Québec, province du Canada, le français est la langue officielle, parlée par° 80% (quatre-vingts pour cent) de la population. Les Québécois, pour° préserver l'usage de la langue, ont° une loi qui oblige l'affichage° en français dans les lieux° publics. Le français est aussi la langue co-officielle du Canada: les employés du gouvernement doivent° être bilingues.

## Les gens

### Les francophones d'Algérie

Depuis° 1830 (mille huit cent trente), date de l'acquisition de l'Algérie par la France, l'influence culturelle française y° est très importante. À présent ancienne° colonie, l'Algérie est un des plus grands° pays francophones au monde. L'arabe est la langue officielle, mais le français est la deuxième langue parlée et est compris° par la majorité de la population algérienne.

## Les destinations

### La Louisiane

Ce territoire au sud° des États-Unis a été nommé «Louisiane» en l'honneur du Roi° de France Louis XIV. En 1803 (mille huit cent trois), Napoléon Bonaparte vend° la colonie aux États-Unis pour 15 millions de dollars, pour empêcher° son acquisition par les Britanniques. Aujourd'hui° en Louisiane, 200.000 (deux cent mille) personnes parlent° le français cajun. La Louisiane est connue° pour sa° cuisine cajun, comme° le jambalaya, ici sur° la photo avec le chef Paul Prudhomme.

## Les traditions

### La Journée internationale de la Francophonie

Chaque année°, l'Organisation internationale de la Francophonie (O.I.F.) coordonne la Journée internationale de la Francophonie. Dans plus de° 100 (cent) pays et sur cinq continents, on célèbre la langue française et la diversité culturelle francophone avec des festivals de musique, de gastronomie, de théâtre, de danse et de cinéma. Le rôle principal de l'O.I.F. est la promotion de la langue française et la défense de la diversité culturelle et linguistique du monde francophone.

JOURNÉE INTERNATIONALE DE LA FRANCOPHONIE
LA FRANCOPHONIE AU CŒUR

---

**Qu'est-ce que vous avez appris?** Complete the sentences.

1. <u>Ousmane Sembène</u> est un cinéaste africain.

2. <u>200 millions</u> de personnes parlent français dans le monde.

3. <u>L'Organisation internationale de la Francophonie</u> est responsable de la promotion de la diversité culturelle francophone.

4. Les employés du gouvernement du Canada parlent <u>anglais et français</u>.

5. En Algérie, la langue officielle est <u>l'arabe</u>.

6. Une majorité d'Algériens comprend (understands) <u>le français</u>.

7. Le nom «Louisiane» vient du (comes from the) nom de <u>Louis XIV</u>.

8. Plus de 100 pays célèbrent <u>la Journée internationale de la Francophonie</u>.

9. Le français est parlé sur <u>cinq</u> continents.

10. En 1803, Napoléon Bonaparte vend <u>la Louisiane</u> aux États-Unis.

Practice more at **daccord1.vhlcentral.com.**

### SUR INTERNET

 Go to **daccord1.vhlcentral.com** to find more cultural information related to this **PANORAMA**.

1. Les États-Unis célèbrent la Journée internationale de la Francophonie. Faites (Make) une liste de trois événements (events) et dites (say) où ils ont lieu (take place).

2. Trouvez des informations sur un(e) chanteur/chanteuse francophone célèbre aux États-Unis. Citez (Cite) trois titres de chanson (song titles).

**parlée par** spoken by **pour** in order to **ont** have **loi** law **affichage** posting **lieux** places **doivent** must **Depuis** Since **y** there **ancienne** former **un des plus grands** one of the largest **compris** understood **au sud** in the South **a été nommé** was named **Roi** King **vend** sells **empêcher** to prevent **Aujourd'hui** Today **parlent** speak **connue** known **sa** its **comme** such as **sur** in **Chaque année** Each year **dans plus de** in more than

ressources

CE
pp. 13–14    daccord1.vhlcentral.com

---

Since Jacques Cartier first arrived in the Gaspé and claimed the land for the French king in 1534, the people of Quebec have maintained their language and culture, despite being outnumbered and surrounded by English speakers. French became an official language of Canada in 1867. Ask students if they know of any places in the United States where people speak two languages or they can see bilingual signs.

**Les francophones d'Algérie** Algeria gained its independence from France in 1962, but French is still taught from primary school through high school. French is principally used in business relations, some social situations, and in the information industries. Some newspapers, as well as several television and radio broadcasts, are produced in French.

**La Louisiane** The early settlers of Louisiana came from France and Acadia (now Nova Scotia and adjacent areas) during the seventeenth and eighteenth centuries. The Acadian settlers were descendents of French Canadians who were exiled from Acadia by the English and eventually settled in the bayou region. Cajun French evolved over time borrowing terms from American Indian, German, English, African, and Spanish speakers.

**La Journée internationale de la Francophonie**
- The members of **l'Organisation internationale de la Francophonie** comprise 63 states and governments. The celebrations in the various Francophone regions take place throughout the month of March. The name **20 mars** was chosen to commemorate the signature of a treaty which created **l'Agence intergouvernementale de la Francophonie.**
- Point out the symbol of **l'Organisation internationale de la Francophonie** on page 30 next to the heading **Les pays en chiffres.**

---

**Using Maps** Have students work in pairs. Tell them to look at the maps in the frontmatter and make a list of the Francophone countries and capitals that do not appear in the section **Villes capitales.** Point out that they need to find eighteen countries.

**Cultural Comparison** In groups of three, have students compare **la Journée internationale de la Francophonie** to a cultural celebration held in their town, city, or country. Tell them to discuss the purpose of each celebration, the reasons why people attend them, and the types of events or activities that are part of the celebration.

## Section Goals

In this section, students will:
• learn to recognize cognates
• use context to guess the meaning of new words
• read some pages from an address book in French

## Key Standards

1.3, 3.1, 5.1

**Stratégie** Tell students that cognates are words in one language that have identical or similar counterparts in another language. True cognates are close in meaning, so recognizing French words that are cognates of English words can help them read French. To help students recognize cognates, write these common correspondences between French and English on the board: **-ie** = *-y* (**sociologie**); **-ique** = *-ic* (**fantastique**); **-if(-ive)** = *-ive* (**active**).

**Successful Language Learning** Tell students that reading in French will be less anxiety provoking if they follow the advice in the **Stratégie** sections, which are designed to reinforce and improve reading comprehension skills.

**Examinez le texte** Ask students to tell you what type of text this is and how they can tell. (It's an excerpt from an address book. You can tell because it contains names and telephone numbers.)

**Mots apparentés**
• Check to see if students found all of the cognates from the **Stratégie** box in the reading: **pharmacie, dentiste, télévision, médecin, banque,** and **restaurant.**
• If students are having trouble finding other cognates, point out a few to get them started: **route** (*route*), **avenue** (*avenue*), **boulevard** (*boulevard*), **théâtre** (*theater*), **comédie** (*comedy*), **dîner** (*dinner*), and **municipale** (*municipal*).

**Devinez** Ask volunteers to share their responses with the class. Find out how many were able to guess the meanings correctly: **horaires** (*schedule [hours open]*), **lundi** (*Monday*), **ouvert** (*open*), **soirs** (*evenings; nights*), and **tous** (*all; every*).

# Lecture Ⓢ Reading

## Avant la lecture

### STRATÉGIE

#### Recognizing cognates

Cognates are words that share similar meanings and spellings in two or more languages. When reading in French, it's helpful to look for cognates and use them to guess the meaning of what you're reading. However, watch out for false cognates. For example, **librairie** means *bookstore*, not *library*, and **coin** means *corner*, not *coin*. Look at this list of French words. Can you guess the meaning of each word?

| | |
|---|---|
| important | banque |
| pharmacie | culture |
| intelligent | actif |
| dentiste | sociologie |
| décision | fantastique |
| télévision | restaurant |
| médecine | police |

### Examinez le texte

Briefly look at the document. What kind of information is listed? In what order is it listed? Where do you usually find such information? Can you guess what this document is?

### Mots apparentés

Read the list of cognates in the **Stratégie** box again. How many cognates can you find in the reading selection? Are there additional cognates in the reading? Which ones? Can you guess their English equivalents?

### Devinez

In addition to using cognates and words you already know, you can also use context to guess the meaning of words you do not know. Find the following words in the reading selection and try to guess what they mean. Compare your answers with those of a classmate.

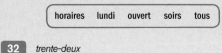

| horaires | lundi | ouvert | soirs | tous |

*Carnet d'adresses*

**Carnet d'adresses**

Recherche ▶

A B C D E F G H I J K L

☑ **DAMERY Jean-Claude**
dentiste
✉ 18, rue des Lilas
45000 Orléans
02 38 23 45 46

☐ **Café de la Poste**
Ouvert° tous les jours°, de 7h00° à 22h00
✉ 25, place de la Poste
45000 Orléans
02 38 27 18 00

☐ **Librairie Balzac**
Horaires: 9h00–12h00 et 14h00–18h00
✉ 18, route de Lorient
45000 Orléans
02 38 18 60 36

☐ **DANTEC Pierre-Henri**
médecin généraliste
✉ 23, rue du Lac
45000 Orléans
02 38 47 34 20

☑ **Banque du Centre**
Ouvert de 9h00 à 17h00 du lundi° au vendredi°
✉ 17, boulevard Giroud
45000 Orléans
02 38 58 35 00

Dîner vendredi 8h00
Restaurant du Chat qui dort

**O P T I O N S**

**Cognates** Write these words on the board and have students guess the English meaning: **un agent** (*agent*), **un concert** (*concert*), **la géographie** (*geography*), **une guitare** (*guitar*), **la musique** (*music*), **un réfrigérateur** (*refrigerator*), **confortable** (*comfortable*), **courageux** (*courageous*), **riche** (*rich*), and **typique** (*typical*). Then have them look at the **Vocabulaire** on page 36 and identify all the cognates they have learned.

**Using Lists** Have students work in groups of three or four. Assign four letters of the alphabet to each group. (Adjust the number of letters according to your class size so that the entire alphabet is covered.) Tell students to use a French-English dictionary and make a list of all the cognates they find beginning with their assigned letters. Have groups read their list of cognates to the rest of the class.

# Après la lecture

**Où aller?** Tell where each of these people should go based on what they need or want to do.

**MODÈLE**

Camille's daughter is starting high school.
*Lycée Molière*

1. Mrs. Leroy needs to deposit her paycheck.
   Banque du Centre

2. Laurent would like to take his girlfriend out for a special dinner.
   Restaurant du Chat qui dort

3. Marc has a toothache.
   DAMERY Jean-Claude, dentiste

4. Céleste would like to go see a play tonight.
   Théâtre de la Comédie

5. Pauline's computer is broken.
   Messier et fils, Réparations ordinateurs et télévisions

6. Mr. Duchemin needs to buy some aspirin for his son.
   Pharmacie Vidal

7. Jean-Marie needs a book on French history but he doesn't want to buy one.
   Bibliothèque municipale

8. Noémie thinks she has the flu.
   DANTEC Pierre-Henri, médecin généraliste

9. Mr. and Mrs. Prudhomme want to go out for breakfast this morning.
   Café de la Poste

10. Jonathan wants to buy a new book for his sister's birthday.
    Librairie Balzac

**Notre annuaire** With a classmate, select three of the listings from the reading and use them as models to create similar listings in French advertising places or services in your area.

**MODÈLE**

Restaurant du Chat qui dort
Ouvert tous les soirs pour le dîner
Horaires: 19h00 à 23h00
29, avenue des Rosiers
45000 Orléans
02 38 45 35 08

*Always Good Eats Restaurant*
*Ouvert tous les jours*
*Horaires: 6h00 à 19h00*
*1250 9th Avenue*
*San Diego, CA 92108*
*224-0932*

---

**11:29 AM**   **Contacts**   **Éditer**

**P Q R S T U V W X Y Z**

**Messier et fils°**
Réparations ordinateurs et télévisions
56, boulevard Henri IV    02 38 44 42 59
**45000 Orléans**

**Théâtre de la Comédie**
11, place de la Comédie    02 38 45 32 11
**45000 Orléans**

**Pharmacie Vidal**
45, rue des Acacias    02 38 13 57 53
**45000 Orléans**

**Restaurant du Chat qui dort°**
Ouvert tous les soirs pour le dîner / Horaires: 19h00 à 23h00
29, avenue des Rosiers    02 38 45 35 08
**45000 Orléans**

**Bibliothèque municipale**
Place de la gare    02 38 56 43 22
**45000 Orléans**

**Lycée Molière**
15, rue Molière    02 38 29 23 04
**45000 Orléans**

Ouvert *Open* tous les jours *every day* 7h00 (sept heures) *7:00* lundi *Monday* vendredi *Friday* fils *son(s)* Chat qui dort *Sleeping cat*

**Où aller?** Go over the activity with the class. If students have trouble inferring the answer to any question, help them identify the cognate or provide additional context clues.

**Notre annuaire**
- Before beginning the activity, have students brainstorm places and services in the area, and write a list on the board. You might also want to bring in a few local telephone books for students to use as references for addresses and phone numbers.
- You may wish to have students include e-mail addresses (**les adresses e-mail**) in their lists.

**OPTIONS**

**Addresses** To review numbers 0–60, have students work in pairs and take turns asking each other the phone numbers and addresses of the people and places listed in the reading. Example: **Élève 1: Le numéro de téléphone du dentiste Jean-Claude DAMERY? Élève 2: C'est le zéro deux, trente-huit, vingt-trois, quarante-cinq, quarante-six. Élève 1: Et l'adresse? Élève 2: Dix-huit, rue des Lilas, Orléans.**

**Reading Aloud** Have several students select one of the three listings they created for the **Notre annuaire** activity to read aloud. Instruct the rest of the class to write down the information they hear. To check students' work, have the students who read the listings write the information on the board.

## Section Goals

In this section, students will:
- learn strategies for writing in French
- learn to write a telephone/address book in French
- integrate vocabulary and structures taught in **Leçons 1A–1B**

## Key Standards

**1.3, 3.1, 5.1**

**Stratégie** Have students focus on the final point under the "Do" section. Ask them to think about the types of writing that most interests them as readers. Why? Is it that the writer supplies vivid detail? Interesting anecdotes? An easy-to-read style? Is it simply that the subject is important to them? This shows the value of putting themselves in their reader's place.

**Thème** Introduce students to standard headings used in a telephone/address list: **Nom**, **Adresse**, **Numéro de téléphone**, **Numéro de portable**, and **Adresse e-mail**. Students may wish to add notes pertaining to home (**Numéro de domicile**) or office (**Numéro de bureau**) telephone numbers, fax numbers (**Numéro de fax**), or office hours (**Horaires de bureau**).

# Écriture

### Writing in French

Why do we write? All writing has a purpose. For example, we may write a poem to reveal our innermost feelings, a letter to impart information, or an essay to persuade others to accept a point of view. Proficient writers are not born, however. Writing requires time, thought, effort, and a lot of practice. Here are some tips to help you write more effectively in French.

**DO**

▶ Write your ideas in French.

▶ Make an outline of your ideas.

▶ Decide what the purpose of your writing will be.

▶ Use the grammar and vocabulary that you know.

▶ Use your textbook for examples of style, format, and expressions in French.

▶ Use your imagination and creativity to make your writing more interesting.

▶ Put yourself in your reader's place to determine if your writing is interesting.

**DON'T**

▶ Translate your ideas from English to French.

▶ Repeat what is in the textbook or on a web page.

▶ Use a bilingual dictionary until you have learned how to use one effectively.

## Thème

# Faites une liste!

### Avant l'écriture

1. Imagine that several students from a French-speaking country will be spending a year at your school. You've been asked to put together a list of people and places that might be useful and of interest to them. Your list should include:

■ Your name, address, phone number(s) (home and/or cell), and e-mail address

■ The names of four other students in your French class, their addresses, phone numbers, and e-mail addresses

■ Your French teacher's name, office and/or cell phone number(s), and e-mail address

■ Your school library's phone number and hours

■ The names, addresses, and phone numbers of three places near your school where students like to go

2. Write down the names of the classmates you want to include.

3. Interview your classmates and your teacher to find out the information you need to include. Use the following questions and write down their responses.

| Informal | Formal |
|---|---|
| Comment t'appelles-tu? | Comment vous appelez-vous? |
| Quel est ton numéro de téléphone? | Quel est votre numéro de téléphone? |
| Quelle est ton adresse e-mail? | Quelle est votre adresse e-mail? |

**Stratégie** Review the **Do** list with students. Ask them if they have tried any of these tips. Tell them that they should refer back to this list as they complete the **Écriture** tasks in each lesson. Students may also find it helpful to keep track of which tips work best for them.

**Avant l'écriture** Before students begin writing, brainstorm a list of popular places where students frequently go. Group them by name in different categories, such as **bibliothèques, cafés, restaurants, magasins, théâtres, parcs, librairies**, and so on. Encourage students to incorporate these category headings into their lists, along with the specific names of different businesses that fall into the categories.

4. Think of three places in your community that a group of students from a French-speaking country would enjoy visiting. They could be a library, a bookstore, a coffee shop, a restaurant, a theater, or a park. Find out their addresses, telephone numbers, and e-mail addresses/URLs and write them down.

5. Go online and do a search for two websites that promote your town or area's history, culture, and attractions. Write down their URLs.

## Écriture

Write your complete list, making sure it includes all the relevant information. It should include at least five people (with their phone numbers and e-mail addresses), four places (with phone numbers and addresses), and two websites (with URLs). Avoid using a dictionary and just write what you can in French.

## Après l'écriture

1. Exchange your list with a partner's. Comment on his or her work by answering these questions.

   - Did your partner include the correct number of people, places, and websites?

   - Did your partner include the pertinent information for each?

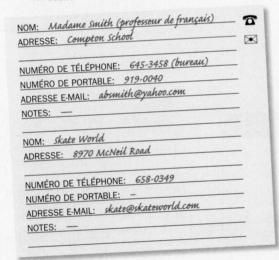

NOM: Madame Smith (professeur de français) ☎

ADRESSE: Compton School ✉

NUMÉRO DE TÉLÉPHONE: 645-3458 (bureau)

NUMÉRO DE PORTABLE: 919-0040

ADRESSE E-MAIL: absmith@yahoo.com

NOTES: —

NOM: Skate World

ADRESSE: 8970 McNeil Road

NUMÉRO DE TÉLÉPHONE: 658-0349

NUMÉRO DE PORTABLE: —

ADRESSE E-MAIL: skate@skateworld.com

NOTES: —

2. Edit your partner's work, pointing out any spelling or content errors. Notice the use of these editing symbols:

   - ℐ   delete

   - ∧   insert letter or word(s) written in margin

   - |   replace letter or word(s) with one(s) in margin

   - ≡   change to uppercase

   - /   change to lowercase

   - ∿   transpose indicated letters or words

Now look at this model of what an edited draft looks like:

o   Nm: Sally Wagner
     ∧
é   Téléphone: 655–8888

    Adresse e-mail: sally@uru.edu

    Nom: Madame Nancy smith
                        ≡
Téléphone: 655–8090

    Adresse e-mail: nsmith@uru.edu

3. Revise your list according to your partner's comments and corrections. After writing the final version, read it one more time to eliminate these kinds of problems:

   - spelling errors
   - punctuation errors
   - capitalization errors
   - use of incorrect verb forms
   - use of incorrect adjective agreement
   - use of incorrect definite and indefinite articles

## EVALUATION

### Criteria

**Content** Includes all the information mentioned in the five parts of the task description.
Scale: 1  2  3  4  5

**Organization** Organizes the list similarly to the model provided.
Scale: 1  2  3  4  5

**Accuracy** Spells the French words used to designate the list categories correctly, including correct accentuation.
Scale: 1  2  3  4  5

**Creativity** Includes extra information (such as home, office, and fax numbers), more than three students, more than three places.
Scale: 1  2  3  4  5

### Scoring

| | |
|---|---|
| Excellent | 18-20 points |
| Good | 14-17 points |
| Satisfactory | 10-13 points |
| Unsatisfactory | < 10 points |

## Key Standards

**4.1**

**Teacher Resources**
Vocabulary MP3s/CD

**Suggestions**

- Tell students that this is active vocabulary for which they are responsible and that it will appear on tests and exams.
- Tell them that an easy way to study from **Vocabulaire** is to cover up the French half of each section, leaving only the English equivalents exposed. They can then quiz themselves on the French items. To focus on the English equivalents of the French entries, they simply reverse this process.

### En classe

| | |
|---|---|
| une bibliothèque | library |
| un café | café |
| une faculté | university; faculty |
| une librairie | bookstore |
| un lycée | high school |
| une salle de classe | classroom |
| une université | university |
| un dictionnaire | dictionary |
| une différence | difference |
| un examen | exam, test |
| la littérature | literature |
| un livre | book |
| un problème | problem |
| un résultat | result |
| la sociologie | sociology |
| un bureau | desk; office |
| une carte | map |
| une chaise | chair |
| une fenêtre | window |
| une horloge | clock |
| un ordinateur | computer |
| une porte | door |
| une table | table |
| un tableau | blackboard; picture |
| la télévision | television |
| un cahier | notebook |
| une calculatrice | calculator |
| une chose | thing |
| une corbeille (à papier) | wastebasket |
| un crayon | pencil |
| une feuille (de papier) | sheet of paper |
| un instrument | instrument |
| une montre | watch |
| un objet | object |
| un sac à dos | backpack |
| un stylo | pen |

### Les personnes

| | |
|---|---|
| un(e) ami(e) | friend |
| un(e) camarade de chambre | roommate |
| un(e) camarade de classe | classmate |
| une classe | class (group of students) |
| un copain/une copine (fam.) | friend |
| un(e) élève | pupil, student |
| un(e) étudiant(e) | student |
| un(e) petit(e) ami(e) | boyfriend/girlfriend |
| une femme | woman |
| une fille | girl |
| un garçon | boy |
| un homme | man |
| une personne | person |
| un acteur/une actrice | actor |
| un chanteur/ une chanteuse | singer |
| un professeur | teacher, professor |

### Les présentations

| | |
|---|---|
| Comment vous appelez-vous? (form.) | What is your name? |
| Comment t'appelles-tu? (fam.) | What is your name? |
| Enchanté(e). | Delighted. |
| Et vous/toi? (form./fam.) | And you? |
| Je m'appelle... | My name is... |
| Je vous/te présente... (form./fam.) | I would like to introduce (name) to you. |

### Identifier

| | |
|---|---|
| c'est/ce sont | it's/they are |
| Combien...? | How much/many...? |
| ici | here |
| Il y a... | There is/are... |
| là | there |
| là-bas | over there |
| Qu'est-ce que c'est? | What is it? |
| Qui est-ce? | Who is it? |
| Quoi? | What? |
| voici | here is/are |
| voilà | there is/are |

### Bonjour et au revoir

| | |
|---|---|
| À bientôt. | See you soon. |
| À demain. | See you tomorrow. |
| À plus tard. | See you later. |
| À tout à l'heure. | See you later. |
| Au revoir. | Good-bye. |
| Bonne journée! | Have a good day! |
| Bonjour. | Good morning.; Hello. |
| Bonsoir. | Good evening.; Hello. |
| Salut! | Hi!; Bye! |

### Comment ça va?

| | |
|---|---|
| Ça va? | What's up?; How are things? |
| Comment allez-vous? (form.) | How are you? |
| Comment vas-tu? (fam.) | How are you? |
| Comme ci, comme ça. | So-so. |
| Je vais bien/mal. | I am doing well/badly. |
| Moi aussi. | Me too. |
| Pas mal. | Not badly. |
| Très bien. | Very well. |

### Expressions de politesse

| | |
|---|---|
| De rien. | You're welcome. |
| Excusez-moi. (form.) | Excuse me. |
| Excuse-moi. (fam.) | Excuse me. |
| Il n'y a pas de quoi. | You're welcome. |
| Je vous/t'en prie. (form./fam.) | You're welcome.; It's nothing. |
| Merci beaucoup. | Thank you very much. |
| Monsieur (M.) | Sir (Mr.) |
| Madame (Mme) | Ma'am (Mrs.) |
| Mademoiselle (Mlle) | Miss |
| Pardon. | Pardon (me). |
| S'il vous plaît. (form.) | Please. |
| S'il te plaît. (fam.) | Please. |

| | |
|---|---|
| *Expressions utiles* | See pp. 7 and 21. |
| Numbers 0–60 | See p. 12. |
| Subject pronouns | See p. 24. |
| *être* | See p. 25. |
| Descriptive adjectives | See p. 26. |
| Adjectives of nationality | See p. 27. |

daccord1.vhlcentral.com

# Au lycée

### Pour commencer
- What object is on the table?
  a. une montre   b. un stylo   c. un tableau
- What is Rachid looking at?
  a. un cahier   b. un ordinateur   c. un livre
- How does Rachid look in this photo?
  a. intelligent   b. sociable   c. égoïste
- Which word describes what he is doing?
  a. arriver   b. voyager   c. étudier

## Unit Goals

**Leçon 2A**

In this lesson, students will learn:
- terms for academic subjects
- to express likes and dislikes
- about liaisons
- about French high schools and the Canadian French immersion program
- the present tense of regular **-er** verbs
- about spelling changes in **-cer** and **-ger** verbs
- to ask questions and express negation
- about the French company Clairefontaine

**Leçon 2B**

In this lesson, students will learn:
- terms for talking about schedules and when things happen
- to pronounce the French **r**
- about **le bac** and higher education in France
- more about university life through specially shot video footage
- the present tense of **avoir**
- some expressions with **avoir**
- to tell time
- to listen for cognates

**Savoir-faire**

In this section, students will learn:
- cultural, economic, geographical, and historical information about France
- to use text formats to predict content
- to brainstorm before writing
- to write a personal description

**Pour commencer**
- b. un stylo
- b. un ordinateur
- a. intelligent
- c. étudier

---

**RESOURCES**

**Student Materials**
**Print:** Student Book, Workbooks (*Cahier d'exercices, Cahier d'activités*)
**Technology:** MAESTRO® *Cahier interactif* and Supersite (Audio, Video, Practice)

**Teacher Materials**
DVDs (*Roman-photo, Flash culture*)
Teacher's Resources (Scripts, Answer Keys, Testing Program)
Audio CDs (Testing Program, Textbook, Audio Program)

MAESTRO® Supersite: Student Supersite Content; Planning and Teaching Resources (Overheads, *PowerPoints*, Lesson Plans, Information Gaps and *Feuilles d'activités*); Learning Management System (Gradebook, Assignments); Audio MP3s and Streaming Video
**D'ACCORD! 1 Supersite:** daccord1.vhlcentral.com

# Leçon 2A

**You will learn how to...**
- talk about your classes
- ask questions and express negation

# Les cours

## Section Goals

In this section, students will learn and practice vocabulary related to:
- academic subjects
- places around school
- expressing likes and dislikes

## Key Standards
1.1, 1.2, 4.1

### Student Resources
*Cahier d'exercices*, pp. 15-16;
*Cahier d'activités*, pp. 2, 123;
Supersite: Activities,
*Cahier interactif*

### Teacher Resources
Answer Keys; Overhead #17;
Audio Script; Textbook & Audio
Activity MP3s/CD; *Feuilles
d'activités*; Testing program:
Vocabulary Quiz

## Suggestions

- Have students look at the new vocabulary and identify cognates. Say the words and have students guess the meaning. Point out that the words **lettres** and **note** are **faux amis** in this context.
- Call students' attention to the pronunciation of **ps** in **psychologie**.
- Point out that abbreviations such as **sciences po** are common. For more examples, see **Le français quotidien** on page 45.
- To review classroom objects and practice new vocabulary, show items and ask what courses they might be used for. Example: **Un dictionnaire, c'est pour quel cours?**
- Explain that many of the adjectives they learned for nationalities in **Leçon 1B** are also used for languages and language classes. Examples: **le cours de français (d'anglais, d'italien, d'espagnol)**
- Introduce vocabulary for expressing likes and dislikes by talking about your own. Use facial and hand gestures to convey meaning. Examples: **J'adore la littérature française. J'aime bien l'histoire. Je n'aime pas tellement la biologie. Je déteste l'informatique.**

## Vocabulaire

| | |
|---|---|
| J'aime bien... | *I like...* |
| Je n'aime pas tellement... | *I don't like... very much* |
| être reçu(e) à un examen | *to pass an exam* |
| | |
| l'architecture (f.) | *architecture* |
| l'art (m.) | *art* |
| le droit | *law* |
| l'éducation physique (f.) | *physical education* |
| la gestion | *business administration* |
| les lettres (f.) | *humanities* |
| la philosophie | *philosophy* |
| les sciences (politiques / po) (f.) | *(political) science* |
| le stylisme | *fashion design* |
| | |
| une bourse | *scholarship, grant* |
| une cantine | *cafeteria* |
| un cours | *class, course* |
| un devoir | *homework* |
| un diplôme | *diploma, degree* |
| l'école (f.) | *school* |
| les études (supérieures) (f.) | *(higher) education; studies* |
| le gymnase | *gymnasium* |
| une note | *grade* |
| un restaurant universitaire (un resto U) | *university cafeteria* |
| | |
| difficile | *difficult* |
| facile | *easy* |
| inutile | *useless* |
| utile | *useful* |
| | |
| surtout | *especially; above all* |

la biologie
la chimie
Je déteste la physique! (détester)
J'adore la géographie! (adorer)
J'aime bien... I like...
la géographie
la physique
les mathématiques (f.)
l'informatique (f.)

**OPTIONS**

**Oral Practice** Ask students questions using the new vocabulary words. Examples: **La physique, c'est facile ou difficile? L'informatique, c'est utile ou inutile?**

**Brainstorming** Have them brainstorm adjectives that can describe their courses and write them: **facile, difficile, utile, inutile, intéressant, amusant, agréable, différent,** and **important**.

Ask students to describe various courses. Example: **Le cours de philosophie est difficile.**

**Using Games** Divide the class into teams. Say the name of a course in English and ask one team to say it in French. If the team is correct, it gets a point. If not, the other team gets a chance to say it and "steal" the point. Alternate giving words to the two teams.

# Mise en pratique

**1 Associez** Which classes, activities, or places do you associate with these words? Not all items in the second column will be used.

| | | |
|---|---|---|
| _d_ | 1. manger | a. les mathématiques |
| _e_ | 2. un ordinateur | b. la physique |
| _i_ | 3. le français | c. l'histoire |
| _a_ | 4. une calculatrice | d. une cantine |
| _f_ | 5. le sport | e. l'informatique |
| _h_ | 6. Socrate | f. l'éducation physique |
| _b_ | 7. E=MC² | g. la biologie |
| _c_ | 8. Napoléon | h. la philosophie |
| | | i. les langues étrangères |
| | | j. l'art |

**2 Écoutez** 🎧 On their first day back to school, Aurélie and Hassim are discussing their classes, likes, and dislikes. Indicate who is most likely to use the books listed: Aurélie (**A**), Hassim (**H**), both (**A & H**), or neither (**X**). Not all items will be used.

1. Informatique et statistiques ___A & H___
2. L'économie de la France ___A___
3. L'architecture japonaise ___X___
4. Histoire de France ___H___
5. Études Freudiennes ___H___
6. La géographie de l'Europe ___H___
7. L'italien, c'est facile! ___A & H___
8. Le droit international ___A___

**3 Qu'est-ce que j'aime?** Read each statement and indicate whether you think it is **vrai** or **faux**. Compare your answers with a classmate's. Do you agree? Why? Answers will vary.

| | Vrai | Faux |
|---|---|---|
| 1. C'est facile d'être reçu à l'examen de mathématiques. | ☐ | ☐ |
| 2. Je déteste manger à la cantine. | ☐ | ☐ |
| 3. Je vais recevoir (*receive*) une bourse; c'est très utile. | ☐ | ☐ |
| 4. Le stylisme, c'est inutile. | ☐ | ☐ |
| 5. Avoir un diplôme de l'université, c'est facile. | ☐ | ☐ |
| 6. La chimie, c'est un cours difficile. | ☐ | ☐ |
| 7. Je déteste les lettres. | ☐ | ☐ |
| 8. Les notes sont très importantes. | ☐ | ☐ |
| 9. Je n'aime pas tellement les études. | ☐ | ☐ |
| 10. J'adore les langues étrangères. | ☐ | ☐ |

Practice more at **daccord1.vhlcentral.com**.

*trente-neuf* **39**

**Illustration labels:**
les langues étrangères (f.)
FRANÇAIS · ESPAGNOL · ANGLAIS
l'économie (f.)
l'histoire (f.)
La Révolution française
la psychologie
Jung · Lacan · FREUD

---

**1 Expansions**
- Items g. and j. were not used. Ask the class what words they associate with **la biologie** and **l'art**.
- Have students brainstorm a list of famous people that they associate with the following fields: **la physique** (Isaac Newton, Albert Einstein); **l'informatique** (Bill Gates, Michael Dell); and **la gestion** (Donald Trump, Martha Stewart). Then have the class guess the field associated with each of the following people: Louis Pasteur (**la biologie**), Alan Greenspan (**l'économie**).

**2 Script** AURÉLIE: Bonjour, Hassim. Comment ça va?
HASSIM: Bien. Et toi?
A: Pas mal, merci.
H: Tu aimes le cours d'informatique?
A: Oui, j'adore et j'aime bien l'économie et le droit aussi.
H: Moi, je n'aime pas tellement l'informatique, c'est difficile. J'aime l'histoire, la géographie et la psychologie. C'est très intéressant.
A: Tu aimes la gestion?
H: Ah non, je déteste!
A: Mais c'est très utile!
H: Mais non! Les langues, oui, sont utiles. J'aime bien l'italien.
A: Oui, j'adore l'italien, moi aussi!
H: Bon, à tout à l'heure, Aurélie!
A: Oui, à bientôt!
*(On Textbook Audio)*

**2 Expansion** Play the recording again and ask students these true/false statements or write them on the board. **1. Aurélie n'aime pas le cours d'économie. (Faux.) 2. Hassim déteste le cours de gestion. (Vrai.) 3. Pour Hassim, le cours d'informatique est facile. (Faux.) 4. Hassim aime la psychologie et la géographie. (Vrai.) 5. Aurélie et Hassim aiment bien l'italien. (Vrai.)**

**3 Expansion** Take a class survey of students' responses to each question and tally the results on the board. Ask students which questions are most controversial. Then ask them on which questions they agree. You might want to introduce the expression **être d'accord**, which will be presented later in **Leçon 2A**.

---

**Categories** Write the names of different fields of study across the board (for example, **les langues**, **les sciences naturelles**, **les sciences humaines**, **les cours techniques**). Working in groups of three or four, have students list the courses under the appropriate category.

**Using Visuals** Using **Overhead #17**, point to various people in the drawing and ask general questions about them. Examples: **Les élèves sont à la cantine? Il aime la physique?**

## Communication

**4** **Conversez** In pairs, fill in the blanks according to your own situations. Then, act out the conversation for the class. Answers will vary.

Élève A: _____, comment ça va?
Élève B: _____. Et toi?
Élève A: _____ merci.
Élève B: Est-ce que tu aimes le cours de _____?

Élève A: J'adore le cours de _____.
Élève B: Moi aussi. Tu aimes _____?
Élève A: Non, j'aime mieux (better) _____.
Élève B: Bon, à bientôt.
Élève A: À _____.

**5** **Qu'est-ce que c'est?** Write a caption for each image, stating where the students are and how they feel about the classes they are attending. Then, in pairs, take turns reading your captions for your partner to guess about whom you are talking. Answers will vary. Suggested answers.

**MODÈLE**
C'est le cours de français.
Le français, c'est facile.

1. C'est le cours d'informatique. Je déteste l'informatique.

2. Être reçu à l'examen / Avoir le diplôme de l'université, c'est difficile.

3. C'est la philosophie. J'adore la philosophie.

4. C'est le cours de chimie. La chimie, c'est facile.

5. C'est le cours d'éducation physique / la cantine. Je n'aime pas tellement...

6. C'est un devoir d'architecture / de stylisme. J'aime bien...

**6** **Vous êtes...** Imagine what subjects these celebrities liked and disliked as students. In pairs, take turns playing the role of each one and guessing the answer. Answers will vary.

**MODÈLE**
Élève 1: J'aime la physique et la chimie, mais je n'aime pas tellement les cours d'économie.
Élève 2: Vous êtes Albert Einstein!

• Albert Einstein
• Louis Pasteur
• Donald Trump
• Bill Clinton
• Christian Dior
• Le docteur Phil
• Bill Gates
• Frank Lloyd Wright

**7** **Sondage** Your teacher will give you a worksheet to conduct a survey (**un sondage**). Go around the room to find people that study the subjects listed. Ask what your classmates think about their subjects. Keep a record of their answers to discuss with the class. Answers will vary.

**MODÈLE**
Élève 1: Jean, est-ce que tu étudies (do you study) la chimie?
Élève 2: Oui. J'aime bien la chimie. C'est un cours utile.

# Les sons et les lettres

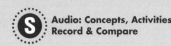 **Audio: Concepts, Activities Record & Compare**

## Liaisons

Consonants at the end of French words are generally silent but are usually pronounced when the word that follows begins with a vowel sound. This linking of sounds is called a liaison.

**À tout à l'heure!** **Comment allez-vous?**

An **s** or an **x** in a liaison sounds like the letter **z**.

**les étudiants** **trois élèves** **six élèves** **deux hommes**

Always make a liaison between a subject pronoun and a verb that begins with a vowel sound; always make a liaison between an article and a noun that begins with a vowel sound.

**nous aimons** **ils ont** **un étudiant** **les ordinateurs**

Always make a liaison between **est** (a form of **être**) and a word that begins with a vowel or a vowel sound. Never make a liaison with the final consonant of a proper name.

**Robert est anglais.** **Paris est exceptionnelle.**

Never make a liaison with the conjunction **et** (*and*).

**Carole et Hélène** **Jacques et Antoinette**

Never make a liaison between a singular noun and an adjective that follows it.

**un cours horrible** **un instrument élégant**

---

**Prononcez** Practice saying these words and expressions aloud.

1. un examen
2. des étudiants
3. les hôtels
4. dix acteurs
5. Paul et Yvette
6. cours important
7. des informations
8. les études
9. deux hommes
10. Bernard aime
11. chocolat italien
12. Louis est

**Articulez** Practice saying these sentences aloud.

1. Nous aimons les arts.
2. Albert habite à Paris.
3. C'est un objet intéressant.
4. Sylvie est avec Anne.
5. Ils adorent les deux universités.

**Dictons** Practice reading these sayings aloud.

*Un hôte non invité doit apporter son siège.*[2]

*Les amis de nos amis sont nos amis.*[1]

¹ Friends of our friends are our friends.
² An uninvited guest must bring his own chair.

**ressources**

CA
p. 124

daccord1.vhlcentral.com

*quarante et un* **41**

---

---

**Section Goals**

In this section, students will learn about liaisons.

**Key Standards**

4.1

**Student Resources**
*Cahier d'activités*, p. 124;
Supersite: Activities,
*Cahier interactif*
**Teacher Resources**
Answer Keys; Audio Script;
Textbook & Audio Activity
MP3s/CD

**Suggestions**

• Model the pronunciation of each phrase and have students repeat. Explain the liaison for each case.

• Point out expressions with liaison in **Contextes** or ask students to find them. Have them repeat after you. Example: **les études.**

• Ask students to provide expressions from **Leçons 1A–1B** that contain a liaison. Examples: **les États-Unis** and **Comment allez-vous?**

• Write the sentences in **Articulez** on the board or a transparency. Have students listen to the recording and tell you where they hear liaisons. Alternately, have students write the sentences on a sheet of paper, draw lines linking letters that form liaisons, and cross out silent final consonants.

• **Liaisons obligatoires** and **liaisons interdites** will be formally presented in **Level 2.**

• The explanation and exercises are available on the Supersite. You may want to play them in class so students practice listening to French speakers other than yourself.

**Dictons** Tell students to pronounce the liaison between **n** and **in** in **non invité**. Have students compare the saying **«Un hôte non invité doit apporter son siège»** with its literal translation. Ask what they think it means figuratively. (Possible answer: People who show up unexpectedly have no right to complain about the service.) Ask: What do the two sayings in this section reveal about French culture?

# ROMAN-PHOTO

## Trop de devoirs!  Video: *Roman-photo* Record & Compare

## Section Goals

In this section, students will learn functional phrases for talking about their courses.

## Key Standards

1.2, 2.1, 2.2, 4.1, 4.2

**Student Resources**
*Cahier d'activités*, pp. 71-72;
Supersite: Activities,
*Cahier interactif*
**Teacher Resources**
Answer Keys; Video Script & Translation; *Roman-photo* video

**Video Recap: Leçon 1B**
Before doing this **Roman-photo**, review the previous one.
**1. Le cours d'histoire est difficile pour Stéphane, n'est-ce pas?**
**(Non, les maths et le français sont difficiles pour Stéphane.)**
**2. Comment est Sandrine? (égoïste, sociable et charmante)**
**3. De quelle origine est Amina? (sénégalaise) Et Rachid? (algérienne)**
**4. Comment est Amina? (charmante, sincère et élégante)**
**5. Comment est Rachid? (intelligent, poli, modeste, réservé et brillant)**

**Video Synopsis** Rachid and Antoine discuss their political science class. As they are walking, David joins them, and Rachid introduces him. Then Antoine leaves. When the two roommates get to Rachid's car, Sandrine and Amina are waiting for them. The girls ask David about school and his classes. Later, at **Le P'tit Bistrot**, Stéphane joins the four friends and they continue their discussion about classes. Stéphane hates all of his courses.

## Suggestions

• Have students predict what they think the episode will be about. Record predictions on the board.
• Have students work in groups of six. Tell them to choose a role and read the **Roman-photo** conversation aloud. Ask one or two groups to act out the conversation for the class.
• After students read the **Roman-photo**, review their predictions and ask which ones were correct. Then ask a few questions to guide them in summarizing this episode.

**PERSONNAGES**

Amina

Antoine

David

Rachid

Sandrine

Stéphane

**ANTOINE** Je déteste le cours de sciences po.
**RACHID** Oh? Mais pourquoi? Je n'aime pas tellement le prof, Monsieur Dupré, mais c'est un cours intéressant et utile!
**ANTOINE** Tu crois? Moi, je pense que c'est très difficile, et il y a beaucoup de devoirs. Avec Dupré, je travaille, mais je n'ai pas de bons résultats.

**RACHID** Si on est optimiste et si on travaille, on est reçu à l'examen.
**ANTOINE** Toi, oui, mais pas moi! Toi, tu es un étudiant brillant! Mais moi, les études, oh là là.
**DAVID** Eh! Rachid! Oh! Est-ce que tu oublies ton coloc?

**RACHID** Pas du tout, pas du tout. Antoine, voilà, je te présente David, mon colocataire américain.
**DAVID** Nous partageons un des appartements du P'tit Bistrot.
**ANTOINE** Le P'tit Bistrot? Sympa!

**SANDRINE** Salut! Alors, ça va l'université française?
**DAVID** Bien, oui. C'est différent de l'université américaine, mais c'est intéressant.
**AMINA** Tu aimes les cours?
**DAVID** J'aime bien les cours de littérature et d'histoire françaises. Demain, on étudie *Les Trois Mousquetaires* d'Alexandre Dumas.

**SANDRINE** J'adore Dumas. Mon livre préféré, c'est *Le Comte de Monte-Cristo*.
**RACHID** Sandrine! S'il te plaît! *Le Comte de Monte-Cristo*?
**SANDRINE** Pourquoi pas? Je suis chanteuse, mais j'adore les classiques de la littérature.
**DAVID** Donne-moi le sac à dos, Sandrine.

*Au P'tit Bistrot...*
**RACHID** Moi, j'aime le cours de sciences po, mais Antoine n'aime pas Dupré. Il pense qu'il donne trop de devoirs.

**1** **Vrai ou faux?** Choose whether each statement is  vrai or faux. **Correct the false statements.**
Answers may vary slightly.
1. Rachid et Antoine n'aiment pas le professeur Dupré. Vrai.
2. Antoine aime bien le cours de sciences po.
   Faux. Antoine déteste le cours de sciences po.
3. Rachid et Antoine partagent (*share*) un appartement.
   Faux. Rachid et David partagent un appartement.
4. David et Rachid cherchent (*look for*) Amina et Sandrine après (*after*) les cours. Vrai.
5. Le livre préféré de Sandrine est *Le Comte de Monte-Cristo*.
   Vrai.

6. L'université française est très différente de l'université américaine. Vrai.
7. Stéphane aime la chimie.
   Faux. Stéphane n'aime pas la chimie.
8. Monsieur Dupré est professeur de maths.
   Faux. Monsieur Dupré est professeur de sciences po.
9. Antoine a (*has*) beaucoup de devoirs. Vrai.
10. Stéphane adore l'anglais. Faux. Stéphane déteste l'anglais.

 Practice more at **daccord1.vhlcentral.com.**

**A C T I V I T É S**

**OPTIONS**

**Avant de regarder la vidéo** Before showing the video episode, have students brainstorm some expressions people might use when talking about their classes and teachers.

**Regarder la vidéo** Download and print the videoscript and white out ten words or expressions in order to create a master for a cloze activity. Hand out the photocopies and tell students to fill in the missing words as they watch the video episode. You may want to show the episode twice if students have difficulty with the activity. Then have students compare their answers in small groups.

Antoine, David, Rachid et Stéphane parlent (*talk*)
de leurs (*their*) cours.

**RACHID** Ah… on a rendez-vous avec
Amina et Sandrine. On y va?
**DAVID** Ah, oui, bon, ben, salut,
Antoine!
**ANTOINE** Salut, David. À demain,
Rachid!

**SANDRINE** Bon, Pascal, au revoir,
chéri.
**RACHID** Bonjour, chérie. Comme
j'adore parler avec toi au téléphone!
Comme j'adore penser à toi!

**STÉPHANE** Dupré? Ha! C'est Madame
Richard, mon prof de français. Elle,
elle donne trop de devoirs.
**AMINA** Bonjour, comment ça va?
**STÉPHANE** Plutôt mal. Je n'aime
pas Madame Richard. Je déteste
les maths. La chimie n'est pas
intéressante. L'histoire-géo,
c'est l'horreur. Les études, c'est
le désastre.

**DAVID** Le français, les maths, la
chimie, l'histoire-géo… mais on
n'étudie pas les langues étrangères
au lycée en France?
**STÉPHANE** Si, malheureusement!
Moi, j'étudie l'anglais. C'est une
langue très désagréable! Oh, non,
non, ha, ha, c'est une blague, ha,
ha. L'anglais, j'adore l'anglais. C'est
une langue charmante….

## Expressions utiles

### Talking about classes

- **Tu aimes les cours?**
  *Do you like the classes?*
- **Antoine n'aime pas Dupré.**
  *Antoine doesn't like Dupré.*
- **Il pense qu'il donne trop de devoirs.**
  *He thinks he gives too much homework.*
- **Tu crois? Mais pourquoi?**
  *You think? But why?*
- **Avec Dupré, je travaille, mais je n'ai pas
  de bons résultats.**
  *With Dupré, I work, but I don't get good
  results (grades).*
- **Demain, on étudie *Les Trois Mousquetaires*.**
  *Tomorrow we're studying The Three
  Musketeers.*
- **C'est mon livre préféré.**
  *It's my favorite book.*

### Additional vocabulary

- **On a rendez-vous.**
  *We have a meeting.*
- **Comme j'adore…**
  *How I love…*
- **parler au téléphone**
  *to talk on the phone*
- **C'est une blague.**
  *It's a joke.*
- **Si, malheureusement!**
  *Yes, unfortunately!*
- **On y va? / On y va.**
  *Are you ready? / Let's go.*
- **Eh!**
  *Hey!*
- **pas du tout**
  *not at all*
- **chéri(e)**
  *darling*

---

**2 Complétez** Match the people in the second column with the
verbs in the first. Refer to a dictionary, the dialogue, and the video
stills as necessary. Use each option once.

| | | |
|---|---|---|
| b/e | 1. travailler | a. Sandrine is very forgetful. |
| c | 2. partager | b. Rachid is very studious. |
| a | 3. oublier | c. David can't afford his own apartment. |
| b/e | 4. étudier | d. Amina is very generous. |
| d | 5. donner | e. Stéphane needs to get good grades. |

**3 Conversez** In this episode, Rachid, Antoine, David, and Stéphane
talk about the subjects they are studying. Get together with a partner.
Do any of the characters' complaints or preferences remind you of your
own? Whose opinions do you agree with? Whom do you disagree with?

ressources

CA
pp. 71–72

daccord1.vhlcentral.com

**A C T I V I T É S**

## Expressions utiles

- Model the pronunciation of the
  **Expressions utiles** and have
  students repeat after you.
- As you work through the list,
  point out forms of **-er** verbs.
  Also identify examples of
  negation. Tell students that
  **-er** verbs and negation will
  be formally presented in
  **Structures**.
- Ask students a few questions
  about their classes and
  teachers. Examples: **Vous
  aimez le cours de sciences
  po? Comment s'appelle le prof
  de sciences po? Est-ce que
  _____ donne trop de devoirs?**
- Point out that **si** is used
  instead of **oui** to contradict
  a negative statement or
  question. Example: **Si,
  malheureusement!**

**1 Suggestion** Have students
correct the false statements.

**1 Expansion** For additional
practice, give students these
items. **11. Rachid pense que le
cours de sciences po est inutile.
(Faux.) 12. Madame Richard est
prof de français. (Vrai.) 13. Pour
Stéphane, les études, c'est le
désastre. (Vrai.)**

**2 Expansion** Write these
verbs on the board: **aimer,
détester, adorer,** and **penser.**
Have students create additional
statements about the video
characters that relate to
each verb.

**3 Suggestion** Encourage
students to express their
opinions in simple French.
Write a few sentence starters
on the board. Example: **Comme
Stéphane, je n'aime pas…**

---

**O P T I O N S**

**Alexandre Dumas** Alexandre Dumas (**père**) (1802–1870) was a
prolific French novelist and dramatist. With the assistance of a
group of collaborators, he wrote almost 300 works. *The Three
Musketeers* (**Les Trois Mousquetaires**), *The Count of Monte
Cristo* (**Le Comte de Monte-Cristo**), and *The Black Tulip* (**La
Tulipe noire**) are among his most famous and popular novels.
These historical romances feature swashbuckling characters.

Ask students if they have read any of these books or seen any
movies based on them.

**Small Groups** Working in groups of four, have students create a
short skit similar to the scenes in video stills 6–10 in which some
students are talking about their classes and teachers. Give
students about ten minutes to prepare, and then call on groups
to perform their skits for the class.

# CULTURE

 Video: *Flash culture*

## CULTURE À LA LOUPE

# Au lycée

**What is high school like in France?** At the end of middle school (**le collège**), French students begin three years of high-school study at the **lycée.** Beginning in **seconde** (10th grade), students pass into **première** (11th grade) and end with **la terminale** (12th grade).

The **lycée** experience is quite different from American high school. For example, the days are much longer: 8:00 am until 5:00 pm, except on Wednesdays, when classes end at noon. Students in some **lycées** may also have class on Saturday morning. French schools do not have sports teams, but students who want to play an organized sport can join **l'Association sportive scolaire.** Every public **lycée** must offer this option to its students. Music or art classes must also be taken outside the school. All such extra-curricular activities take place after school hours or on Wednesday afternoons.

Grades are based on a 20-point scale, with 10 being the average grade. As students advance in their studies, it becomes harder for them to achieve a grade of 16/20 or even 14/20. A student can receive a below-average score in one or more courses and still advance to the next level as long as their overall grade average is at least 10/20.

Another important difference is that French students must choose a specialization while in high school, at the end of the **classe de seconde.** That choice is likely to influence the rest of their studies and, later, their job choice. While they can change their mind after the first trimester of **première,** by then students are already set on a course towards the **baccalauréat** or **bac,** the terminal exam that concludes their **lycée** studies.

### Système français de notation

| NOTE FRANÇAISE | NOTE AMÉRICAINE | % | NOTE FRANÇAISE | NOTE AMÉRICAINE | % |
|---|---|---|---|---|---|
| 0 | F | 0 | 11 | B- | 82 |
| 2 | F | 3 | 12 | B+ | 88 |
| 3 | F | 8 | 13 | A- | 93 |
| 4 | F | 18 | 14 | A | 95 |
| 5 | F | 28 | 15 | A | 96 |
| 6 | F | 38 | 16 | A+ | 98 |
| 7 | D- | 60 | 17 | A+ | 98 |
| 8 | D- | 65 | 18 | A+ | 99 |
| 9 | D+ | 68 | 19 | A+ | 99 |
| 10 | C | 75 | 20 | A+ | 100 |

## ACTIVITÉS

**1 Vrai ou faux?** Indicate whether each statement is **vrai** or **faux.**

1. The **lycée** comes after **collège.**
   Vrai.
2. It takes 4 years to complete **lycée.**
   Faux. It takes three years.
3. The grade order in the **lycée** is **terminale, première,** and lastly **seconde.**
   Faux. The order is seconde, première, terminale.
4. **Lycées** never have classes on Saturday.
   Faux. Some lycées have classes Saturday mornings.
5. French students have class from Monday to Friday all day long.
   Faux. Wednesdays are half days.
6. French students have to specialize in a field of study while in high school.
   Vrai.
7. In **seconde,** all the students study the same subjects.
   Vrai.
8. The French grading system resembles the US grading system.
   Faux. The American grading system is based on 100 points.
9. The highest grade that a French student can get is 20/20.
   Vrai.
10. To obtain a grade of 20/20 is common in France.
    Faux. A grade of 20/20 is very rare.

Practice more at **daccord1.vhlcentral.com.**

## LE FRANÇAIS QUOTIDIEN

### Les cours

| | |
|---|---|
| être fort(e) en... | to be good at |
| être nul(le) en... | to stink at |
| sécher un cours | to skip a class |
| potasser | to cram |
| piger | to get it |
| l'emploi du temps | class schedule |
| l'histoire-géo | history-geography |
| les maths | math |
| la philo | philosophy |
| le prof | teacher |
| la récré(ation) | recess |

## LE MONDE FRANCOPHONE

### Le lycée

Le «lycée» n'existe pas partout°.

**En Afrique francophone**, on utilise° les termes de *lycée* et de *baccalauréat*.

**En Belgique**, le lycée public s'appelle une *école secondaire* ou un *athénée*. Un lycée privé° s'appelle un *collège*. Le bac n'existe pas°.

**Au Canada**, le lycée français s'appelle un *Cégep* et les élèves reçoivent° un diplôme d'études collégiales.

**En Suisse**, les lycées s'appellent *gymnases*, *écoles préparant à la maturité* ou *écoles de culture générale*. Les élèves reçoivent un certificat du secondaire II.

**partout** *everywhere* **on utilise** *one uses* **privé** *private* **n'existe pas** *does not exist* **reçoivent** *receive*

## PORTRAIT

# Immersion française au Canada

Au Canada, l'anglais et le français sont les langues officielles, mais les provinces ne sont pas nécessairement bilingues — New Brunswick est la seule province officiellement bilingue. Seulement 17,4% des Canadiens parlent le français et l'anglais. Pourtant°, il existe un programme d'immersion française qui encourage le bilinguisme: certains élèves d'école primaire ou secondaire (lycée) choisissent de suivre leurs cours° en français. Pendant° trois années ou plus, les élèves ont tous° les cours uniquement en français. À New Brunswick, 32% des élèves y sont matriculés°. À Québec, province majoritairement Francophone, mais avec une communauté anglophone importante, 22% des élèves sont matriculés dans le programme d'immersion française.

**Pourtant** *However* **suivre leurs cours** *take their classes*
**Pendant** *For* **ont tous** *take all* **matriculés** *enrolled*

### Coup de main

To read decimal places in French, use the French word **virgule** (*comma*) where you would normally say *point* in English. To say *percent*, use **pour cent**.

17,4% dix-sept virgule quatre
pour cent
*seventeen point four percent*

### SUR INTERNET

Qu'est-ce une journée (*day*) typique dans un lycée français?

Go to daccord1.vhlcentral.com to find more information related to this **CULTURE** section.

---

**2** Complete each statement.

1. L'anglais et le français sont les langues officielles du ___Canada___.
2. Le programme d'immersion existe dans les écoles primaires et ___secondaires___.
3. Le programme d'immersion est pour une période de ___trois.___ ans ou plus.
4. À New Brunswick, la communauté ___francophone___ est importante.
5. Au Canada, le lycée français s'appelle un ___Cégep___.

**3** **Les cours** Research what classes are taught in the **lycée** and how long each course is. How does this compare to your class schedule? You may search in your library or online.

ressources

daccord1.vhlcentral.com

**ACTIVITÉS**

---

**OPTIONS**

**Numbers** Point students to the information in the chart **Coup de main**. Model how to say percentages. Example: 32% (**trente-deux pour cent**). Then write on the board the percentages of students enrolled in the French immersion program in these provinces and ask students to say the figures out loud: Prince Edward Island - 20%, Nova Scotia - 12%, British Columbia - 2%.

**Cultural Comparison** Ask students if they know of any bilingual or immersion programs at school districts in the United States. Have them list advantages and disadvantages to enrolling in an immersion program that begins in high school.

---

**Le français quotidien** Have students work in pairs. Tell them to take turns describing the courses they are good and bad at using the vocabulary in this section. Examples: **Je suis nul(le) en maths. Je suis fort(e) en géo.**

**Portrait**
- Ask students if they know of any areas of the U.S. that are officially bilingual. (Puerto Rico)
- Point out the **Coup de main**. Explain that commas are used instead of periods when speaking percentages aloud.

**1** **Expansion** For additional practice, give students these items. 11. French schools have sports teams just like in the United States. (**Faux.** Students must join an outside club if they want to participate in a sport.) 12. A 10/10 is the minimum passing grade. (**Vrai.**) 13. The last chance for students to change their specialization is at the end of **seconde**. (**Faux.** It is after the first trimester of **première**.)

**2** **Suggestion** Have students compare their answers with a classmate.

**3** **Expansion** Have students find out the following information as part of their research: how many courses a typical student takes at one time, what foreign language requirements exist, and what electives are available.

CULTURE **45**

## Section Goals

In this section, students will learn:
- the present tense of regular -er verbs
- spelling changes in -cer and -ger verbs

## Key Standards

**4.1, 5.1**

**Student Resources**
*Cahier d'exercices*, pp. 17-18;
*Cahier d'activités*, p. 125;
Supersite: Activities,
*Cahier interactif*

**Teacher Resources**
Answer Keys; Audio Script;
Audio Activity MP3s/CD; Testing
program: Grammar Quiz

## Suggestions

- Point out that students have been using verbs from the start: **Comment t'appelles-tu?, il y a**, forms of **être**, etc. Ask the class: **Quels cours aimez-vous?** Model the response **J'aime….** Ask a student: _____ **aime quels cours?** Model **Il/Elle aime….** Give other subjects.
- Introduce the idea of a "boot verb." Write the conjugation of a common -er verb on the board with the singular forms in the first column and the plural forms in the second column. Draw a line around **je, tu, il/elle**, and **ils/elles**, forming the shape of a boot. The four verb forms inside the "boot" are pronounced alike.
- Create sentences with **j'aime…** and **j'adore…** followed by infinitives. Stress that **je** changes to **j'** before verbs starting with a vowel and most verbs starting with **h**. Ask if students like some of the activities. Example: **Vous aimez voyager?**
- Explain that the French present tense equals four English present tenses. Ask volunteers to translate examples like these: **Au lycée, je mange bien.** (*At school, I eat well.*) **Excusez-moi, je mange.** (*Excuse me, I'm eating.*)
- Point out that verbs ending in -cer and -ger have a spelling change in the **nous** form. Write **commençons** and **mangeons** on the board, and circle the change.
- Tell students they can find the complete explanation of the **impératif** in **Appendice B**.
- Model the pronunciation of adverbs in **Boîte à outils**. Have students repeat after you.

## 2A.1 Present tense of regular -er verbs

**Point de départ** The infinitives of most French verbs end in -er. To form the present tense of regular -er verbs, drop the -er from the infinitive and add the corresponding endings for the different subject pronouns. This chart demonstrates how to conjugate regular -er verbs.

| Parler (to speak) | | | |
|---|---|---|---|
| je parle | *I speak* | nous parlons | *we speak* |
| tu parles | *you speak* | vous parlez | *you speak* |
| il/elle parle | *he/she/it speaks* | ils/elles parlent | *they speak* |

- Here are some other verbs that are conjugated the same way as **parler**.

| Common -er verbs | | | |
|---|---|---|---|
| adorer | *to love* | habiter (à/en) | *to live in* |
| aimer | *to like; to love* | manger | *to eat* |
| aimer mieux | *to prefer (to like better)* | oublier | *to forget* |
| | | partager | *to share* |
| arriver | *to arrive* | penser (que/qu'…) | *to think (that…)* |
| chercher | *to look for* | regarder | *to look (at)* |
| commencer | *to begin, to start* | rencontrer | *to meet* |
| dessiner | *to draw* | retrouver | *to meet up with; to find (again)* |
| détester | *to hate* | | |
| donner | *to give* | travailler | *to work* |
| étudier | *to study* | voyager | *to travel* |

- Note that **je** becomes **j'** when it appears before a verb that begins with a vowel sound.

**J'habite** à Bruxelles.       **J'étudie** la psychologie.
*I live in Brussels.*            *I study psychology.*

- With the verbs **adorer, aimer**, and **détester**, use the definite article before a noun to tell what someone loves, likes, prefers, or hates.

J'aime mieux **l'**art.       Marine déteste **les** devoirs.
*I prefer art.*               *Marine hates homework.*

- Use infinitive forms after the verbs **adorer, aimer**, and **détester** to say that you like (or hate, etc.) to do something. Only the first verb should be conjugated.

Ils **adorent travailler** ici.       Ils **détestent étudier** ensemble.
*They love to work here.*            *They hate to study together.*

**1** **Complétez** Complete the conversation with the correct forms of the verbs.

ARTHUR   Tu (1) __parles__ (parler) bien français!

OLIVIER   Merci! Mon ami Marc et moi, nous (2) __retrouvons__ (retrouver) un professeur de français et nous (3) __étudions__ (étudier) ensemble. Et toi, tu (4) __aimes__ (aimer) les langues étrangères?

ARTHUR   Non, j' (5) __étudie__ (étudier) l'art et l'économie. Je (6) __dessine__ (dessiner) bien et j' (7) __aime__ (aimer) beaucoup l'art moderne. Marc et toi, vous (8) __voyagez__ (voyager) beaucoup?

**2** **Phrases** Form sentences using the words provided. Conjugate the verbs and add any necessary words.

1. je / oublier / devoir de littérature
   J'oublie le devoir de littérature.
2. nous / commencer / études supérieures
   Nous commençons des études supérieures.
3. vous / rencontrer / amis / à / lycée
   Vous rencontrez des amis au lycée.
4. Hélène / détester / travailler
   Hélène déteste travailler.
5. tu / chercher / cours / facile
   Tu cherches un cours facile.
6. élèves / arriver / avec / dictionnaires
   Les élèves arrivent avec des dictionnaires.

**3** **Après l'école** Say what Stéphanie and her friends are doing after (**après**) school.
Answers may vary.

**MODÈLE**

*Nathalie cherche un livre.*

1. André __travaille__ à la bibliothèque.

2. Maxime __retrouve__ Caroline au café.

3. Jérôme et moi, nous __dessinons__.

4. Julien et Audrey __parlent__ avec Simon.

5. Alexis et toi, vous __voyagez__ avec la classe.

6. Je __mange__ à la cantine.

**Practice more at daccord1.vhlcentral.com.**

---

**OPTIONS**

**Rapid Drill** Do a rapid-response drill. Write an infinitive from the list of -er verbs on the board. Call out subject pronouns and/or names, and have students respond with the correct verb form. Then reverse the drill; write a verb form on the board and have students say the subject pronouns.

**Using Games** Divide the class into two teams. Choose one team member at a time to go to the board, alternating between teams. Say an infinitive and a subject pronoun. The person at the board must write and say the correct present tense form. Example: **parler: vous (vous parlez).** Give a point for each correct answer. The team with the most points at the end of the game wins.

## COMMUNICATION

**4** **Activités** In pairs, say which of these activities you and your best friend both do. Be prepared to share your partner's answers with the class. Then, get together with another partner and report to the class again. *Answers will vary.*

**MODÈLE**

To your partner: *Nous parlons au téléphone, nous…*
To the class: *Ils/Elles travaillent, ils/elles…*

| | |
|---|---|
| manger à la cantine | étudier une langue étrangère |
| oublier les devoirs | regarder la télévision |
| retrouver des amis au café | aimer les cours |
| travailler | voyager |

**5** **Les études** In pairs, take turns asking your partner if he or she likes one academic subject or another. If you don't like a subject, mention one you do like. Then, use **tous/toutes les deux** (*both of us*) to tell the class what subjects both of you like or hate. *Answers will vary.*

**MODÈLE**

Élève 1: *Tu aimes la chimie?*
Élève 2: *Non, je déteste la chimie. J'aime mieux les langues. Et toi?*
Élève 1: *Moi aussi… Nous adorons tous les deux les langues.*

**6** **Adorer, aimer, détester** In groups of four, ask each other if you like to do these activities. Then, use an adjective to tell why you like them or not and say whether you do them often (**souvent**), sometimes (**parfois**), or rarely (**rarement**). *Answers will vary.*

**MODÈLE**

Élève 1: *Tu aimes voyager?*
Élève 2: *Oui, j'adore voyager. C'est amusant! Je voyage souvent.*
Élève 3: *Moi, je n'aime pas tellement voyager. C'est désagréable! Je voyage rarement.*

| | |
|---|---|
| dessiner | partager une chambre |
| étudier le week-end | retrouver des amis |
| manger au restaurant | travailler à la bibliothèque |
| oublier les devoirs | voyager |
| parler avec les professeurs | |

---

• The present tense in French can be translated in different ways in English. The English equivalent depends on the context.

Ils **étudient** la physique.
*They study physics.*
*They are studying physics.*
*They do study physics.*

Nous **travaillons** ici demain.
*We work here tomorrow.*
*We are working here tomorrow.*
*We will work here tomorrow.*

• Verbs ending in -ger (**manger, partager, voyager**) and -cer (**commencer**) have a spelling change in the **nous** form.

manger ▶ nous mangeons          commencer ▶ nous commençons

Nous **voyageons** avec une amie.
*We are traveling with a friend.*

Nous **commençons** les devoirs.
*We are starting the homework.*

• Unlike the English *to look for*, the French **chercher** requires no preposition before the noun that follows it.

Nous **cherchons les stylos**.
*We are looking for the pens.*

Vous **cherchez la montre**?
*Are you looking for the watch?*

• Use present tense verb forms to give commands. The **nous** and **vous** command forms are identical to those of the present tense. The **tu** command form of -**er** verbs drops the -**s** from the present tense form. The command forms of **être** are irregular: **sois, soyons, soyez**.

| | | | |
|---|---|---|---|
| **Regarde!** | **Travaillons.** | **Parlez** français. | **Sois** patiente! |
| *Look!* | *Let's work.* | *Speak French.* | *Be patient!* |

*Est-ce que tu oublies ton coloc?*

*Nous partageons un des appartements du P'tit Bistrot.*

**BOÎTE À OUTILS**

To express yourself with greater accuracy, use these adverbs: **assez** (*enough*), **d'habitude** (*usually*), **de temps en temps** (*from time to time*), **parfois** (*sometimes*), **rarement** (*rarely*), **souvent** (*often*), **toujours** (*always*).

**Essayez!** Complete the sentences with the correct present tense forms of the verbs in parentheses.

1. Je __parle__ (parler) français en classe.
2. Nous __habitons__ (habiter) près de (*near*) l'université.
3. Ils __aiment__ (aimer) le cours de sciences politiques.
4. Élodie! __Regarde__ (regarder) le professeur!
5. Le cours __commence__ (commencer) à huit heures (*at eight o'clock*).
6. Claire et Sylvain, __partagez__ (partager) le livre.

---

**Essayez!** Have students create new sentences orally or in writing by changing the subject of the sentence.

**1** Suggestion Go over the answers quickly in class, then ask several pairs of students to act out the conversation and add at least two lines of their own at the end.

**2** Suggestion To check students' answers, have volunteers write the sentences on the board and read them aloud.

**2** Expansion For additional practice, change the subjects of the sentences and have students restate or write the sentences. Examples: **1. Tu** (Tu oublies le devoir de littérature.) **2. Chantal** (Chantal commence des études supérieures.) **3. Je** (Je rencontre des amis à l'école.) **4. Les élèves** (Les élèves détestent travailler.) **5. Nous** (Nous cherchons un cours facile.) **6. Pascale** (Pascale arrive avec des dictionnaires.)

**3** Expansion Have students add additional sentences to the captions below the drawings. Example: **1. Il étudie l'histoire. Il y a un examen.**

**4** Suggestion Encourage students to personalize the information and to add additional information. Examples: **étudier** *a different subject*, **travailler dans** *a place*, and **regarder la télé.**

**5** Suggestion Before beginning the activity, tell students to jot down a list of academic subjects that they can ask their partner about and to note their partner's responses. Examples: **Il/Elle aime** or **Il/Elle déteste.**

**6** Suggestion Before beginning the activity, have students brainstorm adjectives they can use and write them on the board.

---

**Using Video** Show the **Roman-photo** video episode again to give students additional input on verbs. Pause the video where appropriate to discuss how certain verbs were used and to ask comprehension questions.

**Using Games** Have students play a game of pantomime in groups of four or five. Tell students to pick a verb from the list on page 46 and act out the word. The other members of the group have to guess what the person is doing. Example: **Tu travailles?** The first person to guess correctly acts out the next pantomime.

## Section Goals

In this section, students will learn:
- to form questions
- to express negation
- expressions for agreeing and disagreeing

## Key Standards
4.1, 5.1

**Student Resources**
*Cahier d'exercices*, pp. 19–20;
*Cahier d'activités*, p. 126;
Supersite: Activities,
*Cahier interactif*

**Teacher Resources**
Answer Keys; Audio Script;
Audio Activity MP3s/CD; Testing
program: Grammar Quiz

## Suggestions

- Model the pronunciation and intonation of the different types of example questions. Point out that the questions on page 48 signal yes-no responses.
- Explain how to form inverted questions. Point out that inversion is usually used in written and formal language. Inversion with **je** is rare in spoken French, but seen in literary language, especially questions. Examples: **Ai-je le droit? Qui suis-je?**
- Point out that any question word can go before **est-ce que.** Example: **Que** as in **Qu'est-ce que c'est?**
- Explain the positions of **ne (n')** and **pas** in negative phrases and in inverted questions. If an infinitive follows a conjugated verb, **ne (n')** and **pas** surround the conjugated verb. Example: **Tu n'aimes pas regarder la vidéo?**
- Tell students that **ne (n')** in negative sentences is sometimes dropped in informal speech.
- Model the expressions indicating agreement and disagreement. Show how **mais** can precede **oui** as well as **non** if you want to say yes or no more emphatically.
- Make sure students grasp when to say **si** instead of **oui** by asking questions like these: **Tu n'études pas le français? (Si, j'étudie le français.) Je ne suis pas le professeur? (Si, vous êtes le professeur.)** Choose two students that are friends and ask: ____ et ____ **ne sont pas copains/copines? (Si, nous sommes copains/copines.)** Tell students to say, **Mais si!** if they want to contradict a negative question more forcefully.

## 2A.2 Forming questions and expressing negation

**Point de départ** You have learned how to make affirmative and declarative statements in French. Now you will learn how to form questions and make negative statements.

### Forming questions

- There are several ways to ask a question in French. The simplest way is to use the same wording as for a statement but with rising intonation (when speaking) or setting a question mark at the end (when writing). This method is considered informal.

  **Vous habitez à Bordeaux?**
  *You live in Bordeaux?*

  **Tu aimes le cours de français?**
  *You like French class?*

- A second way is to place the phrase **Est-ce que...** directly before a statement. If the next word begins with a vowel sound, use **Est-ce qu'**. Questions with **est-ce que** are somewhat formal.

  **Est-ce que** vous parlez français?
  *Do you speak French?*

  **Est-ce qu'**il aime dessiner?
  *Does he like to draw?*

- A third way is to place a tag question at the end of a statement. This method can be formal or informal.

  On commence à deux heures, **d'accord**?
  *We're starting at two o'clock, OK?*

  Nous mangeons à midi, **n'est-ce pas**?
  *We eat at noon, don't we?*

- A fourth way is to invert the order of the subject pronoun and the verb and hyphenate them. If the verb ends in a vowel and the subject pronoun is **il**, **elle**, or **on**, **-t-** is inserted between the verb and the pronoun. Inversion is considered more formal.

  **Parlez-vous** français?
  *Do you speak French?*

  **Mange-t-il** à midi?
  *Does he eat at noon?*

  **Est-elle** élève?
  *Is she a student?*

- If the subject is a noun rather than a pronoun, invert the pronoun and the verb, and place the noun before them.

  **Le professeur parle-t-il** français?
  *Does the teacher speak French?*

  **Nina arrive-t-elle** demain?
  *Does Nina arrive tomorrow?*

- The inverted form of **il y a** is **y a-t-il**. **C'est** becomes **est-ce**.

  **Y a-t-il** une horloge dans la classe?
  *Is there a clock in the class?*

  **Est-ce** le professeur de lettres?
  *Is he the humanities professor?*

- Use **pourquoi** to ask *why?* Use **parce que** (**parce qu'** before a vowel sound) in the answer to express *because*.

  **Pourquoi** retrouves-tu Sophie ici?
  *Why are you meeting Sophie here?*

  **Parce qu'**elle habite près d'ici.
  *Because she lives near here.*

### MISE EN PRATIQUE

**1** **L'inversion** Restate the questions using inversion.

1. Est-ce que vous parlez espagnol?
   Parlez-vous espagnol?
2. Est-ce qu'il étudie à Paris?
   Étudie-t-il à Paris?
3. Est-ce qu'ils voyagent avec des amis?
   Voyagent-ils avec des amis?
4. Est-ce que tu aimes les cours de langues?
   Aimes-tu les cours de langues?
5. Est-ce que le professeur parle anglais?
   Le professeur parle-t-il anglais?
6. Est-ce que les élèves aiment dessiner?
   Les élèves aiment-ils/elles dessiner?

**2** **Les questions** Ask the questions that correspond to the answers. Use **est-ce que/qu'** and inversion for each item.

**MODÈLE**

Nous habitons loin (*far away*).
*Est-ce que vous habitez loin? / Habitez-vous loin?*

1. Il mange à la cantine.
   Est-ce qu'il mange à la cantine? / Mange-t-il à la cantine?
2. J'oublie les examens.
   Est-ce que tu oublies les examens? / Oublies-tu les examens?
3. François déteste les maths.
   Est-ce que François déteste les maths? / François déteste-t-il les maths?
4. Nous adorons voyager.
   Est-ce que vous adorez voyager? / Adorez-vous voyager?
5. Les cours ne commencent pas demain. Est-ce que les cours
   ne commencent pas demain? / Les cours ne commencent-ils pas demain?
6. Les élèves arrivent en classe. Est-ce que
   les élèves arrivent en classe? / Les élèves arrivent-ils/elles en classe?

**3** **Complétez** Complete the conversation with the correct questions for the answers given. Act it out with a partner. Suggested answers

MYLÈNE   Salut, Arnaud. Ça va?

ARNAUD   Oui, ça va. Alors (*So*)... (1) Tu aimes les cours?

MYLÈNE   J'adore le cours de sciences po, mais je déteste l'informatique.

ARNAUD   (2) Pourquoi est-ce que tu détestes l'informatique?

MYLÈNE   Parce que le prof est très strict.

ARNAUD   (3) Il y a des élèves sympathiques, n'est-ce pas?

MYLÈNE   Oui, il y a des élèves sympathiques... Et demain? (4) Tu retrouves Béatrice?

ARNAUD   Peut-être, mais demain je retrouve aussi Dominique.

MYLÈNE   (5) Tu cherches une petite amie?

ARNAUD   Pas du tout!

 Practice more at **daccord1.vhlcentral.com.**

---

**O P T I O N S**

**Inversion** Write ten statements on the board or a transparency. Have students work in pairs. Tell them to convert the statements into questions by inverting the subject and verb. When they have finished writing the questions, call on volunteers to read their questions aloud. This activity can also be done orally with the class.

**Tag Questions** Using the same ten statements from the previous activity, ask students to form tag questions. Encourage them to use both **d'accord?** and **n'est-ce pas?** Have students answer some of the questions. Then add a few negative statements so that students will have to respond with **si**.

## COMMUNICATION

**4  Au café** In pairs, take turns asking each other questions about the drawing. Use verbs from the list.
*Answers will vary.*

**MODÈLE**

Élève 1: *Monsieur Laurent parle à Madame Martin, n'est-ce pas?*
Élève 2: *Mais non. Il déteste parler!*

| arriver | dessiner | manger | partager |
|---------|----------|--------|----------|
| chercher | étudier | oublier | rencontrer |

Anne et Sylvie    Didier    André

Madame Martin    Monsieur Laurent

**5  Questions** You and your partner want to know each other better. Take turns asking each other questions. Modify or add elements as needed. *Some answers will vary.*

**MODÈLE** aimer / l'art

Élève 1: *Est-ce que tu aimes l'art?*
Élève 2: *Oui, j'adore l'art.*

1. détester / devoirs
   *Est-ce que tu détestes les devoirs?*
2. étudier / avec / amis
   *Est-ce que tu étudies avec des amis?*
3. penser que / cours / au lycée / être / intéressant
   *Est-ce que tu penses que les cours au lycée sont intéressants?*
4. cours de sciences / être / facile
   *Est-ce que les cours de sciences sont faciles?*
5. aimer mieux / biologie / ou / physique
   *Est-ce que tu aimes mieux la biologie ou la physique?*
6. retrouver / copains / à la cantine
   *Est-ce que tu retrouves des copains à la cantine?*

**6  Confirmez** In groups of three, confirm whether the statements are true of your school. Correct any untrue statements by making them negative. *Answers will vary.*

**MODÈLE**

Les profs sont désagréables.
*Pas du tout. Les profs ne sont pas désagréables.*

1. Le cours d'informatique est inutile.
2. Il y a des élèves de nationalité allemande.
3. Nous mangeons une cuisine excellente à la cantine.
4. Tous (*All*) les élèves étudient à la bibliothèque.
5. Le cours de chimie est facile.
6. Nous adorons le gymnase.

## Expressing negation

- To make a sentence negative in French, place **ne** (**n'** before a vowel sound) before the conjugated verb and **pas** after it.

  Je **ne dessine pas** bien.          **Ne parlez pas** en cours.
  *I don't draw well.*                 *Don't talk in class.*

- In the construction [*conjugated verb + infinitive*], **ne** (**n'**) comes before the conjugated verb and **pas** after it.

  Abdel **n'aime pas** étudier.        Vous **ne détestez pas** travailler?
  *Abdel doesn't like to study.*       *You don't hate to work?*

- In questions with inversion, place **ne** before the inversion and **pas** after it.

  Abdel **n'aime-t-il pas** étudier?   **Ne détestez-vous pas** travailler?
  *Doesn't Abdel like to study?*       *Don't you hate to work?*

- Use these expressions to respond to a statement or a question that requires a *yes* or *no* answer.

### Expressions of agreement and disagreement

| oui | yes | (mais) non | no (but of course not) |
|-----|-----|------------|------------------------|
| bien sûr | of course | pas du tout | not at all |
| moi/toi non plus | me/you neither | peut-être | maybe, perhaps |

Vous mangez souvent à la cantine?    **Non, pas du tout.**
*Do you eat often in the cafeteria?*  *No, not at all.*

- Use **si** instead of **oui** to contradict a negative question.

  Il **ne cherche pas** le sac à dos?  **Si.** Il cherche aussi les crayons.
  *Isn't he looking for the backpack?* *Yes. He's looking for the pencils too.*

**Essayez!**  Make questions out of these statements. Use **est-ce que/qu'** in items 1–6 and inversion in 7–12.

| Statement | Question |
|-----------|----------|
| 1. Vous mangez à la cantine. | *Est-ce que vous mangez à la cantine?* |
| 2. Ils adorent les devoirs. | Est-ce qu'ils adorent les devoirs? |
| 3. La biologie est difficile. | Est-ce que la biologie est difficile? |
| 4. Tu travailles. | Est-ce que tu travailles? |
| 5. Elles cherchent le prof. | Est-ce qu'elles cherchent le prof? |
| 6. Aude voyage beaucoup. | Est-ce qu'Aude voyage beaucoup? |
| 7. Vous arrivez demain. | Arrivez-vous demain? |
| 8. L'élève oublie le livre. | L'élève oublie-t-il/elle le livre? |
| 9. La physique est utile. | La physique est-elle utile? |
| 10. Il y a deux salles de classe. | Y a-t-il deux salles de classe? |
| 11. Ils n'habitent pas à Québec. | N'habitent-ils pas à Québec? |
| 12. C'est le professeur d'art. | Est-ce le professeur d'art? |

**Essayez!** Have students repeat using inversion for items 1–6 and **est-ce que/qu'** in 7–12.

**1 Expansion** Have students work in pairs, and take turns asking and answering the questions in the negative.

**2 Expansion** Have students write two additional statements. Tell them to exchange papers with a partner who will ask the questions that would elicit those statements.

**3 Expansion** Have pairs of students create a similar conversation, replacing the answers and some of the questions with information that is true for them. Then have volunteers act out their conversations for the class.

**4 Suggestion** Tell students to vary the method of asking questions instead of always using a tag question as in the **modèle**.

**5 Suggestions**
- Have two volunteers read the **modèle** aloud.
- After students have completed the activity, ask volunteers to report what they learned about their partner.

**6 Suggestion** Encourage students to use as many expressions indicating agreement or disagreement as they can.

**6 Expansion** Have groups write three additional true/false statements about their school. Ask several groups to read their statements and have the class respond to them. Encourage students to respond with **Mais oui!** or **Mais non!** where appropriate.

**Using Video** Replay the video episode, having students focus on the different forms of questions used. Tell them to write down each question they hear. Stop the video where suitable to give students time to write and to discuss what was heard.

**Questions** Prepare eight questions. Write their answers on the board in random order. Then read your questions aloud, having students match the question to the appropriate answer. Make sure that only one of the possible answers corresponds logically to the questions you ask. Example: **Pourquoi _____ déteste-t-il les maths? (Il n'aime pas le prof.)**

# SYNTHÈSE
# Révision

**Key Standards**

**1.1**

**Student Resources**
*Cahier d'activités*, pp. 25–26;
Supersite: Activities,
*Cahier interactif*

**Teacher Resources**
Answer Keys; Info Gap
Activities; Testing Program:
Lesson Test (Testing Program
Audio MP3s/CD)

**1 Expansion** Have students compare two of their own classes that are very different, such as an English literature class and an art class, and explain which one they prefer. This activity can be done orally or in writing.

**2 Suggestion** Have two volunteers read the **modèle** aloud. Tell students to add at least two more items to the list, one that applies to both of them and one that does not.

**3 Suggestion** As students share their responses with the class, make a list of their likes and dislikes on the board under the headings **Nous aimons** and **Nous n'aimons pas.**

**4 Suggestion** Tell students they may use adjectives that are not in the list.

**5 Suggestion** Before beginning the activity, have the class decide on names for the people in the drawings. Also have them brainstorm possible relationships between the people, for example, strangers meeting for the first time.

**6 Suggestion** Divide the class into pairs and distribute the Info Gap Handouts on the Supersite for this activity. Give students ten minutes to complete the activity.

**6 Expansion** Have pairs compare their answers with another pair to confirm the people's likes and dislikes. Then ask a few groups to share some of their sentences with the class

---

**1 Des styles différents** In pairs, compare these two very different classes. Then, tell your partner which class you prefer and why. Answers will vary.

**2 Les activités** In pairs, discuss whether these expressions apply to both of you. React to every answer you hear. Answers will vary.

> **MODÈLE**
>
> **Élève 1:** *Est-ce que tu étudies le week-end?*
> **Élève 2:** *Non! Je n'aime pas étudier le week-end.*
> **Élève 1:** *Moi non plus. J'aime mieux étudier le soir.*

1. adorer la cantine
2. aimer le cours d'art
3. étudier à la bibliothèque
4. manger souvent (*often*) des sushis
5. oublier les devoirs
6. parler espagnol
7. travailler le soir
8. voyager souvent

**3 Le lycée** In pairs, prepare ten questions inspired by the list and what you know about your school. Together, survey as many classmates as possible to find out what they like and dislike. Answers will vary.

> **MODÈLE**
>
> **Élève 1:** *Est-ce que tu aimes étudier à la bibliothèque?*
> **Élève 2:** *Non, pas trop. J'aime mieux étudier...*

| bibliothèque | élève | cantine |
|---|---|---|
| bureau | gymnase | salle de classe |
| cours | librairie | salle d'ordinateurs |

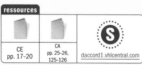

**ressources**

| CE pp. 17–20 | CA pp. 25–26, 125–126 | (S) daccord1.vhlcentral.com |

**4 Pourquoi?** Survey as many classmates as possible to find out if they like these subjects and why. Ask what adjective they would pick to describe them. Tally the most popular answers for each subject. Answers will vary.

> **MODÈLE**
>
> **Élève 1:** *Est-ce que tu aimes la philosophie?*
> **Élève 2:** *Pas tellement.*
> **Élève 1:** *Pourquoi?*
> **Élève 2:** *Parce que c'est trop difficile.*

1. la biologie
2. la chimie
3. l'histoire
4. l'éducation physique
5. l'informatique
6. les langues
7. les mathématiques
8. la psychologie

a. agréable
b. amusant
c. désagréable
d. difficile
e. facile
f. important
g. inutile
h. utile

**5 Les conversations** In pairs, act out a short conversation between the people shown in each drawing. They should greet each other, describe what they are doing, and discuss their likes or dislikes. Choose your favorite skit and role-play it for another pair. Answers will vary.

> **MODÈLE**
>
> **Élève 1:** *Bonjour, Aurélie.*
> **Élève 2:** *Salut! Tu travailles, n'est-ce pas?*

**6 Les portraits** Your teacher will give you and a partner a set of drawings showing the likes and dislikes of eight people. Discuss each person's tastes. Do not look at each other's worksheet. Answers will vary.

> **MODÈLE**
>
> **Élève 1:** *Sarah n'aime pas travailler.*
> **Élève 2:** *Mais elle adore manger.*

---

**OPTIONS**

**Writing Practice** Have students write a brief paragraph describing the activities they like or don't like to do. Collect the descriptions and read a few of them to the class. Have the class guess who wrote each description by asking: **Est-ce que c'est...?**

**Video Expansion** Tell students to turn to the **Roman-photo** on pages 42–43 and write five comprehension questions based on the dialogue. Then have them get together in groups of three or four, and take turns asking and answering each other's questions.

**S** : Video: TV Clip

# Le Zapping

## Clairefontaine: l'écrit du cœur

In 1858, Jean-Baptiste Bichelberger founded a paper factory in eastern France. Soon the company became Clairefontaine and started making envelopes and notebooks. In 1950, Charles Nusse took over the company, offering schoolchildren notebooks made of high-quality paper. He was the creator of the Clairefontaine logo, which became famous. Today, the company has branches all over Europe and even in the United States. It manufactures school supplies, accounting ledgers, and stationery.

—C'est pas vrai°...!

—Je suis votre° nouveau prof d'histoire.

**Compréhension** Answer these questions. Answers will vary.

1. What school-related vocabulary did you understand?
2. Why did one of the girls throw the notebook on the ground?

**Discussion** In pairs, discuss the answers to these questions. Answers will vary.

1. If the commercial were to continue, what would the characters say next?
2. Do you know of any TV commercials advertising stationery?

**vrai** *true* **votre** *your*

 Practice more at **daccord1.vhlcentral.com**.

*cinquante et un* **51**

---

**Le papier Clairefontaine** People love Clairefontaine notebooks for the quality of their paper. The company uses ultra-smooth, brushed vellum paper that it manufactures itself. This paper weighs 90 grams per square meter. It is also very white and anti-glare. Clairefontaine is currently the only manufacturer making its own paper for its stationery products. This helps the company maintain consistent paper quality and also controls the environmental impact of the paper manufacturing process. The company uses pulp exclusively from trees grown in certified sustainable forests.

---

## Section Goals

In this section, students will:
- read about the company Clairefontaine
- watch a commercial for Clairefontaine notebooks
- answer questions about the commercial and Clairefontaine

## Key Standards

1.2, 2.2, 4.2, 5.2

**Student Resources**
Supersite: Video, Activities
**Teacher Resources**
Video Script & Translation;
Supersite: Video

**Introduction**
To check students' comprehension, ask these questions.
1. What was the origin of the Clairefontaine company? (It was a paper factory founded in 1858 in eastern France.)
2. What product did Clairefontaine start making after Charles Nusse took over? (It started to make notebooks with high-quality paper.)
3. Is Clairefontaine a successful brand? (Yes. It has a famous logo, and the company has branches in Europe and the United States.)

**Avant de regarder la vidéo**
- Have students look at the video stills, read the captions, and predict what is happening in the commercial for each visual. (1. Two teenage girls are chatting at school. 2. They meet their new teacher.)
- Before showing the video, explain to students that they do not need to understand every word they hear. Tell them to listen for cognates, school-related vocabulary, and the slogan.

**Compréhension** Have students work in pairs or groups for this activity. Tell them to write their answers. Then show the video again so that they can check their work and add any missing information.

**Discussion** After discussing the questions, ask volunteers to report their comments and ideas to the class.

## Section Goals

In this section, students will learn and practice vocabulary related to:
• talking about schedules
• the days of the week
• sequencing events

## Key Standards
**1.1, 1.2, 4.1**

**Student Resources**
*Cahier d'exercices*, pp. 21-22;
*Cahier d'activités*, pp. 3, 127;
Supersite: Activities,
*Cahier interactif*
**Teacher Resources**
Answer Keys; Overhead #18;
Audio Script; Textbook & Audio
Activity MP3s/CD; *Feuilles d'activités*; Testing program:
Vocabulary Quiz

## Suggestions

• Write days of the week across the board and present them like this: **Aujourd'hui, c'est _____. Demain, c'est _____. Après-demain, c'est _____?**
• Write the following questions and answers on the board, explaining their meaning:
—**Quel jour sommes-nous?**
—**Nous sommes _____.**
—**C'est quel jour demain?**
—**Demain, c'est _____.**
—**C'est quand l'examen?**
—**L'examen est _____.**
Ask students the questions.
• Tell students Monday is the first day of the week in France.
• Point out that days of the week are masculine and lowercase.
• Explain the differences between **le matin/la matinée, le soir/la soirée,** and **le jour/ la journée.**
• Introduce new vocabulary using **Overhead #18.** Give the student a name, for example, Henri. Ask students picture-based questions. Examples: **Quel jour Henri assiste-t-il au cours d'économie? Il assiste au cours d'économie le matin ou le soir? Quels jours visite-t-il Paris avec Annette?**
• Point out that **visiter** is used with places, not people.

**Leçon 2B**

(S) **Talking Picture Audio: Activity**

**You will learn how to...**
▪ say when things happen
▪ discuss your schedule

# Une semaine au lycée

## Vocabulaire

| | |
|---|---|
| demander | to ask |
| échouer | to fail |
| écouter | to listen (to) |
| enseigner | to teach |
| expliquer | to explain |
| trouver | to find; to think |
| Quel jour sommes-nous? | What day is it? |
| un an | year |
| une/cette année | one/this year |
| après | after |
| après-demain | day after tomorrow |
| un/cet après-midi | an/this afternoon |
| aujourd'hui | today |
| demain (matin/ après-midi/soir) | tomorrow (morning/ afternoon/evening) |
| un jour | day |
| une journée | day |
| un/ce matin | a/this morning |
| la matinée | morning |
| un mois/ce mois-ci | month/this month |
| une/cette nuit | a/this night |
| une/cette semaine | a/this week |
| un/ce soir | an/this evening |
| une soirée | evening |
| un/le/ce week-end | a/the/this weekend |
| dernier/dernière | last |
| premier/première | first |
| prochain(e) | next |

**ressources**

CE pp. 21-22 | CA pp. 3, 127 | (S) daccord1.vhlcentral.com

**semaine**

| lundi | mardi | mercredi | jeudi | vendredi |
|---|---|---|---|---|

*matin*

*après-midi*

*soir*

assister au cours d'économie

passer l'examen de maths

téléphoner à Marc

préparer l'examen de maths

dîner en famille

**52** *cinquante-deux*

## Mise en pratique

**Attention!**

Use the masculine definite article **le** + [*day of the week*] when an activity is done on a weekly basis. Omit **le** when it is done on a specific day.

**Le prof enseigne le lundi.**
*The teacher teaches on Mondays.*

**Je passe un examen lundi.**
*I'm taking a test on Monday.*

**1** **Écoutez** 🎧 You will hear Lorraine describing her schedule. Listen carefully and indicate whether the statements are **vrai** or **faux**.

|  | Vrai | Faux |
|---|---|---|
| 1. Lorraine étudie à l'université le soir. | ☐ | ☑ |
| 2. Elle trouve le cours de mathématiques facile. | ☐ | ☑ |
| 3. Elle étudie le week-end. | ☐ | ☑ |
| 4. Lorraine étudie la chimie le mardi et le jeudi matin. | ☐ | ☑ |
| 5. Le professeur de mathématiques explique bien. | ☐ | ☑ |
| 6. Lorraine regarde la télévision, écoute de la musique ou téléphone à Claire et Anne le soir. | ☑ | ☐ |
| 7. Lorraine travaille dans (*in*) une librairie. | ☐ | ☑ |
| 8. Elle étudie l'histoire le mardi et le jeudi matin. | ☑ | ☐ |
| 9. Lorraine adore dîner avec sa famille le week-end. | ☑ | ☐ |
| 10. Lorraine rentre à la maison le soir. | ☐ | ☑ |

**2** **La classe de Mme Arnaud** Complete this paragraph by selecting the correct verb from the list below. Make sure to conjugate the verb. Some verbs will not be used.

| | | |
|---|---|---|
| demander | expliquer | rentrer |
| écouter | passer un examen | travailler |
| enseigner | préparer | trouver |
| étudier | regarder | visiter |

Madame Arnaud (1) ____travaille____ au lycée. Elle (2) ____enseigne____ le français. Elle (3) ____explique____ les verbes et la grammaire aux élèves. Le vendredi, en classe, les élèves (4) ____regardent____ une vidéo en français ou (*or*) (5) ____écoutent____ de la musique française. Ce week-end, ils (6) ____étudient/travaillent____ pour (*for*) (7) ____préparer____ l'examen très difficile de lundi matin. Je/J' (8) ____travaille/étudie____ beaucoup pour ce cours, mais mes (*my*) amis et moi, nous (9) ____trouvons____ la classe sympa.

**3** **Quel jour sommes-nous?** Complete each statement with the correct day of the week.

1. Aujourd'hui, c'est ____Answers will vary.____
2. Demain, c'est ____Answers will vary.____
3. Après-demain, c'est ____Answers will vary.____
4. Le week-end, c'est ____le samedi et le dimanche____
5. Le premier jour de la semaine en France, c'est ____le lundi____
6. Les jours du cours de français sont ____Answers will vary.____
7. Mon (*My*) jour préféré de la semaine, c'est ____Answers will vary.____
8. Je travaille à la bibliothèque ____Answers will vary.____

🎵 Practice more at **daccord1.vhlcentral.com.**

*cinquante-trois* **53**

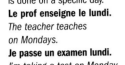
samedi | dimanche

**visiter Paris avec une amie**

**rentrer à la maison**

**1** **Script** Cette année à l'université j'étudie: la chimie, le lundi et le mercredi matin; l'histoire, le mardi et le jeudi matin; l'art, le vendredi matin et les mathématiques, le lundi et le mercredi après-midi. Je déteste les mathématiques; le professeur n'explique pas bien et je trouve le cours difficile. J'étudie l'après-midi quand je rentre à la maison. Le soir, je ne travaille pas, alors je regarde la télévision, j'écoute de la musique ou je téléphone à mes amies, Claire et Anne. Le week-end, j'adore rendre visite à ma famille pour dîner!
(*On Textbook Audio*)

**1** **Suggestions**
• Before playing the recording, have students read the statements and identify the expressions that describe when things occur. Examples: **le soir**, **le week-end**, and **le jeudi matin**.
• Go over the answers with the class. If students have difficulty, replay the recording.

**2** **Expansion** Have pairs write original sentences about Madame Arnaud and her class using the verbs that weren't in this paragraph. Ask volunteers to read their sentences aloud.

**3** **Expansions**
• Give these items for more practice. **9. Le jour après lundi, c'est ____. 10. Il n'y a pas de cours de français le ____.**
• Have students repeat items 1–5 from the perspective of a different day of the week.

**Using Movement** Create a schedule for an imaginary student using the whole class. Assign each day of the week to a different student and assign each of the remaining students a different activity. As you describe the schedule, students arrange themselves as a page in a weekly day-planner, starting with the day of the week and then each activity you mention. Example: **Le lundi** matin, j'assiste au cours. L'après-midi, je passe un examen de français. Le soir, je dîne avec ma famille.

**Writing Practice** Have students write a paragraph similar to the one in **Activité 2** describing your French class or a different class. They should use as many verbs from the list as possible. Ask volunteers to read their paragraph aloud.

## Communication

**4**   **Conversez** Interview a classmate. Answers will vary.

1. Quel jour sommes-nous?
2. Quand (*When*) est le prochain cours de français?
3. Quand rentres-tu à la maison?
4. Est-ce que tu prépares un examen cette année?
5. Est-ce que tu écoutes la radio? Quel genre de musique aimes-tu?
6. Quand téléphones-tu à des amis?
7. Est-ce que tu regardes la télévision l'après-midi ou (*or*) le soir?
8. Est-ce que tu dînes dans un restaurant ce mois-ci?

**5**   **Le premier jour** You make a new friend in your French class and want to know what his or her class schedule is like this semester. With a partner, prepare a conversation to perform for the class where you: Answers will vary.

- ask his or her name
- ask what classes he or she is taking
- ask on which days of the week he or she has French class
- ask at which times of day (morning or afternoon) he or she has English and History classes

**6**   **Bataille navale** Your teacher will give you a worksheet. Choose four spaces on your chart and mark them with a battleship. In pairs, formulate questions by using the subjects in the first column and the verbs in the first row to find out where your partner has placed his or her battleships. Whoever "sinks" the most battleships wins. Answers will vary.

**MODÈLE**

**Élève 1:** Est-ce que Luc et Sabine téléphonent à Jérôme?
**Élève 2:** Oui, ils téléphonent à Jérôme.
*(if you marked that square)*
Non, ils ne téléphonent pas à Jérôme.
*(if you didn't mark that square)*

| | enseigner | téléphoner |
|---|---|---|
| Marie | | |
| Luc et Sabine | | 🚢 |

**7**   **Le week-end** Write a schedule to show what you do during a typical weekend. Use the verbs you know. Compare your schedule with a classmate's, and talk about the different activities that you do and when. Be prepared to discuss your results with the class.
Answers will vary.

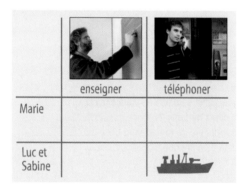

**OPTIONS**

**Using Games** Play a memory game in which the first player says one activity he or she does on a particular day of the week. The next player repeats what the first person said, then adds what he or she does on the following day. The third player must remember what the first two people said before saying what he or she does on the next day. Continue until the end of a week. If someone makes a mistake, then choose another student to continue.

**Oral Practice** Have students work in groups of three. Tell them to take turns asking and answering what days of the week different TV shows are on. Example: **Quel(s) jour(s) est la série *CSI*?**

# Les sons et les lettres

 Audio: Concepts, Activities
Record & Compare

🎧 **The letter r**

The French **r** is very different from the English *r*. The English *r* is pronounced by placing the tongue in the middle and toward the front of the mouth. The French **r** is pronounced in the throat. You have seen that an **-er** at the end of a word is usually pronounced **-ay**, as in the English word *way*, but without the glide sound.

| chant**er** | mang**er** | expliqu**er** | aim**er** |

In most other cases, the French **r** has a very different sound. Pronunciation of the French **r** varies according to its position in a word. Note the different ways the **r** is pronounced in these words.

| **r**ivière | litté**r**ature | ordinateu**r** | devoi**r** |

If an **r** falls between two vowels or before a vowel, it is pronounced with slightly more friction.

| **r**a**r**e | ga**r**age | Eu**r**ope | **r**ose |

An **r** sound before a consonant or at the end of a word is pronounced with slightly less friction.

| po**r**te | bou**r**se | ado**r**e | jou**r** |

🔊 **Prononcez** Practice saying these words aloud.

1. crayon
2. professeur
3. plaisir
4. différent
5. terrible
6. architecture
7. trouver
8. restaurant
9. rentrer
10. regarder
11. lettres
12. réservé
13. être
14. dernière
15. arriver
16. après

🔊 **Articulez** Practice saying these sentences aloud.

1. Au revoir, Professeur Colbert!
2. Rose arrive en retard mardi.
3. Mercredi, c'est le dernier jour des cours.
4. Robert et Roger adorent écouter la radio.
5. La corbeille à papier, c'est quarante-quatre euros!
6. Les parents de Richard sont brillants et très agréables.

🔊 **Dictons** Practice reading these sayings aloud.

*Quand le renard prêche, gare aux oies.*[2]

*Qui ne risque rien n'a rien.*[1]

[1] Nothing ventured, nothing gained.
[2] When the fox preaches, watch your geese.

**ressources**

CA
p. 128

daccord1.vhlcentral.com

*cinquante-cinq* **55**

**Section Goals**
In this section, students will learn about the letter **r**.

**Key Standards**
4.1

**Student Resources**
*Cahier d'activités*, p. 128;
Supersite: Activities,
*Cahier interactif*
**Teacher Resources**
Answer Keys; Audio Script;
Textbook & Audio Activity
MP3s/CD

**Suggestions**
- Model the pronunciation of words and expressions with **r** from **Contextes**. Then have students repeat. Examples: **regarder, préparer un examen**, etc.
- Explain that the French **r** has more in common with a **k** sound than it does with the English *r*. The **k** sound is velar, produced when the back of the tongue touches the soft palate. The French **r** is uvular, produced a bit farther back in the mouth with the back of the tongue and the uvula.
- Model the pronunciation of each example word and have students repeat.
- Ask students to provide words or expressions from previous lessons that contain the letter **r**. Examples: **au revoir**, **très bien**, **professeur**, and **merci**.
- The explanation and exercises are available on the Supersite. You may want to play them in class so students hear French speakers other than yourself.

**Dictons** Ask students if they can think of an English saying that is similar to «**Quand le renard prêche, gare aux oies.**» (*Don't let a fox guard the hen house.*)

**OPTIONS**

**Mini-dictée** Dictate five familiar words with the **r** in different places, saying each one at least two times. Examples: **librairie**, **résultat**, **jour**, **chercher**, and **montre**. Then write them on the board or a transparency and have students check their spelling.

**Mini-dictée** Use these sentences with the letter **r** for additional oral practice or dictation. 1. **Renée regarde un garçon américain.** 2. **Le grand-père de Grégoire est réservé.** 3. **Je travaille le mercredi après-midi et le vendredi soir.** 4. **Nous trouvons le cours d'histoire très intéressant.**

# ROMAN-PHOTO

## On trouve une solution.  Video: *Roman-photo* Record & Compare

**PERSONNAGES**

 Amina

 Astrid

 David

 Rachid

 Sandrine

 Stéphane

*À la terrasse du café...*

**RACHID** Alors, on a rendez-vous avec David demain à cinq heures moins le quart pour rentrer chez nous.
**SANDRINE** Aujourd'hui, c'est mercredi. Demain... jeudi. Le mardi et le jeudi, j'ai cours de chant de trois heures vingt à quatre heures et demie. C'est parfait!
**AMINA** Pas de problème. J'ai cours de stylisme...

**AMINA** Salut, Astrid!
**ASTRID** Bonjour.
**RACHID** Astrid, je te présente David, mon (*my*) coloc américain.
**DAVID** Alors, cette année, tu as des cours très difficiles, n'est-ce pas?

**ASTRID** Oui? Pourquoi?
**DAVID** Ben, Stéphane pense que les cours sont très difficiles.
**ASTRID** Ouais, Stéphane, il assiste au cours, mais... il ne fait pas ses (*his*) devoirs et il n'écoute pas les profs. Cette année est très importante, parce que nous avons le bac...
**DAVID** Ah, le bac...

*Au parc...*

**ASTRID** Stéphane! Quelle heure est-il? Tu n'as pas de montre?
**STÉPHANE** Oh, Astrid, excuse-moi! Le mercredi, je travaille avec Astrid au café sur le cours de maths...
**ASTRID** Et le mercredi après-midi, il oublie! Tu n'as pas peur du bac, toi!

**STÉPHANE** Tu as tort, j'ai très peur du bac! Mais je n'ai pas envie de passer mes (*my*) journées, mes soirées et mes week-ends avec des livres!
**ASTRID** Je suis d'accord avec toi, Stéphane! J'ai envie de passer les week-ends avec mes copains... des copains qui n'oublient pas les rendez-vous!

**RACHID** Écoute, Stéphane, tu as des problèmes avec ta (*your*) mère, avec Astrid aussi.
**STÉPHANE** Oui, et j'ai d'énormes problèmes au lycée. Je déteste le bac.
**RACHID** Il n'est pas tard pour commencer à travailler pour être reçu au bac.
**STÉPHANE** Tu crois, Rachid?

**A C T I V I T É S**

**1 Vrai ou faux?** Choose whether each statement is **vrai** or **faux.** Correct the false statements.
Answers may vary slightly.
1. Le mardi et le mercredi, Sandrine a (*has*) cours de chant. Faux. Sandrine a cours de chant le mardi et le jeudi.
2. Le jeudi, Amina a cours de stylisme. Vrai.
3. Astrid pense qu'il est impossible de réussir (*pass*) le bac. Faux. Astrid pense que ce n'est pas impossible.
4. La famille de David est allemande. Faux. La famille de David est française.
5. Le mercredi, Stéphane travaille avec Astrid au café sur le cours de maths. Vrai.

6. Stéphane a beaucoup de problèmes. Vrai.
7. Rachid est optimiste. Vrai.
8. Stéphane dîne chez Rachid samedi. Faux. Stéphane dîne chez Rachid dimanche.
9. Le sport est très important pour Stéphane. Vrai.
10. Astrid est fâchée (*angry*) contre Stéphane. Vrai.

 Practice more at **daccord1.vhlcentral.com.**

**56** *cinquante-six*

**Les amis organisent des rendez-vous.**

**RACHID** C'est un examen très important que les élèves français passent la dernière année de lycée pour continuer en études supérieures.

**DAVID** Euh, n'oublie pas, je suis de famille française.

**ASTRID** Oui, et c'est difficile, mais ce n'est pas impossible. Stéphane trouve que les études ne sont pas intéressantes. Le sport, oui, mais pas les études.

**RACHID** Le sport? Tu cherches Stéphane, n'est-ce pas? On trouve Stéphane au parc! Allons-y, Astrid.

**ASTRID** D'accord. À demain!

**RACHID** Oui. Mais le sport, c'est la dernière des priorités. Écoute, dimanche prochain, tu dînes chez moi et on trouve une solution.

**STÉPHANE** Rachid, tu n'as pas envie de donner des cours à un lycéen nul comme moi!

**RACHID** Mais si, j'ai très envie d'enseigner les maths...

**STÉPHANE** Bon, j'accepte. Merci, Rachid. C'est sympa.

**RACHID** De rien. À plus tard!

## Expressions utiles

### Talking about your schedule

- **Alors, on a rendez-vous demain à cinq heures moins le quart pour rentrer chez nous.**
  *So, we're meeting tomorrow at quarter to five to go home (our home).*
- **J'ai cours de chant de trois heures vingt à quatre heures et demie.**
  *I have voice (singing) class from three-twenty to four-thirty.*
- **J'ai cours de stylisme de deux heures à quatre heures vingt.**
  *I have fashion design class from two o'clock to four-twenty.*
- **Quelle heure est-il?** • **Tu n'as pas de montre?**
  *What time is it?* *You don't have a watch?*

### Talking about school

- **Nous avons le bac.**
  *We have the bac.*
- **Il ne fait pas ses devoirs.**
  *He doesn't do his homework.*
- **Tu n'as pas peur du bac!**
  *You're not afraid of the bac!*
- **Tu as tort, j'ai très peur du bac!**
  *You're wrong, I'm very afraid of the bac!*
- **Je suis d'accord avec toi.**
  *I agree with you.*
- **J'ai d'énormes problèmes.**
  *I have big/enormous problems.*
- **Tu n'as pas envie de donner des cours à un(e) lycéen(ne) nul(le) comme moi.**
  *You don't want to teach a high school student as bad as myself.*

### Useful expressions

- **C'est parfait!**
  *That's perfect!*
- **Allons-y!**
  *Let's go!*
- **D'accord.**
  *OK./All right.*
- **Ouais.**
  *Yeah.*
- **C'est sympa.**
  *That's nice/fun.*

---

**2** **Répondez** Answer these questions. Refer to the video scenes and use a dictionary as necessary. You do not have to answer in complete sentences. Answers will vary.

1. Où est-ce que tu as envie de voyager?
2. Est-ce que tu as peur de quelque chose? De quoi?
3. Qu'est-ce que tu dis (*say*) quand tu as tort?

**3** **À vous!** With a partner, describe someone you know whose personality, likes, or dislikes resemble those of Rachid or Stéphane.

**MODÈLE**

*Paul est comme (like) Rachid... il est sérieux.*

ressources

CA
pp. 73-74

daccord1.vhlcentral.com

ACTIVITÉS

---

# CULTURE

## CULTURE À LA LOUPE

# Le bac

**The three years of** lycée **culminate in a high-stakes exam called the** baccalauréat **or** bac. Students begin preparing for this exam by the end of **seconde** (10th grade), when they must decide the type of **bac** they will take. This choice determines their coursework during the last two years of **lycée**; for example, a student who plans to take the **bac S** will study mainly physics, chemistry, and math. Most students take **le bac économique et sociale (ES)**, **le bac littéraire (L)**, or **le bac scientifique (S)**. Others, though, choose to follow a more technical path and take the **bac sciences et technologies industrielles (STI)**, the **bac sciences et technologies de la santé et du social (ST2S)**, or the **bac sciences et techniques médico-sociales (SMS)**. There is even a **bac technique** for hotel management, and music/dance!

The **bac** has both oral and written sections, which are weighted differently according to the type of **bac**. This means that, for example, a bad grade on the math section would lower a student's grade significantly on a **bac S** but to a lesser degree on a **bac L**. In all cases the highest possible grade is 20/20. If a student's overall score on the **bac** is below 10/20 (the minimum passing grade) but above 8/20, he can take the **rattrapage**, or make-up exam. If the student fails again, then he can **redoubler**, or repeat the school year and take the **bac** again.

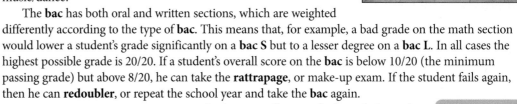

| Students can pass the **bac** with: | |
|---|---|
| 18/20 - 20/20 | mention Très bien et félicitation du jury |
| 16/20 - 18/20 | mention Très bien |
| 14/20 - 16/20 | mention Bien |
| 12/20 - 14/20 | mention Assez bien |
| 10/20 - 12/20 | no special mention |

Students usually go to find out their results with friends and classmates just a few days after they take the exam. This yearly ritual is full of emotion: it's common to see groups of students frantically looking for their results posted on bulletin boards at the **lycée**. Over 80% of students pass the **bac** every year, granting them access to France's higher education system.

**Coup de main**

In French, a superscript <sup>e</sup> following a numeral tells you that it is an ordinal number. It is the equivalent of a <sup>th</sup> after a numeral in English: 10<sup>e</sup> (**dixième**) = *10th*.

### ACTIVITÉS

**1 Vrai ou faux?** Indicate whether each statement is **vrai** or **faux**.

1. The **bac** is an exam that students take at the end of **terminale**.
   Vrai.
2. The **bac** has only oral exams.
   Faux. It also has written exams.
3. The highest possible grade on the **bac** is 20/20.
   Vrai.
4. Students decide which **bac** they will take at the beginning of **terminale**.
   Faux. Students must decide which bac they will take by the end of seconde.
5. Most students take the **bac technique**.
   Faux. Most students take le bac ES, le bac L, or le bac S.
6. All the grades of the **bac** are weighted equally.
   Faux. The different sections are weighted differently in each bac.
7. A student with an average grade of 14.5 on the **bac** receives his diploma with **mention bien**.
   Vrai.
8. A student who fails the **bac** but has an overall grade of 8/20 can take a make-up exam.
   Vrai.
9. A student who fails the **bac** and the **rattrapage** cannot repeat the year.
   Faux. He can repeat the year and attempt the bac again.
10. Passing the **bac** enables students to register for college or to apply for the **grandes écoles**.
    Vrai.

 Practice more at **daccord1.vhlcentral.com**.

## LE FRANÇAIS QUOTIDIEN

### Les examens

| | |
|---|---|
| **assurer/cartonner** (à un examen) | *to ace (an exam)* |
| **bachoter** | *to cram for the bac* |
| **bosser** | *to work hard* |
| **une moyenne** | *an average* |
| **rater (un examen)** | *to fail (an exam)* |
| **réviser** | *to study, to review* |
| **un(e) surveillant(e)** | *a proctor* |
| **tricher** | *to cheat* |

## LE MONDE FRANCOPHONE

### Le français langue étrangère

Voici quelques° écoles du monde francophone où vous pouvez étudier° le français.

**En Belgique** Université de Liège

**En France** Université de Franche-Comté–Centre de linguistique appliquée, Université de Grenoble, Université de Paris IV-Sorbonne

**À la Martinique** Institut Supérieur d'Études Francophones, à Schoelcher

**En Nouvelle-Calédonie** Centre de Rencontres et d'Échanges Internationaux du Pacifique, à Nouméa

**Au Québec** Université Laval, Université de Montréal

**Aux îles Saint-Pierre et Miquelon** Le FrancoForum, à Saint-Pierre

**En Suisse** Université Populaire de Lausanne, Université de Neuchâtel

**quelques-unes** *some* **où vous pouvez étudier** *where you can study*

## PORTRAIT

### Les études supérieures en France

Après qu'ils passent le bac, les étudiants français ont le choix° de plusieurs° types d'étude: les meilleurs° entrent en classe préparatoire pour passer les concours d'entrée aux° grandes écoles. Les grandes écoles forment l'élite de l'enseignement supérieur en France. Les plus connues° sont l'ENA (école nationale d'administration), Polytechnique, HEC (école des hautes études commerciales) et Sciences Po (institut des sciences politiques). Certains étudiants choisissent° une école spécialisée, comme une école de commerce ou de journalisme. Ces écoles proposent une formation° et un diplôme très spécifiques. L'autre° possibilité est l'entrée à l'université. Les étudiants d'université se spécialisent dans un domaine dès° la première année. Les études universitaires durent° trois ou quatre ans en général, et plus pour un doctorat.

**choix** *choice* **plusieurs** *several* **meilleurs** *best* **concours d'entrée aux** *entrance tests to the* **plus connues** *most well known* **choisissent** *choose* **formation** *education* **autre** *other* **dès** *starting in* **durent** *last*

## SUR INTERNET

**Quel** *(Which)* bac aimeriez-vous *(would you like)* passer?

Go to **daccord1.vhlcentral.com** to find more information related to this **CULTURE** section.

---

**2** **Les études supérieures en France** What kind of higher education might these students seek?

1. Une future journaliste   *une école spécialisée*
2. Un élève exceptionnel   *une grande école*
3. Une étudiante en anglais   *l'université*
4. Un étudiant en affaires   *une école spécialisée*
5. Un étudiant de chimie   *l'université*

**3** **Et les cours?** In French, name two courses you might take in preparation for each of these baccalauréat exams. *Answers will vary. Possible answers shown.*

1. un bac L
   *le français et la philosophie*
2. un bac SMS
   *la biologie et la psychologie*
3. un bac ES
   *l'économie et la sociologie*
4. un bac STI
   *la physique et les maths*

**ressources**

CA pp. 101–102

daccord1.vhlcentral.com

**A C T I V I T É S**

---

**O P T I O N S**

**Cultural Comparison** Have students compare entrance to university in France and the United States. Ask them what determines a student's ability to enroll in a university in France versus in the United States. Which system do they prefer?

**Pairs** Have students work in pairs. Tell them to take turns asking and answering questions using the expressions in **Le français quotidien**. Examples: **Tu bosses pour le cours de français?**

---

**Le français quotidien** Model the pronunciation of each term and have students repeat it. You might also add these words to this list: **une dissert(ation)** *(writing assignment)*, **réussir à un examen** *(to pass an exam)*, and **recaler** *(to fail)*.

**Portrait** Show the class the photo of **la Sorbonne**. Ask: **Qu'est-ce que c'est? (une université) Comment s'appelle-t-elle?** Then ask students if they know why it is famous.

**Le monde francophone** Have students read the list. Use this as an opportunity to explain the importance of language immersion in a French-speaking country and to encourage students to start thinking about study abroad. If possible, bring in brochures or refer students to websites for study abroad programs.

**2** **Expansion** For each item, ask students where an American student with these interests might choose to study. Have them name either a type of school or a specific university.

**CULTURE**   **59**

## Section Goals

In this section, students will learn:
- the verb **avoir**
- some common expressions with **avoir**

## Key Standards

4.1, 5.1

**Student Resources**
*Cahier d'exercices*, pp. 23-24;
*Cahier d'activités*, pp. 4, 129;
Supersite: Activities,
*Cahier interactif*

**Teacher Resources**
Answer Keys; Audio Script;
Audio Activity MP3s/CD;
*Feuilles d'activités*; Testing
program: Grammar Quiz

## Suggestions

- Model **avoir** by asking questions such as: **Avez-vous un examen cette semaine? Avez-vous une calculatrice? ____ a-t-il/elle une calculatrice?** Point out that forms of **avoir** were in the **Roman-photo**.
- Explain that **avoir** is irregular and must be memorized. Begin a paradigm for **avoir** by writing **j'ai** on the board and asking volunteers questions that elicit **j'ai**. Examples: **J'ai un stylo. Qui a un crayon?**
- Add **tu as** and **il/elle a** to the paradigm on the board. Point out that **as** and **a** are pronounced alike. Tell students that **avoir** has no real stem apart from the letter **a**.
- Write **nous avons** and **vous avez**. Point out that **-ons** and **-ez** are the same endings as in **-er** verbs. Add **ils/elles ont**.
- Remind students of liaisons in the plural forms of **avoir** and have them pronounce these forms again.
- Tell the class that many French expressions use **avoir** + *noun* instead of **être** to say *to be* + *adjective* in English. Also point out that, to ask people if they feel like doing something, use **avoir envie de** + *infinitive*.
- Model the use of the expressions by talking about yourself while gesturing and asking students questions about themselves. Examples: **J'ai froid ce matin/ cet après-midi. Vous avez froid aussi ou vous avez chaud? J'ai besoin d'un dictionnaire. Avez-vous un dictionnaire?**

## 2B.1 Present tense of *avoir*

**Point de départ** The verb **avoir** (*to have*) is used frequently. You will have to memorize each of its present tense forms because they are irregular.

### Present tense of *avoir*

| | | | |
|---|---|---|---|
| j'ai | *I have* | nous avons | *we have* |
| tu as | *you have* | vous avez | *you have* |
| il/elle a | *he/she/it has* | ils/elles ont | *they have* |

On a rendez-vous avec David demain.

Cette année, nous avons le bac.

- Liaison is required between the final consonants of **on**, **nous**, **vous**, **ils**, and **elles** and the forms of **avoir** that follow them. When the final consonant is an **-s**, pronounce it as a *z* before the verb forms.

On a un prof sympa.
*We have a nice teacher.*

Nous avons un cours d'art.
*We have an art class.*

- Keep in mind that an indefinite article, whether singular or plural, usually becomes **de/d'** after a negation.

J'ai **un** cours difficile.
*I have a difficult class.*

Je n'ai pas **de** cours difficile.
*I do not have a difficult class.*

Il a **des** examens.
*He has exams.*

Il n'a pas **d'**examens.
*He does not have exams.*

---

**1** **On a...** Use the correct forms of **avoir** to form questions from these elements. Use inversion and provide an affirmative or negative answer as cued.

**MODÈLE**

tu / devoirs (oui)
*As-tu des devoirs? Oui, j'ai des devoirs.*

1. nous / dictionnaire (oui)
   Avons-nous un dictionnaire? Oui, nous avons un dictionnaire.
2. Luc / diplôme (non)
   Luc a-t-il un diplôme? Non, il n'a pas de diplôme.
3. elles / montre (non)
   Ont-elles une montre? Non, elles n'ont pas de montre.
4. vous / copains (oui)
   Avez-vous des copains? Oui, j'ai/nous avons des copains.
5. Thérèse / téléphone (oui)
   Thérèse a-t-elle un téléphone? Oui, elle a un téléphone.
6. Charles et Jacques / calculatrice (non)
   Charles et Jacques ont-ils une calculatrice? Non, ils n'ont pas de calculatrice.

**2** **C'est évident** Describe these people using expressions with **avoir**. Answers may vary.

1. J' ___ai besoin d'___ étudier.

3. Vous ___avez froid___.

2. Tu ___as honte___.

4. Elles ___ont sommeil___.

**3** **Assemblez** Use the verb **avoir** and combine elements from the two columns to create sentences about yourself, your class, and your school. Make any necessary changes or additions. Answers will vary.

| A | B |
|---|---|
| Je | cours utiles |
| Le lycée | bonnes notes |
| Les profs | professeurs brillants |
| Mon (*My*) petit ami | ami(e) mexicain(e) |
| Ma (*My*) petite amie | / anglais(e) |
| Nous | / canadien(ne) |
| | / vietnamien(ne) |
| | élèves intéressants |
| | cantine agréable |
| | cours d'informatique |

 Practice more at **daccord1.vhlcentral.com**.

---

**Rapid Drill** Do a quick substitution drill with **avoir**. Write a sentence on the board and have students read it aloud. Then say a new subject and have students repeat the sentence, substituting the new subject. Examples: **1. J'ai des problèmes. (Éric et moi, tu, Stéphane, vous, les hommes) 2. Pierre a cours de chimie le mardi et le jeudi. (Pierre et Julie, nous, je, vous, tu)**

**Using Games** Divide the class into two teams. Choose one team member at a time to go to the board, alternating between teams. Say a subject pronoun. The person at the board must write and say the correct form of **avoir**. Example: **elle (elle a)**. Give a point for each correct answer. The team with the most points at the end of the game wins.

## COMMUNICATION

**4  Besoins** Your teacher will give you a worksheet. Ask different classmates if they need to do these activities. Find at least one person to answer **Oui** and at least one to answer **Non** for each item. Answers will vary.

**MODÈLE**  regarder la télé

**Élève 1:** Tu as besoin de regarder la télé?
**Élève 2:** Oui, j'ai besoin de regarder la télé.
**Élève 3:** Non, je n'ai pas besoin de regarder la télé.

| Activités | Oui | Non |
|---|---|---|
| 1. regarder la télé | Anne | Louis |
| 2. étudier ce soir | | |
| 3. passer un examen cette semaine | | |
| 4. retrouver des amis demain | | |
| 5. travailler à la bibliothèque | | |
| 6. commencer un devoir important | | |
| 7. téléphoner à un(e) copain/copine ce week-end | | |
| 8. parler avec le professeur | | |

**5  C'est vrai?** Interview a classmate by transforming each of these statements into a question. Be prepared to report the results of your interview to the class. Answers will vary.

**MODÈLE**  J'ai deux ordinateurs.

**Élève 1:** Tu as deux ordinateurs?
**Élève 2:** Non, je n'ai pas deux ordinateurs.

1. J'ai peur des examens.
2. J'ai seize ans.
3. J'ai envie de visiter Montréal.
4. J'ai un cours de biologie.
5. J'ai sommeil le lundi matin.
6. J'ai un(e) petit(e) ami(e) égoïste.

**6  Interview** You are talking to a college admissions advisor. Answer his or her questions. In pairs, practice the scene and role-play it for the class. Answers will vary.

1. Qu'est-ce que (*What*) tu as envie d'étudier?
2. Est-ce que tu as d'excellentes notes?
3. Est-ce que tu as envie de partager une chambre?
4. Est-ce que tu as un ordinateur?
5. Est-ce que tu aimes retrouver des amis au lycée?
6. Est-ce que tu écoutes de la musique?

---

• The verb **avoir** is used in certain idiomatic or set expressions where English generally uses *to be* or *to feel.*

### Expressions with *avoir*

| | | | |
|---|---|---|---|
| avoir... ans | to be... years old | avoir froid | to be cold |
| avoir besoin (de) | to need | avoir honte (de) | to be ashamed (of) |
| avoir de la chance | to be lucky | avoir l'air | to look like |
| | | avoir peur (de) | to be afraid (of) |
| avoir chaud | to be hot | avoir raison | to be right |
| | | avoir sommeil | to be sleepy |
| avoir envie (de) | to feel like | avoir tort | to be wrong |

Il a chaud.

Ils ont froid.

Elle a sommeil.

Il a de la chance.

• The command forms of **avoir** are irregular: **aie, ayons, ayez.**

**Aie** un peu de patience.          N'**ayez** pas peur.
*Be a little patient.*          *Don't be afraid.*

**Essayez!**  Complete the sentences with the correct forms of **avoir.**

1. La température est de 35 degrés Celsius. Nous ___avons___ chaud.
2. En Alaska, en décembre, vous ___avez___ froid.
3. Martine écoute la radio et elle ___a___ envie de danser.
4. Ils ___ont___ besoin d'une calculatrice pour le devoir.
5. N' ___aie/ayez___ pas peur des insectes.
6. Sébastien pense que je travaille aujourd'hui. Il ___a___ raison.
7. J' ___ai___ cours d'économie le lundi et le mercredi.
8. Mes amis voyagent beaucoup. Ils ___ont___ de la chance.
9. Mohammed ___a___ deux cousins à Marseille.
10. Vous ___avez___ un grand appartement.

---

**Essayez!** Ask students to identify the idiomatic expressions in the sentences. (All are idiomatic expressions, except items 7, 9, and 10.)

**1  Suggestion** This activity can be done in pairs. Tell students to alternate asking and answering the questions.

**2  Expansion** For each drawing, ask students how many people there are, their names, and their ages. Example: **Combien de personnes y a-t-il sur le dessin numéro 4? Comment s'appellent-elles? Quel âge a ____?**

**3  Suggestion** This activity can be done orally or in writing in pairs or groups.

**4  Suggestions**
• Have three volunteers read the **modèle** aloud. Then distribute the **Feuilles d'activités** from the Supersite.
• Have students add at least two activities of their own.

**5  Suggestion** Have two volunteers read the **modèle** aloud. Remind students that an indefinite article becomes **de (d')** if it follows **avoir** in the negative.

**6  Suggestions**
• Remind students to do the interview twice so each person asks and answers the questions.
• Ask volunteers to summarize their partners' responses. Record the responses on the board as a survey (**un sondage**) about the class' characteristics. Then ask questions like this: **Combien d'élèves dans la classe étudient la physique?**

---

**Using Movement** Assign gestures to expressions with **avoir**. Examples: **avoir chaud**: *wipe brow;* **avoir froid**: *wrap arms around oneself and shiver;* **avoir peur**: *hold one's hand over mouth in fear;* **avoir faim**: *rub stomach;* **avoir sommeil**: *yawn and stretch.* Have students stand. Say an expression at random as you point to a student who performs the appropriate gesture. Vary by indicating more than one student at a time.

**Sentences** Have students work in groups of three. Tell them to write nine sentences, each of which uses a different expression with **avoir**. Call on volunteers to write some of their group's best sentences on the board. Have the class read the sentences aloud and correct any errors.

## Section Goals

In this section, students will learn:
- to tell time
- some time expressions
- the 24-hour system of telling time

## Key Standards

4.1, 5.1

**Student Resources**
*Cahier d'exercices*, pp. 25-26;
*Cahier d'activités*, p. 130;
Supersite: Activities,
*Cahier interactif*
**Teacher Resources**
Answer Keys; Overhead #19;
Audio Script; Audio Activity
MP3s/CD; Testing program:
Grammar Quiz

## Suggestions

- To prepare for telling time, review the meanings of **il est** and numbers 0–60.
- Introduce: **Il est sept heures (huit heures, neuf heures…).**
- Explain to students that **heures** refers to *hours* when telling time, but can also mean *o'clock.*
- Introduce: **Il est _____ heure(s) cinq, dix, et quart,** and **et demie.**
- Using a paper plate clock, display various times on the hour. Ask: **Quelle heure est-il?**
- Introduce and explain: **Il est _____ heure(s) moins cinq, moins dix, moins le quart,** and **moins vingt.** Repeat the procedure above using your movable-hands clock.
- Explain that the French view times of day differently from Americans. In France, they say «**bonjour**» until about 4:00 or 5:00 p.m. After that, they use the greeting «**bonsoir**». They say «**bonne nuit**» only when going to sleep.
- Explain the use of the 24-hour clock. Have students practice saying times this way by adding 12.
- Model the pronunciation of the time expressions in the box and have students repeat. Point out that a.m. and p.m. are not used in France or most francophone regions. Instead, they use **du matin, de l'après midi,** and **du soir.**
- Tell students that **et demi(e)** agrees in gender with the noun it follows, but not in number. After **midi** and **minuit,** both **et demi** and **et demie** are accepted.

---

### 2B.2 Telling time

**Point de départ** Use the verb **être** with numbers to tell time.

- There are two ways to ask what time it is.

  **Quelle heure est-il?**    **Est-ce que vous avez l'heure?**
  *What time is it?*    *Do you have the time?*

- Use **heures** by itself to express time on the hour. Use **heure** for one o'clock.

Il est **six heures**.    Il est **une heure**.

- Express time from the hour to the half-hour by adding minutes.

Il est quatre heures **cinq**.    Il est onze heures **vingt**.

- Use **et quart** to say that it is fifteen minutes past the hour. Use **et demie** to say that it is thirty minutes past the hour.

Il est une heure **et quart**.    Il est sept heures **et demie**.

- To express time from the half hour to the hour, subtract minutes or a portion of an hour from the next hour.

Il est trois heures **moins dix**.    Il est une heure **moins le quart**.

- To express at what time something happens, use the preposition **à**.

  Céline travaille **à sept**    On passe un examen
    **heures moins vingt**.    **à une heure**.
  *Céline works at 6:40.*    *We take a test at one o'clock.*

**62** *soixante-deux*

---

**1** **Quelle heure est-il?** Give the time shown on each clock or watch. *Some answers may vary.*

**MODÈLE**

Il est quatre heures et quart de l'après-midi.

1. Il est midi/minuit et demi.  2. Il est une heure du matin.  3. Il est huit heures dix.  4. Il est onze heures moins le quart.

5. Il est deux heures douze.  6. Il est sept heures cinq.  7. Il est quatre heures moins cinq.  8. Il est minuit moins vingt-cinq.

**2** **À quelle heure?** Find out when you and your friends are going to do certain things.

**MODÈLE**

À quelle heure est-ce qu'on étudie? (about 8 p.m.)
*On étudie vers huit heures du soir.*

À quelle heure…

1. … est-ce qu'on arrive au cours? (at 10:30 a.m.)
   On arrive au cours à dix heures et demie du matin.
2. … est-ce que vous parlez avec le professeur? (at noon)
   Nous parlons avec le professeur à midi.
3. … est-ce que tu rentres? (late, at 11:15 p.m.)
   Je rentre tard, à onze heures et quart du soir.
4. … est-ce qu'on regarde la télé? (at 9:00 p.m.)
   On regarde la télé à neuf heures du soir.
5. … est-ce que Marlène et Nadine mangent? (around 1:45 p.m.)
   Elles mangent vers deux heures moins le quart de l'après-midi.
6. … est-ce que le cours commence? (very early, at 8:20 a.m.)  Il commence très tôt, à huit heures vingt du matin.

**3** **Départ à…** Tell what each of these times would be on a 24-hour clock.

**MODÈLE**

Il est trois heures vingt de l'après-midi.
*Il est quinze heures vingt.*

1. Il est dix heures et demie du soir.
   Il est vingt-deux heures trente.
2. Il est deux heures de l'après-midi.
   Il est quatorze heures.
3. Il est huit heures et quart du soir.
   Il est vingt heures quinze.
4. Il est minuit moins le quart.
   Il est vingt-trois heures quarante-cinq.
5. Il est six heures vingt-cinq du soir.
   Il est dix-huit heures vingt-cinq.
6. Il est trois heures moins cinq du matin.
   Il est deux heures cinquante-cinq.

 Practice more at **daccord1.vhlcentral.com.**

---

**O P T I O N S**

**Clocks** Draw a large clock face on the board with its numbers but without the hands. Say a time and ask a volunteer to come up and draw the hands to indicate that time. The rest of the class verifies whether or not the person has written the correct time, saying: **Il/Elle a raison/tort.** Repeat this a number of times.

**Oral Practice** Have pairs take turns telling each other what time their classes are this semester/term. Example: **J'ai un cours à _____ heures….** For each time given, the other student draws a clock face with the corresponding time. The first student verifies if the clock is correct.

## COMMUNICATION

**4 Télémonde** Look at this French TV guide. In pairs, ask questions about program start times. Answers will vary.

**MODÈLE**

**Élève 1:** À quelle heure commence Télé-ciné?
**Élève 2:** Télé-ciné commence à dix heures dix du soir.

| | |
|---|---|
| dessins animés | cartoons |
| feuilleton télévisé | soap opera |
| film policier | detective film |
| informations | news |
| jeu télévisé | game show |

### VENDREDI

| Antenne 2 | Antenne 4 | Antenne 5 |
|---|---|---|
| **15h30** Pomme d'Api (dessins animés) | **14h00** Football: match France-Italie | **18h25** Montréal: une ville à visiter |
| **17h35** Reportage spécial: le sport dans les lycées | **19h45** Les informations | **19h30** Des chiffres et des lettres (jeu télévisé) |
| **20h15** La famille Menet (feuilleton télévisé) | **20h30** Concert: Orchestre de Nice | **21h05** Reportage spécial: les Sénégalais |
| **21h35** Télé-ciné: L'inspecteur Duval (film policier) | **22h10** Télé-ciné: Une chose difficile (comédie dramatique) | **22h05** Les informations |

**5 Où es-tu?** In pairs, take turns asking where (où) your partner usually is on these days at these times. Choose from the places listed. Answers will vary.

| | |
|---|---|
| au lit (bed) | chez mes (at my) |
| à la cantine | parents |
| à la bibliothèque | chez mes copains |
| en ville (town) | au lycée |
| au parc | au restaurant |
| en cours | |

1. Le samedi: à 8h00 du matin; à midi; à minuit
2. En semaine: à 9h00 du matin; à 3h00 de l'après-midi; à 7h00 du soir
3. Le dimanche: à 4h00 de l'après-midi; à 6h30 du soir; à 10h00 du soir
4. Le vendredi: à 11h00 du matin; à 5h00 de l'après-midi; à 11h00 du soir

**6 Le suspect** A student at your school is a suspect in a crime. You and a partner are detectives. Keeping a log of the student's activities, use the 24-hour clock to say what he or she is doing when. Answers will vary.

**MODÈLE**

À vingt-deux heures trente-trois, il parle au téléphone.

---

- **Liaison** occurs between numbers and the word **heure(s)**. Final **-s** and **-x** in **deux, trois, six,** and **dix** are pronounced like a z. The final **-f** of **neuf** is pronounced like a v.

Il est **deux heures**.
*It's two o'clock.*

Il est **neuf heures** et quart.
*It's 9:15.*

- You do not usually make a **liaison** between the verb form **est** and a following number that starts with a vowel sound.

Il est onze heures.
*It's eleven o'clock.*

Il est une heure vingt.
*It's 1:20.*

Il est huit heures et demie.
*It's 8:30.*

### Expressions for telling time

| À quelle heure? | (At) what time/ when? | midi | noon |
|---|---|---|---|
| de l'après-midi | in the afternoon | minuit | midnight |
| du matin | in the morning | pile | on the dot |
| du soir | in the evening | presque | almost |
| en avance | early | tard | late |
| en retard | late | tôt | early |
| | | vers | about |

Il est **minuit** à Paris.
*It's midnight in Paris.*

Il est six heures **du soir** à New York.
*It's six o'clock in the evening in New York.*

- The 24-hour clock is often used to express official time. Departure times, movie times, and store hours are expressed in this fashion. Only numbers are used to tell time this way. Expressions like **et demie, moins le quart,** etc. are not used.

Le train arrive à **dix-sept heures six**.
*The train arrives at 5:06 p.m.*

Le film est à **vingt-deux heures trente sept**.
*The film is at 10:37 p.m.*

J'ai cours de trois heures vingt à quatre heures et demie.

Stéphane! Quelle heure est-il?

**Essayez!** Complete the sentences by writing out the correct times according to the cues.

1. (1:00 a.m.) Il est _une heure_ du matin.
2. (2:50 a.m.) Il est _trois heures moins dix_ du matin.
3. (8:30 p.m.) Il est _huit heures et demie_ du soir.
4. (12:00 p.m.) Il est _midi_.
5. (4:05 p.m.) Il est _quatre heures cinq_ de l'après-midi.
6. (4:45 a.m.) Il est _cinq heures moins le quart_ du matin.

---

**Essayez!** For additional practice, give students these items.
7. 6:20 p.m.   8. 9:10 a.m.
9. 2:15 p.m.   10. 10:35 a.m.
11. 12:00 a.m.   12. 9:55 p.m.

**1 Expansion** At random, say the times shown and have students say the number of the clock or watch described. Example: **Il est sept heures cinq. (C'est le numéro six.)**

**2 Suggestion** Read the **modèle** aloud with a volunteer. Working in pairs, have students take turns asking and answering the questions.

**3 Expansion** Create a train schedule and write it on the board or use photocopies of a real one. Ask students questions based on the schedule. Example: **À quelle heure est le train Paris-Bordeaux le vendredi soir?**

**4 Suggestion** Before starting this activity, have students read the TV guide, point out cognates, and predict their meaning. Provide examples for non-cognate categories so students can guess their meaning. Examples: **dessins animés, feuilleton télévisé,** and **jeu télévisé**.

**4 Expansion** Have pairs ask each other additional questions based on the TV guide. Examples: **Est-ce qu'il y a un reportage à vingt heures dix? (Non, les reportages sont à dix-sept heures trente-cinq et à vingt et une heures cinq.) J'ai envie de regarder le film policier. À quelle heure est-il? (Le film policier est à vingt et une heures trente-cinq.)**

**5 Suggestion** Before beginning the activity, provide students with a model. Example: **Élève 1: Où es-tu le samedi à midi? Élève 2: Le samedi à midi, je suis au parc.**

**6 Expansion** After completing the activity, ask students if the suspect has an alibi at certain times. Tell them to respond using the information on their logs. Example: **Le suspect a-t-il un alibi à vingt-trois heures? (Oui, à vingt-trois heures il étudie avec un ami.)**

---

**OPTIONS**

**Using Video** Play the video episode again to give students additional input on telling time and the verb **avoir**. Pause the video where appropriate to discuss how time or **avoir** were used and to ask comprehension questions. Example: **Est-ce que Stéphane a peur de parler à Astrid? (Mais non, il a peur du bac.)**

**Oral Practice** Have students work in groups of three. Tell them to take turns asking what time various TV shows start. Example: **À quelle heure est *60 Minutes*? (C'est à dix-neuf heures.)** Remind students to use the 24-hour system when talking about TV shows.

# SYNTHÈSE
# Révision

**Key Standards**
1.1

**Student Resources**
*Cahier d'activités*, pp. 27-28;
Supersite: Activities,
*Cahier interactif*
**Teacher Resources**
Answer Keys; Info Gap
Activities; Testing Program:
Lesson Test (Testing Program
Audio MP3s/CD)

**1 Suggestion** Have two
volunteers read the **modèle**
aloud. Encourage students to
add other items to the list.

**2 Suggestion** Before beginning
the activity, tell students to
choose two language classes,
a science class, and an elective
in the list. Then read the **modèle**
aloud with a volunteer.

**3 Expansion** Have volunteers
report their findings to the class.
Then do a quick class survey to
find out how many students are
taking the same courses. Example:
**Combien d'élèves ont l'éducation
physique ce semestre?**

**4 Suggestion** Before doing
the activity, point out the use of
the construction **avoir envie de**
+ *infinitive*. Encourage students
to add activities to the list.
Examples: **regarder un film,
manger/partager une pizza,
parler au téléphone,** and
**voyager en France/Europe.**

**5 Suggestion** Ask what
expressions express likes
and dislikes, and write them
on the board before assigning
this activity.

**6 Suggestions**
• Divide the class into pairs and
distribute the Info Gap Handouts
on the Supersite for this activity.
Have two volunteers read the
**modèle**. Give students ten
minutes to complete the activity.
• After completing the activity, ask
students what activities Patrick
would like to do this weekend.

---

**1 J'ai besoin de...** In pairs, take turns saying which items
you need. Your partner will guess why you need them. How
many times did each of you guess correctly? Answers will vary.

**MODÈLE**

**Élève 1:** *J'ai besoin d'un cahier et d'un dictionnaire
pour demain.*
**Élève 2:** *Est-ce que tu as un cours de français?*
**Élève 1:** *Non. J'ai un examen d'anglais.*

| | |
|---|---|
| un cahier | un livre de physique |
| une calculatrice | une montre |
| une carte | un ordinateur |
| un dictionnaire | un stylo |
| une feuille de papier | un téléphone |

**2 À la fac** To complete your degree, you need two language
classes, a science class, and an elective of your choice. Take
turns deciding what classes you need or want to take. Your
partner will tell you the days and times so you can set up
your schedule. Answers will vary.

**MODÈLE**

**Élève 1:** *J'ai besoin d'un cours de maths, peut-être
«Initiation aux maths».*
**Élève 2:** *C'est le mardi et le jeudi après-midi, de deux
heures à trois heures et demie.*
**Élève 1:** *J'ai aussi besoin d'un cours de langue...*

| Les cours | Jours et heures |
|---|---|
| Allemand | mardi, jeudi; 14h00-15h30 |
| Biologie II | mardi, jeudi; 9h00-10h30 |
| Chimie générale | lundi, mercredi; 11h00-12h30 |
| Espagnol | lundi, mercredi; 11h00-12h30 |
| Gestion | mercredi; 13h00-14h30 |
| Histoire des États-Unis | jeudi; 12h15-14h15 |
| Initiation à la physique | lundi, mercredi; 12h00-13h30 |
| Initiation aux maths | mardi, jeudi; 14h00-15h30 |
| Italien | lundi, mercredi; 12h00-13h30 |
| Japonais | mardi, jeudi; 9h00-10h30 |
| Les philosophes grecs | lundi; 15h15-16h45 |
| Littérature moderne | mardi; 10h15-11h15 |

**3 Les cours** Your partner will tell you what classes he or
she is currently taking. Make a list, including the times and
days of the week. Then, talk to as many classmates as you
can, and find at least two students who take at least two of
the same classes as your partner. Answers will vary.

**4 On y va?** Walk around the room and find at least one
classmate who feels like doing each of these activities with
you. For every affirmative answer, record the name of your
classmate and agree on a time and date. Do not speak to
the same classmate twice. Answers will vary.

**MODÈLE**

**Élève 1:** *Tu as envie de retrouver des amis avec moi?*
**Élève 2:** *Oui, pourquoi pas? Samedi, à huit heures
du soir, peut-être?*
**Élève 1:** *D'accord!*

| | |
|---|---|
| chercher un café sympa | regarder la télé française |
| manger à la cantine | retrouver des amis |
| écouter des CD | travailler à la bibliothèque |
| étudier le français cette semaine | visiter un musée |

**5 Au téléphone** Two former high school friends are
attending different universities. In pairs, imagine a conversation
where they discuss the time, their classes, and likes or dislikes
about campus life. Then, role-play the conversation for the
class and vote for the best skit. Answers will vary.

**MODÈLE**

**Élève 1:** *J'ai cours de chimie à dix heures et demie.*
**Élève 2:** *Je n'ai pas de cours de chimie cette année.*
**Élève 1:** *N'aimes-tu pas les sciences?*
**Élève 2:** *Si, mais...*

**6 La semaine de Patrick** Your teacher will give you
and a partner different incomplete pages from Patrick's day
planner. Do not look at each other's worksheet while you
complete your own. Answers will vary.

**MODÈLE**

**Élève 1:** *Lundi matin, Patrick a cours de géographie à dix
heures et demie.*
**Élève 2:** *Lundi, il a cours de sciences po à deux heures de
l'après-midi.*

**ressources**

| CE pp. 23–26 | CA pp. 4, 27–28, 129–130 | (S) daccord1.vhlcentral.com |
|---|---|---|

---

**OPTIONS**

**Skits** Working in groups of three or four, have students create a
short skit similar to the scene in video still 1 of the **Roman-photo**.
Tell them that they have to decide on a day, time, and place to
meet for a study session in order to prepare for the next French
test. Have groups perform their skits for the class.

**Oral Practice** Have students make a list of six items that
students normally carry in their backpacks to class. Then tell
them to circulate around the room asking their classmates if
they have those items in their backpacks. Also tell them to ask
how many they have. Example: **As-tu un cahier dans le sac à
dos? Combien de cahiers as-tu?**

# À l'écoute

 **Audio: Activities**

## Listening for cognates

You already know that cognates are words that have similar spellings and meanings in two or more languages: for example *group* and **groupe** or *activity* and **activité**. Listen for cognates to increase your comprehension of spoken French.

 To help you practice this strategy, you will listen to two sentences. Make a list of all the cognates you hear.

## Préparation

Based on the photograph, who and where do you think Marie-France and Dominique are? Do you think they know each other well? Where are they probably going this morning? What do you think they are talking about?

## À vous d'écouter

Listen to the conversation and list any cognates you hear. Listen again and complete the highlighted portions of Marie-France's schedule.

| 28 OCTOBRE | lundi | | |
|---|---|---|---|
| 8H00 | *jogging* | 14H00 | psychologie |
| 8H30 | | 14H30 | |
| 9H00 | | 15H00 | |
| 9H30 | biologie | 15H30 | physique |
| 10H00 | | 16H00 | |
| 10H30 | | 16H30 | |
| 11H00 | chimie | 17H00 | |
| 11H30 | | 17H30 | *étudier* |
| 12H00 | resto U | 18H00 | |
| 12H30 | | 18H30 | |
| 13H00 | *bibliothèque* | 19H00 | *téléphoner à papa* |
| 13H30 | | 19H30 | *Sophie:* restaurant vietnamien |

 Practice more at **daccord1.vhlcentral.com**.

## Compréhension

**Vrai ou faux?** Indicate whether each statement is **vrai** or **faux**. Then correct the false statements.

1. D'après Marie-France, la biologie est facile.
   Vrai.

2. Marie-France adore la chimie.
   Faux. Marie-France déteste la chimie.

3. Marie-France et Dominique mangent au restaurant vietnamien à midi.
   Faux. Marie-France et Dominique mangent au restaurant vietnamien à sept heures et demie du soir.

4. Dominique aime son cours de sciences politiques.
   Faux. Dominique aime son cours d'informatique.

5. Monsieur Meyer est professeur de physique.
   Vrai.

6. Monsieur Meyer donne des devoirs faciles.
   Faux. Monsieur Meyer donne des devoirs très difficiles.

7. Le lundi après-midi, Marie-France a psychologie et physique.
   Vrai.

8. Aujourd'hui, Dominique mange au resto U.
   Faux. Aujourd'hui, Marie-France mange au resto U.

**Votre emploi du temps** With a partner, discuss the classes you're taking. Be sure to say when you have each one, and give your opinion of at least three courses.

*soixante-cinq* **65**

## Section Goals

In this section, students will:
- learn to listen for cognates
- listen to sentences containing familiar and unfamiliar vocabulary
- listen to a conversation, complete a schedule, and answer true/false questions

## Key Standards

1.2, 2.1

**Student Resources**
Supersite: Activities, Audio
**Teacher Resources**
Answer Keys; Audio Script; Audio Activity MP3s/CD

**Stratégie**
**Script** 1. Dans certaines institutions d'études supérieures, les étudiants reçoivent un salaire. 2. Ma cousine étudie la médecine vétérinaire. C'est sa passion!

**Préparation** Have students describe the photo. Ask them to justify their descriptions based on the visual clues.

**Suggestion** To check answers for the **À vous d'écouter** activity, have students work in pairs and take turns asking questions about Marie-France's schedule. Example: **Est-ce que Marie-France a cours de biologie à 14h00? (Non, elle a cours de biologie à 9h30.)**

**À vous d'écouter**
**Script** DOMINIQUE: Tiens, bonjour, Marie-France. Comment ça va?
MARIE-FRANCE: Salut, Dominique. Ça va bien. Et toi?
D: Très bien, merci. Tu vas en cours?
M: Oui, j'ai cours toute la journée, le lundi. Ce matin, j'ai biologie à neuf heures et demie.
D: Tu aimes la biologie?
M: Oui, j'aime bien. C'est facile. Après, à onze heures, j'ai chimie. Ça, je déteste! C'est difficile! À midi, je mange au resto U avec des copains.
D: Et cet après-midi?
M: Alors, à deux heures, j'ai psychologie et à trois heures et demie, j'ai physique.
D: Est-ce que tu aimes ça, la physique?
M: Oui, mais cette année, le prof n'est pas très intéressant.

D: Ah bon? Qui est-ce?
M: Monsieur Meyer.
D: Ah oui! Tu as raison. Il n'est pas très intéressant. Et il donne des devoirs et des examens très difficiles.
M: C'est vrai. Et toi, tu aimes tes cours cette année?
D: Oui, beaucoup. J'adore l'informatique. Le prof est amusant et il explique bien.

M: Tu as de la chance! Dis, est-ce que tu as envie de dîner au restaurant avec Sophie et moi ce soir? On va au restaurant vietnamien près de l'université.
D: Oui, avec plaisir. À quelle heure?
M: À sept heures et demie.
D: Bon, d'accord. À ce soir.
M: Salut.

# Panorama

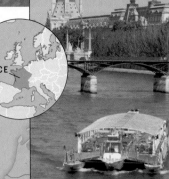
LA FRANCE

## La France

### Le pays en chiffres

▶ **Superficie:** 549.000 km²
(cinq cent quarante-neuf mille kilomètres carrés°)

▶ **Population:** 62.106.000 (soixante-deux millions cent six mille)
SOURCE: INSEE

▶ **Industries principales:** agro-alimentaires°, assurance°, banques, énergie, produits pharmaceutiques, produits de luxe, télécommunications, tourisme, transports
La France est le pays° le plus° visité du monde° avec plus de° 60 millions de touristes chaque° année. Son histoire, sa culture et ses monuments–plus de 12.000 (douze mille)–et musées–plus de 1.200 (mille deux cents)–attirent° des touristes d'Europe et de partout° dans le monde.

▶ **Villes principales:** Paris, Lille, Lyon, Marseille, Toulouse

▶ **Monnaie°:** l'euro
La France est un pays membre de l'Union européenne et, en 2002, l'euro a remplacé° le franc français comme° monnaie nationale.

### Français célèbres

▶ **Jeanne d'Arc,** héroïne française° (1412–1431)

▶ **Émile Zola,** écrivain° (1840–1902)

▶ **Auguste Renoir,** peintre° (1841–1919)

▶ **Claude Debussy,** compositeur et musicien (1862–1918)

▶ **Camille Claudel,** femme sculpteur (1864–1943)

▶ **Claudie André-Deshays,** médecin, première astronaute française (1957– )

carrés *square* agro-alimentaires *food processing* assurance *insurance* pays *country* le plus *the most* monde *world* plus de *more than* chaque *each* attirent *attract* partout *everywhere* Monnaie *Currency* a remplacé *replaced* comme *as* écrivain *writer* peintre *painter* élus à vie *elected for life* Depuis *Since* mots *words* courrier *mail* pont *bridge*

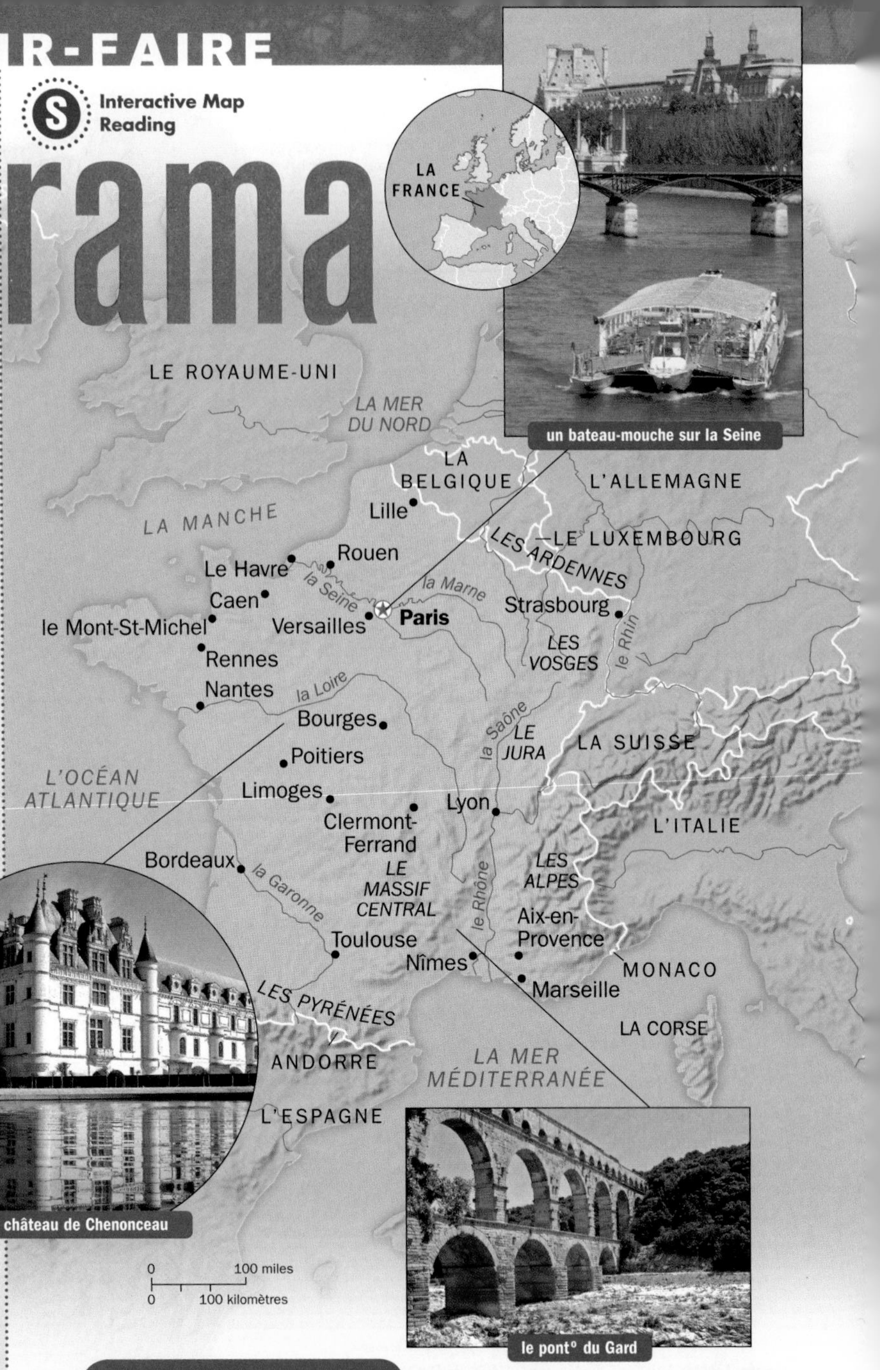

**66** *soixante-six*

---

LE ROYAUME-UNI
LA MER DU NORD
LA MANCHE
LA BELGIQUE
L'ALLEMAGNE
LE LUXEMBOURG
LES ARDENNES
Lille
Rouen
Le Havre
la Seine
la Marne
Caen
★ **Paris**
Strasbourg
le Mont-St-Michel
Versailles
LES VOSGES
le Rhin
Rennes
Nantes
la Loire
Bourges
la Saône
LE JURA
LA SUISSE
Poitiers
L'OCÉAN ATLANTIQUE
Limoges
Lyon
L'ITALIE
Clermont-Ferrand
Bordeaux
la Garonne
LE MASSIF CENTRAL
le Rhône
LES ALPES
Aix-en-Provence
Toulouse
Nîmes
MONACO
Marseille
LES PYRÉNÉES
LA CORSE
ANDORRE
LA MER MÉDITERRANÉE
L'ESPAGNE

0    100 miles
0    100 kilomètres

un bateau-mouche sur la Seine

le château de Chenonceau

le pont° du Gard

### Incroyable mais vrai!

Être «immortel», c'est réguler et défendre le bon usage du français! Les académiciens de l'Académie française sont élus à vie° et s'appellent les «Immortels». Depuis° 1635 (mille six cent trente-cinq), ils décident de l'orthographe correcte des mots° et publient un dictionnaire. Attention, c'est «courrier° électronique», pas «e-mail»!

---

## Teacher's annotations (left margin)

**Carte de la France**
• Have students look at the map of France or use **Overhead #20**. Ask volunteers to read the cities' names aloud.
• Have students identify the location of the place or object in each photo.

**Le pays en chiffres**
• Have students read the section headings. Point out the type of information contained in each section and clarify unfamiliar words.
• Have volunteers read the sections aloud. After each section, ask questions about the content.
• Ask students to share any additional information they might know about the people in **Français célèbres.**

**Incroyable mais vrai!**
**L'Académie française** was founded by Cardinal Richelieu during the reign of Louis XIII. In the beginning, the Academy's primary role was to standardize the language for French-speaking people by establishing rules to make it pure, eloquent, and capable of dealing with the arts and sciences.

---

## Bottom options bar

**O P T I O N S**

**Le pays en chiffres** France is the third largest country in Europe. It is divided into 22 **régions** (*regions*), which include **la Corse** (*Corsica*). The **régions** are divided into 95 **départements** (*departments*). France also has four overseas **Départements et régions d'outre-mer (DROM): la Guadeloupe, la Guyane française, la Réunion,** and **la Martinique.** Using the map of France in **Appendice A** that shows the **régions** and **départements,** have students locate various cities as

you say the names. Example: **Marseille (C'est dans le département des Bouches-du-Rhône.)**

**Oral Presentation** If a student has visited France (preferably outside Paris), ask him or her to prepare a short presentation about his or her experiences there. Encourage the student to bring in photos and souvenirs of France.

## La géographie

### L'Hexagone

Surnommé° l'Hexagone à cause de° sa forme géométrique, le territoire français a trois fronts maritimes: l'océan Atlantique, la mer° Méditerranée et la Manche°; et trois frontières° naturelles: les Pyrénées, les Ardennes, les Alpes et le Jura. À l'intérieur du pays°, le Massif central et les Vosges ponctuent° un relief composé de vastes plaines et de forêts. La Loire, la Seine, la Garonne, le Rhin et le Rhône sont les fleuves° principaux de l'Hexagone.

## La technologie

### Le Train à Grande Vitesse

Le chemin de fer° existe en France depuis° 1827 (mille huit cent vingt-sept). Aujourd'hui, la SNCF (Société nationale des chemins de fer français) offre la possibilité aux voyageurs de se déplacer° dans tout° le pays et propose des tarifs° avantageux aux élèves et aux moins de 25 ans°. Le TGV (Train à Grande Vitesse°) roule° à plus de 300 (trois cent) km/h (kilomètres/heure) et emmène° les voyageurs jusqu'à° Londres et Bruxelles.

## Les arts

### Le cinéma, le 7<sup>e</sup> art!

L'invention du cinématographe par les frères° Lumière en 1895 (mille huit cent quatre-vingt-quinze) marque le début° du «7<sup>e</sup> (septième) art». Le cinéma français donne naissance° aux prestigieux César° en 1976 (mille neuf cent soixante-seize), à des cinéastes talentueux comme° Jean Renoir, François Truffaut et Luc Besson, et à des acteurs mémorables comme Brigitte Bardot, Catherine Deneuve, Olivier Martinez et Audrey Tautou (*Amélie*, *The Da Vinci Code*).

## L'économie

### L'industrie

Avec la richesse de la culture française, il est facile d'oublier que l'économie en France n'est pas limitée à l'artisanat°, à la gastronomie ou à la haute couture°. En fait°, la France est une véritable puissance° industrielle et se classe° parmi° les économies les plus° importantes du monde. Ses° activités dans des secteurs comme la construction automobile (Peugeot, Citroën, Renault), l'industrie aérospatiale (Airbus) et l'énergie nucléaire (Électricité de France) sont considérables.

---

 **Qu'est-ce que vous avez appris?** Complete these sentences.

1. __Camille Claudel__ est une femme sculpteur française.
2. Les Académiciens sont élus __à vie__.
3. Pour «e-mail», on utilise aussi l'expression __courrier électronique__
4. À cause de sa forme, la France s'appelle aussi __«l'Hexagone»__.
5. La __SNCF__ offre la possibilité de voyager dans tout le pays.

6. Avec le __TGV__, on voyage de Paris à Londres.
7. Les __frères Lumière__ sont les inventeurs du cinéma.
8. __Answers will vary.__ est un grand cinéaste français.
   Possible answer: Jean Renoir
9. La France est une grande puissance __industrielle__.
10. Électricité de France produit (*produces*) __l'énergie nucléaire__

 Practice more at **daccord1.vhlcentral.com.**

**ressources**

CE
pp. 27-28

daccord1.vhlcentral.com

---

### SUR INTERNET

Go to **daccord1.vhlcentral.com** to find more cultural information related to this **PANORAMA**.

1. Cherchez des informations sur l'Académie française. Faites (*Make*) une liste de mots ajoutés à la dernière édition du dictionnaire de l'Académie française.
2. Cherchez des informations sur l'actrice Catherine Deneuve. Quand a-t-elle commencé (*did she begin*) sa (*her*) carrière? Trouvez ses (*her*) trois derniers films.

**Surnommé** *Nicknamed* **à cause de** *because of* **mer** *sea* **Manche** *English Channel* **frontières** *borders* **pays** *country* **ponctuent** *punctuate* **fleuves** *rivers* **chemin de fer** *railroad* **depuis** *since* **se déplacer** *travel* **dans tout** *throughout* **tarifs** *fares* **moins de 25 ans** *people under 25* **Train à Grande Vitesse** *high speed train* **roule** *rolls, travels* **emmène** *takes* **jusqu'à** *all the way to* **frères** *brothers* **début** *beginning* **donne naissance** *gives birth* **César** *equivalent of the Oscars in France* **comme** *such as* **artisanat** *craft industry* **haute couture** *high fashion* **En fait** *In fact* **puissance** *power* **se classe** *ranks* **parmi** *among* **les plus** *the most* **Ses** *Its*

---

### Le Train à Grande Vitesse

- The first **TGV** service was from Paris to Lyon in 1981. Since then, its service has expanded. Presently, the high-speed network has over 30,000 kilometers of track that connect over 150 cities and towns in France.
- Have students look at the photo and compare the **TGV** to the trains they have traveled on or seen in the United States. Then have them figure out the speed of the **TGV** in miles per hour (1 km = 0.62 mile). (300 km/h = 186 mph)

### Le cinéma, le 7e art!

- Each year the members of **l'Académie des Arts et Techniques du Cinéma** choose the actors, actresses, directors, and others involved in film-making to receive the **César** awards for their outstanding achievements. The ceremony was named after the artist who designed the award trophies.
- The six traditional arts are **architecture**, **sculpture**, **peinture** (painting), **littérature**, **musique**, and **danse**.

### L'industrie

- The craft industry, **l'Artisanat**, can be found throughout France. Using traditional methods that are centuries old, French artisans craft products, such as pottery and figurines, but also work as bakers, carpenters, confectioners, butchers, or masons. Each region's products reflect the history and culture of that particular area.
- Bring in some French craft items or magazine photos of items to show the class.

---

**O P T I O N S**

**Using Games** Create categories for the newly learned information on France: **Géographie, Français célèbres, Technologie,** etc. Make index cards with a question on one side and category on the other. Tape cards to the board under the appropriate categories with questions face down. Teams take turns picking a card and answering the question. Give a point for each right answer. The team with the most points at the end wins.

**Cultural Comparison** Distribute a list in French of the award categories for the **César** from the website of **l'Académie des Arts et Techniques du Cinéma** (www.lescesarducinema.com). Ask if the same categories exist for the Oscars. Show them pictures of a **César** and an Oscar. Have students compare the trophies. Ask what other film festivals occur in France. (Cannes Film Festival and the American Film Festival)

## Teacher's Annotation (left margin)

**...oals**

...ction, students will:
- ...to use text formats to ...edict content
- read a brochure for a French language school

### Key Standards
**1.2, 2.1, 3.2, 5.2**

**Stratégie**
Tell students that many documents have easily identifiable formats that can help them predict the content. Have them look at the document in the **Stratégie** box and ask them to identify the recognizable elements:
- days of the week
- times
- classes

Ask what kind of document it is. (a student's weekly schedule)

**Examinez le texte** Have students look at the headings and ask them what type of information is contained in **École de français (pour étrangers) de Lille**. (lists of courses by level and specialization, a list of supplementary activities, and a list of types of housing available) Then ask students what types of documents contain these elements. (brochures)

**Mots apparentés**
- In pairs, have students scan the brochure, identify cognates, and guess their meanings.
- Ask students what this document is and its purpose. (It's a brochure. It's advertising a French language and culture immersion program. Its purpose is to attract students.)

## Main Content

# Lecture 🆂 Reading

## Avant la lecture

### STRATÉGIE

#### Predicting content through formats

Recognizing the format of a document can help you to predict its content. For instance, invitations, greeting cards, and classified ads follow an easily identifiable format, which usually gives you a general idea of the information they contain. Look at the text and identify it based on its format.

|  | lundi | mardi | mercredi | jeudi | vendredi |
|---|---|---|---|---|---|
| 8h30 | biologie | littérature | biologie | littérature | biologie |
| 9h00 |  |  |  |  |  |
| 9h30 | anglais | anglais | anglais | anglais | anglais |
| 10h00 |  |  |  |  |  |
| 10h30 | maths | histoire | maths | histoire | maths |
| 11h00 |  |  |  |  |  |
| 11h30 | français |  | français |  | français |
| 12h00 |  |  |  |  |  |
| 12h30 |  |  |  |  |  |
| 1h00 | art | économie | art | économie | art |

If you guessed that this is a page from a student's schedule, you are correct. You can now infer that the document contains information about a student's weekly schedule, including days, times, and activities.

### Examinez le texte

Briefly look at the document. What is its format? What kind of information is given? How is it organized? Are there any visuals? What kind? What type(s) of documents usually contain these elements?

### Mots apparentés

As you have already learned, in addition to format, you can use cognates to help you predict the content of a document. With a classmate, make a list of all the cognates you find in the reading selection. Based on these cognates and the format of the document, can you guess what this document is and what it's for?

# ÉCOLE DE FRANÇAIS
*(pour étrangers°)* DE LILLE

| COURS DE FRANÇAIS POUR TOUS° | COURS DE SPÉCIALISATION |
|---|---|
| Niveau° débutant° | Français pour enfants° |
| Niveau élémentaire | Français des affaires° |
| Niveau intermédiaire | Droit° français |
| Niveau avancé | Français pour le tourisme |
| Conversation | Culture et civilisation |
| Grammaire française | Histoire de France |
|  | Art et littérature |
|  | Arts culinaires |

26, place d'Arsonval • 59000 Lille
Tél. 03.20.52.48.17 • Fax. 03.20.52.48.18 • www.efpelille.fr

## Options (bottom)

**O P T I O N S**

**Schedules** Have students write a friend's or family member's weekly schedule as homework. Tell them to label the days of the week in French and add notes for that person's appointments and activities. In class, ask students questions about the schedules they wrote. Examples: **Quel cours est-ce que _____ a aujourd'hui? Combien de jours est-ce que _____ travaille cette semaine?**

**Cultural Activity** Ask students what aspects of this school they find appealing or interesting: **Qu'est-ce que vous trouvez intéressant à l'école?** Jot down their responses on the board. Then do a quick class survey to find out which aspect is the most appealing.

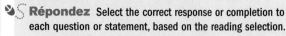

**Programmes de 2 à 8 semaines,**

**4 à 8 heures par jour**

**Immersion totale**

**Professeurs diplômés**

le Musée des Beaux-Arts, Lille

## GRAND CHOIX° D'ACTIVITÉS SUPPLÉMENTAIRES

- Excursions à la journée dans la région
- Visites de monuments et autres sites touristiques
- Sorties° culturelles (théâtre, concert, opéra et autres spectacles°)
- Sports et autres activités de loisir°

## HÉBERGEMENT°

- En cité universitaire°
- Dans° une famille française
- À l'hôtel

pour étrangers *for foreigners* tous *all* Niveau *Level* débutant *beginner* enfants *children* affaires *business* Droit *Law* choix *choice* Sorties *Outings* spectacles *shows* loisir *leisure* hébergement *lodging* cité universitaire *university dormitories (on campus)* Dans *In*

# Après la lecture

**Répondez** Select the correct response or completion to each question or statement, based on the reading selection.

1. C'est une brochure pour...
   - a. des cours de français pour étrangers.
   - b. une université française.
   - c. des études supérieures en Belgique.

2. «Histoire de France» est...
   - a. un cours pour les professeurs diplômés.
   - b. un cours de spécialisation.
   - c. un cours pour les enfants.

3. Le cours de «Français pour le tourisme» est utile pour...
   - a. une étudiante qui (*who*) étudie les sciences po.
   - b. une femme qui travaille dans un hôtel de luxe.
   - c. un professeur d'administration des affaires.

4. Un étudiant étranger qui commence le français assiste probablement à quel (*which*) cours?
   - a. Cours de français pour tous, Niveau avancé
   - b. Cours de spécialisation, Art et littérature
   - c. Cours de français pour tous, Niveau débutant

5. Quel cours est utile pour un homme qui parle assez bien français et qui travaille dans l'économie?
   - a. Cours de spécialisation, Français des affaires
   - b. Cours de spécialisation, Arts culinaires
   - c. Cours de spécialisation, Culture et civilisation

6. Le week-end, les étudiants...
   - a. passent des examens.
   - b. travaillent dans des hôtels.
   - c. visitent la ville et la région.

7. Les étudiants qui habitent dans une famille...
   - a. ont envie de rencontrer des Français.
   - b. ont des bourses.
   - c. ne sont pas reçus aux examens.

8. Un étudiant en architecture va aimer...
   - a. le cours de droit français.
   - b. les visites de monuments et de sites touristiques.
   - c. les activités sportives.

**Complétez** Complete these sentences.

1. Le numéro de téléphone est le ___03.20.52.48.17___.

2. Le numéro de fax est le ___03.20.52.48.18___.

3. L'adresse de l'école est ___26, place d'Arsonval, 59000 Lille___

4. L'école offre des programmes de Français de ___2 à 8___ semaines et de ___4 à 8 heures___ par jour.

*soixante-neuf* **69**

**Répondez** Go over the answers with the whole class or have students check their answers in pairs.

**Complétez** For additional practice, give students these items.
5. L'école est à____. (Lille)
6. L'adresse Internet de l'école est ____. (www.efpelille.fr)
7. «Grammaire française» est un cours de ____. (français pour tous) 8. Les professeurs de l'école sont ____. (diplômés)
9. On habite en cité universitaire, ____ ou à l'hôtel. (dans une famille française)

**Suggestion** Encourage students to record unfamiliar words and phrases that they learn in **Lecture** in their notebooks.

# Écriture

## STRATÉGIE

### Brainstorming

How do you find ideas to write about? In the early stages of writing, brainstorming can help you generate ideas on a specific topic. You should spend ten to fifteen minutes brainstorming and jotting down any ideas about the topic that occur to you. Whenever possible, try to write down your ideas in French. Express your ideas in single words or phrases, and jot them down in any order. While brainstorming, do not worry about whether your ideas are good or bad. Selecting and organizing ideas should be the second stage of your writing. Remember that the more ideas you write down while brainstorming, the more options you will have to choose from later when you start to organize your ideas.

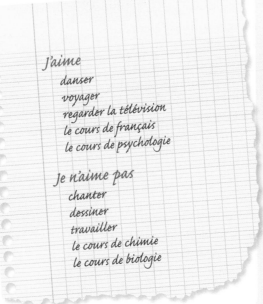

J'aime
   danser
   voyager
   regarder la télévision
   le cours de français
   le cours de psychologie

Je n'aime pas
   chanter
   dessiner
   travailler
   le cours de chimie
   le cours de biologie

## Thème

## Une description personnelle

### Avant l'écriture

1. Write a description of yourself to post on a website in order to find a francophone e-pal. Your description should include:

- your name and where you are from
- the name of your school and where it is located
- the courses you are currently taking and your opinion of each one
- some of your likes and dislikes
- where you work if you have a job
- any other information you would like to include

Use a chart like this one to brainstorm information about your likes and dislikes.

| J'aime | Je n'aime pas |
|---|---|
|  |  |

**2.** Now take the information about your likes and dislikes and fill out this new chart to help you organize the content of your description.

| | |
|---|---|
| Je m'appelle... | (name). |
| Je suis de... | (where you are from). |
| J'étudie... | (names of classes) à/au/à la (name of school). |
| Je ne travaille pas./ Je travaille à/au/ à la/chez... | (place where you work). |
| J'aime... | (activities you like). |
| Je n'aime pas... | (activities you dislike). |

## Écriture

Use the information from the second chart to write a paragraph describing yourself. Make sure you include all the information from the chart in your paragraph. Use the structures provided for each topic.

**Bonjour!**

Je m'appelle Stacy Adams. Je suis américaine. J'étudie au lycée à New York. Je travaille à la bibliothèque le samedi. J'aime parler avec des amis, lire (*read*), écouter de la musique et voyager, parce que j'aime rencontrer des gens. Par contre, je n'aime pas le sport...

## Après l'écriture

**1.** Exchange a rough draft of your description with a partner. Comment on his or her work by answering these questions:

- Did your partner include all the necessary information (at least six facts)?

- Did your partner use the structures provided in the chart?

- Did your partner use the vocabulary of the unit?

- Did your partner use the grammar of the unit?

**2.** Revise your description according to your partner's comments. After writing the final version, read it one more time to eliminate these kinds of problems:

- spelling errors

- punctuation errors

- capitalization errors

- use of incorrect verb forms

- use of incorrect adjective agreement

- use of incorrect definite and indefinite articles

## EVALUATION

**Criteria**

**Content**  Includes all the information mentioned in the six bulleted items in the description of the task.
Scale: 1  2  3  4  5

**Organization**  Organizes the description similarly to the model provided.
Scale: 1  2  3  4  5

**Accuracy**  Uses **j'aime/je n'aime pas**, regular **-er** verbs, and negation patterns correctly. Words are spelled correctly and adjectives agree with the nouns they modify.
Scale: 1  2  3  4  5

**Creativity**  Includes additional information that is not specified in the task and makes an effort to create longer sentences with a number of items.
Scale: 1  2  3  4  5

**Scoring**

| | |
|---|---|
| Excellent | 18–20 points |
| Good | 14–17 points |
| Satisfactory | 10–13 points |
| Unsatisfactory | < 10 points |

**OPTIONS**

**Écriture**  Before students begin writing, give them some transition words they may want to incorporate into their descriptions. Words and expressions such as **mais**, **parce que**, **alors**, **pourtant**, **par contre**, **ou**, and **et** can be used to make sentences longer and to make transitions between them.

**Après l'écriture**  Once students have written their descriptions, choose several among those and ask the authors for their permission to read them aloud. As you read each one, see if the class can guess whom it is describing, based on the likes, dislikes, and other information included.

## Key Standards

**4.1**

**Teacher Resources**
Vocabulary MP3s/CD

**Suggestion** Tell students that an easy way to study from **Vocabulaire** is to cover up the French half of each section, leaving only the English equivalents exposed. They can then quiz themselves on the French items. To focus on the English equivalents of the French entries, they simply reverse this process.

### Verbes

| | |
|---|---|
| adorer | to love |
| aimer | to like; to love |
| aimer mieux | to prefer |
| arriver | to arrive |
| chercher | to look for |
| commencer | to begin, to start |
| dessiner | to draw |
| détester | to hate |
| donner | to give |
| étudier | to study |
| habiter (à/en) | to live in |
| manger | to eat |
| oublier | to forget |
| parler (au téléphone) | to speak (on the phone) |
| partager | to share |
| penser (que/qu') | to think (that) |
| regarder | to look (at), to watch |
| rencontrer | to meet |
| retrouver | to meet up with; to find (again) |
| travailler | to work |
| voyager | to travel |

### Vocabulaire supplémentaire

| | |
|---|---|
| J'adore... | I love... |
| J'aime bien... | I like... |
| Je n'aime pas tellement... | I don't like... very much. |
| Je déteste... | I hate... |
| être reçu(e) à un examen | to pass an exam |

### Des questions et des opinions

| | |
|---|---|
| bien sûr | of course |
| d'accord | OK, all right |
| Est-ce que/qu'...? | question phrase |
| (mais) non | no (but of course not) |
| moi/toi non plus | me/you neither |
| ne... pas | no, not |
| n'est-ce pas? | isn't that right? |
| oui/si | yes |
| parce que | because |
| pas du tout | not at all |
| peut-être | maybe, perhaps |
| pourquoi? | why? |

ressources

daccord1.vhlcentral.com

### Les cours

| | |
|---|---|
| assister | to attend |
| demander | to ask |
| dîner | to have dinner |
| échouer | to fail |
| écouter | to listen (to) |
| enseigner | to teach |
| expliquer | to explain |
| passer un examen | to take an exam |
| préparer | to prepare (for) |
| rentrer (à la maison) | to return (home) |
| téléphoner à | to telephone |
| trouver | to find; to think |
| visiter | to visit (a place) |
| l'architecture (f.) | architecture |
| l'art (m.) | art |
| la biologie | biology |
| la chimie | chemistry |
| le droit | law |
| l'économie (f.) | economics |
| l'éducation physique (f.) | physical education |
| la géographie | geography |
| la gestion | business administration |
| l'histoire (f.) | history |
| l'informatique (f.) | computer science |
| les langues (étrangères) (f.) | (foreign) languages |
| les lettres (f.) | humanities |
| les mathématiques (maths) (f.) | mathematics |
| la philosophie | philosophy |
| la physique | physics |
| la psychologie | psychology |
| les sciences (politiques/po) (f.) | (political) science |
| le stylisme | fashion design |
| une bourse | scholarship, grant |
| une cantine | cafeteria |
| un cours | class, course |
| un devoir | homework |
| un diplôme | diploma, degree |
| l'école (f.) | school |
| les études (supérieures) (f.) | (higher) education; studies |
| le gymnase | gymnasium |
| une note | grade |
| un restaurant universitaire (un resto U) | university cafeteria |

| | |
|---|---|
| *Expressions utiles* | See pp. 43 and 57. |
| Telling time | See pp. 62-63. |

### Expressions de temps

| | |
|---|---|
| Quel jour sommes-nous? | What day is it? |
| un an | year |
| une/cette année | one/this year |
| après | after |
| après-demain | day after tomorrow |
| un/cet après-midi | an/this afternoon |
| aujourd'hui | today |
| demain (matin/après-midi/soir) | tomorrow (morning/afternoon/evening) |
| un jour | day |
| une journée | day |
| (le) lundi, mardi, mercredi, jeudi, vendredi, samedi, dimanche | (on) Monday(s), Tuesday(s), Wednesday(s), Thursday(s), Friday(s), Saturday(s), Sunday(s) |
| un/ce matin | a/this morning |
| la matinée | morning |
| un mois/ce mois-ci | a month/this month |
| une/cette nuit | a/this night |
| une/cette semaine | a/this week |
| un/ce soir | an/this evening |
| une soirée | evening |
| un/le/ce week-end | a/the/this weekend |
| dernier/dernière | last |
| premier/première | first |
| prochain(e) | next |

### Adjectifs et adverbes

| | |
|---|---|
| difficile | difficult |
| facile | easy |
| inutile | useless |
| utile | useful |
| surtout | especially; above all |

### Expressions avec avoir

| | |
|---|---|
| avoir | to have |
| avoir... ans | to be... years old |
| avoir besoin (de) | to need |
| avoir chaud | to be hot |
| avoir de la chance | to be lucky |
| avoir envie (de) | to feel like |
| avoir froid | to be cold |
| avoir honte (de) | to be ashamed (of) |
| avoir l'air | to look like |
| avoir peur (de) | to be afraid (of) |
| avoir raison | to be right |
| avoir sommeil | to be sleepy |
| avoir tort | to be wrong |

# La famille et les copains

## Pour commencer

- Combien de personnes y a-t-il?
- Où sont ces personnes?
- Que font-elles?
- Ont-elles l'air agréables ou désagréables?

## Unit Goals

**Leçon 3A**
In this lesson, students will learn:

- words for family members and marital status
- some words for pets
- usage of **l'accent aigu** and **l'accent grave**
- about the French family
- more about families and friends through specially shot video footage
- descriptive adjectives
- possessive adjectives
- about the Belgian company **Pages d'Or**

**Leçon 3B**
In this lesson, students will learn:

- words for some professions and occupations
- more descriptive adjectives
- usage of **l'accent circonflexe, la cédille,** and **le tréma**
- about different types of friendships and relationships
- the numbers 61–100
- some prepositions of location
- disjunctive pronouns
- to ask for repetition in oral communication

**Savoir-faire**
In this section, students will learn:

- historical and cultural information about Paris
- to use visuals and graphic elements to predict content
- to use idea maps to organize information
- to write an informal letter

**Pour commencer**

- **Il y a trois personnes.**
- **Elles sont dans un café.**
- **Elles ne mangent pas. Elles parlent.**
- **Elles ont l'air agréables.**

---

**RESOURCES**

**Student Materials**
**Print:** Student Book, Workbooks (*Cahier d'exercices, Cahier d'activités*)
**Technology:** MAESTRO® *Cahier interactif* and Supersite (Audio, Video, Practice)

**Teacher Materials**
DVDs (*Roman-photo, Flash culture*)
Teacher's Resources (Scripts, Answer Keys, Testing Program)
Audio CDs (Testing Program, Textbook, Audio Program)

MAESTRO® Supersite: Student Supersite Content; Planning and Teaching Resources (Overheads, *PowerPoints*, Lesson Plans, Information Gaps and *Feuilles d'activités*); Learning Management System (Gradebook, Assignments); Audio MP3s and Streaming Video
**D'ACCORD! 1 Supersite:** daccord1.vhlcentral.com

## Section Goals

In this section, students will learn and practice vocabulary related to:
- family members
- some pets
- marital status

## Key Standards

1.1, 1.2, 4.1

**Student Resources**
*Cahier d'exercices*, pp. 29-30;
*Cahier d'activités*, pp. 5, 131;
Supersite: Activities,
*Cahier interactif*
**Teacher Resources**
Answer Keys; Overheads #21,
#22; Audio Script; Textbook
& Audio Activity MP3s/CD;
*Feuilles d'activités*; Testing
program: Vocabulary Quiz

## Suggestions

- Introduce active lesson vocabulary with questions and gestures. Ask: **Comment s'appelle ton frère?** Ask a different student: **Comment s'appelle le frère de ____?** Work your way through various family relationships.
- Point out the meanings of plural family terms so students understand that the masculine plural forms can refer to mixed groups of males and females:
**les enfants** *male children; male and female children*
**les cousins** *male cousins; male and female cousins*
**les petits-enfants** *male grandchildren; male and female grandchildren*
- Point out the difference in meaning between the noun **mari** (*husband*) and the adjective **marié(e)** (*married*).
- Use **Overhead #21**. Point out that the family tree is drawn from the point of view of Marie Laval. Have students refer to the family tree to answer your questions about it. Example: **Comment s'appelle la mère de Marie?**

**Leçon** **3A**

**Talking Picture
Audio: Activity**

### You will learn how to...
- discuss family, friends, and pets
- express ownership

# La famille de Marie Laval

## Vocabulaire

| | |
|---|---|
| divorcer | *to divorce* |
| épouser | *to marry* |
| aîné(e) | *elder* |
| cadet(te) | *younger* |
| un beau-frère | *brother-in-law* |
| un beau-père | *father-in-law; stepfather* |
| une belle-mère | *mother-in-law; stepmother* |
| un demi-frère | *half-brother; stepbrother* |
| une demi-sœur | *half-sister; stepsister* |
| les enfants (*m., f.*) | *children* |
| un(e) époux/épouse | *husband/wife* |
| une famille | *family* |
| une femme | *wife; woman* |
| une fille | *daughter; girl* |
| les grands-parents (*m.*) | *grandparents* |
| les parents (*m.*) | *parents* |
| un(e) voisin(e) | *neighbor* |
| un chat | *cat* |
| un oiseau | *bird* |
| un poisson | *fish* |
| célibataire | *single* |
| divorcé(e) | *divorced* |
| fiancé(e) | *engaged* |
| marié(e) | *married* |
| séparé(e) | *separated* |
| veuf/veuve | *widowed* |

**ressources**

| CE pp. 29-30 | CA pp. 5, 131 | daccord1.vhlcentral.com |

**Luc Garneau**

**mon grand-père**

**Juliette Laval** **Robert Laval**

**ma mère, fille de Luc et d'Hélène** | **mon père, mari de Juliette**

**Véronique Laval** **Guillaume Laval** **Marie Laval**

**ma belle-sœur, femme de mon frère** | **mon frère** | **moi, Marie Laval, fille de Juliette et de Robert**

**Matthieu Laval** **Émilie Laval**

**mon neveu** | **ma nièce**

**petits-enfants de mes parents**

**OPTIONS**

**Family Tree** Draw your own family tree on a transparency or the board and label it with names. Ask students questions about it. Examples: **Est-ce que ____ est ma sœur ou ma tante? Comment s'appelle ma grand-mère? ____ est le neveu ou le frère de ____ ? Qui est le grand-père de ____ ?** Help them identify the relationships between members. Then invite them to ask you questions.

**Les noms de famille français** Ask for a show of hands to see if any students' last names are French in origin. Examples: names that begin with **Le____** or **La____** such as **Leblanc** or **Larose**, or even names such as **Fitzgerald** or **Fitzpatrick** (**Fitz-** = **fils de**). Ask these students what they know about their French heritage or family history.

**Hélène Garneau**

ma grand-mère

**Sophie Garneau**          **Marc Garneau**

ma tante,          mon oncle, fils de
femme de Marc          Luc et d'Hélène

**Jean Garneau      Isabelle Garneau      Virginie Garneau**

mon cousin,      ma cousine, sœur      ma cousine,
petit-fils de Luc      de Jean et de      sœur de Jean et
et d'Hélène      Virginie, petite-fille      d'Isabelle,
     de Luc et d'Hélène      petite-fille de Luc
          et d'Hélène

**Bambou**

le chien de
mes cousins

# Mise en pratique

**1  Qui est-ce?** Match the definition in the first list with the correct item from the second list. Not all the items will be used.

1. __d__ le frère de ma cousine
2. __g__ le père de mon cousin
3. __a__ le mari de ma grand-mère
4. __e__ le fils de mon frère
5. __c__ la fille de mon grand-père
6. __i__ le fils de ma mère
7. __h__ la fille de mon fils
8. __f__ le fils de ma belle-mère

a. mon grand-père
b. ma sœur
c. ma tante
d. mon cousin
e. mon neveu
f. mon demi-frère
g. mon oncle
h. ma petite-fille
i. mon frère

**2  Choisissez** Fill in the blank by selecting the most appropriate answer.

1. Voici le frère de mon père. C'est mon ___oncle___ (oncle, neveu, fiancé).
2. Voici la mère de ma cousine. C'est ma ___tante___ (grand-mère, voisine, tante).
3. Voici la petite-fille de ma grand-mère. C'est ma ___cousine___ (cousine, nièce, épouse).
4. Voici le père de ma mère. C'est mon ___grand-père___ (grand-père, oncle, cousin).
5. Voici le fils de mon père, mais ce n'est pas le fils de ma mère. C'est mon ___demi-frère___ (petit-fils, demi-frère, voisin).

**3  Complétez** Complete each sentence with the appropriate word.

1. Voici ma nièce. C'est la ___petite-fille___ de ma mère.
2. Voici la mère de ma tante. C'est ma ___grand-mère___.
3. Voici la sœur de mon oncle. C'est ma ___tante___.
4. Voici la fille de mon père, mais pas de ma mère. C'est ma ___demi-sœur___.
5. Voici le mari de ma mère, mais ce n'est pas mon père. C'est mon ___beau-père___.

**4  Écoutez** 🎧 Listen to each statement made by Marie Laval. Based on her family tree, indicate whether it is **vrai** or **faux**.

|  | Vrai | Faux |  | Vrai | Faux |
|---|---|---|---|---|---|
| 1. | ☑ | ☐ | 6. | ☐ | ☑ |
| 2. | ☐ | ☑ | 7. | ☐ | ☑ |
| 3. | ☑ | ☐ | 8. | ☑ | ☐ |
| 4. | ☐ | ☑ | 9. | ☑ | ☐ |
| 5. | ☐ | ☑ | 10. | ☑ | ☐ |

Practice more at **daccord1.vhlcentral.com.**

*soixante-quinze* **75**

**Successful Language Learning**
Tell students that it isn't necessary to understand every word they hear in French. They will feel less anxious if they listen for general meaning.

**1 Suggestion** Mention that adjectives such as **beau** and **petit** in hyphenated family terms must agree in gender. Exceptions: **la grand-mère, la demi-sœur.**

**2 & 3 Expansion** Have students provide additional examples for the class to identify.

**4 Script**
1. Marc est mon oncle.
2. Émilie est la nièce de Véronique.
3. Jean est le petit-fils d'Hélène.
4. Robert est mon grand-père.
5. Luc est le père de Sophie.
6. Isabelle est ma tante.
7. Matthieu est le fils de Jean.
8. Émilie est la fille de Guillaume.
9. Juliette est ma mère.
10. Virginie est ma cousine.
*(On Textbook Audio)*

**4 Expansion** Play Marie's statements again, stopping at the end of each. Where the statements are true, have students repeat. Where the statements are false, have students correct them by referring to Marie Laval's family tree.

**O P T I O N S**

**Using Games** As a class or group activity, have students state the relationship between people on Marie Laval's family tree. Their classmates will guess which person on the family tree they are describing. Example: **C'est la sœur de Jean et la fille de Sophie. (Isabelle ou Virginie)** Take turns until each member of the class or group has had a chance to state a relationship.

**My Family Tree** Have students draw their own family tree as homework. Tell them to label each position on the tree with the appropriate French term and the person's name. Also tell them to write five fill-in-the-blank statements based on their family tree. Examples: **Je suis la fille de ____. Mon frère s'appelle ____.** In the next class, have students exchange papers with a classmate and complete the activity.

# CONTEXTES

## Communication

**5** **L'arbre généalogique** With a classmate, identify the members of the family by asking how each one is related to Anne Durand. Answers will vary.

**MODÈLE**

Élève 1: *Qui est Louis Durand?*
Élève 2: *C'est le grand-père d'Anne.*

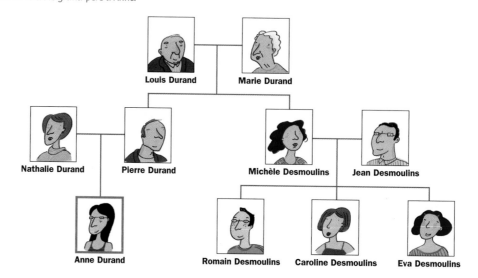

**6** **Entrevue** With a classmate, take turns asking each other these questions. Answers will vary.

1. Combien de personnes y a-t-il dans ta famille?
2. Comment s'appellent tes parents?
3. As-tu des frères et sœurs?
4. Combien de cousins/cousines as-tu? Comment s'appellent-ils/elles? Où habitent-ils/elles?
5. Quel(le) (*Which*) est ton cousin préféré/ta cousine préférée?
6. As-tu des neveux/des nièces?
7. Comment s'appellent tes grands-parents? Où habitent-ils?
8. Combien de petits-enfants ont tes grands-parents?

### Coup de main

Use these words to help you complete this activity.

ton *your (m.)* → mon *my (m.)*
ta *your (f.)* → ma *my (f.)*
tes *your (pl.)* → mes *my (pl.)*

**7** **Qui suis-je?** Your teacher will give you a worksheet. Walk around the class and ask your classmates questions about their families. When a classmate gives one of the answers on the worksheet, write his or her name in the corresponding space. Be prepared to discuss the results with the class. Answers will vary.

**MODÈLE** J'ai un chien.

Élève 1: *Est-ce que tu as un chien?*
Élève 2: *Oui, j'ai un chien (You write the student's name.)/Non, n'ai pas de chien. (You ask another classmate.)*

# Les sons et les lettres

**Audio: Concepts, Activities Record & Compare**

## L'accent aigu and l'accent grave

In French, diacritical marks (*accents*) are an essential part of a word's spelling. They indicate how vowels are pronounced or distinguish between words with similar spellings but different meanings. **L'accent aigu** ( ´ ) appears only over the vowel **e**. It indicates that the **e** is pronounced similarly to the vowel *a* in the English word *cake*, but shorter and crisper.

| **é**tudier | r**é**serv**é** | **é**l**é**gant | t**é**l**é**phone |

**L'accent aigu** also signals some similarities between French and English words. Often, an **e** with **l'accent aigu** at the beginning of a French word marks the place where the letter *s* would appear at the beginning of the English equivalent.

| **é**ponge | **é**pouse | **é**tat | **é**tudiante |
| *sponge* | *spouse* | *state* | *student* |

**L'accent grave** ( ` ) appears only over the vowels **a**, **e**, and **u**. Over the vowel **e**, it indicates that the **e** is pronounced like the vowel *e* in the English word *pet*.

| tr**è**s | apr**è**s | m**è**re | ni**è**ce |

Although **l'accent grave** does not change the pronunciation of the vowels **a** or **u**, it distinguishes words that have a similar spelling but different meanings.

| la | là | ou | où |
| *the* | *there* | *or* | *where* |

**Prononcez** Practice saying these words aloud.

1. agréable
2. sincère
3. voilà
4. faculté
5. frère
6. à
7. déjà
8. éléphant
9. lycée
10. poème
11. là
12. élève

**Articulez** Practice saying these sentences aloud.

1. À tout à l'heure!
2. Thérèse, je te présente Michèle.
3. Hélène est très sérieuse et réservée.
4. Voilà mon père, Frédéric, et ma mère, Ségolène.
5. Tu préfères étudier à la fac demain après-midi?

**Dictons** Practice reading these sayings aloud.

Tel père, tel fils.¹

À vieille mule, frein doré.²

¹ Like father, like son.
² For an old mule, a golden bit.

**ressources**

CA p. 132

daccord1.vhlcentral.com

*soixante-dix-sept* **77**

**Section Goals**

In this section, students will learn about:
• l'accent aigu
• l'accent grave
• a strategy for recognizing cognates

**Key Standards**
4.1

**Student Resources**
*Cahier d'activités*, p. 132; Supersite: Activities, *Cahier interactif*

**Teacher Resources**
Answer Keys; Audio Script; Textbook & Audio Activity MP3s/CD

**Suggestions**

• Write **é** on the board. Tell students to watch your mouth as you pronounce the sound. Explain that when **é** appears at the beginning of a word, the corners of your mouth are slightly turned up and your tongue is low behind your bottom teeth. Have students repeat **é** after you several times.

• Write words and/or French names from the Laval family with **l'accent aigu** on the board. Pronounce each word as you point to it and have students repeat it after you. Examples: **époux, célibataire, fiancé, séparé, Émilie,** and **Véronique.**

• Give students some sample sentences with **la, là, ou,** or **où** and ask them what the words mean to demonstrate how context clarifies meaning. Examples: **1. Où est la fille? 2. La fille est là. 3. Est-ce que Sophie est la tante ou la grand-mère de Marie Laval?**

• Ask students to provide more examples of words they know with these accents.

• The explanation and exercises are available on the Supersite. You may want to play them in class so students hear French speakers besides yourself.

**Dictons** Explain to students that the saying **«À vieille mule, frein doré»** applies to a situation in which someone tries to sell something old by dressing it up or decorating it. For example, to have a better chance at selling an old car, give it a new paint job.

**OPTIONS**

**Mini-dictée** Here are additional sentences to use for extra practice with **l'accent aigu** and **l'accent grave**. 1. Étienne est mon frère préféré. 2. Ma sœur aînée est très occupée avec les études. 3. André et Geneviève sont séparés. 4. Vous êtes marié ou célibataire? 5. Éric et Sabine sont fiancés.

**Using Games** Have a spelling bee using words with **l'accent aigu** and/or **l'accent grave** from **Leçon 3A** or previous lessons. Divide the class into two teams. Call on one team member at a time, alternating between teams. Give a point for each correct answer. The team with the most points at the end of the game wins. Before students begin, remind them that they must indicate the accent marks in the words. Give them an example: **très T-R-E accent grave-S.**

# ROMAN-PHOTO

## L'album de photos

 Video: *Roman-photo*
Record & Compare

**PERSONNAGES**

Amina

Michèle

Stéphane

Valérie

**MICHÈLE** Mais, qui c'est? C'est ta sœur? Tes parents?
**AMINA** C'est mon ami Cyberhomme.
**MICHÈLE** Comment est-il? Est-ce qu'il est beau? Il a les yeux de quelle couleur? Marron ou bleue? Et ses cheveux? Ils sont blonds ou châtains?
**AMINA** Je ne sais pas.
**MICHÈLE** Toi, tu es timide.

**VALÉRIE** Stéphane, tu as dix-sept ans. Cette année, tu passes le bac, mais tu ne travailles pas!
**STÉPHANE** Écoute, ce n'est pas vrai, je déteste mes cours, mais je travaille beaucoup. Regarde, mon cahier de chimie, mes livres de français, ma calculatrice pour le cours de maths, mon dictionnaire anglais-français...

**STÉPHANE** Oh, et qu'est-ce que c'est? Ah, oui, les photos de tante Françoise.
**VALÉRIE** Des photos? Mais où?
**STÉPHANE** Ici! Amina, on peut regarder des photos de ma tante sur ton ordinateur, s'il te plaît?

**AMINA** Ah, et ça, c'est toute la famille, n'est-ce pas?
**VALÉRIE** Oui, ça, c'est Henri, sa femme, Françoise, et leurs enfants: le fils aîné, Bernard, et puis son frère, Charles, sa sœur, Sophie, et leur chien, Socrate.
**STÉPHANE** J'aime bien Socrate. Il est vieux, mais il est amusant!

**VALÉRIE** Ah! Et Bernard, il a son bac aussi et sa mère est très heureuse.
**STÉPHANE** Moi, j'ai envie d'habiter avec oncle Henri et tante Françoise. Comme ça, pas de problème pour le bac!

**STÉPHANE** Pardon, maman. Je suis très heureux ici, avec toi. Ah, au fait, Rachid travaille avec moi pour préparer le bac.
**VALÉRIE** Ah, bon? Rachid est très intelligent... un étudiant sérieux.

---

**A C T I V I T É S**

**1** **Vrai ou faux?** Are these sentences **vrai** or **faux**? Correct the false ones.

1. Amina communique avec sa (*her*) tante par ordinateur. Faux. Elle communique avec Cyberhomme.
2. Stéphane n'aime pas ses (*his*) cours au lycée. Vrai.
3. Ils regardent des photos de vacances. Faux. Ils regardent les photos de tante Françoise.
4. Henri est le frère aîné de Valérie. Vrai.
5. Bernard est le cousin de Stéphane. Vrai.

6. Charles a déjà son bac. Vrai.
7. La tante de Stéphane s'appelle Françoise. Vrai.
8. Stéphane travaille avec Amina pour préparer le bac. Faux. Il travaille avec Rachid.
9. Socrate est le fils d'Henri et de Françoise. Faux. C'est le chien d'Henri et de Françoise.
10. Rachid n'est pas un bon étudiant. Faux. C'est un étudiant sérieux.

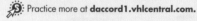 Practice more at **daccord1.vhlcentral.com**.

---

**Avant de regarder la vidéo** Before students view the video episode **L'album de photos**, ask them to brainstorm a list of things someone might say when describing his or her family photos.

**Regarder la vidéo** Play the first half of the video episode and have students describe what happened. Write their observations on the board. Then ask them to guess what will happen in the second half of the episode. Write their ideas on the board. Play the entire video episode; then help the class summarize the plot.

**Stéphane et Valérie regardent des photos de famille avec Amina.**

*À la table d'Amina...*

**AMINA** Alors, voilà vos photos. Qui est-ce?

**VALÉRIE** Oh, c'est Henri, mon frère aîné!

**AMINA** Quel âge a-t-il?

**VALÉRIE** Il a cinquante ans. Il est très sociable et c'est un très bon père.

**VALÉRIE** Ah! Et ça, c'est ma nièce Sophie et mon neveu Charles! Regarde, Stéphane, tes cousins!

**STÉPHANE** Je n'aime pas Charles. Il est tellement sérieux.

**VALÉRIE** Il est peut-être trop sérieux, mais, lui, il a son bac!

**AMINA** Et Sophie, qu'elle est jolie!

**VALÉRIE** ... et elle a déjà son bac.

**AMINA** Ça, oui, préparer le bac avec Rachid, c'est une idée géniale!

**VALÉRIE** Oui, c'est vrai. En théorie, c'est une excellente idée. Mais tu prépares le bac avec Rachid, hein? Pas le prochain match de foot!

## Expressions utiles

### Talking about your family

- **C'est ta sœur? Ce sont tes parents?**
  *Is that your sister? Are those your parents?*
- **C'est mon ami.**
  *That's my friend.*
- **Ça, c'est Henri, sa femme, Françoise, et leurs enfants.**
  *That's Henri, his wife, Françoise, and their kids.*

### Describing people

- **Il a les yeux de quelle couleur? Marron ou bleue?**
  *What color are his eyes? Brown or blue?*
- **Il a les yeux bleus.**
  *He has blue eyes.*
- **Et ses cheveux? Ils sont blonds ou châtains? Frisés ou raides?**
  *And his hair? Is it blond or brown? Curly or straight?*
- **Il a les cheveux châtains et frisés.**
  *He has curly brown hair.*

### Additional vocabulary

- **On peut regarder des photos de ma tante sur ton ordinateur?**
  *Can/May we look at some photos from my aunt on your computer?*
- **C'est toute la famille, n'est-ce pas?**
  *That's the whole family, right?*
- **Je ne sais pas (encore).**
  *I (still) don't know.*

| | |
|---|---|
| **Alors...** *So...* | **peut-être** *maybe* |
| **vrai** *true* | **au fait** *by the way* |
| **une photo(graphie)** *a photograph* | **Hein?** *Right?* |
| **une idée** *an idea* | **déjà** *already* |

*soixante-dix-neuf* **79**

---

**2 Vocabulaire** Choose the adjective that describes how Stéphane would feel on these occasions. Refer to a dictionary as necessary.

1. on his 87th birthday _____ vieux
2. after finding 20€ _____ heureux
3. while taking the **bac** _____ sérieux
4. after getting a good grade _____ heureux
5. after dressing for a party _____ beau

| beau |
| heureux |
| sérieux |
| vieux |

**3 Conversez** In pairs, describe which member of your family is most like Stéphane. How are they alike? Do they both like sports? Do they take similar courses? How do they like school? How are their personalities? Be prepared to describe your partner's "Stéphane" to the class.

**ressources**

CA pp. 75–76 | daccord1.vhlcentral.com

**ACTIVITÉS**

---

**Valérie's Family Tree** Working in pairs, have students draw a family tree based on Valérie's description of her brother's family. Tell them to use the family tree on page 74 as a model. Remind them to include Valérie and Stéphane. Then have them get together with another pair of students and compare their drawings.

**Writing Questions** Have students write four questions about Henri's family based on the conversation and video still #6. Then have them get together in groups of three and take turns asking and answering each other's questions. Examples: **Combien de personnes y a-t-il dans la famille d'Henri? Comment s'appelle le fils aîné? Combien de frères a Sophie?**

---

**Expressions utiles**
- Point out the various forms of possessive adjectives and descriptive adjectives in the captions and the **Expressions utiles.** Tell students that this material will be formally presented in the **Structures** section. Do not expect students to produce the forms correctly at this time.
- Model the pronunciation of the **Expressions utiles** and have students repeat them.
- To practice new vocabulary, ask students to describe their classmates' eyes and hair. Examples: _____ **a les yeux de quelle couleur? Marron ou bleue? Avez-vous les yeux bleus?** _____ **a-t-il/elle les cheveux blonds ou châtains? Qui a les cheveux blonds/châtains dans la classe? Est-ce que les cheveux de** _____ **sont frisés ou raides?**

**1 Suggestion** Have students correct the false statements.

**1 Expansion** For additional practice, give students these items. **11. Valérie n'aime pas son frère, Henri. (Faux.) 12. Stéphane aime les gens très sérieux. (Faux.) 13. Socrate est un chien. (Vrai.) 14. Stéphane et Rachid préparent le prochain match de foot. (Faux.)**

**2 Suggestion** Before students begin the activity, you might want to introduce the adjectives in the word list using pictures or people in the video stills, rather than having students look them up in the dictionary.

**2 Expansion** Have students describe Rachid, Charles, and Henri using the adjectives in the word list. At this point, avoid asking students to describe people that would require a feminine or plural form of these adjectives.

**3 Suggestion** If time is limited, this activity may be assigned as a written composition for homework.

Video: *Flash culture*

## CULTURE À LA LOUPE

# La famille en France

**Comment est la famille française?** Est-elle différente de la famille américaine? La majorité des Français sont-ils mariés, divorcés ou célibataires?

Il n'y a pas de réponse simple à ces questions. Les familles françaises sont très diverses. Le mariage est toujours° très populaire: la majorité des hommes et des femmes sont mariés. Mais attention! Les nombres° de personnes divorcées et de personnes célibataires augmentent chaque° année.

La structure familiale traditionnelle existe toujours en France, mais il y a des structures moins traditionnelles, comme les familles monoparentales, où° l'unique parent est divorcé, séparé ou veuf. Il y a aussi des familles recomposées, c'est-à-dire qui combinent deux familles, avec un beau-père, une belle-mère, des demi-frères et des demi-sœurs. Certains couples choisissent° le Pacte Civil de Solidarité (PACS), qui offre certains droits° et protections aux couples non-mariés.

Géographiquement, les membres d'une famille d'immigrés peuvent° habiter près ou loin° les uns des autres°. Mais en général, ils préfèrent habiter les uns près des autres parce que l'intégration est parfois° difficile. Il existe aussi des familles d'immigrés séparées entre° la France et le pays d'origine.

Alors, oubliez les stéréotypes des familles en France. Elles sont grandes et petites, traditionnelles et non-conventionnelles; elles changent et sont toujours les mêmes°.

**toujours** *still* **nombres** *numbers* **chaque** *each* **où** *where* **choisissent** *choose* **droits** *rights* **peuvent** *can* **près ou loin** *near or far from* **les uns des autres** *one another* **parfois** *sometimes* **entre** *between* **mêmes** *same* **tranche** *bracket*

### Coup de main

Remember to read decimal places in **French** using the French word **virgule** (*comma*) where you would normally say *point* in English. To say *percent*, use **pour cent**.

**64,3% soixante-quatre virgule trois pour cent**

*sixty-four point three percent*

### La situation familiale des Français
*(par tranche° d'âge)*

| ÂGE | CÉLIBATAIRE | EN COUPLE SANS ENFANTS | EN COUPLE AVEC ENFANTS | PARENT D'UNE FAMILLE MONOPARENTALE |
|---|---|---|---|---|
| < 25 ans | 3,6% | 2,8% | 1% | 0,3% |
| 25–29 ans | 16,7% | 26,5% | 26,2% | 2,6% |
| 30–44 ans | 10,9% | 9,8% | 64,3% | 6,2% |
| 45–59 ans | 11,7% | 29,9% | 47,2% | 5,9% |
| > 60 ans | 20,3% | 59,2% | 11,7% | 2,9% |

SOURCE: INSEE

## ACTIVITÉS

**1 Complétez** Provide logical answers, based on the reading.

1. Si on regarde la population française d'aujourd'hui, on observe que les familles françaises sont très ___diverses___.
2. Le ___mariage___ est toujours très populaire en France.
3. La majorité des hommes et des femmes sont ___mariés___.
4. Le nombre de Français qui sont ___célibataires___ augmente.
5. Dans les familles ___monoparentales___, l'unique parent est divorcé, séparé ou veuf.
6. Il y a des familles qui combinent ___deux___ familles.
7. Le ___PACS___ offre certains droits et protections aux couples qui ne sont pas mariés.
8. Les immigrés aiment ___habiter___ les uns près des autres.
9. Oubliez les ___stéréotypes___ des familles en France.
10. Les familles changent et sont toujours ___les mêmes___.

Practice more at **daccord1.vhlcentral.com**.

## LE FRANÇAIS QUOTIDIEN

### La famille

| | |
|---|---|
| un frangin | *brother* |
| une frangine | *sister* |
| maman | *Mom* |
| mamie | *Nana, Grandma* |
| un minou | *kitty* |
| papa | *Dad* |
| papi | *Grandpa* |
| tata | *Auntie* |
| tonton | *Uncle* |
| un toutou | *doggy* |

## LE MONDE FRANCOPHONE

### Les fêtes et la famille

Les États-Unis ont quelques fêtes° en commun avec le monde francophone, mais les dates et les traditions de ces fêtes diffèrent d'un pays° à l'autre°. Voici deux fêtes associées à la famille.

**La Fête des mères**

**En France** le dernier° dimanche de mai ou le premier° dimanche de juin

**En Belgique** le deuxième° dimanche de mai

**À l'île Maurice** le dernier dimanche de mai

**Au Canada** le deuxième dimanche de mai

**La Fête des pères**

**En France** le troisième° dimanche de juin

**En Belgique** le deuxième° dimanche de juin

**Au Canada** le troisième dimanche de juin

**quelques fêtes** *some holidays* **pays** *country* **autre** *other*
**dernier** *last* **premier** *first* **deuxième** *second* **troisième** *third*

## PORTRAIT

### Les Noah

Dans° la famille Noah, le sport est héréditaire. À chacun son° sport: pour° Yannick, né° en France, c'est le tennis; pour son père, Zacharie, né à Yaoundé, au Cameroun, c'est le football°; pour son fils, Joakim, né aux États-Unis, c'est le basket-ball. Yannick est champion junior à Wimbledon en 1977 et participe aux championnats° du Grand Chelem° dans les années 1980. Son fils, Joakim, est un joueur° de basket-ball aux États-Unis. Il gagne° la

finale du *Final Four NCAA* en 2006 et en 2007 avec les Florida Gators. Il est aujourd'hui joueur professionnel avec les Chicago Bulls. Le sport est dans le sang° chez les Noah!

**Dans** *In* **À chacun son** *To everybody his* **pour** *for* **né** *born* **football** *soccer* **championnats** *championships* **Chelem** *Slam* **joueur** *player* **gagne** *wins* **sang** *blood*

## SUR INTERNET

**Yannick Noah: célébrité du tennis et... de la chanson?°**

Go to daccord1.vhlcentral.com to find more information related to this **CULTURE** section. Then watch the corresponding **Flash culture.**

Tennis star and singing sensation?

---

**2** **Vrai ou faux?** Indicate if these statements are **vrai** or **faux.**

1. Le tennis est héréditaire chez les Noah. Faux. Le sport est héréditaire chez les Noah.
2. Zacharie Noah est né au Cameroun. Vrai.
3. Zacharie Noah était (*was*) un joueur de basket-ball. Faux. Zacharie Noah était un joueur de football.
4. Yannick gagne à l'US Open. Faux. Yannick gagne à Wimbledon.
5. Joakim joue (*plays*) pour les Lakers. Faux. Joakim joue pour les Chicago Bulls.
6. Le deuxième dimanche de mai, c'est la Fête des mères en Belgique et au Canada. Vrai.

**3** **À vous...** With a partner, write six sentences describing another celebrity family whose members all share a common field or profession. Be prepared to share your sentences with the class.

**ressources**

CA pp. 103–104

daccord1.vhlcentral.com

**ACTIVITÉS**

---

**O P T I O N S**

**Les fêtes de la famille** Explain to students that many countries around the world have a special day to honor mothers. **La Fête des mères** and **La Fête des pères** are celebrated somewhat similarly in France, Belgium, and Canada to the way Mother's Day and Father's Day are celebrated in the United States. Children create cards, write poems, and make handicrafts in school to give to their parents on these holidays. Older sons and daughters often give a small gift. On **l'île Maurice**, they do not officially celebrate Father's Day. In other francophone regions, such as North and West Africa, there is no official holiday for either Mother's or Father's Day.

---

**Le français quotidien** Point out that this vocabulary, while quite common in day-to-day language, is very familiar. These words are usually used in informal conversations with family members, children, and close friends.

**Portrait** Show the class a photo of Yannick Noah. Ask: **Qui est-ce? Comment s'appelle-t-il?** Ask students what they know about him. Explain that thanks to his active involvement in charity work, Noah is often referred to as **Tonton Yannick.**

**Le monde francophone** Explain that Mother's Day and Father's Day did not originate in France. The first **Journée des mères** took place in France in 1926; it became an official holiday, **La Fête des mères,** in 1950.

**2 Suggestion** Have students correct the false statements.

**2 Expansion** Have students write three more true/false statements based on **Portrait** and **Le monde francophone.** Then have them work in groups of three and take turns reading their statements while the other group members respond **vrai** or **faux.**

**3 Expansion** Have students work in pairs. Tell them to create a brief conversation in which they talk about their families and pets, using vocabulary in **Le français quotidien.** Example: **Est-ce que tu as un minou? Non, mais ma tata, elle a des minous.** Remind students that this level of language is only appropriate when talking to small children.

**Flash culture** Tell students that they will learn more about family and friends by watching a variety of real-life images narrated by Csilla. Show the video segment, then have students jot down in French at least three examples of people or things they saw. You can also use the activities in the video manual in class to reinforce this **Flash culture** or assign them as homework.

# STRUCTURES

## 3A.1 Descriptive adjectives

**Point de départ** As you learned in **Leçon 1B**, adjectives describe people, places, and things. In French, most adjectives agree in gender and number with the nouns or pronouns they modify.

| SINGULAR MASCULINE NOUN ⟷ SINGULAR MASCULINE ADJECTIVE | PLURAL MASCULINE NOUN ⟷ PLURAL MASCULINE ADJECTIVE |
|---|---|
| Le **père** est **américain**. | As-tu des **cours faciles**? |
| *The father is American.* | *Do you have easy classes?* |

- You've already learned several adjectives of nationality and some adjectives to describe your classes. Here are some adjectives used to describe physical characteristics.

### Adjectives of physical description

| | | | |
|---|---|---|---|
| bleu(e) | *blue* | joli(e) | *pretty* |
| blond(e) | *blond* | laid(e) | *ugly* |
| brun(e) | *dark (hair)* | marron | *brown (not for hair)* |
| châtain | *brown (hair)* | noir(e) | *black* |
| court(e) | *short* | petit(e) | *small, short (stature)* |
| grand(e) | *tall, big* | raide | *straight* |
| jeune | *young* | vert(e) | *green* |

- Notice that, in the examples below, the adjectives agree in gender and number with the subjects.

**Elles** sont **blondes** et **petites**.
*They are blond and short.*

**L'examen** est **long**.
*The exam is long.*

- Use the expression **de taille moyenne** to describe someone or something of medium size.

Victor est un homme **de taille moyenne**.
*Victor is a man of medium height.*

C'est une université **de taille moyenne**.
*It's a medium-sized university.*

- The adjective **marron** is invariable; that is, it does not agree in gender and number with the noun it modifies. The adjective **châtain** is almost exclusively used to describe hair color.

Mon neveu a les **yeux marron**.
*My nephew has brown eyes.*

Ma nièce a les **cheveux châtains**.
*My niece has brown hair.*

---

## MISE EN PRATIQUE

**1** **Ressemblances** Family members often look and behave alike. Describe these family members.

**MODÈLE**

Caroline est intelligente. Elle a un frère.
*Il est intelligent aussi.*

1. Jean est curieux. Il a une sœur. Elle est curieuse aussi.
2. Carole est blonde. Elle a un cousin. Il est blond aussi.
3. Albert est gros. Il a trois tantes. Elles sont grosses aussi.
4. Sylvie est fière et heureuse. Elle a un fils. Il est fier et heureux aussi.
5. Christophe est vieux. Il a une demi-sœur. Elle est vieille aussi.
6. Martin est laid. Il a une petite-fille. Elle est laide aussi.
7. Sophie est intellectuelle. Elle a deux grands-pères. Ils sont intellectuels aussi.
8. Céline est naïve. Elle a deux frères. Ils sont naïfs aussi.
9. Anne est belle. Elle a cinq neveux. Ils sont beaux aussi.
10. Anissa est rousse. Elle a un oncle. Il est roux aussi.

**2** **Une femme heureuse** Christine has a happy life. To know why, complete these sentences. Make any necessary changes.

**MODÈLE**

Christine / avoir / trois enfants (beau)
*Christine a trois beaux enfants.*

1. Elle / avoir / des amis (sympathique)
   Elle a des amis sympathiques.
2. Elle / habiter / dans un appartement (nouveau)
   Elle habite dans un nouvel appartement.
3. Son (*Her*) mari / avoir / un travail (bon)
   Son mari a un bon travail.
4. Ses (*Her*) filles / être / des étudiantes (sérieux)
   Ses filles sont des étudiantes sérieuses.
5. Christine / être (fier) / de son succès
   Christine est fière de son succès.
6. Son mari / être / un homme (beau)
   Son mari est un bel homme.
7. Elle / avoir / des collègues (amusant)
   Elle a des collègues amusants.
8. Sa (*Her*) secrétaire / être / une fille (jeune/intellectuel)
   Sa secrétaire est une jeune fille intellectuelle.
9. Elle / avoir / des chiens (bon)
   Elle a de bons chiens.
10. Ses voisins / être (poli)
    Ses voisins sont polis.

Practice more at **daccord1.vhlcentral.com**.

---

---

Language Note  Point out that the adjective **châtain** comes from the noun **une châtaigne**, which is a type of sweet chestnut. The adjective **marron** is also a noun; **un marron** means horse chestnut.

## COMMUNICATION

**3  Comparaisons** In pairs, take turns comparing these brothers and their sister. Make as many comparisons as possible, then share them with the class. *Answers will vary.*

**Jean-Paul      Tristan      Géraldine**

**MODÈLE**

*Géraldine et Jean-Paul sont grands, mais Tristan est petit.*

**4  Qui est-ce?** Choose a classmate. Your partner must guess the person's name by asking up to 10 **oui** or **non** questions. Then, switch roles. *Answers will vary.*

**MODÈLE**

Élève 1: *C'est un garçon?*
Élève 2: *Oui.*
Élève 1: *Il est de taille moyenne?*
Élève 2: *Non.*

**5  Les bons copains** Interview two classmates to learn about one of their friends, using these questions and descriptive adjectives. Be prepared to report to the class what you learned. *Answers will vary.*

- Est-ce que tu as un(e) bon(ne) copain/copine?
- Comment est-ce qu'il/elle s'appelle?
- Quel âge a-t-il/elle?
- Comment est-il/elle?
- Il/Elle est de quelle origine?
- Quels cours est-ce qu'il/elle aime?
- Quels cours est-ce qu'il/elle déteste?

### Some irregular adjectives

| masculine singular | feminine singular | masculine plural | feminine plural | |
|---|---|---|---|---|
| beau | belle | beaux | belles | *beautiful; handsome* |
| bon | bonne | bons | bonnes | *good; kind* |
| fier | fière | fiers | fières | *proud* |
| gros | grosse | gros | grosses | *fat* |
| heureux | heureuse | heureux | heureuses | *happy* |
| intellectuel | intellectuelle | intellectuels | intellectuelles | *intellectual* |
| long | longue | longs | longues | *long* |
| naïf | naïve | naïfs | naïves | *naïve* |
| roux | rousse | roux | rousses | *red-haired* |
| vieux | vieille | vieux | vieilles | *old* |

- The forms of the adjective **nouveau** (*new*) follow the same pattern as those of **beau**.

- Other adjectives that follow the pattern of **heureux** are **curieux** (*curious*), **malheureux** (*unhappy*), **nerveux** (*nervous*), and **sérieux** (*serious*).

### Position of adjectives

- These adjectives are usually placed before the noun they modify: **beau**, **bon**, **grand**, **gros**, **jeune**, **joli**, **long**, **nouveau**, **petit**, and **vieux**.

    J'aime bien les **grandes familles**.       Joël est un **vieux copain**.
    *I like large families.*       *Joël is an old friend.*

- These forms are used before masculine singular nouns that begin with a vowel sound.

    beau → bel → un **bel** appartement
    nouveau → nouvel → un **nouvel** ami
    vieux → vieil → un **vieil** homme

- These adjectives are also generally placed before a noun: **mauvais(e)** (*bad*), **pauvre** (*poor, unfortunate*), **vrai(e)** (*true, real*).

- The plural indefinite article **des** changes to **de** before an adjective followed by a noun.

    J'habite avec **des amis sympathiques**.       J'habite avec **de bons amis**.
    *I live with nice friends.*       *I live with good friends.*

### Essayez!   Provide all four forms of these adjectives.

1. grand *grand, grande, grands, grandes*
2. nerveux *nerveux, nerveuse, nerveux, nerveuses*
3. roux *roux, rousse, roux, rousses*
4. bleu *bleu, bleue, bleus, bleues*
5. naïf *naïf, naïve, naïfs, naïves*
6. gros *gros, grosse, gros, grosses*
7. long *long, longue, longs, longues*
8. fier *fier, fière, fiers, fières*

**Essayez!** Have students create sentences using these adjectives. Examples: **La tour Eiffel est grande. Les étudiants ne sont pas naïfs.**

**1 Expansion** Have students restate the answers, except #3, #7, #8 and #9, using the phrase **les deux** to practice plural forms. Example: 1. **Les deux sont curieux.**

**2 Suggestion** To check students' work, have volunteers write their sentences on the board and read them aloud.

**2 Expansion** For additional practice, change the adjective(s) and have students restate or write the sentences. Examples: 1. **bon (Elle a de bons amis.)** 2. **beau (Elle habite dans un bel appartement.)** 3. **agréable (Son mari a un travail agréable.)** 4. **bon (Ses filles sont de bonnes étudiantes.)** 5. **indépendant/élégant (Christine est indépendante et élégante.)** 6. **fier (Son mari est un homme fier.)** 7. **poli (Elle a des collègues polis.)** 8. **joli/intelligent (Sa secrétaire est une jolie fille intelligente.)**

**3 Expansion** To practice negation, have students say what the people in the drawings are not. Example: **Géraldine et Jean-Paul ne sont pas petits.**

**4 Suggestion** This activity can also be done in small groups or with the whole class.

**5 Suggestions**
- To model this activity, have students look at the photo and respond as you ask the interview questions. Tell them to invent answers, where necessary.
- Tell students to add two questions of their own to the list and to jot down notes during their interviews.
- If time is limited, have students write a description of one of their classmates' friends as written homework.

**Brainstorming** Have students brainstorm and make a list of adjectives in French that describe their ideal friend (**Mon copain idéal/Ma copine idéale**). Tell them to rank each adjective in terms of its importance to them. Then take a quick class survey to find out what the most important and least important qualities are in the ideal friend. Tally the results on the board.

**Mini-dictée** Prepare short descriptions of five easily recognizable people. Write their names on the board in random order. Tell students to write your descriptions as you dictate them. Then have them match the description to the appropriate name. Example: **Elle est jeune, brune, athlétique et intellectuelle. (Serena Williams)**

## 3A.2 Possessive adjectives

**Point de départ** In both English and French, possessive adjectives express ownership or possession.

**BOÎTE À OUTILS**
In CONTEXTES, you learned a few possessive adjectives with family vocabulary: **mon grand-père, ma sœur, mes cousins.**

### Possessive adjectives

| masculine singular | feminine singular | plural | |
|---|---|---|---|
| mon | ma | mes | *my* |
| ton | ta | tes | *your* (fam. and sing.) |
| son | sa | ses | *his, her, its* |
| notre | notre | nos | *our* |
| votre | votre | vos | *your* (form. or pl.) |
| leur | leur | leurs | *their* |

*C'est ta sœur?*
*Ce sont tes parents?*

*Voilà vos photos.*

- Possessive adjectives are always placed before the nouns they modify.

| C'est **ton** père? | Non, c'est **mon** oncle. |
|---|---|
| *Is that your father?* | *No, that's my uncle.* |

- In French, unlike English, possessive adjectives agree in gender and number with the nouns they modify.

| **mon** frère | **ma** sœur | **mes** grands-parents |
|---|---|---|
| *my brother* | *my sister* | *my grandparents* |

- Note that **notre, votre,** and **leur** agree in number only.

| **notre** neveu | **notre** famille | **nos** enfants |
|---|---|---|
| *our nephew* | *our family* | *our children* |
| **leur** cousin | **leur** cousine | **leurs** cousins |
| *their cousin* | *their cousin* | *their cousins* |

- The masculine singular forms **mon, ton,** and **son** are used with feminine singular nouns that begin with a vowel sound.

| **mon** amie | **ton** étudiante | **son** histoire |
|---|---|---|
| *my friend* | *your student* | *his story* |

**1 Complétez** Complete the sentences with the correct possessive adjectives.

1. ____Ma____ (*My*) sœur est très patiente.
2. Marc et Julien adorent ____leurs____ (*their*) cours de philosophie et de maths.
3. Nadine et Gisèle, qui est ____votre____ (*your*) amie?
4. C'est une belle photo de ____leur____ (*their*) grand-mère.
5. Est-ce que tu as ____ta____ (*your*) montre?
6. Nous voyageons en France avec ____nos____ (*our*) enfants.
7. Est-ce que tu travailles beaucoup sur ____ton____ (*your*) ordinateur?
8. ____Ses____ (*Her*) cousins habitent à Paris.
9. J'aime bien ____son____ (*his*) livre, il est très intéressant.
10. Bonjour, M. Martin. Comment sont ____vos____ (*your*) élèves cette année?

**2 Identifiez** Identify the owner of each object.

**MODÈLE**
*Ce sont les cahiers de Sophie.*

**Sophie**

**Christophe**
1. C'est la télévision de Christophe.

**Virginie**
4. Ce sont les stylos de Virginie.

**Paul**
2. C'est l'ordinateur de Paul.

**Jacqueline**
5. C'est l'université de Jacqueline.

**Stéphanie**
3. C'est la calculatrice de Stéphanie.

**Christine**
6. Ce sont les dictionnaires de Christine.

 Practice more at **daccord1.vhlcentral.com.**

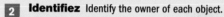

## COMMUNICATION

**3** **Ma famille** Use these cues to interview as many classmates as you can to learn about their family members. Then, tell the class what you found out.

Answers will vary.

**MODÈLE**

mère / parler / espagnol
**Élève 1:** Est-ce que ta mère parle espagnol?
**Élève 2:** Oui, ma mère parle espagnol.

1. sœur / travailler / en Californie
   _____

2. frère / être / célibataire
   _____

3. neveux / avoir / un chien
   _____

4. cousin / voyager / beaucoup
   _____

5. père / adorer / les ordinateurs
   _____

6. parents / être / divorcés
   _____

7. tante / avoir / les yeux marron
   _____

8. grands-parents / habiter / en Floride
   _____

**4** **Portrait de famille** In groups of three, take turns describing your family. Listen carefully to your partners' descriptions without taking notes. After everyone has spoken, two of you describe the other's family to see how well you remember. Answers will vary.

**MODÈLE**

**Élève 1:** Ma mère est timide et elle a les cheveux châtains.
**Élève 2:** Sa mère est sociable.
**Élève 3:** Sa mère est blonde.
**Élève 1:** Mais non! Ma mère est timide et elle a les cheveux châtains.

---

- The choice of **son**, **sa**, and **ses** depends on the gender and number of the noun possessed, not the gender and number of the owner. Context usually makes the meaning clear.

  **son** frère = *his/her brother*
  **sa** sœur = *his/her sister*
  **ses** parents = *his/her parents*

### Possession with *de*

- In English, you use *'s* to express relationships or ownership. In French, use **de (d')** + [*the noun or proper name*] instead.

  C'est le petit ami **d'Élisabeth**.        C'est le petit ami **de ma sœur**.
  *That's Élisabeth's boyfriend.*        *That's my sister's boyfriend.*

- When the preposition **de** is followed by the definite articles **le** and **les**, they contract to form **du** and **des**, respectively. There is no contraction when **de** is followed by **la** and **l'**.

  de + le ▶ du        de + les ▶ des

  L'opinion **du** grand-père        La fille **des** voisins a
  est importante.        les cheveux châtains.
  *The grandfather's opinion*        *The neighbors' daughter*
  *is important.*        *has brown hair.*

On peut regarder des photos de ma tante?

Sophie, c'est la nièce de Valérie.

---

**Essayez!** Provide the appropriate form of each possessive adjective.

**mon, ma, mes**

1. _mon_ livre
2. _ma_ librairie
3. _mes_ professeurs

**ton, ta, tes**

4. _tes_ ordinateurs
5. _ta_ télévision
6. _ton_ stylo

**son, sa, ses**

7. _sa_ table
8. _ses_ problèmes
9. _son_ école

**notre, nos**

10. _notre_ cahier
11. _nos_ études
12. _notre_ bourse

**votre, vos**

13. _vos_ soirées
14. _votre_ lycée
15. _vos_ devoirs

**leur, leurs**

16. _leur_ résultat
17. _leur_ classe
18. _leurs_ notes

---

**Essayez!** Have students create sentences using these phrases. Examples: **C'est mon livre. Mes professeurs sont patients.**

**1 Suggestion** To check answers, call on volunteers to read the completed sentences aloud.

**1 Expansion** For additional practice, give students these items. **11. Est-ce que _____** (*your, form.*) **famille est française? (votre) 12. _____** (*My*) **femme est italienne. (Ma) 13. _____** (*Our*) **professeur est américain. (Notre) 14. Est-ce que _____** (*her*) **cousins sont espagnols? (ses) 15. _____** (*Their*) **parents sont canadiens. (Leurs) 16. _____** (*Your, fam.*) **amis sont anglais? (Tes)**

**2 Suggestion** Have students work in pairs. Tell them to take turns identifying the owners of the items.

**2 Expansion** To reinforce the relationship between possessive adjectives and possession with **de**, have students restate the answers using **son**, **sa**, or **ses**. Example: **C'est sa télévision.**

**3 Suggestion** Have two volunteers read the **modèle**. Explain to students that they use the cues to create the questions.

**3 Expansion** To practice asking questions with the formal *you* forms, tell students that they are going to interview the head of the Foreign Language Department about his or her family. Then have students restate the questions.

**4 Suggestion** Before students begin the activity, tell them to make a list of the family members they plan to describe. Call on three volunteers to read the **modèle**. Explain that one student will describe his or her own family (using **mon**, **ma**, **mes**) and then the other two will describe the first student's family (using **son**, **sa**, **ses**).

---

**Role-playing** To practice plural possessive adjectives, have pairs describe the family on pages 74–75 from the point of view of Luc and Hélène Garneau. Encourage them to include descriptive adjectives and be creative in their sentences. You might want to introduce the term **les arrière-petits-enfants** (*great-grandchildren*) for this activity. Examples: **Juliette et Marc sont nos enfants. Juliette est blonde,**

**mais Marc est brun. Juliette et son époux, Robert, ont trois enfants. Leurs enfants s'appellent Véronique, Guillaume et Marie.**

**Interviewing** To practice **votre** and **vos**, have students ask you questions about your family. Examples: **Comment s'appellent vos parents? Est-ce que vous avez des enfants? Comment s'appellent-ils? Est-ce que vous avez des neveux ou des nièces? Comment s'appellent-ils?**

# SYNTHÈSE
# Révision

**1** **Suggestion** You may also do this activity with the whole class using **Overhead #21**. Have two students do the **modèle** beforehand. The first student will read **Élève 1**. The second student [**Élève 2**] will point to the people on the overhead as he or she states the relationship.

**2** **Suggestion** Have students brainstorm a list of adjectives that describe personality traits and write them on the board.

**3** **Suggestion** Before students begin the activity, show them pictures of the families listed for identification purposes. You might also wish to add a few names. Examples: **la famille Noah, la famille Bush, la famille Clinton, la famille Soprano, la famille Skywalker,** or **la famille Barone.**

**4** **Expansion** Do a class survey to find out how many students think a large or small family is ideal and the ideal number of children. Ask: **La famille idéale est grande? Petite? Combien d'enfants a la famille idéale? Un? Deux? Trois? Plus?** Tally the results.

**5** **Suggestion** Before students begin the activity, have two volunteers read the **modèle**. Make sure students understand that **Élève 1** is the agent and **Élève 2** is the casting director. Then ask students to describe the family in the comedy. Example: **Comment est le fils? (Il est brun et grand.)**

**6** **Suggestion** Divide the class into pairs and distribute the Info Gap Handouts on the Supersite for this activity.

**6** **Expansion** Ask students questions based on the artwork. Examples: **Le grand-père est-il grand? Les filles sont-elles heureuses?**

---

**1** **Expliquez** In pairs, take turns randomly calling out one person from column A and one from column B. Your partner will explain how they are related. Answers will vary.

**MODÈLE**
**Élève 1:** *ta sœur et ta mère*
**Élève 2:** *Ma sœur est la fille de ma mère.*

| A | B |
|---|---|
| 1. sœur | a. cousine |
| 2. tante | b. mère |
| 3. cousins | c. grand-père |
| 4. frère | d. neveux |
| 5. père | e. oncle |

**2** **Les yeux de ma mère** List seven physical or personality traits that you share with other members of your family. Be specific. Then, in pairs, compare your lists and be ready to present your partner's list to the class. Answers will vary.

**MODÈLE**
**Élève 1:** *J'ai les yeux bleus de mon père et je suis fier/fière comme mon grand-père.*
**Élève 2:** *Moi, je suis impatient(e) comme ma mère.*

**3** **Les familles célèbres** In groups of four, play a guessing game. Imagine that you belong to one of these famous families or one of your choice. Start describing your new family to your partners. The first person who guesses which family you are describing and where you fit in is the winner. He or she should describe another family. Answers will vary.

> La famille Adams
> La famille Griswold
> La famille Kennedy
> La famille Osborne
> La famille Simpson

**4** **La famille idéale** Walk around the room to survey your classmates. Ask them to describe their ideal family. Record their answers. Then, in pairs, compare your results. Answers will vary.

**MODÈLE**
**Élève 1:** *Comment est ta famille idéale?*
**Élève 2:** *Ma famille idéale est petite, avec deux enfants et beaucoup de chiens et de chats.*

**5** **Le casting** A casting director is on the phone with an agent to find actors for a new comedy about a strange family. In pairs, act out their conversation and find an actor to play each character, based on these illustrations. Answers will vary.

**MODÈLE**
**Élève 1 (agent):** *Pour la mère, il y a Émilie. Elle est rousse et elle a les cheveux courts.*
**Élève 2 (casting director):** *Ah, non. La mère est brune et elle a les cheveux longs. Avez-vous une actrice brune?*

La famille

le fils   la fille   le père   la mère   le cousin

Les acteurs et les actrices

Michelle   Patrick
Annick
Julie

Laurent

Émilie

Stéphane   Robert

**6** **Les différences** Your teacher will give you and a partner each a similar drawing of a family. Identify and name the six differences between your picture and your partner's.

**MODÈLE**
**Élève 1:** *La mère est blonde.*
**Élève 2:** *Non, la mère est brune.*

**ressources**

| CE pp. 31-34 | CA pp. 29-30, 133-134 | S daccord1.vhlcentral.com |
|---|---|---|

---

**OPTIONS**

**Mini-dictée** Use this paragraph as a dictation. Read each sentence twice, pausing to give students time to write.
**Ma famille est très grande. Mes parents sont divorcés. Mon beau-père a une fille. La mère de mon demi-frère cadet est française. Leur père est américain. Leurs enfants sont franco-américains. Ma demi-sœur et son frère sont blonds,** **grands et beaux. Il y a aussi ma sœur aînée. Elle est jolie et de taille moyenne. Notre mère est très fière.**

Call on volunteers to write the sentences on the board. Then ask students to draw a family tree based on this description. You can also ask a few comprehension questions. Examples: **Combien de filles a son beau-père? (Il a une fille.) Qui est franco-américain? (la demi-sœur et le demi-frère)**

**Video: TV Clip**

# Le Zapping

## Pages d'Or

The **Pages d'Or** (*Golden Pages*) of Belgium offer a range of services that connect businesses with potential customers. In addition to the traditional printed telephone book, the **Pages d'Or** use technology to reach a wide customer base. The **Pages d'Or** website, listings on CD-ROM or DVD, and digital television allow consumers to find businesses quickly for the services they need.

—Papa, combien tu m'aimes?

—Pour toi, je décrocherais° la Lune°.

**Pages d'Or**
www.pagesdor.be

**Compréhension** Answer these questions. Some answers will vary.

1. Qui (*Who*) sont les deux personnes dans la publicité (*ad*)? C'est un père et son fils.
2. Pourquoi l'homme téléphone-t-il pour obtenir une grue (*crane*)? Il aime beaucoup son fils.
3. Comment trouve-t-il le numéro de téléphone? Il cherche dans les Pages d'Or.

**Discussion** In groups of three, discuss the answers to these questions. Answers will vary.

1. Pourquoi est-il facile de trouver un numéro de téléphone aujourd'hui? Comment le faites-vous?
2. Employez le vocabulaire de cette leçon pour décrire les parents idéaux.

**décrocherais** *would take down* **Lune** *Moon*

 Practice more at **daccord1.vhlcentral.com**.

## Section Goals

In this section, students will:
- read about the **Pages d'Or** of Belgium
- watch a commercial for their information services
- answer questions about the commercial and the **Pages d'Or**

## Key Standards

**1.2, 2.2, 4.2, 5.2**

**Student Resources**
Supersite: Video, Activities
**Teacher Resources**
Video Script & Translation; Supersite: Video

**Introduction**
Have students compare and contrast the **Pages d'Or** to the Yellow Pages. Have them visit each company's website and ask them to compare the range of services each offers.

**Avant de regarder la vidéo**
- Have students look at the video stills, read the captions, and predict what is happening in the commercial for each visual. **(1. Le petit garçon parle à son père. Le père écoute son fils. 2. Le garçon regarde la Lune. Il est heureux.)**
- Before showing the video, explain to students that they do not need to understand every word they hear. Tell them to listen for the text in the captions and for cognates or any familiar words from this lesson.

**Compréhension** Have students work in pairs or groups for this activity. Tell them to write their answers. Then show the video again so that they can check their answers and add any missing information.

**Discussion**
- Ask volunteers to share their group's answers to the first item with the class.
- Write on the board the students' descriptions of the ideal parents. Determine the three most common answers and discuss why it is so important for a good parent to have these particular skills.

**Les Pages d'Or** Obtaining a business telephone listing has come a long way since the printed phone book. The **Pages d'Or** website offers customers an attractive and user-friendly interface for finding a specific number, of course. However, its services go a great deal beyond that. Depending on the time of year, for instance, the site might provide lists of seasonal tasks that people typically need to accomplish around that time. A selection of categories not only reminds the user that it is spring and time to plant a new garden, but also provides links to business throughout Belgium for starting the job.

**O P T I O N S**

## Section Goals

In this section, students will learn and practice vocabulary related to:
- professions and occupations
- character traits and some emotional states

## Key Standards

1.1, 1.2, 4.1

**Student Resources**
*Cahier d'exercices*, pp. 35-36;
*Cahier d'activités*, p. 135;
Supersite: Activities,
*Cahier interactif*

**Teacher Resources**
Answer Keys; Overhead #23;
Audio Script; Textbook & Audio Activity MP3s/CD; Testing program: Vocabulary Quiz

## Suggestions

- Use magazine pictures to introduce occupations. As you show each picture identify the occupation and write it on the board. Example: **Il/Elle est architecte.**
- To introduce the adjectives, pantomime the emotions or character traits using facial expressions and/or body language. Example: **Je suis triste.** (Make a sad face.) Then ask a few students if they feel or are the same way. Example: ____, **êtes-vous triste aujourd'hui?**
- Point out that **paresseux** and **travailleur** follow the patterns of **généreux** and **coiffeur**, respectively, to form the feminine **paresseuse** and **travailleuse**.
- Point out that the masculine noun **médecin** is also used to refer to a female doctor. The expression **une femme médecin** is also common.
- Project **Overhead #23.** Ask students yes/no or either/or questions using the new vocabulary. Examples: **Est-ce que la petite fille est drôle? (Non, elle n'est pas drôle.) Le petit garçon est-il heureux ou triste? (Il est triste.)**

---

**Leçon 3B**

Talking Picture
Audio: Activity

**You will learn how to...**
- describe people
- talk about occupations

# Comment sont-ils?

Il est fort.

Il est rapide.

Il est travailleur.

Ils sont paresseux.

discrète (discret *m.*)

fatiguée (fatigué *m.*)

jaloux (jalouse *f.*)

inquiète (inquiet *m.*)

triste

### Vocabulaire

| | |
|---|---|
| actif/active | active |
| antipathique | unpleasant |
| courageux/courageuse | courageous, brave |
| cruel(le) | cruel |
| doux/douce | sweet; soft |
| ennuyeux/ennuyeuse | boring |
| étranger/étrangère | foreign |
| faible | weak |
| favori(te) | favorite |
| fou/folle | crazy |
| généreux/généreuse | generous |
| génial(e) (géniaux *pl.*) | great |
| gentil(le) | nice |
| lent(e) | slow |
| méchant(e) | mean |
| modeste | modest, humble |
| pénible | tiresome |
| prêt(e) | ready |
| sportif/sportive | athletic |
| | |
| un(e) architecte | architect |
| un(e) artiste | artist |
| un(e) athlète | athlete |
| un(e) avocat(e) | lawyer |
| un(e) dentiste | dentist |
| un homme/une femme d'affaires | businessman/woman |
| un ingénieur | engineer |
| un(e) journaliste | journalist |
| un médecin | doctor |

**ressources**

CE pp. 35-36

CA p. 135

S daccord1.vhlcentral.com

**88** *quatre-vingt-huit*

---

**OPTIONS**

**Using Games** Have students play a miming game in groups of four or five. Tell them that each person should think of an adjective presented in this lesson and act out the word. The first person to guess correctly acts out the next one. Example: **Es-tu fatigué(e)?** Then have each group pick out the best mime. Ask students to act out their mimes while the class guesses what they are doing.

**Word Association** Say the French term for a profession, for example, **un médecin**. Tell students to write down as many words as possible, especially the new adjectives, that they associate with this job. Then call on volunteers to read their lists as you write the words on the board, or have students compare their lists in pairs.

# Mise en pratique

la coiffeuse
(coiffeur *m.*)

Il est drôle.

## 1  Les célébrités  Match these famous people with their professions. Not all of the professions will be used.

| h | 1. Donald Trump | a. médecin |
|---|---|---|
| e | 2. Claude Monet | b. journaliste |
| d | 3. Paul Mitchell | c. musicien(ne) |
| a | 4. Dr. Phil C. McGraw | d. coiffeur/coiffeuse |
| i | 5. Serena Williams | e. artiste |
| b | 6. Katie Couric | f. architecte |
| c | 7. Beethoven | g. avocat(e) |
| f | 8. Frank Lloyd Wright | h. homme/femme d'affaires |
| | | i. athlète |
| | | j. dentiste |

## 2  Les contraires  Complete each sentence with the opposite adjective.

1. Ma grand-mère n'est pas cruelle, elle est __douce/gentille__.
2. Mon frère n'est pas travailleur, il est __paresseux__.
3. Mes cousines ne sont pas faibles, elles sont __fortes__.
4. Ma tante n'est pas drôle, elle est __ennuyeuse__.
5. Mon oncle est un bon athlète. Il n'est pas lent, il est __rapide__.
6. Ma famille et moi, nous ne sommes pas antipathiques, nous sommes __sympathiques__.
7. Mes parents ne sont pas méchants, ils sont __gentils/doux__.
8. Mon oncle n'est pas heureux, il est __triste__.

## 3  Écoutez 🎧  You will hear descriptions of three people. Listen carefully and indicate whether the statements about them are **vrai** or **faux**.

**Nora**        **Ahmed**        **Françoise**

| | Vrai | Faux |
|---|---|---|
| 1. L'architecte aime le sport. | ☐ | ☑ |
| 2. L'artiste est paresseuse. | ☐ | ☑ |
| 3. L'artiste aime son travail. | ☑ | ☐ |
| 4. Ahmed est médecin. | ☐ | ☑ |
| 5. Françoise est gentille. | ☑ | ☐ |
| 6. Nora est avocate. | ☐ | ☑ |
| 7. Nora habite au Québec. | ☐ | ☑ |
| 8. Ahmed est travailleur. | ☑ | ☐ |
| 9. Françoise est mère de famille. | ☑ | ☐ |
| 10. Ahmed habite avec sa femme. | ☐ | ☑ |

Practice more at **daccord1.vhlcentral.com**.

un musicien
(musicienne *f.*)

---

**1 Suggestion**  To check students' answers, tell them to form complete sentences using the verb **être**. Example: **Donald Trump est un homme d'affaires.** You might also have them include the person's nationality. Example: **Claude Monet est un artiste français.**

**1 Expansion**  Have students provide additional names of famous people for each profession listed. Example: **Henri Matisse est un artiste.**

**2 Expansion**  Ask students to write two more fill-in-the-blank statements modeled on the activity. Then have them exchange papers with a classmate and complete the sentences.

**3 Script**  NORA: Moi, c'est Nora. J'ai 27 ans. Je suis artiste. Je suis mexicaine et j'habite à Paris. Je ne suis pas paresseuse. Je suis active, sportive et sympa. J'adore les animaux et l'art, bien sûr!
AHMED: Moi, je m'appelle Ahmed. J'ai 30 ans. Je suis architecte. Je suis discret, travailleur et un peu jaloux. Je ne suis pas sportif; je trouve le sport ennuyeux. J'habite avec mes parents au Québec.
FRANÇOISE: Moi, c'est Françoise. J'ai 51 ans. Je suis médecin. Je suis généreuse et gentille. Je travaille dans un hôpital. J'ai deux enfants, une fille et un fils. Les deux sont étudiants à l'université.
*(On Textbook Audio)*

**3 Suggestions**
• Before students begin the activity, have them describe the people in the photos.
• To check students' answers, call on volunteers to read the sentences and answers.

---

OPTIONS

**Using Games**  Divide the class into two teams. Indicate one team member at a time, alternating between teams. Give a certain form of an adjective and name another form which the team member should say. Example: **fou**; feminine singular (**folle**). Give a point for each correct answer. Deduct a point for each wrong answer. The team with the most points at the end of the game wins.

**Using Categories**  Have students work in groups of three. Tell them to decide which of the character traits presented in **Contextes** are positive qualities and which ones are negative or undesirable qualities. Have groups list the adjectives under the headings **Qualités** and **Défauts**.

# Communication

**4** **Les professions** In pairs, say what the real professions of these people are. Alternate reading and answering the questions.

**MODÈLE**
**Élève 1:** *Est-ce que Sabine et Sarah sont femmes d'affaires?*
**Élève 2:** *Non, elles sont avocates.*

1. Est-ce que Louis est architecte?
Non, il est dentiste.

2. Est-ce que Jean est professeur?
Non, il est coiffeur.

3. Est-ce que Juliette est ingénieur?
Non, elle est journaliste.

4. Est-ce que Charles est médecin?
Non, il est homme d'affaires.

5. Est-ce que Pauline est musicienne?
Non, elle est architecte.

6. Est-ce que Jacques et Brigitte sont avocats?
Non, ils sont athlètes.

7. Est-ce qu'Édouard est dentiste?
Non, il est artiste.

8. Est-ce que Martine et Sophie sont dentistes?
Non, elles sont musiciennes.

**5** **Conversez** Interview a classmate. Your partner should answer **pourquoi** questions with  **parce que** (*because*). Answers will vary.

1. Quel âge ont tes parents? Comment sont-ils?
2. Quelle est la profession de tes parents?
3. Qui est ton/ta cousin(e) préféré(e)? Pourquoi?
4. Qui n'est pas ton/ta cousin(e) préféré(e)? Pourquoi?
5. As-tu des animaux de compagnie (*pets*)? Quel est ton animal de compagnie favori? Pourquoi?
6. Qui est ton professeur préféré? Pourquoi?
7. Qui est gentil dans la classe?
8. Quelles professions aimes-tu?

**6** **Les petites annonces** Write a **petite annonce** (*personal ad*) where you describe yourself and your ideal significant other. Include details such as profession, age, physical characteristics, and personality, both for yourself and for the person you hope reads the ad. Your teacher will post the ads. In groups, take turns reading them and then vote for the most interesting one. Answers will vary.

**7** **Quelle surprise!** You run into your best friend from high school ten years after you graduated and want to know what his or her life is like today. With a partner, prepare a conversation where you: Answers will vary.

• greet each other
• ask each other's ages
• ask what each other's professions are
• ask about marital status and for a description of your significant others
• ask if either of you have children, and if so, for a description of them

# Les sons et les lettres  Audio: Concepts, Activities Record & Compare

🎧 L'accent circonflexe, la cédille, and le tréma

L'accent circonflexe (^) can appear over any vowel.

| pâté | prêt | aîné | drôle | croûton |

L'accent circonflexe is also used to distinguish between words with similar spellings but different meanings.

| **mûr** | **mur** | **sûr** | **sur** |
|---------|---------|---------|---------|
| *ripe* | *wall* | *sure* | *on* |

L'accent circonflexe indicates that a letter, frequently an **s**, has been dropped from an older spelling. For this reason, **l'accent circonflexe** can be used to identify French cognates of English words.

*hospital* → h**ô**pital          *forest* → for**ê**t

La cédille ( ¸ ) is only used with the letter **c**. A **c** with a **cédille** is pronounced with a soft **c** sound, like the *s* in the English word *yes*. Use a **cédille** to retain the soft **c** sound before an **a**, **o**, or **u**. Before an **e** or an **i**, the letter **c** is always soft, so a **cédille** is not necessary.

| gar**ç**on | fran**ç**ais | **ç**a | le**ç**on |

Le tréma ( ¨ ) is used to indicate that two vowel sounds are pronounced separately. It is always placed over the second vowel.

| égo**ï**ste | na**ï**ve | No**ë**l | Ha**ï**ti |

🔊 **Prononcez** Practice saying these words aloud.

1. naïf      3. châtain    5. français    7. théâtre    9. égoïste
2. reçu      4. âge        6. fenêtre     8. garçon     10. château

🔊 **Articulez** Practice saying these sentences aloud.

1. Comment ça va?
2. Comme ci, comme ça.
3. Vous êtes française, Madame?
4. C'est un garçon cruel et égoïste.
5. J'ai besoin d'être reçu à l'examen.
6. Caroline, ma sœur aînée, est très drôle.

🔊 **Dictons** Practice reading these sayings aloud.

Impossible n'est pas français.[1]

Plus ça change, plus c'est la même chose.[2]

[1] There's no such thing as "can't". (lit. Impossible is not French.)
[2] The more things change, the more they stay the same.

ressources

CA p. 136

daccord1.vhlcentral.com

*quatre-vingt-onze* **91**

# ROMAN-PHOTO

## On travaille chez moi!

 **Video:** *Roman-photo* Record & Compare

## Section Goals

In this section, students will learn through comprehensible input functional phrases for making complaints, expressing location, and reading numbers.

## Key Standards

1.2, 2.1, 2.2, 4.1, 4.2

**Student Resources**
*Cahier d'activités*, pp. 77-78;
Supersite: Activities,
*Cahier interactif*
**Teacher Resources**
Answer Keys; Video Script & Translation; *Roman-photo* video

## Video Recap: Leçon 3A

Before doing this **Roman-photo**, review the previous one with this activity.

**1. Qui a un ami Cyberhomme sur Internet? (Amina)**

**2. Pourquoi est-ce que Valérie est très inquiète? (Parce que Stéphane ne travaille pas pour le bac.)**

**3. Qu'est-ce que Stéphane, Valérie et Amina regardent sur l'ordinateur portable? (les photos de la famille de Valérie et de Stéphane)**

**4. Qui travaille avec Stéphane pour préparer le bac? (Rachid)**

## Video Synopsis

In the café, Sandrine searches frantically for her ringing cell phone, only to find that Stéphane is playing a joke on her. Rachid and Stéphane leave to go study. At Rachid's and David's apartment, Stéphane and Rachid complain about how tiresome it is to hear David constantly talk about Sandrine. They also look at photos of Rachid's parents. Finally, they start studying math. Stéphane says he wants to be an architect.

## Suggestions

• Have students scan the captions under the video stills and find four phrases with descriptive adjectives and two that mention professions.

• Have the class read through the scenes that correspond to video stills 1–4 with volunteers playing character roles. Then have small groups read scenes 5–10.

• Have students locate **Algérie** on the world map in **Appendice A**.

**PERSONNAGES**

**Amina**

**David**

**Rachid**

**Sandrine**

**Stéphane**

**Valérie**

**SANDRINE** Alors, Rachid, où est David?

*Un portable sonne (a cell phone rings)...*

**VALÉRIE** Allô.

**RACHID** Allô.

**AMINA** Allô.

**SANDRINE** C'est Pascal! Je ne trouve pas mon téléphone!

**AMINA** Il n'est pas dans ton sac à dos?

**SANDRINE** Non!

**RACHID** Ben, il est sous tes cahiers.

**SANDRINE** Non plus!

**AMINA** Il est peut-être derrière ton livre... ou à gauche.

**SANDRINE** Mais non! Pas derrière! Pas à gauche! Pas à droite! Et pas devant!

**RACHID** Non! Il est là... sur la table. Mais non! La table à côté de la porte.

**SANDRINE** Ce n'est pas vrai! Ce n'est pas Pascal! Numéro de téléphone 06.62.70.94.87. Mais qui est-ce?

**DAVID** Sandrine? Elle est au café?

**RACHID** Oui... pourquoi?

**DAVID** Ben, j'ai besoin d'un bon café, oui, d'un café très fort. D'un espresso! À plus tard!

**RACHID** Tu sais, David, lui aussi, est pénible. Il parle de Sandrine. Sandrine, Sandrine, Sandrine.

**RACHID ET STÉPHANE** C'est barbant!

**STÉPHANE** C'est ta famille? C'est où?

**RACHID** En Algérie, l'année dernière chez mes grands-parents. Le reste de ma famille — mes parents, mes sœurs et mon frère, habitent à Marseille.

**STÉPHANE** C'est ton père, là?

**RACHID** Oui. Il est médecin. Il travaille beaucoup.

**RACHID** Et là, c'est ma mère. Elle, elle est avocate. Elle est très active... et très travailleuse aussi.

**ACTIVITÉS**

**1** **Identifiez** Indicate which character would make each statement. The names may be used more than once. Write **D** for David, **R** for Rachid, **S** for Sandrine, and **St** for Stéphane.

1. J'ai envie d'être architecte. _____St_____

2. Numéro de téléphone 06.62.70.94.87. _____S_____

3. David est un colocataire pénible. _____R_____

4. Stéphane! Tu n'es pas drôle! _____S_____

5. Que c'est ennuyeux! _____St_____

6. On travaille chez moi! _____R_____

7. Sandrine, elle est tellement pénible. _____St_____

8. Sandrine? Elle est au café? _____D_____

9. J'ai besoin d'un café très fort. _____D_____

10. C'est pour ça qu'on prépare le bac. _____R_____

**S** Practice more at **daccord1.vhlcentral.com**.

**OPTIONS**

**Avant de regarder la vidéo** Write the episode title **On travaille chez moi!** on the board and have students guess its meaning. Then ask them to predict who might say this phrase in the video and to explain their reasons. Also ask them to guess in what context or situation the person might say this phrase.

**Regarder la vidéo** Show the video episode and have students give you a play-by-play description of the action. Write their descriptions on the board. Then show the episode again so students can add more details to the description.

Sandrine perd (*loses*) son téléphone.
Rachid aide Stéphane à préparer le bac.

**STÉPHANE** Qui est-ce? C'est moi!

**SANDRINE** Stéphane! Tu n'es pas drôle!

**AMINA** Oui, Stéphane. C'est cruel.

**STÉPHANE** C'est génial...

**RACHID** Bon, tu es prêt? On travaille chez moi!

*À l'appartement de Rachid et de David...*

**STÉPHANE** Sandrine, elle est tellement pénible. Elle parle de Pascal, elle téléphone à Pascal... Pascal, Pascal, Pascal! Que c'est ennuyeux!

**RACHID** Moi aussi, j'en ai marre.

**STÉPHANE** Avocate? Moi, j'ai envie d'être architecte.

**RACHID** Architecte? Alors, c'est pour ça qu'on prépare le bac.

*Rachid et Stéphane au travail...*

**RACHID** Allez, si *x* égale 83 et *y* égale 90, la réponse, c'est...

**STÉPHANE** Euh... 100?

**RACHID** Oui! Bravo!

---

## Expressions utiles

### Making complaints

- **Sandrine, elle est tellement pénible.**
  *Sandrine is so tiresome.*
- **J'en ai marre.**
  *I'm fed up.*
- **Tu sais, David, lui aussi, est pénible.**
  *You know, David, he's tiresome, too.*
- **C'est barbant!/C'est la barbe!**
  *What a drag!*

### Reading numbers

- **Numéro de téléphone 06.62.70.94.87 (zéro six, soixante-deux, soixante-dix, quatre-vingt-quatorze, quatre-vingt-sept).**
  *Phone number 06.62.70.94.87.*
- **Si *x* égale 83 (quatre-vingt-trois) et *y* égale 90 (quatre-vingt-dix)...**
  *If x equals 83 and y equals 90...*
- **La réponse, c'est 100 (cent).**
  *The answer is 100.*

### Expressing location

- **Où est le téléphone de Sandrine?**
  *Where is Sandrine's telephone?*
- **Il n'est pas dans son sac à dos.**
  *It's not in her backpack.*
- **Il est sous ses cahiers.**
  *It's under her notebooks.*
- **Il est derrière son livre, pas devant.**
  *It's behind her book, not in front.*
- **Il est à droite ou à gauche?**
  *Is it to the right or to the left?*
- **Il est sur la table à côté de la porte.**
  *It's on the table next to the door.*

---

---

**2** **Vocabulaire** Refer to the video stills and dialogues to match these people and objects with their locations.

<u>a/c/e</u> 1. sur la table     a. le téléphone de Sandrine

<u>a</u> 2. pas sous les cahiers     b. Sandrine

<u>b/c/e</u> 3. devant Rachid     c. l'ordinateur de Rachid

<u>b</u> 4. au café     d. la famille de Rachid

<u>a/f</u> 5. à côté de la porte     e. le café de Rachid

<u>d</u> 6. en Algérie     f. la table

**3** **Écrivez** In pairs, write a brief description in French of one of the video characters. Do not mention the character's name. Describe his or her personality traits, physical characteristics, and career path. Be prepared to read your description aloud to your classmates, who will guess the identity of the character.

ressources

CA pp. 77–78

daccord1.vhlcentral.com

**A C T I V I T É S**

---

**OPTIONS**

**Using Visuals** To practice the terms **à droite** and **à gauche**, ask students to describe the people's positions in reference to each other in the video stills of the **Roman-photo**. Example: **1. Amina est à droite de Sandrine.**

**Mini-skit** Have groups create a short skit similar to the scenes in video stills 1–4 in which someone is searching for a lost object. Provide suggestions for objects. Examples: a notebook (**un cahier**), their homework (**leurs devoirs**), a calculator (**une calculatrice**), a dictionary (**un dictionnaire**), a pen (**un stylo**), and a pencil (**un crayon**). Give students ten minutes to prepare, then call on groups to act out their skits for the class.

# Section Goals

In this section, students will:
- learn to distinguish between different types of friendships
- learn some commonly used adjectives to describe people
- learn about some marriage traditions in the francophone world
- read about the Depardieu family

# Key Standards

2.1, 2.2, 3.1, 3.2, 4.2

Student Resources
Supersite: Activities
Teacher Resources
Answer Keys

**Culture à la loupe**

**Avant la lecture**
- Introduce the reading topic by asking: **Avez-vous beaucoup de copains? Combien d'amis avez-vous? De quoi parlez-vous avec vos copains? Et avec vos amis?**
- Have students look at the photos and describe the people.
- Tell students to scan the reading, identify the cognates, and guess their meanings.

**Lecture**
- Point out that **un(e) petit(e) ami(e)** is the main term for boyfriend and girlfriend, but **mon ami(e)** or **mon copain/ma copine** alone without **petit(e)** can also imply a romantic relationship.
- Tell students that it is not uncommon to hear people describe their significant others as **fiancé(e)** even if they are not officially engaged.

**Après la lecture**
- Have students classify the following people as **copains**, **amis**, **petits amis**, or **fiancés**.
  1. two classmates (**copains**) 2. an engaged couple (**fiancés**)
  3. two coworkers (**copains**) 4. you and your best friend (**ami[e]s**)
  5. a boyfriend and girlfriend in junior high (**petits amis**)
- Have students identify some differences in French and American dating customs. Ask: **Quelles sont les différences entre les coutumes françaises et américaines des jeunes couples?**

**1 Expansion** Have students write two more true/false statements. Then tell them to exchange their papers with a classmate and complete the activity.

## CULTURE À LA LOUPE

# L'amitié

**Quelle est la différence entre un copain et un ami? Un petit ami, qu'est-ce que c'est?** Avoir plus de copains que° d'amis, c'est normal. Des copains sont des personnes qu'on voit assez souvent°, comme° des gens de l'université ou du travail°, et avec qui on parle de sujets ordinaires. L'amitié° entre copains est souvent éphémère et n'est pas très profonde. D'habitude°, ils ne parlent pas de problèmes très personnels.

Par contre°, des amis parlent de choses plus importantes et plus intimes. L'amitié est plus profonde, solide et stable, même si° on ne voit pas ses amis très souvent. Un ami, c'est une personne très proche° qui vous écoute quand vous avez un problème.

Un(e) petit(e) ami(e) est une personne avec qui on a une relation très intime et établie°, basée sur l'amour. Les jeunes couples français sortent° souvent en groupe avec d'autres° couples plutôt que° seuls; même si un jeune homme et une jeune femme sortent ensemble°, normalement chaque personne paie sa part.

plus de... que *more... than* voit assez souvent *sees rather often* comme *such as* du travail *from work*
L'amitié *Friendship* D'habitude *Usually* Par contre *On the other hand* même si *even if* proche *close*
établie *established* sortent *go out* d'autres *other* plutôt que *rather than* ensemble *together*

### Coup de main

To ask *what is* or *what are*, you can use **quel** and a form of the verb **être**. The different forms of **quel** agree in gender and number with the nouns to which they refer:

**Quel/Quelle est...?**
*What is...?*

**Quels/Quelles sont...?**
*What are...?*

---

**ACTIVITÉS**

**1 Vrai ou faux?** Are these statements **vrai** or **faux**? Correct the false statements.

1. D'habitude, on a plus d'amis que de copains. Faux. On a plus de copains que d'amis.
2. Un copain est une personne qu'on ne voit pas souvent. Faux. C'est une personne qu'on voit souvent.
3. On parle de sujets intimes avec un copain. Faux. On parle de sujets ordinaires.
4. Un ami est une personne avec qui on a une relation très solide. Vrai.
5. Normalement, on ne parle pas de ses problèmes personnels avec ses copains. Vrai.

6. Un ami vous écoute quand vous avez un problème. Vrai.
7. L'amitié entre amis est plus profonde que l'amitié entre copains. Vrai.
8. En général, les jeunes couples français vont au café ou au cinéma en groupe. Vrai.
9. Un petit ami est comme un copain. Faux. Un petit ami est une personne avec qui on a une relation intime.
10. En France, les femmes ne paient pas quand elles sortent. Faux. Chaque personne paie sa part.

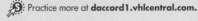 Practice more at **daccord1.vhlcentral.com.**

**OPTIONS**

**Using Categories** In small groups, have students draw a chart with three columns. Tell them to label the columns with the three main types of relationships between people: fellow students or coworkers (**les copains, les collègues**); intimate, platonic friends (**les amis**); and people that are boyfriend and girlfriend (**un[e] petit[e] ami[e]**). Then have students list at least five adjectives in each column in French that apply to the people in that type of relationship. Tell them that they can use adjectives from the reading or others that they know. Examples: **normal, ordinaire, intime, personnel, établi, profond, stable, solide,** and **éphémère.** When students have finished, ask different groups to read their lists of adjectives and compile the results on the board.

## LE FRANÇAIS QUOTIDIEN

### Pour décrire les gens

| | |
|---|---|
| **bête** | stupid |
| **borné(e)** | narrow-minded |
| **canon** | good-looking |
| **coincé(e)** | inhibited |
| **cool** | relaxed |
| **dingue** | crazy |
| **malin/maligne** | clever |
| **marrant(e)** | funny |
| **mignon(ne)** | cute |
| **zarbi** | weird |

## LE MONDE FRANCOPHONE

### Le mariage et les traditions

Voici des objets et traditions associés au mariage dans le monde francophone.

**En France** Les jeunes mariés boivent° dans une coupe de mariage°, un objet de famille°.

**En Belgique** Une femme, à l'occasion de son mariage, porte° le mouchoir° familial où son nom et le nom de toutes les femmes mariées de sa famille sont brodés°.

**Au Maroc** Les amies de la mariée lui appliquent° du henné sur les mains°.

**Au Québec** Les jeunes mariés et leurs invités boivent le caribou°.

**boivent** drink **dans une coupe de mariage** from an engraved, double-handled wedding goblet **objet de famille** family heirloom **porte** carries **mouchoir** handkerchief **brodés** embroidered **lui appliquent** apply **henné sur les mains** henna to the hands **caribou** red wine with whisky

## PORTRAIT

# Les Depardieu

**Gérard**

**Guillaume**

**Julie**

Les Depardieu sont une famille d'acteurs français. Gérard, le père, est l'acteur le plus célèbre° de France. Lauréat° de deux César°, un pour *Le Dernier Métro*° et l'autre° pour *Cyrano de Bergerac*, et d'un Golden Globe pour le film américain *Green Card*, il joue depuis plus de trente ans° et a tourné dans° plus de 120 (cent vingt) films. Sa fille, Julie, a aussi du succès dans la profession: elle a déjà° deux César et a joué° dans *Un long dimanche de fiançailles*°. Son fils, Guillaume (1971–2008), a joué dans beaucoup de films dont° *Tous les matins du monde*° avec son père. Les deux enfants ont joué avec leur père dans *Le Comte de Monte-Cristo*.

**le plus célèbre** most famous **Lauréat** Winner **César** César awards (the equivalent of the Oscars in France) **Le Dernier Métro** The Last Metro **l'autre** the other **Il joue depuis plus de trente ans** he has been acting for more than thirty years **a tourné dans** has been in **déjà** already **a joué** has acted **Un long dimanche de fiançailles** A Very Long Engagement **dont** including **Tous les matins du monde** All the Mornings of the World

### SUR INTERNET

Quand ils sortent (*go out*), où vont (*go*) les jeunes couples français?

Go to **daccord1.vhlcentral.com** to find more information related to this **CULTURE** section.

---

**2** **Les Depardieu** Complete these statements with the correct information.

1. Gérard Depardieu a joué dans plus de ___120___ films.
2. Guillaume était (*was*) ___le fils___ de Gérard Depardieu.
3. Julie est ___la fille___ de Gérard Depardieu.
4. Julie joue avec Gérard dans ___Le Comte de Monte-Cristo___.
5. Guillaume a joué avec Gérard dans ___Tous les matins du monde/___ ___Le Comte de Monte-Cristo___.
6. Julie a déjà ___deux___ César.

**3** **Comment sont-ils?** Look at the photos of the Depardieu family. With a partner, take turns describing each person in detail in French. How old do you think they are? What do you think their personalities are like? Do you see any family resemblances?

**ressources**

**S**

daccord1.vhlcentral.com

**A C T I V I T É S**

---

**Le mariage et les traditions** Here are some other wedding customs or traditions.

• In France, many couples have two wedding ceremonies on the same day. By law, there must be a civil ceremony, and it has to take place before any religious ceremony.

• A traditional Moroccan wedding ceremony lasts from four to seven days. After the couple exchanges vows, the bride walks around the exterior of her new home three times.

• In Belgium, wedding invitations are traditionally printed on two sheets of paper—one sheet is from the bride's family and the other sheet is from the groom's family. The two sheets of paper symbolize the union of two families.

---

**Le français quotidien** Have students work in pairs. Tell them to take turns describing their friends or classmates using these words.

**Portrait** Show the class a photo of Gérard Depardieu. Ask: **Qui est-ce? Comment s'appelle-t-il? Quelle est sa profession?** Repeat the questions with a photo of his son and/or daughter. Then ask students to name any movies starring one or more of the Depardieus that they have seen, for example, *Jean de Florette* (1986), *The Man in the Iron Mask* (1998), *Last Holiday* (2006), or one of the *Astérix* movies.

**Le monde francophone** Ask students which tradition they find most interesting. Then explain that not everyone in these countries follows these customs. As in the United States, the wedding traditions a couple chooses to follow often depend upon their religion. For example, a Jewish couple might observe Jewish traditions at their wedding, and an Algerian or Moroccan couple might follow Islamic traditions.

**2** **Expansion** To check students' answers, have them work in pairs. Tell students to take turns asking the questions that would elicit each statement and responding with the completed sentence.

**3** **Expansions**
• Give students these dates of birth and have them calculate each person's age: Gérard (1948), Julie (1973)
• You might want to tell students that Gérard was born in Châteauroux, France, and that Depardieu is a typical name from the center of France.
• In October 2008, Guillaume Depardieu passed away in France at the age of 37. He had contracted severe pneumonia in Romania on the set of a new film.

## Section Goals

In this section, students will learn numbers 61–100.

## Key Standards

4.1, 5.1

**Student Resources**
*Cahier d'exercices*, pp. 37–38;
*Cahier d'activités*, p. 137;
Supersite: Activities,
*Cahier interactif*

**Teacher Resources**
Answer Keys; Audio Script;
Audio Activity MP3s/CD; Testing
program: Grammar Quiz

## Suggestions

- Review numbers 0–20 by having the class count with you. Then have them count by tens to 60.
- Model the pronunciation of numbers 61–100 and have students repeat them.
- Explain that the numbers 70–99 follow a slightly different pattern than the numbers 21–69. Point out that 61 and 71 use the conjunction **et**, while 81 and 91 need hyphens.
- Write a few numbers on the board, such as 68, 72, 85, and 99. Have students say each number in French as you point to it. Then have students count by fives from 60–100.
- Numbers 101 and greater are presented in **Leçon 5B**.

**Essayez!** Have students write five more numbers between 61–100. Then tell them to get together with a classmate and take turns dictating their numbers to each other and writing them down. Remind students to check each other's answers.

# 3B.1 Numbers 61–100

### Numbers 61–100

**61–69**
61 soixante et un
62 soixante-deux
63 soixante-trois
64 soixante-quatre
65 soixante-cinq
66 soixante-six
67 soixante-sept
68 soixante-huit
69 soixante-neuf

**80–89**
80 quatre-vingts
81 quatre-vingt-un
82 quatre-vingt-deux
83 quatre-vingt-trois
84 quatre-vingt-quatre
85 quatre-vingt-cinq
86 quatre-vingt-six
87 quatre-vingt-sept
88 quatre-vingt-huit
89 quatre-vingt-neuf

**70–79**
70 soixante-dix
71 soixante et onze
72 soixante-douze
73 soixante-treize
74 soixante-quatorze
75 soixante-quinze
76 soixante-seize
77 soixante-dix-sept
78 soixante-dix-huit
79 soixante-dix-neuf

**90–100**
90 quatre-vingt-dix
91 quatre-vingt-onze
92 quatre-vingt-douze
93 quatre-vingt-treize
94 quatre-vingt-quatorze
95 quatre-vingt-quinze
96 quatre-vingt-seize
97 quatre-vingt-dix-sept
98 quatre-vingt-dix-huit
99 quatre-vingt-dix-neuf
100 cent

 **BOÎTE À OUTILS**
**STUDY TIP:** To say numbers **70–99**, remember the arithmetic behind them. For example, **quatre-vingt-douze (92)** is 4 (quatre) x 20 (vingt) + 12 (douze).

- Numbers that end in the digit **1** are not usually hyphenated. They use the conjunction **et** instead.

trente et un          cinquante et un          soixante et un

- Note that **81** and **91** are exceptions:

quatre-vingt-un          quatre-vingt-onze

- The number **quatre-vingts** ends in **-s**, but there is no **-s** when it is followed by another number.

quatre-vingts          quatre-vingt-cinq          quatre-vingt-dix-huit

### Essayez!   What are these numbers in French?

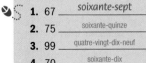

1. 67 _soixante-sept_
2. 75 _soixante-quinze_
3. 99 _quatre-vingt-dix-neuf_
4. 70 _soixante-dix_
5. 82 _quatre-vingt-deux_
6. 91 _quatre-vingt-onze_
7. 66 _soixante-six_
8. 87 _quatre-vingt-sept_
9. 52 _cinquante-deux_
10. 60 _soixante_

**96** *quatre-vingt-seize*

## MISE EN PRATIQUE

**1  Les numéros de téléphone** Write down these phone numbers, then read them aloud in French.

**MODÈLE**
C'est le zéro un, quarante-trois, soixante-quinze, quatre-vingt-trois, seize.
01.43.75.83.16

1. C'est le zéro deux, soixante-cinq, trente-trois, quatre-vingt-quinze, zéro six.
02.65.33.95.06

2. C'est le zéro un, quatre-vingt-dix-neuf, soixante-quatorze, quinze, vingt-cinq.
01.99.74.15.25

3. C'est le zéro cinq, soixante-cinq, onze, zéro huit, quatre-vingts.
05.65.11.08.80

4. C'est le zéro trois, quatre-vingt-dix-sept, soixante-dix-neuf, cinquante-quatre, vingt-sept.
03.97.79.54.27

5. C'est le zéro quatre, quatre-vingt-cinq, soixante-neuf, quatre-vingt-dix-neuf, quatre-vingt-onze.
04.85.69.99.91

6. C'est le zéro un, vingt-quatre, quatre-vingt-trois, zéro un, quatre-vingt-neuf.
01.24.83.01.89

**2  Les maths** Read these math problems aloud, then write out each answer in words.

**MODÈLE**
65 + 3 = _soixante-huit_
Soixante-cinq plus trois font (equals) soixante-huit.

1. 70 + 15 = quatre-vingt-cinq
2. 82 + 10 = quatre-vingt-douze
3. 76 + 3 = soixante-dix-neuf
4. 88 + 12 = cent
5. 40 + 27 = soixante-sept
6. 67 + 6 = soixante-treize
7. 43 + 54 = quatre-vingt-dix-sept
8. 78 + 5 = quatre-vingt-trois
9. 70 + 20 = quatre-vingt-dix
10. 64 + 16 = quatre-vingts

**3  Comptez** Read the following numbers aloud in French, then follow the pattern to provide the missing numbers.

1. 60, 62, 64, ... 80   66, 68, 70, 72, 74, 76, 78
2. 76, 80, 84, ... 100   88, 92, 96
3. 100, 95, 90, ... 60   85, 80, 75, 70, 65
4. 99, 96, 93, ... 69   90, 87, 84, 81, 78, 75, 72

Practice more at **daccord1.vhlcentral.com**.

**Using Games** Play a game of Bingo. Have students draw a square on a sheet of paper with three horizontal and three vertical rows. Tell them to write nine different numbers between 61–100 in the boxes. Explain that they should cross out the numbers as they hear them and that they should say "Bingo!" if they have three numbers in a horizontal, vertical, or diagonal row. Then call out numbers at random and write them down to verify.

**Using Movement** Assign ten students a number from 0–100 and line them up in front of the class. As you call out a number at random, that student should take a step forward. When two students have stepped forward, ask them to repeat their numbers. Then ask volunteers to add or subtract the two numbers given. Make sure the resulting sum is not greater than 100.

## COMMUNICATION

**4 Questions indiscrètes** With a partner, take turns asking how old these people are. Answers will vary.

M. Hubert
Mme Hubert
M. Moreau
Mme Moreau
M. Durand
Mme Durand

> **MODÈLE**
> **Élève 1:** *Madame Hubert a quel âge?*
> **Élève 2:** *Elle a 70 ans.*

**5 Qui est-ce?** Interview as many classmates as you can in five minutes to find out the name, relationship, and age of their oldest family member. Identify the student with the oldest family member to the class. Answers will vary.

> **MODÈLE**
> **Élève 1:** *Qui est le plus vieux (the oldest) dans ta famille?*
> **Élève 2:** *C'est ma tante Julie. Elle a soixante-dix ans.*

**6 Les pourcentages** Tally your classmates' responses to the questions below, then calculate the percentages for each affirmative answer. (To figure percentages, divide the number of affirmative answers by the number of people in your class.) Answers will vary.

> **MODÈLE**
> *Soixante-seize pour cent des élèves ont un chien.*

1. Tu as un chien?
2. Tu as un chat?
3. Tu as un frère ou des frères?
4. Tu as une sœur ou des sœurs?
5. Tu as des cousins?
6. Tu as des oncles et des tantes?

## Le français vivant

**A**s-tu envie d'être
- ingénieur,
- musicien,
- architecte,
- professeur?

la calculatrice
61€

le sac à dos
70€

la chaise
82€

le bureau
96€

Tu as besoin d'une calculatrice intelligente, d'un beau bureau, d'une chaise confortable et d'un bon sac à dos.

Tu trouves tout dans le
**Catalogue VPC!**

**Identifiez** Scan this catalogue page, and identify the instances where the numbers 61–100 are used. Answers will vary.

**Questions** Answers will vary.

1. Quels objets trouve-t-on sur cette page du Catalogue VPC?
2. Quels sont leurs prix (*their prices*)?
3. Quels autres (*other*) objets trouve-t-on dans le Catalogue VPC? (Imaginez.)
4. Quels sont les prix des autres objets?
5. Le mois prochain, les prix des objets dans le catalogue seront réduits (*will be reduced*) de 25 pour cent. Quels seront les nouveaux prix?

*quatre-vingt-dix-sept* **97**

**1 Expansions**
- Model the question: **Quel est ton numéro de téléphone?** Then have students circulate around the room asking each other their phone numbers. Tell them to write the person's number next to his or her name and have the person verify it.
- Dictate actual phone numbers to the class and tell them to write the numerals.

**2 Expansion** Have each student write five more addition or subtraction problems. Then have students work in pairs and take turns reading their problems aloud while the other person says the answer.

**3 Expansion** Tell students to write three additional series of numbers. Then have them exchange papers with a classmate and take turns reading the series and filling in the numbers.

**4 Expansion** To review descriptive adjectives, have students describe the people in the drawing.

**5 Suggestions**
- Have two volunteers read the **modèle**.
- You may wish to provide a few supplementary terms for family members, such as **l'arrière-grand-mère** and **l'arrière-grand-père**.
- Ask various students to identify the person who has the oldest family member from their interviews. Continue this until students identify the oldest person among all the families.

**6 Expansion** Have students make a pie chart or bar graph that shows the percentages of affirmative answers to each question. Call on volunteers to present their graphs to the class and to explain them in French.

**Le français vivant**
- Call on a volunteer to read the catalogue page aloud. Point out the prices in euros.
- Ask students: **Combien d'objets y a-t-il sur la photo?**

**OPTIONS**

**Using Games** Ask for two volunteers and station them at opposite ends of the board so neither one can see what the other is writing. Say a number from 0–100 and tell them to write it on the board. If both students are correct, continue to give numbers until one writes an incorrect number. The winner continues on to play against another student.

**Mini-dictée** Ask students to write a number between 61 and 100 on a slip of paper. Collect the papers. Tell students to say **«C'est mon numéro!»** when they hear their number. Then proceed to read the numbers aloud at random.

## Section Goals

In this section, students will learn:
- prepositions of location
- disjunctive pronouns

## Key Standards

4.1, 5.1

Student Resources
*Cahier d'exercices*, pp. 39–40;
*Cahier d'activités*, p. 138;
Supersite: Activities,
*Cahier interactif*
Teacher Resources
Answer Keys; Audio Script;
Audio Activity MP3s/CD; Testing
program: Grammar Quiz

## Suggestions

- Explain that prepositions typically indicate where one thing or person is in relation to another: *near, far, on, between, under*. Model the pronunciation of the prepositions and have students repeat.
- Remind students that they may need to use the contractions **du** and **des**.
- Take a book or other object and place it in various locations in relation to your desk or a student's desk as you ask individual students about its location. Examples: **Où est le livre? Est-ce qu'il est derrière le bureau? Quel objet est à côté du livre?** Work through various locations, eliciting all prepositions of location.
- Ask where different students are in relation to one another. Example: ____, où est ____? **(Il/Elle est à côté de [à droite de, à gauche de, derrière] ____.)**
- Model the pronunciation of the disjunctive pronouns and have students repeat them. Explain that these pronouns are used in prepositional phrases. Examples: 1. **Ma famille vient** (*comes*) **souvent chez moi.** 2. **Je suis en face de toi.** Then ask volunteers for examples.
- Write the following in a column on the board and explain each usage of **chez**: **chez** + *person's name or person* (**chez Rachid, chez des amis**); **chez** + *professional's office or business* (**chez le docteur**); and **chez** + *disjunctive pronoun* (**chez toi**).

### 3B.2 Prepositions of location and disjunctive pronouns

**Point de départ** You have already learned expressions in French containing prepositions like **à**, **de**, and **en**. Prepositions of location describe the location of something or someone in relation to something or someone else.

| Prepositions of location | | | |
|---|---|---|---|
| à côté de | *next to* | en face de | *facing, across from* |
| à droite de | *to the right of* | entre | *between* |
| à gauche de | *to the left of* | loin de | *far from* |
| dans | *in* | par | *by* |
| derrière | *behind* | près de | *close to, near* |
| devant | *in front of* | sous | *under* |
| en | *in* | sur | *on* |

La librairie est **derrière** l'école.
*The bookstore is behind the school.*

Ma maison est **loin de** la ville.
*My house is far from the city.*

- Use the preposition **à** before the name of any city to express *in* or *to*. The preposition that accompanies the name of a country varies, but you can use **en** in many cases. In **Leçon 7A**, you will learn more names of countries and their corresponding prepositions.

Il étudie **à Nice**.
*He studies in Nice.*

Je voyage **en France** et **en Belgique**.
*I'm traveling in France and Belgium.*

- Use the contractions **du** and **des** in prepositional expressions when they are appropriate.

La cantine est **à côté du** gymnase.
*The cafeteria is next to the gym.*

Notre chien aime manger **près des** enfants.
*Our dog likes to eat close to the children.*

- You can further modify prepositions of location by using intensifiers such as **tout** (*very, really*) and **juste** (*just, right*).

Ma sœur habite **juste à côté de** l'université.
*My sister lives right next to the university.*

Jules et Alain travaillent **tout près de** la fac.
*Jules and Alain work really close to the (university) campus.*

- You may use prepositions without the word **de** when they are not followed by a noun.

Ma sœur habite **juste à côté**.
*My sister lives right next door.*

Elle travaille **tout près**.
*She works really close by.*

### MISE EN PRATIQUE

**1** **Où est ma montre?** Claude has lost her watch. Choose the appropriate prepositions to complete her friend Pauline's questions.

1. Elle est (sur / entre) le bureau? sur
2. Elle est (par / derrière) la télévision? derrière
3. Elle est (entre / dans) le lit et la table? entre
4. Elle est (en / sous) la chaise? sous
5. Elle est (sur / à côté de) la fenêtre? à côté de
6. Elle est (près du / entre le) sac à dos? près du
7. Elle est (devant / sur) la porte? devant
8. Elle est (dans / sous) la corbeille? dans

**2** **Complétez** Complete these sentences with the appropriate prepositions, based on what you see in the illustration. Suggested answers

**MODÈLE**

Nous sommes *chez* nos cousins.

1. Nous sommes _devant_ la maison de notre tante.
2. Michel est _loin de_ Béatrice.
3. _Entre_ Jasmine et Laure, il y a le petit cousin, Adrien.
4. Béatrice est juste _à côté de_ Jasmine.
5. Jasmine est tout _près de_ Béatrice.
6. Michel est _derrière_ Laure.
7. Un oiseau est _sur_ la maison.
8. Laure est _à droite d'_ Adrien.

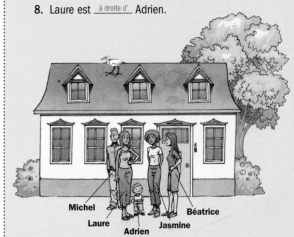

Michel
Laure
Adrien
Jasmine
Béatrice

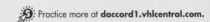
Practice more at **daccord1.vhlcentral.com**.

**OPTIONS**

**Using Video** Show the video episode again to give students more input containing prepositions and disjunctive pronouns. Stop the video where appropriate to discuss how the prepositions of location and disjunctive pronouns were used. Ask comprehension questions.

**Using Movement** Have one student start with a small beanbag or rubber ball. You call out another student identified only by his or her location with reference to other students. Example: **C'est la personne derrière ____.** The student with the beanbag or ball has to throw it to the student identified. The latter student must then throw the object to the next person you identify.

## COMMUNICATION

**3** **Où est l'objet?** In pairs, take turns asking where these items are in the classroom. Use prepositions of location. *Answers will vary.*

**MODÈLE** la carte
Élève 1: *Où est la carte?*
Élève 2: *Elle est devant la classe.*

1. l'horloge
2. l'ordinateur
3. le tableau
4. la fenêtre
5. le bureau du professeur
6. ton livre de français
7. la corbeille
8. la porte

**4** **Qui est-ce?** Choose someone in the room. The class will guess whom you chose by asking yes/no questions that use prepositions of location. *Answers will vary.*

**MODÈLE**
*Est-ce qu'il/elle est derrière Dominique?*
*Est-ce qu'il/elle est entre Jean-Pierre et Suzanne?*

**5** **S'il vous plaît...?** A tourist stops someone on the street to ask where certain places are located. In pairs, play these roles using the map to locate the places.
*Answers will vary.*

**MODÈLE** la banque
Élève 1: *La banque, s'il vous plaît?*
Élève 2: *Elle est en face de l'hôpital.*

1. le cinéma Ambassadeur
2. le restaurant Chez Marlène
3. la librairie Antoine
4. le lycée Camus
5. l'hôtel Royal
6. le café de la Place

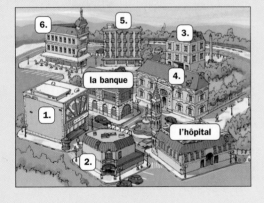

---

- The preposition **chez** has no exact English equivalent. It expresses the idea of *at* or *to someone's house* or *place.*

  > Louise n'aime pas étudier **chez** Arnaud parce qu'il parle beaucoup.
  > *Louise doesn't like studying at Arnaud's because he talks a lot.*

  > Ce matin, elle n'étudie pas parce qu'elle est **chez** sa cousine.
  > *This morning she's not studying because she's at her cousin's.*

- The preposition **chez** is also used to express the idea of *at* or *to a professional's office* or *business.*

  **chez** le docteur          **chez** la coiffeuse
  *at the doctor's*            *to the hairdresser's*

*On travaille chez moi!*

*Stéphane est chez Rachid.*

### Disjunctive pronouns

- Use disjunctive pronouns after prepositions instead of subject pronouns:

| singular | | plural | |
|---|---|---|---|
| je | moi | nous | nous |
| tu | toi | vous | vous |
| il | lui | ils | eux |
| elle | elle | elles | elles |

Maryse travaille **à côté de moi.**
*Maryse is working next to me.*

J'aime mieux dîner **chez eux.**
*I prefer to dine at their house.*

Nous pensons **à lui.**
*We're thinking about him.*

**Essayez!** **Provide the preposition indicated in parentheses.**

1. La librairie est _derrière_ (*behind*) la banque.
2. J'habite _près de_ (*close to*) leur lycée.
3. Le laboratoire est _à côté de_ (*next to*) ma résidence.
4. Tu retournes _chez_ (*to the house of*) tes parents ce soir?
5. La fenêtre est _en face de_ (*across from*) la porte.
6. Mon sac à dos est _sous_ (*under*) la chaise.
7. Ses crayons sont _sur_ (*on*) la table.
8. Votre ordinateur est _dans_ (*in*) la corbeille!

---

**Essayez!** Have students write three more fill-in-the-blank sentences describing where certain objects are located in their dorm room or apartment. Then tell them to exchange papers with a classmate and complete the sentences.

**1** **Suggestion** To check students' answers, have them work in pairs and take turns asking the completed questions and answering them in the affirmative or negative.

**2** **Suggestion** Before students begin the activity, have them identify the people, places, and other objects in the drawing. Example: **Il y a un oiseau.**

**2** **Expansion** Have students create additional sentences about the location of the people or objects in the drawing. To practice negation, have students describe where the people and other objects are not located. Example: **La famille n'est pas devant la bibliothèque.**

**3** **Suggestion** Have two volunteers read the **modèle** aloud. Remind students to pay attention to the gender of the nouns when responding.

**3** **Expansion** For additional practice, give students these items if they are present in the classroom. **9. le dictionnaire de français 10. la calculatrice 11. les examens**

**4** **Suggestion** To continue this activity, allow the student who guessed the correct person to choose another person and have the class ask the student yes/no questions.

**5** **Suggestion** Before students begin this activity, make sure they understand that the numbers on the illustration correspond to the places on the list. Have two volunteers read the **modèle** aloud.

---

**OPTIONS**

**Using Maps** Have students look at the world map in the **Front Matter** or use **Overheads #1** and **#2**. Make true/false statements about the locations of various countries. Examples: **1. La Chine est près des États-Unis. (Faux.) 2. Le Luxembourg est entre la France et l'Allemagne. (Vrai.)** For variation, you can make statements or ask true/false questions about the location of various cities in France.

**My Region** In groups of three or four, have students think of a city or town within a 100-mile radius of your city or town. They need to figure out how many miles away it is and what other cities or towns are nearby (**La ville est près de...**). Then have them get together with another group and read their descriptions. The other group has to guess which city or town is being described.

# Révision

## Key Standards
1.1

**Student Resources**
*Cahier d'activités*, pp. 31-32;
Supersite: Activities,
*Cahier interactif*
**Teacher Resources**
Answer Keys; Info Gap Activities;
Testing Program: Lesson Test
(Testing Program Audio MP3s/CD)

**1 Suggestion** Point out that in France and most francophone countries (except Canada) it is not common for universities to have sports teams. If they do, their fans are usually limited to university students. The general public doesn't usually follow college sports.

**2 Expansion** To review descriptive adjectives, ask students to give physical descriptions of the people.

**3 Suggestion** You might want to draw a simple map on the board to assist students visualize the location of important places in your town.

**4 Suggestion** To practice listening skills, tell students to cover the phone numbers with one hand and write the phone numbers down as their partner says them.

**5 Suggestion** Encourage students to ask questions when they are playing the role of the customer. For example, they can ask if the store has certain brands of an item, backpacks and notebooks in certain colors, or a specific type of dictionary.

**6 Suggestion** Divide the class into pairs and distribute the Info Gap Handouts on the Supersite for this activity. Give students ten minutes to complete the activity.

**6 Expansion** Ask students questions based on the artwork. Example: **Est-ce que le neveu est à côté de la mère?**

---

**1 Le basket** These basketball rivals are competing for the title. In pairs, predict the missing playoff scores. Then, compare your predictions with those of another pair. Be prepared to share your predictions with the class. Answers will vary.

1. Ohio State 76, Michigan _____
2. Florida _____, Florida State 84
3. Stanford _____, UCLA 79
4. Purdue 81, Indiana _____
5. Duke 100, Virginia _____
6. Kansas 95, Colorado _____
7. Texas _____, Oklahoma 88
8. Kentucky 98, Tennessee _____

**2 La famille d'Édouard** In pairs, take turns guessing how the members of Édouard's family are related to him and to each other by describing their locations in the photo. Compare your answers with those of another pair. Answers will vary.

**MODÈLE**

*Son père est derrière sa mère.*

Édouard

**3 La ville** In pairs, take turns describing the location of a building (**un bâtiment**) somewhere in your town or city. Your partner must guess which building you are describing in three tries. Keep score to determine the winner after several rounds. Answers will vary.

**MODÈLE**

**Élève 1:** *C'est un bâtiment entre la banque et le lycée.*
**Élève 2:** *C'est l'hôpital?*
**Élève 1:** *C'est ça!*

**ressources**

| | | |
|---|---|---|
| CE pp. 37–40 | CA pp. 31-32, 137-138 | daccord1.vhlcentral.com |

---

**4 C'est quel numéro?** What courses would you take if you were studying at a French university? Take turns deciding and having your partner give you the phone number for enrollment information. Answers will vary.

**MODÈLE**

**Élève 1:** *Je cherche un cours de philosophie.*
**Élève 2:** *C'est le zéro quatre...*

| Département | Numéro de téléphone |
|---|---|
| Architecture | 04.76.65.74.92 |
| Biologie | 04.76.72.63.85 |
| Chimie | 04.76.84.79.64 |
| Littérature anglaise | 04.76.99.90.82 |
| Mathématiques | 04.76.86.66.93 |
| Philosophie | 04.76.75.99.80 |
| Psychologie | 04.76.61.88.91 |
| Sciences politiques | 04.76.68.96.81 |
| Sociologie | 04.76.70.83.97 |

**5 À la librairie** In pairs, role-play a customer at a bookstore and a clerk who points out where supplies are located. Then, switch roles. Each turn, the customer picks four items from the list. Use the drawing to find the supplies. Answers will vary.

**MODÈLE**

**Élève 1:** *Je cherche des stylos.*
**Élève 2:** *Ils sont à côté des cahiers.*

| | |
|---|---|
| des cahiers | un dictionnaire |
| une calculatrice | un iPhone® |
| une carte | du papier |
| des crayons | un sac à dos |

**6 Trouvez** Your teacher will give you and your partner each a drawing of a family picnic. Ask each other questions to find out where all of the family members are located. Answers will vary.

**MODÈLE**

**Élève 1:** *Qui est à côté du père?*
**Élève 2:** *Le neveu est à côté du père.*

---

**OPTIONS**

**Using Games** Divide the class into two teams. Select a student from the first team to choose an item in the classroom and to write it down. Call on five students from the other team one at a time to ask questions in French about where this item is. The first student can respond only with **oui**, **non**, **chaud** (*hot*), or **froid** (*cold*). If a team guesses the item within five tries, give them a point. The team with the most points wins.

**Mini-dictée** Have students work in pairs. Tell them to take turns reading phone numbers at random from the list in **Activité 4** without mentioning the department. The person who responds should say the name of the department. Example: **Élève 1:** 04.76.65.74.92 **Élève 2: C'est le département d'architecture.**

# À l'écoute

**S** Audio: Activities

## STRATÉGIE

### Asking for repetition/ Replaying the recording

Sometimes it is difficult to understand what people say, especially in a noisy environment. During a conversation, you can ask someone to repeat by asking **Comment?** (*What?*) or **Pardon?** (*Pardon me?*). In class, you can ask your teacher to repeat by saying, **Répétez, s'il vous plaît** (*Repeat, please*). If you don't understand a recorded activity, you can simply replay it.

 To help you practice this strategy, you will listen to a short paragraph. Ask your teacher to repeat it or replay the recording, and then summarize what you heard.

## Préparation

Based on the photograph, where do you think Suzanne and Diane are? What do you think they are talking about?

## À vous d'écouter 🎧

Now you are going to hear Suzanne and Diane's conversation. Use **R** to indicate adjectives that describe Suzanne's boyfriend, Robert. Use **E** for adjectives that describe Diane's boyfriend, Édouard. Some adjectives will not be used.

| | | | |
|---|---|---|---|
| _E_ | brun | _R_ | optimiste |
| ___ | laid | _E_ | intelligent |
| _E_ | grand | ___ | blond |
| _E_ | intéressant | _E_ | beau |
| _E_ | gentil | _R_ | sympathique |
| _R_ | drôle | _R_ | patient |

 Practice more at **daccord1.vhlcentral.com**.

## Compréhension

**Identifiez-les** Whom do these statements describe?

1. Elle a un problème avec un garçon. <u>Diane</u>

2. Il ne parle pas à Diane. <u>Édouard</u>

3. Elle a de la chance. <u>Suzanne</u>

4. Ils parlent souvent. <u>Suzanne et Robert</u>

5. Il est sympa. <u>Robert</u>

6. Il est timide. <u>Édouard</u>

**Vrai ou faux?** Indicate whether each sentence is **vrai** or **faux**, then correct any false statements.

1. Édouard est un garçon très patient et optimiste.

   <u>Faux. Robert est très patient et optimiste.</u>

2. Diane pense que Suzanne a de la chance.

   <u>Vrai.</u>

3. Suzanne et son petit ami parlent de tout.

   <u>Vrai.</u>

4. Édouard parle souvent à Diane.

   <u>Faux. Édouard ne parle pas à Diane.</u>

5. Robert est peut-être un peu timide.

   <u>Faux. Édouard est peut-être un peu timide.</u>

6. Suzanne parle de beaucoup de choses avec Robert.

   <u>Vrai.</u>

*cent un* **101**

## Section Goals

In this section, students will:
- learn to ask for repetition in oral communication
- listen to and summarize a short paragraph
- listen to a conversation and complete several activities

## Key Standards

**1.2, 2.1**

**Student Resources**
Supersite: Activities, Audio
**Teacher Resources**
Answer Keys; Audio Script; Audio Activity MP3s/CD

**Stratégie**
**Script** Bonjour, je m'appelle Christine Dupont. Je suis médecin et mère de famille. Mon mari, Richard, est ingénieur. Il est intelligent et très drôle aussi. Nous avons trois enfants charmants: deux fils et une fille. Les garçons sont roux et notre fille est blonde. Notre fils aîné, Marc, a 17 ans. Le cadet, Pascal, a 15 ans. Leur petite sœur, Véronique, a 12 ans.

**Préparation** Before students do the activity, tell them to look at the photo and describe what they see. Ask students to justify their responses based on visual clues in the photo.

**Suggestion** To check students' answers for the **À vous d'écouter** activity, have them work in pairs and take turns asking and answering questions using the adjectives listed. Example: **Est-ce que Robert est brun? Non, Édouard est brun.**

**À vous d'écouter**
**Script**
SUZANNE: Salut, Diane. Est-ce que ça va?
DIANE: Oh, comme ci, comme ça. J'ai un petit problème. Ce n'est pas grand-chose, mais...
S: Quel genre de problème?
D: Tu sais que j'aime bien Édouard.

S: Oui.
D: Le problème, c'est qu'il ne me parle pas!
S: Il t'aime bien aussi. Il est peut-être un peu timide?
D: Tu crois? ...Il est si beau! Grand, brun... Et puis, il est gentil, très intelligent et aussi très intéressant. Et Robert et toi, comment ça va?
S: Euh... plutôt bien. Robert est sympa. Je l'aime

beaucoup. Il est patient, optimiste et très drôle.
D: Vous parlez souvent?
S: Oui. Nous parlons deux à trois heures par jour. Nous parlons de beaucoup de choses! De nos cours, de nos amis, de nos familles... de tout.
D: C'est super! Tu as de la chance.

# Panorama

**Interactive Map Reading**

Paris
LA FRANCE

l'Arc de Triomphe

Basilique du Sacré-Cœur

Place du Tertre

Le Moulin Rouge

Parc Monceau

BOULEVARD HAUSSMANN

Opéra Garnier

BLVD. DES ITALIENS

Arc de Triomphe

AVENUE DES CHAMPS-ELYSÉES

La Madeleine

BLVD. DES CAPUCINES

RUE DE L'OPÉRA

BOULEVARD DE SEBASTOPOL

Bois de Boulogne

Grand Palais

Place de la Concorde

Jeu de Paume

RUE DE RIVOLI

Jardin des Tuileries

Les Halles

Beaubourg/Centre Georges Pompidou-Centre National d'Art et de Culture

Jardins du Trocadéro

QUAI D'ORSAY

Seine

Orangerie

Musée du Louvre

RUE DE RIVOLI

Tour Eiffel

Assemblée Nationale

BLVD ST-GERMAIN

Musée d'Orsay

Conciergerie

Île de la Cité

Hôtel de Ville

Place des Vosges

Parc du Champ de Mars

Hôtel des Invalides

BOULEVARD RASPAIL

BOULEVARD ST. GERMAIN

Cathédrale Notre-Dame

Île St-Louis

Opéra de Paris Bastille

École Militaire

BOULEVARD SAINT-MICHEL

Sorbonne

Jardin du Luxembourg

Panthéon

Seine

Tour Montparnasse

0        0.5 mile
0      0.5 kilomètre

## Paris

### La ville en chiffres

▶ **Superficie:** *105 km² (cent cinq kilomètres carrés°)*

▶ **Population:** *plus de° 9.828.000 (neuf millions huit cent vingt-huit mille)*
SOURCE: Population Division, UN Secretariat

*Paris est la capitale de la France. On a l'impression que Paris est une grande ville—et c'est vrai si on compte° ses environs°. Néanmoins°, Paris mesure moins de° 10 kilomètres de l'est à l'ouest°. On peut ainsi° très facilement visiter la ville à pied°. Paris est divisée en 20 arrondissements°. Chaque° arrondissement a son propre maire° et son propre caractère.*

▶ **Industries principales:** *haute couture, finances, transports, technologie, tourisme*

▶ **Musées:** *plus de 150 (cent cinquante): le musée° du Louvre, le musée d'Orsay, le centre Georges Pompidou et le musée Rodin*

### Parisiens célèbres

▶ **Victor Hugo,** *écrivain° et activiste (1802–1885)*

▶ **Charles Baudelaire,** *poète (1821–1867)*

▶ **Auguste Rodin,** *sculpteur (1840–1917)*

▶ **Jean-Paul Sartre,** *philosophe (1905–1980)*

▶ **Simone de Beauvoir,** *écrivain (1908–1986)*

▶ **Édith Piaf,** *chanteuse (1915–1963)*

▶  **Emmanuelle Béart,** *actrice (1965– )*

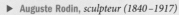

carrés *square* plus de *more than* si on compte *if one counts* environs *surrounding areas* Néanmoins *Nevertheless* moins de *less than* de l'est à l'ouest *from east to west* ainsi *in this way* à pied *on foot* arrondissements *districts* Chaque *Each* son propre maire *its own mayor* musée *museum* écrivain *writer* rues *streets* reposent *lie; rest* provenant *from* repos *rest*

l'opéra Garnier

une terrasse de café

### Incroyable mais vrai!

Sous les rues° de Paris, il y a une autre ville: les catacombes. Ici reposent° les squelettes d'environ 7.000.000 (sept millions) de personnes provenant° d'anciens cimetières de Paris et de ses environs. Plus de 250.000 (deux cent cinquante mille) touristes par an visitent cette ville de repos° éternel.

---

## Section Goals

In this section, students will learn historical and cultural information about the city of Paris.

## Key Standards

2.2, 3.1, 3.2, 5.1

**Student Resources**
*Cahier d'exercices*, pp. 41-42;
Supersite: Activities,
*Cahier interactif*
**Teacher Resources**
Answer Keys; Overhead #24

## Plan de Paris

- Have students look at the map of Paris or use **Overhead #24**. Point out that **Paris** and its surrounding areas (**la banlieue**) are called **l'Île-de-France**. This area is also known as **la Région parisienne**. Ask students to locate places mentioned in the **Panorama** on the map. Examples: **le musée du Louvre, le musée d'Orsay, le centre Georges Pompidou, l'Arc de Triomphe,** and **la tour Eiffel.**
- Point out that the Seine River (**la Seine**) divides Paris into two parts: the left bank (**la rive gauche**) and the right bank (**la rive droite**).

## La ville en chiffres

- Point out the city's coat of arms.
- Call on volunteers to read the sections. After each section, ask questions about content.
- Point out that the population figure for Paris includes the city and the surrounding areas.
- Tell students that there is a Rodin Museum in Paris and one in Philadelphia. If possible, show students pictures of two of Rodin's most famous sculptures: *The Kiss* (**le Baiser**) and *The Thinker* (**le Penseur**).

**Incroyable mais vrai!** The miles of tunnels and catacombs under Paris used to be quarries; the city was built with much of the stone dug from them. Some of these quarries date back to Roman times. The skeletons in the catacombs are Parisians who were moved from overcrowded cemeteries in the late 1700s.

---

**OPTIONS**

**Oral Presentation** If a student has visited Paris, ask the person to prepare a short presentation about his or her experiences there. Encourage the student to bring in photos and souvenirs. Tell the presenter to include what his or her favorite place or activity is in Paris and to explain why.

**Parisiens célèbres** **Jean-Paul Sartre** and **Simone de Beauvoir** had a personal and professional relationship. Sartre became famous as the leader of a group of intellectuals who used to gather regularly at the **Café de Flore**. This group included Simone de Beauvoir and **Albert Camus**. Ask students to name some works they may have read or heard of by Sartre, de Beauvoir, or Camus.

## Les monuments

### La tour Eiffel

La tour Eiffel a été construite° en 1889 (mille huit cent quatre-vingt-neuf) pour l'Exposition universelle, à l'occasion du centenaire° de la Révolution française. Elle mesure 324 (trois cent vingt-quatre) mètres de haut et pèse° 10.100 (dix mille cent) tonnes. La tour attire près de° 7.000.000 (sept millions) de visiteurs par an°.

## Les gens

### Paris-Plages

Pour les Parisiens qui ne voyagent pas pendant l'été°, la ville de Paris a créé° Paris-Plages pour apporter la plage° aux Parisiens! Inauguré en 2001 et installé sur les quais° de la Seine, Paris-Plages consiste en trois kilomètres de sable et d'herbe°, plein° d'activités comme la natation° et le volley. Ouvert en° juillet et en août, près de 4.000.000 (quatre millions) de personnes visitent Paris-Plages chaque° année.

## Les musées

### Le musée du Louvre

Ancien° palais royal, le musée du Louvre est aujourd'hui un des plus grands musées du monde° avec sa vaste collection de peintures°, de sculptures et d'antiquités orientales, égyptiennes, grecques et romaines. L'œuvre° la plus célèbre de la collection est La Joconde° de Léonard de Vinci. La pyramide de verre°, créée par l'architecte américain I.M. Pei, marque l'entrée° principale du musée.

## Les transports

### Le métro

L'architecte Hector Guimard a commencé à réaliser° des entrées du métro de Paris en 1898 (mille huit cent quatre-vingt-dix-huit). Ces entrées sont construites dans le style Art Nouveau: en forme de plantes et de fleurs°. Le métro est aujourd'hui un système très efficace° qui permet aux passagers de traverser° Paris rapidement.

---

**Qu'est-ce que vous avez appris?** Complétez les phrases.

1. La ville de Paris est divisée en vingt __arrondissements__.
2. Chaque arrondissement a ses propres __maire__ et __caractère__.
3. Charles Baudelaire est le nom d'un __poète__ français.
4. Édith Piaf est une __chanteuse__ française.
5. Plus de 250.000 personnes par an visitent __les catacombes__ sous les rues de Paris.
6. La tour Eiffel mesure __324__ mètres de haut.
7. En 2001, la ville de Paris a créé __Paris-Plages__ au bord (banks) de la Seine.
8. Le musée du Louvre est un ancien __palais__.
9. __La pyramide de verre__ est une création de I.M. Pei.
10. Certaines entrées du métro sont de style __Art Nouveau__.

Practice more at **daccord1.vhlcentral.com**.

**ressources**

CE
pp. 41–42

daccord1.vhlcentral.com

---

## SUR INTERNET

Go to **daccord1.vhlcentral.com** to find more cultural information related to this **PANORAMA**.

1. Quels sont les monuments les plus importants à Paris? Qu'est-ce qu'on peut faire (can do) dans la ville?
2. Trouvez des informations sur un des musées de Paris.
3. Recherchez la vie (Research the life) d'un(e) Parisien(ne) célèbre.
4. Cherchez un plan du métro de Paris et trouvez comment voyager du Louvre à la tour Eiffel.

**construite** built **centenaire** 100-year anniversary **pèse** weighs **attire près de** attracts nearly **par an** per year **pendant l'été** during the summer **a créé** created **apporter la plage** bring the beach **quais** banks **de sable et d'herbe** of sand and grass **plein** full **natation** swimming **Ouvert en** Open in **chaque** each **Ancien** Former **monde** world **peintures** paintings **L'œuvre** The work (of art) **La Joconde** The Mona Lisa **verre** glass **entrée** entrance **a commencé à réaliser** began to create **fleurs** flowers **efficace** efficient **traverser** to cross

---

**La tour Eiffel** Constructed of wrought iron, the architectural design of the Eiffel Tower was an engineering masterpiece for its time. Critics of Gustave Eiffel's design said it couldn't be built, but he proved them wrong. Later, some of the engineering techniques employed would be used to build the first steel skyscrapers. The Eiffel Tower remained the world's tallest building until 1930.

**Paris-Plages** To create this manmade beach, each year about 2,000 tons of sand are spread over what is a busy highway the rest of the year. In 2007, it cost more than two million euros to create the beach. A swimming pool was added in 2004 because the Seine is too dirty to swim in. When it is open, **Paris-Plages** is a popular center for relaxation and fun, with numerous organized sports activities and concerts. Ask students if they think that **Paris-Plages** is worth the money.

**Le musée du Louvre** Bring in photos or slides of the **Louvre** and some of the most famous artwork in its collection, such as the *Mona Lisa*, the *Venus de Milo*, the *Winged Victory of Samothrace*, *Vermeer's Lacemaker*, and *Delacroix's Liberty Leading the People* (**La Liberté guidant le peuple**). Ask students to describe the woman in the *Mona Lisa*. Point out that only a fraction of the 300,000 works owned by the museum are on display.

**Le métro** The Paris public transportation system, **le métro** (short for **le Métropolitain**), has 14 lines. It is the most convenient and popular means of transportation in the city since every building in Paris is within 500 meters of a **métro** station. Ask students what cities in the United States have metro or subway systems.

---

**Mini-report** Assign each student a famous site in Paris. Examples: **l'Île de la Cité, la Sainte-Chapelle, le quartier latin**, etc. Tell students to research the site and write a brief description. Encourage them to include photos from the Internet or magazines. Ask a few volunteers to share their descriptions with the class.

**My itinerary** Have students work in pairs. Tell them that they have three days in Paris, and they have to make a list of places they want to see or visit each day so that they can make the most of their time there. Remind students that many famous sights, other than those mentioned in the text, appear on the map. Example: **Jour 1: visiter le musée du Louvre.** Ask volunteers to share their lists with the class.

## Section Goals

In this section, students will:
• learn to use visuals and graphic elements to predict content
• read an article about pets in France

## Key Standards
1.3, 3.1, 5.1

**Stratégie** Tell students that they can infer a great deal of information about the content of an article or text by examining the visual and graphic elements. Some items they should look at are:
• titles and headings
• photos
• photo captions
• graphs, tables, and diagrams
To practice this strategy, have students read the headings in the chart **Le Top 10 des chiens de race.** Ask: What information does this chart contain? (It lists the top ten dog breeds and the percentage of households that owns each breed.)

**Examinez le texte** After students have finished the activity, tell them to look at the visual elements in the article again. Then ask them the following questions and have them explain their answers.
1. What is the article about? (It is about dogs as family pets. The title of the article and the photos of dogs indicate the main topic.)
2. What information does the table on page 105 contain? (It lists the reasons why people have pets and shows the percentages of people who own dogs, cats, birds, and fish for each reason.)
3. What can you learn from the photo on page 105? (Answers will vary.)

# Lecture ⓈReading

## Avant la lecture

### STRATÉGIE

### Predicting content from visuals

When you are reading in French, be sure to look for visual clues that will orient you as to the content and purpose of what you are reading. Photos and illustrations, for example, will often give you a good idea of the main points that the reading covers. You may also encounter helpful visuals that summarize large amounts of data in a way that is easy to comprehend; these visuals include bar graphs, pie charts, flow charts, lists of percentages, and other diagrams.

| Le Top 10 des chiens de race° |
| --- |
| **% DE FOYERS° POSSESSEURS** |
| les caniches° **9,3%** |
| les labradors **7,8%** |
| les yorkshires **5,6%** |
| les épagneuls bretons° **4,6%** |
| les bergers allemands° **4,1%** |
| les autres bergers **3,3%** |
| les bichons **2,7%** |
| les cockers/fox-terriers **2,2%** |
| les boxers **2%** |
| les colleys **1,6%** |

### Examinez le texte

Take a quick look at the visual elements of the article in order to generate a list of ideas about its content. Then, compare your list with a classmate's. Are your lists the same or are they different? Discuss your lists and make any changes needed to produce a final list of ideas.

**race** *breed* **foyers** *households* **caniches** *poodles* **épagneuls bretons** *Brittany Spaniels* **bergers allemands** *German Shepherds*

104 *cent quatre*

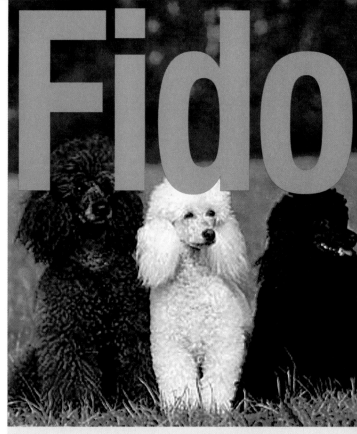

# Fido

Les Français adorent les animaux. Plus de la moitié° des foyers en France ont un chien, un chat ou un autre animal de compagnie°. Les chiens sont particulièrement appréciés et intégrés dans la famille et la société françaises.

Qui possède un chien en France et pourquoi? Souvent°, la présence d'un chien en famille suit l'arrivée° d'enfants, parce que les parents pensent qu'un chien contribue positivement à leur développement. Il est aussi commun de trouver deux chiens ou plus dans le même° foyer.

Les chiens sont d'excellents compagnons. Leurs maîtres° sont moins seuls° et déclarent avoir moins de stress. Certaines personnes possèdent un chien pour avoir plus d'exercice

**OPTIONS**

**Reading Aloud** Working in pairs, students should read the article aloud and write four questions about it. After they have finished, tell them to exchange their papers with another pair and answer the questions.

**Reading Charts** Tell students to read the chart **Le Top 10 des chiens de race**. Then pronounce the name of each dog breed and have students repeat it after you. To check comprehension, give students these true/false statements. **1. Le caniche est la race de chien la plus populaire. (Vrai.) 2. Les boxers n'existent pas en France. (Faux.) 3. Les labradors sont moins populaires que les épagneuls. (Faux.) 4. Les Français aiment mieux les yorkshires que les bergers. (Faux.) 5. Les colleys sont le numéro dix sur la liste. (Vrai.)**

# en famille

physique. Et il y a aussi des personnes qui possèdent un chien parce qu'elles en ont toujours eu un° et n'imaginent pas une vie° sans° chien.

Les chiens ont parfois° les mêmes droits° que les autres membres de la famille, et parfois des droits spéciaux. Bien sûr, ils accompagnent leurs maîtres pour les courses en ville° et les promenades dans le parc, et ils entrent même dans certains magasins°. Ne trouvez-vous pas parfois un caniche ou un labrador, les deux races les plus° populaires en France, avec son maître dans un restaurant?

En France, il n'est pas difficile d'observer que les chiens ont une place privilégiée au sein de° la famille.

### Pourquoi avoir un animal de compagnie?

| RAISON | CHIENS | CHATS | OISEAUX | POISSONS |
|--------|--------|-------|---------|----------|
| Pour l'amour des animaux | 61,4% | 60,5% | 61% | 33% |
| Pour avoir de la compagnie | 43,5% | 38,2% | 37% | 10% |
| Pour s'occuper* | 40,4% | 37,7% | 0% | 0% |
| Parce que j'en ai toujours eu un* | 31,8% | 28,9% | 0% | 0% |
| Pour le bien-être* personnel | 29,2% | 26,2% | 0% | 0% |
| Pour les enfants | 23,7% | 21,3% | 30% | 48% |

**Plus de la moitié** *More than half* **animal de compagnie** *pet* **Souvent** *Often* **suit l'arrivée** *follows the arrival* **même** *same* **maîtres** *owners* **moins** *less* **seuls** *lonely* **en ont toujours eu un** *have always had one* **vie** *life* **sans** *without* **parfois** *sometimes* **droits** *rights* **courses en ville** *errands in town* **magasins** *stores* **les plus** *the most* **au sein de** *in the heart of* **s'occuper** *keep busy* **Parce que j'en ai toujours eu un** *Because I've always had one* **bien-être** *well-being*

## Après la lecture

**Vrai ou faux?** Indicate whether these items are **vrai** or **faux**, based on the reading. Correct the false ones.

| | Vrai | Faux |
|---|---|---|
| 1. Les chiens accompagnent leurs maîtres pour les promenades dans le parc. | ☑ | ☐ |
| 2. Parfois, les chiens accompagnent leurs maîtres dans les restaurants. | ☑ | ☐ |
| 3. Le chat n'est pas un animal apprécié en France. En France, plus de la moitié des foyers ont un chien, un chat ou un autre animal de compagnie. | ☐ | ☑ |
| 4. Certaines personnes déclarent posséder un chien pour avoir plus d'exercice physique. | ☑ | ☐ |
| 5. Certaines personnes déclarent posséder un chien pour avoir plus de stress. Certaines personnes déclarent avoir moins de stress avec un chien. | ☐ | ☑ |
| 6. En France, les familles avec enfants n'ont pas de chien. Souvent, la présence d'un chien dans une famille suit l'arrivée d'enfants. | ☐ | ☑ |

**Fido en famille** Choose the correct response according to the article.

1. Combien de foyers en France ont au moins (*at least*) un animal de compagnie?
   a. 20%–25%
   b. 40%–45%
   c. 50%–55%

2. Pourquoi est-ce une bonne idée d'avoir un chien?
   a. pour plus de compagnie et plus de stress
   b. pour l'exercice physique et être seul
   c. pour la compagnie et le développement des enfants

3. Que pensent les familles françaises de leurs chiens?
   a. Les chiens sont plus importants que les enfants.
   b. Les chiens font partie (*are part*) de la famille et participent aux activités quotidiennes (*daily*).
   c. Le rôle des chiens est limité aux promenades.

4. Quelles races de chien les Français préfèrent-ils?
   a. les caniches et les oiseaux
   b. les labradors et les bergers allemands
   c. les caniches et les labradors

5. Y a-t-il des familles avec plus d'un chien?
   a. non
   b. oui
   c. les caniches et les labradors

**Mes animaux** In groups of three, say why you own or someone you know owns a pet. Give one of the reasons listed in the table on the left or a different one. Use the verb **avoir** and possessive adjectives.

**MODÈLE**

*Mon grand-père a un chien pour son bien-être personnel.*

---

**Vrai ou faux?** Have students correct the false statements and check their answers with a partner.

**Fido en famille** Go over the answers with the class. Ask students to read the corresponding line(s) of the text that contain the answer to each question.

**Suggestion** Encourage students to record unfamiliar words and phrases that they learn in **Lecture** in their notebooks.

**Expansions**
- Ask students to describe their pets. If they don't own a pet, then tell them to describe someone else's pet. Example: **Mon chat s'appelle Tyler. Il est très gentil avec tout le monde. Il est noir et c'est un bon copain.**
- Write these headings on the board: **animaux de compagnie, chiens, chats, oiseaux, poissons**, and **autres animaux**. Do a quick class survey to find out how many have pets in general and how many have dogs, cats, birds, fish, and other animals. Record the results on the board. Then ask them why they have a pet. If students need help expressing their reasons, tell them to look at the reasons in the chart on this page.

**Mes animaux** Ask students to report their partners' answers to the class.

---

**OPTIONS**

**Cultural Comparison** Have students work in pairs or groups of three. Tell them to draw a two-column chart and write the headings **Similitudes** (*Similarities*) and **Différences** (*Differences*). Then, tell them to list the similarities and differences between the French and American attitudes toward dogs based on the facts in the reading and what they know about Americans and their pets. Allow students to use their books for this activity. After pairs have completed their charts, call on volunteers to read their lists. Ask the class if they agree or disagree with the similarities.

# Section Goals

In this section, students will:
- learn to use idea maps to organize information
- learn to write an informal letter in French

## Key Standards

1.3, 3.1, 5.1

**Stratégie** Tell students that they might find it helpful to use note cards to create idea maps. Writing each detail on a separate card will allow them to rearrange ideas and experiment with organization. Remind students to write their ideas in French, since they may not have the vocabulary or structures for some English terms they generate.

**Thème** Introduce the common salutations and closings used in informal letters in French. Point out the difference between **cher** (masculine) and **chère** (feminine). Model the pronunciation to show students that the two words sound the same. Explain that the closings **Grosses bises!** and **Bisous!** are often used with close friends. If the relationship is informal but the person is not a close friend, then **À plus** is an appropriate choice. **Amitiés** and **Cordialement** are less familiar than the other options.

# Écriture

## STRATÉGIE

### Using idea maps

How do you organize ideas for a first draft? Often, the organization of ideas represents the most challenging part of the writing process. Idea maps are useful for organizing pertinent information. Here is an example of an idea map you can use when writing.

**SCHÉMA D'IDÉES**

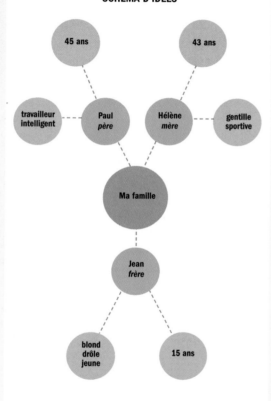

## Thème

# Écrivez une lettre

### Avant l'écriture

1. A French-speaking friend wants to know about your family. Using some of the verbs and adjectives you learned in this lesson, write a brief letter describing your own family or an imaginary one. Be sure to include information from each of these categories for each family member:

- Names, ages, and relationships
- Physical characteristics
- Hobbies and interests

Before you begin, create an idea map like the one on the left, with a circle for each member of your family.

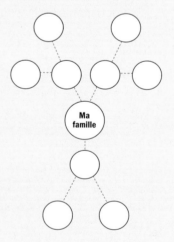

**Avant l'écriture** Remind students that they used a word web to brainstorm ideas in Unit 2. Tell them that an idea map is similar, but that it links various ideas to a central topic and breaks those ideas down into smaller categories. Point out the colors used in the idea map on page 106 and how they are used to group similar levels of information.

Help students create an outline for a typical letter: a salutation, an introductory paragraph with greetings, a second paragraph with the family description, a third paragraph with a request for a response, a closing, and a signature. Tell them their first paragraph should include an inquiry into how the person is doing, along with a similar comment about themselves.

**2.** Once you have completed your idea map, compare it with the one created by a classmate. Did you both include the same kind of information? Did you list all your family members? Did you include information from each of the three categories for each person?

**3.** Here are some useful expressions for writing a letter in French:

| Salutations | |
|---|---|
| Cher Fabien, | Dear Fabien, |
| Chère Joëlle, | Dear Joëlle, |

| Asking for a response | |
|---|---|
| Réponds-moi vite. | Write back soon. |
| Donne-moi de tes nouvelles. | Tell me all your news. |

| Closings | |
|---|---|
| Grosses bises! | Big kisses! |
| Je t'embrasse! | Kisses! |
| Bisous! | Kisses! |
| À bientôt! | See you soon! |
| Amitiés, | In friendship, |
| Cordialement, | Cordially, |
| À plus (tard), | Until later, |

## Écriture

Use your idea map and the list of letter-writing expressions to write a letter that describes your family to a friend. Be sure to include some of the verbs and adjectives you have learned in this lesson.

*Cher Christophe,*

*Mon père s'appelle Gabriel. Il a 42 ans. Il est grand, a les cheveux châtains et les yeux marron. Il est architecte et travaille à Paris. Il aime dessiner, lire (to read) et voyager. Ma mère, Nicole, a 37 ans. Elle est petite, blonde et a les yeux bleus. Elle est professeur d'anglais à l'université. Comme mon père, elle aime voyager. Elle aime aussi faire (to do) du sport. Ma sœur, Élodie, a 17 ans. Elle est grande, a les cheveux châtains et les yeux verts. Elle est encore au lycée. Elle adore écouter de la musique et aller au (to go to) cinéma. Mon oncle, ...*
*Et ta famille, comment est-elle? Donne-moi vite de tes nouvelles!*
*À bientôt!*
*Caroline*

## Après l'écriture

**1.** Exchange rough drafts with a partner. Comment on his or her work by answering these questions:

- Did your partner make the adjectives agree with the person described?

- Did your partner include the age, family relationship, physical characteristics, and hobbies and interests of each family member?

- Did your partner use verb forms correctly?

- Did your partner use the letter-writing expressions correctly?

**2.** Revise your description according to your partner's comments. After writing the final version, read it once more to eliminate these kinds of problems:

- spelling errors

- punctuation errors

- capitalization errors

- use of incorrect verb forms

- adjectives that do not agree with the nouns they modify

## EVALUATION

**Criteria**

**Content** Includes all the information mentioned in the three bulleted items in the task description as well as some of the expressions in the list of salutations, requests for response, and closings.
Scale: 1 2 3 4 5

**Organization** Organizes the letter into a salutation, a family description, a request for a response, and a closing.
Scale: 1 2 3 4 5

**Accuracy** Uses possessive and descriptive adjectives and modifies them accordingly. Spells words and conjugates verbs correctly throughout.
Scale: 1 2 3 4 5

**Creativity** The student includes additional information that is not included in the task and/or provides detailed information about numerous family members.
Scale: 1 2 3 4 5

**Scoring**

| | |
|---|---|
| Excellent | 18–20 points |
| Good | 14–17 points |
| Satisfactory | 10–13 points |
| Unsatisfactory | < 10 points |

## Key Standards

**4.1**

**Teacher Resources**
Vocabulary MP3s/CD

**Suggestion** Tell students that an easy way to study from **Vocabulaire** is to cover up the French half of each section, leaving only the English equivalents exposed. They can then quiz themselves on the French items. To focus on the English equivalents of the French entries, they simply reverse this process.

### La famille

| | |
|---|---|
| aîné(e) | elder |
| cadet(te) | younger |
| un beau-frère | brother-in-law |
| un beau-père | father-in-law; stepfather |
| une belle-mère | mother-in-law; stepmother |
| une belle-sœur | sister-in-law |
| un(e) cousin(e) | cousin |
| un demi-frère | half-brother; stepbrother |
| une demi-sœur | half-sister; stepsister |
| les enfants (m., f.) | children |
| un époux/ une épouse | spouse |
| une famille | family |
| une femme | wife; woman |
| une fille | daughter; girl |
| un fils | son |
| un frère | brother |
| une grand-mère | grandmother |
| un grand-père | grandfather |
| les grands-parents (m.) | grandparents |
| un mari | husband |
| une mère | mother |
| un neveu | nephew |
| une nièce | niece |
| un oncle | uncle |
| les parents (m.) | parents |
| un père | father |
| une petite-fille | granddaughter |
| un petit-fils | grandson |
| les petits-enfants (m.) | grandchildren |
| une sœur | sister |
| une tante | aunt |
| un chat | cat |
| un chien | dog |
| un oiseau | bird |
| un poisson | fish |

### Adjectifs descriptifs

| | |
|---|---|
| antipathique | unpleasant |
| bleu(e) | blue |
| blond(e) | blond |
| brun(e) | dark (hair) |
| court(e) | short |
| drôle | funny |
| faible | weak |
| fatigué(e) | tired |
| fort(e) | strong |
| frisé(e) | curly |
| génial(e) (géniaux pl.) | great |
| grand(e) | big; tall |
| jeune | young |
| joli(e) | pretty |
| laid(e) | ugly |
| lent(e) | slow |
| mauvais(e) | bad |
| méchant(e) | mean |
| modeste | modest, humble |
| noir(e) | black |
| pauvre | poor, unfortunate |
| pénible | tiresome |
| petit(e) | small, short (stature) |
| prêt(e) | ready |
| raide | straight |
| rapide | fast |
| triste | sad |
| vert(e) | green |
| vrai(e) | true; real |

### Vocabulaire supplémentaire

| | |
|---|---|
| divorcer | to divorce |
| épouser | to marry |
| célibataire | single |
| divorcé(e) | divorced |
| fiancé(e) | engaged |
| marié(e) | married |
| séparé(e) | separated |
| veuf/veuve | widowed |
| un(e) voisin(e) | neighbor |

| | |
|---|---|
| *Expressions utiles* | See pp. 79 and 93. |
| Possessive adjectives | See p. 84. |
| Numbers 61–100 | See p. 96. |
| Prepositions of location | See p. 98. |

### Professions et occupations

| | |
|---|---|
| un(e) architecte | architect |
| un(e) artiste | artist |
| un(e) athlète | athlete |
| un(e) avocat(e) | lawyer |
| un coiffeur/ une coiffeuse | hairdresser |
| un(e) dentiste | dentist |
| un homme/une femme d'affaires | businessman/ woman |
| un ingénieur | engineer |
| un(e) journaliste | journalist |
| un médecin | doctor |
| un(e) musicien(ne) | musician |

### Adjectifs irréguliers

| | |
|---|---|
| actif/active | active |
| beau/belle | beautiful; handsome |
| bon(ne) | kind; good |
| châtain | brown (hair) |
| courageux/ courageuse | courageous, brave |
| cruel(le) | cruel |
| curieux/curieuse | curious |
| discret/discrète | discreet; unassuming |
| doux/douce | sweet; soft |
| ennuyeux/ennuyeuse | boring |
| étranger/étrangère | foreign |
| favori(te) | favorite |
| fier/fière | proud |
| fou/folle | crazy |
| généreux/généreuse | generous |
| gentil(le) | nice |
| gros(se) | fat |
| inquiet/inquiète | worried |
| intellectuel(le) | intellectual |
| jaloux/jalouse | jealous |
| long(ue) | long |
| (mal)heureux/ (mal)heureuse | (un)happy |
| marron | brown |
| naïf/naïve | naïve |
| nerveux/nerveuse | nervous |
| nouveau/nouvelle | new |
| paresseux/paresseuse | lazy |
| roux/rousse | red-haired |
| sérieux/sérieuse | serious |
| sportif/sportive | athletic |
| travailleur/ travailleuse | hard-working |
| vieux/vieille | old |

**ressources**

daccord1.vhlcentral.com

# Au café

## Pour commencer

- Quelle heure est-il?
  a. 6h00 du matin   b. midi   c. minuit
- Qu'est-ce que Sandrine et Amina ont envie de faire (do)?
  a. manger   b. partager   c. échouer
- Que vont-elles (are they going to) manger?
  a. un café       b. une limonade
  c. des sandwichs

## Unit Goals

**Leçon 4A**

In this lesson, students will learn:
- names for places around town
- terms for activities around town
- to pronounce oral vowels
- about pastimes of young French people and **le verlan**
- the verb **aller** and to express future actions with it
- the preposition **à** and contractions with it
- interrogative words
- about the Swiss national airline

**Leçon 4B**

In this lesson, students will learn:
- terms for food items at a café
- expressions of quantity
- to pronounce nasal vowels
- about the role of the café in France and the cafés of North Africa
- more about cafés and food items through specially shot video footage
- the present tense of **prendre** and **boire**
- the formation and use of partitive articles
- regular **-ir** verbs
- to listen for the gist in oral communication

**Savoir-faire**

In this section, students will learn:
- cultural and historical information about the French regions of **Normandie** and **Bretagne**
- to scan a text to improve comprehension
- to add details in French to make writing more interesting

**Pour commencer**
- b. midi
- a. manger
- c. des sandwichs

---

## Section Goals

In this section, students will learn and practice vocabulary related to:
- places in a city
- pastimes

## Key Standards

**1.1, 1.2, 4.1**

### Student Resources
*Cahier d'exercices*, pp. 43–44;
Cahier d'activités, pp. 33–34, 139;
Supersite: Activities,
*Cahier interactif*

### Teacher Resources
Answer Keys; Overhead #25;
Audio Script; Textbook & Audio Activity MP3s/CD; Info Gap Activities; Testing program: Vocabulary Quiz

## Suggestions

- Have students look at the new vocabulary and identify the cognates.
- Use **Overhead #25**. As you point to different people, describe where they are and what they are doing. Examples: **Ils sont à la terrasse d'un café. Elles bavardent.** Follow up with simple questions based on your narrative.
- Ask students yes/no and either/or questions about their preferences using the new vocabulary. Examples: **Aimez-vous nager? Préférez-vous regarder un film au cinéma ou à la maison?**
- Tell students that proper names of places, like adjectives, usually follow generic nouns. Examples: **le cinéma Rex** and **le parc Monceau.**
- Point out that the term **une boîte de nuit** is familiar and usually used among young people. **Une discothèque** is the more formal word for *nightclub*.
- Point out that **un gymnase** in France generally has a track, exercise equipment, basketball or tennis courts, showers, but no pool.

**Leçon** **4A**

S **Talking Picture**
**Audio: Activity**

You will learn how to...
- say where you are going
- say what you are going to do

# Où allons-nous?

une montagne
une maison
Il passe chez quelqu'un. (passer)
Elle quitte la maison. (quitter)
Ils déjeunent. (déjeuner)
une place
une terrasse de café
Elles bavardent. (bavarder)

### Vocabulaire

| | |
|---|---|
| danser | to dance |
| explorer | to explore |
| fréquenter | to frequent; to visit |
| inviter | to invite |
| nager | to swim |
| patiner | to skate |
| | |
| une banlieue | suburbs |
| une boîte (de nuit) | nightclub |
| un bureau | office; desk |
| un centre commercial | shopping center, mall |
| un centre-ville | city/town center, downtown |
| un cinéma (ciné) | movie theater, movies |
| un endroit | place |
| un grand magasin | department store |
| un gymnase | gym |
| un hôpital | hospital |
| un lieu | place |
| un magasin | store |
| un marché | market |
| un musée | museum |
| un parc | park |
| une piscine | pool |
| un restaurant | restaurant |
| une ville | city, town |

**ressources**

CE
pp. 43–44

CA
p. 33–34, 139

S
daccord1.vhlcentral.com

**110** *cent dix*

**O P T I O N S**

**Using Games** Divide the class into two teams. Put objects related to different places in a box (for example, movie ticket stubs, sunglasses, and a coffee cup). Without looking, have a student reach into the box and pick out an object. The next player on that person's team has five seconds to name a place associated with the object. If the person cannot do so within the time limit, the other team may "steal" the point by giving a correct response. When the box is empty, the team with the most points wins.

**Flash Cards** Use magazine photos or clip art from the Internet to make flash cards representing places in and around town. As you show each image, students should say the name of the place and as many activities associated with it as they can think of.

## Mise en pratique

### Attention!

Remember that nouns that end in –al have an irregular plural. Replace –al with –aux.

un hôpital → deux hôpitaux

À (to, at) before le or les makes these contractions:
à + le = au     à + les = aux
le musée → au musée
les endroits → aux endroits
À does NOT contract with l' or la.

une église

une épicerie

euromarché

JOURNAUX

un kiosque

Il dépense de l'argent (m.). (dépenser)

**1** **Associez** Quels lieux associez-vous à ces activités?

1. nager _____ une piscine
2. danser _____ une boîte (de nuit)
3. dîner _____ un restaurant
4. travailler _____ un bureau
5. habiter _____ une maison
6. épouser _____ une église
7. voir (to see) un film _____ un cinéma
8. acheter (to buy) des fruits _____ un marché, une épicerie

**2** **Écoutez** 🎧 Djamila parle de sa journée à son amie Samira. Écoutez la conversation et mettez (put) les lieux de la liste dans l'ordre chronologique. Il y a deux lieux en trop (extra).

_3_ **a.** à l'hôpital
_8_ **b.** à la maison
_1_ **c.** à la piscine
_5_ **d.** au centre commercial
_6_ **e.** au cinéma
_NA_ **f.** à l'église
_2_ **g.** au musée
_7_ **h.** au bureau
_NA_ **i.** au parc
_4_ **j.** au restaurant

### Coup de main

Note that the French **Je vais à...** is the equivalent of the English *I am going to...*

**3** **Logique ou illogique** Lisez chaque phrase et déterminez si l'action est logique ou illogique. Corrigez si nécessaire. Suggested answers

| | logique | illogique |
|---|---|---|
| 1. Maxime invite Delphine à une épicerie. <br> Maxime invite Delphine au musée. | ☐ | ☑ |
| 2. Caroline et Aurélie bavardent au marché. | ☑ | ☐ |
| 3. Nous déjeunons à l'épicerie. <br> Nous déjeunons au restaurant. | ☐ | ☑ |
| 4. Ils dépensent beaucoup d'argent au centre commercial. | ☑ | ☐ |
| 5. Vous explorez une ville. | ☑ | ☐ |
| 6. Vous escaladez (climb) une montagne. | ☑ | ☐ |
| 7. J'habite en banlieue. | ☑ | ☐ |
| 8. Tu danses dans un marché. <br> Tu danses dans une boîte (de nuit). | ☐ | ☑ |

🖱️ Practice more at **daccord1.vhlcentral.com.**

*cent onze* **111**

**1** **Expansion**
• For additional practice, give students these items.
**9.** chanter (une église)
**10.** manger (un restaurant/un café) **11.** dessiner (un musée)
• Do this activity in reverse. Name places and have students say what activities can be done there.

**2** **Script** DJAMILA: Allô, Samira. Comment ça va?
SAMIRA: Très bien, et toi?
D: Aujourd'hui, très bien, mais alors demain, quelle journée!
S: Comment ça?
D: Eh bien… demain matin, je vais à la piscine avec mon frère, Hassan, à 8h00. À 10h00, je vais au musée Rodin avec ma classe. À 11h00, je passe un moment avec grand-mère à l'hôpital. À midi, je vais au restaurant Chez Benoît, près de la place Carnot. L'après-midi, je vais au centre commercial et au cinéma voir le dernier film de Jean Reno. Pour terminer, à 17h00, je vais au bureau de maman pour travailler un peu et nous rentrons à la maison ensemble.
S: Quel programme! Bon, courage Djamila et à bientôt.
D: Merci, bonne soirée.
*(On Textbook Audio)*

**2** **Suggestion** Before beginning the activity, have students read the list of places and the **Coup de main**.

**3** **Suggestion** Tell students to write their corrections. Then have volunteers write their sentences on the board.

**3** **Expansion** For additional practice, give students these items. **9. Vous dansez au magasin. (illogique) 10. Je nage au musée. (illogique) 11. Madame Ducharme habite dans une maison. (logique)**

**OPTIONS**

**Using Movement** Have students represent various stores and places in town by giving them signs to hold. Ask them where one does various activities. Examples: **Où est-ce qu'on regarde un film/mange/nage?** The student with the appropriate sign should step forward and answer. Examples: **On regarde un film au cinéma. On mange au restaurant. On nage à la piscine.**

**Oral Practice** Ask students about their favorite places. Tell them to use generic place names in front of proper nouns, such as **le parc Zilker** and **le musée du Louvre.** Ask: **Quel est votre restaurant/musée préféré?**

# Communication

**4**   **Conversez** Avec un(e) partenaire, échangez vos opinions sur ces activités. Utilisez un élément de chaque colonne dans vos réponses.   Answers will vary.

**MODÈLE**

**Élève 1:** Moi, j'adore bavarder au restaurant, mais je déteste parler au musée.
**Élève 2:** Moi aussi, j'adore bavarder au restaurant. Je ne déteste pas parler au musée, mais j'aime mieux bavarder au parc.

| Opinion | Activité | Lieu |
|---|---|---|
| adorer | bavarder | au bureau |
| aimer (mieux) | danser | au centre commercial |
| ne pas tellement aimer | déjeuner | au centre-ville |
| détester | dépenser de l'argent | au cinéma |
| | étudier | au gymnase |
| | inviter | au musée |
| | nager | au parc |
| | parler | à la piscine |
| | patiner | au restaurant |

**5**   **La journée d'Anne** Votre professeur va vous donner, à vous et à votre partenaire, une feuille d'activités partiellement illustrée. À tour de rôle, posez-vous des questions pour compléter vos feuilles respectives. Utilisez le vocabulaire de la leçon. Attention! Ne regardez pas la feuille de votre partenaire.   Answers will vary.

**MODÈLE**

**Élève 1:** À 7h30, Anne quitte la maison. Qu'est-ce qu'elle fait ensuite (do next)?
**Élève 2:** À 8h00, elle…

**Anne**

**6**   **Une lettre** Écrivez une lettre à un(e) ami(e) dans laquelle (in which) vous décrivez vos activités de la semaine. Utilisez les expressions de la liste.   Answers will vary.

| | |
|---|---|
| bavarder | passer chez quelqu'un |
| déjeuner | travailler |
| dépenser de l'argent | quitter la maison |
| étudier | un centre commercial |
| manger au restaurant | un cinéma |

*Cher Paul,*

*Comment vas-tu? Pour (For) moi, tout va bien. Je suis très actif/active. Je travaille beaucoup et j'ai beaucoup d'amis. En général, le samedi, après les cours, je déjeune chez moi et l'après-midi, je bavarde avec mes amis…*

# Les sons et les lettres

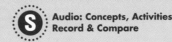

**Audio: Concepts, Activities
Record & Compare**

🎧 **Oral vowels**

French has two basic kinds of vowel sounds: oral vowels, the subject of this discussion, and nasal vowels, presented in **Leçon 4B**. Oral vowels are produced by releasing air through the mouth. The pronunciation of French vowels is consistent and predictable.

In short words (usually two-letter words), **e** is pronounced similarly to the *a* in the English word *about*.

| l**e** | qu**e** | c**e** | d**e** |
|---|---|---|---|

The letter **a** alone is pronounced like the *a* in *father*.

| l**a** | ç**a** | m**a** | t**a** |
|---|---|---|---|

The letter **i** by itself and the letter **y** are pronounced like the vowel sound in the word *bee*.

| **i**c**i** | l**i**vre | st**y**lo | l**y**cée |
|---|---|---|---|

The letter combination **ou** sounds like the vowel sound in the English word *who*.

| v**ou**s | n**ou**s | **ou**blier | éc**ou**ter |
|---|---|---|---|

The French **u** sound does not exist in English. To produce this sound, say *ee* with your lips rounded.

| t**u** | d**u** | **u**ne | ét**u**dier |
|---|---|---|---|

**Prononcez** Répétez les mots suivants à voix haute.

1. je
2. chat
3. fou
4. ville
5. utile
6. place
7. jour
8. triste
9. mari
10. active
11. Sylvie
12. rapide
13. gymnase
14. antipathique
15. calculatrice
16. piscine

**Articulez** Répétez les phrases suivantes à voix haute.

1. Salut, Luc. Ça va?
2. La philosophie est difficile.
3. Brigitte est une actrice fantastique.
4. Suzanne va à son cours de physique.
5. Tu trouves le cours de maths facile?
6. Viviane a une bourse universitaire.

**Dictons** Répétez les dictons à voix haute.

*Plus on est de fous, plus on rit.*[2]

*Qui va à la chasse perd sa place.*[1]

[2] The more the merrier.

[1] He who steps out of line loses his place.

**ressources**

CA
p. 140

daccord1.vhlcentral.com

*cent treize* **113**

---

---

CONTEXTES **113**

## Star du cinéma

 Video: *Roman-photo*
Record & Compare

**PERSONNAGES**

Amina

David

Pascal

Sandrine

*À l'épicerie...*
**DAVID** Juliette Binoche? Pas possible! Je vais chercher Sandrine!

*Au café...*
**PASCAL** Alors, chérie, tu vas faire quoi de ton week-end?
**SANDRINE** Euh, demain je vais déjeuner au centre-ville.
**PASCAL** Bon... et quand est-ce que tu vas rentrer?
**SANDRINE** Euh, je ne sais pas. Pourquoi?

**PASCAL** Pour rien. Et demain soir, tu vas danser?
**SANDRINE** Ça dépend. Je vais passer chez Amina pour bavarder avec elle.
**PASCAL** Combien d'amis as-tu à Aix-en-Provence?
**SANDRINE** Oh, Pascal...
**PASCAL** Bon, moi, je vais continuer à penser à toi jour et nuit.

**DAVID** Mais l'actrice! Juliette Binoche!
**SANDRINE** Allons-y! Vite! C'est une de mes actrices préférées! J'adore le film *Chocolat*!
**AMINA** Et comme elle est chic! C'est une vraie star!
**DAVID** Elle est à l'épicerie! Ce n'est pas loin d'ici!

*Dans la rue...*
**AMINA** Mais elle est où, cette épicerie? Nous allons explorer toute la ville pour rencontrer Juliette Binoche?
**SANDRINE** C'est là, l'épicerie Pierre Dubois, à côté du cinéma?
**DAVID** Mais non, elle n'est pas à l'épicerie Pierre Dubois, elle est à l'épicerie près de l'église, en face du parc.

**AMINA** Et combien d'églises est-ce qu'il y a à Aix?
**SANDRINE** Il n'y a pas d'église en face du parc!
**DAVID** Bon, hum, l'église sur la place.
**AMINA** D'accord, et ton église sur la place, elle est ici au centre-ville ou en banlieue?

**1**  **Vrai ou faux?** Indiquez pour chaque phrase si l'affirmation est vraie ou fausse et corrigez si nécessaire.

1. David va chercher Pascal. Faux. David va chercher Sandrine.
2. Sandrine va déjeuner au centre-ville. Vrai.
3. Pascal va passer chez Amina. Faux. Sandrine va passer chez Amina.
4. Pascal va continuer à penser à Sandrine jour et nuit. Vrai.
5. Pascal va bien. Vrai.

6. Juliette Binoche est l'actrice préférée de Sandrine. Vrai.
7. L'épicerie est loin du café. Faux. L'épicerie n'est pas loin.
8. L'épicerie Pierre Dubois est à côté de l'église. Faux. L'épicerie Pierre Dubois est à côté du cinéma.
9. Il n'y a pas d'église en face du parc. Vrai.
10. Juliette Binoche fréquente le P'tit Bistrot. Faux. Juliette Binoche ne fréquente pas le P'tit Bistrot.

 Practice more at **daccord1.vhlcentral.com.**

**David et les filles à la recherche de (*in search of*) leur actrice préférée**

**SANDRINE**  Oui. Génial.
Au revoir, Pascal.
**AMINA**  Salut, Sandrine. Comment
va Pascal?
**SANDRINE**  Il va bien, mais il
adore bavarder.

**DAVID**  Elle est là, elle est là!
**SANDRINE**  Mais, qui est là?
**AMINA**  Et c'est où, «là»?
**DAVID**  Juliette Binoche! Mais non,
pas ici!
**SANDRINE ET AMINA**  Quoi? Qui? Où?

*Devant l'épicerie...*
**DAVID**  C'est elle, là! Hé, JULIETTE!
**AMINA**  Oh, elle est belle!
**SANDRINE**  Elle est jolie, élégante!
**AMINA**  Elle est... petite?
**DAVID**  Elle, elle... est... vieille?!?

**AMINA**  Ce n'est pas du tout
Juliette Binoche!
**SANDRINE**  David, tu es complètement
fou! Juliette Binoche, au
centre-ville d'Aix?
**AMINA**  Pourquoi est-ce qu'elle ne
fréquente pas le P'tit Bistrot?

## Expressions utiles

### Talking about your plans

- **Tu vas faire quoi de ton week-end?**
  *What are you doing this weekend?*
- **Je vais déjeuner au centre-ville.**
  *I'm going to have lunch downtown.*
- **Quand est-ce que tu vas rentrer?**
  *When are you coming back?*
- **Je ne sais pas.**
  *I don't know.*
- **Je vais passer chez Amina.**
  *I am going to Amina's (house).*
- **Nous allons explorer toute la ville.**
  *We're going to explore the whole city.*

### Additional vocabulary

- **C'est une de mes actrices préférées.**
  *She's one of my favorite actresses.*
- **Comme elle est chic!**
  *She is so chic!*
- **Ce n'est pas loin d'ici!**
  *It's not far from here!*
- **Ce n'est pas du tout...**
  *It's not... at all.*
- **Ça dépend.**
  *It depends.*
- **Pour rien.**
  *No reason.*
- **Vite!**
  *Quick!, Hurry!*

---

**2**  **Questions**  À l'aide (*the help*) d'un dictionnaire, choisissez le bon mot pour chaque question.

1. (Avec qui, Quoi) Sandrine parle-t-elle au téléphone?
2. (Où, Parce que) Sandrine va-t-elle déjeuner?
3. (Qui, Pourquoi) Pascal demande-t-il à Sandrine quand elle va rentrer?
4. (Combien, Comment) d'amis Sandrine a-t-elle?
5. (Combien, À qui) Amina demande-t-elle comment va Pascal?
6. (Quand, Où) est Juliette Binoche?

**3**  **Écrivez**  Pensez à votre acteur ou actrice préféré(e) et préparez un paragraphe où vous décrivez son apparence, sa personnalité et sa carrière. Comment est-il/elle? Dans quel(s) (*which*) film(s) joue-t-il/elle? Si un jour vous rencontrez cet acteur/cette actrice, qu'est-ce que vous allez lui dire (*say to him or her*)?

**ressources**

CA
pp. 79–80

daccord1.vhlcentral.com

A
C
T
I
V
I
T
É
S

*cent quinze*   **115**

---

**Expressions utiles**
- Model the pronunciation of the **Expressions utiles** and have students repeat after you.
- As you work through the list, point out forms of **aller** and the interrogative words. Tell students that these concepts will be formally presented in **Structures**.
- Point out that, like the English verb *to go*, the verb **aller** is used to express future actions.
- Write **je vais** and **tu vas** on the board. Ask students the questions in the **Expressions utiles** and have them respond. Examples: **Tu vas faire quoi de ton week-end? Quand est-ce que tu vas rentrer?**
- Have students scan the video-still captions for interrogative words that are not in the list and read the sentences. Examples: **combien de, comment, qui, où,** and **pourquoi**.

**1**  **Suggestion**  Have students write the correct answers to the false statements on the board.

**1**  **Expansion**  For additional practice, give students these items. **11. Juliette Binoche est vieille. (Faux. Elle n'est pas vieille.) 12. Amina pense que Juliette Binoche est chic. (Vrai.)**

**2**  **Expansion**
- For additional practice, give students these items. **7. (Qui, Comment) est-ce que David voit (*see*) à l'épicerie? (Qui) 8. (Pourquoi, Comment) est Juliette Binoche? (Comment) 9. (Quand, Où) est-ce que Pascal va penser à Sandrine? (Quand)**
- Have students answer the questions.

**3**  **Suggestion**  Have students exchange papers for peer editing. Remind them to pay particular attention to adjective agreement and subject-verb agreement.

---

O
P
T
I
O
N
S

**Juliette Binoche**  Juliette Binoche (1964– ), often referred to by the French press simply as "La Binoche", was born in Paris. In addition to being an actress, she is a poster designer and avid painter. Her first film was *Liberty Belle* (1983). She has now acted in more that 30 films. She won a César for "Best actress" in *Bleu* (1983) and an Oscar for "Best Supporting Actress" in

*The English Patient* (1996). *Chocolat* (2000) is the film version of the novel *Chocolat* by Joanne Harris.

**Skits**  Working in groups of three, have students create a short skit similar to the scenes in video stills 5–10 in which someone thinks they have seen a famous person. Give students ten minutes to prepare, then call on groups to perform their skits for the class.

---

### CULTURE À LA LOUPE

# Les passe-temps des jeunes Français

**Comment est-ce que les jeunes occupent leur temps libre° en France?**
Les jeunes de 15 à 25 ans passent beaucoup de temps à regarder la télévision: environ° 12 heures par° semaine. Ils écoutent aussi beaucoup de musique: environ 16 heures par semaine, et surfent souvent° sur Internet (11 heures). Environ 25% des jeunes Français ont même° déjà° un blog sur Internet. Les jeux° vidéo sont aussi très populaires: les jeunes jouent° en moyenne° 15 heures par semaine.

En France, les jeunes aiment également° les activités culturelles, en particulier le cinéma: en moyenne, ils y° vont une fois° par semaine. Ils aiment aussi la littérature et l'art: presque° 50% (pour cent) visitent des musées ou des monuments historiques chaque année et plus de° 40% vont au théâtre ou à des concerts. Un jeune sur cinq° joue d'un instrument de musique ou chante°, et environ 20% d'entre eux° pratiquent une activité artistique, comme la danse, le théâtre, la sculpture, le dessin° ou la peinture°. La photographie et la vidéo sont aussi très appréciées.

Il ne faut pas° oublier de mentionner que les jeunes Français sont aussi très sportifs. Bien sûr, comme tous les jeunes, ils préfèrent parfois° simplement se détendre° et bavarder avec des amis.

Finalement, les passe-temps des jeunes Français sont similaires aux activités des jeunes Américains!

### Les activités culturelles des Français

*(% des Français qui les° pratiquent)*

| | |
|---|---|
| le dessin | 7% |
| la peinture | 4% |
| le piano | 3% |
| autre instrument de musique | 3% |
| la danse | 2% |
| la guitare | 2% |
| la sculpture | 1% |
| le théâtre | 1% |

SOURCE: Francoscopie

**temps libre** *free time* **environ** *around* **par** *per* **souvent** *often* **même** *even* **déjà** *already* **jeux** *games* **jouent** *play* **en moyenne** *on average* **également** *also* **y** *there* **fois** *time* **presque** *almost* **plus de** *more than* **un... sur cinq** *one... in five* **chante** *sings* **d'entre eux** *of them* **dessin** *drawing* **peinture** *painting* **Il ne faut pas** *One must not* **parfois** *sometimes* **se détendre** *relax* **les** *them*

---

**A C T I V I T É S**

**1** **Vrai ou faux?** Indiquez si les phrases sont **vraies** ou **fausses**. Corrigez les phrases fausses. Some answers may vary.

1. Les jeunes Français n'écoutent pas de musique. Faux. Les jeunes Français écoutent de la musique environ 16 heures par semaine.
2. Ils n'utilisent pas Internet. Faux. Ils utilisent Internet 11 heures par semaine.
3. Ils aiment aller au musée. Vrai.
4. Ils n'aiment pas beaucoup les livres. Faux. Ils aiment la littérature.
5. Ils n'aiment pas pratiquer d'activités artistiques. Faux. Possible answer: Ils aiment la danse, le théâtre et le dessin.
6. Les Français entre 15 et 25 ans ne font pas de sport. Faux. Les jeunes Français sont très sportifs.

7. Les passe-temps des jeunes Américains sont similaires aux passe-temps des jeunes Français. Vrai.
8. L'instrument de musique le plus (*the most*) populaire en France est le piano. Vrai.
9. Plus de (*More*) gens pratiquent la peinture que la sculpture. Vrai.
10. Environ 10% des jeunes Français pratiquent la sculpture. Faux. 1% des jeunes Français pratiquent la sculpture.

**S** Practice more at **daccord1.vhlcentral.com**.

---

## LE FRANÇAIS QUOTIDIEN

### Le verlan

En France, on entend parfois° des jeunes parler en **verlan**. En verlan, les syllabes des mots sont inversées° :

l'envers° → vers-l'en → verlan.

Voici quelques exemples :

| français | verlan | anglais |
|----------|--------|---------|
| louche | chelou | *shady* |
| café | féca | *café* |
| mec | keum | *guy* |
| femme | meuf | *woman* |

**parfois** *sometimes* **inversées** *inverted* **l'envers** *the reverse*

## LE MONDE FRANCOPHONE

### Où passer le temps

Voici quelques endroits typiques où les jeunes francophones aiment se restaurer° et passer du temps.

#### En Afrique de l'Ouest

**Le maquis** Commun dans beaucoup de pays° d'Afrique de l'Ouest°, le maquis est un restaurant où on peut manger à bas prix°. Situé en ville ou en bord de route°, le maquis est typiquement en plein air°.

#### Au Sénégal

**Le tangana** Le terme «tang» signifie «chaud» en wolof, une des langues nationales du Sénégal. Le tangana est un lieu populaire pour se restaurer. On trouve souvent les tanganas au coin de la rue°, en plein air, avec des tables et des bancs°.

**se restaurer** *have something to eat* **pays** *countries* **ouest** *west* **à bas prix** *inexpensively* **en bord de route** *on the side of the road* **en plein air** *outdoors* **coin de la rue** *street corner* **bancs** *benches*

# Le parc Astérix

Situé° à 30 kilomètres de Paris, en Picardie, le parc Astérix est le premier parc à thème français. Le parc d'attractions°, ouvert° en 1989, est basé sur la bande dessinée° française, *Astérix le Gaulois*. Création de René Goscinny et d'Albert Uderzo, Astérix est un guerrier gaulois° qui lutte° contre l'invasion des Romains. Au parc Astérix, il y a des montagnes russes°, des petits trains et des spectacles, tous° basés sur les aventures d'Astérix et de son meilleur ami, Obélix. Une des attractions, *le Tonnerre° de Zeus*, est la plus grande° montagne russe en bois° d'Europe.

**Situé** *Located* **parc d'attractions** *amusement park* **ouvert** *opened* **bande dessinée** *comic strip* **guerrier gaulois** *Gallic warrior* **lutte** *fights* **montagnes russes** *roller coasters* **tous** *all* **Tonnerre** *Thunder* **la plus grande** *the largest* **en bois** *wooden*

### SUR INTERNET

Comment sont les parcs d'attractions dans les autres pays francophones?

Go to **daccord1.vhlcentral.com** to find more information related to this **CULTURE** section.

---

**2** **Compréhension** Complétez les phrases.

1. Le parc Astérix est basé sur Astérix le Gaulois, une <u>bande dessinée</u>.
2. Astérix le Gaulois est une <u>création</u> de René Goscinny et d'Albert Uderzo.
3. Le parc Astérix est près de la ville de <u>Paris</u>.
4. Astérix est un <u>guerrier</u> gaulois.
5. En verlan, on peut passer du temps avec ses copains au <u>féca</u>.
6. Au Sénégal, on parle aussi le <u>wolof</u>.

**3** **Vos activités préférées** Posez des questions à trois ou quatre de vos camarades de classe à propos de leurs activités favorites. Comparez vos résultats avec ceux (*those*) d'un autre groupe.

**ressources**

Ⓢ

daccord1.vhlcentral.com

**A C T I V I T É S**

---

**Le français quotidien** Model the pronunciation of each term and have students repeat it. Ask students what language or jargon in English is similar to **verlan**. (pig latin)

**Portrait** Point out Astérix and Obélix in the photo. If possible, bring in an Astérix comic strip to show the students.

**Le monde francophone** Have students read the text. Then ask a few comprehension questions. Examples: **1. Pourquoi les jeunes fréquentent-ils les maquis et les tanganas? (pour manger et passer le temps) 2. On trouve les maquis en ville ou en bord de route? (les deux) Et les tanganas? (Ils sont souvent au coin d'une rue.) 3. On mange à l'intérieur ou en plein air dans le maquis et le tangana? (en plein air)**

**2** **Expansion** For additional practice, give students these items. **7. Le parc Astérix est le premier _____ à thème français. (parc) 8. Astérix lutte (*fights*) contre les _____. (Romains) 9. Au parc Astérix, il y a des montagnes _____. (russes) 10. L'ami d'Astérix s'appelle _____. (Obélix)**

**3** **Expansion** Do a quick class survey to find out how many students like each activity and which one is the most popular. Tally the results on the board. Example: **Combien d'élèves surfent sur Internet?**

---

**O P T I O N S**

**Le verlan** Write on the board: **1. une bande 2. la musique 3. le métro 4. manger 5. bonjour 6. fou** Have students work in pairs. Tell them to copy the words and write the equivalents in verlan. Answers: **1. une deban 2. la siquemu/sicmu 3. le tromé 4. géman 5. jourbon 6. ouf**

**Le parc Astérix** Some other popular attractions at the park are **La Galère** (a giant swinging ship), **Les Chaises Volantes** (flying chairs), **Le Cheval de Troie** (the Trojan horse), and **Transdemonium** (a ghost train through a castle dungeon). Have students take a virtual tour of the park by going to **www.parcasterix.com**.

## 4A.1 The verb *aller*

**Point de départ** In **Leçon 1A**, you saw a form of the verb **aller** (*to go*) in the expression **ça va**. Now you will use this verb to talk about going places and to express actions that take place in the immediate future.

| Aller | | | |
|---|---|---|---|
| je vais | *I go* | nous allons | *we go* |
| tu vas | *you go* | vous allez | *you go* |
| il/elle va | *he/she/it goes* | ils/elles vont | *they go* |

- Note that **aller** is irregular. Only the **nous** and **vous** forms resemble the infinitive.

Tu **vas** souvent au cinéma?
*Do you go often to the movies?*

Je **vais** à la piscine.
*I'm going to the pool.*

Nous **allons** au marché le samedi.
*We go to the market on Saturdays.*

Vous **allez** au parc aussi?
*Are you going to the park too?*

- **Aller** can also be used with another verb to tell what is going to happen. This construction is called **le futur proche** (*immediate future*). Conjugate **aller** in the present tense and place the other verb's infinitive form directly after it.

Nous **allons déjeuner** sur la terrasse.
*We're going to eat lunch on the terrace.*

Marc et Julie **vont explorer** le centre-ville.
*Marc and Julie are going to explore downtown.*

Demain, je vais déjeuner au centre-ville.

Et quand est-ce que tu vas rentrer?

- To negate an expression in **le futur proche**, place **ne/n'** before the conjugated form of **aller** and **pas** after it.

Je **ne vais pas** faire mes devoirs.
*I'm not going to do my homework.*

Nous **n'allons pas** quitter la maison.
*We're not going to leave the house.*

- Note that this construction can be used with the infinitive of **aller** to mean *going to go (somewhere)*.

Elle **va aller** à la piscine.
*She's going to go to the pool.*

Vous **allez aller** au gymnase ce soir?
*You're going to go to the gym tonight?*

**1** **Questions parentales** Votre père est très curieux. Trouvez les questions qu'il pose.

**MODÈLE**

tes frères / piscine  *Tes frères vont à la piscine?*

1. tu / cinéma / ce soir
   Tu vas au cinéma ce soir?
2. tes amis et toi, vous / café
   Tes amis et toi, vous allez au café?
3. ta mère et moi, nous / ville / vendredi
   Ta mère et moi, nous allons en ville vendredi?
4. ton ami(e) / souvent / marché
   Ton ami(e) va souvent au marché?
5. je / musée / avec toi / demain
   Je vais au musée avec toi demain?
6. tes amis / parc
   Tes amis vont au parc?

**2** **Samedi prochain** Voici ce que (*what*) vous et vos amis faites (*are doing*) aujourd'hui. Indiquez que vous allez faire les mêmes (*same*) choses samedi prochain.

**MODÈLE**

Je nage.  *Samedi prochain aussi, je vais nager.*

1. Paul bavarde avec ses copains.
   Samedi prochain aussi, Paul va bavarder avec ses copains.
2. Nous dansons.
   ... nous allons danser.
3. Je dépense de l'argent dans un magasin.
   ... je vais dépenser de l'argent dans un magasin.
4. Luc et Sylvie déjeunent au restaurant.
   ... Luc et Sylvie vont déjeuner au restaurant.
5. Vous explorez le centre-ville.
   ... vous allez explorer le centre-ville.
6. Tu patines.
   ... tu vas patiner.

**3** **Où vont-ils?** Avec un(e) partenaire, regardez les images et indiquez où vont les personnages. Answers will vary.

**MODÈLE**

Henri va au cinéma.

**Henri**

**1. je**

**3. Paul et Luc**

**2. nous**

**4. vous**

Practice more at **daccord1.vhlcentral.com**.

## COMMUNICATION

**4 Activités du week-end** Avec un(e) partenaire, assemblez les éléments des colonnes pour poser des questions. Rajoutez (*Add*) d'autres éléments utiles.
Answers will vary.

**MODÈLE**

Élève 1: Est-ce que tu vas déjeuner avec tes copains?
Élève 2: Oui, je vais déjeuner avec mes copains.

| A | B | C | D |
|---|---|---|---|
| ta sœur | aller | voyager | professeur |
| vous | | aller | cinéma |
| tes copains | | déjeuner | boîte de nuit |
| nous | | bavarder | piscine |
| tu | | nager | centre commercial |
| ton petit ami | | danser | café |
| ta petite amie | | parler | parents |
| tes grands-parents | | | copains |
| | | | petit(e) ami(e) |

**5 À Deauville** Votre professeur va vous donner, à vous et à votre partenaire, un plan (*map*) de Deauville. Attention! Ne regardez pas la feuille de votre partenaire. Answers will vary.

**MODÈLE**

Élève 1: Où va Simon?
Élève 2: Il va au kiosque.

**6 Le grand voyage** Vous partez (*leave*) en voyage dans un lieu de votre choix. Par groupes de trois, expliquez à vos camarades ce que vous allez faire pendant (*during*) le voyage. Vos camarades vont deviner (*to guess*) où vous allez. Answers will vary.

**MODÈLE**

Élève 1: Je vais visiter le musée du Louvre.
Élève 2: Est-ce que tu vas aller à Paris?

### The preposition *à*

- The preposition **à** contracts with the definite articles **le** and **les**. It does not contract with **la** or **l'**.

| à + le ▸ au | à + les ▸ aux |
|---|---|

Nous allons **au** magasin.
*We're going to the store.*

Je rentre **à la** maison.
*I'm going back home.*

Ils parlent **aux** profs.
*They speak to the teachers.*

Il va **à l'**épicerie.
*He's going to the grocery store.*

- The preposition **à** can be translated in various ways in English: *to, in, at*. It often indicates a physical location, as with **aller à** and **habiter à**. However, it can have other meanings depending on the verb used.

**Verbs with the preposition *à***

| commencer à [+ infinitive] | to start (doing something) | penser à | to think about |
|---|---|---|---|
| parler à | to talk to | téléphoner à | to phone (someone) |

Elle va **parler au** professeur.
*She's going to talk to the teacher.*

Il **commence à travailler** demain.
*He starts working tomorrow.*

- In general, **à** is used to mean *at* or *in*, whereas **dans** is used to mean *inside*. When learning a place name in French, learn the preposition that accompanies it.

**Prepositions with place names**

| à la maison | at home | dans la maison | inside the house |
|---|---|---|---|
| à Paris | in Paris | dans Paris | inside Paris |
| en ville | in town | dans la ville | inside the town |
| sur la place | in the square | à la/sur la/ en terrasse | on the terrace |

Il travaille **à la maison**?
*Is he working at home?*

On mange **dans la maison**.
*We'll eat inside the house.*

**Essayez!** Utilisez la forme correcte du verbe **aller**.

1. Comment ça __va__?
2. Tu __vas__ à la piscine pour nager.
3. Ils __vont__ au centre-ville.
4. Nous __allons__ bavarder au parc.
5. Vous __allez__ aller au restaurant ce soir?
6. Elle __va__ aller à l'église dimanche matin.
7. Ce soir, je __vais__ danser en boîte.
8. On ne __va__ pas passer par l'épicerie cet après-midi.

# 4A.2 Interrogative words

**Point de départ** In **Leçon 2A**, you learned four ways to formulate yes or no questions in French. However, many questions seek information that can't be provided by a simple yes or no answer.

- Use these words with **est-ce que** or inversion.

## Interrogative words

| | | | |
|---|---|---|---|
| **à quelle heure?** | *at what time?* | **quand?** | *when?* |
| **combien (de)?** | *how many?;* | **que/qu'...?** | *what?* |
| | *how much?* | **quel(le)(s)?** | *which?; what?* |
| **comment?** | *how?; what?* | **(à/avec/pour)** | *(to/with/for)* |
| **où?** | *where?* | **qui?** | *who(m)?* |
| **pourquoi?** | *why?* | **quoi?** | *what?* |

**À qui** le professeur **parle-t-il** ce matin?
*Whom is the teacher talking to this morning?*

**Combien de** villes **y a-t-il** en Suisse?
*How many cities are there in Switzerland?*

**Pourquoi est-ce que** tu danses?
*Why are you dancing?*

**Que** vas-tu manger?
*What are you going to eat?*

- Although **quand?** and **à quelle heure?** can be translated as *when?* in English, they are not interchangeable. Use **quand** to talk about a day or date, and **à quelle heure** to talk about a particular time of day.

**Quand** est-ce que le cours commence?
*When does the class start?*

**À quelle heure** est-ce qu'il commence?
*At what time does it begin?*

Il commence **le lundi 28 août**.
*It starts Monday, August 28.*

Il commence **à dix heures et demie**.
*It starts at 10:30.*

- Another way to formulate questions with most interrogative words is by placing them after a verb. This kind of formulation is very informal but very common.

Tu t'appelles **comment**?
*What's your name?*

Tu habites **où**?
*Where do you live?*

- Note that **quoi?** (*what?*) must immediately follow a preposition in order to be used with **est-ce que** or inversion. If no preposition is necessary, place **quoi** after the verb.

**À quoi** pensez-vous?
*What are you thinking about?*

Elle étudie **quoi**?
*What does she study?*

**De quoi** est-ce qu'il parle?
*What is he talking about?*

Tu regardes **quoi**?
*What are you looking at?*

## MISE EN PRATIQUE

**1** **Le français familier** Utilisez l'inversion pour refaire les questions.

**MODÈLE**
Tu t'appelles comment?
*Comment t'appelles-tu?*

1. Tu habites où? Où habites-tu?
2. Le film commence à quelle heure? À quelle heure le film commence-t-il?
3. Il est quelle heure? Quelle heure est-il?
4. Tu as combien de frères? Combien de frères as-tu?
5. Le prof parle quand? Quand le prof parle-t-il?
6. Vous aimez quoi? Qu'aimez-vous?
7. Elle téléphone à qui? À qui téléphone-t-elle?
8. Il étudie comment? Comment étudie-t-il?

**2** **La paire** Trouvez la paire et formez des phrases complètes. Utilisez chaque (*each*) phrase une fois (*once*). Answers may vary.

1. À quelle heure  d
2. Comment  f
3. Combien de  g
4. Avec qui  h
5. Où  b
6. Pourquoi  c
7. Qu'  a
8. Quelle  e

a. est-ce que tu regardes?
b. habitent-ils?
c. est-ce que tu habites dans le centre-ville?
d. est-ce que le cours commence?
e. heure est-il?
f. vous appelez-vous?
g. villes est-ce qu'il y a aux États-Unis?
h. parlez-vous?

**3** **La question** Vous avez les réponses. Quelles sont les questions? Some answers will vary.

**MODÈLE**
Il est midi.
*Quelle heure est-il?*

1. Les cours commencent à huit heures.
À quelle heure est-ce que les cours commencent?
2. Stéphanie habite à Paris.
Où est-ce que Stéphanie habite?
3. Julien danse avec Caroline.
Avec qui est-ce que Julien danse?
4. Elle s'appelle Julie.
Comment s'appelle-t-elle?
5. Laëtitia a deux chiens.
Combien de chiens Laëtitia a-t-elle?
6. Elle déjeune dans ce restaurant parce qu'il est à côté de son bureau.
Pourquoi déjeune-t-elle dans ce restaurant?
7. Nous allons bien, merci.
Comment allez-vous?
8. Je vais au marché mardi.
Quand est-ce que tu vas au marché?

Practice more at **daccord1.vhlcentral.com**.

---

## COMMUNICATION

**4  Questions et réponses** À tour de rôle, posez une question à un(e) partenaire au sujet de chaque (*each*) thème de la liste. Posez une deuxième (*second*) question basée sur sa réponse. Answers will vary.

**MODÈLE**

Élève 1: *Où est-ce que tu vas après les cours?*
Élève 2: *Je vais au gymnase.*
Élève 1: *Pourquoi est-ce que tu vas au gymnase?*

**Thèmes**

- où vous habitez
- ce que vous faites (*do*) le week-end
- à qui vous téléphonez
- combien de frères et sœurs vous avez
- les endroits que vous fréquentez avec vos copains

**5  La montagne** Par groupes de quatre, lisez (*read*) avec attention la lettre de Céline. Fermez votre livre. Une personne du groupe va poser une question basée sur l'information donnée. La personne qui répond pose une autre question au groupe, etc.

Answers will vary.

*Bonjour. Je m'appelle Céline. J'ai 17 ans. Je suis grande, mince et sportive. J'habite à Grenoble dans une maison agréable. Je suis en première. J'adore la montagne.*

*Tous les week-ends, je vais skier à Chamrousse avec mes trois amis Théo, Catherine et Pascal. Nous skions de midi à cinq heures. À six heures, nous prenons un chocolat chaud chez moi ou nous allons manger des crêpes chez Théo. Nous allons au cinéma tous ensemble.*

---

- To answer a question formulated with **pourquoi**, use **parce que/qu'** (*because*).

**Pourquoi** habites-tu en banlieue?
*Why do you live in the suburbs?*

**Parce que** je n'aime pas le centre-ville.
*Because I don't like downtown.*

- It's impolite to use **Quoi?** to indicate that you don't understand what's being said. Use **Comment?** or **Pardon?** instead.

Vous allez voyager cette année?
*Are you going to travel this year?*

**Comment?**
*I beg your pardon?*

- Note that when **qui** is used as a subject, the verb that follows is always singular.

**Qui** fréquente le café?
*Who goes to the café?*

Nora et Angélique fréquentent le café.
*Nora and Angélique go to the café.*

- **Quel(le)(s)** agrees in gender and number with the noun it modifies.

### The interrogative adjective *quel(le)(s)*

| | singular | | plural | |
|---|---|---|---|---|
| masculine | **quel** hôpital? | *which hospital?* | **quels** restaurants? | *which restaurants?* |
| feminine | **quelle** place? | *which public square?* | **quelles** montagnes? | *which mountains?* |

- **Quel(le)(s)** can be placed before a form of the verb **être**.

**Quels** problèmes as-tu?     *but*     **Quels sont** tes problèmes?
*What problems do you have?*          *What are your problems?*

*Tu es de quelle origine?*

*Quel jour sommes-nous?*

**Essayez!**    Donnez les mots (*words*) interrogatifs.

1. <u>Comment</u> allez-vous? Moi, je vais très bien, merci.
2. <u>Qu'</u> est-ce que vous allez faire (*do*) après le cours?
3. Le cours de français commence à <u>quelle</u> heure?
4. <u>Pourquoi</u> est-ce que tu ne travailles pas aujourd'hui?
5. Avec <u>qui</u> est-ce qu'on va au cinéma ce soir?
6. <u>Combien</u> d'élèves y a-t-il dans la salle de classe?

---

**Essayez!** Have one student read the question aloud, then call on another student to respond.

**1 Suggestion** Have students compare their answers with a classmate.

**2 Suggestion** Have one student say the question and call on another student to answer it.

**3 Suggestion** Before beginning the activity, point out that there is more than one way to form some of the questions. Have students work in pairs. Tell them to take turns asking and answering the questions.

**4 Suggestion** Have two volunteers read the **modèle** aloud. Tell students to jot down their partner's responses.

**5 Suggestion** Circulate among the groups, lending help where necessary. You might want to have one person in each group keep the book open to verify answers.

---

**OPTIONS**

**Using Visuals** Bring in pictures or magazine photos of people doing various activities. Have students, as a class, create as many questions as they can about the pictures. Also, call on individuals to answer each question.

**Pourquoi?** Tell students to write a simple statement about something they like, love, or hate. Have the first student say the statement. The next student asks **Pourquoi?** and the first student answers. Then the second student says his or her statement, and a third student asks why. Examples: **Élève 1: Je déteste étudier le samedi soir. Élève 2: Pourquoi? Élève 1: Parce que c'est la barbe/barbant!**

# SYNTHÈSE

# Révision

**1 Suggestion** Model the activity with a volunteer by asking questions about **le café**. Tell students to jot down notes during the interviews. Encourage them to add other places to the list.

**2 Suggestion** Photocopy and distribute a page from a French day planner so that students can make a note of the activities in the appropriate place. To review telling time, tell students to say the time at which they do the activities as well as the day.

**3 Suggestion** Before beginning the activity, have students make a list of possible activities for the weekend.

**4 Suggestion** Before beginning the activity, give students a few minutes to make a list of possible activities in their hometown to discuss.

**5 Suggestion** Have two volunteers to read the **modèle** aloud. Then have students brainstorm places they could go and things they could do in each city. Write their suggestions on the board.

**6 Suggestion** Divide the class into pairs and distribute the Info Gap Handouts for this activity. Give students ten minutes to complete the activity.

**6 Expansion** Call on volunteers to read their descriptions aloud and have the class compare them.

**1 En ville** Par groupes de trois, interviewez vos camarades. Où allez-vous en ville? Quand ils mentionnent un endroit de la liste, demandez des détails (quand? avec qui? pourquoi? etc.). Présentez les réponses à la classe. *Answers will vary.*

| | |
|---|---|
| le centre commercial | le musée |
| le cinéma | le parc |
| le gymnase | la piscine |
| le marché | le restaurant |

**2 La semaine prochaine** Voici votre agenda (*day planner*). Parlez de votre semaine avec un(e) partenaire. Mentionnez trois activités associées au travail et trois activités d'un autre type. Deux des activités doivent (*must*) être des activités de groupe. *Answers will vary.*

**MODÈLE**

*Lundi, je vais préparer un examen, mais samedi, je vais danser en boîte.*

| | L | M | M | J | V | S | D |
|---|---|---|---|---|---|---|---|
| 8h30 | | | | | | | |
| 9h00 | | | | | | | |
| 9h30 | | | | | | | |
| 10h00 | | | | | | | |
| 10h30 | | | | | | | |
| 11h00 | | | | | | | |
| 11h30 | | | | | | | |
| 12h00 | | | | | | | |
| 12h30 | | | | | | | |

**3 Le week-end** Par groupes de trois, posez-vous des questions sur vos projets (*plans*) pour le week-end prochain. Donnez des détails. Mentionnez aussi des activités faites (*made*) pour deux personnes. *Answers will vary.*

**MODÈLE**

**Élève 1:** *Quels projets avez-vous pour ce week-end?*
**Élève 2:** *Nous allons au marché samedi.*
**Élève 3:** *Et nous allons au cinéma dimanche.*

**4 Ma ville** À tour de rôle, vous invitez votre partenaire dans une ville pour une visite d'une semaine. Préparez une liste d'activités variées et proposez-les (*them*) à votre partenaire. Ensuite (*Then*), comparez vos villes et vos projets (*plans*) avec ceux (*those*) d'un autre groupe. *Answers will vary.*

**MODÈLE**

**Élève 1:** *Samedi, on va au centre-ville.*
**Élève 2:** *Nous allons dépenser de l'argent!*

**5 Où passer un long week-end?** Vous et votre partenaire avez la possibilité de passer un long week-end à Montréal ou à La Nouvelle-Orléans, mais vous préférez chacun(e) (*each one*) une ville différente. Jouez la conversation pour la classe. *Answers will vary.*

**MODÈLE**

**Élève 1:** *À Montréal, on va aller dans les librairies!*
**Élève 2:** *Oui, mais à La Nouvelle-Orléans, je vais aller à des concerts de musique cajun!*

**Montréal**
- le jardin (*garden*) botanique
- le musée des Beaux-Arts
- le parc du Mont-Royal
- le Vieux-Montréal

**La Nouvelle-Orléans**
- le Café du Monde
- la cathédrale Saint-Louis
- la route des plantations
- le vieux carré, quartier (*neighborhood*) français

**6 La semaine de Martine** Votre professeur va vous donner, à vous et à votre partenaire, des informations sur la semaine de Martine. Attention! Ne regardez pas la feuille de votre partenaire. *Answers will vary.*

**MODÈLE**

*Lundi matin, Martine va dessiner au parc.*

**ressources**

CE pp. 45-48 | CA pp. 35-38, 141-142 | daccord1.vhlcentral.com

**OPTIONS**

**Cultural Activity** Invite a native French speaker to class. Before the person arrives, have students prepare a list of questions that they would like to ask this person. For example, they could ask about the person's job, family, leisure-time activities, weekend plans, and the places he or she frequents. Have students use their questions to interview the person.

**Writing Practice** Give pairs three minutes to write as many questions as they can using interrogative words. Then have them get together with another pair and take turns asking and answering the questions.

**Video: TV Clip**

# Le Zapping

**Section Goals**
In this section, students will:
• read about Swiss International Airlines
• watch a commercial for a Swiss airline
• answer questions about the commercial and Swiss International Airlines

**Key Standards**
1.2, 2.2, 4.2, 5.2

Student Resources
Supersite: Video, Activities
Teacher Resources
Video Script & Translation;
Supersite: Video

## SWISS made

La compagnie Swiss International Air Lines offre à ses passagers une alternative aux compagnies aériennes° contemporaines. En général, le public a une mauvaise opinion des compagnies: les gens° se plaignent° constamment du mauvais service et de la mauvaise cuisine. Voilà pourquoi Swiss International Air Lines propose à ses clients l'élégance et le confort. Sa stratégie de marketing bénéficie de l'excellente réputation des produits et des services suisses, dont° la qualité supérieure est reconnue° dans le monde entier.

—Le ventilateur doucement° murmure...    —Au micro° parle le copilote...

### Compréhension Répondez aux questions.

1. Quels endroits d'une ville trouve-t-on dans la publicité (*ad*)? Dans la publicité, on trouve un parc, un bureau, un restaurant et une piscine.
2. Quels types de personnes y a-t-il dans la publicité? Pourquoi est-ce important? Answers will vary.

 **Discussion** Par groupes de quatre, répondez aux questions. Answers will vary.

1. Avez-vous un produit fabriqué en Suisse? Si oui, quel produit? Décrivez sa qualité. Sinon, quel produit suisse avez-vous envie de posséder? Pourquoi?
2. Vous allez fonder une compagnie aérienne différente des autres (*from the others*). Comment est-elle différente? Quelles destinations va-t-elle proposer?

**compagnies aériennes** *airlines* **les gens** *people* **se plaignent** *complain* **dont** *whose*
**reconnue** *recognized* **avion** *plane* **Le ventilateur doucement** *The fan gently* **micro** *microphone*

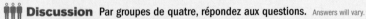 Practice more at **daccord1.vhlcentral.com.**

**Introduction**
To check comprehension, ask these questions. **1. Que propose Swiss International Airlines à ses passagers? (Elle propose une alternative aux compagnies aériennes contemporaines.) 2. Quelle opinion le public a-t-il des compagnies aériennes? (Le public a une mauvaise opinion des compagnies aériennes.) 3. Pourquoi la stratégie de marketing bénéficie-t-elle de l'excellente réputation des produits suisses? (La qualité supérieure des produits suisses est reconnue dans le monde entier.)**

**Avant de regarder la vidéo**
• Have students look at the video stills, read the captions, and predict what is happening in the commercial for each visual.
• Tell students to listen for the sentences in the video still captions, and then try to understand the rest of the song.

**Compréhension** Have students work in pairs or groups for this activity. Tell them to write their answers. Then show the video again so that they can check their answers and add any missing information.

**Discussion** Have volunteers explain how their airline would be different. Have them name the airline's destinations and say how their group came to choose them.

*cent vingt-trois* **123**

**Swiss International Airlines** Also known as SWISS, the airline was founded in 2001, after Swissair, the former Swiss national airline, filed for bankruptcy. During its first few years, SWISS struggled financially until 2005, when it made a profit after several consecutive years of losses. This coincided with the airline's takeover by the German Lufthansa. SWISS, however, maintains a high degree of autonomy from its parent company and retains its headquarters in Switzerland. Although the vast majority of the airline's destinations are in Europe, SWISS also flies to destinations all around the world. This includes service to Boston, Chicago, Los Angeles, Miami, and New York City in the United States, and to Montreal in Canada.

# Section Goals

In this section, students will learn and practice vocabulary related to:
- foods and beverages
- eating at a café or restaurant

## Key Standards
**1.1, 1.2, 4.1**

**Student Resources**
*Cahier d'exercices*, pp. 49-50; *Cahier d'activités*, pp. 39-40, 143; Supersite: Activities, *Cahier interactif*

**Teacher Resources**
Answer Keys; Overhead #26; Audio Script; Textbook & Audio Activity MP3s/CD; Info Gap Activities; Testing program: Vocabulary Quiz

## Suggestions

- Use **Overhead #26**. Ask students to describe where the scene takes place and what people are doing. Have students identify items they know.
- Have students look at the new vocabulary and identify the cognates.
- Model the pronunciation of the words and have students repeat after you. Then ask students a few questions about the people in the drawing. Examples: **Qui a faim? Que mange l'homme? Qui a soif?**
- Point out the menu in the illustration. Explain the difference between **un menu** and **une carte**. Ask students what **soupe du jour** and **plat du jour** mean. Then ask: **Combien coûte le plat du jour? Et la soupe du jour?**
- Tell students that a 15% tip is usually included in the price of a meal in a café or restaurant. If the service is particularly good, it is customary to leave a little bit extra.

## Leçon 4B

**You will learn how to...**
- order food and beverages
- ask for your check

**S** Talking Picture
Audio: Activity

# J'ai faim!

### Vocabulaire

| | |
|---|---|
| apporter | to bring, to carry |
| coûter | to cost |
| Combien coûte(nt)...? | How much is/are...? |
| une baguette | baguette (long, thin loaf of bread) |
| le beurre | butter |
| des frites (f.) | French fries |
| un fromage | cheese |
| le jambon | ham |
| un pain (de campagne) | (country-style) bread |
| un sandwich | sandwich |
| une boisson (gazeuse) | (soft) (carbonated) drink/ beverage |
| un chocolat (chaud) | (hot) chocolate |
| une eau (minérale) | (mineral) water |
| un jus (d'orange, de pomme, etc.) | (orange, apple, etc.) juice |
| le lait | milk |
| une limonade | lemon soda |
| un thé (glacé) | (iced) tea |
| (pas) assez (de) | (not) enough (of) |
| beaucoup (de) | a lot (of) |
| d'autres | others |
| un morceau (de) | piece, bit (of) |
| un peu (plus/moins) (de) | a little (more/less) (of) |
| plusieurs | several |
| quelque chose | something; anything |
| quelques | some |
| tous (m. pl.) | all |
| tout (m. sing.) | all |
| tout le/tous les (m.) | all the |
| toute la/toutes les (f.) | all the |
| trop (de) | too many/much (of) |
| un verre (de) | glass (of) |

Illustration labels: un serveur (serveuse f.); le prix; menu du jour / soupe du jour 3,50€ / plat du jour 12€; une bouteille d'eau; l'addition (f.); une soupe; les croissants (m.); Elle laisse un pourboire. (laisser); Il a faim.

**ressources**
CE pp. 49-50
CA p. 39-40, 143
**S** daccord1.vhlcentral.com

**124** cent vingt-quatre

**OPTIONS**

**Food and Drink** Write **le matin**, **à midi**, and **le soir** on the board or on a transparency. Then ask students when they prefer to have various foods and beverages. Example: **Préférez-vous manger des frites le matin ou à midi?** Other items you can mention are **un éclair**, **un sandwich**, **une soupe**, and **un croissant**.

**Categories** Have students work in pairs. Tell them to classify the foods and drinks under the headings **Manger** and **Boire** (*To drink*). After pairs have completed the activity, tell them to compare their lists with another pair and to resolve any differences.

**Attention!**

To read prices in French, say the number of euros (**euros**) followed by the number of cents (**centimes**). French decimals are marked with a comma, not a period.

8,10€ = huit euros dix (**centimes**)

# Mise en pratique

### 1 Chassez l'intrus Trouvez le mot qui ne va pas avec les autres.

1. un croissant, le pain, (le fromage), une baguette
2. une limonade, un jus de pomme, un jus d'orange, (le beurre)
3. des frites, un sandwich, (le sucre), le jambon
4. (le jambon), un éclair, un croissant, une baguette
5. l'eau, la boisson, l'eau minérale, (la soupe)
6. l'addition, (un chocolat), le pourboire, coûter
7. (apporter), d'autres, plusieurs, quelques
8. (un morceau), une bouteille, un verre, une tasse

### 2 Reliez Choisissez les expressions de quantité qui correspondent le mieux (*the best*) aux produits.

**MODÈLE**

*un morceau de* baguette

| une bouteille de | une tasse de |
|---|---|
| un morceau de | un verre de |

1. <u>un verre d'/une bouteille d'</u> eau
2. <u>un morceau de</u> sandwich
3. <u>un morceau de</u> fromage
4. <u>une tasse de</u> chocolat
5. <u>une tasse de</u> café
6. <u>un verre de/une bouteille de</u> jus de pomme
7. <u>une tasse de</u> thé
8. <u>un verre de</u> limonade

### 3 Écoutez 🎧 Écoutez la conversation entre André et le serveur du café Gide, et décidez si les phrases sont **vraies** ou **fausses**.

| | Vrai | Faux |
|---|---|---|
| 1. André n'a pas très soif. | ☑ | ☐ |
| 2. André n'a pas faim. | ☐ | ☑ |
| 3. Au café, on peut commander (*one may order*) un jus d'orange, une limonade, un café ou une boisson gazeuse. | ☑ | ☐ |
| 4. André commande un sandwich au jambon avec du fromage. | ☐ | ☑ |
| 5. André commande une tasse de chocolat. | ☐ | ☑ |
| 6. André déteste le lait et le sucre. | ☐ | ☑ |
| 7. André n'a pas beaucoup d'argent. | ☑ | ☐ |
| 8. André ne laisse pas de pourboire. | ☑ | ☐ |

🔎 Practice more at **daccord1.vhlcentral.com**.

le sucre

le thé

Il a soif.

une tasse

Il mange quelque chose. (manger)

un café

un éclair

---

**1 Expansion** For additional practice, give students these items. **9.** beaucoup de, un verre de, assez de, un peu de (un verre de) **10.** le café, le jus, le thé, le chocolat chaud (le jus) **11.** l'addition, le prix, le serveur, le pourboire (le serveur)

**2 Suggestion** You may wish to introduce words for other types of containers, such as **une assiette, un bol,** and **un paquet.**

**2 Expansion** For additional practice, give students these items. **9.** lait (une bouteille de, un verre de) **10.** beurre (un morceau de)

**3 Script** SERVEUR: Bonjour, Monsieur! Vous désirez?
ANDRÉ: Bonjour! Combien coûtent les sandwichs?
S: Ça dépend. Un sandwich au jambon coûte 3€, mais un sandwich au jambon avec du fromage et des frites coûtent 5,50€.
A: Et combien coûte le café?
S: Une tasse de café coûte 3€ et avec du lait 3,50€.
A: Y a-t-il d'autres boissons?
S: Bien sûr, il y a du jus d'orange, des boissons gazeuses, de la limonade et de l'eau.
A: Je n'ai pas beaucoup d'argent sur moi, mais j'ai très faim. J'ai envie d'un sandwich au jambon. Je n'ai pas très soif, alors une tasse de café au lait avec un peu de sucre, s'il vous plaît.
S: Très bien, Monsieur.
A: Excusez-moi, c'est combien?
S: C'est 6,50€.
A: Voici. Merci et bonne journée!
S: Merci, Monsieur, au revoir. Oh là là! Pas de pourboire!
(*On Textbook Audio*)

**3 Suggestion** Have students correct the false items.

---

**Using Games** Write these categories on the board: **Boissons froides / chaudes** and **Nourriture froide / chaude.** Toss a beanbag to a student at random and call out a category. The student has four seconds to name a food or beverage that fits the category. He or she then tosses the beanbag to another student and calls out a category. Players who cannot think of an item in time or repeat an item are eliminated. The last person standing wins.

**Oral Practice** For additional practice, ask students questions about their food and drink preferences. Examples: **Préférez-vous le thé ou le chocolat? Le lait ou l'eau minérale? Le jus d'orange ou le jus de pomme? Le jambon ou le fromage? Les sandwichs ou les éclairs? La soupe ou les frites? Les baguettes ou les croissants?**

# CONTEXTES

## Communication

**4** 👥 🔁 **Combien coûte...?** Regardez la carte et, à tour de rôle, demandez à votre partenaire combien coûte chaque élément. Répondez par des phrases complètes.

> **MODÈLE**
> **Élève 1:** *Combien coûte un sandwich?*
> **Élève 2:** *Un sandwich coûte 3,50€.*

1. Combien coûtent les frites? Les frites coûtent 2€.
2. Combien coûte une boisson gazeuse? Une boisson gazeuse coûte 2€.
3. Combien coûte une limonade? Une limonade coûte 1,75€.
4. Combien coûte une bouteille d'eau? Une bouteille d'eau coûte 2€.
5. Combien coûte une tasse de café? Une tasse de café coûte 3€.
6. Combien coûte une tasse de thé? Une tasse de thé coûte 2,50€.
7. Combien coûte un croissant? Un croissant coûte 1€.
8. Combien coûte un éclair? Un éclair coûte 1,95€.

Café de la Fleur
menu
prix prix
3,50€  3€
2€  2,50€
2€  1€
1,75€
2€  1,95€

**5** 👥 🔁 **Conversez** Interviewez un(e) camarade de classe. *Answers will vary.*

1. Qu'est-ce que tu aimes boire (*drink*) quand tu as soif? Quand tu as froid? Quand tu as chaud?
2. Quand tu as faim, est-ce que tu manges un sandwich? Qu'est-ce que tu aimes manger?
3. Est-ce que tu aimes le café ou le thé? Combien de tasses est-ce que tu aimes boire par jour?
4. Comment est-ce que tu aimes le café? Avec du lait? Avec du sucre? Noir (*Black*)?
5. Comment est-ce que tu aimes le thé? Avec du lait? Avec du sucre? Nature (*Black*)?
6. Dans ta famille, qui aime le thé? Et le café?
7. Est-ce que tu aimes les boissons gazeuses ou l'eau minérale?
8. Quand tu manges avec ta famille dans un restaurant, est-ce que vous laissez un pourboire au serveur/à la serveuse?

**6** 👥 **Au restaurant** Choisissez deux partenaires et écrivez une conversation entre deux client(e)s et leur serveur/serveuse. Préparez-vous à jouer (*perform*) la scène devant la classe. *Answers will vary.*

**Client(e)s**

- Demandez des détails sur le menu et les prix.
- Choisissez des boissons et des plats (*dishes*).
- Demandez l'addition.

**Serveur/Serveuse**

- Parlez du menu et répondez aux questions.
- Apportez les plats et l'addition.

> **Coup de main**
>
> **Vous désirez?**
> *What can I get you?*
>
> **Je voudrais...**
> *I would like...*
>
> **C'est combien?**
> *How much is it/this/that?*

**7** 👥 **Sept différences** Votre professeur va vous donner, à vous et à votre partenaire, deux feuilles d'activités différentes. Attention! Ne regardez pas la feuille de votre partenaire.

> 🔁 **MODÈLE**
> **Élève 1:** *J'ai deux tasses de café.*
> **Élève 2:** *Oh, j'ai une tasse de thé!*

---

**Side notes (left margin):**

**4 Suggestion** Tell students that in conversation, the word **euro** is often omitted when giving prices that contain whole euros and cents. Example: **10,50€ = dix, cinquante.**

**5 Suggestion** Tell students to jot down notes during their interviews. Then have volunteers report their findings to the class.

**6 Suggestion** Distribute photocopies of actual café menus for students to use or have students base their conversation on the menu in **Activité 4.**

**7 Suggestion** Divide the class into pairs and distribute the Info Gap Handouts found on the Supersite.

---

**OPTIONS**

**Using Games** Divide the class into two teams. At the same time, give one person on each team a set of scrambled words that form a sentence about foods and/or beverages. The first person to unscramble the words and write the sentence on the board correctly scores a point for his or her team. The team with the most points at the end of the game wins.

**Using Visuals** To review vocabulary, bring in pictures or magazine photos of the foods and drinks listed. Ask students to identify the items. Example: **Qu'est-ce que c'est? (C'est _____.)** Or you can make false statements about the pictures and have students correct them. Example: **C'est un(e) _____, n'est-ce pas? (Non, c'est _____.)** When plural, remind students to say **Ce sont _____.**

# Les sons et les lettres

 **Audio: Concepts, Activities Record & Compare**

## 🎧 Nasal vowels

In French, when vowels are followed by an **m** or an **n** in a single syllable, they usually become nasal vowels. Nasal vowels are produced by pushing air through both the mouth and the nose.

The nasal vowel sound you hear in **français** is usually spelled **an** or **en**.

| an | français | enchanté | enfant |
|----|----------|----------|--------|

The nasal vowel sound you hear in **bien** may be spelled **en**, **in**, **im**, **ain**, or **aim**. The nasal vowel sound you hear in **brun** may be spelled **un** or **um**.

| examen | américain | lundi | parfum |
|--------|-----------|-------|--------|

The nasal vowel sound you hear in **bon** is spelled **on** or **om**.

| ton | allons | combien | oncle |
|-----|--------|---------|-------|

When **m** or **n** is followed by a vowel sound, the preceding vowel is not nasal.

| image | inutile | ami | amour |
|-------|---------|-----|-------|

🔊 **Prononcez** Répétez les mots suivants à voix haute.

1. blond
2. dans
3. faim
4. entre
5. garçon
6. avant
7. maison
8. cinéma
9. quelqu'un
10. différent
11. amusant
12. télévision
13. impatient
14. rencontrer
15. informatique
16. comment

🔊 **Articulez** Répétez les phrases suivantes à voix haute.

1. Mes parents ont cinquante ans.
2. Tu prends une limonade, Martin?
3. Le Printemps est un grand magasin.
4. Lucien va prendre le train à Montauban.
5. Pardon, Monsieur, l'addition s'il vous plaît!
6. Jean-François a les cheveux bruns et les yeux marron.

🔊 **Dictons** Répétez les dictons à voix haute.

*L'appétit vient en mangeant.*[1]

*N'allonge pas ton bras au-delà de ta manche.*[2]

[1] Appétite comes from eating.
[2] Don't bite off more than you can chew. (lit. Don't stretch your arm out farther than your sleeve.)

**ressources**

CA p. 144

daccord1.vhlcentral.com

---

## Section Goals

In this section, students will learn about nasal vowels.

## Key Standards

4.1

**Student Resources**
*Cahier d'activités*, p. 144; Supersite: Activities, *Cahier interactif*

**Teacher Resources**
Answer Keys; Audio Script; Textbook & Audio Activity MP3s/CD

## Suggestions

- Model the pronunciation of each nasal vowel sound and have students repeat after you. Then pronounce each of the example words and have students repeat them.
- Tell students that when an **m** or an **n** is followed by an unaccented **e** at the end of a word, the preceding vowel is not nasalized. Have them compare these words: **un/une**, **brun/brune**, and **faim/femme**.
- Ask students to provide more examples of words they know with nasal vowels. Examples: **croissant**, **boisson**, **jambon**, **inviter**, **quand**, **dépenser**, and **danser**.
- Dictate five simple sentences with words containing nasal vowels to the class, repeating each one at least two times. Then write them on the board or on a transparency and have students check their spelling.

**Dictons** Ask students if they can think of a saying in English that is similar to **«L'appétit vient en mangeant.»** (*The more one has, the more one wants.*)

---

**OPTIONS**

**Tongue Twisters** Teach students these French tongue-twisters that contain nasal vowel sounds. **1.** Son chat chante sa chanson. **2.** Un chasseur sachant chasser sait chasser sans son chien de chasse. **3.** Dans la gendarmerie, quand un gendarme rit, tous les gendarmes rient dans la gendarmerie.

**Mini-dictée** Use these sentences with nasal vowels for additional practice or dictation. **1.** Raymond mange un sandwich au jambon. **2.** Martin invite ses cousins au restaurant. **3.** Tante Blanche a soixante-cinq ans. **4.** Mon oncle Quentin a envie de danser.

# ROMAN-PHOTO

## L'heure du déjeuner

 **Video: Roman-photo**
Record & Compare

**PERSONNAGES**

Amina

David

Michèle

Rachid

Sandrine

Valérie

*Près du café...*
**AMINA** J'ai très faim. J'ai envie de manger un sandwich.
**SANDRINE** Moi aussi, j'ai faim, et puis j'ai soif. J'ai envie d'une bonne boisson. Eh, les garçons, on va au café?

**RACHID** Moi, je rentre à l'appartement étudier pour un examen de sciences po. David, tu vas au café avec les filles?
**DAVID** Non, je rentre avec toi. J'ai envie de dessiner un peu.
**AMINA** Bon, alors, à tout à l'heure.

*Au café...*
**VALÉRIE** Bonjour, les filles! Alors, ça va, les études?
**AMINA** Bof, ça va. Qu'est-ce qu'il y a de bon à manger, aujourd'hui?
**VALÉRIE** Eh bien, j'ai une soupe de poisson maison délicieuse! Il y a aussi des sandwichs jambon-fromage, des frites... Et, comme d'habitude, j'ai des éclairs, euh...

**VALÉRIE** Et pour toi, Amina?
**AMINA** Hmm... Pour moi, un sandwich jambon-fromage avec des frites.
**VALÉRIE** Très bien, et je vous apporte du pain tout de suite.
**SANDRINE ET AMINA** Merci!

*Au bar...*
**VALÉRIE** Alors, pour la table d'Amina et Sandrine, une soupe du jour, un sandwich au fromage... Pour la table sept, une limonade, un café, un jus d'orange et trois croissants.
**MICHÈLE** D'accord! Je prépare ça tout de suite. Mais Madame Forestier, j'ai un problème avec l'addition de la table huit.

**VALÉRIE** Ah, bon?
**MICHÈLE** Le monsieur ne comprend pas pourquoi ça coûte onze euros cinquante. Je ne comprends pas non plus. Regardez.
**VALÉRIE** Ah, non! Avec tout le travail que nous avons cet après-midi, des problèmes d'addition aussi?!

**A C T I V I T É S**

**1** **Identifiez** Trouvez à qui correspond chacune (*each*) des phrases. Écrivez **A** pour Amina, **D** pour David, **M** pour Michèle, **R** pour Rachid, **S** pour Sandrine et **V** pour Valérie.

__M__ 1. Je ne comprends pas non plus.

__V__ 2. Vous prenez du jus d'orange uniquement le matin.

__S__ 3. Tu bois de l'eau aussi?

__M__ 4. Je prépare ça tout de suite.

__A__ 5. Je ne bois pas de limonade.

__S__ 6. Je vais apprendre à préparer des éclairs.

__D__ 7. J'ai envie de dessiner un peu.

__V__ 8. Je vous apporte du pain tout de suite.

__R__ 9. Moi, je rentre à l'appartement étudier pour un examen de sciences po.

__A__ 10. Qu'est-ce qu'il y a de bon à manger, aujourd'hui?

 Practice more at **daccord1.vhlcentral.com.**

**Avant de regarder la vidéo** Before viewing the video, have students work in pairs and write a list of words and expressions that they might hear in a video episode entitled **L'heure du déjeuner**.

**Regarder la vidéo** Show the video episode and tell students to check off the words or expressions they hear on their lists. Then show the episode again and have students give you a play-by-play description of the action. Write their descriptions on the board.

Amina et Sandrine déjeunent au café.

**SANDRINE** Oh, Madame Forestier, j'adore! Un jour, je vais apprendre à préparer des éclairs. Et une bonne soupe maison. Et beaucoup d'autres choses.
**AMINA** Mais pas aujourd'hui. J'ai trop faim!
**SANDRINE** Alors, je choisis la soupe et un sandwich au fromage.

**VALÉRIE** Et comme boisson?
**SANDRINE** Une bouteille d'eau minérale, s'il vous plaît. Tu bois de l'eau aussi? Avec deux verres, alors.

**VALÉRIE** Ah, ça y est! Je comprends! La boisson gazeuse coûte un euro vingt-cinq, pas un euro soixante-quinze. C'est noté, Michèle?
**MICHÈLE** Merci, Madame Forestier. Excusez-moi. Je vais expliquer ça au monsieur. Et voilà, tout est prêt pour la table d'Amina et Sandrine.
**VALÉRIE** Merci, Michèle.

*À la table des filles...*
**VALÉRIE** Voilà, une limonade, un café, un jus d'orange et trois croissants.
**AMINA** Oh? Mais Madame Forestier, je ne bois pas de limonade!
**VALÉRIE** Et vous prenez du jus d'orange uniquement le matin, n'est-ce pas? Ah! Excusez-moi, les filles!

## Expressions utiles

### Talking about food

- **Moi aussi, j'ai faim, et puis j'ai soif.**
  *Me too, I am hungry, and I am thirsty as well.*
- **J'ai envie d'une bonne boisson.**
  *I feel like having a nice drink.*
- **Qu'est-ce qu'il y a de bon à manger, aujourd'hui?**
  *What looks good on the menu today?*
- **Une soupe de poisson maison délicieuse.**
  *A delicious homemade fish soup.*
- **Je vais apprendre à préparer des éclairs.**
  *I am going to learn (how) to prepare éclairs.*
- **Je choisis la soupe.**
  *I choose the soup.*
- **Tu bois de l'eau aussi?**
  *Are you drinking water too?*
- **Vous prenez du jus d'orange uniquement le matin.**
  *You only have orange juice in the morning.*

### Additional vocabulary

- **On va au café?**
  *Shall we go to the café?*
- **Bof, ça va.**
  *So-so.*
- **comme d'habitude**
  *as usual*
- **Le monsieur ne comprend pas pourquoi ça coûte onze euros cinquante.**
  *The gentleman doesn't understand why this costs 11,50€.*
- **Je ne comprends pas non plus.**
  *I don't understand either.*
- **Je prépare ça tout de suite.**
  *I am going to prepare this right away.*
- **Ça y est! Je comprends!**
  *That's it! I get it!*
- **C'est noté?**
  *Understood?/Got it?*
- **Tout est prêt.**
  *Everything is ready.*

---

**Expressions utiles**
- Model the pronunciation of the **Expressions utiles** and have students repeat after you.
- As you work through the list, point out the forms of the verbs **prendre** and **boire** and the partitive articles. Tell students that these verbs and the partitive articles will be formally presented in the **Structures** section.
- Ask students questions about foods and beverages using the vocabulary in the **Expressions utiles.** Examples: **Vous prenez du jus d'orange uniquement le matin? Quand est-ce que vous avez envie de boire de l'eau?**

**1 Expansion**
- For additional practice, give students these items. **11. Le monsieur ne comprend pas pourquoi ça coûte 11,50€. (M) 12. J'ai faim et puis j'ai soif. (S) 13. Mais pas aujourd'hui. J'ai trop faim! (A) 14. Non, je rentre avec toi. (D)**
- Write these adverbial expressions on the board: **non plus, aussi,** and **tout de suite.** Have students create sentences with them.

**2 Suggestion** Have students work in groups of six. Write each sentence on a strip of paper. Make a set of sentences for each group, then distribute them to students. Tell them to read their sentences aloud and arrange them in the proper order.

**2 Expansion** Have students create sentences to fill in the missing parts of the story.

**3 Suggestion** Before doing this activity, have the class brainstorm vocabulary and expressions they might use in this activity and write their ideas on the board.

---

**2 Mettez dans l'ordre** Numérotez les phrases suivantes dans l'ordre correspondant à l'histoire.

5 a. Michèle a un problème avec l'addition.
3 b. Amina prend (*gets*) un sandwich jambon-fromage.
1 c. Sandrine dit qu'elle (*says that she*) a soif.
2 d. Rachid rentre à l'appartement.
4 e. Valérie va chercher du pain.
6 f. Tout est prêt pour la table d'Amina et Sandrine.

**3 Conversez** Au moment où Valérie apporte le plateau (*tray*) de la table sept à Sandrine et Amina, Michèle apporte le plateau de Sandrine et Amina à la table sept. Avec trois partenaires, écrivez la conversation entre Michèle et les client(e)s et jouez-la devant la classe.

**ressources**

CA pp. 81-82

daccord1.vhlcentral.com

A C T I V I T É S

*cent vingt-neuf* **129**

---

**Mini-dialogues** Have students work in pairs. Tell them to combine sentences in **Expressions utiles** with other words and expressions they know to create mini-dialogues. Example:
—**Qu'est-ce qu'il y a de bon aujourd'hui?**
—**Il y a une soupe de poisson maison délicieuse.**

**Skits** Ask volunteers to ad-lib the **Roman-photo** episode for the class. Tell them that it is not necessary to memorize the episode or to stick strictly to its content. They should try to get the general meaning across with the vocabulary and expressions they know, and they should also feel free to be creative. Give them time to prepare.

Video: *Flash culture*

## Section Goals

In this section, students will:
- learn about the role of the café in French life
- learn some terms for describing how people eat and drink
- learn about some common snacks in different francophone countries
- read about the cafés of **North Africa**
- view authentic cultural footage

## Key Standards
**2.1, 2.2, 3.1, 3.2, 4.2**

**Student Resources**
*Cahier d'activités*, pp. 105-106;
Supersite: Activities,
*Cahier interactif*
**Teacher Resources**
Answer Keys; Video Script & Translation; *Flash culture* video

**Culture à la loupe**
**Avant la lecture** Have students look at the photos and describe what they see.

**Lecture** Point out that you can order a drink or food at the bar (**le comptoir**) and pay less than sitting at a table. Sitting on the **terrasse** is even more expensive. The menu posted outside a café usually indicates the different **tarifs**.

**Après la lecture** Ask students what aspects of French cafés they find interesting.

**1 Expansion** For additional practice, give students these items. **11. Aller au café est une tradition récente en France. (Faux.) 12. Les étudiants et les adultes fréquentent les cafés en France. (Vrai.)**

CULTURE À LA LOUPE

# Le café français

**À Toute Heure**

| | |
|---|---|
| Quiches | 3,50€ |
| Pâtisseries | 3,50€ |
| Omelettes | 5,25€ |
| Thé | 1,50€ |
| Glaces | 5,50€ |
| Café | 1,50€ |
| Cappuccino | 2,00€ |
| Chocolat chaud | 2,30€ |

**Le premier café français, le Procope, a ouvert° ses portes à Paris en 1686.** Depuis°, passer du temps° au café est une tradition. C'est un lieu de rendez-vous pour beaucoup de personnes: le matin, on y° va pour un café et un croissant; à midi, on y déjeune pour le plaisir ou pour des rendez-vous d'affaires, parce que c'est moins cher° et plus rapide qu'°au restaurant. Après le travail, les gens° y vont pour prendre l'apéritif°. Les étudiants ont souvent «leur» café où ils vont déjeuner, étudier ou se détendre° avec des amis.

Les cafés servent une grande variété de boissons: café, thé, chocolat chaud, eau minérale, sodas, jus de fruit, etc. En général, les cafés proposent aussi un menu: sandwichs, omelettes, quiches, soupes, salades, hot-dogs et, pour le dessert, des pâtisseries° et des glaces°. La terrasse d'un café est l'endroit° idéal pour se détendre, lire° ou pour observer la vie° de tous les jours et regarder passer les gens. Benjamin Franklin et Napoléon Bonaparte fréquentaient° le Procope. Alors, qui sait° sur qui vous allez tomber°!

**a ouvert** *opened* **Depuis** *Since* **passer du temps** *spending time* **gens** *people* **y** *there* **moins cher** *less expensive* **plus rapide qu'** *faster than* **les gens** *people* **apéritif** *before-dinner drink* **se détendre** *relax* **pâtisseries** *pastries* **glaces** *ice cream* **endroit** *place* **lire** *read* **vie** *life* **fréquentaient** *used to frequent* **sait** *knows* **allez tomber** *are going to run into*

**A C T I V I T É S**

**1 Vrai ou faux?** Indiquez si les phrases sont vraies ou fausses. Corrigez les phrases fausses. Some answers may vary.

1. Le premier café parisien date des années 1600. Vrai.
2. Les Français vont au café uniquement aux grandes occasions. Faux. Les Français vont aussi au café après le travail.
3. Le matin, les Français prennent du jambon et du fromage. Faux. Les Français prennent un café et un croissant.
4. En général, les cafés en France sont plus chers que les restaurants. Faux. Les cafés sont moins chers que les restaurants.
5. Les étudiants ont souvent un café où ils vont tous les jours (*every day*). Vrai.

6. Au café, on trouve des sandwichs et des salades, mais pas de desserts. Faux. On trouve aussi des desserts.
7. En France, on mange rarement (*rarely*) dans les cafés. Faux. Dans les cafés, on déjeune pour le plaisir ou pour des rendez-vous d'affaires.
8. Les cafés ont une grande variété de boissons. Vrai.
9. On peut se détendre au café et observer la vie de tous les jours. Vrai.
10. Napoléon Bonaparte et Benjamin Franklin sont d'anciens clients du Procope. Vrai.

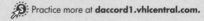 Practice more at **daccord1.vhlcentral.com**.

**O P T I O N S**

**Cultural Comparison** Have students work in groups of three and compare French cafés to the cafés they know about. Tell them to list the similarities and differences in a two-column chart under the headings **Similitudes** and **Différences**. After completing their charts, have two groups get together and compare their lists.

**Using Visuals** Have students look at the **À Toute Heure** menu. Ask them what they are having and how much it costs. Examples: **Qu'est-ce que vous prenez? Combien coûte le chocolat chaud?** Alternatively, this activity can be done in pairs.

## LE FRANÇAIS QUOTIDIEN

### J'ai faim!

| | |
|---|---|
| avoir les crocs | to be hungry |
| avoir un petit creux | to be slightly hungry |
| boire à petites gorgées | to sip |
| bouffer | to eat |
| dévorer | to devour |
| grignoter | to snack on |
| mourir de faim | to be starving |
| siroter | to sip (with pleasure) |

## LE MONDE FRANCOPHONE

### Des spécialités à grignoter

Voici quelques spécialités à grignoter dans les pays et régions francophones.

**En Afrique du Nord** la merguez (saucisse épicée°) et le makroud (pâtisserie° au miel° et aux dattes)

**En Côte d'Ivoire** l'aloco (bananes plantains frites°)

**En France** le pan-bagnat (sandwich avec de la salade, des tomates, des oeufs durs° et du thon°) et les crêpes (pâte° cuite° composée de farine°, d'œufs et de lait, de forme ronde)

**À la Martinique** les accras de morue° (beignets° à la morue)

**Au Québec** la poutine (frites avec du fromage fondu° et de la sauce)

**Au Sénégal** le chawarma (de la viande°, des oignons et des tomates dans le pain pita)

saucisse épicée *spicy sausage* pâtisserie *pastry* miel *honey* frites *fried* oeufs durs *hard-boiled eggs* thon *tuna* pâte *batter* cuite *cooked* farine *flour* morue *cod* beignets *fritters* fondu *melted* viande *meat*

## PORTRAIT

# Les cafés nord-africains

Comme en France, les cafés ont une grande importance culturelle en Afrique du Nord. C'est le lieu où les amis se rencontrent pour discuter° ou pour jouer aux cartes° ou aux dominos. Les cafés ont une variété de boissons, mais ils n'offrent° pas d'alcool. La boisson typique, au café comme à la maison, est le thé à la menthe°. Il a peu de caféine, mais il a des vertus énergisantes et il favorise la digestion. En général, ce sont les hommes qui le° préparent. C'est la boisson qu'on vous sert° quand vous êtes invité, et ce n'est pas poli de refuser!

**pour discuter** *to chat* **jouer aux cartes** *play cards* **offrent** *offer* **menthe** *mint* **le** *it* **on vous sert** *you are served*

## SUR INTERNET

Comment prépare-t-on le thé à la menthe au Maghreb?

Go to **daccord1.vhlcentral.com** to find more information related to this **CULTURE** section. Then watch the corresponding **Flash culture.**

**2 Compréhension** Complétez les phrases.

1. Quand on a un peu soif, on a tendance à (*tends to*) boire _à petites gorgées_
2. On ne peut pas boire de/d' _alcool_ dans un café nord-africain.
3. Les hommes préparent _le thé à la menthe_ en Afrique du Nord.
4. Il n'est pas poli de _refuser_ une tasse de thé en Afrique du Nord.
5. Si vous aimez les frites, vous allez aimer _la poutine_ au Québec.

**3 Un café francophone** Par groupes de quatre, préparez une liste de suggestions pour un nouveau café francophone: noms pour le café, idées (*ideas*) pour le menu, prix, heures, etc. Indiquez où le café va être situé et qui va fréquenter ce café.

**ressources**

CA pp. 105–106

daccord1.vhlcentral.com

**ACTIVITÉS**

*cent trente et un* **131**

## Section Goals

In this section, students will learn:
- the verbs **prendre**, **apprendre**, and **comprendre**
- the verb **boire**
- partitive articles

## Key Standards

4.1, 5.1

**Student Resources**
*Cahier d'exercices*, pp. 51–52;
*Cahier d'activités*, pp. 6, 145;
Supersite: Activities,
*Cahier interactif*

**Teacher Resources**
Answer Keys; Audio Script;
Audio Activity MP3s/CD;
*Feuilles d'activités*; Testing
program: Grammar Quiz

## Suggestions

- Point out that **prendre** means *to have* when saying what one is having to eat or drink, but it cannot be used to express possession. For possession, **avoir** must be used.
- Work through the forms of **boire**, asking students what they drink most often or rarely. Model a response by first saying what you drink: **Je bois souvent _____. Qu'est-ce que vous buvez?**
- Write the conjugation of **boire** on the board with the singular forms in one column and the plural forms in another column. Draw a line around the forms that have **oi**. Tell students that **boire** is a "boot verb."
- Write a summary chart of the articles on the board with these headings: Definite Articles, Indefinite Articles, and Partitive Articles. Briefly review definite and indefinite articles.
- Make sure students understand the idea of count nouns and non-count nouns. Have students classify vocabulary from **Contextes.**
- Point out that the use of partitives differs whether you are at home or in a café/restaurant. It is preferable to use **de** + [definite article] when at home or at someone's house, and indefinite articles when in a restaurant. Examples: **Bois-tu du café?** (at home) **Je prends un café.** (in a restaurant)

### 4B.1 The verbs *prendre* and *boire*; Partitives

**Point de départ** The verbs **prendre** (*to take, to have*) and **boire** (*to drink*), like **être**, **avoir**, and **aller**, are irregular.

| *Prendre* | | | |
|---|---|---|---|
| **je prends** | *I take* | **nous prenons** | *we take* |
| **tu prends** | *you take* | **vous prenez** | *you take* |
| **il/elle prend** | *he/she/it takes* | **ils/elles prennent** | *they take* |

Brigitte **prend** le métro le soir.
*Brigitte takes the subway in the evening.*

Nous **prenons** un café chez moi.
*We are having a coffee at my house.*

- The forms of the verbs **apprendre** (*to learn*) and **comprendre** (*to understand*) follow the same pattern as that of **prendre**.

Tu ne **comprends** pas l'espagnol?
*Don't you understand Spanish?*

Elles **apprennent** beaucoup en classe.
*They're learning a lot in class.*

Je ne comprends pas non plus.

Je ne bois pas de limonade.

| *Boire* | | | |
|---|---|---|---|
| **je bois** | *I drink* | **nous buvons** | *we drink* |
| **tu bois** | *you drink* | **vous buvez** | *you drink* |
| **il/elle boit** | *he/she/it drinks* | **ils/elles boivent** | *they drink* |

Ton père **boit** un jus d'orange.
*Your father is drinking an orange juice.*

Vous **buvez** un chocolat, M. Dion?
*Are you drinking hot chocolate, Mr. Dion?*

Nous ne **buvons** pas pendant le repas.
*We don't drink during the meal.*

Je **bois** toujours du lait froid au petit-déjeuner.
*I always drink cold milk for breakfast.*

**132** *cent trente-deux*

**1 Au restaurant** Alain est au restaurant avec toute sa famille. Il note les préférences de tout le monde. Utilisez le verbe indiqué.

**MODÈLE**
Oncle Lucien aime bien le café. (prendre) *Il prend un café.*

1. Marie-Hélène et papa adorent le thé. (prendre)
   Ils prennent un thé.
2. Tu adores le chocolat chaud. (boire)
   Tu bois un chocolat chaud.
3. Vous aimez bien le jus de pomme. (prendre)
   Vous prenez un jus de pomme.
4. Mes nièces aiment la limonade. (boire)
   Elles boivent une limonade.
5. Tu aimes les boissons gazeuses. (prendre)
   Tu prends une boisson gazeuse.
6. Vous adorez le café. (boire)
   Vous buvez un café.

**2 Au café** Indiquez l'article correct.

**MODÈLE**
Prenez-vous ___du___ thé glacé?

1. Avez-vous ___du___ lait froid?
2. Je voudrais ___une___ baguette, s'il vous plaît.
3. Elle prend ___un___ croissant.
4. Nous ne prenons pas ___de___ sucre avec le café.
5. Thérèse ne laisse pas ___de___ pourboire.
6. Vous mangez ___des___ frites.
7. Zeina boit ___une___ boisson gazeuse.
8. Voici ___de l'___ eau minérale.
9. Nous mangeons ___du___ pain.
10. Je ne prends pas ___de___ fromage.

**3 Des suggestions** Laurent est au café avec des amis et il fait (*makes*) des suggestions. Que suggère-t-il?

**MODÈLE**
*On prend du jus d'orange?*

1.  On prend de la limonade?

2.  On prend de l'eau minérale?

3. _____ On prend du thé?

4.  On prend des sandwichs?

⚡ Practice more at **daccord1.vhlcentral.com.**

## COMMUNICATION

**4  Échanges** Posez les questions à un(e) partenaire.

1. Qu'est-ce que tu bois quand tu as très soif?
2. Qu'est-ce que tu apprends au lycée?
3. Quelles langues est-ce que tes parents comprennent?
4. Est-ce que tu bois beaucoup de café? Pourquoi?
5. Qu'est-ce que tu prends à manger à midi?
6. Quelle langue est-ce que ton/ta meilleur(e) ami(e) apprend?
7. Où est-ce que tu prends tes repas (meals)?
8. Qu'est-ce que tu bois le matin? À midi? Le soir?

**5  Je bois, je prends** Votre professeur va vous donner une feuille d'activités. Circulez dans la classe pour demander à vos camarades s'ils prennent rarement, une fois (once) par semaine ou tous les jours la boisson ou le plat (dish) indiqués. Écrivez (Write) les noms sur la feuille, puis présentez vos réponses à la classe.

*Answers will vary.*

### MODÈLE

**Élève 1:** Est-ce que tu bois du café?
**Élève 2:** Oui, je bois du café une fois par semaine. Et toi?

| boisson ou plat | rarement | une fois par semaine | tous les jours |
|---|---|---|---|
| 1. café | | Didier | |
| 2. fromage | | | |
| 3. thé | | | |
| 4. soupe | | | |
| 5. chocolat chaud | | | |
| 6. jambon | | | |

**6  Après les cours** Des amis se retrouvent au café. Par groupes de quatre, jouez (play) les rôles d'un(e) serveur/serveuse et de trois clients. Utilisez les mots de la liste et présentez la scène à la classe.

*Answers will vary.*

| | | |
|---|---|---|
| addition | chocolat chaud | frites |
| avoir faim | coûter | prix |
| avoir soif | croissant | sandwich |
| boisson | eau minérale | soupe |

## Partitives

- Use partitive articles in French to express *some* or *any*. To form the partitive, use the preposition **de** followed by a definite article. Although the words *some* and *any* are often omitted in English, the partitive must always be used in French.

  Je bois **du** thé chaud.
  *I drink (some) hot tea.*

  Elle prend **de l'**eau?
  *Is she having (some) water?*

- Note that partitive articles are only used with non-count nouns (nouns whose quantity cannot be expressed by a number).

  | PARTITIVE ARTICLE | NON-COUNT NOUN | | INDEFINITE ARTICLE | COUNT NOUN |
  |---|---|---|---|---|

  Tu prends **de la** soupe tous les jours.
  *You have (some) soup every day.*

  Tu prends **une** banane, aussi.
  *You have a banana, too.*

- The article **des** also means *some*, but it is the plural form of the indefinite article, not the partitive.

  PARTITIVE ARTICLE

  Vous prenez **de la** limonade.
  *You're having (some) lemon soda.*

  INDEFINITE ARTICLE

  Nous prenons **des** croissants.
  *We're having (some) croissants.*

- To give a negative response to a question asked using the partitive structure, as with indefinite articles, always use **ne... pas de**.

  Est-ce qu'il y a **du** lait?
  *Is there (any) milk?*

  Non, il **n'y** a **pas de** lait.
  *No, there isn't (any) milk.*

  Prends-tu **de la** soupe?
  *Will you have (some) soup?*

  Non, je **ne** prends **pas de** soupe.
  *No, I'm not having (any) soup.*

**Essayez!** Complétez les phrases. Utilisez la forme correcte du verbe entre parenthèses et l'article qui convient.

1. Ma sœur ____prend____ (prendre) ____des____ éclairs.
2. Tes parents ____boivent____ (boire) ____du____ café?
3. Louise ne ____boit____ (boire) pas ____de____ thé.
4. Est-ce qu'il y ____a____ (avoir) ____du____ sucre?
5. Nous ____buvons____ (boire) ____de la____ limonade.
6. Non, merci. Je ne ____prends____ (prendre) pas ____de____ frites.
7. Vous ____prenez____ (prendre) ____un____ taxi?
8. Nous ____apprenons____ (apprendre) ____le____ français.

---

**Essayez!** Have students create new sentences orally or in writing by changing the subjects of the sentences.

**1 Suggestion** This activity can also be done in pairs. One person should say the sentence and the other person responds. Remind students to switch roles after items 1–3.

**2 Expansion** Have students write two more fill-in-the-blank sentences. Tell them to exchange papers with a partner and complete the sentences.

**3 Suggestion** Have students say the questions, then call on other individuals to answer them. Examples: **Oui, on prend ____. Non, on ne prend pas de/d' ____.**

**4 Suggestion** Have students create two additional questions with **boire, apprendre, prendre,** or **comprendre** to ask their partner.

**5 Suggestion** Have two volunteers read the **modèle** aloud. Then distribute the **Feuilles d'activités** found on the Supersite.

**6 Suggestions**
- Bring in a few props, such as cups, bottles, and plates, for students to use in their role-plays.
- Have volunteers perform their role-plays for the class, then vote on the best one.

---

**OPTIONS**

**Using Games** Arrange students in rows of six. The first person in each row has a piece of paper. Call out the infinitive of **boire, prendre, apprendre,** or **comprendre.** Silently, the first student writes the **je** form and passes the paper to the student behind him or her. That student writes the **tu** form and passes the paper on. The last person holds up the completed paper. Have students rotate places before the next verb.

**Writing Practice** Write this activity on the board. Tell students to add the missing words and form complete sentences.
1. Marc / boire / eau / et / prendre / sandwich / jambon
2. Solange / prendre / soupe / et / boire / boisson gazeuse
3. Nous / boire / café / lait / et / prendre / éclairs
4. Henri et Paul / prendre / hot-dogs / et / frites
5. Anne / prendre / soupe / poisson / et / verre / thé glacé

## Section Goals

In this section, students will learn regular **-ir** verbs.

## Key Standards

**4.1, 5.1**

**Student Resources**
*Cahier d'exercices,* pp. 53-54;
*Cahier d'activités,* p. 146;
Supersite: Activities,
*Cahier interactif*
**Teacher Resources**
Answer Keys; Audio Script;
Audio Activity MP3s/CD; Testing
program: Grammar Quiz

## Suggestions

- Model the pronunciation of **-ir** verbs and have students repeat them.
- Introduce the verbs by saying what time you finish teaching today and asking students what time they finish classes. Examples: **Aujourd'hui, je finis d'enseigner à quatre heures. Et vous, à quelle heure finissez-vous les cours?** Then ask students to ask a classmate: **Et toi, à quelle heure finis-tu, aujourd'hui?**
- Point out that the singular forms of **-ir** verbs all sound the same.
- Call students' attention to the **-iss-** in the plural forms of **-ir** verbs.
- Remind students that **-ss-** sounds like an *s,* but a single **s** between vowels is pronounced like a *z.*
- Tell students that many **-ir** verbs are derived from adjectives, such as **grand**, **rouge, gros,** or **vieux.**
- Ask students questions using **-ir** verbs in the present and also with the **futur proche.** Examples: **Quand allez-vous finir vos études? Réussissez-vous vos examens?**

**Essayez!** For additional practice, give students these items. **9. Comment _____ (réagir)-vous quand vous avez peur? (réagissez) 10. Vos grands-parents _____ (vieillir) ensemble. (vieillissent)**

---

### 4B.2 Regular *-ir* verbs

**Point de départ** In **Leçon 2A**, you learned the pattern of **-er** verbs. Verbs that end in **-ir** follow a different pattern.

#### *Finir (to finish)*

| | |
|---|---|
| je finis | nous finissons |
| tu finis | vous finissez |
| il/elle finit | ils/elles finissent |

Je **finis** mon sandwich avant tout le monde.
*I am finishing my sandwich before everyone else.*

Alain et Chloé **finissent** leur déjeuner.
*Alain and Chloé are finishing their lunch.*

- Here are some other verbs that follow the same pattern as **finir.**

#### Other regular *-ir* verbs

| | | | |
|---|---|---|---|
| choisir | to choose | réfléchir (à) | to think (about), to reflect (on) |
| grandir | to grow | | |
| grossir | to gain weight | réussir (à) | to succeed (in doing something) |
| maigrir | to lose weight | | |
| obéir (à) | to obey | rougir | to blush |
| réagir | to react | vieillir | to grow old |

Nous **grossissons** quand nous mangeons beaucoup d'éclairs.
*We gain weight when we eat a lot of eclairs.*

Je **choisis** un croissant avec du chocolat chaud.
*I choose a croissant with hot chocolate.*

- Like for **–er** verbs, use present tense verb forms to give commands.

**Réagis** vite!
*React quickly!*

**Obéissez**-moi.
*Obey me.*

**Réfléchissons** bien.
*Let's think well.*

Ne **rougis** pas.
*Don't blush.*

#### Essayez!    Complétez les phrases.

1. Quand je mange de la salade, je <u>maigris</u> (maigrir).
2. Il <u>réussit</u> (réussir) son examen.
3. Nous <u>finissons</u> (finir) notre déjeuner.
4. Quand les enfants mangent beaucoup de frites, ils <u>grossissent</u> (grossir)!
5. Tu <u>choisis</u> (choisir) le fromage ou le dessert?
6. <u>Réfléchis/ Réfléchissez</u> (réfléchir) au problème.
7. Mes enfants <u>grandissent</u> (grandir) très vite (*fast*).
8. Vous ne m' <u>obéissez</u> (obéir) jamais (*never*)!

**134**   *cent trente-quatre*

---

**1**   **Au restaurant** Complétez le dialogue avec la forme correcte du verbe entre parenthèses.

**SERVEUR**   Vous désirez?

**LISE**   Nous (1) <u>réfléchissons</u> (réfléchir) encore.

**FANNY**   Je pense savoir ce que je veux (*know what I want*).

**SERVEUR**   Que (2) <u>choisissez</u> (choisir)-vous, Mademoiselle?

**FANNY**   Je (3) <u>choisis</u> (choisir) un hamburger avec des frites. Et toi?

**LISE**   Euh... je (4) <u>réfléchis</u> (réfléchir). La soupe ou la salade, je pense... Oui, je prends la salade.

**SERVEUR**   Très bien, Mesdemoiselles. Je vous apporte ça tout de suite (*right away*).

**FANNY**   Tu n'as pas très faim?

**LISE**   Non, pas trop. Et je suis au régime (*on a diet*). J'ai besoin de (5) <u>maigrir</u> (maigrir) un peu.

**FANNY**   Tu (6) <u>réussis</u> (réussir) déjà. Ton jean est trop grand. Tu n'as pas envie de partager mon éclair?

**LISE**   Mais non! Je vais (7) <u>grossir</u> (grossir)!

**FANNY**   Alors, je (8) <u>finis</u> (finir) l'éclair.

**2**   **Complétez** Complétez les phrases avec la forme correcte des verbes de la liste. N'utilisez les verbes qu'une seule fois.

| | |
|---|---|
| choisir | maigrir |
| finir | obéir |
| grandir | rougir |
| grossir | vieillir |

1. Nous <u>choisissons</u> l'endroit où nous allons déjeuner.
2. Corinne <u>rougit</u> quand elle a honte.
3. Mes frères cadets <u>grandissent</u> encore. Ils sont déjà (*already*) très grands!
4. Vous ne mangez pas assez et vous <u>maigrissez</u>. Attention!
5. Nous <u>obéissons</u> aux profs.
6. Sylvie <u>finit</u> ses études cette année.
7. Mes grands-parents <u>vieillissent</u>. Mais c'est la vie (*life*).
8. Quand on mange beaucoup de chocolat, on <u>grossit</u>.

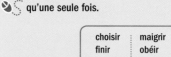 Practice more at **daccord1.vhlcentral.com.**

---

**Using Games** Divide the class into two teams. Choose one team member at a time to go to the board, alternating between teams. Say a subject pronoun and an infinitive. The person at the board must write and say the correct verb form. Example: **tu: choisir (tu choisis).** Give a point for each correct answer. The team with the most points at the end of the game wins.

**Writing Practice** Have students write fill-in-the-blank or dehydrated sentences for each of the **-ir** verbs. Then tell them to exchange papers with a partner and complete the activity. Remind students to verify their answers.

## COMMUNICATION

**3 Réactions** Avec un(e) partenaire, dites ce que ces (*Say what these*) personnes font (*do*) dans ces situations. Utilisez un verbe en **-ir** dans vos réponses. Answers may vary. Possible answers suggested

1. Il fait 35°C et Paul a très soif. Il est dans un café. Il choisit une boisson froide.
2. Nous sommes en classe. Le prof nous donne un problème de maths. Nous réfléchissons à la solution du problème.
3. Tes parents te demandent d'aller chercher ta sœur à l'école. Tu obéis à tes parents.
4. M. Lepic va avoir 84 ans. Il vieillit.
5. Florent mange deux sandwichs et boit un soda tous les midis. Il grossit beaucoup.

**4 Assemblez** Avec un(e) partenaire, assemblez les éléments des trois colonnes pour créer des phrases logiques. Answers will vary.

| A | B | C |
|---|---|---|
| je | choisir | aujourd'hui |
| tu | finir | beaucoup |
| notre prof | grandir | cette (*this*) année |
| mes parents | grossir | cours |
| mon frère | maigrir | devoirs |
| ma sœur | réfléchir | diplôme |
| mon/ma petit(e) ami(e) | réussir | encore |
| mon/ma cousin(e) | rougir | problème |
| mes camarades de classe | vieillir | vite |
| ? | | ? |

**5 Qui...?** Posez (*Ask*) des questions pour trouvez une personne dans la classe qui fait ces (*does these*) choses.

**MODÈLE**
**Élève 1:** Est-ce que tu rougis facilement?
**Élève 2:** Non, je ne rougis pas facilement.

1. rougir facilement (*easily*)
2. réagir vite
3. obéir à ses parents
4. finir toujours ses devoirs
5. choisir bien sa nourriture (*food*)
6. grandir cette année

## Le français vivant

Café du Marché

Formule petit-déjeuner simple    **5,50€**

boisson chaude + croissant +
jus de fruits (au choix°) ou
boisson chaude + mini-baguette avec
du beurre + jus de fruits (au choix)

❖❖❖

Formule petit-déjeuner complet    **7,50€**

boisson chaude +
sandwich jambon-fromage +
jus de fruits (au choix)

Boissons

| | |
|---|---|
| Café ..................... 1,50€ | |
| Café déca ............. 1,60€ | |
| Café crème ........... 2,00€ | Eau minérale ......... 2,50€ |
| Chocolat chaud ..... 2,20€ | Jus de fruits .......... 2,80€ |
| Thé ...................... 2,20€ | Limonade .............. 2,80€ |

**au choix** *your choice of*

**Répondez** Avec un(e) partenaire, discutez de la carte et de ces (*these*) situations. Utilisez des verbes en **-ir**. Answers may vary.

1. Je prends quatre croissants. Tu grossis.
2. J'ai très faim. Tu choisis le petit-déjeuner complet.
3. Je ne mange pas beaucoup. Tu maigris./Tu choisis le petit-déjeuner simple.
4. Je ne commande pas encore. Tu réfléchis.
5. Je bois toute la bouteille d'eau minérale. Tu finis la bouteille d'eau.

**1 Suggestion** Go over the correct answers with the class. Then ask two volunteers to act out the conversation.

**2 Expansion** Have students create additional sentences using these verbs with different subjects.

**3 Expansion** Have students imagine themselves in these situations and tell what they do using **-ir** verbs.

**4 Suggestion** Give students five minutes to write as many sentences as they can using **-ir** verbs. Then have volunteers read some of their sentences aloud or write them on the board.

**5 Suggestion** Remind students to ask and answer using complete sentences. Have them write the name of the person they find for each question. Follow up with questions about what they found out. Example: **Qui finit toujours ses devoirs?**

**Le français vivant**
- Ask volunteers to share their responses with the class.
- Have students act out a scene in which they order from the café menu. Encourage them to use as many **-ir** verbs as possible. Ask volunteers to perform their scene for the class.

**1 Suggestion** Have two
volunteers read the **modèle** aloud.

**1 Expansion** Have students
write three things they are
learning to do. Then have them
exchange papers with a partner
and ask each other why they are
learning to do those things.

**2 Suggestions**
• Tell students to jot down notes
during their interviews.
• Have students report some
of their findings to the rest
of the class.

**3 Suggestion** Tell students
that a few **centimes** are almost
always added to the price of
each item if the people sit on
the **terrasse**.

**4 Suggestion** After completing
the activity, call on volunteers
to state one difference until all
options are exhausted.

**5 Suggestion** Give students
five minutes to work with a
partner. Then ask volunteers
to share their responses with
the class.

**6 Suggestion** Divide the class
into pairs and distribute the
Info Gap Handouts found on the
Supersite for this activity. Give
students ten minutes to complete
the activity.

---

**1 Ils aiment apprendre** Vous demandez à Sylvie et à
Jérôme pourquoi ils aiment apprendre. Un(e) partenaire va
poser des questions et l'autre partenaire va jouer les rôles
de Jérôme et de Sylvie. Answers will vary.

**MODÈLE**

**Élève 1:** *Pourquoi est-ce que tu
apprends à travailler sur l'ordinateur?*
**Élève 2:** *J'apprends parce
que j'aime les ordinateurs.*

1.

4.

2.

5.

3.

6.

**2 Quelle boisson?** Interviewez une personne de votre
classe. Que boit-on dans ces circonstances? Ensuite (*Then*),
posez les questions à une personne différente. Utilisez des
articles partitifs dans vos réponses. Answers will vary.

1. au café
2. au cinéma
3. en classe
4. le dimanche matin
5. le matin très tôt
6. quand il/elle passe des examens
7. quand il/elle a très soif
8. quand il/elle étudie toute la nuit

**3 Notre café** Vous et votre partenaire allez créer un café
français. Choisissez le nom du café et huit boissons. Pour
chaque (*each*) boisson, inventez deux prix, un pour
le comptoir (*bar*) et un pour la terrasse. Comparez votre
café au café d'un autre groupe. Answers will vary.

---

**4 La terrasse du café** Avec un(e) partenaire, observez
les deux dessins et trouvez au minimum quatre différences.
Comparez votre liste à la liste d'un autre groupe. Ensuite,
écrivez (*write*) un paragraphe sur ces trois personnages en
utilisant (*by using*) des verbes en **-ir**. Answers will vary.

**MODÈLE**

**Élève 1:** *Mylène prend une limonade.*
**Élève 2:** *Mylène prend de la soupe.*

Patrick    Mylène    Djamel

**5 Dialogue** Avec un(e) partenaire, créez un dialogue avec les
éléments de la liste. Answers will vary.

| choisir | du chocolat |
| grossir | de l'eau minérale |
| maigrir | un sandwich au jambon |
| réagir | des frites |
| réfléchir (à) | de la soupe |
| réussir (à) | du jus de pomme |

**6 La famille Arnal au café** Votre professeur va vous
donner, à vous et à votre partenaire, des photos de la famille
Arnal. Attention! Ne regardez pas la feuille de votre partenaire.
Answers will vary.

**MODÈLE**

**Élève 1:** *Qui prend un sandwich?*
**Élève 2:** *La grand-mère prend un sandwich.*

ressources

| CE pp. 51–54 | CA pp. 6, 41–42, 145–146 | S daccord1.vhlcentral.com |

---

**OPTIONS**

**Writing Practice** Have students write a brief story about some
friends who go to a café and what happens when they are
there. Tell students that the story can be real or imaginary.
Encourage them to be creative.

**Questions** Have students write five questions that they would
like to ask you using the verbs **apprendre, comprendre, boire,
prendre,** and **-ir** verbs. Then allow each student the opportunity
to ask you one question.

# À l'écoute

**S** Audio: Activities

## STRATÉGIE

### Listening for the gist

Listening for the general idea, or gist, can help you follow what someone is saying even if you can't hear or understand some of the words. When you listen for the gist, you try to capture the essence of what you hear without focusing on individual words.

 To help you practice this strategy, you will listen to three sentences. Jot down a brief summary of what you hear.

## Préparation

Regardez la photo. Combien de personnes y a-t-il? Où sont Charles et Gina? Qu'est-ce qu'ils vont manger? Boire? Quelle heure est-il? Qu'est-ce qu'ils vont faire (*to do*) cet après-midi?

## À vous d'écouter 🎧

Écoutez la conversation entre Charles, Gina et leur serveur. Écoutez une deuxième fois (*a second time*) et indiquez quelles activités ils vont faire.

✓ 1. acheter un livre

✓ 2. aller à la librairie

___ 3. aller à l'église

✓ 4. aller chez des grands-parents

___ 5. boire un coca

✓ 6. danser

✓ 7. dépenser de l'argent

___ 8. étudier

✓ 9. manger au restaurant

✓ 10. manger un sandwich

 Practice more at **daccord1.vhlcentral.com.**

## Compréhension

**Un résumé** Complétez ce résumé (*summary*) de la conversation entre Charles et Gina avec des mots et expressions de la liste.

| | |
|---|---|
| aller au cinéma | une eau minérale |
| aller au gymnase | en boîte de nuit |
| avec son frère | faim |
| café | un jus d'orange |
| chez ses grands-parents | manger au restaurant |
| des copains | du pain |
| un croissant | soif |

Charles et Gina sont au (1) ___café___. Charles va boire (2) ___une eau minérale___. Gina n'a pas très (3) ___faim___. Elle va manger (4) ___un croissant___. Cet après-midi, Charles va (5) ___aller au gymnase___. Ce soir, il va (6) ___manger au restaurant___ avec (7) ___des copains___. Cet après-midi, Gina va peut-être (8) ___aller au cinéma___. Ce soir, elle va manger (9) ___chez ses grands-parents___. À onze heures, elle va aller (10) ___en boîte de nuit___ avec Charles.

**Et vous?** 👥 Avec un(e) camarade, discutez de vos projets (*plans*) pour ce week-end. Où est-ce que vous allez aller? Qu'est-ce que vous allez faire (*to do*)?

au centre-ville, près du parc. Tu as envie d'y aller?
G: Au restaurant, non. Je vais manger chez mes grands-parents ce soir, mais en boîte de nuit, oui, pourquoi pas. À quelle heure?
C: Ben, je passe chez toi après le restaurant, vers onze heures, d'accord?
G: D'accord.
C: Excusez-moi, Monsieur, l'addition, s'il vous plaît.

S: Voilà.
G: C'est combien, pour mon croissant et mon café?
C: Alors, c'est 2,50 pour le croissant et pour le café, c'est... Oh, allez, je t'invite.
G: Merci. C'est gentil.

# Panorama

S Interactive Map Reading

## La Normandie

### La région en chiffres

▶ **Superficie:** *29.906 km² (vingt-neuf mille neuf cent six kilomètres carrés°)*

▶ **Population:** *3.248.000 (trois millions deux cent quarante-huit mille)*
SOURCE: Institut National de la Statistique et des Études Économiques (INSEE)

▶ **Industries principales:** *élevage bovin°, énergie nucléaire, raffinage° du pétrole*

▶ **Villes principales:** *Alençon, Caen, Évreux, Le Havre, Rouen*

### Personnes célèbres

▶ **la comtesse de Ségur,** *femme écrivain° (1799–1874)*

▶ **Guy de Maupassant,** *écrivain (1850–1893)*

▶ **Christian Dior,** *couturier° (1905–1957)*

## La Bretagne

### La région en chiffres

▶ **Superficie:** *27.208 km² (vingt-sept mille deux cent huit kilomètres carrés)*

▶ **Population:** *3.011.000 (trois millions onze mille)*

▶ **Industries principales:** *agriculture, élevage°, pêche°, tourisme*

▶ **Villes principales:** *Brest, Quimper, Rennes, Saint-Brieuc, Vannes*

### Personnes célèbres

▶ **Anne de Bretagne,** *reine° de France (1477–1514)*

▶ **Jacques Cartier,** *explorateur (1491–1557)*

▶ **Bernard Hinault,** *cycliste (1954– )*

**carrés** *squared* **élevage bovin** *cattle raising* **raffinage** *refining* **femme écrivain** *writer* **couturier** *fashion designer* **élevage** *livestock raising* **pêche** *fishing* **reine** *queen* **les plus grandes marées** *the highest tides* **presqu'île** *peninsula* **entourée de sables mouvants** *surrounded by quicksand* **basse** *low* **île** *island* **haute** *high* **chaque** *each* **onzième siècle** *11th century* **pèlerinage** *pilgrimage* **falaises** *cliffs* **faire** *make* **moulin** *mill*

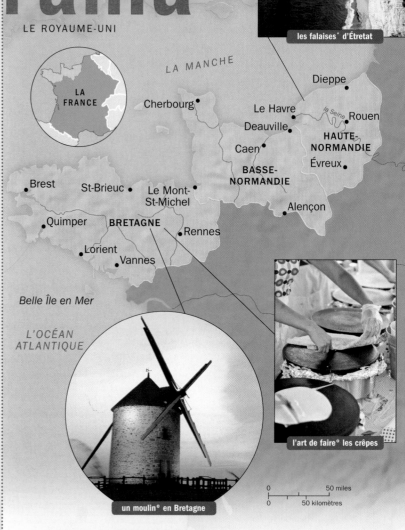

LE ROYAUME-UNI
LA FRANCE
LA MANCHE
Cherbourg
Le Havre
Deauville
Caen
Brest
St-Brieuc
Le Mont-St-Michel
Quimper
BRETAGNE
Lorient
Vannes
Rennes
Belle Île en Mer
L'OCÉAN ATLANTIQUE
Dieppe
la Seine
Rouen
HAUTE-NORMANDIE
BASSE-NORMANDIE
Évreux
Alençon

les falaises° d'Étretat

l'art de faire° les crêpes

un moulin° en Bretagne

0 50 miles
0 50 kilomètres

### Incroyable mais vrai!

C'est au Mont-Saint-Michel qu'il y a les plus grandes marées° d'Europe. Le Mont-Saint-Michel, presqu'île° entourée de sables mouvants° à marée basse°, est transformé en île° à marée haute°. Trois millions de touristes visitent chaque° année l'église du onzième siècle°, centre de pèlerinage° depuis 1000 (mille) ans.

## La gastronomie

### Les crêpes et galettes bretonnes et le camembert normand

Les crêpes et les galettes sont une des spécialités culinaires de Bretagne; en Normandie, c'est le camembert. Les crêpes sont appréciées sucrées, salées°, flambées... Dans les crêperies°, le menu est complètement composé de galettes et de crêpes! Le camembert normand est un des grands symboles gastronomiques de la France. Il est vendu° dans la fameuse boîte en bois ronde° pour une bonne conservation.

## Les monuments

### Les menhirs et les dolmens

À Carnac, en Bretagne, il y a 3.000 (trois mille) menhirs et dolmens. Les menhirs sont d'énormes pierres° verticales. Alignés ou en cercle, ils ont une fonction rituelle associée au culte de la fécondité ou à des cérémonies en

l'honneur du soleil°. Les plus anciens° datent de 4.500 (quatre mille cinq cents) ans avant J.-C.° Les dolmens servent de° sépultures collectives et ont une fonction culturelle comme° le rite funéraire du passage de la vie° à la mort°.

## Les arts

### Giverny et les impressionnistes

La maison° de Claude Monet, maître du mouvement impressionniste, est à Giverny, en Normandie. Après des rénovations, la résidence et les deux jardins° ont aujourd'hui leur ancienne° splendeur. Le légendaire jardin d'eau est la source d'inspiration pour les célèbres peintures° «Les Nymphéas°» et «Le pont japonais°». Depuis la fin° du dix-neuvième siècle°, beaucoup d'artistes américains, influencés par les techniques impressionnistes, font de la peinture à Giverny.

## Les destinations

### Deauville: station balnéaire de réputation internationale

Deauville, en Normandie, est une station balnéaire° de luxe et un centre de thalassothérapie°. La ville est célèbre pour sa marina, ses courses hippiques°, son casino, ses grands hôtels et son festival du film américain. La clientèle internationale apprécie beaucoup la plage°, le polo et le golf. L'hôtel le Royal Barrière est un palace° du début° du vingtième° siècle.

---

### Compréhension Complétez ces phrases.

1. <u>Jacques Cartier</u> est un explorateur breton.
2. Le Mont-Saint-Michel est une <u>île</u> à marée haute.
3. <u>Les crêpes</u> sont une spécialité bretonne.
4. Dans <u>les crêperies</u>, on mange uniquement des crêpes.
5. <u>Le camembert</u> est vendu dans une boîte en bois ronde.
6. Le <u>jardin d'eau</u> de Monet est la source d'inspiration de beaucoup de peintures.
7. Beaucoup d'artistes <u>américains</u> font de la peinture à Giverny.
8. Les menhirs ont une fonction <u>rituelle</u>.
9. Les dolmens servent de <u>sépultures</u>.
10. Deauville est une <u>station balnéaire</u> de luxe.

 Practice more at **daccord1.vhlcentral.com**.

**ressources**

CE pp. 55-56

daccord1.vhlcentral.com

### SUR INTERNET

Go to **daccord1.vhlcentral.com** to find more cultural information related to this **PANORAMA**.

1. Cherchez des informations sur les marées du Mont-Saint-Michel. À quelle heure est la marée haute aujourd'hui?
2. Cherchez des informations sur deux autres impressionnistes. Trouvez deux peintures que vous aimez et dites (say) pourquoi.

**salées** salty  **crêperies** crêpes restaurants  **vendu** sold  **boîte en bois ronde** round, wooden box  **maison** house  **jardins** gardens  **ancienne** former  **peintures** paintings  **Nymphéas** Waterlilies  **pont japonais** Japanese Bridge  **Depuis la fin** Since the end  **dix-neuvième siècle** 19th century  **pierres** stones  **soleil** sun  **Les plus anciens** The oldest  **avant J.-C.** B.C.  **servent de** serve as  **sépultures** graves  **comme** such as  **vie** life  **mort** death  **station balnéaire** seaside resort  **thalassothérapie** seawater therapy  **courses hippiques** horse races  **plage** beach  **palace** luxury hotel  **début** beginning  **vingtième** twentieth

---

### Les crêpes bretonnes et le camembert normand

- There are various types of crêpes. In Brittany, the **galettes de blé noir** (buckwheat crêpes) are filled with foods such as egg, ham and cheese, or mushrooms. The **crêpes de froment** (wheat flour crêpes) frequently have sweet fillings such as honey, sugar, jam, or chocolate. Normandy has been known for its cheeses since the sixteenth century. Created in 1890, the wooden container permitted Camembert to be exported worldwide.

- Ask students if they have eaten crêpes or Camembert and if they like them. Or bring in some Camembert and a baguette for students to sample.

### Giverny et les impressionnistes
Considered one of the greatest landscape painters, Claude Monet lived in the village of Giverny from 1883 until his death in 1926. Bring in photos of *Les Nymphéas* or *Le pont japonais* and briefly comment on the style and colors.

### Les menhirs et les dolmens
The megaliths, which are ancient granite blocks, can be found all over Brittany. The **menhir** is the most common form of megalith. The **dolmen** has two upright stones with a flat stone on top, like a table. The words **menhir** and **dolmen** come from Breton; **men** means *stone*, **hir** means *long*, and **dol** means *table*.

### Deauville: station balnéaire de réputation internationale
Founded by the Duke of Normandy in the 1860s, Deauville is famous for its **Promenade des Planches**, the wooden boardwalk alongside the beach, which was created so women wouldn't have to walk in the sand. Ask students: **Avez-vous envie de visiter Deauville? Pourquoi?**

---

**OPTIONS**

**Cultural Comparison** Working in small groups, have students compare Deauville to a famous American seaside resort. Tell them to list the similarities and differences in a two-column chart under the headings **Similitudes** and **Différences**. After completing their charts, call on volunteers to read their lists.

**La Chandeleur** On February 2, friends and family gather to celebrate the holiday **la Chandeleur** by cooking and eating crêpes and hoping for a prosperous year. Originally a religious celebration, **la Chandeleur** attracted pilgrims to Rome, and according to legend, the pope gave the pilgrims crêpes. Since then, crêpes have been associated with the holiday.

## Section Goals

In this section, students will:
- learn to scan a text for specific information
- read an advertisement for a cybercafé

## Key Standards
1.2, 2.1, 3.2, 5.2

**Stratégie** Tell students that a good way to get an idea of what an article or other text is about is to scan it before reading. Scanning means running one's eyes over a text in search of specific information that can be used to infer the text's content. Explain that scanning a text before reading it is a good way to improve reading comprehension.

**Examinez le texte** Call on volunteers to identify the cognates. Then ask the class what the text is about. (a cybercafé)

**Trouvez** Have students give details about the information they found in the document. Examples: **une adresse (24, place des Terreaux 69001 LYON), les noms des propriétaires (Bernard et Marie-Claude Fouchier), les heures d'ouverture (7h à 20h), and le numéro de téléphone (04.72.45.87.90).**

**Décrivez** Tell students to proofread each other's descriptions for spelling, verb agreement, and accuracy of information.

# Lecture (S) Reading

## Avant la lecture

### STRATÉGIE

#### Scanning

Scanning involves glancing over a document in search of specific information. For example, you can scan a document to identify its format, to find cognates, to locate visual clues about the document's content, or to find specific facts. Scanning allows you to learn a great deal about a text without having to read it word-for-word.

### Examinez le texte

Regardez le texte et indiquez huit mots apparentés (*cognates*) que vous trouvez. Answers may vary.

| | | | |
|---|---|---|---|
| 1. | Chocolat | 5. | Salade |
| 2. | Cybercafé | 6. | Tarte |
| 3. | Accès Internet | 7. | Soupe |
| 4. | Omelette | 8. | Snack |

### Trouvez

Regardez le document. Indiquez si les informations suivantes sont présentes dans le texte.

✓ 1. une adresse
___ 2. le nombre d'ordinateurs
___ 3. un plat du jour (*daily special*)
✓ 4. une terrasse
✓ 5. les noms des propriétaires
___ 6. des prix réduits pour les jeunes
___ 7. de la musique *live*
✓ 8. les heures d'ouverture (*business hours*)
✓ 9. un numéro de téléphone
___ 10. une librairie à l'intérieur

### Décrivez

Regardez les photos. Écrivez un paragraphe succinct pour décrire (*describe*) le cybercafé. Comparez votre paragraphe avec le paragraphe d'un(e) camarade.

# Cybercafé Le

- Ouvert° du lundi au samedi, de 7h00 à 20h00
- Snack et restauration rapide
- Accès Internet et jeux° vidéo

## Cybercafé Le connecté

### MENU

| | | | |
|---|---|---|---|
| **PETIT-DÉJEUNER° FRANÇAIS** | 12,00€ | **PETIT-DÉJEUNER ANGLAIS** | 15,00€ |
| Café, thé, chocolat chaud ou lait | | Café, thé, chocolat chaud ou lait | |
| Pain, beurre et confiture° | | Œufs° (au plat° ou | |
| Orange pressée | | brouillés°), bacon, toasts | |
| | | Orange pressée | |
| **VIENNOISERIES°** | 3,00€ | | |
| Croissant, pain au chocolat, | | **DESSERTS** | |
| brioche°, pain aux raisins | | Tarte aux fruits | 7,50€ |
| | | Banana split | 6,40€ |
| **SANDWICHS ET SALADES** | | | |
| Sandwich (jambon ou | 7,50€ | **AUTRES SÉLECTIONS CHAUDES** | |
| fromage; baguette ou pain | | Frites | 4,30€ |
| de campagne) | | Soupe à l'oignon | 6,40€ |
| Croque-monsieur° | 7,80€ | Omelette au fromage | 8,50€ |
| Salade verte° | 6,20€ | Omelette au jambon | 8,50€ |
| **BOISSONS CHAUDES** | | **BOISSONS FROIDES** | |
| Café/Déca | 3,80€ | Eau minérale non gazeuse | 3,00€ |
| Grand crème | 5,50€ | Eau minérale gazeuse | 3,50€ |
| Chocolat chaud | 5,80€ | Jus de fruits (orange...) | 5,80€ |
| Thé | 5,50€ | Soda, limonade | 5,50€ |
| Lait chaud | 4,80€ | Café, thé glacé° | 5,20€ |

**Propriétaires:** Bernard et Marie-Claude Fouchier

**OPTIONS**

**Using Games** Have students work in pairs and play a game of **Dix questions**. The first person thinks of a food or beverage listed in the **Cybercafé Le connecté** menu. The second person must guess the item by asking yes/no questions. Remind students that they may only ask ten questions.

**Mini-project** Have students work in groups of three or four. Tell them that they are going to open up a new cybercafé and they need to create a "must-have" list of services and foods for their establishment. After groups have completed their lists, have them describe their café to the class. Then have the class vote on the cybercafé with the best features.

# connecté

- **Le connecté, le cybercafé préféré des étudiants**
- **Ordinateurs disponibles° de 10h00 à 18h00, 1,50€ les 10 minutes**

24, place des Terreaux
69001 LYON
Tél. 04.72.45.87.90
www.leconnecte.fr

Place des Terreaux

Rue d'Algérie

Rue Paul Chenavard

Musée des
Beaux-Arts
de Lyon

Rue de Constantine

**Situé en face du musée des Beaux-Arts**

**Ouvert** *Open* **jeux** *games* **Petit-déjeuner** *Breakfast* **confiture** *jam* **Viennoiseries** *Breakfast pastries* **brioche** *a light, slightly-sweet bread* **Croque-monsieur** *Grilled sandwich with cheese and ham* **verte** *green* **Œufs** *Eggs* **au plat** *fried* **brouillés** *scrambled* **glacé** *iced* **disponibles** *available*

## Après la lecture

**Répondez** Répondez aux questions par des phrases complètes.

1. Combien coûte un sandwich?
   Un sandwich coûte 7,50€.

2. Quand est-ce qu'on peut (*can*) surfer sur Internet?
   On peut surfer sur Internet de 10h00 à 18h00.

3. Qui adore ce cybercafé?
   Les étudiants adorent ce cybercafé.

4. Quelles sont les deux boissons gazeuses? Combien coûtent-elles?
   L'eau minérale gazeuse coûte 3,50€. Un soda coûte 5,50€.

5. Combien de desserts sont proposés?
   Deux desserts sont proposés.

6. Vous aimez le sucre. Qu'est-ce que vous allez manger?
   (2 sélections) Answers may vary. Je vais manger... Any two of the following: un croissant, un pain au chocolat, une brioche, un pain aux raisins, une tarte aux fruits, un banana split.

**Choisissez** Indiquez qui va prendre quoi. Écrivez des phrases complètes. Answers may vary. Possible answers provided.

> **MODÈLE**
>
> Julie a soif. Elle n'aime pas les boissons gazeuses. Elle a 6 euros.
> *Julie va prendre un jus d'orange.*

1. Lise a froid. Elle a besoin d'une boisson chaude. Elle a 4 euros et 90 centimes.
   Lise va prendre un café.

2. Nathan a faim et soif. Il a 14 euros.
   Nathan va prendre un croque-monsieur et un soda.

3. Julien va prendre un plat chaud. Il a 8 euros et 80 centimes.
   Julien va prendre une omelette au jambon.

4. Annie a chaud et a très soif. Elle a 5 euros et 75 centimes.
   Annie va prendre un thé glacé.

5. Martine va prendre une boisson gazeuse. Elle a 4 euros et 20 centimes.
   Martine va prendre une eau minérale gazeuse.

6. Ève va prendre un dessert. Elle n'aime pas les bananes. Elle a 8 euros.
   Ève va prendre une tarte aux fruits.

**L'invitation** Avec un(e) camarade, jouez (*play*) cette scène: vous invitez un ami à déjeuner au cybercafé Le connecté. Parlez de ce que vous allez manger et boire. Puis (*Then*), bavardez de vos activités de l'après-midi et du soir.

**Répondez** Go over the answers with the class. Take a quick class poll to find out what is the most popular food chosen for question 6.

**Choisissez** Have students write two more situations similar to those in the activity. Then tell them to exchange papers with a partner, write the answers, and verify the answers.

**L'invitation** Before beginning the activity, tell students that they only have 20€ to spend at the **Cybercafé Le connecté**.

# Écriture

## STRATÉGIE

### Adding details

How can you make your writing more informative or more interesting? You can add details by answering the "W" questions: Who? What? When? Where? Why? The answers to these questions will provide useful and interesting details that can be incorporated into your writing. You can use the same strategy when writing in French. Here are some useful question words that you have already learned:

| | |
|---|---|
| (À/Avec) Qui? | À quelle heure? |
| Quoi? | Où? |
| Quand? | Pourquoi? |

Compare these two sentences.

> Je vais aller nager.

> Aujourd'hui, à quatre heures, je vais aller nager à la piscine du parc avec mon ami Paul, parce que nous avons chaud.

While both sentences give the same basic information (the writer is going to go swimming), the second, with its detail, is much more informative.

## Thème

## Un petit mot

### Avant l'écriture

1. Vous passez un an en France et vous vivez (*are living*) dans une famille d'accueil (*host family*). C'est samedi, et vous allez passer la journée en ville avec des amis. Écrivez un petit mot (*note*) pour informer votre famille de vos projets (*plans*) pour la journée.

2. D'abord (*First*), choisissez (*choose*) cinq activités que vous allez faire (*to do*) avec vos amis aujourd'hui.

Activité 1:

Activité 2:

Activité 3:

Activité 4:

Activité 5:

3. Ensuite (*Then*), complétez ce tableau (*this chart*) pour organiser vos idées. Répondez à (*Answer*) tous les pronoms interrogatifs.

|  | Activité 1 | Activité 2 | Activité 3 | Activité 4 | Activité 5 |
|---|---|---|---|---|---|
| Qui? |  |  |  |  |  |
| Quoi? |  |  |  |  |  |
| Quand? |  |  |  |  |  |
| Où? |  |  |  |  |  |
| Comment? |  |  |  |  |  |
| Pourquoi? |  |  |  |  |  |

4. Maintenant (*Now*), comparez votre tableau à celui (*to the one*) d'un(e) partenaire. Avez-vous tous les deux (*both of you*) cinq activités? Avez-vous des informations dans toutes les colonnes? Avez-vous répondu à tous les pronoms interrogatifs?

## Écriture

Écrivez la note à votre famille d'accueil. Référez-vous au tableau que vous avez créé (*have created*) et incluez toutes les informations. Utilisez les verbes **aller**, **boire** et **prendre**, et le vocabulaire de l'unité. Organisez vos idées de manière logique.

*Chère famille,*
*Aujourd'hui, je vais visiter*
*la ville avec Xavier et*
*Laurent, deux élèves belges*
*du lycée...*

## Après l'écriture

1. Échangez votre tableau et votre note avec ceux (*the ones*) d'un(e) partenaire. Faites des commentaires sur son travail (*work*) d'après (*according to*) ces questions:

   - Votre partenaire a-t-il/elle inclus dans la note toutes les informations du tableau?

   - A-t-il/elle correctement (*correctly*) utilisé le vocabulaire de l'unité?

   - A-t-il/elle utilisé la forme correcte des verbes **aller**, **boire** et **prendre**?

   - A-t-il/elle présenté ses informations de manière logique?

2. Corrigez (*Correct*) votre note d'après les commentaires de votre partenaire. Relisez votre travail pour éliminer ces (*these*) problèmes:

   - des fautes (*errors*) d'orthographe

   - des fautes de ponctuation

   - des fautes de conjugaison

   - des fautes d'accord (*agreement*) des adjectifs

## EVALUATION

**Criteria**
**Content** Contains a greeting, describes the five planned activities, answers the questions: **qui? quoi? quand? où? pourquoi?**, and includes supporting detail without redundancy.
Scale: 1 2 3 4 5

**Organization** Organizes the note into a salutation, a description, and a signature.
Scale: 1 2 3 4 5

**Accuracy** Uses forms of **aller** and places in town correctly. Spells words, conjugates verbs, and modifies adjectives correctly throughout. Avoids redundant language.
Scale: 1 2 3 4 5

**Creativity** The student includes additional information that is not included in the task, mentions more than five activities and/or includes a closing (not shown in the model).
Scale: 1 2 3 4 5

**Scoring**
| | |
|---|---|
| Excellent | 18–20 points |
| Good | 14–17 points |
| Satisfactory | 10–13 points |
| Unsatisfactory | < 10 points |

### Key Standards

4.1

**Teacher Resources**
Vocabulary MP3s/CD

**Suggestion** Tell students that an easy way to study from **Vocabulaire** is to cover up the French half of each section, leaving only the English equivalents exposed. They can then quiz themselves on the French items. To focus on the English equivalents of the French entries, they simply reverse this process.

#### Dans la ville

| | |
|---|---|
| une boîte (de nuit) | nightclub |
| un bureau | office; desk |
| un centre commercial | shopping center, mall |
| un cinéma (ciné) | movie theater, movies |
| une église | church |
| une épicerie | grocery store |
| un grand magasin | department store |
| un gymnase | gym |
| un hôpital | hospital |
| un kiosque | kiosk |
| un magasin | store |
| une maison | house |
| un marché | market |
| un musée | museum |
| un parc | park |
| une piscine | pool |
| une place | square; place |
| un restaurant | restaurant |
| une terrasse de café | café terrace |
| une banlieue | suburbs |
| un centre-ville | city/town center, downtown |
| un endroit | place |
| un lieu | place |
| une montagne | mountain |
| une ville | city, town |

#### Les questions

| | |
|---|---|
| à quelle heure? | at what time? |
| à qui? | to whom? |
| avec qui? | with whom? |
| combien (de)? | how many?; how much? |
| comment? | how?; what? |
| où? | where? |
| parce que | because |
| pour qui? | for whom? |
| pourquoi? | why? |
| quand? | when? |
| quel(le)(s)? | which?; what? |
| que/qu'...? | what? |
| qui? | who?; whom? |
| quoi? | what? |

#### À table

| | |
|---|---|
| avoir faim | to be hungry |
| avoir soif | to be thirsty |
| manger quelque chose | to eat something |
| une baguette | baguette (long, thin loaf of bread) |
| le beurre | butter |
| un croissant | croissant (flaky, crescent-shaped roll) |
| un éclair | éclair (pastry filled with cream) |
| des frites (f.) | French fries |
| un fromage | cheese |
| le jambon | ham |
| un pain (de campagne) | (country-style) bread |
| un sandwich | sandwich |
| une soupe | soup |
| le sucre | sugar |
| une boisson (gazeuse) | (soft) (carbonated) drink/beverage |
| un café | coffee |
| un chocolat (chaud) | (hot) chocolate |
| une eau (minérale) | (mineral) water |
| un jus (d'orange, de pomme, etc.) | (orange, apple, etc.) juice |
| le lait | milk |
| une limonade | lemon soda |
| un thé (glacé) | (iced) tea |

#### Activités

| | |
|---|---|
| bavarder | to chat |
| danser | to dance |
| déjeuner | to eat lunch |
| dépenser de l'argent (m.) | to spend money |
| explorer | to explore |
| fréquenter | to frequent; to visit |
| inviter | to invite |
| nager | to swim |
| passer chez quelqu'un | to stop by someone's house |
| patiner | to skate |
| quitter la maison | to leave the house |

| | |
|---|---|
| Expressions utiles | See pp. 115 and 129. |
| Prepositions | See p. 119. |
| Partitives | See p. 133. |

#### Expressions de quantité

| | |
|---|---|
| (pas) assez (de) | (not) enough (of) |
| beaucoup (de) | a lot (of) |
| d'autres | others |
| une bouteille (de) | bottle (of) |
| un morceau (de) | piece, bit (of) |
| un peu (plus/moins) (de) | little (more/less) (of) |
| plusieurs | several |
| quelque chose | something; anything |
| quelques | some |
| une tasse (de) | cup (of) |
| tous (m. pl.) | all |
| tout (m. sing.) | all |
| tout le/tous les (m.) | all the |
| toute la/toutes les (f.) | all the |
| trop (de) | too many/much (of) |
| un verre (de) | glass (of) |

#### Au café

| | |
|---|---|
| apporter | to bring, to carry |
| coûter | to cost |
| laisser un pourboire | to leave a tip |
| l'addition (f.) | check, bill |
| Combien coûte(nt)...? | How much is/are...? |
| un prix | price |
| un serveur/une serveuse | server |

#### Verbes

| | |
|---|---|
| aller | to go |
| apprendre | to learn |
| boire | to drink |
| comprendre | to understand |
| prendre | to take; to have |

#### Verbes réguliers en -ir

| | |
|---|---|
| choisir | to choose |
| finir | to finish |
| grandir | to grow |
| grossir | to gain weight |
| maigrir | to lose weight |
| obéir (à) | to obey |
| réagir | to react |
| réfléchir (à) | to think (about), to reflect (on) |
| réussir (à) | to succeed (in doing something) |
| rougir | to blush |
| vieillir | to grow old |

**ressources**

daccord1.vhlcentral.com

# Les loisirs

## Unit Goals

**Leçon 5A**

In this lesson, students will learn:
- terms for sports and leisure activities
- adverbs of frequency
- about intonation
- about **le football**
- more about sports and leisure activities through specially shot video footage
- the verb **faire**
- expressions with **faire**
- the expression **il faut**
- irregular **-ir** verbs
- about the insurance company SwissLife

**Leçon 5B**

In this lesson, students will learn:
- terms for seasons and months
- weather expressions
- to tell the date
- differences between open and closed vowels
- about public gardens and parks in the francophone world
- the numbers 101 and higher
- **-er** verbs with spelling changes
- to listen for key words in oral communication

**Savoir-faire**

In this section, students will learn:
- cultural and historical information about the French regions of **Pays de la Loire** and **Centre**
- to skim a text
- to use a French-English dictionary

**Pour commencer**
- **Il est dans le parc.**
- **Non, il n'a pas froid.**
- **Oui, je pense qu'il aime le sport.**
- **Il pratique le football.**
- **Nous sommes en septembre.**

### Pour commencer
- Où est Stéphane?
- A-t-il froid?
- Pensez-vous qu'il aime le sport?
- Quel sport pratique-t-il? Le football ou le basket-ball?
- Quel mois sommes-nous? En septembre ou en décembre?

---

**RESOURCES**

**Student Materials**
**Print:** Student Book, Workbooks (*Cahier d'exercices, Cahier d'activités*)
**Technology:** MAESTRO® *Cahier interactif* and Supersite (Audio, Video, Practice)

**Teacher Materials**
DVDs (*Roman-photo, Flash culture*)
Teacher's Resources (Scripts, Answer Keys, Testing Program)
Audio CDs (Testing Program, Textbook, Audio Program)

MAESTRO® Supersite: Student Supersite Content; Planning and Teaching Resources (Overheads, *PowerPoints*, Lesson Plans, Information Gaps and *Feuilles d'activités*); Learning Management System (Gradebook, Assignments); Audio MP3s and Streaming Video
**D'ACCORD! 1 Supersite:** daccord1.vhlcentral.com

## Section Goals

In this section, students will learn and practice vocabulary related to:
• sports and leisure activities
• adverbs of frequency

## Key Standards

1.1, 1.2, 4.1

**Student Resources**
*Cahier d'exercices*, pp. 57-58;
*Cahier d'activités*, pp. 7, 147;
Supersite: Activities,
*Cahier interactif*
**Teacher Resources**
Answer Keys; Overhead #28;
Audio Script; Textbook & Audio
Activity MP3s/CD; *Feuilles
d'activités*; Testing program:
Vocabulary Quiz

## Suggestions

• Have students look over the new vocabulary, covering the translations. Guide them to notice the numerous cognates for sports terms. See how many words students know without looking at the English.
• Use **Overhead #28** to describe what people are doing. Examples: **Ils jouent au football. Elles jouent au tennis.** Encourage students to add their remarks.
• Teach students the expression **aider quelqu'un à... (étudier, bricoler, travailler).** Pointing to the person toward the right helping his injured friend, say: **Il aide son copain à marcher.**
• Point out the differences between the words **un jeu, jouer, un joueur,** and **une joueuse.**
• Ask students closed-ended questions about their favorite activities: **Tu préfères jouer au tennis ou aller à la pêche? Aller à un spectacle ou jouer au golf?**
• Call out sports and other activities from this section and have students classify them as either **un sport** or **un·loisir.** List them on the board in two columns.

---

**Leçon 5A**

**S** Talking Picture
Audio: Activity

You will learn how to...
▪ talk about activities
▪ tell how often and how well you do things

# Le temps libre

### Vocabulaire

| | |
|---|---|
| aller à la pêche | to go fishing |
| bricoler | to tinker; to do odd jobs |
| désirer | to want |
| jouer (à/de) | to play |
| pratiquer | to play regularly, to practice |
| skier | to ski |
| le baseball | baseball |
| le cinéma | movies |
| le foot(ball) | soccer |
| le football américain | football |
| le golf | golf |
| un jeu | game |
| un loisir | leisure activity |
| un passe-temps | pastime, hobby |
| un spectacle | show |
| un stade | stadium |
| le temps libre | free time |
| le volley(-ball) | volleyball |
| une/deux fois | one/two time(s) |
| par jour, semaine, mois, an, etc. | per day, week, month, year, etc. |
| déjà | already |
| encore | again, still |
| jamais | never |
| longtemps | long time |
| maintenant | now |
| parfois | sometimes |
| rarement | rarely |
| souvent | often |

**ressources**

| CE pp. 57-58 | CA pp. 7, 147 | **S** daccord1.vhlcentral.com |
|---|---|---|

les joueuses (f.)

un match de tennis (m.)

Elle marche. (marcher)

le sport

une équipe

les joueurs (m.)

Il joue au foot. (jouer)

Il gagne. (gagner)

les cartes (f.)

une bande dessinée (B.D.)

---

**O P T I O N S**

**Brainstorming** Have students give their opinions about activities in **Contextes**. Brainstorm pairs of adjectives that apply to activities and write them on the board or on a transparency. Examples: **agréable/désagréable, intéressant/ennuyeux, utile/ inutile, génial/nul, facile/difficile.** Then ask questions like these: **Le football, c'est intéressant ou c'est ennuyeux? Les échecs, c'est facile ou difficile?**

**Using Games** Play a game of **Jacques a dit** (*Simon says*) using the activities in this section. Tell students to mime each activity only if they hear the words **Jacques a dit.** If a student mimes an activity not preceded by **Jacques a dit,** he or she is eliminated from the game. The last person standing wins. You might want students to take turns calling out activities.

# Mise en pratique

## Attention!

Use **jouer à** with games and sports.

Elle joue aux cartes/au baseball.
*She plays cards/baseball.*

Use **jouer de** with musical instruments.

Vous jouez de la guitare/du piano.
*You play the guitar/piano.*

**1　Remplissez** Choisissez dans la liste le mot qui convient (*the word that fits*) pour compléter les phrases. N'oubliez pas de conjuguer les verbes.

| | | |
|---|---|---|
| aider | jeu | pratiquer |
| bande dessinée | jouer | skier |
| bricoler | marcher | sport |
| équipe | | |

1. Notre ___équipe___ joue un match cet après-midi.
2. Le tarot est un ___jeu___ de cartes.
3. Mon livre préféré, c'est une ___bande dessinée___ de Tintin, *Le sceptre d'Ottokar*.
4. J'aime ___jouer___ aux cartes avec ma grand-mère.
5. Pour devenir (*To become*) champion de volley, je ___pratique___ tous les jours.
6. Le dimanche, nous ___marchons___ beaucoup, environ (*about*) cinq kilomètres.
7. Mon ___sport___ préféré, c'est le foot.
8. Mon père ___aide___ mon frère à préparer son match de tennis.
9. J'aime mieux ___skier___ dans les Alpes que dans le Colorado.
10. Il faut réparer la table, mais je n'aime pas ___bricoler___.

**2　Écoutez** 🎧 Écoutez Sabine et Marc parler de leurs passe-temps préférés. Dans le tableau suivant, écrivez un **S** pour Sabine et un **M** pour Marc pour indiquer s'ils pratiquent ces activités **souvent**, **parfois**, **rarement** ou **jamais**. Attention, toutes les activités ne sont pas utilisées.

| Activités | Souvent | Parfois | Rarement | Jamais |
|---|---|---|---|---|
| 1. chanter | S | | | |
| 2. le basket | S | M | | |
| 3. les cartes | | | | |
| 4. le tennis | M | S | | |
| 5. aller à la pêche | | | M | S |
| 6. le golf | | | | M |
| 7. le cinéma | M, S | | | |
| 8. le spectacle | M | | S | |

**3　Les loisirs** Utilisez un élément de chaque colonne pour former huit phrases au sujet des loisirs de ces personnes. N'oubliez pas les accords (*agreements*). Answers will vary.

| Personnes | Activités | Fréquence |
|---|---|---|
| Je | jouer aux échecs | maintenant |
| Ma sœur | chanter | parfois |
| Mes parents | jouer au tennis | rarement |
| Christian | gagner le match | souvent |
| Sandrine et Cédric | skier | déjà |
| Les élèves | regarder un spectacle | une fois par semaine |
| Élise | jouer au basket | une fois par mois |
| Mon ami(e) | aller à la pêche | encore |

✏️ Practice more at **daccord1.vhlcentral.com**.

*cent quarante-sept* **147**

le basket(-ball)

Il aide le joueur. (aider)

Il chante. (chanter)

Il indique. (indiquer)

les échecs (*m.*)

---

**1　Suggestions**
- To review **-er** verb forms, conjugate on the board one of the verbs from the list.
- Tell students to use each item in the word box only once.

**2　Script** SABINE: Bonjour, Marc, comment ça va?
MARC: Pas mal. Et toi?
S: Très bien, merci. Est-ce que tu joues au golf?
M: Non, jamais. Je n'aime pas ce sport. Je préfère jouer au tennis. En général, je joue au tennis trois fois par semaine. Et toi?
S: Moi? Jouer au tennis? Oui, parfois, mais j'aime mieux le basket. C'est un sport que je pratique souvent.
M: Ah le basket, je n'aime pas tellement. Je joue parfois avec des amis, mais ce n'est pas mon sport préféré. Le soir, j'aime bien aller au spectacle ou au cinéma. Et toi, qu'est-ce que tu aimes faire le soir?
S: Oh, je vais rarement au spectacle mais j'adore aller au cinéma. J'y vais très souvent.
M: C'est quoi, ton passe-temps préféré?
S: Mon passe-temps préféré, c'est le chant. J'aime chanter tous les jours.
M: Moi, j'adore aller à la pêche quand j'ai du temps libre, mais ce n'est que très rarement.
S: La pêche? Oh, moi, jamais. Je trouve ça ennuyeux.
M: Et est-ce que tu aimes le baseball?
S: Je ne sais pas; je n'ai jamais regardé un match de baseball.
M: Il y a un match toutes les semaines. C'est très intéressant. (On Textbook Audio)

**2　Expansion** Have students tell a partner how often they, themselves, do these activities.

**3　Suggestion** Ask volunteers to write one of their sentences on the board, making sure to have one example sentence for each of the verbs listed in this activity.

**3　Expansion** Ask students how frequently they do each of the activities listed. Encourage them to use as many different adverbial expressions as possible.

---

**OPTIONS**

**Making Associations** Call out names of famous athletes and have students say: **Ils jouent au ___sport___**. Examples: Tiger Woods, Arnold Palmer (**golf**), David Beckham, Zinédine Zidane (**football**), Serena Williams, André Agassi (**tennis**), Donovan McNabb, Troy Aikman (**football américain**), Shaquille O'Neal, Larry Bird (**basketball**), and Babe Ruth, Mark McGwire (**baseball**).

**Using Games** Write each of the words or expressions in **Activité 3** on an index card. Label three boxes **Personnes**, **Activités**, and **Fréquence**. Then place the cards in their respective boxes. Divide the class into two teams. Students take turns drawing one card from each box. Each player has five seconds to form a sentence using all of the words on the three cards. If they do not make a mistake, they score a point for their team.

# CONTEXTES

## Communication

**4** **Répondez** Avec un(e) partenaire, posez-vous (*ask each other*) ces (*these*) questions et répondez (*answer*) à tour de rôle. Answers will vary.

1. Quel est votre loisir préféré?
2. Quel est votre sport préféré à la télévision?
3. Êtes-vous sportif/sportive? Si oui, quel sport pratiquez-vous?
4. Qu'est-ce que vous désirez faire (*to do*) ce week-end?
5. Combien de fois par mois allez-vous au cinéma?
6. Que faites-vous (*do you do*) quand vous avez du temps libre?
7. Est-ce que vous aidez quelqu'un? Qui? À faire quoi? Comment?
8. Quel est votre jeu de société (*board game*) préféré? Pourquoi?

**5** **Sondage** Avec la feuille d'activités que votre professeur va vous donner, circulez dans la classe et demandez à vos camarades s'ils pratiquent ces activités et si oui (*if so*), à quelle fréquence. Quelle est l'activité la plus pratiquée (*the most practiced*) de la classe? Answers will vary.

**MODÈLE**

aller à la pêche
**Élève 1:** Est-ce que tu vas à la pêche?
**Élève 2:** Oui, je vais parfois à la pêche.

| Activités | Noms | Fréquence |
|---|---|---|
| 1. aller à la pêche | François | parfois |
| 2. jouer au tennis | _____ | _____ |
| 3. jouer au foot | _____ | _____ |
| 4. skier | _____ | _____ |

**6** **Conversez** Avec un(e) partenaire, utilisez les expressions de la liste et les mots de **CONTEXTES** et écrivez une conversation au sujet de vos loisirs. Présentez votre travail au reste de la classe. Answers will vary.

**MODÈLE**

**Élève 1:** Que fais-tu (*do you do*) comme sport?
**Élève 2:** Je joue au volley.
**Élève 1:** Tu joues souvent?
**Élève 2:** Oui, trois fois par semaine, avec mon amie Julie. C'est un sport que j'adore. Et toi, quel est ton passe-temps préféré?

| | |
|---|---|
| Avec qui? | Pourquoi? |
| Combien de fois par...? | Quand? |
| Comment? | Quel(le)(s)? |
| Où? | Quoi? |

**7** **La lettre** Écrivez une lettre à un(e) ami(e). Dites ce que vous faites (*do*) pendant vos loisirs, quand, avec qui et à quelle fréquence.

Cher Marc,

Pendant (*During*) mon temps libre, j'aime bien jouer au basket et au tennis. J'aime gagner, mais ça n'arrive pas souvent! Je joue au tennis avec mes amis deux fois par semaine, le mardi et le vendredi, et au basket le samedi. J'adore les films et je vais souvent au cinéma avec ma sœur ou mes amis. Le soir...

# Les sons et les lettres

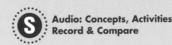
Audio: Concepts, Activities
Record & Compare

## Intonation

In short, declarative sentences, the pitch of your voice, or intonation, falls on the final word or syllable.

**Nathalie est française.** **Hector joue au football.**

In longer, declarative sentences, intonation rises, then falls.

**À trois heures et demie, j'ai sciences politiques.**

In sentences containing lists, intonation rises for each item in the list and falls on the last syllable of the last one.

**Martine est jeune, blonde et jolie.**

In long, declarative sentences, such as those containing clauses, intonation may rise several times, falling on the final syllable.

**Le samedi, à dix heures du matin, je vais au centre commercial.**

Questions that require a yes or no answer have rising intonation. Information questions have falling intonation.

**C'est ta mère?** **Est-ce qu'elle joue au tennis?**

**Quelle heure est-il?** **Quand est-ce que tu arrives?**

**Prononcez** Répétez les phrases suivantes à voix haute.

1. J'ai dix-neuf ans.
2. Tu fais du sport?
3. Quel jour sommes-nous?
4. Sandrine n'habite pas à Paris.
5. Quand est-ce que Marc arrive?
6. Charlotte est sérieuse et intellectuelle.

**Articulez** Répétez les dialogues à voix haute.

1. —Qu'est-ce que c'est?
   —C'est un ordinateur.
2. —Tu es américaine?
   —Non, je suis canadienne.
3. —Qu'est-ce que Christine étudie?
   —Elle étudie l'anglais et l'espagnol.
4. —Où est le musée?
   —Il est en face de l'église.

**Dictons** Répétez les dictons à voix haute.

Petit à petit, l'oiseau fait son nid.[2]

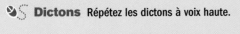
Si le renard court, le poulet a des ailes.[1]

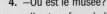

[1] Though the fox runs, the chicken has wings.
[2] Little by little, a bird builds its nest.

ressources

CA
p. 148

daccord1.vhlcentral.com

---

In this section, students will learn about using intonation.

**Key Standards**
4.1

**Student Resources**
*Cahier d'activités*, p. 148;
Supersite: Activities,
*Cahier interactif*
**Teacher Resources**
Answer Keys; Audio Script;
Textbook & Audio Activity
MP3s/CD

**Suggestions**
• Model the intonation of each of the example sentences and have students repeat them after you.
• Make sure students can recognize an information question. Tell them that information questions contain question words: **qui**, **qu'est-ce que**, **quand**, **comment**, **pourquoi**, etc. Remind students that the question word is not always the first word of the sentence. Examples: **À qui parles-tu? Ils arrivent quand?**
• Contrast the intonation of various types of declarative sentences (short, long, and those containing lists).
• Point out that the sentences without question words in the **Prononcez** activity (all except items 3 and 5) can be changed from a question to a statement and vice-versa simply by changing the intonation.

**Dictons**
• Ask students if they can think of sayings in English that are similar to «**Petit à petit, l'oiseau fait son nid.**» (*Slow and steady wins the race.*)
• Have students discuss the meaning of «**Si le renard court, le poulet a des ailes.**»

---

**OPTIONS**

**Intonation** Here are some sentences to use for additional practice with intonation: **1. Il a deux frères? 2. Il a deux frères. 3. Combien de frères est-ce qu'il a? 4. Vous jouez au tennis? 5. Vous jouez au tennis. 6. Avec qui est-ce que vous jouez au tennis?** Make sure students hear the difference between declarative and interrogative statements.

**Using Games** Divide the class into small groups. Pronounce ten phrases based on those in the examples and in **Prononcez**. Have students silently pass one piece of paper, numbered 1–10, around their group. Members of each group take turns recording whether the statements are declarative or interrogative. Collect the papers, one per group, when you finish saying the phrases. The group with the most correct answers wins.

# ROMAN-PHOTO

## Au parc  Video: *Roman-photo*
Record & Compare

## Section Goals

In this section, students will learn functional phrases for talking about leisure activities through comprehensible input.

## Key Standards

1.2, 2.1, 2.2, 4.1, 4.2

**Student Resources**
*Cahier d'activités*, pp. 83-84;
Supersite: Activities,
*Cahier interactif*

**Teacher Resources**
Answer Keys; Video Script & Translation; *Roman-photo* video

**Video Recap: Leçon 4B**
Before doing this **Roman-photo**, review the previous episode.
**1. Amina et Sandrine vont au café, mais David et Rachid… (rentrent à l'appartement/chez eux)**
**2. Rachid va étudier et David a envie de… (dessiner un peu)**
**3. Sandrine a envie d'apprendre à… (préparer des éclairs)**
**4. Amina commande… (un sandwich jambon-fromage et des frites)**

**Video Synopsis** In a park, Rachid, David, and Sandrine talk about their favorite pastimes. David likes to draw; Rachid plays soccer. They run into Stéphane. He and Rachid talk about Stéphane's studies. Stéphane doesn't like his classes; he prefers sports. Sandrine tells David she doesn't like sports, but prefers movies and concerts. She also wants to be singer.

**Suggestions**
• Ask students to predict what the episode will be about.
• Have pairs of students list words they expect to hear in a video about sports and activities. As they watch, have them mark the words and expressions they hear.
• Have students scan the captions to find phrases used to talk about sports and activities. Examples: **Rachid, lui, c'est un grand sportif. Je fais du ski, de la planche à voile, du vélo… et j'adore nager.**
• Ask students to read the **Roman-photo** in groups of four. Ask groups to present their dramatic readings to the class.
• Review the predictions and confirm the correct ones. Have students summarize this episode.

**PERSONNAGES**

David

Rachid

Sandrine

Stéphane

**DAVID** Oh là là… On fait du sport aujourd'hui!
**RACHID** C'est normal! On est dimanche. Tous les week-ends à Aix, on fait du vélo, on joue au foot…
**SANDRINE** Oh, quelle belle journée! Faisons une promenade!
**DAVID** D'accord.

**DAVID** Moi, le week-end, je sors souvent. Mon passe-temps favori, c'est de dessiner la nature et les belles femmes. Mais Rachid, lui, c'est un grand sportif.
**RACHID** Oui, je joue au foot très souvent et j'adore.

**RACHID** Tiens, Stéphane! Déjà? Il est en avance.
**SANDRINE** Salut.
**STÉPHANE** Salut. Ça va?
**DAVID** Ça va.
**STÉPHANE** Salut.
**RACHID** Salut.

**STÉPHANE** Pfft! Je n'aime pas l'histoire-géo.
**RACHID** Mais, qu'est-ce que tu aimes alors, à part le foot?
**STÉPHANE** Moi? J'aime presque tous les sports. Je fais du ski, de la planche à voile, du vélo… et j'adore nager.
**RACHID** Oui, mais tu sais, le sport ne joue pas un grand rôle au bac.

**RACHID** Et puis, les études, c'est comme le sport. Pour être bon, il faut travailler!
**STÉPHANE** Ouais, ouais.
**RACHID** Allez, commençons. En quelle année Napoléon a-t-il…

**SANDRINE** Dis-moi David, c'est comment chez toi, aux États-Unis? Quels sont les sports favoris des Américains?
**DAVID** Euh… chez moi? Beaucoup pratiquent le baseball ou le basket et surtout, on adore regarder le football américain. Mais toi, Sandrine, qu'est-ce que tu fais de tes loisirs? Tu aimes le sport? Tu sors?

**A C T I V I T É S**

**1** **Les événements** Mettez ces (*these*) événements dans l'ordre chronologique.

___10___ a. David dessine un portrait de Sandrine.

___6___ b. Stéphane se plaint (*complains*) de ses cours.

___4___ c. Rachid parle du match de foot.

___9___ d. David complimente Sandrine.

___2___ e. David mentionne une activité que Rachid aime faire.

___7___ f. Sandrine est curieuse de savoir (*to know*) quels sont les sports favoris des Américains.

___5___ g. Stéphane dit (*says*) qu'il ne sait (*knows*) pas s'il va gagner son prochain match.

___3___ h. Stéphane arrive.

___1___ i. David parle de son passe-temps favori.

___8___ j. Sandrine parle de sa passion.

 Practice more at **daccord1.vhlcentral.com.**

**O P T I O N S**

**Avant de regarder la vidéo** Before viewing the **Au parc** episode, ask students to consider both the title and video still 1. Then brainstorm what David, Sandrine, and Rachid might talk about in an episode set in a park. Examples: sports and activities: **On fait du sport aujourd'hui!** or the weather: **Quelle belle journée!**

**Regarder la vidéo** Play the video episode once without sound and have the class create a plot summary based on the visual cues. Afterward, show the video with sound and have the class correct any mistaken guesses and fill in any gaps in the plot summary they created.

**Les amis parlent de leurs loisirs.**

**RACHID** Alors, Stéphane, tu crois que tu vas gagner ton prochain match?
**STÉPHANE** Hmm, ce n'est pas garanti! L'équipe de Marseille est très forte.
**RACHID** C'est vrai, mais tu es très motivé, n'est-ce pas?
**STÉPHANE** Bien sûr.

**RACHID** Et, pour les études, tu es motivé? Qu'est-ce que vous faites en histoire-géo en ce moment?
**STÉPHANE** Oh, on étudie Napoléon.
**RACHID** C'est intéressant! Les cent jours, la bataille de Waterloo...

**SANDRINE** Bof, je n'aime pas tellement le sport, mais j'aime bien sortir le week-end. Je vais au cinéma ou à des concerts avec mes amis. Ma vraie passion, c'est la musique. Je désire être chanteuse professionnelle.

**DAVID** Mais tu es déjà une chanteuse extraordinaire! Eh! J'ai une idée. Je peux faire un portrait de toi?
**SANDRINE** De moi? Vraiment? Oui, si tu insistes!

## Expressions utiles

### Talking about your activities

- **Qu'est-ce que tu fais de tes loisirs? Tu sors?**
  *What do you do in your free time? Do you go out?*
- **Le week-end, je sors souvent.**
  *On weekends I often go out.*
- **J'aime bien sortir.**
  *I like to go out.*
- **Tous les week-ends, on/tout le monde fait du sport.**
  *Every weekend, people play/everyone plays sports.*
- **Qu'est-ce que tu aimes alors, à part le foot?**
  *What else do you like then, besides soccer?*
- **J'aime presque tous les sports.**
  *I like almost all sports.*
- **Je peux faire un portrait de toi?**
  *Can/May I do a portrait of you?*
- **Qu'est-ce que vous faites en histoire-géo en ce moment?**
  *What are you doing in history-geography at this moment?*
- **Les études, c'est comme le sport. Pour être bon, il faut travailler!**
  *Studies are like sports. To be good, you have to work!*
- **Faisons une promenade!**
  *Let's take a walk!*

### Additional vocabulary

- **Dis-moi.**
  *Tell me.*
- **Tu sais.**
  *You know.*
- **Ce n'est pas garanti!**
  *It's not guaranteed!*
- **Vraiment?**
  *Really?*
- **Bien sûr.**
  *Of course.*
- **Tiens.**
  *Hey, look./Here you are.*

---

**2** **Questions** Choisissez la traduction (*translation*) qui convient pour chaque activité. Essayez de ne pas utiliser de dictionnaire. Combien de traductions y a-t-il pour le verbe **faire**?

_c_ 1. faire du ski          a. to play sports
_d_ 2. faire une promenade   b. to go biking
_b_ 3. faire du vélo         c. to ski
_a_ 4. faire du sport        d. to take a walk

**3** **À vous!** David et Rachid parlent de faire des projets (*plans*) pour le week-end, mais les loisirs qu'ils aiment sont très différents. Ils discutent de leurs préférences et finalement choisissent (*choose*) une activité qu'ils vont pratiquer ensemble (*together*). Avec un(e) partenaire, écrivez la conversation et jouez la scène devant la classe.

**ressources**

CA
pp. 83–84

daccord1.vhlcentral.com

**ACTIVITÉS**

---

**Expressions utiles**

- Draw attention to the forms of the verb **faire** and irregular **-ir** verbs in the captions, in the **Expressions utiles** box, and as they occur in your conversation with students. Tell students that this material will be presented in **Structures**.
- Respond briefly to questions about **faire** and irregular **-ir** verbs. Reinforce correct forms, but do not expect students to produce them consistently at this time.
- Work through the **Expressions utiles** by asking students about their activities. As you do, respond to the content of their responses and ask other students questions about their classmates' answers. Example: **Qu'est-ce que tu fais de tes loisirs? Tu sors?**
- Remind students that the **nous** form of a verb can be used to say *Let's...* Example: **Faisons une promenade!** = *Let's take a walk!*

**1** **Suggestion** Form several groups of eight students. Write each of these sentences on individual strips of paper and distribute them among the students in each group. Make a set of sentences for each group. Have students read their sentences aloud in the correct order.

**1** **Expansion** Have students make sentences to fill in parts of the story not mentioned in this activity.

**2** **Suggestion** Remind students that **faire** has several English translations.

**3** **Suggestion** Remind students of expressions like **On...?** for suggesting activities and **D'accord** and **Non, je préfère...** for accepting or rejecting suggestions. As students write their scenes, circulate around the room to help with unfamiliar vocabulary and expressions.

---

**OPTIONS**

**Mini-conversations** Have pairs of students create two-line mini-conversations using as many **Expressions utiles** as they can. Example: —**Qu'est-ce que tu aimes alors, à part le foot?** —**J'aime presque tous les sports.** Then have them use the vocabulary in this section to talk about their own activities and those of their friends and family.

**Improvisation** Ask volunteers to ad-lib the **Roman-photo** episode for the class. Assure them that it is not necessary to memorize the episode or to stick strictly to its content. They should try to get the general meaning across with the vocabulary and expressions they know. Encourage creativity. Give them time to prepare. You may want to assign this as homework and do it the next class period as a review activity.

**CULTURE**

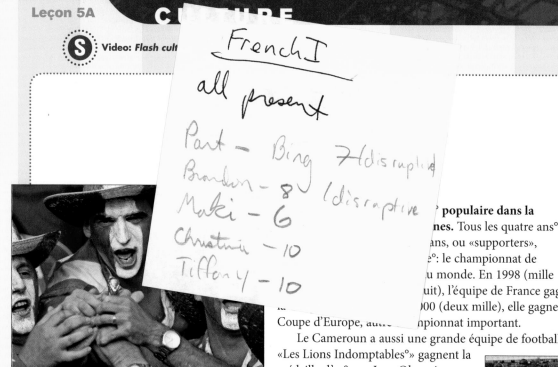

⑤ Video: *Flash culture*

---

Handwritten note:

French I

all present

Part — Bing 7 (disruptid)
Brandon — 8 (disruptive)
Maki — 6
Christine — 10
Tiffany — 10

---

### Section Goals

In this section, students will:
• learn about a popular sport
• learn sports terms
• learn names of champions from French-speaking regions
• read about two celebrated French athletes
• view authentic video footage

### Key Standards

2.1, 2.2, 3.1, 3.2, 4.2

**Student Resources**
*Cahier d'activités*, pp. 107-108;
Supersite: Activities,
*Cahier interactif*
**Teacher Resources**
Answer Keys; Video Script & Translation; *Flash culture* video

**Culture à la loupe**
**Avant la lecture** Before opening their books, ask students to call out as many sports-related words as they can remember in French. Ask them to name the most popular sports in the United States and those that they associate with the French.

**Lecture**
• Point out the chart **Nombre de membres des fédérations sportives en France**. Ask students what information the chart shows. (The number of members of athletic federations in France for each sport listed.)
• Point out that the term **le foot** is a common abbreviation for **le football**. Make sure your class understands that **le football américain** is *football* and **le foot** is *soccer*.

**Après la lecture** Have students prepare a list of questions with **jouer** and frequency expressions to ask a classmate. Have them present the other person's preferences to the class. Example: **Élève 1: Est-ce que tu joues parfois au volley-ball? Élève 2: Non, je joue rarement au volley-ball.**

**1** **Expansion** Continue the activity with these true/false statements.
**11. En France, le basket-ball est plus populaire que la natation. (Vrai.) 12. On fait moins de rugby que de vélo en France. (Faux.) 13. L'équipe de foot de Marseille est très populaire. (Vrai.)**

---

... populaire dans la ...nes. Tous les quatre ans°, ...ans, ou «supporters», ...e°: le championnat de ...u monde. En 1998 (mille ...uit), l'équipe de France gagne ... 000 (deux mille), elle gagne la Coupe d'Europe, aut... ...npionnat important.

Le Cameroun a aussi une grande équipe de football. «Les Lions Indomptables°» gagnent la médaille d'or° aux Jeux Olympiques de Sydney en 2000. En 2007, l'équipe camerounaise est la première équipe africaine à être dans le classement mondial° de la FIFA (Fédération Internationale de Football Association). Certains «Lions» jouent dans les clubs français et européens.

**les Lions Indomptables**

En France, il y a deux ligues professionnelles de vingt équipes chacune°. Ça fait° quarante équipes professionnelles de football pour un pays plus petit que° le Texas! Certaines équipes, comme le Paris Saint-Germain («le PSG») ou l'Olympique de Marseille («l'OM»), ont beaucoup de supporters.

Les Français, comme les Camerounais, adorent regarder le football, mais ils sont aussi des joueurs très sérieux: aujourd'hui en France, il y a plus de 19.000 (dix-neuf mille) clubs amateurs de football et plus de deux millions de joueurs.

| Nombre° de membres des fédérations sportives en France | |
|---|---|
| Football | 2.066.000 |
| Tennis | 1.068.000 |
| Judo-jujitsu | 577.000 |
| Basket-ball | 427.000 |
| Hand-ball | 334.000 |
| Golf | 325.000 |
| Voile° | 279.000 |
| Rugby | 253.000 |
| Natation° | 214.000 |
| Ski | 152.000 |

SOURCE: Ministère de la Jeunesse et des Sports

**le plus** *the most* **pays** *countries* **Tous les quatre ans** *Every four years* **centaines de milliers de** *hundreds of thousands of* **Coupe du Monde** *World Cup* **Indomptables** *Untamable* or *gold* **classement mondial** *world ranking* **chacune** *each* **Ça fait** *That makes* **un pays plus petit que** *a country smaller than* **Nombre** *Number* **Voile** *Sailing* **Natation** *Swimming*

---

**A C T I V I T É S**

**1** **Vrai ou faux?** Indiquez si ces phrases sont **vraies** ou **fausses**. Corrigez les phrases fausses.

1. Le football est le sport le plus populaire en France. Vrai.
2. La Coupe du Monde a lieu (*takes place*) tous les deux ans. Faux. Elle a lieu tous les quatre ans.
3. En 2000, l'équipe de France gagne la Coupe du Monde. Faux. En 2000, elle gagne la Coupe d'Europe.
4. Le Cameroun gagne le tournoi de football aux Jeux Olympiques de Sydney. Vrai.
5. L'équipe du Cameroun est la première équipe africaine à être au classement mondial de la FIFA. Vrai.

6. Certains «Tigres Indomptables» jouent dans des clubs français et européens. Faux. Certains «Lions Indomptables» jouent dans des clubs français et européens.
7. En France, il y a vingt équipes professionnelles de football. Faux. Il y a quarante équipes professionnelles de football.
8. La France est plus petite que le Texas. Vrai.
9. L'Olympique de Marseille est un célèbre stade de football. Faux. L'OM est une célèbre équipe de football.
10. Les Français aiment jouer au football. Vrai.

⑤ Practice more at **daccord1.vhlcentral.com**.

---

**OPTIONS**

**Writing Practice** Provide groups of three students with a list of words that are relevant to **Le football** like **gagner, longtemps, courir** from the **Leçon 5A** vocabulary list. Ask them to work together to create sentences about the reading by incorporating the lexical items you have prompted. Example: **gagner (En 1998, la France gagne la Coupe du Monde.)** Answers will vary in an open-ended activity like this, but remind the class to stick to learned material. Follow up by creating a column on the board for each word that you prompted so students can share sentences they consider successful. After at least one student has written a response for each word, correct the sentences as a class.

## LE FRANÇAIS QUOTIDIEN

### Le sport

| | |
|---|---|
| **arbitre** (*m./f.*) | *referee* |
| **ballon** (*m.*) | *ball* |
| **coup de sifflet** (*m.*) | *whistle* |
| **entraîneur/-euse** | *coach* |
| **maillot** (*m.*) | *jersey* |
| **terrain** (*m.*) | *playing field* |
| **hors-jeu** | *off-side* |
| **marquer** | *to score* |

## LE MONDE FRANCOPHONE

### Des champions

Voici quelques champions olympiques récents.

**Algérie** Nouria Merah-Benida, athlétisme°, or°, Sydney, 2000

**Burundi** Venuste Niyongabo, athlétisme, or, Atlanta, 1996

**Cameroun** Françoise Mbango-Etone, athlétisme, or, Pékin, 2008

**Canada** Éric Lamaze, équitation°, or, Pékin, 2008

**France** Alain Bernard, natation, or, Pékin, 2008

**Maroc** Hicham El Guerrouj, athlétisme, or, Athènes, 2004

**Suisse** Stéphane Lambiel, patinage artistique°, argent°, Turin, 2006

**Tunisie** Oussama Mellouli, natation, or, Pékin, 2008

**athlétisme** *track and field* **or** *gold* **équitation** *horseback riding* **patinage artistique** *figure skating* **argent** *silver*

## PORTRAIT

### Zinédine Zidane et Laura Flessel

**Zinédine Zidane**, ou «Zizou», est un footballeur français. Né° à Marseille de parents algériens, il joue dans différentes équipes françaises. Nommé trois fois «Joueur de l'année» par la FIFA (la Fédération Internationale de Football Association), il gagne la Coupe du Monde avec l'équipe de France en 1998 (mille neuf cent quatre-vingt-dix-huit). Pendant° sa carrière, il joue aussi pour une équipe italienne et pour le Real Madrid, en Espagne°.

Née à la Guadeloupe, **Laura Flessel** commence l'escrime à l'âge de sept ans. Après plusieurs titres° de championne de Guadeloupe, elle va en France pour continuer sa carrière. En 1991 (mille neuf cent quatre-vingt-onze), à 20 ans, elle est championne de France et cinq ans plus tard, elle est double championne olympique à Atlanta en 1996.

**Né** *Born* **Pendant** *During* **Espagne** *Spain* **plusieurs titres** *several titles*

### SUR INTERNET

**Qu'est-ce que le «free-running»?**

Go to **daccord1.vhlcentral.com** to find more information related to this **CULTURE** section. Then watch the corresponding **Flash culture.**

---

**Le français quotidien** You might extend this list to include **le poteau de but** (*goalpost*), **le coup d'envoi** (*kickoff*), **un penalty** (*penalty kick*), and **une faute** (*foul*).

**Portrait** Zinédine Zidane became the most expensive player in the history of soccer when Real Madrid acquired him for the equivalent of about $66 million American dollars. «Zizou» also made history as Christian Dior's first male model. Laura Flessel is a left-handed fencer called «**la Guêpe**» (*Wasp*) because of her competitive and dangerous attack.

**Le monde francophone** Model the pronunciation of names and places in this box. Then ask students if they know of any other athletes from the francophone world.

**2 Expansion** Continue the activity with additional fill-in-the-blank statements such as these.
7. _____ joue aussi pour une équipe espagnole. (**Zinédine**)
8. _____ est championne aux Jeux Olympiques de 1996. (**Laura**)

**3 Expansion** Have students prepare five sentences in the first person for homework, describing themselves as a well-known athlete. Ask students to introduce themselves to the class. The class tries to guess the presenter's identity.

**Flash culture** Tell students that they will learn more about sports and leisure activities by watching a variety of real-life images narrated by Csilla. Show the video, and then have students close their eyes and describe from memory what they saw. Write their descriptions on the board. You can also use the activities in the video manual in class to reinforce this **Flash culture** or assign them as homework.

---

**2** **Zinédine ou Laura?** Indiquez de qui on parle.

1. _Zinédine_ est de France métropolitaine.
2. _Laura_ est née à la Guadeloupe.
3. _Zinédine_ gagne la Coupe du Monde pour la France en 1998.
4. _Laura_ est championne de Guadeloupe en 1991.
5. _Laura_ est double championne olympique en 1996.
6. _Zinédine_ a été trois fois joueur de l'année.

**3** **Une interview** Avec un(e) partenaire, préparez une interview entre un(e) journaliste et un(e) athlète que vous aimez. Jouez la scène devant la classe. Est-ce que vos camarades peuvent deviner (*can guess*) le nom de l'athlète?

**ressources**

CA
pp. 107–108 | daccord1.vhlcentral.com

**A C T I V I T É S**

---

**O P T I O N S**

**Des champions** Look at the map of the world in the front matter to remind students where francophone countries featured in **Le monde francophone** are located. Ask students to pick one of the athletes from this list to research for homework. They should come to the next class with five French sentences about that athlete's life and career. You may want to have students bring an image from the Internet of the athlete they chose to research. Collect the photos and gather different images of the same athlete. Have students who researched the same champion work together as a group to present that athlete while the rest of the class looks at the images they found.

# STRUCTURES

## Section Goals

In this section, students will learn:
- the verb **faire**
- expressions with **faire**
- the expression **il faut**

### Key Standards
4.1, 5.1

---

**Student Resources**
*Cahier d'exercices*, pp. 59-60;
*Cahier d'activités*, pp. 8, 149;
Supersite: Activities,
*Cahier interactif*

**Teacher Resources**
Answer Keys; Overhead #28;
Audio Script; Audio Activity
MP3s/CD; *Feuilles d'activités*;
Testing program: Grammar Quiz

---

### Suggestions

- Point out that students have seen **faire** in previous lessons. Example: **faire ses devoirs** in **Leçon 2B Roman-photo**.
- Model **faire** with the whole class by asking: **Qu'est-ce que vous faites? Je fais…** Then, using **Overhead #28**, ask what people in the image are doing.
- Write the forms of **faire** on the board as students hear them in your questions. If **tu** and **nous** forms are missing, complete the conjugation by asking a student: **Tu fais attention?** Then ask: **Qu'est-ce que nous faisons? (Nous apprenons/ faisons attention.)**
- Point out that **fai-** in **nous faisons** is pronounced differently than **fai-** in all other forms. Underline the first syllable of the **nous** form and have students repeat.
- Ask students where they have seen the **-s, -s, -t** pattern. (**boire: je bois, tu bois, il/elle boit**)
- To facilitate memorization, have students compare **faire** with **aller, avoir,** and **être**, noting similarities in the forms. Examples: **tu fais, vas, as, es; nous faisons, avons, allons; vous êtes, faites;** etc.
- Explain that **il faut** is a very common expression in French even though its English translations are not as widely used in everyday language.

---

### 5A.1 The verb *faire*

**Point de départ** Like other commonly used verbs, the verb **faire** (*to do, to make*) is irregular in the present tense.

| Faire | |
|---|---|
| je fais | nous faisons |
| tu fais | vous faites |
| il/elle fait | ils/elles font |

Il ne **fait** pas ses devoirs.
*He's not doing his homework.*

Qu'est-ce que vous **faites** ce soir?
*What are you doing this evening?*

*On fait du sport aujourd'hui!*

*Qu'est-ce que vous faites en histoire-géo?*

- Use the verb **faire** in these idiomatic expressions. Note that it is not always translated into English as *to do* or *to make*.

| Expressions with *faire* | | | |
|---|---|---|---|
| faire de l'aérobic | to do aerobics | faire de la planche à voile | to go windsurfing |
| faire attention (à) | to pay attention (to) | faire une promenade | to go for a walk |
| faire du camping | to go camping | faire une randonnée | to go for a hike |
| faire du cheval | to go horseback riding | faire du ski | to go skiing |
| faire la connaissance de… | to meet (someone) for the first time | faire du sport | to do sports |
| faire la cuisine | to cook | faire un tour (en voiture) | to go for a walk (drive) |
| faire de la gym | to work out | faire du vélo | to go bike riding |
| faire du jogging | to go jogging | | |

Tu **fais** souvent **du sport**?
*Do you do sports often?*

Nous **faisons attention** en classe.
*We pay attention in class.*

Elles **font du camping**.
*They go camping.*

Yves **fait la cuisine**.
*Yves is cooking.*

Je **fais de la gym**.
*I'm working out.*

**Faites**-vous **une promenade**?
*Are you going for a walk?*

---

### MISE EN PRATIQUE

**1 Chassez l'intrus** Quelle activité ne fait pas partie du groupe?

1. a. faire du jogging   b. faire une randonnée
   c. faire de la planche à voile
2. a. faire du vélo   b. faire du camping
   c. faire du jogging
3. a. faire une promenade   b. faire la cuisine
   c. faire un tour
4. a. faire du sport   b. faire du vélo
   c. faire la connaissance de quelqu'un
5. a. faire ses devoirs   b. faire du ski
   c. faire du camping
6. a. faire la cuisine   b. faire du sport
   c. faire de la planche à voile

**2 La paire** Reliez (*Link*) les éléments des deux colonnes et ajoutez (*add*) la forme correcte du verbe **faire**.

1. Elle aime courir (*to run*), alors elle…
   e. fait du jogging.
2. Ils adorent les animaux. Ils…
   d. font du cheval.
3. Quand j'ai faim, je…
   b. fais la cuisine.
4. L'hiver, vous…
   g. faites du ski.
5. Pour marcher, nous…
   f. faisons une promenade.
6. Tiger Woods…
   a. fait du golf.

a. du golf.
b. la cuisine.
c. les devoirs.
d. du cheval.
e. du jogging.
f. une promenade.
g. du ski.
h. de l'aérobic.

**3 Que font-ils?** Regardez les dessins. Que font les personnages?

**MODÈLE**

*Julien fait du jogging.*

**Julien**

1. **je**  Je fais du cheval.     3. **Anne**  Anne fait de l'aérobic.

2. **tu**  Tu fais de la planche à voile.     4. **Louis et Paul**  Louis et Paul font du camping.

**Practice more at daccord1.vhlcentral.com.**

---

**Using Movement** Assign gestures to pantomime some of the expressions with **faire**. Examples: **faire de l'aérobic, la connaissance de…, du jogging, du ski**. Signal to individuals or pairs to gesture appropriately as you cue activities by saying: **Vous faites… _____ fait…** Then ask for a few volunteers to take your place calling out the activities.

**Brainstorming** Write on the board two headings: **Il faut…** and **Il ne faut pas…** Have students think of as many general pieces of advice (**les conseils**) as possible. Tell them to use **être**, any **-er** verbs, **avoir** and expressions with **avoir, aller, prendre, boire,** and **faire** to formulate the sentences. Examples: **Il faut souvent boire de l'eau. Il ne faut pas manger trop de sucre.** See how many sentences the class can write.

## COMMUNICATION

**4 Ce week-end** Que faites-vous ce week-end? Avec un(e) partenaire, posez les questions à tour de rôle. *Some answers will vary.*

**MODÈLE**

tu / jogging

**Élève 1:** Est-ce que tu fais du jogging ce week-end?

**Élève 2:** Non, je ne fais pas de jogging. Je fais du cheval.

1. tu / le vélo
   Est-ce que tu fais du vélo ce week-end?
2. tes amis / la cuisine
   Est-ce que tes amis font la cuisine ce week-end?
3. ton/ta petit(e) ami(e) et toi, vous / le jogging
   Est-ce que ton/ta petit(e) ami(e) et toi, vous faites du jogging ce week-end?
4. toi et moi, nous / une randonnée
   Est-ce que toi et moi, nous faisons une randonnée ce week-end?
5. tu / la gym
   Est-ce que tu fais de la gym ce week-end?
6. ton/ta cousin(e) / le sport
   Est-ce que ton/ta cousin(e) fait du sport ce week-end?

**5 De bons conseils** Avec un(e) partenaire, donnez de bons conseils (*advice*). À tour de rôle, posez des questions et utilisez les éléments de la liste. Présentez vos idées à la classe. *Answers will vary.*

**MODÈLE**

**Élève 1:** Qu'est-ce qu'il faut faire pour avoir de bonnes notes?

**Élève 2:** Il faut étudier jour et nuit.

| | |
|---|---|
| être en pleine forme (*great shape*) | avoir de bonnes notes |
| avoir de l'argent | gagner une course (*race*) |
| avoir beaucoup d'amis | bien manger |
| être champion de ski | réussir (*succeed*) aux examens |

**6 Les activités** Votre professeur va vous donner une feuille d'activités. Faites une enquête sur le nombre d'élèves qui pratiquent certaines activités dans votre classe. Présentez les résultats à la classe. *Answers will vary.*

**MODÈLE**

**Élève 1:** Est-ce que tu fais du jogging?

**Élève 2:** Oui, je fais du jogging.

| Activités | Noms |
|---|---|
| 1. jogging | Carole |
| 2. vélo | |
| 3. planche à voile | |
| 4. cuisine | |
| 5. camping | |
| 6. cheval | |

---

- Make sure to learn the correct article with each **faire** expression that calls for one. For **faire** expressions requiring a partitive or indefinite article, the article is replaced with **de** when the expression is negated.

Elles font **de la** gym trois fois par semaine.
*They work out three times a week.*

Elles ne font pas **de** gym le dimanche.
*They don't work out on Sundays.*

- Use **faire la connaissance de** before someone's name or another noun that identifies a person.

Je vais **faire la connaissance de Martin**.
*I'm going to meet Martin for the first time.*

Je vais **faire la connaissance des joueurs**.
*I'm going to meet the players for the first time.*

### The expression *il faut*

Pour être bon, il faut travailler!

Il ne faut pas regarder la télé.

- When followed by a verb in the infinitive, the expression **il faut...** means *it is necessary to...* or *one must...*

**Il faut faire** attention en cours de maths.
*It is necessary to pay attention in math class.*

**Il ne faut pas manger** après dix heures.
*One must not eat after 10 o'clock.*

**Faut-il laisser** un pourboire?
*Is it necessary to leave a tip?*

**Il faut gagner** le match!
*We must win the game!*

**Essayez!** Complétez chaque phrase avec la forme correcte du verbe **faire** au présent.

 1. Tu ____*fais*____ tes devoirs le samedi?
2. Vous ne ____*faites*____ pas attention au professeur.
3. Nous ____*faisons*____ du camping.
4. Ils ____*font*____ du jogging.
5. On ____*fait*____ une promenade au parc.
6. Il ____*fait*____ du ski en montagne.
7. Je ____*fais*____ de l'aérobic.
8. Elles ____*font*____ un tour en voiture.
9. Est-ce que vous ____*faites*____ la cuisine?
10. Nous ne ____*faisons*____ pas de sport.

---

**Essayez!** Have students check each other's answers.

**1 Suggestion** Have pairs of students drill each other on the meanings of expressions with **faire** (that are not cognates). Then tell them to cover that half of the page with paper or a book before doing this activity.

**2 Suggestion** Have students check their answers with a partner. If partners disagree, have them say: **Mais non, il ne fait pas...** Remind students that any expression with the partitive must use **pas de** when negative.

**3 Suggestion** Bring in images of people doing other activities with **faire** expressions. Ask: **Que fait-il/elle?**

**4 Expansion** Have students come up with four more activities using expressions with **faire** that they would like to ask their partner about. Encourage students to include adverbs or other logical additions in their answers.

**5 Expansion** Write **Qu'est-ce qu'il faut faire pour...** on the board followed by a few of the most talked about expressions from the box. Have volunteers write their ideas under each expression, forming columns of categories. Accept several answers for each. Ask: **Êtes-vous d'accord? Pourquoi?**

**6 Suggestions**
- Read the **modèle** aloud with a volunteer. Then distribute the **Feuilles d'activités**.
- Have students say how popular these activities are among classmates. Tell them to be prepared to justify their statements by citing how many students participate in each. Example: **Faire du jogging, c'est très populaire. Quinze élèves de notre classe font du jogging.**

---

# STRUCTURES

## 5A.2 Irregular -ir verbs

**Point de départ** You are already familiar with regular verbs whose infinitives end in **-er** and **-ir**. Some of the most commonly used **-ir** verbs are irregular.

- **Sortir** is used to express leaving a room or a building. It also expresses the idea of going out, as with friends or on a date. The preposition **de** is used after **sortir** when the place someone is leaving is expressed.

### Sortir

| | |
|---|---|
| je sors | nous sortons |
| tu sors | vous sortez |
| il/elle sort | ils/elles sortent |

Tu **sors** souvent avec tes copains?
*Do you go out often with your friends?*

Pierre et moi **sortons de** la salle de classe.
*Pierre and I leave the classroom.*

Le week-end, je sors souvent.

Ils partent pour la fac.

- **Partir** is generally used to say someone is leaving a large place such as a city, country, or region. Often, a form of **partir** is accompanied by the preposition **pour** and a destination name to say *to leave for (a place).*

### Partir

| | |
|---|---|
| je pars | nous partons |
| tu pars | vous partez |
| il/elle part | ils/elles partent |

Je **pars pour** l'Algérie.
*I'm leaving for Algeria.*

Ils **partent pour** Genève demain.
*They're leaving for Geneva tomorrow.*

> **BOÎTE À OUTILS**
> As you learned in **Leçon 4A**, **quitter** is used to say that someone leaves a place or another person: **Tu quittes la maison?** (*Are you leaving the house?*)

## MISE EN PRATIQUE

**1 Choisissez** Monique et ses amis aiment bien sortir. Choisissez la forme correcte des verbes **partir** ou **sortir** pour compléter la description de leurs activités.

1. Samedi soir, je _____ sors _____ avec mes copains.
2. Mes copines Magali et Anissa _____ partent _____ pour New York.
3. Nous _____ sortons _____ du cinéma.
4. Nicolas _____ part _____ pour Dakar vers 10 heures du soir.
5. Samedi matin, vous _____ partez _____ pour Londres.
6. Je _____ pars _____ pour le Maroc dans une semaine.
7. Tu _____ sors _____ avec ton petit ami ce week-end.
8. Olivier et Bernard _____ sortent _____ tard du bureau.

**2 Vos habitudes** Utilisez les éléments des colonnes pour décrire (*describe*) les habitudes de votre famille et de vos amis. Answers will vary.

| A | B | C |
|---|---|---|
| je | (ne pas) courir | jusqu'à (*until*) midi |
| mon frère | (ne pas) dormir | |
| ma sœur | (ne pas) partir | tous les week-ends |
| mes parents | (ne pas) sortir | |
| mes cousins | | tous les jours |
| mon petit ami | | souvent |
| ma petite amie | | rarement |
| mes copains | | jamais |
| ? | | une (deux, etc.) fois par jour/ semaine |
| | | ? |

**3 La question** Vincent parle au téléphone avec sa mère. Vous entendez (*hear*) ses réponses, mais pas les questions. Avec un(e) partenaire, reconstruisez la conversation. Answers will vary.

> **MODÈLE**
> Comment vas-tu? Ça va bien, merci.

1. _____ Oui, je sors avec mes amis ce soir.
2. _____ Nous partons à six heures.
3. _____ Oui, nous allons jouer au tennis.
4. _____ Après, nous allons au restaurant.
5. _____ Nous sortons du restaurant à neuf heures.
6. _____ Marc et Audrey partent pour Nice le week-end prochain.

 Practice more at **daccord1.vhlcentral.com.**

**Section Goals**

In this section, students will learn:
- the verbs **sortir** and **partir**
- other irregular **-ir** verbs

**Key Standards**
4.1, 5.1

**Student Resources**
*Cahier d'exercices*, pp. 61-62;
*Cahier d'activités*, p. 150;
Supersite: Activities,
*Cahier interactif*
**Teacher Resources**
Answer Keys; Audio Script;
Audio Activity MP3s/CD;
Testing program: Grammar Quiz

**Suggestions**

- Ask students where they have heard irregular **-ir** verbs before. (They heard **sortir** in this lesson's **Roman-photo**. If students have been to French-speaking places, they may have noticed the noun derived from **sortir**, **la sortie**, on **SORTIE** signs.)
- Model the pronunciation of forms for **sortir** and **partir**. Ask students simple questions. Example: **Je sors d'habitude le vendredi soir. Quand sortez-vous? (Je sors le samedi soir.)** As you elicit responses, write the present-tense forms of **sortir** on the board until the conjugation is complete. Underline the endings.
- Point out the recurrence of the **-s, -s, -t** pattern in singular forms.
- Reiterate that **sortir** is used as *to go out* or *to exit* while **partir** means *to leave*. Ask students to think of more examples comparing the two verbs. Then remind them of the note about **quitter** in the **Boîte à outils**. Using ideas from students, write on the board a short paragraph (two to three sentences) that contains at least one form of each of the three verbs mentioned above. Make sure the context defines the meanings well.
- Go over other irregular **-ir** verbs, pointing out that they are all in the same grammatical "verb family" as **sortir** and **partir**. Note that all verbs of this type have two stems: **sortir**: singular stem **sor-** and plural stem **sort-**.

**OPTIONS**

**Using Movement** Tell students that they will act out the appropriate gestures when you say what certain people in the class are doing. Examples: _____ **dort.** (The student gestures sleeping.) _____ **et** _____ **courent.** (The two students indicated run in place briefly.) Repeat verbs and vary forms as much as possible.

**Mini-dictée** Dictate sentences like these to the class, saying each one twice and pausing between. **1. Je pars pour la France la semaine prochaine. 2. Mon copain et moi, nous sortons ce soir. 3. Les élèves ne dorment jamais en classe. 4. Le café sent bon. 5. Tu cours vite. 6. Que servez-vous au restaurant?** Advise students to pay attention to the verbs.

## COMMUNICATION

**4 Descriptions** Avec un(e) partenaire, complétez les phrases avec la forme correcte d'un verbe de la liste.

| courir | dormir | partir | sentir | servir | sortir |

1. Véronique /  / tard
   Véronique dort tard.

2. je /  / sandwichs
   Je sers des sandwichs.

3. les enfants /  / le chocolat chaud
   Les enfants sentent le chocolat chaud.

4. nous /  / souvent
   Nous courons souvent.

5. tu /  / de l'hôpital
   Tu sors de l'hôpital.

6. vous / 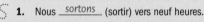 / pour la France demain
   Vous partez pour la France demain.

**5 Indiscrétions** Votre partenaire est curieux/curieuse et désire savoir (*to know*) ce que vous faites chez vous. Répondez à ses questions. *Answers will vary.*

1. Jusqu'à (*Until*) quelle heure dors-tu le week-end?
2. Dors-tu pendant (*during*) les cours au lycée? Pendant quels cours? Pourquoi?
3. À quelle heure sors-tu le samedi soir?
4. Avec qui sors-tu le samedi soir?
5. Que sers-tu quand tu as des copains à la maison?
6. Pars-tu bientôt en vacances (*vacation*)? Où?

**6 Dispute** Laëtitia est très active. Son petit ami Bertrand ne sort pas beaucoup, alors ils ont souvent des disputes. Avec un(e) partenaire, jouez les deux rôles. Utilisez les mots et les expressions de la liste.
*Answers will vary.*

| | |
|---|---|
| dormir | partir |
| faire des promenades | un passe-temps |
| | sentir |
| faire un tour (en voiture) | sortir |
| | rarement |
| par semaine | souvent |

• Here is a list of verbs that are conjugated like **sortir** and **partir**.

### Other irregular -ir verbs

| | dormir (*to sleep*) | servir (*to serve*) | sentir (*to feel*) | courir (*to run*) |
|---|---|---|---|---|
| je | dors | sers | sens | cours |
| tu | dors | sers | sens | cours |
| il/elle | dort | sert | sent | court |
| nous | dormons | servons | sentons | courons |
| vous | dormez | servez | sentez | courez |
| ils/elles | dorment | servent | sentent | courent |

*Rachid dort.*

*Nous courons.*

Nous **servons** du thé glacé aux enfants.
*We are serving iced tea to the children.*

Vous **courez** vite!
*You run fast!*

Je **sers** du fromage aux invités.
*I'm serving cheese to the guests.*

Elles **dorment** jusqu'à midi.
*They sleep until noon.*

• **Sentir** can mean *to feel*, *to smell*, or *to sense*.

Je **sens** qu'il va arriver dans quelques minutes.
*I sense that he's going to arrive in a few minutes.*

Ça **sent** bon!
*That smells good!*

Vous **sentez** l'odeur de ce bouquet de fleurs?
*Do you smell the scent of these flowers?*

Ils **sentent** sa présence.
*They feel his presence.*

### Essayez!    Complétez les phrases avec la forme correcte du verbe.

1. Nous _sortons_ (sortir) vers neuf heures.
2. Je _sers_ (servir) des boissons gazeuses aux invités.
3. Tu _pars_ (partir) quand pour le Canada?
4. Nous ne _dormons_ (dormir) pas en cours.
5. Ils _courent_ (courir) pour attraper (*to catch*) le bus.
6. Tu manges des oignons? Ça _sent_ (sentir) mauvais.
7. Vous _sortez_ (sortir) avec des copains ce soir.
8. Elle _part_ (partir) pour Dijon ce week-end.

*cent cinquante-sept* **157**

**Essayez!** Give these items for additional practice, having students choose which -ir verb(s) to use. 1. J'adore ____. Je ____ vingt à trente kilomètres par semaine. (courir, cours) 2. Les enfants ne ____ pas parce qu'ils ne sont pas fatigués. (dorment) 3. Qu'est-ce qu'on ____ au restaurant en face de chez toi? (sert) 4. Merci pour les fleurs. Elles ____ très bon. (sentent)

**1 Suggestion** Give a tip on how to choose between **sortir** and **partir**. Remind students that **partir** is often followed by the preposition **pour**. **Partir pour** always implies leaving for a certain amount of time and distance.

**2 Suggestions**
• Have students write at least five sentences describing their family's and friends' habits.
• In pairs, have students compare the information. Example: **Élève 1: Est-ce que tu dors jusqu'à midi? Élève 2: Oui, mais rarement. Élève 1: Moi, jamais!**
• Ask for volunteers to share some of their sentences with the class.

**3 Expansion** Ask students to imagine they are on the telephone and a classmate can overhear them. Have students write three answers to say in front of a partner who will guess the questions. Example: **Non, je ne cours pas dans le parc demain. (Est-ce que tu cours dans le parc demain?)**

**4 Suggestion** Find a photo to use for a **modèle**. Example: Put on the board **Les chiens** / image of dogs sleeping / **beaucoup**. Have students ask **Que fait Véronique? Qu'est-ce que je fais?** etc. before partners answer.

**5 Suggestion** Remind students to answer in complete sentences.

**6 Suggestion** Have a couple of volunteer pairs act out their conversations for the class.

**Using Games** Divide the class into two teams. Announce an infinitive and a subject pronoun. Example: **dormir; elle.** At the board, have the first member of Team A say and write down the given subject and the conjugated form of the verb. If the team member answers correctly, Team A gets one point. If not, give the first member of Team B the same example. The team with the most points at the end of the game wins.

**Writing Stories** Have small groups of students create a short story in the present tense or a conversation in which they logically mention as many verb forms as possible of **sortir**, **partir**, **dormir**, **servir**, **sentir**, and **courir**. If the class is advanced, add **mentir**. Call on groups to tell their story to the class or act out their conversation. Have students vote on the best story or conversation.

# SYNTHÈSE
# Révision

## Key Standards
1.1

**Student Resources**
*Cahier d'activités*, pp. 43–44;
Supersite: Activities,
*Cahier interactif*
**Teacher Resources**
Answer Keys; Info Gap Activities;
Testing Program: Lesson Test
(Testing Program Audio MP3s/CD)

**1** **Suggestion** After collaborating on their efforts, ask groups how many activities they described. Have the group with most sentences share them with the class.

**2** **Suggestion** Remind students that adverbs like **rarement**, **souvent**, and **toujours** should be placed immediately after the verb, not at the end of a sentence or anywhere else as one can say in English. Example: **Je fais rarement du cheval.** They should never say: **je fais du cheval rarement** or **je rarement fais du cheval.**

**3** **Suggestion** Have students say what their partners are going to do on vacation, when, where, and with whom.

**4** **Suggestion** Call on two volunteers to do the **modèle**.

**4** **Expansion** Have students continue the activity with additional places, such as **au lycée, à la cantine, au centre-ville**, etc.

**5** **Suggestion** Tell students to use as many irregular **-ir** verbs and **faire** expressions as possible.

**6** **Suggestion** Divide the class into pairs and distribute the Info Gap Handouts found on the Supersite for this activity. Give students ten minutes to complete the activity.

---

**1** **Au parc** C'est dimanche. Avec un(e) partenaire, décrivez les activités de tous les personnages. Comparez vos observations avec les observations d'un autre groupe pour compléter votre description. Answers will vary.

**2** **Mes habitudes** Avec un(e) partenaire, parlez de vos habitudes de la semaine. Que faites-vous régulièrement? Utilisez tous les mots de la liste. Answers will vary.

 **MODÈLE**

**Élève 1:** *Je fais parfois de la gym le lundi. Et toi?*
**Élève 2:** *Moi, je fais parfois la cuisine le lundi.*

| | |
|---|---|
| parfois le lundi | souvent à midi |
| le mercredi à midi | toujours le vendredi |
| le jeudi soir | tous les jours |
| le vendredi matin | trois fois par semaine |
| rarement le matin | une fois par semaine |

**3** **Mes vacances** Parlez de vos prochaines vacances (*vacation*) avec un(e) partenaire. Mentionnez cinq de vos passe-temps habituels en vacances et cinq nouvelles activités que vous allez essayer (*to try*). Comparez votre liste avec la liste de votre partenaire, puis présentez les réponses à la classe. Answers will vary.

**4** **Que faire ici?** Avec un(e) partenaire, trouvez au minimum quatre choses à faire dans chaque (*each*) endroit. Quel endroit préférez-vous et pourquoi? Comparez votre liste avec un autre groupe et parlez de vos préférences avec la classe. Answers will vary.

**MODÈLE**

**Élève 1:** *À la campagne, on fait des randonnées à cheval.*
**Élève 2:** *Oui, et il faut marcher.*

**1. à la campagne**

**3. au parc**

**2. à la plage**

**4. au gymnase**

**5** **Le conseiller** Un(e) conseiller/conseillère au lycée suggère des stratégies à un(e) élève pour l'aider (*help him or her*) à préparer les examens. Avec un(e) partenaire, jouez les deux rôles. Vos camarades vont sélectionner les meilleurs conseils (*best advice*). Answers will vary.

**MODÈLE**

*Il faut faire tous ses devoirs.*

**6** **Quelles activités?** Votre professeur va vous donner, à vous et à votre partenaire, deux feuilles d'activités différentes pour le week-end. Attention! Ne regardez pas la feuille de votre partenaire. Answers will vary.

**MODÈLE**

**Élève 1:** *Est-ce que tu fais une randonnée dimanche après-midi?*
**Élève 2:** *Oui, je fais une randonnée dimanche après-midi.*

| ressources | | |
|---|---|---|
| CE pp. 59–62 | CA pp. 8, 43–44, 149–150 | daccord1.vhlcentral.com |

---

**O P T I O N S**

**Mini-dictée** Ask students to write five sentences individually, at least two with **faire**, at least one with **il faut**, and at least three with different irregular **-ir** verbs. Tell them to try to include more than one requirement in each sentence. Have students dictate their sentences to their partner. After both students in each pair have finished dictating their sentences, have them exchange papers for correction.

**Telling Stories** Have students take turns telling their partners about a memorable vacation experience, who they were with, what they did, etc. Encourage students to express themselves using as much variety as possible in terms of vocabulary and grammar structures. Have students take notes as their partner narrates to reveal to the class later what was said.

 Video: TV Clip

 *Le Zapping*

## Sponsors de demain

Fondée en 1857, SwissLife est la plus grande° compagnie d'assurance vie° de Suisse, avec des filiales° aussi dans d'autres pays européens. C'est une entreprise° consciente de l'importance de la vie culturelle et sportive des communautés. SwissLife sponsorise des associations et des programmes aux niveaux° national et communautaire parce qu'elle reconnaît° qu'ils ont un effet positif sur les générations futures. En 2004, SwissLife commence à soutenir° l'équipe nationale suisse de football et, en 2007, le Kids Festival, tournois de football pour les enfants de six à dix ans.

Sponsor officiel des équipes nationales suisses de football

—Gagner la Ligue des Champions...

—Jouer en finale de la Coupe du Monde...

###  Compréhension  Répondez aux questions.  Some answers will vary.

1. Qui sont les personnes dans la publicité (*ad*)?  Ce sont des joueurs de football.
2. Quel âge le narrateur a-t-il à peu près (*approximately*)?  Il a entre six et dix ans.
3. Qu'est-ce que le narrateur a envie de faire un jour?  Some answers will vary.
   Suggested answers: Il a envie de gagner la Ligue des Champions et de jouer en finale de la Coupe du Monde.

### Discussion  Par groupes de trois, répondez aux questions.  Answers will vary.

1. Pourquoi est-ce un enfant qui parle dans la pub, et non un adulte? Quel est le rôle des adultes?
2. Quelle personne est un modèle pour vous? Que fait-elle?

**la plus grande** *the largest* **assurance vie** *life insurance* **filiales** *branches*
**entreprise** *company* **niveaux** *levels* **reconnaît** *recognizes* **soutenir** *to support*

 Practice more at **daccord1.vhlcentral.com**.

---

**SwissLife**  As Switzerland's largest life insurance company and one of Europe's largest, SwissLife also operates in France, Belgium, Germany, the Netherlands, and other European countries. It also partners with other insurance companies around the world, thereby extending its market on a global scale. It takes community sponsorship seriously and practices it actively. In addition to the Swiss national soccer team and the Kids Festival tournaments, SwissLife also sponsors the Zurich Chamber Orchestra, the Swiss National Circus, running marathons, and the Swiss film festival, among others.

---

### Section Goals

In this section, students will:
• read about the insurance company SwissLife
• watch a commercial for the company
• answer questions about the commercial and SwissLife

### Key Standards

1.2, 2.2, 4.2, 5.2

**Student Resources**
Supersite: Video, Activities
**Teacher Resources**
Video Script & Translation; Supersite: Video

**Introduction**
To check comprehension, ask these questions:
**1. En quelle année SwissLife est-elle fondée? (SwissLife est fondée en 1857.)**
**2. De quoi la compagnie est-elle consciente? (Elle est consciente de l'importance de la vie culturelle et sportive des communautés.)**
**3. Que commence à faire SwissLife en 2007? (Elle commence à soutenir le Kids Festival.)**

**Avant de regarder la vidéo**
• Have students look at the video stills, read the captions, and predict what is happening in the commercial for each visual.
**(1. L'homme joue au football.
2. Le garçon désire être joueur de foot professionnel.)**
• Before showing the video, explain to students that they do not need to understand every word they hear. Tell them to listen for vocabulary from this lesson as well as cognates that indicate the boy's wish to become a soccer hero.

**Compréhension**  Have students work in pairs or groups for this activity. Tell them to write their answers. Then show the video again so that they can check their answers and add any missing information.

**Discussion**  Ask students if they believe that a large company that sponsors cultural activities genuinely does so for the community's sake. Have them explain their answers.

## Leçon 5B

**You will learn how to...**
- talk about seasons and the date
- discuss the weather

Talking Picture
Audio: Activity

# Quel temps fait-il?

## Vocabulaire

| | |
|---|---|
| Il fait 18 degrés. | *It is 18 degrees.* |
| Il fait beau. | *The weather is nice.* |
| Il fait bon. | *The weather is good/warm.* |
| Il fait mauvais. | *The weather is bad.* |
| Il fait un temps épouvantable. | *The weather is dreadful.* |
| Le temps est orageux. | *It is stormy.* |
| Quel temps fait-il? | *What is the weather like?* |
| Quelle température fait-il? | *What is the temperature?* |
| une saison | *season* |
| en automne | *in the fall* |
| en été | *in the summer* |
| en hiver | *in the winter* |
| au printemps | *in the spring* |
| Quelle est la date? | *What's the date?* |
| C'est le 1ᵉʳ (premier) octobre. | *It's the first of October.* |
| C'est quand votre/ton anniversaire? | *When is your birthday?* |
| C'est le 2 mai. | *It's the second of May.* |
| C'est quand l'anniversaire de Paul? | *When is Paul's birthday?* |
| C'est le 15 mars. | *It's March 15ᵗʰ.* |
| un anniversaire | *birthday* |

**ressources**

CE
pp. 63–64

CA
p. 45–46, 151

S
daccord1.vhlcentral.com

Il neige. (neiger)

Il fait froid.

L'hiver (*m.*): décembre, janvier, février

Il fait (du) soleil.

Bal du 14 juillet

Il fait chaud.

Quelle est la date d'aujourd'hui? C'est le 14 juillet.

L'été (*m.*): juin, juillet, août

---

**OPTIONS**

**Using Visuals** Distribute a set of illustrations of various weather conditions to pairs of students. Choose images with variety and have students write detailed descriptions of each one. They should describe the weather, the season, and any activities represented.

**Using Visuals** Distribute a calendar that shows **les fêtes**. First, call out dates and have students give the corresponding name on the calendar. Then call out names on the calendar and have students provide the date. Example: **la Saint-Valentin (le 14 février).**

## Mise en pratique

**Il pleut.** (pleuvoir)

**un parapluie**

**un imperméable**

**Le printemps (m.): mars, avril, mai**

**1** **Les fêtes et les jours fériés** Indiquez la date et la saison de chaque fête et jour férié (*holiday*).

|  | | Date | Saison |
|---|---|---|---|
| 1. | la fête nationale française | le 14 juillet | l'été |
| 2. | l'indépendance des États-Unis | le 4 juillet | l'été |
| 3. | Poisson d'avril (*April Fool's Day*) | le 1er avril | le printemps |
| 4. | Noël | le 25 décembre | l'hiver |
| 5. | la Saint-Valentin | le 14 février | l'hiver |
| 6. | le Nouvel An | le 1er janvier | l'hiver |
| 7. | Halloween | le 31 octobre | l'automne |
| 8. | l'anniversaire de Washington | le 22 février | l'hiver |

**2** **Quel temps fait-il?** Répondez aux questions par des phrases complètes. *Answers will vary.*

1. Quel temps fait-il en été?
2. Quel temps fait-il en automne?
3. Quel temps fait-il au printemps?
4. Quel temps fait-il en hiver?
5. Où est-ce qu'il neige?
6. Quel est votre mois préféré de l'année? Pourquoi?
7. Quand est-ce qu'il pleut où vous habitez?
8. Quand est-ce que le temps est orageux où vous habitez?

janvier

octobre

mai

décembre

**Le temps est nuageux.**

**Il fait frais.**

**Il fait du vent.**

**L'automne (m.): septembre, octobre, novembre**

**3** **Écoutez** 🎧 Écoutez le bulletin météorologique et répondez aux questions suivantes.

|  | | Vrai | Faux |
|---|---|---|---|
| 1. | C'est l'été. | ☐ | ☑ |
| 2. | Le printemps commence le 21 mars. | ☑ | ☐ |
| 3. | Il fait 11 degrés vendredi. | ☑ | ☐ |
| 4. | Il fait du vent vendredi. | ☐ | ☑ |
| 5. | Il va faire soleil samedi. | ☐ | ☑ |
| 6. | Il faut utiliser le parapluie et l'imperméable vendredi. | ☐ | ☑ |
| 7. | Il va faire un temps épouvantable dimanche. | ☑ | ☐ |
| 8. | Il ne va pas faire chaud samedi. | ☑ | ☐ |

Practice more at **daccord1.vhlcentral.com.**

*cent soixante et un* **161**

**1** **Suggestions**
- Remind students to give the date in the correct order (day before month) and to include **le** before the day.
- Point out that the day always precedes the month in French when the date is written with numbers. Examples: **14 avril 2011**, **14/04/2011**

**1** **Expansion** Using this year's calendar, have students find the dates of these holidays. **9. la fête du travail aux États-Unis 10.** *Thanksgiving* **11.** *Easter* **(Pâques) 12.** *Memorial Day* You may ask students to look up dates of other secular celebrations or religious holidays from various faiths. Answers will vary from year to year.

**2** **Suggestions**
- Have students work in pairs or small groups to answer these questions.
- Tell students they may also encounter the phrase **à l'automne**, meaning *this fall*. For other seasons, make sure they know to use **en** before those starting with a vowel sound and **au** with **printemps**, as it starts with a consonant.

**3** **Script** Aujourd'hui, vendredi 21 mars, nous commençons le printemps avec une température de 11 degrés; il n'y a pas de vent, mais il y a quelques nuages. Votre météo du week-end: samedi, il ne va pas faire soleil; il va faire frais avec une température de 13 degrés; dimanche, encore 13 degrés, mais il va faire un temps épouvantable; il va pleuvoir toute la journée, alors, n'oubliez pas votre parapluie et votre imperméable! *(On Textbook Audio)*

**3** **Suggestion** Have students correct the false items.

**OPTIONS**

**Le calendrier républicain** During the French Revolution, the official calendar was changed. The New Year began on September 22 (the autumnal equinox), and the year was divided into 30-day months named as follows: **Vendémiaire** (*Vintage*), **Brumaire** (*Mist*), **Frimaire** (*Frost*), **Nivôse** (*Snow*), **Pluviôse** (*Rain*), **Ventôse** (*Wind*), **Germinal** (*Seed time*), **Floréal** (*Flower*), **Prairial** (*Meadow*), **Messidor** (*Harvest*), **Thermidor** (*Heat*), and **Fructidor** (*Fruits*).

**Using Games** Have students take turns guessing another student's birthday. He or she responds by saying **avant** or **après** until someone guesses correctly. The class then tries to guess the winning student's birthday. Play several rounds of this game to give all students as many opportunities as possible to guess.

# CONTEXTES

## Communication

**4** | **Conversez** Interviewez un(e) camarade de classe. Answers will vary.

1. C'est quand ton anniversaire? C'est quand l'anniversaire de ton père? Et de ta mère?
2. En quelle saison est ton anniversaire? Quel temps fait-il?
3. Quelle est ta saison préférée? Pourquoi? Quelles activités aimes-tu pratiquer?
4. En quelles saisons utilises-tu un parapluie et un imperméable? Pourquoi?
5. À quel moment de l'année es-tu en vacances? Précise les mois. Pendant (During) quels mois de l'année préfères-tu voyager? Pourquoi?
6. À quelle période de l'année étudies-tu? Précise les mois.
7. Quelle saison détestes-tu le plus (the most)? Pourquoi?
8. Quand est l'anniversaire de mariage de tes parents?

**5** | **Une lettre** Vous avez un(e) correspondant(e) (pen pal) en France qui veut (wants) vous rendre visite (to visit you). Écrivez (Write) une lettre à votre ami(e) où vous décrivez (describe) le temps qu'il fait à chaque saison et les activités que vous pouvez (can) pratiquer ensemble (together). Comparez votre lettre avec la lettre d'un(e) camarade de classe. Answers will vary.

> Cher Thomas,
>
> Ici à Boston, il fait très froid en hiver et il neige souvent. Est-ce que tu aimes la neige? Moi, j'adore parce que je fais du ski tous les week-ends.
>
> Et toi, tu fais du ski? ...

**6** | **Quel temps fait-il en France?** Votre professeur va vous donner, à vous et à votre partenaire, deux feuilles d'activités différentes. Attention! Ne regardez pas la feuille de votre partenaire.

**MODÈLE**

Élève 1: *Quel temps fait-il à Paris?*
Élève 2: *À Paris, le temps est nuageux et la température est de dix degrés.*

**7** | **La météo** Préparez avec un(e) camarade de classe une présentation où vous: Answers will vary.

- mentionnez le jour, la date et la saison.
- présentez la météo d'une ville francophone.
- présentez les prévisions météo (weather forecasts) pour le reste de la semaine.
- préparez une affiche pour illustrer votre présentation.

**La météo d'Haïti en juillet — Port-au-Prince**

| samedi 23 | dimanche 24 | lundi 25 |
|---|---|---|
| 27°C | 35°C | 37°C |
| ☀ | ⛅ | ⛈ |
| soleil | nuageux | orageux |

Aujourd'hui samedi, c'est le 23 juillet. C'est l'été. Il va faire soleil...

---

### Teacher's Annotated Edition sidebar

**4 Suggestion** Have students share what they've learned about their partners with another pair of students or with the rest of the class.

**5 Suggestion** Encourage students to use a wide variety of expressions for seasons and activities. Have them exchange papers for peer editing.

**6 Suggestions**
- Divide the class into pairs and distribute the Info Gap Handouts found on the Supersite for this activity. Give students ten minutes to complete the activity.
- Have two volunteers read the **modèle**.

**7 Expansion** Assign a different francophone location to each pair of students and have them research its weather forecast on the Internet. Hold a vote without revealing names of students, and give prizes for the best presentation in various categories (**le plus amusant, créateur, utile,** and so on).

**Successful Language Learning** Tell students that when looking at materials intended for native speakers like weather forecasts, they should pay attention to visual cues and use their background knowledge about the subject to help them understand. They should try to anticipate vocabulary they might hear, listen for familiar sounding words, and make intelligent guesses.

---

**OPTIONS**

**Using Movement** Write **C'est quand ton anniversaire?** on the board or on a transparency. Make a "human calendar" using students to represent various days. Have them form 12 rows (one for each month) and put themselves in order according to their birthdays by asking and answering the question. Give the person with the first birthday in each month a sign for that month. Call out each month and have students give their birthdays in order.

**Guessing Dates** Have students form groups of two to four. Hand out cards with the name of a holiday or other annual event. Instruct each group to hide their card from other groups. Groups come up with three sentences to describe the holiday or occasion without mentioning its name. They can mention the season. The other groups must first guess the month and day on which the event takes place, then name the event itself.

# Les sons et les lettres

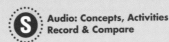 **Audio: Concepts, Activities**
**Record & Compare**

🎧 Open vs. closed vowels: Part 1

You have already learned that **é** is pronounced like the vowel *a* in the English word *cake*.
This is a closed **e** sound.

| **étudiant** | **agréable** | **nationalité** | **enchanté** |

The letter combinations **-er** and **-ez** at the end of a word are pronounced the same way, as
is the vowel sound in single-syllable words ending in **-es**.

| **travailler** | **avez** | **mes** | **les** |

The vowels spelled **è** and **ê** are pronounced like the vowel in the English word *pet*, as is an **e**
followed by a double consonant. These are open **e** sounds.

| **répète** | **première** | **pêche** | **italienne** |

The vowel sound in *pet* may also be spelled **et**, **ai**, or **ei**.

| **secret** | **français** | **fait** | **seize** |

Compare these pairs of words. To make the vowel sound in *cake*, your mouth should be
slightly more closed than when you make the vowel sound in *pet*.

| **mes  mais** | **ces  cette** | **théâtre  thème** |

◉S **Prononcez** Répétez les mots suivants à voix haute.

| 1. thé | 4. été | 7. degrés | 10. discret |
| 2. lait | 5. neige | 8. anglais | 11. treize |
| 3. belle | 6. aider | 9. cassette | 12. mauvais |

◉S **Articulez** Répétez les phrases suivantes à voix haute.

1. Hélène est très discrète.
2. Céleste achète un vélo laid.
3. Il neige souvent en février et en décembre.
4. Désirée est canadienne; elle n'est pas française.

◉S **Dictons** Répétez les dictons à voix haute.

Qui sème le vent récolte la tempête.[2]

Péché avoué est à demi pardonné.[1]

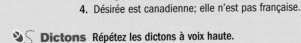

[1] An offense admitted is half pardoned.
[2] You reap what you sow. (lit. He who sows the wind reaps a storm.)

**ressources**

CA
p. 152

daccord1.vhlcentral.com

---

## Section Goals
In this section, students will learn about open and closed vowels.

## Key Standards
4.1

**Student Resources**
*Cahier d'activités*, p. 152;
Supersite: Activities,
*Cahier interactif*
**Teacher Resources**
Answer Keys; Audio Script;
Textbook & Audio Activity
MP3s/CD

## Suggestions
• Model the pronunciation of these open and closed vowel sounds and have students watch the shape of your mouth, then repeat each sound after you. Then pronounce each of the example words and have students repeat them.
• Mention words and expressions from the **Vocabulaire** on page 160 that contain the open and closed vowels presented on this page. Alternately, ask students to recall such vocabulary. Then have them repeat after you. Examples: **février**, **Il fait frais**, etc. See if a volunteer is able to recall any expression from previous lessons. Examples: **seize**, **vélo**, **aérobic**.
• Dictate five familiar words containing the open and closed vowels presented on this page, repeating each one at least two times. Then write them on the board or on a transparency and have students check and correct their spelling.
• Remind students that **ai** and **ei** are nasalized when followed by **m** or **n**. Compare the following words: **français** / **faim**, **seize** / **hein**.
• Point out that, unlike English, there is no diphthong or glide in these vowel sounds. To illustrate this, contrast the pronunciation of the English word *may* with that of the French word **mai**.

---

**Extra Practice** Here are some sentences to use for additional practice with these open and closed vowel sounds. **1. Il fait soleil. 2. En janvier, il neige et il fait mauvais. 3. Toute la journée, j'aide ma mère. 4. Didier est français, mais Hélène est belge.**

**Using Games** Have a spelling bee using vocabulary words from **Leçons 1A–5B** that contain the two open and closed vowel sounds featured on this page. Pronounce each word, use it in a sentence, and then say the individual word again. Tell students that they must spell the words in French and include all diacritical marks.

# ROMAN-PHOTO

## Quel temps!  Video: *Roman-photo*
Record & Compare

**PERSONNAGES**

David

Rachid

Sandrine

Stéphane

*Au parc...*

**RACHID** Napoléon établit le Premier Empire en quelle année?
**STÉPHANE** Euh... mille huit cent quatre?
**RACHID** Exact! On est au mois de novembre et il fait toujours chaud.
**STÉPHANE** Oui, il fait bon!... dix-neuf, dix-huit degrés!

**RACHID** Et on a chaud aussi parce qu'on court.
**STÉPHANE** Bon, allez, je rentre faire mes devoirs d'histoire-géo.
**RACHID** Et moi, je rentre boire une grande bouteille d'eau.

**RACHID** À demain, Stéph! Et n'oublie pas: le cours du jeudi avec ton professeur, Monsieur Rachid Kahlid, commence à dix-huit heures, pas à dix-huit heures vingt!
**STÉPHANE** Pas de problème! Merci et à demain!

**SANDRINE** Et puis, en juillet, le Tour de France commence. J'aime bien le regarder à la télévision. Et après, c'est mon anniversaire, le 20. Cette année, je fête mes vingt et un ans. Tous les ans, pour célébrer mon anniversaire, j'invite mes amis et je prépare une super soirée. J'adore faire la cuisine, c'est une vraie passion!
**DAVID** Ah, oui?

**SANDRINE** En parlant d'anniversaire, Stéphane célèbre ses dix-huit ans samedi prochain. C'est un anniversaire important. ...On organise une surprise. Tu es invité!
**DAVID** Hmm, c'est très gentil, mais... Tu essaies de ne pas parler deux minutes, s'il te plaît? Parfait!

**SANDRINE** Pascal! Qu'est-ce que tu fais aujourd'hui? Il fait beau à Paris?
**DAVID** Encore un peu de patience! Allez, encore dix secondes... Voilà!

A C T I V I T É S

**1** **Qui?** Identifiez les personnages pour chaque phrase.
 Écrivez **D** pour David, **R** pour Rachid, **S** pour Sandrine et **St** pour Stéphane

1. Cette personne aime faire la cuisine. S
2. Cette personne sort quand il fait froid. D
3. Cette personne aime le Tour de France. S
4. Cette personne n'aime pas la pluie. S

5. Cette personne va boire de l'eau. R
6. Ces personnes ont rendez-vous tous les jeudis. R, St
7. Cette personne fête son anniversaire en janvier. D
8. Ces personnes célèbrent un joli portrait. D, R, S
9. Cette personne fête ses dix-huit ans samedi prochain. St
10. Cette personne prépare des crêpes pour le dîner. S

 Practice more at **daccord1.vhlcentral.com**.

## Les anniversaires à travers (*through*) les saisons

*À l'appartement de David et de Rachid...*

**SANDRINE** C'est quand, ton anniversaire?

**DAVID** Qui, moi? Oh, c'est le quinze janvier.

**SANDRINE** Il neige en janvier, à Washington?

**DAVID** Parfois... et il pleut souvent à l'automne et en hiver.

**SANDRINE** Je déteste la pluie. C'est pénible. Qu'est-ce que tu aimes faire quand il pleut, toi?

**DAVID** Oh, beaucoup de choses! Dessiner, écouter de la musique. J'aime tellement la nature, je sors même quand il fait très froid.

**SANDRINE** Moi, je préfère l'été. Il fait chaud. On fait des promenades.

**RACHID** Oh là là, j'ai soif! Mais... qu'est-ce que vous faites, tous les deux?

**DAVID** Oh, rien! Je fais juste un portrait de Sandrine.

**RACHID** Bravo, c'est pas mal du tout! Hmm, mais quelque chose ne va pas, David. Sandrine n'a pas de téléphone dans la main!

**SANDRINE** Oh, Rachid, ça suffit! C'est vrai, tu as vraiment du talent, David. Pourquoi ne pas célébrer mon joli portrait? Vous avez faim, les garçons?

**RACHID ET DAVID** Oui!

**SANDRINE** Je prépare le dîner. Vous aimez les crêpes ou vous préférez une omelette?

**RACHID ET DAVID** Des crêpes... Miam!

### Expressions utiles

#### Talking about birthdays

- **Cette année, je fête mes vingt et un ans.**
  *This year, I celebrate my twenty-first birthday.*
- **Pour célébrer mon anniversaire, je prépare une super soirée.**
  *To celebrate my birthday, I plan a great party.*
- **Stéphane célèbre ses dix-huit ans samedi prochain.**
  *Stéphane celebrates his eighteenth birthday next Saturday.*
- **On organise une surprise.**
  *We are planning a surprise.*

#### Talking about hopes and preferences

- **Tu essaies de ne pas parler deux minutes, s'il te plaît?**
  *Could you try not to talk for two minutes, please?*
- **J'aime tellement la nature, je sors même quand il fait très froid.**
  *I like nature so much, I go out even when it's very cold.*
- **Moi, je préfère l'été.**
  *Me, I prefer summer.*
- **Vous aimez les crêpes ou vous préférez une omelette?**
  *Do you like crêpes or do you prefer an omelette?*

#### Additional vocabulary

- **encore un peu**
  *a little more*
- **Quelque chose ne va pas.**
  *Something's not right/working.*
- **Allez.**
  *Come on.*
- **main**
  *hand*
- **Ça suffit!**
  *That's enough!*
- **Miam!**
  *Yum!*

---

**2** **Faux!** Toutes ces phrases contiennent une information qui est fausse. Corrigez chaque phrase. Answers will vary. Suggested answers below.

1. Stéphane a dix-huit ans. Stéphane a dix-sept ans.

2. David et Rachid préfèrent une omelette. Ils préfèrent des crêpes.

3. Il fait froid et il pleut. Il fait beau/bon.

4. On n'organise rien (*anything*) pour l'anniversaire de Stéphane. On organise une surprise pour l'anniversaire de Stéphane.

5. L'anniversaire de Stéphane est au printemps. L'anniversaire de Stéphane est en automne.

6. Rachid et Stéphane ont froid. Ils ont chaud.

**3** **Conversez** Parlez avec vos camarades de classe pour découvrir (*find out*) qui a l'anniversaire le plus proche du vôtre (*closest to yours*). Qui est-ce? Quand est son anniversaire? En quelle saison? Quel mois? En général, quel temps fait-il le jour de son anniversaire?

**ressources**

CA
pp. 85–86 | daccord1.vhlcentral.com

A C T I V I T É S

---

**Expressions utiles**

- Draw attention to numbers 101 and higher and spelling-change **-er** verbs in the video-still captions, in the **Expressions utiles** box, and as they occur in your conversation with students.
- Have students scan the video-still captions and the **Expressions utiles** box for expressions related to hopes and preferences.
- Ask students about their own preferences. You might ask questions like: **Vous préférez l'été ou l'hiver? l'automne ou le printemps? janvier ou juillet? regarder la télé ou aller au cinéma?** For a more challenging activity, follow up by asking **Pourquoi?**

**1** **Expansion**

- Continue the activity with more statements like these. **11. Cette personne fête son anniversaire samedi prochain. (St) 12. Cette personne parle souvent au téléphone. (S) 13. Cette personne aime écouter de la musique. (D)**
- Assign one of the four main characters in this episode to a small group. Each group should write a brief description of their character's likes, dislikes, and preferences.

**2** **Suggestion** Have students correct false statements on the board.

**2** **Expansion** Give these false items for extra practice. **1. Sandrine n'aime pas parler au téléphone (Faux.) 2. Stéphane et Rachid étudient la psychologie aujourd'hui. (Faux.) 3. Sandrine n'aime pas regarder la télé. (Faux.) 4. Sur son portrait, Sandrine a un téléphone dans la main. (Faux.)**

**3** **Suggestion** Brainstorm questions students might ask to find the person whose birthday is closest to their own. Once they have found that person, have them do this activity in pairs. Ask volunteers to tell the class what they learned about their partner.

---

**OPTIONS**

**Improvisation** Ask volunteers to ad-lib the episode for the class. Assure them that it is not necessary to memorize the episode or to stick strictly to its content. They should try to get the general meaning across with the vocabulary and expressions they know, and they should feel free to be creative. Give them time to prepare. You may want to assign this as homework and do it the next class period as a review activity.

**Using Games** Play a memory game. The first player tells his or her birthday. The next player repeats what the first said, then adds his or her birthday. The third player must state the first two birthdays, then his or her own. Continue until someone makes an error. Replay the game until everyone has had a turn. Or, form teams and alternate sides. If a player makes a mistake, that team gets a strike. After three strikes, the game is over.

CULTURE À LA LOUPE

# Les jardins publics français

le jardin du Luxembourg

**Dans les villes françaises, on trouve des jardins° publics, la plupart du° temps au centre-ville.** Ils sont en général entourés° d'une grille° et ouverts° au public pendant° la journée. Certains sont très petits et très simples; d'autres sont très grands avec d'immenses pelouses°, des plantes, des arbres° et de jolis parterres de fleurs°. Il y a aussi des sentiers° pour faire des promenades, des bancs°, des aires de jeux° pour les enfants, des statues, des fontaines ou des bassins°. On y° trouve des parents avec leurs enfants, des personnes qui font un pique-nique, qui jouent à la pétanque° ou au football, etc.

À Paris, le jardin des Tuileries et le jardin du Luxembourg sont deux jardins publics de style classique, très appréciés des Parisiens. Il y a aussi deux grands parcs à côté de Paris: le bois° de Vincennes, à l'est°, qui a un zoo, un jardin tropical et la foire° du Trône, la plus grande fête foraine° de France; et le bois de Boulogne, à l'ouest°, qui a un parc d'attractions° pour les enfants. Tous les deux ont aussi des cafés et des restaurants. Quand il fait beau, on peut faire du canotage° sur leurs lacs° ou pratiquer des activités sportives diverses.

### Le bois de Vincennes et le bois de Boulogne

| VINCENNES | BOULOGNE |
|---|---|
| • une superficie° totale de 995 hectares | • une superficie totale de 863 hectares |
| • un zoo de 15 hectares | • cinq entrées° |
| • 19 km de sentiers pour les promenades à cheval et à vélo | • 95 km d'allées |
| • 32 km d'allées pour le jogging | • une cascade° de 10 mètres de large° et 14 mètres de haut° |
| • la Ferme° de Paris, une ferme de 5 hectares | • deux hippodromes° |

*jardins* gardens/parks **la plupart du** most of **entourés** surrounded **grille** fence **ouverts** open **pendant** during **pelouses** lawns **arbres** trees **parterres de fleurs** flower beds **sentiers** paths **bancs** benches **aires de jeux** playgrounds **bassins** ponds **y** there **pétanque** a popular game similar to the Italian game of bocce **bois** forest/wooded park **est** east **foire** fair **fête foraine** carnival **ouest** west **parc d'attractions** amusement park **canotage** boating **lacs** lakes **superficie** area **Ferme** Farm **entrées** entrances **cascade** waterfall **de large** wide **de haut** high **hippodromes** horse racetracks

### Coup de main

In France and in most other countries, units of measurement are different than those used in the United States.

**1 hectare** = *2.47 acres*

**1 kilomètre** = *0.62 mile*

**1 mètre** = *approximately 1 yard (3 feet)*

**A C T I V I T É S**

**1** **Répondez** Répondez aux questions par des phrases complètes.

1. Où trouve-t-on, en général, les jardins publics des villes françaises?
   En général, on trouve les jardins publics des villes françaises au centre-ville.
2. Quel type de végétation y a-t-il dans les jardins publics français?
   Il y a des pelouses, des arbres, des plantes et des parterres de fleurs.
3. Qu'y a-t-il pour les enfants dans les jardins et les parcs français?
   Il y a des aires de jeux, des parcs d'attractions et des zoos.
4. Où va-t-on, à Paris, si on a envie de voir des animaux?
   On va au zoo du bois de Vincennes.
5. Quel type de plantes, en particulier, peut-on trouver au bois de Vincennes? On peut trouver des plantes tropicales au bois de Vincennes.

6. Comment s'appelle la plus grande fête foraine de France?
   Elle s'appelle la foire du Trône.
7. Où les enfants peuvent-ils visiter un parc d'attractions?
   Les enfants peuvent visiter un parc d'attractions au bois de Boulogne.
8. Que peut-on faire au bois de Vincennes? Answers may vary. Possible answers: On peut faire du jogging, ou des promenades à cheval ou à vélo.
9. Citez deux activités que les Français aiment faire dans les jardins publics. Answers may vary. Possible answers: Ils font des promenades et des pique-niques.
10. Est-il possible de manger dans les jardins et les parcs?
    Expliquez votre réponse. Answers may vary. Possible answer: Oui. Il y a parfois des restaurants et des cafés, et des personnes font aussi des pique-niques.

**O P T I O N S**

**Les jardins publics français** Explain the longstanding reputations of **le bois de Vincennes** and **le bois de Boulogne**. **Le bois de Vincennes** was a working-class destination where marginal characters did their business. **Le bois de Boulogne** was a place where the well-heeled hoped to be seen. Eighteenth-century associations say it all: **le Marquis de Sade** was imprisoned at **le bois de Vincennes**, and **Marie-Antoinette** lived in **le château de Bagatelle**, which she commissioned at the western end of **le bois de Boulogne**. There is no longer a socio-economic status attached to either of these green spaces, but many Parisians are familiar with their reputations.

## LE FRANÇAIS QUOTIDIEN

### Les catastrophes naturelles

| | |
|---|---|
| tempête (f.) de neige | blizzard |
| canicule (f.) | heat wave |
| inondation (f.) | flood |
| ouragan (m.) | hurricane |
| raz-de-marée (m.) | tidal wave, tsunami |
| sécheresse (f.) | drought |
| tornade (f.) | tornado |
| tremblement (m.) de terre | earthquake |

## LE MONDE FRANCOPHONE

### Des parcs publics

Voici quelques parcs publics du monde francophone.

**Bruxelles, Belgique**
le bois de la Cambre 123 hectares, un lac° avec une île° au centre

**Casablanca, Maroc**
le parc de la Ligue Arabe des palmiers°, un parc d'attractions pour enfants, des cafés et restaurants

**Québec, Canada**
le parc des Champs de Batailles («Plaines d'Abraham») 107 hectares, 6.000 arbres°

**Tunis, Tunisie**
le parc du Belvédère 110 hectares, un zoo de 13 hectares, 230.000 arbres (80 espèces° différentes), situé° sur une colline°

lac *lake* île *island* palmiers *palm trees* arbres *trees* espèces *species* situé *located* colline *hill*

## PORTRAIT

# Les Français et le vélo

Tous les étés, la course° cycliste du Tour de France attire° un grand nombre de spectateurs, Français et étrangers, surtout lors de° son arrivée sur les Champs-Élysées, à Paris. C'est le grand événement° sportif de l'année pour les amoureux du cyclisme. Les Français adorent aussi faire du vélo pendant° leur temps libre. Beaucoup de clubs organisent des randonnées en vélo de course° le week-end. Pour les personnes qui préfèrent le vélo tout terrain (VTT)°, il y a des sentiers° adaptés dans les parcs régionaux et nationaux. Certaines agences de voyages proposent aussi des vacances «vélo» en France ou à l'étranger°.

course *race* attire *attracts* lors de *at the time of* événement *event* pendant *during* vélo de course *road bike* vélo tout terrain (VTT) *mountain biking* sentiers *paths* à l'étranger *abroad*

le Tour de France sur les Champs-Élysées

### SUR INTERNET

Qu'est-ce que Jacques Anquetil, Eddy Merckx et Bernard Hinault ont en commun?

Go to daccord1.vhlcentral.com to find more information related to this **CULTURE** section.

### ACTIVITÉS

**2 Vrai ou faux?** Indiquez si les phrases sont vraies ou fausses. Corrigez les phrases fausses.

1. Les Français ne font pas de vélo. Faux. Les Français adorent faire du vélo pendant leur temps libre.
2. Les membres de clubs de vélo font des promenades le week-end. Vrai.
3. Les agences de voyages offrent des vacances «vélo». Vrai.
4. On utilise un VTT quand on fait du vélo sur la route. Faux. On utilise un vélo de course.
5. Le Tour de France arrive sur les Champs-Élysées à Paris. Vrai.

**3 Les catastrophes naturelles** Avec un(e) partenaire, parlez de trois catastrophes naturelles. Quel temps fait-il, en général, pendant (*during*) chaque catastrophe? Choisissez une catastrophe et décrivez-la à vos camarades. Peuvent-ils deviner (*Can they guess*) de quelle catastrophe vous parlez?

**ressources**

Practice more at daccord1.vhlcentral.com.

S

daccord1.vhlcentral.com

---

**Le français quotidien** After studying the vocabulary, ask students to close their books and to number from one to five on a piece of paper. Describe five of these **catastrophes naturelles** with new lexical items from **Leçon 5B**. Have the class write down the event you are describing. Go over the answers as a class.

**Portrait**
- Ask students what they know about the **Tour de France**. They may mention Lance Armstrong, **le maillot jaune** (*yellow jersey*), etc.
- Find out if the class has heard of stereotypes about the French and cycling. Have them list ideas in small groups.
- The importance of the bicycle has increased in France as a response to environmental issues. Cities like Paris, Lyon, Nantes, and Aix-en-Provence have created systems of **vélopartage**, large-scale bike renting whereby people take and leave a "citybike" whenever they want. Also, many municipalities have increased the number of bike paths (**pistes cyclables**).

**Le monde francophone**
- Look at the francophone world map in the front matter to remind students where these countries are located.
- Practice pronunciation with the descriptions of these parks.

**2 Expansion** Continue the activity with more true/false statements like these.
**6. Le Tour de France est une grande course cycliste. (Vrai.)**
**7. Le Tour de France est au printemps. (Faux, en été)**
**8. Les Français et les étrangers sont spectateurs du Tour de France. (Vrai.)**

**3 Expansion** Students can use this as an opportunity to practice contradicting while quizzing each other about weather in the context of these new expressions. Example: **Élève 1: Quand il y a un ouragan, fait-il soleil? Élève 2: Pas du tout! Il pleut beaucoup.**

**OPTIONS**

**Des parcs publics** Assign a francophone country to several students in class. Have everyone do individual research on gardens or a park in the country he or she has been assigned. Students should be prepared to present their findings about the park in at least three clear sentences in French and an image from the Internet, if possible.

**Les Français et le vélo** Bring in an example of francophone music or film about cycling. For example, play the song ***Mon vélo est blanc*** by Anne Sylvestre. Screen part of the Belgian film ***Le vélo de Ghislain Lambert***. There are also scenes with Charlotte Gainsbourg riding a bicycle in ***La petite voleuse***.

**Leçon 5B**

## 5B.1 Numbers 101 and higher

| Numbers 101 and higher | |
|---|---|
| **101** cent un | **800** huit cents |
| **125** cent vingt-cinq | **900** neuf cents |
| **198** cent quatre-vingt-dix-huit | **1.000** mille |
| **200** deux cents | **1.100** mille cent |
| **245** deux cent quarante-cinq | **2.000** deux mille |
| **300** trois cents | **5.000** cinq mille |
| **400** quatre cents | **100.000** cent mille |
| **500** cinq cents | **550.000** cinq cent cinquante mille |
| **600** six cents | **1.000.000** un million |
| **700** sept cents | **8.000.000** huit millions |

- Note that French uses a period, rather than a comma, to indicate thousands and millions.

- The word **cent** does not take a final **-s** when it is followed by the numbers **1–99**.

| | | |
|---|---|---|
| Il y a **deux cent cinquante** jours de soleil. | *but* | J'ai **quatre cents** bandes dessinées. |
| *There are 250 sunny days.* | | *I have 400 comic books.* |

- The number **un** is not used before the word **mille** to mean *a/one thousand*. It is used, however, before **million** to say *a/one million*.

| | | |
|---|---|---|
| **Mille** personnes habitent le village. | *but* | **Un million** de personnes habitent la région. |
| *One thousand people live in the village.* | | *One million people live in the region.* |

- **Mille**, unlike **cent** and **million**, is invariable. It never takes an **-s**.

| | |
|---|---|
| Aimez-vous *Les **Mille** et Une Nuits*? | **Onze mille** étudiants sont inscrits. |
| *Do you like "The Thousand and One Nights"?* | *Eleven thousand students are registered.* |

- Before a noun, **million** and **millions** are followed by **de/d'**.

| | |
|---|---|
| **Deux millions de personnes** sont en vacances. | Il y a **onze millions d'habitants** dans la capitale. |
| *Two million people are on vacation.* | *There are 11,000,000 inhabitants in the capital.* |

- When writing out years, the word **mille** is usually shortened to **mil**.

**mil** huit cent soixante-cinq
*eighteen (hundred) sixty-five*

---

### MISE EN PRATIQUE

**1** **Quelle adresse?** Vous allez distribuer des journaux (*newspapers*) et vous téléphonez aux clients pour avoir leur adresse. Écrivez les adresses.

**MODÈLE**

cent deux, rue Lafayette
*102, rue Lafayette*

1. deux cent cinquante-deux, rue de Bretagne
   252, rue de Bretagne
2. quatre cents, avenue Malbon
   400, avenue Malbon
3. cent soixante-dix-sept, rue Jeanne d'Arc
   177, rue Jeanne d'Arc
4. cinq cent quarante-six, boulevard St. Marc
   546, boulevard St. Marc
5. six cent quatre-vingt-huit, avenue des Gaulois
   688, avenue des Gaulois
6. trois cent quatre-vingt-douze, boulevard Micheline
   392, boulevard Micheline
7. cent vingt-cinq, rue des Pierres
   125, rue des Pierres
8. trois cent quatre, avenue St. Germain
   304, avenue St. Germain

**2** **Les maths** Faites les opérations et écrivez les réponses. Answers may vary slightly.

**MODÈLE**

200 + 300 =
*Deux cents plus trois cents font cinq cents.*

1. 650 + 750 = Six cent cinquante plus sept cent cinquante font mille quatre cents.
2. 2.000.000 + 3.000.000 = Deux millions plus trois millions font cinq millions.
3. 966 – 342 = Neuf cent soixante-six moins trois cent quarante-deux égale six cent vingt-quatre.
4. 155 + 310 = Cent cinquante-cinq plus trois cent dix font quatre cent soixante-cinq.
5. 2.000 – 150 = Deux mille moins cent cinquante font mille huit cent cinquante.
6. 375 × 2 = Trois cent soixante-quinze multiplié par deux égale sept cent cinquante.
7. 1.250 + 2.250 = Mille deux cent cinquante plus deux mille deux cent cinquante font trois mille cinq cents.
8. 4.444 ÷ 4 = Quatre mille quatre cent quarante-quatre divisé par quatre égale mille cent onze.

**3** **Combien d'habitants?** À tour de rôle, demandez à votre partenaire combien d'habitants il y a dans chaque ville d'après (*according to*) les statistiques.

**MODÈLE**

Dijon: 153.813
**Élève 1:** Combien d'habitants y a-t-il à Dijon?
**Élève 2:** Il y a cent cinquante-trois mille huit cent treize habitants.

1. Toulouse: 398.423 Il y a trois cent quatre-vingt-dix-huit mille quatre cent vingt-trois habitants.
2. Abidjan: 2.877.948 Il y a deux millions huit cent soixante-dix-sept mille neuf cent quarante-huit habitants.
3. Lyon: 453.187 Il y a quatre cent cinquante-trois mille cent quatre-vingt-sept habitants.
4. Québec: 510.559 Il y a cinq cent dix mille cinq cent cinquante-neuf habitants.
5. Marseille: 807.071 Il y a huit cent sept mille soixante et onze habitants.
6. Papeete: 26.181 Il y a vingt-six mille cent quatre-vingt-un habitants.

 Practice more at **daccord1.vhlcentral.com**.

---

## COMMUNICATION

**4 Quand?** Avec un(e) partenaire, regardez les dates et dites quand ces événements ont lieu (*take place*).

1776  1789  1914-1918  1939-1945  1968  1997
l'Indépendance des États-Unis | La Révolution française | la Première Guerre mondiale | la Seconde Guerre mondiale | Martin Luther King, Jr. est assassiné. | Le Pathfinder arrive sur la planète Mars.

1. Le Pathfinder arrive sur la planète Mars.
   Il arrive en mille neuf cent quatre-vingt-dix-sept.
2. La Première Guerre mondiale commence.
   Elle commence en mille neuf cent quatorze.
3. La Seconde Guerre mondiale prend fin (*ends*).
   Elle prend fin en mille neuf cent quarante-cinq.
4. L'Amérique déclare son indépendance.
   Elle déclare son indépendance en mille sept cent soixante-seize.
5. Martin Luther King, Jr. est assassiné.
   Il est assassiné en mille neuf cent soixante-huit.
6. La Première Guerre Mondiale prend fin.
   Elle prend fin en mille neuf cent dix-huit.

**5 Combien ça coûte?** Vous regardez un catalogue avec un(e) ami(e). À tour de rôle, demandez à votre partenaire le prix des choses. Answers will vary.

**MODÈLE**
Élève 1: Combien coûte l'ordinateur?
Élève 2: Il coûte mille huit cents euros.

1. É1: ... la montre?
   É2: Elle ... quatre cent trente-deux ...

   **1.** 432€

3. É1: ... le sac à dos?
   É2: Il ... cent dix-huit ...

   **3.** 116€

2. É1: ... les dictionnaires?
   É2: Ils ... cent seize ...

   **2.** 116€

4. É1: ... le vélo?
   É2: Il ... six cent soixante-quinze ...

   **4.** 675€

**6 Dépensez de l'argent** Vous et votre partenaire avez 100.000€. Décidez quels articles de la liste vous allez prendre. Justifiez vos choix à la classe. Answers will vary.

**MODÈLE**
Élève 1: On prend un rendez-vous avec Brad Pitt.
Élève 2: Alors, nous n'avons pas assez d'argent pour la voiture!

| | |
|---|---|
| un ordinateur... 2.000€ | des vacances à Tahiti... 7.000€ |
| un rendez-vous avec Brad Pitt... 50.000€ | un vélo... 1.000€ |
| un rendez-vous avec Madonna... 50.000€ | une voiture de luxe... 60.000€ |

---

- In French, years before 2000 may be written out in two ways. Notice that in English, the word *hundred* can be omitted, but in French, the word **cent** is required.

**mil neuf cent treize** *or* **dix-neuf cent treize**
*one thousand nine hundred (and) thirteen* / *nineteen (hundred) thirteen*

- You can talk about mathematical operations both formally and informally.

### Mathematical terms

| | informal | formal |
|---|---|---|
| *plus* | et | plus |
| *minus* | moins | moins |
| *multiplied by* | fois | multiplié par |
| *divided by* | sur | divisé par |
| *equals* | font | égale |

- The verb **égaler** (*to equal*) is expressed in the singular, but the verb **faire** is plural.

**110 et 205 font 315**
$110 + 205 = 315$

**110 plus 205 égale 315**
$110 + 205 = 315$

**60 fois 3 font 180**
$60 \times 3 = 180$

**60 multiplié par 3 égale 180**
$60 \times 3 = 180$

**999 sur 9 font 111**
$999 \div 9 = 111$

**999 divisé par 9 égale 111**
$999 \div 9 = 111$

- In French, decimal punctuation is inverted. Use **une virgule** (*comma*) instead of **un point** (*period*).

**5.419,32** — cinq mille quatre cent dix-neuf virgule trente-deux
*5,419.32* — *five thousand four hundred nineteen point thirty-two*

- The expression **pour cent** (*percent*) is two words, not one.

Le magasin offre une réduction de soixante **pour cent**.
*The store is offering a sixty percent discount.*

### Essayez! Donnez les équivalents en français.

1. 10.000 — *dix mille*
2. 620 — six cent vingt
3. 365 — trois cent soixante-cinq
4. 42.000 — quarante-deux mille
5. 200.000.000 — deux cents millions
6. 480 — quatre cent quatre-vingts
7. 1.789 — mille sept cent quatre-vingt-neuf
8. 400 — quatre cents
9. 150% — cent cinquante pour cent
10. 1.250,50 — mille deux cent cinquante virgule cinquante

---

**Essayez!** Have students think of four more numbers for their partner to write out in French.

**1 Suggestion** For listening comprehension, have students read numbers from the activity to a partner.

**1 Expansion** Give students these real addresses in regions **Centre** and **Pays de la Loire**. Model how to pronounce the postal codes. Example: 45000: **quarante-cinq mille**. (1) Préfecture de la Région Centre et du Loiret: 181, rue de Bourgogne - 45042 ORLÉANS (2) Espace Région Centre de Tours: 1, rue des Ursulines - 37000 TOURS (3) Auberge de Jeunesse: 23, Avenue Neigre - 28000 CHARTRES (4) Médiathèque Louis Aragon: 54, rue du Port - 72015 LE MANS

**2 Suggestions**
- Call on pairs of students to say some of the calculations aloud.
- Give additional math problems if more practice is needed.

**2 Expansion** Have pairs convert a **calcul** into a word problem. Example: **J'ai deux cents dollars. Ma sœur a trois cents dollars. Combien de dollars avons-nous?**

**3 Expansion** Write on the board some well-known American cities and your high school's city or town. Ask students: **Combien d'habitants…?** Have them guess if they don't know. Then write the accurate number next to each city. Have students come to the board to write out the populations in French.

**4 Expansion** Ask students to brainstorm other famous years throughout history.

**5 & 6 Suggestions**
- Before beginning each activity, make sure students know the vocabulary.
- Do the **modèles** with a volunteer to make sure students understand the activities.

---

## Section Goals

In this section, students will learn **-er** verbs with spelling changes.

## Key Standards

4.1, 5.1

**Student Resources**
*Cahier d'exercices*, pp. 67-68;
*Cahier d'activités*, pp. 9, 154;
Supersite: Activities,
*Cahier interactif*
**Teacher Resources**
Answer Keys; Audio Script;
Audio Activity MP3s/CD; *Feuilles d'activités*; Testing program:
Grammar Quiz

## Suggestions

• Model pronunciations of forms of **acheter**, **espérer**, and **envoyer**. Go over the example statements as a class.

• Guide students to notice that, like regular **-er** verbs, spelling-change **-er** verbs are "boot verbs."

• Point out that infinitives often follow forms of **espérer**. Example: **Il espère gagner.**

• Ask questions using verbs from this section, encouraging student responses. Examples: **Où est-ce que vous achetez du pain? Quelle saison préférez-vous: l'été ou l'hiver?**

• Explain that when the letter **e** is followed by one pronounced consonant and a silent **e**, you need to add an **accent grave** over the first **e**. If the first **e** already has an **accent aigu**, it becomes an **accent grave**. This causes spelling changes in some verbs, adjectives, and nouns. Remind students to apply this rule whenever this pattern of letters occurs. Exception: **e** with an **accent circonflexe**.

• Go through the meanings of verbs. Note the number of cognates. Make sure students understand that **amener** and **emmener** are only used for people. Ask: What verbs would you use to say *to take* and *to bring* objects? (**prendre; apporter**)

---

# 5B.2 Spelling-change -er verbs

**Point de départ** Some **-er** verbs, though regular with respect to their verb endings, have spelling changes that occur in the verb stem (what remains after the **-er** is dropped).

• Most infinitives whose next-to-last syllable contains an **e** (no accent) change this letter to **è** in all forms except **nous** and **vous**.

### Acheter (to buy)

| | |
|---|---|
| j'achète | nous achetons |
| tu achètes | vous achetez |
| il/elle achète | ils/elles achètent |

Où est-ce que tu **achètes** des skis?
*Where do you buy skis?*

Ils **achètent** beaucoup sur Internet.
*They buy a lot on the Internet.*

• Infinitives whose next-to-last syllable contains an **é** change this letter to **è** in all forms except **nous** and **vous**.

### Espérer (to hope)

| | |
|---|---|
| j'espère | nous espérons |
| tu espères | vous espérez |
| il/elle espère | ils/elles espèrent |

Elle **espère** arriver tôt aujourd'hui.
*She hopes to arrive early today.*

Nos profs **espèrent** commencer les cours.
*Our teachers hope to start classes.*

**Elle achète quelque chose.**

**Ils répètent.**

• Infinitives ending in **-yer** change **y** to **i** in all forms except **nous** and **vous**.

### Envoyer (to send)

| | |
|---|---|
| j'envoie | nous envoyons |
| tu envoies | vous envoyez |
| il/elle envoie | ils/elles envoient |

J'**envoie** une lettre.
*I'm sending a letter.*

Tes amis **envoient** un e-mail.
*Your friends send an e-mail.*

---

**1 Passe-temps** Chaque membre de la famille Desrosiers a son passe-temps préféré. Utilisez les éléments pour dire ce qu'ils (*what they*) font.

**MODÈLE**

Tante Manon fait une randonnée. (acheter / sandwichs)
*Elle achète des sandwichs.*

1. Nous faisons du vélo. (essayer / vélo)
   Nous essayons le vélo.
2. Christiane aime chanter. (répéter)
   Elle répète.
3. Les filles jouent au foot. (espérer / gagner)
   Elles espèrent gagner.
4. Vous allez à la pêche. (emmener / enfants)
   Vous emmenez les enfants.
5. Papa fait un tour en voiture. (nettoyer / voiture)
   Il nettoie la voiture.
6. Mes frères font du camping. (préférer / partir tôt)
   Ils préfèrent partir tôt.

**2 Invitation au cinéma** Avec un(e) partenaire, jouez les rôles de Halouk et de Thomas. Ensuite, présentez la scène à la classe.

THOMAS J'ai envie d'aller au cinéma.

HALOUK Bonne idée. Nous (1) ____emmenons____ (emmener, protéger) Véronique avec nous?

THOMAS J' (2) ____espère____ (acheter, espérer) qu'elle a du temps libre.

HALOUK Peut-être, mais je/j' (3) ____envoie____ (envoyer, payer) des e-mails tous les jours et elle ne répond pas.

THOMAS Parce que son ordinateur ne fonctionne pas. Elle (4) ____préfère____ (essayer, préférer) parler au téléphone.

HALOUK D'accord. Alors toi, tu (5) ____achètes____ (acheter, répéter) les tickets au cinéma et moi, je vais chercher Véronique.

**3 Que font-ils?** Dites ce que (*Say what*) font les personnages. Answers will vary.

**MODÈLE**

*Il achète une baguette.*

**acheter**

**1. envoyer**

**3. répéter**

**2. payer**

**4. nettoyer**

Practice more at daccord1.vhlcentral.com.

---

**Using Games** Divide the class into two teams. Announce one of the infinitives and a subject pronoun. Example: **emmener; ils**. At the board, have the first member of Team A say and write the given subject and the conjugated form of the verb. If the team member answers correctly, Team A gets one point. If not, give the first member of Team B the same example. The team with the most points at the end of the game wins.

**Using Video** Replay the video episode, having students focus on **-er** verbs with spelling changes. Have them note each one they hear, with subjects if conjugated. Find out how many occurrences students heard before pointing out these examples: **je préfère, célébrer, célèbre, tu essaies,** and **préférer**. Ask for remarks with spelling-change **-er** verbs that describe the characters. Example: **Rachid possède un ordinateur.**

## COMMUNICATION

**4 Questions** À tour de rôle, posez les questions à un(e) partenaire. *Answers will vary.*

1. Qu'est-ce que tu achètes pour la Fête des mères?
2. Qu'est-ce que tu achètes au supermarché?
3. Comment célèbres-tu l'anniversaire de ton/ta meilleur(e) ami(e)?
4. Et quand tu sors avec des copains, qui paie quoi?
5. Quelle marque (*make*) de voiture préfères-tu?
6. Qui nettoie ta chambre?
7. À qui est-ce que tu envoies des e-mails?
8. Qu'est-ce que tu espères faire cet été?

**5 Réponses affirmatives** Votre professeur va vous donner une feuille d'activités. Trouvez au moins un(e) camarade de classe qui réponde oui à chaque question. Et si vous aussi, vous répondez oui aux questions, écrivez votre nom. *Answers will vary.*

**MODÈLE**

**Élève 1:** Est-ce que tu achètes exclusivement sur Internet?
**Élève 2:** Oui, j'achète exclusivement sur Internet.

| Questions | Noms |
|---|---|
| 1. acheter exclusivement sur Internet | Virginie, Éric |
| 2. posséder un ordinateur | |
| 3. envoyer des lettres à ses grands-parents | |
| 4. célébrer une occasion spéciale demain | |

**6 E-mail à l'oncle Marcel** Xavier va écrire un e-mail à son oncle pour raconter (*to tell*) ses activités de la semaine prochaine. Il prépare une liste des choses qu'il veut dire (*wants to say*). Avec un(e) partenaire, écrivez son e-mail. *Answers will vary.*

- lundi: emmener maman chez le médecin
- mercredi: cours de français envoyer notes
- jeudi: répéter rôle Roméo et Juliette
- vendredi: célébrer anniversaire papa
- vendredi: essayer faire gym
- samedi: parents acheter voiture

---

- The change of **y** to **i** is optional in verbs whose infinitives end in **-ayer**.

Comment est-ce que tu **payes**?
*How do you pay?*

Je **paie** avec une carte de crédit.
*I pay with a credit card.*

### Other spelling-change *-er* verbs

| like *espérer* | | | like *acheter* | |
|---|---|---|---|---|
| célébrer | to celebrate | | amener | to bring (someone) |
| considérer | to consider | | emmener | to take (someone) |
| posséder | to possess, to own | | | like *envoyer* |
| préférer | to prefer | | | |
| protéger | to protect | | employer | to use; to employ |
| répéter | to repeat; to rehearse | | essayer (de + inf.) | to try (to) |
| | | | nettoyer | to clean |
| | | | payer | to pay |

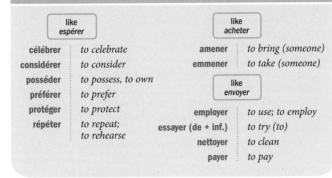

Je préfère l'été. Il fait chaud.

Tu essaies de ne pas parler?

- Note that the **nous** and **vous** forms of the verbs presented in this section have no spelling changes.

Vous **achetez** des sandwichs aussi.
*You're buying sandwiches, too.*

Nous **espérons** partir à huit heures.
*We hope to leave at 8 o'clock.*

Nous **envoyons** les enfants à l'école.
*We're sending the children to school.*

Vous **payez** avec une carte de crédit.
*You pay with a credit card.*

### Essayez! Complétez les phrases avec la forme correcte du verbe.

1. Les bibliothèques __emploient__ (employer) beaucoup d'étudiants.
2. Vous __répétez__ (répéter) les phrases en français.
3. Nous __payons__ (payer) assez pour les livres.
4. Mon frère ne __nettoie__ (nettoyer) pas son bureau.
5. Est-ce que tu __espères__ (espérer) gagner?
6. Vous __essayez__ (essayer) parfois d'arriver à l'heure.
7. Tu __préfères__ (préférer) prendre du thé ou du café?
8. Elle __emmène__ (emmener) sa mère au cinéma.
9. On __célèbre__ (célébrer) une occasion spéciale.
10. Les parents __protègent__ (protéger) leurs enfants.

---

**Essayez!** For additional drills with spelling-change **-er** verbs for the whole class or those who need extra practice, do this activity orally and on the board with different subjects.

**1 Suggestion** Ask for a volunteer to demonstrate the **modèle**.

**1 Expansion** Have students write four additional statements modeled on the activity about their own family members.

**2 Suggestion** Explain that students must first choose the logical verb, then write the correct form.

**3 Expansion** Show additional pictures of people cleaning, using something, trying, sending, etc. Ask a yes/no question about each picture. Example: Showing an image of someone sending a letter, ask: **Est-ce qu'il nettoie?** Students answer: **Mais non, il envoie une lettre.**

**4 Expansion** Have students write two more questions containing spelling-change **-er** verbs that they would like to ask their partner.

**5 Suggestion** Call on two volunteers to read the **modèle** aloud. Then distribute the **Feuilles d'activités** found on the Supersite.

**6 Expansion** Have students think of a family member or friend to whom they would likely write an e-mail. Tell them to first list at least five ideas using as many spelling-change **-er** verbs as possible. Then have them write an e-mail of at least five sentences.

---

**OPTIONS**

**Using Games** Arrange students in rows of six. The first person in each row has a piece of paper. Call out an infinitive. The first student writes the **je** form and passes the paper to the student behind him or her. That student writes the **tu** form and passes the paper on. The last person in the row holds up the paper to show completion. The first team to finish accurately wins a point. Have students rotate places before calling out another verb.

**Using Word Play** Have small groups write dehydrated sentences with only subjects and infinitives. Examples: **1. tu / amener / ???** **2. Sylvie et Véronique / espérer / ???** Tell groups to switch with another group, who will form a complete sentence by conjugating the verb and inventing an appropriate ending. Ask for volunteers to write one of their group's sentences on the board.

**1** **Expansion** Have students write a story about their preferred sport modeled on the paragraph in this activity.

**2** **Suggestion** Have pairs get together to form groups of four to review each others' sentences. Have students explain any corrections or suggested changes.

**3** **Suggestion** Encourage students to choose places from the French-speaking world that they have learned about in **Culture** and **Panorama** sections.

**3** **Expansion** Have students create more questions based on those in the activity to ask their partner. Guide the class to ask about where the partner hopes or prefers to go for various vacations throughout the year. Students may combine reusing weather conditions described in the box and using additional weather descriptions.

**4** **Expansion** For additional numbers practice, have students ask each other: **Combien coûte _____ (type de voyage) avec la commission?**

**5** **Suggestion** Ask for volunteers to do the **modèle** and auction off a few more items to set further examples.

**6** **Suggestions**
• Divide the class into pairs and distribute the Info Gap Handouts found on the Supersite for this activity. Give students ten minutes to complete the activity.
• Act out the **modèle** with a student volunteer playing the role of **Élève 2**.

---

**1** **Le basket** Avec un(e) partenaire, utilisez les verbes de la liste pour compléter le paragraphe.

| acheter | considérer | envoyer | essayer | préférer |
|---|---|---|---|---|
| amener | employer | espérer | payer | répéter |

Je m'appelle Stéphanie et je joue au basket. Je/J'
(1) _amène_ toujours (*always*) mes parents avec moi aux matchs le samedi. Ils (2) _considèrent_ que les filles sont de très bonnes joueuses. Mes parents font aussi du sport. Ma mère fait du vélo et mon père (3) _espère_ gagner son prochain match de foot! Le vendredi matin, je/j' (4) _envoie_ un e-mail à ma mère pour lui rappeler (*remind her of*) le match. Mais elle n'oublie jamais! Ils ne/n' (5) _achètent_ pas de tickets pour les matchs, parce que les parents des joueurs ne/n' (6) _paient_ pas. Nous (7) _essayons_ toujours d'arriver une demi-heure avant le match, parce que maman et papa (8) _préfèrent, espèrent_ s'asseoir (*to sit*) tout près du terrain (*court*). Ils sont tellement fiers!

**2** **Que font-ils?** Avec un(e) partenaire, parlez des activités des personnages et écrivez une phrase par illustration. *Answers will vary.*

1. _____  2. _____  3. _____

4. _____  5. _____  6. _____

**3** **Où partir?** Avec un(e) partenaire, choisissez cinq endroits intéressants à visiter où il fait le temps indiqué sur la liste. Ensuite, répondez aux questions. *Answers will vary.*

| Il fait chaud. | Il fait soleil. | Il fait du vent. | Il neige. | Il pleut. |

1. Où essayez-vous d'aller cet été? Pourquoi?
2. Où préférez-vous partir cet hiver? Pourquoi?
3. Quelle est la première destination que vous espérez visiter? La dernière? Pourquoi?
4. Qui emmenez-vous avec vous? Pourquoi?

---

**4** **Quelle générosité!** Vous allez payer un voyage aux membres de votre famille et à vos amis. À tour de rôle, choisissez un voyage et donnez à votre partenaire la liste des personnes qui partent. Votre partenaire va vous donner le prix à payer. *Answers will vary.*

**MODÈLE**

**Élève 1:** *J'achète un voyage de dix jours dans les Pays de la Loire à ma cousine Pauline et à mon frère Alexandre.*
**Élève 2:** *D'accord. Tu paies deux mille cinq cent soixante-deux euros.*

| Voyages | Prix par personne | Commission |
|---|---|---|
| Dix jours dans les Pays de la Loire .......... 1.250€ .................. | | 62€ |
| Deux semaines de camping........................ 660€ ................ | | 35€ |
| Sept jours au soleil en hiver .................... 2.100€ ............. | | 78€ |
| Trois jours à Paris en avril........................ 500€ ................ | | 55€ |
| Trois mois en Europe en été ................. 10.400€ ............... | | 47€ |
| Un week-end à Nice en septembre............ 350€ ................. | | 80€ |
| Une semaine à la montagne en juin............ 990€ ................ | | 66€ |
| Une semaine à la neige .......................... 1.800€ ................ | | 73€ |

**5** **La vente aux enchères** Par groupes de quatre, organisez une vente aux enchères (*auction*) pour vendre les affaires (*things*) du professeur. À tour de rôle, un(e) élève joue le rôle du vendeur/de la vendeuse et les autres élèves jouent le rôle des enchérisseurs (*bidders*). Vous avez 5.000 euros et toutes les enchères (*bids*) commencent à cent euros. *Answers will vary.*

**MODÈLE**

**Élève 1:** *J'ai le cahier du professeur. Qui paie cent euros?*
**Élève 2:** *Moi, je paie cent euros.*
**Élève 1:** *Qui paie cent cinquante euros?*

**6** **À la bibliothèque** Votre professeur va vous donner, à vous et à votre partenaire, deux feuilles d'activités différentes. Attention! Ne regardez pas la feuille de votre partenaire. *Answers will vary.*

**MODÈLE**

**Élève 1:** *Est-ce que tu as le livre «Candide»?*
**Élève 2:** *Oui, son numéro de référence est P, Q, deux cent soixante-six, cent quarante-sept, cent dix.*

| ressources | | |
|---|---|---|
| CE pp. 65-68 | CA pp. 9, 47-48, 153-154 | **S** daccord1.vhlcentral.com |

---

**OPTIONS**

**Conversations** Have students write a conversation between two friends. One tries to convince the other to go out. The other makes excuses to not go. Students should include as many spelling-change -er verbs and weather expressions as possible. Example: **Élève 1: Faisons une randonnée! Élève 2: Mais je nettoie ma chambre. Élève 1: Mais il fait beau. Élève 2: Il va pleuvoir plus tard.**

**Using Lists** Ask students to imagine they are going on an extended trip. Have them make a list of at least five things they are to do (buy things, take someone somewhere, send mail, etc.) before leaving. Examples: **Je vais acheter un nouveau parapluie. J'espère envoyer une carte d'anniversaire.**

# À l'écoute  Audio: Activities

## Préparation

Regardez l'image. Où trouve-t-on ce type d'image? Manque-t-il des éléments (*Is anything missing*) sur cette carte? Faites une liste de mots-clés qui vont vous aider à trouver ces informations quand vous allez écouter la météo (*the forecast*).

## À vous d'écouter

Écoutez la météo. Puis, écoutez une deuxième fois et complétez le tableau. Notez la température et écrivez un **X** pour indiquer le temps qu'il fait dans chaque ville.

| Ville | ☀️ | 🌤️ | ☁️ | 🌧️ | 🌬️ | ❄️ | Température |
|---|---|---|---|---|---|---|---|
| Paris | | | X | | | | 8°C |
| Lille | | | | X | | | 6°C |
| Strasbourg | | | | | | X | 5°C |
| Brest | | | X | | | | 10°C |
| Lyon | | | | X | | | 9°C |
| Bordeaux | | X | | | | | 11°C |
| Toulouse | X | | | | | | 12°C |
| Marseille | | | X | | | | 12°C |
| Nice | | | | | X | | 13°C |

 Practice more at **daccord1.vhlcentral.com**.

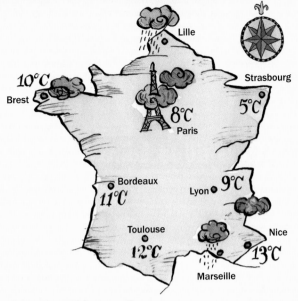

## Compréhension

**Probable ou improbable?** Indiquez si ces (*these*) phrases sont probables ou improbables, d'après la météo d'aujourd'hui.

| | Probable | Improbable |
|---|---|---|
| **MODÈLE** Ève va nager à Strasbourg. | | ✓ |
| 1. Lucie fait du vélo à Lille. | | ✓ |
| 2. Il fait un temps épouvantable à Toulouse. | | ✓ |
| 3. Émilien joue aux cartes à la maison à Lyon. | ✓ | |
| 4. Il va neiger à Marseille. | | ✓ |
| 5. Jérome et Yves jouent au golf à Bordeaux. | ✓ | |
| 6. À Lyon, on a besoin d'un imperméable. | ✓ | |
| 7. Il fait froid à Strasbourg. | ✓ | |
| 8. Nous allons nager à Nice cet après-midi. | | ✓ |

**Quelle ville choisir?** Imaginez qu'aujourd'hui vous êtes en France. Décidez dans quelle ville vous avez envie de passer la journée. Pourquoi? Décrivez le temps qu'il fait et citez des activités que vous allez peut-être faire.

**MODÈLE**

J'ai envie d'aller à Strasbourg parce que j'aime l'hiver et la neige. Aujourd'hui, il fait froid et il neige. Je vais faire une promenade en ville et après, je vais boire un chocolat chaud au café.

---

# SAVOIR-FAIRE

Interactive Map
Reading

# Panorama

## Les Pays de la Loire

### La région en chiffres

- ▶ **Superficie:** *32.082 km²°*
- ▶ **Population:** *3.344.000*
  SOURCE: INSEE
- ▶ **Industries principales:** *aéronautique, agriculture, informatique, tourisme, viticulture°*
- ▶ **Villes principales:** *Angers, Laval, Le Mans, Nantes, Saint Nazaire*

### Personnes célèbres

- ▶ Claire Bretécher, *dessinatrice de bandes dessinées (1940– )*
- ▶ Léon Bollée, *inventeur d'automobiles (1870–1913)*
- ▶ Jules Verne, *écrivain° (1828–1905)*

## Le Centre

### La région en chiffres

- ▶ **Superficie:** *39.152 km²*
- ▶ **Population:** *2.480.000*
- ▶ **Industrie principale:** *tourisme*
- ▶ **Villes principales:** *Bourges, Chartres, Orléans, Tours, Vierzon*

### Personnes célèbres

- ▶ Honoré de Balzac, *écrivain (1799–1850)*
- ▶ George Sand, *femme écrivain (1804–1876)*
- ▶ Gérard Depardieu, *acteur (1948– )*

**km² (kilomètres carrés)** *square kilometers* **viticulture** *wine-growing* **écrivain** *writer* **Construit** *Constructed* **siècle** *century* **pièces** *rooms* **escaliers** *staircases* **chaque** *each* **logis** *living area* **hélice** *helix* **même** *same* **ne se croisent jamais** *never cross* **pèlerinage** *pilgrimage* **course** *race*

un pèlerinage° à la cathédrale de Chartres

LA FRANCE

Laval
Le Mans
Chartres
la Mayenne
la Sarthe
le Loir
Orléans
PAYS DE LA LOIRE
Angers
St.-Nazaire
Tours
la Loire
Chambord
la Loire
Nantes
Cholet
Saumur
Chenonceaux
le Cher
Vierzon
L'île de
Noirmoutier
CENTRE
Bourges
L'île d'Yeu
La Roche-
sur-Yon
Châteauroux
Les Sables-
d'Olonne
la Vienne
l'Indre

L'OCÉAN
ATLANTIQUE

le Vendée Globe, course° nautique

la Loire

| 0 | | 50 miles |
| 0 | | 50 kilomètres |

### Incroyable mais vrai!

Construit° au XVI$^e$ (seizième) siècle°, l'architecture du château de Chambord est influencée par Léonard de Vinci. Le château a 440 pièces°, 84 escaliers° et 365 cheminées (une pour chaque° jour de l'année). Le logis° central a deux escaliers en forme de double hélice°. Les escaliers vont dans la même° direction, mais ne se croisent jamais°.

---

## Les monuments

### La vallée des rois

La vallée de la Loire, avec ses châteaux, est appelée la vallée des rois°. C'est au XVIᵉ (seizième) siècle° que les Valois° quittent Paris pour habiter dans la région, où ils construisent° de nombreux° châteaux de style Renaissance. François Iᵉʳ inaugure le siècle des «rois voyageurs»: ceux° qui vont d'un château à l'autre avec leur cour° et toutes leurs possessions. Chenonceau, Chambord et Amboise sont aujourd'hui les châteaux les plus° visités.

## Les festivals

### Le Printemps de Bourges

Le Printemps de Bourges est un festival de musique qui a lieu° chaque année, en avril. Pendant° une semaine, tous les styles de musique sont représentés: variété française, musiques du monde°, rock, musique électronique, reggae, hip-hop, etc... Il y a des dizaines° de spectacles, de nombreux artistes, des milliers de spectateurs et des noms légendaires comme Serge Gainsbourg, Yves Montand, Ray Charles et Johnny Clegg.

## Les sports

### Les 24 heures du Mans

Les 24 heures du Mans, c'est la course° d'endurance automobile la plus célèbre° du monde. Depuis° 1923, de prestigieuses marques° y° participent. C'est sur ce circuit de 13,6 km que Ferrari gagne neuf victoires et que Porsche détient° le record de 16 victoires avec une vitesse moyenne° de 222 km/h sur 5.335 km. Il existe aussi les 24 heures du Mans moto°.

## Les destinations

### La route des vins

La vallée de la Loire est réputée pour ses vignobles°, en particulier pour ses vins blancs°. Le Sauvignon et le Chardonnay, par exemple, constituent environ° 75% (pour cent) de la production. La vigne est cultivée dans la vallée depuis l'an 380. Aujourd'hui, les vignerons° de la région produisent 400 millions de bouteilles par an.

---

### La vallée des rois

François Iᵉʳ (1515–1547) and his court resided and traveled between his châteaux in Amboise, Blois, and Chambord. The castles were first built as defense structures but later evolved into decorative palaces. With less of a need for defense, elements like moats and towers remained as symbols of rank and ancestry. Other magnificent châteaux of the area are Azay-le-Rideau, Chenonceau, Villandry, Saumur, Ussé, Chaumont, Beauregard, and Cour-Cheverny.

### Le Printemps de Bourges

This music festival has been taking place every spring since its creation in 1977. Festival goers can listen to the music of the latest up-and-coming talent as well as world-renowned artists. Music shows can be found close to downtown. Musicians also play in restaurants, bars, and at outdoor and indoor stages. Some shows are free to the public.

### Les 24 heures du Mans

The biggest names in sports car racing come to test their speed, endurance, and reliability on the 13.6 km (8.5 mile) track. The driver of the car to travel the greatest distance within the 24-hour period is the champion. Close to 200,000 fans and 2,000 journalists come to Le Mans in June for one of the best-known automobile races in the world.

### La route des vins

The Loire River flows through the heart of the Loire Valley, connecting many of the major wine-producing towns. Nantes, home of the Muscadet grape, produces dry white wines. There is a concentration of vineyards closer to the center of the Loire Valley in Saumur, Vouvray, Azay-le-Rideau, Chinon, Bourgueil, among others. Classic white wines are found further east in Pouilly-sur-Loire. The Loire Valley is known for all sorts of white wines, but also produces some red and rosé wines.

---

 **Qu'est-ce que vous avez appris?** Répondez aux questions par des phrases complètes.

1. Quel événement peut-on voir aux Sables d'Olonne?
   On peut voir le Vendée Globe, une course nautique, aux Sables d'Olonne.
2. Au seizième siècle, qui influence le style de construction de Chambord?
   Léonard de Vinci influence le style de construction de Chambord.
3. Combien de cheminées y a-t-il à Chambord?
   Il y a 365 cheminées à Chambord.
4. De quel style sont les châteaux de la Loire?
   Les châteaux de la Loire sont de style Renaissance.
5. Pourquoi les Valois sont-ils «les rois voyageurs»?
   Ils sont «les rois voyageurs» parce qu'ils vont d'un château à l'autre avec toutes leurs possessions.

6. Combien de spectateurs vont au Printemps de Bourges chaque année? Des milliers de spectateurs vont au Printemps de Bourges chaque année.
7. Qu'est-ce que les 24 heures du Mans?
   C'est une course d'endurance automobile.
8. Quel autre type de course existe-t-il au Mans?
   Il existe aussi une course de moto.
9. Quels vins sont produits dans la vallée de la Loire?
   Les vins blancs sont principalement produits dans la vallée de la Loire.
10. Combien de bouteilles y sont produites chaque année? 400 millions de bouteilles de vin sont produites chaque année dans la vallée de la Loire.

**ressources**

CE pp. 69–70

daccord1.vhlcentral.com

**Practice more at daccord1.vhlcentral.com.**

### SUR INTERNET

Go to **daccord1.vhlcentral.com** to find more cultural information related to this **PANORAMA**.

1. Trouvez des informations sur le Vendée Globe. Quel est l'itinéraire de la course? Combien de bateaux (*boats*) y participent chaque année?

2. Qui étaient (*were*) les artistes invités au dernier Printemps de Bourges? En connaissez-vous quelques-uns? (*Do you know some of them?*)

**rois** *kings* **siècle** *century* **les Valois** *name of a royal dynasty* **construisent** *build* **de nombreux** *numerous* **ceux** *those* **cour** *court* **les plus** *the most* **a lieu** *takes place* **Pendant** *For* **monde** *world* **dizaines** *dozens* **course** *race* **célèbre** *famous* **Depuis** *Since* **marques** *brands* **y** *there* **détient** *holds* **vitesse moyenne** *average speed* **moto** *motorcycle* **vignobles** *vineyards* **vins blancs** *white wines* **environ** *around* **vignerons** *wine-growers*

*cent soixante-quinze* **175**

---

**Section Goals**

In this section, students will:
• learn to skim a text
• read a weekly city guide about Montreal

**Key Standards**
1.2, 2.1, 3.2, 5.2

**Stratégie** Tell students that they can often predict the content of an unfamiliar document in French by skimming it and looking for recognizable format elements.

**Examinez le texte** Have students skim the text at the top of this calendar of events in and around Montreal. Point out the cognates **arts, culture, festival, musique classique,** and **manifestations culturelles**. Ask them to predict what type of document it is (city guide/calendar of events in a newspaper/weekly). Then ask students to scan the rest of the calendar of events.

**Catégories** Before students do this activity, ask them to think of three words or expressions that fit each of the three given categories (**les loisirs culturels, les activités sportives, les activités de plein air**) in English.

**Trouvez** Go over answers with the whole class by pointing out where in the text each piece of information is found. Expand the activity by having students write additional entries for the calendar of events that include information for the unchecked items (**où manger cette semaine, le temps qu'il va faire cette semaine, des prix d'entrée, des adresses**).

**Language Note** Point out that French-speaking Canadians say **la fin de semaine** instead of **le week-end**.

# Lecture  Reading

## Avant la lecture

### STRATÉGIE

#### Skimming

Skimming involves quickly reading through a document to absorb its general meaning. This allows you to understand the main ideas without having to read word for word. When you skim a text, look at its title and subtitles and read the first sentence of each paragraph.

### Examinez le texte

Regardez rapidement le texte. Quel est le titre (*title*) du texte? En combien de parties le texte est-il divisé? Quels sont les titres des parties? Maintenant, regardez les photos. Quel est le sujet de l'article?

### Catégories

Dans le texte, trouvez trois mots ou expressions qui représentent chaque catégorie. Answers will vary. Suggested answers below.

les loisirs culturels

| musique classique | cinéma africain | musée des Beaux-Arts |

les activités sportives

| golf | ski | tennis |

les activités de plein air (*outdoor*)

| camping | randonnées | équitation |

### Trouvez

Regardez le document. Indiquez si vous trouvez ces informations.

_____ 1. où manger cette semaine
_____ 2. le temps qu'il va faire cette semaine
__✓__ 3. où aller à la pêche
_____ 4. des prix d'entrée (*entrance*)
__✓__ 5. des numéros de téléphone
__✓__ 6. des sports
__✓__ 7. des spectacles
_____ 8. des adresses

# CETTE SEMAINE À MONTRÉAL
## ET DANS LA RÉGION

## ARTS ET CULTURE

*Festivals et autres manifestations culturelles à explorer:*

• Festival de musique classique, samedi de 16h00 à 22h00, à la Salle de concerts Richelieu, à Montréal

• Festival du cinéma africain, dans tous les cinémas de Montréal

• Journée de la bande dessinée, samedi toute la journée, à la Librairie Rochefort, à Montréal

• Festival de reggae, dimanche tout l'après-midi, à l'Espace Lemay, à Montréal

**Spectacle à voir°**

• *La Cantatrice chauve*, pièce° d'Eugène Ionesco, samedi et dimanche à 20h00, au Théâtre du Chat Bleu, à Montréal

**À ne pas oublier°**

• Le musée des Beaux-Arts de Montréal, avec sa collection de plus de° 30.000 objets d'art du monde entier°

**Using Movement** Write activities from the calendar of events (**aller à la pêche, jouer au baseball, faire de l'équitation,** etc.) on slips of paper. Divide the class into two teams. Have a member of one team draw a paper. That team member mimes the chosen activity. The other team guesses what it is. Give points for correct answers. The team with the most points wins.

**Reading Aloud** Have groups of three students work together to read aloud each section of the calendar of events (**Arts et culture, Sports et jeux, Exploration**). Each student will then write two questions about the section that he or she read. After they have finished, ask groups to exchange their questions with another group. Have groups read the questions to the class and ask volunteers to answer them.

# SPORTS ET JEUX

- L'Académie de golf de Montréal organise un grand tournoi° le mois prochain. Pour plus d'informations, contactez le (514) 846-1225.
- Tous les dimanches, le Club d'échecs de Montréal organise des tournois d'échecs en plein air° dans le parc Champellier. Pour plus d'informations, appelez le (514) 846-1085.
- Skiez! Passez la fin de semaine dans les Laurentides° ou dans les Cantons-de-l'Est!
- Et pour la famille sportive: essayez le parc Lafontaine, un centre d'amusement pour tous qui offre: volley-ball, tennis, football et baseball.

PASSIONNÉ° DE PÊCHE?
N'OUBLIEZ PAS LES NOMBREUX
LACS° OÙ LA PÊCHE EST AUTORISÉE.

# EXPLORATION

*Redécouvrez la nature grâce à° ces activités à ne pas manquer°:*

### Visite du parc national de la Jacques-Cartier°
- Camping
- Promenades et randonnées
- Observation de la faune et de la flore

### Région des Laurentides et Gaspésie°
- Équitation°
- Randonnées à cheval de 2 à 5 jours en camping

**voir** *see* **pièce (de théâtre)** *play* **À ne pas oublier** *Not to be forgotten* **plus de** *more than* **du monde entier** *from around the world* **tournoi** *tournament* **en plein air** *outdoor* **Laurentides** *region of eastern Quebec* **Passionné** *Enthusiast* **lacs** *lakes* **grâce à** *thanks to* **à ne pas manquer** *not to be missed* **la Jacques-Cartier** *the Jacques-Cartier river in Quebec* **Gaspésie** *peninsula of Quebec* **Équitation** *Horseback riding*

# Après la lecture

**Répondez** Répondez aux questions avec des phrases complètes.

1. Citez deux activités sportives qu'on peut pratiquer à l'extérieur.
   Answers will vary.

2. À quel jeu est-ce qu'on joue dans le parc Champellier?
   On joue aux échecs dans le parc Champellier.

3. Où va peut-être aller un passionné de lecture et de dessin?
   Un passionné de lecture et de dessin va peut-être aller à la Journée de la bande dessinée.

4. Où pratique-t-on des sports d'équipe?
   On pratique des sports d'équipe au parc Lafontaine.

5. Où y a-t-il de la neige au Québec en cette saison?
   Il y a de la neige dans les Laurentides et dans les Cantons-de-l'Est.

6. Si on aime beaucoup la musique, où peut-on aller?
   On peut aller au Festival de musique classique ou au Festival de reggae.

**Suggestions** Lucille passe une année dans un lycée du Québec. Ce week-end, elle invite sa famille à explorer la région. Choisissez une activité à faire ou un lieu à visiter que chaque membre de sa famille va aimer.

**MODÈLE**

La sœur cadette de Lucille adore le ski.
*Elle va aimer les Laurentides et les Cantons-de-l'Est.*

1. La mère de Lucille est artiste.
   Elle va aimer le musée des Beaux-Arts de Montréal.

2. Le frère de Lucille joue au volley-ball à l'université.
   Il va aimer le parc Lafontaine.

3. La sœur aînée de Lucille a envie de voir un film sénégalais.
   Elle va aimer le Festival du cinéma africain.

4. Le grand-père de Lucille joue souvent aux échecs.
   Il va aimer les tournois d'échecs en plein air dans le parc Champellier.

5. La grand-mère de Lucille est fan de théâtre.
   Elle va aimer *La Cantatrice chauve* au Théâtre du Chat Bleu.

6. Le père de Lucille adore la nature et les animaux, mais il n'est pas très sportif.
   Answers will vary. Possible answer: Il va aimer les promenades dans le parc national de la Jacques-Cartier.

**Une invitation** 👥 Vous allez passer le week-end au Québec. Qu'est-ce que vous allez faire? Par groupes de quatre, discutez des activités qui vous intéressent (*that interest you*) et essayez de trouver trois ou quatre activités que vous avez en commun. Attention! Il va peut-être pleuvoir ce week-end, alors ne choisissez pas (*don't choose*) uniquement des activités de plein air!

---

**Répondez** Present these as items 7–10. **7. Où peut-on voir des films africains?** (On peut voir des films africains dans tous les cinémas de Montréal.) **8. Combien d'objets d'art y a-t-il au musée des Beaux-Arts de Montréal?** (Il y a plus de 30.000 objets d'art.) **9. Quels sports pratique-t-on au parc Lafontaine?** (On propose le volley-ball, le tennis, le football et le baseball.) **10. Si on aime beaucoup les animaux et les fleurs, où peut-on aller?** (On peut aller au parc national de la Jacques-Cartier.)

**Suggestions** Ask students to write about three more members of Lucille's family. They should model their sentences after the ones in the activity, saying what each person enjoys doing. Then have students read their sentences to a partner. The partner will come up with a suggested activity or place to visit that will suit each person.

**Une invitation** Give students a couple of minutes to review the **Vocabulaire** on page 146, **Expressions utiles** on page 151, and Expressions with **faire** on page 154. Add activities, such as **faire du surf des neiges, prendre des photos, faire des arts martiaux**, and **faire du skateboard**.

**Expansion** Have one or two groups act out their conversation from **Une invitation** for the rest of the class. Before the groups begin, have the listeners in the class write a list of ten activities that they think will be mentioned in each of the presentations. As students listen, have them check off on their list the activities they hear.

---

**OPTIONS**

**True-False Statements** Give students true or false statements about the **Lecture**. Example: **On peut faire des randonnées à cheval au parc national de la Jacques-Cartier.** (Faux. On peut faire des randonnées à cheval en Région des Laurentides et Gaspésie.)

**Writing Practice** Ask students to go through the selection and locate all of the activities that require usage of **faire**. (Encourage them to use their dictionaries, if necessary.) Then have them write sentences saying whether or not they like doing those activities. Example: **Activités avec faire: faire du vélo, faire de l'équitation**, etc. **J'aime faire du vélo. Je n'aime pas faire d'équitation.**

## Section Goals

In this section, students will:
- learn to use a French-English dictionary
- write a brochure including weather-related information and seasonal activities

## Key Standards

1.3, 3.1, 5.1

**Stratégie** Explain to students that when they look up a translation of an English word in a French-English dictionary, they will frequently find more than one translation. They must decide which one best fits the context. Discuss the meanings of *racket* that might be found in an entry in a French-English dictionary and the usefulness of the explanatory notes and abbreviations found in dictionary entries.

**Thème** Remind students of some of the common graphic features used in brochures: headings, times and places, brief descriptions of events, and prices.

# Écriture

## STRATÉGIE

### Using a dictionary

A common mistake made by beginning language learners is to embrace the dictionary as the ultimate resource for reading, writing, and speaking. While it is true that the dictionary is a useful tool that can provide valuable information about vocabulary, using the dictionary correctly requires that you understand the elements of each entry.

If you glance at a French-English dictionary, you will notice that the format is similar to that of an English dictionary. The word is listed first, usually followed by its pronunciation. Then come the definitions, organized by parts of speech. Sometimes, the most frequently used meanings are listed first.

To find the best word for your needs, you should refer to the abbreviations and the explanatory notes that appear next to the entries. For example, imagine that you are writing about your pastimes. You want to write *I want to buy a new racket for my match tomorrow*, but you don't know the French word for *racket*.

In the dictionary, you might find an entry like this one:

> **racket** n 1. boucan; 2. raquette (sport)

The abbreviation key at the front of the dictionary says that *n* corresponds to **nom** (*noun*). Then, the first word you see is **boucan**. The definition of **boucan** is *noise or racket,* so **boucan** is probably not the word you want. The second word is **raquette**, followed by the word *sport*, which indicates that it is related to **sports**. This detail indicates that the word **raquette** is the best choice for your needs.

## Thème

## Écrire une brochure

### Avant l'écriture

1. Choisissez le sujet de votre brochure:

   A. Vous travaillez à la Chambre de Commerce de votre région pour l'été. Des hommes et des femmes d'affaires québécois vont visiter votre région cette année, mais ils n'ont pas encore décidé (*have not yet decided*) quand. La Chambre de Commerce vous demande de créer (*asks you to create*) une petite brochure sur le temps qu'il fait dans votre région aux différentes saisons de l'année. Dites quelle saison, à votre avis (*in your opinion*), est idéale pour visiter votre région et expliquez pourquoi.

   B. Vous avez une réunion familiale pour décider où aller en vacances cette année, mais chaque membre de la famille suggère un endroit différent. Choisissez un lieu de vacances où vous avez envie d'aller et créez une brochure pour montrer à votre famille pourquoi vous devriez (*should*) tous y aller (*go there*). Décrivez la météo de l'endroit et indiquez les différentes activités culturelles et sportives qu'on peut y faire.

   C. Vous passez un semestre/trimestre dans le pays francophone de votre choix (*of your choice*). Deux élèves de votre cours de français ont aussi envie de visiter ce pays. Créez une petite brochure pour partager vos impressions du pays. Présentez le pays, donnez des informations météorologiques et décrivez vos activités préférées.

**OPTIONS**

**Avant l'écriture** Reinforce to students that when they look up a word in a French-English dictionary, not all of the translations listed will have the same meaning. Tell them that a good way to check a possible translation of an English word is to look up the French word and see how it is translated back into English.

Discuss the three topics students may wish to write about. Introduce terms such as **comité**, **guide d'orientation**, and **chambre de commerce**. Evaluate the level of formality of each of the brochures described. (The chamber of commerce brochure will be more formal than the family and student brochures.) Remind students to keep this in mind when they create their brochures.

**2.** Choisissez le sujet de votre brochure et pensez au vocabulaire utile à son écriture. Utilisez le tableau (*chart*) pour noter tous les mots (*words*) en français qui vous viennent à l'esprit (*you can think of*). Ensuite (*Then*), révisez (*review*) la liste de vocabulaire des unités 1–4 et ajoutez (*add*) le vocabulaire utile pour le sujet. Enfin (*Finally*), regardez votre tableau. Quels sont les mots en anglais que vous pourriez (*could*) ajouter? Créez une nouvelle liste et cherchez les mots dans un dictionnaire.

| Mots en français (de moi) | Mots en français (des listes) | Mots en anglais |
|---|---|---|
| | | anglais / français: |
| | | |

**3.** Cherchez les mots dans le dictionnaire. N'oubliez pas d'utiliser la procédure de **Stratégie**.

## Écriture

Utilisez le vocabulaire du tableau pour créer votre brochure. N'oubliez pas de penser à un titre (*title*). Ensuite, créez des sections et donnez-leur (*them*) aussi un titre, comme **Printemps, Été, …; Ville, Campagne (Countryside), …; France, Tunisie, …** Vous pouvez (*can*) utiliser des photos pour illustrer.

## Après l'écriture

**1.** Échangez votre brochure avec celle (*the one*) d'un(e) partenaire. Répondez à ces questions pour commenter son travail.

- Votre partenaire a-t-il/elle couvert (*did cover*) le sujet?

- A-t-il/elle donné (*did give*) un titre à la brochure et aux sections?

- S'il (*If there*) y a des photos, illustrent-elles le texte?

- Votre partenaire a-t-il/elle utilisé (*did use*) le vocabulaire approprié?

- A-t-il/elle correctement conjugué (*did conjugate*) les verbes?

**2.** Corrigez votre brochure d'après (*according to*) les commentaires de votre partenaire. Relisez votre travail pour éliminer ces problèmes:

- des fautes (*errors*) d'orthographe

- des fautes de ponctuation

- des fautes de conjugaison

- des fautes d'accord (*agreement*) des adjectifs

- un mauvais emploi (*use*) de la grammaire

*cent soixante-dix-neuf* **179**

## EVALUATION

### Criteria
**Content** Contains all the information included in the subject description the student chose.
Scale: 1 2 3 4 5

**Organization** Follows a typical brochure organization with a major head, text, and at least one visual.
Scale: 1 2 3 4 5

**Accuracy** Uses possessive and descriptive adjectives and modifies them accordingly. Spells words and conjugates verbs correctly throughout.
Scale: 1 2 3 4 5

**Creativity** The student includes additional information that is not included in the task, adds extra features to the brochure such as bulleted lists and boxed text, and/or spends extra time on design and presentation.
Scale: 1 2 3 4 5

### Scoring
| | |
|---|---|
| Excellent | 18–20 points |
| Good | 14–17 points |
| Satisfactory | 10–13 points |
| Unsatisfactory | < 10 points |

**OPTIONS**

**Avant l'écriture** Group students who have chosen to work on the same brochures and encourage them to share their ideas and personalized vocabulary from step 2 before they begin writing. As a group, have them brainstorm additional vocabulary they may need to look up before they begin writing.

Before students begin writing, have the class discuss some of the features that are typically found in brochures, such as headings, schedules, lists, boxed/highlighted text, photos, graphics, and other visuals. Bring in some brochures for students to analyze before they create their own.

## Key Standards

**4.1**

**Teacher Resources**
Vocabulary MP3s/CD

**Suggestion** Tell students that an easy way to study from **Vocabulaire** is to cover up the French half of each section, leaving only the English equivalents exposed. They can then quiz themselves on the French items. To focus on the English equivalents of the French entries, they simply reverse this process.

### Activités sportives et loisirs

| | |
|---|---|
| aider | to help |
| aller à la pêche | to go fishing |
| bricoler | to tinker; to do odd jobs |
| chanter | to sing |
| désirer | to want |
| gagner | to win |
| indiquer | to indicate |
| jouer (à/de) | to play |
| marcher | to walk (person); to work (thing) |
| pratiquer | to play regularly, to practice |
| skier | to ski |
| une bande dessinée (B.D.) | comic strip |
| le baseball | baseball |
| le basket(-ball) | basketball |
| les cartes (f.) | cards |
| le cinéma | movies |
| les échecs (m.) | chess |
| une équipe | team |
| le foot(ball) | soccer |
| le football américain | football |
| le golf | golf |
| un jeu | game |
| un joueur/ une joueuse | player |
| un loisir | leisure activity |
| un match | game |
| un passe-temps | pastime, hobby |
| un spectacle | show |
| le sport | sport |
| un stade | stadium |
| le temps libre | free time |
| le tennis | tennis |
| le volley(-ball) | volleyball |

### Verbes irréguliers en –ir

| | |
|---|---|
| courir | to run |
| dormir | to sleep |
| partir | to leave |
| sentir | to feel; to smell; to sense |
| servir | to serve |
| sortir | to go out, to leave |

### Le temps qu'il fait

| | |
|---|---|
| Il fait 18 degrés. | It is 18 degrees. |
| Il fait beau. | The weather is nice. |
| Il fait bon. | The weather is good/warm. |
| Il fait chaud. | It is hot (out). |
| Il fait (du) soleil. | It is sunny. |
| Il fait du vent. | It is windy. |
| Il fait frais. | It is cool. |
| Il fait froid. | It is cold. |
| Il fait mauvais. | The weather is bad. |
| Il fait un temps épouvantable. | The weather is dreadful. |
| Il neige. (neiger) | It is snowing. (to snow) |
| Il pleut. (pleuvoir) | It is raining. (to rain) |
| Le temps est nuageux. | It is cloudy. |
| Le temps est orageux. | It is stormy. |
| Quel temps fait-il? | What is the weather like? |
| Quelle température fait-il? | What is the temperature? |
| un imperméable | rain jacket |
| un parapluie | umbrella |

### Verbes

| | |
|---|---|
| acheter | to buy |
| amener | to bring (someone) |
| célébrer | to celebrate |
| considérer | to consider |
| emmener | to take (someone) |
| employer | to use; to employ |
| envoyer | to send |
| espérer | to hope |
| essayer (de + inf.) | to try (to) |
| nettoyer | to clean |
| payer | to pay |
| posséder | to possess, to own |
| préférer | to prefer |
| protéger | to protect |
| répéter | to repeat; to rehearse |

### La fréquence

| | |
|---|---|
| une/deux fois | one/two time(s) |
| par jour, semaine, mois, an, etc. | per day, week, month, year, etc. |
| déjà | already |
| encore | again, still |
| jamais | never |
| longtemps | long time |
| maintenant | now |
| parfois | sometimes |
| rarement | rarely |
| souvent | often |

### Les saisons, les mois, les dates

| | |
|---|---|
| une saison | season |
| l'automne (m.)/ en automne | fall/in the fall |
| l'été (m.)/en été | summer/in the summer |
| l'hiver (m.)/en hiver | winter/in the winter |
| le printemps (m.)/ au printemps | spring/in the spring |
| Quelle est la date? | What's the date? |
| C'est le 1er (premier) octobre. | It's the first of October. |
| C'est quand votre/ ton anniversaire? | When is your birthday? |
| C'est le 2 mai. | It's the second of May. |
| C'est quand l'anniversaire de Paul? | When is Paul's birthday? |
| C'est le 15 mars. | It's March 15th. |
| un anniversaire | birthday |
| janvier | January |
| février | February |
| mars | March |
| avril | April |
| mai | May |
| juin | June |
| juillet | July |
| août | August |
| septembre | September |
| octobre | October |
| novembre | November |
| décembre | December |

| | |
|---|---|
| *Expressions utiles* | *See pp. 151 and 165.* |
| Expressions with *faire* | *See p. 154.* |
| *faire* | *See p. 154.* |
| *Il faut...* | *See p. 155.* |
| Numbers 101 and higher | *See p. 168.* |

**ressources**

daccord1.vhlcentral.com

**180** *cent quatre-vingts*

# Les fêtes

## Unit Goals

**Leçon 6A**

In this lesson, students will learn:

- terms for parties and celebrations
- terms for the stages of life
- more differences between open and closed vowels
- about **carnaval** and France's Bastille Day
- more about festivals and holiday celebrations through specially shot video footage
- demonstrative adjectives
- the **passé composé** with **avoir**
- some irregular past participles
- about the Belgian postal service

**Leçon 6B**

In this lesson, students will learn:

- terms for clothing, shopping, and colors
- more about open and closed vowels
- about the fashion industry in France
- indirect object pronouns
- more uses of disjunctive pronouns
- regular and irregular -re verbs
- to listen for linguistic cues in oral communication

**Savoir-faire**

In this section, students will learn:

- cultural and historical information about the French regions of **Aquitaine, Midi-Pyrénées**, and **Languedoc-Roussillon**
- to recognize word families
- how to report an interview

**Pour commencer**

- **Amina est l'invitée.**
- **Elles vont faire la fête.**
- **Elles vont manger une mousse au chocolat.**
- **Son tee-shirt est orange.**

### Pour commencer

- Qui est l'invitée sur la photo?
- Qu'est-ce qu'Amina et Valérie vont faire?
- Qu'est-ce qu'elles vont manger? Du pain ou une mousse au chocolat?
- De quelle couleur est le tee-shirt d'Amina? Orange ou violet?

---

**RESOURCES**

**Student Materials**
**Print:** Student Book, Workbooks (*Cahier d'exercices, Cahier d'activités*)
**Technology:** MAESTRO® *Cahier interactif* and Supersite (Audio, Video, Practice)

**Teacher Materials**
DVDs (*Roman-photo, Flash culture*)
Teacher's Resources (Scripts, Answer Keys, Testing Program)
Audio CDs (Testing Program, Textbook, Audio Program)

MAESTRO® Supersite: Student Supersite Content; Planning and Teaching Resources (Overheads, *PowerPoints*, Lesson Plans, Information Gaps and *Feuilles d'activités*); Learning Management System (Gradebook, Assignments); Audio MP3s and Streaming Video
**D'ACCORD! 1 Supersite:** daccord1.vhlcentral.com

## Section Goals

In this section, students will learn and practice vocabulary related to:
- parties and celebrations
- stages of life and interpersonal relationships

## Key Standards

**1.1, 1.2, 4.1**

**Student Resources**
*Cahier d'exercices*, pp. 71–72;
*Cahier d'activités*, pp. 49–50, 155;
Supersite: Activities,
*Cahier interactif*
**Teacher Resources**
Answer Keys; Overhead #31;
Audio Script; Textbook & Audio
Activity MP3s/CD; Info Gap
Activities; Testing program:
Vocabulary Quiz

## Suggestions

- Have students look over the new vocabulary and identify the cognates. Examples: **organiser**, **fiancé(e)**, **mariage**, and **divorce**.
- Describe what people are doing in the drawing using **Overhead #31**. Follow up with simple questions based on your narrative.
- Point out the banner and the cake in the illustration. Ask students what **Bon anniversaire** and **Joyeux anniversaire** mean. (*Happy birthday*)
- Point out the similarities and differences between these related words: **aimer, ami(e), l'amitié, un amour, amoureux,** and **amoureuse**.

**Leçon** **6A**

**Talking Picture**
**Audio: Activity**

You will learn how to...
- talk about celebrations
- talk about the stages of life

# Surprise!

### Vocabulaire

| | |
|---|---|
| faire la fête | to party |
| faire une surprise (à quelqu'un) | to surprise (someone) |
| fêter | to celebrate |
| organiser une fête | to organize a party |
| une fête | party; celebration |
| un jour férié | holiday |
| une bière | beer |
| le vin | wine |
| l'amitié | friendship |
| l'amour | love |
| le bonheur | happiness |
| un(e) fiancé(e) | fiancé |
| des jeunes mariés (m.) | newlyweds |
| un rendez-vous | date; appointment |
| l'adolescence (f.) | adolescence |
| l'âge adulte (m.) | adulthood |
| un divorce | divorce |
| l'enfance (f.) | childhood |
| une étape | stage |
| l'état civil (m.) | marital status |
| la jeunesse | youth |
| un mariage | marriage; wedding |
| la mort | death |
| la naissance | birth |
| la vie | life |
| la vieillesse | old age |
| prendre sa retraite | to retire |
| tomber amoureux/ amoureuse | to fall in love |
| ensemble | together |

les invitées (f.)

les invités (m.)

l'hôte (m.)

l'hôtesse (f.)

le gâteau

la glace

les biscuits (m.)

les bonbons (m.)

le champagne

les desserts (m.)

les glaçons (m.)

**ressources**

| CE pp. 71–72 | CA pp. 49–50, 155 | daccord1.vhlcentral.com |

**Les fêtes** Point out that, in addition to celebrating birthdays, many people in French-speaking cultures celebrate **la fête**, or saint's day, which is based upon their given name. Bring in a French calendar that has the names of **fêtes** and have students find their own saint's day. You may need to help students find the name that most closely resembles their own.

**Writing Practice** Have students write three fill-in-the-blank sentences based on the drawing above, using the new vocabulary. Then have each student exchange papers with a classmate and complete the sentences. Remind them to verify their answers.

# Mise en pratique

**BON ANNIVERSAIRE, MARC!**

**1  Chassez l'intrus** Indiquez le mot ou l'expression qui n'appartient pas (*doesn't belong*) à la liste.

1. l'amour, tomber amoureux, un fiancé, (un divorce)
2. un mariage, un couple, (un jour férié,) un fiancé
3. un biscuit, (une bière,) un dessert, un gâteau
4. (une glace,) une bière, le champagne, le vin
5. (la vieillesse,) la naissance, l'enfance, la jeunesse
6. faire la fête, un hôte, des invités, (une étape)
7. fêter, un cadeau, (la vie,) une surprise
8. (l'état civil,) la naissance, la mort, l'adolescence

**la surprise**   **le couple**

**2  Écoutez** Écoutez la conversation entre Anne et Nathalie. Indiquez si les affirmations sont **vraies** ou **fausses**.

|  | Vrai | Faux |
|---|---|---|
| 1. Jean-Marc va prendre sa retraite dans six mois. | ☐ | ☑ |
| 2. Nathalie a l'idée d'organiser une fête pour Jean-Marc. | ☐ | ☑ |
| 3. Anne va acheter un gâteau. | ☑ | ☐ |
| 4. Nathalie va apporter de la glace. | ☐ | ☑ |
| 5. La fête est une surprise. | ☑ | ☐ |
| 6. Nathalie va envoyer les invitations par e-mail. | ☑ | ☐ |
| 7. La fête va avoir lieu (*take place*) dans le bureau d'Anne. | ☐ | ☑ |
| 8. La maison d'Anne n'est pas belle. | ☐ | ☑ |
| 9. Tout le monde va donner des idées pour le cadeau. | ☑ | ☐ |
| 10. Les invités vont acheter le cadeau. | ☐ | ☑ |

**3  Associez** Faites correspondre les mots et expressions de la colonne de gauche avec les définitions de la colonne de droite. Notez que tous les éléments ne sont pas utilisés. Ensuite (*Then*), avec un(e) partenaire, donnez votre propre définition de quatre expressions de la première colonne. Votre partenaire doit deviner (*must guess*) de quoi vous parlez.

_b_ 1. la naissance
___ 2. l'enfance
_c_ 3. l'adolescence
___ 4. l'âge adulte
_e_ 5. tomber amoureux
_a_ 6. un jour férié
_g_ 7. le mariage
_f_ 8. le divorce
_h_ 9. prendre sa retraite
_d_ 10. la mort

a. C'est une date importante, comme le 4 juillet aux États-Unis.
b. C'est la fin de l'étape prénatale.
c. C'est l'étape de la vie pendant laquelle (*during which*) on va au lycée.
d. C'est un événement très triste.
e. C'est soudain (*suddenly*) aimer une personne.
f. C'est le futur probable d'un couple qui se dispute (*fights*) tout le temps.
g. C'est un jour de bonheur et de célébration de l'amour.
h. C'est quand une personne décide de ne plus travailler.

**le cadeau**

Practice more at **daccord1.vhlcentral.com.**

**Expansion**
- For additional practice, give students these items. **9. la vieillesse, la jeunesse, la fête, l'âge adulte (la fête) 10. l'amour, le bonheur, l'amitié, la retraite (la retraite)**
- Have students create one or two additional items using at least three of the new vocabulary words in each one. Collect their papers and write some of the items on the board.

**2 Script** ANNE: Nathalie, je vais organiser une fête pour Jean-Marc. Il va prendre sa retraite dans un mois. Ça va être une surprise. Je vais acheter un gâteau.
NATHALIE: Oh, et moi, qu'est-ce que je fais pour aider, Anne? J'apporte des biscuits?
A: Oui, c'est une bonne idée. Il faut aussi trouver un cadeau original.
N: D'accord, mais je vais avoir besoin d'un peu de temps pour y penser.
A: Qu'est-ce qu'on fait pour les invités?
N: Pour faire une vraie surprise à Jean-Marc, il faut être discrètes. Je propose d'envoyer un e-mail à tout le monde. En plus, comme ça, c'est rapide.
A: Et qu'est-ce qu'on fait pour la décoration?
N: Pourquoi ne pas fêter sa retraite chez toi? Ta maison est belle, et on n'a pas besoin de beaucoup de décoration.
A: Oui, pourquoi pas! Maintenant, il ne reste plus qu'à trouver un cadeau. Pourquoi est-ce qu'on ne demande pas aux autres de donner des idées par e-mail?
N: Oui, et quel beau cadeau pour Jean-Marc si tout le monde participe et donne un peu d'argent!
(*On Textbook Audio*)

**2 Suggestion** Play the conversation again, stopping at the end of each sentence that contains the answer to one of these items. Have students verify true statements and correct the false ones.

**3 Suggestion** Have volunteers share their definitions with the class.

**4 Suggestions**
- Go over the answers to the activity with the class before students write their own sentences.
- Ask volunteers to write their sentences on the board and have the class make corrections as needed.

**5 Suggestion** Have two volunteers read the **modèle** aloud. Then divide the class into pairs and distribute the Info Gap Handouts found on the Supersite for this activity. Give students ten minutes to complete the activity.

**6 Suggestion** Tell students that they should plan the party first by answering the questions. Then they should use those answers to write the conversation discussing the details of the party.

## Communication

**4 Le mot juste** Complétez les phrases par le mot illustré. Faites les accords nécessaires. Ensuite (*Then*), avec un(e) partenaire, créez (*create*) une phrase pour laquelle (*for which*) vous illustrez trois mots de **CONTEXTES**. Échangez votre phrase avec celle d'un autre groupe et résolvez le rébus.

1. Caroline est une amie d' __enfance__ . Je vais lui faire une __surprise__ samedi. C'est son anniversaire.

2. Marc et Sophie sont inséparables. Ils sont toujours __ensemble__ . C'est le bonheur et le grand __amour__ .

3. Les __invités__ aiment beaucoup les desserts: un __gâteau__ au chocolat et des __bonbons__ .

4. Les __(jeunes) mariés__ ont beaucoup de __cadeaux__ .

5. La __naissance__ de ma sœur est un grand __bonheur__ pour mes parents.

**5 Sept différences** Votre professeur va vous donner, à vous et à votre partenaire, deux feuilles d'activités différentes. À tour de rôle, posez-vous des questions pour trouver les sept différences entre les illustrations de l'anniversaire des jumeaux (*twins*) Boniface. Attention! Ne regardez pas la feuille de votre partenaire.

**MODÈLE**

**Élève 1:** *Sur mon image, il y a trois cadeaux. Combien de cadeaux y a-t-il sur ton image?*
**Élève 2:** *Sur mon image, il y a quatre cadeaux.*

**6 C'est la fête!** Vous venez de passer le bac, et vous allez organiser une fête! Avec un(e) partenaire, écrivez une conversation au sujet de la préparation de cette fête. N'oubliez pas de répondre aux questions suivantes. Ensuite (*Then*), jouez (*act out*) votre dialogue devant la classe. Answers will vary.

1. Quand allez-vous organiser la fête?
2. Qui vont être les invités?
3. Où la fête va-t-elle avoir lieu (*take place*)?
4. Qu'allez-vous manger? Qu'allez-vous boire?
5. Qui va apporter quoi?
6. Qui est responsable de la musique? De la décoration?
7. Qu'allez-vous faire pendant (*during*) la fête?
8. Qui va nettoyer après la fête?

**OPTIONS**

**Skits** In groups of three or four, have students plan and perform a skit in which they depict a particular stage of life (youth, old age, etc.) or marital status (engaged, single, divorced). The rest of the class tries to guess which stage of life or marital status the skit represents.

**Vrai ou faux** Have students write four or five true/false statements based on the illustration on pages 182–183. Then have them get together with a partner and take turns saying their statements and responding **C'est vrai** or **C'est faux**. Call on volunteers to correct the false statements, pointing out the changes on **Overhead #31**.

# Les sons et les lettres

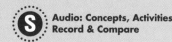

**Audio:** Concepts, Activities
Record & Compare

## Open vs. closed vowels: Part 2

The letter combinations **au** and **eau** are pronounced like the vowel sound in the English word *coat*, but without the glide heard in English. These are closed **o** sounds.

| ch**au**d | **au**ssi | b**eau**coup | tabl**eau** |
|---|---|---|---|

When the letter **o** is followed by a consonant sound, it is usually pronounced like the vowel in the English word *raw*. This is an open **o** sound.

| h**o**mme | téléph**o**ne | **o**rdinateur | **o**range |
|---|---|---|---|

When the letter **o** occurs as the last sound of a word or is followed by a *z* sound, such as a single **s** between two vowels, it is usually pronounced with the closed **o** sound.

| tr**o**p | hér**o**s | r**o**se | ch**o**se |
|---|---|---|---|

When the letter **o** has an **accent circonflexe**, it is usually pronounced with the closed **o** sound.

| dr**ô**le | bient**ô**t | p**ô**le | c**ô**té |
|---|---|---|---|

**Prononcez** Répétez les mots suivants à voix haute.

1. rôle
2. porte
3. dos
4. chaud
5. prose
6. gros
7. oiseau
8. encore
9. mauvais
10. nouveau
11. restaurant
12. bibliothèque

**Articulez** Répétez les phrases suivantes à voix haute.

1. En automne, on n'a pas trop chaud.
2. Aurélie a une bonne note en biologie.
3. Votre colocataire est d'origine japonaise?
4. Sophie aime beaucoup l'informatique et la psychologie.
5. Nos copains mangent au restaurant marocain aujourd'hui.
6. Comme cadeau, Robert et Corinne vont préparer un gâteau.

**Dictons** Répétez les dictons à voix haute.

La fortune vient en dormant.[2]

Tout nouveau, tout beau.[1]

[1] Shiny and new.
[2] Fortune comes while you sleep.

**ressources**

CA
p. 156

daccord1.vhlcentral.com

*cent quatre-vingt-cinq* **185**

---

**Section Goals**

In this section, students will learn more about open and closed vowels.

**Key Standards**
4.1

**Student Resources**
*Cahier d'activités*, p. 156;
Supersite: Activities,
*Cahier interactif*

**Teacher Resources**
Answer Keys; Audio Script;
Textbook & Audio Activity
MP3s/CD

**Suggestions**

• Model the pronunciation of each open and closed vowel sound. Have students watch the shape of your mouth, then repeat the sound after you. Pronounce each of the example words and have students repeat them.

• Remind students that **o** is sometimes nasalized when followed by a single **m** or **n**. Compare the following words: **bon, nom**, and **bonne, homme**.

• Ask students to provide more examples of words from this lesson or previous lessons with these vowel sounds. Examples: **cadeau, gâteau, hôte, octobre,** and **beau.**

• Dictate five familiar words containing the open and closed vowels presented here, repeating each one at least two times. Then write them on the board or on a transparency and have students check their spelling.

**Dictons** Ask students if they can think of sayings in English that are similar to **«La fortune vient en dormant.»** (*Good things come to those who wait. Patience is a virtue.*)

---

**OPTIONS**

**Mini-dictée** Use these sentences with open and closed vowel sounds for additional practice or dictation. **1. Octobre est en automne. 2. Est-ce qu'il fait mauvais aujourd'hui? 3. En août, il fait beau, mais il fait chaud. 4. Aurélie est aussi drôle que Paul.**

**Tongue Twister** Teach students this French tongue-twister that contains a variety of vowel sounds. **Paul se pèle au pôle dans sa pile de pulls et polos pâles. Pas plus d'appel de la poule à l'Opel que d'opale dans la pelle à Paul.**

CONTEXTES **185**

# ROMAN-PHOTO

## Les cadeaux

 Video: *Roman-photo*
Record & Compare

**PERSONNAGES**

Amina

Astrid

Rachid

Sandrine

Valérie

Vendeuse

*À l'appartement de Sandrine...*
**SANDRINE** Allô, Pascal? Tu m'as téléphoné? Écoute, je suis très occupée, là. Je prépare un gâteau d'anniversaire pour Stéphane... Il a dix-huit ans aujourd'hui... On organise une fête surprise au P'tit Bistrot.

**SANDRINE** J'ai fait une mousse au chocolat, comme pour ton anniversaire. Stéphane adore ça! J'ai aussi préparé des biscuits que David aime bien.

**SANDRINE** Quoi? David!... Mais non, il n'est pas marié. C'est un bon copain, c'est tout!... Désolée, je n'ai pas le temps de discuter. À bientôt.

**RACHID** Écoute, Astrid. Il faut trouver un cadeau... un *vrai* cadeau d'anniversaire.
**ASTRID** Excusez-moi, Madame. Combien coûte cette montre, s'il vous plaît?
**VENDEUSE** Quarante euros.
**ASTRID** Que penses-tu de cette montre, Rachid?
**RACHID** Bonne idée.

**VENDEUSE** Je fais un paquet cadeau?
**ASTRID** Oui, merci.
**RACHID** Eh, Astrid, il faut y aller!
**VENDEUSE** Et voilà dix euros. Merci, Mademoiselle, bonne fin de journée.

*Au café...*
**VALÉRIE** Ah, vous voilà! Astrid, aide-nous avec les décorations, s'il te plaît. La fête commence à six heures. Sandrine a tout préparé.
**ASTRID** Quelle heure est-il? Zut, déjà? En tout cas, on a trouvé des cadeaux.
**RACHID** Je vais chercher Stéphane.

---

 **1** **Vrai ou faux?** Indiquez si ces (*these*) affirmations sont vraies ou fausses. Corrigez les phrases fausses.

1. Sandrine prépare un gâteau d'anniversaire pour Stéphane. Vrai.
2. Sandrine est désolée parce qu'elle n'a pas le temps de discuter avec Rachid. Faux. Elle n'a pas le temps de discuter avec Pascal.
3. Rachid ne comprend pas la blague. Vrai.
4. Pour aider Sandrine, Valérie va apporter les desserts. Vrai.

5. Rachid et Astrid trouvent un cadeau pour Valérie. Faux. Ils trouvent un cadeau pour Stéphane.
6. Rachid n'aime pas l'idée de la montre pour Stéphane. Faux. Rachid aime l'idée de la montre pour Stéphane.
7. La fête d'anniversaire pour Stéphane commence à huit heures. Faux. Elle commence à six heures.
8. Sandrine va chercher Stéphane. Faux. Rachid va chercher Stéphane.
9. Amina a apporté de la glace au chocolat. Vrai.
10. Les parents d'Amina vont passer l'été à Aix-en-Provence. Vrai.

Practice more at **daccord1.vhlcentral.com.**

---

**OPTIONS**

**Avant de regarder la vidéo** Before viewing the video, have students brainstorm a list of words or expressions that someone might say when preparing for a party and discussing gifts. Write their ideas on the board.

**Regarder la vidéo** Show the video in three parts, pausing the video before each location change. Have students describe what happens in each place. Write their observations on the board. Then show the entire episode again without pausing and have the class fill in any missing details to summarize the plot.

**Tout le monde prépare la surprise pour Stéphane.**

**VALÉRIE** Oh là là! Tu as fait tout ça pour Stéphane?!

**SANDRINE** Oh, ce n'est pas grand-chose.

**VALÉRIE** Tu es un ange! Stéphane va bientôt arriver. Je t'aide à apporter ces desserts?

**SANDRINE** Oh, merci, c'est gentil.

*Dans un magasin...*

**ASTRID** Eh Rachid, j'ai eu une idée géniale... Des cadeaux parfaits pour Stéphane. Regarde! Ce matin, j'ai acheté cette calculatrice et ces livres.

**RACHID** Mais enfin, Astrid, Stéphane n'aime pas les livres.

**ASTRID** Oh, Rachid, tu ne comprends rien. C'est une blague.

**AMINA** Bonjour! Désolée, je suis en retard!

**VALÉRIE** Ce n'est pas grave. Tu es toute belle ce soir!

**AMINA** Vous trouvez? J'ai acheté ce cadeau pour Stéphane. Et j'ai apporté de la glace au chocolat aussi.

**VALÉRIE** Oh, merci! Il faut aider Astrid avec les décorations.

**ASTRID** Salut, Amina. Ça va?

**AMINA** Oui, super. Mes parents ont téléphoné du Sénégal ce matin! Ils vont passer l'été ici. C'est le bonheur!

---

## Expressions utiles

### Talking about celebrations

- **J'ai fait une mousse au chocolat, comme pour ton anniversaire.**
  *I made a chocolate mousse, (just) like for your birthday.*
- **J'ai aussi préparé des biscuits que David aime bien.**
  *I have also prepared some cookies that David likes.*
- **Je fais un paquet cadeau?**
  *Shall I wrap the present?*
- **En tout cas, on a trouvé des cadeaux.**
  *In any case, we have found some presents.*
- **Et j'ai apporté de la glace au chocolat.**
  *And I brought some chocolate ice cream.*

### Talking about the past

- **Tu m'as téléphoné?**
  *Did you call me?*
- **Tu as fait tout ça pour Stéphane?!**
  *You did all that for Stéphane?!*
- **J'ai eu une idée géniale.**
  *I had a great idea.*
- **Sandrine a tout préparé.**
  *Sandrine prepared everything.*

### Pointing out things

- **Je t'aide à apporter ces desserts?**
  *Can I help you to carry these desserts?*
- **J'ai acheté cette calculatrice et ces livres.**
  *I bought this calculator and these books.*
- **J'ai acheté ce cadeau pour Stéphane.**
  *I bought this present for Stéphane.*

### Additional vocabulary

- **Ce n'est pas grave.**
  *It's okay./No problem.*
- **Tu ne comprends rien.**
  *You don't understand a thing.*
- **désolé(e)**
  *sorry*
- **discuter**
  *to talk*
- **zut**
  *darn*

---

## ACTIVITÉS

**2  Le bon mot** Choisissez le bon mot entre **ce** (*m.*), **cette** (*f.*) et **ces** (*pl.*) pour compléter les phrases. Attention, les phrases ne sont pas identiques aux dialogues!

1. Je t'aide à apporter __ce__ gâteau?
2. Ce matin, j'ai acheté __ces__ calculatrices et __ce__ livre.
3. Rachid ne comprend pas __cette__ blague.
4. Combien coûtent __ces__ montres?
5. À quelle heure commence __cette__ classe?

**3  Imaginez** Avec un(e) partenaire, imaginez qu'Amina soit (*is*) dans un grand magasin et qu'elle téléphone à Valérie pour l'aider à choisir le cadeau idéal pour Stéphane. Amina propose plusieurs possibilités de cadeaux et Valérie donne son avis (*opinion*) sur chacune d'entre elles (*each of them*).

ressources

CA pp. 87-88

daccord1.vhlcentral.com

*cent quatre-vingt-sept* **187**

---

Video: *Flash culture*

CULTURE À LA LOUPE

# Le carnaval

le roi du carnaval de Nice

**Tous les ans, beaucoup de pays° et de régions francophones célèbrent le carnaval.** Cette tradition est l'occasion de fêter la fin° de l'hiver et l'arrivée° du printemps. En général, la période de fête commence la semaine avant le Carême° et se termine° le jour du Mardi gras. Le carnaval demande très souvent des mois de préparation. La ville organise des défilés° de musique, de masques, de costumes et de chars fleuris°. La fête finit souvent par la crémation du roi° Carnaval, personnage de papier qui représente le carnaval et l'hiver.

Certaines villes et certaines régions sont réputées° pour leur carnaval: Nice, en France, la ville de Québec, au Canada, la Nouvelle-Orléans, aux États-Unis, et la Martinique. Chaque ville a ses traditions particulières. La ville de Nice, lieu du plus grand carnaval français, organise une grande bataille de fleurs° où des jeunes, sur des chars, envoient des milliers° de fleurs aux spectateurs. À Québec, le climat intense transforme le carnaval en une célébration de l'hiver. Le symbole officiel de la fête est le «Bonhomme» (de neige°) et les gens font du ski, de la pêche sous la glace° ou des courses de traîneaux à chiens°. À la Martinique, le carnaval continue jusqu'au° mercredi des Cendres°, à minuit: les gens, tout en noir et blanc°,

le carnaval de Québec

regardent la crémation de Vaval, le roi Carnaval. Le carnaval de la Nouvelle-Orléans est célébré avec de nombreux bals° et défilés costumés. Ses couleurs officielles sont l'or°, le vert° et le violet.

**pays** *countries* **fin** *end* **arrivée** *arrival* **Carême** *Lent* **se termine** *ends* **défilés** *parades* **chars fleuris** *floats decorated with flowers* **roi** *king* **réputées** *famous* **bataille de fleurs** *flower battle* **milliers** *thousands* **«Bonhomme» (de neige)** *snowman* **pêche sous la glace** *ice-fishing* **courses de traîneaux à chiens** *dogsled races* **jusqu'au** *until* **mercredi des Cendres** *Ash Wednesday* **noir et blanc** *black and white* **bals** *balls (dances)* **or** *gold* **vert** *green* **reine** *queen* **a eu lieu** *took place* **pendant** *during*

### Le carnaval en détail

| Martinique | Chaque ville choisit une reine°. |
|---|---|
| Nice | La première bataille de fleurs a eu lieu° en 1876. Chaque année, on envoie entre 80.000 et 100.000 fleurs aux spectateurs. |
| la Nouvelle-Orléans | Il y a plus de 70 défilés pendant° le carnaval. |
| la ville de Québec | Le premier carnaval a eu lieu en 1894. |

**A C T I V I T É S**

**1 Compréhension** Répondez par des phrases complètes.

1. En général, quel est le dernier jour du carnaval?
   En général, le dernier jour du carnaval est le jour du Mardi gras.
2. Dans quelle ville des États-Unis est-ce qu'on célèbre le carnaval?
   On célèbre le carnaval à la Nouvelle-Orléans.
3. Où a lieu le plus grand carnaval français?
   Le plus grand carnaval français a lieu à Nice.
4. Qu'est-ce que les jeunes envoient aux spectateurs du carnaval de Nice?
   Les jeunes envoient des fleurs aux spectateurs.
5. Quel est le symbole officiel du carnaval de Québec?
   Le «Bonhomme» est le symbole officiel du carnaval de Québec.

6. Que fait-on pendant (*during*) le carnaval de Québec?
   On pratique des activités d'hiver pendant le carnaval de Québec.
7. Qu'est-ce qui est différent au carnaval de la Martinique?
   Il continue jusqu'au mercredi des Cendres.
8. Qui est Vaval?
   Vaval est le roi du carnaval à la Martinique.
9. Comment est-ce qu'on célèbre le carnaval à la Nouvelle-Orléans?
   On célèbre le carnaval à la Nouvelle-Orléans avec des bals et des défilés.
10. Quelles sont les couleurs officielles du carnaval de la Nouvelle-Orléans?
    Les couleurs officielles du carnaval de la Nouvelle-Orléans sont l'or, le vert et le violet.

## LE FRANÇAIS QUOTIDIEN

### Les vœux

| | |
|---|---|
| **À votre santé!** | *To your health!* |
| **Bonne année!** | *Happy New Year!* |
| **Bravo! Félicitations!** | *Bravo! Congratulations!* |
| **Joyeuses fêtes!** | *Have a good holiday!* |
| **Meilleurs vœux!** | *Best wishes!* |
| **Santé!** | *Cheers!* |
| **Tous mes vœux de bonheur!** | *All the best!* |

## LE MONDE FRANCOPHONE

### Fêtes et festivals

Voici d'autres fêtes et festivals francophones.

**En Côte d'Ivoire**
**La fête des Ignames (plusieurs dates)** On célèbre la fin° de la récolte° des ignames°, une ressource très importante pour les Ivoiriens.

**Au Maroc**
**La fête du Trône (le 30 juillet)** Tout le pays honore le roi° avec des parades et des spectacles.

**À la Martinique/À la Guadeloupe**
**La fête des Cuisinières (en août)** Les femmes défilent° en costumes traditionnels et présentent des spécialités locales qu'elles ont préparées pour la fête.

**Dans de nombreux pays**
**L'Aïd el-Fitr** C'est la fête musulmane° de la rupture du jeûne° à la fin du Ramadan.

**fin** *end* **récolte** *harvest* **ignames** *yams* **roi** *king* **défilent** *parade* **musulmane** *Muslim* **jeûne** *fast*

## PORTRAIT

# Le 14 juillet

Le 14 juillet 1789, sous le règne° de Louis XVI, les Français se sont rebellés contre° la monarchie et ont pris° la Bastille, une forteresse utilisée comme prison. Cette date est très importante dans l'histoire de France parce qu'elle représente le début de la Révolution. Le 14 juillet symbolise la fondation de la République française et a donc° été sélectionné comme date de la Fête nationale. Tous les ans, il y a un grand défilé° militaire sur les Champs-Élysées, la plus grande° avenue parisienne. Partout° en France, les gens assistent à des défilés et à des fêtes dans les rues°. Le soir, il y a de nombreux bals populaires° où les Français dansent et célèbrent cette date historique. Le soir, on assiste aux feux d'artifices° traditionnels.

**règne** *reign* **se sont rebellés contre** *rebelled against* **ont pris** *stormed* **donc** *therefore* **défilé** *parade* **la plus grande** *the largest* **Partout** *Everywhere* **rues** *streets* **bals populaires** *public dances* **feux d'artifices** *fireworks*

### SUR INTERNET

**Qu'est-ce que c'est, la fête des Rois?** Go to daccord1.vhlcentral.com to find more cultural information related to this **CULTURE** section. Then watch the corresponding **Flash culture.**

---

**2** **Les fêtes** Complétez les phrases.

1. Le 14 juillet 1789 est la date <u>du début de la Révolution française</u>
2. Aujourd'hui, le 14 juillet est la <u>Fête nationale de la République française</u>
3. En France, le soir du 14 juillet, il y a a <u>des bals populaires et des feux d'artifices</u>
4. À plusieurs dates, les Ivoiriens fêtent <u>la fin de la récolte des ignames</u>
5. Au Maroc, il y a un festival au mois de <u>juillet</u>
6. Dans les pays musulmans, l'Aïd el-Fitr célèbre <u>la fin du Ramadan</u>

Practice more at **daccord1.vhlcentral.com.**

**3** **Faisons la fête ensemble!** Vous êtes en vacances dans un pays francophone et vous invitez un(e) ami(e) à aller à une fête ou à un festival francophone avec vous. Expliquez à votre partenaire ce que vous allez faire. Votre partenaire va vous poser des questions.

**ressources**

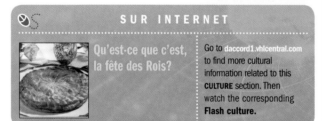

CA pp. 109–110   daccord1.vhlcentral.com

**A C T I V I T É S**

*cent quatre-vingt-neuf* **189**

---

---

# STRUCTURES

## 6A.1 Demonstrative adjectives

**Point de départ** To identify or point out a noun with the French equivalent of *this/these* and *that/those*, use a demonstrative adjective before the noun.

### Demonstrative adjectives

| | singular | | plural |
|---|---|---|---|
| | Before consonant | Before vowel sound | |
| masculine | ce café | cet éclair | ces cafés, ces éclairs |
| feminine | cette surprise | cette amie | ces surprises, ces amies |

**Ce** copain organise une fête.
*This friend is organizing a party.*

**Cet** hôpital est trop loin du centre-ville.
*That hospital is too far from downtown.*

**Cette** glace est excellente.
*This ice cream is excellent.*

Je préfère **ces** cadeaux.
*I prefer those gifts.*

Combien coûte cette montre?

J'ai ce cadeau pour Stéphane.

• Although the forms of **ce** can refer to a noun that is near (*this/these*) and one that is far (*that/those*), the meaning will usually be clear from context.

**Ce** dessert est délicieux.
*This dessert is delicious.*

Joël préfère **cet** éclair.
*Joël prefers that éclair.*

Ils vont aimer **cette** surprise.
*They're going to like this surprise.*

**Ces** glaçons sont pour la limonade.
*Those ice cubes are for the lemon soda.*

La maison Julien

Pour toutes ces occasions...

pour célébrer tout ce bonheur...

nous pensons à tous les détails.

---

**1 Remplacez** Remplacez les noms au singulier par des noms au pluriel et vice versa.

**MODÈLE**

J'aime mieux ce dessert.
*J'aime mieux ces desserts.*

1. Ces glaces au chocolat sont délicieuses.
   Cette glace au chocolat est délicieuse.
2. Ce gâteau est énorme.
   Ces gâteaux sont énormes.
3. Ces biscuits ne sont pas bons.
   Ce biscuit n'est pas bon.
4. Ces invitées sont gentilles.
   Cette invitée est gentille.
5. Ces hôtes parlent japonais.
   Cet hôte parle japonais.
6. Cette fille est allemande.
   Ces filles sont allemandes.

**2 Monsieur Parfait** Avant la fête, l'hôte donne à sa femme son opinion sur les préparations. Complétez ce texte avec ce, cette ou ces.

Mmm! (1) __Cette__ glace est parfaite. Ah! (2) __Ces__ gâteaux sont magnifiques, (3) __ces__ biscuits sont délicieux et j'adore (4) __ces__ chocolats. Bah! (5) __Ces__ bonbons sont originaux, mais pas très bons. Ouvre (*Open*) (6) __cette__ bouteille. (7) __Ce__ café sur (8) __cette__ table sent très bon. (9) __Cette__ plante a besoin d'eau. (10) __Ce__ tableau (*painting*) n'est pas droit (*straight*)! Oh là là! Arrange (11) __ces__ chaises autour de (*around*) (12) __ces__ trois tables!

**3 Magazine** Complétez les phrases.

**MODÈLE**

Ce cheval est très grand.

1. Ce gâteau au chocolat et cette glace sont délicieux.
3. Ces jeunes mariés sont très heureux.

2. Cette fille aime beaucoup ces bonbons.
4. Cet homme est à la retraite.

 Practice more at **daccord1.vhlcentral.com**.

---

---

## COMMUNICATION

**4 Comparez** Avec un(e) partenaire, comparez le contenu (content) à tour de rôle. Answers will vary.

**MODÈLE**

Élève 1: Comment sont ces hommes?
Élève 2: Cet homme-ci est petit et cet homme-là est grand.

l'homme

1. la femme

3. le chien

2. l'automobile (f.)

4. la fille

**5 Préférences** Demandez à votre partenaire ses préférences, puis donnez votre opinion. Employez des adjectifs démonstratifs et présentez vos réponses à la classe. Answers will vary.

**MODÈLE**

Élève 1: Quel film est-ce que tu aimes?
Élève 2: J'aime bien Casablanca.
Élève 1: Moi, je n'aime pas du tout ce vieux film.

| | |
|---|---|
| acteur/actrice | passe-temps |
| chanteur/chanteuse | restaurant |
| dessert | saison |
| film | sport |
| magasin | ville |
| ? | ? |

**6 Invitation** Nathalie est au supermarché avec une amie. Elles organisent une fête, mais elles ne sont pas d'accord sur ce qu'elles vont acheter. Avec un(e) partenaire, jouez les rôles. Answers will vary.

**MODÈLE**

Élève 1: On achète cette glace-ci?
Élève 2: Je n'aime pas cette glace-ci. Je préfère cette glace-là!
Élève 1: Mais cette glace-là coûte dix euros!
Élève 2: D'accord! On prend cette glace-ci.

---

- To make it especially clear that you're referring to something near versus something far, add **-ci** or **-là**, respectively, to the noun following the demonstrative adjective.

**ce** couple-**ci**
*this couple (here)*

**cette** invitée-**là**
*that guest (there)*

**ces** biscuits-**ci**
*these cookies (here)*

**ces** fêtes-**là**
*those parties (there)*

- Use **-ci** and **-là** in the same sentence to contrast similar items.

On prend **cette glace-ci**, pas **cette glace-là**.
*We'll have this ice cream, not that ice cream.*

Tu achètes **ce fromage-ci** ou **ce fromage-là**?
*Are you buying this cheese or that cheese?*

J'aime bien **cette jupe-ci**.
*I like this skirt.*

Je n'aime pas **ces chaussures-là**.
*I don't like those shoes.*

**Essayez!** Complétez les phrases avec la forme correcte de l'adjectif démonstratif.

1. __Cette__ glace au chocolat est très bonne!
2. Qu'est-ce que tu penses de __ce__ cadeau?
3. __Cet__ homme-là est l'hôte de la fête.
4. Tu préfères __ces__ biscuits-ci ou __ces__ biscuits-là?
5. Vous aimez mieux __ce__ dessert-ci ou __ce__ dessert-là?
6. __Cette__ année-ci, on va fêter l'anniversaire de mariage de nos parents en famille.
7. Tu achètes __cet__ éclair-là.
8. Vous achetez __cette__ montre?
9. __Cette__ surprise va être géniale!
10. __Cet__ invité-là est antipathique.

---

**Essayez!** Have students create new sentences orally by changing the singular nouns to the plural or vice versa in items 1–5.

**1 Expansion** For additional practice, give students these items. **7. Ces bonbons sont trop sucrés. 8. Ces vins sont rouges.**

**2 Suggestion** Tell students to underline the nouns that will correspond to the demonstrative adjectives and identify their number and gender before they write the demonstrative adjective.

**3 Suggestion** Before beginning the activity, have students identify in French the items pictured.

**4 Suggestion** Have two volunteers read the **modèle** aloud. Remind students to take turns asking and answering the questions.

**5 Suggestion** Have two volunteers read the **modèle** aloud. Tell students to add at least two items of their own to the list.

**6 Suggestion** Before beginning the activity, have students brainstorm items they might buy for the party and write them on the board.

---

## 6A.2 The *passé composé* with *avoir*

**Point de départ** In order to talk about events in the past, French uses two principal tenses: the **passé composé** and the imperfect. In this lesson, you will learn how to form the **passé composé**, which is used to express actions or states of being completed in the past. You will learn about the imperfect in **Leçon 7B**.

• The **passé composé** of most verbs is formed with a present-tense form of **avoir** (the auxiliary verb) followed by the past participle of the verb expressing the action.

AUXILIARY  PAST
VERB  PARTICIPLE
Nous **avons fêté**.
*We celebrated / have celebrated.*

• The past participle of a regular **-er** verb is formed by replacing the **-er** ending of the infinitive with **-é**.

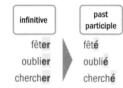

| infinitive | past participle |
|---|---|
| fêt**er** | fêt**é** |
| oubli**er** | oubli**é** |
| cherch**er** | cherch**é** |

• Most regular **-er** verbs are conjugated in the **passé composé** like the verb **parler** shown below.

### The *passé composé*

| | | | |
|---|---|---|---|
| j'ai parlé | *I spoke/have spoken* | nous avons parlé | *we spoke/ have spoken* |
| tu as parlé | *you spoke/ have spoken* | vous avez parlé | *you spoke/ have spoken* |
| il/elle a parlé | *he/she/it spoke/ has spoken* | ils/elles ont parlé | *they spoke/ have spoken* |

• To make a verb negative in the **passé composé**, place **ne/n'** and **pas** around the conjugated form of **avoir**.

On **n'**a **pas** fêté
mon anniversaire.
*We didn't celebrate
my birthday.*

Elles **n'**ont **pas** acheté
de biscuits hier?
*They didn't buy any cookies
yesterday?*

• To ask questions using inversion in the **passé composé**, invert the subject pronoun and the conjugated form of **avoir**.

**Avez-vous** fêté votre
anniversaire?
*Did you celebrate your birthday?*

Est-ce qu'elles **ont acheté**
des biscuits?
*Did they buy any cookies?*

### MISE EN PRATIQUE

**1 Qu'est-ce qu'ils ont fait?** Laurent parle de son week-end en ville avec sa famille. Complétez ses phrases avec le **passé composé** du verbe correct.

1. Nous ___avons mangé___ (nager, manger) des escargots.
2. Papa ___a acheté___ (acheter, apprendre) une nouvelle montre.
3. J'___ai pris___ (prendre, oublier) une glace à la terrasse d'un café.
4. Vous ___avez essayé___ (enseigner, essayer) un nouveau restaurant.
5. Mes parents ___ont célébré___ (dessiner, célébrer) leur anniversaire de mariage.
6. Ils ___ont fait___ (fréquenter, faire) une promenade.
7. Ma sœur ___a bu___ (boire, nettoyer) un chocolat chaud.
8. Le soir, nous ___avons eu___ (écouter, avoir) sommeil.

**2 Pas encore** Un copain pose des questions pénibles. Écrivez ses questions, puis donnez des réponses négatives.

**MODÈLE**

inviter vos amis (vous)
*Vous avez invité vos amis?*
*Non, nous n'avons pas invité nos amis.*

1. écouter mon CD (tu)
Tu as écouté mon CD? Non, je n'ai pas écouté ton CD.
2. faire ses devoirs (Matthieu)
Matthieu a fait ses devoirs? Non, il n'a pas fait ses devoirs.
3. courir dans le parc (elles)
Elles ont couru dans le parc? Non, elles n'ont pas couru dans le parc.
4. parler aux profs (tu)
Tu as parlé aux profs? Non, je n'ai pas parlé aux profs.
5. apprendre les verbes irréguliers (Yassim) Yassim a appris les verbes irréguliers? Non, il n'a pas appris les verbes irréguliers.
6. être à la piscine (Marie et Lise) Marie et Lise ont été à la piscine? Non, elles n'ont pas été à la piscine.
7. emmener André au cinéma (vous) Vous avez emmené André au cinéma? Non, nous n'avons pas emmené André au cinéma.
8. avoir le temps d'étudier (tu) Tu as eu le temps d'étudier? Non, je n'ai pas eu le temps d'étudier.

**3 La semaine** À tour de rôle, assemblez les éléments des colonnes pour raconter (*to tell*) à votre partenaire ce que (*what*) tout le monde (*everyone*) a fait cette semaine. Answers will vary.

| A | B | C |
|---|---|---|
| je | acheter | bonbons |
| Luc | apprendre | café |
| mon prof | boire | l'espagnol |
| Sylvie | faire | famille |
| mes parents | jouer | foot |
| mes copains et moi | manger | glace |
| tu | parler | jogging |
| vous | prendre | promenade |

 Practice more at **daccord1.vhlcentral.com**.

## COMMUNICATION

**4** **Vendredi soir** Vous et votre partenaire avez assisté à une fête vendredi soir. Parlez de la fête à tour de rôle. Qu'est-ce que les invités ont fait? Quelle a été l'occasion? Answers will vary.

**5** **L'été dernier** Vous avez passé l'été dernier avec deux amis, mais vos souvenirs (*memories*) diffèrent. Par groupes de trois, utilisez les expressions de la liste et imaginez le dialogue. Answers will vary.

**MODÈLE**

Élève 1: *Nous avons fait du cheval tous les matins.*
Élève 2: *Mais non! Moi, j'ai fait du cheval. Vous deux, vous avez fait du jogging.*
Élève 3: *Je n'ai pas fait de jogging. J'ai dormi!*

| | | |
|---|---|---|
| acheter | essayer | faire une promenade |
| courir | faire du cheval | |
| dormir | faire du jogging | jouer aux cartes |
| emmener | faire la fête | jouer au foot |
| | | manger |

**6** **Qu'est-ce que tu as fait?** Avec un(e) partenaire, posez-vous les questions à tour de rôle. Ensuite, présentez vos réponses à la classe. Answers will vary.

1. As-tu fait la fête samedi dernier? Où? Avec qui?
2. Est-ce que tu as célébré une occasion importante cette année? Quelle occasion?
3. As-tu organisé une fête? Pour qui?
4. Qui est-ce que tu as invité à ta dernière fête?
5. Qu'est-ce que tu as fait pour fêter ton dernier anniversaire?
6. Est-ce que tu as préparé quelque chose à manger pour une fête ou un dîner? Quoi?

---

● The adverbs **hier** (*yesterday*) and **avant-hier** (*the day before yesterday*) are used often with the **passé composé**.

● Place the adverbs **déjà, encore, bien, mal**, and **beaucoup** between the auxiliary verb or **pas** and the past participle.

Tu as **déjà** mangé ta part de gâteau.
*You already ate your piece of cake.*

Elle n'a pas **encore** visité notre ville.
*She hasn't visited our town yet.*

● The past participle of spelling-change **-er** verbs has no spelling changes.

Laurent a-t-il **acheté** le champagne?
*Did Laurent buy the champagne?*

Vous avez **envoyé** des bonbons.
*You sent candy.*

● The past participle of most **-ir** verbs is formed by replacing the **-ir** ending with **-i**.

Sylvie a **dormi** jusqu'à dix heures.
*Sylvie slept until 10 o'clock.*

On a **senti** leurs regards.
*We felt their stares.*

### Some irregular past participles

| | | | |
|---|---|---|---|
| apprendre | appris | être | été |
| avoir | eu | faire | fait |
| boire | bu | pleuvoir | plu |
| comprendre | compris | prendre | pris |
| courir | couru | surprendre | surpris |

Nous avons **bu** de la limonade.
*We drank lemonade.*

Ils ont **été** très en retard.
*They were very late.*

● The **passé composé** of **il faut** is **il a fallu**; that of **il y a** is **il y a eu**.

**Il a fallu** passer par le supermarché.
*It was necessary to stop by the supermarket.*

**Il y a eu** deux fêtes hier soir.
*There were two parties last night.*

**BOÎTE À OUTILS**
Some verbs, like **aller**, use **être** instead of **avoir** to form the **passé composé**. You will learn more about these verbs in **Leçon 7A**.

### Essayez!  Indiquez les formes du passé composé des verbes.

1. j' _ai commencé, ai payé, ai bavardé_ (commencer, payer, bavarder)
2. tu _as servi, as compris, as donné_ (servir, comprendre, donner)
3. on _a parlé, a eu, a dormi_ (parler, avoir, dormir)
4. nous _avons adoré, avons fait, avons amené_ (adorer, faire, amener)
5. vous _avez pris, avez employé, avez couru_ (prendre, employer, courir)
6. elles _ont espéré, ont bu, ont appris_ (espérer, boire, apprendre)

---

**Essayez!** For additional practice, have students create complete sentences orally or in writing using the subjects and verbs given.

**1 Expansion** Ask follow-up questions about Laurent's weekend. Examples: **1. Qu'est-ce qu'ils ont mangé? 2. Qui a acheté une montre? 3. Qui a pris une glace à la terrasse d'un café? 4. Qu'est-ce que leurs parents ont célébré? 5. Quand est-ce que Laurent et sa famille ont eu sommeil?**

**2 Suggestion** To check answers, have one student ask the question and call on another student to answer it. This activity can also be done in pairs.

**2 Expansion** For additional practice, give students these items. **9. parler à ses parents (Stéphane) 10. boire du café (toi et ton copain)**

**3 Suggestion** Before beginning this activity, call on volunteers to give the past participles of verbs listed.

**4 Suggestion** Before beginning the activity, have students describe what the people are doing in the present tense.

**5 Suggestion** Have three volunteers read the **modèle** aloud. Encourage students to be creative.

**6 Suggestion** Tell students to jot down notes on their partner's responses and to add two of their own questions to the list.

*cent quatre-vingt-treize* **193**

---

**OPTIONS**

**Using Movement** Working in groups of three, have students write three sentences in the **passé composé**, each with a different verb. After they have finished, have each group mime its sentences for the class. When someone guesses the mimed action, the group writes the sentence on the board.

**Writing Practice** For homework, have students write a paragraph about what they did yesterday or last weekend. Then, in class, have them exchange papers with a classmate and peer edit each other's work.

# SYNTHÈSE
# Révision

**Key Standards**
1.1

**Student Resources**
*Cahier d'activités*, pp. 10, 51-52;
Supersite: Activities,
*Cahier interactif*
**Teacher Resources**
Answer Keys; *Feuilles d'activités*;
Info Gap Activities; Testing
Program: Lesson Test (Testing
Program Audio MP3s/CD)

**1 Suggestion** Before beginning this activity, give students a few minutes to jot down some notes about the previous Thanksgiving.

**2 Expansion** Have a few volunteers report the common activities they and their partner did.

**3 Suggestion** Before beginning the activity, have students identify the items on the table.

**4 Suggestion** Distribute the **Feuilles d'activités** found on the Supersite.

**5 Suggestion** Tell students that they can talk about a real or imaginary dinner. Encourage students to be creative.

**6 Suggestion** Divide the class into pairs and distribute the Info Gap Handouts found on the Supersite for this activity. Give students ten minutes to complete the activity.

---

**1 L'année dernière et cette année** Décrivez vos dernières fêtes de Thanksgiving à votre partenaire. Utilisez les verbes de la liste. Parlez aussi de vos projets (*plans*) pour le prochain Thanksgiving. Answers will vary.

**MODÈLE**

**Élève 1:** *L'année dernière, nous avons fêté Thanksgiving chez mes grands-parents. Cette année, je vais manger au restaurant avec mes parents.*

**Élève 2:** *Moi, j'ai fait la fête avec mes amis l'année dernière. Cette année, je vais visiter New York avec ma sœur.*

| aller | donner | fêter | préparer |
|-------|--------|-------|----------|
| acheter | dormir | manger | regarder |
| boire | faire | prendre | téléphoner |

**2 Ce musée, cette ville** Faites par écrit (*Write*) une liste de cinq lieux (villes, musées, restaurants, etc.) que vous avez visités. Avec un(e) partenaire, comparez vos listes. Utilisez des adjectifs démonstratifs dans vos phrases. Answers will vary.

**MODÈLE**

**Élève 1:** *Ah, tu as visité Bruxelles. Moi aussi, j'ai visité cette ville. Elle est belle.*

**Élève 2:** *Tu as mangé au restaurant La Douce France. Je n'aime pas du tout ce restaurant!*

**3 La fête** Vous et votre partenaire avez préparé une fête avec vos amis. Vous avez acheté des cadeaux, des boissons et des snacks. À tour de rôle, parlez de ce qu'il y a sur l'illustration. Answers will vary.

**MODÈLE**

**Élève 1:** *J'aime bien ces biscuits-là.*

**Élève 2:** *Moi, j'ai apporté cette glace-ci.*

**4 Enquête** Qu'est-ce que vos camarades ont fait de différent dans leur vie? Votre professeur va vous donner une feuille d'activités. Parlez à vos camarades pour trouver une personne différente pour chaque expérience, puis écrivez son nom. Answers will vary.

**MODÈLE**

**Élève 1:** *As-tu parlé à un acteur?*

**Élève 2:** *Oui! Une fois, j'ai parlé à Bruce Willis!*

| Expérience | Noms |
|------------|------|
| 1. parler à un(e) acteur/actrice | Julien |
| 2. passer une nuit entière sans dormir | |
| 3. dépenser plus de $100 pour de la musique en une fois | |
| 4. faire la fête un lundi soir | |
| 5. courir cinq kilomètres ou plus | |
| 6. faire une surprise à un(e) ami(e) pour son anniversaire | |

**5 Conversez** Avec un(e) partenaire, imaginez une conversation entre deux ami(e)s qui ont mangé dans un restaurant le week-end dernier. À tour de rôle, racontez: Answers will vary.

- où ils ont mangé
- les thèmes de la conversation
- qui a parlé de quoi
- qui a payé
- la date du prochain dîner

**6 Magali fait la fête** Votre professeur va vous donner, à vous et à votre partenaire, deux feuilles d'activités différentes. Attention! Ne regardez pas la feuille de votre partenaire. Answers will vary.

**MODÈLE**

**Élève 1:** *Magali a parlé avec un homme. Cet homme n'a pas l'air intéressant du tout!*

**Élève 2:** *Après, ...*

**ressources**

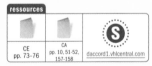

CE
pp. 73-76

CA
pp. 10, 51-52,
157-158

daccord1.vhlcentral.com

---

**OPTIONS**

**Narration** Have students create a continuous narration about a person who had a very bad day. Begin the story by saying: **Hier, Robert a passé une très mauvaise journée.** Call on one student to continue the story by telling how Robert began his day. The second person tells what happened next. Students continue adding sentences until only one student remains. He or she must conclude the story.

**Using Lists** Have students make a "to do" list (**à faire...**) at the beginning of their day. Then, tell students to review their list at the end of the day and write down which activities they completed and which ones they didn't complete. Example: **acheter de la nourriture: Non, je n'ai pas acheté de nourriture.**

 Video: TV Clip

# Le Zapping

## La Poste

La Poste, le service postal belge, distribue tous les jours les cartes de vœux° (et le reste du courrier°) chez ses clients, comme la poste des États-Unis et celle (*the one*) du Canada. Pourtant°, en Belgique, La Poste offre aussi à ses clients une vaste gamme° de services pour la gestion° de leur argent. Par l'intermédiaire de° la Banque de La Poste, les Belges ont la possibilité d'ouvrir° des comptes° chèques et de posséder des cartes de crédit comme avec une banque traditionnelle. Il existe aussi des prêts° variés pour les grandes dépenses, comme des vacances ou même une maison. Tout ça à La Poste!

*Envoyez vos cartes de voeux.*

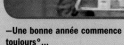

—Une bonne année commence toujours°...

—... par quelqu'un qui vous la souhaite°.

### Compréhension  Répondez aux questions.  Some answers will vary.

1. Qui est l'homme dans la publicité (*ad*)? Comment est son année?
   C'est un jeune père. Il a beaucoup de chance cette année.
2. Que fête-t-il cette année?
   Il fête la naissance de son enfant. Il gagne un match de football et un gros contrat au bureau.
3. Pourquoi l'année commence-t-elle par la fin (*end*)?
   C'est pour indiquer que l'homme a eu de la chance toute l'année, parce que quelqu'un a envoyé une carte de vœux.

### Discussion  Avec un(e) partenaire, répondez aux questions et discutez.  Answers will vary.

1. Quelles sortes d'événements fêtez-vous? Comment?
2. Envoyez-vous des cartes de vœux? Quel effet ont-elles sur le/la destinataire (*recipient*)?

cartes de vœux *greeting cards* courrier *mail* Pourtant *However* gamme *range* gestion *management*
Par l'intermédiaire de *Through* ouvrir *to open* comptes *accounts* prêts *loans*
toujours *always* par quelqu'un qui vous la souhaite *with someone who wishes it for you*

 Practice more at **daccord1.vhlcentral.com.**

*cent quatre-vingt-quinze* **195**

---

## Section Goals

In this section, students will:
• read about **La Poste**, the Belgian postal service
• watch a commercial for **La Poste**
• answer questions about the commercial and **La Poste**

## Key Standards
**1.2, 2.2, 4.2, 5.2**

Student Resources
Supersite: Video, Activities
Teacher Resources
Video Script & Translation;
Supersite: Video

**Introduction**
To check comprehension, ask these questions:
**1. Que fait La Poste belge comme les services postaux d'autres pays? (Elle distribue les cartes de voeux.)**
**2. Qu'offre-t-elle aussi à ses clients? (Elle offre des services pour la gestion de leur argent.)**
**3. Qu'existe-t-il pour les grandes dépenses? (Il existe des prêts variés.)**

**Avant de regarder la vidéo**
• Have students look at the video stills, read the captions, and predict what is happening in the commercial for each visual. **(1. Cet homme fête la naissance de son enfant. C'est le grand bonheur. 2. Il va avoir une très bonne année, parce qu'un ami a envoyé une carte de voeux.)**
• Before showing the video, explain to students that they do not need to understand every word they hear. Tell them to listen for the text in the captions and for any familiar words. They should also look out for scenes depicting this lesson's vocabulary.

**Compréhension** Have students work in pairs or groups for this activity. Tell them to write their answers. Then show the video again so that they can check their answers and add any missing information.

**Discussion** Ask students to share their partner's answers. Keep track of them on the board to determine how many of the same special occasions they celebrate and which one is most common.

---

**O P T I O N S**

**Postal History** Belgium has long played a key role in postal history. In the early sixteenth century, François de Tassis, whose ancestors had operated mail delivery services between Italian city states since the late thirteenth century, was appointed by the Holy Roman Emperor Maximilian I to run the first pan-European postal service. François de Tassis consequently moved his family to Brussels, where the operation was to be headquartered. Mail delivery now covered a vast expanse, from Belgium and the Low Countries to modern-day France and Germany, reaching as far south as Spain and Naples. The logo of the Belgian postal service depicts the horn traditionally blown by mail carriers along the extensive routes to announce the arrival or departure of the mail.

## Section Goals

In this section, students will learn and practice vocabulary related to:
- clothing and accessories
- shopping
- colors

## Key Standards

1.1, 1.2, 4.1

**Student Resources**
*Cahier d'exercices*, pp. 77-78;
*Cahier d'activités*, p. 159;
Supersite: Activities,
*Cahier interactif*

**Teacher Resources**
Answer Keys; Overhead #32;
Audio Script; Textbook &
Audio Activity MP3s/CD;
Testing program: Vocabulary Quiz

## Suggestions

- Use **Overhead #32**. Point out clothing items in the store and describe what the people in the illustration are wearing. Examples: **Cette femme porte une robe. Ce tee-shirt est bon marché.**
- After presenting the new vocabulary, briefly describe what you are wearing.
- Have students name one item of clothing they are wearing today. Then ask: **Que porte ____? De quelle couleur est ____?**
- Point out the difference between **une écharpe** (a heavier scarf or wrap worn in fall or winter) and **un foulard** (a lighter scarf usually worn in spring or summer).
- Tell students that the word **taille** is used to talk about *clothing sizes*. **Pointure** refers to *shoe sizes*.
- Point out the title of this lesson. Tell students that **chic** is an invariable adjective.
- Tell students that the verb **porter** means *to wear* or *to carry*. The verb **mettre** (*to put on*) is presented on page 207.

**Leçon 6B**

**You will learn how to...**
- describe clothing
- offer and accept gifts

**Talking Picture Audio: Activity**

# Très chic!

### Vocabulaire

| | |
|---|---|
| aller avec | to go with |
| un anorak | ski jacket, parka |
| une chaussette | sock |
| une chemise (à manches courtes/longues) | shirt (short-/long-sleeved) |
| un chemisier | blouse |
| un gant | glove |
| un jean | jeans |
| une jupe | skirt |
| un manteau | coat |
| un pantalon | pants |
| un pull | sweater |
| un sous-vêtement | underwear |
| une taille | clothing size |
| un tailleur | (woman's) suit; tailor |
| un tee-shirt | tee shirt |
| un vendeur/une vendeuse | salesman/saleswoman |
| des vêtements (m.) | clothing |
| De quelle couleur...? | In what color...? |
| des soldes (m.) | sales |
| chaque | each |
| large | loose; big |
| serré(e) | tight |

**ressources**

CE pp. 77-78 | CA p. 159 | daccord1.vhlcentral.com

**OPTIONS**

**Using Games** Have students stand. Toss a beanbag to a student at random and say the name of a sport, place, or activity. The person has four seconds to name a clothing item or accessory that goes with it. That person then tosses the beanbag to another student and says a sport, place, or activity. Students who cannot think of an item in time or repeat an item that has already been mentioned are eliminated. The last person standing wins.

**Oral Practice** Review the weather and seasons by asking students what they wear in various circumstances. Examples: **Que portez-vous quand il fait chaud/quand il fait frais/quand il neige/au printemps/en hiver?**

## Attention!

Note that the adjectives **orange** and **marron** are invariable; they do not vary in gender or number to match the noun they modify.

J'aime l'anorak orange.

Il porte des chaussures marron.

**des lunettes (de soleil) (f.)**

**une casquette**

**une écharpe**

**un blouson**

**bon marché**

# Mise en pratique

### 1 Les vêtements Choisissez le mot qui ne va pas avec les autres.

1. des baskets, (une cravate,) une chaussure
2. un jean, un pantalon, (une jupe)
3. un tailleur, un costume, (un short)
4. (des lunettes,) un chemisier, une chemise
5. (un tee-shirt,) un pull, un anorak
6. une casquette, (une ceinture,) un chapeau
7. un sous-vêtement, une chaussette, (un sac à main)
8. une jupe, une robe, (une écharpe)

### 2 Écoutez 🎧 Guillaume prépare ses vacances d'hiver (*winter vacation*). Indiquez quels vêtements il va acheter pour son voyage.

|   |   | Oui | Non |
|---|---|:---:|:---:|
| 1. | des baskets | ☑ | ☐ |
| 2. | un maillot de bain | ☐ | ☑ |
| 3. | des chemises | ☐ | ☑ |
| 4. | un pantalon noir | ☑ | ☐ |
| 5. | un manteau | ☑ | ☐ |
| 6. | un anorak | ☐ | ☑ |
| 7. | un jean | ☑ | ☐ |
| 8. | un short | ☐ | ☑ |
| 9. | un pull | ☐ | ☑ |
| 10. | une robe | ☐ | ☑ |

**Guillaume**

### 3 De quelle couleur? Indiquez de quelle(s) couleur(s) sont ces choses.

**MODÈLE**

l'océan
*Il est bleu.*
la statue de la Liberté
*Elle est verte.*

1. le drapeau français  Il est bleu, blanc et rouge.
2. les dollars américains  Ils sont verts.
3. les pommes (*apples*)  Answers will vary. Elles sont rouges, vertes ou jaunes.
4. le soleil  Il est jaune.
5. la nuit  Elle est noire.
6. le zèbre  Il est blanc et noir.
7. la neige  Elle est blanche.
8. les oranges  Elles sont orange.
9. le café  Il est marron ou noir.
10. les bananes  Elles sont jaunes.

Practice more at **daccord1.vhlcentral.com.**

**1 Expansion**

- For additional practice, give students these items. **9. un sac à main, une ceinture, une robe (une robe) 10. un pull, un gant, un tee-shirt (un gant) 11. un pantalon, un blouson, un anorak (un pantalon) 12. des chaussettes, des baskets, un chapeau (un chapeau)**
- Have students create one or two additional items using at least three new vocabulary words in each one. Collect their papers and write some of the items on the board.

**2 Script** Bonjour! Je m'appelle Guillaume. Je vais aller en Suisse pour mes vacances d'hiver. J'ai besoin d'acheter un manteau parce qu'il va faire froid. J'ai déjà acheté un pull gris. J'ai aussi un bel anorak bleu qui est un peu vieux, mais chaud. Pour faire des randonnées, j'ai besoin d'un jean et de nouvelles baskets. Pour aller en boîte, je vais acheter un pantalon noir qui va aller avec toutes mes chemises: j'ai des chemises de toutes les couleurs, des chemises à manches longues, à manches courtes. Bien sûr, je ne vais pas avoir besoin d'un short parce qu'il ne va pas faire chaud.
*(On Textbook Audio)*

**2 Expansion** Play the recording again. Ask students why Guillaume is not going to buy the items marked **Non**. Example: **Pourquoi Guillaume ne va-t-il pas acheter un maillot de bain? (parce qu'il va faire froid en Suisse)**

**3 Expansion**

- Point out items in the classroom and have students tell what color they are. Examples: **le tableau, ce sac à dos,** and **mon stylo.**
- Have students name items of various colors. Example: **Nommez** (*Name*) **quelque chose de rouge. (le chemisier de ____)**

**OPTIONS**

**Using Movement** Play a game of **Jacques a dit** (*Simon says*). Write **asseyez-vous** and **levez-vous** on the board and model them by sitting and standing as you say them. Start by saying: **Jacques a dit: Si vous portez un jean noir, levez-vous.** Students wearing black jeans stand up and remain standing until further instruction. Work through various items of clothing. Give instructions without saying **Jacques a dit…** once in a while.

**Vacations** Divide the class into small groups. Assign each group a season and a vacation destination. Have groups brainstorm a list of items to pack and write a brief explanation for each item. You might want to have groups write two lists, one for a female traveler and one for a male.

## Communication

**4 Qu'est-ce qu'ils portent?** Avec un(e) camarade de classe, regardez les images et à tour de rôle, décrivez ce que les personnages portent. *Answers will vary.*

**MODÈLE**

*Elle porte un maillot de bain rouge.*

1.                2.                3.                4.

**5 On fait du shopping** Choisissez deux partenaires et préparez une conversation. Deux client(e)s et un vendeur/une vendeuse sont dans un grand magasin; les client(e)s sont invité(e)s à un événement très chic, mais ils ou elles ne veulent pas *(don't want)* dépenser beaucoup d'argent. *Answers will vary.*

**Client(e)s**
- Décrivez l'événement auquel *(to which)* vous êtes invité(e)s.
- Parlez des vêtements que vous cherchez, de vos couleurs préférées, de votre taille. Trouvez-vous le vêtement trop large, trop serré, etc.?
- Demandez les prix et dites si vous trouvez que c'est cher, bon marché, etc.

**Vendeur/Vendeuse**
- Demandez les tailles, préférences, etc. des client(e)s.
- Répondez à toutes les questions de vos client(e)s.
- Suggérez des vêtements appropriés.

> **Coup de main**
>
> To compare French and American sizes, see the chart on p. 202.

**6 Conversez** Interviewez un(e) camarade de classe. *Answers will vary.*
1. Qu'est-ce que tu portes l'hiver? Et l'été?
2. Qu'est-ce que tu portes pour aller au lycée?
3. Qu'est-ce que tu portes pour aller à la plage *(beach)*?
4. Qu'est-ce que tu portes pour faire une randonnée?
5. Qu'est-ce que tu portes pour aller en boîte de nuit?
6. Qu'est-ce que tu portes quand il pleut?
7. Quelle est ta couleur préférée? Pourquoi?
8. Qu'est-ce que tu portes pour aller dans un restaurant très élégant?
9. Où est-ce que tu achètes tes vêtements? Pourquoi?
10. Est-ce que tu prêtes *(lend)* tes vêtements à tes ami(e)s?

**7 Défilé de mode** Votre classe a organisé un défilé de mode *(fashion show)*. Votre partenaire est mannequin *(model)* et vous représentez la marque *(brand)* de vêtements. Pendant que votre partenaire défile, vous décrivez à la classe les vêtements qu'il ou elle porte. Après, échangez les rôles. *Answers will vary.*

**MODÈLE**

*Et voici la charmante Julie, qui porte les modèles de la dernière collection H&M®: une chemise à manches courtes et un pantalon noir, ensemble idéal pour sortir le soir. Ses chaussures blanches vont parfaitement avec l'ensemble. Cette collection H&M est très à la mode et très bon marché.*

**4 Suggestion** Tell students to write their descriptions. Then have volunteers write a description on the board for each picture.

**4 Expansion** Have students describe what they are wearing in detail, including accessories and colors of each item.

**5 Suggestion** Remind students to include greetings and other polite expressions in their role-plays. Have volunteers perform their role-plays for the rest of the class.

**6 Expansion** Take a quick class survey to find out students' clothing preferences. Tally the results on the board.

**7 Suggestion** Have a volunteer read the **modèle** aloud.

**OPTIONS**

**Dream Trip** Have students write a paragraph about a real or imaginary vacation they plan to take and the clothing they will take with them. Tell them to include what kind of weather they expect at their destination and any weather-specific clothing they will need. Ask volunteers to share their paragraphs with the class.

**Writing Practice** Have students write descriptions of an article of clothing or a complete outfit that best describes them without indicating who they are. Collect the papers and read the descriptions aloud. The rest of the class has to guess who wrote each one.

# Les sons et les lettres

 **Audio: Concepts, Activities Record & Compare**

🎧 Open vs. closed vowels: Part 3

The letter combination **eu** can be pronounced two different ways, open and closed. Compare the pronunciation of the vowel sounds in these words.

| cheveux | neveu | heure | meilleur |
|---------|-------|-------|----------|

When **eu** is followed by a pronounced consonant, it has an open sound. The open **eu** sound does not exist in English. To pronounce it, say **è** with your lips only slightly rounded.

| peur | jeune | chanteur | beurre |
|------|-------|----------|--------|

The letter combination **œu** is usually pronounced with an open **eu** sound.

| sœur | bœuf | œuf | chœur |
|------|------|-----|-------|

When **eu** is the last sound of a syllable, it has a closed vowel sound, similar to the vowel sound in the English word *full*. While this exact sound does not exist in English, you can make the closed **eu** sound by saying **é** with your lips rounded.

| deux | bleu | peu | mieux |
|------|------|-----|-------|

When **eu** is followed by a *z* sound, such as a single **s** between two vowels, it is usually pronounced with the closed **eu** sound.

| chanteuse | généreuse | sérieuse | curieuse |
|-----------|-----------|----------|----------|

🔊 **Prononcez** Répétez les mots suivants à voix haute.

1. leur
2. veuve
3. neuf
4. vieux
5. curieux
6. acteur
7. monsieur
8. coiffeuse
9. ordinateur
10. tailleur
11. vendeuse
12. couleur

🔊 **Articulez** Répétez les phrases suivantes à voix haute.

1. Le professeur Heudier a soixante-deux ans.
2. Est-ce que Matthieu est jeune ou vieux?
3. Monsieur Eustache est un chanteur fabuleux.
4. Eugène a les yeux bleus et les cheveux bruns.

🔊 **Dictons** Répétez les dictons à voix haute.

Qui vole un œuf, vole un bœuf.[1]

Les conseillers ne sont pas les payeurs.[2]

[1] He who steals an egg would steal an ox. [2] Those who give advice are not the ones who pay the price.

**ressources**

CA p. 160

daccord1.vhlcentral.com

*cent quatre-vingt-dix-neuf* **199**

**Section Goals**

In this section, students will learn about additional open and closed vowel sounds.

**Key Standards**

4.1

**Student Resources**
*Cahier d'activités*, p. 160; Supersite: Activities, *Cahier interactif*

**Teacher Resources**
Answer Keys; Audio Script; Textbook & Audio Activity MP3s/CD

**Suggestions**

• Model the pronunciation of each open and closed vowel sound. Have students watch the shape of your mouth, then repeat each sound after you. Pronounce each of the example words and have students repeat them.

• Point out that the letters **o** and **e** together are usually written as the single character **œ**.

• Ask students to provide more examples of words from this lesson or previous lessons with these vowel sounds. Examples: **tailleur, vendeuse, ordinateur, feuille,** and **chanteuse.**

• Dictate five familiar words containing the open and closed vowels presented in this section to the class, repeating each one at least two times. Then write them on the board or on a transparency and have students check their spelling.

**Dictons** Ask students to explain the two sayings in their own words.

**OPTIONS**

**Mini-dictée** Use these sentences with open and closed vowel sounds for additional practice or dictation. **1. Elle a deux ordinateurs neufs. 2. Ma sœur est jeune et sérieuse. 3. J'aime mieux être coiffeur ou ingénieur. 4. Tu veux ce vieux tailleur?**

**Tongue Twisters** Teach students these French tongue-twisters that contain the open and closed vowel sounds on this page. **Pépé paie peu, mémé m'émeut. Je veux un feutre bleu.**

# L'anniversaire

 Video: *Roman-photo*
Record & Compare

**PERSONNAGES**

Amina

Astrid

Rachid

Sandrine

Stéphane

Valérie

*Au café...*

**VALÉRIE, SANDRINE, AMINA, ASTRID ET RACHID** Surprise! Joyeux anniversaire, Stéphane!
**STÉPHANE** Alors là, je suis agréablement surpris!
**VALÉRIE** Bon anniversaire, mon chéri!
**SANDRINE** On a organisé cette surprise ensemble...

**VALÉRIE** Pas du tout! C'est Sandrine qui a presque tout préparé.
**SANDRINE** Oh, je n'ai fait que les desserts et ton gâteau d'anniversaire.
**STÉPHANE** Tu es un ange.
**RACHID** Bon anniversaire, Stéphane. Tu sais, à ton âge, il ne faut pas perdre son temps. Alors cette année, tu travailles sérieusement, c'est promis?
**STÉPHANE** Oui, oui.

**AMINA** Rachid a raison. Dix-huit ans, c'est une étape importante dans la vie! Il faut fêter ça.
**ASTRID** Joyeux anniversaire, Stéphane.
**STÉPHANE** Oh, et en plus, vous m'avez apporté des cadeaux!

**AMINA** Oui. J'ai tout fait moi-même: ce tee-shirt, cette jupe et j'ai acheté ces chaussures.
**SANDRINE** Tu es une véritable artiste, Amina! Ta jupe est très originale! J'adore!
**AMINA** J'ai une idée. Tu me prêtes ta robe grise samedi et je te prête ma jupe. D'accord?
**SANDRINE** Bonne idée!

**STÉPHANE** Eh! C'est super cool, ce blouson en cuir noir. Avec des gants en plus! Merci, maman!
**AMINA** Ces gants vont très bien avec le blouson! Très à la mode!
**STÉPHANE** Tu trouves?

**RACHID** Tiens, Stéphane.
**STÉPHANE** Mais qu'est-ce que c'est? Des livres?
**RACHID** Oui, la littérature, c'est important pour la culture générale!
**VALÉRIE** Tu as raison, Rachid.
**STÉPHANE** Euh oui... euh... c'est gentil... euh... merci, Rachid.

**A C T I V I T É S**

**1** **Vrai ou faux?** Indiquez si ces affirmations sont **vraies** ou **fausses**. Corrigez les phrases fausses.

1. David ne veut pas (*doesn't want*) aller à la fête.
   Faux. David est désolé de ne pas être là.
2. Sandrine porte une jupe bleue.
   Faux. Sandrine porte une robe grise.
3. Amina a fait sa jupe elle-même (*herself*).
   Vrai.
4. Le tee-shirt d'Amina est en soie.
   Vrai.
5. Valérie donne un blouson en cuir et une ceinture à Stéphane.
   Faux. Valérie donne un blouson en cuir et des gants à Stéphane.

6. Sandrine n'aime pas partager ses vêtements.
   Faux. Sandrine va prêter sa robe à Amina.
7. Pour Amina, 18 ans, c'est une étape importante.
   Vrai.
8. Sandrine n'a rien fait (*didn't do anything*) pour la fête.
   Faux. Sandrine a fait le gâteau et les desserts.
9. Rachid donne des livres de littérature à Stéphane.
   Vrai.
10. Stéphane pense que ses amis sont drôles.
    Faux. Stéphane pense que ses amis ne sont pas drôles.

 Practice more at **daccord1.vhlcentral.com**.

**200** *deux cents*

**Les amis fêtent l'anniversaire de Stéphane.**

**SANDRINE** Ah au fait, David est désolé de ne pas être là. Ce week-end, il visite Paris avec ses parents. Mais il pense à toi.

**STÉPHANE** Je comprends tout à fait. Les parents de David sont de Washington, n'est-ce pas?

**SANDRINE** Oui, c'est ça.

**AMINA** Merci, Sandrine. Je trouve que tu es très élégante dans cette robe grise! La couleur te va très bien.

**SANDRINE** Vraiment? Et toi, tu es très chic. C'est du coton?

**AMINA** Non, de la soie.

**SANDRINE** Cet ensemble, c'est une de tes créations, n'est-ce pas?

**STÉPHANE** Une calculatrice rose... pour moi?

**ASTRID** Oui, c'est pour t'aider à répondre à toutes les questions en maths, et avec le sourire.

**STÉPHANE** Euh, merci beaucoup! C'est très... utile.

**ASTRID** Attends! Il y a encore un cadeau pour toi...

**STÉPHANE** Ouah, cette montre est géniale, merci!

**ASTRID** Tu as aimé notre petite blague? Nous, on a bien ri.

**RACHID** Eh Stéphane! Tu as vraiment aimé tes livres et ta calculatrice?

**STÉPHANE** Ouais, vous deux, ce que vous êtes drôles.

## Expressions utiles

### Talking about your clothes

- **Et toi, tu es très chic. C'est du coton/de la soie?**
  *And you, you are very chic. Is it cotton/silk?*
- **J'ai tout fait moi-même.**
  *I did/made everything myself.*
- **La couleur te va très bien.**
  *The color suits you well.*
- **Tu es une véritable artiste! Ta jupe est très originale!**
  *You are a true artist! Your skirt is very original!*
- **Tu me prêtes ta robe grise samedi et je te prête ma jupe.**
  *You lend me your gray dress Saturday and I'll lend you my skirt.*
- **C'est super cool, ce blouson en cuir/laine/velours noir(e). Avec des gants en plus!**
  *It's really cool, this black leather/wool/velvet jacket. With gloves as well!*

### Additional vocabulary

- **Vous m'avez apporté des cadeaux!**
  *You brought me gifts!*
- **Tu sais, à ton âge, il ne faut pas perdre son temps.**
  *You know, at your age, one should not waste time.*
- **C'est pour t'aider à répondre à toutes les questions en maths, et avec le sourire.**
  *It's to help you answer all the questions in math, with a smile.*
- **agréablement surpris(e)**
  *pleasantly surprised*
- **C'est promis?**
  *Promise?*
- **Il pense à toi.**
  *He's thinking of you.*
- **tout à fait**
  *absolutely*
- **Vraiment?**
  *Really?*
- **véritable**
  *true, genuine*
- **Pour moi?**
  *For me?*
- **Attends!**
  *Wait!*
- **On a bien ri.**
  *We had a good laugh.*

---

**2 Identifiez** Indiquez qui a dit (*said*) ces phrases: Amina (A), Astrid (As), Rachid (R), Sandrine (S), Stéphane (St) ou Valérie (V).

- _S_ 1. Tu es une véritable artiste.
- _As_ 2. On a bien ri.
- _A_ 3. Très à la mode.
- _St_ 4. Je comprends tout à fait.
- _V_ 5. C'est Sandrine qui a presque tout préparé.
- _R_ 6. C'est promis?

**3 À vous!** Ce sont les soldes. Sandrine, David et Amina vont dans un magasin pour acheter des vêtements. Ils essaient différentes choses, donnent leur avis (*opinion*) et parlent de leurs préférences, des prix et des matières (*fabrics*). Avec un(e) partenaire, écrivez la conversation et jouez la scène devant la classe.

**ressources**

CA pp. 89–90

daccord1.vhlcentral.com

A C T I V I T É S

---

**Expressions utiles**
- Model the pronunciation of the **Expressions utiles** and have students repeat them.
- As you work through the list, point out expressions with indirect object pronouns, disjunctive pronouns, and **-re** verbs. Tell students that these grammar structures will be formally presented in **Structures**.
- Respond briefly to questions about indirect object pronouns and -re verbs. Reinforce correct forms, but do not expect students to produce them consistently at this time.
- Point out that the pronouns **tu**, **te**, and **toi** all mean *you*, but they cannot be used interchangeably because they are different parts of speech.
- To practice different fabrics and other materials, ask students yes/no and either/or questions about their clothing. Examples: _____, votre chemisier, c'est du coton ou de la soie? _____, votre blouson, c'est du cuir ou de la laine? Avez-vous des gants en cuir noir?

**1 Suggestion** Have students write their corrections for false statements on the board.

**1 Expansion** For additional practice, give students these items. **11. Stéphane n'est pas content de la fête. (Faux.) 12. David est à Paris avec ses parents. (Vrai.) 13. Sandrine aime bien la jupe d'Amina. (Vrai.) 14. Stéphane n'aime pas la montre. (Faux.)**

**2 Expansion** In addition to identifying the speaker, have students give the name of the person to whom each one is speaking. **1. Amina 2. Stéphane 3. Stéphane 4. Sandrine 5. Stéphane 6. Stéphane**

**3 Suggestion** Tell students to use an idea map or outline to plan their conversation before they begin to write it.

*deux cent un* **201**

---

**O P T I O N S**

**Using Games** Divide the class into two teams. Give one team member a card with the name of an item of clothing or an accessory. This person has 30 seconds to draw the item and one player on his or her team has to guess what it is. Give a point for each correct answer. If a player cannot guess the item within the time limit, the next player on the opposing team may "steal" the point.

**Magazines** Bring in photos from French fashion magazines or catalogues, such as *3 Suisses* or *La Redoute*, and have students give their opinions about the clothing and accessories.

# CULTURE

## CULTURE À LA LOUPE

# La mode en France

Paris est la capitale de la mode et les maisons de haute couture° françaises, comme Chanel, Yves Saint Laurent, Dior ou Christian Lacroix, sont connues° dans le monde entier°. Pendant° une semaine, en été et en hiver, elles présentent leurs collections à la presse et à un public privilégié, au cours de° défilés de mode°. Les modèles° sont uniques et très chers. Certains couturiers° dessinent° aussi des modèles pour le prêt-à-porter°. Ils vendent° ces collections plus abordables° dans leurs boutiques et parfois dans les grands magasins, comme les Galeries Lafayette ou le Printemps à Paris.

Pour la majorité des Français, la mode est un moyen° d'expression. Beaucoup de jeunes, par exemple, personnalisent leurs vêtements «basiques», ce qu'on appelle «customiser». Les magasins préférés des Français sont les boutiques indépendantes et, pour les jeunes, les chaînes de magasins spécialisés, comme Naf Naf ou Kookaï. Les Français achètent également° des vêtements dans les hypermarchés° et les centres commerciaux, comme Auchan ou Carrefour. Des vêtements sont aussi vendus° sur les marchés aux puces°, et par correspondance, dans des catalogues et sur Internet.

**maisons de haute couture** *high fashion houses* **connues** *known* **monde entier** *entire world* **Pendant** *For* **au cours de** *during* **défilés de mode** *fashion shows* **modèles** *creations (clothing)* **couturiers** *fashion designers* **dessinent** *design* **prêt-à-porter** *ready-to-wear* **vendent** *sell* **plus abordables** *more affordable* **moyen** *means* **également** *also* **hypermarchés** *large supermarkets* **vendus** *sold* **marchés aux puces** *flea markets*

### Coup de main

**Comparaison des tailles**

| FEMMES | | | | | | |
|---|---|---|---|---|---|---|
| France | 32 | 34 | 36 | 38 | 40 | 42 |
| USA | 2 | 4 | 6 | 8 | 10 | 12 |

| HOMMES (PANTALONS) | | | | | | |
|---|---|---|---|---|---|---|
| France | 36 | 38 | 40 | 42 | 44 | 46 |
| USA | 26 | 28 | 30 | 32 | 34 | 36 |

**Évolution des dépenses des Français pour la mode (en % du budget)**

10,0
8,0
6,0
4,0
2,0

1960  1970  1980  1990  2000

SOURCE: Francoscopie

## ACTIVITÉS

**1 Vrai ou faux?** Indiquez si les phrases sont **vraies** ou **fausses**. Corrigez les phrases fausses.

1. Les grands couturiers français dessinent des modèles de haute couture. Vrai.
2. Les défilés de haute couture ont lieu (*take place*) en mai. Faux. Ils ont lieu en été et en hiver.
3. Le prêt-à-porter est plus cher que (*more expensive than*) la haute couture. Faux. La haute couture est plus chère.
4. Les vêtements de prêt-à-porter sont parfois vendus dans les grands magasins. Vrai.

5. Les jeunes Français aiment personnaliser leurs vêtements. Vrai.
6. En France, on vend des vêtements par correspondance. Vrai.
7. Aujourd'hui, les Français dépensent plus (*more*) d'argent pour leurs vêtements qu'en (*than in*) 1980. Faux. Ils dépensent moins d'argent aujourd'hui.
8. Naf Naf est une maison de haute couture française. Faux. Naf Naf est une chaîne de magasins.
9. On vend des vêtements dans les hypermarchés en France. Vrai.
10. Les Français n'achètent pas de vêtements sur Internet. Faux. Ils achètent des vêtements sur Internet.

Practice more at **daccord1.vhlcentral.com**.

## LE FRANÇAIS QUOTIDIEN

### Les vêtements et la mode

| | |
|---|---|
| fringues (*f.*) | *clothes* |
| look (*m.*) | *style* |
| vintage (*m.*) | *vintage clothing* |
| BCBG (bon chic bon genre) | *chic and conservative* |
| ringard(e) | *out-of-style* |
| être bien/ mal sapé(e) | *to be well/ badly dressed* |
| être sur son 31 | *to be well dressed* |

## LE MONDE FRANCOPHONE

### Vêtements et tissus

Voici quelques vêtements et tissus° traditionnels du monde francophone.

**En Afrique centrale et de l'Ouest**
**Le boubou** tunique plus ou moins° longue et souvent très colorée
**Les batiks** tissus traditionnels très colorés

**En Afrique du Nord**
**La djellaba** longue tunique à capuche°
**Le kaftan** sorte de djellaba portée à la maison

**À la Martinique**
**Le madras** tissu typique aux couleurs vives

**À Tahiti**
**Le paréo** morceau° de tissu attaché au-dessus de la poitrine° ou à la taille°

**tissus** *fabrics* **plus ou moins** *more or less* **à capuche** *hooded* **morceau** *piece* **poitrine** *chest* **taille** *waist*

## PORTRAIT

# Coco Chanel, styliste parisienne

«La mode se démode°, le style jamais.» —Coco Chanel

Coco Chanel (1883–1971) est considérée comme étant° l'icône du parfum et de la mode du vingtième siècle°. Dans les années 1910, elle a l'idée audacieuse° d'intégrer la mode «à la garçonne» dans ses créations: les lignes féminines empruntent aux° éléments de la mode masculine. C'est la naissance du fameux tailleur Chanel. Pour «Mademoiselle Chanel», l'important dans la mode, c'est que les vêtements permettent de bouger°; ils doivent° être simples et confortables. Son invention de «la petite robe noire» illustre l'esprit° classique et élégant de ses collections. De nombreuses célébrités ont immortalisé le nom de Chanel: Jacqueline Kennedy avec le tailleur et Marilyn Monroe avec le parfum No. 5, par exemple.

**se démode** *goes out of fashion* **étant** *being* **vingtième siècle** *twentieth century* **idée audacieuse** *daring idea* **empruntent aux** *borrow* **bouger** *move* **doivent** *have to* **esprit** *spirit*

### SUR INTERNET

Combien de couturiers présentent leurs collections dans les défilés de mode, à Paris, chaque hiver?

Go to daccord1.vhlcentral.com to find more cultural information related to this **CULTURE** section.

---

**2 Coco Chanel** Complétez les phrases.

1. Coco Chanel était (*was*) ___styliste de mode___
2. Le style Chanel est inspiré de ___la mode masculine___
3. Les vêtements Chanel sont ___simples et confortables___
4. Jacqueline Kennedy portait souvent des ___tailleurs___ Chanel.
5. D'après «Mademoiselle Chanel», il est très important de pouvoir (*to be able to*) ___bouger___ dans ses vêtements.
6. C'est Coco Chanel qui a inventé ___la petite robe noire___

**3 Le «relookage»** Vous êtes conseiller/conseillère en image (*image counselors*), spécialisé(e) dans le «relookage». Votre nouveau (nouvelle) client(e), une célébrité, vous demande de l'aider à sélectionner un nouveau style. Discutez de ce nouveau look avec un(e) partenaire.

**ressources**
Ⓢ
daccord1.vhlcentral.com

**A C T I V I T É S**

---

---

## Section Goals

In this section, students will learn:
- indirect object pronouns
- some additional uses of disjunctive pronouns

## Key Standards

**4.1, 5.1**

**Student Resources**
*Cahier d'exercices*, pp. 79-80;
*Cahier d'activités*, p. 161;
Supersite: Activities,
*Cahier interactif*

**Teacher Resources**
Answer Keys; Audio Script;
Audio Activity MP3s/CD;
Testing program: Grammar Quiz

## Suggestions

- Say and write on the board: **Valérie achète un blouson à Stéphane.** Tell students that an indirect object is a noun or pronoun that answers the question *to whom* or *for whom* an action is done. Ask them what the indirect object of the verb is in the sentence. (Stéphane) Explain that indirect object nouns are introduced by the preposition **à.** Point out that **un blouson** is the direct object of the verb.
- Write the indirect object pronouns on the board. Show students some photos and say: **Je vous montre mes photos.** Give a student an object, such as a book, and say: **Je vous prête mon livre.** Continue the same procedure with the remaining indirect object pronouns.
- Emphasize that, in French, indirect object pronouns do not follow verbs as they do in English.
- Ask students to call out the disjunctive pronouns. Explain the use of **-même(s)** and provide a few examples. Then have students create some sentences with the disjunctive pronouns.

---

**Leçon 6B**

# 6B.1 Indirect object pronouns

- An indirect object expresses *to whom* or *for whom* an action is done. In the example below, the indirect object answers this question: **À qui parle Claire?** (*To whom does Claire speak?*)

SUBJECT    VERB    INDIRECT OBJECT NOUN

**Claire parle à sa mère.**
*Claire speaks to her mother.*

| Indirect object pronouns | | | | | |
|---|---|---|---|---|---|
| **singular** | | | **plural** | | |
| me | te | lui | nous | vous | leur |

- Indirect object pronouns replace indirect object nouns.

Claire parle à **sa mère**.
*Claire speaks to her mother.*

J'envoie des cadeaux à **mes nièces**.
*I send gifts to my nieces.*

Claire **lui** parle.
*Claire speaks to her.*

Je **leur** envoie des cadeaux.
*I send them gifts.*

Vous m'avez apporté des cadeaux!

Je te prête ma jupe. D'accord?

- The indirect object pronoun usually precedes the conjugated verb.

Antoine, je **te** parle.
*Antoine, I'm speaking to you.*

Notre père **nous** a envoyé un e-mail.
*Our father sent us an e-mail.*

- In a negative statement, place the indirect object pronoun between **ne** and the conjugated verb.

Antoine, je **ne te parle** pas de ça.
*Antoine, I'm not speaking to you about that.*

Notre père **ne nous a** pas envoyé d'e-mail.
*Our father didn't send us an e-mail.*

- When an infinitive follows a conjugated verb, the indirect object pronoun precedes the infinitive.

Nous allons **lui donner** la cravate.
*We're going to give him the tie.*

Ils espèrent **vous prêter** le costume.
*They hope to lend you the suit.*

---

**MISE EN PRATIQUE**

**1** **Complétez** Corinne fait du shopping avec sa copine Célia. Trouvez le bon pronom d'objet indirect pour compléter ses phrases.

1. Je __leur__ achète des baskets. (à mes cousins)
2. Je __te__ prends une ceinture. (à toi, Célia)
3. Nous __lui__ achetons une jupe. (à notre copine Christelle)
4. Célia __nous__ prend des lunettes de soleil. (à ma mère et à moi)
5. Je __vous__ achète des gants. (à ta mère et à toi, Célia)
6. Célia __m'__ achète un pantalon. (à moi)

**2** **Dialogues** Complétez les dialogues.

1. **M. SAUNIER** Tu m'as posé une question, chérie?
   **MME SAUNIER** Oui. Je __t'__ ai demandé l'heure.
2. **CLIENT** Je cherche un beau pull.
   **VENDEUSE** Je vais __vous__ montrer ce pull noir.
3. **PROF 1** Mes élèves ont passé l'examen.
   **PROF 2** Tu __leur__ envoies les résultats?
4. **MÈRE** Qu'est-ce que vous allez faire?
   **ENFANTS** On va aller au cinéma. Tu __nous__ donnes de l'argent?
5. **PIERRE** Tu __me__ téléphones ce soir?
   **CHARLOTTE** D'accord. Je te téléphone.
6. **GÉRARD** Christophe a oublié son pull. Il a froid!
   **VALENTIN** Je __lui__ prête mon blouson.

**3** **Assemblez** Avec un(e) partenaire, assemblez les éléments des colonnes pour comparer vos familles et vos amis. Answers will vary.

**MODÈLE**

**Élève 1:** *Mon père me prête souvent ses pulls.*
**Élève 2:** *Mon père, lui, nous prête de l'argent.*

| A | B | C |
|---|---|---|
| je | acheter | argent |
| tu | apporter | biscuits |
| mon père | envoyer | cadeaux |
| ma mère | expliquer | devoirs |
| mon frère | faire | e-mails |
| ma sœur | montrer | problèmes |
| mon/ma | parler | vêtements |
| petit(e) ami(e) | payer | voiture |
| mes copains | prêter | |

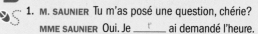
Practice more at **daccord1.vhlcentral.com.**

---

**Indirect Objects** Write sentences with indirect objects on the board. Examples: **Anne-Laure ne te donne pas de biscuits. Pierre ne me parle pas. Loïc prête de l'argent à Louise. Marie nous pose une question. Je téléphone à mes amis.** Have students come to the board and circle the indirect objects.

**Oral Practice** Working in groups of three, the first student lends an object to the second and says: **Je te prête mon/ma….** The second student responds: **Tu me prêtes ton/ta….** The third student says: **Marc lui prête son/sa….** Groups repeat the procedure until everyone has begun the chain twice. To practice plural pronouns, have two groups get together. Then two students lend something to two other students.

## COMMUNICATION

**4**  **Qu'allez-vous faire?** Avec un(e) partenaire, dites ce que vous allez faire pour aider ces personnes. Employez les verbes de la liste et présentez vos réponses à la classe. Answers will vary.

**MODÈLE**

Un ami a soif.
*On va lui donner de l'eau.*

| apporter | parler |
|----------|--------|
| demander | poser des questions |
| donner | préparer |
| envoyer | prêter |
| faire | téléphoner |

1. Une personne âgée (*old*) a froid.
2. Des touristes sont perdus (*lost*).
3. Un homme est sans abri (*homeless*).
4. Votre professeur est à l'hôpital.
5. Des amis vous invitent à manger chez eux.
6. Vos nièces ont faim.
7. Votre petit(e) ami(e) fête son anniversaire.
8. Votre meilleur(e) (*best*) ami(e) a des problèmes.

**5**  **Les cadeaux de l'année dernière** Par groupes de trois, parlez des cadeaux que vous avez achetés à votre famille et à vos amis l'année dernière. Que vous ont-ils acheté? Présentez vos réponses à la classe.
Answers will vary.

**MODÈLE**

**Élève 1:** *Qu'est-ce que tu as acheté à ta mère?*
**Élève 2:** *Je lui ai acheté un ordinateur.*
**Élève 3:** *Ma copine Dominique m'a acheté une montre.*

**6**  **Au grand magasin** Par groupes de trois, jouez les rôles de deux client(e)s et d'un(e) vendeur/vendeuse. Les client(e)s cherchent des vêtements pour faire des cadeaux. Ils parlent de ce qu'ils (*what they*) cherchent et le/la vendeur/vendeuse leur fait des suggestions.
Answers will vary.

### Verbs used with indirect object pronouns

| demander à | to ask, to request | parler à | to speak to |
|------------|--------------------|----------|-------------|
| donner à | to give to | poser une question à | to pose/ ask a question (to) |
| envoyer à | to send to | prêter à | to lend to |
| montrer à | to show to | téléphoner à | to phone, to call |

● The indirect object pronouns **me** and **te** become **m'** and **t'** before a verb beginning with a vowel sound.

Ton petit ami **t'envoie** des fleurs.
*Your boyfriend sends you flowers.*

Isabelle **m'a** prêté son sac à main.
*Isabelle lent me her handbag.*

### Disjunctive pronouns

**BOÎTE À OUTILS**
In Leçon 3B, you learned to use disjunctive pronouns (**moi, toi, lui, elle, nous, vous, eux, elles**) after prepositions: **J'ai une écharpe pour ton frère/ pour lui.** (*I have a scarf for your brother/for him.*)

● Disjunctive pronouns can also be used alone or in phrases without a verb.

Qui prend du café?     **Moi**!     **Eux** aussi?
*Who's having coffee?*   *Me!*   *Them, too?*

● Disjunctive pronouns emphasize the person to whom they refer.

**Moi**, je porte souvent une casquette.
*Me, I often wear a cap.*

Mon frère, **lui**, déteste les casquettes.
*My brother, on the other hand, hates caps.*

● To say *myself*, *ourselves*, etc., add **-même(s)** after the disjunctive pronoun.

Tu fais ça **toi-même**?
*Are you doing that yourself?*

Ils organisent la fête **eux-mêmes**.
*They're organizing the party themselves.*

**Essayez!**  Complétez les phrases avec le pronom d'objet indirect approprié.

1. Tu ___nous___ montres tes photos? (*us*)
2. Luc, je __te__ donne ma nouvelle adresse. (*you, fam.*)
3. Vous __me__ posez de bonnes questions. (*me*)
4. Nous __leur__ avons demandé. (*them*)
5. On __vous__ achète une nouvelle robe. (*you, form.*)
6. Ses parents __lui__ ont acheté un tailleur. (*her*)
7. Je vais __lui__ téléphoner à dix heures. (*him*)
8. Elle va __me__ prêter sa jupe. (*me*)

**Essayez!** Have students restate items 1, 2, 4, 5, and 6 using the **futur proche**. Example: **1. Tu vas nous montrer tes photos?**

**1** Expansion  Have students write four more sentences with indirect objects (not pronouns). Tell them to exchange papers with a classmate and rewrite the sentences, replacing the indirect object with the corresponding indirect object pronoun.

**2** Suggestion  To check students' answers, have volunteers read different roles aloud.

**3** Expansion  Have students convert three of their statements into questions for their partner, using **Qui…?** or **À qui…?** Example: **Qui te prête ses livres?**

**4** Suggestion  Have pairs write their suggestions. Encourage them to come up with multiple responses for each item.

**5** Suggestion  Before beginning the activity, give students a few minutes to jot down a list of gifts they bought for their family last year. Then have three volunteers read the **modèle** aloud.

**6** Suggestions
● Before beginning the activity, have students describe what is happening in the photo.
● Videotape the scenes in class or have students videotape themselves outside of class. Show the videos so students can critique their role-plays.

**OPTIONS**

**Using Video** Have students read along as you show the video episode again. Tell them to note each time an indirect object pronoun or a disjunctive pronoun is used. After the video, ask them to read the sentences they identified and to say to whom each pronoun refers.

**Interview** Have students work in pairs. Tell them to write five questions they would like to ask their partner that require an indirect object pronoun in the answer. They should then take turns asking and answering each other's questions.

**Leçon 6B**

## Section Goals

In this section, students will learn:
- regular **-re** verbs
- irregular **-re** verbs

## Key Standards

4.1, 5.1

**Student Resources**
*Cahier d'exercices*, pp. 81-82;
*Cahier d'activités*, pp. 53-54, 162;
Supersite: Activities,
*Cahier interactif*

**Teacher Resources**
Answer Keys; Audio Script;
Audio Activity MP3s/CD;
Info Gap Activities; Testing
program: Grammar Quiz

## Suggestions

- Model the pronunciation of the **-re** verbs and have students repeat them.
- Introduce the verbs by talking about yourself and asking students follow-up questions. Examples: **Je réponds à tous mes e-mails. Et vous, répondez-vous à tous vos e-mails? D'habitude, je mets un pantalon. Aujourd'hui, j'ai mis une jupe/un costume. Et vous, que mettez-vous, en général? Je rends visite à ma grand-mère le week-end. Rendez-vous visite à vos grands-parents le week-end?**
- Ask a volunteer to go to the board and write the conjugation of **donner** as you write the conjugation of **attendre**. Have students compare the endings of the two verb conjugations, noting the similarities and differences.
- Follow the same procedure with the conjugations of **conduire** and **mettre**. Point out that many irregular **-re** verbs have two stems. Examples: **conduire (condui-, conduis-)** and **mettre (met-, mett-)**.
- Explain that the past participles of regular **-re** verbs add **-u** to the stem. Example: **attendre: attendu**. Then say the verbs listed and have students respond with the past participles.
- Point out the irregular past participles.

### 6B.2 Regular and irregular -re verbs

**Point de départ** You've already seen infinitives that end in **-er** and **-ir**. The infinitive forms of some French verbs end in **-re**.

- Many **-re** verbs, such as **attendre** (*to wait*), follow a regular pattern of conjugation, as shown below.

| Attendre | |
|---|---|
| j'**attends** | nous **attendons** |
| tu **attends** | vous **attendez** |
| il/elle **attend** | ils/elles **attendent** |

Tu **attends** les soldes?
*Are you waiting for the sales?*

Nous **attendons** dans le magasin.
*We're waiting in the store.*

| Other regular -re verbs | | | |
|---|---|---|---|
| descendre (de) | to go downstairs; to get off; to take down | rendre (à) | to give back, to return (to) |
| | | rendre visite (à) | to visit someone |
| entendre | to hear | répondre (à) | to respond, to answer (to) |
| perdre (son temps) | to lose (to waste one's time) | vendre | to sell |

- The verb **attendre** means *to wait* or *to wait for*. Unlike English, it does not require a preposition.

Marc **attend** le bus.
*Marc is waiting for the bus.*

Ils **attendent** Robert.
*They're waiting for Robert.*

- To form the past participle of regular **-re** verbs, drop the **-re** from the infinitive and add **-u**.

Les étudiants ont **vendu** leurs livres.
*The students sold their books.*

Il a **entendu** arriver la voiture de sa femme.
*He heard his wife's car arrive.*

J'ai **répondu** à ton e-mail.
*I answered your e-mail.*

Nous avons **perdu** patience.
*We lost patience.*

- **Rendre visite à** means *to visit a person*, while **visiter** means *to visit a place*.

Tu **rends visite à** ta grand-mère le lundi.
*You visit your grandmother on Mondays.*

Cécile va **visiter** le musée aujourd'hui.
*Cécile is going to visit the museum today.*

**1** **Qui fait quoi?** Quelles phrases vont avec les illustrations?

1.        3.

2.        4.

   3    a. Martin attend ses copains.

   4    b. Nous rendons visite à notre grand-mère.

   1    c. Tu vends de jolis vêtements.

   2    d. Je ris en regardant un film.

**2** **Les clients difficiles** Florian et Vincent travaillent dans un grand magasin. Complétez leur conversation.

**VINCENT** Tu n'as pas encore mangé?

**FLORIAN** Non, j' (1) ___attends___ (attendre) Jérémy.

**VINCENT** Il ne (2) ___descend___ (descendre) pas tout de suite. Il (3) ___perd___ (perdre) son temps avec un client difficile. Il (4) ___met___ (mettre) des cravates, des costumes, des chaussures...

**FLORIAN** Nous ne (5) ___vendons___ (vendre) pas souvent à des clients comme ça.

**VINCENT** C'est vrai. Ils (6) ___promettent___ (promettre) d'acheter quelque chose, puis ils partent les mains vides (*empty*).

**3** **La journée de Béatrice** Hier, Béatrice a fait une liste des choses à faire. Avec un(e) partenaire, utilisez les verbes de la liste au passé composé pour dire (*to say*) tout ce qu'elle a fait. *Answers will vary.*

| attendre | mettre |
|---|---|
| conduire | rendre visite |
| entendre | traduire |

1. *devoir d'espagnol*     4. *tante Albertine*
2. *mon nouveau CD*     5. *gants dans mon sac*
3. *e-mail de Sébastien*     6. *vieille voiture (car)*

Practice more at **daccord1.vhlcentral.com**.

---

**O P T I O N S**

**Oral Practice** Do a rapid-response drill. Write an infinitive from the list of **-re** verbs on the board. Call out subject pronouns and/or names, and have students respond with the correct verb form. Then repeat the drill, having students respond with the correct forms of the **passé composé**.

**Making Lists** Have students make a list of five things their parents allow them to do and five things their parents don't allow them to do. Then have them get together in pairs and compare their lists. Have volunteers report to the class the items they have in common. Example: **Mes parents ne me permettent pas de mettre des vêtements trop serrés. Ils me permettent parfois de conduire leur voiture.**

## COMMUNICATION

**4 Fréquence** Employez les verbes de la liste et d'autres verbes pour dire (*to tell*) à un(e) partenaire ce que (*what*) vous faites tous les jours, une fois par mois et une fois par an. Alternez les rôles. Answers will vary.

**MODÈLE**

**Élève 1:** *J'attends mes copains à la cantine tous les jours.*
**Élève 2:** *Moi, je rends visite à mes grands-parents une fois par mois.*

| | |
|---|---|
| attendre | perdre |
| conduire | rendre |
| entendre | répondre |
| mettre | sourire |
| ? | ? |

**5 La journée des vendeuses** Votre professeur va vous donner, à vous et à votre partenaire, une série d'illustrations qui montrent la journée d'Aude et d'Aurélie. Attention! Ne regardez pas la feuille de votre partenaire. Answers will vary.

**MODÈLE**

**Élève 1:** *Le matin, elles ont conduit pour aller au magasin.*
**Élève 2:** *Après, ...*

**6 Les charades** Par groupes de quatre, jouez aux charades. Chaque élève pense à une phrase différente avec un des verbes en **-re**. La première personne qui devine (*guesses*) propose la charade suivante. Answers will vary.

• Some verbs whose infinitives end in **-re** are irregular.

### Irregular -re verbs

| | conduire (to drive) | mettre (to put (on)) | rire (to laugh) |
|---|---|---|---|
| je | conduis | mets | ris |
| tu | conduis | mets | ris |
| il/elle | conduit | met | rit |
| nous | conduisons | mettons | rions |
| vous | conduisez | mettez | riez |
| ils/elles | conduisent | mettent | rient |

Je **conduis** bien. | Il **met** ses gants. | Elles **rient** toujours.
*I drive well.* | *He puts on his gloves.* | *They always laugh.*

### Other irregular -re verbs

like *conduire*

| | |
|---|---|
| construire | to build, to construct |
| détruire | to destroy |
| produire | to produce |
| réduire | to reduce |
| traduire | to translate |

like *mettre*

| | |
|---|---|
| permettre | to allow |
| promettre | to promise |

like *rire*

| | |
|---|---|
| sourire | to smile |

• The past participle of the verb **mettre** is **mis**. Verbs derived from **mettre** (**permettre, promettre**) follow the same pattern: **permis, promis**.

• The past participle of **conduire** is **conduit**. Verbs like it follow the same pattern: **construire → construit; détruire → détruit; produire → produit; réduire → réduit; traduire → traduit.**

• The past participle of **rire** is **ri**. The past participle of **sourire** is **souri**.

• Like for the other verb groups, use present tense verb forms to give commands.

**Conduis** moins vite! | **Promettez**-moi. | **Réponds**-lui.
*Drive more slowly!* | *Promise me.* | *Answer him.*

**Essayez!** Complétez les phrases avec la forme correcte du présent du verbe.

1. Ils _attendent_ (attendre) l'arrivée du train.
2. Nous _répondons_ (répondre) aux questions du professeur.
3. Je _souris_ (sourire) quand je suis heureuse.
4. Si on _construit_ (construire) trop, on _détruit_ (détruire) la nature.
5. Quand il fait froid, vous _mettez_ (mettre) un pull.
6. Est-ce que les élèves _entendent_ (entendre) le professeur?

**Essayez!** For additional practice, change the subjects of the sentences and have students restate them.

**1 Expansion** Have students create short descriptions of the people, places, and objects in the drawings by putting in additional information.

**2 Expansion** Ask students comprehension questions about the dialogue. Examples: **1. Pourquoi Henri n'a-t-il pas encore mangé? (Il attend Jean-Michel.) 2. Où est Jean-Michel? (Il est avec un client difficile.) 3. Pourquoi ce client est-il difficile? (parce qu'il met tout, mais il part les mains vides)**

**3 Expansion** Have students also say what Béatrice did not do.

**4 Suggestion** Have two volunteers read the **modèle** aloud.

**4 Expansion** To practice the **passé composé**, have students specify when they did these things. Example: **J'ai rendu visite à mes grands-parents en avril.**

**5 Suggestion** Divide the class into pairs and distribute the Info Gap Handouts found on the Supersite for this activity.

**6 Suggestion** This activity can also be used as a game by dividing the class into two teams with players from each team acting out the charades.

**OPTIONS**

**Questions** Ask students personalized questions using **-re** verbs. Examples: **1. Comment les élèves perdent-ils leur temps? 2. Est-ce que l'argent rend les gens heureux? 3. Que vend-on dans une boutique? 4. Vos parents vous permettent-ils d'avoir une carte de crédit? 5. Répondez-vous toujours à vos e-mails? 6. Où mettez-vous vos livres en classe?**

**Writing Practice** Have students work in pairs. Tell them to write a conversation between a clerk in a clothing store and a customer who has lost some item like sunglasses, a scarf, or gloves. The customer should explain the situation, and the clerk should ask for details, such as when the item was lost and a description. Alternatively, pairs can role-play this situation.

# SYNTHÈSE
# Révision

## Key Standards
**1.1**

**Student Resources**
*Cahier d'activités*, pp. 55-56;
Supersite: Activities,
*Cahier interactif*
**Teacher Resources**
Answer Keys; Info Gap Activities;
Testing Program: Lesson Test
(Testing Program Audio MP3s/CD)

**1 Suggestion** Have two volunteers read the **modèle** aloud. Remind students that they need to use the preposition **à** before the indirect object in the questions.

**2 Expansion** Take a quick class survey of students' reactions to each type of e-mail. Tally the results on the board.

**3 Suggestion** Before beginning the activity, have students jot down a list of clothes and accessories.

**4 Suggestion** Before beginning, have the class identify the items in each **ensemble**.

**4 Expansion** Have students think of two new destinations. Tell them to switch roles and repeat the activity.

**5 Suggestion** Encourage students to use some of the comments in the **Expressions utiles** on page 201 in their role-plays.

**6 Suggestion** Divide the class into pairs and distribute the Info Gap Handouts found on the Supersite for this activity.

---

**1 Je leur téléphone** Par groupes de quatre, interviewez vos camarades. Préparez dix questions avec un verbe et une personne de la liste. Écrivez les réponses. Answers will vary.

**MODÈLE**

**Élève 1:** *Est-ce que tu parles souvent à tes cousines?*
**Élève 2:** *Oui, je leur parle toutes les semaines.*

| verbes | personnes |
|---|---|
| donner un cadeau | copain ou copine d'enfance |
| envoyer une carte/un e-mail | cousin ou cousine |
| parler | grands-parents |
| rendre visite | petit(e) ami(e) |
| téléphoner | sœur ou frère |

**2 Mes e-mails** Ces personnes vous envoient des e-mails. Que faites-vous? Vous ne répondez pas, vous attendez quelques jours, vous leur téléphonez? Par groupes de trois, comparez vos réactions. Answers will vary.

**MODÈLE**

**Élève 1:** *Ma sœur m'envoie un e-mail tous les jours.*
**Élève 2:** *Tu lui réponds tout de suite?*
**Élève 3:** *Tu préfères ne pas lui répondre?*

1. un e-mail anonyme
2. un e-mail d'un(e) camarade de classe
3. un e-mail d'un professeur
4. un e-mail d'un(e) ami(e) d'enfance
5. un e-mail d'un(e) ex-petit(e) ami(e)
6. un e-mail de vos parents

**3 Une liste** Des membres de votre famille ou des amis vous ont donné ou acheté des vêtements que vous n'aimez pas du tout. Faites une liste de quatre ou cinq de ces vêtements. Comparez votre liste à la liste d'un(e) camarade. Answers will vary.

**MODÈLE**

**Élève 1:** *Ma sœur m'a donné une écharpe verte et laide et mon père m'a acheté des chaussettes marron trop petites!*
**Élève 2:** *L'année dernière, mon petit ami m'a donné...*

---

**4 Quoi mettre?** Vous et votre partenaire allez faire des choses différentes. Un(e) partenaire va fêter la retraite de ses grands-parents à Tahiti. L'autre va skier dans les Alpes. Qu'allez-vous porter? Demandez des vêtements à votre partenaire si vous n'aimez pas tous les vêtements de votre ensemble. Answers will vary.

**MODÈLE**

**Élève 1:** *Est-ce que tu me prêtes ton tee-shirt violet?*
**Élève 2:** *Ah non, j'ai besoin de ce tee-shirt. Tu me prêtes ton pantalon?*

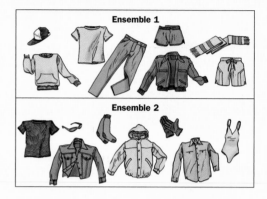

Ensemble 1

Ensemble 2

**5 S'il te plaît** Votre ami(e) a acheté un nouveau vêtement que vous aimez beaucoup. Vous essayez de convaincre (*to convince*) cet(te) ami(e) de vous prêter ce vêtement. Préparez un dialogue avec un(e) partenaire où vous employez tous les verbes. Jouez la scène pour la classe. Answers will vary.

| | |
|---|---|
| aller avec | montrer |
| aller bien | prêter |
| donner | promettre |
| mettre | rendre |

**6 Bon anniversaire, Nicolas!** Votre professeur va vous donner, à vous et à votre partenaire, deux feuilles d'activités différentes. Attention! Ne regardez pas la feuille de votre partenaire. Answers will vary.

**MODÈLE**

**Élève 1:** *Les amis de Nicolas lui téléphonent.*
**Élève 2:** *Ensuite, ...*

**ressources**

| CE pp. 79-82 | CA pp. 53-56, 161-162 | **S** daccord1.vhlcentral.com |
|---|---|---|

---

**O P T I O N S**

**Commercial** Have students work in groups of three. Tell them to imagine that it is the holiday season. They have to create a radio commercial for a clothing store. The commercials should include gift ideas for prospective customers, such as what they can buy, for whom, and at what price.

**Conversation** Have students write a conversation between two people sitting at a busy sidewalk café in the city. They are watching the people who walk by, asking each other questions about what the passersby are doing, and making comments about their clothing. Tell students to use as many **-re** verbs and verbs that take indirect object pronouns as possible.

# À l'écoute

 **Audio: Activities**

**Section Goals**

In this section, students will:
• learn to listen for specific linguistic cues
• listen for temporal cues in sentences
• listen to a conversation and complete several activities

**Key Standards**

1.2, 2.1

**Student Resources**
Supersite: Activities, Audio
**Teacher Resources**
Answer Keys; Audio Script; Audio Activity MP3s/CD

## STRATÉGIE

### Listening for linguistic cues

You can enhance your listening comprehension by listening for specific linguistic cues. For example, if you listen for the endings of conjugated verbs, or for familiar constructions, such as the **passé composé** with **avoir**, **avoir envie de** + [*infinitive*] or **aller** + [*infinitive*], you can find out whether a person did something in the past, wants to do something, or will do something in the future.

🎧 To practice listening for linguistic cues, you will listen to four sentences. As you listen, note whether each sentence refers to a past, present, or future action.

## Préparation

Regardez la photo. Où sont Pauline et Sarah? Que font-elles? Décrivez les vêtements qu'elles regardent. À votre avis, pour quelle occasion cherchent-elles des vêtements?

## 🎧 À vous d'écouter 🎧

Écoutez la conversation entre Pauline et Sarah. Après une deuxième écoute, indiquez si les actions suivantes sont du **passé (p)**, du **présent (pr)** ou du **futur (f)**.

_p_ 1. aller à la fête de la cousine de Pauline

_p_ 2. beaucoup danser

_p_ 3. rencontrer un musicien

_f_ 4. déjeuner avec un garçon intéressant

_pr_ 5. chercher de nouveaux vêtements

_f_ 6. mettre des chaussures en cuir noir

_pr_ 7. aimer une robe bleue

_f_ 8. acheter la robe bleue

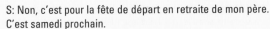 Practice more at **daccord1.vhlcentral.com**.

## Compréhension

**Complétez** Complétez les phrases.

1. Pauline cherche des vêtements pour _c_.
   a. un dîner   b. une fête   c. un rendez-vous

2. Pauline va acheter un pantalon noir et _b_.
   a. un tee-shirt   b. une chemise rose   c. un maillot de bain

3. Sarah pense que _b_ ne vont pas avec les nouveaux vêtements.
   a. l'écharpe verte   b. les baskets roses   c. les lunettes de soleil

4. D'après Sarah, les chaussures _a_ sont élégantes.
   a. en cuir noir   b. roses   c. en soie

5. La couleur préférée de Sarah n'est pas le _c_.
   a. rose   b. jaune   c. vert

6. Sarah cherche un vêtement pour _b_.
   a. un déjeuner   b. la fête de retraite de son père   c. un mariage

7. Sarah va acheter une robe en soie _a_.
   a. à manches courtes   b. à manches longues   c. rouge

8. La robe existe en vert, en bleu et en _c_.
   a. noir   b. marron   c. blanc

**Une occasion spéciale** Décrivez la dernière fois que vous avez fêté une occasion spéciale. Qu'est-ce que vous avez fêté? Où? Comment? Avec qui? Qu'est-ce que vous avez mis comme vêtements? Et les autres?

**MODÈLE**

*Samedi, nous avons fêté l'anniversaire de mon frère. Mes parents ont invité nos amis Paul, Marc, Julia et Naomi dans un restaurant élégant. Moi, j'ai mis une belle robe verte en coton. Mon frère a mis un costume gris. Paul a mis...*

*deux cent neuf* **209**

**Stratégie**
**Script** 1. Est-ce que tu vas aller au mariage de tes cousins? (*future*) 2. Elles ont acheté dix nouveaux maillots de bain pour cet été! (*past*) 3. Noémie a envie de parler à Martha de son rendez-vous avec Julien. (*present*) 4. Vous avez vendu tous les tee-shirts? (*past*)

**Préparation** Have students look at the photo of Pauline and Sarah, describe what they see, and predict what they are talking about.

**À vous d'écouter**
**Script** PAULINE: Tiens, bonjour, Sarah. Ça va?
SARAH: Ah, bonjour Pauline! Oui, très bien et toi?
P: Bien, merci. Dis, je t'ai cherchée hier soir à la fête de ma cousine...
S: Excuse-moi. J'ai passé une mauvaise journée hier et j'ai complètement oublié. Mais... Et toi? Tu as aimé la fête?
P: Oui, j'ai beaucoup dansé et j'ai rencontré un garçon intéressant. Il s'appelle Boris et il est musicien. Je vais déjeuner avec lui demain midi, alors je cherche de nouveaux vêtements pour notre rendez-vous. Qu'est-ce que tu penses de ce pantalon noir avec cette chemise rose?
S: Oui, c'est bien. Et qu'est-ce que tu vas mettre comme chaussures?
P: Ben, ces baskets roses, non?
S: Ah non. Des chaussures en cuir noir, c'est plus élégant.
P: Oui, tu as raison. Et toi, qu'est-ce que tu cherches?
S: Une jolie robe pas trop chère.
P: Tu as un rendez-vous, toi aussi?

S: Non, c'est pour la fête de départ en retraite de mon père. C'est samedi prochain.
P: Regarde cette robe rouge en coton. Elle est jolie, non?
S: Oui, mais elle a l'air un peu serrée. Je préfère les robes larges.

P: Et cette belle robe en soie à manches courtes?
S: Je déteste le vert. Ils l'ont en bleu?
P: Oui, et en blanc aussi.
S: Super. Je vais prendre la bleue.

# Panorama

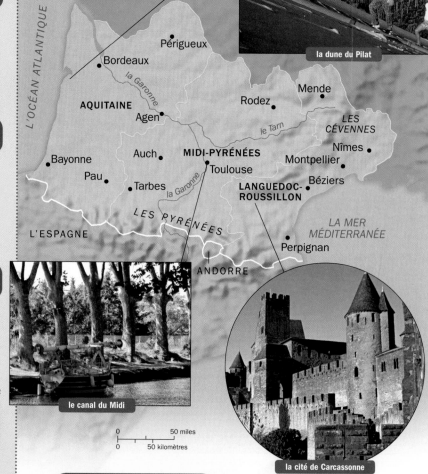

**Interactive Map Reading**

LA FRANCE

la dune du Pilat

## Section Goals

In this section, students will read historical and cultural information about **Aquitaine**, **Midi-Pyrénées**, and **Languedoc-Roussillon**.

## Key Standards
2.2, 3.1, 3.2, 5.1

**Student Resources**
*Cahier d'exercices*, pp. 83-84;
Supersite: Activities,
*Cahier interactif*
**Teacher Resources**
Answer Keys; Overhead #33

**Carte des régions Aquitaine, Midi-Pyrénées et Languedoc-Roussillon**
- Have students look at the map or use **Overhead #33**. Ask volunteers to read aloud the names of cities and geographical features. Model French pronunciation as necessary. Point out the locations of Spain and Andorra.
- Have students identify the locations of the places in the photos.

**La région en chiffres**
- Point out the three different coats of arms for the regions.
- Have volunteers read the sections aloud. After each section, ask questions about the content.
- Ask students to share any information they might know about the **Personnes célèbres**.

**Incroyable mais vrai!** The original cave at Lascaux was closed in 1963 in order to save the paintings from deterioration. A replica of the cave, known as Lascaux II, was built nearby and contains reproductions of the Great Hall of Bulls and the Painted Gallery.

## Aquitaine

### La région en chiffres

▸ **Superficie:** *41.308 km²*
▸ **Population:** *3.049.000*
▸ **Industrie principale:** *agriculture*
▸ **Villes principales:** *Bordeaux, Pau, Périgueux*

## Midi-Pyrénées

### La région en chiffres

▸ **Superficie:** *45.348 km²*
▸ **Population:** *2.687.000*
▸ **Industries principales:** *aéronautique, agriculture*
▸ **Villes principales:** *Auch, Toulouse, Rodez*

## Languedoc-Roussillon

### La région en chiffres

▸ **Superficie:** *27.376 km²*
▸ **Population:** *2.458.000*
▸ **Industrie principale:** *agriculture*
▸ **Villes principales:** *Montpellier, Nîmes, Perpignan*

### Personnes célèbres

▸ **Aliénor d'Aquitaine**, *Aquitaine, reine° de France (1122–1204)*
▸ **Jean Jaurès**, *Midi-Pyrénées, homme politique (1859–1914)*
▸ **Henri de Toulouse-Lautrec**, *Midi-Pyrénées, peintre et lithographe (1864–1901)*
▸ **Georges Brassens**, *Languedoc-Roussillon, chanteur (1921–1981)*
▸ **Francis Cabrel**, *Aquitaine, chanteur (1953– )*

**reine** *queen* **grotte** *cave* **gravures** *carvings* **peintures** *paintings* **découvrent** *discover*

le canal du Midi

la cité de Carcassonne

### Incroyable mais vrai!

Appelée parfois «la chapelle Sixtine préhistorique», la grotte° de Lascaux, en Aquitaine, est décorée de 1.500 gravures° et de 600 peintures°, vieilles de plus de 17.000 ans. En 1940, quatre garçons découvrent° ce sanctuaire. Les fresques, composées de plusieurs animaux, ont jusqu'à ce jour une signification mystérieuse.

---

**O P T I O N S**

**Personnes célèbres  Eleanor of Aquitaine** was one of the most powerful women in Europe during her time. Her first husband was King Louis VII of France. She later became Queen of England when she married Henry II. She was also the mother of Richard the Lionheart. **Francis Cabrel** is a guitarist, composer, and singer of blues-rock, pop, and contemporary folk music.

**Jean Jaurès** was a leader of the French socialist movement. **Toulouse-Lautrec** established lithography as a major art form with his vivid posters depicting Parisian nightlife in Montmartre. **Georges Brassens** was a poetic songwriter and performer who used his lyrics to address social issues.

## La gastronomie

### Le foie gras et le cassoulet

Le foie gras° et le cassoulet sont des spécialités du sud-ouest° de la France. Le foie gras est un produit° de luxe, en général réservé aux grandes occasions. On le mange sur du pain grillé ou comme ingrédient d'un plat° élaboré. Le cassoulet est un plat populaire, préparé à l'origine dans une «cassole°». Les ingrédients varient, mais en général, cette spécialité est composée d'haricots° blancs, de viande° de porc et de canard, de saucisses°, de tomates, d'ail° et d'herbes.

## Les monuments

### Les arènes de Nîmes

Inspirées du Colisée de Rome, les arènes° de Nîmes, en Languedoc-Roussillon, datent de la fin du premier siècle. C'est l'amphithéâtre le plus grand° de France et le mieux° conservé de l'ère° romaine. Les spectacles de gladiateurs d'autrefois°, appréciés par plus de° 20.000 spectateurs, sont aujourd'hui remplacés° par des corridas° et des spectacles musicaux pour le plaisir de 15.000 spectateurs en été et 7.000 spectateurs en hiver.

## Le sport

### La pelote basque

L'origine de la pelote est ancienne°: on retrouve des versions du jeu chez les Mayas, les Grecs et les Romains. C'est au Pays Basque, à la frontière° entre la France et l'Espagne, en Aquitaine, que le jeu se transforme en véritable sport. La pelote basque existe sous sept formes différentes; le principe de base est de lancer° une balle en cuir°, la «pelote», contre un mur° avec la «paleta», une raquette en bois°, et le «chistera», un grand gant en osier°.

## Les traditions

### La langue d'Oc

La langue d'Oc (l'occitan) est une langue romane° née° dans le sud de la France. Cette langue a donné son nom à la région: Languedoc-Roussillon. La poésie lyrique occitane et l'idéologie des troubadours° du Moyen Âge° influencent les valeurs° culturelles et intellectuelles européennes. Il existe plusieurs dialectes de l'occitan. «Los cats fan pas de chins» (les chats ne font pas des chiens) et «la bornicarié porta pas pa a casa» (la beauté n'apporte pas de pain à la maison) sont deux proverbes occitans connus°.

---

**Qu'est-ce que vous avez appris?** Répondez aux questions par des phrases complètes.

1. Qui était (*was*) peintre, lithographe et d'origine midi-pyrénéenne?
   Henri de Toulouse-Lautrec était peintre, lithographe et d'origine midi-pyrénéenne.
2. Quel est le surnom (*nickname*) de la grotte de Lascaux?
   Le surnom de la grotte de Lascaux est «la chapelle Sixtine préhistorique».
3. Que trouve-t-on dans la grotte de Lascaux?
   On trouve des peintures et des gravures dans la grotte de Lascaux.
4. Quand mange-t-on du foie gras, en général?
   En général, le foie gras est réservé aux grandes occasions.
5. Quels ingrédients utilise-t-on pour le cassoulet?
   On utilise des haricots blancs, de la viande, des saucisses, des tomates, de l'ail et des herbes.
6. Quand les arènes de Nîmes ont-elles été construites?
   Les arènes de Nîmes datent de la fin du premier siècle.

7. Combien de spectateurs y a-t-il dans les arènes de Nîmes en hiver?
   Il y a 7.000 personnes dans les arènes de Nîmes en hiver.
8. Quelles civilisations ont une version de la pelote?
   Les civilisations des Mayas, des Romains et des Grecs ont une version de la pelote.
9. Combien de formes différentes de pelote basque y a-t-il?
   Il y a sept formes différentes de pelote basque.
10. Qu'est-ce qui influence les valeurs culturelles et intellectuelles européennes?
    Ce sont la poésie occitane et l'idéologie des troubadours du Moyen Âge.

**S:** Practice more at **daccord1.vhlcentral.com**.

---

### SUR INTERNET

Go to **daccord1.vhlcentral.com** to find more cultural information related to this **PANORAMA**.

1. Il existe une forme de la pelote basque aux États-Unis. Comment s'appelle ce sport?
2. Cherchez des peintures de la grotte de Lascaux. Quelles sont vos préférées? Pourquoi?
3. Cherchez plus d'informations sur Henri de Toulouse-Lautrec. Avez-vous déjà vu quelques-unes de ses peintures? Où?

**ressources**

CE
pp. 83–84    daccord1.vhlcentral.com

**foie gras** *fatted liver of an animal served in the form of a pâté* **sud-ouest** *southwest* **produit** *product* **plat** *dish* **cassole** *pottery dish* **haricots** *beans* **viande** *meat* **saucisses** *sausages* **ail** *garlic* **arènes** *amphitheaters* **le plus grand** *the largest* **le mieux** *the most* **ère** *era* **autrefois** *long ago* **plus de** *more than* **remplacés** *replaced* **corridas** *bullfights* **ancienne** *ancient* **frontière** *border* **lancer** *throw* **cuir** *leather* **mur** *wall* **bois** *wood* **osier** *wicker* **langue romane** *romance language* **née** *born* **troubadours** *minstrels* **Moyen Âge** *Middle Ages* **valeurs** *values* **connus** *well-known*

---

**Le foie gras et le cassoulet**
- The raising of geese and ducks for **foie gras** dates back to ancient Egypt, Greece, Rome, and Gaul. There is a rivalry amongst the southwestern regions for the best variety of **cassoulet**. The differences occur mostly in the type of meat used.
- Ask students to name some regional dishes in the United States. Also ask if they know of a dish similar to **cassoulet**.

**Les arènes de Nîmes**
- Throughout the centuries the amphitheater always remained in use. At one time, residences were built within the arena and during another period it was used as a fortress and refuge. In 1909, it was restored to its original design as an arena for entertainment.
- Have students compare today's amphitheaters or arenas to the amphitheaters of the Romans.

**La pelote basque**
- The courts, gear, and rules used to play **pelote basque** can vary from village to village. But no matter which variety of the game is played, it is always lively and fast. The speed of the **pelote** can get up to 250–300 km/hr or about 155–186 mph.
- Ask students what sports are similar to **pelote basque**.

**La langue d'Oc**  **La langue d'Oc** is spoken by approximately 1.5 million people in the south of France. Although the Occitan dialects have been influenced by modern French, they still strongly resemble dialects of the Middle Ages in which the phonology and grammar are more closely related to Spanish.

**OPTIONS**

**La langue d'Oc** The troubadours of southern France were traveling poet-musicians. They wrote and performed courtly love poems or songs for the ladies of the courts in the Occitan dialect Provençal. Eleanor of Aquitaine, a patron of troubadours, used her influence to introduce Provençal poetry at the courts in northern France. This type of poetry thrived in the twelfth and thirteenth centuries, and had a great influence on later lyric poetry.

**Cultural Activity** Point out that France and Spain share a border. Ask students to give some examples of cross-cultural influences. (**les corridas à Nîmes, la pelote basque**, or jai-alai, and **la poésie lyrique des troubadours**)

## Section Goals

In this section, students will:
- learn to recognize word families
- read an invitation to an engagement celebration

## Key Standards

**1.2, 2.1, 3.2, 5.2**

**Stratégie** Write **inviter** on the board and ask students what it means in English. Next to it, write **invitation** and **invité(e)**, then ask them the meaning of these words. Point out that all three words have the same root and belong to a word family. Explain that recognizing the relationship between a known word and unfamiliar words can help them infer the meaning of words they don't know.

**Examinez le texte** Tell students to scan the text for the new words and try to guess their meaning based on the root and context before they look them up in the dictionary.

**Familles de mots** Point out the three categories of words. You might want to tell students to look for the words in the **Vocabulaire** on page 216.

# Lecture Ⓢ Reading

## Avant la lecture

### STRATÉGIE

#### Recognizing word families

Recognizing related words can help you guess the meaning of words in context, ensuring better comprehension of a reading selection. Using this strategy will enrich your French vocabulary.

### Examinez le texte

Voici quelques mots que vous avez déjà appris. Pour chaque mot, trouvez un terme de la même famille dans le texte et utilisez un dictionnaire pour donner son équivalent en anglais.

**MODÈLE**

| ami | *amitié* | *friendship* |
|-----|----------|--------------|
| 1. diplôme | diplômés | graduates |
| 2. commencer | le commencement | beginning |
| 3. sortir | la sortie | exit |
| 4. timide | la timidité | shyness |
| 5. difficile | les difficultés | difficulties |
| 6. préférer | les préférences | preferences |

### Familles de mots

Avec un(e) partenaire, trouvez le bon mot pour compléter chaque famille de mots. (Note: vous avez appris tous les mots qui manquent (*all the missing words*) dans cette unité et il y a un mot de chaque famille dans le texte.)

**MODÈLE**

| *attendre* | *l'attente* | *attendu(e)* |
|------------|-------------|--------------|
| **VERBE** | **NOM** | **ADJECTIF** |
| 1. boire | la boisson | bu(e) |
| 2. fêter | la fête | festif/festive |
| 3. vivre | la vie | vif/vive |
| 4. rajeunir | la jeunesse | jeune |
| 5. surprendre | la surprise | surpris(e) |
| 6. répondre | la réponse | répondu(e) |

## Ça y est, c'est officiel.

**Bravo, jeunes diplômés°!** C'est le commencement d'une nouvelle vie. Il est maintenant temps de fêter ça!

**Pour faire retomber la pression°, Mathilde, Christophe, Alexandre et Laurence vous invitent à fêter entre amis votre diplôme bien mérité°!**

À laisser chez vous:
**La timidité, la fatigue, les soucis° et les difficultés des études et de la vie quotidienne° pour une ambiance festive**

Quoi d'autre?
**Un groupe de musique (le frère de Mathilde et sa bande) va venir° jouer pour nous!**

**Word Relationships** Write these words on the board. At least one form will be familiar to students. Have them discuss the relationship between the words and their meanings. **1. idée, idéal(e), idéaliste, idéalement, idéaliser 2. organiser, organisateur/organisatrice, organisation, organisationnel(le) 3. chanter, chanteur/chanteuse, chansonnette, chanson, chantable**

**Party** Working in pairs, have students discuss whether or not they would attend a party like the one in the selection. Tell them to talk about the aspects of the activities that they do and do not like. Afterwards, ask them if they have ever attended a similar event and what types of activities were planned for the guests.

**À apporter:**
Nourriture° et boissons: Chaque invité apporte quelque chose pour le buffet: salades, plats° froids/chauds, fruits, desserts, boissons
Activités: Jeux de cartes, ballons°, autres jeux selon° vos préférences, chaises pliantes°, maillot de bain (pour la piscine), crème solaire
Surprenez-nous!

**Quand:**
Le samedi 16 juillet (de 16h00 à minuit)

**Où:**
Chez les parents de Laurence, 14 route des Mines, Allouagne, Nord-Pas-de-Calais

**Comment y aller°:**
À la sortie d'Allouagne, prenez la route de Lozinghem. Tournez à gauche sur la route des Mines. Le numéro 14 est la grande maison sur la droite. (Nous allons mettre des ballons° de couleurs sur la route pour indiquer l'endroit.)

**Au programme:**
Faire la fête, bien sûr! Manger (buffet et barbecue), rire, danser et fêter la fin des cours! Attendez-vous à passer un bon moment!

**Autres activités:**
Activités en plein air° (football, badminton, volley, piscine... et surtout détente°!)

**Pour répondre à cette invitation:**
Téléphonez à Laurence (avant le 6 juillet, SVP°) au 06.14.55.85.80 ou par e-mail: **laurence@courriel.fr**

---

**Ça y est!** *That's it!* **diplômés** *graduates* **faire retomber la pression** *to unwind* **bien mérité** *well deserved* **soucis** *worries* **vie quotidienne** *daily life* **va venir** *is going to come* **Nourriture** *Food* **plats** *dishes* **ballons** *balls* **selon** *depending on* **pliantes** *folding* **y aller** *get there* **ballons** *balloons* **en plein air** *outdoor* **détente** *relaxation* **svp** *please*

---

# Après la lecture

 **Vrai ou faux?** Indiquez si les phrases sont **vraies** ou **fausses**. Corrigez les phrases fausses. Answers may vary slightly.

1. C'est une invitation à une fête d'anniversaire.
   Faux. C'est une invitation pour fêter le diplôme.
2. Les invités vont passer un mauvais moment.
   Faux. Les invités vont passer un bon moment.
3. On va manger des salades et des desserts.
   Vrai.
4. Les invités vont faire toutes les activités dans la maison.
   Faux. Les invités vont faire des activités en plein air.
5. Un groupe de musique va jouer à la fête.
   Vrai.
6. La fête commence à 16h00.
   Vrai.

**Conseillez** Vous êtes Laurence, un des organisateurs de la fête. Les invités veulent (*want*) assister à la fête, mais ils vous contactent pour parler de leurs soucis respectifs. Donnez-leur des conseils (*advice*) pour les mettre à l'aise (*at ease*).
Answers may vary. Suggested answers:

**MODÈLE**

Isabelle: J'ai beaucoup de soucis cette semaine.
Vous: *Tu vas laisser tes soucis à la maison et venir (come) à la fête.*

1. Thomas: Je ne sais (*know*) pas quoi apporter.
   Vous: Tu vas apporter des boissons gazeuses.

2. Sarah: Je me perds (*get lost*) facilement quand je conduis.
   Vous: Tu vas chercher les ballons de couleurs sur la route.

3. Sylvie: Je ne fais pas de sport.
   Vous: Tu vas jouer aux cartes et discuter.

4. Salim: Je veux (*want*) répondre à l'invitation, mais je n'ai pas d'ordinateur.
   Vous: Tu vas me téléphoner.

5. Sandra: Je n'aime pas le barbecue.
   Vous: Tu vas manger des salades.

6. Véronique: J'aime faire du sport en plein air, mais je n'aime pas le football.
   Vous: Tu vas faire du badmington et du volley.

**On va à la fête?** 👥 Vous êtes invité(e) à cette fête et vous allez amener un(e) ami(e). Téléphonez à cet(te) ami(e) (votre partenaire) pour l'inviter. Donnez des détails et répondez aux questions de votre ami(e) sur les hôtes, les invités, les activités de l'après-midi et de la soirée, les choses à apporter, etc.

---

**Vrai ou faux?** Go over the answers with the class. For the false items, have students point out where they found the correct answer in the text.

**Conseillez**
• This activity can be done in pairs. Remind students to switch roles after items 1–3.
• Have pairs write two more situations for the activity. Then have them exchange papers with another pair and complete the situations.

**On va à la fête?** After students have completed the activity, take a quick class poll. Ask: **Qui va assister à la fête? Qui ne va pas assister à la fête? Pourquoi?**

---

**OPTIONS**

**Project** Have students write an invitation to a birthday party, an anniversary party, or a holiday celebration. Tell them to include the name(s) of the host(s); date, time, and place of the event; what is being celebrated; and any other important details. If possible, provide students with examples of other invitations in French to use as models.

**Oral Practice** Working in pairs, have students write three content questions based on the reading. When they have finished, have them get together with another pair and take turns asking and answering each other's questions.

## Section Goals

In this section, students will:
• learn to report an interview
• learn to conduct an interview

## Key Standards

1.3, 3.1, 5.1

**Stratégie** Play the role of an interviewee. Tell students to interview you about your clothing preferences. Allow recording so students can transcribe the interview. Then choose volunteers to report on the interview, transcribing it verbatim, summarizing it, or summarizing and quoting you occasionally.

**Proofreading Activity** Have the class correct these sentences.
**1. Quand est-ce vous avez achete ces vetements? 2. Cette blouson-la est tres cher, mais c'est parfait. 3. Est-ce que vous déjà avez travaille comme styliste? 4. Vous allez parler moi de votre travail?**

# Écriture

## STRATÉGIE

### How to report an interview

There are several ways to prepare a written report about an interview. For example, you can transcribe the interview verbatim, or you can summarize it. In any event, the report should begin with an interesting title and a brief introduction including the five *W*'s (*who, what, when, where, why*) and the *H* (*how*) of the interview. The report should end with an interesting conclusion. Note that when you transcribe a conversation in French, you should pay careful attention to format and punctuation.

### Écrire une conversation en français

● Pour indiquer qui parle dans une conversation, on peut mettre le nom de la personne qui parle devant sa phrase.

MONIQUE Lucie, qu'est-ce que tu vas mettre pour l'anniversaire de Julien?

LUCIE Je vais mettre ma robe en soie bleue à manches courtes. Et toi, tu vas mettre quoi?

MONIQUE Eh bien, une jupe en coton et un chemisier, je pense. Ou peut-être mon pantalon en cuir avec... Tiens, tu me prêtes ta chemise jaune et blanche?

LUCIE Oui, si tu me la rends (*return it to me*) dimanche. Elle va avec le pantalon que je vais porter la semaine prochaine.

● On peut aussi commencer les phrases avec des tirets (*dashes*) pour indiquer quand une nouvelle personne parle.

— Qu'est-ce que tu as acheté comme cadeau pour Julien?

— Une cravate noire et violette. Elle est très jolie. Et toi?

— Je n'ai pas encore acheté son cadeau. Des lunettes de soleil peut-être?

— Oui, c'est une bonne idée! Et il y a des soldes à Saint-Louis Lunettes.

## Thème

## Écrire une interview

### Avant l'écriture

**1.** Clarisse Deschamps est une styliste suisse. Elle dessine des vêtements pour les jeunes et va présenter sa nouvelle collection sur votre campus. Vous allez interviewer Clarisse pour le journal de votre lycée.

Préparez une liste de questions à poser à Clarisse Deschamps sur sa nouvelle collection. Vous pouvez (*can*) poser des questions sur:

■ les types de vêtements

■ les couleurs

■ le style

■ les prix

| Quoi? | 1.<br>2. |
| Comment? | 1.<br>2. |
| Pour qui? | 1.<br>2. |
| Combien? | 1.<br>2. |
| Pourquoi? | 1.<br>2. |
| Où? | 1.<br>2. |
| Quand? | 1.<br>2. |

**O P T I O N S**

**Avant l'écriture** As a preparation, have each student write a short paragraph or list of their ideas about Clarisse Deschamps. What is she like? What does she look like? What kinds of clothes does she like and dislike? Have them write a short profile to use when they write the answers.

Once students have written the answers, discuss various techniques they can use to organize their information. One way is to go back to the chart they used to ask their questions and add the answers to it. Another is to prioritize by level of interest, with the most interesting information first. Ask students if they have other ideas on how to organize their facts.

2. Une fois que vous avez rempli (*filled out*) le tableau (*chart*), choisissez les questions à poser pendant (*during*) l'interview.

3. Une fois (*Once*) vos questions finalisées, notez les réponses. Ensuite (*Then*), organisez les informations en catégories telles que (*such as*) les types de vêtements, les couleurs et les styles, la clientèle, le prix, etc.

## Écriture

Écrivez un compte rendu (*report*) de l'interview.

- Commencez par une courte introduction.

  **MODÈLE** *Voici une interview de Clarisse Deschamps, styliste suisse.*

- Résumez (*Summarize*) les informations obtenues (*obtained*) pour chaque catégorie et présentez ces éléments de manière cohérente. Citez la personne interviewée au moins deux fois (*at least twice*).

  **MODÈLE** *Je lui ai demandé: —Quel genre de vêtements préférez-vous porter pour sortir? Elle m'a répondu: —Moi, je préfère porter une robe noire. C'est très élégant.*

- Terminez par une brève (*brief*) conclusion.

  **MODÈLE** *On vend la collection de Clarisse Deschamps à Vêtements & Co à côté du lycée. Cette semaine, il y a des soldes!*

### Tête-à-tête avec Clarisse Deschamps

Voici une interview de Clarisse Deschamps, styliste suisse.

Je lui ai demandé:
- Quel genre de vêtements préférez-vous porter pour sortir?
Elle m'a répondu:
- Moi, je préfère porter une robe noire. C'est très élégant...

On vend la collection de Clarisse Deschamps à Vêtements & Co dans le magasin qui est à côté de notre lycée. Cette semaine, il y a des soldes!

## Après l'écriture

1. Échangez votre compte rendu avec celui (*the one*) d'un(e) partenaire. Répondez à ces questions pour commenter son travail.

   - Votre partenaire a-t-il/elle organisé les informations en plusieurs catégories?

   - A-t-il/elle inclu au moins deux citations (*quotes*) dans son compte rendu?

   - A-t-il/elle utilisé le bon style pour écrire les citations?

   - A-t-il/elle utilisé les bonnes formes verbales?

2. Corrigez votre compte rendu d'après (*according to*) les commentaires de votre partenaire. Relisez votre travail pour éliminer ces problèmes:

   - des fautes (*errors*) d'orthographe

   - des fautes de ponctuation

   - des fautes de conjugaison

   - des fautes d'accord (*agreement*) des adjectifs

   - un mauvais emploi (*use*) de la grammaire

**Criteria**

**Content** Contains all the information included in bulleted list of tasks.
Scale: 1  2  3  4  5

**Organization** Includes a short introduction, a 10-12 line conversation that represents the interview and a brief conclusion.
Scale: 1  2  3  4  5

**Accuracy** Uses forms of the **passé composé** (when applicable) and new unit verbs correctly. Spells words, conjugates verbs, and modifies adjectives correctly throughout.
Scale: 1  2  3  4  5

**Creativity** The student includes additional information that is not included in the task and/or creates a conversation that is longer than 10-12 lines.
Scale: 1  2  3  4  5

**Scoring**

| | |
|---|---|
| Excellent | 18–20 points |
| Good | 14–17 points |
| Satisfactory | 10–13 points |
| Unsatisfactory | < 10 points |

*deux cent quinze*  **215**

**OPTIONS**

**Écriture** On the board, demonstrate other ways to report direct quotations in writing. One is the name with a colon after it, followed by the quote (dialogue style). Another is the person's name, followed by a comma and a direct quote using quotation marks (**guillemets**).

Bring in some magazines and newspapers showing how interviews are transcribed and presented. Ask students to choose one example and to follow the model.

## Les vêtements

| | |
|---|---|
| aller avec | to go with |
| porter | to wear |
| un anorak | ski jacket; parka |
| des baskets (f.) | tennis shoes |
| un blouson | jacket |
| une casquette | (baseball) cap |
| une ceinture | belt |
| un chapeau | hat |
| une chaussette | sock |
| une chaussure | shoe |
| une chemise (à manches courtes/longues) | shirt (short-/long-sleeved) |
| un chemisier | blouse |
| un costume | (man's) suit |
| une cravate | tie |
| une écharpe | scarf |
| un gant | glove |
| un jean | jeans |
| une jupe | skirt |
| des lunettes (de soleil) (f.) | (sun)glasses |
| un maillot de bain | swimsuit, bathing suit |
| un manteau | coat |
| un pantalon | pants |
| un pull | sweater |
| une robe | dress |
| un sac à main | purse, handbag |
| un short | shorts |
| un sous-vêtement | underwear |
| une taille | clothing size |
| un tailleur | (woman's) suit; tailor |
| un tee-shirt | tee shirt |
| des vêtements (m.) | clothing |
| des soldes (m.) | sales |
| un vendeur/ une vendeuse | salesman/ saleswoman |
| bon marché | inexpensive |
| chaque | each |
| cher/chère | expensive |
| large | loose; big |
| serré(e) | tight |

## Les fêtes

| | |
|---|---|
| faire la fête | to party |
| faire une surprise (à quelqu'un) | to surprise (someone) |
| fêter | to celebrate |
| organiser une fête | to organize a party |
| une bière | beer |
| un biscuit | cookie |
| un bonbon | candy |
| le champagne | champagne |
| un dessert | dessert |
| un gâteau | cake |
| la glace | ice cream |
| un glaçon | ice cube |
| le vin | wine |
| un cadeau | gift |
| une fête | party; celebration |
| un hôte/une hôtesse | host(ess) |
| un(e) invité(e) | guest |
| un jour férié | holiday |
| une surprise | surprise |

## Périodes de la vie

| | |
|---|---|
| l'adolescence (f.) | adolescence |
| l'âge adulte (m.) | adulthood |
| un divorce | divorce |
| l'enfance (f.) | childhood |
| une étape | stage |
| l'état civil (m.) | marital status |
| la jeunesse | youth |
| un mariage | marriage; wedding |
| la mort | death |
| la naissance | birth |
| la vie | life |
| la vieillesse | old age |
| prendre sa retraite | to retire |
| tomber amoureux/ amoureuse | to fall in love |
| avant-hier | the day before yesterday |
| hier | yesterday |

| | |
|---|---|
| *Expressions utiles* | See pp. 187 and 201. |
| Demonstrative adjectives | See p. 190. |
| Indirect object pronouns | See p. 204. |
| Disjunctive pronouns | See p. 205. |

## Les relations

| | |
|---|---|
| une amitié | friendship |
| un amour | love |
| le bonheur | happiness |
| un couple | couple |
| un(e) fiancé(e) | fiancé |
| des jeunes mariés (m.) | newlyweds |
| un rendez-vous | date; appointment |
| ensemble | together |

## Les couleurs

| | |
|---|---|
| De quelle couleur...? | In what color...? |
| blanc(he) | white |
| bleu(e) | blue |
| gris(e) | gray |
| jaune | yellow |
| marron | brown |
| noir(e) | black |
| orange | orange |
| rose | pink |
| rouge | red |
| vert(e) | green |
| violet(te) | purple; violet |

## Verbes en –re

| | |
|---|---|
| attendre | to wait |
| conduire | to drive |
| construire | to build; to construct |
| descendre (de) | to go down; to get off; to take down |
| détruire | to destroy |
| entendre | to hear |
| mettre | to put (on); to place |
| perdre (son temps) | to lose (to waste one's time) |
| permettre | to allow |
| produire | to produce |
| promettre | to promise |
| réduire | to reduce |
| rendre (à) | to give back; to return (to) |
| rendre visite (à) | to visit someone |
| répondre (à) | to respond; to answer (to) |
| rire | to laugh |
| sourire | to smile |
| traduire | to translate |
| vendre | to sell |

**ressources**

daccord1.vhlcentral.com

**216** *deux cent seize*

# En vacances

## Pour commencer
- Indiquez les couleurs qu'on voit (*sees*) sur la photo.
- Quel temps fait-il?
- Quel(s) vêtement(s) Stéphane porte-t-il?
- Quelle(s) activité(s) Stéphane peut-il pratiquer là où il se trouve?

## Unit Goals
**Leçon 7A**
In this lesson, students will learn:
- terms for travel and vacation
- names of countries and nationalities
- the role of diacriticals
- about Tahiti and **le musée d'Orsay**
- more about transportation and lodging through specially shot video footage
- the **passé composé** with **être**
- direct object pronouns
- about **TER** regional train service

**Leçon 7B**
In this lesson, students will learn:
- terms related to hotels and accommodations
- ordinal numbers
- expressions for sequencing events
- the pronunciation of **ti**, **sti**, and **ssi**
- how and where the French vacation
- the formation and usage of adverbs
- the **imparfait**
- the verbs **dire**, **écrire**, **lire**, and **décrire**
- to recognize the genre of spoken discourse

**Savoir-faire**
In this section, students will learn:
- cultural and historical information about the French regions of **Provence-Alpes-Côte d'Azur** and **Rhône-Alpes**
- to predict the content of a text from its title
- to make an outline
- to write a brochure

**Pour commencer**
- jaune, bleu, vert, noir, blanc
- Il fait beau./Il fait (du) soleil./ Il fait chaud.
- Il porte un maillot de bain.
- Il peut nager.

---

**Student Materials**
**Print:** Student Book, Workbooks (*Cahier d'exercices, Cahier d'activités*)
**Technology:** MAESTRO® *Cahier interactif* and Supersite (Audio, Video, Practice)

**Teacher Materials**
DVDs (*Roman-photo, Flash culture*)
Teacher's Resources (Scripts, Answer Keys, Testing Program)
Audio CDs (Testing Program, Textbook, Audio Program)

MAESTRO® Supersite: Student Supersite Content; Planning and Teaching Resources (Overheads, *PowerPoints*, Lesson Plans, Information Gaps and *Feuilles d'activités*); Learning Management System (Gradebook, Assignments); Audio MP3s and Streaming Video
**D'ACCORD! 1 Supersite:** daccord1.vhlcentral.com

## Section Goals

In this section, students will learn and practice vocabulary related to:
• travel and vacations
• names of countries and nationalities

## Key Standards
1.1, 1.2, 4.1

**Student Resources**
*Cahier d'exercices*, pp. 85-86;
*Cahier d'activités*, pp. 57-58, 163;
Supersite: Activities,
*Cahier interactif*

**Teacher Resources**
Answer Keys; Overhead #34;
Audio Script; Textbook & Audio
Activity MP3s/CD; Info Gap
Activities; Testing program:
Vocabulary Quiz

### Suggestions

• Use **Overhead #34** and describe what the people are doing. Examples: **Cette femme achète un billet. Cet homme utilise un plan.**

• Ask students questions about travel and transportation using the vocabulary. **Aimez-vous voyager? Comment préférez-vous voyager? Aimez-vous prendre le train? Aimez-vous prendre l'avion? Préférez-vous rouler en voiture ou prendre l'autobus? Quels pays avez-vous visités?** At this time, introduce additional countries, states, provinces, and their prepositions as needed.

• Point out that **faire des achats** also means *to go shopping*.

• Point out that **un (auto)bus** is a local bus; a bus that goes from town to town is **un (auto) car**. Then explain the nuance between **une station de train** and **une gare**.

• Point out that **les vacances** is always plural.

• Tell students that **un plan** is a city or town map; **une carte** is a map of a larger area, such as a region or country.

• Explain that the word **un ticket** is used for a bus, subway, or other small ticket. A plane or train ticket or a ticket to an event, such as a concert, is called **un billet**.

## Leçon 7A

**Talking Picture**
**Audio: Activity**

### You will learn how to...
▪ describe trips you have taken
▪ tell where you went

# Bon voyage!

### Vocabulaire

| | |
|---|---|
| faire du shopping | to go shopping |
| faire les valises | to pack one's bags |
| faire un séjour | to spend time (somewhere) |
| partir en vacances | to go on vacation |
| prendre un train (un taxi, un (auto)bus, un bateau) | to take a train (taxi, bus, boat) |
| rouler en voiture | to ride in a car |
| | |
| un aéroport | airport |
| un arrêt d'autobus (de bus) | bus stop |
| un billet aller-retour | round-trip ticket |
| un billet (d'avion, de train) | (plane, train) ticket |
| un (jour de) congé | day off |
| une douane | customs |
| une gare (routière) | train station (bus terminal) |
| une station (de métro) | (subway) station |
| une station de ski | ski resort |
| un ticket (de bus, de métro) | (bus, subway) ticket |
| des vacances (f.) | vacation |
| un vol | flight |
| | |
| à l'étranger | abroad, overseas |
| | |
| la campagne | country(side) |
| une capitale | capital |
| un pays | country |
| | |
| (en/l') Allemagne (f.) | (to/in) Germany |
| (en/l') Angleterre (f.) | (to/in) England |
| (en/la) Belgique (belge) | (to/in) Belgium (Belgian) |
| (au/le) Brésil (brésilien(ne)) | (to/in) Brazil (Brazilian) |
| (en/la) Chine (chinois(e)) | (to/in) China (Chinese) |
| (en/l') Irlande (irlandais(e)) (f.) | (to/in) Ireland (Irish) |
| (en/l') Italie (f.) | (to/in) Italy |
| (au/le) Japon | (to/in) Japan |
| (en/la) Suisse | (to/in) Switzerland |

Labels in illustration: une sortie · Il utilise un plan. (utiliser) · le soleil! · Elle bronze. (bronzer) · la plage · la mer · les gens (m.) · Le Figaro · le journal

**ressources**

CE
pp. 85-86

CA
p. 57-58, 163

daccord1.vhlcentral.com

---

**OPTIONS**

**Oral Drill** Call out names of countries and nationalities at random, including adjectives of nationality from previous lessons. Have students classify them as either **un pays** or **une nationalité**. You might want to list the words on the board in two columns or have students write them on the board.

**Using Games** Write vocabulary for means of transportation on index cards. On another set of cards, draw or paste pictures to match each term. Tape them face down on the board in random order. Divide the class into two teams. Play a game of Concentration in which students match words with pictures. When a match is made, that player's team collects those cards. When all pairs have been matched, the team with the most cards wins.

# Mise en pratique

**1** **Chassez l'intrus** Indiquez le mot ou l'expression qui ne convient pas.

1. faire un séjour, partir en vacances, un jour de congé, (une station de ski)
2. un aéroport, une station de métro, (une arrivée,) une gare routière
3. (une douane,) un départ, une arrivée, une sortie
4. le monde, un pays, (le journal,) une capitale
5. la campagne, la mer, la plage, (des gens)
6. prendre un bus, un arrêt de bus, (utiliser un plan,) une gare routière
7. (bronzer,) prendre un avion, un vol, un aéroport
8. prendre un taxi, rouler en voiture, (un vol,) une gare routière

**2** **Écoutez** 🎧 Écoutez Cédric et Nathalie parler de leurs vacances. Ensuite (*Then*), complétez les phrases avec un mot ou une expression de la section **CONTEXTES**. Notez que toutes les options ne sont pas utilisées.

_f_ 1. Nathalie va partir...
_b_ 2. Nathalie a déjà...
_i_ 3. Nathalie va peut-être...
_g_ 4. La famille de Cédric...
_h_ 5. Paul pense que l'Espagne est...
_a_ 6. Pour Cédric, les plages du Brésil...
_e_ 7. Un jour, Cédric va faire...
_c_ 8. Nathalie va utiliser...

a. sont idéales pour bronzer.
b. son billet d'avion.
c. le plan de Paris de Cédric.
d. la capitale du Mexique.
e. le tour du monde.
f. à l'étranger.
g. n'a pas encore décidé entre l'Espagne, le Mexique et le Brésil.
h. un pays superbe.
i. faire un séjour en Italie.

**3** **Les vacances** Justine va partir en vacances demain. Complétez le paragraphe avec les mots et expressions de la liste. Toutes les options ne sont pas utilisées.

| | | |
|---|---|---|
| aller-retour | faire ma valise | sortie |
| une arrivée | pays | station |
| faire un séjour | plage | taxi |
| faire du shopping | prendre un bus | vol |

Demain, je pars en vacances. Je vais (1) ___faire un séjour___ avec mon frère à l'île Maurice, une petite île (*island*) tropicale dans l'océan Indien. Nous allons (2) ___prendre un bus___ pour l'aéroport à 7h00. Mon frère veut (*wants*) prendre un (3) ___taxi___, mais moi, je pense qu'il faut économiser parce que j'ai envie de (4) ___faire du shopping___ au marché et dans les boutiques de Port-Louis, la capitale. Le (5) ___vol___ est à 10h. Nous n'avons pas besoin de visa pour le voyage; pour entrer dans le (6) ___pays___, il faut seulement montrer un passeport et un billet (7) ___aller-retour___. J'ai acheté un nouveau maillot de bain pour aller à la (8) ___plage___. Et maintenant je vais (9) ___faire ma valise___!

🔊 Practice more at **daccord1.vhlcentral.com**.

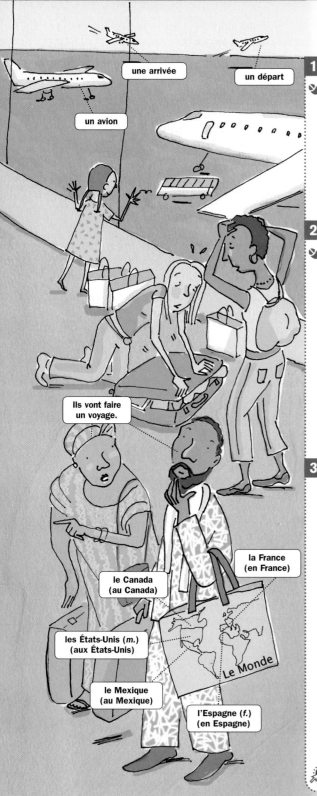

une arrivée

un départ

un avion

Ils vont faire un voyage.

le Canada (au Canada)

les États-Unis (m.) (aux États-Unis)

le Mexique (au Mexique)

la France (en France)

l'Espagne (f.) (en Espagne)

Le Monde

**1** **Suggestion** Have students put **l'intrus** with other expressions like it. Example: **une station de ski** goes with item 5. If the word does not fit another set, have students create a set of at least three related words.

**2** **Script** CÉDRIC: Nathalie, où est-ce que tu vas aller en vacances cet été?
NATHALIE: Je vais partir à l'étranger.
C: Moi aussi. Où est-ce que tu vas?
N: Je vais en France pour quinze jours. C'est un pays tellement intéressant. J'ai déjà mon billet d'avion. J'attends le départ avec beaucoup d'impatience. Je vais aller à Paris et aussi à Nice. On va peut-être faire un court séjour en Italie. Ça va être super! Et toi, où est-ce que tu pars en vacances?
C: Moi, je vais faire un voyage mais je ne sais pas où. Ma famille n'a pas encore décidé entre l'Espagne, le Mexique et le Brésil. Qu'en penses-tu?
N: Mon frère Paul fait ses études en Espagne, à Grenade. Il trouve que c'est un pays superbe et que les gens sont très gentils.
C: Moi, je pense que le Brésil, c'est plus exotique et les plages sont idéales pour bronzer.
N: Mexico, la capitale du Mexique, a beaucoup de musées très intéressants.
C: Un jour, je vais faire le tour du monde, mais pour ça, il faut trouver un vol bon marché. Nathalie, tu as besoin de quelqu'un pour t'aider à faire tes valises et te conduire à l'aéroport?
N: Oh oui, merci. C'est vraiment gentil. Est-ce que tu as un plan de Paris à me prêter?
C: Bien sûr, pas de problème.
(*On Textbook Audio*)

**2** **Suggestion** Before students listen, have them scan the sentence fragments in this activity and pick out new words. Examples: **bronzer, aéroport, séjour,** and **pays.**

**3** **Expansion** Have pairs of students add to Justine's paragraph by creating sentences using the three unused words (**arrivée, station, sortie**). Have them rewrite the paragraph, logically adding their sentences. Ask volunteers to read their paragraphs aloud.

**OPTIONS**

**Class Discussion** Ask students what means of transportation one might take to go from one place to another. Example: **Quel(s) moyen(s) de transport est-ce qu'on prend pour aller de Paris à Rome? Des États-Unis en Angleterre? Du lycée au supermarché? De la tour Eiffel à l'Arc de Triomphe?**

**Using Games** Play a game of **Dix questions**. Ask a volunteer to think of a country. Other students get one chance to ask a yes/no question and guess the country. Encourage students to ask questions about languages spoken there and location. You might want to brainstorm prepositions of location on the board. Examples: **près de, loin de, à côté de,** etc. Limit attempts to ten questions per place.

**4 Suggestion** After completing this activity in pairs, combine pairs of students to form groups of four. Have students share what they learned about their partners with the other pair.

**4 Expansion** Ask each student question 8: **Dans quel pays as-tu envie de voyager?** Accept simple answers like **la France.** Follow up each answer by asking **Pourquoi?**

**5 Suggestion** Ask volunteers to write their descriptions on the board.

**6 Suggestion** Before distributing the Info Gap Handouts found on the Supersite, you might want to brainstorm some questions that will elicit the missing information and write them on the board.

**7 Suggestion** Have students exchange letters for peer editing. Editors should make sure all required elements are included in the letter and underline, rather than correct, grammar and spelling errors.

## Communication

**4** **Répondez** Avec un(e) partenaire, posez-vous ces questions et répondez-y (them) à tour de rôle. Answers will vary.

1. Où pars-tu en vacances cette année? Quand?
2. Quand fais-tu tes valises? Avec combien de valises voyages-tu?
3. Préfères-tu la mer, la campagne ou les stations de ski?
4. Comment vas-tu à l'aéroport? Prends-tu l'autobus? Le métro?
5. Quelles sont tes vacances préférées?
6. Quand utilises-tu un plan?
7. Quel est ton pays favori? Pourquoi?
8. Dans quel(s) pays as-tu envie de voyager?

**5** **Décrivez** Avec un(e) partenaire, écrivez (write) une description des images. Donnez autant de (as many) détails que possible. Ensuite (Then), rejoignez un autre groupe et lisez vos descriptions. L'autre groupe doit deviner (must guess) quelle image vous décrivez (describe). Answers will vary.

1.

2.

3.

4.

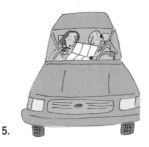
5.

6.

**6** **Conversez** Votre professeur va vous donner, à vous et à votre partenaire, une feuille d'activités. L'un de vous est un(e) client(e) qui a besoin de faire une réservation pour des vacances, l'autre est l'agent de voyages. Travaillez ensemble pour finaliser la réservation et compléter vos feuilles respectives. Attention! Ne regardez pas la feuille de votre partenaire. Answers will vary.

**7** **Un voyage** Vous allez faire un voyage en Europe et rendre visite à votre cousin, Jean-Marc, qui étudie en Belgique. Écrivez-lui (Write him) une lettre et utilisez les mots de la liste. Answers will vary.

| | |
|---|---|
| un aéroport | la France |
| la Belgique | prendre un taxi |
| un billet | la Suisse |
| faire un séjour | un vol |
| faire les valises | un voyage |

- Parlez des détails de votre départ.
- Expliquez votre tour d'Europe.
- Organisez votre arrivée en Belgique.
- Parlez de ce que (what) vous allez faire ensemble.

**OPTIONS**

**Word Games** Have students work in groups of three to write riddles about people, places, or objects from **Contextes**. For each riddle, the group must come up with at least three hints or descriptions. Have students from each group read hints to the rest of the class. Example: **Je suis fait de papier. Je suis souvent en noir et blanc. Je vous donne beaucoup d'informations. (Je suis un journal.)**

**Using Games** Write **Dans quel pays parle-t-on…?** on the board. Have students stand. Toss a beanbag to a student and ask where a language is spoken. The player has four seconds to name a country. He or she then tosses the beanbag to a classmate and asks where a language is spoken. Players who cannot think of a country in time are eliminated. Languages may be repeated, but countries may not. The last person standing wins.

# Les sons et les lettres

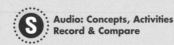

**Audio:** Concepts, Activities
Record & Compare

## 🎧 Diacriticals for meaning

Some French words with different meanings have nearly identical spellings except for a diacritical mark (*accent*). Sometimes a diacritical does not affect pronunciation at all.

| **ou** | **où** | **a** | **à** |
|---|---|---|---|
| *or* | *where* | *has* | *to, at* |

Sometimes, you can clearly hear the difference between the words.

| **côte** | **côté** | **sale** | **salé** |
|---|---|---|---|
| *coast* | *side* | *dirty* | *salty* |

Very often, two similar-looking words are different parts of speech. Many similar-looking word pairs are those with and without an **-é** at the end.

| **âge** | **âgé** | **entre** | **entré (entrer)** |
|---|---|---|---|
| *age* (n.) | *elderly* (adj.) | *between* (prep.) | *entered* (p.p.) |

In such instances, context should make their meaning clear.

**Tu as quel âge?**
*How old are you? / What is your age?*

**C'est un homme âgé.**
*He's an elderly man.*

### 🎾 Prononcez  Répétez les mots suivants à voix haute.

1. la (*the*)    là (*there*)
2. êtes (*are*)    étés (*summers*)
3. jeune (*young*)    jeûne (*fasting*)
4. pêche (*peach*)    pêché (*fished*)

### 🎾 Articulez  Répétez les phrases suivantes à voix haute.

1. J'habite dans une ferme (*farm*).
   Le magasin est fermé (*closed*).
2. Les animaux mangent du maïs (*corn*).
   Je suis suisse, mais il est belge.
3. Est-ce que tu es prête?
   J'ai prêté ma voiture (*car*) à Marcel.
4. La lampe est à côté de la chaise.
   J'adore la côte ouest de la France.

### 🎾 Dictons  Répétez les dictons à voix haute.

À vos marques, prêts, partez! ¹

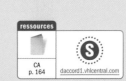

C'est un prêté pour un rendu.²

---

² One good turn deserves another. (lit. It is one loaned for one returned.)

¹ On your mark, get set, go!

*deux cent vingt et un*  **221**

ressources

CA
p. 164

daccord1.vhlcentral.com

---

**Section Goals**

In this section, students will learn about the use of diacriticals to distinguish between words with the same or similar spellings.

**Key Standards**
4.1

**Student Resources**
*Cahier d'activités*, p. 164;
Supersite: Activities,
*Cahier interactif*

**Teacher Resources**
Answer Keys; Audio Script;
Textbook & Audio Activity
MP3s/CD

**Suggestions**
• Model the pronunciation of the example words and have students repeat after you.
• Write examples of other past participles that are used as adjectives on the board. Examples: **réservé** and **préparé**. Ask students to provide more examples.
• Have students give you the English equivalents for the following words in the **Articulez**: 2. **mais** 3. **prête** and **prêté** 4. **côté** and **côte**.
• Dictate five simple sentences with words that have diacriticals that distinguish meaning, repeating each one at least two times. Then write the sentences on the board or a transparency and have students check their spelling.

**Dictons**  Have students compare the pronunciation and meaning of **prêts** and **prêté**. Then have them identify their parts of speech.

---

**OPTIONS**

**Mini-dictée**  Use these sentences that contain words with and without diacriticals for additional practice or as a dictation. **1. Quel âge a-t-il? Mon grand-père est âgé. 2. Le bureau est entre le lit et la porte. Marcel est entré dans la salle. 3. La ligne est occupée. Suzanne s'occupe des enfants. 4. J'ai réservé une table au restaurant. Sylvain est réservé.**

**Tongue Twister**  Teach students this French tongue-twister that contains diacriticals that affect meaning. **Un pêcheur pêchait sous un pêcher, le pêcher empêchait le pêcheur de pêcher, le pêcheur coupa le pêcher, le pêcher n'empêcha plus le pêcheur de pêcher.**

# ROMAN-PHOTO

## De retour au P'tit Bistrot

 Video: *Roman-photo*
Record & Compare

## Section Goals

In this section, students will learn functional phrases for talking about vacations.

## Key Standards

1.2, 2.1, 2.2, 4.1, 4.2

**Student Resources**
*Cahier d'activités*, pp. 91-92;
Supersite: Activities,
*Cahier interactif*
**Teacher Resources**
Answer Keys; Video Script & Translation; *Roman-photo* video

### Video Recap: Leçon 6B

Before doing this **Roman-photo**, review the previous one with this activity.
1. _____ a fêté ses dix-huit ans. (Stéphane)
2. _____ a fait un gâteau d'anniversaire. (Sandrine)
3. _____ a visité Paris avec ses parents. (David)
4. _____ a fait une jupe originale. (Amina)
5. _____ ont donné une montre à Stéphane. (Rachid et Astrid)
6. _____ lui a donné un blouson en cuir noir. (Valérie)

### Video Synopsis

At the train station, David tells Rachid about his trip to Paris. At the café, he tells Stéphane about his trip and that he loved the museums. Stéphane wants to go to Tahiti. David gives Stéphane sunglasses for his birthday. When Sandrine hears about David's trip, she remembers she needs to make reservations for her ski trip to Albertville.

### Suggestions

• Ask students to read the title, glance at the video stills, and predict what the episode will be about. Record their predictions.
• Have students read the **Roman-photo** aloud in groups of four.
• Point out the expressions **bon voyage** and **bon séjour**. Explain that **un voyage** refers to travel to and from a destination; **un séjour** is extended time spent at the place itself.
• Review predictions and ask which ones were correct.

**PERSONNAGES**

David

Rachid

Sandrine

Stéphane

*À la gare...*

**RACHID** Tu as fait bon voyage?
**DAVID** Salut! Excellent, merci.
**RACHID** Tu es parti pour Paris avec une valise et te voici avec ces énormes sacs en plus!
**DAVID** Mes parents et moi sommes allés aux Galeries Lafayette. On a acheté des vêtements et des trucs pour l'appartement aussi.

**RACHID** Ah ouais?
**DAVID** Mes parents sont arrivés des États-Unis jeudi soir. Ils ont pris une chambre dans un bel hôtel, tout près de la tour Eiffel.
**RACHID** Génial!
**DAVID** Moi, je suis arrivé à la gare vendredi soir. Et nous sommes allés dîner dans une excellente brasserie. Mmm!

**DAVID** Samedi, on a pris un bateau-mouche sur la Seine. J'ai visité un musée différent chaque jour: le musée du Louvre, le musée d'Orsay...
**RACHID** En résumé, tu as passé de bonnes vacances dans la capitale... Bon, on y va?
**DAVID** Ah, euh, oui, allons-y!

**STÉPHANE** Pour moi, les vacances idéales, c'est un voyage à Tahiti. Ahhh... la plage, et moi en maillot de bain avec des lunettes de soleil... et les filles en bikini!
**DAVID** Au fait, je n'ai pas oublié ton anniversaire.
**STÉPHANE** Ouah! Super, ces lunettes de soleil! Merci, David, c'est gentil.

**DAVID** Désolé de ne pas avoir été là pour ton anniversaire, Stéphane. Alors, ils t'ont fait la surprise?
**STÉPHANE** Oui, et quelle belle surprise! J'ai reçu des cadeaux trop cool. Et le gâteau de Sandrine, je l'ai adoré.
**DAVID** Ah, Sandrine... elle est adorable... Euh, Stéphane, tu m'excuses une minute?

**DAVID** Coucou! Je suis de retour!
**SANDRINE** Oh! Salut, David. Alors, tu as aimé Paris?
**DAVID** Oui! J'ai fait plein de choses... de vraies petites vacances! On a fait...

**A C T I V I T É S**

**1** **Les événements** Mettez ces événements dans l'ordre chronologique.

_1_ a. Rachid va chercher David.
_6_ b. Stéphane parle de son anniversaire.
_10_ c. Sandrine va faire une réservation.
_5_ d. David donne un cadeau à Stéphane.
_2_ e. Rachid mentionne que David a beaucoup de sacs.
_7_ f. Stéphane met les lunettes de soleil.
_4_ g. Stéphane décrit (*describes*) ses vacances idéales.
_8_ h. David parle avec Sandrine.
_9_ i. Sandrine pense à ses vacances.
_3_ j. Rachid et David repartent en voiture.

 Practice more at **daccord1.vhlcentral.com**.

**O P T I O N S**

**Avant de regarder la vidéo** Before viewing the video episode **De retour au P'tit Bistrot**, have pairs of students make a list of things someone might say when describing a trip and talking about means of transportation.

**Regarder la vidéo** Download and print the videoscript on the Supersite, and white out words related to travel and transportation. Distribute the scripts to pairs or groups to complete as cloze paragraphs as they watch the video.

## David parle de ses vacances.

**STÉPHANE** Alors, ces vacances? Tu as fait un bon séjour?
**DAVID** Oui, formidable!
**STÉPHANE** Alors, vous êtes restés combien de temps à Paris?
**DAVID** Quatre jours. Ce n'est pas très long, mais on a visité pas mal d'endroits.
**STÉPHANE** Comment est-ce que vous avez visité la ville? En voiture?

**DAVID** En voiture!? Tu es fou! On a pris le métro, comme tout le monde.
**STÉPHANE** Tes parents n'aiment pas conduire?
**DAVID** Si, à la campagne, mais pas en ville, surtout une ville comme Paris. On a visité les monuments, les musées...
**STÉPHANE** Et Monsieur l'artiste a aimé les musées de Paris?
**DAVID** Je les ai adorés!

**SANDRINE** Oh! Des vacances!
**DAVID** Oui... Des vacances? Qu'est-ce qu'il y a?
**SANDRINE** Je vais à Albertville pour les vacances d'hiver. On va faire du ski!

**SANDRINE** Est-ce que tu skies?
**DAVID** Un peu, oui...
**SANDRINE** Désolée, je dois partir. J'ai une réservation à faire! Rendez-vous ici demain, David. D'accord? Ciao!

---

## Expressions utiles

### Talking about vacations

- **Tu es parti pour Paris avec une valise et te voici avec ces énormes sacs en plus!**
  *You left for Paris with one suitcase and here you are with these huge extra bags!*
- **Nous sommes allés aux Galeries Lafayette.**
  *We went to the Galeries Lafayette.*
- **On a acheté des trucs pour l'appartement aussi.**
  *We also bought some things for the apartment.*
- **Moi, je suis arrivé à la gare vendredi soir et nous sommes allés dîner.**
  *I got to/arrived at the station Friday night and we went to dinner.*
- **On a pris un bateau-mouche sur la Seine.**
  *We took a sightseeing boat on the Seine.*
- **Vous êtes restés combien de temps à Paris?**
  *How long did you stay in Paris?*
- **On a pris le métro, comme tout le monde.**
  *We took the subway, like everyone else.*
- **J'ai fait plein de choses.**
  *I did a lot of things.*
- **Les musées de Paris, je les ai adorés!**
  *The museums in Paris, I loved them!*

### Additional vocabulary

- **Alors, ils t'ont fait la surprise?**
  *So, they surprised you?*
- **J'ai reçu des cadeaux trop cool.**
  *I got the coolest gifts.*
- **Le gâteau, je l'ai adoré.**
  *I loved the cake.*
- **Tu m'excuses une minute?**
  *Would you excuse me a minute?*
- **Oui, formidable!**
  *Yes, wonderful!*
- **Qu'est-ce qu'il y a?**
  *What is the matter?*
- **Désolé(e), je dois partir.**
  *Sorry, I have to leave.*

---

**Expressions utiles**
- Model the pronunciation of the **Expressions utiles** and have students repeat them after you.
- Draw attention to expressions with direct object pronouns and the **passé composé** with **être** in the video still captions, in the **Expressions utiles** box, and as they occur in your conversation with students. Point out that this material will be formally presented in **Structures**.
- Respond briefly to questions about direct object pronouns and the **passé composé** with **être**. Reinforce correct forms, but do not expect students to produce them consistently at this time.
- Point out that **cool** is invariable since it is an adopted word.
- Point out to students that the word **formidable** is a **faux ami**, meaning *wonderful*, not *formidable*.
- Remind students that **désolée** in the last sentence is feminine because Sandrine is talking about herself. A man would say, **(je suis) désolé**.

**1** **Suggestion** Form several groups of five students. Write each of these sentences on individual strips of paper and distribute them among the students in each group (two per student). Copy a set of sentences for each group. Have students read their sentences aloud in the proper order.

**1** **Expansion** Have students write sentences to fill in parts of the story not mentioned in this activity.

**2** **Expansion** Give students time to write out their answers to these questions. Then ask volunteers to write them on the board.

**3** **Suggestion** Before starting this activity, review vocabulary for weather, clothing, and activities by asking questions. Examples: **Quel temps fait-il à Paris en été? à Albertville en hiver? Qu'est-ce que vous aimez faire à la plage? à la montagne? Qu'est-ce que vous mettez quand il fait chaud? quand il fait froid?**

---

**2** **Questions** Répondez aux questions. <small>Answers may vary slightly.</small>

1. David est parti pour Paris avec combien de valises? À son retour (*Upon his return*), est-ce qu'il a le même nombre de valises?
   <small>Il est parti avec une valise. Non, à son retour, il a des sacs en plus.</small>
2. Qu'est-ce que David a fait pour ses vacances?
   <small>Il a visité Paris avec ses parents.</small>
3. Qu'est-ce que David donne à Stéphane comme cadeau d'anniversaire? Stéphane aime-t-il le cadeau?
   <small>Il donne des lunettes de soleil à Stéphane. Oui, Stéphane aime beaucoup le cadeau.</small>
4. Quelles sont les vacances idéales de Stéphane? <small>C'est un voyage à Tahiti.</small>
   <small>Stéphane est à la plage en maillot de bain avec des lunettes de soleil.</small>
5. Qu'est-ce que Sandrine va faire pour ses vacances d'hiver?
   <small>Elle va faire du ski à Albertville.</small>

**3** **Écrivez** Imaginez: vous êtes David, Stéphane ou Sandrine et vous allez en vacances à Paris, Tahiti ou Albertville. Écrivez un e-mail à Valérie. Quel temps fait-il? Où est-ce que vous séjournez? Quels vêtements est-ce que vous avez apportés? Qu'est-ce que vous faites chaque jour?

 ressources

CA
pp. 91-92    daccord1.vhlcentral.com

**ACTIVITÉS**

---

**Les bateaux-mouches** Touring by **bateau-mouche** is an excellent way to see the famous sights along the River Seine. Tourists can listen to narrations in various languages as they pass by **la cathédrale de Notre-Dame**, **la Conciergerie**, under the ornate **pont Alexandre III**, under the oldest bridge in Paris **le Pont Neuf**, **la tour Eiffel**, and even a miniature version of the **statue de la Liberté**.

**Skits** Have students work in groups of four to prepare a skit to present to the class. In the skit, the group of friends checks into a hotel and decides what they feel like doing for the rest of the day. Tell them to describe what city they are visiting, describe the hotel and their rooms, and explain what activities they want to do while they are visiting the city.

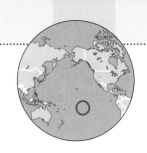

# CULTURE

**Leçon 7A**

**Video:** *Flash culture*

## CULTURE À LA LOUPE

# Tahiti

## Section Goals

In this section, students will:
- learn about Tahiti
- learn terms related to train travel
- find out some unusual facts about transportation in the francophone world
- read about **le musée d'Orsay**
- view authentic video footage

## Key Standards
2.1, 2.2, 3.1, 3.2, 4.2

**Student Resources**
*Cahier d'activités*, pp. 111–112;
Supersite: Activities,
*Cahier interactif*
**Teacher Resources**
Answer Keys; Video Script & Translation; *Flash culture* video

**Culture à la loupe**

**Avant la lecture** Ask students: **Où est Tahiti? Quelle(s) langue(s) parle-t-on à Tahiti?** Ask if anyone can explain Tahiti's relationship to France.

**Lecture** Pointing out the **Coup de main** box, explain the relationship between the verb tenses in the two clauses. Discourage students from experimenting with **si** clauses except those with both verbs in the present or one in the present and the other in **le futur proche**. **Si** clauses with the conditional are presented in **Level 2**.

**Après la lecture**
- Ask students to say something they learned from the passage that inspires them to visit Tahiti or that dissuades them from visiting. Examples: **J'ai envie de visiter Tahiti parce que j'adore la montagne et la plage. Moi, je n'ai pas envie d'aller à Tahiti parce que je déteste le temps très chaud.**
- You might also ask students to identify any review vocabulary in the passage. Examples: **la pêche, la planche à voile, faire des randonnées**, etc.

**1 Expansion** Continue the activity with these questions.
**11. Comment est le climat de Tahiti? (C'est un climat chaud.)**
**12. À part les plages, que peut-on visiter? (des montagnes, des lagons, des spas, Papeete)**
**13. Quelles attractions trouve-t-on à Papeete? (des restaurants, des boîtes de nuit, des boutiques variées et un marché)**

**Tahiti, dans le sud° de l'océan Pacifique, est la plus grande île° de la Polynésie française.** Elle devient° un protectorat français en 1842, puis° une colonie française en 1880. Depuis 1959, elle fait partie de la collectivité d'outre-mer° de Polynésie française. Les langues officielles de Tahiti sont le français et le tahitien.

Le tourisme est une source d'activité très importante pour l'île. Ses hôtels de luxe et leurs fameux bungalows sur l'eau accueillent° près de 200.000 visiteurs par an. Les touristes apprécient Tahiti pour son climat chaud, ses plages superbes et sa culture riche en traditions. À Tahiti, il y a la possibilité de faire toutes sortes d'activités aquatiques comme du bateau, de la pêche, de la planche à voile ou de la plongée°. On peut aussi faire des randonnées en montagne ou explorer les nombreux lagons bleus de l'île. Si on n'a pas envie de faire de sport, on peut

se détendre° dans un spa, bronzer à la plage ou se promener° sur l'île. Papeete, capitale de la Polynésie française et ville principale de Tahiti, offre de bons restaurants, des boîtes de nuit, des boutiques variées et un marché.

sud *south* la plus grande île *the largest island* devient *becomes* puis *then* collectivité d'outre-mer *overseas territory* accueillent *welcome* plongée *scuba diving* se détendre *relax* se promener *go for a walk*

### Coup de main

**Si** introduces a hypothesis. It may come at the beginning or at the middle of a sentence.

**si** + *subject* + *verb* + *subject* + *verb*

**Si on n'a pas envie de faire de sport, on peut se détendre dans un spa.**

*subject* + *verb* + **si** + *subject* + *verb*

**On peut se détendre dans un spa si on n'a pas envie de faire de sport.**

## ACTIVITÉS

**1 Répondez** Répondez aux questions par des phrases complètes.

1. Où est Tahiti?
Tahiti est dans le sud de l'océan Pacifique.
2. Quand est-ce que Tahiti devient une colonie française?
Tahiti devient une colonie en 1880.
3. De quoi fait partie Tahiti?
Tahiti fait partie de la collectivité d'outre-mer de Polynésie française.
4. Quelles langues parle-t-on à Tahiti?
On parle français et tahitien.
5. Quelle particularité ont les hôtels de luxe à Tahiti?
Les hôtels de luxe ont des bungalows sur l'eau.

6. Combien de personnes par an visitent Tahiti?
Près de 200.000 touristes par an visitent Tahiti.
7. Pourquoi est-ce que les touristes aiment visiter Tahiti? Les touristes aiment visiter Tahiti parce qu'il fait chaud et parce que les plages sont superbes.
8. Quelles sont deux activités sportives que les touristes aiment faire à Tahiti?
Answers may vary. Possible answer: Ils aiment faire du bateau et de la plongée.
9. Comment s'appelle la ville principale de Tahiti?
La ville principale de Tahiti s'appelle Papeete.
10. Où va-t-on à Papeete pour acheter un cadeau pour un ami?
On va au marché ou dans les boutiques.

**224** *deux cent vingt-quatre*

**OPTIONS**

**Oral Practice** Have students imagine arriving in Tahiti to meet a friend who lives there. The "visitor" should ask about possible ways to spend time during the visit and the "resident" should propose activities (basing information on the reading and the vocabulary from **Contextes**).

Then combine two pairs for a reflection on each pair's experiences while together in Tahiti. One pair should ask the other pair what they did, using **les pronoms disjoints** for emphasis and contrast. Encourage students to use an array of verbs conjugated in the **passé composé** with **être** and **avoir**.

## LE FRANÇAIS QUOTIDIEN

### À la gare

| | |
|---|---|
| **contrôleur** | *ticket inspector* |
| **couchette** | *berth* |
| **guichet** | *ticket window* |
| **horaire** | *schedule* |
| **quai** | *train/metro platform* |
| **voie** | *track* |
| **wagon-lit** | *sleeper car* |
| **composter** | *to punch one's (train) ticket* |

## LE MONDE FRANCOPHONE

### Les transports

Voici quelques faits insolites° dans les transports.
**Au Canada** Inauguré en 1966, le métro de Montréal est le premier du monde à rouler° sur des pneus° et non sur des roues° en métal. Chaque station a été conçue° par un architecte différent.
**En France** L'Eurotunnel (le tunnel sous la Manche°) permet aux trains Eurostar de transporter des voyageurs et des marchandises entre la France et l'Angleterre.
**En Mauritanie** Le train du désert, en Mauritanie, en Afrique, est peut-être le train de marchandises le plus long° du monde. Long de 2 à 3 km en général, le train fait deux ou trois voyages chaque jour du Sahara à la côte ouest°. C'est un voyage de plus de 600 km qui dure jusqu'à° 18 heures. Un des seuls moyens° de transport dans la région, ce train est aussi un train de voyageurs.

**faits insolites** *unusual facts* **rouler** *ride* **pneus** *tires* **roues** *wheels* **conçue** *designed* **Manche** *English Channel* **le plus long** *the longest* **côte ouest** *west coast* **dure jusqu'à** *lasts up to* **seuls moyens** *only means*

## PORTRAIT

# Le musée d'Orsay

Le musée d'Orsay est un des musées parisiens les plus° visités. Le lieu n'a pourtant° pas toujours été un musée. À l'origine, ce bâtiment° est une gare, construite par l'architecte Victor Laloux et inaugurée en 1900 à l'occasion de l'Exposition universelle. Les voies° de la gare d'Orsay deviennent° trop courtes et en 1939, on décide de limiter le service aux trains de banlieue. Plus tard, la gare sert de décor à des films, comme *Le Procès* de Kafka adapté par Orson Welles, puis° elle devient théâtre, puis salle de ventes aux enchères°. En 1986, le bâtiment est transformé en musée. Il est principalement dédié° à l'art du dix-neuvième siècle°, avec une magnifique collection d'art impressionniste.

**les plus** *the most* **pourtant** *however* **bâtiment** *building* **voies** *tracks* **deviennent** *become* **puis** *then* **ventes aux enchères** *auction* **principalement dédié** *mainly dedicated* **siècle** *century*

*Danseuses en bleu,*
Edgar Degas

### SUR INTERNET

Qu'est-ce que le funiculaire de Montmartre?

Go to **daccord1.vhlcentral.com** to find more information related to this **CULTURE** section. Then watch the corresponding **Flash culture**.

---

**2** **Vrai ou faux?** Indiquez si les phrases sont **vraies** ou **fausses**. Corrigez les phrases fausses.

1. Le musée d'Orsay a été un théâtre.
   Vrai.
2. Le musée d'Orsay a été une station de métro.
   Faux. Il a été une gare.
3. Le musée d'Orsay est dédié à la sculpture moderne.
   Faux. Le musée d'Orsay est dédié à l'art du dix-neuvième siècle.
4. Il y a un tunnel entre la France et la Guyane française.
   Faux. Il y a un tunnel entre la France et l'Angleterre.
5. Le métro de Montréal roule sur des roues en métal.
   Faux. Le métro de Montréal roule sur des pneus.
6. Le train du désert transporte aussi des voyageurs.
   Vrai.

**3** **Comment voyager?** Vous allez passer deux semaines en France. Vous avez envie de visiter Paris et deux autres régions. Par petits groupes, parlez des moyens (*means*) de transport que vous allez utiliser pendant votre voyage. Expliquez vos choix (*choices*).

**ressources**

CA
pp. 111–112

daccord1.vhlcentral.com

Practice more at **daccord1.vhlcentral.com.**

**A C T I V I T É S**

---

**Le français quotidien** Explain that French people visit **la SNCF (Société nationale des chemins de fer français)** to get information about rates and to buy train tickets (just as Americans go to an Amtrak station). Bring in a map showing train routes, so students understand the viability of train travel to and from big cities and small towns alike. Remind students of what they learned about **le TGV** in **Unité 2, Panorama**, page 67.

**Portrait** Show photos of Claude Monet's train paintings *La Gare Saint-Lazare*, *Train dans la neige*, and *Train dans la campagne*, the last of which is in **le musée d'Orsay**.

**Le monde francophone** Have students work in pairs to ask each other content questions. Examples: **1. Quel est le nom du tunnel entre la France et l'Angleterre?** (L'Eurotunnel/ le tunnel sous la Manche) **2. Quelle est une des différences entre le métro de Montréal et le métro de Paris?** (Le métro de Montréal roule sur des pneus.)

**2** **Expansion** Continue the activity with these true/false statements.
**7. La gare d'Orsay a servi de décor à des films.** (Vrai.)
**8. Quand les voies deviennent trop courtes, la gare d'Orsay est limitée au métro.** (Faux, aux trains de banlieue)

**3** **Expansion** Once students have agreed on the areas they would like to visit, they should consult road and train maps to see which **moyen de transport** would work best.

**Flash culture** Tell students that they will learn more about transportation and lodging by watching a variety of real-life images narrated by Csilla. Show the video segment without sound and tell students to call out what they see. Then show the video segment again with sound. You can also use the activities in the video manual in class to reinforce this **Flash culture** or assign them as homework.

---

**OPTIONS**

**Cultural Comparison** Bring in maps of the Paris **métro** and **RER** along with maps of a well-known American public transportation system, such as the New York City subway. Ask students: **Quel moyen de transport préférez-vous à Paris? à New York?** Then have them discuss their answers and plan mock commutes to various destinations in the two cities. Tell them to list similarities (**Similitudes**) and differences

(**Différences**) between the two subway systems. Have groups compare lists.
**Les transports** You may want to supplement this section by telling students about travel between **Tanger (Maroc)** and **Algésiras (Espagne)** via hydrofoil; between **la Corse**, **l'Italie**, and **la Tunisie** by ferry; **le funiculaire de Montmartre**; **les canaux** in France; and **le bus amphibie** in **Montréal**.

# STRUCTURES

## 7A.1 The *passé composé* with *être*

**Point de départ** In **Leçon 6A**, you learned to form the **passé composé** with **avoir**. Some verbs, however, form the **passé composé** with **être**.

- To form the **passé composé** of these verbs, use a present-tense form of **être** and the past participle of the verb that expresses the action.

| PRESENT TENSE | PAST PARTICIPLE | | PRESENT TENSE | PAST PARTICIPLE |
|---|---|---|---|---|
| Je **suis** | **allé**. | Il **est** | **sorti**. |

- Many of the verbs that take **être** in the **passé composé** involve motion. You have already learned a few of them: **aller, arriver, descendre, partir, passer, rentrer, sortir,** and **tomber.**

Jean-Luc **est parti** en vacances.
*Jean-Luc left on vacation.*

Je **suis tombé** de la chaise.
*I fell off the chair.*

*Tu es parti pour Paris.*

*Mes parents sont arrivés des États-Unis.*

- The past participles of verbs conjugated with **être** agree with their subjects in number and gender.

Charles, tu **es allé** à Montréal?
*Charles, did you go to Montreal?*

Florence **est partie** en vacances.
*Florence left on vacation.*

Mes frères **sont rentrés**.
*My brothers came back.*

Elles **sont arrivées** hier soir.
*They arrived last night.*

- To make a verb negative in the **passé composé**, place **ne/n'** and **pas** around the auxiliary verb, in this case, **être**.

Emma et Élodie **ne sont pas sorties**?
*Emma and Élodie didn't go out?*

Nous **ne sommes pas allées** à la plage.
*We didn't go to the beach.*

Je **ne suis pas passé** chez mon amie.
*I didn't stop by my friend's house.*

Vous **n'êtes pas rentrés** à la maison hier.
*You didn't come home yesterday.*

---

## MISE EN PRATIQUE

**1** **Un week-end sympa** Carole raconte son week-end à Paris. Complétez l'histoire avec les formes correctes des verbes au passé composé.

Thomas et moi, nous (1) __sommes partis__ (partir) de Lyon samedi et nous (2) __sommes arrivés__ (arriver) à Paris à onze heures. Nous (3) __sommes passés__ (passer) à l'hôtel et puis, je (4) __suis allée__ (aller) au Louvre. En route, je (5) __suis tombée__ (tomber) sur un vieil ami, et nous (6) __sommes allés__ (aller) prendre un café. Ensuite, je (7) __suis entrée__ (entrer) dans le musée. Samedi soir, Thomas et moi (8) __sommes montés__ (monter) au sommet de la tour Eiffel et après, nous (9) __sommes sortis__ (sortir) en boîte. Dimanche, nous (10) __sommes retournés__ (retourner) au Louvre. Ouf... je suis fatiguée!

**2** **Dimanche dernier** Dites ce que (*what*) ces personnes ont fait dimanche dernier. Utilisez les verbes de la liste. Suggested answers

**MODÈLE**

*Laure est allée à la piscine.*

| aller | monter |
|---|---|
| arriver | rentrer |
| descendre | sortir |

**Laure**

**1. je** Je suis rentré tard.

**3. nous** Nous sommes allés à l'église.

**2. tu** Tu es descendue à l'hôtel.

**4. Pamela et Caroline** Pamela et Caroline sont sorties.

**3** **L'accident** Le mois dernier, Djénaba et Safiatou sont allées au Sénégal. Racontez (*Tell*) leur histoire. Avec un(e) partenaire, complétez les phrases au passé composé. Ensuite, mettez-les dans l'ordre chronologique.

__1__ a. les filles / partir pour Dakar en avion
Les filles sont parties pour Dakar en avion.

__5__ b. Djénaba / tomber de vélo
Djénaba est tombée de vélo.

__4__ c. elles / aller faire du vélo dimanche matin
Elles sont allées faire du vélo dimanche matin.

__2__ d. elles / arriver à Dakar tard le soir
Elles sont arrivées à Dakar tard le soir.

__3__ e. elles / descendre à l'hôtel Sofitel
Elles sont descendues à l'hôtel Sofitel.

__6__ f. elle / aller à l'hôpital
Elle est allée à l'hôpital.

Practice more at **daccord1.vhlcentral.com.**

---

## Section Goals

In this section, students will learn the **passé composé** with **être**.

## Key Standards

**4.1, 5.1**

**Student Resources**
*Cahier d'exercices*, pp. 87-88;
*Cahier d'activités*, pp. 11, 165;
Supersite: Activities,
*Cahier interactif*

**Teacher Resources**
Answer Keys; Overhead #34;
Audio Script; Audio Activity
MP3s/CD; *Feuilles d'activités*;
Testing program: Grammar Quiz

## Suggestions

- Quickly review the **passé composé** with **avoir**.
- Introduce the **passé composé** with **être** by describing where you went yesterday. Example: **Hier, je suis allé(e) à la bibliothèque. Ensuite, je suis allé(e) chez moi.** Then ask students: **Et vous, où êtes-vous allé(e) hier?**
- Write the **passé composé** of **donner** and **aller** on the board. Have students compare the forms of the **passé composé** with **avoir** and **être**.
- Explain the agreement of past participles in the **passé composé** with **être**.
- Point out the verbs that form the **passé composé** with **être** as well as the irregular past participles **mort** and **né**.
- Tell students that the present tense forms of **naître** and **mourir** are rarely used.
- Have students turn to the illustration on pages 218–219 or use **Overhead #34** and have them describe the scene in the past.
- Tell students they will learn about adverbs in Structures 7B.1
- Point out that the verb **rester** means *to stay* in the sense of *not leaving*. One uses the verb **descendre** (with **être** in the p.c.) when referring to staying in a hotel. Example: **Nous sommes descendus dans un hôtel pour la nuit.** (*We stayed in a hotel for the night.*) **Loger** and **séjourner** (with **avoir** in the p.c.) are also common and acceptable ways to express the same idea.

**Oral Drill** To practice choosing between the **passé composé** with **être** and the **passé composé** with **avoir**, call out infinitives and have students respond with **avoir** or **être** and the past participle. Examples: **1. voyager (avoir voyagé) 2. entrer (être entré) 3. aller (être allé) 4. parler (avoir parlé) 5. retourner (être retourné)**

**Using Games** Divide the class into two teams. Choose one team member at a time to go to the board, alternating between teams. Say a subject pronoun and an infinitive. The person at the board must write and say the correct **passé composé** form. Example: **je: aller (je suis allé[e])**. Give a point for each correct answer. The team with the most points at the end of the game wins.

## COMMUNICATION

**4 Les vacances de printemps** Avec un(e) partenaire, parlez de vos dernières vacances de printemps. Répondez à toutes ses questions. *Answers will vary.*

### MODÈLE

quand / partir
**Élève 1:** *Quand es-tu parti(e)?*
**Élève 2:** *Je suis parti(e) vendredi soir.*

1. où / aller
2. avec qui / partir
3. comment / voyager
4. à quelle heure / arriver
5. où / descendre
6. combien de temps / rester
7. que / visiter
8. sortir / souvent le soir
9. que / acheter
10. quand / rentrer

**5 Enquête** Votre professeur va vous donner une feuille d'activités. Circulez dans la classe et demandez à différents camarades s'ils ont fait ces choses récemment (*recently*). Présentez les résultats de votre enquête à la classe. *Answers will vary.*

### MODÈLE

**Élève 1:** *Es-tu allé(e) au musée récemment?*
**Élève 2:** *Oui, je suis allé(e) au musée jeudi dernier.*

| Questions | Noms |
|---|---|
| 1. aller au musée | François |
| 2. passer chez ses amis | |
| 3. sortir en boîte | |
| 4. rester à la maison pour écouter de la musique | |
| 5. partir en week-end | |
| 6. monter dans un avion | |

**6 À l'aéroport** Par groupes de quatre, parlez d'une mauvaise expérience dans un aéroport. À tour de rôle, racontez (*tell*) vos aventures et posez le plus (*most*) de questions possible. Utilisez les expressions de la liste et d'autres. *Answers will vary.*

### MODÈLE

**Élève 1:** *Quand je suis rentré(e) de la Martinique, j'ai attendu trois heures à la douane.*
**Élève 2:** *Quelle horreur! Pourquoi?*

| arriver | partir |
|---|---|
| attendre | perdre |
| avion | prendre un avion |
| billet (aller-retour) | sortir |
| douane | vol |

---

- Here are a few more verbs that take **être** instead of **avoir** in the **passé composé**.

### Some verbs used with *être*

| entrer | to enter | naître | to be born |
|---|---|---|---|
| monter | to go up; to get in/on | rester | to stay |
| mourir | to die | retourner | to return |

Mes parents **sont nés** en 1958 à Paris.
*My parents were born in 1958 in Paris.*

Ma grand-mère maternelle **est morte** l'année dernière.
*My maternal grandmother died last year.*

- Note that the verb **passer** takes **être** when it means *to pass by*, but it takes **avoir** when it means *to spend time*.

Maryse **est passée** par la douane.
*Maryse passed through customs.*

Maryse **a passé** trois jours à la campagne.
*Maryse spent three days in the country.*

- To form a question using inversion in the **passé composé**, invert the subject pronoun and the conjugated form of **être**.

**Est-elle descendue** à l'hôtel Aquabella?
*Did she stay at the Hotel Aquabella?*

**Vous êtes arrivée** ce matin, Madame Roch?
*Did you arrive this morning, Mrs. Roch?*

- Place short adverbs such as **déjà**, **encore**, **bien**, **mal**, and **beaucoup** between the auxiliary verb **être** or **pas** and the past participle.

Elle **est déjà rentrée** de vacances?
*She already came back from vacation?*

Nous **ne sommes pas encore arrivés** à Aix-en-Provence.
*We haven't arrived in Aix-en-Provence yet.*

**Essayez!** Choisissez le participe passé approprié.

1. Vous êtes (nés/né) en 1959, Monsieur?
2. Les élèves sont (partis/parti) le 2 juin.
3. Les filles sont (rentrées/rentrés) de vacances.
4. Simone de Beauvoir est-elle (mort/morte) en 1986?
5. Mes frères sont (sortis/sortie).
6. Paul n'est pas (resté/restée) chez sa grand-mère.
7. Tu es (arrivés/arrivée) avant dix heures, Sophie.
8. Jacqueline a (passée/passé) une semaine en Suisse.

---

**Essayez!** For additional practice, change the subjects of the sentences (except items 1 and 7), and have students restate or rewrite them.

**1 Suggestion** Before beginning the activity, have students identify the past participles of the verbs in parentheses.

**2 Expansion** Ask students what they did last Sunday.

**3 Expansion** Have two volunteers play the roles of Djénaba and Safiatou. Tell the rest of the class to ask them questions about their trip. Example: **Quand êtes-vous arrivées à Dakar?**

**4 Suggestion** Have two volunteers read the **modèle** aloud.

**5 Suggestion** Distribute the **Feuilles d'activités** found on the Supersite.

**6 Suggestion** Before beginning the activity, ask the students about their travel experiences. Example: **Êtes-vous déjà allé(e)s dans un autre pays?**

---

**OPTIONS**

**Using Video** Show the video episode again to give students more input regarding the **passé composé** with **être** and **avoir**. Pause the video where appropriate to discuss how certain verbs were used and to ask comprehension questions.

**Writing Practice** Using the information in the **Roman-photo**, have students write a summary of David's trip to Paris. Then have students get together with a partner and exchange papers. Tell them to peer edit each other's work. Remind them to check for the correct usage of **avoir** and **être** in the **passé composé**, subject-verb agreement, and the correct forms of past participles.

## Section Goals

In this section, students will learn direct object pronouns.

## Key Standards

4.1, 5.1

---

**Student Resources**
*Cahier d'exercices*, pp. 89–90;
*Cahier d'activités*, p. 166;
Supersite: Activities,
*Cahier interactif*
**Teacher Resources**
Answer Keys; Audio Script;
Audio Activity MP3s/CD;
Testing program: Grammar Quiz

---

## Suggestions

- Write these sentences on the board: **Qui a les tickets? Roger les a.** Underline **les tickets** and explain that it is the direct object. The direct object receives the action of the verb. It answers the questions *what?* or *whom?* Then underline **les** and explain that it is the plural direct object pronoun. Translate both sentences, pointing out the word order. Follow the same procedure with these sentences.
  —**Qui prend le bus?**
  —**Les élèves le prennent.**
  —**Qui écrit la lettre?**
  —**Mon père l'écrit.**
- Take various objects from students' desks and ask: **Qui a _____?** Have students respond using the direct object pronoun: **Vous _____ avez.**
- Point out that direct objects are never preceded by a preposition.
- Continue asking questions to elicit other direct object pronouns. Examples: **M'entendez-vous? (Oui, nous vous entendons.) Qui achète vos vêtements? (Mes parents les achètent.)**
- Explain the agreement of past participles with direct object pronouns in the **passé composé**.

---

## 7A.2 Direct object pronouns

**Point de départ** In **Leçon 6B**, you learned about indirect objects. You are now going to learn about direct objects.

DIRECT OBJECT    INDIRECT OBJECT
J'ai fait **un cadeau à ma sœur**.
*I gave a gift to my sister.*

- Note that a direct object receives the action of a verb directly and an indirect object receives the action of a verb indirectly. While indirect objects are frequently preceded by the preposition à, no preposition is needed before the direct object.

  J'emmène **mes parents**.    *but*    Je parle **à mes parents**.
  *I'm taking my parents.*      *I'm speaking to my parents.*

- You can use a direct object pronoun in the place of a direct object noun.

  Tu fais **les valises**?     Tu **les** fais?
  *Are you packing the suitcases?*    *Are you packing them?*

  Ils retrouvent **Luc** à la gare.    Ils **le** retrouvent à la gare.
  *They're meeting Luc at*     *They're meeting him at*
  *the station.*       *the station.*

### Direct object pronouns

| singular | | plural | |
|---|---|---|---|
| me/m' | *me* | nous | *us* |
| te/t' | *you* | vous | *you* |
| le/la/l' | *him/her/it* | les | *them* |

*Tes parents sont allés te chercher?*

*Tu m'excuses une minute?*

- Place a direct object pronoun before the conjugated verb.

  Les langues? Laurent et Xavier **les** étudient.    Les élèves **vous** ont entendu(e)(s).
  *Languages? Laurent and Xavier study them.*    *The students heard you.*

---

## MISE EN PRATIQUE

**1** **Des activités** Dites ce que (*what*) ces gens font le week-end. Employez les pronoms d'objet direct.

**MODÈLE**
Il l'écoute.

Dominique écoute ce CD.

**1. Benoît regarde ses DVD.**
Il les regarde.

**3. Il mange son gâteau.**
Il le mange.

**2. Ma mère admire cette robe.**
Elle l'admire.

**4. Ils achètent ces lunettes.**
Ils les achètent.

**2** **À la plage** La famille de Dalila a passé une semaine à la mer. Dalila parle de ce que (*what*) chaque membre de sa famille a fait. Employez des pronoms d'objet direct.

**MODÈLE**
J'ai conduit Ahmed à la plage. *Je l'ai conduit à la plage.*

1. Mon père a acheté le journal tous les matins.
   Il l'a acheté tous les matins.
2. Ma sœur a retrouvé son petit ami au café.
   Elle l'a retrouvé au café.
3. Mes parents ont emmené les enfants au cinéma.
   Ils les ont emmenés au cinéma.
4. Mon frère a invité sa fiancée au restaurant.
   Il l'a invitée au restaurant.
5. Anissa a porté ses lunettes de soleil.
   Elle les a portées.
6. À midi, Chekib a acheté les baguettes pour le repas (*meal*). À midi, il les a achetées.

**3** **Des doutes** Julie et son amie Caroline sont au parc. Elle répond à ses questions sur leurs vacances chez ses parents. Formez les questions que pose Caroline. Avec un(e) partenaire, jouez les deux rôles. Ensuite, présentez la scène à la classe. Suggested answers

1. Oui, mes parents t'invitent au bord de la mer.
   Tes parents m'invitent au bord de la mer?
2. Oui, je vais t'attendre à l'aéroport.
   Quelqu'un va m'attendre à l'aéroport?
3. Oui, mon frère va nous emmener sur son bateau.
   Ton frère va-t-il nous emmener sur son bateau?
4. Oui, je pense que ma famille va bien t'aimer.
   Penses-tu que ta famille va bien m'aimer?
5. J'ai choisi d'emporter (*take*) les chaussures vertes.
   Quelles chaussures as-tu choisies d'emporter?
6. J'ai pris le maillot de bain bleu.
   Quel maillot de bain as-tu pris?

💲 Practice more at **daccord1.vhlcentral.com**.

---

## COMMUNICATION

**4** **À Tahiti** Vous allez partir à Tahiti. Avec un(e) partenaire, posez-vous ces questions. Il/Elle vous répond en utilisant (*by using*) le pronom d'objet direct approprié. Ensuite, alternez les rôles. Answers will vary.

**MODÈLE**

Est-ce que tu prends le bus pour aller à la plage?
*Non, je ne le prends pas.*

1. Est-ce que tu prends l'avion?
2. Qui va t'attendre à l'aéroport?
3. Quand as-tu fait tes valises?
4. Est-ce que tu as acheté ton maillot de bain?
5. Est-ce que tu prends ton appareil photo?
6. Quels vêtements as-tu achetés?
7. Tu vas regarder la télévision tahitienne?
8. Vas-tu essayer les plats typiques de Tahiti?

**5** **Le départ** Clémentine va partir au Cameroun chez sa correspondante (*pen pal*) Léa. Sa mère veut (*wants*) être sûre qu'elle n'a pas oublié un objet important, mais sa fille n'a presque rien (*nothing*) fait. Avec un(e) partenaire, jouez leur conversation en utilisant les phrases de la liste. Answers will vary.

**MODÈLE**

**Élève 1:** *Tu as acheté le cadeau pour ton amie?*
**Élève 2:** *Non, je ne l'ai pas encore acheté.*
**Élève 1:** *Quand vas-tu l'acheter?*
**Élève 2:** *Je vais l'acheter cet après-midi.*

| | |
|---|---|
| acheter ton billet d'avion | faire tes valises |
| avoir l'adresse de Léa | prendre tes lunettes |
| chercher ton maillot de bain | préparer tes vêtements |
| confirmer l'heure d'arrivée | trouver ton passeport |

---

• In a negative statement, place the direct object pronoun between **ne/n'** and the conjugated verb.

Le chinois? Je **ne le parle pas**.
*Chinese? I don't speak it.*

Elle **ne l'a pas** pris à 14 heures?
*She didn't take it at 2 o'clock?*

• When an infinitive follows a conjugated verb, the direct object pronoun precedes the infinitive.

Marcel va **nous écouter**.
*Marcel is going to listen to us.*

Tu ne préfères pas **la porter** demain?
*Don't you prefer to wear it tomorrow?*

• When a direct object pronoun is used with the **passé composé**, the past participle must agree with it in both gender and number.

J'ai mis **la valise** dans la voiture ce matin.
*I put the suitcase in the car this morning.*

Je **l'ai mise** dans la voiture ce matin.
*I put it in the car this morning.*

J'ai attendu **les filles** à la gare.
*I waited for the girls at the station.*

Je **les ai attendues** à la gare.
*I waited for them at the station.*

• In questions using **Quel(s)/Quelle(s)** and the **passé composé**, the past participle must agree with the gender and number of **Quel(s)/Quelle(s)**.

**Quel** hôtel avez-vous **choisi**?
*Which hotel did you choose?*

**Quels** pays as-tu **visités**?
*Which countries did you visit?*

**Quelle** plage as-tu **préférée**?
*Which beach did you prefer?*

**Quelles** valises as-tu **apportées**?
*Which suitcases did you bring?*

---

**Essayez!** Répondez aux questions en remplaçant (*by replacing*) l'objet direct par un pronom d'objet direct.

1. Thierry prend le train? Oui, il __le__ prend.
2. Tu attends ta mère? Oui, je __l'__ attends.
3. Vous entendez Olivier et Vincent? Oui, on __les__ entend.
4. Le professeur te cherche? Oui, il __me__ cherche.
5. Quels copains retrouves-tu au parc? Marc et Cyril? Oui, je __les__ retrouve au parc.
6. Vous m'invitez? Oui, nous __t'/vous__ invitons.
7. Tu nous comprends? Oui, je __vous__ comprends.
8. Quelle valise prends-tu pour aller en vacances? La rouge? Oui, je __la__ prends.
9. Chloé aime écouter la musique classique? Oui, elle aime __l'__ écouter.
10. Vous avez regardé le film *Chacun cherche son chat*? Oui, nous __l'__ avons regardé.

---

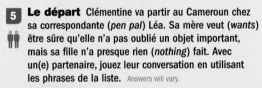

**Essayez!** For additional practice, have students restate or rewrite the answers in the negative.

**1** **Suggestion** Have students ask questions with a direct object pronoun for each item. Example: **Qui l'écoute?**

**2** **Suggestion** Before beginning the activity, have students identify the direct objects.

**3** **Suggestion** Tell students to add two of their own questions to the list.

**4** **Suggestions**
• Before beginning the activity, have students describe the photo.
• Tell students to add three of their own questions with direct objects to the list.

**5** **Suggestions**
• Before beginning the activity, have students underline the direct objects in the phrases.
• Have two volunteers read the **modèle** aloud.

---

**O P T I O N S**

**Questions** Make a list of twenty questions requiring direct object pronouns in the answer. Arrange students in two concentric circles. Students in the inner circle ask questions from the list to those in the outer circle until you say stop (**Arrêtez-vous**). The outer circle then moves one person to the right and the questions begin again. Continue for five minutes, and then have the students in the outer circle ask the questions.

**Skit** Have students work in pairs. Tell them to invent a romantic dialogue between Simone and Jean-Claude, two protagonists of a soap opera. They should include direct object pronouns in their dialogues and these verbs: **adorer, aimer, détester,** and **attendre**. Example: **Jean-Claude: Simone, je t'adore.**

STRUCTURES **229**

# SYNTHÈSE
# Révision

## Key Standards
1.1

**Student Resources**
*Cahier d'activités*, pp. 12, 59-60;
Supersite: Activities,
*Cahier interactif*

**Teacher Resources**
Answer Keys; *Feuilles d'activités*;
Info Gap Activities; Testing
Program: Lesson Test (Testing
Program Audio MP3s/CD)

**1 Suggestion** Tell students to write their sentences. Remind them that verbs that indicate motion often require the **passé composé** with **être**.

**2 Suggestions**
• Distribute the **Feuilles d'activités** found on the Supersite.
• Have two volunteers read the **modèle** aloud. Remind students to use direct object pronouns in their responses.

**3 Suggestion** Tell students to jot down notes during their interviews.

**4 Suggestion** Before beginning the activity, have the class identify the items.

**4 Expansion** To practice **vous** forms, bring in a small suitcase with various items and tell the class you just returned from a trip. Students must ask you questions about your vacation based on the items and figure out where you went. Example: a suitcase with gloves, a hat, a parka, and ski goggles.

**5 Expansion** Have groups decide who had the best or most interesting weekend, then ask them to tell the class about it.

**6 Suggestion** Divide the class into pairs and distribute the Info Gap Handouts found on the Supersite for this activity. Give students ten minutes to complete the activity.

---

**1 Il y a dix minutes** Avec un(e) partenaire, décrivez (*describe*) dans cette scène les actions qui se sont passées (*happened*) il y a dix minutes. Utilisez les verbes de la liste pour écrire (*write*) des phrases. Ensuite, comparez vos phrases avec les phrases d'un autre groupe. Answers will vary.

**MODÈLE**

**Élève 1:** *Il y a dix minutes, M. Hamid est parti.*
**Élève 2:** *Il y a dix minutes, …*

| aller | partir |
| arriver | rentrer |
| descendre | sortir |
| monter | tomber |

**2 Qui aime quoi?** Votre professeur va vous donner une feuille d'activités. Circulez dans la classe pour trouver un(e) camarade différent(e) qui aime ou qui n'aime pas chaque lieu de la liste. Answers will vary.

**MODÈLE**

**Élève 1:** *Est-ce que tu aimes les aéroports?*
**Élève 2:** *Je ne les aime pas du tout; je les déteste.*

**3 À l'étranger** Par groupes de quatre, interviewez vos camarades. Dans quels pays sont-ils déjà allés? Dans quelles villes? Comparez vos destinations, puis présentez toutes les réponses à la classe. N'oubliez pas de demander: Answers will vary.

• quand vos camarades sont parti(e)s
• où ils/elles sont allé(e)s
• où ils/elles sont resté(e)s
• combien de temps ils/elles ont passé là-bas

**4 La valise** Sandra et John sont partis en vacances. Voici leur valise. Avec un(e) partenaire, faites une description écrite (*written*) de leurs vacances. Où sont-ils allés? Comment sont-ils partis? Answers will vary.

**5 Un long week-end** Avec un(e) partenaire, préparez huit questions sur le dernier long week-end. Utilisez les verbes de la liste. Ensuite, par groupes de quatre, répondez à toutes les questions. Answers will vary.

**MODÈLE**

**Élève 1:** *Où es-tu allé(e) vendredi soir?*
**Élève 2:** *Vendredi soir, je suis resté(e) chez moi. Mais samedi, je suis sorti(e)!*

| aller | rentrer |
| arriver | rester |
| partir | retourner |
| passer | sortir |

**6 Mireille et les Girard** Votre professeur va vous donner, à vous et à votre partenaire, une feuille sur le week-end de Mireille et de la famille Girard. Attention! Ne regardez pas la feuille de votre partenaire. Answers will vary.

**MODÈLE**

**Élève 1:** *Qu'est-ce que Mireille a fait vendredi soir?*
**Élève 2:** *Elle est allée au cinéma.*

| ressources | | |
|---|---|---|
| CE pp. 87-90 | CA pp. 11-12, 59-60, 165-166 | ⓢ daccord1.vhlcentral.com |

---

OPTIONS

**Dehydrated Sentences** Write these phrases on the board. Tell students to write complete sentences, using the **passé composé**. **1.** Janine et moi / faire du shopping **2.** Nous / partir / une heure **3.** Nous / prendre / métro / Galeries Lafayette / et / nous / passer / après-midi / là **4.** Nous / arriver / chez Janine / fatigué **5.** Elle / ne pas / avoir besoin / sortir / pour manger / et / nous / rester / la maison

**Narrative** Have students write a composition about a memorable vacation they took with friends or family. Remind them to use the **passé composé**. They should also use object pronouns to avoid unnecessary repetition.

**Video: TV Clip**

# Le Zapping

## Le TER

En 1984, la SNCF (Société nationale des chemins de fer° français) met en place dans 20 régions le TER (Transport Express Régional). Les trains TER relient° les villes d'une même région ou de différentes régions. Il y a, entre autres, le TER Picardie et le TER Alsace. Ces trains sont rapides, confortables et pratiques pour éviter° les embouteillages° du matin et du soir. Les TER concrétisent la décentralisation des chemins de fer français, parce que ce sont les Conseils Régionaux qui financent et décident des trajets°, des dessertes° et des horaires°.

**ter** avec votre Région

—On devrait° parfois réfléchir avant de° prendre sa voiture.

—Pour être bien, bougeons mieux°.

**Compréhension** Répondez aux questions. Some answers will vary.

1. Comment le guépard (*cheetah*) chasse-t-il la gazelle? Il roule en voiture.
2. Quelle mauvaise surprise rencontre-t-il? Il rencontre un énorme embouteillage.
3. Pourquoi l'autre guépard va-t-il attraper la gazelle? Il prend le train et évite l'embouteillage.

**Discussion** Par groupes de trois, répondez aux questions. Answers will vary.

1. Quelle est l'importance du guépard dans cette publicité (*ad*)? Pourquoi pas un autre animal?
2. Quels moyens (*means*) de transport prenez-vous souvent? Pourquoi? Quels sont leurs avantages?

**chemins de fer** *railroads* **relient** *link* **éviter** *avoid* **embouteillages** *traffic jams* **trajets** *routes* **dessertes** *service* **horaires** *schedules* **devrait** *should* **réfléchir avant de** *think before* **bougeons mieux** *let's move better*

 Practice more at **daccord1.vhlcentral.com**.

**SNCF** In 1997, new European Union regulations required the **SNCF** to transfer the management of its network of tracks as well as other components of its infrastructure to a separate, government-subsidized company called the **RFF** (**Réseau ferré de France**). The **SNCF** still operates and maintains the trains themselves. Of course, the **SNCF** for years has collaborated with other rail entities. It has worked with the **RER** (suburban Paris commuter trains) for the purpose of sharing tracks and negotiating rail traffic and schedules. Furthermore, the **SNCF** has long collaborated with the **RATP** (Paris **Métro**) for running its trains on the subway network's lower-voltage tracks.

---

## Section Goals

In this section, students will:
- read about the network of regional **TER** trains
- watch a commercial for the regional trains
- answer questions about the commercial and traveling by train

## Key Standards

**1.2, 2.2, 4.2, 5.2**

**Student Resources**
Supersite: Video, Activities
**Teacher Resources**
Video Script & Translation; Supersite: Video

**Introduction**
To check comprehension, ask these questions: 1. **Quelle fonction ont les trains TER? (Ils relient les villes d'une même région ou de différentes régions.) 2. Pourquoi sont-ils pratiques? (On évite les embouteillages du matin et du soir.)**

**Avant de regarder la vidéo**
- Have students look at the video stills, read the captions, and predict what is happening in the commercial for each visual. (**1. Parfois, prendre la voiture n'est pas une bonne idée. 2. Pour être bien et ne pas perdre de temps, le train est une option intelligente.**)
- Before showing the video, explain to students that they do not need to understand every word they hear. Introduce the verb **réfléchir** and ask them to guess the English cognate (*to reflect*). Use the verb **bouger** in a few sample sentences and have students guess its meaning and create sentences of their own with it.

**Compréhension** Have students work in pairs or groups for this activity. Tell them to write their answers. Then show the video again so that they can check their answers and add any missing information.

**Discussion** Ask students if they have ever found themselves in a situation where riding in a car turned out unexpectedly to be the slowest option. What type of public transportation would they have picked instead?

## Section Goals

In this section, students will learn and practice vocabulary related to:
• hotels
• ordinal numbers
• sequencing events

## Key Standards

1.1, 1.2, 4.1

**Student Resources**
*Cahier d'exercices*, pp. 91-92;
*Cahier d'activités*, p. 167;
Supersite: Activities,
*Cahier interactif*
**Teacher Resources**
Answer Keys; Overhead #35;
Audio Script; Textbook & Audio
Activity MP3s/CD; Testing
program: Vocabulary Quiz

## Suggestions

• Use **Overhead #35**. Point out people and things in the illustration and describe what the people are doing. Example: **Ils sont à la réception d'un hôtel. Ils ont une réservation. Voici la clé de leur chambre.**

• Have students look over the new vocabulary. They should notice that many terms related to hotels and travel are cognates (**réservation, réception, passeport,** and **passager**).

• Point out that **passeport** has an **e** and **passager/passagère** have no **n**.

• Model the difference in pronunciation between **deuxième** and **douzième**, and have students repeat.

• Point out that the word **libre** means *free*, as in *available*, not *free of charge*.

• Emphasize that, in this context, **complet/complète** means *full*, not *complete*.

• Tell students that the word **second(e)** is used instead of **deuxième** when there are only two items to list. Example: **La Seconde Guerre mondiale.**

**Leçon 7B**

**You will learn how to...**
▪ make hotel reservations
▪ give instructions

S Talking Picture
Audio: Activity

# À l'hôtel

la réception

Bienvenue!

le lit

l'hôtelière (f.)

l'hôtelier (m.)

le passeport

la clé

les client(e)s

### Vocabulaire

| | |
|---|---|
| annuler une réservation | to cancel a reservation |
| réserver | to reserve, to book |
| premier/première | first |
| cinquième | fifth |
| neuvième | ninth |
| vingt et unième | twenty-first |
| vingt-deuxième | twenty-second |
| trente et unième | thirty-first |
| centième | hundredth |
| une agence de voyages | travel agency |
| un agent de voyages | travel agent |
| une auberge de jeunesse | youth hostel |
| une chambre individuelle | single room |
| un hôtel | hotel |
| un passager/une passagère | passenger |
| complet/complète | full (no vacancies) |
| libre | available |
| alors | so, then; at that moment |
| après (que) | after |
| avant (de) | before |
| d'abord | first |
| donc | therefore |
| enfin | finally, at last |
| ensuite | then, next |
| finalement | finally |
| pendant (que) | during, while |
| puis | then |
| tout à coup | suddenly |
| tout de suite | right away |

**ressources**

CE
pp. 91-92

CA
p. 167

S
daccord1.vhlcentral.com

232    *deux cent trente-deux*

---

**O P T I O N S**

**Using Movement** Ask ten volunteers to line up facing the class. Make sure students know what number they are in line. Call out ordinal numbers at random. The student whose cardinal number corresponds to the called ordinal number has three seconds to step forward. If that student is too slow, he or she sits down. The order changes for the rest of the students standing further down the line. The last students standing win.

**Les étages** Point out to students that a second floor in the U.S. would be called **le premier étage** in the Francophone world. Tell them that an **étage** is a floor above another floor. Elevators usually indicate the ground floor by the letter **R** (or other abbreviation of **rez-de-chaussée**) or the number **0**. Add that, in buildings with only two floors, people say **à l'étage** for *on the second floor*.

## Attention!

In French, form ordinal numbers by placing –ième at the end of the cardinal number. If the cardinal number ends in an –e, drop it before adding –ième. Note the spelling changes in cinquième and neuvième. Also note that the French word for first, premier/première (1er/1ère), is an exception.

onze → onzième (11e)
vingt → vingtième (20e)

le premier étage

le rez-de-chaussée

l'ascenseur (m.)

les étages (m.)

le troisième

le premier

1er. 100-110
2e. 200-210
3e. 300-310
4e. 400-410

le deuxième

le quatrième

# Mise en pratique

## 1 Remplissez Complétez les phrases avec le nombre ordinal qui convient (fits).

**MODÈLE**

B est la ___deuxième___ lettre de l'alphabet.

1. Décembre est le ___douzième___ mois de l'année.
2. Mercredi est le ___troisième___ jour de la semaine.
3. Aux États-Unis, le rez-de-chaussée est le ___premier___ étage.
4. Ma classe de français est au _Answers will vary._ (étage).
5. Octobre est le ___dixième___ mois de l'année.
6. Z est la ___vingt-sixième___ lettre de l'alphabet.
7. Samedi est le ___sixième___ jour de la semaine.
8. Barack Obama est le ___quarante-quatrième___ président des États-Unis.
9. Mon prénom (first name) commence avec la _Answers will vary._ lettre de l'alphabet.
10. La fête nationale américaine est le ___quatrième___ jour du mois de juillet.

## 2 Écoutez 🎧 Écoutez la conversation entre Mme Renoir et un hôtelier et décidez si les phrases sont vraies ou fausses.

| | Vrai | Faux |
|---|---|---|
| 1. Mme Renoir est à l'agence de voyages. | ☐ | ☑ |
| 2. Mme Renoir a fait une réservation. | ☑ | ☐ |
| 3. Mme Renoir prend la chambre au cinquième étage. | ☐ | ☑ |
| 4. Il y a un ascenseur dans l'hôtel. | ☐ | ☑ |
| 5. Mme Renoir a réservé une chambre à deux lits. | ☐ | ☑ |
| 6. La cliente s'appelle Margot Renoir. | ☑ | ☐ |
| 7. L'hôtel a des chambres libres. | ☐ | ☑ |
| 8. L'hôtelier donne à Mme Renoir la clé de la chambre 27. | ☑ | ☐ |

## 3 Hôtel Paradis Virginie téléphone à l'hôtel Paradis pour faire une réservation. Mettez les phrases dans l'ordre chronologique.

__6__ a. Finalement, il me demande le numéro de ma carte de crédit (credit card) pour finaliser la réservation.

__2__ b. Pendant la conversation, je demande une chambre individuelle au troisième étage.

__1__ c. D'abord, j'appelle l'hôtel Paradis pour faire une réservation.

__4__ d. Je ne veux (want) pas dormir au rez-de-chaussée, donc je demande une chambre au deuxième étage.

__3__ e. Ensuite, l'hôtel me rappelle (calls me back) pour annoncer qu'il n'y a plus de chambre libre au troisième étage, donc ma réservation est annulée.

__5__ f. C'est alors que l'hôtelier me donne une chambre au deuxième étage à côté de l'ascenseur.

🔎 Practice more at **daccord1.vhlcentral.com.**

*deux cent trente-trois* **233**

**1 Expansion**
• Point out that the French calendar begins the week with Monday.
• Give students these items. **11. Aujourd'hui, c'est le ____ jour de la semaine. 12. Ce cours est mon ____ cours aujourd'hui. 13. Ma chambre est au ____ étage. 14. Mon anniversaire est pendant le ____ mois de l'année.** (Answers will vary.)
• Have students invent riddles using ordinal numbers. Example: **Je suis le seizième président des États-Unis. Qui suis-je?** (Abraham Lincoln)

**2 Script** L'HÔTELIER: Bonjour, Madame. Bienvenue à l'hôtel Casablanca! Avez-vous une réservation?
LA CLIENTE: Bonjour, Monsieur. Oui, mon mari et moi avons fait une réservation.
H: Et c'est à quel nom?
C: Je l'ai faite à mon nom, Renoir.
H: Excellent! Vous avez réservé une chambre avec un grand lit. Votre chambre est la numéro 57 au cinquième étage.
C: Ah non, il y a une erreur. J'ai réservé la chambre numéro 27 au deuxième étage. Je refuse de prendre cette chambre, il n'y a pas d'ascenseur dans votre hôtel. Est-ce que vous avez une autre solution?
H: Madame Renoir, je suis désolé, mais l'hôtel est complet.
C: Oh là là. Ce n'est pas possible! Qu'est-ce que je vais faire?
H: Un instant, êtes-vous Marguerite Renoir?
C: Non, je suis Margot Renoir.
H: Madame Renoir, pardonnez-moi. Voici votre clé, chambre 27 au deuxième étage.
*(On Textbook Audio)*

**3 Suggestion** Call students' attention to the sequencing words in these sentences. Examples: **Finalement, Pendant, D'abord**, etc.

**3 Expansion** Have pairs of students rewrite the story using the sequencing words, but changing the details. Example: reserve a different kind of room, encounter a different problem, and find a different solution.

**OPTIONS**

**Questions** Review seasons, months, and days while practicing ordinal numbers by asking questions like the following: **Quel est le septième mois de l'année? Quelle est la troisième saison de l'année? Quel est le dernier jour de la semaine?**

**Oral Practice** Ask questions about the **À l'hôtel** illustration. Examples: **Cet hôtel a combien d'étages? Le passeport est de quel pays? Qu'est-ce que l'homme à la réception donne aux clients?** Then ask students personalized questions. Examples: **À votre avis, est-ce mieux (better) d'aller à une agence de voyages ou de faire les réservations sur Internet? Aimez-vous voyager avec votre famille ou en groupe? Avez-vous un hôtel préféré?**

## Communication

**4** **Conversez** Un(e) camarade passe des vacances idéales dans un hôtel. Interviewez-le/la (*him/her*). Answers will vary.

1. Quelles sont les dates de ton séjour?
2. Où vas-tu? Dans quel pays, quelle région ou quelle ville? Vas-tu à la mer, à la campagne, ...?
3. À quel hôtel descends-tu (*do you stay*)?
4. Qui fait la réservation?
5. Comment est l'hôtel? Est-ce que l'hôtel a un ascenseur, une piscine, ...?
6. À quel étage est ta chambre?
7. Combien de lits a ta chambre?
8. Laisses-tu ton passeport à la réception?

**5** **Notre réservation** Par groupes de trois, travaillez pour préparer une présentation où deux touristes font une réservation dans un hôtel ou une auberge de jeunesse francophone. N'oubliez pas d'ajouter (*add*) les informations de la liste. Answers will vary.

- le nom de l'hôtel
- le nombre de lits
- le type de chambre(s)
- les dates
- l'étage
- le prix

**6** **Mon hôtel** Vous allez ouvrir (*open*) votre propre hôtel. Par groupes de quatre, créez une affiche (*poster*) pour le promouvoir (*promote*) avec l'information de la liste et présentez votre hôtel au reste de la classe. Votre professeur va ensuite donner à chaque groupe un budget. Avec ce budget, vous allez faire la réservation à l'hôtel qui convient le mieux (*best suits*) à votre groupe. Answers will vary.

- le nom de votre hôtel
- le nombre d'étoiles (*stars*)
- les services offerts
- le prix pour une nuit

| ★ | ★★ | ★★★ | ★★★★ | ★★★★★ |
|---|---|---|---|---|
| une étoile | deux étoiles | trois étoiles | quatre étoiles | cinq étoiles |

**7** **Votre dernière réservation** Écrivez un paragraphe où vous décrivez (*describe*) ce qu'un touriste doit (*must*) faire pour réserver une chambre. Utilisez au moins cinq mots de la liste. Échangez et comparez votre paragraphe avec celui (*the one*) d'un camarade de classe. Answers will vary.

| alors | d'abord | puis |
|---|---|---|
| après (que) | donc | tout à coup |
| avant (de) | enfin | tout de suite |

**Expansion**
- After students have answered the questions, have them make up a conversation between a customer and a travel agent to arrange the trip.
- Ask volunteers to describe their **vacances idéales** to the class.

**5** **Suggestion** Have students consider other details that might come up while making a hotel reservation and include them in their conversation. Examples: **Est-ce qu'il y a un ascenseur? Il y a une télévision dans la chambre?**

**6** **Expansion** Assign each group a different francophone location. Tell students to include any nearby attractions (**la plage, la campagne, le centre-ville**) and hotel amenities (**la piscine, le restaurant**) in their poster. For inspiration, show some French language brochures from actual hotels.

**7** **Suggestion** Before starting this activity, have students brainstorm a list of steps involved in making a hotel reservation. Have them make up a scenario that includes at least one complication, for instance, their first choice of hotel is full.

**Successful Language Learning** Remind students to accept some corrections without explanation, especially when they are attempting to use language and structures above their current level. Tell them not to overanalyze and to trust that it will make more sense as their language skills develop.

**OPTIONS**

**Logical Associations** Give each student a card with either (1) a noun from the **Vocabulaire**, such as **chambre, clé,** or **passeport** or (2) a related verb, such as **réserver, prendre, oublier,** or **perdre**. Tell students to find someone whose word can be combined logically with their own. Then have them write an original sentence in the **passé composé**. Compile the sentences on the board. Then use sequencing expressions to combine them into a story.

**Combien d'étoiles préférez-vous?** Tell students that the French government regulates hotel ratings and requires that they be posted. Hotels must meet standards to qualify for a certain number of stars. A two-star hotel is a comfortable budget hotel. A five-star hotel is luxurious. While the level of comfort is standardized, prices are not.

# Les sons et les lettres

 **Audio: Concepts, Activities Record & Compare**

🎧 ti, sti, and ssi

The letters **ti** followed by a consonant are pronounced like the English word *tea*, but without the puff released in the English pronunciation.

| ac**ti**f | pe**ti**t | **ti**gre | u**ti**les |

When the letter combination **ti** is followed by a vowel sound, it is often pronounced like the sound linking the English words *miss you*.

| dic**ti**onnaire | pa**ti**ent | ini**ti**al | addi**ti**on |

Regardless of whether it is followed by a consonant or a vowel, the letter combination **sti** is pronounced *stee*, as in the English word *steep*.

| ges**ti**on | ques**ti**on | Séba**sti**en | arti**sti**que |

The letter combination **ssi** followed by another vowel or a consonant is usually pronounced like the sound linking the English words *miss you*.

| pa**ssi**on | expre**ssi**on | mi**ssi**on | profe**ssi**on |

Words that end in **-sion** or **-tion** are often cognates with English words, but they are pronounced quite differently. In French, these words are never pronounced with a *sh* sound.

| compre**ssi**on | na**ti**on | atten**ti**on | addi**ti**on |

🔊Ⓢ **Prononcez** Répétez les mots suivants à voix haute.

1. artiste
2. mission
3. réservation
4. impatient
5. position
6. initiative
7. possession
8. nationalité
9. compassion
10. possible

🔊Ⓢ **Articulez** Répétez les phrases suivantes à voix haute.

1. L'addition, s'il vous plaît.
2. Christine est optimiste et active.
3. Elle a fait une bonne première impression.
4. Laëtitia est impatiente parce qu'elle est fatiguée.
5. Tu cherches des expressions idiomatiques dans le dictionnaire.

🔊Ⓢ **Dictons** Répétez les dictons à voix haute.

*Il n'est de règle sans exception.*[2]

*De la discussion jaillit la lumière.*[1]

**ressources**

CA p. 168

daccord1.vhlcentral.com

[1] Discussion brings light.
[2] The exception proves the rule.

*deux cent trente-cinq* **235**

## Section Goals

In this section, students will learn about the letter combinations **ti**, **sti**, and **ssi**.

## Key Standards

4.1

**Student Resources**
*Cahier d'activités*, p. 168;
Supersite: Activities,
*Cahier interactif*
**Teacher Resources**
Answer Keys; Audio Script;
Textbook & Audio Activity
MP3s/CD

**Suggestions**

- Pronounce each of the example words and have students repeat them after you.
- To practice **ti**, have students put the palm of their hand in front of their lips and say the English word *tea*. Ask them if they felt the puff of air when they pronounced the letter **t**. Then have them pronounce the French word **petit** holding their hand in front of their mouth. Explain that they should not feel a puff of air when they pronounce the letters **ti** in French.
- Point out that **-sion** as in the word **télévision** has a [z] sound. Additionally, **-cia** as in the name **Patricia** has an unvoiced [s] sound.
- Many words that end in **-sion**, **-ssion**, **-stion**, and **-tion** are cognates. Contrast the French and English pronunciation of words such as **attention** and **mission**.
- Mention words from the **Vocabulaire** that contain **ti**, **sti**, or **ssi**. Then have students repeat after you. Alternatively, ask students to recall such vocabulary. Examples: **réception, réservation, vingtième**. See if a volunteer is able to recall any words from previous lessons. Examples: **pessimiste, dessiner, l'addition**, and **attention**.

**Dictons** Tell students that the word **lumière** is used figuratively in the proverb «**De la discussion jaillit la lumière.**» Ask students what they think it means in this context (*clarity, ideas*).

# ROMAN-PHOTO

## La réservation d'hôtel

 **Video:** *Roman-photo*
**Record & Compare**

**PERSONNAGES**

Agent de voyages

Amina

Pascal

Sandrine

*À l'agence de voyages...*

**SANDRINE** J'ai besoin d'une réservation d'hôtel, s'il vous plaît. C'est pour les vacances de Noël.
**AGENT** Où allez-vous? En Italie?
**SANDRINE** Nous allons à Albertville.
**AGENT** Et c'est pour combien de personnes?
**SANDRINE** Nous sommes deux, mais il nous faut deux chambres individuelles.

**AGENT** Très bien. Quelles sont les dates du séjour, Mademoiselle?
**SANDRINE** Alors, le 25, c'est Noël, donc je fête en famille. Disons du 26 décembre au 2 janvier.
**AGENT** Ce n'est pas possible à Albertville, mais à Megève, j'ai deux chambres à l'hôtel Le Vieux Moulin pour 143 euros par personne. Ou alors, à l'hôtel Le Mont Blanc pour 171 euros par personne.

**SANDRINE** Oh non, mais Megève, ce n'est pas Albertville... et ces prix! C'est vraiment trop cher.
**AGENT** C'est la saison, Mademoiselle. Les hôtels les moins chers sont déjà complets.
**SANDRINE** Oh là là. Je ne sais pas quoi faire... J'ai besoin de réfléchir. Merci, Monsieur. Au revoir!
**AGENT** Au revoir, Mademoiselle.

*Chez Sandrine...*

**SANDRINE** Oui, Pascal. Amina nous a trouvé une auberge à Albertville. C'est génial, non? En plus, c'est pas cher!
**PASCAL** Euh, en fait... Albertville, maintenant, c'est impossible.
**SANDRINE** Qu'est-ce que tu dis?

**PASCAL** C'est que... j'ai du travail.
**SANDRINE** Du travail! Mais c'est Noël! On ne travaille pas à Noël! Et Amina a déjà tout réservé... Oh! C'est pas vrai!
**PASCAL** *(à lui-même)* Elle n'est pas très heureuse maintenant, mais quelle surprise en perspective!

*Un peu plus tard...*

**AMINA** On a réussi, Sandrine! La réservation est faite. Tu as de la chance! Mais, qu'est-ce qu'il y a?
**SANDRINE** Tu es super gentille, Amina, mais Pascal a annulé pour Noël. Il dit qu'il a du travail... Lui et moi, c'est fini. Tu as fait beaucoup d'efforts pour faire la réservation, je suis désolée.

---

**A C T I V I T É S**

**1 Vrai ou faux?** Indiquez si ces affirmations sont **vraies** ou **fausses**. Corrigez les phrases fausses. *Answers may vary.*

1. Sandrine fait une réservation à l'agence de voyages.
   Faux. Sandrine ne fait pas de réservation à l'agence de voyages.
2. Pascal dit un mensonge (*lie*).
   Vrai.
3. Amina fait une réservation à l'hôtel Le Mont Blanc.
   Faux. Amina fait une réservation à l'auberge de la Costaroche.
4. Il faut annuler la réservation à l'auberge de la Costaroche.
   Vrai.
5. Amina est fâchée (*angry*) contre Sandrine.
   Faux. Amina n'est pas fâchée contre Sandrine.

6. Pascal est fâché contre Sandrine.
   Faux. Pascal n'est pas fâché contre Sandrine.
7. Sandrine est fâchée contre Pascal.
   Vrai.
8. Sandrine a envie de voyager le 25 décembre.
   Faux. Sandrine a envie de voyager le 26 décembre.
9. Cent soixante et onze euros, c'est beaucoup d'argent pour Sandrine.
   Vrai.
10. Il y a beaucoup de touristes à Albertville en décembre.
    Vrai.

 Practice more at **daccord1.vhlcentral.com**.

---

**O P T I O N S**

**Avant de regarder la vidéo** Before viewing the video episode **La réservation d'hôtel**, have students brainstorm a list of things people might say when arranging a hotel reservation. For example, what questions might a travel agent ask? How might the traveler respond?

**Regarder la vidéo** Play the video episode once without sound and have the class create a plot summary based on the visual cues. Afterward, show the video with sound and have the class correct any mistaken guesses and fill in any gaps in the plot summary they created.

**Sandrine essaie d'organiser son voyage.**

*Au P'tit Bistrot...*

**SANDRINE** Amina, je n'ai pas réussi à faire une réservation pour Albertville. Tu peux m'aider?

**AMINA** C'est que... je suis connectée avec Cyberhomme.

**SANDRINE** Avec qui?

**AMINA** J'écris un e-mail à... Bon, je t'explique plus tard. Dis-moi, comment est-ce que je peux t'aider?

*Un peu plus tard...*

**AMINA** Bon, alors... Sandrine m'a demandé de trouver un hôtel pas cher à Albertville. Pas facile à Noël... Je vais essayer... Voilà! L'auberge de la Costaroche... 39 euros la nuit pour une chambre individuelle. L'hôtel n'est pas complet et il y a deux chambres libres. Quelle chance, cette Sandrine! Bon, nom... Sandrine Aubry...

**AMINA** Bon, la réservation, ce n'est pas un problème. C'était facile de réserver. Mais toi, Sandrine, c'est évident, ça ne va pas.

**SANDRINE** C'est vrai. Mais, alors, c'est qui, ce «Cyberhomme»?

**AMINA** Oh, c'est juste un ami virtuel. On correspond sur Internet, c'est tout. Ce soir, c'est son dixième message!

**SANDRINE** Lis-le-moi!

**AMINA** Euh non, c'est personnel...

**SANDRINE** Alors, dis-moi comment il est!

**AMINA** D'accord... Il est étudiant, sportif mais sérieux. Très intellectuel.

**SANDRINE** S'il te plaît, écris-lui: «Sandrine cherche aussi un cyberhomme»!

## Expressions utiles

### Getting help

- **Je ne sais pas quoi faire... J'ai besoin de réfléchir.**
  *I don't know what to do... I have to think.*
- **Je n'ai pas réussi à faire une réservation pour Albertville.**
  *I didn't manage to make a reservation for Albertville.*
- **Tu peux m'aider?**
  *Can you help me?*
- **Dis-moi, comment est-ce que je peux t'aider?**
  *Tell me, how can I help you?*
- **Qu'est-ce que tu dis?**
  *What are you saying/did you say?*
- **On a réussi.**
  *We succeeded./We got it.*
- **S'il te plaît, écris-lui.**
  *Please, write to him.*

### Additional vocabulary

- **C'est trop tard?**
  *Is it too late?*
- **Disons...**
  *Let's say...*
- **La réservation est faite.**
  *The reservation has been made.*
- **C'est fini.**
  *It's over.*
- **Je suis connectée avec...**
  *I am online with...*
- **Lis-le-moi.**
  *Read it to me.*
- **Il dit que...**
  *He says that...*
- **les moins chers**
  *the least expensive*
- **en fait**
  *in fact*

---

**2 Questions** Répondez aux questions.

1. Pourquoi est-il difficile de faire une réservation pour Albertville?
   C'est difficile parce que c'est Noël.
2. Pourquoi est-ce que Sandrine ne veut pas (*doesn't want*) rester à l'hôtel Le Vieux Moulin?
   L'hôtel Le Vieux Moulin est très cher.
3. Pourquoi Pascal dit-il qu'il ne peut pas (*can't*) aller à Albertville?
   Il dit qu'il a du travail.
4. Qui est Cyberhomme?
   C'est l'ami virtuel d'Amina.
5. À votre avis (*In your opinion*), Sandrine va-t-elle rester (*stay*) avec Pascal? Answers will vary.

**3 Devinez** Inventez-vous une identité virtuelle. Écrivez un paragraphe dans lequel (*in which*) vous vous décrivez, vous et vos loisirs préférés. Donnez votre nom d'internaute (*cybername*). Votre professeur va afficher (*post*) vos messages. Devinez (*Guess*) à qui correspondent les descriptions.

**ressources**

CA pp. 93–94 | daccord1.vhlcentral.com

**ACTIVITÉS**

---

## Expressions utiles

- Draw attention to **-ir** verbs and expressions used to ask for help in the captions, in the **Expressions utiles** box, and as they occur in your conversation with students. Point out that this material will be formally presented in **Structures**.
- Respond briefly to questions about regular and irregular **-ir** verbs. Reinforce correct forms, but do not expect students to produce them consistently at this time.
- Contrast the pronunciation of the following expressions: **en fait, on fait**.
- Point out the differences between direct and indirect discourse by writing these two sentences on the board: **Il dit qu'il a du travail. Il dit: «J'ai du travail.»**

**1 Suggestion** Have students correct the items that are false.

**1 Expansion** Give these statements to the class. **11. Sandrine a besoin de deux chambres individuelles. (Vrai.) 12. Amina ne fait pas de réservation. (Faux.) 13. Cyberhomme est l'ami virtuel de Sandrine. (Faux.)**

**2 Suggestion** Have students discuss these questions in small groups.

**2 Expansion** Discuss question #5 as a class. Have students make other predictions about what will happen. Ask what kind of surprise they think Pascal has in mind.

**3 Suggestion** Without revealing students' identities, match students with common interests and have them write back to one another.

---

**Skits** Ask volunteers to act out the **Roman-photo** episode for the class. Assure them that it is not necessary to memorize the episode or to stick strictly to its content. Give them time to prepare. You may want to assign this as homework and do it the next class period as a review activity.

**Writing Practice** Have students write a brief paragraph recapping the major events in this episode and using sequencing expressions, such as **d'abord, donc, ensuite, avant de, alors,** etc. Ask volunteers to read their synopses aloud.

# CULTURE

## Section Goals

In this section, students will:
• learn about how and where the French vacation
• learn some terms used in youth hostels
• find out about vacation spots in the francophone world
• read about the Alps, a popular destination for skiers

## Key Standards

**2.1, 2.2, 3.1, 3.2, 4.2**

**Student Resources**
Supersite: Activities
**Teacher Resources**
Answer Keys

**Culture à la loupe**
**Avant la lecture** Ask students how much vacation their parents can take annually, how much is typical in this country, and how much they think working people need to be happy in their work. You might also ask what vacation activities Americans enjoy and what the students imagine is popular in France.

**Lecture**
• Mention to students that when experts anticipate the **grands départs** on the **autoroutes**, these days are labeled **rouge** throughout France.
• Explain the **Coup de main** box on superlatives to help students understand the text.

**Après la lecture** Ask students to compare American and French vacation habits. Example: **Les étudiants à l'université ici commencent leurs vacances en mai, mais les étudiants en France terminent leurs études en juin.**

**1 Expansion** Continue the activity with these fill-in-the-blank statements.
**11. Les Français d'aujourd'hui prennent des vacances qui durent _____ en moyenne. (sept jours) 12. Les vacances les moins populaires à l'étranger sont _____. (en Asie) 13. Les étudiants commencent leurs vacances d'été en _____. (juin)**

---

### CULTURE À LA LOUPE

# Les vacances des Français

une plage à Biarritz, en France

**Les Français, aujourd'hui, ont beaucoup de vacances.** En 1936, les Français obtiennent° leurs premiers congés payés: deux semaines par an. En 1956, les congés payés passent à trois semaines, puis à quatre en 1969, et enfin à cinq semaines en 1982. Aujourd'hui, les Français sont parmi ceux qui° ont le plus de vacances en Europe. Pendant longtemps, les Français prenaient° un mois de congés l'été, en août, et beaucoup d'entreprises°, de bureaux et de magasins ferment° tout le mois (la fermeture annuelle). Aujourd'hui, les Français ont tendance à prendre des vacances plus courtes (sept jours en moyenne°), mais plus souvent. Quant aux° destinations de vacances, 90% (pour cent) des Français restent en France. S'ils partent à l'étranger, leurs destinations préférées sont l'Espagne, l'Afrique et l'Italie. Environ° 35% des Français vont à la campagne, 30% vont en ville, 25% vont à la mer et 10% vont à la montagne.

Ce sont les personnes âgées et les agriculteurs° qui partent le moins souvent en vacances et les étudiants qui voyagent le plus, parce qu'ils ont beaucoup de congés. Pour eux, les cours commencent en septembre ou octobre avec la rentrée des classes. Puis, il y a deux semaines de vacances plusieurs fois dans l'année: les vacances de Noël en décembre-janvier, les vacances d'hiver en février-mars et les vacances de printemps en avril-mai. Les élèves (de la maternelle° au lycée) ont une semaine en plus pour les vacances de la Toussaint en octobre-novembre. L'été, les étudiants et les élèves ont les grandes vacances de juin jusqu'à° la rentrée.

### Les destinations de vacances des Français aujourd'hui

| PAYS / CONTINENT | SÉJOURS |
|---|---|
| France | 90,1% |
| Espagne | 1,9% |
| Afrique | 1,8% |
| Italie | 1,6% |
| Amérique | 1,3% |
| Belgique / Luxembourg | 0,9% |
| Grande-Bretagne / Irlande | 0,9% |
| Allemagne | 0,8% |
| Asie / Océanie | 0,7% |

SOURCE: TNS Sofres

**obtiennent** obtain **parmi ceux qui** among the ones who **prenaient** took **entreprises** companies **ferment** close **en moyenne** on average **Quant aux** As for **Environ** Around **agriculteurs** farmers **maternelle** pre-school **jusqu'à** until

### Coup de main

To form the superlative of nouns, use **le plus (de)** + (noun) to say the most and **le moins (de)** + (noun) to say the least.

**Les étudiants ont le plus de congés.**

**Les personnes âgées prennent le moins de congés.**

---

**A C T I V I T É S**

**1 Complétez** Complétez les phrases.

1. C'est en 1936 que les Français obtiennent leurs premiers <u>congés payés</u>.

2. Depuis (Since) 1982, les Français ont <u>cinq semaines</u> de congés payés.

3. Pendant longtemps, les Français prennent leurs vacances au mois <u>d'août</u>.

4. Pendant <u>la fermeture annuelle</u>, beaucoup de magasins sont fermés.

5. <u>La France</u> est le lieu de vacances préféré de 90% des Français.

6. Les destinations étrangères préférées des Français sont <u>l'Espagne, l'Afrique et l'Italie</u>.

7. Le lieu de séjour favori des Français est <u>la campagne</u>.

8. <u>Les personnes âgées et les agriculteurs</u> ne partent pas souvent en vacances.

9. Ce sont <u>les étudiants</u> qui ont le plus de vacances.

10. Les étudiants ont <u>deux semaines de vacances</u> plusieurs fois par an.

Practice more at daccord1.vhlcentral.com.

---

**O P T I O N S**

**Using Visuals** Ask students what they can learn in the chart **Les destinations de vacances des Français aujourd'hui**. (percentages showing where the French spend their vacations today) Have students quiz each other on the chart, so they can practice geography and percentages.

**Oral Presentation** Ask students to work with a partner to tell in their own words three main points described in **Les vacances des Français**. You might brainstorm a list on the board: the history of employee vacations, the change in how the French take their vacations, and the time periods of student vacations.

## LE FRANÇAIS QUOTIDIEN

### À l'auberge de jeunesse

| | |
|---|---|
| **bagagerie** (*f.*) | *baggage check room* |
| **cadenas** (*m.*) | *padlock* |
| **casier** (*m.*) | *locker* |
| **couvre-feu** (*m.*) | *curfew* |
| **dortoir** (*m.*) | *dormitory* |
| **sac** (*m.*) **de couchage** | *sleeping bag* |
| **mixte** | *coed* |

## LE MONDE FRANCOPHONE

### Des vacances francophones

Voici quelques idées de vacances francophones:

#### Au soleil
- un séjour ou une croisière (un voyage en bateau) aux Antilles, dans la mer des Caraïbes: la Martinique, la Guadeloupe
- un séjour ou une croisière en Polynésie française, dans l'océan Pacifique: l'archipel de la Société (avec Tahiti), les Marquises, les Tuamotu, les îles Gambier et les îles Australes

#### Pour de l'aventure
- un trekking (une randonnée à pied) ou une randonnée à dos de chameau° dans le désert du Sahara: Maroc, Tunisie, Algérie
- un circuit-aventure dans les forêts de Madagascar, dans l'océan Indien ou dans la forêt équatoriale de la Guyane française, en Amérique du Sud°

**à dos de chameau** *camelback* **Sud** *South*

## PORTRAIT

# Les Alpes et le ski

Près de 11% des Français partent à la montagne pendant les vacances d'hiver. Soixante-dix pour cent d'entre eux° choisissent° une station de ski des Alpes françaises. La chaîne° des Alpes est la plus grande chaîne de montagnes d'Europe. Elle fait plus de 1.000 km de long et va de la Méditerranée à l'Autriche°. Plusieurs pays la partagent: entre autres° la France, la Suisse, l'Allemagne et l'Italie. Le Mont-Blanc, le sommet° le plus haut° d'Europe occidentale°, est à 4.811 mètres d'altitude. On trouve d'excellentes pistes° de ski dans les Alpes, comme à Chamonix, Tignes, Val d'Isère et aux Trois Vallées.

**d'entre eux** *of them* **choisissent** *choose* **chaîne** *range* **l'Autriche** *Austria* **entre autres** *among others* **sommet** *peak* **le plus haut** *the highest* **occidentale** *Western* **pistes** *trails*

### SUR INTERNET

Chaque année, depuis (*since*) 1982, plus de 4 millions de Français utilisent des Chèques-Vacances pour payer leurs vacances. Qu'est-ce que c'est, un Chèque-Vacances?

Go to **daccord1.vhlcentral.com** to find more information related to this **CULTURE** section.

---

**2** **Répondez** Répondez aux questions par des phrases complètes.

1. Que peut-on utiliser à la place des draps?
   On peut utiliser un sac de couchage.
2. Quand on passe la nuit dans le dortoir d'une auberge de jeunesse, où met-on ses affaires (*belongings*)?
   On les met dans un casier.
3. Qu'est-ce que c'est, les Alpes?
   C'est une grande chaîne de montagnes partagée entre plusieurs pays d'Europe.
4. Quel est le sommet le plus haut d'Europe occidentale?
   Le Mont-Blanc est le sommet le plus haut d'Europe occidentale.
5. Quel séjour est-ce que vous suggérez à un(e) jeune Américain(e) qui aime l'aventure et qui a envie de pratiquer son français?
   Answers will vary.

**3** **À l'agence de voyages** Vous travaillez dans une agence de voyages en France. Votre partenaire, un(e) client(e), va vous parler des activités et du climat qu'il/elle aime. Faites quelques suggestions de destinations. Votre client(e) va vous poser des questions sur les différents voyages que vous suggérez.

**ressources**

Ⓢ

daccord1.vhlcentral.com

**ACTIVITÉS**

---

---

**Le français quotidien** Encourage students to try an **auberge de jeunesse** if they travel overseas. They have no frills, sometimes have curfews, can be noisy, and meals (if offered) are during limited hours. **L'auberge de jeunesse** is the best deal, though; many travelers find lifelong international friends and traveling companions there.

**Portrait** Explain that the Pyrenees are another important ski destination in France. Show their geographical relationship to the Alps on a map and point out that the Pyrenees create a natural border between France and Spain.

**Le monde francophone** Call on volunteers to read each bulleted item. Then ask for other volunteers to point out each francophone place mentioned on **Overheads #2** or **#4**.

**2** **Expansion** Continue the activity with these questions.
**6. Quel pourcentage de Français part pour la montagne pendant les vacances d'hiver? (près de 11%) 7. Quels pays partagent les Alpes? (la France, l'Allemagne, la Suisse, l'Autriche et l'Italie) 8. Où trouve-t-on de bonnes pistes de ski? (à Chamonix, Tignes, Val d'Isère et aux Trois Vallées)**

**3** **Expansion** After the trip, the **client(e)** returns to the **agent** to discuss what he or she did on the trip. The **agent** asks: **Qu'est-ce que vous avez fait? Et puis, qu'est-ce que vous avez vu? Ensuite, où êtes-vous allé(e)?** The **client(e)** then volunteers as much information as possible about the trip.

---

**Les vacances** Have students imagine that, while studying in France, they are planning a trip for an upcoming vacation. They can speak **au présent** and **au futur proche**. Examples: **Où est-ce qu'on va aller? Qui va réserver l'hôtel/l'auberge de jeunesse? Qu'est-ce qu'on a envie de faire?** Encourage them to consult **Les vacances des Français** to plan a trip when French schools are actually on break. Then have them refer to **Le monde** **francophone** to discuss which type of vacation they would like best, **au soleil** or **pour de l'aventure**. You might want to come up with some questions as a class before students continue in pairs. Examples: **Que préférez-vous, la plage ou le désert? Entre le Maroc et la Martinique, que préférez-vous? Moi, j'ai envie de faire une croisière, et vous?**

## Section Goals

In this section, students will learn:

- the formation of adverbs using [adjective] + **-ment**
- irregular adverbs
- adverb placement

## Key Standards

**4.1, 5.1**

**Student Resources**
*Cahier d'exercices*, pp. 93-94;
*Cahier d'activités*, pp. 13, 169;
Supersite: Activities,
*Cahier interactif*

**Teacher Resources**
Answer Keys; Audio Script;
Audio Activity MP3s/CD;
*Feuilles d'activités*; Testing
program: Grammar Quiz

## Suggestions

- To start the lesson, ask volunteers to give examples of adverbs already learned and use them in a sentence. Examples: **Je vais très bien/ mal. Ils ont déjà fait leurs devoirs. Elle travaille souvent le samedi.**
- Use magazine pictures of people doing various things to further review known adverbs and introduce a few new ones. Examples: **Ce chien mange beaucoup. Cette fille-ci nettoie rarement sa chambre. Cet homme-là se sent mal.**
- Brainstorm a list of masculine adjectives with the whole class. Have students write the feminine forms, reminding them that some do not change. Examples: **heureux (heureuse), facile (facile).**
- Point out that many adverbs are formed by adding **-ment** to the end of feminine forms of adjectives. Call attention to the exception for adjectives that already end in a vowel. Then ask questions with adverbs that correspond to the adjectives mentioned. Example: **Faites- vous facilement vos devoirs?**
- Write sentences using regular adverbs with **-ment** on the board. Have volunteers underline the adverb. Example: **Le professeur parle rapidement.**

### 7B.1 Adverbs

**Point de départ** Adverbs describe how, when, and where actions take place. They modify verbs, adjectives, and even other adverbs. You've already learned some adverbs such as **bien**, **déjà**, **surtout**, and **très**.

- To form an adverb from an adjective that ends in a consonant, take the feminine singular form and add **-ment**. This ending is equivalent to the English *-ly*.

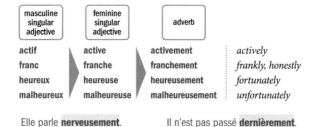

| masculine singular adjective | feminine singular adjective | adverb | |
|---|---|---|---|
| actif | active | activement | *actively* |
| franc | franche | franchement | *frankly, honestly* |
| heureux | heureuse | heureusement | *fortunately* |
| malheureux | malheureuse | malheureusement | *unfortunately* |

Elle parle **nerveusement**.
*She speaks nervously.*

Il n'est pas passé **dernièrement**.
*He hasn't stopped by lately.*

- If the masculine singular form of an adjective ends in a vowel, just add **-ment** to the end.

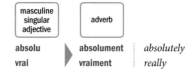

| masculine singular adjective | adverb | |
|---|---|---|
| absolu | absolument | *absolutely* |
| vrai | vraiment | *really* |

Martin répond **poliment**.
*Martin answers politely.*

Ils réservent **facilement** la chambre.
*They reserve the room easily.*

- To form an adverb from an adjective that ends in **-ant** or **-ent** in the masculine singular, replace the ending with **-amment** or **-emment**, respectively. Both endings are pronounced identically, like **femme**.

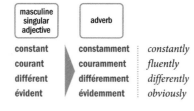

| masculine singular adjective | adverb | |
|---|---|---|
| constant | constamment | *constantly* |
| courant | couramment | *fluently* |
| différent | différemment | *differently* |
| évident | évidemment | *obviously* |

Les élèves lisent **patiemment**.
*The students are reading patiently.*

Je préfère travailler **indépendamment**.
*I prefer to work independently.*

Elle parle **couramment** français.
*She speaks French fluently.*

Vous pensez **différemment**.
*You think differently.*

### MISE EN PRATIQUE

**1 Assemblez** Trouvez l'adverbe opposé.

| | | | |
|---|---|---|---|
| f | 1. gentiment | a. | difficilement |
| e | 2. bien | b. | rarement |
| h | 3. heureusement | c. | faiblement |
| g | 4. lentement | d. | impatiemment |
| a | 5. facilement | e. | mal |
| d | 6. patiemment | f. | méchamment |
| b | 7. fréquemment | g. | vite |
| c | 8. fortement | h. | malheureusement |

**2 Invitation aux vacances** Béatrice parle de ses vacances chez sa cousine. Complétez les phrases avec les adverbes qui correspondent aux adjectifs entre parenthèses.

Ma cousine Caroline m'a invitée à passer les vacances chez elle, à Nice. (1) __Évidemment__ (Évident), j'ai été très contente et j'ai (2) __rapidement__ (rapide) accepté son invitation. J'ai (3) __attentivement__ (attentif) lu les brochures touristiques et j'ai (4) __constamment__ (constant) parlé de mon voyage. (5) __Finalement__ (Final), le jour de mon départ est arrivé. J'ai (6) __prudemment__ (prudent) fait ma valise. À Paris, j'ai attendu le train très (7) __impatiemment__ (impatient). (8) __Franchement__ (Franc), j'avais hâte (*was eager*) d'arriver!

**3 Les activités** Avec un(e) partenaire, assemblez les éléments des colonnes pour décrire à tour de rôle comment on fait ces activités. *Answers will vary.*

**MODÈLE**
**Élève 1:** *Je travaille sérieusement.*
**Élève 2:** *Mon frère joue constamment.*

| A | B | C |
|---|---|---|
| je | aider | constamment |
| mon frère | dormir | facilement |
| ma sœur | faire la cuisine | franchement |
| mon ami(e) | jouer | gentiment |
| mes profs | parler | patiemment |
| ma mère | travailler | rapidement |
| mon père | voyager | sérieusement |
| ? | ? | ? |

Practice more at **daccord1.vhlcentral.com**.

**O P T I O N S**

**Using Video** Replay the video episode, having students focus on the use of adverbs. Tell them to jot down a list of all of the adverbs they hear. Make two columns on the board, one for adverbs with **-ment** and another for all other adverbs. Have students write the adverbs under the appropriate column. Then have them create original sentences using each adverb.

**Using Games** Divide the class into small groups. Say the name of a famous person or historical figure. Give groups three minutes to write down as many short sentences as possible about that person, using adverbs and adverbial expressions. At the end of each round, have groups read their answers aloud. Award one point after each round to the group with the highest number of correct adverbs. The first group to earn five points wins.

## COMMUNICATION

**4 Au lycée** Vous désirez mieux connaître (*know better*) vos camarades de classe. Répondez aux questions de votre partenaire avec les adverbes de la liste ou avec d'autres.

*Answers will vary.*

| | | |
|---|---|---|
| attentivement | mal | rapidement |
| bien | parfois | rarement |
| facilement | patiemment | sérieusement |
| lentement | prudemment | souvent |

1. Quand vas-tu à la cantine?
2. Comment étudies-tu en général?
3. Quand tes amis et toi étudiez-vous ensemble?
4. Comment les élèves écoutent-ils leur prof?
5. Comment ton prof de français parle-t-il?
6. Comment vas-tu au lycée?
7. Quand fais-tu du sport?
8. Quand allez-vous au cinéma, tes amis et toi?

**5 Fréquences** Votre professeur va vous donner une feuille d'activités. Circulez dans la classe et demandez à vos camarades à quelle fréquence ils/elles font ces choses. Trouvez une personne différente pour chaque réponse, puis présentez les réponses à la classe.

*Answers will vary.*

**MODÈLE**

**Élève 1:** À quelle fréquence pars-tu en vacances?
**Élève 2:** Je pars fréquemment en vacances.

**6 Notre classe** Par groupes de quatre, choisissez les camarades de votre classe qui correspondent à ces descriptions. Trouvez le plus de (*the most*) personnes possible. *Answers will vary.*

Qui dans la classe...

1. bavarde constamment avec ses voisins?
2. parle bien français?
3. chante bien?
4. apprend facilement les langues?
5. écoute attentivement le prof?
6. travaille sérieusement après les cours?
7. aime beaucoup les maths?
8. travaille trop?
9. dessine souvent pendant les cours?
10. dort parfois pendant les cours?

---

● Some adverbs are irregular.

| masculine singular adjective | adverb | |
|---|---|---|
| bon | bien | *well* |
| gentil | gentiment | *nicely* |
| mauvais | mal | *badly* |

Son français est bon; il le parle **bien**.
*His French is good; he speaks it well.*

Leurs devoirs sont mauvais; ils écrivent **mal**.
*Their homework is bad; they write badly.*

● Although the adverb **rapidement** can be formed from the adjective **rapide**, you can also use the adverb **vite** to say *fast/quickly*. Note that when you use **vite** with a verb in the **passé composé** when meaning *fast*, the adverb needs to be placed after the past participle.

Bérénice a gagné la course? Oui, elle a couru **vite**.
*Did Bérénice win the race? Yes, she ran fast.*

● You've learned **jamais**, **parfois**, **rarement**, and **souvent**. Here are three more adverbs of frequency: **de temps en temps** (*from time to time*), **en général** (*in general*), **quelquefois** (*sometimes*).

Elle lit **souvent**.
*She often reads.*

**En général**, ils prennent le bus.
*In general, they take the bus.*

● Place an adverb that modifies an adjective or another adverb before the word it modifies.

La chambre est **assez** grande.
*The room is pretty big.*

Ils font très **vite** les réservations.
*They make reservations very quickly.*

● Place an adverb that modifies a verb immediately after the verb.

Il parle **bien** le français?
*Does he speak French well?*

Elles parlent **constamment**.
*They talk constantly.*

● In the **passé composé**, place short adverbs before the past participle.

Ils sont **vite** partis.
*They left quickly.*

Ils ont **bien** travaillé.
*They worked well.*

**Essayez!** Donnez les adverbes qui correspondent à ces adjectifs.

1. complet _complètement_
2. sérieux _sérieusement_
3. séparé _séparément_
4. constant _constamment_
5. mauvais _mal_
6. actif _activement_
7. impatient _impatiemment_
8. bon _bien_
9. franc _franchement_
10. difficile _difficilement_
11. vrai _vraiment_
12. gentil _gentiment_

*deux cent quarante et un* **241**

---

---

## Section Goals

In this section, students will learn:
- the imperfect tense
- être in the imperfect tense

## Key Standards

4.1, 5.1

---

**Student Resources**
*Cahier d'exercices,* pp. 95-96;
*Cahier d'activités,* p. 170;
Supersite: Activities,
*Cahier interactif*

**Teacher Resources**
Answer Keys; Audio Script;
Audio Activity MP3s/CD; Testing
program: Grammar Quiz

---

## Suggestions

- Remind students that they can already express the past using the **passé composé**. Now they will learn another tense needed to express themselves in the past. Mention that the **imparfait** expresses the past in a different way.

- Introduce the **imparfait** by describing something you used to do when you were little. Example: **Quand j'étais petit(e), je passais souvent les vacances chez mes grands-parents. Quand il faisait froid, nous jouions aux cartes à la maison. En été, ma famille louait une maison au bord de la mer.** Then ask students: **Et vous, que faisiez-vous quand vous étiez petits?** Encourage student responses.

- Ask volunteers to answer questions about their childhood. Example: **Quand vous étiez jeune, où alliez-vous en vacances avec votre famille? Aimiez-vous aller au cinéma? Au musée?**

- Review the present-tense **nous** forms of various verbs and explain that the stem without **-ons** is also the **imparfait** stem. Mention the exception with verbs ending in **-ger** and **-cer**.

---

### 7B.2 The *imparfait*

**Point de départ** You've learned how the **passé composé** can express past actions. Now you'll learn another past tense, the **imparfait** (*imperfect*).

- The **imparfait** can be translated several ways into English.

| | |
|---|---|
| Hakim **voyageait**. | Nina **chantait**. |
| *Hakim traveled.* | *Nina sang.* |
| *Hakim used to travel.* | *Nina used to sing.* |
| *Hakim was traveling.* | *Nina was singing.* |

- The **imparfait** is used to talk about actions that took place repeatedly or habitually during an unspecified period of time.

| | |
|---|---|
| Je **prenais** le bus en ville. | Vous m'**appeliez** tous les jours. |
| *I used to take the bus to town.* | *You used to call me every day.* |
| Nous **réservions** la même chambre. | Il **faisait** toujours du shopping. |
| *We reserved the same room.* | *He was always going shopping.* |

- To form the **imparfait**, drop the **-ons** ending from the **nous** form of the present tense and replace it with these endings.

**The *imparfait***

| | parler (parl~~ons~~) | finir (finiss~~ons~~) | vendre (vend~~ons~~) | boire (buv~~ons~~) |
|---|---|---|---|---|
| je | parlais | finissais | vendais | buvais |
| tu | parlais | finissais | vendais | buvais |
| il/elle | parlait | finissait | vendait | buvait |
| nous | parlions | finissions | vendions | buvions |
| vous | parliez | finissiez | vendiez | buviez |
| ils/elles | parlaient | finissaient | vendaient | buvaient |

- Verbs whose infinitives end in **-ger** add an **e** before all endings of the **imparfait** except in the **nous** and **vous** forms. Verbs whose infinitives end in **-cer** change **c** to **ç** before all endings except in the **nous** and **vous** forms.

| tu **voyageais** | *but* | nous **voyagions** |
|---|---|---|
| les invités **commençaient** | *but* | vous **commenciez** |

- Note that the **nous** and **vous** forms of infinitives ending in **-ier** contain a double **i** in the **imparfait**.

| Vous **skiiez** en janvier. | Nous **étudiions** jusqu'à minuit. |
|---|---|
| *You used to ski in January.* | *We studied until midnight.* |

---

### MISE EN PRATIQUE

**1** **Nos voyages** La famille d'Emmanuel voyageait souvent quand il était petit. Complétez son histoire en mettant (*by putting*) à l'imparfait les verbes entre parenthèses.

Quand j' (1) __étais__ (être) jeune, mon père (2) __travaillait__ (travailler) pour une société canadienne et nous (3) __voyagions__ (voyager) souvent. Quand nous (4) __partions__ (partir), je (5) __faisais__ (faire) ma valise et je (6) __préparais__ (préparer) toutes mes affaires. Ma petite sœur (7) __détestait__ (détester) voyager. Elle (8) __disait__ (dire) qu'elle (9) __aimait__ (aimer) rester chez nous près de ses amis et que ce n' (10) __était__ (être) pas juste!

**2** **Le samedi** Dites ce que (*what*) ces personnes faisaient habituellement le samedi.

**MODÈLE**
*Paul dormait.*

**Paul / dormir**

**1. je / faire / jogging**
Je faisais du jogging.

**3. vous / manger / glace**
Vous mangiez des glaces/une glace.

**2. ils / finir / devoirs**
Ils finissaient leurs devoirs.

**4. tu / prendre / café**
Tu prenais du café.

**3** **Maintenant et avant** Qu'est-ce qu'Emmanuel et sa famille font différemment aujourd'hui? Avec un(e) partenaire, écrivez des phrases à l'imparfait et trouvez les adverbes opposés. Suggested answers

**MODÈLE**

beaucoup travailler (je)
*Maintenant, je travaille beaucoup, mais avant je travaillais peu.*

1. rarement voyager (je)
   ... je voyage rarement, ... je voyageais constamment.
2. facilement prendre le train (nous)
   ... nous prenons facilement le train., ... nous prenions difficilement le train.
3. souvent aller à la piscine (on)
   ... on va souvent à la piscine, ... on allait rarement à la piscine.
4. parfois acheter des cartes postales (mes parents)
   ... ils achètent parfois des cartes postales, ... ils achetaient souvent...
5. bien bricoler (vous)
   ... vous bricolez bien, ... vous bricoliez mal.
6. patiemment attendre son anniversaire (ma sœur)
   ... elle attend patiemment..., ... elle attendait impatiemment...

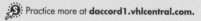 Practice more at **daccord1.vhlcentral.com.**

---

**Using Games** Divide the class into two teams. Choose one team member at a time to go to the board, alternating between teams. Say a subject pronoun and an infinitive. The student at the board must write and say the correct **imparfait** form. Example: **je: parler (je parlais)**. Give a point for each correct answer. Play to five or ten points, depending on how much time you have.

**True/False Sentences** Have students write five true/false sentences with the **imparfait** describing things they did while on vacation when they were younger. Have pairs read their descriptions aloud, one sentence at a time, listening for the **imparfait** and guessing what is true or false. Encourage follow-up discussion. Example: **L'hôtel où je suis descendu avait 99 étages.** The other students might say: **Ce n'est pas vrai! Combien d'étages avait-il vraiment?**

## COMMUNICATION

**4** **Quand tu avais dix ans** À tour de rôle, posez ces questions à votre partenaire pour savoir *(to know)* les détails de sa vie quand il/elle avait dix ans. Answers will vary.

1. Où habitais-tu?
2. Est-ce que tu faisais beaucoup de vélo?
3. Où est-ce que ta famille et toi alliez en vacances?
4. Pendant combien de temps partiez-vous en vacances?
5. Est-ce que tes amis et toi, vous jouiez ensemble après l'école?
6. Que faisaient tes parents le week-end?
7. Quels sports pratiquais-tu?
8. Quel genre de musique écoutais-tu?
9. Comment était ton école?
10. Aimais-tu l'école? Pourquoi?

**5** **Discutez** Regardez l'image. Un(e) partenaire et vous avez passé vos vacances à Saint-Barthélemy. Avec votre partenaire, écrivez un paragraphe d'au moins six phrases. Décrivez le temps qu'il faisait et ce que *(what)* vous faisiez quand vous étiez là-bas. Utilisez l'imparfait dans votre description.

**6** **Une énigme** La nuit dernière, quelqu'un est entré dans le bureau de votre professeur et a emporté *(took away)* l'examen de français. Vous devez *(must)* trouver qui. Qu'est-ce que vos camarades de classe faisaient hier soir? Relisez vos notes et dites qui est le voleur *(thief)*. Ensuite, présentez vos conclusions à la classe. Answers will vary.

---

• The **imparfait** is used for description, often with the verb **être**, which is irregular in this tense.

### The *imparfait* of *être*

| | |
|---|---|
| j'étais | nous étions |
| tu étais | vous étiez |
| il/elle était | ils/elles étaient |

J'**étais** dans la chambre.
*I was in the bedroom.*

Vous **étiez** à l'hôtel.
*You were at the hotel.*

• Note the imperfect forms of these expressions.

Il **pleuvait** chaque matin.
*It rained each morning.*

Il **neigeait** parfois au printemps.
*It snowed sometimes in the spring.*

Il y **avait** deux clés.
*There were two keys.*

Il **fallait** payer le repas.
*It was necessary to pay for the meal*

### The verbs *dire, lire,* and *écrire*

• The verbs **dire** *(to say)*, **lire** *(to read)*, and **écrire** *(to write)* are conjugated as follows: **je dis, tu dis, il dit, nous disons, vous dites, ils disent; je lis, tu lis, il lit, nous lisons, vous lisez, ils lisent; j'écris, tu écris, il écrit, nous écrivons, vous écrivez, ils écrivent.** The verb **décrire** *(to describe)* is conjugated like **écrire**.

Elle m'**écrit**.
*She writes to me.*

Ne **dis** pas ton secret.
*Don't tell your secret.*

**Lisez** cet e-mail.
*Read that e-mail.*

• The past participle of **dire, écrire,** and **décrire**, respectively, are **dit, écrit,** and **décrit**. The past participle of **lire** is **lu**.

Ils l'**ont dit**.
*They said it.*

Tu l'**as écrit**.
*You wrote it.*

Nous l'**avons** lu.
*We read it.*

• In the **imparfait**, these verbs have regular endings.

Je le **disais**.
*I used to say it.*

Ils **lisaient** souvent.
*They read often.*

Tu **écrivais** rarement.
*You wrote rarely.*

**Essayez!**  Choisissez la réponse correcte pour compléter les phrases.

1. Muriel (réservais/(réservait)) une chambre en ville.
2. Vous (partageait/(partagiez)) une chambre avec un autre étudiant.
3. Nous (écrivait/(écrivions)) beaucoup à nos amis.
4. Il y (avait)/était) un bon restaurant au premier étage.
5. Il (neigeait/(fallait)) mettre le chauffage *(heat)* quand il (faisaient/(faisait)) froid.
6. Qu'est-ce que tu (faisait/(faisais)) à la plage?
7. Vous ((lisiez)/lisaient) beaucoup avant?
8. Nous (étaient/(étions)) trois dans la petite chambre.

---

**Essayez!** Have students identify the infinitive of each verb in the activity. Examples: **1. réserver 2. partager**

**1 Suggestion** Before assigning the activity, review the forms of the imperfect by calling out an infinitive and a series of subject pronouns. Ask volunteers to give the corresponding forms. Example: **détester, nous (nous détestions)**.

**2 Expansion** After completing the activity, have students complete the sentences using the **passé composé**. Compare the meanings of each sentence.

**3 Suggestion** Divide the class into two groups, **l'imparfait** and **le présent**. Have the first group give one phrase about what Emmanuel and his family used to do. The second group should describe what he and his family do differently now, using an opposite verb in the present tense.

**4 Expansion** Have students share their partner's answers with the class using the third person pronouns **il/elle**.

**5 Suggestion** Write a few descriptive sentences using the imperfect on the board before having students work in pairs. Examples: **Nous ne partagions pas de chambre. Tous les jours, nous allions à la plage.**

**5 Expansion** Have pairs of students present their imaginary vacations to another pair or to the whole class. Using the imperfect, compile a list of activities on the board.

**6 Suggestion** Before doing this activity, remind students that the imperfect form of **être** is irregular.

---

**Using Games** Label the four corners of the room with different historical periods. Examples: **la Préhistoire, le Moyen Âge, la Renaissance,** and **le Dix-Neuvième siècle**. Tell students to go to the corner that best represents the historical period they would visit if they could. Each group then discusses their reasons for picking that period using the **imparfait**. A spokesperson will summarize his or her group's responses to the class.

**Using Video** Bring in, or choose a few students to bring in, video clips from popular movies. Show clips to the class. Brainstorm important vocabulary. After viewing each clip, have students use the **imparfait** to describe what was happening and what people in the clip were doing.

**Key Standards**

1.1

**Student Resources**
*Cahier d'activités*, pp. 14, 61-62;
Supersite: Activities,
*Cahier interactif*
**Teacher Resources**
Answer Keys; *Feuilles d'activités*;
Info Gap Activities; Testing
Program: Lesson Test (Testing
Program Audio MP3s/CD)

**1** **Suggestion** Have students write out the questions and answers. Check use of subject pronouns and the **imparfait** forms of **être**.

**2** **Suggestion** Have two volunteers model a question and answer for the class.

**2** **Expansion** After group members finish questioning each other, have a student from each group read the answers from another student. The class will then guess which student's childhood birthday celebration was described.

**3** **Suggestions**
• Ask two students to read the **modèle** aloud. Then distribute the **Feuilles d'activités** found on the Supersite.
• Encourage students to add sports and leisure activities not already found in their survey.

**4** **Suggestion** Before beginning the activity, have students describe what the people in the drawing are doing in the present tense.

**5** **Expansion** Tell students to imagine they are the **ancien(ne) patron(ne)** and have decided to give the employee a second chance. It is time for the three-month review. Have them draft a brief letter to the employee discussing his or her past versus present performance on the job.

**6** **Suggestion** Divide the class into pairs and distribute the Info Gap Handouts for this activity

---

**1** **Mes affaires** Vous cherchez vos affaires (*belongings*). À tour de rôle, demandez de l'aide à votre partenaire. Où étaient-elles la dernière fois? Answers will vary.

**MODÈLE**

**Élève 1:** Je cherche mes clés. Où sont-elles?

**Élève 2:** Tu n'as pas cherché à la réception? Elles étaient à la réception.

| | |
|---|---|
| baskets | passeport |
| journal | pull |
| livre | sac à dos |
| parapluie | valise |

| | |
|---|---|
| à la réception | sur la chaise |
| au rez-de-chaussée | sous le lit |
| dans la chambre | dans ton sac |
| au deuxième étage | à l'auberge de jeunesse |

**2** **Les anniversaires** Avec un(e) partenaire, préparez huit questions pour savoir (*know*) comment vos camarades de classe célébraient leur anniversaire quand ils étaient enfants. Employez l'imparfait et des adverbes dans vos questions, puis posez-les à un autre groupe. Answers will vary.

**MODÈLE**

**Élève 1:** Que faisais-tu souvent pour ton anniversaire?

**Élève 2:** Quand j'étais petit, mes parents organisaient souvent une fête.

**3** **Sports et loisirs** Votre professeur va vous donner une feuille d'activités. Circulez dans la classe et demandez à vos camarades s'ils pratiquaient ces activités avant d'entrer au lycée. Trouvez une personne différente qui dise (*says*) oui pour chaque activité. Présentez les réponses à la classe. Answers will vary.

**MODÈLE**

**Élève 1:** Est-ce que tu faisais souvent du jogging avant d'entrer au lycée?

**Élève 2:** Oui, je courais souvent le matin.

---

**4** **Pendant les vacances** Par groupes de trois, créez le texte d'un article qui décrit ce que (*what*) faisaient ces gens. Utilisez des verbes à l'imparfait et des adverbes dans vos descriptions. Ensuite, présentez vos articles à la classe. Answers will vary.

**5** **Mes mauvaises habitudes** Vous aviez de mauvaises habitudes, mais vous les avez changées. Maintenant, vous parlez avec votre ancien prof de français que vous rencontrez dans la rue. Avec un(e) partenaire, préparez la conversation. Answers will vary.

**MODÈLE**

**Élève 1:** Vous dormiez tout le temps en cours!

**Élève 2:** Je dormais souvent, mais je travaillais aussi. Maintenant, je travaille sérieusement.

**6** **Un week-end en vacances** Votre professeur va vous donner, à vous et à votre partenaire, une feuille de dessins sur le week-end de M. et Mme Bardot et de leur fille Alexandra. Attention! Ne regardez pas la feuille de votre partenaire. Answers will vary.

**MODÈLE**

**Élève 1:** En général, ils logeaient dans un hôtel.

**Élève 2:** Tous les jours, …

| ressources | | |
|---|---|---|
| CE pp. 93-96 | CA pp. 13-14, 61-62, 169-170 | **S** daccord1.vhlcentral.com |

---

**OPTIONS**

**Mini-dictée** Use these sentences containing adverbs and regular and irregular verbs in the **imparfait** as a dictation. Read each sentence twice, pausing after the second time for students to write. **1. Heureusement, il y avait beaucoup d'élèves dans la classe. 2. Conduisait-il vite la voiture? 3. J'étais vraiment très heureuse de te voir. 4. Il fallait constamment travailler le samedi.**

**Skits** Have small groups organize a skit about a birthday or other party that took place recently. Guide them to first make general comments about the party, such as **C'était vraiment amusant!** Then describe a few specific things that were going on, what people were talking about, what they were wearing, and any other appropriate details. After the skits are performed, have students vote for their favorite.

# À l'écoute  S Audio: Activities

## Préparation

Quand vous partez en vacances, qui décide où aller? Qui fait les réservations? Est-ce que vous utilisez les services d'une agence de voyages? Internet?

## ◑S À vous d'écouter 🎧

Écoutez la publicité. Puis écoutez une deuxième fois et notez les informations qui manquent (*that are missing*). Notez aussi un détail supplémentaire pour chaque voyage.

| Pays (ville/région) | Nombre de jours/semaines | Prix par personne | Détail supplémentaire |
|---|---|---|---|
| 1. Italie (Venise) | 3 jours | 395 euros | Answers will vary. |
| 2. Brésil | 1 semaine | 1.500 euros | Answers will vary. |
| 3. Irlande (Dublin) | 5 jours | 575 euros | Answers will vary. |
| 4. Amérique du Nord (États-Unis, Canada, Mexique) | 14 jours | 2.000 euros | Answers will vary. |
| 5. France (Avignon) | 7 jours | 487 euros | Answers will vary. |

 Practice more at **daccord1.vhlcentral.com.**

## Compréhension

**Où vont-ils?** Vous travaillez pour l'agence Vacances Pour Tous cet été. Indiquez où chaque personne va aller.

1. Madame Dupuis n'a pas envie d'aller à l'étranger.

   Madame Dupuis va aller à Avignon.

2. Le fils de Monsieur Girard a besoin de pratiquer son espagnol et son anglais.

   Il va aller en Amérique du Nord.

3. Madame Leroy a envie de visiter une capitale européenne.

   Elle va aller en Irlande.

4. Yves Marignaud a seulement trois jours de congé.

   Il va aller en Italie (Venise).

5. Justine adore la plage et le soleil.

   Elle va aller au Brésil.

6. La famille Abou a envie de passer ses vacances à la campagne.

   Ils vont aller à Avignon.

**Votre voyage** Vous avez fait un des voyages proposés par l'agence Vacances Pour Tous. C'est le dernier jour et vous écrivez une carte postale (*postcard*) à un(e) ami(e) francophone. Parlez-lui de votre séjour. Quel voyage avez-vous fait? Pourquoi? Comment avez-vous voyagé? Qu'est-ce que vous avez fait pendant votre séjour? Est-ce que vous avez aimé vos vacances? Expliquez pourquoi.

*deux cent quarante-cinq* **245**

---

Découvrez la capitale irlandaise avec un séjour de 5 jours à Dublin; 575 euros par personne. En train et bateau.
Autre super promotion pour étudiants: un voyage de deux semaines en Amérique. Une semaine aux États-Unis, quatre jours au Canada et trois jours au Mexique; 2.000 euros par personne. En avion et autobus. Logement en auberge de jeunesse.

Vous n'avez pas envie de partir à l'étranger, mais vous avez une semaine de congé? Nous avons une promotion incroyable sur la France. Sept jours à la campagne. Voyage en train. Logement dans un petit hôtel près d'Avignon; 487 euros par personne.
Appelez tout de suite le 01.42.46.46.46 pour faire vos réservations!

Interactive Map
Reading

# Panorama

le ski dans les Alpes

## Provence-Alpes-Côte d'Azur

### La région en chiffres

▶ **Superficie:** *31.400 km²*

▶ **Population:** *4.818.000*
SOURCE: INSEE

▶ **Industries principales:** *agriculture, industries agro-alimentaires°, métallurgiques et mécaniques, parfumerie, tourisme*

▶ **Villes principales:** *Avignon, Gap, Marseille, Nice, Toulon*

### Personnes célèbres

▶ **Nostradamus,** *astrologue et médecin (1503–1566)*

▶ **Marcel Pagnol,** *cinéaste° et écrivain (1895–1974)*

▶ **Surya Bonaly,** *athlète olympique (1973– )*

## Rhône-Alpes

### La région en chiffres

▶ **Superficie:** *43.698 km²*

▶ **Population:** *6.058.000*

▶ **Industries principales:** *agriculture, élevage°, tourisme, industries chimiques, métallurgiques et textiles*

▶ **Villes principales:** *Annecy, Chambéry, Grenoble, Lyon, Saint-Étienne*

### Personnes célèbres

▶ **Louise Labé,** *poétesse (1524–1566)*

▶ **Stendhal,** *écrivain (1783–1842)*

▶ **Antoine de Saint-Exupéry,** *écrivain, auteur° du Petit Prince (1900–1944)*

**agro-alimentaires** *food-processing* **cinéaste** *filmmaker* **élevage** *livestock raising* **auteur** *author* **confrérie** *brotherhood* **gardians** *herdsmen* **depuis** *since* **sud** *south* **chevaux** *horses* **taureaux** *bulls* **flamants** *flamingos* **Montés** *Riding* **Papes** *Popes*

246 *deux cent quarante-six*

LA SUISSE

L'ITALIE

LA FRANCE

Annecy • Chamonix
▲ Mont-Blanc
Lyon • le Rhône • Albertville
Chambéry •
St-Étienne • RHÔNE-ALPES
la Saône
l'Isère
Grenoble •
Valence •
la Drôme
Montélimar • Gap •
le Rhône la Durance
PROVENCE-ALPES-
CÔTE D'AZUR
(PACA)
le Var
Avignon • le Verdon
la Durance
Arles • Grasse • Nice
LA CAMARGUE Cannes • MONACO
Aix-en-Provence Antibes
Marseille • Toulon •
Les îles d'Hyères

0 — 50 miles
0 — 50 kilomètres

LA MER
MÉDITERRANÉE

le palais des Papes° à Avignon

PROMENADE des ANGLAIS

la promenade des Anglais à Nice

### Incroyable mais vrai!

Tous les cow-boys ne sont pas américains. En Camargue, la confrérie° des gardians° perpétue depuis° 1512 les traditions des cow-boys français. C'est dans le sud° que cohabitent les chevaux° blancs camarguais, des taureaux° noirs et des flamants° roses. Montés° sur des chevaux blancs, les gardians gardent les taureaux noirs.

---

## Section Goals

In this section, students will learn about the history and culture of **Provence-Alpes-Côte d'Azur** and **Rhône-Alpes**.

## Key Standards

2.2, 3.1, 3.2, 5.1

**Student Resources**
*Cahier d'exercices,* pp. 97-98;
Supersite: Activities,
*Cahier interactif*
**Teacher Resources**
Answer Keys; Overhead #36

### Carte des régions Provence-Alpes-Côte d'Azur et Rhône-Alpes

• Have students look at the map of the regions **Provence-Alpes-Côte d'Azur (PACA)** and **Rhône-Alpes** or use **Overhead #36**. Point out that **Provence-Alpes-Côte d'Azur** and **Rhône-Alpes** are popular tourist destinations year-round. Ask students to cite the geographic features that likely make these locations such attractive and diverse vacation spots. (**les Alpes, les plages,** etc.)
• Ask students if they are familiar with any of the location names and to share what they know about or associate with these places. Students should recognize Aix-en-Provence for the references in **Roman-photo**.
• Have students find **Mont-Blanc**. It is Europe's highest mountain, reaching 15,780 ft.

### La région en chiffres

• Ask volunteers to read the sections. Then ask students questions about the content.
• Point out cognates and clarify any unfamiliar words.
• Tell students that Grenoble was the site of the 1968 Winter Olympics. Ask what other towns of these regions have hosted the Olympic Games. (Chamonix, 1924 and Albertville, 1992)

**Incroyable mais vrai!** Have students reference the map to see where **la Camargue** is located. **Le parc naturel régional de Camargue** was created to protect the rich flora and fauna found in the region and encompasses 211,740 acres. See if students remember how to convert that into hectares. (211,740 acres ÷ 2.47 = 85,690 hectares)

**OPTIONS**

**Personnes célèbres Surya Bonaly** has competed in three Olympic Games and has won medals in many national and international figure skating competitions. **Marcel Pagnol** was the first filmmaker to be elected to the **Académie française**. Two of **Stendhal**'s best-known novels are *Le Rouge et le Noir* and *La Chartreuse de Parme*. **Louise Labé** wrote passionate poetry in the style of

Petrarch. **Antoine de Saint-Exupéry** is the only French author to have three books among the top ten best sellers of the period. He is best known for writing and illustrating *Le Petit Prince*, which has been translated into numerous languages.

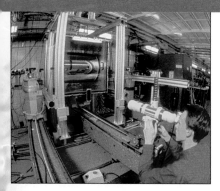

## Les destinations
### Grenoble

La ville de Grenoble, dans la région Rhône-Alpes, est surnommée «Capitale des Alpes» et «Ville Technologique». Située° à la porte des Alpes, elle donne accès aux grandes stations de ski alpin et est le premier centre de recherche° en France après Paris, avec plus de° 15.000 chercheurs°. Le synchrotron de Grenoble, un des plus grands° accélérateurs de particules du monde, permet à 5.000 chercheurs d'étudier la matière°. Grenoble est également° une ville universitaire avec quatre universités et 60.000 étudiants.

## Les arts
### Le festival de Cannes

Chaque année depuis° 1946, au mois de mai, de nombreux acteurs, réalisateurs° et journalistes viennent à Cannes, sur la Côte d'Azur, pour le Festival International du Film. Avec près de 4.000 films (courts et longs métrages°), 4.500 journalistes et plus de 90 pays représentés, c'est la manifestation cinématographique annuelle la plus médiatisée°. Après deux semaines de projections, de fêtes, d'expositions et de concerts, le jury international du festival choisit le meilleur° des vingt films présentés en compétition officielle.

## La gastronomie
### La raclette et la fondue

La Savoie, dans la région Rhône-Alpes, est très riche en fromages et deux de ses spécialités sont à base de fromage. Pour la raclette, on met du fromage à raclette sur un appareil° à raclette pour le faire fondre°. Chaque personne racle° du fromage dans son assiette° et le mange avec des pommes de terre° et de la charcuterie°. La fondue est un mélange° de fromages fondus°. Avec un bâton°, on trempe° un morceau° de pain dans la fondue. Ne le faites pas tomber!

## Les traditions
### Grasse, France

La ville de Grasse, sur la Côte d'Azur, est le centre de la parfumerie° française. Capitale mondiale du parfum depuis le dix-huitième siècle, Grasse cultive les fleurs depuis le Moyen Âge°: violette, lavande, rose, plantes aromatiques, etc. Au dix-neuvième siècle, ses parfumeurs, comme Molinard, ont conquis° les marchés du monde grâce à° la fabrication industrielle.

**Grenoble** There are a vast number of educational institutions in the city of Grenoble. The city is considered a center for chemical, electronic, and nuclear research. Have students search Grenoble's city web site for information about how many universities are located in Grenoble and in what areas of study they specialize.

**Le festival de Cannes** Only accredited film industry professionals can attend **le festival de Cannes**. Those not involved in the film industry can obtain invitations to the **Cinéma de la Plage**. Each evening at the **Cinéma de la Plage**, films that are not in the running for the **Palme d'Or** may be viewed on a large open-air screen.

**La raclette et la fondue** Invented by the Swiss, fondue has become an international dish, and each region has adapted the dish to its own taste. In Savoie, instead of the traditional Gruyère cheese, people use Comté and Beaufort as well as Emmental cheeses. Kirsch and dry white wine, preferably from Savoie, are added to the cheese.

**Grasse, France** Each summer, people in Grasse celebrate the **Fête du Jasmin**. Over 150,000 flowers are used to decorate the floats and to throw in the battle of flowers. Women throw flowers from the floats and spray the audience with jasmine water. Folk dancers, bands, and artists come from all over Europe to celebrate this festival.

**Qu'est-ce que vous avez appris?** Répondez aux questions par des phrases complètes.

1. Comment s'appelle la région où les gardians perpétuent les traditions des cow-boys français?
   La région s'appelle la Camargue.
2. Qui a écrit *Le Petit Prince*?
   Antoine de Saint-Exupéry a écrit *Le Petit Prince.*
3. Quel est le rôle des gardians?
   Ils gardent les taureaux.
4. Où est située Grenoble?
   Grenoble est située dans la région Rhône-Alpes.
5. À Grenoble, qui vient étudier la matière?
   À Grenoble, les chercheurs viennent étudier la matière.
6. Depuis quand existe le festival de Cannes?
   Le festival de Cannes existe depuis 1946.
7. Qui choisit le meilleur film au festival de Cannes?
   Le jury international choisit le meilleur film.
8. Avec quoi mange-t-on la raclette?
   On mange la raclette avec des pommes de terre et de la charcuterie.
9. Quelle ville est le centre de la parfumerie française?
   La ville de Grasse est le centre de la parfumerie française.
10. Pourquoi Grasse est-elle le centre de la parfumerie française?
    Grasse est le centre de la parfumerie française parce que la ville cultive les fleurs. / grâce à la fabrication industrielle.

 Practice more at **daccord1.vhlcentral.com.**

### SUR INTERNET

Go to **daccord1.vhlcentral.com** to find more cultural information related to this **PANORAMA**.

1. Quels films étaient (*were*) en compétition au dernier festival de Cannes? Qui composait (*made up*) le jury?
2. Trouvez des informations sur la parfumerie à Grasse. Quelles sont deux autres parfumeries qu'on trouve à Grasse?

**ressources**

CE pp. 97-98

daccord1.vhlcentral.com

**Située** *Located* **recherche** *research* **plus de** *more than* **chercheurs** *researchers* **des plus grands** *of the largest* **matière** *matter* **également** *also* **depuis** *since* **réalisateurs** *filmmakers* **métrages** *films* **la plus médiatisée** *the most publicized* **meilleur** *best* **appareil** *machine* **fondre** *melt* **racle** *scrapes* **assiette** *plate* **pommes de terre** *potatoes* **charcuterie** *cooked pork meats* **mélange** *mix* **fondus** *melted* **bâton** *stick* **trempe** *dips* **morceau** *piece* **parfumerie** *perfume industry* **Moyen Âge** *Middle Ages* **ont conquis** *conquered* **grâce à** *thanks to*

SAVOIR-FAIRE **247**

**OPTIONS**

**Cultural Activity** Have students look at the web sites for **le festival de Cannes**, **les César du Cinéma**, and a major award show or film festival from their region. Ask students to compare and contrast the award categories, the selection process, the event, and the winners. Have each student share his or her findings with the class.

**Narrative** Have students imagine that they have gone on vacation in **Provence-Alpes-Côte d'Azur**, **Rhône-Alpes**, or both. Students will work with a partner telling about their experience. Ask students to tell where they went, talk about at least two activities they did there, and what the weather was like. The partner should then ask a question about the trip and tell about his or her vacation.

## Section Goals

In this section, students will:
• learn to predict content from the title
• read a travel brochure in French

## Key Standards

1.2, 2.1, 3.2, 5.2

**Stratégie** Tell students that they can often predict the content of a newspaper article from its headline. Display or make up several cognate-rich headlines from French newspapers. Examples: **L'ONU critique le changement de règle du vote pour le référendum en Irak; Huit clubs de football français rattrapés par la justice; À la télé américaine, le président est une femme.** Ask students to predict the content of each article.

**Examinez le texte** Ask volunteers to share their ideas about what type of document it is, and what information they think each section will have. Then go over the correct answers with the entire class.

**Des titres** Working in pairs to compare their answers, have students discuss how they are able to tell where these titles were found.

# Lecture  Ⓢ Reading

## Avant la lecture

### STRATÉGIE

#### Predicting content from the title

Prediction is an invaluable strategy in reading for comprehension. We can usually predict the content of a newspaper article from its headline, for example. More often than not, we decide whether or not to read the article based on its headline. Predicting content from the title will help you increase your reading comprehension in French.

### Examinez le texte

Regardez le titre (*title*) et les sous-titres (*subtitles*) du texte. À votre avis, quel type de document est-ce? Avec un(e) camarade, faites une liste des informations que vous allez probablement trouver dans chaque section du document.

### Des titres

Regardez ces titres et indiquez en quelques mots le sujet possible du texte qui suit (*follows*) chaque titre. Où pensez-vous qu'on a trouvé ces titres (dans un journal, un magazine, une brochure, un guide, etc.)?

**Cette semaine à Paris:**
un journal

**Encore un nouveau restaurant pour chiens**
un journal, un magazine

**L'Égypte des pyramides en 8 jours**
une brochure, un guide

**L'AÉROPORT CHARLES-DE-GAULLE A PERDU LES VALISES D'UN VOL DE TOURISTES ALLEMANDS**
un journal

*Plan du centre-ville*
un guide

**Résultats du septième match de football entre la France et l'Angleterre**
un journal

**Hôtel confortable près de la gare routière**
une brochure

# TOUR DE CORSE

## Voyage organisé de 12 jours

**3.000 euros tout compris°
Promotion spéciale de
Vacances–Voyages,
agence de voyages certifiée**

## ITINÉRAIRE

### JOUR 1  Paris–Ajaccio

Vous partez de Paris en avion pour Ajaccio, en Corse. Vous prenez tout de suite le bus pour aller à votre hôtel. Vous commencez par visiter la ville d'Ajaccio à pied°, puis vous dînez à l'hôtel.

### JOUR 2  Ajaccio–Bonifacio

Le matin, vous partez en autobus pour Bonifacio, la belle ville côtière° où vous déjeunez dans un petit restaurant italien avant de visiter la ville. L'après-midi, vous montez à bord° d'un bateau pour une promenade en mer, occasion idéale pour observer les falaises rocailleuses° et les plages blanches de l'île°. Ensuite, vous rentrez à l'hôtel pour dîner et y (*there*) passer la nuit.

### JOUR 3  Bonifacio–Corte

La forêt de l'Ospédale est l'endroit idéal pour une randonnée à pied. Vous pique-niquez à Zonza, petite ville montagneuse, avant de continuer vers Corte, l'ancienne° capitale de la Corse. Vous passez la soirée et la nuit à Corte.

### JOUR 4  Corte–Bastia

Vous avez la journée pour visiter la ville de Bastia. Vous assistez à un spectacle de danse, puis vous passez la soirée à l'hôtel.

### JOUR 5  Bastia–Calvi

Vous visitez d'abord le Cap Corse, la péninsule au nord° de la Corse. Puis, vous continuez vers le désert des Agriates, zone de montagnes désertiques où la chaleur est très forte. Ensuite, c'est l'Île-Rousse et une promenade à vélo dans la ville de Calvi. Vous dînez à votre hôtel.

---

**Brainstorming** Have five students work together to brainstorm a list of what would constitute an ideal vacation for them. Each student should contribute at least one idea. Opinions will vary. Ask the group to designate one student to take notes and another to present the information to the class. When each group has its list, ask the presenters to share the group's ideas. How are the group's ideas? Similar or different?

**Interviews** Ask students if they have ever been on an organized tour. If students have not been on a tour similar to the one to Corsica described in **Lecture**, have them interview someone they know who has. Have students answer questions like these: **Où êtes-vous allé(e)? Avec quelle agence? Avez-vous aimé toutes les activités organisées? Expliquez pourquoi.**

# Après la lecture

**Les questions du professeur** Vous avez envie de faire ce voyage en Corse et vous parlez du voyage organisé avec votre professeur de français. Répondez à ses questions par des phrases complètes, d'après la brochure.

1. Comment allez-vous aller en Corse?
   *Je vais prendre l'avion à Paris.*

2. Où le vol arrive-t-il en Corse?
   *Le vol arrive à Ajaccio.*

3. Combien de temps est-ce que vous allez passer en Corse?
   *Je vais passer douze jours en Corse.*

4. Est-ce que vous allez dormir dans des auberges de jeunesse?
   *Non. Je vais dormir à l'hôtel./dans des hôtels.*

5. Qu'est-ce que vous allez faire à Bastia?
   *Je vais visiter la ville, aller à un spectacle de danse, puis passer la soirée à l'hôtel.*

6. Est-ce que vous retournez à Ajaccio le neuvième jour?
   *Non. Je retourne à Ajaccio le septième jour.*

7. Qu'est-ce que vous allez prendre comme transports en Corse?
   *Je vais prendre l'autobus et des bateaux.*

8. Avez-vous besoin de faire toutes les réservations?
   *Non. Le voyage est organisé par une agence de voyages.*

**Partons en Corse!** Vous allez en France avec votre famille pour trois semaines et vous aimeriez *(would like)* faire le voyage organisé en Corse au départ de Paris. Vous téléphonez à l'agence de voyages pour avoir plus de détails pour convaincre *(convince)* votre famille. Posez des questions sur le voyage et demandez des précisions sur les villes visitées, les visites et les activités au programme, les hôtels, les transports, etc.

- Vous aimez faire des randonnées, mais votre frère/sœur préfère voir *(to see)* des spectacles et faire du shopping.

- L'agent va expliquer pourquoi vous allez aimer ce voyage en Corse.

- Demandez à l'agent de vous trouver des billets d'avion aller-retour pour aller de votre ville à Paris.

- Demandez aussi un hôtel à Paris pour la troisième semaine de votre séjour en France.

- L'agent va aussi suggérer des visites et des activités intéressantes à faire à Paris.

- Vous expliquez à l'agent que votre famille veut *(wants)* avoir du temps libre pendant le voyage.

## JOUR 6 Calvi–Porto
Vous partez en bus le matin pour la vallée du Fango et le golfe de Galéria à l'ouest° de l'île. Puis, vous visitez le parc naturel régional et le golfe de Porto. Ensuite, vous faites une promenade en bateau avant de passer la soirée dans la ville de Porto.

## JOUR 7 Porto–Ajaccio
En bateau, vous visitez des calanques°, particularité géographique de la région méditerranéenne, avant de retourner à Ajaccio.

## JOURS 8 à 11 Ajaccio
À Ajaccio, vous avez trois jours pour explorer la ville. Vous avez la possibilité de visiter la cathédrale, la maison natale° de Napoléon ou des musées, et aussi de faire du shopping ou d'aller à la plage.

## JOUR 12 Ajaccio–Paris
Vous retournez à Paris en avion.

**tout compris** *all-inclusive* **à pied** *on foot* **côtière** *coastal* **à bord** *aboard*
**falaises rocailleuses** *rocky cliffs* **île** *island* **ancienne** *former* **nord** *north*
**ouest** *west* **calanques** *rocky coves or creeks* **natale** *birth*

---

**Les questions du professeur** Have students quickly review the brochure before answering the questions. Suggest that pairs take turns answering them. The student who does not answer a question should find the line of text that contains the answer.

**C'est sûr, je pars en Corse!** Have groups act out their conversations for the rest of the class.

**Expansion** Tell students that the travel agency is planning to create additional brochures to help them promote their **Tour de Corse** excursion. Their goal is to have several slightly different brochures about the same trip that may appeal to different types of people. Ask students to come up with 3 or 4 short, interesting titles for these new brochures.

---

**OPTIONS**

**Narrative** Have students work together in pairs. Tell them to divide the twelve-day **Tour de Corse** itinerary between them. Each student will then write at least five questions asking about their chosen parts of the trip. They will then answer each other's questions.

**Les journaux** Bring in additional short, simple French-language magazine or newspaper articles you have read. Have pairs scan the headlines/titles of the articles to determine their content. Have them write down all the clues that help them come to these conclusions. Then ask pairs to present their findings to the class. Confirm the correct predictions.

# Écriture

## STRATÉGIE

### Making an outline

When we write to share information, an outline can serve to separate topics and subtopics, providing a framework for presenting the data. Consider the following excerpt from an outline of the tourist brochure on pages 248–249.

I. Itinéraire et description du voyage
    A. Jour 1
        1. ville: Ajaccio
        2. visites: visite de la ville à pied
        3. activités: dîner
    B. Jour 2
        1. ville: Bonifacio
        2. visites: la ville de Bonifacio
        3. activités: promenade en bateau, dîner
II. Description des hôtels et des transports
    A. Hôtels
    B. Transports

### Schéma d'idées

Idea maps can be used to create outlines. The major sections of an idea map correspond to the Roman numerals in an outline. The minor sections correspond to the outline's capital letters, and so on. Consider the idea map that led to the outline above.

## Thème

## Écrivez une brochure

### Avant l'écriture

1. Vous allez préparer une brochure pour un voyage organisé que vous avez fait ou que vous avez envie de faire dans un pays francophone. Utilisez un schéma d'idées pour vous aider. Voici des exemples d'informations que votre brochure peut (*can*) donner.

■ le pays et la ville

■ le nombre de jours

■ la date et l'heure du départ et du retour

■ les transports utilisés (train, avion, …) et le lieu de départ (aéroport JFK, gare de Lyon, …)

■ le temps qu'il va probablement faire et quelques suggestions de vêtements à porter

■ où on va dormir (hôtel, auberge de jeunesse, camping, …)

■ où on va manger (restaurant, café, pique-nique dans un parc, …)

■ les visites culturelles (monuments, musées, …)

■ les autres activités au programme (explorer la ville, aller au marché, faire du sport, …)

■ le prix du voyage par personne

**2.** Complétez le schéma d'idées pour vous aider à visualiser ce que (*what*) vous allez présenter dans votre brochure.

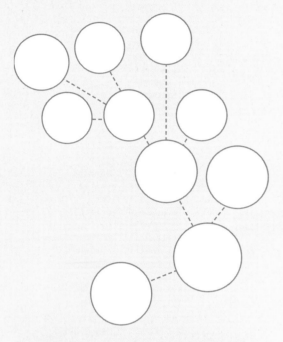

**3.** Une fois (*Once*) votre schéma d'idées créé, pensez à d'autres informations qui pourraient (*could*) être importantes pour la création de votre brochure.

## Écriture

Utilisez votre schéma d'idées pour créer la brochure de votre voyage. Donnez un titre (*title*) à la présentation et aux différentes catégories. Chaque section et sous-section (*minor section*) doit (*must*) avoir son titre et être présentée séparément. Incorporez au moins (*at least*) quatre sous-sections. Vous pouvez inclure (*can include*) des visuels. Faites attention à bien les placer dans les sections correspondantes. Utilisez les constructions grammaticales et le vocabulaire que vous avez appris dans cette unité.

## Après l'écriture

**1.** Échangez votre brochure avec celle (*the one*) d'un(e) partenaire. Répondez à ces questions pour commenter son travail.

- La brochure de votre partenaire correspond-elle au schéma d'idées qu'il/elle a créé?

- Votre partenaire a-t-il/elle inclu au moins quatre sections?

- Toutes les sections et sous-sections ont-elles un titre?

- Votre partenaire a-t-il/elle décrit en détail chaque catégorie?

- Chaque sous-section présente-t-elle des informations supplémentaires sur le sujet?

- Si votre partenaire a ajouté (*added*) des visuels, illustrent-ils vraiment le texte qu'ils accompagnent?

- Votre partenaire a-t-il/elle correctement utilisé les constructions grammaticales et le vocabulaire de l'unité?

**2.** Corrigez votre brochure d'après (*according to*) les commentaires de votre partenaire. Relisez votre travail pour éliminer ces problèmes:

- des fautes (*errors*) d'orthographe

- des fautes de ponctuation

- des fautes de conjugaison

- des fautes d'accord (*agreement*) des adjectifs

- un mauvais emploi (*use*) de la grammaire

## EVALUATION

**Criteria**

**Content** Contains both an idea map and an outline that provide all the information requested in bulleted list of tasks.
Scale: 1 2 3 4 5

**Organization** An outline or idea map that is then converted into a brochure with a title and minor sections that correspond to the outline or idea map.
Scale: 1 2 3 4 5

**Accuracy** Uses forms of **aller** and direct object pronouns correctly. Spells words, conjugates verbs, and modifies adjectives correctly throughout.
Scale: 1 2 3 4 5

**Creativity** Includes additional information that is not included in the task and/or designs a brochure with photos, drawings, or extra embellishments.
Scale: 1 2 3 4 5

**Scoring**

| | |
|---|---|
| Excellent | 18–20 points |
| Good | 14–17 points |
| Satisfactory | 10–13 points |
| Unsatisfactory | < 10 points |

**OPTIONS**

**Écriture** Students may need help converting the bulleted information into an outline/idea map. As a class, brainstorm ways to organize the facts. For example: (1st level): **Un voyage à** _____, (2nd level): **Généralités, Que faire et voir** (to see). Then have students associate the following with one of the 2nd level categories: number of days, dates, travel times, transportation, weather, price, hotels, restaurants, cultural visits, other activities.

Review the kind of neutral and formal language typically used in a travel brochure. Have students review command forms from Lessons 2A, 4B, and 6B. You may want to get them started with some useful expressions such as **Nous donnons...** and **Vous allez** [+ *infinitive*], along with a number of adjectives such as **fascinant(e), intéressant(e), beau/belle, historique, ancien(ne), confortable, agréable, délicieux/délicieuse,** and so on.

Ⓢ Flashcards
Audio: Vocabulary

## Key Standards

4.1

**Suggestion** Tell students that an easy way to study from **Vocabulaire** is to cover up the French half of each section, leaving only the English equivalents exposed. They can then quiz themselves on the French items. To focus on the English equivalents of the French entries, they simply reverse this process.

### Partir en voyage

| | |
|---|---|
| un aéroport | airport |
| un arrêt d'autobus (de bus) | bus stop |
| une arrivée | arrival |
| un avion | plane |
| un billet aller-retour | round-trip ticket |
| un billet (d'avion, de train) | (plane, train) ticket |
| un départ | departure |
| une douane | customs |
| une gare (routière) | train station (bus terminal) |
| une sortie | exit |
| une station (de métro) | (subway) station |
| une station de ski | ski resort |
| un ticket (de bus, de métro) | (bus, subway) ticket |
| un vol | flight |
| un voyage | trip |
| | |
| à l'étranger | abroad, overseas |
| | |
| la campagne | country(side) |
| une capitale | capital |
| des gens (m.) | people |
| le monde | world |
| un pays | country |

### Les pays

| | |
|---|---|
| (en/l') Allemagne (f.) | (to/in) Germany |
| (en/l') Angleterre (f.) | (to/in) England |
| (en/la) Belgique (belge) | (to/in) Belgium (Belgian) |
| (au/le) Brésil (brésilien(ne)) | (to/in) Brazil (Brazilian) |
| (au/le) Canada | (to/in) Canada |
| (en/la) Chine (chinois(e)) | (to/in) China (Chinese) |
| (en/l') Espagne (f.) | (to/in) Spain |
| (aux/les) États-Unis (m.) | (to/in) United States |
| (en/la) France | (to/in) France |
| (en/l') Irlande (f.) (irlandais(e)) | (to/in) Ireland (Irish) |
| (en/l') Italie (f.) | (to/in) Italy |
| (au/le) Japon | (to/in) Japan |
| (au/le) Mexique | (to/in) Mexico |
| (en/la) Suisse | (to/in) Switzerland |

### Les vacances

| | |
|---|---|
| bronzer | to tan |
| faire du shopping | to go shopping |
| faire les valises | to pack one's bags |
| faire un séjour | to spend time (somewhere) |
| partir en vacances | to go on vacation |
| prendre un train (un avion, un taxi, un (auto)bus, un bateau) | to take a train (plane, taxi, bus, boat) |
| rouler en voiture | to ride in a car |
| utiliser un plan | to use/read a map |
| | |
| un (jour de) congé | day off |
| le journal | newspaper |
| la mer | sea |
| une plage | beach |
| des vacances (f.) | vacation |

### Adverbes

| | |
|---|---|
| absolument | absolutely |
| activement | actively |
| bien | well |
| constamment | constantly |
| couramment | fluently |
| différemment | differently |
| évidemment | obviously, evidently; of course |
| franchement | frankly, honestly |
| gentiment | nicely |
| heureusement | fortunately |
| mal | badly |
| malheureusement | unfortunately |
| vraiment | really |

### Verbes

| | |
|---|---|
| aller | to go |
| arriver | to arrive |
| descendre | to go/take down |
| entrer | to enter |
| monter | to go/come up; to get in/on |
| mourir | to die |
| naître | to be born |
| partir | to leave |
| passer | to pass by; to spend time |
| rentrer | to return |
| rester | to stay |
| retourner | to return |
| sortir | to go out |
| tomber (sur quelqu'un) | to fall (to run into somebody) |

### Faire une réservation

| | |
|---|---|
| annuler | to cancel |
| une réservation | a reservation |
| réserver | to reserve, to book |
| | |
| une agence de voyages | travel agency |
| un agent de voyages | travel agent |
| un ascenseur | elevator |
| une auberge de jeunesse | youth hostel |
| une chambre individuelle | single room |
| une clé | key |
| un(e) client(e) | client; guest |
| un étage | floor |
| un hôtel | hotel |
| un hôtelier/ une hôtelière | hotel keeper |
| un lit | bed |
| un passager/ une passagère | passenger |
| un passeport | passport |
| la réception | reception desk |
| le rez-de-chaussée | ground floor |
| | |
| complet/complète | full (no vacancies) |
| libre | available |

### Verbes irréguliers

| | |
|---|---|
| décrire | to describe |
| dire | to say |
| écrire | to write |
| lire | to read |

| | |
|---|---|
| *Expressions utiles* | See pp. 223 and 237. |
| Direct object pronouns | See pp. 228–229. |
| Ordinal numbers | See pp. 232–233. |

# Chez nous

## Unit Goals

**Leçon 8A**

In this lesson, students will learn:

- terms for parts of the house
- terms for furniture
- the pronunciation of **s** and **ss**
- about housing in France and **le château Frontenac**
- more about housing in France through specially shot video footage
- the uses of the **passé composé** and the **imparfait**
- about Century 21 in France

**Leçon 8B**

In this lesson, students will learn:

- terms for household chores
- terms for appliances
- the pronunciation of semi-vowels
- about the interiors of French homes and the French Quarter in New Orleans
- more about the uses of the **passé composé** and the **imparfait**
- the uses of **savoir** and **connaître**
- to use visual cues to understand spoken French

**Savoir-faire**

In this section, students will learn:

- cultural and historical information about **Alsace** and **Lorraine**
- to guess the meaning of unknown words from context
- to write a narrative using the **passé composé** and the **imparfait**

**Pour commencer**

- a. dans le salon
- c. une télévision
- b. Ils passent un bon moment.

---

**Pour commencer**

- Où sont David et Rachid?
  a. dans le salon  b. dans la cuisine
  c. dans la chambre
- Qu'est-ce qu'il n'y a pas sur la photo?
  a. un canapé  b. une table  c. une télévision
- Que font David et Rachid?
  a. Ils étudient.  b. Ils passent un bon moment.
  c. Ils regardent la télé.

**Savoir-faire**

**Panorama:** **L'Alsace** and **la Lorraine**
**Lecture:** Read an article about Versailles.
**Écriture:** Write a story about your dream house.

---

**Student Materials**
**Print:** Student Book, Workbooks (*Cahier d'exercices*, *Cahier d'activités*)
**Technology:** MAESTRO® *Cahier interactif* and Supersite (Audio, Video, Practice)

**Teacher Materials**
DVDs (*Roman-photo, Flash culture*)
Teacher's Resources (Scripts, Answer Keys, Testing Program)
Audio CDs (Testing Program, Textbook, Audio Program)

MAESTRO® Supersite: Student Supersite Content; Planning and Teaching Resources (Overheads, *PowerPoints*, Lesson Plans, Information Gaps and *Feuilles d'activités*); Learning Management System (Gradebook, Assignments); Audio MP3s and Streaming Video
**D'ACCORD! 1 Supersite:** daccord1.vhlcentral.com

RESOURCES

## Section Goals

In this section, students will learn and practice vocabulary related to:
• housing
• rooms and home furnishings

## Key Standards
**1.1, 1.2, 4.1**

**Student Resources**
*Cahier d'exercices*, pp. 99-100; *Cahier d'activités*, pp. 63-64, 171; Supersite: Activities, *Cahier interactif*

**Teacher Resources**
Answer Keys; Overhead #37; Audio Script; Textbook & Audio Activity MP3s/CD; Info Gap Activities; Testing program: Vocabulary Quiz

## Suggestions

• Use **Overhead #37**. Point out rooms and furnishings in the illustration. Examples: **Ça, c'est la salle de bains. Voici un canapé.**

• Ask students questions about their homes using the new vocabulary. Examples: **Habitez-vous dans une maison ou dans un appartement? Avez-vous un balcon? Un garage? Combien de salles de bains avez-vous?**

• Point out the difference between **le loyer** (*the rent*) and **louer** (*to rent*).

• Explain that **une chambre** is *a bedroom*, but **une pièce** is the generic term for *a room*.

• Explain that **un salon** is a more formal room used primarily for entertaining guests. Generally, it is not used for watching television or other leisure activities. **Une salle de séjour** is a more functional room, similar to an American family room or den.

• Point out that **un studio** is *a studio apartment*, usually equipped with a couch that converts into a bed and a kitchenette.

**Leçon 8A**

**Talking Picture Audio: Activity**

You will learn how to...
▪ describe your home
▪ talk about habitual past actions

# La maison

le balcon

la salle de bains

les toilettes (f.)/ les W.C. (m.)

le miroir

la lampe

la baignoire

le canapé

le tapis

une fleur

le fauteuil

le sous-sol

la salle de séjour

### Vocabulaire

| | |
|---|---|
| déménager | to move out |
| emménager | to move in |
| louer | to rent |
| un appartement | apartment |
| une cave | cellar; basement |
| un couloir | hallway |
| une cuisine | kitchen |
| un escalier | staircase |
| un immeuble | building |
| un jardin | garden; yard |
| un logement | housing |
| un loyer | rent |
| une pièce | room |
| un quartier | area, neighborhood |
| une résidence universitaire | dorm |
| une salle à manger | dining room |
| un salon | formal living/sitting room |
| un studio | studio (apartment) |
| une armoire | armoire, wardrobe |
| une douche | shower |
| un lavabo | bathroom sink |
| un meuble | piece of furniture |
| un placard | closet, cupboard |
| un tiroir | drawer |
| un(e) propriétaire | owner |

**ressources**

| CE pp. 99–100 | CA pp.63–64,171 | daccord1.vhlcentral.com |
|---|---|---|

**OPTIONS**

**Asking Questions** Ask students what activities they do in various rooms. Examples: **Dans quelle pièce... mangez-vous? étudiez-vous? dormez-vous? faites-vous la cuisine? travaillez-vous sur l'ordinateur? parlez-vous au téléphone?**

**Using Movement** Make signs for various rooms in a house and for other parts of a home, such as **le garage** or **le balcon**. Also make several signs for bedrooms and bathrooms. Distribute the signs to students. As other students describe their homes (one floor at a time), those holding signs arrange themselves according to the descriptions. Tell students to use prepositions of location in their descriptions.

les rideaux (m.)

le mur

les affiches (f.)

les étagères (f.)

la commode

la chambre

le garage

# Mise en pratique

## 1 Chassez l'intrus
Indiquez le mot ou l'expression qui ne va pas avec les autres (*that doesn't belong*).

1. un appartement, (un quartier,) un logement, un studio
2. une baignoire, une douche, (un sous-sol,) un lavabo
3. un salon, une salle à manger, une salle de séjour, (un jardin)
4. un meuble, un canapé, une armoire, (une affiche)
5. (un placard,) un balcon, un jardin, un garage
6. une chambre, une cuisine, (un rideau,) une pièce
7. un meuble, une commode, (un couloir,) un lit
8. un miroir, (un tapis,) une fenêtre, une affiche

## 2 Écoutez 🎧
Patrice cherche un appartement. Écoutez sa conversation téléphonique et dites si les affirmations sont **vraies** ou **fausses**.

|  | Vrai | Faux |
|---|---|---|
| 1. Madame Dautry est la propriétaire de l'appartement. | ☑ | ☐ |
| 2. L'appartement est au 24, rue Pasteur. | ☑ | ☐ |
| 3. L'appartement est au cinquième étage. | ☐ | ☑ |
| 4. L'appartement est dans un vieil immeuble. | ☐ | ☑ |
| 5. L'appartement n'a pas de balcon, mais il a un garage. | ☐ | ☑ |
| 6. Il y a une baignoire dans la salle de bains. | ☐ | ☑ |
| 7. Les toilettes ne sont pas dans la salle de bains. | ☑ | ☐ |
| 8. L'appartement est un studio. | ☐ | ☑ |
| 9. Le loyer est de 490€. | ☑ | ☐ |
| 10. Patrice va tout de suite emménager. | ☐ | ☑ |

## 3 Définitions
Lisez les définitions et trouvez les mots ou expressions de **CONTEXTES** qui correspondent. Ensuite, avec un(e) partenaire, donnez votre propre définition de cinq mots ou expressions. Rejoignez un autre groupe et lisez vos définitions. L'autre groupe doit deviner (*must guess*) de quoi vous parlez.

1. C'est ce que (*what*) vous payez chaque mois quand vous n'êtes pas propriétaire de votre appartement. _____un loyer_____
2. Vous passez par ici pour aller d'une pièce à une autre. _____un couloir_____
3. C'est le fait de (*act of*) partir de votre appartement. _____déménager_____
4. C'est là que vous mettez vos livres. _____une étagère_____
5. En général, il y en a quatre dans une pièce et ils séparent les pièces de votre appartement. _____les murs_____
6. C'est ce que vous utilisez pour lire le soir. _____une lampe_____
7. C'est là que vous mettez votre voiture. _____un garage_____
8. C'est ce que vous utilisez pour aller du premier au deuxième étage d'un immeuble. _____un escalier/un ascenseur_____
9. Quand vous avez des invités, c'est la pièce dans laquelle (*in which*) vous dînez. _____la salle à manger_____
10. En général, il est sur le sol (*floor*) d'une pièce. _____un tapis_____

🔍 Practice more at **daccord1.vhlcentral.com.**

*deux cent cinquante-cinq* **255**

**1 Expansion** Have students create one or two additional sets using at least three of the new vocabulary words in each one. Collect their papers and write some of the items on the board.

**2 Script** PATRICE: Allô, Madame Dautry, s'il vous plaît.
MADAME: Oui, c'est moi. J'écoute.
P: Mon nom est Patrice Leconte. Je vous appelle au sujet de votre appartement du 24, rue Pasteur. Est-ce qu'il est toujours libre?
M: Oui, jeune homme. Il est toujours libre.
P: Parfait. Comment est-il?
M: Il est au quatrième étage d'un immeuble moderne. Il y a un balcon, mais pas de garage. La chambre est plutôt petite, mais il y a beaucoup de placards.
P: Et la salle de bains?
M: Elle est petite aussi, avec une douche, un lavabo et un grand miroir. Les toilettes sont séparées.
P: Et le salon?
M: C'est la pièce principale. Elle est plutôt grande. La cuisine est juste à côté.
P: C'est combien, le loyer?
M: Le loyer est de 490€.
P: Oh, c'est cher!
M: Mais vous êtes à côté de l'université et l'appartement est libre le premier septembre.
P: Bon, je vais y penser. Merci beaucoup. Au revoir, Madame.
M: Au revoir, Monsieur.
(*On Textbook Audio*)

**2 Expansion** Play the recording again, stopping at the end of each sentence that contains an answer. Have students verify true statements and correct the false ones.

**3 Suggestion** Before beginning this activity, you might want to teach your students expressions for circumlocution. Examples: **C'est un objet qu'on utilise pour... C'est une pièce où...**

**OPTIONS**

**Using Games** Write vocabulary words related to home furnishings on index cards. On another set of cards, draw or paste pictures to match each term. Tape them face down on the board in random order. Divide the class into two teams. Play a game of Concentration in which students match words with pictures. When a player has a match, his or her team collects those cards. When all cards are matched, the team with the most cards wins.

**Classifying Words** Write **Logements** and **Meubles** at the top of two columns on the board or on a transparency. Say vocabulary words and have students classify them in the correct category. Examples: **un appartement (logement), une résidence (logement), un studio (logement), un canapé (meuble), un lit (meuble),** and **une armoire (meuble).**

## Communication

**4 Répondez** À tour de rôle avec un(e) partenaire, posez-vous ces questions et répondez-y (*them*). Answers will vary.

1. Où est-ce que tu habites?
2. Quelle est la taille de ton appartement ou de ta maison? Combien de pièces y a-t-il?
3. Quand as-tu emménagé?
4. Est-ce que tu as un jardin? Un garage?
5. Combien de placards as-tu? Où sont-ils?
6. Quels meubles as-tu? Comment sont-ils?
7. Quels meubles est-ce que tu voudrais (*would like*) avoir dans ta chambre?
   (Répondez: **Je voudrais...**)
8. Qu'est-ce que tu n'aimes pas au sujet de ta chambre?

**5 Votre chambre** Écrivez une description de votre chambre. À tour de rôle, lisez votre description à votre partenaire. Il/Elle va vous demander d'autres détails et dessiner un plan. Ensuite, regardez le dessin (*drawing*) de votre partenaire et dites s'il correspond à votre chambre ou non. N'oubliez pas d'inclure (*include*) des prépositions pour indiquer où sont certains meubles et objets. Answers will vary.

**6 Sept différences** Votre professeur va vous donner, à vous et à votre partenaire, deux feuilles d'activités différentes. Il y a sept différences entre les deux images. Comparez vos dessins et faites une liste de ces différences. Quel est le groupe le plus rapide (*the quickest*) de la classe? Attention! Ne regardez pas la feuille de votre partenaire. Answers will vary.

**MODÈLE**
**Élève 1:** *Dans mon appartement, il y a un lit. Il y a une lampe à côté du lit.*
**Élève 2:** *Dans mon appartement aussi, il y a un lit, mais il n'y a pas de lampe.*

**7 La décoration** Formez un groupe de trois. L'un de vous est un décorateur d'intérieur qui a rendez-vous avec deux clients qui veulent (*want*) redécorer leur maison. Les clients sont très difficiles. Imaginez votre conversation et jouez la scène devant la classe. Utilisez les mots de la liste. Answers will vary.

| | |
|---|---|
| un canapé | un fauteuil |
| une chambre | un meuble |
| une cuisine | un mur |
| un escalier | un placard |
| une étagère | un tapis |

**OPTIONS**

**Finding the Correct Room** Call out words for furnishings and other objects, and have students write or say the room(s) where they might be found. Examples: **la télévision (la salle de séjour), le lit (la chambre)**, and **la table (la salle à manger)**.

**Skits** Have the class label various parts of the classroom with the names of rooms one would typically find in a house. Then have groups of three perform a skit in which the owner is showing the house to two exchange students who are going to spend the semester there.

# Les sons et les lettres

Audio: Concepts, Activities
Record & Compare

## 🎧 s and ss

You've already learned that an **s** at the end of a word is usually silent.

| lavabo**s** | copain**s** | va**s** | placard**s** |

An **s** at the beginning of a word, before a consonant, or after a pronounced consonant is pronounced like the s in the English word *set*.

| **s**oir | **s**alon | **s**tudio | ab**s**olument |

A double **s** is pronounced like the ss in the English word *kiss*.

| gro**ss**e | a**ss**ez | intére**ss**ant | rou**ss**e |

An **s** at the end of a word is often pronounced when the following word begins with a vowel sound. An **s** in a liaison sounds like a *z*, like the s in the English word *rose*.

| très élégant | trois hommes |

The other instance where the French **s** has a *z* sound is when there is a single **s** between two vowels within the same word. The **s** is pronounced like the s in the English word *music*.

| mu**s**ée | amu**s**ant | oi**s**eau | be**s**oin |

These words look alike, but have different meanings. Compare the pronunciations of each word pair.

| poi**s**on | poi**ss**on | dé**s**ert | de**ss**ert |

### 🔊 Prononcez  Répétez les mots suivants à voix haute.

1. sac
2. triste
3. suisse
4. chose
5. bourse
6. passer
7. surprise
8. assister
9. magasin
10. expressions
11. sénégalaise
12. sérieusement

### 🔊 Articulez  Répétez les phrases suivantes à voix haute.

1. Le spectacle est très amusant et la chanteuse est superbe.
2. Est-ce que vous habitez dans une résidence universitaire?
3. De temps en temps, Suzanne assiste à l'inauguration d'expositions au musée.
4. Heureusement, mes professeurs sont sympathiques, sociables et très sincères.

*Les oiseaux de même plumage s'assemblent sur le même rivage.*[2]

### 🔊 Dictons  Répétez les dictons à voix haute.

*Si jeunesse savait, si vieillesse pouvait.*[1]

[1] Youth is wasted on the young.
(lit. If youth but knew, if old age but could.)
[2] Birds of a feather flock together.

ressources

CA p. 172

daccord1.vhlcentral.com

---

**Section Goals**
In this section, students will learn about the sounds of **s** and **ss**.

**Key Standards**
4.1

**Student Resources**
*Cahier d'activités*, p. 172;
Supersite: Activities,
*Cahier interactif*
**Teacher Resources**
Answer Keys; Audio Script;
Textbook & Audio Activity
MP3s/CD

**Suggestions**
- Model the pronunciation of the example words and have students repeat them after you.
- Ask students to provide more examples of words from this lesson or previous lessons with these sounds. Examples: **cuisine, salon, résidence,** and **expression.**
- Dictate five familiar words containing **s** and **ss**, repeating each one at least two times. Then write them on the board or on a transparency and have students check their spelling.

---

**O P T I O N S**

**Mini-dictée**  Use these sentences for additional practice or dictation. **1. Serge est professeur de sociologie. 2. Solange est paresseuse et pessimiste. 3. Ces étudiants sénégalais sont très intelligents. 4. Sylvain essaie les chaussures sans chaussettes.**

**Tongue-twisters**  Teach students these French tongue-twisters that contain the **s** and **ss** sounds. **1. Ces six saucissons-ci sont si secs qu'on ne sait si c'en sont. 2. Zazie causait avec sa cousine en cousant.**

# ROMAN-PHOTO

## La visite surprise

 Video: *Roman-photo*
Record & Compare

**PERSONNAGES**

David

Pascal

Rachid

Sandrine

*En ville, Pascal fait tomber (drops) ses fleurs.*

**PASCAL** Aïe!
**RACHID** Tenez. (*Il aide Pascal.*)
**PASCAL** Oh, merci.
**RACHID** Aïe!
**PASCAL** Oh pardon, je suis vraiment désolé!
**RACHID** Ce n'est rien.
**PASCAL** Bonne journée!

*Chez Sandrine...*

**RACHID** Eh, salut, David! Dis donc, ce n'est pas un logement d'étudiants ici! C'est grand chez toi! Tu ne déménages pas, finalement?
**DAVID** Heureusement, Sandrine a décidé de rester.
**SANDRINE** Oui, je suis bien dans cet appartement. Seulement, les loyers sont très chers au centre-ville.

**RACHID** Oui, malheureusement! Tu as combien de pièces?
**SANDRINE** Il y a trois pièces: le salon, la salle à manger, ma chambre. Bien sûr, il y a une cuisine et j'ai aussi une grande salle de bains. Je te fais visiter?

**SANDRINE** Et voici ma chambre.
**RACHID** Elle est belle!
**SANDRINE** Oui... j'aime le vert.

**RACHID** Dis, c'est vrai, Sandrine, ta salle de bains est vraiment grande.
**DAVID** Oui! Et elle a un beau miroir au-dessus du lavabo et une baignoire!
**RACHID** Chez nous, on a seulement une douche.
**SANDRINE** Moi, je préfère les douches, en fait.

*Le téléphone sonne (rings).*

**RACHID** Comparé à cet appartement, le nôtre, c'est une cave! Pas de décorations, juste des affiches, un canapé, des étagères et mon bureau.
**DAVID** C'est vrai. On n'a même pas de rideaux.

---

**A C T I V I T É S**

**1** **Vrai ou faux?** Indiquez si ces affirmations sont **vraies** ou **fausses**. Corrigez les phrases fausses. Answers may vary.

1. C'est la première fois que Rachid visite l'appartement. Vrai.
2. Sandrine ne déménage pas. Vrai.
3. Les loyers au centre-ville ne sont pas chers. Faux. Les loyers au centre-ville sont très chers.
4. Sandrine invite ses amis chez elle. Vrai.
5. Rachid préfère son appartement à l'appartement de Sandrine. Faux. Rachid préfère l'appartement de Sandrine.

6. Chez les garçons, il y a une baignoire et des rideaux. Faux. Les garçons ont une douche et n'ont pas de rideaux.
7. Quand Pascal arrive, Sandrine est contente (*pleased*). Faux. Sandrine n'est pas contente.
8. Pascal doit (*must*) travailler ce week-end. Faux. Pascal ne travaille pas ce week-end.

 Practice more at **daccord1.vhlcentral.com**.

---

## Pascal arrive à Aix-en-Provence.

**SANDRINE** Voici la salle à manger.
**RACHID** Ça, c'est une pièce très importante pour nous, les invités.

**SANDRINE** Et puis, la cuisine.
**RACHID** Une pièce très importante pour Sandrine...
**DAVID** Évidemment!

**SANDRINE** Mais Pascal... je pensais que tu avais du travail... Quoi? Tu es ici, maintenant? C'est une blague!
**PASCAL** Mais ma chérie, j'ai pris le train pour te faire une surprise...

**SANDRINE** Une surprise! Nous deux, c'est fini! D'abord, tu me dis que les vacances avec moi, c'est impossible et ensuite tu arrives à Aix sans me téléphoner!
**PASCAL** Bon, si c'est comme ça, reste où tu es. Ne descends pas. Moi, je m'en vais. Voilà tes fleurs. Tu parles d'une surprise!

### Expressions utiles

#### Talking about your home

- **Tu ne déménages pas, finalement?**
  *You are not moving, after all?*
- **Heureusement, Sandrine a décidé de rester.**
  *Thankfully/Happily, Sandrine has decided to stay.*
- **Seulement, les loyers sont très chers au centre-ville.**
  *However, rents are very expensive downtown.*
- **Je te fais visiter?**
  *Shall I give you a tour?*
- **Ta salle de bains est vraiment grande.**
  *Your bathroom is really big.*
- **Elle a un beau miroir au-dessus du lavabo.**
  *It has a nice mirror above the sink.*
- **Chez nous, on a seulement une douche.**
  *At our place, we only have a shower.*

#### Additional vocabulary

- **Aïe!**
  *Ouch!*
- **Tenez.**
  *Here.*
- **Je pensais que tu avais du travail.**
  *I thought you had work to do.*
- **Mais ma chérie, j'ai pris le train pour te faire une surprise.**
  *But sweetie, I took the train to surprise you.*
- **sans**
  *without*
- **Moi, je m'en vais.**
  *I am leaving/getting out of here.*

---

**2** **Quel appartement?** Indiquez si ces objets sont dans l'appartement de Sandrine (S) ou dans l'appartement de David et Rachid (D & R).

1. baignoire  S
2. douche  D & R
3. rideaux  S
4. canapé  D & R, S
5. trois pièces  S
6. étagères  D & R
7. miroir  S
8. affiches  D & R

**3** **Conversez** Sandrine décide que son loyer est vraiment trop cher. Elle cherche un appartement à partager avec Amina. Avec deux partenaires, écrivez leur conversation avec un agent immobilier (*real estate agent*). Elles décrivent l'endroit idéal, le prix et les meubles qu'elles préfèrent. L'agent décrit plusieurs possibilités.

ressources

CA
pp. 95-96

daccord1.vhlcentral.com

A C T I V I T É S

---

**Expressions utiles**
- Model the pronunciation of the **Expressions utiles** and have students repeat them.
- As you work through the list, point out adverbs ending in **-ment** and verbs in the **imparfait.** You might want to tell students that the ending **-ment** usually corresponds to the English ending *-ly.* Then tell them that these grammar structures will be formally presented in the **Structures** section.
- Respond briefly to questions about the **imparfait.** Reinforce correct forms, but do not expect students to produce them consistently at this time.

**1** Suggestion Have students write their corrections for false statements on the board.

**1** Expansion For additional practice, give students these items. **9. Rachid et Pascal sont de bons amis. (Faux.) 10. La chambre de Sandrine est rose. (Faux.) 11. L'appartement de Sandrine est une cave. (Faux.)**

**2** Expansion For additional practice, give students these items. **9. bureau (D & R) 10. grande salle de bains (S) 11. douche (D & R)**

**3** Suggestions
- Before writing the conversation, tell students that the person playing the real estate agent should make a list of questions to ask prospective clients, and the two people playing Sandrine and Amina should decide on the features they are looking for in an apartment.
- You might want to bring in some real estate ads in French from newspapers or the Internet for the agents to use.

---

O P T I O N S

**Interviews** Have groups of three interview each other about their dream house, with one student conducting the interview, one answering, and one taking notes. At three-minute intervals, have students switch roles until each has been interviewer, interviewee, and note-taker. Then have two groups get together and take turns describing their dream houses to one another using their notes.

**Writing Practice** Have students work in pairs. Tell them to write an alternate ending to this episode, in which Sandrine is pleased to see Pascal and invites him upstairs to meet Rachid and David. Encourage students to use some of the **Expressions utiles.** Then have volunteers perform their role-plays for the class.

# CULTURE

**S** Video: *Flash culture*

## CULTURE À LA LOUPE

# Le logement en France

**Les trois quarts des gens habitent en ville et un Français sur cinq habite la région parisienne.** Quinze pour cent de la population habitent en banlieue dans des HLM (habitations à loyer modéré°), des appartements réservés aux familles qui n'ont pas beaucoup d'argent. Plus de la moitié des Français habitent une maison individuelle et l'autre partie habite un appartement. Cinquante pour cent des Français sont propriétaires, dont° dix pour cent ont une résidence secondaire.

Le type et la taille° des logements varient. Dans les grandes villes, beaucoup d'anciens hôtels particuliers° ont été transformés en appartements. En banlieue, on trouve de grands ensembles°, des groupes d'immeubles assez° modernes qui bénéficient de certains équipements collectifs°. En général, dans les petites villes et les villages, les gens habitent de petites maisons qui sont souvent assez anciennes.

Le style et l'architecture varient d'une région à l'autre. La région parisienne a de nombreux pavillons (maisons avec de petits jardins). Dans le nord°, on habite souvent des maisons en briques° avec des toits en ardoise°. En Alsace-Lorraine, il y a de vieilles maisons à colombages° avec des parties de mur en bois°. Les maisons traditionnelles de l'ouest° ont des toits de chaume°. Dans le sud°, il y a des villas de style méditerranéen avec des toits en tuiles° rouges et des mas° provençaux (vieilles maisons en pierres°).

### Coup de main

Here are some terms commonly used in statistics.

**un quart** = *one quarter*
**un tiers** = *one third*
**la moitié** = *half*
**la plupart de** = *most of*
**un sur cinq** = *one in five*

### Évolution de la taille des logements en France

| TAILLE | 1999 | 2005 |
|---|---|---|
| 1 pièce | 6,5% | 6,0% |
| 2 pièces | 12,0% | 11,5% |
| 3 pièces | 22,0% | 20,5% |
| 4 pièces et plus | 58,5% | 61,0% |

SOURCE: INSEE

habitations à loyer modéré *low-cost government housing* **dont** *of which* **taille** *size* **anciens hôtels particuliers** *former private mansions* **grands ensembles** *high-rise buildings* **assez** *rather* **bénéficient de certains équipements collectifs** *benefit from certain shared facilities* **nord** *north* **briques** *bricks* **toits en ardoise** *slate roofs* **maisons à colombages** *half-timbered houses* **bois** *wood* **ouest** *west* **chaume** *thatch* **sud** *south* **tuiles** *tiles* **mas** *farmhouses* **pierres** *stones*

**ACTIVITÉS**

**1** **Vrai ou faux?** Indiquez si les phrases sont **vraies** ou **fausses**. Corrigez les phrases fausses. Answers may vary slightly.

1. Il n'y a pas beaucoup de Français qui habitent la région parisienne.
   Faux. Un Français sur cinq habite la région parisienne.
2. Les familles sans beaucoup d'argent habitent souvent dans des HLM. Vrai.
3. La moitié des Français ont une résidence secondaire.
   Faux. Peu de Français qui sont propriétaires ont une résidence secondaire.
4. On a transformé beaucoup d'anciens hôtels particuliers en appartements. Vrai.
5. Les grands ensembles sont des maisons en pierres.
   Faux. Les grands ensembles sont des groupes d'immeubles assez modernes.

6. Les maisons françaises ont des styles d'architecture différents d'une région à l'autre. Vrai.
7. En général, les maisons dans les villages sont assez vieilles. Vrai.
8. Dans le sud de la France, il y a beaucoup de pavillons. Faux. Dans le sud de la France, il y a des villas de style méditerranéen et des mas provençaux.
9. Dans le nord de la France, il y a beaucoup de vieilles maisons à colombages. Faux. Dans le nord de la France, il y a des maisons en briques.
10. En France, en 1999, presque (*almost*) un quart des maisons et des appartements avaient (*had*) seulement trois pièces. Vrai.

**S** Practice more at **daccord1.vhlcentral.com**.

## LE FRANÇAIS QUOTIDIEN

### Location d'un logement

| | |
|---|---|
| agence (f.) de location | rental agency |
| bail (m.) | lease |
| caution (f.) | security deposit |
| charges (f.) | basic utilities |
| chauffage (m.) | heating |
| électricité (f.) | electricity |
| locataire (m./f.) | tenant |
| petites annonces (f.) | (rental) ads |

## LE MONDE FRANCOPHONE

### L'architecture

Voici quelques exemples d'habitations traditionnelles.

**En Afrique centrale et de l'Ouest** des maisons construites sur pilotis°, avec un grenier à riz°

**En Afrique du Nord** des maisons en pisé (de la terre° rouge mélangée° à de la paille°) construites autour d'un patio central et avec, souvent, une terrasse sur le toit°

**Aux Antilles** des maisons en bois de toutes les couleurs avec des toits en métal

**En Polynésie française** des bungalows, construits sur pilotis ou sur le sol, souvent en bambou avec des toits en paille ou en feuilles de cocotier°

**Au Viêt-nam** des maisons sur pilotis construites sur des lacs, des rivières ou simplement au-dessus du sol°

pilotis *stilts* grenier à riz *rice loft* terre *clay* mélangée *mixed* paille *straw* toit *roof* feuilles de cocotier *coconut palm leaves* au-dessus du sol *off the ground*

## PORTRAIT

# Le château Frontenac

Le château Frontenac est un hôtel de luxe et un des plus beaux° sites touristiques de la ville de Québec. Construit entre la fin° du

XIXᵉ siècle et le début° du XXᵉ siècle sur le Cap Diamant, dans le quartier du Vieux-Québec, le château offre une vue° spectaculaire sur la ville. Aujourd'hui, avec ses 618 chambres sur 18 étages, ses restaurants gastronomiques, sa piscine et son centre sportif, le château Frontenac est classé parmi° les 500 meilleurs° hôtels du monde.

un des plus beaux *one of the most beautiful* fin *end* début *beginning* vue *view* classé parmi *ranked among* meilleurs *best*

## SUR INTERNET

Qu'est-ce qu'une pendaison de crémaillère? D'où vient cette expression?

Go to **daccord1.vhlcentral.com** to find more information related to this **CULTURE** section. Then watch the corresponding **Flash culture**.

**2 Répondez** Répondez aux questions, d'après les informations données dans les textes.

1. Qu'est-ce que le château Frontenac?
   C'est un hôtel de luxe.
2. De quel siècle date le château Frontenac?
   Le château Frontenac date du XIXᵉ siècle.
3. Dans quel quartier de la ville de Québec le trouve-t-on?
   On le trouve dans le quartier du Vieux-Québec.
4. Où trouve-t-on les maisons sur pilotis?
   On les trouve en Afrique centrale et de l'Ouest, au Viêt-nam et en Polynésie française.
5. Quelles sont les caractéristiques des maisons d'Afrique du Nord?
   Le patio central et la terrasse sur le toit sont des caractéristiques des maisons d'Afrique du Nord.

**3 Une année en France** Vous allez habiter en France. Téléphonez à un agent immobilier (*real estate*) (votre partenaire) et expliquez-lui le type de logement que vous recherchez. Il/Elle va vous donner des renseignements sur les logements disponibles (*available*). Posez des questions pour avoir plus de détails.

ressources

CA pp. 113–114 | daccord1.vhlcentral.com

A C T I V I T É S

*deux cent soixante et un* **261**

**Le français quotidien** Model the pronunciation of each term and have students repeat it. Point out that the word **location** is a **faux ami**; it means *rental*. You might also wish to add these terms to the list: **un particulier** (*a private seller/buyer*), **une chambre de bonne** (*a small room, usually on the top floor, to rent in someone's home; originally it was the maid's room*), **un deux-pièces** (*a two-room apartment*), and **un(e) concierge** (*doorman*).

**Portrait**
- **Le château Frontenac** is located on a hill overlooking the St. Lawrence River. It is considered the symbol of Quebec City. Have students locate Quebec City on the map of North America and point out its strategic location.
- Ask students: **Désirez-vous faire un séjour au château Frontenac? Pourquoi?**

**Le monde francophone** Bring in photos of the various types of houses from magazines or the Internet. After students have read the text, show them the photos and have them identify the location.

**2 Expansion** For additional practice, give students these items. **6. Combien de chambres y a-t-il au château? (618) 7. Où trouve-t-on les maisons en bois de toutes les couleurs? (aux Antilles)**

**3 Suggestion** Have students sit back-to-back and pretend they are holding a phone to their ear to simulate a phone conversation.

**Flash culture** Tell students that they will learn more about housing by watching a variety of real-life images narrated by Benjamin. Show the video segment, then have students jot down in French at least three types of residences they saw. You can also use the activities in the video manual in class to reinforce this **Flash culture** or assign them as homework.

**OPTIONS**

**Location d'un logement** Distribute photocopies of apartment rental ads from a French newspaper or the Internet. Have students guess the meanings of abbreviations, such as **sdb**, **cuis.** and **pisc.**, and explain unfamiliar ones, such as **T3** or **m²**. Then tell students to work in pairs and write five comprehension questions based on the ads. Have volunteers read their questions aloud, and ask other students to answer them.

**Cultural Comparison** Have students work in groups of three and compare **le château Frontenac** to the hotels in their city or town. Tell them to list the similarities and differences in a two-column chart under the headings **Similitudes** and **Différences**. After completing their charts, have two groups get together and compare their lists.

## 8A.1 The *passé composé* vs. the *imparfait* (Part 1)

**Point de départ** Although the **passé composé** and the **imparfait** are both past tenses, they have very distinct uses and are not interchangeable. The choice between these two tenses depends on the context and on the point of view of the speaker.

### The *passé composé*

| Uses of the *passé composé* | |
|---|---|
| To express specific actions that started and ended in the past and are viewed by the speaker as completed | J'**ai nettoyé** la salle de bains deux fois. *I cleaned the bathroom twice.* <br><br> Nous **avons acheté** un tapis. *We bought a rug.* <br><br> L'enfant **est né** à la maison. *The child was born at home.* <br><br> Il **a plu** hier. *It rained yesterday.* |
| To tell about events that happened at a specific point in time or within a specific length of time in the past | Je **suis allé** à la pêche avec papa il y a deux ans. *I went fishing with dad two years ago.* <br><br> Elle **a étudié** à Paris pendant six mois. *She studied in Paris for six months.* |
| To express the beginning or end of a past action | Le film **a commencé** à huit heures. *The movie began at 8 o'clock.* <br><br> Ils **ont fini** les devoirs samedi matin. *They finished the homework Saturday morning.* |
| To narrate a series of past actions or events | Ce matin, j'**ai fait** du jogging, j'**ai nettoyé** la chambre et j'**ai rangé** la cuisine. *This morning, I jogged, I cleaned my bedroom, and I tidied up the kitchen.* <br><br> Pour la fête d'anniversaire de papa, maman **a envoyé** les invitations, elle **a acheté** un cadeau et elle **a fait** les décorations. *For dad's birthday party, mom sent out the invitations, bought a gift, and did the decorations.* |
| To signal a change in physical or mental state | Il **est mort** dans un accident. *He died in an accident.* <br><br> Tout à coup, elle **a eu** peur. *All of a sudden, she got frightened.* |

### MISE EN PRATIQUE

**1** **Une surprise désagréable** Récemment, Benoît a fait un séjour à Strasbourg avec un collègue. Complétez son récit (*narration*) avec l'imparfait ou le passé composé.

Ce matin, il (1) _faisait_ (faire) chaud. J' (2) _étais_ (être) content de partir pour Strasbourg. Je (3) _suis parti_ (partir) pour la gare, où j' (4) _ai retrouvé_ (retrouver) Franck. Le train (5) _est arrivé_ (arriver) à Strasbourg à midi. Nous (6) _avons commencé_ (commencer) notre promenade en ville. Nous (7) _avions_ (avoir) besoin d'un plan. J' (8) _ai cherché_ (chercher) mon portefeuille (*wallet*), mais il (9) _était_ (être) toujours dans le train! Franck et moi, nous (10) _avons couru_ (courir) à la gare!

**2** **Le week-end dernier** Qu'est-ce que Lucie a fait samedi dernier? Créez des phrases complètes au passé composé ou à l'imparfait pour décrire sa soirée.

> **MODÈLE** finir / je / mes tâches ménagères / tôt
> J'ai fini mes tâches ménagères tôt.

1. froid / faire / et / neiger
   *Il faisait froid et il neigeait.*
2. cinéma / mes amis / aller / je / avec / alors
   *Alors, je suis allée au cinéma avec mes amis.*
3. film / sept heures / commencer
   *Le film a commencé à sept heures.*
4. Audrey Tautou / film / dans / être
   *Audrey Tautou était dans le film.*
5. après / film / aller / café / mes amis et moi
   *Après le film, mes amis moi sommes allés au café.*
6. nous / prendre / éclairs / limonades / et
   *Nous avons pris des éclairs et des limonades.*
7. rentrer / je / chez / minuit / moi
   *Je suis rentrée chez moi à minuit.*
8. fatigué / avoir / sommeil / je / être
   *J'étais fatiguée et j'avais sommeil.*

**3** **Vacances à la montagne** Hugo raconte ses vacances. Complétez ses phrases avec un des verbes de la liste au passé composé ou à l'imparfait.

| | | |
|---|---|---|
| aller | neiger | retourner |
| avoir | passer | skier |
| faire | rester | venir |

1. L'hiver dernier, nous _avons passé_ les vacances à la montagne.
2. Quand nous sommes arrivés sur les pistes de ski, il _neigeait_ beaucoup et il _faisait_ un temps épouvantable.
3. Ce jour-là, nous _sommes restés_ à l'hôtel tout l'après-midi.
4. Le jour suivant, nous _sommes retournés_ sur les pistes.
5. Nous _avons skié_ et papa _est allé_ faire une randonnée.
6. Quand ils _avaient_ mon âge, papa et oncle Hervé _venaient_ tous les hivers à la montagne.

Practice more at **daccord1.vhlcentral.com**.

## COMMUNICATION

**4  Situations** Avec un(e) partenaire, parlez de ces situations en utilisant (*by using*) le passé composé ou l'imparfait. Comparez vos réponses, puis présentez-les à la classe. Answers will vary.

**MODÈLE**

Le premier jour de cours...
**Élève 1:** *Le premier jour de cours, j'étais tellement nerveux que j'ai oublié mes livres.*
**Élève 2:** *Moi, j'étais nerveux aussi, alors j'ai quitté la maison très tôt.*

1. Quand j'étais petit(e), ...
2. L'été dernier, ...
3. Hier soir, mon père/ma mère...
4. Hier, le professeur...
5. La semaine dernière, mon/ma copain/copine...
6. Ce matin, au lycée, ...
7. Quand j'étais au collège, ...
8. La dernière fois que j'étais en vacances, ...

**5  Votre premier/première ami(e)**
Posez ces questions à un(e) partenaire. Ajoutez (*Add*) d'autres questions si vous le voulez (*want*). Answers will vary.

1. Qui a été ton/ta premier/première ami(e)?
2. Quel âge avais-tu quand tu as fait sa connaissance?
3. Comment était-il/elle?
4. Est-ce que tu as fait la connaissance de sa famille?
5. Combien de temps êtes-vous resté(e)s ami(e)s?
6. À quoi jouiez-vous ensemble?
7. Aviez-vous les mêmes (*same*) centres d'intérêt?
8. Avez-vous perdu contact?

**6  Dialogue** Sébastien, qui a seize ans, est sorti avec des amis hier soir. Quand il est rentré à trois heures du matin, sa mère était furieuse parce que ce n'était pas la première fois qu'il rentrait tard. Avec un(e) partenaire, préparez le dialogue entre Sébastien et sa mère. Answers will vary.

**MODÈLE**

**Élève 1:** *Que faisais-tu à minuit?*
**Élève 2:** *Mes copains et moi, nous sommes allés manger une pizza...*

## The *imparfait*

### Uses of the *imparfait*

| To describe an ongoing past action with no reference to its beginning or end | Vous **dormiez** sur le canapé. *You were sleeping on the couch.* |
| --- | --- |
| | Tu **attendais** dans le café? *You were waiting in the café?* |
| | Nous **regardions** la télé chez Fanny. *We were watching TV at Fanny's house.* |
| | Les enfants **lisaient** tranquillement. *The children were reading peacefully.* |
| To express habitual or repeated past actions and events | Nous **faisions** un tour en voiture le dimanche matin. *We used to go for a drive on Sunday mornings.* |
| | Elle **mettait** toujours la voiture dans le garage. *She always put the car in the garage.* |
| | Maman **travaillait** souvent dans le jardin. *Mom would often work in the garden.* |
| | Quand j'**étais** jeune, j'**aimais** faire du camping. *When I was young, I used to like to go camping.* |
| To describe mental, physical, and emotional states or conditions | Karine **était** très inquiète. *Karine was very worried.* |
| | Simon et Marion **étaient** fatigués et ils **avaient** sommeil. *Simon and Marion were tired and sleepy.* |
| | Mon ami **avait** faim et il **avait** envie de manger quelque chose. *My friend was hungry and felt like eating something.* |

**Essayez!**    Donnez les formes correctes des verbes.

**passé composé**

1. commencer (il) *il a commencé*
2. acheter (tu) ___tu as acheté___
3. boire (nous) ___nous avons bu___
4. apprendre (ils) ___ils ont appris___
5. répondre (je) ___j'ai répondu___

**imparfait**

1. jouer (nous) *nous jouions*
2. être (tu) ___tu étais___
3. prendre (elles) ___elles prenaient___
4. avoir (vous) ___vous aviez___
5. conduire (il) ___il conduisait___

**Essayez!** Give items like these as additional practice. For the **passé composé: 6. descendre: elle (elle est descendue) 7. lire: je (j'ai lu)** For the **imparfait: 6. écrire: je (j'écrivais) 7. dire: on (on disait)**

**1 Expansion** Have volunteers explain why they chose the **passé composé** or **imparfait** in each case. Ask them to point out any words or expressions that triggered one tense or the other.

**2 Suggestion** Before assigning the activity, remind students that actions viewed as completed by the speaker take the **passé composé.** Have students give personal examples of actions in the past using this verb tense.

**3 Expansion** Have students use this activity as a model to write a short journal entry about a vacation of their own using the **passé composé** and the **imparfait.**

**4 Expansion** Have students choose one of these sentences to begin telling a short story in the past. Encourage students to use both the **passé composé** and the **imparfait.**

**5 Expansion** After completing the pair work, assign this activity as a short written composition.

**6 Suggestion** Act out the **modèle** with a volunteer before assigning this activity. Have pairs role-play their dialogues in front of the class.

**OPTIONS**

**Using Cards** Make cards that contain a verb or noun and an expression that signals a past tense. Example: **hier / parc** or **Quand j'étais jeune / voyager.** Mix them up in a hat and have each student pick a card at random. Have each student state the cues on his or her card and use them in a sentence with the **passé composé** or **imparfait.** Have the student say which tense he or she will use before formulating the sentence.

**Writing Practice** Have students work in groups to pick a popular holiday and write a few sentences in the past tense to describe it. Students might talk about typical activities they did that day, the weather, or how they felt on that day. Then, have them share their description with the class without revealing the holiday and have their classmates guess what holiday it is.

## Section Goals

In this section, students will learn:

- the use of the **passé composé** vs. the **imparfait** in a narration, interrupted actions, and cause and effect
- common expressions indicating the past tense
- the verb **vivre**

## Key Standards

4.1, 5.1

**Student Resources**
*Cahier d'exercices*, pp. 103-104;
*Cahier d'activités*, p. 174;
Supersite: Activities,
*Cahier interactif*

**Teacher Resources**
Answer Keys; Audio Script;
Audio Activity MP3s/CD;
Testing program: Grammar Quiz

## Suggestions

- Tell students that the choice of the **passé composé** vs. the **imparfait** is very important since the meaning conveyed can be different based on which tense you use. Example: **J'ai téléphoné quand ma mère est arrivée. Je téléphonais quand ma mère est arrivée.** In the first case, I called after my mother arrived. In the second case, I was in the process of calling when my mother arrived. Have students come up with other similar examples.

- Point out that if both actions in a sentence are ongoing or completed simultaneously, then both verbs can be either in the **passé composé** or the **imparfait**. Example: **Je suis sorti quand tu es entré. Je sortais quand tu entrais.** They will need to pay close attention to the meaning they want to convey.

- Give personalized examples as you contrast the **passé composé** and the **imparfait**. Examples: **La semaine dernière quand je répétais dans le salon, quelqu'un m'a téléphoné. Je n'ai pas entendu le téléphone parce que je jouais du piano.**

- Give students these other expressions that signal the **imparfait**: **de temps en temps** (*from time to time*), **en général** (*in general, usually*), **quelquefois** (*sometimes*), **autrefois** (*in the past*).

---

## 8A.2 The *passé composé* vs. the *imparfait* (Part 2)

**Point de départ** You have already seen some uses of the **passé composé** versus the **imparfait** while talking about things and events in the past. Here are some other contexts in which the choice of the tense you use is important.

- The **passé composé** and the **imparfait** are often used together to narrate a story or an incident. In such cases, the imparfait is usually used to set the scene or the background while the **passé composé** moves the story along.

### Uses of the *passé composé* and the *imparfait*

| passé composé | imparfait |
|---|---|
| *It is used to talk about:* | *It is used to describe:* |
| • main facts | • the framework of the story: *weather, date, time, background scenery* |
| • specific, completed events | • descriptions of people: *age, physical and personality traits, clothing, feelings, state of mind* |
| • actions that advance the plot | • background setting: *what was going on, what others were doing* |

Il **était** minuit et le temps **était** orageux. J'**avais** peur parce que j'**étais** seule dans la maison. Soudain, quelqu'un **a frappé** à la porte. J'**ai regardé** par la fenêtre et j'**ai vu** un vieil homme habillé en noir...
*It was midnight and it was stormy. I was afraid because I was alone at home. Suddenly, someone knocked on the door. I looked through the window and I saw an old man dressed in black...*

Il **était** deux heures de l'après-midi et il **faisait** beau dehors. Les élèves **attendaient** impatiemment la sortie. C'**était** le dernier jour d'école! Finalement, le prof **est entré** dans la salle pour nous donner les résultats...
*It was 2 o'clock and it was nice outside. The students were waiting impatiently for dismissal. It was the last day of school! Finally, the teacher came into the classroom to give us our results...*

- When the **passé composé** and the **imparfait** occur in the same sentence, the action in the **passé composé** often interrupts the ongoing action in the **imparfait**.

| ACTION IN PROGRESS | INTERRUPTING ACTION |
|---|---|
| Je **chantais** | quand mon ami **est arrivé**. |
| *I was singing* | *when my friend arrived.* |
| Céline et Maxime **dormaient** | quand le téléphone **a sonné**. |
| *Céline and Maxime were sleeping* | *when the phone rang.* |

---

## MISE EN PRATIQUE

**1 Pourquoi?** Expliquez pourquoi Sabine a fait ou n'a pas fait ces choses.

**MODÈLE** ne pas faire de tennis / être fatigué
*Sabine n'a pas fait de tennis parce qu'elle était fatiguée.*

1. aller au centre commercial / avoir des soldes
les soldes *Sabine est allée au centre commercial parce qu'il y avait des soldes.*
2. ne pas travailler / avoir sommeil
*Sabine n'a pas travaillé parce qu'elle avait sommeil.*
3. ne pas sortir / pleuvoir
*Sabine n'est pas sortie parce qu'il pleuvait.*
4. mettre un pull / faire froid
*Sabine a mis un pull parce qu'il faisait froid.*
5. manger une pizza / avoir faim
*Sabine a mangé une pizza parce qu'elle avait faim.*
6. acheter une nouvelle robe / sortir avec des amis
*Sabine a acheté une nouvelle robe parce qu'elle sortait avec des amis.*
7. vendre son fauteuil / déménager
*Sabine a vendu son fauteuil parce qu'elle déménageait.*
8. ne pas bien dormir / être inquiet
*Sabine n'a pas bien dormi parce qu'elle était inquiète.*

**2 Qu'est-il arrivé quand...?** Dites ce qui (*what*) est arrivé quand ces personnes faisaient ces activités. Utilisez les mots donnés et d'autres mots. Suggested answers

**MODÈLE**

*Tu nageais quand ton oncle est arrivé.*

**tu / oncle / arriver**

**1. Tristan / entendre / chien**
*Tristan nettoyait sa chambre quand il a entendu le chien.*

**3. vous / perdre / billet**
*Vous partiez pour la France quand vous avez perdu votre billet.*

**2. nous / petite fille / tomber**
*Nous patinions quand la petite fille est tombée.*

**4. Paul et Éric / téléphone / sonner**
*Paul et Éric déjeunaient dans la salle à manger quand le téléphone a sonné.*

**3 Rien d'extraordinaire** Matthieu a passé une journée assez banale. Réécrivez ce paragraphe au passé.

Il est 6h30. Il pleut. Je prends mon petit-déjeuner, je mets mon imperméable et je quitte la maison. J'attends une demi-heure à l'arrêt de bus et finalement, je cours au restaurant où je travaille. J'arrive en retard. Le patron (*boss*) n'est pas content. Le soir, après mon travail, je rentre à la maison et je vais directement au lit.
*Il était 6h30. Il pleuvait. J'ai pris mon petit-déjeuner, j'ai mis mon imperméable et j'ai quitté la maison. J'ai attendu une demi-heure à l'arrêt de bus et finalement, j'ai couru au restaurant où je travaillais. Je suis arrivé en retard. Le patron n'était pas content. Le soir, après mon travail, je suis rentré à la maison et je suis directement allé au lit.*

 Practice more at **daccord1.vhlcentral.com.**

---

**Oral Practice** Ask students to narrate an embarrassing moment. Tell them to describe what happened and how they felt, using the **passé composé** and **imparfait.** Then have volunteers retell their partner's embarrassing moment using the third person. You may want to let students make up a fake embarrassing moment.

**Writing Practice** Have students work in groups of four to write a short article about an imaginary road trip they took last summer. Students should use the **imparfait** to set the scene and the **passé composé** to narrate events. Each student should contribute three sentences to the article. When finished, have students read their article to the class.

## COMMUNICATION

**4** **La curiosité** Votre tante Louise veut tout savoir. Elle vous pose beaucoup de questions. Avec un(e) partenaire, répondez aux questions d'une manière logique et échangez les rôles. Answers will vary.

**MODÈLE** retourner au bureau

**Élève 1:** *Pourquoi est-ce que tu es retourné(e) au bureau?*
**Élève 2:** *Je suis retourné(e) au bureau parce que j'avais beaucoup de travail.*

1. aller à la bibliothèque
2. aller au magasin
3. sortir avec des amis
4. téléphoner à ton cousin
5. rentrer tard
6. aller au parc
7. inviter des gens
8. être triste

**5** **Une entrevue** Avec un(e) partenaire, posez-vous ces questions à tour de rôle. Answers will vary.

1. Où allais-tu souvent quand tu étais petit(e)?
2. Qu'est-ce que tu aimais lire?
3. Est-ce que tu as vécu dans un autre pays?
4. Comment étais-tu quand tu avais dix ans?
5. Qu'est-ce que ta sœur/ton frère faisait quand tu es rentré(e) hier?
6. Qu'est-ce que tu as fait hier soir?
7. Qu'est-ce que tu as pris au petit-déjeuner ce matin?
8. Qu'est-ce que tu as porté aujourd'hui?

**6** **Scénario** Par groupes de trois, créez une histoire au passé. La première personne commence par une phrase. La deuxième personne doit (*must*) continuer l'histoire. La troisième personne reprend la suite d'une manière logique. Continuez l'histoire une personne à la fois jusqu'à ce que vous ayez (*until you have*) un petit scénario. Soyez créatif! Ensuite, présentez votre scénario à la classe. Answers will vary.

---

- Depending on how you want to express the actions, either the **passé composé** or the **imparfait** can follow **quand**.

  Mes parents **sont arrivés** quand nous **répétions** dans le sous-sol.
  *My parents arrived when we were rehearsing in the basement.*

- Sometimes the use of the **passé composé** and the **imparfait** in the same sentence expresses a cause and effect.

  J'**avais** faim, alors j'**ai mangé** un sandwich.
  *I was hungry so I ate a sandwich.*

- Certain adverbs often indicate a particular past tense.

### Expressions that signal a past tense

| passé composé | | imparfait | |
|---|---|---|---|
| soudain | suddenly | d'habitude | usually |
| tout d'un coup/ tout à coup | all of a sudden | parfois | sometimes |
| | | souvent | often |
| une (deux, etc.) fois | once (twice, etc.) | toujours | always |
| un jour | one day | tous les jours | every day |

- While talking about the past or narrating a tale, you might use the verb **vivre** (*to live*) which is irregular.

### Present tense of *vivre*

| je vis | nous vivons |
|---|---|
| tu vis | vous vivez |
| il/elle vit | ils/elles vivent |

Les enfants **vivent** avec leurs grands-parents.
*The children live with their grandparents.*

- The past participle of **vivre** is **vécu**. The **imparfait** is formed like regular **–re** verbs by taking the **nous** form, dropping the **–ons**, and adding the endings.

  Rémi **a** toujours **vécu** à Nice.        Nous **vivions** avec mon oncle.
  *Rémi always lived in Nice.*        *We used to live with my uncle.*

### Essayez!        Choisissez la forme correcte du verbe au passé.

1. Lise (a étudié /étudiait) toujours avec ses amis.
2. Maman (a fait /faisait) du yoga hier.
3. Ma grand-mère (passait /a passé) par là tous les jours.
4. D'habitude, ils (arrivaient /sont arrivés) toujours en retard.
5. Tout à coup, le professeur (entrait /est entré) dans la classe.
6. Ce matin, Camille (a lavé /lavait) le chien.

*deux cent soixante-cinq* **265**

---

Essayez! Give the following items as additional practice: **9. Autrefois, Nathan (a amené / amenait) sa sœur au cours de danse. (amenait) 10. Je/J' (ai parlé / parlais) deux fois à ma cousine la semaine dernière. (ai parlé) 11. Parfois, nous (faisions / avons fait) une randonnée en montagne. (faisions) 12. Elle (voyait / a vu) mes parents une fois à la mairie. (a vu)**

**1 Expansion** Have students redo this activity, this time coming up with their own explanations for why Sabine did or did not do the activities.

**2 Suggestion** Have students come up with different sentences using the same illustrations.

**3 Suggestion** Have students compare their answers with a partner's. For sentences where their answers differ, they should explain why they chose the **passé composé** or the **imparfait** and decide which tense is appropriate.

**4 Expansion** Have pairs repeat the activity, reframing the questions in the negative. Example: **Pourquoi est-ce que tu n'es pas allé(e) en boîte de nuit?**

**5 Suggestion** Have students do questions 1, 2, 3, 6, 7, and 8 as a survey by circulating around the classroom and interviewing at least five classmates. Have them tabulate the responses in a chart and see how similar or different they were.

**6 Suggestion** This activity can be done either orally or in writing.

---

**OPTIONS**

**Using Games** Divide the class into teams. Make a list of all the adverbs or expressions that signal a past tense. As you read out each expression, a member from each team should come to the board and write a sentence in the past using that expression. The team that completes a correct sentence first gets a point.

**Oral Practice** Have students work in small groups to discuss their favorite movie or book. Students should use appropriate past tense forms to describe the main characters and give a brief summary of the plot. Encourage students to ask their classmates questions about the film or text.

# SYNTHÈSE
# Révision

**Key Standards**
1.1

**Student Resources**
Supersite: Activities
**Teacher Resources**
Answer Keys; Testing Program:
Lesson Test (Testing Program
Audio MP3s/CD)

**1 Expansion** Have students add an adjective to each object they ask about. Example: **Je cherche mes nouvelles baskets. Où sont-elles? Je cherche mon pull jaune. Où est-il?**

**2 Expansion** You can expand this activity by having students do this in groups of three or four where one student plays the role of the detective and the others are possible witnesses who all claim to have seen the suspects. When questioned, the witnesses give the detective conflicting information about the suspects.

**3 Suggestion** As the students take turns being the interviewer and interviewee, have one of them answer the questions as if he or she had a wonderful vacation, the house was lovely, the weather was great, and everything went well while the other person had a negative experience where nothing was satisfactory.

**4 Expansion** Expand this activity by showing the class an **avant** and **après** picture of a person or place in a magazine. Divide the students into two groups. Have one group describe the person or place in the before picture. Have the other group describe the after picture using the present tense.

**5 Suggestion** Remind students that the floors are counted differently in France than in the U.S. The first floor in the U.S. would be the **rez-de-chaussée** in France while the second floor would be the **premier étage**. Ask students if they know other countries which refer to floors in the same way as the French do.

---

**1 Mes affaires** Vous cherchez vos affaires (*belongings*). À tour de rôle, demandez de l'aide à votre partenaire. Où étaient-elles pour la dernière fois? Utilisez l'illustration pour les trouver. Answers will vary.

**MODÈLE**

**Élève 1:** *Je cherche mes baskets. Où sont-elles?*
**Élève 2:** *Tu n'as pas cherché sur l'étagère? Elles étaient sur l'étagère.*

| | |
|---|---|
| baskets | ordinateur |
| casquette | parapluie |
| journal | pull |
| livre | sac à dos |

**2 Un bon témoin** Il y a eu un cambriolage (*burglary*) chez votre voisin M. Cachetout. Le détective vous interroge parce que vous avez vu deux personnes suspectes sortir de la maison du voisin. Avec un(e) partenaire, créez ce dialogue et jouez cette scène devant la classe. Utilisez ces éléments dans votre scène. Answers will vary.

- une description physique des suspects
- leurs attitudes
- leurs vêtements
- ce que (*what*) vous faisiez quand vous avez vu les suspects

**MODÈLE**

**Élève 1:** *À quelle heure est-ce que vous avez vu les deux personnes sortir?*
**Élève 2:** *À dix heures. Elles sont sorties du garage.*

---

**3 Quel séjour!** Le magazine *Campagne décoration* a eu un concours et vous avez gagné le prix, une semaine de vacances dans une maison à la campagne. Vous venez de revenir de (*just came back from*) vos vacances et vous donnez une interview à propos de (*about*) votre séjour. Avec un(e) partenaire, posez-vous des questions sur la maison, le temps, les activités dans la région et votre opinion en général. Utilisez l'imparfait et le passé composé. Answers will vary.

**MODÈLE**

**Élève 1:** *Combien de pièces y avait-il dans cette maison?*
**Élève 2:** *Il y avait six pièces dans la maison.*

**4 Avant et après** Voici la chambre d'Annette avant et après une visite de sa mère. Comment était sa chambre à l'origine? Avec un(e) partenaire, décrivez la pièce et cherchez les différences entre les deux illustrations. Answers will vary.

**MODÈLE**

*Avant, la lampe était à côté de l'ordinateur. Maintenant, elle est à côté du canapé.*

**5 La maison de mon enfance** Décrivez l'appartement ou la maison de votre enfance à un(e) partenaire. Où se trouvait-il/elle? Comment les pièces étaient-elles orientées? Y avait-il une piscine, un sous-sol? Qui vivait avec vous dans cet appartement ou cette maison? Racontez (*Tell*) des anecdotes. Answers will vary.

**MODÈLE**

*Ma maison se trouvait au bord de la mer. C'était une maison à deux étages (floors). Au rez-de-chaussée, il y avait...*

| ressources | | |
|---|---|---|
| CE pp. 101–104 | CA pp. 173–174 | daccord1.vhlcentral.com |

---

**OPTIONS**

**Floor Plan** Have students work in pairs to draw the floor plan of their dream home on a sheet of paper or cardboard. Have them cut out the floor plan into pieces by individual rooms. Then have them give these pieces to their partner who will reassemble the floor plan based on their description of the house.

**Skits** Have small groups organize a skit about a birthday or other party that took place recently. Guide them to first make general comments about the party, such as **C'était vraiment amusant!** Then describe a few specific things that were going on, what people were talking about, what they were wearing, and what happened. After the skits are performed, have students vote on their favorite one.

**Video: TV Clip**

## Century 21 France

La société immobilière° Century 21 France commence ses opérations en 1987. Ses agences franchisées ont bientôt un grand succès, et Century 21 devient° une des principales sociétés immobilières de France. Cette société est connue° pour son marketing innovateur, qui diffuse à la télévision et sur Internet des publicités° d'un humour contemporain et parfois hors norme°. Century 21 France crée, par exemple, une campagne publicitaire pour montrer les risques de ne pas utiliser un agent immobilier quand on vend ou quand on achète une maison.

**L'IMMOBILIER, C'EST PLUS SIMPLE AVEC UN AGENT IMMOBILIER**

www.century21france.fr

—Alors, d'abord le salon...

—Des pièces, des pièces, des pièces...

**Compréhension** Répondez aux questions. Some answers will vary.

1. Quelles pièces le propriétaire de l'appartement montre-t-il au couple? Il leur montre le salon, la chambre et les toilettes.
2. Comment est sa description de l'appartement? Elle est trop courte et superficielle.
3. Que ne mentionne-t-il pas du tout? Sample answer: Il ne parle pas du tout de la cuisine.

**Discussion** Par groupes de trois, répondez aux questions et discutez. Answers will vary.

1. Un agent immobilier est-il vraiment nécessaire pour vendre ou acheter une maison? Pourquoi?
2. Jouez les rôles d'un agent immobilier très compétent qui montre une maison à deux clients. Quelles pièces montrez-vous? Quels détails donnez-vous? Jouez la scène devant la classe.

société immobilière *real estate company* devient *becomes*
connue *known* publicités *ads* hors norme *unconventional*

 Practice more at **daccord1.vhlcentral.com.**

## Section Goals

In this section, students will:
• read about the real estate franchise Century 21 France
• watch a commercial for the franchise
• answer questions about the commercial and Century 21 France

## Key Standards
1.2, 2.2, 4.2, 5.2

**Student Resources**
Supersite: Video, Activities
**Teacher Resources**
Video Script & Translation;
Supersite: Video

**Introduction**
To check comprehension, ask these questions:
**1. Comment sont les publicités de la société immobilière? (Elles sont d'un humour contemporain.)
2. Que montre une de ses campagnes publicitaires? (Elle montre les risques de ne pas utiliser un agent immobilier.)**

**Avant de regarder la vidéo**
• Have students look at the video stills, read the captions, and predict what is happening (**1. Les clients sont dans l'appartement avec le propriétaire. Il leur montre le salon. 2. Les clients sont dans le couloir avec le propriétaire. Ils n'entrent pas dans toutes les pièces.**)
• Explain to students that they do not need to understand every word they hear. Tell them to listen for the text in the captions, cognates, and house-related vocabulary.

**Compréhension** Have students work in pairs or groups for this activity. Tell them to write their answers. Then show the video again so that they can check their answers and add any missing information.

**Discussion** After students watch each role-play, ask them to say what the competent real estate agent did right.

**Pierre Palmade** French actor and comedian Pierre Palmade plays the owner of the apartment in this Century 21 France commercial. Born in Bordeaux in 1968, Palmade moved to Paris at 19 to launch his career as a stand-up comic. Soon he was appearing on television with other well-known comics, among them the now popular Michèle Laroque. However, it was his first co-writing experience with comic Muriel Robin that not only forged a strong professional and personal friendship between them, but also led to their collaboration on multiple other projects and helped secure his celebrity status. Although Palmade has starred in a few films, most of his creative output has involved writing material for other actors. Today he is an enormously popular comedian known for playing unpleasant characters.

# Section Goals

In this section, students will learn and practice vocabulary related to:
• household chores
• home appliances

## Key Standards

**1.1, 1.2, 4.1**

**Student Resources**
*Cahier d'exercices*, pp. 105-106;
*Cahier d'activités*, pp. 15, 175;
Supersite: Activities,
*Cahier interactif*
**Teacher Resources**
Answer Keys; Overhead #38;
Audio Script; Textbook & Audio
Activity MP3s/CD; *Feuilles
d'activités*; Testing program:
Vocabulary Quiz

## Suggestions

• Use **Overhead #38.** Point out appliances and talk about what people in the illustration are doing. Examples: **Ça, c'est un four à micro-ondes. Cette fille balaie.**

• Ask students questions about chores using the new vocabulary. Examples: **Préférez-vous balayer ou passer l'aspirateur? Faire la cuisine ou faire la lessive? Mettre la table ou sortir la poubelle?**

• Say vocabulary words and tell students to write or say the opposite terms. Examples: **sale (propre), débarrasser la table (mettre la table),** and **salir les vêtements (faire la lessive).**

• Point out the difference between **un évier** (*kitchen sink*) and **un lavabo** (*bathroom sink*).

• Point out the expressions that use **faire: faire la lessive, faire la poussière, faire le ménage, faire le lit,** and **faire la vaisselle.**

• Tell students that the names of several appliances are compounds of verbs and nouns. Examples: **grille-pain, lave-vaisselle,** and **sèche-linge.** Other appliances use the preposition à: **un fer à repasser, un four à micro-ondes.**

---

**Leçon 8B**

 **Talking Picture**
**Audio: Activity**

You will learn how to...
▪ talk about chores
▪ talk about appliances

# Les tâches ménagères

### Vocabulaire

| | |
|---|---|
| débarrasser la table | to clear the table |
| enlever/faire la poussière | to dust |
| essuyer la vaisselle/ la table | to dry the dishes/ to wipe the table |
| faire la lessive | to do the laundry |
| faire le ménage | to do the housework |
| laver | to wash |
| mettre la table | to set the table |
| passer l'aspirateur | to vacuum |
| ranger | to tidy up; to put away |
| salir | to soil, to make dirty |
| | |
| propre | clean |
| sale | dirty |
| | |
| un appareil électrique/ ménager | electrical/household appliance |
| une cafetière | coffeemaker |
| une cuisinière | stove |
| un grille-pain | toaster |
| un lave-linge | washing machine |
| un lave-vaisselle | dishwasher |
| un sèche-linge | clothes dryer |
| une tâche ménagère | household chore |

**ressources**

| CE pp. 105-106 | CA pp. 15, 175 | daccord1.vhlcentral.com |

**268** *deux cent soixante-huit*

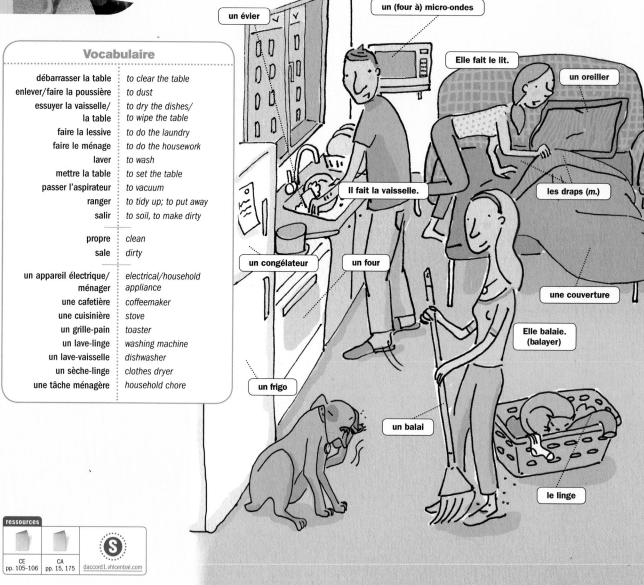

un évier

un (four à) micro-ondes

Elle fait le lit.

un oreiller

Il fait la vaisselle.

les draps (m.)

un congélateur

un four

une couverture

Elle balaie. (balayer)

un frigo

un balai

le linge

---

**Using Games** Write vocabulary words for appliances on index cards. On another set of cards, draw or paste pictures to match each term. Tape them face down on the board in random order. Divide the class into two teams. Then play a game of Concentration in which students match words with pictures. When a player has a match, that player's team collects those cards. When all the cards have been matched, the team with the most cards wins.

**Oral Practice** Ask students what chores they do in various rooms. Examples: **Dans quelle pièce... faites-vous la vaisselle? faites-vous le lit? mettez-vous la table? passez-vous l'aspirateur? repassez-vous? balayez-vous?**

---

# Mise en pratique

**1** **On fait le ménage** Complétez les phrases avec le bon mot.

1. On balaie avec _____un balai_____.
2. On repasse le linge avec _____un fer à repasser_____.
3. On fait la lessive avec _____un lave-linge_____.
4. On lave la vaisselle avec _____un lave-vaisselle_____.
5. On prépare le café avec _____une cafetière_____.
6. On sèche les vêtements avec _____un sèche-linge_____.
7. On met la glace dans _____un congélateur_____.
8. Pour faire le lit, on doit arranger _____les draps_____, _____la couverture_____ et _____l'oreiller/les oreillers_____

**2** **Écoutez** 🎧 Écoutez la conversation téléphonique (*phone call*) entre Édouard, un étudiant, et un conseiller à la radio (*radio psychologist*). Ensuite, indiquez les tâches ménagères que faisaient Édouard et Paul au début du semestre.

|  | Édouard | Paul |
|---|---|---|
| 1. Il faisait la cuisine. | ☑ | ☐ |
| 2. Il faisait les lits. | ☐ | ☑ |
| 3. Il passait l'aspirateur. | ☑ | ☐ |
| 4. Il sortait la poubelle. | ☐ | ☑ |
| 5. Il balayait. | ☐ | ☑ |
| 6. Il faisait la lessive. | ☑ | ☐ |
| 7. Il faisait la vaisselle. | ☐ | ☑ |
| 8. Il nettoyait le frigo. | ☑ | ☐ |

**3** **Les tâches ménagères** Avec un(e) partenaire, indiquez quelles tâches ménagères vous faites dans chaque pièce ou partie de votre logement. Il y a plus d'une réponse possible. *Answers will vary.*

1. La chambre: _____
2. La cuisine: _____
3. La salle de bains: _____
4. La salle à manger: _____
5. La salle de séjour: _____
6. Le garage: _____

🔊 Practice more at **daccord1.vhlcentral.com.**

*deux cent soixante-neuf* **269**

**Il sort la poubelle. (sortir)**

**un fer à repasser**

**Il repasse. (repasser)**

---

**1** **Expansion** Reverse this activity and ask students what each appliance is used for. Example: **Que fait-on avec une cuisinière? (On fait la cuisine.)**

**2** **Script** J'ai un problème avec Paul, mon colocataire, parce qu'il ne m'aide pas à faire le ménage. Quand le semestre a commencé, il faisait la vaisselle, il sortait la poubelle et il balayait. Parfois, il faisait même mon lit. Paul ne faisait jamais la cuisine parce qu'il détestait ça, c'est moi qui la faisais. Je faisais aussi la lessive, je passais l'aspirateur et je nettoyais le frigo. Maintenant, Paul ne fait jamais son lit et il ne m'aide pas. C'est moi qui fais tout. Qu'est-ce que vous me suggérez de faire?
*(On Textbook Audio)*

**2** **Suggestion** After listening to the recording, have students identify Paul and Édouard in the photo and describe what they are doing.

**2** **Expansion** Have students describe how they share household chores with their siblings or others at home.

**3** **Suggestion** Have students get together with another pair and compare their answers.

---

## Communication

**4 Qui fait quoi?** Votre professeur va vous donner une feuille d'activités. Dites si vous faites les tâches indiquées en écrivant (by writing) **Oui** ou **Non** dans la première colonne. Ensuite, posez des questions à vos camarades de classe; écrivez leur nom dans la deuxième colonne quand ils répondent **Oui**. Présentez vos réponses à la classe. Answers will vary.

**MODÈLE**

mettre la table pour prendre le petit-déjeuner
**Élève 1:** Est-ce que tu mets la table pour prendre le petit-déjeuner?
**Élève 2:** Oui, je mets la table chaque matin./ Non, je ne prends pas de petit-déjeuner, donc je ne mets pas la table.

| Activités | Moi | Mes camarades de classe |
|---|---|---|
| 1. mettre la table pour prendre le petit-déjeuner | | |
| 2. passer l'aspirateur tous les jours | | |
| 3. salir ses vêtements quand on mange | | |
| 4. nettoyer les toilettes | | |
| 5. balayer la cuisine | | |
| 6. débarrasser la table après le dîner | | |
| 7. souvent enlever la poussière sur son ordinateur | | |
| 8. laver les vitres (windows) | | |

**5 Conversez** Interviewez un(e) camarade de classe. Answers will vary.

1. Qui fait la vaisselle chez toi?
2. Qui fait la lessive chez toi?
3. Fais-tu ton lit tous les jours?
4. Quelles tâches ménagères as-tu faites le week-end dernier?
5. Repasses-tu tous tes vêtements?
6. Quelles tâches ménagères détestes-tu faire?
7. Quels appareils électriques as-tu chez toi?
8. Ranges-tu souvent ta chambre?

**6 Au pair** Vous partez dans un pays francophone pour vivre dans une famille pendant un an. Travaillez avec deux camarades de classe et préparez un dialogue dans lequel (in which) vous: Answers will vary.

- parlez des tâches ménagères que vous détestez/aimez faire.
- posez des questions sur vos nouvelles responsabilités.
- parlez de vos passions et de vos habitudes.
- décidez si cette famille vous convient.

**7 Écrivez** L'appartement de Martine est un désastre: la cuisine est sale et le reste de l'appartement est encore pire (worse). Préparez un paragraphe où vous décrivez les problèmes que vous voyez (see) et que vous imaginez. Ensuite, écrivez la liste des tâches que Martine va faire pour tout nettoyer. Answers will vary.

**Riddles** Have groups of three write riddles about furnishings or appliances. For each riddle, the group comes up with at least three hints. Example: **Je suis très doux. On me met sur le lit. Je vous aide à bien dormir. (Je suis un oreiller.)** Ask them to read their riddles to the class, who will guess the answer.

**Completion** Have students complete this paragraph.
**L'appartement de Roger est un désastre. Il a rarement le temps de faire le _____ (ménage). Il _____ (passe) l'aspirateur une fois par semestre et il ne/n'_____ (fait/enlève) pas la poussière. Il y a des tasses et des verres dans l'_____ (évier) parce qu'il oublie de les mettre dans le _____ (lave-vaisselle). L'appartement sent mauvais parce qu'il ne sort pas la _____ (poubelle).**

# Les sons et les lettres

 **Audio: Concepts, Activities Record & Compare**

## 🎧 Semi-vowels

French has three semi-vowels. Semi-vowels are sounds that are produced in much the same way as vowels, but also have many properties in common with consonants. Semi-vowels are also sometimes referred to as *glides* because they glide from or into the vowel they accompany.

| Luc**i**en | ch**i**en | s**oi**f | n**ui**t |

The semi-vowel that occurs in the word **bien** is very much like the *y* in the English word *yes*. It is usually spelled with an **i** or a **y** (pronounced *ee*), then glides into the following sound. This semi-vowel sound is also produced when **ll** follows an **i**.

| nat**i**on | bala**y**er | b**i**en | bri**ll**ant |

The semi-vowel that occurs in the word **soif** is like the *w* in the English words *was* and *we*. It usually begins with **o** or **ou**, then glides into the following vowel.

| tr**oi**s | fr**oi**d | **ou**i | **ou**istiti |

The third semi-vowel sound occurs in the word **nuit**. It is spelled with the vowel **u**, as in the French word **tu**, then glides into the following sound.

| l**ui** | s**ui**s | cr**u**el | intellect**u**el |

### 🖉S Prononcez Répétez les mots suivants à voix haute.

1. oui
2. taille
3. suisse
4. fille
5. mois
6. cruel
7. minuit
8. jouer
9. cuisine
10. juillet
11. échouer
12. croissant

### 🖉S Articulez Répétez les phrases suivantes à voix haute.

1. Voici trois poissons noirs.
2. Louis et sa famille sont suisses.
3. Parfois, Grégoire fait de la cuisine chinoise.
4. Aujourd'hui, Matthieu et Damien vont travailler.
5. Françoise a besoin de faire ses devoirs d'histoire.
6. La fille de Monsieur Poirot va conduire pour la première fois.

### 🖉S Dictons Répétez les dictons à voix haute.

*Vouloir, c'est pouvoir.²*

*La nuit, tous les chats sont gris.¹*

¹ All cats are gray in the dark.
² Where there's a will, there's a way.

**ressources**

CA p. 176

daccord1.vhlcentral.com

---

## Section Goals

In this section, students will learn about semi-vowels.

## Key Standards
**4.1**

**Student Resources**
*Cahier d'activités*, p. 176;
Supersite: Activities,
*Cahier interactif*
**Teacher Resources**
Answer Keys; Audio Script;
Textbook & Audio Activity
MP3s/CD

## Suggestions

- Model the pronunciation of the example words and have students repeat them after you.
- Ask students to provide more examples of words from this or previous lessons with these sounds. Examples: **balayer, essuyer, évier**
- Dictate five familiar words containing semi-vowels, repeating each one at least two times. Then write them on the board or on a transparency and have students check their spelling.
- Remind students that many vowels combine to make a single sound with no glide. Examples: **ai** and **ou**
- Explain that **un ouistiti** is a marmoset.

---

**Mini-dictée** Use these sentences with semi-vowels for additional practice or dictation. **1. Nous balayons bien la cuisine. 2. J'ai soif, mais tu as froid. 3. Une fois, ma fille a oublié son parapluie. 4. Parfois, mon chien aime jouer entre minuit et trois heures du matin.**

**Tongue-twisters** Teach students these French tongue-twisters that contain semi-vowels. **1. Trois petites truites non cuites, trois petites truites crues. 2. Une bête noire se baigne dans une baignoire noire.**

CONTEXTES **271**

# ROMAN-PHOTO

## La vie sans Pascal

Video: *Roman-photo*
Record & Compare

**PERSONNAGES**

Amina

Michèle

Sandrine

Stéphane

Valérie

*Au P'tit Bistrot...*
**MICHÈLE** Tout va bien, Amina?
**AMINA** Oui, ça va, merci. *(Au téléphone)* Allô?... Qu'est-ce qu'il y a, Sandrine?... Non, je ne le savais pas, mais franchement, ça ne me surprend pas... Écoute, j'arrive chez toi dans quinze minutes, d'accord? ... À tout à l'heure!

**MICHÈLE** Je débarrasse la table?
**AMINA** Oui, merci, et apporte-moi l'addition, s'il te plaît.
**MICHÈLE** Tout de suite.

**VALÉRIE** Tu as fait ton lit, ce matin?
**STÉPHANE** Oui, maman.
**VALÉRIE** Est-ce que tu as rangé ta chambre?
**STÉPHANE** Euh... oui, ce matin, pendant que tu faisais la lessive.

*Chez Sandrine...*
**SANDRINE** Salut, Amina! Merci d'être venue.
**AMINA** Mmmm. Qu'est-ce qui sent si bon?
**SANDRINE** Il y a des biscuits au chocolat dans le four.
**AMINA** Oh, est-ce que tu les préparais quand tu m'as téléphoné?

**SANDRINE** Tu as soif?
**AMINA** Un peu, oui.
**SANDRINE** Sers-toi, j'ai des jus de fruits au frigo.

*Sandrine casse (breaks) une assiette.*
**SANDRINE** Et zut!
**AMINA** Ça va, Sandrine?
**SANDRINE** Oui, oui... passe-moi le balai, s'il te plaît.
**AMINA** N'oublie pas de balayer sous la cuisinière.
**SANDRINE** Je sais! Excuse-moi, Amina. Comme je t'ai dit au téléphone, Pascal et moi, c'est fini.

### ACTIVITÉS

**1** **Questions** Répondez aux questions par des phrases complètes. *Answers may vary slightly.*

1. Avec qui Amina parle-t-elle au téléphone?
Elle parle avec Sandrine.
2. Comment va Sandrine aujourd'hui? Pourquoi?
Elle est de mauvaise humeur parce que c'est fini avec Pascal.
3. Est-ce que Stéphane a fait toutes ses tâches ménagères? Non, il n'a pas fait toutes ses tâches ménagères.
4. Qu'est-ce que Sandrine préparait quand elle a téléphoné à Amina? Elle préparait des biscuits au chocolat.

5. Amina a faim et a soif. À votre avis *(opinion)*, que va-t-elle prendre? Elle va prendre un jus de fruits et elle va manger des biscuits.
6. Pourquoi Amina n'est-elle pas fâchée *(angry)* contre Sandrine? Elle comprend pourquoi Sandrine est un peu triste/de mauvaise humeur.
7. Pourquoi Amina pense-t-elle que Sandrine aimerait *(would like)* un cyberhomme américain? Amina pense que Sandrine aime David.
8. Sandrine pense qu'Amina devrait *(should)* rencontrer Cyberhomme, mais Amina pense que ce n'est pas une bonne idée. À votre avis, qui a raison? *Answers will vary.*

## Amina console Sandrine.

**VALÉRIE** Hmm... et la vaisselle? Tu as fait la vaisselle?
**STÉPHANE** Non, pas encore, mais...
**MICHÈLE** Il me faut l'addition pour Amina.
**VALÉRIE** Stéphane, tu dois faire la vaisselle avant de sortir.
**STÉPHANE** Bon, ça va, j'y vais!

**VALÉRIE** Ah, Michèle, il faut sortir les poubelles pour ce soir!
**MICHÈLE** Oui, comptez sur moi, Madame Forestier.
**VALÉRIE** Très bien! Moi, je rentre, il est l'heure de préparer le dîner.

**SANDRINE** Il était tellement pénible. Bref, je suis de mauvaise humeur aujourd'hui.
**AMINA** Ne t'en fais pas, je comprends.
**SANDRINE** Toi, tu as de la chance.
**AMINA** Pourquoi tu dis ça?
**SANDRINE** Tu as ton Cyberhomme. Tu vas le rencontrer un de ces jours?
**AMINA** Oh... Je ne sais pas si c'est une bonne idée.

**SANDRINE** Pourquoi pas?
**AMINA** Sandrine, il faut être prudent dans la vie, je ne le connais pas vraiment, tu sais.
**SANDRINE** Comme d'habitude, tu as raison. Mais finalement, un cyberhomme, c'est peut-être mieux qu'un petit ami. Ou alors, un petit ami artistique, charmant et beau garçon.
**AMINA** Et américain?

### Expressions utiles

#### Talking about what you know

- Je ne le savais pas, mais franchement, ça ne me surprend pas.
  *I didn't know that, but frankly, I'm not surprised.*
- Je sais!
  *I know!*
- Je ne sais pas si c'est une bonne idée.
  *I don't know if that's a good idea.*
- Je ne le connais pas vraiment, tu sais.
  *I don't really know him, you know.*

#### Additional vocabulary

- **Comptez sur moi.**
  *Count on me.*
- **Ne t'en fais pas.**
  *Don't worry about it.*
- **J'y vais!**
  *I'm going there!/I'm on my way!*
- **pas encore**
  *not yet*
- **tu dois**
  *you must*
- **être de bonne/mauvaise humeur**
  *to be in a good/bad mood*

**Expressions utiles**
- Model the pronunciation of the **Expressions utiles** and have students repeat them.
- As you work through the list, point out the forms of **savoir** and **connaître**. See if students can discern the difference in meaning between the two verbs from the example sentences. Respond briefly to their questions, but tell them that these verbs will be formally presented in **Structures 8B.2**.

**1 Suggestion** Have volunteers write their answers on the board. Go over them as a class.

**2 Expansion** Ask students who works the hardest of all these people. Have them support their opinion with details from this episode and previous ones.

**3 Suggestion** Have students use commands in their lists for review.

---

**2** **Le ménage** Indiquez qui a fait ou va faire ces tâches ménagères: Amina (**A**), Michèle (**M**), Sandrine (**S**), Stéphane (**St**), Valérie (**V**) ou personne (*no one*) (**P**).

1. sortir la poubelle M
2. balayer S & A
3. passer l'aspirateur P
4. faire la vaisselle St
5. faire le lit St
6. débarrasser la table M
7. faire la lessive V
8. ranger sa chambre St

 Practice more at **daccord1.vhlcentral.com**.

**3** **Écrivez** Vous avez gagné un pari (*bet*) avec votre grande sœur et elle doit faire (*must do*) en conséquence toutes les tâches ménagères que vous lui indiquez pendant un mois. Écrivez une liste de dix tâches minimum. Pour chaque tâche, précisez la pièce du logement et combien de fois par semaine elle doit l'exécuter.

**ressources**

CA
pp. 97–98

daccord1.vhlcentral.com

**A C T I V I T É S**

---

**O P T I O N S**

**Debate** Divide the class into two groups based on their answers to question 8 on page 272 (whether or not Amina should meet Cyberhomme) and have a debate about who is right. Tell groups to brainstorm a list of arguments to support their point of view and anticipate rebuttals for what the other team might say.

**Predicting Future Episodes** Have students work in pairs. Tell them to reread the last lines of the **Roman-photo** and write a short paragraph predicting what will happen in future episodes. Do they think Amina will meet Cyberhomme in person? What do they think will happen in Sandrine's love life? Have volunteers read their paragraphs aloud to the class.

## Section Goals

In this section, students will:
- learn about the interior of French homes
- learn some colloquial terms for describing a home or room
- learn the names of some famous homes in the francophone world
- read about the French Quarter in New Orleans

## Key Standards

2.1, 2.2, 3.1, 3.2, 4.2

**Student Resources**
Supersite: Activities
**Teacher Resources**
Answer Keys

**Culture à la loupe**
**Avant la lecture**
- Have students look at the photos and describe what they see.
- Tell students to read the first sentence of the text. Then ask: **Quel est le sujet du texte?**

**Lecture**
- Point out the **Coup de main** and have two volunteers read the examples. Demonstrative pronouns will be presented in **D'accord!** Level 2.
- Point out the statistics chart. Ask students what information the chart shows (the percentage of French residences that have the appliances listed).

**Après la lecture** Ask students: **Quelles sont les différences entre l'intérieur des logements français et l'intérieur des logements américains?**

**1** **Suggestion** Go over the answers with the class.

## CULTURE À LA LOUPE

# L'intérieur des logements français

L'intérieur des maisons et des appartements français est assez° différent de celui des Américains. Quand on entre dans un immeuble ancien en France, on est dans un hall° où il y a des boîtes aux lettres°. Ensuite, il y a souvent une deuxième porte. Celle-ci conduit à° l'escalier. Il n'y a pas souvent d'ascenseur, mais s'il y en a un°, en général, il est très petit et il est au milieu de° l'escalier. Le hall de l'immeuble peut aussi avoir une porte qui donne sur une cour° ou un jardin, souvent derrière le bâtiment°.

À l'intérieur des logements, les pièces sont en général plus petites que° les pièces américaines, surtout les cuisines et les salles de bains. Dans la cuisine, on trouve tous les appareils ménagers nécessaires (cuisinière, four, four à micro-ondes, frigo), mais ils sont plus petits qu'aux États-Unis. Les lave-vaisselle sont assez rares dans les appartements et plus communs dans les maisons. On a souvent une seule° salle de bains et les toilettes sont en général dans une autre petite pièce séparée°. Les lave-linge sont aussi assez petits et on les trouve, en général, dans la cuisine ou dans la salle de bains. Dans les chambres, en France, il n'y a pas de grands placards et les vêtements sont rangés la plupart° du temps dans une armoire ou une commode. Les fenêtres s'ouvrent° sur l'intérieur, un peu comme des portes, et il est très rare d'avoir des moustiquaires°. Par contre°, il y a toujours des volets°.

### Combien de logements ont ces appareils ménagers?

| | |
|---|---|
| Réfrigérateur | 96% |
| Lave-linge | 95% |
| Cuisinière/Four | 94% |
| Four à micro-ondes | 72% |
| Congélateur | 55% |
| Lave-vaisselle | 45% |
| Sèche-linge | 27% |

SOURCE: GIFAM/Francoscopie

### Coup de main

Demonstrative pronouns help to avoid repetition.

| | S. | P. |
|---|---|---|
| M. | **celui** | **ceux** |
| F. | **celle** | **celles** |

Ce lit est grand, mais le lit de Monique est petit.

Ce lit est grand, mais **celui** de Monique est petit.

**assez** *rather* **hall** *entryway* **boîtes aux lettres** *mailboxes* **conduit à** *leads to* **s'il y en a un** *if there is one* **au milieu de** *in the middle of* **cour** *courtyard* **bâtiment** *building* **plus petites que** *smaller than* **une seule** *only one* **séparée** *separate* **la plupart** *most* **s'ouvrent** *open* **moustiquaires** *screens* **Par contre** *On the other hand* **volets** *shutters*

**ACTIVITÉS**

**1** **Complétez** Complétez chaque phrase logiquement.
Answers will vary. Possible answers provided.
1. Dans le hall d'un immeuble français, on trouve... des boîtes aux lettres et des portes.
2. Au milieu de l'escalier, dans les vieux immeubles français, ... il y a parfois un ascenseur.
3. Derrière les vieux immeubles, on trouve souvent... une cour ou un jardin.
4. Les cuisines et les salles de bains françaises sont... assez petites.
5. Dans les appartements français, il est assez rare d'avoir... un lave-vaisselle.
6. Les logements français ont souvent une seule... salle de bains.
7. En France, les toilettes sont souvent... dans une pièce séparée.
8. Les Français rangent souvent leurs vêtements dans une armoire parce qu'ils... n'ont pas souvent de placards.
9. On trouve souvent le lave-linge... dans la cuisine ou dans la salle de bains.
10. En général, les fenêtres dans les logements français... ont des volets.

**OPTIONS**

**Cultural Comparison** Take a quick class survey to find out how many students have the appliances listed in the chart in their homes. Tally the results on the board and have students calculate the percentages. Example: **Combien de personnes ont un réfrigérateur à la maison?**

Then have students compare the results of this survey with those in the chart. Examples: **Plus d'Américains ont un sèche-linge dans leur maison./Moins de Français ont un sèche-linge dans leur maison.**

## LE FRANÇAIS QUOTIDIEN

### Quelles conditions!

| | |
|---|---|
| **boxon** (*m.*) | *shambles* |
| **gourbis** (*m.*) | *pigsty* |
| **piaule** (*f.*) | *pad, room* |
| **souk** (*m.*) | *mess* |
| | |
| **impeccable** | *spic-and-span* |
| **ringard** | *cheesy, old-fashioned* |
| **crécher** | *to live* |
| **semer la pagaille** | *to make a mess* |

## LE MONDE FRANCOPHONE

### Résidences célèbres

Voici quelques résidences célèbres.

**En France**
**l'hôtel Matignon** la résidence du Premier ministre°

**Au Maroc**
**le Palais royal de Rabat** la résidence du roi°
et de sa famille

**À la Martinique**
**la Pagerie** la maison natale° de Joséphine de
Beauharnais (femme de Napoléon Bonaparte)

**À Monaco**
**le Palais du Prince** la résidence de la famille
princière° de Monaco (la famille Grimaldi)

**Au Sénégal**
**le Palais présidentiel de Dakar** la résidence du
président du Sénégal, dans un jardin tropical

**Premier ministre** *Prime Minister* **roi** *king* **la maison natale** *birthplace*
**la famille princière** *the prince and his family*

## PORTRAIT

# Le Vieux Carré

Le Quartier Français, ou Vieux Carré, est le centre historique de la Nouvelle-Orléans. Il est connu pour sa culture créole, sa vie nocturne°, sa musique et sa fameuse «joie de vivre». Beaucoup de visiteurs viennent° participer à ses fêtes, comme le carnaval de Mardi Gras ou le festival de jazz, en avril. Ils aiment aussi admirer ses nombreux bâtiments° classés monuments historiques, comme le Cabildo ou la cathédrale Saint-Louis, la plus vieille° cathédrale des États-Unis. On ne doit pas quitter le Vieux Carré sans avoir exploré les jardins et les patios cachés° de ses vieilles maisons de planteurs.

**vie nocturne** *night life* **viennent** *come* **bâtiments** *buildings*
**la plus vieille** *the oldest* **cachés** *hidden*

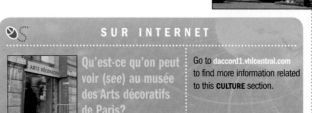

### SUR INTERNET

Qu'est-ce qu'on peut voir (see) au musée des Arts décoratifs de Paris?

Go to **daccord1.vhlcentral.com** to find more information related to this **CULTURE** section.

---

**2** **Complétez** Complétez les phrases.

1. Le Vieux Carré est <u>le centre historique de la Nouvelle-Orléans</u>
2. Il est connu pour <u>sa culture créole, sa vie nocturne, sa musique et sa «joie de vivre»</u>
3. Dans le Vieux Carré, il faut explorer <u>les jardins et les patios cachés des vieilles maisons de planteurs</u>
4. Les Grimaldi habitent <u>dans le Palais du Prince à Monaco</u>
5. L'hôtel Matignon est <u>la résidence du Premier ministre français</u>
6. L'impératrice Joséphine est née <u>à la Pagerie, à la Martinique</u>

Practice more at **daccord1.vhlcentral.com.**

**3** **C'est le souk!** Votre oncle favori vient vous rendre visite et votre petit frère a semé la pagaille dans votre chambre. C'est le souk! Avec un(e) partenaire, inventez une conversation où vous lui donnez des ordres pour nettoyer avant l'arrivée de votre oncle. Jouez la scène devant la classe.

**ressources**

daccord1.vhlcentral.com

**A C T I V I T É S**

---

**Le français quotidien**
• Model the pronunciation of each term and have students repeat it.
• Have volunteers create sentences using these words.

**Portrait** Ask students: **Que désirez-vous faire ou visiter dans le Vieux Carré de la Nouvelle-Orléans?**

**Le monde francophone**
• Bring in photos from magazines, books, or the Internet of these famous homes to show the class.
• Ask a few content questions based on the text. Examples: **1. Où est le Palais du Prince?** (à Monaco) **2. Où habite le Premier ministre de la France?** (à l'hôtel Matignon) **3. Qui habite le Palais du Prince?** (la famille princière de Monaco) **4. Comment s'appelle la maison natale de la femme de Napoléon?** (la Pagerie)

**2** **Expansion** For additional practice, give students these items. **7. _____ sont deux fêtes célèbres à la Nouvelle-Orléans.** (Le carnaval de Mardi Gras et le festival de jazz) **8. Le palais du Cabildo est à _____.** (la Nouvelle-Orléans) **9. Le roi du Maroc habite _____.** (le Palais royal de Rabat)

**3** **Suggestion** Encourage students to use terms in **Le français quotidien** in their role-plays.

---

**O P T I O N S**

**Le Vieux Carré** **Le Cabildo** was completed in 1799. The ceremonies finalizing the Louisiana Purchase were held there in 1803. Since 1903, it has been the Louisiana State Museum. The museum contains a number of objects from Napoleonic history. The present-day **cathédrale Saint-Louis** was completed in 1851. Made of bricks, the cathedral is dedicated to King Louis IX of France (1214–1270), who was canonized in 1297. His life is depicted in ten of the stained glass windows. This building is actually the third cathedral to occupy this site. The first cathedral was completed in 1727, but it burned down in 1788. The second was completed in 1794, but collapsed in 1849.

## Section Goals

In this section, students will learn:
- to compare and contrast the uses and meanings of the **passé composé** and the **imparfait**
- common expressions indicating past tenses

## Key Standards

**4.1, 5.1**

**Student Resources**
*Cahier d'exercices*, pp. 107–108;
*Cahier d'activités*, p. 177;
Supersite: Activities,
*Cahier interactif*

**Teacher Resources**
Answer Keys; Audio Script;
Audio Activity MP3s/CD;
Testing program: Grammar Quiz

## Suggestions

- To practice contrasting the **passé composé** vs. the **imparfait**, first do a quick review of each tense and its uses. Then write the following sentences on the board: **1. Je vais au cinéma avec un ami. 2. Nous prenons le bus. 3. Après le film, nous mangeons au restaurant. 4. Ensuite, nous faisons une promenade. 5. Nous rentrons tard à la maison.** Have students change the sentences above first to the **passé composé** and then to the **imparfait**. Have them add adverbs or expressions they've learned that signal a past tense.

- As you review the **passé composé** vs. the **imparfait**, have students focus on the pronunciation of these tenses since it is important to distinguish between the respective sounds. You might have them practice the following sentences: **J'ai travaillé. / Je travaillais. Il parlait. / Il a parlé. Tu allais. / Tu es allé(e). Elle chantait. / Elle a chanté.** You could also add the present tense of these sentences and have them practice pronouncing all three tenses.

- Have students interview each other about their childhood activities using the following question: **Quand tu étais petit(e), qu'est-ce que tu faisais... a) après l'école? b) le week-end? c) pendant les grandes vacances** (*summer vacation*)?

### 8B.1 The *passé composé* vs. the *imparfait* (Summary)

**Point de départ** You have learned the uses of the **passé composé** versus the **imparfait** to talk about things and events in the past. These tenses are distinct and are not used in the same way. Remember always to keep the context and the message you wish to convey in mind while deciding which tense to use.

#### Uses of the *passé composé*

| | |
|---|---|
| To talk about events that happened at a specific moment or that took place for a precise duration in the past | Je **suis allé** au concert vendredi. *I went to the concert on Friday.* |
| To relate a sequence of events or tell about isolated actions that started and ended in the past and are completed from the speaker's viewpoint | Tu **as fait** le lit, tu **as sorti** la poubelle et tu **as mis** la table. *You made the bed, took out the trash, and set the table.* |
| To indicate a change in the mental, emotional or physical state of a person | Tout à coup, elle **a eu** soif. *Suddenly, she got thirsty.* |
| To narrate the facts in a story | Nous **avons passé** une journée fantastique à la plage. *We spent a fantastic day at the beach.* |
| To describe actions that move the plot forward in a narration | Soudain, Thomas **a trouvé** la réponse à leur question. *Suddenly, Thomas found the answer to their question.* |

#### Uses of the *imparfait*

| | |
|---|---|
| To talk about actions that lasted for an unspecified duration of time | Elle **dormait** tranquillement. *She was sleeping peacefully.* |
| To relate events that occurred habitually or repeatedly in the past or tell how things used to be | Nous **faisions** une promenade au parc tous les dimanches matins. *We used to walk in the park every Sunday morning.* |
| To describe an ongoing mental, emotional or physical state of a person | Elle **avait** toujours soif. *She was always thirsty.* |
| To describe the background scene and setting of a story | Il **faisait** beau et le ciel **était** bleu. *The weather was nice and the sky was blue.* |
| To describe people and things | C'**était** une photo d'une jolie fille. *It was a photograph of a pretty girl.* |

### MISE EN PRATIQUE

**1** **À l'étranger!** Racontez (*Tell*) cette histoire au passé en choisissant (*by choosing*) l'imparfait ou le passé composé.

Lise (1) _avait_ (avoir) vraiment envie de travailler en France après l'université. Alors, un jour, elle (2) _a quitté_ (quitter) son petit village près de Bruxelles et elle (3) _a pris_ (prendre) le train pour Paris. Elle (4) _est arrivée_ (arriver) à Paris. Elle (5) _a trouvé_ (trouver) une chambre dans un petit hôtel. Pendant six mois, elle (6) _a balayé_ (balayer) le couloir et (7) _a nettoyé_ (nettoyer) les chambres. Au bout de (*After*) six mois, elle (8) _a pris_ (prendre) des cours au Cordon Bleu et maintenant, elle est chef dans un petit restaurant!

**2** **Explique-moi!** Dites pourquoi vous et vos amis n'avez pas fait les choses que vous deviez faire. Faites des phrases complètes en disant ce que (*by saying what*) vous n'avez pas fait au passé composé et en donnant (*by giving*) la raison à l'imparfait.

**MODÈLE** Élise / étudier / avoir sommeil
*Élise n'a pas étudié parce qu'elle avait sommeil.*

1. Carla / faire une promenade / pleuvoir
   Carla n'a pas fait de promenade parce qu'il pleuvait.
2. Alexandre et Mia / ranger la chambre / regarder la télé
   Alexandre et Mia n'ont pas rangé la chambre parce qu'ils regardaient la télé.
3. nous / répondre au prof / ne pas faire attention
   Nous n'avons pas répondu au prof parce que nous ne faisions pas attention.
4. Jade et Noémie / venir au café / nettoyer la maison
   Jade et Noémie ne sont pas venues au café parce qu'elles nettoyaient la maison.
5. Léo / mettre un short / aller à un entretien (*interview*)
   Léo n'a pas mis son short parce qu'il allait à un entretien.

**3** **Qu'est-ce qu'ils faisaient quand...?** Que faisaient ces personnes au moment de l'interruption?
Suggested answers

**MODÈLE**

*Papa débarrassait la table quand mon frère est arrivé.*

**débarrasser / arriver**

Ils sortaient la poubelle quand le voisin a dit bonjour.

**1. sortir / dire**

Sa mère faisait la lessive quand Anne est partie.

**3. faire / partir**

Michel passait l'aspirateur quand l'enfant est tombé.

**2. passer / tomber**

Ils lavaient la voiture quand il a commencé à pleuvoir.

**4. laver / commencer**

**Practice more at daccord1.vhlcentral.com.**

**Oral Practice** Have students recall a memorable day from their childhood. Ask them to narrate this day, giving as many details as possible: the weather, who was there, what happened, how they felt etc. Alternatively, you could do this as a written activity and have students create a journal entry about their memorable day.

**Using Visuals** Distribute illustrations or photos from magazines of everyday activities and vacation activities. Have students arrange the pictures in pairs and create sentences to say that one activity was going on when the other one interrupted it. You might call on pairs to hold up their pictures and present their sentences to the class.

## COMMUNICATION

**4  Situations** Avec un(e) partenaire, complétez ces phrases avec le passé composé ou l'imparfait. Comparez vos réponses, puis présentez-les à la classe. *Answers will vary.*

1. Autrefois, ma famille...
2. Je faisais une promenade quand...
3. Mon/Ma meilleur(e) ami(e)... tous les jours.
4. D'habitude, au petit-déjeuner, je...
5. Une fois, mon copain et moi...
6. Hier, je rentrais du lycée quand...
7. Parfois, ma mère...
8. Hier, il faisait mauvais. Soudain, ...

**5  À votre tour** Demandez à un(e) partenaire de compléter ces phrases avec le passé composé ou l'imparfait. Ensuite, présentez ses phrases à la classe. *Answers will vary.*

1. Mes profs au collège...
2. Quand je suis rentré(e) chez moi hier, ...
3. Le week-end dernier, ...
4. Quand j'ai fait la connaissance de mon/ma meilleur(e) ami(e), ...
5. La première fois que mon/ma meilleur(e) ami(e) et moi sommes sortis, ...
6. Quand j'avais dix ans, ...
7. Le jour où la tragédie du 11 septembre est arrivée, ...
8. Pendant les vacances d'été, ...
9. Quand M. Barack Obama est devenu président des États-Unis, ...
10. Hier soir, je regardais la télé quand...

**6  Je me souviens!** Racontez à votre partenaire un événement spécial de votre vie qui s'est déjà passé. Votre partenaire vous pose des questions pour avoir plus de détails sur cet événement. Vous pouvez (*can*) parler d'un anniversaire, d'une fête familiale, d'un mariage ou d'un concert. *Answers will vary.*

**MODÈLE**

Élève 1: *Nous avons fait une grande fête d'anniversaire pour ma grand-mère l'année dernière.*
Élève 2: *Quel âge a-t-elle eu?*

---

• The **imparfait** and the **passé composé** are sometimes used in the same sentence where the former is used to say what was going on when something else happened. To say what happened that interrupted the ongoing activity, use the **passé composé**.

> Je **travaillais** dans le jardin quand mon amie **a téléphoné**.
> *I was working in the garden when my friend called.*

> Ils **faisaient** de la planche à voile quand j'**ai pris** cette photo.
> *They were wind-surfing when I took this photo.*

• A cause and effect relationship is sometimes expressed by using the **passé composé** and the **imparfait** in the same sentence.

> Marie **avait** envie de faire du shopping, alors elle **est allée** au centre commercial.
> *Marie felt like shopping so she went to the mall.*

> Mon ami **a balayé** la maison parce qu'elle **était** sale.
> *My friend swept the house because it was dirty.*

• The verb **avoir** has a different meaning when used in the **imparfait** versus the **passé composé**.

> J'**avais** sommeil.
> *I was sleepy.*

> J'**ai eu** sommeil.
> *I got sleepy.*

• Certain expressions like **soudain, tout à coup, autrefois, une fois, d'habitude, souvent, toujours**, etc. serve as clues to signal a particular past tense.

> Autrefois, mes parents et moi **vivions** en Belgique.
> *In the past, my parents and I used to live in Belgium.*

> Un jour, j'**ai rencontré** Nathalie au cinéma.
> *One day, I met Nathalie at the movies.*

> D'habitude, j'**allais** au centre-ville avec mes amis.
> *Usually, I used to go downtown with my friends.*

> J'**ai fait** du cheval deux fois dans ma vie.
> *I have gone horseback riding two times in my life.*

---

**Essayez!**  Écrivez la forme correcte du verbe au passé.

1. D'habitude, vous _mangiez_ (manger) dans la salle à manger.
2. Quand mes copines étaient petites, elles _jouaient_ (jouer) de la guitare.
3. Tout à coup, ma sœur _est arrivée_ (arriver) à l'école.
4. Ce matin, Matthieu _a repassé_ (repasser) le linge.
5. Ils _ont vécu_ (vivre) en France pendant un mois.
6. Les chats _dormaient_ (dormir) toujours sur le tapis.
7. Je/J' _ai loué_ (louer) un studio en ville pendant trois semaines.
8. Vous _laviez_ (laver) toujours les rideaux?

---

**Essayez!**  Give the following items as additional practice.
9. La semaine dernière, mon ami et moi _____ (faire) de la planche à voile. (avons fait)
10. Avant, ils _____ (répondre) toujours aux questions du prof. (répondaient)
11. Papa _____ (acheter) un nouveau frigo hier. (a acheté)
12. D'habitude, nous _____ (mettre) nos vêtements dans le placard. (mettions)

**1 & 2 Expansions** Have volunteers explain why they chose the **passé composé** or **imparfait** in each case. Ask them to point out any words or expressions that triggered one tense or the other.

**3 Expansion** Have students come up with a short story for each illustration.

**4 Expansion** Have students choose one of these sentences to begin telling a short story in the past. Encourage students to use both the **passé composé** and the **imparfait**.

**5 Expansion** You could also have students do this activity as a survey by turning the phrases into questions and adding additional questions in the past. Examples: **Comment étaient tes profs au collège? Que faisait ta mère quand tu es rentré(e) chez toi hier? Qu'est-ce que tu as fait le week-end dernier?**

**6 Suggestions**
• Act out the **modèle** with a volunteer before assigning this activity to pairs.
• Encourage students to use key adverbs to indicate the appropriate verb tenses in the dialogue. Examples: **soudain, tout à coup, autrefois**, etc.

---

## 8B.2 The verbs *savoir* and *connaître*

**Point de départ** The verbs **savoir** and **connaître** both mean *to know*. The verb you use will depend on the context.

### Savoir

| Savoir | |
|---|---|
| je | sais |
| tu | sais |
| il/elle | sait |
| nous | savons |
| vous | savez |
| ils/elles | savent |

- Use the verb **savoir** to say you know factual information.

  Je **sais** tout sur lui.
  *I know everything about him.*

  Vous **savez** qui est venu hier?
  *Do you know who came yesterday?*

- While talking about facts, the verb **savoir** may often be followed by **que, qui, où, quand, comment,** or **pourquoi**.

  Nous **savons que** tu arrives mardi.
  *We know that you are arriving on Tuesday.*

  Ils **savent comment** aller à la gare.
  *They know how to get to the train station.*

  Je **sais où** je vais.
  *I know where I am going.*

  Tu **sais qui** a fait la lessive?
  *Do you know who did the laundry?*

- Use the verb **savoir** to say how to do something.

  Il **sait** jouer du piano.
  *He knows how to play the piano.*

  **Savez**-vous faire la cuisine?
  *Do you know how to cook?*

  Je **sais** jouer au tennis.
  *I know how to play tennis.*

  Ils **savent** parler espagnol.
  *They know how to speak Spanish.*

- The forms of **savoir** are regular in the **imparfait**. The past participle of **savoir** is **su**. When used in the **passé composé**, **savoir** implies *to find out* or *to discover*.

  Je **savais** qu'il allait venir.
  *I knew he was coming.*

  J'**ai su** qu'il allait venir.
  *I found out (discovered) he was coming.*

  Nous **savions** qu'il y avait une fête.
  *We knew that there was a party.*

  Nous **avons su** qu'il y avait une fête.
  *We found out that there was a party.*

---

**1** **Les passe-temps** Qu'est-ce que ces personnes savent faire?

**MODÈLE**

*Patrick sait skier.*

**Patrick**

**1. Halima**
Halima sait faire du roller.

**3. tu**
Tu sais jouer au tennis.

**2. vous**
Vous savez nager.

**4. nous**
Nous savons jouer au foot.

**2** **Dialogues** Complétez les conversations avec le présent du verbe **savoir** ou **connaître**.

1. Marie ___sait___ faire la cuisine?
   Oui, mais elle ne ___connaît___ pas beaucoup de recettes (*recipes*).
2. Vous ___connaissez___ les parents de François?
   Non, je ___connais___ seulement sa cousine.
3. Tes enfants ___savent___ nager dans la mer.
   Et mon fils aîné ___connaît___ toutes les espèces de poissons.
4. Je ___sais___ que le train arrive à trois heures.
   Est-ce que tu ___sais___ à quelle heure il part?

**3** **Assemblez** Assemblez les éléments des colonnes pour construire des phrases. Answers will vary.

**MODÈLE** *Je sais parler une langue étrangère.*

| A | B | C |
|---|---|---|
| Gérard Depardieu | (ne pas) connaître | des célébrités |
| Oprah | (ne pas) savoir | faire la cuisine |
| je | | jouer au basket |
| ton/ta camarade de classe | | Julia Roberts |
| | | parler une langue étrangère |

Practice more at **daccord1.vhlcentral.com**.

---

## COMMUNICATION

**4** **Enquête** Votre professeur va vous donner une feuille d'activités. Circulez dans la classe pour trouver au moins une personne différente qui répond oui à chaque question. Answers will vary.

| Sujets | Noms |
|---|---|
| 1. Sais-tu faire une mousse au chocolat? | Jacqueline |
| 2. Connais-tu New York? | |
| 3. Connais-tu le nom des sénateurs de cet état (state)? | |
| 4. Connais-tu quelqu'un qui habite en Californie? | |

**5** **Questions** À tour de rôle, posez ces questions à un(e) partenaire. Ensuite, présentez vos réponses à la classe. Answers will vary.

1. Quel bon restaurant connais-tu près d'ici? Est-ce que tu y (there) manges souvent?
2. Dans ta famille, qui sait chanter le mieux (best)?
3. Connais-tu l'Europe? Quelles villes connais-tu?
4. Reconnais-tu toutes les chansons (songs) que tu entends à la radio?
5. Tes parents savent-ils utiliser Internet? Le font-ils bien?
6. Connais-tu un(e) acteur/actrice célèbre? Une autre personne célèbre?
7. Ton/Ta meilleur(e) (best) ami(e) sait-il/elle écouter quand tu lui racontes (tell) tes problèmes?
8. Connais-tu la date d'anniversaire de tous les membres de ta famille et de tous tes amis? Donne des exemples.

**6** **Je sais le faire** Michelle et Maryse étudient avec un(e) nouvel/nouvelle ami(e). Par groupes de trois, jouez les rôles. Chacun(e) (Each one) essaie de montrer toutes les choses qu'il/elle sait faire. Answers will vary.

### MODÈLE

**Élève 1:** Alors, tu sais faire la vaisselle?
**Élève 2:** Je sais faire la vaisselle, et je sais faire la cuisine aussi.
**Élève 3:** Moi, je sais faire la cuisine, mais il/elle ne sait pas passer l'aspirateur.

## Connaître

| | Connaître |
|---|---|
| je | connais |
| tu | connais |
| il/elle | connaît |
| nous | connaissons |
| vous | connaissez |
| ils/elles | connaissent |

• Use the verb **connaître** to say that you *know, have a knowledge of,* or *are familiar with* people.

Mes parents ne **connaissent** pas mon prof de maths.
*My parents don't know my math teacher.*

Tu **connais** la fille qui vend l'appartement?
*Do you know the girl who is selling the apartment?*

• Use the verb **connaître** to say that you *know, have a knowledge of,* or *are familiar with* places or things.

Sébastien **connaît** ce quartier de Rome.
*Sébastien knows (is familiar with) this neighborhood of Rome.*

Je ne **connais** pas bien la cuisine marocaine.
*I am not familiar with Moroccan cuisine.*

• The forms of **connaître** are regular in the **imparfait**. The past participle of **connaître** is **connu**. When used in the **passé composé**, **connaître** implies *met (for the first time)*.

Luca **a connu** Élodie au lycée.
*Luca met Élodie in high school.*

Luca **connaissait** Élodie au lycée.
*Luca knew Élodie in high school.*

• **Reconnaître** means *to recognize*. It follows the same conjugation pattern as **connaître**.

Mes profs de collège me **reconnaissent** encore.
*My middle school teachers still recognize me.*

Nous avons **reconnu** vos enfants à la soirée.
*We recognized your children at the party.*

**Essayez!** Complétez les phrases avec les formes correctes des verbes **savoir** et **connaître**.

1. Je __connais__ de bons restaurants.
2. Ils ne __savent__ pas parler allemand.
3. Vous __savez__ faire du cheval?
4. Tu __connais__ une bonne coiffeuse?
5. Nous ne __connaissons__ pas Jacques.
6. Caroline __sait__ jouer aux échecs.
7. Vous ne __connaissez__ pas cet artiste?
8. Nous __savons__ faire le ménage.

**Essayez!** Have students change the sentences to the past tense. Examples: 1. Je connaissais de bons restaurants. 2. Ils ne savaient pas parler allemand.

**1** **Expansion** Ask individual students questions about what they know how to do. Example: **Savez-vous parler espagnol? (Non, je ne sais pas parler espagnol.)**

**2** **Expansion** Have students work in pairs to write three more sentences similar to those in the activity. Call on volunteers to present their sentences to the class.

**3** **Expansion** Ask students questions about what certain celebrities know how to do or whom they know. Examples: **Est-ce que Brad Pitt connaît Jennifer Aniston? (Oui, il la connaît.) Est-ce que Jennifer Lopez sait parler espagnol? (Oui, elle sait le parler.)**

**4** **Suggestions**
• Distribute the **Feuilles d'activités** found on the Supersite.
• Have students read through the list of questions using **savoir** and **connaître** for comprehension before completing the activity.

**5** **Expansion** Ask these questions of the whole class. Ask students who answer in the affirmative for additional information. Examples: **Qui sait chanter? Chantez-vous bien? Chantiez-vous souvent quand vous étiez plus jeune?**

**6** **Suggestion** Ask for three volunteers to act out the **modèle** for the class.

**O P T I O N S**

**Savoir bien** Have students write down three things they know how to do well (using **savoir bien** + [*infinitive*]). Collect the papers, and then read the sentences. Tell students that they must not identify themselves when they hear their sentence. The rest of the class takes turns trying to guess who wrote each sentence. Repeat this activity with **connaître**.

**Writing Practice** Ask students to write brief, but creative, paragraphs in which they use **savoir** and **connaître**. Then have them exchange their papers with a partner. Tell students to help each other, through peer editing, to make the paragraphs as error-free as possible. Collect the papers for grading.

# SYNTHÈSE
# Révision

**1** **Expansion** Tell students to imagine they are hosting their own dinner party. Have them make a list of the tasks they completed and another one of the tasks left to complete before the guests arrive. Have them use the **passé composé**.

**2** **Suggestions**
• Have two students say the **modèle** before distributing the **Feuilles d'activités** found on the Supersite.
• Before doing the activity, have students practice creating sentences using **connaître** in the **passé composé** and in the **imparfait**. Example: **J'ai connu la sœur de Jacques en 2010. Je connais sa meilleure amie.**

**3** **Suggestion** Review the **imparfait** with the verb phrases listed in this activity. Ask volunteers to supply the correct verb forms for the subjects you suggest. Example: **repasser le linge: je (je repassais le linge).**

**4** **Suggestion** Have students bring photos from magazines or newspapers to supplement this activity. Or, students may prefer to sketch drawings of events.

**5** **Expansion** Ask students to imagine that they are writing an e-mail home to their family expressing what they have learned and whom they have met since starting the school year. Instruct them to use sentence constructions similar to those presented in this activity.

**6** **Suggestion** Divide the class into pairs and distribute the Info Gap Handouts found on the Supersite for this activity. Give students ten minutes to complete the activity.

---

**1** **Un grand dîner** Émilie et son mari Vincent ont invité des amis à dîner ce soir. Qu'ont-ils fait cet après-midi pour préparer la soirée? Que vont-ils faire ce soir après le départ des invités? Conversez avec un(e) partenaire. Answers will vary.

**MODÈLE**

**Élève 1:** *Cet après-midi, Émilie et Vincent ont mis la table.*

**Élève 2:** *Ce soir, ils vont faire la vaisselle.*

**2** **Mes connaissances** Votre professeur va vous donner une feuille d'activités. Interviewez vos camarades. Pour chaque activité, trouvez un(e) camarade différent(e) qui réponde affirmativement. Answers will vary.

**Élève 1:** *Connais-tu une personne qui aime faire le ménage?*

**Élève 2:** *Oui, autrefois, mon père aimait bien faire le ménage.*

| Activités | Noms |
|---|---|
| 1. ne pas souvent faire la vaisselle | |
| 2. aimer faire le ménage | Farid |
| 3. dormir avec une couverture en été | |
| 4. faire son lit tous les jours | |
| 5. rarement repasser ses vêtements | |

**3** **Qui faisait le ménage?** Par groupes de trois, interviewez vos camarades. Qui faisait le ménage à la maison quand ils étaient plus petits? Préparez des questions avec ces expressions et comparez vos réponses. Answers will vary.

| | |
|---|---|
| balayer | mettre et débarrasser la table |
| faire la lessive | passer l'aspirateur |
| faire le lit | ranger |
| faire la vaisselle | repasser le linge |

**4** **Soudain!** Tout était calme quand soudain... Avec un(e) partenaire, choisissez l'une des deux photos et écrivez un texte de dix phrases. Faites cinq phrases pour décrire la photo, et cinq autres pour raconter (*to tell*) un événement qui s'est passé soudainement (*that suddenly happened*). Employez des adverbes et soyez imaginatifs. Answers will vary.

**5** **J'ai appris...** Qu'avez-vous appris ou qui connaissez-vous depuis que (*since*) vous êtes au lycée? Avec un(e) partenaire, faites une liste de cinq choses et de cinq personnes. À chaque fois, utilisez un imparfait et un passé composé dans vos explications. Answers will vary.

**MODÈLE**

**Élève 1:** *Avant, je ne savais pas comment dire bonjour en français, et puis j'ai commencé ce cours, et maintenant, je sais le dire.*

**Élève 2:** *Avant, je ne connaissais pas tous les pays francophones, et maintenant, je les connais.*

**6** **Élise fait sa lessive** Votre professeur va vous donner, à vous et à votre partenaire, une feuille avec des dessins représentant (*representing*) Élise et sa journée d'hier. Attention! Ne regardez pas la feuille de votre partenaire. Answers will vary.

**MODÈLE**

**Élève 1:** *Hier matin, Élise avait besoin de faire sa lessive.*

**Élève 2:** *Mais, elle...*

**ressources**

| | | |
|---|---|---|
| CE pp. 107–110 | CA pp. 16–17, 65–66, 177–178 | **S** daccord1.vhcentral.com |

---

**OPTIONS**

**Assigning Verbs** Divide the class into three groups. One group is **savoir** (present tense with infinitive, **imparfait**), the second group is **connaître** (present tense, **imparfait**), and the third group is **savoir** and **connaître** (**passé composé**). Have each group brainstorm a list of phrases using their assigned verbs and tenses. A volunteer from each group should present their results to the class.

Example: Group 1 – **Je sais chanter.** (présent) **Ma mère savait parler français.** (imparfait) Group 2 – **Nous connaissons les nouveaux élèves.** (présent) **Il connaissait le président des États-Unis.** (imparfait) Group 3 – **J'ai su que l'examen de français était très difficile.** (passé composé) **Mon père a connu mon petit ami.** (passé composé)

# À l'écoute  Audio: Activities

## STRATÉGIE

### Using visual cues

Visual cues like illustrations and headings provide useful clues about what you will hear.

To practice this strategy, you will listen to a passage related to the image. Jot down the clues the image gives you as you listen. Answers will vary.

## Préparation

Qu'est-ce qu'il y a sur les trois photos à droite? À votre avis, quel va être le sujet de la conversation entre M. Duchemin et Mme Lopez?

## À vous d'écouter

Écoutez la conversation. M. Duchemin va proposer trois logements à Mme Lopez. Regardez les annonces et écrivez le numéro de référence de chaque possibilité qu'il propose.

1. Possibilité 1: Réf. 521
2. Possibilité 2: Réf. 522
3. Possibilité 3: Réf. 520

---

### À LOUER

Appartement en ville, moderne, avec balcon
1.200 €
**(Réf. 520)**

5 pièces, jardin, proche parc
Victor Hugo
950 €
**(Réf. 521)**

Maison meublée en banlieue, grande, tt confort, cuisine équipée
1.200 €
**(Réf. 522)**

## Compréhension

**Les détails** Après une deuxième écoute, complétez le tableau (*chart*) avec les informations données dans la conversation.

| | Où? | Maison ou appartement? | Meublé ou non? | Nombre de chambres? | Garage? | Jardin? |
|---|---|---|---|---|---|---|
| **Logement 1** | ville | maison | non | trois | non | oui |
| **Logement 2** | banlieue | maison | oui | quatre | oui | oui |
| **Logement 3** | centre-ville | appartement | non | deux | oui | non |

**Quel logement pour les Lopez?** Lisez cette description de la famille Lopez. Décidez quel logement cette famille va probablement choisir et expliquez votre réponse.

M. Lopez travaille au centre-ville. Le soir, il rentre tard à la maison et il est souvent fatigué parce qu'il travaille beaucoup. Il n'a pas envie de passer son temps à travailler dans le jardin. Mme Lopez adore le cinéma et le théâtre. Elle n'aime pas beaucoup faire le ménage. Les Lopez ont une fille qui a seize ans. Elle adore retrouver ses copines pour faire du shopping en ville. Les Lopez ont beaucoup de beaux meubles modernes. Ils ont aussi une nouvelle voiture: une grosse BMW qui a coûté très cher!

*deux cent quatre-vingt-un* **281**

---

### Section Goals

In this section, students will:
- use visual cues to understand an oral description
- listen to a conversation and complete several activities

### Key Standards
1.2, 2.1

**Student Resources**
Supersite: Activities, Audio
**Teacher Resources**
Answer Keys; Audio Script; Audio Activity MP3s/CD

**Stratégie**
**Script** Nous avons trouvé un appartement super dans le quartier du Marais. Il est au premier étage, dans un immeuble très calme. Il y a une salle de séjour assez grande, une cuisine avec frigo, cuisinière et lave-linge, une petite salle de bains et deux chambres très jolies. Il y a aussi des placards dans toutes les pièces et un garage en sous-sol pour notre voiture. On peut emménager la semaine prochaine et le loyer n'est pas très cher. Nous sommes vraiment heureux, tu sais!

**À vous d'écouter**
**Script** AGENT: Allô, bonjour. Madame Lopez, s'il vous plaît.
CLIENTE: C'est elle-même.
A: Ah, bonjour, Madame. Ici Monsieur Duchemin de l'agence immobilière. Vous cherchez un logement à louer à Avignon ou dans la banlieue, c'est bien ça?
C: Oui, Monsieur, c'est exact. Vous avez une maison à me proposer?
A: Oui, j'ai trois possibilités. La première est une maison en ville, dans un quartier calme près du parc Victor Hugo. Elle n'est pas très grande, mais elle est très jolie et elle a un petit jardin. Il y a un salon, une salle à manger, une grande cuisine avec beaucoup de placards, une salle de bains, les W.-C. et trois chambres.
C: Il y a un garage?
A: Non, Madame, mais il y a toujours des places dans le quartier.
C: Bon. Et qu'est-ce que vous avez d'autre?
A: J'ai aussi une très grande maison meublée avec jardin et garage en banlieue, à une demi-heure de la ville.
C: C'est un peu loin, mais bon... Il y a combien de chambres?
A: Quatre chambres.

---

C: Et qu'est-ce qu'il y a comme meubles?
A: Un canapé, des fauteuils et des étagères dans le salon, un grand lit et une commode dans la grande chambre... et voyons, quoi d'autre? Ah, oui! La cuisine est équipée avec tout le nécessaire: frigo, congélateur, cuisinière, four à micro-ondes, lave-linge et sèche-linge.
C: Très bien. Et la troisième possibilité?
A: C'est un grand appartement dans le centre-ville, sur la place des

Halles. Il n'y a pas de jardin.
C: Et combien de chambres y a-t-il?
A: Deux chambres avec des balcons. Si vous aimez le moderne, cet appartement est parfait pour vous. Et il a un garage.
C: Bon, je vais en parler avec mon mari.
A: Très bien, Madame. Au revoir.
C: Au revoir, Monsieur Duchemin.

# Panorama

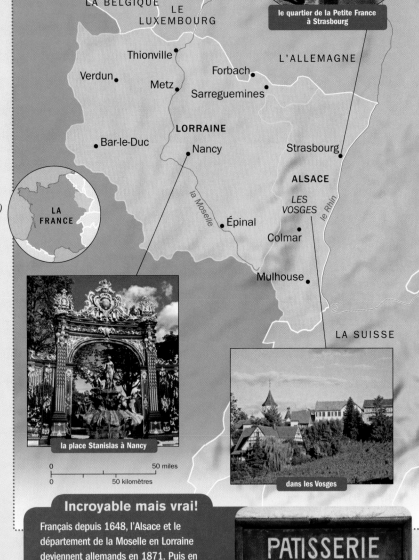

le quartier de la Petite France à Strasbourg

## L'Alsace

### La région en chiffres

▶ **Superficie:** *8.280 km²*

▶ **Population:** *1.829.000*
SOURCE: INSEE

▶ **Industries principales:** *viticulture, culture du houblon° et brassage° de la bière, exploitation forestière°, industrie automobile, tourisme*

▶ **Villes principales:** *Colmar, Mulhouse, Strasbourg*

### Personnes célèbres

▶ Gustave Doré, *dessinateur° et peintre° (1832–1883)*

▶ Auguste Bartholdi, *sculpteur, statue de la Liberté à New York, (1834–1904)*

▶  Albert Schweitzer, *médecin, prix Nobel de la paix en 1952 (1875–1965)*

## La Lorraine

### La région en chiffres

▶ **Superficie:** *23.547 km²*

▶ **Population:** *2.343.000*

▶ **Industries principales:** *industrie automobile, agroalimentaire°, bois° pour le papier, chimie et pétrochimie, métallurgie, verre et cristal*

▶ **Villes principales:** *Épinal, Forbach, Metz, Nancy*

### Personnes célèbres

▶ Georges de La Tour, *peintre (1593–1652)*

▶ Bernard-Marie Koltès, *dramaturge° (1948–1989)*

▶  Patricia Kaas, *chanteuse (1966– )*

**houblon** *hops* **brassage** *brewing* **exploitation forestière** *forestry* **dessinateur** *illustrator* **peintre** *painter* **agroalimentaire** *food processing* **bois** *wood* **dramaturge** *playwright* **traité** *treaty* **envahit** *invades* **à nouveau** *once again*

**282** *deux cent quatre-vingt-deux*

**LA BELGIQUE** **LE LUXEMBOURG**

**L'ALLEMAGNE**

Thionville

Verdun

Metz

Forbach

Sarreguemines

**LORRAINE**

Bar-le-Duc

Nancy

Strasbourg

**ALSACE**

**LA FRANCE**

*la Moselle*

Épinal

*LES VOSGES*

*le Rhin*

Colmar

Mulhouse

**LA SUISSE**

la place Stanislas à Nancy

dans les Vosges

0 — 50 miles
0 — 50 kilomètres

### Incroyable mais vrai!

Français depuis 1648, l'Alsace et le département de la Moselle en Lorraine deviennent allemands en 1871. Puis en 1919, le traité° de Versailles les rend à la France. Ensuite, en 1939, l'Allemagne envahit° la région qui redevient allemande entre 1940 et 1944. Depuis, l'Alsace et la Lorraine sont à nouveau° françaises.

**PATISSERIE**
**CAKES**
**TEE-KAFFEE**
**CHOCOLAT**

## La gastronomie

### La choucroute

La choucroute est typiquement alsacienne et son nom vient de l'allemand «sauerkraut». Du chou râpé° fermente dans un baril° avec du gros sel° et des baies de genièvre°. Puis, le chou est cuit° dans du vin blanc ou de la bière et mangé avec de la charcuterie° alsacienne et des pommes de terre°. La choucroute, qui se conserve longtemps° grâce à° la fermentation, est une nourriture appréciée° des marins° pendant leurs longs voyages.

## L'histoire

### Jeanne d'Arc

Jeanne d'Arc est née en 1412, en Lorraine, dans une famille de paysans°. En 1429, quand la France est en guerre avec l'Angleterre, Jeanne d'Arc décide de partir au combat pour libérer son pays. Elle prend la tête° d'une armée et libère la ville d'Orléans des Anglais. Cette victoire permet de sacrer° Charles VII roi de France. Plus tard, Jeanne d'Arc perd ses alliés° pour des raisons politiques. Vendue aux Anglais, elle est condamnée pour hérésie. Elle est exécutée à Rouen, en 1431. En 1920, l'Église catholique la canonise.

## Les destinations

### Strasbourg

Strasbourg, capitale de l'Alsace, est le siège° du Conseil de l'Europe depuis 1949 et du Parlement européen depuis 1979. Le Conseil de l'Europe est responsable de la promotion des valeurs démocratiques et des droits de l'homme°, de l'identité culturelle européenne et de la recherche de solutions° aux problèmes de société. Les membres du Parlement sont élus° dans chaque pays de l'Union européenne. Le Parlement contribue à l'élaboration de la législation européenne et à la gestion de l'Europe.

## La société

### Un mélange de cultures

L'Alsace a été enrichie° par de multiples courants° historiques et culturels grâce à sa position entre la France et l'Allemagne. La langue alsacienne vient d'un dialecte germanique et l'allemand est maintenant enseigné dans les écoles primaires. Quand la région est rendue à la France en 1919, les Alsaciens continuent de bénéficier des lois° sociales allemandes. Le mélange° des cultures est visible à Noël avec des traditions allemandes et françaises (le sapin de Noël, Saint Nicolas, les marchés).

 **Qu'est-ce que vous avez appris?** Répondez aux questions par des phrases complètes.

1. En 1919, quel document rend l'Alsace et la Moselle à la France?
   Le traité de Versailles les rend à la France.
2. Combien de fois l'Alsace et la Moselle ont-elles changé de nationalité depuis 1871?
   Elles ont changé quatre fois de nationalité depuis 1871.
3. Quel est l'ingrédient principal de la choucroute?
   L'ingrédient principal de la choucroute est le chou.
4. De qui la choucroute est-elle particulièrement appréciée?
   Elle est appréciée des marins.
5. Pourquoi Strasbourg est-elle importante?
   C'est le siège du Conseil de l'Europe et du Parlement européen.
6. Quel est un des rôles du Conseil de l'Europe?
   Answers will vary. Suggested answer: Il est responsable de la promotion des valeurs démocratiques.
7. Contre qui Jeanne d'Arc a-t-elle défendu la France?
   Elle a défendu la France contre les Anglais.
8. Comment est-elle morte?
   Elle a été exécutée.
9. Quelle langue étrangère enseigne-t-on aux petits Alsaciens?
   On leur enseigne l'allemand.
10. À quel moment de l'année le mélange des cultures est-il particulièrement visible en Alsace?
    Il est particulièrement visible à Noël.

 Practice more at **daccord1.vhlcentral.com.**

**ressources**

| |
|---|
| CE pp. 111–112 |

(S) daccord1.vhlcentral.com

---

### SUR INTERNET

Go to **daccord1.vhlcentral.com** to find more cultural information related to this **PANORAMA**.

1. Quelle est la différence entre le Conseil européen et le Conseil de l'Europe?
2. Trouvez d'autres informations sur Jeanne d'Arc. Quel est son surnom?
3. Pourquoi l'Alsace et le département de la Moselle sont-ils devenus allemands en 1871?

**chou râpé** grated cabbage **baril** cask **gros sel** coarse sea salt **baies de genièvre** juniper berries **cuit** cooked **charcuterie** cooked pork meats **pommes de terre** potatoes **qui se conserve longtemps** which keeps for a long time **grâce à** thanks to **appréciée** valued **marins** sailors **paysans** peasants **prend la tête** takes the lead **sacrer** crown **alliés** allies **siège** headquarters **droits de l'homme** human rights **recherche de solutions** finding solutions **élus** elected **enrichie** enriched **courants** trends, movements **lois** laws **mélange** mix

---

### La choucroute
- In other regions, **la choucroute** may be garnished with smoked beef, goose, and occasionally fish.
- Ask students: **Avez-vous déjà mangé de la choucroute? A-t-on déjà servi de la choucroute chez vous? L'aimez-vous?**

### Jeanne d'Arc
- Joan of Arc was accused of witchcraft, wantonness in cutting her hair and wearing men's clothes, and blasphemous pride. She was burned at the stake at the age of 19. In 1456, she was officially declared innocent, and later canonized for her bravery and martyrdom. Her life has been the subject of many famous literary works.
- Ask students if they think it was common for a woman to lead an army into battle in the fifteenth century.

**Strasbourg** **Le Conseil de l'Europe** is Europe's oldest political organization. It has 47 member countries. Have students research the **Conseil de l'Europe** website to find out what countries were the original members and what countries are more recent members.

**Un mélange de cultures** The traditional costumes worn by the Protestant Alsatian women have either a red or black bonnet tied with a bow. The traditional costumes of the Catholic Alsatian women have a white bonnet made of tulle bordered with flowers.

---

**O P T I O N S**

**Cultural Activity** Have students work in pairs. Tell them to make a list of examples of Germanic influences in these regions, including those shown in the photos and map. After completing their lists, ask various volunteers to give examples until all are mentioned.

**La Petite France** This picturesque part of old Strasbourg used to be the fishers', millers', and tanners' district. The half-timbered houses (**les maisons à colombages**) in the alleys, dating from the sixteenth century, have the traditional interior courtyards, sloped roofs, and open attic areas where the pelts used to dry. The covered bridges and the Vauban Barrage played critical roles in uniting Strasbourg to France in 1681.

## Section Goals

In this section, students will:
- learn to guess meaning from context
- read an article about **le château de Versailles**

## Key Standards

**1.2, 2.1, 3.2, 5.2**

**Stratégie** Tell students that they can often infer the meaning of an unfamiliar word by looking at the word's context and by using their common sense. Five types of context clues are:
- synonyms
- antonyms
- clarifications
- definitions
- additional details

Have students read this sentence from the letter: **Je cherchais un studio, mais j'ai trouvé un appartement plus grand: un deux-pièces près de mon travail!** Point out that the meaning of **un deux-pièces** can be inferred since they already know the words **deux** and **une pièce**. The explanation that follows in the note also helps to clarify the meaning.

**Examinez le texte**
- Write this sentence on the board: **La pièce la plus célèbre du château de Versailles est la galerie des Glaces.** Point out the phrase **la plus célèbre** and ask a volunteer to explain how the context might give clues to its meaning.
- Go over the answers to the activity with the class.

**Expérience personnelle**
Before beginning the activity, have students brainstorm the names of famous or historic homes they can talk about.

# Lecture (S) Reading

## Avant la lecture

### STRATÉGIE

#### Guessing meaning from context

As you read in French, you will often see words you have not learned. You can guess what they mean by looking at surrounding words. Read this note and guess what **un deux-pièces** means.

> Johanne,
> Je cherchais un studio, mais j'ai trouvé un appartement plus grand: un deux-pièces près de mon travail! Le salon est grand et la chambre a deux placards. La cuisine a un frigo et une cuisinière, et la salle de bains a une baignoire. Et le loyer? Seulement 450 euros par mois!

If you guessed *a two-room apartment*, you are correct. You can conclude that someone is describing an apartment he or she will rent.

### Examinez le texte

Regardez le texte et décrivez les photos. Quel va être le sujet de la lecture? Puis, trouvez ces mots et expressions dans le texte. Essayez de deviner leur sens (*to guess their meaning*).

| ont été rajoutées<br>*were added* | autour du<br>*around* | de haut<br>*in height* |
| de nombreux bassins<br>*numerous pools/fountains* | légumes<br>*vegetables* | roi<br>*King* |

### Expérience personnelle 👥

Avez-vous visité une résidence célèbre ou historique? Où? Quand? Comment était-ce? Un personnage historique a-t-il habité là? Qui? Parlez de cette visite à un(e) camarade.

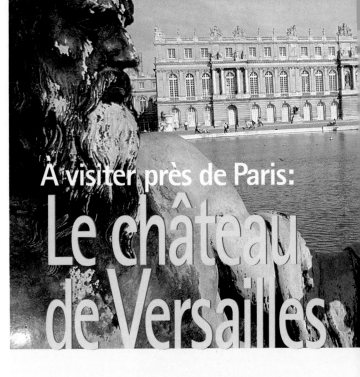

## À visiter près de Paris:
# Le château de Versailles

**La construction du célèbre° château de Versailles a commencé en 1623 sous le roi Louis XIII.** Au départ, c'était un petit château où le roi logeait° quand il allait à la chasse°. Plus tard, en 1678, Louis XIV, aussi appelé le Roi-Soleil, a décidé de faire de Versailles sa résidence principale. Il a demandé à son architecte, Louis Le Vau, d'agrandir° le château, et à son premier peintre°, Charles Le Brun, de le décorer. Le Vau a fait construire, entre autres°, le Grand Appartement du Roi. La décoration de cet appartement de sept pièces était à la gloire du Roi-Soleil. La pièce la plus célèbre du château de Versailles est la galerie des Glaces°. C'est une immense pièce de 73 mètres de long, 10,50 mètres de large et 12,30 mètres de haut°. D'un côté, 17 fenêtres donnent° sur les jardins, et de l'autre côté, il y a 17 arcades embellies de miroirs immenses. Au nord° de la galerie des Glaces, on trouve le salon de la Guerre°, et, au sud°, le salon de la Paix°. Quand on visite le château de Versailles, on peut également° voir de nombreuses autres pièces, ajoutées à différentes périodes, comme la chambre de la Reine°,

À l'intérieur du palais

---

**O P T I O N S**

**Le château de Versailles** Located in the **Île-de-France** region, **le château de Versailles** is about twelve miles from Paris. **Le château et les jardins de Versailles** are classified as a UNESCO World Heritage Site. Hundreds of masterpieces of seventeenth-century French sculpture can be viewed in the gardens, and it is estimated that seven million people visit the gardens each year.

**Using Lists** Ask students to make a list of words from the text whose meanings they guessed. Then have them work with partners and compare their lists. Students should explain to each other what clues they used in the text to help them guess the meanings. Help the class confirm the predictions, or have students confirm the meanings in a dictionary.

**Le château de Versailles et une fontaine**

plusieurs cuisines et salles à manger d'hiver et d'été, des bibliothèques, divers salons et cabinets, et plus de 18.000 m²° de galeries qui racontent° l'histoire de France en images. L'opéra, une grande salle où plus de° 700 personnes assistaient souvent à divers spectacles et bals, a aussi été ajouté plus tard. C'est dans cette salle que le futur roi Louis XVI et Marie-Antoinette ont été mariés. Partout° dans le château, on peut admirer une collection unique de meubles (lits, tables, fauteuils et chaises, bureaux, etc.) et de magnifiques tissus° (tapis, rideaux et tapisseries°). Le château de Versailles a aussi une chapelle et d'autres bâtiments, comme le Grand et le Petit Trianon. Autour du château, il y a des serres° et de magnifiques jardins avec de nombreux bassins°, fontaines et statues. Dans l'Orangerie, on trouve plus de 1.000 arbres°, et de nombreux fruits et légumes sont toujours cultivés dans le Potager° du Roi. L'Arboretum de Chèvreloup était le terrain de chasse des rois et on y° trouve aujourd'hui des arbres du monde entier°.

---

**célèbre** famous **logeait** stayed **chasse** hunting **agrandir** enlarge **peintre** painter **entre autres** among other things **Glaces** Mirrors **haut** high **donnent** open **nord** north **Guerre** War **sud** south **Paix** Peace **également** also **Reine** Queen **m²** (mètres carrés) square meters **racontent** tell **plus de** more than **Partout** Everywhere **tissus** fabrics **tapisseries** tapestries **serres** greenhouses **bassins** ponds **arbres** trees **Potager** vegetable garden **y** there **entier** entire

## Après la lecture

**Vrai ou faux?** Indiquez si les phrases sont **vraies** ou **fausses**. Corrigez les phrases fausses.

1. Louis XIII habitait à Versailles toute l'année.
   Faux. Louis XIII logeait à Versailles quand il allait à la chasse.

2. Louis Le Vau est appelé le Roi-Soleil.
   Faux. Louis XIV est appelé le Roi-Soleil.

3. La galerie des Glaces est une grande pièce avec beaucoup de miroirs et de fenêtres.
   Vrai.

4. Il y a deux salons près de la galerie des Glaces.
   Vrai.

5. Aujourd'hui, au château de Versailles, il n'y a pas de meubles.
   Faux. Il y a une collection unique de meubles (lits, tables, fauteuils et chaises, bureaux, etc.).

6. Le château de Versailles n'a pas de jardins parce qu'il a été construit en ville.
   Faux. Il a des jardins: l'Orangerie, le Potager et l'Arboretum de Chèvreloup.

**Répondez** Répondez aux questions par des phrases complètes.

1. Comment était Versailles sous Louis XIII? Quand logeait-il là?
   C'était un petit château où le roi logeait quand il allait à la chasse.

2. Qu'est-ce que Louis XIV a fait du château?
   Il a fait de Versailles sa résidence principale. Il l'a agrandi et l'a décoré.

3. Qu'est-ce que Louis Le Vau a fait à Versailles?
   Il a construit, entre autres, le Grand Appartement du Roi.

4. Dans quelle salle Louis XVI et Marie-Antoinette ont-ils été mariés? Comment est cette salle?
   Ils ont été mariés dans l'Opéra. C'est une grande salle où plus de 700 personnes assistaient souvent à divers spectacles et bals.

5. Louis XVI est-il devenu roi avant ou après son mariage?
   Il est devenu roi après son mariage.

6. Le château de Versailles est-il composé d'un seul bâtiment? Expliquez.
   Non, le château a aussi une chapelle et d'autres bâtiments comme le Grand et le Petit Trianon.

### Les personnages célèbres de Versailles 👤👤👤

Par groupes de trois ou quatre, choisissez une des personnes mentionnées dans la lecture et faites des recherches (*research*) à son sujet. Préparez un rapport écrit (*written report*) à présenter à la classe. Vous pouvez (*may*) utiliser les ressources de votre bibliothèque ou Internet.

*deux cent quatre-vingt-cinq* **285**

# Écriture

## STRATÉGIE

### Mastering the past tenses

In French, when you write about events that occurred in the past, you need to know when to use the **passé composé** and when to use the **imparfait**. A good understanding of the uses of each tense will make it much easier to determine which one to use as you write.

Look at the following summary of the uses of the **passé composé** and the **imparfait**. Write your own example sentence for each of the rules described.

### Passé composé vs. imparfait

### Passé composé

1. Actions viewed as completed

   _____

2. Beginning or end of past actions

   _____

3. Series of past actions

   _____

### Imparfait

1. Ongoing past actions

   _____

2. Habitual past actions

   _____

3. Mental, physical, and emotional states and characteristics of the past

   _____

With a partner, compare your example sentences. Use the sentences as a guide to help you decide which tense to use as you are writing a story about something that happened in the past.

## Thème

## Écrire une histoire

### Avant l'écriture

1. Quand vous étiez petit(e), vous habitiez dans la maison ou l'appartement de vos rêves (*of your dreams*).

   - Vous allez décrire cette maison ou cet appartement.

   - Vous allez écrire sur la ville où vous habitiez et sur votre quartier.

   - Vous allez décrire les différentes pièces, les meubles et les objets décoratifs.

   - Vous allez parler de votre pièce préférée et de ce que (*what*) vous aimiez faire dans cette pièce.

   Ensuite, imaginez qu'il y ait eu (*was*) un cambriolage (*burglary*) dans cette maison ou dans cet appartement. Vous allez alors décrire ce qui est arrivé (*what happened*).

### Coup de main

Here are some terms that you may find useful in your narration.

| | |
|---|---|
| le voleur | *thief* |
| cassé(e) | *broken* |
| j'ai vu | *I saw* |
| manquer | *to be missing* |

**2.** Utilisez le diagramme pour vous aider à analyser les éléments de votre histoire. Écrivez les éléments qui se rapportent à (*that are related to*) l'imparfait dans la partie IMPARFAIT et ceux (*the ones*) qui se rapportent au passé composé dans les parties PASSÉ COMPOSÉ.

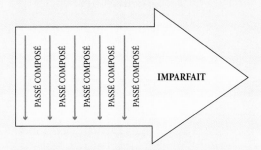

**3.** Après avoir complété le diagramme, échangez-le avec celui d'un(e) partenaire. Votre partenaire doit-il (*does he/she have to*) changer quelque chose? Expliquez pourquoi.

## Écriture

Utilisez le diagramme pour écrire votre histoire. Écrivez trois paragraphes:

- le premier sur la présentation générale de la maison ou de l'appartement et de la ville où vous habitiez,

- le deuxième sur votre pièce préférée et la raison pour laquelle (*the reason why*) vous l'avez choisie,

- le troisième sur le cambriolage, sur ce qui s'est passé (*what happened*) et sur ce que vous avez fait (*what you did*).

> *Quand j'étais petit(e), j'habitais dans un château, en France. Le château était dans une petite ville près de Paris. Il y avait un grand jardin, avec beaucoup d'animaux. Il y avait douze pièces...*
>
> *Ma pièce préférée était la cuisine parce que j'aimais faire la cuisine et que j'aidais souvent ma mère...*
>
> *Un jour, mes parents et moi sommes rentrés de vacances...*

## Après l'écriture

**1.** Échangez votre histoire avec celle (*the one*) d'un(e) partenaire. Répondez à ces questions pour commenter son travail.

- Votre partenaire a-t-il/elle correctement utilisé l'imparfait et le passé composé?

- A-t-il/elle écrit trois paragraphes qui correspondent aux descriptions de sa maison ou de son appartement et de la ville, de sa pièce préférée et du cambriolage?

- Quel(s) détail(s) ajouteriez-vous (*would you add*)? Lequel/Lesquels enlèveriez-vous (*Which one(s) would you delete*)? Quel(s) autre(s) commentaire(s) avez-vous pour votre partenaire?

**2.** Corrigez votre histoire d'après (*according to*) les commentaires de votre partenaire. Relisez votre travail pour éliminer ces problèmes:

- des fautes (*errors*) d'orthographe

- des fautes de ponctuation

- des fautes de conjugaison

- des fautes d'accord (*agreement*) des adjectifs

- un mauvais emploi (*use*) de la grammaire

**Criteria**

**Content** Contains a complete description of a house or apartment, its furnishings, and the place where it was located, followed by a complete past-tense narration about a robbery that took place there.
Scale: 1 2 3 4 5

**Organization** Contains two parts: a complete past-tense description of a place that uses **imparfait** forms followed by a past-tense narration using the **passé composé**.
Scale: 1 2 3 4 5

**Accuracy** Uses **passé composé** and **imparfait** forms correctly and in the correct context. Spells words, conjugates verbs, and modifies adjectives correctly throughout.
Scale: 1 2 3 4 5

**Creativity** Includes additional information that is not included in the task and/or uses adjectives and descriptive verbs to make the scene more vivid.
Scale: 1 2 3 4 5

**Scoring**

| | |
|---|---|
| Excellent | 18–20 points |
| Good | 14–17 points |
| Satisfactory | 10–13 points |
| Unsatisfactory | < 10 points |

**OPTIONS**

**Écriture** Supply students with some useful expressions to use for their compositions. 1. Ongoing past-tense description: **toujours, tous les jours, d'habitude, normalement, en général/ généralement, chaque fois, de temps en temps** 2. Completed past actions: **tout à coup, tous ensemble, dans un moment, à ce moment-là, puis, ensuite, après, plus tard, enfin, finalement**

**Après l'écriture** When students have completed their stories, have them work in pairs or small groups to create a dramatic reenactment of the story. They can use voiceover narration for the descriptive part, then act out the completed actions that are part of the robbery and its aftermath. Encourage students to be creative and to use props and posters to set the stage and tell the story.

## Key Standards
4.1

**Suggestion** Tell students that an easy way to study from **Vocabulaire** is to cover up the French half of each section, leaving only the English equivalents exposed. They can then quiz themselves on the French items. To focus on the English equivalents of the French entries, they simply reverse this process.

### Les parties d'une maison

| | |
|---|---|
| un balcon | balcony |
| une cave | cellar; basement |
| une chambre | bedroom |
| un couloir | hallway |
| une cuisine | kitchen |
| un escalier | staircase |
| un garage | garage |
| un jardin | garden; yard |
| un mur | wall |
| une pièce | room |
| une salle à manger | dining room |
| une salle de bains | bathroom |
| une salle de séjour | living/family room |
| un salon | formal living/ sitting room |
| un sous-sol | basement |
| un studio | studio (apartment) |
| les toilettes (f.)/ les W.-C. (m.) | restrooms/toilet |

### Les appareils ménagers

| | |
|---|---|
| un appareil électrique/ménager | electrical/household appliance |
| une cafetière | coffeemaker |
| un congélateur | freezer |
| une cuisinière | stove |
| un fer à repasser | iron |
| un four | oven |
| un (four à) micro-ondes | microwave oven |
| un frigo | refrigerator |
| un grille-pain | toaster |
| un lave-linge | washing machine |
| un lave-vaisselle | dishwasher |
| un sèche-linge | clothes dryer |

### Chez soi

| | |
|---|---|
| un(e) propriétaire | owner |
| un appartement | apartment |
| un immeuble | building |
| un logement | housing |
| un loyer | rent |
| un quartier | area, neighborhood |
| une résidence universitaire | dorm |
| une affiche | poster |
| une armoire | armoire, wardrobe |
| une baignoire | bathtub |
| un balai | broom |
| un canapé | couch |
| une commode | dresser, chest of drawers |
| une couverture | blanket |
| une douche | shower |
| les draps (m.) | sheets |
| une étagère | shelf |
| un évier | kitchen sink |
| un fauteuil | armchair |
| une fleur | flower |
| une lampe | lamp |
| un lavabo | bathroom sink |
| un meuble | piece of furniture |
| un miroir | mirror |
| un oreiller | pillow |
| un placard | closet, cupboard |
| un rideau | drape, curtain |
| un tapis | rug |
| un tiroir | drawer |
| déménager | to move out |
| emménager | to move in |
| louer | to rent |

### Les tâches ménagères

| | |
|---|---|
| une tâche ménagère | household chore |
| balayer | to sweep |
| débarrasser la table | to clear the table |
| enlever/faire la poussière | to dust |
| essuyer la vaisselle/ la table | to dry the dishes/ to wipe the table |
| faire la lessive | to do the laundry |
| faire le lit | to make the bed |
| faire le ménage | to do the housework |
| faire la vaisselle | to do the dishes |
| laver | to wash |
| mettre la table | to set the table |
| passer l'aspirateur | to vacuum |
| ranger | to tidy up; to put away |
| repasser (le linge) | to iron (the laundry) |
| salir | to soil, to make dirty |
| sortir la/les poubelle(s) | to take out the trash |
| propre | clean |
| sale | dirty |

### Verbes

| | |
|---|---|
| connaître | to know, to be familiar with |
| reconnaître | to recognize |
| savoir | to know (facts), to know how to do something |
| vivre | to live |

| | |
|---|---|
| *Expressions utiles* | See pp. 259 and 273. |
| Expressions that signal a past tense | See p. 265. |

# The *impératif*

**Point de départ** The **impératif** is the form of a verb that is used to give commands or to offer directions, hints, and suggestions. With command forms, you do not use subject pronouns.

- Form the **tu** command of -**er** verbs by dropping the -**s** from the present tense form. Note that **aller** also follows this pattern.

  | **Réserve** deux chambres. | **Ne travaille pas.** | **Va** au marché. |
  |---|---|---|
  | *Reserve two rooms.* | *Don't work.* | *Go to the market.* |

- The **nous** and **vous** command forms of -**er** verbs are the same as the present tense forms.

  | **Nettoyez** votre chambre. | **Mangeons** au restaurant ce soir. |
  |---|---|
  | *Clean your room.* | *Let's eat at the restaurant tonight.* |

- For -**ir** verbs, -**re** verbs, and most irregular verbs, the command forms are identical to the present tense forms.

  | **Finis** la salade. | **Attendez** dix minutes. | **Faisons** du yoga. |
  |---|---|---|
  | *Finish the salad.* | *Wait ten minutes.* | *Let's do some yoga.* |

### The *impératif* of *avoir* and *être*

|  | avoir | être |
|---|---|---|
| (tu) | aie | sois |
| (nous) | ayons | soyons |
| (vous) | ayez | soyez |

- The forms of **avoir** and **être** in the **impératif** are irregular.

  | **Aie** confiance. | Ne **soyons** pas en retard. |
  |---|---|
  | *Have confidence.* | *Let's not be late.* |

- An object pronoun can be added to the end of an affirmative command. Use a hyphen to separate them. Use **moi** and **toi** for the first- and second-person object pronouns.

  | **Permettez-moi** de vous aider. | Achète le dictionnaire et **utilise-le**. |
  |---|---|
  | *Allow me to help you.* | *Buy the dictionary and use it.* |

- In negative commands, place object pronouns between **ne** and the verb. Use **me** and **te** for the first- and second-person object pronouns.

  | Ne **me montre** pas les réponses, **s'il te plaît.** | Cette photo est fragile. Ne **la touchez** pas. |
  |---|---|
  | *Please don't show me the answers.* | *That picture is fragile. Don't touch it.* |

# Glossary of Grammatical Terms

**ADJECTIVE** A word that modifies, or describes, a noun or pronoun.

| des livres **amusants** | une **jolie** fleur |
|---|---|
| *some **funny** books* | *a **pretty** flower* |

**Demonstrative adjective** An adjective that specifies which noun a speaker is referring to.

| **cette** chemise | **ce** placard |
|---|---|
| *this shirt* | *this closet* |
| **cet** hôtel | **ces** boîtes |
| *this hotel* | *these boxes.* |

**Possessive adjective** An adjective that indicates ownership or possession.

| **ma** belle montre | C'est **son** cousin. |
|---|---|
| *my beautiful watch* | *This is **his/her** cousin.* |
| **tes** crayons | Ce sont **leurs** tantes. |
| *your pencils* | *Those are **their** aunts.* |

**ADVERB** A word that modifies, or describes, a verb, adjective, or other adverb.

Michael parle **couramment** français.
*Michael speaks French **fluently**.*

Elle lui parle **très** franchement.
*She speaks to him **very** candidly.*

**ARTICLE** A word that points out a noun in either a specific or a non-specific way.

**Definite article** An article that points out a noun in a specific way.

| **le** marché | **la** valise |
|---|---|
| *the market* | *the suitcase* |
| **les** dictionnaires | **les** mots |
| *the dictionaries* | *the words* |

**Indefinite article** An article that points out a noun in a general, non-specific way.

| **un** vélo | **une** fille |
|---|---|
| *a bike* | *a girl* |
| **des** oiseaux | **des** affiches |
| *some birds* | *some posters* |

**CLAUSE** A group of words that contains both a conjugated verb and a subject, either expressed or implied.

**Main (or Independent) clause** A clause that can stand alone as a complete sentence.

**J'ai un manteau vert.**
*I have a green coat.*

**Subordinate (or Dependent) clause** A clause that does not express a complete thought and therefore cannot stand alone as a sentence.

Je travaille dans un restaurant **parce que j'ai besoin d'argent**.
*I work in a restaurant **because I need money.***

**COMPARATIVE** A construction used with an adjective or adverb to express a comparison between two people, places, or things.

Thomas est **plus petit** qu'Adrien.
*Thomas is **shorter than** Adrien.*

En Corse, il pleut **moins souvent qu'**en Alsace.
*In Corsica, it rains **less often than** in Alsace.*

Cette maison n'a pas **autant de fenêtres** que l'autre.
*This house does not have **as many windows as** the other one.*

**CONJUGATION** A set of the forms of a verb for a specific tense or mood, or the process by which these verb forms are presented.

**Imparfait** conjugation of **chanter**:
| | |
|---|---|
| je chant**ais** | nous chant**ions** |
| tu chant**ais** | vous chant**iez** |
| il/elle chant**ait** | ils/elles chant**aient** |

**CONJUNCTION** A word used to connect words, clauses, or phrases.

Suzanne **et** Pierre habitent en Suisse.
*Suzanne **and** Pierre live in Switzerland.*

Je ne dessine pas très bien, **mais** j'aime les cours de dessin.
*I don't draw very well, **but** I like art classes.*

**CONTRACTION** The joining of two words into one. In French, the contractions are **au**, **aux**, **du**, and **des**.

Ma sœur est allée **au** concert hier soir.
*My sister went **to a** concert last night.*

Il a parlé **aux** voisins cet après-midi.
*He talked **to the** neighbors this afternoon.*

Je retire de l'argent **du** distributeur automatique.
*I withdraw money **from the** ATM machine.*

Nous avons campé près **du** village.
*We camped **near the** village.*

**DIRECT OBJECT** A noun or pronoun that directly receives the action of the verb.

| | |
|---|---|
| Thomas lit **un livre**. | Je **l'**ai vu hier. |
| *Thomas reads **a book**.* | *I saw **him** yesterday.* |

**GENDER** The grammatical categorizing of certain kinds of words, such as nouns and pronouns, as masculine, feminine, or neuter.

**Masculine**
*articles* **le, un**
*pronouns* **il, lui, le, celui-ci, celui-là, lequel**
*adjective* **élégant**

**Feminine**
*articles* **la, une**
*pronouns* **elle, la, celle-ci, celle-là, laquelle**
*adjective* **élégante**

**IMPERSONAL EXPRESSION** A third-person expression with no expressed or specific subject.

| | |
|---|---|
| **Il** pleut. | **C'est** très important. |
| *It's raining.* | *It's very important.* |

**INDIRECT OBJECT** A noun or pronoun that receives the action of the verb indirectly; the object, often a living being, to or for whom an action is performed.

Éric donne un livre **à Linda**.
*Éric gave a book **to Linda**.*

Le professeur **m'**a donné une bonne note.
*The teacher gave **me** a good mark.*

**INFINITIVE** The basic form of a verb. Infinitives in French end in **-er**, **-ir**, **-oir**, or **-re**.

| **parler** | **finir** | **savoir** | **prendre** |
|---|---|---|---|
| *to speak* | *to finish* | *to know* | *to take* |

**INTERROGATIVE** An adjective or pronoun used to ask a question.

**Qui** parle?
***Who** is speaking?*

**Combien** de biscuits as-tu achetés?
***How many** cookies did you buy?*

**Que** penses-tu faire aujourd'hui?
***What** do you plan to do today?*

**INVERSION** Changing the word order of a sentence, often to form a question.

*Statement:* Elle a vendu sa voiture.

*Inversion:* A-t-elle vendu sa voiture?

**MOOD** A grammatical distinction of verbs that indicates whether the verb is intended to make a statement or command or to express a doubt, emotion, or condition contrary to fact.

**Conditional mood** Verb forms used to express what would be done or what would happen under certain circumstances, or to make a polite request, soften a demand, express what someone could or should do, or to state a contrary-to-fact situation.

**Il irait** se promener s'il avait le temps.
*He would go for a walk if he had the time.*

**Pourrais-tu** éteindre la lumière, s'il te plaît?
*Would you turn off the light, please?*

**Je devrais** lui parler gentiment.
*I should talk to her nicely.*

**Imperative mood** Verb forms used to make commands or suggestions.

**Parle** lentement.       **Venez** avec moi.
*Speak slowly.*            *Come with me.*

**Indicative mood** Verb forms used to state facts, actions, and states considered to be real.

**Je sais** qu'**il a** un chat.
*I know that he has a cat.*

**Subjunctive mood** Verb forms used principally in subordinate (dependent) clauses to express wishes, desires, emotions, doubts, and certain conditions, such as contrary-to-fact situations.

Il est important que **tu finisses** tes devoirs.
*It's important that **you finish** your homework.*

Je doute que **Louis ait** assez d'argent.
*I doubt that **Louis has** enough money.*

**NOUN** A word that identifies people, animals, places, things, and ideas.

| | | |
|---|---|---|
| **homme** | **chat** | **Belgique** |
| *man* | *cat* | *Belgium* |
| **maison** | **livre** | **amitié** |
| *house* | *book* | *friendship* |

**NUMBER** A grammatical term that refers to singular or plural. Nouns in French and English have number. Other parts of a sentence, such as adjectives, articles, and verbs, can also have number.

| Singular | Plural |
|---|---|
| **une** chose | **des** choses |
| *a thing* | *some things* |
| **le** professeur | **les** professeurs |
| *the professor* | *the professors* |

**NUMBERS** Words that represent amounts.

**Cardinal numbers** Words that show specific amounts.

| | |
|---|---|
| **cinq** minutes | l'année **deux mille six** |
| *five minutes* | *the year **2006*** |

**Ordinal numbers** Words that indicate the order of a noun in a series.

| | |
|---|---|
| le **quatrième** joueur | la **dixième** fois |
| *the **fourth** player* | *the **tenth** time* |

**PAST PARTICIPLE** A past form of the verb used in compound tenses. The past participle may also be used as an adjective, but it must then agree in number and gender with the word it modifies.

Ils ont beaucoup **marché**.
*They have **walked** a lot.*

Je n'ai pas **préparé** mon examen.
*I haven't **prepared** for my exam.*

Il y a une fenêtre **ouverte** dans le salon.
*There is an **open** window in the living room.*

**PERSON** The form of the verb or pronoun that indicates the speaker, the one spoken to, or the one spoken about. In French, as in English, there are three persons: first, second, and third.

| Person | Singular | | Plural | |
|---|---|---|---|---|
| 1st | **je** | *I* | **nous** | *we* |
| 2nd | **tu** | *you* | **vous** | *you* |
| 3rd | **il/elle** | *he/she/it* | **ils/elles** | *they* |
| | **on** | *one* | | |

**PREPOSITION** A word or words that describe(s) the relationship, most often in time or space, between two other words.

Annie habite **loin de** Paris.
*Annie lives **far from** Paris.*

Le blouson est **dans** la voiture.
*The jacket is **in** the car.*

Martine s'est coiffée **avant de** sortir.
*Martine combed her hair **before** going out.*

**PRONOUN** A word that takes the place of a noun or nouns.

**Demonstrative pronoun** A pronoun that takes the place of a specific noun.

Je veux **celui-ci**.
*I want **this one**.*

Marc préférait **ceux-là**.
*Marc preferred **those**.*

**Object pronoun** A pronoun that functions as a direct or indirect object of the verb.

Elle **lui** donne un cadeau.  Frédéric **me l'**a apporté.
*She gives **him** a present.*  *Frédéric brought **it** to me.*

**Reflexive pronoun** A pronoun that indicates that the action of a verb is performed by the subject on itself. These pronouns are often expressed in English with -*self*: *myself, yourself,* etc.

Je **me lave** avant de sortir.
*I **wash (myself)** before going out.*

Marie **s'est couchée** à onze heures et demie.
*Marie **went to bed** at eleven-thirty.*

**Relative pronoun** A pronoun that connects a subordinate clause to a main clause.

Le garçon **qui** nous a écrit vient nous voir demain.
*The boy **who** wrote us is coming to visit tomorrow.*

Je sais **que** nous avons beaucoup de choses à faire.
*I know **that** we have a lot of things to do.*

**Subject pronoun** A pronoun that replaces the name or title of a person or thing, and acts as the subject of a verb.

**Tu** vas partir.  **Il** arrive demain.
***You** are going to leave.*  ***He** arrives tomorrow.*

**SUBJECT** A noun or pronoun that performs the action of a verb and is often implied by the verb.

**Marine** va au supermarché.
***Marine** goes to the supermarket.*

**Ils** travaillent beaucoup.
***They** work a lot.*

**Ces livres** sont très chers.
***Those books** are very expensive.*

**SUPERLATIVE** A word or construction used with an adjective, adverb or a noun to express the highest or lowest degree of a specific quality among three or more people, places, or things.

Le cours de français est **le plus intéressant**.
*The French class is **the most interesting**.*

Romain court **le moins rapidement**.
*Romain runs **the least fast**.*

C'est son jardin qui a **le plus d'arbres**.
*It is her garden that has **the most trees**.*

**TENSE** A set of verb forms that indicates the time of an action or state: past, present, or future

**Compound tense** A two-word tense made up of an auxiliary verb and a present or past participle. In French, there are two auxiliary verbs: **être** and **avoir**.

Le colis n'**est** pas encore **arrivé**.
*The package **has** not **arrived** yet.*

Elle **a réussi** son examen.
*She **has passed** her exam.*

**Simple tense** A tense expressed by a single verb form.

Timothée **jouait** au volley-ball pendant les vacances.
*Timothée **played** volleyball during his vacation.*

Joëlle **parlera** à sa mère demain.
*Joëlle **will speak** with her mom tomorrow.*

**VERB** A word that expresses actions or states-of-being.

**Auxiliary verb** A verb used with a present or past participle to form a compound tense. **Avoir** is the most commonly used auxiliary verb in French.

Ils **ont** vu les éléphants.
*They **have** seen the elephants.*

J'espère que tu **as** mangé.
*I hope you **have** eaten.*

**Reflexive verb** A verb that describes an action performed by the subject on itself and is always used with a reflexive pronoun.

Je **me suis acheté** une voiture neuve.
*I **bought myself** a new car.*

Pierre et Adeline **se lèvent** très tôt.
*Pierre and Adeline **get (themselves) up** very early.*

**Spelling-change verb** A verb that undergoes a predictable change in spelling in the various conjugations.

| **acheter** | e → è | nous achetons | j'achète |
| **espérer** | é → è | nous espérons | j'espère |
| **appeler** | l → ll | nous appelons | j'appelle |
| **envoyer** | y → i | nous envoyons | j'envoie |
| **essayer** | y → i | nous essayons | j'essaie/ j'essaye |

# Verb Conjugation Tables

Each verb in this list is followed by a model verb conjugated according to the same pattern. The number in parentheses indicates where in the verb tables you can find the conjugated forms of the model verb. Reminder: All reflexive (pronominal) verbs use **être** as their auxiliary verb in the **passé composé**. The infinitives of reflexive verbs begin with **se (s')**.

\* = This verb, unlike its model, takes **être** in the **passé composé**.

† = This verb, unlike its model, takes **avoir** in the **passé composé**.

In the tables you will find the infinitive, past participles, and all the forms of each model verb you have learned.

**abolir** like finir (2)
**aborder** like parler (1)
**abriter** like parler (1)
**accepter** like parler (1)
**accompagner** like parler (1)
**accueillir** like ouvrir (31)
**acheter** (7)
**adorer** like parler (1)
**afficher** like parler (1)
**aider** like parler (1)
**aimer** like parler (1)
**aller** (13) **p.c.** with **être**
**allumer** like parler (1)
**améliorer** like parler (1)
**amener** like acheter (7)
**animer** like parler (1)
**apercevoir** like recevoir (36)
**appeler** (8)
**applaudir** like finir (2)
**apporter** like parler (1)
**apprendre** like prendre (35)
**arrêter** like parler (1)
**arriver\*** like parler (1)
**assister** like parler (1)
**attacher** like parler (1)
**attendre** like vendre (3)
**attirer** like parler (1)
**avoir** (4)
**balayer** like essayer (10)
**bavarder** like parler (1)
**boire** (15)
**bricoler** like parler (1)
**bronzer** like parler (1)
**célébrer** like préférer (12)
**chanter** like parler (1)
**chasser** like parler (1)

**chercher** like parler (1)
**choisir** like finir (2)
**classer** like parler (1)
**commander** like parler (1)
**commencer** (9)
**composer** like parler (1)
**comprendre** like prendre (35)
**compter** like parler (1)
**conduire** (16)
**connaître** (17)
**consacrer** like parler (1)
**considérer** like préférer (12)
**construire** like conduire (16)
**continuer** like parler (1)
**courir** (18)
**coûter** like parler (1)
**couvrir** like ouvrir (31)
**croire** (19)
**cuisiner** like parler (1)
**danser** like parler (1)
**débarrasser** like parler (1)
**décider** like parler (1)
**découvrir** like ouvrir (31)
**décrire** like écrire (22)
**décrocher** like parler (1)
**déjeuner** like parler (1)
**demander** like parler (1)
**démarrer** like parler (1)
**déménager** like manger (11)
**démissionner** like parler (1)
**dépasser** like parler (1)
**dépendre** like vendre (3)
**dépenser** like parler (1)
**déposer** like parler (1)
**descendre\*** like vendre (3)
**désirer** like parler (1)

**dessiner** like parler (1)
**détester** like parler (1)
**détruire** like conduire (16)
**développer** like parler (1)
**devenir** like venir (41)
**devoir** (20)
**dîner** like parler (1)
**dire** (21)
**diriger** like parler (1)
**discuter** like parler (1)
**divorcer** like commencer (9)
**donner** like parler (1)
**dormir†** like partir (32)
**douter** like parler (1)
**durer** like parler (1)
**échapper** like parler (1)
**échouer** like parler (1)
**écouter** like parler (1)
**écrire** (22)
**effacer** like commencer (9)
**embaucher** like parler (1)
**emménager** like manger (11)
**emmener** like acheter (7)
**employer** like essayer (10)
**emprunter** like parler (1)
**enfermer** like parler (1)
**enlever** like acheter (7)
**enregistrer** like parler (1)
**enseigner** like parler (1)
**entendre** like vendre (3)
**entourer** like parler (1)
**entrer\*** like parler (1)
**entretenir** like tenir (40)
**envahir** like finir (2)
**envoyer** like essayer (10)
**épouser** like parler (1)

**espérer** like préférer (12)
**essayer** (10)
**essuyer** like essayer (10)
**éteindre** (24)
**éternuer** like parler (1)
**étrangler** like parler (1)
**être** (5)
**étudier** like parler (1)
**éviter** like parler (1)
**exiger** like manger (11)
**expliquer** like parler (1)
**explorer** like parler (1)
**faire** (25)
**falloir** (26)
**fermer** like parler (1)
**fêter** like parler (1)
**finir** (2)
**fonctionner** like parler (1)
**fonder** like parler (1)
**freiner** like parler (1)
**fréquenter** like parler (1)
**fumer** like parler (1)
**gagner** like parler (1)
**garder** like parler (1)
**garer** like parler (1)
**gaspiller** like parler (1)
**enfler** like parler (1)
**goûter** like parler (1)
**graver** like parler (1)
**grossir** like finir (2)
**guérir** like finir (2)
**habiter** like parler (1)
**imprimer** like parler (1)
**indiquer** like parler (1)
**interdire** like dire (21)
**inviter** like parler (1)

**jeter** like appeler (8)

**jouer** like parler (1)

**laisser** like parler (1)

**laver** like parler (1)

**lire** (27)

**loger** like manger (11)

**louer** like parler (1)

**lutter** like parler (1)

**maigrir** like finir (2)

**maintenir** like tenir (40)

**manger** (11)

**marcher** like parler (1)

**mêler** like préférer (12)

**mener** like parler (1)

**mettre** (28)

**monter*** like parler (1)

**montrer** like parler (1)

**mourir** (29); **p.c.** with **être**

**nager** like manger (11)

**naître** (30); **p.c.** with **être**

**nettoyer** like essayer (10)

**noter** like parler (1)

**obtenir** like tenir (40)

**offrir** like ouvrir (31)

**organiser** like parler (1)

**oublier** like parler (1)

**ouvrir** (31)

**parler** (1)

**partager** like manger (11)

**partir** (32); **p.c.** with **être**

**passer** like parler (1)

**patienter** like parler (1)

**patiner** like parler (1)

**payer** like essayer (10)

**penser** like parler (1)

**perdre** like vendre (3)

**permettre** like mettre (28)

**pleuvoir** (33)

**plonger** like manger (11)

**polluer** like parler (1)

**porter** like parler (1)

**poser** like parler (1)

**posséder** like préférer (12)

**poster** like parler (1)

**pouvoir** (34)

**pratiquer** like parler (1)

**préférer** (12)

**prélever** like parler (1)

**prendre** (35)

**préparer** like parler (1)

**présenter** like parler (1)

**préserver** like parler (1)

**prêter** like parler (1)

**prévenir** like tenir (40)

**produire** like conduire (16)

**profiter** like parler (1)

**promettre** like mettre (28)

**proposer** like parler (1)

**protéger** like préférer (12)

**provenir** like venir (41)

**publier** like parler (1)

**quitter** like parler (1)

**raccrocher** like parler (1)

**ranger** like manger (11)

**réaliser** like parler (1)

**recevoir** (36)

**recommander** like parler (1)

**reconnaître** like connaître (17)

**recycler** like parler (1)

**réduire** like conduire (16)

**réfléchir** like finir (2)

**regarder** like parler (1)

**régner** like préférer (12)

**remplacer** like parler (1)

**remplir** like finir (2)

**rencontrer** like parler (1)

**rendre** like vendre (3)

**rentrer*** like parler (1)

**renvoyer** like essayer (10)

**réparer** like parler (1)

**repasser** like parler (1)

**répéter** like préférer (12)

**repeupler** like parler (1)

**répondre** like vendre (3)

**réserver** like parler (1)

**rester*** like parler (1)

**retenir** like tenir (40)

**retirer** like parler (1)

**retourner*** like parler (1)

**retrouver** like parler (1)

**réussir** like finir (2)

**revenir** like venir (41)

**revoir** like voir (42)

**rire** (37)

**rouler** like parler (1)

**salir** like finir (2)

**s'amuser** like se laver (6)

**s'asseoir** (14)

**sauvegarder** like parler (1)

**sauver** like parler (1)

**savoir** (38)

**se brosser** like se laver (6)

**se coiffer** like se laver (6)

**se composer** like se laver (6)

**se connecter** like se laver (6)

**se coucher** like se laver (6)

**se croiser** like se laver (6)

**se dépêcher** like se laver (6)

**se déplacer*** like commencer (9)

**se déshabiller** like se laver (6)

**se détendre*** like vendre (3)

**se disputer** like se laver (6)

**s'embrasser** like se laver (6)

**s'endormir** like partir (32)

**s'énerver** like se laver (6)

**s'ennuyer*** like essayer (10)

**s'excuser** like se laver (6)

**se fouler** like se laver (6)

**s'installer** like se laver (6)

**se laver** (6)

**se lever*** like acheter (7)

**se maquiller** like se laver (6)

**se marier** like se laver (6)

**se promener*** like acheter (7)

**se rappeler*** like appeler (8)

**se raser** like se laver (6)

**se rebeller** like se laver (6)

**se réconcilier** like se laver (6)

**se relever*** like acheter (7)

**se reposer** like se laver (6)

**se réveiller** like se laver (6)

**servir†** like partir (32)

**se sécher*** like préférer (12)

**se souvenir** like venir (41)

**se tromper** like se laver (6)

**s'habiller** like se laver (6)

**sentir†** like partir (32)

**signer** like parler (1)

**s'inquiéter*** like préférer (12)

**s'intéresser** like se laver (6)

**skier** like parler (1)

**s'occuper** like se laver (6)

**sonner** like parler (1)

**s'orienter** like se laver (6)

**sortir** like partir (32)

**sourire** like rire (37)

**souffrir** like ouvrir (31)

**souhaiter** like parler (1)

**subvenir†** like venir (41)

**suffire** like lire (27)

**suggérer** like préférer (12)

**suivre** (39)

**surfer** like parler (1)

**surprendre** like prendre (35)

**télécharger** like parler (1)

**téléphoner** like parler (1)

**tenir** (40)

**tomber*** like parler (1)

**tourner** like parler (1)

**tousser** like parler (1)

**traduire** like conduire (16)

**travailler** like parler (1)

**traverser** like parler (1)

**trouver** like parler (1)

**tuer** like parler (1)

**utiliser** like parler (1)

**valoir** like falloir (26)

**vendre** (3)

**venir** (41); **p.c.** with **être**

**vérifier** like parler (1)

**visiter** like parler (1)

**vivre** like suivre (39)

**voir** (42)

**vouloir** (43)

**voyager** like manger (11)

# Regular verbs

| Infinitive<br>Past participle | Subject<br>Pronouns | INDICATIVE | | | | | CONDITIONAL | SUBJUNCTIVE | IMPERATIVE |
|---|---|---|---|---|---|---|---|---|---|
| | | Present | Passé<br>composé | Imperfect | Future | Present | Present | |
| **1** parler<br>(to speak)<br>parlé | je (j') | parle | ai parlé | parlais | parlerai | parlerais | parle | |
| | tu | parles | as parlé | parlais | parleras | parlerais | parles | parle |
| | il/elle/on | parle | a parlé | parlait | parlera | parlerait | parle | |
| | nous | parlons | avons parlé | parlions | parlerons | parlerions | parlions | parlons |
| | vous | parlez | avez parlé | parliez | parlerez | parleriez | parliez | parlez |
| | ils/elles | parlent | ont parlé | parlaient | parleront | parleraient | parlent | |
| **2** finir<br>(to finish)<br>fini | je (j') | finis | ai fini | finissais | finirai | finirais | finisse | |
| | tu | finis | as fini | finissais | finiras | finirais | finisses | finis |
| | il/elle/on | finit | a fini | finissait | finira | finirait | finisse | |
| | nous | finissons | avons fini | finissions | finirons | finirions | finissions | finissons |
| | vous | finissez | avez fini | finissiez | finirez | finiriez | finissiez | finissez |
| | ils/elles | finissent | ont fini | finissaient | finiront | finiraient | finissent | |
| **3** vendre<br>(to sell)<br>vendu | je (j') | vends | ai vendu | vendais | vendrai | vendrais | vende | |
| | tu | vends | as vendu | vendais | vendras | vendrais | vendes | vends |
| | il/elle/on | vend | a vendu | vendait | vendra | vendrait | vende | |
| | nous | vendons | avons vendu | vendions | vendrons | vendrions | vendions | vendons |
| | vous | vendez | avez vendu | vendiez | vendrez | vendriez | vendiez | vendez |
| | ils/elles | vendent | ont vendu | vendaient | vendront | vendraient | vendent | |

## Auxiliary verbs: *avoir* and *être*

| Infinitive / Past participle | Subject Pronouns | INDICATIVE Present | Passé composé | Imperfect | Future | CONDITIONAL Present | SUBJUNCTIVE Present | IMPERATIVE |
|---|---|---|---|---|---|---|---|---|
| **4** avoir *(to have)* | j' | ai | ai eu | avais | aurai | aurais | aie | |
| | tu | as | as eu | avais | auras | aurais | aies | aie |
| | il/elle/on | a | a eu | avait | aura | aurait | ait | |
| eu | nous | avons | avons eu | avions | aurons | aurions | ayons | ayons |
| | vous | avez | avez eu | aviez | aurez | auriez | ayez | ayez |
| | ils/elles | ont | ont eu | avaient | auront | auraient | aient | |
| **5** être *(to be)* | je (j') | suis | ai été | étais | serai | serais | sois | |
| | tu | es | as été | étais | seras | serais | sois | sois |
| | il/elle/on | est | a été | était | sera | serait | soit | |
| été | nous | sommes | avons été | étions | serons | serions | soyons | soyons |
| | vous | êtes | avez été | étiez | serez | seriez | soyez | soyez |
| | ils/elles | sont | ont été | étaient | seront | seraient | soient | |

## Reflexive (Pronominal)

| Infinitive / Past participle | Subject Pronouns | INDICATIVE Present | Passé composé | Imperfect | Future | CONDITIONAL Present | SUBJUNCTIVE Present | IMPERATIVE |
|---|---|---|---|---|---|---|---|---|
| **6** se laver *(to wash oneself)* | je | me lave | me suis lavé(e) | me lavais | me laverai | me laverais | me lave | |
| | tu | te laves | t'es lavé(e) | te lavais | te laveras | te laverais | te laves | lave-toi |
| | il/elle/on | se lave | s'est lavé(e) | se lavait | se lavera | se laverait | se lave | |
| lavé | nous | nous lavons | nous sommes lavé(e)s | nous lavions | nous laverons | nous laverions | nous lavions | lavons-nous |
| | vous | vous lavez | vous êtes lavé(e)s | vous laviez | vous laverez | vous laveriez | vous laviez | lavez-vous |
| | ils/elles | se lavent | se sont lavé(e)s | se lavaient | se laveront | se laveraient | se lavent | |

# Verb Conjugation Tables

## Verbs with spelling changes

| Infinitive / Past participle | Subject Pronouns | INDICATIVE Present | Passé composé | Imperfect | Future | CONDITIONAL Present | SUBJUNCTIVE Present | IMPERATIVE |
|---|---|---|---|---|---|---|---|---|
| **7** acheter (*to buy*) acheté | j' | achète | ai acheté | achetais | achèterai | achèterais | achète | |
| | tu | achètes | as acheté | achetais | achèteras | achèterais | achètes | achète |
| | il/elle/on | achète | a acheté | achetait | achètera | achèterait | achète | |
| | nous | achetons | avons acheté | achetions | achèterons | achèterions | achetions | achetons |
| | vous | achetez | avez acheté | achetiez | achèterez | achèteriez | achetiez | achetez |
| | ils/elles | achètent | ont acheté | achetaient | achèteront | achèteraient | achètent | |
| **8** appeler (*to call*) appelé | j' | appelle | ai appelé | appelais | appellerai | appellerais | appelle | |
| | tu | appelles | as appelé | appelais | appelleras | appellerais | appelles | appelle |
| | il/elle/on | appelle | a appelé | appelait | appellera | appellerait | appelle | |
| | nous | appelons | avons appelé | appelions | appellerons | appellerions | appelions | appelons |
| | vous | appelez | avez appelé | appeliez | appellerez | appelleriez | appeliez | appelez |
| | ils/elles | appellent | ont appelé | appelaient | appelleront | appelleraient | appellent | |
| **9** commencer (*to begin*) commencé | je (j') | commence | ai commencé | commençais | commencerai | commencerais | commence | |
| | tu | commences | as commencé | commençais | commenceras | commencerais | commences | commence |
| | il/elle/on | commence | a commencé | commençait | commencera | commencerait | commence | |
| | nous | commençons | avons commencé | commencions | commencerons | commencerions | commencions | commençons |
| | vous | commencez | avez commencé | commenciez | commencerez | commenceriez | commenciez | commencez |
| | ils/elles | commencent | ont commencé | commençaient | commenceront | commenceraient | commencent | |
| **10** essayer (*to try*) essayé | j' | essaie | ai essayé | essayais | essaierai | essaierais | essaie | |
| | tu | essaies | as essayé | essayais | essaieras | essaierais | essaies | essaie |
| | il/elle/on | essaie | a essayé | essayait | essaiera | essaierait | essaie | |
| | nous | essayons | avons essayé | essayions | essaierons | essaierions | essayions | essayons |
| | vous | essayez | avez essayé | essayiez | essaierez | essaieriez | essayiez | essayez |
| | ils/elles | essayent | ont essayé | essayaient | essaieront | essaieraient | essaient | |
| **11** manger (*to eat*) mangé | je (j') | mange | ai mangé | mangeais | mangerai | mangerais | mange | |
| | tu | manges | as mangé | mangeais | mangeras | mangerais | manges | mange |
| | il/elle/on | mange | a mangé | mangeait | mangera | mangerait | mange | |
| | nous | mangeons | avons mangé | mangions | mangerons | mangerions | mangions | mangeons |
| | vous | mangez | avez mangé | mangiez | mangerez | mangeriez | mangiez | mangez |
| | ils/elles | mangent | ont mangé | mangeaient | mangeront | mangeraient | mangent | |

**12**

| Infinitive / Past participle | Subject Pronouns | INDICATIVE Present | Passé composé | Imperfect | Future | CONDITIONAL Present | SUBJUNCTIVE Present | IMPERATIVE |
|---|---|---|---|---|---|---|---|---|
| préférer (to prefer) préféré | je (j') | préfère | ai préféré | préférais | préférerai | préférerais | préfère | |
| | tu | préfères | as préféré | préférais | préféreras | préférerais | préfères | préfère |
| | il/elle/on | préfère | a préféré | préférait | préférera | préférerait | préfère | |
| | nous | préférons | avons préféré | préférions | préférerons | préférerions | préférions | préférons |
| | vous | préférez | avez préféré | préfériez | préférerez | préféreriez | préfériez | préférez |
| | ils/elles | préfèrent | ont préféré | préféraient | préféreront | préféreraient | préfèrent | |

## Irregular verbs

| Infinitive / Past participle | Subject Pronouns | INDICATIVE Present | Passé composé | Imperfect | Future | CONDITIONAL Present | SUBJUNCTIVE Present | IMPERATIVE |
|---|---|---|---|---|---|---|---|---|
| **13** aller (to go) allé | je (j') | vais | suis allé(e) | allais | irai | irais | aille | |
| | tu | vas | es allé(e) | allais | iras | irais | ailles | va |
| | il/elle/on | va | est allé(e) | allait | ira | irait | aille | |
| | nous | allons | sommes allé(e)s | allions | irons | irions | allions | allons |
| | vous | allez | êtes allé(e)s | alliez | irez | iriez | alliez | allez |
| | ils/elles | vont | sont allé(e)s | allaient | iront | iraient | aillent | |
| **14** s'asseoir (to sit down, to be seated) assis | je | m'assieds | me suis assis(e) | m'asseyais | m'assiérai | m'assiérais | m'asseye | |
| | tu | t'assieds | t'es assis(e) | t'asseyais | t'assiéras | t'assiérais | t'asseyes | assieds-toi |
| | il/elle/on | s'assied | s'est assis(e) | s'asseyait | s'assiéra | s'assiérait | s'asseye | |
| | nous | nous asseyons | nous sommes assis(e)s | nous asseyions | nous assiérons | nous assiérions | nous asseyions | asseyons-nous |
| | vous | vous asseyez | vous êtes assis(e)s | vous asseyiez | vous assiérez | vous assiériez | vous asseyiez | asseyez-vous |
| | ils/elles | s'asseyent | se sont assis(e)s | s'asseyaient | s'assiéront | s'assiéraient | s'asseyent | |
| **15** boire (to drink) bu | je (j') | bois | ai bu | buvais | boirai | boirais | boive | |
| | tu | bois | as bu | buvais | boiras | boirais | boives | bois |
| | il/elle/on | boit | a bu | buvait | boira | boirait | boive | |
| | nous | buvons | avons bu | buvions | boirons | boirions | buvions | buvons |
| | vous | buvez | avez bu | buviez | boirez | boiriez | buviez | buvez |
| | ils/elles | boivent | ont bu | buvaient | boiront | boiraient | boivent | |

| | Infinitive / Past participle | Subject Pronouns | INDICATIVE Present | Passé composé | Imperfect | Future | CONDITIONAL Present | SUBJUNCTIVE Present | IMPERATIVE |
|---|---|---|---|---|---|---|---|---|---|
| 16 | conduire (to drive; to lead) conduit | je (j') | conduis | ai conduit | conduisais | conduirai | conduirais | conduise | |
| | | tu | conduis | as conduit | conduisais | conduiras | conduirais | conduises | conduis |
| | | il/elle/on | conduit | a conduit | conduisait | conduira | conduirait | conduise | |
| | | nous | conduisons | avons conduit | conduisions | conduirons | conduirions | conduisions | conduisons |
| | | vous | conduisez | avez conduit | conduisiez | conduirez | conduiriez | conduisiez | conduisez |
| | | ils/elles | conduisent | ont conduit | conduisaient | conduiront | conduiraient | conduisent | |
| 17 | connaître (to know, to be acquainted with) connu | je (j') | connais | ai connu | connaissais | connaîtrai | connaîtrais | connaisse | |
| | | tu | connais | as connu | connaissais | connaîtras | connaîtrais | connaisses | connais |
| | | il/elle/on | connaît | a connu | connaissait | connaîtra | connaîtrait | connaisse | |
| | | nous | connaissons | avons connu | connaissions | connaîtrons | connaîtrions | connaissions | connaissons |
| | | vous | connaissez | avez connu | connaissiez | connaîtrez | connaîtriez | connaissiez | connaissez |
| | | ils/elles | connaissent | ont connu | connaissaient | connaîtront | connaîtraient | connaissent | |
| 18 | courir (to run) couru | je (j') | cours | ai couru | courais | courrai | courrais | coure | |
| | | tu | cours | as couru | courais | courras | courrais | coures | cours |
| | | il/elle/on | court | a couru | courait | courra | courrait | coure | |
| | | nous | courons | avons couru | courions | courrons | courrions | courions | courons |
| | | vous | courez | avez couru | couriez | courrez | courriez | couriez | courez |
| | | ils/elles | courent | ont couru | couraient | courront | courraient | courent | |
| 19 | croire (to believe) cru | je (j') | crois | ai cru | croyais | croirai | croirais | croie | |
| | | tu | crois | as cru | croyais | croiras | croirais | croies | crois |
| | | il/elle/on | croit | a cru | croyait | croira | croirait | croie | |
| | | nous | croyons | avons cru | croyions | croirons | croirions | croyions | croyons |
| | | vous | croyez | avez cru | croyiez | croirez | croiriez | croyiez | croyez |
| | | ils/elles | croient | ont cru | croyaient | croiront | croiraient | croient | |
| 20 | devoir (to have to; to owe) dû | je (j') | dois | ai dû | devais | devrai | devrais | doive | |
| | | tu | dois | as dû | devais | devras | devrais | doives | dois |
| | | il/elle/on | doit | a dû | devait | devra | devrait | doive | |
| | | nous | devons | avons dû | devions | devrons | devrions | devions | devons |
| | | vous | devez | avez dû | deviez | devrez | devriez | deviez | devez |
| | | ils/elles | doivent | ont dû | devaient | devront | devraient | doivent | |

| Infinitive / Past participle | Subject Pronouns | INDICATIVE Present | Passé composé | Imperfect | Future | CONDITIONAL Present | SUBJUNCTIVE Present | IMPERATIVE |
|---|---|---|---|---|---|---|---|---|
| **21** dire (*to say, to tell*) | je (j') | dis | ai dit | disais | dirai | dirais | dise | |
| | tu | dis | as dit | disais | diras | dirais | dises | dis |
| | il/elle/on | dit | a dit | disait | dira | dirait | dise | |
| dit | nous | disons | avons dit | disions | dirons | dirions | disions | disons |
| | vous | dites | avez dit | disiez | direz | diriez | disiez | dites |
| | ils/elles | disent | ont dit | disaient | diront | diraient | disent | |
| **22** écrire (*to write*) | j' | écris | ai écrit | écrivais | écrirai | écrirais | écrive | |
| | tu | écris | as écrit | écrivais | écriras | écrirais | écrives | écris |
| | il/elle/on | écrit | a écrit | écrivait | écrira | écrirait | écrive | |
| écrit | nous | écrivons | avons écrit | écrivions | écrirons | écririons | écrivions | écrivons |
| | vous | écrivez | avez écrit | écriviez | écrirez | écririez | écriviez | écrivez |
| | ils/elles | écrivent | ont écrit | écrivaient | écriront | écriraient | écrivent | |
| **23** envoyer (*to send*) | j' | envoie | ai envoyé | envoyais | enverrai | enverrais | envoie | |
| | tu | envoies | as envoyé | envoyais | enverras | enverrais | envoies | envoie |
| | il/elle/on | envoie | a envoyé | envoyait | enverra | enverrait | envoie | |
| envoyé | nous | envoyons | avons envoyé | envoyions | enverrons | enverrions | envoyions | envoyons |
| | vous | envoyez | avez envoyé | envoyiez | enverrez | enverriez | envoyiez | envoyez |
| | ils/elles | envoient | ont envoyé | envoyaient | enverront | enverraient | envoient | |
| **24** éteindre (*to turn off*) | j' | éteins | ai éteint | éteignais | éteindrai | éteindrais | éteigne | |
| | tu | éteins | as éteint | éteignais | éteindras | éteindrais | éteignes | éteins |
| | il/elle/on | éteint | a éteint | éteignait | éteindra | éteindrait | éteigne | |
| éteint | nous | éteignons | avons éteint | éteignions | éteindrons | éteindrions | éteignions | éteignons |
| | vous | éteignez | avez éteint | éteigniez | éteindrez | éteindriez | éteigniez | éteignez |
| | ils/elles | éteignent | ont éteint | éteignaient | éteindront | éteindraient | éteignent | |
| **25** faire (*to do; to make*) | je (j') | fais | ai fait | faisais | ferai | ferais | fasse | |
| | tu | fais | as fait | faisais | feras | ferais | fasses | fais |
| | il/elle/on | fait | a fait | faisait | fera | ferait | fasse | |
| fait | nous | faisons | avons fait | faisions | ferons | ferions | fassions | faisons |
| | vous | faites | avez fait | faisiez | ferez | feriez | fassiez | faites |
| | ils/elles | font | ont fait | faisaient | feront | feraient | fassent | |
| **26** falloir (*to be necessary*) | il | faut | a fallu | fallait | faudra | faudrait | faille | |
| fallu | | | | | | | | |

| Infinitive / Past participle | Subject Pronouns | INDICATIVE Present | Passé composé | Imperfect | Future | CONDITIONAL Present | SUBJUNCTIVE Present | IMPERATIVE |
|---|---|---|---|---|---|---|---|---|
| **27** lire (*to read*) lu | je (j') | lis | ai lu | lisais | lirai | lirais | lise | |
| | tu | lis | as lu | lisais | liras | lirais | lises | lis |
| | il/elle/on | lit | a lu | lisait | lira | lirait | lise | |
| | nous | lisons | avons lu | lisions | lirons | lirions | lisions | lisons |
| | vous | lisez | avez lu | lisiez | lirez | liriez | lisiez | lisez |
| | ils/elles | lisent | ont lu | lisaient | liront | liraient | lisent | |
| **28** mettre (*to put*) mis | je (j') | mets | ai mis | mettais | mettrai | mettrais | mette | |
| | tu | mets | as mis | mettais | mettras | mettrais | mettes | mets |
| | il/elle/on | met | a mis | mettait | mettra | mettrait | mette | |
| | nous | mettons | avons mis | mettions | mettrons | mettrions | mettions | mettons |
| | vous | mettez | avez mis | mettiez | mettrez | mettriez | mettiez | mettez |
| | ils/elles | mettent | ont mis | mettaient | mettront | mettraient | mettent | |
| **29** mourir (*to die*) mort | je | meurs | suis mort(e) | mourais | mourrai | mourrais | meure | |
| | tu | meurs | es mort(e) | mourais | mourras | mourrais | meures | meurs |
| | il/elle/on | meurt | est mort(e) | mourait | mourra | mourrait | meure | |
| | nous | mourons | sommes mort(e)s | mourions | mourrons | mourrions | mourions | mourons |
| | vous | mourez | êtes mort(e)s | mouriez | mourrez | mourriez | mouriez | mourez |
| | ils/elles | meurent | sont mort(e)s | mouraient | mourront | mourraient | meurent | |
| **30** naître (*to be born*) né | je | nais | suis né(e) | naissais | naîtrai | naîtrais | naisse | |
| | tu | nais | es né(e) | naissais | naîtras | naîtrais | naisses | nais |
| | il/elle/on | naît | est né(e) | naissait | naîtra | naîtrait | naisse | |
| | nous | naissons | sommes né(e)s | naissions | naîtrons | naîtrions | naissions | naissons |
| | vous | naissez | êtes né(e)s | naissiez | naîtrez | naîtriez | naissiez | naissez |
| | ils/elles | naissent | sont né(e)s | naissaient | naîtront | naîtraient | naissent | |
| **31** ouvrir (*to open*) ouvert | j' | ouvre | ai ouvert | ouvrais | ouvrirai | ouvrirais | ouvre | |
| | tu | ouvres | as ouvert | ouvrais | ouvriras | ouvrirais | ouvres | ouvre |
| | il/elle/on | ouvre | a ouvert | ouvrait | ouvrira | ouvrirait | ouvre | |
| | nous | ouvrons | avons ouvert | ouvrions | ouvrirons | ouvririons | ouvrions | ouvrons |
| | vous | ouvrez | avez ouvert | ouvriez | ouvrirez | ouvririez | ouvriez | ouvrez |
| | ils/elles | ouvrent | ont ouvert | ouvraient | ouvriront | ouvriraient | ouvrent | |

| | | INDICATIVE | | | | CONDITIONAL | SUBJUNCTIVE | IMPERATIVE |
|---|---|---|---|---|---|---|---|---|
| Infinitive / Past participle | Subject Pronouns | Present | Passé composé | Imperfect | Future | Present | Present | |
| **32** partir (to leave) / parti | je | pars | suis parti(e) | partais | partirai | partirais | parte | |
| | tu | pars | es parti(e) | partais | partiras | partirais | partes | pars |
| | il/elle/on | part | est parti(e) | partait | partira | partirait | parte | |
| | nous | partons | sommes parti(e)s | partions | partirons | partirions | partions | partons |
| | vous | partez | êtes parti(e)(s) | partiez | partirez | partiriez | partiez | partez |
| | ils/elles | partent | sont parti(e)s | partaient | partiront | partiraient | partent | |
| **33** pleuvoir (to rain) / plu | il | pleut | a plu | pleuvait | pleuvra | pleuvrait | pleuve | |
| **34** pouvoir (to be able) / pu | je (j') | peux | ai pu | pouvais | pourrai | pourrais | puisse | |
| | tu | peux | as pu | pouvais | pourras | pourrais | puisses | |
| | il/elle/on | peut | a pu | pouvait | pourra | pourrait | puisse | |
| | nous | pouvons | avons pu | pouvions | pourrons | pourrions | puissions | |
| | vous | pouvez | avez pu | pouviez | pourrez | pourriez | puissiez | |
| | ils/elles | peuvent | ont pu | pouvaient | pourront | pourraient | puissent | |
| **35** prendre (to take) / pris | je (j') | prends | ai pris | prenais | prendrai | prendrais | prenne | |
| | tu | prends | as pris | prenais | prendras | prendrais | prennes | prends |
| | il/elle/on | prend | a pris | prenait | prendra | prendrait | prenne | |
| | nous | prenons | avons pris | prenions | prendrons | prendrions | prenions | prenons |
| | vous | prenez | avez pris | preniez | prendrez | prendriez | preniez | prenez |
| | ils/elles | prennent | ont pris | prenaient | prendront | prendraient | prennent | |
| **36** recevoir (to receive) / reçu | je (j') | reçois | ai reçu | recevais | recevrai | recevrais | reçoive | |
| | tu | reçois | as reçu | recevais | recevras | recevrais | reçoives | reçois |
| | il/elle/on | reçoit | a reçu | recevait | recevra | recevrait | reçoive | |
| | nous | recevons | avons reçu | recevions | recevrons | recevrions | recevions | recevons |
| | vous | recevez | avez reçu | receviez | recevrez | recevriez | receviez | recevez |
| | ils/elles | reçoivent | ont reçu | recevaient | recevront | recevraient | reçoivent | |
| **37** rire (to laugh) / ri | je (j') | ris | ai ri | riais | rirai | rirais | rie | |
| | tu | ris | as ri | riais | riras | rirais | ries | ris |
| | il/elle/on | rit | a ri | riait | rira | rirait | rie | |
| | nous | rions | avons ri | riions | rirons | ririons | riions | rions |
| | vous | riez | avez ri | riiez | rirez | ririez | riiez | riez |
| | ils/elles | rient | ont ri | riaient | riront | riraient | rient | |

| Infinitive / Past participle | Subject Pronouns | INDICATIVE Present | Passé composé | Imperfect | Future | CONDITIONAL Present | SUBJUNCTIVE Present | IMPERATIVE |
|---|---|---|---|---|---|---|---|---|
| **38** savoir (*to know*) su | je (j') | sais | ai su | savais | saurai | saurais | sache | |
| | tu | sais | as su | savais | sauras | saurais | saches | sache |
| | il/elle/on | sait | a su | savait | saura | saurait | sache | |
| | nous | savons | avons su | savions | saurons | saurions | sachions | sachons |
| | vous | savez | avez su | saviez | saurez | sauriez | sachiez | sachez |
| | ils/elles | savent | ont su | savaient | sauront | sauraient | sachent | |
| **39** suivre (*to follow*) suivi | je (j') | suis | ai suivi | suivais | suivrai | suivrais | suive | |
| | tu | suis | as suivi | suivais | suivras | suivrais | suives | suis |
| | il/elle/on | suit | a suivi | suivait | suivra | suivrait | suive | |
| | nous | suivons | avons suivi | suivions | suivrons | suivrions | suivions | suivons |
| | vous | suivez | avez suivi | suiviez | suivrez | suivriez | suiviez | suivez |
| | ils/elles | suivent | ont suivi | suivaient | suivront | suivraient | suivent | |
| **40** tenir (*to hold*) tenu | je (j') | tiens | ai tenu | tenais | tiendrai | tiendrais | tienne | |
| | tu | tiens | as tenu | tenais | tiendras | tiendrais | tiennes | tiens |
| | il/elle/on | tient | a tenu | tenait | tiendra | tiendrait | tienne | |
| | nous | tenons | avons tenu | tenions | tiendrons | tiendrions | tenions | tenons |
| | vous | tenez | avez tenu | teniez | tiendrez | tiendriez | teniez | tenez |
| | ils/elles | tiennent | ont tenu | tenaient | tiendront | tiendraient | tiennent | |
| **41** venir (*to come*) venu | je | viens | suis venu(e) | venais | viendrai | viendrais | vienne | |
| | tu | viens | es venu(e) | venais | viendras | viendrais | viennes | viens |
| | il/elle/on | vient | est venu(e) | venait | viendra | viendrait | vienne | |
| | nous | venons | sommes venu(e)s | venions | viendrons | viendrions | venions | venons |
| | vous | venez | êtes venu(e)(s) | veniez | viendrez | viendriez | veniez | venez |
| | ils/elles | viennent | sont venu(e)s | venaient | viendront | viendraient | viennent | |
| **42** voir (*to see*) vu | je (j') | vois | ai vu | voyais | verrai | verrais | voie | |
| | tu | vois | as vu | voyais | verras | verrais | voies | vois |
| | il/elle/on | voit | a vu | voyait | verra | verrait | voie | |
| | nous | voyons | avons vu | voyions | verrons | verrions | voyions | voyons |
| | vous | voyez | avez vu | voyiez | verrez | verriez | voyiez | voyez |
| | ils/elles | voient | ont vu | voyaient | verront | verraient | voient | |
| **43** vouloir (*to want, to wish*) voulu | je (j') | veux | ai voulu | voulais | voudrai | voudrais | veuille | |
| | tu | veux | as voulu | voulais | voudras | voudrais | veuilles | veuille |
| | il/elle/on | veut | a voulu | voulait | voudra | voudrait | veuille | |
| | nous | voulons | avons voulu | voulions | voudrons | voudrions | voulions | veuillons |
| | vous | voulez | avez voulu | vouliez | voudrez | voudriez | vouliez | veuillez |
| | ils/elles | veulent | ont voulu | voulaient | voudront | voudraient | veuillent | |

# Guide to Vocabulary

This glossary contains the words and expressions listed on the **Vocabulaire** page found at the end of each unit in **D'ACCORD!** Levels 1 & 2. The number following an entry indicates the **D'ACCORD!** level and unit where the term was introduced. For example, the first entry in the glossary, **à**, was introduced in **D'ACCORD!** Level 1, Unit 4. Note that **II–P** refers to the **Unité Préliminaire** in **D'ACCORD!** Level 2.

## Abbreviations used in this glossary

| | | | | | | | |
|---|---|---|---|---|---|---|---|
| *adj.* | adjective | *f.* | feminine | *i.o.* | indirect object | *prep.* | preposition |
| *adv.* | adverb | *fam.* | familiar | *m.* | masculine | *pron.* | pronoun |
| *art.* | article | *form.* | formal | *n.* | noun | *refl.* | reflexive |
| *comp.* | comparative | *imp.* | imperative | *obj.* | object | *rel.* | relative |
| *conj.* | conjunction | *indef.* | indefinite | *part.* | partitive | *sing.* | singular |
| *def.* | definite | *interj.* | interjection | *p.p.* | past participle | *sub.* | subject |
| *dem.* | demonstrative | *interr.* | interrogative | *pl.* | plural | *super.* | superlative |
| *disj.* | disjunctive | *inv.* | invariable | *poss.* | possessive | *v.* | verb |
| *d.o.* | direct object | | | | | | |

## French-English

### A

**à** *prep.* at; in; to I-4
  **À bientôt.** See you soon. I-1
  **à condition que** on the condition that, provided that II-7
  **à côté de** *prep.* next to I-3
  **À demain.** See you tomorrow. I-1
  **à droite (de)** *prep.* to the right (of) I-3
  **à gauche (de)** *prep.* to the left (of) I-3
  **à … heure(s)** at … (o'clock) I-4
  **à la radio** on the radio II-7
  **à la télé(vision)** on television II-7
  **à l'étranger** abroad, overseas I-7
  **à mi-temps** half-time (*job*) II-5
  **à moins que** unless II-7
  **à plein temps** full-time (*job*) II-5
  **À plus tard.** See you later. I-1
  **À quelle heure?** What time?; When? I-2
  **À qui?** To whom? I-4
  **À table!** Let's eat! Food is on! II-1
  **à temps partiel** part-time (*job*) II-5
  **À tout à l'heure.** See you later. I-1
  **au bout (de)** *prep.* at the end (of) II-4

**au contraire** on the contrary II-7
**au fait** by the way I-3
**au printemps** in the spring I-5
**Au revoir.** Good-bye. I-1
**au secours** help II-3
**au sujet de** on the subject of, about II-6
**abolir** *v.* to abolish II-6
**absolument** *adv.* absolutely I-8, II-P
**accident** *m.* accident II-3
  **avoir un accident** to have/to be in an accident II-3
**accompagner** *v.* to accompany II-4
**acheter** *v.* to buy I-5
**acteur** *m.* actor I-1
**actif/active** *adj.* active I-3
**activement** *adv.* actively I-8, II-P
**actrice** *f.* actress I-1
**addition** *f.* check, bill I-4
**adieu** farewell II-6
**adolescence** *f.* adolescence I-6
**adorer** *v.* to love I-2
  **J'adore…** I love… I-2
**adresse** *f.* address II-4
**aérobic** *m.* aerobics I-5
  **faire de l'aérobic** *v.* to do aerobics I-5
**aéroport** *m.* airport I-7
**affaires** *f., pl.* business I-3
**affiche** *f.* poster I-8, II-P
**afficher** *v.* to post II-5
**âge** *m.* age I-6
  **âge adulte** *m.* adulthood I-6
**agence de voyages** *f.* travel agency I-7
**agent** *m.* officer; agent II-3

**agent de police** *m.* police officer II-3
**agent de voyages** *m.* travel agent I-7
**agent immobilier** *m.* real estate agent II-5
**agréable** *adj.* pleasant I-1
**agriculteur/agricultrice** *m., f.* farmer II-5
**aider (à)** *v.* to help (*to do something*) I-5
**aie (avoir)** *imp. v.* have I-7
**ail** *m.* garlic II-1
**aimer** *v.* to like I-2
  **aimer mieux** to prefer I-2
  **aimer que…** to like that… II-6
  **J'aime bien…** I really like… I-2
  **Je n'aime pas tellement…** I don't like … very much. I-2
**aîné(e)** *adj.* elder I-3
**algérien(ne)** *adj.* Algerian I-1
**aliment** *m.* food item; a food II-1
**Allemagne** *f.* Germany I-7
**allemand(e)** *adj.* German I-1
**aller** *v.* to go I-4
  **aller à la pêche** to go fishing I-5
  **aller aux urgences** to go to the emergency room II-2
  **aller avec** to go with I-6
  **aller-retour** *adj.* round-trip I-7
  **billet aller-retour** *m.* round-trip ticket I-7
  **Allons-y!** Let's go! I-2
  **Ça va?** What's up?; How are things? I-1
  **Comment allez-vous?** *form.* How are you? I-1
  **Comment vas-tu?** *fam.* How are you? I-1

**Je m'en vais.** I'm leaving. I-8, II-P

**Je vais bien/mal.** I am doing well/badly. I-1

**J'y vais.** I'm going/coming. I-8, II-P

**Nous y allons.** We're going/coming. II-1

**allergie** *f.* allergy II-2

**Allez.** Come on. I-5

**allô** *(on the phone)* hello I-1

**allumer** *v.* to turn on II-3

**alors** *adv.* so, then; at that moment I-2

**améliorer** *v.* to improve II-5

**amende** *f.* fine II-3

**amener** *v.* to bring *(someone)* I-5

**américain(e)** *adj.* American I-1

   **football américain** *m.* football I-5

**ami(e)** *m., f.* friend I-1

   **petit(e) ami(e)** *m., f.* boyfriend/girlfriend I-1

**amitié** *f.* friendship I-6

**amour** *m.* love I-6

**amoureux/amoureuse** *adj.* in love I-6

   **tomber amoureux/ amoureuse** *v.* to fall in love I-6

**amusant(e)** *adj.* fun I-1

**an** *m.* year I-2

**ancien(ne)** *adj.* ancient, old; former II-7

**ange** *m.* angel I-1

**anglais(e)** *adj.* English I-1

**angle** *m.* corner II-4

**Angleterre** *f.* England I-7

**animal** *m.* animal II-6

**année** *f.* year I-2

   **cette année** this year I-2

**anniversaire** *m.* birthday I-5

   **C'est quand l'anniversaire de ... ?** When is ...'s birthday? I-5

   **C'est quand ton/votre anniversaire?** When is your birthday? I-5

**annuler (une réservation)** *v.* to cancel (a reservation) I-7

**anorak** *m.* ski jacket, parka I-6

**antipathique** *adj.* unpleasant I-3

**août** *m.* August I-5

**apercevoir** *v.* to see, to catch sight of II-4

**aperçu (apercevoir)** *p.p.* seen, caught sight of II-4

**appareil** *m.* (on the phone) telephone II-5

   **appareil (électrique/ ménager)** *m.* (electrical/household) appliance I-8, II-P

**appareil photo (numérique)** *m.* (digital) camera II-3

**C'est M./Mme/Mlle ... à l'appareil.** It's Mr./Mrs./Miss ... on the phone. II-5

**Qui est à l'appareil?** Who's calling, please? II-5

**appartement** *m.* apartment II-7

**appeler** *v.* to call I-7

**applaudir** *v.* to applaud II-7

**applaudissement** *m.* applause II-7

**apporter** *v.* to bring, to carry *(something)* I-4

**apprendre (à)** *v.* to teach; to learn *(to do something)* I-4

**appris (apprendre)** *p.p., adj.* learned I-6

**après (que)** *adv.* after I-2

**après-demain** *adv.* day after tomorrow I-2

**après-midi** *m.* afternoon I-2

   **cet après-midi** this afternoon I-2

   **de l'après-midi** in the afternoon I-2

   **demain après-midi** *adv.* tomorrow afternoon I-2

   **hier après-midi** *adv.* yesterday afternoon I-7

**arbre** *m.* tree II-6

**architecte** *m., f.* architect I-3

**architecture** *f.* architecture I-2

**argent** *m.* money II-4

   **dépenser de l'argent** *v.* to spend money I-4

   **déposer de l'argent** *v.* to deposit money II-4

   **retirer de l'argent** *v.* to withdraw money II-4

**armoire** *f.* armoire, wardrobe I-8, II-P

**arrêt d'autobus (de bus)** *m.* bus stop I-7

**arrêter (de faire quelque chose)** *v.* to stop (doing something) II-3

**arrivée** *f.* arrival I-7

**arriver (à)** *v.* to arrive; to manage *(to do something)* I-2

**art** *m.* art I-2

   **beaux-arts** *m., pl.* fine arts II-7

**artiste** *m., f.* artist I-3

**ascenseur** *m.* elevator I-7

**aspirateur** *m.* vacuum cleaner I-8, II-P

   **passer l'aspirateur** to vacuum I-8, II-P

**aspirine** *f.* aspirin II-2

**Asseyez-vous! (s'asseoir)** *imp. v.* Have a seat! II-2

**assez** *adv. (before adjective or adverb)* pretty; quite I-8, II-P

**assez (de)** *(before noun)* enough (of) I-4

   **pas assez (de)** not enough (of) I-4

**assiette** *f.* plate II-1

**assis (s'asseoir)** *p.p., adj. (used as past participle)* sat down; *(used as adjective)* sitting, seated II-2

**assister** *v.* to attend I-2

**assurance (maladie/vie)** *f.* (health/life) insurance II-5

**athlète** *m., f.* athlete I-3

**attacher** *v.* to attach II-3

   **attacher sa ceinture de sécurité** to buckle one's seatbelt II-3

**attendre** *v.* to wait I-6

**attention** *f.* attention I-5

   **faire attention (à)** *v.* to pay attention (to) I-5

**au (à + le)** *prep.* to/at the I-4

**auberge de jeunesse** *f.* youth hostel I-7

**aucun(e)** *adj.* no; *pron.* none II-2

   **ne... aucun(e)** none, not any II-4

**augmentation (de salaire)** *f.* raise (in salary) II-5

**aujourd'hui** *adv.* today I-2

**auquel (à + lequel)** *pron., m., sing.* which one II-5

**aussi** *adv.* too, as well; as I-1

   **Moi aussi.** Me too. I-1

   **aussi ... que** *(used with an adjective)* as ... as II-1

**autant de ... que** *adv. (used with noun to express quantity)* as much/as many ... as II-6

**auteur/femme auteur** *m., f.* author II-7

**autobus** *m.* bus I-7

   **arrêt d'autobus (de bus)** *m.* bus stop I-7

   **prendre un autobus** to take a bus I-7

**automne** *m.* fall I-5

   **à l'automne** in the fall I-5

**autoroute** *f.* highway II-3

**autour (de)** *prep.* around II-4

**autrefois** *adv.* in the past I-8, II-P

**aux (à + les)** to/at the I-4

**auxquelles (à + lesquelles)** *pron., f., pl.* which ones II-5

**auxquels (à + lesquels)** *pron., m., pl.* which ones II-5

**avance** *f.* advance I-2

   **en avance** *adv.* early I-2

**avant (de/que)** *adv.* before I-7

**avant-hier** *adv.* day before yesterday I-7

**avec** *prep.* with I-1

**Avec qui?** With whom? I-4
**aventure** *f.* adventure II-7
　**film d'aventures** *m.* adventure film II-7
**avenue** *f.* avenue II-4
**avion** *m.* airplane I-7
　**prendre un avion** *v.* to take a plane I-7
**avocat(e)** *m., f.* lawyer I-3
**avoir** *v.* to have I-2
　**aie** *imp. v.* have I-2
　**avoir besoin (de)** to need (*something*) I-2
　**avoir chaud** to be hot I-2
　**avoir de la chance** to be lucky I-2
　**avoir envie (de)** to feel like (*doing something*) I-2
　**avoir faim** to be hungry I-4
　**avoir froid** to be cold I-2
　**avoir honte (de)** to be ashamed (of) I-2
　**avoir mal** to have an ache II-2
　**avoir mal au cœur** to feel nauseated II-2
　**avoir peur (de/que)** to be afraid (of/that) I-2
　**avoir raison** to be right I-2
　**avoir soif** to be thirsty I-4
　**avoir sommeil** to be sleepy I-2
　**avoir tort** to be wrong I-2
　**avoir un accident** to have/to be in an accident II-3
　**avoir un compte bancaire** to have a bank account II-4
　**en avoir marre** to be fed up I-3
**avril** *m.* April I-5
**ayez (avoir)** *imp. v.* have I-7
**ayons (avoir)** *imp. v.* let's have I-7

### B

**bac(calauréat)** *m.* an important exam taken by high-school students in France I-2
**baguette** *f.* baguette I-4
**baignoire** *f.* bathtub I-8, II-P
**bain** *m.* bath I-6
　**salle de bains** *f.* bathroom I-8, II-P
**baladeur CD** *m.* personal CD player II-3
**balai** *m.* broom I-8, II-P
**balayer** *v.* to sweep I-8, II-P
**balcon** *m.* balcony I-8, II-P
**banane** *f.* banana II-1
**banc** *m.* bench II-4
**bancaire** *adj.* banking II-4
　**avoir un compte bancaire** *v.* to have a bank account II-4
**bande dessinée (B.D.)** *f.* comic strip I-5
**banlieue** *f.* suburbs I-4

**banque** *f.* bank II-4
**banquier/banquière** *m., f.* banker II-5
**barbant** *adj.,* **barbe** *f.* drag I-3
**baseball** *m.* baseball I-5
**basket(-ball)** *m.* basketball I-5
**baskets** *f., pl.* tennis shoes I-6
**bateau** *m.* boat I-7
　**prendre un bateau** *v.* to take a boat I-7
**bateau-mouche** *m.* riverboat I-7
**bâtiment** *m.* building II-4
**batterie** *f.* drums II-7
**bavarder** *v.* to chat I-4
**beau (belle)** *adj.* handsome; beautiful I-3
　**faire quelque chose de beau** *v.* to be up to something interesting II-4
　**Il fait beau.** The weather is nice. I-5
**beaucoup (de)** *adv.* a lot (of) 4
　**Merci (beaucoup).** Thank you (very much). I-1
**beau-frère** *m.* brother-in-law I-3
**beau-père** *m.* father-in-law; stepfather I-3
**beaux-arts** *m., pl.* fine arts II-7
**belge** *adj.* Belgian I-7
**Belgique** *f.* Belgium I-7
**belle** *adj., f. (feminine form of* **beau***)* beautiful I-3
**belle-mère** *f.* mother-in-law; stepmother I-3
**belle-sœur** *f.* sister-in-law I-3
**besoin** *m.* need I-2
　**avoir besoin (de)** to need (*something*) I-2
**beurre** *m.* butter 4
**bibliothèque** *f.* library I-1
**bien** *adv.* well I-7
　**bien sûr** *adv.* of course I-2
　**Je vais bien.** I am doing well. I-1
　**Très bien.** Very well. I-1
**bientôt** *adv.* soon I-1
　**À bientôt.** See you soon. I-1
**bienvenu(e)** *adj.* welcome I-1
**bière** *f.* beer I-6
**bijouterie** *f.* jewelry store II-4
**billet** *m. (travel)* ticket I-7; *(money)* bills, notes II-4
　**billet aller-retour** *m.* round-trip ticket I-7
**biologie** *f.* biology I-2
**biscuit** *m.* cookie I-6
**blague** *f.* joke I-2
**blanc(he)** *adj.* white I-6
**blessure** *f.* injury, wound II-2
**bleu(e)** *adj.* blue I-3
**blond(e)** *adj.* blonde I-3
**blouson** *m.* jacket I-6
**bœuf** *m.* beef II-1

**boire** *v.* to drink I-4
**bois** *m.* wood II-6
**boisson (gazeuse)** *f.* (carbonated) drink/beverage I-4
**boîte** *f.* box; can II-1
　**boîte aux lettres** *f.* mailbox II-4
　**boîte de conserve** *f.* can (of food) II-1
　**boîte de nuit** *f.* nightclub I-4
**bol** *m.* bowl II-1
**bon(ne)** *adj.* kind; good I-3
　**bon marché** *adj.* inexpensive I-6
　**Il fait bon.** The weather is good/warm. I-5
**bonbon** *m.* candy I-6
**bonheur** *m.* happiness I-6
**Bonjour.** Good morning.; Hello. I-1
**Bonsoir.** Good evening.; Hello. I-1
**bouche** *f.* mouth II-2
**boucherie** *f.* butcher's shop II-1
**boulangerie** *f.* bread shop, bakery II-1
**boulevard** *m.* boulevard II-4
　**suivre un boulevard** *v.* to follow a boulevard II-4
**bourse** *f.* scholarship, grant I-2
**bout** *m.* end II-4
　**au bout (de)** *prep.* at the end (of) II-4
**bouteille (de)** *f.* bottle (of) I-4
**boutique** *f.* boutique, store II-4
**bras** *m.* arm II-2
**brasserie** *f.* café; restaurant II-4
**Brésil** *m.* Brazil II-2
**brésilien(ne)** *adj.* Brazilian I-7
**bricoler** *v.* to tinker; to do odd jobs I-5
**brillant(e)** *adj.* bright I-1
**bronzer** *v.* to tan I-6
**brosse (à cheveux/à dents)** *f.* (hair/tooth)brush II-2
**brun(e)** *adj. (hair)* dark I-3
**bu (boire)** *p.p.* drunk I-6
**bureau** *m.* desk; office I-1
　**bureau de poste** *m.* post office II-4
**bus** *m.* bus I-7
　**arrêt d'autobus (de bus)** *m.* bus stop I-7
　**prendre un bus** *v.* to take a bus I-7

### C

**ça** *pron.* that; this; it I-1
　**Ça dépend.** It depends. I-4
　**Ça ne nous regarde pas.** That has nothing to do with us.; That is none of our business. II-6

**Ça suffit.** That's enough. I-5
**Ça te dit?** Does that appeal to you? II-6
**Ça va?** What's up?; How are things? I-1
**ça veut dire** that is to say II-2
**Comme ci, comme ça.** So-so. I-1
**cabine téléphonique** *f.* phone booth II-4
**cadeau** *m.* gift I-6
  **paquet cadeau** wrapped gift I-6
**cadet(te)** *adj.* younger I-3
**cadre/femme cadre** *m., f.* executive II-5
**café** *m.* café; coffee I-1
  **terrasse de café** *f.* café terrace I-4
  **cuillére à café** *f.* teaspoon II-1
**cafetière** *f.* coffeemaker I-8, II-P
**cahier** *m.* notebook I-1
**calculatrice** *f.* calculator I-1
**calme** *adj.* calm I-1; *m.* calm I-1
**camarade** *m., f.* friend I-1
  **camarade de chambre** *m., f.* roommate I-1
  **camarade de classe** *m., f.* classmate I-1
**caméra vidéo** *f.* camcorder II-3
**caméscope** *m.* camcorder II-3
**campagne** *f.* country(side) I-7
  **pain de campagne** *m.* country-style bread I-4
  **pâté (de campagne)** *m.* pâté, meat spread II-1
**camping** *m.* camping I-5
  **faire du camping** *v.* to go camping I-5
**Canada** *m.* Canada I-7
**canadien(ne)** *adj.* Canadian I-1
**canapé** *m.* couch I-8, II-P
**candidat(e)** *m., f.* candidate; applicant II-5
**cantine** *f.* (school) cafeteria II-1
**capitale** *f.* capital I-7
**capot** *m.* hood II-3
**carafe (d'eau)** *f.* pitcher (of water) II-1
**carotte** *f.* carrot II-1
**carrefour** *m.* intersection II-4
**carrière** *f.* career II-5
**carte** *f.* map I-1; menu II-1; card II-4
  **payer avec une carte de crédit** to pay with a credit card II-4
  **carte postale** *f.* postcard II-4
  **cartes** *f. pl.* (*playing*) cards I-5

**casquette** *f.* (baseball) cap I-6
**cassette vidéo** *f.* videotape II-3
**catastrophe** *f.* catastrophe II-6
**cave** *f.* basement, cellar I-8, II-P
**CD** *m.* CD(s) II-3
**CD-ROM** *m.* CD-ROM(s) II-3
**ce** *dem. adj., m., sing.* this; that I-6
  **ce matin** this morning I-2
  **ce mois-ci** this month I-2
  **Ce n'est pas grave.** It's no big deal. I-6
  **ce soir** this evening I-2
  **ce sont...** those are... I-1
  **ce week-end** this weekend I-2
**cédérom(s)** *m.* CD-ROM(s) II-3
**ceinture** *f.* belt I-6
  **attacher sa ceinture de sécurité** *v.* to buckle one's seatbelt II-3
**célèbre** *adj.* famous II-7
**célébrer** *v.* to celebrate I-5
**célibataire** *adj.* single I-3
**celle** *pron., f., sing.* this one; that one; the one II-6
**celles** *pron., f., pl.* these; those; the ones II-6
**celui** *pron., m., sing.* this one; that one; the one II-6
**cent** *m.* one hundred I-3
  **cent mille** *m.* one hundred thousand I-5
  **cent un** *m.* one hundred one I-5
  **cinq cents** *m.* five hundred I-5
**centième** *adj.* hundredth I-7
**centrale nucléaire** *f.* nuclear plant II-6
**centre commercial** *m.* shopping center, mall I-4
**centre-ville** *m.* city/town center, downtown I-4
**certain(e)** *adj.* certain II-1
  **Il est certain que...** It is certain that... II-7
  **Il n'est pas certain que...** It is uncertain that... II-7
**ces** *dem. adj., m., f., pl.* these; those I-6
**c'est...** it/that is... I-1
  **C'est de la part de qui?** On behalf of whom? II-5
  **C'est le 1ᵉʳ (premier) octobre.** It is October first. I-5
  **C'est M./Mme/Mlle ... (à l'appareil).** It's Mr./Mrs./Miss ... (on the phone). II-5
  **C'est quand l'anniversaire de... ?** When is ...'s birthday? I-5
  **C'est quand ton/votre anniversaire?** When is your birthday? I-5

**Qu'est-ce que c'est?** What is it? I-1
**cet** *dem. adj., m., sing.* this; that I-6
  **cet après-midi** this afternoon I-2
**cette** *dem. adj., f., sing.* this; that I-6
  **cette année** this year I-2
  **cette semaine** this week I-2
**ceux** *pron., m., pl.* these; those; the ones II-6
**chaîne (de télévision)** *f.* (television) channel 11
**chaîne stéréo** *f.* stereo system I-3
**chaise** *f.* chair I-1
**chambre** *f.* bedroom I-8, II-P
  **chambre (individuelle)** *f.* (single) room I-7
  **camarade de chambre** *m., f.* roommate I-1
**champ** *m.* field II-6
**champagne** *m.* champagne I-6
**champignon** *m.* mushroom II-1
**chance** *f.* luck I-2
  **avoir de la chance** *v.* to be lucky I-2
**chanson** *f.* song II-7
**chanter** *v.* to sing I-5
**chanteur/chanteuse** *m., f.* singer I-1
**chapeau** *m.* hat I-6
**chaque** *adj.* each I-6
**charcuterie** *f.* delicatessen II-1
**charmant(e)** *adj.* charming I-1
**chasse** *f.* hunt II-6
**chasser** *v.* to hunt II-6
**chat** *m.* cat I-3
**châtain** *adj.* (*hair*) brown I-3
**chaud** *m.* heat I-2
  **avoir chaud** *v.* to be hot I-2
  **Il fait chaud.** (*weather*) It is hot. I-5
**chauffeur de taxi/de camion** *m.* taxi/truck driver II-5
**chaussette** *f.* sock I-6
**chaussure** *f.* shoe I-6
**chef d'entreprise** *m.* head of a company II-5
**chef-d'œuvre** *m.* masterpiece II-7
**chemin** *m.* path; way II-4
  **suivre un chemin** *v.* to follow a path II-4
**chemise (à manches courtes/ longues)** *f.* (short-/long-sleeved) shirt I-6
**chemisier** *m.* blouse I-6
**chèque** *m.* check II-4
  **compte-chèques** *m.* checking account II-4
  **payer par chèque** *v.* to pay by check II-4

**cher/chère** *adj.* expensive I-6
**chercher** *v.* to look for I-2
  **chercher un/du travail** to look for work II-4
**chercheur/chercheuse** *m., f.* researcher II-5
**chéri(e)** *adj.* dear, beloved, darling I-2
**cheval** *m.* horse I-5
  **faire du cheval** *v.* to go horseback riding I-5
**cheveux** *m., pl.* hair II-1
  **brosse à cheveux** *f.* hairbrush II-2
  **cheveux blonds** blond hair I-3
  **cheveux châtains** brown hair I-3
  **se brosser les cheveux** *v.* to brush one's hair II-1
**cheville** *f.* ankle II-2
  **se fouler la cheville** *v.* to twist/sprain one's ankle II-2
**chez** *prep.* at (*someone's*) house I-3, at (*a place*) I-3
  **passer chez quelqu'un** *v.* to stop by someone's house I-4
**chic** *adj.* chic I-4
**chien** *m.* dog I-3
**chimie** *f.* chemistry I-2
**Chine** *f.* China I-7
**chinois(e)** *adj.* Chinese 7
**chocolat (chaud)** *m.* (hot) chocolate I-4
**chœur** *m.* choir, chorus II-7
**choisir** *v.* to choose I-4
**chômage** *m.* unemployment II-5
  **être au chômage** *v.* to be unemployed II-5
**chômeur/chômeuse** *m., f.* unemployed person II-5
**chose** *f.* thing I-1
  **quelque chose** *m.* something; anything I-4
**chrysanthèmes** *m., pl.* chrysanthemums II-1
**chut** shh II-7
**-ci** (*used with demonstrative adjective* **ce** *and noun or with demonstrative pronoun* **celui**) here I-6
  **ce mois-ci** this month I-2
**ciel** *m.* sky II-6
**cinéma (ciné)** *m.* movie theater, movies I-4
**cinq** *m.* five I-1
**cinquante** *m.* fifty I-1
**cinquième** *adj.* fifth 7
**circulation** *f.* traffic II-3
**clair(e)** *adj.* clear II-7
  **Il est clair que...** It is clear that... II-7
**classe** *f.* (*group of students*) class I-1

**camarade de classe** *m., f.* classmate I-1
  **salle de classe** *f.* classroom I-1
**clavier** *m.* keyboard II-3
**clé** *f.* key I-7
**client(e)** *m., f.* client; guest I-7
**cœur** *m.* heart II-2
  **avoir mal au cœur** to feel nauseated II-2
**coffre** *m.* trunk II-3
**coiffeur/coiffeuse** *m., f.* hairdresser I-3
**coin** *m.* corner II-4
**colis** *m.* package II-4
**colocataire** *m., f.* roommate (*in an apartment*) I-1
**Combien (de)... ?** *adv.* How much/many... ? I-1
  **Combien coûte... ?** How much is... ? I-4
**combiné** *m.* receiver II-5
**comédie (musicale)** *f.* comedy (musical) II-7
**commander** *v.* to order II-1
**comme** *adv.* how; like, as I-2
  **Comme ci, comme ça.** So-so. I-1
**commencer (à)** *v.* to begin (*to do something*) I-2
**comment** *adv.* how I-4
  **Comment?** *adv.* What? I-4
  **Comment allez-vous?,** *form.* How are you? I-1
  **Comment t'appelles-tu?** *fam.* What is your name? I-1
  **Comment vas-tu?** *fam.* How are you? I-1
  **Comment vous appelez-vous?** *form.* What is your name? I-1
**commerçant(e)** *m., f.* shopkeeper II-1
**commissariat de police** *m.* police station II-4
**commode** *f.* dresser, chest of drawers I-8, II-P
**compact disque** *m.* compact disc II-3
**complet (complète)** *adj.* full (no vacancies) I-7
**composer (un numéro)** *v.* to dial (a number) II-3
**compositeur** *m.* composer II-7
**comprendre** *v.* to understand I-4
**compris (comprendre)** *p.p., adj.* understood; included I-6
**comptable** *m., f.* accountant II-5
**compte** *m.* account (*at a bank*) II-4
  **avoir un compte bancaire** *v.* to have a bank account II-4
  **compte de chèques** *m.* checking account II-4

**compte d'épargne** *m.* savings account II-4
  **se rendre compte** *v.* to realize II-2
**compter sur quelqu'un** *v.* to count on someone I-8, II-P
**concert** *m.* concert II-7
**condition** *f.* condition II-7
  **à condition que** on the condition that..., provided that... II-7
**conduire** *v.* to drive I-6
**conduit (conduire)** *p.p., adj.* driven I-6
**confiture** *f.* jam II-1
**congé** *m.* day off I-7
  **jour de congé** *m.* day off I-7
  **prendre un congé** *v.* to take time off II-5
**congélateur** *m.* freezer I-8, II-P
**connaissance** *f.* acquaintance I-5
  **faire la connaissance de** *v.* to meet (*someone*) I-5
**connaître** *v.* to know, to be familiar with I-8, II-P
**connecté(e)** *adj.* connected II-3
  **être connecté(e) avec quelqu'un** *v.* to be online with someone I-7, II-3
**connu (connaître)** *p.p., adj.* known; famous I-8, II-P
**conseil** *m.* advice II-5
**conseiller/conseillère** *m., f.* consultant; advisor II-5
**considérer** *v.* to consider I-5
**constamment** *adv.* constantly I-8, II-P
**construire** *v.* to build, to construct I-6
**conte** *m.* tale II-7
**content(e)** *adj.* happy II-5
  **être content(e) que...** *v.* to be happy that... II-6
**continuer (à)** *v.* to continue (*doing something*) II-4
**contraire** *adj.* contrary II-7
  **au contraire** on the contrary II-7
**copain/copine** *m., f.* friend I-1
**corbeille (à papier)** *f.* wastebasket I-1
**corps** *m.* body II-2
**costume** *m.* (man's) suit I-6
**côte** *f.* coast II-6
**coton** *m.* cotton II-4
**cou** *m.* neck II-2
**couche d'ozone** *f.* ozone layer II-6
  **trou dans la couche d'ozone** *m.* hole in the ozone layer II-6
**couleur** *f.* color 6
  **De quelle couleur... ?** What color... ? I-6

**couloir** *m.* hallway I-8, II-P
**couple** *m.* couple I-6
**courage** *m.* courage II-5
**courageux/courageuse** *adj.*
 courageous, brave I-3
**couramment** *adv.* fluently
 I-8, II-P
**courir** *v.* to run I-5
**courrier** *m.* mail II-4
**cours** *m.* class, course I-2
**course** *f.* errand II-1
 **faire les courses** *v.* to go
 (grocery) shopping II-1
**court(e)** *adj.* short I-3
 **chemise à manches courtes**
 *f.* short-sleeved shirt I-6
**couru (courir)** *p.p.* run I-6
**cousin(e)** *m., f.* cousin I-3
**couteau** *m.* knife II-1
**coûter** *v.* to cost I-4
 **Combien coûte... ?** How
 much is... ? I-4
**couvert (couvrir)** *p.p.*
 covered II-3
**couverture** *f.* blanket I-8, II-P
**couvrir** *v.* to cover II-3
**covoiturage** *m.* carpooling II-6
**cravate** *f.* tie I-6
**crayon** *m.* pencil I-1
**crème** *f.* cream II-1
 **crème à raser** *f.* shaving
 cream II-2
**crêpe** *f.* crêpe I-5
**crevé(e)** *adj.* deflated; blown
 up II-3
 **pneu crevé** *m.* flat tire II-3
**critique** *f.* review; criticism II-7
**croire (que)** *v.* to believe
 (that) II-7
 **ne pas croire que...** to not
 believe that... II-7
**croissant** *m.* croissant I-4
**croissant(e)** *adj.* growing II-6
 **population croissante** *f.*
 growing population II-6
**cru (croire)** *p.p.* believed II-7
**cruel/cruelle** *adj.* cruel I-3
**cuillère (à soupe/à café)** *f.*
 (soup/tea)spoon II-1
**cuir** *m.* leather II-4
**cuisine** *f.* cooking; kitchen 5
 **faire la cuisine** *v.* to cook 5
**cuisiner** *v.* to cook II-1
**cuisinier/cuisinière** *m., f.*
 cook II-5
**cuisinière** *f.* stove I-8, II-P
**curieux/curieuse** *adj.* curious I-3
**curriculum vitæ (C.V.)** *m.*
 résumé II-5
**cybercafé** *m.* cybercafé II-4

### D

**d'abord** *adv.* first I-7
**d'accord** *(tag question)* all right?
 I-2; *(in statement)* okay I-2
 **être d'accord** to be in
 agreement I-2
**d'autres** *m., f.* others I-4
**d'habitude** *adv.* usually
 I-8, II-P
**danger** *m.* danger, threat II-6
**dangereux/dangereuse** *adj.*
 dangerous II-3
**dans** *prep.* in I-3
**danse** *f.* dance II-7
**danser** *v.* to dance I-4
**danseur/danseuse** *m., f.*
 dancer II-7
**date** *f.* date I-5
 **Quelle est la date?** What is
 the date? I-5
**de/d'** *prep.* of I-3; from I-1
 **de l'après-midi** in the
 afternoon I-2
 **de laquelle** *pron., f., sing.*
 which one II-5
 **De quelle couleur... ?** What
 color... ? I-6
 **De rien.** You're welcome. I-1
 **de taille moyenne** of medium
 height I-3
 **de temps en temps** *adv.*
 from time to time I-8, II-P
**débarrasser la table** *v.* to clear
 the table I-8, II-P
**déboisement** *m.* deforestation II-6
**début** *m.* beginning; debut II-7
**décembre** *m.* December I-5
**déchets toxiques** *m., pl.* toxic
 waste II-6
**décider (de)** *v.* to decide *(to do
 something)* II-3
**découvert (découvrir)** *p.p.*
 discovered II-3
**découvrir** *v.* to discover II-3
**décrire** *v.* to describe I-7
**décrocher** *v.* to pick up II-5
**décrit (décrire)** *p.p., adj.*
 described I-7
**degrés** *m., pl.* *(temperature)*
 degrees I-5
 **Il fait ... degrés.** *(to describe
 weather)* It is ... degrees. I-5
**déjà** *adv.* already I-5
**déjeuner** *m.* lunch II-1; *v.* to eat
 lunch I-4
**de l'** *part. art., m., f., sing.* some I-4
**de la** *part. art., f., sing.* some I-4
**délicieux/délicieuse**
 delicious I-8, II-P
**demain** *adv.* tomorrow I-2

**À demain.** See you
 tomorrow. I-1
 **après-demain** *adv.* day after
 tomorrow I-2
 **demain matin/après-midi/
 soir** *adv.* tomorrow morning/
 afternoon/evening I-2
**demander (à)** *v.* to ask *(someone)*, to make a request *(of
 someone)* I-6
 **demander que...** *v.* to ask
 that... II-6
**démarrer** *v.* to start up II-3
**déménager** *v.* to move out
 I-8, II-P
**demie** half I-2
 **et demie** half past ...
 (o'clock) I-2
**demi-frère** *m.* half-brother,
 stepbrother I-3
**demi-sœur** *f.* half-sister,
 stepsister I-3
**démissionner** *v.* to resign II-5
**dent** *f.* tooth II-1
 **brosse à dents** *f.* tooth
 brush II-2
 **se brosser les dents** *v.* to
 brush one's teeth II-1
**dentifrice** *m.* toothpaste II-2
**dentiste** *m., f.* dentist I-3
**départ** *m.* departure I-7
**dépasser** *v.* to go over; to
 pass II-3
**dépense** *f.* expenditure,
 expense II-4
**dépenser** *v.* to spend I-4
 **dépenser de l'argent** *v.* to
 spend money I-4
**déposer de l'argent** *v.* to
 deposit money II-4
**déprimé(e)** *adj.* depressed II-2
**depuis** *adv.* since; for II-1
**dernier/dernière** *adj.* last I-2
**dernièrement** *adv.* lastly, finally
 I-8, II-P
**derrière** *prep.* behind I-3
**des** *part. art., m., f., pl.* some I-4
**des (de + les)** *m., f., pl.* of the I-3
**dès que** *adv.* as soon as II-5
**désagréable** *adj.* unpleasant I-1
**descendre (de)** *v.* to go
 downstairs; to get off; to take
 down I-6
**désert** *m.* desert II-6
**désirer (que)** *v.* to want (that) I-5
**désolé(e)** *adj.* sorry I-6
 **être désolé(e) que...** to be
 sorry that... II-6
**desquelles (de + lesquelles)**
 *pron., f., pl.* which ones II-5
**desquels (de + lesquels)**
 *pron., m., pl.* which ones II-5

**dessert** *m.* dessert I-6
**dessin animé** *m.* cartoon II-7
**dessiner** *v.* to draw I-2
**détester** *v.* to hate I-2
   **Je déteste...** I hate... I-2
**détruire** *v.* to destroy I-6
**détruit (détruire)** *p.p., adj.*
   destroyed I-6
**deux** *m.* two I-1
**deuxième** *adj.* second I-7
**devant** *prep.* in front of I-3
**développer** *v.* to develop II-6
**devenir** *v.* to become II-1
**devoir** *m.* homework I-2; *v.* to
   have to, must II-1
**dictionnaire** *m.* dictionary I-1
**différemment** *adv.* differently
   I-8, II-P
**différence** *f.* difference I-1
**différent(e)** *adj.* different I-1
**difficile** *adj.* difficult I-1
**dimanche** *m.* Sunday I-2
**dîner** *m.* dinner II-1; *v.* to have
   dinner I-2
**diplôme** *m.* diploma, degree I-2
**dire** *v.* to say I-7
   **Ça te dit?** Does that appeal
   to you? II-6
   **ça veut dire** that is to say II-2
   **veut dire** *v.* means, signifies
   II-1
**diriger** *v.* to manage II-5
**discret/discrète** *adj.* discreet;
   unassuming I-3
**discuter** *v.* discuss I-6
**disque** *m.* disk II-3
   **compact disque** *m.* compact
   disc II-3
   **disque dur** *m.* hard drive II-3
**dissertation** *f.* essay II-3
**distributeur automatique/de
   billets** *m.* ATM II-4
**dit (dire)** *p.p., adj.* said I-7
**divorce** *m.* divorce I-6
**divorcé(e)** *adj.* divorced I-3
**divorcer** *v.* to divorce I-3
**dix** *m.* ten I-1
**dix-huit** *m.* eighteen I-1
**dixième** *adj.* tenth I-7
**dix-neuf** *m.* nineteen I-1
**dix-sept** *m.* seventeen I-1
**documentaire** *m.*
   documentary II-7
**doigt** *m.* finger II-2
**doigt de pied** *m.* toe II-2
**domaine** *m.* field II-5
**dommage** *m.* harm II-6
   **Il est dommage que...** It's a
   shame that... II-6
**donc** *conj.* therefore I-7
**donner (à)** *v.* to give (*to
   someone*) I-2

**dont** *rel. pron.* of which; of
   whom; that II-3
**dormir** *v.* to sleep I-5
**dos** *m.* back II-2
   **sac à dos** *m.* backpack I-1
**douane** *f.* customs I-7
**douche** *f.* shower I-8, II-P
   **prendre une douche** *v.* to
   take a shower II-2
**doué(e)** *adj.* talented, gifted II-7
**douleur** *f.* pain II-2
**douter (que)** *v.* to doubt
   (that) II-7
**douteux/douteuse** *adj.*
   doubtful II-7
   **Il est douteux que...** It is
   doubtful that... II-7
**doux/douce** *adj.* sweet; soft I-3
**douze** *m.* twelve I-1
**dramaturge** *m.* playwright II-7
**drame (psychologique)** *m.*
   (psychological) drama II-7
**draps** *m., pl.* sheets I-8, II-P
**droit** *m.* law I-2
**droite** *f.* the right (side) I-3
   **à droite de** *prep.* to the right
   of I-3
**drôle** *adj.* funny I-3
**du** *part. art., m., sing.* some I-4
**du (de + le)** *m., sing.* of the I-3
**dû (devoir)** *p.p., adj. (used with
   infinitive)* had to; *(used with
   noun)* due, owed II-1
**duquel (de + lequel)** *pron., m.,
   sing.* which one II-5

**E**

**eau (minérale)** *f.* (mineral)
   water I-4
   **carafe d'eau** *f.* pitcher of
   water II-1
**écharpe** *f.* scarf I-6
**échecs** *m., pl.* chess I-5
**échouer** *v.* to fail I-2
**éclair** *m.* éclair I-4
**école** *f.* school I-2
**écologie** *f.* ecology II-6
**écologique** *adj.* ecological II-6
**économie** *f.* economics I-2
**écotourisme** *m.* ecotourism II-6
**écouter** *v.* to listen (to) I-2
**écran** *m.* screen 11
**écrire** *v.* to write I-7
**écrivain/femme écrivain** *m., f.*
   writer II-7
**écrit (écrire)** *p.p., adj.* written I-7
**écureuil** *m.* squirrel II-6
**éducation physique** *f.* physical
   education I-2
**effacer** *v.* to erase II-3

**effet de serre** *m.* greenhouse
   effect II-6
**égaler** *v.* to equal I-3
**église** *f.* church I-4
**égoïste** *adj.* selfish I-1
**Eh!** *interj.* Hey! I-2
**électrique** *adj.* electric I-8, II-P
   **appareil électrique/ménager**
   *m.* electrical/household
   appliance I-8, II-P
**électricien/électricienne** *m., f.*
   electrician II-5
**élégant(e)** *adj.* elegant 1
**élevé** *adj.* high II-5
**élève** *m., f.* pupil, student I-1
**elle** *pron., f.* she; it I-1; her I-3
   **elle est...** she/it is... I-1
**elles** *pron., f.* they I-1; them I-3
   **elles sont...** they are... I-1
**e-mail** *m.* e-mail II-3
**emballage (en plastique)** *m.*
   (plastic) wrapping/
   packaging II-6
**embaucher** *v.* to hire II-5
**embrayage** *m.* (*automobile*)
   clutch II-3
**émission (de télévision)** *f.*
   (television) program II-7
**emménager** *v.* to move in
   I-8, II-P
**emmener** *v.* to take (*someone*) I-5
**emploi** *m.* job II-5
   **emploi à mi-temps/à temps
   partiel** *m.* part-time job II-5
   **emploi à plein temps** *m.*
   full-time job II-5
**employé(e)** *m., f.* employee II-5
**employer** *v.* to use, to employ I-5
**emprunter** *v.* to borrow II-4
**en** *prep.* in I-3
   **en automne** in the fall I-5
   **en avance** early I-2
   **en avoir marre** to be fed up I-6
   **en effet** indeed; in fact II-6
   **en été** in the summer I-5
   **en face (de)** *prep.* facing,
   across (from) I-3
   **en fait** in fact I-7
   **en général** *adv.* in general
   I-8, II-P
   **en hiver** in the winter I-5
   **en plein air** in fresh air II-6
   **en retard** late I-2
   **en tout cas** in any case 6
   **en vacances** on vacation 7
   **être en ligne** to be online II-3
**en** *pron.* some of it/them; about
   it/them; of it/them; from it/
   them II-2
   **Je vous en prie.** *form.*
   Please.; You're welcome. I-1

**Qu'en penses-tu?** What do you think about that? II-6
**enceinte** *adj.* pregnant II-2
**Enchanté(e).** Delighted. I-1
**encore** *adv.* again; still I-3
**endroit** *m.* place I-4
**énergie (nucléaire/solaire)** *f.* (nuclear/solar) energy II-6
**enfance** *f.* childhood I-6
**enfant** *m., f.* child I-3
**enfin** *adv.* finally, at last I-7
**enlever la poussière** *v.* to dust I-8, II-P
**ennuyeux/ennuyeuse** *adj.* boring I-3
**énorme** *adj.* enormous, huge I-2
**enregistrer** *v.* to record II-3
**enseigner** *v.* to teach I-2
**ensemble** *adv.* together I-6
**ensuite** *adv.* then, next I-7
**entendre** *v.* to hear I-6
**entracte** *m.* intermission II-7
**entre** *prep.* between I-3
**entrée** *f.* appetizer, starter II-1
**entreprise** *f.* firm, business II-5
**entrer** *v.* to enter I-7
**entretien: passer un entretien** *to have an interview* II-5
**enveloppe** *f.* envelope II-4
**envie** *f.* desire, envy I-2
**avoir envie (de)** to feel like (*doing something*) I-2
**environnement** *m.* environment II-6
**envoyer (à)** *v.* to send (*to someone*) I-5
**épargne** *f.* savings II-4
**compte d'épargne** *m.* savings account II-4
**épicerie** *f.* grocery store I-4
**épouser** *v.* to marry I-3
**épouvantable** *adj.* dreadful 5
**Il fait un temps épouvantable.** The weather is dreadful. I-5
**époux/épouse** *m., f.* husband/wife I-3
**équipe** *f.* team I-5
**escalier** *m.* staircase I-8, II-P
**escargot** *m.* escargot, snail II-1
**espace** *m.* space II-6
**Espagne** *f.* Spain 7
**espagnol(e)** *adj.* Spanish I-1
**espèce (menacée)** *f.* (endangered) species II-6
**espérer** *v.* to hope I-5
**essayer** *v.* to try I-5
**essence** *f.* gas II-3
**réservoir d'essence** *m.* gas tank II-3

**voyant d'essence** *m.* gas warning light II-3
**essentiel(le)** *adj.* essential II-6
**Il est essentiel que...** It is essential that... II-6
**essuie-glace** *m.* (**essuie-glaces** *pl.*) windshield wiper(s) II-3
**essuyer (la vaiselle/la table)** *v.* to wipe (the dishes/the table) I-8, II-P
**est** *m.* east II-4
**Est-ce que... ?** (*used in forming questions*) I-2
**et** *conj.* and I-1
**Et toi?** *fam.* And you? I-1
**Et vous?** *form.* And you? I-1
**étage** *m.* floor I-7
**étagère** *f.* shelf I-8, II-P
**étape** *f.* stage I-6
**état civil** *m.* marital status I-6
**États-Unis** *m., pl.* United States I-7
**été** *m.* summer I-5
**en été** in the summer I-5
**été (être)** *p.p.* been I-6
**éteindre** *v.* to turn off II-3
**éternuer** *v.* to sneeze II-2
**étoile** *f.* star II-6
**étranger/étrangère** *adj.* foreign I-2
**langues étrangères** *f., pl.* foreign languages I-2
**étranger** *m.* (*places that are*) abroad, overseas I-7
**à l'étranger** abroad, overseas I-7
**étrangler** *v.* to strangle II-5
**être** *v.* to be I-1
**être bien/mal payé(e)** to be well/badly paid II-5
**être connecté(e) avec quelqu'un** to be online with someone I-7, II-3
**être en ligne avec** to be online with II-3
**être en pleine forme** to be in good shape II-2
**études (supérieures)** *f., pl.* studies; (higher) education I-2
**étudiant(e)** *m., f.* student I-1
**étudier** *v.* to study I-2
**eu (avoir)** *p.p.* had I-6
**eux** *disj. pron., m., pl.* they, them I-3
**évidemment** *adv.* obviously, evidently; of course I-8, II-P
**évident(e)** *adj.* evident, obvious II-7
**Il est évident que...** It is evident that... II-7
**évier** *m.* sink I-8, II-P

**éviter (de)** *v.* to avoid (*doing something*) II-2
**exactement** *adv.* exactly II-1
**examen** *m.* exam; test I-1
**être reçu(e) à un examen** *v.* to pass an exam I-2
**passer un examen** *v.* to take an exam I-2
**Excuse-moi.** *fam.* Excuse me. I-1
**Excusez-moi.** *form.* Excuse me. I-1
**exercice** *m.* exercise II-2
**faire de l'exercice** *v.* to exercise II-2
**exigeant(e)** *adj.* demanding II-5
**profession (exigeante)** *f.* a (demanding) profession II-5
**exiger (que)** *v.* to demand (that) II-6
**expérience (professionnelle)** *f.* (professional) experience II-5
**expliquer** *v.* to explain I-2
**explorer** *v.* to explore I-4
**exposition** *f.* exhibit II-7
**extinction** *f.* extinction II-6

**F**

**facile** *adj.* easy I-2
**facilement** *adv.* easily I-8, II-P
**facteur** *m.* mailman II-4
**faculté** *f.* university; faculty I-1
**faible** *adj.* weak I-3
**faim** *f.* hunger I-4
**avoir faim** *v.* to be hungry I-4
**faire** *v.* to do; to make I-5
**faire attention (à)** *v.* to pay attention (to) I-5
**faire quelque chose de beau** *v.* to be up to something interesting II-4
**faire de l'aérobic** *v.* to do aerobics I-5
**faire de la gym** *v.* to work out I-5
**faire de la musique** *v.* to play music II-5
**faire de la peinture** *v.* to paint II-7
**faire de la planche à voile** *v.* to go windsurfing I-5
**faire de l'exercice** *v.* to exercise II-2
**faire des projets** *v.* to make plans II-5
**faire du camping** *v.* to go camping I-5
**faire du cheval** *v.* to go horseback riding I-5
**faire du jogging** *v.* to go jogging I-5

**faire du shopping** *v.* to go shopping I-7

**faire du ski** *v.* to go skiing I-5

**faire du sport** *v.* to do sports I-5

**faire du vélo** *v.* to go bike riding I-5

**faire la connaissance de** *v.* to meet (*someone*) I-5

**faire la cuisine** *v.* to cook I-5

**faire la fête** *v.* to party I-6

**faire la lessive** *v.* to do the laundry I-8, II-P

**faire la poussière** *v.* to dust I-8, II-P

**faire la queue** *v.* to wait in line II-4

**faire la vaisselle** *v.* to do the dishes I-8, II-P

**faire le lit** *v.* to make the bed I-8, II-P

**faire le ménage** *v.* to do the housework I-8, II-P

**faire le plein** *v.* to fill the tank II-3

**faire les courses** *v.* to run errands II-1

**faire les musées** *v.* to go to museums II-7

**faire les valises** *v.* to pack one's bags I-7

**faire mal** *v.* to hurt II-2

**faire plaisir à quelqu'un** *v.* to please someone II-5

**faire sa toilette** *v.* to wash up II-2

**faire une piqûre** *v.* to give a shot 10

**faire une promenade** *v.* to go for a walk I-5

**faire une randonnée** *v.* to go for a hike I-5

**faire un séjour** *v.* to spend time (*somewhere*) I-7

**faire un tour (en voiture)** *v.* to go for a walk (drive) I-5

**faire visiter** *v.* to give a tour I-8, II-P

**fait (faire)** *p.p., adj.* done; made I-6

**falaise** *f.* cliff II-6

**faut (falloir)** *v.* (*used with infinitive*) is necessary to... I-5

**Il a fallu...** It was necessary to... I-6

**Il fallait...** One had to... I-8, II-P

**Il faut que...** One must.../It is necessary that... II-6

**fallu (falloir)** *p.p.* (*used with infinitive*) had to... I-6

**Il a fallu...** It was necessary to... I-6

**famille** *f.* family I-3

**fatigué(e)** *adj.* tired I-3

**fauteuil** *m.* armchair I-8, II-P

**favori/favorite** *adj.* favorite I-3

**fax** *m.* fax (machine) II-3

**félicitations** congratulations II-7

**femme** *f.* woman; wife I-1

**femme d'affaires** businesswoman I-3

**femme au foyer** housewife II-5

**femme auteur** author II-7

**femme cadre** executive II-5

**femme écrivain** writer II-7

**femme peintre** painter II-7

**femme politique** politician II-5

**femme pompier** firefighter II-5

**femme sculpteur** sculptor II-7

**fenêtre** *f.* window I-1

**fer à repasser** *m.* iron I-8, II-P

**férié(e)** *adj.* holiday I-6

**jour férié** *m.* holiday I-6

**fermé(e)** *adj.* closed II-4

**fermer** *v.* to close; to shut off II-3

**festival (festivals pl.)** *m.* festival II-7

**fête** *f.* party; celebration I-6

**faire la fête** *v.* to party I-6

**fêter** *v.* to celebrate I-6

**feu de signalisation** *m.* traffic light II-4

**feuille de papier** *f.* sheet of paper I-1

**feuilleton** *m.* soap opera II-7

**février** *m.* February I-5

**fiancé(e)** *adj.* engaged I-3

**fiancé(e)** *m., f.* fiancé I-6

**fichier** *m.* file II-3

**fier/fière** *adj.* proud I-3

**fièvre** *f.* fever II-2

**avoir de la fièvre** *v.* to have a fever II-2

**fille** *f.* girl; daughter I-1

**film (d'aventures, d'horreur, de science-fiction, policier)** *m.* (adventure, horror, science-fiction, crime) film II-7

**fils** *m.* son I-3

**fin** *f.* end II-7

**finalement** *adv.* finally I-7

**fini (finir)** *p.p., adj.* finished, done, over I-4

**finir (de)** *v.* to finish (*doing something*) I-4

**fleur** *f.* flower I-8, II-P

**fleuve** *m.* river II-6

**fois** *f.* time I-8, II-P

**une fois** *adv.* once I-8, II-P

**deux fois** *adv.* twice I-8, II-P

**fonctionner** *v.* to work, to function II-3

**fontaine** *f.* fountain II-4

**foot(ball)** *m.* soccer I-5

**football américain** *m.* football I-5

**forêt (tropicale)** *f.* (tropical) forest II-6

**formation** *f.* education; training II-5

**forme** *f.* shape; form II-2

**être en pleine forme** *v.* to be in good shape II-2

**formidable** *adj.* great I-7

**formulaire** *m.* form II-4

**remplir un formulaire** to fill out a form II-4

**fort(e)** *adj.* strong I-3

**fou/folle** *adj.* crazy I-3

**four (à micro-ondes)** *m.* (microwave) oven I-8, II-P

**fourchette** *f.* fork II-1

**frais/fraîche** *adj.* fresh; cool I-5

**Il fait frais.** (*weather*) It is cool. I-5

**fraise** *f.* strawberry II-1

**français(e)** *adj.* French I-1

**France** *f.* France I-7

**franchement** *adv.* frankly, honestly I-8, II-P

**freiner** *v.* to brake II-3

**freins** *m., pl.* brakes II-3

**fréquenter** *v.* to frequent; to visit I-4

**frère** *m.* brother I-3

**beau-frère** *m.* brother-in-law I-3

**demi-frère** *m.* half-brother, stepbrother I-3

**frigo** *m.* refrigerator I-8, II-P

**frisé(e)** *adj.* curly I-3

**frites** *f., pl.* French fries I-4

**froid** *m.* cold I-2

**avoir froid** to be cold I-2

**Il fait froid.** (*weather*) It is cold. I-5

**fromage** *m.* cheese I-4

**fruit** *m.* fruit II-1

**fruits de mer** *m., pl.* seafood II-1

**fumer** *v.* to smoke II-2

**funérailles** *f., pl.* funeral II-1

**furieux/furieuse** *adj.* furious II-6

**être furieux/furieuse que...** *v.* to be furious that... II-6

### G

**gagner** *v.* to win I-5; to earn II-5

**gant** *m.* glove I-6

**garage** *m.* garage I-8, II-P

**garanti(e)** *adj.* guaranteed 5

**garçon** *m.* boy I-1

**garder la ligne** *v.* to stay slim II-2

**gare (routière)** *f.* train station (bus station) I-7

**gaspillage** *m.* waste II-6

**gaspiller** *v.* to waste II-6
**gâteau** *m.* cake I-6
**gauche** *f.* the left (side) I-3
  **à gauche (de)** *prep.* to the left (of) I-3
**gazeux/gazeuse** *adj.* carbonated, fizzy 4
  **boisson gazeuse** *f.* carbonated drink/beverage I-4
**généreux/généreuse** *adj.* generous I-3
**génial(e)** *adj.* great I-3
**genou** *m.* knee II-2
**genre** *m.* genre II-7
**gens** *m., pl.* people I-7
**gentil/gentille** *adj.* nice I-3
**gentiment** *adv.* nicely I-8, II-P
**géographie** *f.* geography I-2
**gérant(e)** *m., f.* manager II-5
**gestion** *f.* business administration I-2
**glace** *f.* ice cream I-6
**glaçon** *m.* ice cube I-6
**glissement de terrain** *m.* landslide II-6
**golf** *m.* golf I-5
**enfler** *v.* to swell II-2
**gorge** *f.* throat II-2
**goûter** *m.* afternoon snack II-1; *v.* to taste II-1
**gouvernement** *m.* government II-6
**grand(e)** *adj.* big I-3
  **grand magasin** *m.* department store I-4
**grand-mère** *f.* grandmother I-3
**grand-père** *m.* grandfather I-3
**grands-parents** *m., pl.* grandparents I-3
**gratin** *m.* gratin II-1
**gratuit(e)** *adj.* free II-7
**grave** *adj.* serious II-2
  **Ce n'est pas grave.** It's okay.; No problem. I-6
**graver** *v.* to record, to burn (CD, DVD) II-3
**grille-pain** *m.* toaster I-8, II-P
**grippe** *f.* flu II-2
**gris(e)** *adj.* gray I-6
**gros(se)** *adj.* fat I-3
**grossir** *v.* to gain weight I-4
**guérir** *v.* to get better II-2
**guitare** *f.* guitar II-7
**gym** *f.* exercise I-5
  **faire de la gym** *v.* to work out I-5
**gymnase** *m.* gym I-4

<br>

**             H**

**habitat** *m.* habitat II-6
  **sauvetage des habitats** *m.* habitat preservation II-6

**habiter (à)** *v.* to live (in/at) I-2
**haricots verts** *m., pl.* green beans II-1
**Hein?** *interj.* Huh?; Right? I-3
**herbe** *f.* grass II-6
**hésiter (à)** *v.* to hesitate (*to do something*) II-3
**heure(s)** *f.* hour, o'clock; time I-2
  **à ... heure(s)** at ... (o'clock) I-4
  **À quelle heure?** What time?; When? I-2
  **À tout à l'heure.** See you later. I-1
  **Quelle heure avez-vous?** *form.* What time do you have? I-2
  **Quelle heure est-il?** What time is it? I-2
**heureusement** *adv.* fortunately I-8, II-P
**heureux/heureuse** *adj.* happy I-3
  **être heureux/heureuse que...** to be happy that... II-6
**hier (matin/après-midi/soir)** *adv.* yesterday (morning/afternoon/evening) I-7
  **avant-hier** *adv.* day before yesterday I-7
**histoire** *f.* history; story I-2
**hiver** *m.* winter I-5
  **en hiver** in the winter I-5
**homme** *m.* man I-1
  **homme d'affaires** *m.* businessman I-3
  **homme politique** *m.* politician II-5
**honnête** *adj.* honest II-7
**honte** *f.* shame I-2
  **avoir honte (de)** *v.* to be ashamed (of) I-2
**hôpital** *m.* hospital I-4
**horloge** *f.* clock I-1
**hors-d'œuvre** *m.* hors d'œuvre, appetizer II-1
**hôte/hôtesse** *m., f.* host I-6
**hôtel** *m.* hotel I-7
**hôtelier/hôtelière** *m., f.* hotel keeper I-7
**huile** *f.* oil II-1
  **huile** *f.* (automobile) oil II-3
  **huile d'olive** *f.* olive oil II-1
  **vérifier l'huile** to check the oil II-3
  **voyant d'huile** *m.* oil warning light II-3
**huit** *m.* eight I-1
**huitième** *adj.* eighth I-7
**humeur** *f.* mood I-8, II-P
  **être de bonne/mauvaise humeur** *v.* to be in a good/bad mood I-8, II-P

<br>

**             I**

**ici** *adv.* here I-1
**idée** *f.* idea I-3
**il** *sub. pron.* he; it I-1
  **il est...** he/it is... I-1
  **Il n'y a pas de quoi.** It's nothing.; You're welcome. I-1
  **Il vaut mieux que...** It is better that... II-6
**Il faut (falloir)** *v.* (*used with infinitive*) It is necessary to... I-6
  **Il a fallu...** It was necessary to... I-6
  **Il fallait...** One had to... I-8, II-P
  **Il faut (que)...** One must.../ It is necessary that... II-6
**il y a** there is/are I-1
  **il y a eu** there was/were 6
  **il y avait** there was/were I-8, II-P
  **Qu'est-ce qu'il y a?** What is it?; What's wrong? I-1
  **Y a-t-il... ?** Is/Are there... ? I-2
**il y a...** (*used with an expression of time*) ... ago II-1
**île** *f.* island II-6
**ils** *sub. pron., m., pl.* they I-1
  **ils sont...** they are... I-1
**immeuble** *m.* building I-8, II-P
**impatient(e)** *adj.* impatient I-1
**imperméable** *m.* rain jacket I-5
**important(e)** *adj.* important I-1
  **Il est important que...** It is important that... II-6
**impossible** *adj.* impossible II-7
  **Il est impossible que...** It is impossible that... II-7
**imprimante** *f.* printer II-3
**imprimer** *v.* to print II-3
**incendie** *m.* fire II-6
  **prévenir l'incendie** to prevent a fire II-6
**incroyable** *adj.* incredible II-3
**indépendamment** *adv.* independently I-8, II-P
**indépendant(e)** *adj.* independent I-1
**indications** *f.* directions II-4
**indiquer** *v.* to indicate I-5
**indispensable** *adj.* essential, indispensable II-6
  **Il est indispensable que...** It is essential that... II-6
**individuel(le)** *adj.* single, individual I-7
  **chambre individuelle** *f.* single (hotel) room I-7
**infirmier/infirmière** *m., f.* nurse II-2

**informations (infos)** *f., pl.* news II-7
**informatique** *f.* computer science I-2
**ingénieur** *m.* engineer I-3
**inquiet/inquiète** *adj.* worried I-3
**instrument** *m.* instrument I-1
**intellectuel(le)** *adj.* intellectual I-3
**intelligent(e)** *adj.* intelligent I-1
**interdire** *v.* to forbid, to prohibit II-6
**intéressant(e)** *adj.* interesting I-1
**inutile** *adj.* useless I-2
**invité(e)** *m., f.* guest I-6
**inviter** *v.* to invite I-4
**irlandais(e)** *adj.* Irish I-7
**Irlande** *f.* Ireland I-7
**Italie** *f.* Italy I-7
**italien(ne)** *adj.* Italian I-1

**J**

**jaloux/jalouse** *adj.* jealous I-3
**jamais** *adv.* never I-5
  **ne… jamais** never, not ever II-4
**jambe** *f.* leg II-2
**jambon** *m.* ham I-4
**janvier** *m.* January I-5
**Japon** *m.* Japan I-7
**japonais(e)** *adj.* Japanese I-1
**jardin** *m.* garden; yard I-8, II-P
**jaune** *adj.* yellow I-6
**je/j'** *sub. pron.* I I-1
  **Je vous en prie.** *form.* Please.; You're welcome. I-1
**jean** *m., sing.* jeans I-6
**jeter** *v.* to throw away II-6
**jeu** *m.* game I-5
  **jeu télévisé** *m.* game show II-7
  **jeu vidéo (des jeux vidéo)** *m.* video game(s) II-3
**jeudi** *m.* Thursday I-2
**jeune** *adj.* young I-3
  **jeunes mariés** *m., pl.* newlyweds I-6
**jeunesse** *f.* youth I-6
  **auberge de jeunesse** *f.* youth hostel I-7
**jogging** *m.* jogging I-5
  **faire du jogging** *v.* to go jogging I-5
**joli(e)** *adj.* handsome; beautiful I-3
**joue** *f.* cheek II-2
**jouer (à/de)** *v.* to play (a sport/a musical instrument) I-5
  **jouer un rôle** *v.* to play a role II-7
**joueur/joueuse** *m., f.* player I-5
**jour** *m.* day I-2

**jour de congé** *m.* day off I-7
**jour férié** *m.* holiday I-6
  **Quel jour sommes-nous?** *What day is it?* I-2
**journal** *m.* newspaper; journal I-7
**journaliste** *m., f.* journalist I-3
**journée** *f.* day I-2
**juillet** *m.* July I-5
**juin** *m.* June I-5
**jungle** *f.* jungle II-6
**jupe** *f.* skirt I-6
**jus (d'orange/de pomme)** *m.* (orange/apple) juice I-4
**jusqu'à (ce que)** *prep.* until II-4
**juste** *adv.* just; right I-3
  **juste à côté** right next door I-3

**K**

**kilo(gramme)** *m.* kilo(gram) II-1
**kiosque** *m.* kiosk I-4

**L**

**l'** *def. art., m., f. sing.* the I-1; *d.o. pron., m., f.* him; her; it I-7
**la** *def. art., f. sing.* the I-1; *d.o. pron., f.* her; it I-7
**là(-bas)** (over) there I-1
**-là** *(used with demonstrative adjective* **ce** *and noun or with demonstrative pronoun* **celui***)* there I-6
**lac** *m.* lake II-6
**laid(e)** *adj.* ugly I-3
**laine** *f.* wool II-4
**laisser** *v.* to let, to allow II-3
  **laisser tranquille** *v.* to leave alone II-2
  **laisser un message** *v.* to leave a message II-5
  **laisser un pourboire** *v.* to leave a tip I-4
**lait** *m.* milk I-4
**laitue** *f.* lettuce II-1
**lampe** *f.* lamp I-8, II-P
**langues (étrangères)** *f., pl.* (foreign) languages I-2
**lapin** *m.* rabbit II-6
**laquelle** *pron., f., sing.* which one I-5
  **à laquelle** *pron., f., sing.* which one II-5
  **de laquelle** *pron., f., sing.* which one II-5
**large** *adj.* loose; big I-6
**lavabo** *m.* bathroom sink I-8, II-P
**lave-linge** *m.* washing machine I-8, II-P
**laver** *v.* to wash I-8, II-P

**laverie** *f.* laundromat II-4
**lave-vaisselle** *m.* dishwasher I-8, II-P
**le** *def. art., m. sing.* the I-1; *d.o. pron.* him; it I-7
**lecteur de CD/DVD** *m.* CD/DVD player II-3
**légume** *m.* vegetable II-1
**lent(e)** *adj.* slow I-3
**lequel** *pron., m., sing.* which one II-5
  **auquel (à + lequel)** *pron., m., sing.* which one II-5
  **duquel (de + lequel)** *pron., m., sing.* which one II-5
**les** *def. art., m., f., pl.* the I-1; *d.o. pron., m., f., pl.* them I-7
**lesquelles** *pron., f., pl.* which ones II-5
  **auxquelles (à + lesquelles)** *pron., f., pl.* which ones II-5
  **desquelles (de + lesquelles)** *pron., f., pl.* which ones II-5
**lesquels** *pron., m., pl.* which ones II-5
  **auxquels (à + lesquels)** *pron., m., pl.* which ones II-5
  **desquels (de + lesquels)** *pron., m., pl.* which ones II-5
**lessive** *f.* laundry I-8, II-P
  **faire la lessive** *v.* to do the laundry I-8, II-P
**lettre** *f.* letter II-4
  **boîte aux lettres** *f.* mailbox II-4
  **lettre de motivation** *f.* letter of application II-5
  **lettre de recommandation** *f.* letter of recommendation, reference letter II-5
**lettres** *f., pl.* humanities I-2
**leur** *i.o. pron., m., f., pl.* them I-6
**leur(s)** *poss. adj., m., f.* their I-3
**librairie** *f.* bookstore I-1
**libre** *adj.* available I-7
**lieu** *m.* place I-4
**ligne** *f.* figure, shape II-2
  **garder la ligne** *v.* to stay slim II-2
**limitation de vitesse** *f.* speed limit II-3
**limonade** *f.* lemon soda I-4
**linge** *m.* laundry I-8, II-P
  **lave-linge** *m.* washing machine I-8, II-P
  **sèche-linge** *m.* clothes dryer I-8, II-P
**liquide** *m.* cash (*money*) II-4
  **payer en liquide** *v.* to pay in cash II-4
**lire** *v.* to read I-7
**lit** *m.* bed I-7

**faire le lit** *v.* to make the bed I-8, II-P
**littéraire** *adj.* literary II-7
**littérature** *f.* literature I-1
**livre** *m.* book I-1
**logement** *m.* housing I-8, II-P
**logiciel** *m.* software, program II-3
**loi** *f.* law II-6
**loin de** *prep.* far from I-3
**loisir** *m.* leisure activity I-5
**long(ue)** *adj.* long I-3
**chemise à manches longues** *f.* long-sleeved shirt I-6
**longtemps** *adv.* a long time I-5
**louer** *v.* to rent I-8, II-P
**loyer** *m.* rent I-8, II-P
**lu (lire)** *p.p.* read I-7
**lui** *pron., sing.* he I-1; him I-3; *i.o. pron.* (*attached to imperative*) to him/her II-1
**l'un(e) à l'autre** to one another II-3
**l'un(e) l'autre** one another II-3
**lundi** *m.* Monday I-2
**Lune** *f.* moon II-6
**lunettes (de soleil)** *f., pl.* (sun)glasses I-6
**lycée** *m.* high school I-1
**lycéen(ne)** *m., f.* high school student I-2

**M**

**ma** *poss. adj., f., sing.* my I-3
**Madame** *f.* Ma'am; Mrs. I-1
**Mademoiselle** *f.* Miss I-1
**magasin** *m.* store I-4
**grand magasin** *m.* department store I-4
**magazine** *m.* magazine II-7
**magnétophone** *m.* tape recorder II-3
**magnétoscope** *m.* videocassette recorder (VCR) II-3
**mai** *m.* May I-5
**maigrir** *v.* to lose weight I-4
**maillot de bain** *m.* swimsuit, bathing suit I-6
**main** *f.* hand I-5
**sac à main** *m.* purse, handbag I-6
**maintenant** *adv.* now I-5
**maintenir** *v.* to maintain II-1
**mairie** *f.* town/city hall; mayor's office II-4
**mais** *conj.* but I-1
**mais non** (but) of course not; no I-2
**maison** *f.* house I-4
**rentrer à la maison** *v.* to return home I-2
**mal** *adv.* badly I-7

**Je vais mal.** I am doing badly. I-1
**le plus mal** *super. adv.* the worst II-1
**se porter mal** *v.* to be doing badly II-2
**mal** *m.* illness; ache, pain II-2
**avoir mal** *v.* to have an ache II-2
**avoir mal au cœur** *v.* to feel nauseated II-2
**faire mal** *v.* to hurt II-2
**malade** *adj.* sick, ill II-2
**tomber malade** *v.* to get sick II-2
**maladie** *f.* illness II-5
**assurance maladie** *f.* health insurance II-5
**malheureusement** *adv.* unfortunately I-2
**malheureux/malheureuse** *adj.* unhappy I-3
**manche** *f.* sleeve I-6
**chemise à manches courtes/ longues** *f.* short-/long-sleeved shirt I-6
**manger** *v.* to eat I-2
**salle à manger** *f.* dining room I-8, II-P
**manteau** *m.* coat I-6
**maquillage** *m.* makeup II-2
**marchand de journaux** *m.* newsstand II-4
**marché** *m.* market I-4
**bon marché** *adj.* inexpensive I-6
**marcher** *v.* to walk (*person*) I-5; to work (*thing*) II-3
**mardi** *m.* Tuesday I-2
**mari** *m.* husband I-3
**mariage** *m.* marriage; wedding (*ceremony*) I-6
**marié(e)** *adj.* married I-3
**mariés** *m., pl.* married couple I-6
**jeunes mariés** *m., pl.* newlyweds I-6
**marocain(e)** *adj.* Moroccan I-1
**marron** *adj., inv.* (not for hair) brown I-3
**mars** *m.* March I-5
**martiniquais(e)** *adj.* from Martinique I-1
**match** *m.* game I-5
**mathématiques (maths)** *f., pl.* mathematics I-2
**matin** *m.* morning I-2
**ce matin** *adv.* this morning I-2
**demain matin** *adv.* tomorrow morning I-2
**hier matin** *adv.* yesterday morning I-7
**matinée** *f.* morning I-2
**mauvais(e)** *adj.* bad I-3
**Il fait mauvais.** The weather is bad. I-5

**le/la plus mauvais(e)** *super. adj.* the worst II-1
**mayonnaise** *f.* mayonnaise II-1
**me/m'** *pron., sing.* me; myself I-6
**mec** *m.* guy II-2
**mécanicien** *m.* mechanic II-3
**mécanicienne** *f.* mechanic II-3
**méchant(e)** *adj.* mean I-3
**médecin** *m.* doctor I-3
**médicament (contre/pour)** *m.* medication (against/for) II-2
**meilleur(e)** *comp. adj.* better II-1
**le/la meilleur(e)** *super. adj.* the best II-1
**membre** *m.* member II-7
**même** *adj.* even I-5; same
**-même(s)** *pron.* -self/-selves I-6
**menacé(e)** *adj.* endangered II-6
**espèce menacée** *f.* endangered species II-6
**ménage** *m.* housework I-8, II-P
**faire le ménage** *v.* to do housework I-8, II-P
**ménager/ménagère** *adj.* household I-8, II-P
**appareil ménager** *m.* household appliance I-8, II-P
**tâche ménagère** *f.* household chore I-8, II-P
**mention** *f.* distinction II-5
**menu** *m.* menu II-1
**mer** *f.* sea I-7
**Merci (beaucoup).** Thank you (very much). I-1
**mercredi** *m.* Wednesday I-2
**mère** *f.* mother I-3
**belle-mère** *f.* mother-in-law; stepmother I-3
**mes** *poss. adj., m., f., pl.* my I-3
**message** *m.* message II-5
**laisser un message** *v.* to leave a message II-5
**messagerie** *f.* voicemail II-5
**météo** *f.* weather II-7
**métier** *m.* profession II-5
**métro** *m.* subway I-7
**station de métro** *f.* subway station I-7
**metteur en scène** *m.* director (*of a play*) II-7
**mettre** *v.* to put, to place 6
**mettre la table** to set the table I-8, II-P
**meuble** *m.* piece of furniture I-8, II-P
**mexicain(e)** *adj.* Mexican I-1
**Mexique** *m.* Mexico I-7
**Miam!** *interj.* Yum! I-5
**micro-onde** *m.* microwave oven I-8, II-P
**four à micro-ondes** *m.* microwave oven I-8, II-P
**midi** *m.* noon I-2

**après-midi** *m.* afternoon I-2
**mieux** *comp. adv.* better II-1
  **aimer mieux** *v.* to prefer I-2
  **le mieux** *super. adv.* the best II-1
  **se porter mieux** *v.* to be doing better II-2
**mille** *m.* one thousand I-5
  **cent mille** *m.* one hundred thousand I-5
**million, un** *m.* one million I-5
  **deux millions** *m.* two million I-5
**minuit** *m.* midnight I-2
**miroir** *m.* mirror I-8, II-P
**mis (mettre)** *p.p.* put, placed I-6
**mode** *f.* fashion I-2
**modeste** *adj.* modest II-5
**moi** *disj. pron., sing.* I, me I-3; *pron. (attached to an imperative)* to me, to myself II-1
  **Moi aussi.** Me too. I-1
  **Moi non plus.** Me neither. I-2
**moins** *adv.* before … (o'clock) I-2
**moins (de)** *adv.* less (of); fewer I-4
  **le/la moins** *super. adv. (used with verb or adverb)* the least II-1
  **le moins de…** *(used with noun to express quantity)* the least… II-6
  **moins de… que…** *(used with noun to express quantity)* less… than… II-6
**mois** *m.* month I-2
  **ce mois-ci** this month I-2
**moment** *m.* moment I-1
**mon** *poss. adj., m., sing.* my I-3
**monde** *m.* world I-7
**moniteur** *m.* monitor II-3
**monnaie** *f.* change, coins; money II-4
**Monsieur** *m.* Sir; Mr. I-1
**montagne** *f.* mountain I-4
**monter** *v.* to go up, to come up; to get in/on I-7
**montre** *f.* watch I-1
**montrer (à)** *v.* to show (to someone) I-6
**morceau (de)** *m.* piece, bit (of) I-4
**mort** *f.* death I-6
**mort (mourir)** *p.p., adj. (as past participle)* died; *(as adjective)* dead I-7
**mot de passe** *m.* password II-3
**moteur** *m.* engine II-3
**mourir** *v.* to die I-7
**moutarde** *f.* mustard II-1
**moyen(ne)** *adj.* medium I-3
  **de taille moyenne** of medium height I-3
**mur** *m.* wall I-8, II-P
**musée** *m.* museum I-4

**faire les musées** *v.* to go to museums II-7
**musical(e)** *adj.* musical II-7
  **comédie musicale** *f.* musical II-7
**musicien(ne)** *m., f.* musician I-3
**musique: faire de la musique** *v.* to play music II-7

**N**

**nager** *v.* to swim I-4
**naïf/naïve** *adj.* naïve I-3
**naissance** *f.* birth I-6
**naître** *v.* to be born I-7
**nappe** *f.* tablecloth II-1
**nationalité** *f.* nationality I-1
  **Je suis de nationalité…** I am of … nationality. I-1
  **Quelle est ta nationalité?** *fam.* What is your nationality? I-1
  **Quelle est votre nationalité?** *fam., pl., form.* What is your nationality? I-1
**nature** *f.* nature II-6
**naturel(le)** *adj.* natural II-6
  **ressource naturelle** *f.* natural resource II-6
**né (naître)** *p.p., adj.* born I-7
**ne/n'** no, not I-1
  **ne… aucun(e)** none, not any II-4
  **ne… jamais** never, not ever II-4
  **ne… ni… ni…** neither… nor… II-4
  **ne… pas** no, not I-2
  **ne… personne** nobody, no one II-4
  **ne… plus** no more, not anymore II-4
  **ne… que** only II-4
  **ne… rien** nothing, not anything II-4
  **N'est-ce pas?** *(tag question)* Isn't it? I-2
**nécessaire** *adj.* necessary II-6
  **Il est nécessaire que…** It is necessary that… II-6
**neiger** *v.* to snow I-5
  **Il neige.** It is snowing. I-5
**nerveusement** *adv.* nervously I-8, II-P
**nerveux/nerveuse** *adj.* nervous I-3
**nettoyer** *v.* to clean I-5
**neuf** *m.* nine I-1
**neuvième** *adj.* ninth I-7
**neveu** *m.* nephew I-3
**nez** *m.* nose II-2
**ni** nor II-4

**ne… ni… ni…** neither… nor II-4
**nièce** *f.* niece I-3
**niveau** *m.* level II-5
**noir(e)** *adj.* black I-3
**non** no I-2
  **mais non** (but) of course not; no I-2
**nord** *m.* north II-4
**nos** *poss. adj., m., f., pl.* our I-3
**note** *f. (academics)* grade I-2
**notre** *poss. adj., m., f., sing.* our I-3
**nourriture** *f.* food, sustenance II-1
**nous** *pron.* we I-1; us I-3; ourselves II-2
**nouveau/nouvelle** *adj.* new I-3
**nouvelles** *f., pl.* news II-7
**novembre** *m.* November I-5
**nuage de pollution** *m.* pollution cloud II-6
**nuageux/nuageuse** *adj.* cloudy I-5
  **Le temps est nuageux.** It is cloudy. I-5
**nucléaire** *adj.* nuclear II-6
  **centrale nucléaire** *f.* nuclear plant II-6
  **énergie nucléaire** *f.* nuclear energy II-6
**nuit** *f.* night I-2
  **boîte de nuit** *f.* nightclub I-4
**nul(le)** *adj.* useless I-2
**numéro** *m.* (telephone) number II-3
  **composer un numéro** *v.* to dial a number II-3
  **recomposer un numéro** *v.* to redial a number II-3

**O**

**objet** *m.* object I-1
**obtenir** *v.* to get, to obtain II-5
**occupé(e)** *adj.* busy I-1
**octobre** *m.* October I-5
**œil (les yeux)** *m.* eye (eyes) II-2
**œuf** *m.* egg II-1
**œuvre** *f.* artwork, piece of art II-7
  **chef-d'œuvre** *m.* masterpiece II-7
  **hors-d'œuvre** *m.* hors d'œuvre, starter II-1
**offert (offrir)** *p.p.* offered II-3
**office du tourisme** *m.* tourist office II-4
**offrir** *v.* to offer II-3
**oignon** *m.* onion II-1
**oiseau** *m.* bird I-3
**olive** *f.* olive II-1
  **huile d'olive** *f.* olive oil II-1
**omelette** *f.* omelette I-5
**on** *sub. pron., sing.* one (we) I-1
  **on y va** let's go II-2

**oncle** *m.* uncle I-3
**onze** *m.* eleven I-1
**onzième** *adj.* eleventh I-7
**opéra** *m.* opera II-7
**optimiste** *adj.* optimistic I-1
**orageux/orageuse** *adj.* stormy I-5
    **Le temps est orageux.** It is stormy. I-5
**orange** *adj. inv.* orange I-6; *f.* orange II-1
**orchestre** *m.* orchestra II-7
**ordinateur** *m.* computer I-1
**ordonnance** *f.* prescription II-2
**ordures** *f., pl.* trash II-6
    **ramassage des ordures** *m.* garbage collection II-6
**oreille** *f.* ear II-2
**oreiller** *m.* pillow I-8, II-P
**organiser (une fête)** *v.* to organize/to plan (a party) I-6
**origine** *f.* heritage I-1
    **Je suis d'origine...** I am of... heritage. I-1
**orteil** *m.* toe II-2
**ou** *or* I-3
**où** *adv., rel. pron.* where 4
**ouais** *adv.* yeah I-2
**oublier (de)** *v.* to forget (*to do something*) I-2
**ouest** *m.* west II-4
**oui** *adv.* yes I-2
**ouvert (ouvrir)** *p.p., adj. (as past participle)* opened; *(as adjective)* open II-3
**ouvrier/ouvrière** *m., f.* worker, laborer II-5
**ouvrir** *v.* to open II-3
**ozone** *m.* ozone II-6
    **trou dans la couche d'ozone** *m.* hole in the ozone layer II-6

### P

**page d'accueil** *f.* home page II-3
**pain (de campagne)** *m.* (country-style) bread I-4
**panne** *f.* breakdown, malfunction II-3
    **tomber en panne** *v.* to break down II-3
**pantalon** *m., sing.* pants I-6
**pantoufle** *f.* slipper II-2
**papeterie** *f.* stationery store II-4
**papier** *m.* paper I-1
    **corbeille à papier** *f.* wastebasket I-1
    **feuille de papier** *f.* sheet of paper I-1
**paquet cadeau** *m.* wrapped gift I-6
**par** *prep.* by I-3

**par jour/semaine/mois/an** per day/week/month/year I-5
**parapluie** *m.* umbrella I-5
**parc** *m.* park I-4
**parce que** *conj.* because I-2
**Pardon.** Pardon (me). I-1
**Pardon?** What? I-4
**pare-brise** *m.* windshield II-3
**pare-chocs** *m.* bumper II-3
**parents** *m., pl.* parents I-3
**paresseux/paresseuse** *adj.* lazy I-3
**parfait(e)** *adj.* perfect I-4
**parfois** *adv.* sometimes I-5
**parking** *m.* parking lot II-3
**parler (à)** *v.* to speak (to) I-6
    **parler (au téléphone)** *v.* to speak (on the phone) I-2
**partager** *v.* to share I-2
**partir** *v.* to leave I-5
    **partir en vacances** *v.* to go on vacation I-7
**pas (de)** *adv.* no, none II-4
    **ne... pas** no, not I-2
    **pas de problème** no problem II-4
    **pas du tout** not at all I-2
    **pas encore** not yet I-8, II-P
    **Pas mal.** Not badly. I-1
**passager/passagère** *m., f.* passenger I-7
**passeport** *m.* passport I-7
**passer** *v.* to pass by; to spend time I-7
    **passer chez quelqu'un** *v.* to stop by someone's house I-4
    **passer l'aspirateur** *v.* to vacuum I-8, II-P
    **passer un examen** *v.* to take an exam I-2
**passe-temps** *m.* pastime, hobby I-5
**pâté (de campagne)** *m.* pâté, meat spread II-1
**pâtes** *f., pl.* pasta II-1
**patiemment** *adv.* patiently I-8, II-P
**patient(e)** *m., f.* patient II-2; *adj.* patient I-1
**patienter** *v.* to wait (on the phone), to be on hold II-5
**patiner** *v.* to skate I-4
**pâtisserie** *f.* pastry shop, bakery, pastry II-1
**patron(ne)** *m., f.* boss II-5
**pauvre** *adj.* poor I-3
**payé (payer)** *p.p., adj.* paid II-5
    **être bien/mal payé(e)** *v.* to be well/badly paid II-5
**payer** *v.* to pay I-5
    **payer avec une carte de crédit** *v.* to pay with a credit card II-4

**payer en liquide** *v.* to pay in cash II-4
**payer par chèque** *v.* to pay by check II-4
**pays** *m.* country I-7
**peau** *f.* skin II-2
**pêche** *f.* fishing I-5; peach II-1
    **aller à la pêche** *v.* to go fishing I-5
**peigne** *m.* comb II-2
**peintre/femme peintre** *m., f.* painter II-7
**peinture** *f.* painting II-7
**pendant (que)** *prep.* during, while I-7
    **pendant** *(with time expression) prep.* for II-1
**pénible** *adj.* tiresome I-3
**penser (que)** *v.* to think (that) I-2
    **ne pas penser que...** to not think that... II-7
    **Qu'en penses-tu?** What do you think about that? II-6
**perdre** *v.* to lose I-6
    **perdre son temps** *v.* to lose/to waste time I-6
**perdu** *p.p., adj.* lost II-4
    **être perdu(e)** to be lost II-4
**père** *m.* father I-3
    **beau-père** *m.* father-in-law; stepfather I-3
**permettre (de)** *v.* to allow (*to do something*) I-6
**permis** *m.* permit; license II-3
    **permis de conduire** *m.* driver's license II-3
**permis (permettre)** *p.p., adj.* permitted, allowed I-6
**personnage (principal)** *m.* (main) character II-7
**personne** *f.* person I-1; *pron.* no one II-4
    **ne... personne** nobody, no one II-4
**pessimiste** *adj.* pessimistic I-1
**petit(e)** *adj.* small I-3; short (*stature*) I-3
    **petit(e) ami(e)** *m., f.* boyfriend/girlfriend I-1
**petit-déjeuner** *m.* breakfast II-1
**petite-fille** *f.* granddaughter I-3
**petit-fils** *m.* grandson I-3
**petits-enfants** *m., pl.* grandchildren I-3
**petits pois** *m., pl.* peas II-1
**peu (de)** *adv.* little; not much (of) I-2
**peur** *f.* fear I-2
    **avoir peur (de/que)** *v.* to be afraid (of/that) I-2
**peut-être** *adv.* maybe, perhaps I-2
**phares** *m., pl.* headlights II-3
**pharmacie** *f.* pharmacy II-2

**pharmacien(ne)** *m., f.* pharmacist II-2
**philosophie** *f.* philosophy I-2
**photo(graphie)** *f.* photo (graph) I-3
**physique** *f.* physics I-2
**piano** *m.* piano II-7
**pièce** *f.* room I-8, II-P
**pièce de théâtre** *f.* play II-7
**pièces de monnaie** *f., pl.* change II-4
**pied** *m.* foot II-2
**pierre** *f.* stone II-6
**pilule** *f.* pill II-2
**pique-nique** *m.* picnic II-6
**piqûre** *f.* shot, injection II-2
   **faire une piqûre** *v.* to give a shot II-2
**pire** *comp. adj.* worse II-1
   **le/la pire** *super. adj.* the worst II-1
**piscine** *f.* pool I-4
**placard** *m.* closet; cupboard I-8, II-P
**place** *f.* square; place I-4; *f.* seat II-7
**plage** *f.* beach I-7
**plaisir** *m.* pleasure, enjoyment II-5
   **faire plaisir à quelqu'un** *v.* to please someone II-5
**plan** *m.* map I-7
   **utiliser un plan** *v.* to use a map I-7
**planche à voile** *f.* windsurfing I-5
   **faire de la planche à voile** *v.* to go windsurfing I-5
**planète** *f.* planet II-6
   **sauver la planète** *v.* to save the planet II-6
**plante** *f.* plant II-6
**plastique** *m.* plastic II-6
   **emballage en plastique** *m.* plastic wrapping/packaging II-6
**plat (principal)** *m.* (main) dish II-1
**plein air** *m.* outdoor, open-air II-6
**pleine forme** *f.* good shape, good state of health II-2
   **être en pleine forme** *v.* to be in good shape II-2
**pleurer** *v.* to cry
**pleuvoir** *v.* to rain I-5
   **Il pleut.** It is raining. I-5
**plombier** *m.* plumber II-5
**plu (pleuvoir)** *p.p.* rained I-6
**pluie acide** *f.* acid rain II-6
**plus** *adv. (used in comparatives, superlatives, and expressions of quantity)* more I-4
   **le/la plus ...** *super. adv. (used with adjective)* the most II-1
   **le/la plus mauvais(e)** *super. adj.* the worst II-1

**le plus** *super. adv. (used with verb or adverb)* the most II-1
**le plus de...** *(used with noun to express quantity)* the most... II-6
**le plus mal** *super. adv.* the worst II-1
**plus... que** *(used with adjective)* more... than II-1
**plus de** more of I-4
**plus de... que** *(used with noun to express quantity)* more... than II-6
**plus mal** *comp. adv.* worse II-1
**plus mauvais(e)** *comp. adj.* worse II-1
**plus** *adv.* no more, not any-more II-4
   **ne... plus** no more, not any-more II-4
**plusieurs** *adj.* several I-4
**plutôt** *adv.* rather I-2
**pneu (crevé)** *m.* (flat) tire II-3
   **vérifier la pression des pneus** *v.* to check the tire pressure II-3
**poème** *m.* poem II-7
**poète/poétesse** *m., f.* poet II-7
**point** *m. (punctuation mark)* period II-3
**poire** *f.* pear II-1
**poisson** *m.* fish I-3
**poissonnerie** *f.* fish shop II-1
**poitrine** *f.* chest II-2
**poivre** *m. (spice)* pepper II-1
**poivron** *m. (vegetable)* pepper II-1
**poli(e)** *adj.* polite I-1
**police** *f.* police II-3
   **agent de police** *m.* police officer II-3
   **commissariat de police** *m.* police station II-4
**policier** *m.* police officer II-3
   **film policier** *m.* detective film II-7
**policière** *f.* police officer II-3
**poliment** *adv.* politely I-8, II-P
**politique** *adj.* political I-2
   **femme politique** *f.* politician II-5
   **homme politique** *m.* politician II-5
   **sciences politiques (sciences po)** *f., pl.* political science I-2
**polluer** *v.* to pollute II-6
**pollution** *f.* pollution II-6
   **nuage de pollution** *m.* pollution cloud II-6
**pomme** *f.* apple II-1
**pomme de terre** *f.* potato II-1
**pompier/femme pompier** *m., f.* firefighter II-5
**pont** *m.* bridge II-4

**population croissante** *f.* growing population II-6
**porc** *m.* pork II-1
**portable** *m.* cell phone II-3
**porte** *f.* door I-1
**porter** *v.* to wear I-6
**portière** *f.* car door II-3
**portrait** *m.* portrait I-5
**poser une question (à)** *v.* to ask *(someone)* a question I-6
**posséder** *v.* to possess, to own I-5
**possible** *adj.* possible II-7
   **Il est possible que...** It is possible that... II-6
**poste** *f.* postal service; post office II-4
   **bureau de poste** *m.* post office II-4
**poste** *m.* position II-5
**poste de télévision** *m.* television set II-3
**poster une lettre** *v.* to mail a letter II-4
**postuler** *v.* to apply II-5
**poulet** *m.* chicken II-1
**pour** *prep.* for I-5
   **pour qui?** for whom? I-4
   **pour rien** for no reason I-4
   **pour que** so that II-7
**pourboire** *m.* tip I-4
   **laisser un pourboire** *v.* to leave a tip I-4
**pourquoi?** *adv.* why? I-2
**poussière** *f.* dust I-8, II-P
   **enlever/faire la poussière** *v.* to dust I-8, II-P
**pouvoir** *v.* to be able to; can II-1
**pratiquer** *v.* to play regularly, to practice I-5
**préféré(e)** *adj.* favorite, preferred I-2
**préférer (que)** *v.* to prefer (that) I-5
**premier** *m.* the first *(day of the month)* I-5
   **C'est le 1ᵉʳ (premier) octobre.** It is October first. I-5
**premier/première** *adj.* first I-2
**prendre** *v.* to take I-4; to have I-4
   **prendre sa retraite** *v.* to retire I-6
   **prendre un train/avion/ taxi/autobus/bateau** *v.* to take a train/plane/taxi/bus/ boat I-7
   **prendre un congé** *v.* to take time off II-5
   **prendre une douche** *v.* to take a shower II-2
   **prendre (un) rendez-vous** *v.* to make an appointment II-5
**préparer** *v.* to prepare (for) I-2

**près (de)** *prep.* close (to), near I-3
  **tout près (de)** very close (to) II-4
**présenter** *v.* to present, to introduce II-7
  **Je te présente…** *fam.* I would like to introduce… to you. I-1
  **Je vous présente…** *fam., form.* I would like to introduce… to you. I-1
**préservation** *f.* protection II-6
**préserver** *v.* to preserve II-6
**presque** *adv.* almost I-2
**pressé(e)** *adj.* hurried II-1
**pression** *f.* pressure II-3
  **vérifier la pression des pneus** to check the tire pressure II-3
**prêt(e)** *adj.* ready I-3
**prêter (à)** *v.* to lend (*to someone*) I-6
**prévenir l'incendie** *v.* to prevent a fire II-6
**principal(e)** *adj.* main, principal II-1
  **personnage principal** *m.* main character II-7
  **plat principal** *m.* main dish II-1
**printemps** *m.* spring I-5
  **au printemps** in the spring I-5
**pris (prendre)** *p.p., adj.* taken I-6
**prix** *m.* price I-4
**problème** *m.* problem I-1
**prochain(e)** *adj.* next I-2
**produire** *v.* to produce I-6
**produit** *m.* product II-6
**produit (produire)** *p.p., adj.* produced I-6
**professeur** *m.* teacher, professor I-1
**profession (exigeante)** *f.* (demanding) profession II-5
**professionnel(le)** *adj.* professional II-5
  **expérience professionnelle** *f.* professional experience II-5
**profiter (de)** *v.* to take advantage (of); to enjoy II-7
**programme** *m.* program II-7
**projet** *m.* project II-5
  **faire des projets** *v.* to make plans II-5
**promenade** *f.* walk, stroll I-5
  **faire une promenade** *v.* to go for a walk I-5
**promettre** *v.* to promise I-6
**promis (promettre)** *p.p., adj.* promised I-6
**promotion** *f.* promotion II-5
**proposer (que)** *v.* to propose (that) II-6
  **proposer une solution** *v.* to propose a solution II-6
**propre** *adj.* clean I-8, II-P

**propriétaire** *m., f.* owner I-8, II-P; landlord/landlady I-8, II-P
**protection** *f.* protection II-6
**protéger** *v.* to protect 5
**psychologie** *f.* psychology I-2
**psychologique** *adj.* psychological II-7
**psychologue** *m., f.* psychologist II-5
**pu (pouvoir)** *p.p. (used with infinitive)* was able to 9
**publicité (pub)** *f.* advertisement II-7
**publier** *v.* to publish II-7
**puis** *adv.* then I-7
**pull** *m.* sweater I-6
**pur(e)** *adj.* pure II-6

## Q

**quand** *adv.* when I-4
  **C'est quand l'anniversaire de … ?** When is …'s birthday? I-5
  **C'est quand ton/votre anniversaire?** When is your birthday? I-5
**quarante** *m.* forty I-1
**quart** *m.* quarter I-2
  **et quart** a quarter after… (o'clock) I-2
**quartier** *m.* area, neighborhood I-8, II-P
**quatorze** *m.* fourteen I-1
**quatre** *m.* four I-1
**quatre-vingts** *m.* eighty I-3
**quatre-vingt-dix** *m.* ninety I-3
**quatrième** *adj.* fourth I-7
**que/qu'** *rel. pron.* that; which II-3; *conj.* than II-1, II-6
  **plus/moins … que** (*used with adjective*) more/less … than II-1
  **plus/moins de … que** (*used with noun to express quantity*) more/less … than II-6
**que/qu'…?** *interr. pron.* what? I-4
  **Qu'en penses-tu?** What do you think about that? II-6
  **Qu'est-ce que c'est?** What is it? I-1
  **Qu'est-ce qu'il y a?** What is it?; What's wrong? I-1
**que** *adv.* only II-4
  **ne… que** only II-4
**québécois(e)** *adj.* from Quebec I-1
**quel(le)(s)?** *interr. adj.* which? I-4; what? I-4
  **À quelle heure?** What time?; When? I-2
  **Quel jour sommes-nous?** What day is it? I-2
  **Quelle est la date?** What is the date? I-5

**Quelle est ta nationalité?** *fam.* What is your nationality? I-1
**Quelle est votre nationalité?** *form.* What is your nationality? I-1
**Quelle heure avez-vous?** *form.* What time do you have? I-2
**Quelle heure est-il?** What time is it? I-2
**Quelle température fait-il?** (*weather*) What is the temperature? I-5
**Quel temps fait-il?** What is the weather like? I-5
**quelqu'un** *pron.* someone II-4
**quelque chose** *m.* something; anything I-4
  **Quelque chose ne va pas.** Something's not right. I-5
**quelquefois** *adv.* sometimes I-8, II-P
**quelques** *adj.* some I-4
**question** *f.* question I-6
  **poser une question (à)** to ask (*someone*) a question I-6
**queue** *f.* line II-4
  **faire la queue** *v.* to wait in line II-4
**qui?** *interr. pron.* who? I-4; whom? I-4; *rel. pron.* who, that II-3
  **à qui?** to whom? I-4
  **avec qui?** with whom? I-4
  **C'est de la part de qui?** On behalf of whom? II-5
  **Qui est à l'appareil?** Who's calling, please? II-5
  **Qui est-ce?** Who is it? I-1
**quinze** *m.* fifteen I-1
**quitter (la maison)** *v.* to leave (the house) I-4
  **Ne quittez pas.** Please hold. II-5
**quoi?** *interr. pron.* what? I-1
  **Il n'y a pas de quoi.** It's nothing.; You're welcome. I-1
  **quoi que ce soit** whatever it may be II-5

## R

**raccrocher** *v.* to hang up II-5
**radio** *f.* radio II-7
  **à la radio** on the radio II-7
**raide** *adj.* straight I-3
**raison** *f.* reason; right I-2
  **avoir raison** *v.* to be right I-2
**ramassage des ordures** *m.* garbage collection II-6
**randonnée** *f.* hike I-5
  **faire une randonnée** *v.* to go for a hike I-5
**ranger** *v.* to tidy up, to put away I-8, II-P

**rapide** *adj.* fast I-3
**rapidement** *adv.* rapidly I-8, II-P
**rarement** *adv.* rarely I-5
**rasoir** *m.* razor II-2
**ravissant(e)** *adj.* beautiful; delightful II-5
**réalisateur/réalisatrice** *m., f.* director (*of a movie*) II-7
**récent(e)** *adj.* recent II-7
**réception** *f.* reception desk I-7
**recevoir** *v.* to receive II-4
**réchauffement de la Terre** *m.* global warming II-6
**rechercher** *v.* to search for, to look for II-5
**recommandation** *f.* recommendation II-5
**recommander (que)** *v.* to recommend (that) II-6
**recomposer (un numéro)** *v.* to redial (a number) II-3
**reconnaître** *v.* to recognize I-8, II-P
**reconnu (reconnaître)** *p.p., adj.* recognized I-8, II-P
**reçu** *m.* receipt II-4
**reçu (recevoir)** *p.p., adj.* received I-7
 **être reçu(e) à un examen** to pass an exam I-2
**recyclage** *m.* recycling II-6
**recycler** *v.* to recycle II-6
**redémarrer** *v.* to restart, to start again II-3
**réduire** *v.* to reduce I-6
**réduit (réduire)** *p.p., adj.* reduced I-6
**référence** *f.* reference II-5
**réfléchir (à)** *v.* to think (about), to reflect (on) I-4
**refuser (de)** *v.* to refuse (*to do something*) II-3
**regarder** *v.* to watch I-2
 **Ça ne nous regarde pas.** That has nothing to do with us.; That is none of our business. II-6
**régime** *m.* diet II-2
 **être au régime** *v.* to be on a diet II-1
**région** *f.* region II-6
**regretter (que)** *v.* to regret (that) II-6
**remplir (un formulaire)** *v.* to fill out (a form) II-4
**rencontrer** *v.* to meet I-2
**rendez-vous** *m.* date; appointment I-6
 **prendre (un) rendez-vous** *v.* to make an appointment II-5
**rendre (à)** *v.* to give back, to return (to) I-6

**rendre visite (à)** *v.* to visit I-6
**rentrer (à la maison)** *v.* to return (home) I-2
 **rentrer (dans)** *v.* to hit II-3
**renvoyer** *v.* to dismiss, to let go II-5
**réparer** *v.* to repair II-3
**repartir** *v.* to go back II-7
**repas** *m.* meal II-1
**repasser** *v.* to take again II-7
 **repasser (le linge)** *v.* to iron (the laundry) I-8, II-P
 **fer à repasser** *m.* iron I-8, II-P
**répéter** *v.* to repeat; to rehearse I-5
**répondeur (téléphonique)** *m.* answering machine II-3
**répondre (à)** *v.* to respond, to answer (to) I-6
**réservation** *f.* reservation I-7
 **annuler une réservation** *v.* to cancel a reservation I-7
**réservé(e)** *adj.* reserved I-1
**réserver** *v.* to reserve I-7
**réservoir d'essence** *m.* gas tank II-3
**résidence universitaire** *f.* dorm I-8, II-P
**ressource naturelle** *f.* natural resource II-6
**restaurant** *m.* restaurant I-4
 **restaurant universitaire (resto U)** *m.* university cafeteria I-2
**rester** *v.* to stay I-7
**résultat** *m.* result I-2
**retenir** *v.* to keep, to retain II-1
**retirer (de l'argent)** *v.* to withdraw (money) II-4
**retourner** *v.* to return I-7
**retraite** *f.* retirement I-6
 **prendre sa retraite** *v.* to retire I-6
**retraité(e)** *m., f.* retired person II-5
**retrouver** *v.* to find (again); to meet up with I-2
**rétroviseur** *m.* rear-view mirror II-3
**réunion** *f.* meeting II-5

**réussir (à)** *v.* to succeed (*in doing something*) I-4
**réussite** *f.* success II-5
**réveil** *m.* alarm clock II-2
**revenir** *v.* to come back II-1
**rêver (de)** *v.* to dream about II-3
**revoir** *v.* to see again II-7
 **Au revoir.** Good-bye. I-1
**revu (revoir)** *p.p.* seen again II-7
**rez-de-chaussée** *m.* ground floor I-7

**rhume** *m.* cold II-2
**ri (rire)** *p.p.* laughed I-6
**rideau** *m.* curtain I-8, II-P
**rien** *m.* nothing II-4
 **De rien.** You're welcome. I-1
 **ne... rien** nothing, not anything II-4
 **ne servir à rien** *v.* to be good for nothing II-1
**rire** *v.* to laugh I-6
**rivière** *f.* river II-6
**riz** *m.* rice II-1
**robe** *f.* dress I-6
**rôle** *m.* role II-6
 **jouer un rôle** *v.* to play a role II-7
**roman** *m.* novel II-7
**rose** *adj.* pink I-6
**roue (de secours)** *f.* (emergency) tire II-3
**rouge** *adj.* red I-6
**rouler en voiture** *v.* to ride in a car I-7
**rue** *f.* street II-3
 **suivre une rue** *v.* to follow a street II-4

## S

**s'adorer** *v.* to adore one another II-3
**s'aider** *v.* to help one another II-3
**s'aimer (bien)** *v.* to love (like) one another II-3
**s'allumer** *v.* to light up II-3
**s'amuser** *v.* to play; to have fun II-2
 **s'amuser à** *v.* to pass time by II-3
**s'apercevoir** *v.* to notice; to realize II-4
**s'appeler** *v.* to be named, to be called II-2
 **Comment t'appelles-tu?** *fam.* What is your name? I-1
 **Comment vous appelez-vous?** *form.* What is your name? I-1
 **Je m'appelle...** My name is... I-1
**s'arrêter** *v.* to stop II-2
**s'asseoir** *v.* to sit down II-2
**sa** *poss. adj., f., sing.* his; her; its I-3
**sac** *m.* bag I-1
 **sac à dos** *m.* backpack I-1
 **sac à main** *m.* purse, handbag I-6
**sain(e)** *adj.* healthy II-2
**saison** *f.* season I-5
**salade** *f.* salad II-1
**salaire (élevé/modeste)** *m.* (high/low) salary II-5
 **augmentation de salaire** *f.* raise in salary II-5

**sale** *adj.* dirty I-8, II-P
**salir** *v.* to soil, to make dirty I-8, II-P
**salle** *f.* room I-8, II-P
  **salle à manger** *f.* dining room I-8, II-P
  **salle de bains** *f.* bathroom I-8, II-P
  **salle de classe** *f.* classroom I-1
  **salle de séjour** *f.* living/family room I-8, II-P
**salon** *m.* formal living room, sitting room I-8, II-P
  **salon de beauté** *m.* beauty salon II-4
**Salut!** Hi!; Bye! I-1
**samedi** *m.* Saturday I-2
**sandwich** *m.* sandwich I-4
**sans** *prep.* without I-8, II-P
  **sans que** *conj.* without II-7
**santé** *f.* health II-2
  **être en bonne/mauvaise santé** *v.* to be in good/bad health II-2
**saucisse** *f.* sausage II-1
**sauvegarder** *v.* to save II-3
**sauver (la planète)** *v.* to save (the planet) II-6
**sauvetage des habitats** *m.* habitat preservation II-6
**savoir** *v.* to know (*facts*), to know how to do something I-8, II-P
  **savoir (que)** *v.* to know (that) II-7
  **Je n'en sais rien.** I don't know anything about it. II-6
**savon** *m.* soap II-2
**sciences** *f., pl.* science I-2
  **sciences politiques (sciences po)** *f., pl.* political science I-2
**sculpture** *f.* sculpture II-7
**sculpteur/femme sculpteur** *m., f.* sculptor II-7
**se/s'** *pron., sing., pl. (used with reflexive verb)* himself; herself; itself; 10 (*used with reciprocal verb*) each other II-3
**séance** *f.* show; screening II-7
**se blesser** *v.* to hurt oneself II-2
**se brosser (les cheveux/les dents)** *v.* to brush one's (hair/teeth) II-1
**se casser** *v.* to break II-2
**sèche-linge** *m.* clothes dryer I-8, II-P
**se coiffer** *v.* to do one's hair II-2
**se connaître** *v.* to know one another II-3
**se coucher** *v.* to go to bed II-2
**secours** *m.* help II-3
  **Au secours!** Help! II-3
**s'écrire** *v.* to write one another II-3

**sécurité** *f.* security; safety
  **attacher sa ceinture de sécurité** *v.* to buckle one's seatbelt II-3
**se dépêcher** *v.* to hurry II-2
**se déplacer** *v.* to move, to change location II-4
**se déshabiller** *v.* to undress II-2
**se détendre** *v.* to relax II-2
**se dire** *v.* to tell one another II-3
**se disputer (avec)** *v.* to argue (with) II-2
**se donner** *v.* to give one another II-3
**se fouler (la cheville)** *v.* to twist/to sprain one's (ankle) II-2
**se garer** *v.* to park II-3
**seize** *m.* sixteen I-1
**séjour** *m.* stay I-7
  **faire un séjour** *v.* to spend time (*somewhere*) I-7
  **salle de séjour** *f.* living room I-8, II-P
**sel** *m.* salt II-1
**se laver (les mains)** *v.* to wash oneself (one's hands) II-2
**se lever** *v.* to get up, to get out of bed II-2
**semaine** *f.* week I-2
  **cette semaine** this week I-2
**s'embrasser** *v.* to kiss one another II-3
**se maquiller** *v.* to put on makeup II-2
**se mettre** *v.* to put (*something*) on (yourself) II-2
  **se mettre à** *v.* to begin to II-2
  **se mettre en colère** *v.* to become angry II-2
**s'endormir** *v.* to fall asleep, to go to sleep II-2
**s'énerver** *v.* to get worked up, to become upset II-2
**sénégalais(e)** *adj.* Senegalese I-1
**s'ennuyer** *v.* to get bored II-2
**s'entendre bien (avec)** *v.* to get along well (with one another) II-2
**sentier** *m.* path II-6
**sentir** *v.* to feel; to smell; to sense I-5
**séparé(e)** *adj.* separated I-3
**se parler** *v.* to speak to one another II-3
**se porter mal/mieux** *v.* to be ill/better II-2
**se préparer (à)** *v.* to get ready; to prepare (*to do something*) II-2
**se promener** *v.* to take a walk II-2
**sept** *m.* seven I-1
**septembre** *m.* September I-5
**septième** *adj.* seventh I-7
**se quitter** *v.* to leave one another II-3

**se raser** *v.* to shave oneself II-2
**se réconcilier** *v.* to make up II-7
**se regarder** *v.* to look at oneself; to look at each other II-2
**se relever** *v.* to get up again II-2
**se rencontrer** *v.* to meet one another, to make each other's acquaintance II-3
**se rendre compte** *v.* to realize II-2
**se reposer** *v.* to rest II-2
**se retrouver** *v.* to meet one another (*as planned*) II-3
**se réveiller** *v.* to wake up II-2
**se sécher** *v.* to dry oneself II-2
**se sentir** *v.* to feel II-2
**sérieux/sérieuse** *adj.* serious I-3
**serpent** *m.* snake II-6
**serre** *f.* greenhouse II-6
  **effet de serre** *m.* greenhouse effect II-6
**serré(e)** *adj.* tight I-6
**serveur/serveuse** *m., f.* server I-4
**serviette** *f.* napkin II-1
  **serviette (de bain)** *f.* (bath) towel II-2
**servir** *v.* to serve I-5
**ses** *poss. adj., m., f., pl.* his; her; its I-3
**se souvenir (de)** *v.* to remember II-2
**se téléphoner** *v.* to phone one another II-3
**se tourner** *v.* to turn (oneself) around II-2
**se tromper (de)** *v.* to be mistaken (about) II-2
**se trouver** *v.* to be located II-2
**seulement** *adv.* only I-8, II-P
**s'habiller** *v.* to dress II-2
**shampooing** *m.* shampoo II-2
**shopping** *m.* shopping I-7
  **faire du shopping** *v.* to go shopping I-7
**short** *m., sing.* shorts I-6
**si** *conj.* if II-5
**si** *adv. (when contradicting a negative statement or question)* yes I-2
**signer** *v.* to sign II-4
**S'il te plaît.** *fam.* Please. I-1
**S'il vous plaît.** *form.* Please. I-1
**sincère** *adj.* sincere I-1
**s'inquiéter** *v.* to worry II-2
**s'intéresser (à)** *v.* to be interested (in) II-2
**site Internet/web** *m.* web site II-3
**six** *m.* six I-1
**sixième** *adj.* sixth I-7
**ski** *m.* skiing I-5
  **faire du ski** *v.* to go skiing I-5
  **station de ski** *f.* ski resort I-7
**skier** *v.* to ski I-5

**s'occuper (de)** *v.* to take care (*of something*), to see to II-2
**sociable** *adj.* sociable I-1
**sociologie** *f.* sociology I-1
**sœur** *f.* sister I-3
  **belle-sœur** *f.* sister-in-law I-3
  **demi-sœur** *f.* half-sister, stepsister I-3
**soie** *f.* silk II-4
**soif** *f.* thirst I-4
  **avoir soif** *v.* to be thirsty I-4
**soir** *m.* evening I-2
  **ce soir** *adv.* this evening I-2
  **demain soir** *adv.* tomorrow evening I-2
  **du soir** *adv.* in the evening I-2
  **hier soir** *adv.* yesterday evening I-7
**soirée** *f.* evening I-2
**sois (être)** *imp. v.* be I-2
**soixante** *m.* sixty I-1
**soixante-dix** *m.* seventy I-3
**solaire** *adj.* solar II-6
  **énergie solaire** *f.* solar energy II-6
**soldes** *f., pl.* sales I-6
**soleil** *m.* sun I-5
  **Il fait (du) soleil.** It is sunny. I-5
**solution** *f.* solution II-6
  **proposer une solution** *v.* to propose a solution II-6
**sommeil** *m.* sleep I-2
  **avoir sommeil** *v.* to be sleepy I-2
**son** *poss. adj., m., sing.* his; her; its I-3
**sonner** *v.* to ring II-3
**s'orienter** *v.* to get one's bearings II-4
**sorte** *f.* sort, kind II-7
**sortie** *f.* exit I-7
**sortir** *v.* to go out, to leave I-5; to take out I-8, II-P
  **sortir la/les poubelle(s)** *v.* to take out the trash I-8, II-P
**soudain** *adv.* suddenly I-8, II-P
**souffrir** *v.* to suffer II-3
**souffert (souffrir)** *p.p.* suffered II-3
**souhaiter (que)** *v.* to wish (that) II-6
**soupe** *f.* soup I-4
  **cuillère à soupe** *f.* soupspoon II-1
**sourire** *v.* to smile I-6; *m.* smile II-4
**souris** *f.* mouse II-3
**sous** *prep.* under I-3
**sous-sol** *m.* basement I-8, II-P
**sous-vêtement** *m.* underwear I-6
**souvent** *adv.* often I-5
**soyez (être)** *imp. v.* be I-7

**soyons (être)** *imp. v.* let's be I-7
**spécialiste** *m., f.* specialist II-5
**spectacle** *m.* show I-5
**spectateur/spectatrice** *m., f.* spectator II-7
**sport** *m.* sport(s) I-5
  **faire du sport** *v.* to do sports I-5
**sportif/sportive** *adj.* athletic I-3
**stade** *m.* stadium I-5
**stage** *m.* internship; professional training II-5
**station (de métro)** *f.* (subway) station I-7
**station de ski** *f.* ski resort I-7
**station-service** *f.* service station II-3
**statue** *f.* statue II-4
**steak** *m.* steak II-1
**studio** *m.* studio (*apartment*) I-8, II-P
**stylisme** *m.* **de mode** *f.* fashion design I-2
**stylo** *m.* pen I-1
**su (savoir)** *p.p.* known I-8, II-P
**sucre** *m.* sugar I-4
**sud** *m.* south II-4
**suggérer (que)** *v.* to suggest (that) II-6
**sujet** *m.* subject II-6
  **au sujet de** on the subject of; about II-6
**suisse** *adj.* Swiss I-1
**Suisse** *f.* Switzerland I-7
**suivre (un chemin/une rue/ un boulevard)** *v.* to follow (a path/a street/a boulevard) II-4
**supermarché** *m.* supermarket II-1
**sur** *prep.* on I-3
**sûr(e)** *adj.* sure, certain II-1
  **bien sûr** of course I-2
  **Il est sûr que...** It is sure that... II-7
  **Il n'est pas sûr que...** It is not sure that... II-7
**surfer sur Internet** *v.* to surf the Internet II-1
**surpopulation** *f.* overpopulation II-6
**surpris (surprendre)** *p.p., adj.* surprised I-6
  **être surpris(e) que...** *v.* to be surprised that... II-6
  **faire une surprise à quelqu'un** *v.* to surprise someone I-6
**surtout** *adv.* especially; above all I-2
**sympa(thique)** *adj.* nice I-1
**symptôme** *m.* symptom II-2
**syndicat** *m.* (*trade*) union II-5

**ta** *poss. adj., f., sing.* your I-3
**table** *f.* table I-1
  **À table!** Let's eat! Food is ready! II-1
  **débarrasser la table** *v.* to clear the table I-8, II-P
  **mettre la table** *v.* to set the table I-8, II-P
**tableau** *m.* blackboard; picture I-1; *m.* painting II-7
**tâche ménagère** *f.* household chore I-8, II-P
**taille** *f.* size; waist I-6
  **de taille moyenne** of medium height I-3
**tailleur** *m.* (*woman's*) suit; tailor I-6
**tante** *f.* aunt I-3
**tapis** *m.* rug I-8, II-P
**tard** *adv.* late I-2
  **À plus tard.** See you later. I-1
**tarte** *f.* pie; tart I-8, II-P
**tasse (de)** *f.* cup (of) I-4
**taxi** *m.* taxi I-7
  **prendre un taxi** *v.* to take a taxi I-7
**te/t'** *pron., sing., fam.* you I-7; yourself II-2
**tee-shirt** *m.* tee shirt I-6
**télécarte** *f.* phone card II-5
**télécharger** *v.* to download II-3
**télécommande** *f.* remote control II-3
**téléphone** *m.* telephone I-2
  **parler au téléphone** *v.* to speak on the phone I-2
**téléphoner (à)** *v.* to telephone (*someone*) I-2
**téléphonique** *adj.* (*related to the*) telephone II-4
  **cabine téléphonique** *f.* phone booth II-4
**télévision** *f.* television I-1
  **à la télé(vision)** on television II-7
  **chaîne de télévision** *f.* television channel II-3
**tellement** *adv.* so much I-2
  **Je n'aime pas tellement...** I don't like... very much. I-2
**température** *f.* temperature I-5
  **Quelle température fait-il?** What is the temperature? I-5
**temps** *m., sing.* weather I-5
  **Il fait un temps épouvantable.** The weather is dreadful. I-5
  **Le temps est nuageux.** It is cloudy. I-5
  **Le temps est orageux.** It is stormy. I-5

**Quel temps fait-il?** What is the weather like? I-5

**temps** *m., sing.* time I-5

**de temps en temps** *adv.* from time to time I-8, II-P

**emploi à mi-temps/à temps partiel** *m.* part-time job II-5

**emploi à plein temps** *m.* full-time job II-5

**temps libre** *m.* free time I-5

**Tenez! (tenir)** *imp. v.* Here! II-1

**tenir** *v.* to hold II-1

**tennis** *m.* tennis I-5

**terrasse (de café)** *f.* (café) terrace I-4

**Terre** *f.* Earth II-6

**réchauffement de la Terre** *m.* global warming II-6

**tes** *poss. adj., m., f., pl.* your I-3

**tête** *f.* head II-2

**thé** *m.* tea I-4

**théâtre** *m.* theater II-7

**thon** *m.* tuna II-1

**ticket de bus/métro** *m.* bus/subway ticket I-7

**Tiens! (tenir)** *imp. v.* Here! II-1

**timbre** *m.* stamp II-4

**timide** *adj.* shy I-1

**tiret** *m. (punctuation mark)* dash; hyphen II-3

**tiroir** *m.* drawer I-8, II-P

**toi** *disj. pron., sing., fam.* you I-3; *refl. pron., sing., fam. (attached to imperative)* yourself II-2

**toi non plus** you neither I-2

**toilette** *f.* washing up, grooming II-2

**faire sa toilette** to wash up II-2

**toilettes** *f., pl.* restroom(s) I-8, II-P

**tomate** *f.* tomato II-1

**tomber** *v.* to fall I-7

**tomber amoureux/amoureuse** *v.* to fall in love I-6

**tomber en panne** *v.* to break down II-3

**tomber/être malade** *v.* to get/be sick II-2

**tomber sur quelqu'un** *v.* to run into someone I-7

**ton** *poss. adj., m., sing.* your I-3

**tort** *m.* wrong; harm I-2

**avoir tort** *v.* to be wrong I-2

**tôt** *adv.* early I-2

**toujours** *adv.* always I-8, II-P

**tour** *m.* tour I-5

**faire un tour (en voiture)** *v.* to go for a walk (drive) I-5

**tourisme** *m.* tourism II-4

**office du tourisme** *m.* tourist office II-4

**tourner** *v.* to turn II-4

**tousser** *v.* to cough II-2

**tout** *m., sing.* all I-4

**tous les** *(used before noun)* all the... I-4

**tous les jours** *adv.* every day I-8, II-P

**toute la** *f., sing. (used before noun)* all the... I-4

**toutes les** *f., pl. (used before noun)* all the... I-4

**tout le** *m., sing. (used before noun)* all the... I-4

**tout le monde** everyone II-1

**tout(e)** *adv. (before adjective or adverb)* very, really I-3

**À tout à l'heure.** See you later. I-1

**tout à coup** suddenly I-7

**tout à fait** absolutely; completely II-4

**tout de suite** right away I-7

**tout droit** straight ahead II-4

**tout d'un coup** *adv.* all of a sudden I-8, II-P

**tout près (de)** really close by, really close (to) I-3

**toxique** *adj.* toxic II-6

**déchets toxiques** *m., pl.* toxic waste II-6

**trac** *m.* stage fright II-5

**traduire** *v.* to translate I-6

**traduit (traduire)** *p.p., adj.* translated I-6

**tragédie** *f.* tragedy II-7

**train** *m.* train I-7

**tranche** *f.* slice II-1

**tranquille** *adj.* calm, serene II-2

**laisser tranquille** *v.* to leave alone II-2

**travail** *m.* work II-4

**chercher un/du travail** *v.* to look for work II-4

**trouver un/du travail** *v.* to find a job II-5

**travailler** *v.* to work I-2

**travailleur/travailleuse** *adj.* hard-working I-3

**traverser** *v.* to cross II-4

**treize** *m.* thirteen I-1

**trente** *m.* thirty I-1

**très** *adv. (before adjective or adverb)* very, really I-8, II-P

**Très bien.** Very well. I-1

**triste** *adj.* sad I-3

**être triste que...** *v.* to be sad that... II-6

**trois** *m.* three I-1

**troisième** *adj.* third 7

**trop (de)** *adv.* too many/much (of) I-4

**tropical(e)** *adj.* tropical II-6

**forêt tropicale** *f.* tropical forest II-6

**trou (dans la couche d'ozone)** *m.* hole (in the ozone layer) II-6

**troupe** *f.* company, troupe II-7

**trouver** *v.* to find; to think I-2

**trouver un/du travail** *v.* to find a job II-5

**truc** *m.* thing I-7

**tu** *sub. pron., sing., fam.* you I-1

## U

**un** *m. (number)* one I-1

**un(e)** *indef. art.* a; an I-1

**universitaire** *adj. (related to the)* university I-1

**restaurant universitaire (resto U)** *m.* university cafeteria I-2

**université** *f.* university I-1

**urgences** *f., pl.* emergency room II-2

**aller aux urgences** *v.* to go to the emergency room II-2

**usine** *f.* factory II-6

**utile** *adj.* useful I-2

**utiliser (un plan)** *v.* use (a map) I-7

## V

**vacances** *f., pl.* vacation I-7

**partir en vacances** *v.* to go on vacation I-7

**vache** *f.* cow II-6

**vaisselle** *f.* dishes I-8, II-P

**faire la vaisselle** *v.* to do the dishes I-8, II-P

**lave-vaisselle** *m.* dishwasher I-8, II-P

**valise** *f.* suitcase I-7

**faire les valises** *v.* to pack one's bags I-7

**vallée** *f.* valley II-6

**variétés** *f., pl.* popular music II-7

**vaut (valloir)** *v.*

**Il vaut mieux que** It is better that II-6

**vélo** *m.* bicycle I-5

**faire du vélo** *v.* to go bike riding I-5

**velours** *m.* velvet II-4

**vendeur/vendeuse** *m., f.* seller I-6

**vendre** *v.* to sell I-6

**vendredi** *m.* Friday I-2

**venir** *v.* to come II-1

**venir de** *v. (used with an infinitive)* to have just II-1

**vent** *m.* wind I-5

**Il fait du vent.** It is windy. I-5

**ventre** *m.* stomach II-2

**vérifier (l'huile/la pression des pneus)** *v.* to check (the oil/the tire pressure) II-3
**véritable** *adj.* true, real II-4
**verre (de)** *m.* glass (of) I-4
**vers** *adv.* about I-2
**vert(e)** *adj.* green I-3
 **haricots verts** *m., pl.* green beans II-1
**vêtements** *m., pl.* clothing I-6
 **sous-vêtement** *m.* underwear I-6
**vétérinaire** *m., f.* veterinarian II-5
**veuf/veuve** *adj.* widowed I-3
**veut dire (vouloir dire)** *v.* means, signifies II-1
**viande** *f.* meat II-1
**vie** *f.* life I-6
 **assurance vie** *f.* life insurance II-5
**vieille** *adj., f. (feminine form of* **vieux***)* old I-3
**vieillesse** *f.* old age I-6
**vietnamien(ne)** *adj.* Vietnamese I-1
**vieux/vieille** *adj.* old I-3
**ville** *f.* city; town I-4
**vin** *m.* wine I-6
**vingt** *m.* twenty I-1
**vingtième** *adj.* twentieth I-7
**violet(te)** *adj.* purple; violet I-6
**violon** *m.* violin II-7
**visage** *m.* face II-2
**visite** *f.* visit I-6
 **rendre visite (à)** *v.* to visit (*a person or people*) I-6
**visiter** *v.* to visit (*a place*) I-2
 **faire visiter** *v.* to give a tour I-8, II-P
**vite** *adv.* quickly I-1; quick, hurry I-4
**vitesse** *f.* speed II-3
**voici** here is/are I-1
**voilà** there is/are I-1
**voir** *v.* to see II-7
**voisin(e)** *m., f.* neighbor I-3
**voiture** *f.* car II-3
 **faire un tour en voiture** *v.* to go for a drive I-5
 **rouler en voiture** *v.* to ride in a car I-7
**vol** *m.* flight I-7
**volant** *m.* steering wheel II-3
**volcan** *m.* volcano II-6
**volley(-ball)** *m.* volleyball I-5
**volontiers** *adv.* willingly II-2
**vos** *poss. adj., m., f., pl.* your I-3
**votre** *poss. adj., m., f., sing.* your I-3
**vouloir** *v.* to want; to mean (*with* **dire**) II-1
 **ça veut dire** that is to say II-2
 **veut dire** *v.* means, signifies II-1

**vouloir (que)** *v.* to want (that) II-6
**voulu (vouloir)** *p.p., adj. (used with infinitive)* wanted to… ; (*used with noun*) planned to/for II-1
**vous** *pron., sing., pl., fam., form.* you I-1; *d.o. pron.* you I-7; yourself, yourselves II-2
**voyage** *m.* trip I-7
 **agence de voyages** *f.* travel agency I-7
 **agent de voyages** *m.* travel agent I-7
**voyager** *v.* to travel I-2
**voyant (d'essence/d'huile)** *m.* (gas/oil) warning light 11
**vrai(e)** *adj.* true; real I-3
 **Il est vrai que…** It is true that… II-7
 **Il n'est pas vrai que…** It is untrue that… II-7
**vraiment** *adv.* really, truly I-5
**vu (voir)** *p.p.* seen II-7

## W

**W.-C.** *m., pl.* restroom(s) I-8, II-P
**week-end** *m.* weekend I-2
 **ce week-end** this weekend I-2

## Y

**y** *pron.* there; at (*a place*) II-2
 **j'y vais** I'm going/coming I-8, II-P
 **nous y allons** we're going/coming II-1
 **on y va** let's go II-2
 **Y a-t-il… ?** Is/Are there… ? I-2
**yaourt** *m.* yogurt II-1
**yeux (œil)** *m., pl.* eyes I-3

## Z

**zéro** *m.* zero I-1
**zut** *interj.* darn I-6

# English-French

## A

a **un(e)** *indef. art.* I-1
able: to be able to **pouvoir** *v.* II-1
abolish **abolir** *v.* II-6
about **vers** *adv.* I-2
abroad **à l'étranger** I-7
absolutely **absolument**
    *adv.* I-8, II-P;
    **tout à fait** *adv.* I-6
accident **accident** *m.* II-2
    to have/to be in an accident
    **avoir un accident** *v.* II-3
accompany **accompagner** *v.* II-4
account *(at a bank)* **compte**
    *m.* II-4
    checking account **compte** *m.*
    **de chèques** II-4
    to have a bank account **avoir**
    **un compte bancaire** *v.* II-4
accountant **comptable** *m., f.* II-5
acid rain **pluie acide** *f.* II-6
across from **en face de** *prep.* I-3
acquaintance **connaissance** *f.* I-5
active **actif/active** *adj.* I-3
actively **activement** *adv.* I-8, II-P
actor **acteur/actrice** *m., f.* I-1
address **adresse** *f.* II-4
administration: business
    administration **gestion** *f.* I-2
adolescence **adolescence** *f.* I-6
adore **adorer** I-2
    I love… **J'adore…** I-2
    to adore one another
    **s'adorer** *v.* II-3
adulthood **âge adulte** *m.* I-6
adventure **aventure** *f.* II-7
    adventure film **film** *m.*
    **d'aventures** II-7
advertisement **publicité (pub)**
    *f.* II-7
advice **conseil** *m.* II-5
advisor **conseiller/conseillère**
    *m., f.* II-5
aerobics **aérobic** *m.* I-5
    to do aerobics **faire de**
    **l'aérobic** *v.* I-5
afraid: to be afraid of/that **avoir**
    **peur de/que** *v.* II-6
after **après (que)** *adv.* I-7
afternoon **après-midi** *m.* I-2
    … (o'clock) in the afternoon
    … **heure(s) de l'après-midi** I-2
afternoon snack **goûter** *m.* II-1
again **encore** *adv.* I-3
age **âge** *m.* I-6

agent: travel agent **agent de**
    **voyages** *m.* I-7
    real estate agent **agent**
    **immobilier** *m.* II-5
ago *(with an expression of time)*
    **il y a…** II-1
agree: to agree (with) **être**
    **d'accord (avec)** *v.* I-2
airport **aéroport** *m.* I-7
alarm clock **réveil** *m.* II-2
Algerian **algérien(ne)** *adj.* I-1
all **tout** *m., sing.* I-4
    all of a sudden **soudain** *adv.*
    I-8, II-P; **tout à coup** *adv.*; **tout**
    **d'un coup** *adv.* I-7
    all right? *(tag question)*
    **d'accord?** I-2
allergy **allergie** *f.* II-2
allow *(to do something)* **laisser** *v.*
    II-3; **permettre (de)** *v.* I-6
allowed **permis (permettre)**
    *p.p., adj.* I-6
all the… *(agrees with noun that*
    *follows)* **tout le…** *m., sing;*
    **toute la…** *f., sing;* **tous les…**
    *m., pl.;* **toutes les…** *f., pl.* I-4
almost **presque** *adv.* I-5
a lot (of) **beaucoup (de)** *adv.* I-4
alone: to leave alone **laisser**
    **tranquille** *v.* II-2
already **déjà** *adv.* I-3
always **toujours** *adv.* I-8, II-P
American **américain(e)** *adj.* I-1
an **un(e)** *indef. art.* I-1
ancient *(placed after noun)*
    **ancien(ne)** *adj.* II-7
and **et** *conj.* I-1
    And you? **Et toi?**, *fam.;* **Et**
    **vous?** *form.* I-1
angel **ange** *m.* I-1
angry: to become angry
    **s'énerver** *v.* II-2; **se mettre**
    **en colère** *v.* II-2
animal **animal** *m.* II-6
ankle **cheville** *f.* II-2
answering machine **répondeur**
    **téléphonique** *m.* II-3
apartment **appartement** *m.* I-7
appetizer **entrée** *f.* II-1;
    **hors-d'œuvre** *m.* II-1
applaud **applaudir** *v.* II-7
applause **applaudissement**
    *m.* II-7
apple **pomme** *f.* II-1
appliance **appareil** *m.* I-8, II-P
    electrical/household appliance
    **appareil** *m.* **électrique/**
    **ménager** I-8, II-P
applicant **candidat(e)** *m., f.* II-5
apply **postuler** *v.* II-5

appointment **rendez-vous** *m.* II-5
    to make an appointment
    **prendre (un) rendez-vous**
    *v.* II-5
April **avril** *m.* I-5
architect **architecte** *m., f.* I-3
architecture **architecture** *f.* I-2
Are there… ? **Y a-t-il… ?** I-2
area **quartier** *m.* I-8, II-P
argue (with) **se disputer**
    **(avec)** *v.* II-2
arm **bras** *m.* II-2
armchair **fauteuil** *m.* I-8, II-P
armoire **armoire** *f.* I-8, II-P
around **autour (de)** *prep.* II-4
arrival **arrivée** *f.* I-7
arrive **arriver (à)** *v.* I-2
art **art** *m.* I-2
    artwork, piece of art **œuvre**
    *f.* II-7
    fine arts **beaux-arts** *m., pl.* II-7
artist **artiste** *m., f.* I-3
as *(like)* **comme** *adv.* I-6
    as … as *(used with adjective to*
    *compare)* **aussi … que** II-1
    as much … as *(used with*
    *noun to express comparative*
    *quality)* **autant de … que** II-6
    as soon as **dès que** *adv.* II-5
ashamed: to be ashamed of
    **avoir honte de** *v.* I-2
ask **demander** *v.* I-2
    to ask *(someone)* **demander**
    **(à)** *v.* I-6
    to ask *(someone)* a question
    **poser une question (à)** *v.* I-6
    to ask that… **demander**
    **que…** II-6
aspirin **aspirine** *f.* II-2
at **à** *prep.* I-4
    at … (o'clock) **à … heure(s)** I-4
    at the doctor's office **chez le**
    **médecin** *prep.* I-2
    at (someone's) house **chez…**
    *prep.* I-2
    at the end (of) **au bout (de)**
    *prep.* II-4
    at last **enfin** *adv.* II-3
athlete **athlète** *m., f.* I-3
ATM **distributeur** *m.* **automa-**
    **tique/de billets** *m.* II-4
attend **assister** *v.* I-2
August **août** *m.* I-5
aunt **tante** *f.* I-3
author **auteur/femme auteur**
    *m., f.* II-7
autumn **automne** *m.* I-5
    in autumn **en automne** I-5
available *(free)* **libre** *adj.* I-7
avenue **avenue** *f.* II-4
avoid **éviter de** *v.* II-2

## B

back **dos** *m.* II-2
backpack **sac à dos** *m.* I-1
bad **mauvais(e)** *adj.* I-3
  to be in a bad mood **être de mauvaise humeur** I-8, II-P
  to be in bad health **être en mauvaise santé** II-2
badly **mal** *adv.* I-7
  I am doing badly. **Je vais mal.** I-1
  to be doing badly **se porter mal** *v.* II-2
baguette **baguette** *f.* I-4
bakery **boulangerie** *f.* II-1
balcony **balcon** *m.* I-8, II-P
banana **banane** *f.* II-1
bank **banque** *f.* II-4
  to have a bank account **avoir un compte bancaire** *v.* II-4
banker **banquier/banquière** *m., f.* II-5
banking **bancaire** *adj.* II-4
baseball **baseball** *m.* I-5
baseball cap **casquette** *f.* I-6
basement **sous-sol** *m.;* **cave** *f.* I-8, II-P
basketball **basket(-ball)** *m.* I-5
bath **bain** *m.* I-6
bathing suit **maillot de bain** *m.* I-6
bathroom **salle de bains** *f.* I-8, II-P
bathtub **baignoire** *f.* I-8, II-P
be **être** *v.* I-1
  **sois (être)** *imp. v.* I-7;
  **soyez (être)** *imp. v.* I-7
beach **plage** *f.* I-7
beans **haricots** *m., pl.* II-1
  green beans **haricots verts** *m., pl.* II-1
bearings: to get one's bearings **s'orienter** *v.* II-4
beautiful **beau (belle)** *adj.* I-3
beauty salon **salon** *m.* **de beauté** II-4
because **parce que** *conj.* I-2
become **devenir** *v.* II-1
bed **lit** *m.* I-7
  to go to bed **se coucher** *v.* II-2
bedroom **chambre** *f.* I-8, II-P
beef **bœuf** *m.* II-1
been **été (être)** *p.p.* I-6
beer **bière** *f.* I-6
before **avant (de/que)** *adv.* I-7
  before (*o'clock*) **moins** *adv.* I-2
begin (*to do something*) **commencer (à)** *v.* I-2; **se mettre à** *v.* II-2
beginning **début** *m.* II-7
behind **derrière** *prep.* I-3

Belgian **belge** *adj.* I-7
Belgium **Belgique** *f.* I-7
believe (that) **croire (que)** *v.* II-7
believed **cru (croire)** *p.p.* II-7
belt **ceinture** *f.* I-6
  to buckle one's seatbelt **attacher sa ceinture de sécurité** *v.* II-3
bench **banc** *m.* II-4
best: the best **le mieux** *super. adv.* II-1; **le/la meilleur(e)** *super. adj.* II-1
better **meilleur(e)** *comp. adj.;* **mieux** *comp. adv.* II-1
  It is better that… **Il vaut mieux que/qu'…** II-6
  to be doing better **se porter mieux** *v.* II-2
  to get better (*from illness*) **guérir** *v.* II-2
between **entre** *prep.* I-3
beverage (carbonated) **boisson** *f.* **(gazeuse)** I-4
bicycle **vélo** *m.* I-5
  to go bike riding **faire du vélo** *v.* I-5
big **grand(e)** *adj.* I-3; (*clothing*) **large** *adj.* I-6
bill (*in a restaurant*) **addition** *f.* I-4
bills (*money*) **billets** *m., pl.* II-4
biology **biologie** *f.* I-2
bird **oiseau** *m.* I-3
birth **naissance** *f.* I-6
birthday **anniversaire** *m.* I-5
bit (of) **morceau (de)** *m.* I-4
black **noir(e)** *adj.* I-3
blackboard **tableau** *m.* I-1
blanket **couverture** *f.* I-8, II-P
blonde **blond(e)** *adj.* I-3
blouse **chemisier** *m.* I-6
blue **bleu(e)** *adj.* I-3
boat **bateau** *m.* I-7
body **corps** *m.* II-2
book **livre** *m.* I-1
bookstore **librairie** *f.* I-1
bored: to get bored **s'ennuyer** *v.* II-2
boring **ennuyeux/ennuyeuse** *adj.* I-3
born: to be born **naître** *v.* I-7; **né (naître)** *p.p., adj.* I-7
borrow **emprunter** *v.* II-4
bottle (of) **bouteille (de)** *f.* I-4
boulevard **boulevard** *m.* II-4
boutique **boutique** *f.* II-4
bowl **bol** *m.* II-1
box **boîte** *f.* II-1
boy **garçon** *m.* I-1
boyfriend **petit ami** *m.* I-1
brake **freiner** *v.* II-3
brakes **freins** *m., pl.* II-3
brave **courageux/courageuse** *adj.* I-3

Brazil **Brésil** *m.* I-7
Brazilian **brésilien(ne)** *adj.* I-7
bread **pain** *m.* I-4
  country-style bread **pain** *m.* **de campagne** I-4
bread shop **boulangerie** *f.* II-1
break **se casser** *v.* II-2
breakdown **panne** *f.* II-3
break down **tomber en panne** *v.* II-3
break up (*to leave one another*) **se quitter** *v.* II-3
breakfast **petit-déjeuner** *m.* II-1
bridge **pont** *m.* II-4
bright **brillant(e)** *adj.* I-1
bring (*a person*) **amener** *v.* I-5; (*a thing*) **apporter** *v.* I-4
broom **balai** *m.* I-8, II-P
brother **frère** *m.* I-3
brother-in-law **beau-frère** *m.* I-3
brown **marron** *adj., inv.* I-3
  brown (*hair*) **châtain** *adj.* I-3
brush (hair/tooth) **brosse** *f.* **(à cheveux/à dents)** II-2
  to brush one's hair/teeth **se brosser les cheveux/les dents** *v.* II-1
buckle: to buckle one's seatbelt **attacher sa ceinture de sécurité** *v.* II-3
build **construire** *v.* I-6
building **bâtiment** *m.* II-4; **immeuble** *m.* I-8, II-P
bumper **pare-chocs** *m.* II-3
burn (CD/DVD) **graver** *v.* II-3
bus **autobus** *m.* I-7
bus stop **arrêt d'autobus (de bus)** *m.* I-7
bus terminal **gare** *f.* **routière** I-7
business (*profession*) **affaires** *f., pl.* I-3; (*company*) **entreprise** *f.* II-5
business administration **gestion** *f.* I-2
businessman **homme d'affaires** *m.* I-3
businesswoman **femme d'affaires** *f.* I-3
busy **occupé(e)** *adj.* I-1
but **mais** *conj.* I-1
butcher's shop **boucherie** *f.* II-1
butter **beurre** *m.* I-4
buy **acheter** *v.* I-5
by **par** *prep.* I-3
Bye! **Salut!** *fam.* I-1

## C

cabinet **placard** *m.* I-8, II-P
café **café** *m.* I-1; **brasserie** *f.* II-4
  café terrace **terrasse** *f.* **de café** I-4

cybercafé **cybercafé** *m.* II-4
cafeteria (school) **cantine** *f.* II-1
cake **gâteau** *m.* I-6
calculator **calculatrice** *f.* I-1
call **appeler** *v.* II-5
calm **calme** *adj.* I-1; **calme** *m.* I-1
camcorder **caméra vidéo** *f.* II-3; **caméscope** *m.* II-3
camera **appareil photo** *m.* II-3
   digital camera **appareil photo** *m.* **numérique** II-3
camping **camping** *m.* I-5
   to go camping **faire du camping** *v.* I-5
can (of food) **boîte (de conserve)** *f.* II-1
Canada **Canada** *m.* I-7
Canadian **canadien(ne)** *adj.* I-1
cancel (a reservation) **annuler (une réservation)** *v.* I-7
candidate **candidat(e)** *m., f.* II-5
candy **bonbon** *m.* I-6
cap: baseball cap **casquette** *f.* I-6
capital **capitale** *f.* I-7
car **voiture** *f.* II-3
   to ride in a car **rouler en voiture** *v.* I-7
card (letter) **carte postale** *f.* II-4; credit card **carte** *f.* **de crédit** II-4
   to pay with a credit card **payer avec une carte de crédit** *v.* II-4
   cards (playing) **cartes** *f.* I-5
carbonated drink/beverage **boisson** *f.* **gazeuse** I-4
career **carrière** *f.* II-5
carpooling **covoiturage** *m.* II-6
carrot **carotte** *f.* II-1
carry **apporter** *v.* I-4
cartoon **dessin animé** *m.* II-7
case: in any case **en tout cas** I-6
cash **liquide** *m.* II-4
   to pay in cash **payer en liquide** *v.* II-4
cat **chat** *m.* I-3
catastrophe **catastrophe** *f.* II-6
catch sight of **apercevoir** *v.* II-4
CD(s) **CD** *m.* II-3
CD/DVD player **lecteur de CD/DVD** *m.* II-3
CD-ROM(s) **CD-ROM, cédérom(s)** *m.* II-3
celebrate **célébrer** *v.* I-5; **fêter** *v.* I-6
celebration **fête** *f.* I-6
cellar **cave** *f.* I-8, II-P
cell(ular) phone **portable** *m.* II-3
center: city/town center **centre-ville** *m.* I-4
certain **certain(e)** *adj.* II-1; **sûr(e)** *adj.* II-7

It is certain that… **Il est certain que…** II-7
   It is uncertain that… **Il n'est pas certain que…** II-7
chair **chaise** *f.* I-1
champagne **champagne** *m.* I-6
change (coins) **(pièces** *f. pl.* **de) monnaie** II-4
channel (television) **chaîne** *f.* **(de télévision)** II-3
character **personnage** *m.* II-7
   main character **personnage principal** *m.* II-7
charming **charmant(e)** *adj.* I-1
chat **bavarder** *v.* I-4
check **chèque** *m.* II-4; (bill) **addition** *f.* I-4
   to pay by check **payer par chèque** *v.* II-4;
   to check (the oil/the air pressure) **vérifier (l'huile/la pression des pneus)** *v.* II-3
checking account **compte** *m.* **de chèques** II-4
cheek **joue** *f.* II-2
cheese **fromage** *m.* I-4
chemistry **chimie** *f.* I-2
chess **échecs** *m., pl.* I-5
chest **poitrine** *f.* II-2
   chest of drawers **commode** *f.* I-8, II-P
chic **chic** *adj.* I-4
chicken **poulet** *m.* II-1
child **enfant** *m., f.* I-3
childhood **enfance** *f.* I-6
China **Chine** *f.* I-7
Chinese **chinois(e)** *adj.* I-7
choir **chœur** *m.* II-7
choose **choisir** *v.* I-4
chorus **chœur** *m.* II-7
chrysanthemums **chrysanthèmes** *m., pl.* II-1
church **église** *f.* I-4
city **ville** *f.* I-4
city hall **mairie** *f.* II-4
city/town center **centre-ville** *m.* I-4
class (group of students) **classe** *f.* I-1; (course) **cours** *m.* I-2
classmate **camarade de classe** *m., f.* I-1
classroom **salle** *f.* **de classe** I-1
clean **nettoyer** *v.* I-5; **propre** *adj.* I-8, II-P
clear **clair(e)** *adj.* II-7
   It is clear that… **Il est clair que…** II-7
   to clear the table **débarrasser la table** I-8, II-P
client **client(e)** *m., f.* I-7
cliff **falaise** *f.* II-6
clock **horloge** *f.* I-1
   alarm clock **réveil** *m.* II-2

close (to) **près (de)** *prep.* I-3
   very close (to) **tout près (de)** II-4
close **fermer** *v.* II-3
closed **fermé(e)** *adj.* II-4
closet **placard** *m.* I-8, II-P
clothes dryer **sèche-linge** *m.* I-8, II-P
clothing **vêtements** *m., pl.* I-6
cloudy **nuageux/nuageuse** *adj.* I-5
   It is cloudy. **Le temps est nuageux.** I-5
clutch **embrayage** *m.* II-3
coast **côte** *f.* II-6
coat **manteau** *m.* I-6
coffee **café** *m.* I-1
coffeemaker **cafetière** *f.* I-8, II-P
coins **pièces** *f. pl.* **de monnaie** II-4
cold **froid** *m.* I-2
   to be cold **avoir froid** *v.* I-2
   (weather) It is cold. **Il fait froid.** I-5
cold **rhume** *m.* II-2
color **couleur** *f.* I-6
   What color is… ? **De quelle couleur est… ?** I-6
comb **peigne** *m.* II-2
come **venir** *v.* I-7
come back **revenir** *v.* II-1
Come on. **Allez.** I-2
comedy **comédie** *f.* II-7
comic strip **bande dessinée (B.D.)** *f.* I-5
compact disc **compact disque** *m.* II-3
company (troop) **troupe** *f.* II-7
completely **tout à fait** *adv.* I-6
composer **compositeur** *m.* II-7
computer **ordinateur** *m.* I-1
computer science **informatique** *f.* I-2
concert **concert** *m.* II-7
congratulations **félicitations** II-7
consider **considérer** *v.* I-5
constantly **constamment** *adv.* I-8, II-P
construct **construire** *v.* I-6
consultant **conseiller/ conseillère** *m., f.* II-5
continue (doing something) **continuer (à)** *v.* II-4
cook **cuisiner** *v.* II-1; **faire la cuisine** *v.* I-5; **cuisinier/ cuisinière** *m., f.* II-5
cookie **biscuit** *m.* I-6
cooking **cuisine** *f.* I-5
cool: (weather) It is cool. **Il fait frais.** I-5
corner **angle** *m.* II-4; **coin** *m.* II-4
cost **coûter** *v.* I-4

cotton **coton** *m.* I-6

couch **canapé** *m.* I-8, II-P

cough **tousser** *v.* II-2

count (on someone) **compter (sur quelqu'un)** *v.* I-8, II-P

country **pays** *m.* I-7

    country(side) **campagne** *f.* I-7

country-style **de campagne** *adj.* I-4

couple **couple** *m.* I-6

courage **courage** *m.* II-5

courageous **courageux/ courageuse** *adj.* I-3

course **cours** *m.* I-2

cousin **cousin(e)** *m., f.* I-3

cover **couvrir** *v.* II-3

covered **couvert (couvrir)** *p.p.* II-3

cow **vache** *f.* II-6

crazy **fou/folle** *adj.* I-3

cream **crème** *f.* II-1

credit card **carte** *f.* **de crédit** II-4

    to pay with a credit card **payer avec une carte de crédit** *v.* II-4

crêpe **crêpe** *f.* I-5

crime film **film policier** *m.* II-7

croissant **croissant** *m.* I-4

cross **traverser** *v.* II-4

cruel **cruel/cruelle** *adj.* I-3

cry **pleurer** *v.*

cup (of) **tasse (de)** *f.* I-4

cupboard **placard** *m.* I-8, II-P

curious **curieux/ curieuse** *adj.* I-3

curly **frisé(e)** *adj.* I-3

currency **monnaie** *f.* II-4

curtain **rideau** *m.* I-8, II-P

customs **douane** *f.* I-7

cybercafé **cybercafé** *m.* II-4

### D

dance **danse** *f.* II-7

    to dance **danser** *v.* I-4

danger **danger** *m.* II-6

dangerous **dangereux/ dangereuse** *adj.* II-3

dark (*hair*) **brun(e)** *adj.* I-3

darling **chéri(e)** *adj.* I-2

darn **zut** II-3

dash (*punctuation mark*) **tiret** *m.* II-3

date (*day, month, year*) **date** *f.* I-5; (*meeting*) **rendez-vous** *m.* I-6

    to make a date **prendre (un) rendez-vous** *v.* II-5

daughter **fille** *f.* I-1

day **jour** *m.* I-2; **journée** *f.* I-2

    day after tomorrow **après-demain** *adv.* I-2

day before yesterday **avant-hier** *adv.* I-7

day off **congé** *m.,* **jour de congé** I-7

dear **cher/chère** *adj.* I-2

death **mort** *f.* I-6

December **décembre** *m.* I-5

decide (*to do something*) **décider (de)** *v.* II-3

deforestation **déboisement** *m.* II-6

degree **diplôme** *m.* I-2

degrees (*temperature*) **degrés** *m., pl.* I-5

    It is... degrees. **Il fait... degrés.** I-5

delicatessen **charcuterie** *f.* II-1

delicious **délicieux/délicieuse** *adj.* I-4

Delighted. **Enchanté(e).** *p.p., adj.* I-1

demand (*that*) **exiger (que)** *v.* II-6

demanding **exigeant(e)** *adj.*

    demanding profession **profession** *f.* **exigeante** II-5

dentist **dentiste** *m., f.* I-3

department store **grand magasin** *m.* I-4

departure **départ** *m.* I-7

deposit: to deposit money **déposer de l'argent** *v.* II-4

depressed **déprimé(e)** *adj.* II-2

describe **décrire** *v.* I-7

described **décrit (décrire)** *p.p., adj.* I-7

desert **désert** *m.* II-6

design (*fashion*) **stylisme (de mode)** *m.* I-2

desire **envie** *f.* I-2

desk **bureau** *m.* I-1

dessert **dessert** *m.* I-6

destroy **détruire** *v.* I-6

destroyed **détruit (détruire)** *p.p., adj.* I-6

detective film **film policier** *m.* II-7

detest **détester** *v.* I-2

    I hate... **Je déteste...** I-2

develop **développer** *v.* II-6

dial (*a number*) **composer (un numéro)** *v.* II-3

dictionary **dictionnaire** *m.* I-1

die **mourir** *v.* I-7

died **mort (mourir)** *p.p., adj.* I-7

diet **régime** *m.* II-2

    to be on a diet **être au régime** II-1

difference **différence** *f.* I-1

different **différent(e)** *adj.* I-1

differently **différemment** *adv.* I-8, II-P

difficult **difficile** *adj.* I-1

digital camera **appareil photo** *m.* **numérique** II-3

dining room **salle à manger** *f.* I-8, II-P

dinner **dîner** *m.* II-1

    to have dinner **dîner** *v.* I-2

diploma **diplôme** *m.* I-2

directions **indications** *f.* II-4

director (*movie*) **réalisateur/ réalisatrice** *m., f.;* (*play/show*) **metteur en scène** *m.* II-7

dirty **sale** *adj.* I-8, II-P

discover **découvrir** *v.* II-3

discovered **découvert (découvrir)** *p.p.* II-3

discreet **discret/discrète** *adj.* I-3

discuss **discuter** *v.* II-3

dish (*food*) **plat** *m.* II-1

    to do the dishes **faire la vaisselle** *v.* I-8, II-P

dishwasher **lave-vaisselle** *m.* I-8, II-P

dismiss **renvoyer** *v.* II-5

distinction **mention** *f.* II-5

divorce **divorce** *m.* I-6

    to divorce **divorcer** *v.* I-3

divorced **divorcé(e)** *p.p., adj.* I-3

do (*make*) **faire** *v.* I-5

    to do odd jobs **bricoler** *v.* I-5

doctor **médecin** *m.* I-3

documentary **documentaire** *m.* II-7

dog **chien** *m.* I-3

done **fait (faire)** *p.p., adj.* I-6

door (*building*) **porte** *f.* I-1; (*automobile*) **portière** *f.* II-3

dorm **résidence** *f.* **universitaire** I-8, II-P

doubt (*that*)... **douter (que)...** *v.* II-7

doubtful **douteux/douteuse** *adj.* II-7

    It is doubtful that... **Il est douteux que...** II-7

download **télécharger** *v.* II-3

downtown **centre-ville** *m.* I-4

drag **barbant** *adj.* I-3; **barbe** *f.* I-3

drape **rideau** *m.* I-8, II-P

draw **dessiner** *v.* I-2

drawer **tiroir** *m.* I-8, II-P

dreadful **épouvantable** *adj.* I-5

dream (*about*) **rêver (de)** *v.* II-3

dress **robe** *f.* I-6

    to dress **s'habiller** *v.* II-2

dresser **commode** *f.* I-8, II-P

drink (*carbonated*) **boisson** *f.* **(gazeuse)** I-4

    to drink **boire** *v.* I-4

drive **conduire** *v.* I-6

    to go for a drive **faire un tour en voiture** I-5

driven **conduit (conduire)** *p.p.* I-6

driver (taxi/truck) **chauffeur (de taxi/de camion)** *m.* II-5
driver's license **permis** *m.* **de conduire** II-3
drums **batterie** *f.* II-7
drunk **bu (boire)** *p.p.* I-6
dryer *(clothes)* **sèche-linge** *m.* I-8, II-P
dry oneself **se sécher** *v.* II-2
due **dû(e) (devoir)** *adj.* II-1
during **pendant** *prep.* I-7
dust **enlever/faire la poussière** *v.* I-8, II-P

### E

each **chaque** *adj.* I-6
ear **oreille** *f.* II-2
early **en avance** *adv.* I-2; **tôt** *adv.* I-2
earn **gagner** *v.* II-5
Earth **Terre** *f.* II-6
easily **facilement** *adv.* I-8, II-P
east **est** *m.* II-4
easy **facile** *adj.* I-2
eat **manger** *v.* I-2
  to eat lunch **déjeuner** *v.* I-4
éclair **éclair** *m.* I-4
ecological **écologique** *adj.* II-6
ecology **écologie** *f.* II-6
economics **économie** *f.* I-2
ecotourism **écotourisme** *m.* II-6
education **formation** *f.* II-5
effect: in effect **en effet** II-6
egg **œuf** *m.* II-1
eight **huit** *m.* I-1
eighteen **dix-huit** *m.* I-1
eighth **huitième** *adj.* I-7
eighty **quatre-vingts** *m.* I-3
eighty-one **quatre-vingt-un** *m.* I-3
elder **aîné(e)** *adj.* I-3
electric **électrique** *adj.* I-8, II-P
  electrical appliance **appareil** *m.* **électrique** I-8, II-P
electrician **électricien/électricienne** *m., f.* II-5
elegant **élégant(e)** *adj.* I-1
elevator **ascenseur** *m.* I-7
eleven **onze** *m.* I-1
eleventh **onzième** *adj.* I-7
e-mail **e-mail** *m.* II-3
emergency room **urgences** *f., pl.* II-2
  to go to the emergency room **aller aux urgences** *v.* II-2
employ **employer** *v.* I-5
end **fin** *f.* II-7
endangered **menacé(e)** *adj.* II-6
  endangered species **espèce** *f.* **menacée** II-6
engaged **fiancé(e)** *adj.* I-3
engine **moteur** *m.* II-3

engineer **ingénieur** *m.* I-3
England **Angleterre** *f.* I-7
English **anglais(e)** *adj.* I-1
enormous **énorme** *adj.* I-2
enough (of) **assez (de)** *adv.* I-4
  not enough (of) **pas assez (de)** I-4
enter **entrer** *v.* I-7
envelope **enveloppe** *f.* II-4
environment **environnement** *m.* II-6
equal **égaler** *v.* I-3
erase **effacer** *v.* II-3
errand **course** *f.* II-1
escargot **escargot** *m.* II-1
especially **surtout** *adv.* I-2
essay **dissertation** *f.* II-3
essential **essentiel(le)** *adj.* II-6
  It is essential that... **Il est essentiel/indispensable que...** II-6
even **même** *adv.* I-5
evening **soir** *m.;* **soirée** *f.* I-2
  ... (o'clock) in the evening ... **heures du soir** I-2
every day **tous les jours** *adv.* I-8, II-P
everyone **tout le monde** *m.* II-1
evident **évident(e)** *adj.* II-7
  It is evident that... **Il est évident que...** II-7
evidently **évidemment** *adv.* I-8, II-P
exactly **exactement** *adv.* II-1
exam **examen** *m.* I-1
Excuse me. **Excuse-moi.** *fam.* I-1; **Excusez-moi.** *form.* I-1
executive **cadre/femme cadre** *m., f.* II-5
exercise **exercice** *m.* II-2
  to exercise **faire de l'exercice** *v.* II-2
exhibit **exposition** *f.* II-7
exit **sortie** *f.* I-7
expenditure **dépense** *f.* II-4
expensive **cher/chère** *adj.* I-6
explain **expliquer** *v.* I-2
explore **explorer** *v.* I-4
extinction **extinction** *f.* II-6
eye (eyes) **œil (yeux)** *m.* II-2

### F

face **visage** *m.* II-2
facing **en face (de)** *prep.* I-3
fact: in fact **en fait** I-7
factory **usine** *f.* II-6
fail **échouer** *v.* I-2
fall **automne** *m.* I-5
  in the fall **en automne** I-5
  to fall **tomber** *v.* I-7

to fall in love **tomber amoureux/amoureuse** *v.* I-6
  to fall asleep **s'endormir** *v.* II-2
family **famille** *f.* I-3
famous **célèbre** *adj.* II-7; **connu (connaître)** *p.p., adj.* I-8, II-P
far (from) **loin (de)** *prep.* I-3
farewell **adieu** *m.* II-6
farmer **agriculteur/agricultrice** *m., f.* II-5
fashion **mode** *f.* I-2
  fashion design **stylisme de mode** *m.* I-2
fast **rapide** *adj.* I-3; **vite** *adv.* I-8, II-P
fat **gros(se)** *adj.* I-3
father **père** *m.* I-3
father-in-law **beau-père** *m.* I-3
favorite **favori/favorite** *adj.* I-3; **préféré(e)** *adj.* I-2
fax machine **fax** *m.* II-3
fear **peur** *f.* I-2
  to fear that **avoir peur que** *v.* II-6
February **février** *m.* I-5
fed up: to be fed up **en avoir marre** *v.* I-3
feel *(to sense)* **sentir** *v.* I-5; *(state of being)* **se sentir** *v.* II-2
  to feel like *(doing something)* **avoir envie (de)** I-2
  to feel nauseated **avoir mal au cœur** II-2
festival (festivals) **festival (festivals)** *m.* II-7
fever **fièvre** *f.* II-2
  to have fever **avoir de la fièvre** *v.* II-2
fiancé **fiancé(e)** *m., f.* I-6
field *(terrain)* **champ** *m.* II-6; *(of study)* **domaine** *m.* II-5
fifteen **quinze** *m.* I-1
fifth **cinquième** *adj.* I-7
fifty **cinquante** *m.* I-1
figure *(physique)* **ligne** *f.* II-2
file **fichier** *m.* II-3
fill: to fill out a form **remplir un formulaire** *v.* II-4
  to fill the tank **faire le plein** *v.* II-3
film **film** *m.* II-7
  adventure/crime film **film** *m.* **d'aventures/policier** II-7
finally **enfin** *adv.* I-7; **finalement** *adv.* I-7; **dernièrement** *adv.* I-8, II-P
find (a job) **trouver (un/du travail)** *v.* II-5
  to find again **retrouver** *v.* I-2
fine **amende** *f.* II-3
fine arts **beaux-arts** *m., pl.* II-7
finger **doigt** *m.* II-2

finish (*doing something*) **finir (de)** *v.* I-4, II-3
fire **incendie** *m.* II-6
firefighter **pompier/femme pompier** *m., f.* II-5
firm (*business*) **entreprise** *f.* II-5;
first **d'abord** *adv.* I-7; **premier/première** *adj.* I-2; **premier** *m.* I-5
  It is October first. **C'est le 1ᵉʳ (premier) octobre.** I-5
fish **poisson** *m.* I-3
fishing **pêche** *f.* I-5
  to go fishing **aller à la pêche** *v.* I-5
fish shop **poissonnerie** *f.* II-1
five **cinq** *m.* I-1
flat tire **pneu** *m.* **crevé** II-3
flight (*air travel*) **vol** *m.* I-7
floor **étage** *m.* I-7
flower **fleur** *f.* I-8, II-P
flu **grippe** *f.* II-2
fluently **couramment** *adv.* I-8, II-P
follow (a path/a street/a boulevard) **suivre (un chemin/une rue/un boulevard)** *v.* II-4
food item **aliment** *m.* II-1; **nourriture** *f.* II-1
foot **pied** *m.* II-2
football **football américain** *m.* I-5
for **pour** *prep.* I-5; **pendant** *prep.* II-1
  For whom? **Pour qui?** I-4
forbid **interdire** *v.* II-6
foreign **étranger/étrangère** *adj.* I-2
  foreign languages **langues** *f., pl.* **étrangères** I-2
forest **forêt** *f.* II-6
  tropical forest **forêt tropicale** *f.* II-6
forget (*to do something*) **oublier (de)** *v.* I-2
fork **fourchette** *f.* II-1
form **formulaire** *m.* II-4
former (*placed before noun*) **ancien(ne)** *adj.* II-7
fortunately **heureusement** *adv.* I-8, II-P
forty **quarante** *m.* I-1
fountain **fontaine** *f.* II-4
four **quatre** *m.* I-1
fourteen **quatorze** *m.* I-1
fourth **quatrième** *adj.* I-7
France **France** *f.* I-7
frankly **franchement** *adv.* I-8, II-P
free (*at no cost*) **gratuit(e)** *adj.* II-7
  free time **temps libre** *m.* I-5
freezer **congélateur** *m.* I-8, II-P
French **français(e)** *adj.* I-1
French fries **frites** *f., pl.* I-4
frequent (*to visit regularly*) **fréquenter** *v.* I-4

fresh **frais/fraîche** *adj.* I-5
Friday **vendredi** *m.* I-2
friend **ami(e)** *m., f.* I-1; **copain/copine** *m., f.* I-1
friendship **amitié** *f.* I-6
from **de/d'** *prep.* I-1
  from time to time **de temps en temps** *adv.* I-8, II-P
front: in front of **devant** *prep.* I-3
fruit **fruit** *m.* II-1
full (*no vacancies*) **complet (complète)** *adj.* I-7
full-time job **emploi** *m.* **à plein temps** II-5
fun **amusant(e)** *adj.* I-1
  to have fun (*doing something*) **s'amuser (à)** *v.* II-3
funeral **funérailles** *f., pl.* II-1
funny **drôle** *adj.* I-3
furious **furieux/furieuse** *adj.* II-6
  to be furious that… **être furieux/furieuse que…** *v.* II-6

**G**

gain: gain weight **grossir** *v.* I-4
game (*amusement*) **jeu** *m.* I-5; (*sports*) **match** *m.* I-5
game show **jeu télévisé** *m.* II-7
garage **garage** *m.* I-8, II-P
garbage **ordures** *f., pl.* II-6
garbage collection **ramassage** *m.* **des ordures** II-6
garden **jardin** *m.* I-8, II-P
garlic **ail** *m.* II-1
gas **essence** *f.* II-3
gas tank **réservoir d'essence** *m.* II-3
gas warning light **voyant** *m.* **d'essence** II-3
generally **en général** *adv.* I-8, II-P
generous **généreux/généreuse** *adj.* I-3
genre **genre** *m.* II-7
gentle **doux/douce** *adj.* I-3
geography **géographie** *f.* I-2
German **allemand(e)** *adj.* I-1
Germany **Allemagne** *f.* I-7
get (*to obtain*) **obtenir** *v.* II-5
get along well (with) **s'entendre bien (avec)** *v.* II-2
get off **descendre (de)** *v.* I-6
get up **se lever** *v.* II-2
  get up again **se relever** *v.* II-2
gift **cadeau** *m.* I-6
  wrapped gift **paquet cadeau** *m.* I-6
gifted **doué(e)** *adj.* II-7
girl **fille** *f.* I-1
girlfriend **petite amie** *f.* I-1
give (*to someone*) **donner (à)** *v.* I-2
  to give a shot **faire une piqûre** *v.* II-2

to give a tour **faire visiter** *v.* I-8, II-P
to give back **rendre (à)** *v.* I-6
to give one another **se donner** *v.* II-3
glass (of) **verre (de)** *m.* I-4
glasses **lunettes** *f., pl.* I-6
  sunglasses **lunettes de soleil** *f., pl.* I-6
global warming **réchauffement** *m.* **de la Terre** II-6
glove **gant** *m.* I-6
go **aller** *v.* I-4
  Let's go! **Allons-y!** I-4; **On y va!** II-2
  I'm going. **J'y vais.** I-8, II-P
  to go back **repartir** *v.* II-7
  to go downstairs **descendre (de)** *v.* I-6
  to go out **sortir** *v.* I-7
  to go over **dépasser** *v.* II-3
  to go up **monter** *v.* I-7
  to go with **aller avec** *v.* I-6
golf **golf** *m.* I-5
good **bon(ne)** *adj.* I-3
  Good evening. **Bonsoir.** I-1
  Good morning. **Bonjour.** I-1
  to be good for nothing **ne servir à rien** *v.* II-1
  to be in a good mood **être de bonne humeur** *v.* I-8, II-P
  to be in good health **être en bonne santé** *v.* II-2
  to be in good shape **être en pleine forme** *v.* II-2
  to be up to something interesting **faire quelque chose de beau** *v.* II-4
Good-bye. **Au revoir.** I-1
government **gouvernement** *m.* II-6
grade (*academics*) **note** *f.* I-2
grandchildren **petits-enfants** *m., pl.* I-3
granddaughter **petite-fille** *f.* I-3
grandfather **grand-père** *m.* I-3
grandmother **grand-mère** *f.* I-3
grandparents **grands-parents** *m., pl.* I-3
grandson **petit-fils** *m.* I-3
grant **bourse** *f.* I-2
grass **herbe** *f.* II-6
gratin **gratin** *m.* II-1
gray **gris(e)** *adj.* I-6
great **formidable** *adj.* I-7; **génial(e)** *adj.* I-3
green **vert(e)** *adj.* I-3
green beans **haricots verts** *m., pl.* II-1
greenhouse **serre** *f.* II-6
  greenhouse effect **effet de serre** *m.* II-6
grocery store **épicerie** *f.* I-4

groom: to groom oneself *(in the morning)* **faire sa toilette** *v.* II-2
ground floor **rez-de-chaussée** *m.* I-7
growing population **population** *f.* **croissante** II-6
guaranteed **garanti(e)** *p.p., adj.* I-5
guest **invité(e)** *m., f.* I-6; **client(e)** *m., f.* I-7
guitar **guitare** *f.* II-7
guy **mec** *m.* II-2
gym **gymnase** *m.* I-4

### H

habitat **habitat** *m.* II-6
habitat preservation **sauvetage des habitats** *m.* II-6
had **eu (avoir)** *p.p.* I-6
had to **dû (devoir)** *p.p.* II-1
hair **cheveux** *m., pl.* II-1
to brush one's hair **se brosser les cheveux** *v.* II-1
to do one's hair **se coiffer** *v.* II-2
hairbrush **brosse** *f.* **à cheveux** II-2
hairdresser **coiffeur/coiffeuse** *m., f.* I-3
half **demie** *f.* I-2
half past … (o'clock) **… et demie** I-2
half-brother **demi-frère** *m.* I-3
half-sister **demi-sœur** *f.* I-3
half-time job **emploi** *m.* **à mi-temps** II-5
hallway **couloir** *m.* I-8, II-P
ham **jambon** *m.* I-4
hand **main** *f.* I-5
handbag **sac à main** *m.* I-6
handsome **beau** *adj.* I-3
hang up **raccrocher** *v.* II-5
happiness **bonheur** *m.* I-6
happy **heureux/heureuse** *adj.;* **content(e)** II-5
to be happy that… **être content(e) que…** *v.* II-6; **être heureux/heureuse que…** *v.* II-6
hard drive **disque (dur)** *m.* II-3
hard-working **travailleur/travailleuse** *adj.* I-3
hat **chapeau** *m.* I-6
hate **détester** *v.* I-2
I hate… **Je déteste…** I-2
have **avoir** *v.* I-2; **aie (avoir)** *imp., v.* I-7; **ayez (avoir)** *imp. v.* I-7; **prendre** *v.* I-4
to have an ache **avoir mal** *v.* II-2

to have to *(must)* **devoir** *v.* II-1
he **il** *sub. pron.* I-1
head *(body part)* **tête** *f.* II-2; *(of a company)* **chef** *m.* **d'entreprise** II-5
headache: to have a headache **avoir mal à la tête** *v.* II-2
headlights **phares** *m., pl.* II-3
health **santé** *f.* II-2
to be in good health **être en bonne santé** *v.* II-2
health insurance **assurance** *f.* **maladie** II-5
healthy **sain(e)** *adj.* II-2
hear **entendre** *v.* I-6
heart **cœur** *m.* II-2
heat **chaud** *m.* 2
hello *(on the phone)* **allô** I-1; *(in the evening)* **Bonsoir.** I-1; *(in the morning or afternoon)* **Bonjour.** I-1
help **au secours** II-3
to help *(to do something)* **aider (à)** *v.* I-5
to help one another **s'aider** *v.* II-3
her **la/l'** *d.o. pron.* I-7; **lui** *i.o. pron.* I-6; *(attached to an imperative)* **-lui** *i.o. pron.* II-1
her **sa** *poss. adj., f., sing.* I-3; **ses** *poss. adj., m., f., pl.* I-3; **son** *poss. adj., m., sing.* I-3
Here! **Tenez!** *form., imp. v.* II-1; **Tiens!** *fam., imp., v.* II-1
here **ici** *adv.* I-1; *(used with demonstrative adjective* **ce** *and noun or with demonstrative pronoun* **celui***);* **-ci** I-6; Here is…. **Voici…** I-1
heritage: I am of… heritage. **Je suis d'origine…** I-1
herself *(used with reflexive verb)* **se/s'** *pron.* II-2
hesitate *(to do something)* **hésiter (à)** *v.* II-3
Hey! **Eh!** *interj.* 2
Hi! **Salut!** *fam.* I-1
high **élevé(e)** *adj.* II-5
high school **lycée** *m.* I-1
high school student **lycéen(ne)** *m., f.* 2
higher education **études supérieures** *f., pl.* 2
highway **autoroute** *f.* II-3
hike **randonnée** *f.* I-5
to go for a hike **faire une randonnée** *v.* I-5
him **lui** *i.o. pron.* I-6; **le/l'** *d.o. pron.* I-7; *(attached to imperative)* **-lui** *i.o. pron.* II-1
himself *(used with reflexive verb)* **se/s'** *pron.* II-2
hire **embaucher** *v.* II-5

his **sa** *poss. adj., f., sing.* I-3; **ses** *poss. adj., m., f., pl.* I-3; **son** *poss. adj., m., sing.* I-3
history **histoire** *f.* I-2
hit **rentrer (dans)** *v.* II-3
hold **tenir** *v.* II-1
to be on hold **patienter** *v.* II-5
hole in the ozone layer **trou dans la couche d'ozone** *m.* II-6
holiday **jour férié** *m.* I-6; **férié(e)** *adj.* I-6
home *(house)* **maison** *f.* I-4
at (someone's) home **chez…** *prep.* 4
home page **page d'accueil** *f.* II-3
homework **devoir** *m.* I-2
honest **honnête** *adj.* II-7
honestly **franchement** *adv.* I-8, II-P
hood **capot** *m.* II-3
hope **espérer** *v.* I-5
hors d'œuvre **hors-d'œuvre** *m.* II-1
horse **cheval** *m.* I-5
to go horseback riding **faire du cheval** *v.* I-5
hospital **hôpital** *m.* I-4
host **hôte/hôtesse** *m., f.* I-6
hot **chaud** *m.* I-2
It is hot (weather). **Il fait chaud.** I-5
to be hot **avoir chaud** *v.* I-2
hot chocolate **chocolat chaud** *m.* I-4
hotel **hôtel** *m.* I-7
(single) hotel room **chambre** *f.* **(individuelle)** I-7
hotel keeper **hôtelier/hôtelière** *m., f.* I-7
hour **heure** *f.* I-2
house **maison** *f.* I-4
at (someone's) house **chez…** *prep.* I-2
to leave the house **quitter la maison** *v.* I-4
to stop by someone's house **passer chez quelqu'un** *v.* I-4
household **ménager/ménagère** *adj.* I-8, II-P
household appliance **appareil** *m.* **ménager** I-8, II-P
household chore **tâche ménagère** *f.* I-8, II-P
housewife **femme au foyer** *f.* II-5
housework: to do the housework **faire le ménage** *v.* I-8, II-P
housing **logement** *m.* I-8, II-P
how **comme** *adv.* I-2; **comment?** *interr. adv.* I-4
How are you? **Comment allez-vous?** *form.* I-1; **Comment vas-tu?** *fam.* I-1
How many/How much (of)? **Combien (de)?** I-1

How much is... ? **Combien coûte... ?** I-4
huge **énorme** *adj.* I-2
Huh? **Hein?** *interj.* I-3
humanities **lettres** *f., pl.* I-2
hundred: one hundred **cent** *m.* I-5
    five hundred **cinq cents** *m.* I-5
    one hundred one **cent un** *m.* I-5
    one hundred thousand **cent mille** *m.* I-5
hundredth **centième** *adj.* I-7
hunger **faim** *f.* I-4
hungry: to be hungry **avoir faim** *v.* I-4
hunt **chasse** *f.* II-6
    to hunt **chasser** *v.* II-6
hurried **pressé(e)** *adj.* II-1
hurry **se dépêcher** *v.* II-2
hurt **faire mal** *v.* II-2
    to hurt oneself **se blesser** *v.* II-2
husband **mari** *m.*; **époux** *m.* I-3
hyphen *(punctuation mark)* **tiret** *m.* II-3

## I

I **je** *sub. pron.* I-1; **moi** *disj. pron., sing.* I-3
ice cream **glace** *f.* I-6
ice cube **glaçon** *m.* I-6
idea **idée** *f.* I-3
if **si** *conj.* II-5
ill: to become ill **tomber malade** *v.* II-2
illness **maladie** *f.* II-5
immediately **tout de suite** *adv.* I-4
impatient **impatient(e)** *adj.* I-1
important **important(e)** *adj.* I-1
    It is important that... **Il est important que...** II-6
impossible **impossible** *adj.* II-7
    It is impossible that... **Il est impossible que...** II-7
improve **améliorer** *v.* II-5
in **dans** *prep.* I-3; **en** *prep.* I-3; **à** *prep.* I-4
included **compris (comprendre)** *p.p., adj.* I-6
incredible **incroyable** *adj.* II-3
independent **indépendant(e)** *adj.* I-1
independently **indépendamment** *adv.* I-8, II-P
indicate **indiquer** *v.* 5
indispensable **indispensable** *adj.* II-6
inexpensive **bon marché** *adj.* I-6
injection **piqûre** *f.* II-2

to give an injection **faire une piqûre** *v.* II-2
injury **blessure** *f.* II-2
instrument **instrument** *m.* I-1
insurance (health/life) **assurance** *f.* **(maladie/vie)** II-5
intellectual **intellectuel(le)** *adj.* I-3
intelligent **intelligent(e)** *adj.* I-1
interested: to be interested (in) **s'intéresser (à)** *v.* II-2
interesting **intéressant(e)** *adj.* I-1
intermission **entracte** *m.* II-7
internship **stage** *m.* II-5
intersection **carrefour** *m.* II-4
interview: to have an interview **passer un entretien** II-5
introduce **présenter** *v.* I-1
    I would like to introduce (*name*) to you. **Je te présente...** , *fam.* I-1
    I would like to introduce (*name*) to you. **Je vous présente...** , *form.* I-1
invite **inviter** *v.* I-4
Ireland **Irlande** *f.* I-7
Irish **irlandais(e)** *adj.* I-7
iron **fer à repasser** *m.* I-8, II-P
    to iron (the laundry) **repasser (le linge)** *v.* I-8, II-P
isn't it? *(tag question)* **n'est-ce pas?** I-2
island **île** *f.* II-6
Italian **italien(ne)** *adj.* I-1
Italy **Italie** *f.* I-7
it: It depends. **Ça dépend.** I-4
    It is... **C'est...** I-1
itself *(used with reflexive verb)* **se/s'** *pron.* II-2

## J

jacket **blouson** *m.* I-6
jam **confiture** *f.* II-1
January **janvier** *m.* I-5
Japan **Japon** *m.* I-7
Japanese **japonais(e)** *adj.* I-1
jealous **jaloux/jalouse** *adj.* I-3
jeans **jean** *m. sing.* I-6
jewelry store **bijouterie** *f.* II-4
jogging **jogging** *m.* I-5
    to go jogging **faire du jogging** *v.* I-5
joke **blague** *f.* I-2
journalist **journaliste** *m., f.* I-3
juice (orange/apple) **jus** *m.* **(d'orange/de pomme)** I-4
July **juillet** *m.* I-5
June **juin** *m.* I-5
jungle **jungle** *f.* II-6
just *(barely)* **juste** *adv.* I-3

## K

keep **retenir** *v.* II-1
key **clé** *f.* I-7
keyboard **clavier** *m.* II-3
kilo(gram) **kilo(gramme)** *m.* II-1
kind **bon(ne)** *adj.* I-3
kiosk **kiosque** *m.* I-4
kiss one another **s'embrasser** *v.* II-3
kitchen **cuisine** *f.* I-8, II-P
knee **genou** *m.* II-2
knife **couteau** *m.* II-1
know *(as a fact)* **savoir** *v.* I-8, II-P; *(to be familiar with)* **connaître** *v.* I-8, II-P
    to know one another **se connaître** *v.* II-3
    I don't know anything about it. **Je n'en sais rien.** II-6
    to know that... **savoir que...** II-7
known *(as a fact)* **su (savoir)** *p.p.* I-8, II-P; *(famous)* **connu (connaître)** *p.p., adj.* I-8, II-P

## L

laborer **ouvrier/ouvrière** *m., f.* II-5
lake **lac** *m.* II-6
lamp **lampe** *f.* I-8, II-P
landlord **propriétaire** *m., f.* I-3
landslide **glissement de terrain** *m.* II-6
language **langue** *f.* I-2
    foreign languages **langues** *f., pl.* **étrangères** I-2
last **dernier/dernière** *adj.* I-2
lastly **dernièrement** *adv.* I-8, II-P
late *(when something happens late)* **en retard** *adv.* I-2; *(in the evening, etc.)* **tard** *adv.* I-2
laugh **rire** *v.* I-6
laughed **ri (rire)** *p.p.* I-6
laundromat **laverie** *f.* II-4
laundry: to do the laundry **faire la lessive** *v.* I-8, II-P
law *(academic discipline)* **droit** *m.* I-2; *(ordinance or rule)* **loi** *f.* II-6
lawyer **avocat(e)** *m., f.* I-3
lay off *(let go)* **renvoyer** *v.* II-5
lazy **paresseux/paresseuse** *adj.* I-3
learned **appris (apprendre)** *p.p.* I-6
least **moins** II-1
    the least... *(used with adjective)* **le/la moins...** *super. adv.* II-1
    the least... , *(used with noun to express quantity)* **le moins de...** II-6

the least... *(used with verb or adverb)* **le moins...** *super. adv.* II-1
leather **cuir** *m.* I-6
leave **partir** *v.* I-5; **quitter** *v.* I-4
  to leave alone **laisser tranquille** *v.* II-2
  to leave one another **se quitter** *v.* II-3
  I'm leaving. **Je m'en vais.** I-8, II-P
left: to the left (of) **à gauche (de)** *prep.* I-3
leg **jambe** *f.* II-2
leisure activity **loisir** *m.* I-5
lemon soda **limonade** *f.* I-4
lend *(to someone)* **prêter (à)** *v.* I-6
less **moins** *adv.* I-4
  less of... *(used with noun to express quantity)* **moins de...** I-4
  less ... than *(used with noun to compare quantities)* **moins de... que** II-6
  less... than *(used with adjective to compare qualities)* **moins... que** II-1
let **laisser** *v.* II-3
  to let go *(to fire or lay off)* **renvoyer** *v.* II-5
  Let's go! **Allons-y!** I-4; **On y va!** II-2
letter **lettre** *f.* II-4
  letter of application **lettre** *f.* **de motivation** II-5
  letter of recommendation/ reference **lettre** *f.* **de recommandation** II-5
lettuce **laitue** *f.* II-1
level **niveau** *m.* II-5
library **bibliothèque** *f.* I-1
license: driver's license **permis** *m.* **de conduire** II-3
life **vie** *f.* I-6
life insurance **assurance** *f.* **vie** II-5
light: warning light *(automobile)* **voyant** *m.* II-3
  oil/gas warning light **voyant** *m.* **d'huile/d'essence** II-3
  to light up **s'allumer** *v.* II-3
like *(as)* **comme** *adv.* I-6; to like **aimer** *v.* I-2
  I don't like … very much. **Je n'aime pas tellement...** I-2
  I really like… **J'aime bien...** I-2
  to like one another **s'aimer bien** *v.* II-3
  to like that… **aimer que...** *v.* II-6
line **queue** *f.* II-4
  to wait in line **faire la queue** *v.* II-4
listen (to) **écouter** *v.* I-2

literary **littéraire** *adj.* II-7
literature **littérature** *f.* I-1
little *(not much)* (of ) **peu (de)** *adv.* I-4
live (in) **habiter (à)** *v.* I-2
living room *(informal room)* **salle de séjour** *f.* I-8, II-P; *(formal room)* **salon** *m.* I-8, II-P
located: to be located **se trouver** *v.* II-2
long **long(ue)** *adj.* I-3
  a long time **longtemps** *adv.* I-5
look *(at one another)* **se regarder** *v.* II-3; *(at oneself)* **se regarder** *v.* II-2
look for **chercher** *v.* I-2
  to look for work **chercher du/un travail** II-4
loose *(clothing)* **large** *adj.* I-6
lose: to lose *(time)* **perdre (son temps)** *v.* I-6
  to lose weight **maigrir** *v.* I-4
lost: to be lost **être perdu(e)** *v.* II-4
lot: a lot of **beaucoup de** *adv.* I-4
love **amour** *m.* I-6
  to love **adorer** *v.* I-2
  I love… **J'adore...** I-2
  to love one another **s'aimer** *v.* II-3
  to be in love **être amoureux/ amoureuse** *v.* I-6
luck **chance** *f.* I-2
  to be lucky **avoir de la chance** *v.* I-2
lunch **déjeuner** *m.* II-1
  to eat lunch **déjeuner** *v.* I-4

## M

ma'am **Madame.** *f.* I-1
machine: answering machine **répondeur** *m.* II-3
mad: to get mad **s'énerver** *v.* II-2
made **fait (faire)** *p.p., adj.* I-6
magazine **magazine** *m.* II-7
mail **courrier** *m.* II-4
mailbox **boîte** *f.* **aux lettres** II-4
mailman **facteur** *m.* II-4
main character **personnage principal** *m.* II-7
main dish **plat (principal)** *m.* II-1
maintain **maintenir** *v.* II-1
make **faire** *v.* I-5
makeup **maquillage** *m.* II-2
  to put on makeup **se maquiller** *v.* II-2
make up **se réconcilier** *v.* II-7
malfunction **panne** *f.* II-3
man **homme** *m.* I-1
manage *(in business)* **diriger** *v.* II-5; *(to do something)* **arriver à** *v.* I-2
manager **gérant(e)** *m., f.* II-5

many (of) **beaucoup (de)** *adv.* I-4
  How many (of)? **Combien (de)?** I-1
map *(of a city)* **plan** *m.* I-7; *(of the world)* **carte** *f.* I-1
March **mars** *m.* I-5
marital status **état civil** *m.* I-6
market **marché** *m.* I-4
marriage **mariage** *m.* I-6
married **marié(e)** *adj.* I-3
  married couple **mariés** *m., pl.* I-6
marry **épouser** *v.* I-3
Martinique: from Martinique **martiniquais(e)** *adj.* I-1
masterpiece **chef-d'œuvre** *m.* II-7
mathematics **mathématiques (maths)** *f., pl.* I-2
May **mai** *m.* I-5
maybe **peut-être** *adv.* I-2
mayonnaise **mayonnaise** *f.* II-1
mayor's office **mairie** *f.* II-4
me **moi** *disj. pron., sing.* I-3; *(attached to imperative)* **-moi** *pron.* II-1; **me/m'** *i.o. pron.* I-6; **me/m'** *d.o. pron.* I-7
  Me too. **Moi aussi.** I-1
  Me neither. **Moi non plus.** I-2
meal **repas** *m.* II-1
mean **méchant(e)** *adj.* I-3
  to mean *(with* **dire***)* **vouloir** *v.* II-1
means: that means **ça veut dire** *v.* II-1
meat **viande** *f.* II-1
mechanic **mécanicien/ mécanicienne** *m., f.* II-3
medication (against/ for) **médicament (contre/ pour)** *m., f.* II-2
meet *(to encounter, to run into)* **rencontrer** *v.* I-2; *(to make the acquaintance of)* **faire la connaissance de** *v.* I-5, **se rencontrer** *v.* II-3; *(planned encounter)* **se retrouver** *v.* II-3
meeting **réunion** *f.* II-5; **rendez-vous** *m.* I-6
member **membre** *m.* II-7
menu **menu** *m.* II-1; **carte** *f.* II-1
message **message** *m.* II-5
  to leave a message **laisser un message** *v.* II-5
Mexican **mexicain(e)** *adj.* I-1
Mexico **Mexique** *m.* I-7
microwave oven **four à micro-ondes** *m.* I-8, II-P
midnight **minuit** *m.* I-2
milk **lait** *m.* I-4
mineral water **eau** *f.* **minérale** I-4
mirror **miroir** *m.* I-8, II-P
Miss **Mademoiselle** *f.* I-1

mistaken: to be mistaken (*about something*) **se tromper (de)** *v.* II-2
modest **modeste** *adj.* II-5
moment **moment** *m.* I-1
Monday **lundi** *m.* I-2
money **argent** *m.* II-4; (*currency*) **monnaie** *f.* II-4
    to deposit money **déposer de l'argent** *v.* II-4
monitor **moniteur** *m.* II-3
month **mois** *m.* I-2
    this month **ce mois-ci** I-2
moon **Lune** *f.* I-6
more **plus** *adv.* I-4
    more of **plus de** I-4
    more … than (*used with noun to compare quantities*) **plus de… que** II-6
    more … than (*used with adjective to compare qualities*) **plus… que** II-1
morning **matin** *m.* I-2; **matinée** *f.* I-2
    this morning **ce matin** I-2
Moroccan **marocain(e)** *adj.* I-1
most **plus** II-1
    the most… (*used with adjective*) **le/la plus…** *super. adv.* II-1
    the most… (*used with noun to express quantity*) **le plus de…** II-6
    the most… (*used with verb or adverb*) **le plus…** *super. adv.* II-1
mother **mère** *f.* I-3
mother-in-law **belle-mère** *f.* I-3
mountain **montagne** *f.* I-4
mouse **souris** *f.* II-3
mouth **bouche** *f.* II-2
move (*to get around*) **se déplacer** *v.* II-4
    to move in **emménager** *v.* I-8, II-P
    to move out **déménager** *v.* I-8, II-P
movie **film** *m.* II-7
    adventure/horror/science-fiction/crime movie **film** *m.* **d'aventures/d'horreur/de science-fiction/policier** II-7
movie theater **cinéma (ciné)** *m.* I-4
much (as much … as) (*used with noun to express quantity*) **autant de … que** *adv.* II-6
    How much (*of something*)? **Combien (de)?** I-1
    How much is… ? **Combien coûte… ?** I-4
museum **musée** *m.* I-4

to go to museums **faire les musées** *v.* II-7
mushroom **champignon** *m.* II-1
music: to play music **faire de la musique** II-7
musical **comédie** *f.* **musicale** II-7; **musical(e)** *adj.* II-7
musician **musicien(ne)** *m., f.* I-3
must (*to have to*) **devoir** *v.* II-1
    One must **Il faut…** I-5
mustard **moutarde** *f.* II-1
my **ma** *poss. adj., f., sing.* I-3; **mes** *poss. adj., m., f., pl.* I-3; **mon** *poss. adj., m., sing.* I-3
myself **me/m'** *pron., sing.* II-2; (*attached to an imperative*) **-moi** *pron.* II-1

## N

naïve **naïf (naïve)** *adj.* I-3
name: My name is… **Je m'appelle…** I-1
named: to be named **s'appeler** *v.* II-2
napkin **serviette** *f.* II-1
nationality **nationalité** *f.*
    I am of … nationality. **Je suis de nationalité…** I-1
natural **naturel(le)** *adj.* II-6
natural resource **ressource naturelle** *f.* II-6
nature **nature** *f.* II-6
nauseated: to feel nauseated **avoir mal au cœur** *v.* II-2
near (to) **près (de)** *prep.* I-3
    very near (to) **tout près (de)** II-4
necessary **nécessaire** *adj.* II-6
    It was necessary… (*followed by infinitive or subjunctive*) **Il a fallu…** I-6
    It is necessary…. (*followed by infinitive or subjunctive*) **Il faut que…** I-5
    It is necessary that… (*followed by subjunctive*) **Il est nécessaire que/qu'…** II-6
neck **cou** *m.* II-2
need **besoin** *m.* I-2
    to need **avoir besoin (de)** *v.* I-2
neighbor **voisin(e)** *m., f.* I-3
neighborhood **quartier** *m.* I-8, II-P
neither… nor **ne… ni… ni…** *conj.* II-4
nephew **neveu** *m.* I-3
nervous **nerveux/nerveuse** *adj.* I-3
nervously **nerveusement** *adv.* I-8, II-P
never **jamais** *adv.* I-5; **ne… jamais** *adv.* II-4

new **nouveau/nouvelle** *adj.* I-3
newlyweds **jeunes mariés** *m., pl.* I-6
news **informations (infos)** *f., pl.* II-7; **nouvelles** *f., pl.* II-7
newspaper **journal** *m.* I-7
newsstand **marchand de journaux** *m.* II-4
next **ensuite** *adv.* I-7; **prochain(e)** *adj.* I-2
    next to **à côté de** *prep.* I-3
nice **gentil/gentille** *adj.* I-3; **sympa(thique)** *adj.* I-1
nicely **gentiment** *adv.* I-8, II-P
niece **nièce** *f.* I-3
night **nuit** *f.* I-2
nightclub **boîte (de nuit)** *f.* I-4
nine **neuf** *m.* I-1
nine hundred **neuf cents** *m.* I-5
nineteen **dix-neuf** *m.* I-1
ninety **quatre-vingt-dix** *m.* I-3
ninth **neuvième** *adj.* I-7
no (*at beginning of statement to indicate disagreement*) **(mais) non** I-2; **aucun(e)** *adj.* II-2
    no more **ne… plus** II-4
    no problem **pas de problème** II-4
    no reason **pour rien** I-4
    no, none **pas (de)** II-4
nobody **ne… personne** II-4
none (not any) **ne… aucun(e)** II-4
noon **midi** *m.* I-2
no one **personne** *pron.* II-4
north **nord** *m.* II-4
nose **nez** *m.* II-2
not **ne… pas** *I-2*
    not at all **pas du tout** *adv.* I-2
    Not badly. **Pas mal.** I-1
    to not believe that **ne pas croire que** *v.* II-7
    to not think that **ne pas penser que** *v.* II-7
    not yet **pas encore** *adv.* I-8, II-P
notebook **cahier** *m.* I-1
notes **billets** *m., pl.* II-3
nothing **rien** *indef. pron.* II-4
    It's nothing. **Il n'y a pas de quoi.** I-1
notice **s'apercevoir** *v.* II-4
novel **roman** *m.* II-7
November **novembre** *m.* I-5
now **maintenant** *adv.* I-5
nuclear **nucléaire** *adj.* II-6
nuclear energy **énergie nucléaire** *f.* II-6
nuclear plant **centrale nucléaire** *f.* II-6
nurse **infirmier/infirmière** *m., f.* II-2

## O

object **objet** *m.* I-1
obtain **obtenir** *v.* II-5
obvious **évident(e)** *adj.* II-7
  It is obvious that… **Il est évident que…** II-7
obviously **évidemment** *adv.* I-8, II-P
o'clock: It's… (o'clock). **Il est… heure(s).** I-2
  at … (o'clock) **à … heure(s)** I-4
October **octobre** *m.* I-5
of **de/d'** *prep.* I-3
  of medium height **de taille moyenne** *adj.* I-3
  of the **des (de + les)** I-3
  of the **du (de + le)** I-3
  of which, of whom **dont** *rel. pron.* II-3
of course **bien sûr** *adv.;* **évidemment** *adv.* I-2
  of course not *(at beginning of statement to indicate disagreement)* **(mais) non** I-2
offer **offrir** *v.* II-3
offered **offert (offrir)** *p.p.* II-3
office **bureau** *m.* I-4
  at the doctor's office **chez le médecin** *prep.* I-2
often **souvent** *adv.* I-5
oil **huile** *f.* II-1
  automobile oil **huile** *f.* II-3
  oil warning light **voyant** *m.* **d'huile** II-3
  olive oil **huile** *f.* **d'olive** II-1
  to check the oil **vérifier l'huile** *v.* II-3
okay **d'accord** I-2
old **vieux/vieille** *adj.;* *(placed after noun)* **ancien(ne)** *adj.* I-3
old age **vieillesse** *f.* I-6
olive **olive** *f.* II-1
olive oil **huile** *f.* **d'olive** II-1
omelette **omelette** *f.* I-5
on **sur** *prep.* I-3
  On behalf of whom? **C'est de la part de qui?** II-5
  on the condition that… **à condition que** II-7
  on television **à la télé(vision)** II-7
  on the contrary **au contraire** II-7
  on the radio **à la radio** II-7
  on the subject of **au sujet de** II-6
  on vacation **en vacances** I-7
once **une fois** *adv.* I-8, II-P
one **un** *m.* I-1
  one **on** *sub. pron., sing.* I-1
  one another **l'un(e) à l'autre** II-3

one another **l'un(e) l'autre** II-3
one had to… **il fallait…** I-8, II-P
One must… **Il faut que/qu'…** II-6
One must… **Il faut…** *(followed by infinitive or subjunctive)* I-5
one million **un million** *m.* I-5
  one million *(things)* **un million de…** I-5
onion **oignon** *m.* II-1
online **en ligne** II-3
  to be online **être en ligne** *v.* II-3
  to be online *(with someone)* **être connecté(e) (avec quelqu'un)** *v.* I-7, II-3
only **ne… que** II-4; **seulement** *adv.* I-8, II-P
open **ouvrir** *v.* II-3; **ouvert(e)** *adj.* I-3
opened **ouvert (ouvrir)** *p.p.* II-3
opera **opéra** *m.* II-7
optimistic **optimiste** *adj.* I-1
or **ou** I-3
orange **orange** *f.* II-1; **orange** *inv.adj.* I-6
orchestra **orchestre** *m.* II-7
order **commander** *v.* II-1
organize (a party) **organiser (une fête)** *v.* I-6
orient oneself **s'orienter** *v.* II-4
others **d'autres** I-4
our **nos** *poss. adj., m., f., pl.* I-3; **notre** *poss. adj., m., f., sing.* I-3
outdoor *(open-air)* **plein air** II-6
over **fini** *adj., p.p.* I-7
overpopulation **surpopulation** *f.* II-6
overseas **à l'étranger** *adv.* I-7
over there **là-bas** *adv.* I-1
owed **dû (devoir)** *p.p., adj.* I-1
own **posséder** *v.* I-5
owner **propriétaire** *m., f.* I-3
ozone **ozone** *m.* II-6
  hole in the ozone layer **trou dans la couche d'ozone** *m.* II-6

## P

pack: to pack one's bags **faire les valises** I-7
package **colis** *m.* II-4
paid **payé (payer)** *p.p., adj.* II-5
  to be well/badly paid **être bien/ mal payé(e)** II-5
pain **douleur** *f.* II-2
paint **faire de la peinture** *v.* II-7
painter **peintre/femme peintre** *m., f.* II-7
painting **peinture** *f.* II-7; **tableau** *m.* II-7
Palm Pilot **palm** *m.* I-1

pants **pantalon** *m., sing.* I-6
paper **papier** *m.* I-1
Pardon (me). **Pardon.** I-1
parents **parents** *m., pl.* I-3
park **parc** *m.* I-4
  to park **se garer** *v.* II-3
parka **anorak** *m.* I-6
parking lot **parking** *m.* II-3
part-time job **emploi** *m.* **à mi-temps/à temps partiel** *m.* II-5
party **fête** *f.* I-6
  to party **faire la fête** *v.* I-6
pass **dépasser** *v.* II-3; **passer** *v.* I-7
  to pass an exam **être reçu(e) à un examen** *v.* I-2
passenger **passager/passagère** *m., f.* I-7
passport **passeport** *m.* I-7
password **mot de passe** *m.* II-3
past: in the past **autrefois** *adv.* I-8, II-P
pasta **pâtes** *f., pl.* II-1
pastime **passe-temps** *m.* I-5
pastry **pâtisserie** *f.* II-1
pastry shop **pâtisserie** *f.* II-1
pâté **pâté (de campagne)** *m.* II-1
path **sentier** *m.* II-6; **chemin** *m.* II-4
patient **patient(e)** *adj.* I-1
patiently **patiemment** *adv.* I-8, II-P
pay **payer** *v.* I-5
  to pay by check **payer par chèque** *v.* II-4
  to pay in cash **payer en liquide** *v.* II-4
  to pay with a credit card **payer avec une carte de crédit** *v.* II-4
  to pay attention (to) **faire attention (à)** *v.* I-5
peach **pêche** *f.* II-1
pear **poire** *f.* II-1
peas **petits pois** *m., pl.* II-1
pen **stylo** *m.* I-1
pencil **crayon** *m.* I-1
people **gens** *m., pl.* I-7
pepper *(spice)* **poivre** *m.* II-1; *(vegetable)* **poivron** *m.* II-1
per day/week/month/year **par jour/semaine/mois/ an** I-5
perfect **parfait(e)** *adj.* I-2
perhaps **peut-être** *adv.* I-2
period *(punctuation mark)* **point** *m.* II-3
permit **permis** *m.* II-3
permitted **permis (permettre)** *p.p., adj.* I-6
person **personne** *f.* I-1

personal CD player **baladeur CD** *m.* II-3
pessimistic **pessimiste** *adj.* I-1
pharmacist **pharmacien(ne)** *m., f.* II-2
pharmacy **pharmacie** *f.* II-2
philosophy **philosophie** *f.* I-2
phone booth **cabine téléphonique** *f.* II-4
phone card **télécarte** *f.* II-5
phone one another **se téléphoner** *v.* II-3
photo(graph) **photo(graphie)** *f.* I-3
physical education **éducation physique** *f.* I-2
physics **physique** *f.* I-2
piano **piano** *m.* II-7
pick up **décrocher** *v.* II-5
picnic **pique-nique** *m.* II-6
picture **tableau** *m.* I-1
pie **tarte** *f.* II-1
piece (of) **morceau (de)** *m.* I-4
    piece of furniture **meuble** *m.* I-8, II-P
pill **pilule** *f.* II-2
pillow **oreiller** *m.* I-8, II-P
pink **rose** *adj.* I-6
pitcher (of water) **carafe (d'eau)** *f.* II-1
place **endroit** *m.* I-4; **lieu** *m.* I-4
planet **planète** *f.* II-6
plans: to make plans **faire des projets** *v.* II-5
plant **plante** *f.* II-6
plastic **plastique** *m.* II-6
plastic wrapping **emballage en plastique** *m.* II-6
plate **assiette** *f.* II-1
play **pièce de théâtre** *f.* II-7
play **s'amuser** *v.* II-2; (*a sport/a musical instrument*) **jouer (à/de)** *v.* I-5
    to play regularly **pratiquer** *v.* I-5
    to play sports **faire du sport** *v.* I-5
    to play a role **jouer un rôle** *v.* II-7
player **joueur/joueuse** *m., f.* I-5
playwright **dramaturge** *m.* II-7
pleasant **agréable** *adj.* I-1
please: to please someone **faire plaisir à quelqu'un** *v.* II-5
    Please. **S'il te plaît.** *fam.* I-1
    Please. **S'il vous plaît.** *form.* I-1
    Please. **Je vous en prie.** *form.* I-1
    Please hold. **Ne quittez pas.** II-5
plumber **plombier** *m.* II-5
poem **poème** *m.* II-7
poet **poète/poétesse** *m., f.* II-7
police **police** *f.* II-3; **policier** *adj.* II-7

police officer **agent de police** *m.* II-3; **policier** *m.* II-3; **policière** *f.* II-3
police station **commissariat de police** *m.* II-4
polite **poli(e)** *adj.* I-1
politely **poliment** *adv.* I-8, II-P
political science **sciences politiques (sciences po)** *f., pl.* I-2
politician **homme/femme politique** *m., f.* II-5
pollute **polluer** *v.* II-6
pollution **pollution** *f.* II-6
    pollution cloud **nuage de pollution** *m.* II-6
pool **piscine** *f.* I-4
poor **pauvre** *adj.* I-3
popular music **variétés** *f., pl.* II-7
population **population** *f.* II-6
    growing population **population** *f.* **croissante** II-6
pork **porc** *m.* II-1
portrait **portrait** *m.* I-5
position (*job*) **poste** *m.* II-5
possess (*to own*) **posséder** *v.* I-5
possible **possible** *adj.* II-7
    It is possible that… **Il est possible que…** II-6
post **afficher** *v.* II-5
post office **bureau de poste** *m.* II-4
postal service **poste** *f.* II-4
postcard **carte postale** *f.* II-4
poster **affiche** *f.* I-8, II-P
potato **pomme de terre** *f.* II-1
practice **pratiquer** *v.* I-5
prefer **aimer mieux** *v.* I-2; **préférer (que)** *v.* I-5
pregnant **enceinte** *adj.* II-2
prepare (for) **préparer** *v.* I-2
    to prepare (*to do something*) **se préparer (à)** *v.* II-2
prescription **ordonnance** *f.* II-2
present **présenter** *v.* II-7
preservation: habitat preservation **sauvetage des habitats** *m.* II-6
preserve **préserver** *v.* II-6
pressure **pression** *f.* II-3
    to check the tire pressure **vérifier la pression des pneus** *v.* II-3
pretty **joli(e)** *adj.* I-3; (*before an adjective or adverb*) **assez** *adv.* I-8, II-P
prevent: to prevent a fire **prévenir l'incendie** *v.* II-6
price **prix** *m.* I-4
principal **principal(e)** *adj.* II-4
print **imprimer** *v.* II-3
printer **imprimante** *f.* II-3
problem **problème** *m.* I-1
produce **produire** *v.* I-6

produced **produit (produire)** *p.p., adj.* I-6
product **produit** *m.* II-6
profession **métier** *m.* II-5; **profession** *f.* II-5
    demanding profession **profession** *f.* **exigeante** II-5
professional **professionnel(le)** *adj.* II-5
    professional experience **expérience professionnelle** *f.* II-5
program **programme** *m.* II-7; (*software*) **logiciel** *m.* II-3; (*television*) **émission** *f.* **de télévision** II-7
prohibit **interdire** *v.* II-6
project **projet** *m.* II-5
promise **promettre** *v.* I-6
promised **promis (promettre)** *p.p., adj.* I-6
promotion **promotion** *f.* II-5
propose that… **proposer que…** *v.* II-6
    to propose a solution **proposer une solution** *v.* II-6
protect **protéger** *v.* I-5
protection **préservation** *f.* II-6; **protection** *f.* II-6
proud **fier/fière** *adj.* I-3
psychological **psychologique** *adj.* II-7
psychological drama **drame psychologique** *m.* II-7
psychology **psychologie** *f.* I-2
psychologist **psychologue** *m., f.* II-5
publish **publier** *v.* II-7
pure **pur(e)** *adj.* II-6
purple **violet(te)** *adj.* I-6
purse **sac à main** *m.* I-6
put **mettre** *v.* I-6
    to put (on) (yourself) **se mettre** *v.* II-2
    to put away **ranger** *v.* I-8, II-P
    to put on makeup **se maquiller** *v.* II-2
put **mis (mettre)** *p.p* I-6

## Q

quarter **quart** *m.* I-2
    a quarter after … (o'clock) **… et quart** I-2
Quebec: from Quebec **québécois(e)** *adj.* I-1
question **question** *f.* I-6
    to ask (*someone*) a question **poser une question (à)** *v.* I-6
quick **vite** *adv.* I-4
quickly **vite** *adv.* I-1
quite (*before an adjective or adverb*) **assez** *adv.* I-8, II-P

## R

rabbit **lapin** *m.* II-6
rain **pleuvoir** *v.* I-5
  acid rain **pluie** *f.* **acide** II-6
  It is raining. **Il pleut.** I-5
  It was raining. **Il pleuvait.**
  I-8, II-P
rain forest **forêt tropicale** *f.* II-6
rain jacket **imperméable** *m.* I-5
rained **plu (pleuvoir)** *p.p.* I-6
raise (in salary) **augmentation**
  **(de salaire)** *f.* II-5
rapidly **rapidement** *adv.* I-8, II-P
rarely **rarement** *adv.* I-5
rather **plutôt** *adv.* I-1
ravishing **ravissant(e)** *adj.* II-5
razor **rasoir** *m.* II-2
read **lire** *v.* I-7
read **lu (lire)** *p.p., adj.* I-7
ready **prêt(e)** *adj.* I-3
real (*true*) **vrai(e)** *adj.;* **véritable**
  *adj.* I-3
real estate agent **agent immobilier**
  *m., f.* I-5
realize **se rendre compte** *v.* II-2
really **vraiment** *adv.* I-5; *(before
  adjective or adverb)* **tout(e)**
  *adv.* I-3; *(before adjective or
  adverb)* **très** *adv.* I-8, II-P
  really close by **tout près** I-3
rear-view mirror **rétroviseur**
  *m.* II-3
reason **raison** *f.* I-2
receive **recevoir** *v.* II-4
received **reçu (recevoir)** *p.p.,*
  *adj.* II-4
receiver **combiné** *m.* II-5
recent **récent(e)** *adj.* II-7
reception desk **réception** *f.* I-7
recognize **reconnaître** *v.* I-8, II-P
recognized **reconnu (reconnaître)**
  *p.p., adj.* I-8, II-P
recommend that… **recommander**
  **que…** *v.* II-6
recommendation
  **recommandation** *f.* II-5
record **enregistrer** *v.* II-3
  (*CD, DVD*) **graver** *v.* II-3
recycle **recycler** *v.* II-6
recycling **recyclage** *m.* II-6
red **rouge** *adj.* I-6
redial **recomposer (un numéro)**
  *v.* II-3
reduce **réduire** *v.* I-6
reduced **réduit (réduire)** *p.p.,*
  *adj.* I-6
reference **référence** *f.* II-5
reflect (on) **réfléchir (à)** *v.* I-4
refrigerator **frigo** *m.* I-8, II-P
refuse (*to do something*)
  **refuser (de)** *v.* II-3
region **région** *f.* II-6

regret that… **regretter que…** II-6
relax **se détendre** *v.* II-2
remember **se souvenir (de)**
  *v.* II-2
remote control **télécommande**
  *f.* II-3
rent **loyer** *m.* I-8, II-P
  to rent **louer** *v.* I-8, II-P
repair **réparer** *v.* II-3
repeat **répéter** *v.* I-5
research **rechercher** *v.* II-5
researcher **chercheur/**
  **chercheuse** *m., f.* II-5
reservation **réservation** *f.* I-7
  to cancel a reservation **annuler**
  **une réservation** I-7
reserve **réserver** *v.* I-7
reserved **réservé(e)** *adj.* I-1
resign **démissionner** *v.* II-5
resort (ski) **station** *f.* **(de ski)** I-7
respond **répondre (à)** *v.* I-6
rest **se reposer** *v.* II-2
restart **redémarrer** *v.* II-3
restaurant **restaurant** *m.* I-4
restroom(s) **toilettes** *f., pl.*
  I-8, II-P; **W.-C.** *m., pl.*
result **résultat** *m.* I-2
résumé **curriculum vitæ**
  **(C.V.)** *m.* II-5
retake **repasser** *v.* II-7
retire **prendre sa retraite** *v.* I-6
retired person **retraité(e)** *m.,*
  *f.* II-5
retirement **retraite** *f.* I-6
return **retourner** *v.* I-7
  to return (home) **rentrer (à la**
  **maison)** *v.* I-2
review (*criticism*) **critique** *f.* II-7
rice **riz** *m.* II-1
ride: to go horseback riding
  **faire du cheval** *v.* I-5
  to ride in a car **rouler en**
  **voiture** *v.* I-7
right **juste** *adv.* I-3
  to the right (of) **à droite**
  **(de)** *prep.* I-3
  to be right **avoir raison** I-2
  right away **tout de suite** I-7
  right next door **juste à**
  **côté** I-3
ring **sonner** *v.* II-3
river **fleuve** *m.* II-6; **rivière** *f.* II-6
riverboat **bateau-mouche** *m.* I-7
role **rôle** *m.* II-6
room **pièce** *f.* I-8, II-P; **salle** *f.*
  I-8, II-P
  bedroom **chambre** *f.* I-7
  classroom **salle** *f.* **de classe** I-1
  dining room **salle** *f.* **à manger**
  I-8, II-P
  single hotel room **chambre**
  *f.* **individuelle** I-7

roommate **camarade de**
  **chambre** *m., f.* I-1
  (*in an apartment*) **colocataire**
  *m., f.* I-1
round-trip **aller-retour** *adj.* I-7
  round-trip ticket **billet** *m.*
  **aller-retour** I-7
rug **tapis** *m.* I-8, II-P
run **courir** *v.* I-5; **couru (courir)**
  *p.p., adj.* I-6
  to run into someone **tomber**
  **sur quelqu'un** *v.* I-7

## S

sad **triste** *adj.* I-3
  to be sad that… **être triste**
  **que…** *v.* II-6
safety **sécurité** *f.* II-3
said **dit (dire)** *p.p., adj.* I-7
salad **salade** *f.* II-1
salary (a high, low) **salaire**
  **(élevé, modeste)** *m.* II-5
sales **soldes** *f., pl.* I-6
salon: beauty salon **salon** *m.*
  **de beauté** II-4
salt **sel** *m.* II-1
sandwich **sandwich** *m.* I-4
sat (down) **assis (s'asseoir)**
  *p.p.* II-2
Saturday **samedi** *m.* I-2
sausage **saucisse** *f.* II-1
save **sauvegarder** *v.* II-3
  save the planet **sauver la**
  **planète** *v.* II-6
savings **épargne** *f.* II-4
savings account **compte**
  **d'épargne** *m.* II-4
say **dire** *v.* I-7
scarf **écharpe** *f.* I-6
scholarship **bourse** *f.* I-2
school **école** *f.* I-2
science **sciences** *f., pl.* I-2
  political science
  **sciences politiques**
  **(sciences po)** *f., pl.* I-2
screen **écran** *m.* II-3
screening **séance** *f.* II-7
sculpture **sculpture** *f.* II-7
sculptor **sculpteur/femme**
  **sculpteur** *m., f.* II-7
sea **mer** *f.* I-7
seafood **fruits de mer** *m., pl.* II-1
search for **chercher** *v.* I-2
  to search for work **chercher**
  **du travail** *v.* II-4
season **saison** *f.* I-5
seat **place** *f.* II-7
seatbelt **ceinture de sécurité**
  *f.* II-3
  to buckle one's seatbelt
  **attacher sa ceinture de**
  **sécurité** *v.* II-3

seated **assis(e)** *p.p., adj.* II-2
second **deuxième** *adj.* I-7
security **sécurité** *f.* II-3
see **voir** *v.* II-7; (*catch sight of*) **apercevoir** *v.* II-4
to see again **revoir** *v.* II-7
See you later. **À plus tard.** I-1
See you later. **À tout à l'heure.** I-1
See you soon. **À bientôt.** I-1
See you tomorrow. **À demain.** I-1
seen **aperçu (apercevoir)** *p.p.* II-4; **vu (voir)** *p.p.* II-7
seen again **revu (revoir)** *p.p.* II-7
self/-selves **même(s)** *pron.* I-6
selfish **égoïste** *adj.* I-1
sell **vendre** *v.* I-6
seller **vendeur/vendeuse** *m., f.* I-6
send **envoyer** *v.* I-5
to send (*to someone*) **envoyer (à)** *v.* I-6
to send a letter **poster une lettre** II-4
Senegalese **sénégalais(e)** *adj.* I-1
sense **sentir** *v.* I-5
separated **séparé(e)** *adj.* I-3
September **septembre** *m.* I-5
serious **grave** *adj.* II-2; **sérieux/sérieuse** *adj.* I-3
serve **servir** *v.* I-5
server **serveur/serveuse** *m., f.* I-4
service station **station-service** *f.* II-3
set the table **mettre la table** *v.* I-8, II-P
seven **sept** *m.* I-1
seven hundred **sept cents** *m.* I-5
seventeen **dix-sept** *m.* I-1
seventh **septième** *adj.* I-7
seventy **soixante-dix** *m.* I-3
several **plusieurs** *adj.* I-4
shame **honte** *f.* I-2
It's a shame that… **Il est dommage que…** II-6
shampoo **shampooing** *m.* II-2
shape (*state of health*) **forme** *f.* II-2
share **partager** *v.* I-2
shave (oneself) **se raser** *v.* II-2
shaving cream **crème à raser** *f.* II-2
she **elle** *pron.* I-1
sheet of paper **feuille de papier** *f.* I-1
sheets **draps** *m., pl.* I-8, II-P
shelf **étagère** *f.* I-8, II-P
shh **chut** II-7
shirt (short-/long-sleeved) **chemise (à manches courtes/longues)** *f.* I-6

shoe **chaussure** *f.* I-6
shopkeeper **commerçant(e)** *m., f.* II-1
shopping **shopping** *m.* I-7
to go shopping **faire du shopping** *v.* I-7
to go (grocery) shopping **faire les courses** *v.* II-1
shopping center **centre commercial** *m.* I-4
short **court(e)** *adj.* I-3; (*stature*) **petit(e)** I-3
shorts **short** *m.* I-6
shot (*injection*) **piqûre** *f.* II-2
to give a shot **faire une piqûre** *v.* II-2
show **spectacle** *m.* I-5; (*movie or theater*) **séance** *f.* II-7
to show (*to someone*) **montrer (à)** *v.* I-6
shower **douche** *f.* I-8, II-P
shut off **fermer** *v.* II-3
shy **timide** *adj.* I-1
sick: to get/be sick **tomber/être malade** *v.* II-2
sign **signer** *v.* II-4
silk **soie** *f.* I-6
since **depuis** adv. II-1
sincere **sincère** *adj.* I-1
sing **chanter** *v.* I-5
singer **chanteur/chanteuse** *m., f.* I-1
single (*marital status*) **célibataire** *adj.* I-3
single hotel room **chambre** *f.* **individuelle** I-7
sink **évier** *m.* I-8, II-P; (*bathroom*) **lavabo** *m.* I-8, II-P
sir **Monsieur** *m.* I-1
sister **sœur** *f.* I-3
sister-in-law **belle-sœur** *f.* I-3
sit down **s'asseoir** *v.* II-2
sitting **assis(e)** *adj.* II-2
six **six** *m.* I-1
six hundred **six cents** *m.* I-5
sixteen **seize** *m.* I-1
sixth **sixième** *adj.* I-7
sixty **soixante** *m.* I-1
size **taille** *f.* I-6
skate **patiner** *v.* I-4
ski **skier** *v.* I-5; **faire du ski** I-5
skiing **ski** *m.* I-5
ski jacket **anorak** *m.* I-6
ski resort **station** *f.* **de ski** I-7
skin **peau** *f.* II-2
skirt **jupe** *f.* I-6
sky **ciel** *m.* II-6
sleep **sommeil** *m.* I-2
to sleep **dormir** *v.* I-5
to be sleepy **avoir sommeil** *v.* I-2
sleeve **manche** *f.* I-6

slice **tranche** *f.* II-1
slipper **pantoufle** *f.* II-2
slow **lent(e)** *adj.* I-3
small **petit(e)** *adj.* I-3
smell **sentir** *v.* I-5
smile **sourire** *m.* I-6
to smile **sourire** *v.* I-6
smoke **fumer** *v.* II-2
snack (afternoon) **goûter** *m.* II-1
snake **serpent** *m.* II-6
sneeze **éternuer** *v.* II-2
snow **neiger** *v.* I-5
It is snowing. **Il neige.** I-5
It was snowing… **Il neigeait…** I-8, II-P
so **si** II-3; **alors** *adv.* I-1
so that **pour que** II-7
soap **savon** *m.* II-2
soap opera **feuilleton** *m.* II-7
soccer **foot(ball)** *m.* I-5
sociable **sociable** *adj.* I-1
sociology **sociologie** *f.* I-1
sock **chaussette** *f.* I-6
software **logiciel** *m.* II-3
soil (*to make dirty*) **salir** *v.* I-8, II-P
solar **solaire** *adj.* II-6
solar energy **énergie solaire** *f.* II-6
solution **solution** *f.* II-6
some **de l'** *part. art., m., f., sing.* I-4
some **de la** *part. art., f., sing.* I-4
some **des** *part. art., m., f., pl.* I-4
some **du** *part. art., m., sing.* I-4
some **quelques** *adj.* I-4
some (*of it/them*) **en** *pron.* II-2
someone **quelqu'un** *pron.* II-4
something **quelque chose** *m.* I-4
Something's not right. **Quelque chose ne va pas.** I-5
sometimes **parfois** *adv.* I-5; **quelquefois** *adv.* I-8, II-P
son **fils** *m.* I-3
song **chanson** *f.* II-7
sorry **désolé(e)** II-3
to be sorry that… **être désolé(e) que…** *v.* II-6
sort **sorte** *f.* II-7
So-so. **Comme ci, comme ça.** I-1
soup **soupe** *f.* I-4
soupspoon **cuillère à soupe** *f.* II-1
south **sud** *m.* II-4
space **espace** *m.* II-6
Spain **Espagne** *f.* I-7
Spanish **espagnol(e)** *adj.* I-1
speak (on the phone) **parler (au téléphone)** *v.* I-2
to speak (to) **parler (à)** *v.* I-6
to speak to one another **se parler** *v.* II-3
specialist **spécialiste** *m., f.* II-5
species **espèce** *f.* II-6

endangered species **espèce** *f.*
**menacée** II-6
spectator **spectateur/**
**spectatrice** *m., f.* II-7
speed **vitesse** *f.* II-3
speed limit **limitation de vitesse**
*f.* II-3
spend **dépenser** *v.* I-4
to spend money **dépenser de**
**l'argent** I-4
to spend time **passer** *v.* I-7
to spend time (*somewhere*)
**faire un séjour** I-7
spoon **cuillère** *f.* II-1
sport(s) **sport** *m.* I-5
to play sports **faire du sport**
*v.* I-5
sporty **sportif/sportive** *adj.* I-3
sprain one's ankle **se fouler la**
**cheville** II-2
spring **printemps** *m.* I-5
in the spring **au printemps** I-5
square (*place*) **place** *f.* I-4
squirrel **écureuil** *m.* II-6
stadium **stade** *m.* I-5
stage (*phase*) **étape** *f.* I-6
stage fright **trac** II-5
staircase **escalier** *m.* I-8, II-P
stamp **timbre** *m.* II-4
star **étoile** *f.* II-6
starter **entrée** *f.* II-1
start up **démarrer** *v.* II-3
station **station** *f.* I-7
subway station **station** *f.* **de**
**métro** I-7
train station **gare** *f.* I-7
stationery store **papeterie** *f.* II-4
statue **statue** *f.* II-4
stay **séjour** *m.* I-7; **rester** *v.* I-7
to stay slim **garder la ligne**
*v.* II-2
steak **steak** *m.* II-1
steering wheel **volant** *m.* II-3
stepbrother **demi-frère** *m.* I-3
stepfather **beau-père** *m.* I-3
stepmother **belle-mère** *f.* I-3
stepsister **demi-sœur** *f.* I-3
stereo system **chaîne stéréo**
*f.* II-3
still **encore** *adv.* I-3
stomach **ventre** *m.* II-2
to have a stomach ache **avoir**
**mal au ventre** *v.* II-2
stone **pierre** *f.* II-6
stop (*doing something*) **arrêter**
**(de faire quelque chose)** *v.;*
(*to stop oneself*) **s'arrêter** *v.* II-2
to stop by someone's house
**passer chez quelqu'un** *v.* I-4
bus stop **arrêt d'autobus (de**
**bus)** *m.* I-7
store **magasin** *m.;* **boutique** *f.* II-4

grocery store **épicerie** *f.* I-4
stormy **orageux/orageuse**
*adj.* I-5
It is stormy. **Le temps est**
**orageux.** I-5
story **histoire** *f.* I-2
stove **cuisinière** *f.* I-8, II-P
straight **raide** *adj.* I-3
straight ahead **tout droit**
*adv.* II-4
strangle **étrangler** *v.* II-5
strawberry **fraise** *f.* II-1
street **rue** *f.* II-3
to follow a street **suivre une**
**rue** *v.* II-4
strong **fort(e)** *adj.* I-3
student **étudiant(e)** *m., f.* 1;
**élève** *m., f.* I-1
high school student **lycéen(ne)**
*m., f.* I-2
studies **études** *f.* I-2
studio (*apartment*) **studio**
*m.* I-8, II-P
study **étudier** *v.* I-2
suburbs **banlieue** *f.* I-4
subway **métro** *m.* I-7
subway station **station** *f.* **de**
**métro** I-7
succeed (*in doing something*)
**réussir (à)** *v.* I-4
success **réussite** *f.* II-5
suddenly **soudain** *adv.* I-8, II-P;
**tout à coup** *adv.* I-7.; *tout*
*d'un coup* adv. I-8, II-P
suffer **souffrir** *v.* II-3
suffered **souffert (souffrir)**
*p.p.* II-3
sugar **sucre** *m.* I-4
suggest (that) **suggérer (que)**
*v.* II-6
suit (*man's*) **costume** *m.* I-6;
(*woman's*) **tailleur** *m.* I-6
suitcase **valise** *f.* I-7
summer **été** *m.* I-5
in the summer **en été** I-5
sun **soleil** *m.* I-5
It is sunny. **Il fait (du**
**soleil.** I-5
Sunday **dimanche** *m.* I-2
sunglasses **lunettes de soleil**
*f., pl.* I-6
supermarket **supermarché** *m.* II-1
sure **sûr(e)** II-1
It is sure that... **Il est sûr**
**que...** I-7
It is unsure that... **Il n'est**
**pas sûr que...** II-7
surf on the Internet **surfer sur**
**Internet** II-3
surprise (*someone*) **faire une**
**surprise (à quelqu'un)** *v.* I-6
surprised **surpris (surprendre)**
*p.p., adj.* I-6

to be surprised that... **être**
**surpris(e) que...** *v.* II-6
sweater **pull** *m.* I-6
sweep **balayer** *v.* I-8, II-P
swell **enfler** *v.* II-2
swim **nager** *v.* I-4
swimsuit **maillot de bain** *m.* I-6
Swiss **suisse** *adj.* I-1
Switzerland **Suisse** *f.* I-7
symptom **symptôme** *m.* II-2

## T

table **table** *f.* I-1
to clear the table **débarrasser**
**la table** *v.* I-8, II-P
tablecloth **nappe** *f.* II-1
take **prendre** *v.* I-4
to take a shower **prendre une**
**douche** II-2
to take a train (plane, taxi, bus,
boat) **prendre un train (un**
**avion, un taxi, un autobus,**
**un bateau)** *v.* I-7
to take a walk **se promener**
*v.* II-2
to take advantage of **profiter**
**de** *v.* II-7
to take an exam **passer un**
**examen** *v.* I-2
to take care (of something)
**s'occuper (de)** *v.* II-2
to take out the trash **sortir la/**
**les poubelle(s)** *v.* I-8, II-P
to take time off **prendre un**
**congé** *v.* II-5
to take (*someone*) **emmener**
*v.* I-5
taken **pris (prendre)** *p.p., adj.* I-6
tale **conte** *m.* II-7
talented
(*gifted*) **doué(e)** *adj.* II-7
tan **bronzer** *v.* I-6
tape recorder **magnétophone**
*m.* II-3
tart **tarte** *f.* II-1
taste **goûter** *v.* II-1
taxi **taxi** *m.* I-7
tea **thé** *m.* I-4
teach **enseigner** *v.* I-2
to teach (*to do something*)
**apprendre (à)** *v.* I-4
teacher **professeur** *m.* I-1
team **équipe** *f.* I-5
teaspoon **cuillère à café** *f.* II-1
tee shirt **tee-shirt** *m.* I-6
teeth **dents** *f., pl.* II-1
to brush one's teeth **se brosser**
**les dents** *v.* II-1
telephone (*receiver*) **appareil**
*m.* II-5
to telephone (*someone*)
**téléphoner (à)** *v.* I-2

It's Mr./Mrs./Miss … (on the phone.) **C'est M./Mme/Mlle … (à l'appareil.)** II-5
television **télévision** *f.* I-1
  television channel **chaîne** *f.* **de télévision** II-3
  television program **émission** *f.* **de télévision** II-7
  television set **poste de télévision** *m.* II-3
tell one another **se dire** *v.* II-3
temperature **température** *f.* I-5
ten **dix** *m.* I-1
tennis **tennis** *m.* I-5
tennis shoes **baskets** *f., pl.* I-6
tenth **dixième** *adj.* I-7
terminal (bus) **gare** *f.* **routière** I-7
terrace (café) **terrasse** *f.* **de café** I-4
test **examen** *m.* I-1
than **que/qu'** *conj.* II-1, II-6
thank: Thank you (very much). **Merci (beaucoup).** I-1
that **ce/c', ça** I-1; **que** *rel. pron.* II-3
  Is that… ? **Est-ce… ?** I-2
  That's enough. **Ça suffit.** I-5
  That has nothing to do with us. That is none of our business. **Ça ne nous regarde pas.** II-6
  that is… **c'est…** I-1
  that is to say **ça veut dire** II-2
theater **théâtre** *m.* II-7
their **leur(s)** *poss. adj., m., f.* I-3
them **les** *d.o. pron.* I-7, **leur** *i.o. pron., m., f., pl.* I-6
then **ensuite** *adv.* I-7, **puis** *adv.* I-7, **puis** I-4; **alors** *adv.* I-7
there **là** I-1; **y** *pron.* II-2
  Is there… ? **Y a-t-il… ?** I-2
  over there **là-bas** *adv.* I-1
  (over) there *(used with demonstrative adjective* ce *and noun or with demonstrative pronoun* celui*)* **-là** I-6
  There is/There are… **Il y a…** I-1
  There is/There are…. **Voilà…** I-1
  There was… **Il y a eu…** I-6; **Il y avait…** I-8, II-P
therefore **donc** *conj.* I-7
these/those **ces** *dem. adj., m., f., pl.* I-6
  these/those **celles** *pron., f., pl.* II-6
  these/those **ceux** *pron., m., pl.* II-6
they **ils** *sub. pron., m.* I-1; **elles** *sub. and disj. pron., f.* I-1; **eux** *disj. pron., pl.* I-3
thing **chose** *f.* I-1, **truc** *m.* I-7
think (about) **réfléchir (à)** *v.* I-4
  to think (that) **penser (que)** *v.* I-2

third **troisième** *adj.* I-7
thirst **soif** *f.* I-4
  to be thirsty **avoir soif** *v.* I-4
thirteen **treize** *m.* I-1
thirty **trente** *m.* I-1
thirty-first **trente et unième** *adj.* I-7
this/that **ce** *dem. adj., m., sing.* I-6; **cet** *dem. adj., m., sing.* I-6; **cette** *dem. adj., f., sing.* I-6
  this afternoon **cet après-midi** I-2
  this evening **ce soir** I-2
  this one/that one **celle** *pron., f., sing.* II-6; **celui** *pron., m., sing.* II-6
  this week **cette semaine** I-2
  this weekend **ce week-end** I-2
  this year **cette année** I-2
those are… **ce sont…** I-1
thousand: one thousand **mille** *m.* I-5
  one hundred thousand **cent mille** *m.* I-5
threat **danger** *m.* II-6
three **trois** *m.* I-1
three hundred **trois cents** *m.* I-5
throat **gorge** *f.* II-2
throw away **jeter** *v.* II-6
Thursday **jeudi** *m.* I-2
ticket **billet** *m.* I-7
  round-trip ticket **billet** *m.* **aller-retour** I-7 bus/subway ticket **ticket de bus/de métro** *m.* I-7
tie **cravate** *f.* I-6
tight **serré(e)** *adj.* I-6
time *(occurence)* **fois** *f.;* *(general sense)* **temps** *m., sing.* I-5
  a long time **longtemps** *adv.* I-5
  free time **temps libre** *m.* I-5
  from time to time **de temps en temps** *adv.* I-8, II-P
  to lose time **perdre son temps** *v.* I-6
tinker **bricoler** *v.* I-5
tip **pourboire** *m.* I-4
  to leave a tip **laisser un pourboire** *v.* I-4
tire **pneu** *m.* II-3
  flat tire **pneu** *m.* **crevé** II-3
  (emergency) tire **roue (de secours)** *f.* II-3
  to check the tire pressure **vérifier la pression des pneus** *v.* II-3
tired **fatigué(e)** *adj.* I-3
tiresome **pénible** *adj.* I-3
to **à** *prep.* I-4; **au (à + le)** I-4; **aux (à + les)** I-4
toaster **grille-pain** *m.* I-8, II-P
today **aujourd'hui** *adv.* I-2

toe **orteil** *m.* II-2; **doigt de pied** *m.* II-2
together **ensemble** *adv.* I-6
tomato **tomate** *f.* II-1
tomorrow (morning, afternoon, evening) **demain (matin, après-midi, soir)** *adv.* I-2
  day after tomorrow **après-demain** *adv.* I-2
too **aussi** *adv.* I-1
  too many/much (of) **trop (de)** I-4
tooth **dent** *f.* II-1
  to brush one's teeth **se brosser les dents** *v.* II-1
toothbrush **brosse** *f.* **à dents** II-2
toothpaste **dentifrice** *m.* II-2
tour **tour** *m.* I-5
tourism **tourisme** *m.* II-4
tourist office **office du tourisme** *m.* II-4
towel (bath) **serviette (de bain)** *f.* II-2
town **ville** *f.* I-4
town hall **mairie** *f.* II-4
toxic **toxique** *adj.* II-6
toxic waste **déchets toxiques** *m., pl.* II-6
traffic **circulation** *f.* II-3
traffic light **feu de signalisation** *m.* II-4
tragedy **tragédie** *f.* II-7
train **train** *m.* I-7
train station **gare** *f.* I-7; **station** *f.* **de train** I-7
training **formation** *f.* II-5
translate **traduire** *v.* I-6
translated **traduit (traduire)** *p.p., adj.* I-6
trash **ordures** *f., pl.* II-6
travel **voyager** *v.* I-2
travel agency **agence de voyages** *f.* I-7
travel agent **agent de voyages** *m.* I-7
tree **arbre** *m.* II-6
trip **voyage** *m.* I-7
troop *(company)* **troupe** *f.* II-7
tropical **tropical(e)** *adj.* II-6
  tropical forest **forêt tropicale** *f.* II-6
true **vrai(e)** *adj.* I-3; **véritable** *adj.* I-6
  It is true that… **Il est vrai que…** II-7
  It is untrue that… **Il n'est pas vrai que…** II-7
trunk **coffre** *m.* II-3
try **essayer** *v.* I-5
Tuesday **mardi** *m.* I-2
tuna **thon** *m.* II-1
turn **tourner** *v.* II-4
  to turn off **éteindre** *v.* II-3

to turn on **allumer** *v.* II-3
to turn (oneself) around **se tourner** *v.* II-2
twelve **douze** *m.* I-1
twentieth **vingtième** *adj.* I-7
twenty **vingt** *m.* I-1
twenty-first **vingt et unième** *adj.* I-7
twenty-second **vingt-deuxième** *adj.* I-7
twice **deux fois** *adv.* I-8, II-P
twist one's ankle **se fouler la cheville** *v.* II-2
two **deux** *m.* I-1
two hundred **deux cents** *m.* I-5
two million **deux millions** *m.* I-5
type **genre** *m.* II-7

ugly **laid(e)** *adj.* I-3
umbrella **parapluie** *m.* I-5
uncle **oncle** *m.* I-3
under **sous** *prep.* I-3
understand **comprendre** *v.* I-4
understood **compris (comprendre)** *p.p., adj.* I-6
underwear **sous-vêtement** *m.* I-6
undress **se déshabiller** *v.* II-2
unemployed person **chômeur/ chômeuse** *m., f.* II-5
to be unemployed **être au chômage** *v.* II-5
unemployment **chômage** *m.* II-5
unfortunately **malheureusement** *adv.* I-2
unhappy **malheureux/ malheureuse** *adj.* I-3
union **syndicat** *m.* II-5
United States **États-Unis** *m., pl.* I-7
university **faculté** *f.* I-1; **université** *f.* I-1
university cafeteria **restaurant universitaire (resto U)** *m.* I-2
unless **à moins que** *conj.* II-7
unpleasant **antipathique** *adj.* I-3; **désagréable** *adj.* I-1
until **jusqu'à** *prep.* II-4; **jusqu'à ce que** *conj.* II-7
upset: to become upset **s'énerver** *v.* II-2
us **nous** *i.o. pron.* I-6; **nous** *d.o. pron.* I-7
use **employer** *v.* I-5
to use a map **utiliser un plan** *v.* I-7
useful **utile** *adj.* I-2
useless **inutile** *adj.* I-2; **nul(le)** *adj.* I-2
usually **d'habitude** *adv.* I-8, II-P

vacation **vacances** *f., pl.* I-7
vacation day **jour de congé** *m.* I-7
vacuum **aspirateur** *m.* I-8, II-P
to vacuum **passer l'aspirateur** *v.* I-8, II-P
valley **vallée** *f.* II-6
vegetable **légume** *m.* II-1
velvet **velours** *m.* I-6
very *(before adjective)* **tout(e)** *adv.* I-3; *(before adverb)* **très** *adv.* I-8, II-P
Very well. **Très bien.** I-1
veterinarian **vétérinaire** *m., f.* II-5
videocassette recorder (VCR) **magnétoscope** *m.* II-3
video game(s) **jeu vidéo (des jeux vidéo)** *m.* II-3
videotape **cassette vidéo** *f.* II-3
Vietnamese **vietnamien(ne)** *adj.* I-1
violet **violet(te)** *adj.* I-6
violin **violon** *m.* II-7
visit **visite** *f.* I-6
to visit *(a place)* **visiter** *v.* I-2; *(a person or people)* **rendre visite (à)** *v.* I-6; *(to visit regularly)* **fréquenter** *v.* I-4
voicemail **messagerie** *f.* II-5
volcano **volcan** *m.* II-6
volleyball **volley(-ball)** *m.* I-5

waist **taille** *f.* I-6
wait **attendre** *v.* I-6
to wait *(on the phone)* **patienter** *v.* II-5
to wait in line **faire la queue** *v.* II-4
wake up **se réveiller** *v.* II-2
walk **promenade** *f.* I-5; **marcher** *v.* I-5
to go for a walk **faire une promenade** I-5; **faire un tour** I-5
wall **mur** *m.* I-8, II-P
want **désirer** *v.* I-5; **vouloir** *v.* II-1
wardrobe **armoire** *f.* I-8, II-P
warming: global warming **réchauffement de la Terre** *m.* II-6
warning light (gas/oil) **voyant** *m.* **(d'essence/d'huile)** II-3
wash **laver** *v.* I-8, II-P
to wash oneself (one's hands) **se laver (les mains)** *v.* II-2
to wash up (in the morning) **faire sa toilette** *v.* II-2
washing machine **lave-linge** *m.* I-8, II-P

waste **gaspillage** *m.* II-6; **gaspiller** *v.* II-6
wastebasket **corbeille (à papier)** *f.* I-1
waste time **perdre son temps** *v.* I-6
watch **montre** *f.* I-1; **regarder** *v.* I-2
water **eau** *f.* I-4
mineral water **eau** *f.* **minérale** I-4
way *(by the way)* **au fait** I-3; *(path)* **chemin** *m.* II-4
we **nous** *pron.* I-1
weak **faible** *adj.* I-3
wear **porter** *v.* I-6
weather **temps** *m., sing.* I-5; **météo** *f.* II-7
The weather is bad. **Il fait mauvais.** I-5
The weather is dreadful. **Il fait un temps épouvantable.** I-5
The weather is good/warm. **Il fait bon.** I-5
The weather is nice. **Il fait beau.** I-5
web site **site Internet/web** *m.* II-3
wedding **mariage** *m.* I-6
Wednesday **mercredi** *m.* I-2
weekend **week-end** *m.* I-2
this weekend **ce week-end** *m.* I-2
welcome **bienvenu(e)** *adj.* I-1
You're welcome. **Il n'y a pas de quoi.** I-1
well **bien** *adv.* I-7
I am doing well/badly. **Je vais bien/mal.** I-1
west **ouest** *m.* II-4
What? **Comment?** *adv.* I-4; **Pardon?** I-4; **Quoi?** I-1 *interr. pron.* I-4
What day is it? **Quel jour sommes-nous?** I-2
What is it? **Qu'est-ce que c'est?** *prep.* I-1
What is the date? **Quelle est la date?** I-5
What is the temperature? **Quelle température fait-il?** I-5
What is the weather like? **Quel temps fait-il?** I-5
What is your name? **Comment t'appelles-tu?** *fam.* I-1
What is your name? **Comment vous appelez-vous?** *form.* I-1
What is your nationality? **Quelle est ta nationalité?** *sing., fam.* I-1
What is your nationality? **Quelle est votre nationalité?** *sing., pl., fam., form.* I-1

What time do you have?
**Quelle heure avez-vous?**
*form.* I-2
What time is it? **Quelle heure est-il?** I-2
What time? **À quelle heure?** I-2
What do you think about that? **Qu'en penses-tu?** II-6
What's up? **Ça va?** I-1
whatever it may be **quoi que ce soit** II-5
What's wrong? **Qu'est-ce qu'il y a?** I-1
when **quand** *adv.* I-4
When is …'s birthday? **C'est quand l'anniversaire de …?** I-5
When is your birthday? **C'est quand ton/votre anniversaire?** I-5
where **où** *adv., rel. pron.* I-4
which? **quel(le)(s)?** *adj.* I-4
which one **à laquelle** *pron., f., sing.* II-5
which one **auquel (à + lequel)** *pron., m., sing.* II-5
which one **de laquelle** *pron., f., sing.* II-5
which one **duquel (de + lequel)** *pron., m., sing.* II-5
which one **laquelle** *pron., f., sing.* II-5
which one **lequel** *pron., m., sing.* II-5
which ones **auxquelles (à + lesquelles)** *pron., f., pl.* II-5
which ones **auxquels (à + lesquels)** *pron., m., pl.* II-5
which ones **desquelles (de + lesquelles)** *pron., f., pl.* II-5
which ones **desquels (de + lesquels)** *pron., m., pl.* II-5
which ones **lesquelles** *pron., f., pl.* II-5
which ones **lesquels** *pron., m., pl.* II-5
while **pendant que** *prep.* I-7
white **blanc(he)** *adj.* I-6
who? **qui?** *interr. pron.* I-4; **qui** *rel. pron.* II-3
Who is it? **Qui est-ce?** I-1
Who's calling, please? **Qui est à l'appareil?** II-5
whom? **qui?** *interr.* I-4
For whom? **Pour qui?** I-4
To whom? **À qui?** I-4
why? **pourquoi?** *adv.* I-2, I-4
widowed **veuf/veuve** *adj.* I-3
wife **femme** *f.* I-1; **épouse** *f.* I-3
willingly **volontiers** *adv.* II-2
win **gagner** *v.* I-5

wind **vent** *m.* I-5
It is windy. **Il fait du vent.** I-5
window **fenêtre** *f.* I-1
windshield **pare-brise** *m.* II-3
windshield wiper(s) **essuie-glace (essuie-glaces** *pl.)* *m.* II-3
windsurfing **planche à voile** *v.* I-5
to go windsurfing **faire de la planche à voile** *v.* I-5
wine **vin** *m.* I-6
winter **hiver** *m.* I-5
in the winter **en hiver** I-5
wipe (the dishes/the table) **essuyer (la vaisselle/la table)** *v.* I-8, II-P
wish that… **souhaiter que…** *v.* II-6
with **avec** *prep.* I-1
with whom? **avec qui?** I-4
withdraw money **retirer de l'argent** *v.* II-4
without **sans** *prep.* I-8, II-P; **sans que** *conj.* I-5
woman **femme** *f.* I-1
wood **bois** *m.* II-6
wool **laine** *f.* I-6
work **travail** *m.* II-4
to work **travailler** *v.* I-2; **marcher** *v.* II-3; **fonctionner** *v.* II-3
work out **faire de la gym** *v.* I-5
worker **ouvrier/ouvrière** *m., f.* II-5
world **monde** *m.* I-7
worried **inquiet/inquiète** *adj.* I-3
worry **s'inquiéter** *v.* II-2
worse **pire** *comp. adj.* II-1; **plus mal** *comp. adv.* II-1; **plus mauvais(e)** *comp. adj.* II-1
worst: the worst **le plus mal** *super. adv.* II-1; **le/la pire** *super. adj.* II-1; **le/la plus mauvais(e)** *super. adj.* II-1
wound **blessure** *f.* II-2
wounded: to get wounded **se blesser** *v.* II-2
write **écrire** *v.* I-7
to write one another **s'écrire** *v.* II-3
writer **écrivain/femme écrivain** *m., f.* II-7
written **écrit (écrire)** *p.p., adj.* I-7
wrong **tort** *m.* I-2
to be wrong **avoir tort** *v.* I-2

Y

yeah **ouais** I-2
year **an** *m.* I-2; **année** *f.* I-2
yellow **jaune** *adj.* I-6

yes **oui** I-2; *(when making a contradiction)* **si** I-2
yesterday (morning/afternoon evening) **hier (matin/après-midi/soir)** *adv.* I-7
day before yesterday **avant-hier** *adv.* I-7
yogurt **yaourt** *m.* II-1
you **toi** *disj. pron., sing., fam.* I-3; **tu** *sub. pron., sing., fam.* I-1; **vous** *pron., sing., pl., fam., form.* I-1
you neither **toi non plus** I-2
You're welcome. **De rien.** I-1
young **jeune** *adj.* I-3
younger **cadet(te)** *adj.* I-3
your **ta** *poss. adj., f., sing.* I-3; **tes** *poss. adj., m., f., pl.* I-3; **ton** *poss. adj., m., sing.* I-3; **vos** *poss. adj., m., f., pl.* I-3; **votre** *poss. adj., m., f., sing.* I-3;
yourself **te/t'** *refl. pron., sing., fam.* II-2; **toi** *refl. pron., sing., fam.* II-2; **vous** *refl. pron., form.* II-2
youth **jeunesse** *f.* I-6
youth hostel **auberge de jeunesse** *f.* I-7
Yum! **Miam!** *interj.* I-5

Z

zero **zéro** *m.* I-1

## Mots utiles

**absent(e)** *absent*
**un département** *department*
**une dictée** *dictation*
**une phrase** *sentence*
**une feuille d'activités**
  *activity sheet*
**l'horaire des cours (m.)**
  *class schedule*
**un paragraphe** *paragraph*
**une épreuve** *quiz*
**un examen** *exam; test*
**suivant(e)** *following*

## Expressions utiles

**Asseyez-vous, s'il vous plaît.**
  *Sit down, please.*
**Avez-vous des questions?**
  *Do you have any questions?*
**Comment dit-on _____ en français?** *How do you say _____ in French?*
**Comment écrit-on _____ en français?** *How do you write _____ in French?*
**Écrivez votre nom.** *Write your name.*
**Étudiez la leçon trois.** *Study lesson 3.*
**Fermez votre livre.** *Close your book(s).*
**Je ne comprends pas.** *I don't understand.*
**Je ne sais pas.** *I don't know.*
**Levez la main.** *Raise your hand(s).*
**Lisez la phrase à voix haute.** *Read the sentence aloud.*
**Ouvrez votre livre à la page deux.** *Open your book to page two.*
**Plus lentement, s'il vous plaît.** *Slower, please.*
**Que signifie _____?** *What does _____ mean?*
**Répétez, s'il vous plaît.** *Repeat, please.*
**Répondez à la/aux question(s).** *Answer the question(s).*
**Vous comprenez?** *Do you understand?*

## Titres des sections du livre

**À l'écoute** *Listening*
**Après la lecture** *After Reading*
**Avant la lecture** *Before Reading*
**Coup de main** *Helping Hand*
**Culture à la loupe** *Culture through a magnifying glass*
**Écriture** *Writing*
**Essayez!** *Try it!*
**Incroyable mais vrai!** *Incredible But True!*
**Le français quotidien** *Everyday French*
**Le français vivant** *French Live*
**Lecture** *Reading*
**Les sons et les lettres** *Sounds and Letters*
**Mise en pratique** *Putting it into Practice*
**Le monde francophone** *The Francophone World*
**Pour commencer** *To Begin*
**Projet** *Project*
**Roman-photo** *Story based on photographs*
**Savoir-faire** *Know-how*
**Structures** *Structures; Grammar*
**Le zapping** *Channel-surfing*

## D'autres adjectifs de nationalité en Europe

**autrichien(ne)** *Austrian*
**belge** *Belgian*
**bulgare** *Bulgarian*
**danois(e)** *Danish*
**écossais(e)** *Scottish*
**finlandais(e)** *Finnish*
**grec/grecque** *Greek*
**hongrois(e)** *Hungarian*
**norvégien(ne)** *Norwegian*
**polonais(e)** *Polish*
**portugais(e)** *Portuguese*
**roumain(e)** *Czech*
**russe** *Russian*
**slovaque** *Slovakian*
**slovène** *Slovene; Slovenian*
**suédois(e)** *Swedish*
**tchèque** *Romanian*
**tunisien(ne)** *Tunisian*

## D'autres adjectifs de nationalité en Afrique

**africain(e)** *African*
**angolais(e)** *Angolan*
**béninois(e)** *Beninese*
**camerounais(e)** *Cameroonian*
**congolais(e)** *Congolese*
**égyptien(ne)** *Egyptian*
**éthiopien(ne)** *Ethiopian*
**kenyan(e)** *Kenyan*
**ivoirien(ne)** *of the Ivory Coast*
**nigérien(ne)** *Nigerian*
**somalien(ne)** *Somali*
**soudanais(e)** *Sudanese*
**sud-africain(e)** *South African*
**tchadien(ne)** *Chadian*
**togolais(e)** *Togolese*
**tunisien(ne)** *Tunisian*

## D'autres adjectifs de nationalité dans le monde

**antillais(e)** *Caribbean, West Indian*
**argentin(e)** *Argentinian*
**asiatique** *Asian*
**australien(ne)** *Australian*
**bolivien(ne)** *Bolivian*
**chilien(ne)** *Chilean*
**chinois(e)** *Chinese*
**colombien(ne)** *Colombian*
**cubain(e)** *Cuban*
**haïtien(ne)** *Haitian*
**indien(ne)** *Indian*
**irakien(ne)** *Iraqi*
**iranien(ne)** *Iranian*
**israélien(ne)** *Israeli*
**libanais(e)** *Lebanese*
**néo-zélandais(e)** *New Zealander*
**pakistanais(e)** *Pakistani*
**péruvien(ne)** *Peruvian*
**portoricain(e)** *Puerto Rican*
**syrien(ne)** *Syrian*
**turc/turque** *Turkish*
**vénézuélien(ne)** *Venezuelan*

## D'autres cours

**l'agronomie (f.)** *agriculture*
**l'algèbre (m.)** *algebra*
**l'anatomie (f.)** *anatomy*
**l'anthropologie (f.)** *anthropology*
**l'archéologie (f.)** *archaeology*
**l'architecture (f.)** *architecture*
**l'astronomie (f.)** *astronomy*
**la biochimie** *biochemistry*
**la botanique** *botany*
**le commerce** *business*
**l'éducation physique (f.)**
   *physical education*
**une filière** *course of study*
**le latin** *Latin*
**les langues romanes**
   *romance languages*
**la linguistique** *linguistics*
**le marketing** *marketing*
**les mathématiques**
   **supérieures,**
   **spéciales** *calculus*
**la médecine** *medicine*
**la musique** *music*
**la trigonométrie** *trigonometry*
**la zoologie** *zoology*

## D'autres mots utiles

**une cantine** *cafeteria*
**un classeur** *binder*
**une gomme** *eraser*
**l'infirmerie (f.)** *infirmary*
**une règle** *ruler*

## D'autres animaux familiers

**un cochon d'Inde** *guinea pig*
**un furet** *ferret*
**une gerbille** *gerbil*
**un hamster** *hamster*
**un rongeur** *rodent*
**une souris** *mouse*
**une tortue** *turtle*

## D'autres adjectifs pour décrire les gens

**ambitieux/ambitieuse** *ambitious*
**arrogant(e)** *arrogant*
**calme** *calm*
**compétent(e)** *competent*
**excellent(e)** *excellent*
**franc/franche** *frank, honest*
**(mal)honnête** *(dis)honest*
**idéaliste** *idealistic*
**immature** *immature*
**mûr(e)** *mature*
**(ir)responsable** *(ir)responsible*
**romantique** *romantic*
**séduisant(e)** *attractive*
**sentimental(e)** *sentimental*
**sincère** *sincere*
**souple** *flexible*
**studieux/ieuse** *studious*
**tranquille** *quiet*

## D'autres professions

**un boucher/une**
   **bouchère** *butcher*
**un boulanger/une**
   **boulangère** *baker*
**un caissier/une**
   **caissière** *cashier*
**un cordonnier** *cobbler*
**un dessinateur/une**
   **dessinatrice** *illustrator*
**un fermier/une fermière** *farmer*
**un(e) informaticien(ne)**
   *computer scientist*
**un instituteur/une institutrice**
   *nursery/elementary school teacher*
**un(e) photographe** *photographer*
**un(e) pilote** *pilot*
**un(e) styliste** *fashion designer*
**un tailleur (pour dames)**
   *(ladies') tailor*
**un teinturier** *dry cleaner*

## Au café

**une brioche** *brioche, bun*
**un café crème** *espresso with milk*
**un croque-monsieur** *toasted*
   *ham and cheese sandwich*
**de l'eau gazeuse (f.)** *sparkling*
   *mineral water*
**de l'eau plate (f.)** *plain water*
**un garçon de café** *waiter*
**une omelette au jambon/au**
   **fromage** *omelet with ham/*
   *with cheese*
**des œufs au/sur le plat**
   **(m.)** *fried eggs*
**une part de tarte** *slice of a pie*
**une tartine de beurre** *slice of*
   *bread and butter*

## Quelques fromages

**du bleu des Causses** *blue*
   *cheese made with cow's milk*
**du camembert** *soft cheese made*
   *with cow's milk*
**du fromage de chèvre**
   *goat cheese*
**du gruyère** *Swiss cheese*
**du munster** *semisoft cheese that*
   *can be sharp in flavor, made*
   *with cow's milk*
**du reblochon** *soft cheese made*
   *with cow's milk*
**du roquefort** *blue cheese made*
   *with sheep's milk*
**de la tomme de Savoie**
   *cheese from the Alps made of*
   *scalded curds*

## D'autres loisirs

**une bicyclette** *bicycle*
**bricolage (faire du)** *fixing things*
**collectionner les timbres** *to collect stamps*
**faire des mots croisés** *to do a crossword puzzle*
**une fête foraine/une foire** *fair*
**jouer à la pétanque/aux boules (f.)** *to play the game of petanque*
**jouer aux dames (f.)** *to play checkers*
**louer une vidéo/un DVD** *to rent a video/DVD*
**la natation (faire de)** *swimming*
**un parc d'attractions** *amusement park*
**tapisserie (faire de la)** *needlework*
**tricoter** *knitting*
**un vidéoclub** *video store*

## Des mots liés à la météo

**une averse** *shower*
**la bise** *North wind*
**la brise** *breeze*
**un ciel couvert** *overcast sky*
**un ciel dégagé** *clear sky*
**une éclaircie** *break in the weather; sunny spell*
**la grêle** *hale*
**la grisaille** *grayness*
**de la neige fondue** *sleet*
**un nuage** *cloud*
**un orage** *thunder storm*
**une vague de chaleur** *heat wave*
**le verglas** *black ice*

## Des fêtes de famille

**une bague de fiançailles** *engagement ring*
**un baptême** *christening*
**les fiançailles** *engagement*
**les noces d'argent** *silver wedding anniversary*
**les noces d'or** *golden wedding anniversary*
**un enterrement** *funeral*

## Des jours fériés

**l'Action de grâce** *Thanksgiving*
**la fête de l'Indépendance** *Independence Day*
**une fête nationale** *National holiday*
**le Jour de l'an/la Saint-Sylvestre** *New Year's Day*
**le 14 juillet** *Bastille Day*
**la Saint-Valentin** *Valentine's Day*

## D'autres mots pour faire la fête

**des accessoires de cotillon (m.)** *party accessories*
**des amuse-gueule (m.)** *appetizers; nibbles*
**un bal** *ball*
**des confettis** *confetti*
**une coupe** *glass (champagne)*
**des feux d'artifice** *fireworks*
**une flûte** *flute (champagne)*
**un serpentin** *streamer*

## Quelques vêtements

**une doudoune** *down coat*
**un foulard** *headscarf*
**un gilet** *cardigan; vest*
**un moufle** *mitten*
**un pantacourt** *capri pants*
**un pull à col roulé** *turtleneck*
**un sweat-shirt** *sweatshirt*
**une veste** *jacket*

## Quelques pays d'Europe

**l'/en Autriche (f.)** *Austria*
**la/en Bulgarie** *Bulgaria*
**le/au Danemark** *Denmark*
**l'/en Écosse (f.)** *Scotland*
**la/en Finlande** *Finland*
**la/en Grèce** *Greece*
**la/en Hongrie** *Hungary*
**la/en Norvège** *Norway*
**la/en Pologne** *Poland*
**le/au Portugal** *Portugal*
**la/en République tchèque** *Czech Republic*
**la/en Roumanie** *Romania*
**le/au Royaume-Uni** *United Kingdom*
**la/en Russie** *Russia*
**la/en Slovaquie** *Slovakia*
**la/en Slovénie** *Slovenia*
**la/en Suède** *Sweden*

## Quelques pays d'Afrique

**l'/en Afrique du Sud (f.)** *South Africa*
**l'/en Algérie (f.)** *Algeria*
**l'/en Angola (f.)** *Angola*
**le/au Bénin** *Benin*
**le/au Cameroun** *Cameroon*
**le/au Congo** *Congo*
**la/en Côte d'Ivoire** *Ivory Coast*
**l'/en Égypte (f.)** *Egypt*
**l'/en Éthiopie (f.)** *Ethiopia*
**le/au Kenya** *Kenya*
**le/au Maroc** *Morocco*
**le/au Niger** *Niger*
**le/au Sénégal** *Senegal*
**la/en Somalie** *Somalia*
**le/au Soudan** *Sudan*
**le/au Tchad** *Chad*
**le/au Togo** *Togo*
**la/en Tunisie** *Tunisia*

## D'autres pays

**l'/en Argentine (f.)** *Argentina*
**l'/en Australie (f.)** *Australia*
**la/en Bolivie** *Bolivia*
**le/au Chili** *Chile*
**la/en Colombie** *Colombia*
**(à) Cuba (f.)** *Cuba*
**(à) Haïti** *Haiti*
**l'/en Inde (f.)** *India*
**l'/en Irak (m.)** *Iraq*
**l'/en Iran (m.)** *Iran*
**(en) Israël (m.)** *Israel*
**le/au Liban** *Lebanon*
**la/en Nouvelle-Zélande** *New Zealand*
**le/au Pakistan** *Pakistan*
**le/au Pérou** *Peru*
**(à) Porto Rico (f.)** *Puerto Rico*
**la/en Syrie** *Syria*
**la/en Turquie** *Turkey*
**le/au Venezuela** *Venezuela*

## Partir en vacances

**atterrir** *to land*
**l'atterrissage (m.)** *landing*
**une compagnie aérienne** *airline*
**une crème solaire** *sunscreen*
**une croisière** *cruise*
**le décollage** *take-off*
**décoller** *to take off*
**défaire ses valises** *to unpac*
**un douanier** *customs officer*
**une frontière** *border*
**un groom** *bellhop*
**un numéro de vol** *flight number*
**dormir à la belle étoile** *to sleep
    out in the open*
**une station balnéaire**
    *seaside resort*

## Dans la maison

**allumer la lumière** *to turn on
    the light*
**du bois** *wood*
**le chauffage central**
    *central heating*
**la cheminé** *chimney; fireplace*
**la climatisation** *air-conditioning*
**la décoration intérieure**
    *interior design*
**en bas** *downstairs*
**en haut** *upstairs*
**éteindre la lumière** *to turn off
    the light*
**le fioul** *heating oil*
**le gaz** *natural gas*
**le grenier** *attic*
**la lumière** *light*
**une penderie** *walk-in closet*
**un plafond** *ceiling*
**le sol** *floor*
**le toit** *roof*

## Des tâches ménagères

**aérer une pièce** *to air a room*
**arroser les plantes** *to water
    the plants*
**étendre le linge** *to hang out/
    hang up washing*
**laver les vitres** *to clean
    the windows*
**une vitre** *windowpane*

## Des meubles et des objets de la maison

**une ampoule** *light bulb*
**une bougie** *candle*
**un buffet** *sideboard*
**une corde à linge** *clothesline*
**une couette** *comforter*
**le linge de maison** *linen*
**une persienne** *shutter*
**une pince à linge** *clothes pin*
**un portemanteau** *coat rack*
**un radiateur** *radiator*
**un robot ménager** *food processor*
**un store** *blind*
**un volet** *shutter*

# Index

## Text Credits

**241** © Reprinted by permission of Comité du tourisme des îles de Guadeloupe; ad produced by Comité du tourisme des îles de Guadeloupe in 2005

## Photography Credits

All images ©Vista Higher Learning unless otherwise noted.

**Special thanks to:** Martin Bernetti, Sophie Casson, Tom Delano, Rachel Distler, Janet Dracksdorf, Daniel Finkbeiner, Beth Kramer, Rossy Llano, Anne Loubet, Hermann Mejía, Pascal Pernix and Pere Virgili.

**Front Matter: Cover** (tr) © Lulu Durand Photography/Getty Images; Cover (cr) © Corbis RF/agefotostock; Cover (bl) © David Sanger/Getty Images; Cover (br) © Frans Lemmens/Corbis; **TAE-23** (b) Shutterstock © Monkey Business Images; **v** (right panel: mr) © iStockphoto.com/mddphoto; **vii** (right panel: tr) © Christophe Boisvieux/Corbis; **vii** (right panel: mr) © iStockphoto. com/Dianne Maire; **vii** (tr) © iStockphoto.com/Philip Lange; **ix** (br) © iStockphoto.com/Andreas Karelias; **ix** (tl) © Chromacome/ Stockbyte/Getty Images; **xvi** (bl) © North Wind Picture Archives / Alamy; **xvi** (br) © North Wind Picture Archives / Alamy; **xvii** (bl) © Royalty Free **xviii** (r) © The Gallery Collection/Corbis; **xix** (t) © Fotolia/moodboard; **xix** © Shutterstock/Sean Prior; **xix** (b) © Shutterstock/moshimochi; **xx** (b) © JTB Photo Communications, Inc. / Alamy; **xxi** (l) © Dave & Les Jacobs/Blend Images/ Corbis; **xxi** (r) © Fotolia/Yuri Arcurs; **xxii** (l) © Sébastien Dolidon/Corbis; **xxiii** (t) © Shutterstock/Monkey Business Images; **xxiv** © Dreamstime/Monkey Business Images; **xxiv** © Creasource; **xxv** © H. Schmid/Corbis.

**Unit One: 11** (mr)/#5 © 1996-98 AccuSoft Inc. All Rights Reserved; **22** (r) © Sam Edwards/Getty Images; **24** (right panel: tl)/#1 © Rune Hellestad/Corbis; **24** (right panel: bl)/#3 © 1996-98 AccuSoft Inc.; All rights reserved; **25** (left panel: t) © Reuters/Corbis; **25** (left panel: tl)/#1 © Frank Trapper/Corbis; **25** (left panel: mr)/#5 © Reuters/Lucy Nicholson/Corbis; **25** (left panel: br)/#6 © iStockphoto.com/Rasmus Rasmussen; **28** (tml) © Robert Lerich/Fotolia; **30** (left panel: t) © Hulton-Deutsch Collection/Corbis; **30** (left panel: tm) © Caroline Penn/Corbis; **30** (left panel: bm) © Jean-Pierre Amet/BelOmbra/Corbis; **30** (left panel: b) © Eddy Lemaistre/For Picture/Corbis; **30** (right panel: t) © Tahiti Tourisme; **30** (right panel: mr) © Ariadne Van Zandbergen/ Lonely Planet Images/Getty Images; **30** (right panel: b) © Eddy Lemaistre/For Picture/Corbis; **31** (tl); **31** (tr) © Antoine Gyori/ Corbis Sygma; **31** (bl) © Owen Franken/Corbis; **31** (br) Published with the kind authorization of the Service de communication pour la Francophonie.; **34** (tr) © Inspirestock Royalty-Free/inmagine.

**Unit Two: 38** © Tom Stewart/Corbis; **44** (r) © Jacques Loic/Photolibrary; **45** (t) © Picture Partners/agefotostock, **48** (r) Robert Fried/Alamy, **66** (left panel: t) © Christie's Images/Corbis; **66** (left panel: m) © Bettmann/Corbis; **66** (left panel: b) © Gyori Antoine/Corbis Sygma; **66** (right panel: ml) © Martine Coquilleau/Fotolia; **66** (right panel: mr) © iStockphoto.com/mddphoto; **67** (tl) © David Gregs/Alamy; **67** (br) © iStockphoto.com/Caroline Beecham; **68-69** top © Art Kowalsky/Alamy; **69** inset © Charles Gullung/Corbis.

**Unit Three: 81** (t) © ELISE AMENDOLA/2009 The Associated Press; **81** (m) © NBAE/Getty Images; **81** (b) © Tony Barson/ WireImage/Getty Images; **82** (left panel: r) © FogStock LLC/photolibrary. All rights reserved.; **82** (right panel) © Hemera Technologies/AbleStock.com/Jupiterimages; **84** (tl)/#1 © iStockphoto.com/Dmitry Kutlayev; **85** (t) © iStockphoto; **85** (bl) © Dynamic Graphics/Dynamic Graphics Group/Jupiterimages; **90** (ml)/#1 © 2009 Jupiterimages Corporation; **90** (mr)/#4 © Vstock, LLC/photolibrary. All rights reserved.; **95** (tl) © Henri Tuillio/Corbis; **95** (tr) © Patrick Roncen/Corbis; **95** (m) © Pascalito/Sygma/Corbis; **97** (tr) Jeroen Geeraert/istockphoto, **102** (left panel: t) © Stapleton Collection/Corbis; **102** (left panel: bl) © Kurt Krieger/Corbis; **102** (left panel: br) © Popperfoto/Alamy; **102** (right panel: b) © Benjamin Herzoq/Fotolia; **103** (bl) © Keren Su/Corbis.

**Unit Four: 112** (t) © Buzzshotz / Alamy; **117** (t) © Inge Yspeert/Corbis; **117** (m) © Philippe Cabaret/Sygma/Corbis; **117** (b) © Imgram Publishing/Purestock/Jupiterimages; **124** (tl) © robfood / Alamy; **131** (t) © Yadid Levy/Alamy; **131** (m) © Kevin Foy/ Alamy; **131** (b) © Garcia/photocuisine/Corbis; **138** (left panel: t) © Chris Hellier/Corbis; **138** (left panel: b) © Hulton-Deutsch Collection/Corbis; **138** (right panel: tr) © Christophe Boisvieux/Corbis; **138** (right panel: ml) © David Osborne/Alamy; **138** (right panel: mr) © iStockphoto.com/Dan Moore; **138** (right panel: b) © iStockphoto.com/Daniel Brechwoldt; **139** (bl) © Brian Harris/ Alamy; **143** (c) © Patrick Sheandell O'Carroll/Getty Images.

**Unit Five: 152** (l) © 2009 The Associated Press; **152** (r) © Neil Marchand/Liewig Media Sports/Corbis; **153** (t) © Victor Fraile/Reuters/Corbis; **153** (m) © Arko Datta/Reuters/Corbis; **153** (b) © FogStock LLC/photolibrary. All rights reserved.;

## Video Credits

Production Company: Klic Video Productions, Inc.
Lead Photographer: Pascal Pernix
Photographer, Assistant Director: Barbara Ryan Malcolm
Photography Assistant: Pierre Halart

## *Le zapping* Credits

**15** *La Triplette de Moulinex* © Groupe SEB
**51** © Clairefontaine
**87** © Pages d'Or
**123** © Swiss Airlines International
**159** © SwissLife
**195** *La Poste belge* © La Poste
**231** *Le TER* © SNCF
**267** © Century 21 with the kind authorization of Pierre Palmade